THE ARTS AND MAN

What use to you my ardent mind
Which flames before your eyes?
What good the spell of art that binds
All life in mystic wise?
If you still lack the vital power
How can your life o'erflow,
Or love within you ever flower
That further art may grow?

  —Goethe, "Monologue of the Enthusiast," in *Fragments*.

The Artist and the Critic, by Peter Breughel (*Albertina Facsimile-Schroll*).

THE ARTS
AND MAN

BY RAYMOND S. STITES

CHAIRMAN, DEPARTMENT OF ARTS AND AESTHETICS, ANTIOCH COLLEGE

McGRAW-HILL BOOK COMPANY, INC.

NEW YORK · · · · · 1940 · · · · · LONDON

THE ARTS AND MAN

THE MAPLE PRESS COMPANY, YORK, PA.

Preface

Build thee more stately mansions, O my soul,
　　As the swift seasons roll!
　　　Leave thy low-vaulted past!
　Let each new temple, nobler than the last,
Shut thee from heaven with a dome more vast,
　　　Till thou at length art free,
Leaving thine outgrown shell by life's unresting sea!
　　　　　　"THE CHAMBERED NAUTILUS," 1858[1]

AFTER working almost forty years upon his *Faust*, Goethe wrote a Prologue, staged, significantly, in Heaven. Then, hastily sketching in a preface, he rushed off and paid a printer to publish the work. Needless to say this author is no Goethe; however, this book will also attempt to present, in a way, the drama of man's efforts to organize a more unified world out of the vicissitudes of fortune.

In 1921, *The Dance of Life*, by Havelock Ellis, first suggested to me that art's power to transform life from the material into the spiritual functioned by guiding the energies of the war dance toward the gentler rhythms of peace. In such wise apparently each succeeding human culture has captured excess energy generated during its years of plenty to heal man's spirit after years of war. It appears also that art, studied as a universal language, holds infinite possibilities for penetrating racial and national taboos, thus allowing man to construct a world civilization in which he may live at peace with his neighbors. This thread of a plot which runs through the book was conceived at a time when we first believed idealistically that we had fought a "war to end war" and when we knew that eventually there must be some sort of confederation of peoples in a United States of the World.

The study of the arts as nature's medicine for the disease of war will demonstrate that geography, soil, and race have each played their part in the development of those discrete styles which epitomize various historical culture periods. However, within every culture, certain individuals seem to have created works of universal significance. The following pages will show how these significant discoveries grew from and transcended their stylistic antecedents until at last they became the common heritage of the human race.

Although the facts presented summarize material gathered from sources too numerous for complete mention, some of these call for special acknowledgment. Professor J. Q. Dealey first called attention to those illuminating charts developed by Herbert Spencer in gathering the material from which he wrote his *Principles of Sociology*. Spencer's method was used, with variations traceable to Winckelmann and Wundt, in the Institute for Research in Art History of the University of Vienna. A similar attempt to evaluate the relationship of art to society has recently been published by Pitirim A. Sorokin of Harvard University under the title of *Social and Cultural Dynamics*. The teacher interested in comparing my conclusions with the publications of these other men will dis-

[1] OLIVER WENDELL HOLMES, *Complete Poetical Works,* Houghton Mifflin Company, Boston.

cover that we differ chiefly because, following Emerson, I value more highly man's ability to create eventually a universal culture pattern which will include the best of the past. The a priori assumptions on which this research has been based are more closely allied to the pragmatic realism of James and Dewey than they are to materialism, to aesthetic sensism, or to the purely economic determinism of Karl Marx, which influences much 20th-century writing about the arts.

Since this book was first conceived in the biological laboratory at Brown University, it seems particularly fitting to recall with gratitude the careful scientific method taught there by Professors Walter, Mead, Gorham, and Bumpus. Many helpful thought passages have also stemmed from contacts at Brown with Theodore Collier, L. T. Damon, Alfred Jones, and Dr. Charles McDonald. From Robert Reininger, Karl Bühler, Heinrich Gomperz, Oswald Menghin, and Josef Strzygowski of Vienna likewise has come much material in the fields of the philosophy, history, and psychology of art.

To Professor John Shapley I am particularly grateful for financial assistance in exploring the ancient world, for his masterful translation of Worringer's *Form Problems of the Gothic*, and for continued friendly advice over many years. This friendship has been a distinct inspiration, as has the continued help of Charles E. Leach and Dr. Albert Cohoe throughout the years. I am particularly indebted to Brown University for the fellowships which made possible several years of research in Europe.

The educational philosophies underlying this volume unite three American traditions for teaching the humanities. The first of these is the course in classical civilization, presented by departments of Greek and Latin. This tradition usually more or less unconsciously assumes the primacy of the beautiful as man's most significant ideal. The second, a course in medieval backgrounds, taught by literature and history departments, tends toward a glorifica-

tion of the Gothic, with a suggestion that the energetic is of the highest excellence in art. The third course represents the quasi-anthropological art history and those appreciation of art courses taught by faculties of art or philosophy. These place great emphasis upon the magical or decorative qualities of primitive art or else stress the sublime character of Oriental productions.

It has been my good fortune while teaching to inherit course material of three well-known leaders in each of these fields: the late Professors F. G. Allinson of Brown University, Charles Weller of the University of Iowa, and Dean Hellems of the University of Colorado. I have also profited greatly by the many significant publications of those scholars represented in the pages of *Art Studies*, *The College Art Bulletin*, *Eastern Art*, and *The American Journal of Archaeology* as well as by the monumental works of Springer, Woermann, Mâle, Riemann, and Groves.

Throughout the courses and in the publications appear the above three approaches, more or less unconsciously held by various schools of teaching. They seem to foster three mental attitudes which will be characterized in this book as the Classical, the Gothic, and the Oriental. Each of these may be symbolically represented by a figure: the first a triangle, the second an energetic interweaving of lines, and the third an equilibrated yang-yin. These three symbols, in no sense mystical, represent fundamental composition schemata proper to the plastic and graphic designs of the cultures mentioned. A symbol suggesting synaeresis of the three approaches may be found on the cover.

To make available the gist of the material from these diverse sources, it was decided twelve years ago to incorporate it in the form of an elementary course book. Naturally, where the field was so broad as to cover all the arts it seemed at first an almost impossible task, to present an accurate survey within the space of eight hundred pages. In such a process scholarly accuracy, which insists upon qualifying most of the generally accepted "facts" of art history, of necessity had to be sacrificed to brevity. During an editing process, similar in many respects to the montage of a motion picture, the aesthetic form of the book has undoubtedly gained considerably. For help in this arduous task I am particularly grateful to Professor Albert Schweizer, Alene Little, and L. H. Conrad.

Since one is liable to unintentional errors of both omission and commission, I have gladly accepted the willing help of several qualified scholars who read and suggested corrections in most of the chapters. Where these authorities disagreed markedly concerning a statement, it has been omitted, although in a few instances some partly hypothetical material was retained because no better explanation now exists to bridge the gaps in our knowledge. For this work of scholarly correction I am indebted to Drs. Dorothy Cross and A. S. Arnold; and Professors Edward Capps, Jr., Clarence Ward, Ernst Diez, Dmitros Tselos, and Stowell Goding. Among my colleagues at Antioch College I wish to express gratitude to Vivian Bresnehen, George Geiger, W. Boyd Alexander, Lincoln R. Gibbs, Wilhelm Fiedler, and Ava Champney for reading entire sequences on music, literature, and philosophy. To Walter and Mildred Kahoe I am particularly indebted for many helpful suggestions concerning not only the subject matter but also the formal appearance of the volume.

Illustration of the volume would have been impossible without the assistance of Rudolph Lesch Fine Arts Company, who, by special arrangement with commercial photographers abroad and the Carnegie Corporation of New York, made available several hundred photographs from the Carnegie Art Reference Collection. These have been credited in the legends. I am also indebted for my working library to the Carnegie Corporation's gift of music and graphic art collections with the excellent books which have furnished much of my bibliographi-

cal background. Among other prime sources of photographic illustrations I wish to acknowledge particularly Professors Clarence Kennedy of Smith College and Clarence Ward of Oberlin, Mrs. A. Kingsley Porter, and the Fratelli Alinari of Florence. These and many others who have helped in this way are credited in place, as are the many publishers who made available material from other publications.

I wish here particularly to acknowledge the courtesy and kindness extended by the staffs of the many museums whose collections are represented in the illustrations, particularly the Metropolitan Museum of Art and the American Museum of Natural History in New York, the University of Pennsylvania Museum, the Fogg Museum, the Boston Museum of Fine Arts, the Oriental Institute of Chicago, and the Civic Museums of Dayton, Toledo, Seattle, Detroit, and Worcester. To three libraries—the New York Public Library, the Library of Congress, and that of Columbia University—I am indebted for much assistance, as well as to the librarian and staff of the Antioch College Library. Others who have helped in this way are acknowledged in the legends.

The excellence in the illustration of the book is in great measure due to Myrtle Veal's fine pen renderings of the drawings and the illuminative borders at the beginning of each chapter. Each of these borders, derived from originals belonging to the various cultures, suggests the rhythmical design essential to that culture. A list of the sources of these designs may be found on page xi.

In preparation of material acknowledgment is due particularly to Harold G. Gough, David Dempsey, Marianne Youngblood, Helen Shaver, Jean Dennis, Raymond Brose, Alex Horvath, Janet Wood, Raymond Lanning, and Ralph Krone. To my sister, Frances Stites, I am particularly grateful for typing much of the manuscript. Throughout the work my wife has at every step rendered valuable assistance, helping not only with secretarial work and proofreading but also with many of the architectural drawings and the compilation of the index.

It is hoped that a work completed with so much labor but with a plethora of good will on the part of many helpers will have durable value, that, although later models may call for more delicate streamlining and greater refinement, its essential plan and selection of details, as well as its basic construction, will be found to have been well wrought.

If this volume warrants any dedication, it may well be to both my considerate teachers and my stimulating students. To the latter I can do no more than pass on the spirit with which my old teacher, President W. H. P. Faunce of Brown University, commissioned

ANTIOCH COLLEGE,
YELLOW SPRINGS, OHIO,
November, 1940.

this study: "You are in the very home and by the fireside of the antique civilization with all its wealth—artistic, literary and cultural—all of which makes America seem somewhat crude and fresh. But the world needs both Europe and America, both the memory of Yesterday and the anticipation of Tomorrow. If all Europeans could have our faith in tomorrow, our freedom from the worship of tradition and if all Americans could have that sense of background and perspective which is indigenous to Europeans—we should have a happier world." These words seem today, even more than when I first read them, a proper stimulus for further research.

RAYMOND S. STITES.

Symbolic Borders and Color Plates

WILHELM WUNDT'S *Elements of Folk Psychology* first suggested that the monumental graphic and plastic creations of every culture period seem to be based upon fundamental rhythmical motives. These, it now appears, are always expressed in each culture's earliest linear designs as they first show on its pottery, weaving, or architectural decoration. In a similar fashion man's inherited or unconscious associations with various schemes of color harmony appear to derive from about ten significant designs. Along with the linear designs eight of these are represented in the following plates.

Contents

THE ARTS AND MAN

Introduction

The scientist, dealing as he does with natural phenomena, can at once proceed to analyze them. The humanist, dealing as he does with human actions and creations, has to engage in a mental process of a synthetic and subjective character: he has mentally to *re-enact the actions* and to *re-create the creations*. . . .

Anyone confronted with a work of art, whether aesthetically re-creating or rationally investigating it, is affected by its three constituents: materialized form, idea (that is, in the plastic arts, subject matter) and contents. . . . It is the unity of those three elements which is realized in the aesthetic experience, and all of them enter into what is called aesthetic enjoyment of art.

The re-creative experience of a work of art depends, therefore, not only on the natural *sensitivity* and the visual training of the spectator, but also on his *cultural equipment*. There is no such thing as an entirely "naïve" beholder.[1]

To HELP create an informed and friendly understanding of art is the chief purpose of this book. Art has often been called the most direct language of the soul, the means by which man completely unifies his emotional and intellectual life so that his feelings as well as his thoughts can be transmitted to others. Yet art is more than communication. Through artistic creation and enjoyment—whether in the field of literature, painting, sculpture, or music—man becomes succinctly aware of his oneness with nature and his fellow man. Is this suggestion of a definition too ideal, too abstract for our practical age? Then turn at once to art itself.

Chief Values, Characteristics, and Nomenclature of Art

A Coin That "Talks" of Art. Plato once wrote that art was a language which all nations could understand—a statement something like the one "money talks," which may be most easily demonstrated by the careful inspection of a penny. One side of the coin shows the head of Lincoln; the other, some lettering. It may be said that this piece of money speaks in at least three different ways.

1. As simply a token coin, it claims a certain use value, for it will buy such things as a postage stamp, a piece of chewing gum, or some chocolate. Curiously, in terms of copper, it would actually buy several times its own weight in that metal. That is why it is called a token. Every other work of art, like this penny, has a certain use, or worth, value. This consists of what it will buy in terms of human enjoyment, of instruction, or in some cases, of mystical religious inspiration. One thing to be remembered always is that every significant work of art has some use.

2. The penny, however, has much more than that—its use value. Observe particularly the side bearing in low relief the portrait head. Here Lincoln's rugged, kindly features are a reminder of the highest ideal of a democratic man—a leader of the people—for the people—elected by a free people as a whole. It seems fitting that beside this head should stand the word "Liberty," and above this head, a statement of belief: "In God we trust." Your penny, then, may be regarded as a work of art and

[1] ERWIN PANOFSKY, *The Meaning of the Humanities*, pp. 105*ff*., Princeton University Press, Princeton, 1938.

observed from this second point of view, which has very little to do with what the coin will buy. Anyone who examines this work of art in terms of its subject—Lincoln, "In God we trust," and Liberty—is considering its literary or, as the psychologist would say, its associational value. Practical people are likely to stress the use value; preachers, teachers, and others who are interested particularly in mankind's spiritual welfare tend to cherish the associational values.

3. There is, moreover, still another way in which this work of art may be examined—from the point of view of the professional designer or artist. Notice that the area covered by the portrait head itself is about equal in extent to that occupied by the shoulders and coat. This mass is placed directly on the diameter of the circle. The line "In God we trust" runs around the top border. "Liberty" is so placed in the space at the left that it looks just about right, and the date has its place below the necktie. To improve upon this arrangement would be difficult. The artist who modeled the coin placed these parts so that they constitute what the designer calls an almost perfect "occult," or obscure, balance.

This last, the formal aspect of the work of art, demonstrates what is most truly its international language. In Italy, France, or Germany, your penny would buy nothing, and most of the people would not understand the words. In none of these countries would the face of Lincoln appeal to the emotions of the people in general. But in all these countries there are many who would understand that the coin is well designed.

Has the subject of art previously frightened you? The penny, a common enough object, certainly does not seem very terrifying. Most of us, although we hardly realize it, are artists. When we try to make the rooms in which we live look a little more restful, when we mow the lawn or plant a flower bed, or when—especially if we are young—we array ourselves in extra-attractive garments before going out with someone with whom we are in love, we are arranging or designing our environment. And that is precisely the chief business of the artist.

Possibly most of you have seen the motion picture *Mr. Deeds Goes to Town*, in which Gary Cooper, as the hero, explained the meaning of the term "doodling." I doubt whether anyone who reads these lines has not at some time or other "doodled" on a scrap of paper. Perhaps the "doodling" resulted in little more than dollar signs. This might indicate that the "doodler" was worrying about finances. Probably almost everyone has enjoyed the self-expression found in rearranging one's own initials in a new monogram or in weaving a series of pencil lines together. This "doodling" ability is a mental-physical activity that proves the presence within each of us of a blood brother to the most modern expressive artists. To return to the penny, when the designer first started to arrange the face and the words, he had to do considerable "doodling." Art, after all, is simply "doodling" tempered by need, or social purpose, and design—an instinct for unified arrangement.

To review, three things seem necessary if one is to be an artist or to gain enjoyment from art. (1) One must have faith in both the face and the words of the penny. This means faith in the thoughts suggested by the verse at the beginning of this book. (2) To faith must be added a sympathetic interest for and understanding of human nature. Through these attitudes one's work gains in emotional power. Usually all three are accompanied by a sense of humor, like that suggested in the drawing by farmer Breughel on the frontispiece. (3) Finally, to all these humane intentions the artist or the one who appreciates art must bring either the ability to create and synthesize or the need to find unity or equilibrium within those divergent elements that constitute life.

Every work of art, like the penny, may and should be studied with reference to the three values discussed—its use value, its associational value, and its formal value. Obviously, each value has a primary appeal for some special group. The work of art does not look the same to all people. In what different ways a simple drawing may appear to various observers can be seen in Fig. 1. Some will declare at once that this shows the face of an old woman with a sharp chin, thin lips, a Roman nose, and a rather indistinct eye. Others will find the picture of a pretty young lady whose face is partly turned away so that only one long eyelash shows beyond the contour of her cheek. What would be the eye of the old woman seems to be the ear of the young one.

Personal differences account for the differing associational values discovered in this picture. Only a very objective mind can be aware at once of both faces. Most great works of art, like this simple drawing, combine several aesthetic effects. Thus only long study will reveal the sources of their power. Further, all of us seeking different values bring to these works of art our own personal desires. The careful student of art gains objectivity in examining the works, not by denying his own intuitive reactions, but by recognizing and refining them.

A Thought-provoking Oration. The penny appeals strongly to our sense of use values. Art works created for this appeal—such as clothing and furniture—are usually called "applied" art or crafts, in contrast to painting, sculpture, poetry, and music, which are known as "fine" arts. These categorical terms, "applied art" and "fine art," arose in the 18th and 19th centuries to separate arts with associational and formal values from those that were predominantly useful. Since the principles that dominate the arts remain constant for all forms, no attempt will be made in this book to separate applied and fine arts. A great dramatic speech, such as Lincoln's Gettysburg Address, while richer in associative and formal values than in use values, can still be approached from the practical side.

Lincoln's Gettysburg speech came primarily as a very simple and useful restatement of the purposes for which the Northern states had banded together in the war to preserve the Union. As chief executive of the nation, Lincoln took a very brief "time out" in order to emphasize in his lines the necessity for bringing the war to a victorious conclusion. He spoke

FIG. 1.—Dual aspect of art. (*C. Spearman, Creative Mind, D. Appleton-Century Company, Inc.*)

at the dedication of the battlefield on which, as he saw it, the tide of the war had turned. Thus the speech had the same use value as a prayer or exhortation and continues to have such a value on any occasion when we feel that the democratic principle is at stake.

The associational values to which it owes much of its effect are shown in the opening sentence: "*Four score* and seven years ago *our fathers brought forth* upon this continent a new nation." Contrast this stately line with what might have been said: "Eighty-seven years ago our ancestors founded this country." What makes Lincoln's opening so much finer? The words "our fathers" suggest the beginning of a prayer;

through them our emotions are stirred. The use of the words "fourscore and seven" recalls the Biblical "threescore and ten," the normal span of a man's life. By these words the President linked his hearers with the patriot founders who had lived but a generation before. All these words come from the King James version of the Bible, which still holds a place in our hearts as the chief religious and literary inspiration of our people.

The remainder of the speech has all the elements of aesthetic quality, the formal poetic values of *rhythm*, *harmonious word sounds*, and *alliteration* or *repetition*. These values will be discussed further in succeeding chapters, in connection with the circumstances under which man first consciously used and recognized them.

These formal qualities, which characterize the opening line, recur throughout the speech, binding the more prosaic narration of recent events with the concluding dramatic exhortation: "It is for us, the living, rather, to be dedicated here to the unfinished work . . . and that government of the people, by the people, for the people, shall not perish from the earth."

With the war long past, and North and South firmly united, the speech has a more universal associational value for us than it probably had when it was delivered. This magnificent utterance went almost unnoticed that day at Gettysburg. It was hardly mentioned in the newspapers of the time. Why? Partly because Lincoln's simple words followed a long oration by Edward Everett, "the greatest orator of the day," who gave the crowd the style of speech to which their ears were accustomed. Everett's speech abounds with references to the evils of the conflict and to the iniquities of the Southern states. It made a great hit with the stay-at-homes. Lincoln, in contrast, spoke to the soldiers and to the nation as a whole. It is said that the soldiers liked the speech. Its lines, throughout, suggest *unity*, which was the thing they had fought for. Today the nation is united;

the hatreds of war are gone. So Lincoln's speech, which comprehended that universal idea, still lives, while Everett's long-winded recital of contemporary oratorical platitudes is forgotten. The brief lines of the President had that appropriate combination of formal style and universal sense which constitutes greatness in art. It was rich in use values, associational values, and formal values.

An Inspirational Symphony. Almost everyone has heard, either on the radio or in the concert hall, a symphony by Beethoven. Does it seem like a far cry from the arts of the penny and the dramatic speech to the music of a great composer? The same three values are to be found in all. If we could study together Beethoven's *Fifth Symphony*, we should find it awakening in us the same type of emotion as the Gettysburg Address. The musical qualities that arouse our emotions seem more complex chiefly because musical tones cannot be touched or seen as can the metal and the sculptural masses of a penny. Nor are they precise in meaning, like the words of a speech. The principles by which the symphony is constructed are similar, however, to those on which the other works are built, and the three values of use, association, and form remain inherent.

Unlike the penny and the speech, the music of Beethoven does not have an obvious use value. However, when one studies the historical evolution of some of Beethoven's musical patterns, melodies and rhythms come to light which in a primitive age of magic had a use value. As parts of the Mass in the medieval church, these same melodies were used to symbolize the relationship between man and God. In man's prehistoric past, music had a material use in even giving man courage or helping him in his lovemaking. Indeed, much music still has similar use values. Consider martial music and the commercial value of jazz.

If we listen to the opening bar of the *Fifth Symphony*, we hear first four notes, three of which are on one line, the fourth on the line below— that is, three tones, or a third, below it.

The notes are so timed that the first three are fast, the fourth, longer, and sustained. We may not realize it, of course, but these notes remind us vaguely of two drums. The fact that the

FIG. 2a.

motif is repeated a little lower in the scale in the next four notes has a depressing and somewhat dramatic effect.

This is due to two formal elements in the music—the retarded beat at the end of the sequence of four notes and a tendency to move downward, found almost invariably in primitive music. In music the formal values unite closely with unrecognizable associational values. This fact has led many superficial observers to say that music has no associational values. Critics, indeed, often call music the most purely formal of the arts and warn against searching for associational values. But Beethoven himself once said that these first eight notes represented fate knocking at the door. This interpretation of the line furnishes a dramatic prelude to the meaning of the entire symphony. Beethoven's words and life have become so widely known that we associate his meaning with these notes. Consequently, if we have any musical education whatever, we cannot help thinking of the deafened genius, pitting himself against fate—questioning, first, in this line and receiving his answer in the later development of the symphony.

Music that tends more or less definitely to describe moods or events suggesting tones in nature, such as murmurs of a forest, is called "program" music. Often a definite narrative program is arranged so that the various moods stimulating sounds follow each other to make a connected story.

Use and Abuse of Art Terms. The terms "absolute" and "program" music, like the terms "fine" and "applied" art, have come down to us in part as an inheritance from the highly specialized 19th-century culture, and in part from a certain narrowness in the medieval point of view. The medieval Scholastic philosophers differentiated between the "free" arts, includ-

FIG. 2b.

ing philosophy, arithmetic, geometry, rhetoric, dialectics, astronomy, and music, on the one hand, and the so-called servile arts of architecture, painting, sculpture, and pottery, on the other. Obviously the servile arts were those that demanded a certain degree of manual labor. During the early Florentine Renaissance, debates between scholars and artists led to the acceptance of painting as a "free" art. Music, however, although still considered a free art, functioned as part of what a modern critic would call a "program." Practically all European music then was intended to accompany words, either as part of a church service, as dance music, or as accompaniment for the poems of the troubadours. In the 19th century, an age rich in writings on aesthetic criticism, the aesthetic point of view came, for many cultured people, to take the place of religion. At that time all the old superstitions concerning the priority of one art or the other were elevated to the position of dogmas in the varying aesthetic systems. Then scholars categorically divided the arts into two groups. Those arts which had a maximum of use values fell under the head of crafts or applied arts. Those arts in which associational values seemed to dominate were called the "fine" arts. At the same time, the creation of purely instrumental music—having greatly advanced into the realm of the symphony, or music which did not accompany the voice or theatrical performance—was accorded a place relatively high in the aesthetic hierarchy. The sonata, chamber music in general, and the symphony, under the title "absolute" or "pure" music, were contrasted with program music, that is, music accompanying the dance or theatrical performances. Later this term was applied to music that suggested a program of associational sounds.

In the 20th century, a century in which architecture and motion pictures seem to be dominating art forms, the whole differentiation between fine and applied arts and between absolute and program music no longer has meaning for the masses of people. On the other hand, among the adherents of various art cults or schools of criticism, the lines of demarcation have been drawn even more strictly.

This book, which seeks an objective point of view, will try to show that all art is fine and that no art worthy of the name can lose caste by assisting the other arts. Further, since the element of usefulness connects art with our daily living, and the element of association explains our more personal feeling, it seems necessary in this book to study both the use and the associational values of the subject.

An examination of two works of art—(Fig. 335, Chap. XII) sculpture on the portal of a Romanesque cathedral, which would have been called a "work of applied art," and a modern sculpture by Boccioni (Fig. 589, Chap. XVIII) which would have been called a "work of fine or free art"—shows no essential difference. Both of these, being somewhat abstract, demonstrate clearly formal values that might be thought of as the cement binding the use value to associational value. It is possible, of course, to consider the formal value as the unique value, the *sine qua non* of the work of art. One should not, however, take the point of view of many modern students of aesthetics that it is the sole value worthy of study.

Artistic works created from knowledge of formal values alone, by a person lacking the associational background of culture, invariably must arise from the most primitive level of the common culture around him. This has been demonstrated by experiments with children in Professor Cizech's Viennese class of free art.

The works created by the children are on a level with the Viennese advertising art. American children, working in similar free-art classes, created paintings suspiciously like those of our colored comic sheets (Fig. 632, Chap. XIX). Richness, refinement, and emotional depth in art arise from cultural values; strength develops from the functional demands put upon the artist by having to create something useful.

Recognizing the Paradox of Art. A fundamental paradox demands recognition before one may embark upon any study of art as part of man's social activity. One cannot neglect the useful value of art—its value, that is, as an economic factor in our civilization. On the other hand, it must be recognized that art contains an expression of associational values—the myths, ideals, and dreams of the race—which constitute its ideational aspect.[1] The paradox lies in the fact that the work of art itself, the thing which unites these two contradictory modes of thinking, includes values from both. The formal values resulting from the conflict and ultimate union of these two irreconcilables (use and association) within the artist's mind would seem to be the core of the study of art. If we could but start with the thesis that art is individual and that the solitary struggles of the artist result in formal values, we might allow ourselves to study only the formal values. To build up a philosophy of art in this simple way would lead inevitably to the total withdrawal of art from the very sources of its power, the struggle between the economic or sensate and the ideational forces in life. Further, a study of art from the side of formal values alone, withdrawn from the context of associational and useful values, demands as its basis the a priori assumption that purely formal values exist alone or are based upon a separate aesthetic instinct. Experience does not support this point of view. If the formal values alone are considered worthy of study, then it must follow that that art in which use or associational values play the least

---

[1] The term "ideational" refers to that property of art which enables it to convey thought or meaning as well as to stimulate emotions that might be considered of social value.

part would be the finest or highest form of art. In our brief review of three works of art, it became clear that the art of the musician best filled this requirement. Many years ago Plato advanced this line of argument, stating categorically that "All arts must approach the condition of music." To the musician this may seem quite proper, but, as may be imagined, it appears unfair to architects and potters, whose arts are physically useful.

The Employment of Aesthetic Choice. In considering the selection of an appropriate bit of clothing such as a necktie or hat, we discover that an intelligent choice calls for complicated intellectual and intuitive processes. The selection of a painting for a room, the buying of a motorcar, the planning of a new city hall or railway station would follow the same procedure but would be still more involved. Our brief discussion of Lincoln's Gettysburg Address disclosed something of the mental processes involved when the dramatist plans his play or a community pageant. Finally, on approaching the abstract work of a great musical genius, we found the same values that made the other selections appropriate. The man who arranges or appreciates works of art undergoes, in a lesser degree, the mental processes of the artist, and needs a similar training.

The Substance of Art

From this brief discussion of art and daily living it becomes apparent that art is not something off in the purple hazes which only a few privileged souls may enjoy. Rather, it touches and has touched the life of everyone in almost every direction. As the result of better educational facilities and the conscious use of improved art forms by all sorts of social and business enterprises, the modern man has become more aware of art than were former generations. Even more intelligently, then, than ever before we may ask: "What is art— that is—what is excellent art?" For centuries, philosophers and aestheticians have

been seeking to answer this brief but pointed question.

How Art Gains Significance. As we have seen, the mere fact of formal expression alone cannot

Fig. 3.—The haphazard.

suffice for a definition of art, because our minds are so constituted that some slight desire for use or associational ideas hovers about everything we see or feel. So, in the second place, the desire for expression must be released in some way that makes the end result socially acceptable, either by ministering to or amusing one's fellow men, or else by clarifying the individual's own mind and helping him to grow. That is, it must have significance.

For example, a child thoughtlessly snapping the shutter of a camera might take a fortuitous picture of a segment of life (Fig. 3). Such a photograph could in no measure be called art. In the hands of a Stieglitz or a Bourke-White the same camera would yield a view displaying a pattern or a design, that is, a section of life whose arrangement of detail would have the power to stimulate the imagination, by recalling a grouping of associational values (Fig.

Fig. 4.—Toward the beautiful. (*Photograph by Stevenson.*)

4). By choosing carefully among various papers or developing media, by eliminating lights or shadows in the printing process, the photographer can gain a still higher degree of expressive quality. On occasion, using the technique of the painter, the photographer may even draw lines upon the negative or expunge parts of the image. Beyond this, however, to gain still greater expression in the art of photography, he needs the motion-picture camera, which allows him to enter the dramatic field, or he must turn draftsman and study the works of Dürer or of Rembrandt. These artists not only could eliminate details, but by the manipulation of lines suggested both the physical life of the outer world and the spiritual life or meaning which pulses through all nature. In this way they expressed themselves as parts

of the life of nature in significant objective patterns.

The Triple Character of Artistic Goals. All men grow through artistic expression in one of three

Fig. 5.—The energetic.

ways. Having defined the means by which art arises from the desire for expression toward an objective pattern, we need to define the end results, or goals.

Modern scholars such as Read and Hulme have pointed to the difficulties in attempting to define art in terms of one goal. They call attention to the fact that certain cultures or races have found the end goals to a great extent in the life and energy which almost seem to mirror their own self-confidence. Such art is representational. Other races, however, seek their end goals in more rigid types of geometrical forms, which seem to express a desire for peace or perhaps an escape from the turmoil and bafflement of life. Such arts are nonrepresentational and abstract. To such philosophers,

Here it is proposed that the goals of art are not simply dual but triple. For example, returning to the illustration of the photographs, we see that one picture (Fig. 4) has a fine bal-

FIG. 6.—Toward the sublime.

the ultimate goal, which they call "beauty," is one in which the two elements of passion for life and of order unite to make a balance. With this highly intuitive perception of at least a duality of artistic goals we must agree. But since the word "beauty" has come to have a definite association with the classical (Greek and Roman art) and with certain formal qualities tending toward a feeling of restfulness, we must abandon it here as a term to express the final goal or the definition of the greatest possible ideal of art. Undoubtedly, an unbiased judgment of the great work of art requires a formula of relativity. Since some arts are relatively static and spatial, others dynamic and temporal, they must, by their very nature, strive for differing effects. Necessarily an art, like the opera or the motion picture, that includes both kinds can be judged only in terms of a formula that embraces the temporal and spatial aspects of art.

ance of parts with a grouping of associational values all of which suggest rest. We unconsciously say, "How beautiful!" Another picture (Fig. 5) has a combination of lines and forms all of which tend to make us feel restless and dynamic, perhaps inspiring the imagination to explore new fields of action. Such a picture may be called "energetic." But if the photograph (Fig. 6) gives us a feeling of the immensity of nature, the vast stretches of the prairie, the abiding strength of the mountain, or the awesome aspect of the stormy sky above the wind-tossed seas, we say that it has elements of the Sublime.

Recognizing that art is an expression of man's nature in terms of significant patterns, we must agree that these patterns tend to approximate three general types of perfection—the Beautiful, the Energetic, and the Sublime. Finally, the greatest work of art conceivable would be one in which is contained a complete synthesis of these qualities, resulting in a state of Unity, Harmony, or Equilibrium, depending on which of the three goals—the static, the dynamic, or the awe-inspiring—seemed most significant to the personality experiencing the work of art.

Toward a Tentative Definition of Art. So our definition must finally read: "Art is an expression of the nature of man in significant patterns which tend to induce feelings for the Beautiful, the Energetic, and the Sublime."

The definition above constitutes a small part of what may be called "aesthetic philosophy." If the student finds it difficult, he may be assured that this book will have only as much aesthetic philosophy as is absolutely necessary. Its purpose is to approach the entire subject of art from the bottom, that is, from an observation of phenomena. In pursuit of this purpose, the method of study will be that which Aristotle called "Knowledge on the way up." Aristotle is responsible also for the modern scientific view that man must learn by first observing, then experimenting, and finally by creating a philosophic definition based on the results of his objective labors. Ours is to be a study of art from the scientific (or observational) and creative (or experimental) points of view.

To summarize, we shall observe the evolution of the arts as they resulted from man's partly mental and partly physical activity. In experimental laboratory work, we may, in addition, have pleasurable activity, which is the act of creation itself. And finally, we shall make a scientific study of the theories that led to aesthetics, or the philosophy of art. Thus, this book proposes to help create a more enlightened definition of the term "art" arising from information about and understanding of what man has heretofore called "art." This definition, which will grow from chapter to chapter throughout the book, will take into consideration the personal creation of new ideas, so that we can say with justice that art is the language of the soul; but it will also include an introspective study of the psychological phenomena occurring as the student creates his own art in

the laboratory. We shall see that art is the way in which man unifies the emotional and intellectual aspects of his life so that the results of his struggle may be most successfully transmitted to others. As we examine the environmental factors out of which art grew in the past, it will become apparent that the artist, in his dreams of a more unified mental state, really was connecting two opposing poles of being—the personally useful, or self-preservative, egotistic desires and the desire to make himself socially acceptable.

Expression of Art—Music, Painting, and Literature. We may reach another, more indirect, definition of art by learning what things are commonly called "arts." The arts often have been divided into the categories of spatial, literary, choreutic, and musical. Under the term "spatial" are understood to be the graphic and plastic arts of sculpture, drawing, and painting, as well as an art that seems to combine them, architecture. Under the term "literary" fall the arts of poetry, oratory, and storytelling, or narrative. The term "choreutic," which is derived from the Greek word for the dramatic chorus, comprises the arts of the dance, the pantomime, and the dramatic presentation with words. From time to time, one or the other of these forms absorbs the rest. The drama, for example, draws upon most of the other forms for its most complete emotional expression.

In the course of groping for a definition of art, we found ourselves, without intention, taking a number of points of view. Each of these points of view is one unconsciously held by the artists creating in one of the arts. Sculpture, for example, is an art using forms and masses that seem to "make clear" and "make permanent" our emotions and ideals. Painting is an art that strives to "make simple" or "to make interesting" by means of color patterns the emotional tensions that continually arise in our relationship to our environment. The dance strives to give expression to our feelings in pleasant patterns of bodily movement, which often unite our own personal rhythms to the rhythms and melodies of music from without. Like the drama, the dance calls for a great amount of social interplay. The drama, in turn, strives to capture a few moments of man's "journeying" and to heighten them so that we feel more aware of our relationship to our fellow man and to our natural environment. Architecture makes of our homes more than mere hovels— rather, ceremonial dwellings for family life, places which our friends may enjoy. Poetry and music capture the sounds of words or of many-timbred instruments and arrange them in rhythmical sequences so that they suggest moods or ideas.

The arts of pottery, utensil, or furniture making, as well as the designing of clothing, all contain the values which appear in their essence in the arts of sculpture, painting, architecture, dance, drama, poetry, and music.

Since this book has for its purpose a comprehensive explanation of the term "art," it seems necessary to study all the arts in their relationship to one another. This necessity arises because of the fact that, during a period when one art has dominated the others, its principles have been used to judge the products in the other arts. This situation will be made clear in later chapters. Furthermore, the same descriptive terms are used in several arts. Many of the terms common to music, such as "rhythm" and "harmony," are used to describe elements in painting and design. We find the word "phrase" in both poetry and music. The term "planes" applies to architecture, sculpture, and painting. The term "form," which probably started with the making of pottery or a figure of clay, has run through all the arts, finally coming to describe the tenuous structure of verse. The primary meanings of the descriptive terms used in criticism will also reveal themselves in the following chapters.

The history of the development of the graphic and plastic arts, dealing as it does with the less ephemeral types, has been used in this study to furnish a concrete framework on which the other arts are arranged. This treatment arises from no desire on the part of the author to insinuate a precedence for the spatial arts. Expediency has dictated this practical procedure, since it has been found that the student appreciates a plan of study that he can easily visualize. Musicians who read this book may imagine a musical plot or melody as the central motif, if they wish, using the other arts to demonstrate the rhythm and harmony of the subject.

The Relation of Art to Environment. The artistic products of any culture result from complex conditions determined by race, climate, trade, and physical surroundings. The ideal art forms of a culture, once they have been created in a monumental style through the efforts of the master artists, move, as articles of export, to adjacent cultures. In the new environment they undergo changes and result in a new or hybrid style.

The ultimate bases of all art, however, lie deep in nature. In natural creation man finds the inspiration, as well as some of the tools and materials, for most of his work. The rhythmical sequence of the seasons, the colors of the forests, the deserts, and the changing sky, as well as precious stones, metals, and the pigment earths, influence the artistic production of man much more than he is aware that they do. A few years ago the author was asked by an automobile manufacturer to design appropriate charts of color schemes for use on automobiles to be sold in three different environments— desert regions, fertile plains, and seacoasts. The people in these different regions, it seemed, desired different sets of colors, in accordance with their surroundings.

The Greek temple was in great measure the result of the availability of a large supply of easily worked marble, while skyscrapers are possible only in a land with abundant supplies of iron ore, cheap coal, and the ingredients of glass and cement. Most of the spatial arts depend on natural environment for their stylistic qualities. Particularly is this true where the element of use value ranks relatively high. On the other hand, those elements in the work of art called the "associational" or "ideational" can best be studied in terms of the relationship between the artist at work and the culture pattern that produced him.

Culture and Art

Everyone has heard of culture periods such as the Golden Age of Pericles, the Augustan Age, the Dark Ages, and the Renaissance. These politico-historical concepts, constructed to dramatize periods in which various historians were particularly interested, sometimes mislead the beginning student. The student of art, while recognizing a certain dependence on these politico-historical concepts, should place more emphasis on the long-time cultural and geographic distribution of art than upon the historical.

It must be remembered that, although certain members of the human race have moved through a number of these historical periods, other members have remained on primitive levels of social development. Some of us possess a very sophisticated background transmitted to us by cultured parents and teachers, while others may come from primitive, almost Stone Age surroundings. Those who have aboriginal African or American Indian backgrounds cannot help approaching art from a more vital, colorful, creative angle than does the descendant of a New England Puritan. On the other hand, the student with a Latin inheritance from Italy or France will conceive of art in a way quite different from that of the Scandinavian or the Chinese. In our American communities all types have equal opportunities for study. If, therefore, we are to make art comprehensible to these varying mental patterns, we should recognize four general types of culture, with corresponding mental patterns: the Primitive, the Mediterranean or Classical, the Gothic or Celto-Germanic, and the Oriental. Under these headings the evolution of all man's arts may best be studied.

The Primitive Culture Pattern. Individuals in the primitive state exist unaware of universal culture patterns outside their own tribes. A student without some aesthetic background approaches this course as a Primitive. In the first quarter of his year's study he may learn that several types of art—art as the physically useful, art as personal adornment, and art as a religious fetish—rightfully belong to him as values first recognized by his fellow Primitives in the caves of France thousands of years ago. As he conscientiously experiments with the arts and comes to understand the meaning of the primitive values, the alert student should outgrow his primitivism early in the year, finding new and more advanced values in art through a study of the other three cultures.

The Mediterranean, or Classical-Humanistic, Culture Pattern. As far as we know today, man first left the purely primitive state of culture when he invented writing and recorded his history. This seems to have taken place in either Egypt or Mesopotamia for the Western world and in northwestern India or the valley of the Yangtze Kiang for the Eastern world. Out of a union of the arts of Egypt and Assyria, with fresh primitive infusions from the Danube River valley, arose the Classical-Mediterranean culture. Classical art characteristically displays an underlying geometric quality first found in the hieratic or priestly stiffness of Egyptian sculpture. This style exists in its purest form in the works of the first 400 years of early Greek sculpture, and in the Etruscan, Byzantine, and Romanesque styles. Today it occurs in the works of modern artists like Picasso, Meštrović, Bourdelle, and Lawrie. On this geometric form the Greeks of the Periclean age wove a finely balanced pattern of naturalistic human shapes. The complete classical pattern of art, found in Greek drama and music as well as in sculpture and painting, was taken over by the Romans. Revived in the Italian art of the 15th and 16th centuries, it comes to us today in the so-called academic-classicist productions. The Greeks, who considered art as a narration of historical and legendary events contributing to the development of the perfect individual within the religion of the state, created their art through an idealization of the human form. In the words of Pope, the 18th-century classicist English poet, these humanists held that "the proper study of mankind is man." From this fundamental belief arises the humanist concept of culture. In the second quarter of the year the student studies the classical or humanist origins of our present-day artistic styles, with particular reference to the very interesting relationship between Greek sculpture, drama, painting, architecture, and music.

The Celto-Germanic, or Gothic, Culture Pattern. The men who lived in the forests of northern Europe after the Old Stone Age left the primitive state of culture at about the time of the birth of Christ, bringing with them a pattern of thought different in many ways from that of the classical man. Whereas the classical man saw art as an ideal enchancement of human values, the northerner was conscious particularly of the fact that life is a struggle and a perilous journey. He thought of art as a sort of guidepost on the road to some far-off Utopia. Instead of the constant underlying geometric form, this northern artist used the endless, interwoven melodic line to express his feelings. He, too, adopted the human form at various times in his development, but he twisted this form and elongated it so much that it is often hard to find. (See Fig. 379, Chap. XIII.) The earliest pottery from the lake dwellings of the Danube River valley, as well as designs on vases from Persia, and those on the early Cretan Kamares ware, indicate close relationships with the Celtic iron and bronze works of the La Tène culture, which were produced 500 years before Christ. The La Tène culture, in turn, transmitted these fundamental Celto-Germanic designs to the Gothic sculpture and painting of the 13th century and to the flamboyant architecture of the 15th. Thus the decorative crafts flowered into the monumental paintings and architecture of the baroque. Our own later Romantic painters, finding their newest expression on the American continents through the monumental modern murals of Benton, Rivera, Orozco, and the WPA muralists, mostly create in this style.

In the third period of the study the student discovers how the Christian church captured the imagination of the Celto-Germans. From the church derived the story of the Biblical heroes whose fight for a God of Justice particularly suited the intense Celto-Germanic nature. The Celto-German is seldom completely at home with the purely classical form of art. His development of that Christian mental attitude which is called a "conscience," plus his desire to express struggling inner tensions, has led him to seek an art in which erotic and human elements are subordinate to abstract lines, or, better still, to the rhythms, melodies, and harmonies of music. In this culture pattern, the great Gothic cathedrals and orchestral musical composition give primary meaning to artistic thought. The aesthetic criterion desired is not human beauty but Sublimity and Energy.

The Oriental Culture Pattern. The culture pattern of the Asiatic countries first grew out of the primitive in northwestern India and in the valley of the Yangtze Kiang. Oriental culture differs from the classical in that it does not stress the geometric in art. It differs from the Gothic, in that it does not value the element of tension or struggle. Instead, the Oriental seems to think of art as a very necessary part of his ceremonious daily living. To an Occidental, Oriental art often appears to have retained its primitive simplicity. Further study, however, reveals that it is intricate, and possesses a highly developed ideational meaning. The reason for this continuation of simplicity and subtlety appears to be that Oriental man actually developed out of the primitive without ever passing through an outspokenly humanistic stage. For him man never was so bold or foolish as to conceive of himself as opposed to nature. Consequently, the Oriental thinks of art as one of the healthy functions of nature. Such a point of view, as will be seen, can include both the Gothic and the Classical.

The Oriental culture pattern, as exemplified in its painting and sculpture, usually reduces all appearance to a design of flat, colored surfaces in which both sculptured forms and interwoven lines lose themselves. People, plants, animals, and even the larger elements of the landscape, such as clouds and mountains, appear in a non-spatial or flat world of dreamlike pictures. This method of representation, which with minor variations is native to both Indian and Chinese art, can be found from time to time crossing with the Gothic and classical European modes. In Europe it appears in Byzantine manuscript illumination, in the Gothic stained-glass windows, and in the works of some of the northern German and Flemish masters. In modern art it can be recognized in the paintings of Gauguin, Cézanne, Matisse, and Redon, or in the sculpture of Brancusi.

Our modern style, therefore, is an outcome of the fusion of all the above cultures and styles. In the final part of the book, the reader is asked to examine man's art through Oriental eyes and then to evaluate the art of our modern scienific age, which started with the Italian Renaissance. He does this in terms of the best creations of all four cultures. Lacking acquaintance with all these styles, modern man cannot hope to form an intelligent judgment of the worth of present-day artistic creations. To any great work of art a certain amount of culture must be brought if there is to be any deep appreciation of its finest qualities.

Two Universal Art Types

In science and philosophy words are but tools forged to help hew out new intellectual concepts. In art they act as carriers of emotional energy, with power to sway our feelings. In a study such as this we need a few tool words that will carry with them the least possible amount of old associative emotional energy. Two of these words, "physioplastic" and "ideo-

plastic," invented by the Swiss psychologist Verworn, will be used throughout the book to describe two essentially different points of view from which the artist has approached his un-created work. These points of view, having universal meaning, cut across all the cultural styles. They merit definition here.

Physioplastic, or Representational, Art. Physio-plastic art attempts to reproduce as nearly as possible the appearance of things in nature, de-pending for its effect on the pleasurable ele-ment played by the recognition of objects with which one has become familiar (Fig. 23*b*). The words "representational," "realistic," "natur-alistic," "concrete," and "sensate" have all been used at various times in trying to describe this same fundamental artistic phenomenon. Unfortunately, these words have associated themselves with art movements, and so carry a certain amount of emotional feeling. They can-not serve as sharp tools and will be used only in connection with the historic styles that pro-duced them. Examples of physioplastic art are the paintings of prehistoric bison from Alta-mira (Fig. 19*c*, Chap. II) and the Surrender of Breda, by Velazquez (Fig. 515, Chap. XVI).

Ideoplastic, or Nonrepresentational, Art. Ideo-plastic art attempts to suggest meaning with a minimum amount of recognizable representa-tive material, depending for its effect upon the provocative use of imaginative geometric pat-tern. In creating ideoplastic art, the artist feels very strongly that the material charged with emotional meaning comes from within himself. The work arises in some idea which he wishes to express rather than from the reproduction of a pleasantly perceived object. In this type of art the objects used to express the idea often call to mind recognizable natural forms; still more often, however, they tend to give only such recognizable natural form as is necessary to carry the message. Ideoplastic art frequently seems "abstracted from reality" or "stylized" (Fig. 405*c*, Chap. XIV). It has been called "ab-stract," "ideal," "nonrepresentational," "ide-ological," and even "pure" art, to distinguish it from the physioplastic art. These terms, like those previously discussed in connection with physioplastic art, are not objective enough. Modern writers on aesthetics use them, with all their pleasant or unpleasant connotation, either to praise friends who belong to the same or sympathetic schools of aesthetic thought or to damn critical opponents. Imagine, if you can, an admirer of the works of John Singer Sargent (Fig. 625, Chap. XIX) striving to give an objective criticism of the work of Pablo Picasso (Fig. 575, Chap. XVIII).

Since the mind of modern man inherits both points of view and since his patterns of judgment are based unconsciously upon some slight acquaintance with the art styles of Orient as well as Occident, he should review his inheritance before attempting any critical judgment of present-day art. It may well be that the most useful critical attitude for the 20th century is one that unites both points of view. The belief that this is so gains elaboration with further study throughout the pages of this book.

The Objectives of This Study

An examination of the general background so far presented demonstrates to the inquiring mind that the field of study justly called "the newest of the humanities" holds a vital and timely interest. We may now proceed to a more concise statement of the objectives of this volume. This statement will not only serve as a map or guide to the book, but may prove particularly helpful at a time when our entire concept of education is in a necessary process of remodeling, owing to the vitalizing present-day intermixture of culture patterns.

The four objectives of this book are as follows:

1. To bring the student into close contact with a few great works of art so that he may see how they arose from their pertinent culture patterns. This we shall call "understanding the classics of art."

2. To acquaint the student with the formal principles of composition in the arts illustrated.

This we call "recognition of the formal principles."

3. To demonstrate that intelligent criticism has enhanced rather than destroyed the creation and enjoyment of fine works of art. This we shall call the "critical use of art principles."

4. To encourage the student to take an active part in the creation of the art of our times. This we shall call "enjoyment of art through re-creation."

Understanding the Classics of Art. Any attempt to bring the reader into intimate contact with the greatest works of art through the pages of a book calls for a compromise. Photographic illustrations can never take the place of the originals in size or color. Phonograph records make the matter a little easier for reproductions of music. Whenever possible, the student should seek the originals in art galleries, parks, streets, and concert halls, never forgetting that the common objects of art with which he comes in contact in his daily life partake of the same principles as those examples which man deems more precious. This book, with its illustrations, can only serve to guide the student toward the finest works produced by the greatest artists in the four culture patterns. It can serve to demonstrate or suggest how the works resulted naturally from the dominant thought forms in these different culture patterns. This method of study includes the story of the development of an artistic style in the graphic and plastic arts with reference to similar expressions in architecture, drama, music, and the dance. Wherever possible, the reactions between the artist and the society of his time are suggested. In many cases it can be demonstrated that the artist's productions have been influenced by the social and economic forces that have played upon him; whether, for example, he be a slave or a free man, a member of the community or an outcast.

Recognition of the Formal Principles. To acquaint the reader with the formal principles of the various arts exemplified in the illustrations constitutes the second objective of the book. This necessarily follows the discovery of those principles in nature and their identification as they occur in the works of man. The identification of formal principles through historic examples, however, will not alone suffice. If the reader is to understand formal values, they must be associated in his memory with the social and economic conditions under which the artist used them.

The Critical Use of Art Principles. The third objective of the book—to furnish the reader with some critical insight into art—presents greater difficulty. It follows that the critical analysis of a work of art calls for much more than a knowledge of its historical and formal aspects. Critical analysis demands, in addition, a high degree of imaginative energy. The critic must be able to imagine himself in the place both of the artist and of the person or society for which the art was created. He must feel keenly the needs that called forth the work before he can judge how well the work filled these needs. Secondly and paradoxically, although the art critic must be able to call upon his imagination, he must continually strive to be objective and analytical, so that he may judge the work not only from the standpoint of his likes and dislikes but also according to some general rational principles. How difficult this ideal of criticism can be and how rarely it is achieved may be seen by reading the current art criticisms in daily papers and magazines. These will serve to convince the reader that objectivity plus background and a knowledge of formal principles is rare. Two examples of modern critical essays may serve to make this clear.

The artist-critic Coleridge once wrote as part of his criticism of the poetry of Wordsworth: "Good sense is the body of artistic genius; fancy, its drapery; motion, its life; and imagination, the soul that is everywhere and in each; the last forming all into one graceful and intelligent whole." This definition seems conclusive and unbiased. The mood of the remainder of the essay, however, grows from the idea that good sense constitutes the body—the chief part—of artistic genius. This idea differs considerably from the thesis of Shelley's critical essay in defense of poetry. Shelley wrote:

Poetry in a general sense may be defined to be the expression of the imagination, and poetry is connate with the origins of man. Man is an instrument over which a series of external and internal impressions are driven, like the alternations of an ever-changing wind over an Aeolian lyre, which move it by their motion to ever-changing melody.

In the first definition, the component elements of artistic genius pertain to the nature of man—good sense or intellect representing the body; fancy, its drapery; motion, its life; imagination, its soul. Shelley's definition, however, places no emphasis upon the intellect or intelligence. For him art seems almost altogether a matter of inspiration, with the free air of heaven, like the breath of God, singing itself as an intangible melody. Coleridge has followed the Classic tradition in criticism; Shelley, the Gothic or Romantic tradition. Of course, each of these men, having qualities of unusual genius, eventually developed his point of view until finally it included that of the other. A study of the entire critical essay by Coleridge and of the *Defence of Poetry* by Shelley would make this clear.

The primary objective of all critical study lies in this broadening of the critical or analytic abilities. Unless one is a trained, clear thinker, he usually brings to the work of art only his unconscious, intuitive reactions—in the words of Panofsky, "there is no naïve beholder." The task of critical analysis is to evaluate our intuitive reactions in terms of conscious reason. A full understanding of the chief principles of criticism, which may start at either of the opposite poles of the ideoplastic or the physioplastic points of view, will include a knowledge of the proper weight to be given to the useful, associational, and formal values of art.

Enjoyment of Art through Re-creation. The fourth objective of the book consists in encouraging the student to obtain through laboratory exercises the confidence to enjoy an active participation in the various arts. Expression by means of the arts not only frees one from many personal superstitions concerning them but also leads to a more intelligent critical attitude. Since few students have great talent, there is little or no chance of mastering completely an artistic medium during a brief course of laboratory work. However, the objective knowledge of artistic productions gained through experiments in creation leads to a deeper understanding of the art work of the genius. Only a society with a creative critical consciousness can produce, recognize, and support artists of great genius.

Rationale for the Synthetic Study of Art

Some thirty years before the birth of Christ there lived in Rome the first international art critic. This philosopher, Longinus by name, wrote a short treatise called "On the Sublime." In this treatise, which deals particularly with the literary arts and oratory, Longinus tried to answer the question most perplexing to the thoughtful educator: "Can art ever be taught —or does it not result from some God-given inherited talent?"

The Position of Longinus. Longinus resolved the difficulty by concluding that, although the power to create art depends upon "genuine emotion in the right place, which is a gift, rather than an acquired quality," even people without any great measure of that gift could be educated in what we earlier described as the formal values of art. Thereupon, Longinus listed these formal values, not neglecting to leave a place for an X quality, which he called "a touch of the Sublime." Almost 2,000 years after Longinus, the German philosopher, Immanuel Kant, took up this line of criticism where the earlier man had left it and characterized the formal human values as the "Beautiful." The Sublime, wrote Kant, exists as an eternal, law-abiding quality of the Universe. A mature individual should recognize his innate Sublime inspirational capacities and guide his life by Kant's "categorical imperative": "Act as though by your very action what you do may become a law of the universe." This principle has become the dominant philosophy of the modern artist. Today, in our age of democracy, it appears increasingly that everyone has some capacity for artistic creation, if the field of all the arts be accepted as legitimate creating ground. Today everyone dances; many have fine dramatic and poetic intuitions. Many, perhaps, have inherited skills in the spatial arts, though we cannot be certain of this because, in general, our educational system has not given us the opportunity to develop these skills. It becomes a specific educational task for modern man to review the arts experimentally and to find where in his social group his aesthetic talents may best be used. If he then finds that he lacks the will or the energy to create, he may contribute to the growth of culture by being an intelligent audience.

Longinus advocated that the art of the great masters should be studied for its use and associational values or, if one were desirous of perfection, because these masters had appropriately used the formal values. "The young writer," said he, "should ask, 'How would Homer have listened to this passage of mine?'" Great is the ordeal if we propose such a jury to listen to our utterances, but even more stimulating could it be to add, "If I write this, how would all posterity receive it?"

Striving for an objective, scientific judgment on the efficacy of artistic creations, Longinus proposed the common-sense democratic method of "taking a vote." "To speak generally, you should consider that to be truly beautiful and sublime which pleases all people at all times, for when men differ in their habits, their tastes, their ages, their dates, yet all agree in holding the same view about the same writings, then the unanimous verdict makes our faith in the admired passage strong and indisputable." This is the thought pattern by which the classical critic, at his best, is almost sure to judge the arts. It is essentially the method of the dramatist who believes that his play is good if an intelligent audience likes it.

The Method of Leonardo da Vinci. Artists living and thinking within the Gothic culture pattern placed less emphasis on what men thought about their art. Such artists held their own feelings of integrity to be of highest value; these they judged by the degree of "self-release" or "oneness with God" experienced during the act of creation. Thus the Gothic artists and the critics who followed them became more interested in expression than in formal values of beauty. The power of expression seemed to the Gothic artist to come from a mystical communion with Nature, or from the materials which God put into his hands. Hence, in the Middle Ages, the novice in art apprenticed himself to some master, from whom he absorbed the aesthetic philosophy of the Christian church, along with the formal elements of his craft. He started his career grinding colors and preparing the grounds for his painting. He found spiritual companionship as a member of some monastic community or among his associates in a craft guild.

Growing from this Gothic development, but with some historical background gained by reading the works of classical critics like Longinus, Leonardo da Vinci told his pupils that if they wanted to be really great artists they must study the formal values in the works of the old masters. At other times, speaking as a man with a Gothic background, Leonardo stressed the idea that the student must experiment with artistic techniques, going to nature for his ultimate inspiration. In his life and work Leonardo was one who united the two points of view later to be held by Coleridge and Shelley.

This book attempts to follow the advice of both Longinus and Leonardo da Vinci, bring-ing the reader into contact with the formal values in the work of the masters, while encouraging original creation under the inspiration of those inner drives that arise in nature or out of the reader's relationship to his fellow beings. Every age, as the student will here see demonstrated, has wrought such new artistic forms as were necessary to express the ever-expanding range of emotional experiences. The present-day mind represents in some measure the accumulation of all past thought patterns. If the individual would be well educated, his mind must contain an active, usable selection of the best of that past thought and its concomitant, the record of man's emotional strivings, in his treasury of arts. The student, experimenting for himself, will find that if he wishes to carry his art to a point of perfection, he must measure his experiments against the works of the great masters.

The Modern Pragmatic Approach. Specifically, the pedagogic methods for achieving the four objectives of the book are as follows:

1. Geographical and historical study, using the textbook, with art maps, charts, and illustrations.

2. Discovery of formal values in the illustrations and the creation of art works based upon these values in the laboratory.

3. Critical discussions in the laboratory and by means of test questions, or by written essays designed to exercise the critical faculty.

4. Encouragement of a spirit of communal play in the laboratory work.

Art History as Cultural and Social Geography. After studying each chapter, the student should have an insight into the social or economic and geographic background of culture. In each culture, the ideal appears at first, half consciously, in its poetic mythology, later taking concrete form in its dance, drama, painting, and sculpture.[1] In examining any work of art scientifically, the student should first determine who made it and what the artist wanted to portray

[1] Wundt has demonstrated in his *Völkerpsychologie*, Bd. 1, Teil 1, p. 277, 3d ed., 1911, that this is so for all primitive cultures. See also, Havelock Ellis, *The Dance of Life*, Modern Library, Inc., New York, 1929.

or express. These facts constitute the naming and dating of the work. The work identified, the student proceeds to a discussion of the culture that brought it forth and the relationship of the artist to that culture. This reveals the social purpose that may be said to belong to the work of art. The work may next be examined for the way in which formal values are used to express that social purpose. These formal values, once designed for a given culture, should be weighed against the purpose of the work in order that their effectiveness may be determined. Only in this matter-of-fact, unromantic way can the answer be found for the primary critical question: "Was this art effective for the situation for which it was made?"

In examining for this first objective of historical and geographical research, the following form has been found useful.

Work of art	Culture		Why	Principles involved
What	Where	When		
Name of work and artist	Place of origin	Time of origin	Social purpose	

The Determination of Formal Aesthetic Values. In examining the work of art to determine its formal aesthetic values, sketches or notes should be made by the student during the lecture periods. These notes should be further amplified in connection with the exercises in the laboratory notebook. The examination of the student's knowledge of this material may be reduced to his answers in the end column of the above chart, plus his solution of the laboratory problems.

The Critical Use of Art Principles. In examining the work of art critically, the student should begin with an analysis of his own feelings concerning it. The first question should be "Do I feel drawn to the work of art?" the second, "Does it correspond to my Gothic or classic mood of art criticism?" the third, "How did it appear to the culture which produced it?" and last, "What is the relation between the formal and associational values within the work, that is, do they balance or does one weigh heavier than the other?"

The critical study of art, including both approaches, is the one most difficult for the beginner. Most of us approach works of art as primitives, saying simply, "I like it because it pleases me," thus unconsciously stressing use values. A less primitive attitude is that which accords the work historic or systematic study: "Painting in fresco, by Giotto, 13th century, Bardi Chapel, Santa Croce, Florence, Death of St. Francis." This still ignores the chief values of the work. The approach taken in many art-appreciation courses consists in examining the formal values: "Parthenon pediment, sculpture, absolute balance; Medici tombs, sculpture, absolute balance." Naturally, the mere recognition of the formal values in the last two carries one but little further than the recognition of historical data. The very creative attitude necessary to pull all these things together into an intelligent criticism cannot be easily taught or easily tested. Recently one of the most highly regarded British teachers of art, Professor Herbert Read of the University of Edinburgh, wrote that the greatest difficulty encountered in attempting to teach courses in the appreciation of art arose because he could find no satisfactory way of testing his endeavors. A course given from the point of view of formal values alone, with creative work in the laboratory, succeeds only in making artistic productions that are lacking in taste. Common sense and cultural background, plus a lively imagination, combine in the critic or appreciator of art. The only true test of this ability lies in the production of critical works or essays in criticism or in open debate on the merits of contrasting works of art carried on between teacher and student, or between students, in the laboratory period.

Laboratory Exercises and the Re-creation of Art.
Laboratory exercises have been developed by
the author to reintroduce the student to those
creative activities usually left at fourth- or fifth-
grade levels. These have been based upon the
fact that most students have had in the kinder-
garten, at least, some exercises in artistic play.
The laboratory exercises, beginning with
fundamental forms in music and dancing, appeal to social instincts, which are then concentrated in the exercise of graphic and plastic
arts. Because of recognition of the fact that
fundamental rhythms underlie all artistic
phenomena, the musical background is kept
throughout all the exercises, being heightened
for painting and abstract design and lessened
for the more static arts of pottery and sculpture.
The success of the laboratory work depends
primarily upon the willingness of the teachers
to try all the experiments first, to be able to
laugh at their own mistakes, and to discover
those students whose talents surpass their own.
When the students realize that the teacher can
take just criticism with good spirit, they will
carry the work forward themselves, criticizing
each other and raising the level of the class-
work. The real critics of the art work produced,

in the end, will turn out to be those great masters of the past under whom the students and
teacher alike are working. The chief purpose
of the course is best served when the students
feel that, introduced by the teacher, they are,
through their own endeavors, meeting the artists of the past.

Bibliography

PERRY, KREY, PANOFSKY, CALHOUN, and CHINARD:
Essays: *The Meaning of the Humanities*, by T. M.
Greene, Princeton University Press, Princeton,
1938.
SOROKIN, PITIRIM A.: *Social and Cultural Dynamics*,
Vol. I, "Fluctuation of Forms of Art," American
Book Company, New York, 1937.
COLERIDGE, SAMUEL TAYLOR: "Essay on Art" in
Book of Essays, edited by B. C. Williams, D. C.
Heath & Company, Boston, 1931.
SHELLEY, PERCY BYSSHE: "Defence of Poetry," in
Critical Essays of the Early Nineteenth Century,
edited by R. M. Alden, Charles Scribner's Sons,
New York, 1921.
DEWEY, JOHN: *Art as Experience*, Minton, Balch &
Company, New York, 1934.
READ, HERBERT E.: *Art and Society*, The Macmillan
Company, New York, 1937.

Recordings

Beethoven, *Fifth Symphony*, VM 245 album.

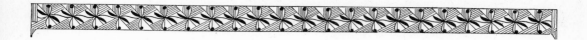

CHAPTER I

Principles and Elements of Art Structure Discovered in Nature

> Nature! . . . . She is the universal artist, creating
> the greatest contrasts from the simplest material,
> while achieving, without seeming to strive for it, an
> ultimate perfection. . . . . Each of her works has its
> own peculiar quality; every one of her manifold ap-
> pearances symbolizes a single concept and yet some-
> how blending they achieve unity. One must obey
> nature's laws even while he denies them: he is forced
> to produce with her aid even when he imagines that
> he is able to work against her.
>
> "NATURE"—A POETIC FRAGMENT[1]

A PRINCIPLE, in the general sense, names the original source or primordial sub-stance of a thing. In science, as usually taught, principles stand either as admitted without proof or as having been proved through man's previous experience. In art, a study continually subject to innovations, there exist two views concerning principles: (1) that a constant number of immutable formal princi-ples underlie all the arts; (2) that the artistic genius may through his work discover and use new principles. The mystic poet Blake de-scribed art in the lines:

> To see a world in a grain of sand,
>   Heaven in a wild flower,
> Hold Infinity in the palm of the hand,
>   Eternity in an hour.

Can so paradoxical a subject as art have fixed principles? The romanticist holds that art principles had best be left undefined, because they are essentially undefinable; the classicist asserts that they should and must be defined before any study of art can be attempted. Our attitude here must be that the essentially unde-finable subject, perfect art, can best be studied by discovering at the start a few tentative form-al principles in nature to which every succeed-ing age of man's culture has attributed new meaning. In greater part our study deals with the evolution of art and its various meanings.

The chief value in a historical approach to art arises from the fact that by this means the formal created art object can be viewed in its proper relation to the useful and associational values that brought it forth. Following the his-torical progression of art forms back to their origins, one arrives eventually in the realm of nature. There the principles and elements of art structure may be found in their simplest condition, before man endowed them with symbolic meaning. Since the purpose of this book is to follow the fortunes of these principles and elements throughout the history of human culture, they should be discovered first as they appear in nature.

A Tentative List of Formal Art Principles Revealed in Nature

Art strives to capture in permanent form the living essence of the growing, changeable spirit.

[1] JOHANN WOLFGANG VON GOETHE, *General Science*, Part I, pp. 5 *ff*.

In this process one principle is fixed—*no work of art can exist without unity.*[1] Because the various arts arise from two great aspects of being, time and space, artistic unity expresses itself in dif-

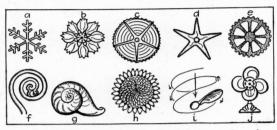

FIG. 7.—Principles underlying spatial arts. *a, b, c, d, e,* symmetry; *f, g, h,* radiation; *i, j,* dynamic source of radiation.

ferent ways, depending on the type of art in which it is sought. The first, or temporal, aspect causes man to express his feelings of growth and advance by means of movement and action in the temporal arts of music and the dance. The second, or spatial, aspect causes man to make harmonious or perfect the ever-changing aspects of nature in substantial form through the spatial arts of painting, sculpture, and architecture.

As the concepts of time and space serve the scientist for first principles under the concept of truth, so rhythm and harmony serve the artist under the concept of unity. The principle of rhythm seems particularly strong in all those arts that aid man to express the concept of time —the temporal arts; the principle of harmony, in those arts which serve to arrange visual phenomena in space—the spatial arts. Arts such as the drama and the modern motion picture, which arise from a union of the two concepts, derive their laws from combinations of the two sets of principles.

Principles Underlying the Spatial Arts

The spatial arts of sculpture, painting, architecture, pottery, and weaving, achieve their

unity through the manipulation of material in space. This manipulation proceeds according to the principles of symmetry and radiation— peculiar to the spatial arts—and balance, emphasis, measure, and harmony—common to both spatial and temporal arts.

Symmetry. The principle of symmetry occurs naturally in the most common inorganic and organic forms. The design of the snowflake (Fig. 7*a*), with its six spicules, or points, arranged around a common center, offers the best illustration from inorganic nature. The petals of a flower around the central organs (Fig. 7*b*) and the rays of the jellyfish and starfish (Fig. 7*c* and 7*d*) demonstrate the same principle in organic nature. From an observation of these may be derived a definition of symmetry as the equal arrangement of lines, forms, or planes, with or without color, around some central space or object (Fig. 7*e*).

Radiation. The principle of radiation appears in nature as a more dynamic aspect of spatial arrangement. The lines suggestive of growth in the unfolding tendril of a plant (Fig. 7*f*) or the shell of a snail (Fig. 7*g*) furnish the most common examples. The two principles of symmetry and radiation unite in the sunflower, whose symmetrical corollas frame a design of seeds in radiation (Fig. 7*h*). Man, appropriating the principle of radiation which he observed in motion when the whirling seed of the maple tree fell to the ground (Fig. 7*i*), invented the screw propeller and the electric fan (Fig. 7*j*), both of which have by some modern art critics been mistakenly considered works of art. As can be seen in these examples, radiation consists in the arrangement of lines, planes, or forms so that they seem to have a relationship suggesting some common origin in a given point, line, or object.

Balance. The principle of balance, like the principles of emphasis, measure, and harmony, belongs to both spatial and temporal arts. In the spatial art forms found in nature, balance

[1] Unity is that principle of a work of art which makes it appear consistent throughout, so that each part, while heightening the total effect, seems completely lost in the whole.

appears as the equal arrangement of lines, planes, or other elements, on each side of a central object, line, or space. Many growing plants put forth leaves equally spaced on both sides of a central stem (Fig. 8b). Minute animal forms and shellfish, such as the horseshoe crab (Fig. 8a) and the lobster, appear to be equally balanced. Man has used this principle of balance in his building to suggest stability, as in the case of the church façade (Fig. 8c) and the automobile illustrated (Fig. 8d). The arrangement of the spout and the handle of the teapot (Fig. 8e) also shows balance, although this balance appears quite different from that of the cathedral façade. The plant stem may have its leaves arranged in such a fashion that a small leaf appears, because of the subtle spacing, to balance a large leaf on the other side—a less obvious type of balance (Fig. 8f). Sometimes the principle of balance appears obvious or absolute, as when objects of equal weight are placed on both sides of a central object; at other times, as obscure or occult, as when two objects of unlike shape or size appear to have equal weight. Occult balance, being irregular, leads us logically to the principle of emphasis or contrast.

Emphasis. Most primitive men desire the regularity produced in nature by the principles of balance and symmetry. Modern man tires of monotonous effects and seeks emphasis and contrast to satisfy his need for progress and his feeling of growth. Fortunately, nature furnishes contrast in abundance. The flaming colors of autumn contrast with the cold blue-white blanket of the winter snow. The flat, desolate spaces of the desert contrast with the towering, pine-covered mountain peaks. Contrast, however, is most conspicuous when it appears as an emphasis upon something out of the ordinary. After becoming used to a long flat stretch of prairie, for example, a rider comes upon a single, tall pine. The tree, by emphasizing the flat, horizontal lines of the land, creates contrast. The amount of emphasis placed upon any one element, such as the

tree, balanced against the amount of contrasting background, such as the prairie, determines whether or not unity has been achieved. The achievement of perfect unity requires a proper

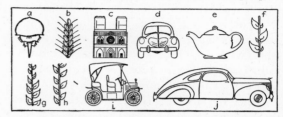

Fig. 8.—Principles underlying the spatial arts. *a, b, c, d,* absolute balance; *e, f,* occult balance; *g,* natural balance; *h,* mechanical measure; *i,* poor proportion; *j,* good proportion.

proportion of one element in relation to the others. Unity cannot be achieved by emphasis alone. Overemphasis, in fact, destroys unity. We come, thus, to a consideration of the principle of measure, or proportion.

Measure. A young plant with all its leaves presents a very nicely balanced but complex relationship of parts. The leaves farther down the stem seem larger than those above (Fig. 8g) —a natural condition in a growing organism. This natural relationship between areas in a composition constitutes its measure, or proportion. A comparison of the two stems illustrated will show that the one with leaves tapering from large to small has a natural measure. The other, because of the purely mechanical repetition of the leaves upon the stem, seems unnatural (Fig. 8h). Man seeks measure, or proportion, in all his works of art. Compare the old-style automobile (Fig. 8i), with its small wheels, short body, and relatively high top, with the newer car, which has greater length and less height (Fig. 8j). The relationship of one part to another in size, shape, or weight constitutes the measure or proportion of a work of art.

Harmony. The principles of symmetry, radiation, balance, emphasis, and measure blend harmoniously in all works of spatial art. The final principle of harmony arises when the relationship of colors, lines, planes, or forms in a design or composition is most satisfactory. The satisfaction, however, must be more than a purely pleasurable sensation; it must be based upon a logical arrangement of parts. In the spatial arts the term "harmony" practically coincides with the term "unity" as a fundamental principle. The difference exists only in the fact that unity to some extent considers associative and use values, whereas harmony has to do only with formal values.

Since the spatial arts include effects of color as well as line and form, one may observe subtle balances of color in nature, changing with the varying seasons of the year. In summer, under the hot sun, the green leaves of the forest seem almost grayed, with only here and there a touch of brilliant color producing an occult balance. In autumn, on the other hand, yellows, reds, and browns contrast in equal areas, so that one may speak of an absolute balance.

The term "harmony" for most people is associated with an effect in music. Harmony in music, as defined by Aristotle and Pythagoras, may be considered that principle involved when two or more parts or notes sound together. In nature, the principle of harmony can be understood only in terms of two or more activities proceeding at once. Any definition of this principle leads inevitably to a discussion of the principles involving the temporal arts.

Principles Underlying the Temporal Arts

The temporal arts of music, poetry, the dance, and drama achieve their unity through the manipulation of sound or moving forms over a duration of time. This manipulation must be undertaken according to the principles of rhythm, repetition, and melodic line, in addition to those of balance, measure, emphasis, and harmony.

Rhythm. The principle of rhythm in the temporal arts arises from the phenomenon of pulsation as it works in nature and in man. This pulsation, starting with the ceaseless ebb and flow of cosmic energy from the stars, may be studied through earthly phenomena in the tides of the sea, the turn of the seasons, and the rising and setting of the sun.

The mighty systole and diastole of external energy, light, and sound, repeat themselves within the body of man in the pulse, the rhythm of breathing, the fluctuations of the electrical impulses within the nerves of the brain, the movements of the visceral organs. All these rhythms of the body influence, without his consciousness, man's tone of expression.

Repetition. Listening to the tapping of the woodpecker or the pounding of the surf upon the shore, one may hear external rhythms which seem like one's own. Repetition, or beat, makes itself felt when there is a regular contrast between sound and nonsound occurring in measured intervals, so that a sequence of sounds in ordered design results. The monotonous beat of the drops from an icicle perhaps suggested to Edgar Allan Poe the beat of the opening lines of "The Raven":

> Once upon a midnight dreary,
> While I pondered, weak and weary, ...

Melodic Line. We find in a melodic line that principle most proper to the temporal arts and most difficult to translate into terms of the spatial arts. Melody is a succession of sounds rising and falling with reference to some given tone. If the student will read the preceding sentence aloud, for example, he will notice that his voice tends to fall naturally at the end. This peculiarity of all animal utterance, heightened and regularized in poetry, forms the basis of melodic line in music. The sensitive ear can distinguish an exact sequence of notes rising and falling in even so ordinary a thing as a prosaic daily greeting. To the musicians, the words, "How are you?" and the answer, "Pretty well, thank you," have definite sound patterns. The reader may have noticed that in some passages of music by Beethoven or Haydn the instruments in the orchestra seem almost to be talking (Fig. 9*a*).

Balance. In the music of nature the principle of balance plays an important role. Balance in music stands for the placing of one complete melodic phrase after another so that there seems

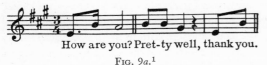

How are you? Pret-ty well, thank you.

Fig. 9a.[1]

to be a distinct question and answer, with perhaps a return to the first phrase after the second. The bird's cry to its mate always merits such an answer. Sometimes the answer comes from the bird itself, balancing in an occult form the first melody or song. The nightingale's song consists of such a question and answer, together suggesting balance (Fig. 9b[1]).

Fig. 9b.

The musician Handel adapted this song as shown in Fig. 9c.[1]

Measure. In the temporal arts, measure, or proportion, consists of the time interval, either between two parts or actions or from the beginning to the end of a series of actions. Measure can be considered as one element of a larger rhythmical pulsation. In terms of the heartbeat, one may notice that the pulse is not always regular but comes in a series of short and then perhaps one or two long beats. Measure may be either the time factor within one series of short and one series of long beats, or the pause between the two series of beats.

Emphasis. The principle of emphasis, sometimes called "contrast," "variety," or "intensity," seems more common than either regular repetition or beat in most of nature's movements and sounds. The woodpecker knocking

upon the tree trunk, tap-tap-tap-tap-tap-tap, suddenly stops to call, "Cre-eek, cre-eek." The difference in tone between the sound of the wooden drumming and the shrill cry consti-

Fig. 9c.

tutes one type of contrast. Poe's line, "the tintinabulation of the bells, bells, bells," is a striking example of contrast in word sound.

A second type of contrast is that between regularity and irregularity of beat. Such contrast is apparent in the difference between the regular repetition of the woodpecker's taps and the irregular notes of his call. This type is familiar in poetry in the interjection of lines of irregular beat into regular rhythmic measures.

The effect of contrast is apparent in music, where diverse tones and instruments have even greater power to stir the emotions. An excellent illustration is furnished in the development of the opening theme of Beethoven's *Fifth Symphony*[2] (Fig. 2, page 7, Intro.). Notice that after the first four notes have been repeated a little lower in the scale the composer accelerates the beat, thus obtaining contrast in rhythmic pulsation. Several more instruments are then introduced, providing contrast in volume and quality of sound.

Harmony. As we said in our discussion of harmony in the spatial arts, most people associate the word with an effect in music. In music, the term "harmony" carries a double meaning, depending upon whether its formal or its associative values are under consideration. To define harmony in terms of its formal values alone, however, is all but impossible, because the associative values are so strong. The physicist says that when two different tones sound simultaneously whose vibrations or wave lengths in the air have a simple ratio— for example, one to two, as in the octave; two

---

[1] WILLIAM GARDINER, *The Music of Nature*, Wilkins, Rice & Kendall, Boston, 1852.
[2] If possible, the first few bars of the symphony should be heard from a phonograph record, or be played on a piano.

to three, as in the third; three to four, as in the fifth—they are in harmony. Yet, even the physicist recognizes that these effects are associated with pleasant sensations. The wind whistling through a grove of pine trees, for example, produces a number of tones simultaneously, which we call "harmonious." This may be because the effect reminds us of a mother singing a lullaby to her child, which is a pleasant association.

The psychologist can demonstrate that the idea of harmony is associated with childhood and racial conditioning, because of which pleasant states of feeling are recalled by certain combinations of sounds. Unharmonious sounds, those, that is, whose wave-length ratios are too complex, unconsciously affect us by suggesting unpleasant or irrational states of being. The term "harmony," one of the most complex and undefinable in art, belongs with such terms as "unity," "beauty," and "perfection."

Summary Showing Apparent Relationship Leading from Static to Dynamic Principles

To summarize, the spatial arts achieve unity through the senses of touch and sight by a use of symmetry, radiation, balance, emphasis, measure, and harmony; whereas the temporal arts achieve unity through the senses of sight and hearing by a use of rhythm, repetition, melodic line, balance, emphasis, measure, and harmony. Starting with the static aspect of complete harmony, one might study these principles in order, proceeding through symmetry, radiation, absolute and occult balance, emphasis, measure, repetition, and melody, to the most dynamic aspect of art, its rhythm. Apparently, unity may be of either the static or the dynamic sort, depending upon what the artist wishes to express—perfection and beauty, or progress and sublimity.

At this point it must be remembered that, since the world of art consists of an infinite number of paradoxes, men have persistently tried to examine the spatial arts, which depend upon the static aspects of symmetry and harmony, in terms of the dynamic principles of melody and rhythm, and vice versa. Plato, Schelling, and Ruskin held that all art should approach the condition of music; and many modern painters, such as Kandinsky and Severini, have tried to capture the melodies and rhythm of music in their panel paintings. The eclectic arts of our day—the opera and the motion picture—must use principles from both extremes, within the time limits of a theatrical performance and on the confined area of stage or screen.

Principles for Judging Useful and Associational Values in Art

Any study of more than two books on the subject of art and aesthetics will serve to convince the student that there exists today the greatest confusion as to the meaning of principles in art. This confusion arises from the fact that since earliest times art critics have applied the body of criticism haphazardly to formal, useful, or associational values, without recognizing the separate functions of each aspect of art. As early as the time of the Egyptian Pharaoh, Akhenaten, in 1450 B.C., a sculptor carved on the walls of his shop: "Art lies in the balance of straight lines, curves, cubes, and cones." Socrates, however, living hundreds of years after Akhenaten, suggested fitness or appropriateness as the first principle of the sculptor's art. Precisely speaking, order, arrangement, and symmetry seem to be principles of formal value. Propriety and economy, on the other hand, may have to do with use and associational values.

While the principles under which useful and associational values may be judged will be applied to numerous examples in the course of later chapters, a brief discussion is in order at this point. Two principles have to do with use values: (1) the fitness of the material or medium of expression and (2) the economical use of the material or medium. The principles that relate to associational values are three: (1) the propriety or fitness of the work of art; (2) its power to stimulate or, conversely, to soothe; and (3) its power to edify or enlighten. Both the useful, or technical, principles and the associational, or social, principles have to do with the way in which the work of art affects an audience; they do not serve as functions of the formal principles merely to suggest unity within the work of art itself.

Principles for Judging Useful Values

1. The principle of the fitness of the material or medium suggests that any work of art must be made of a material or expressed through a medium that will not belie its purpose. In strongly religious ages the icons or sacred objects used in worship seem most fitting if made in a precious metal, such as gold or silver. In general, massive, blocky sculpture seems more appropriate in stone, whereas sculpture in bronze may suitably have attenuated forms that would appear too fragile for stone. In the field of music, likewise, a light, tripping passage would not be appropriate for such instruments as the tuba and the bass viol.

2. The principle of the economic use of material or medium challenges the skill of a fine craftsman. By this principle he is obliged to achieve the greatest effect with the smallest possible amount of material, be the material stone or metal, language or musical theme. Illustrative of this principle is the figure of a Madonna (Fig. 346, Chapter XIII) carved out of a piece of ivory that still preserves the shape of the elephant's tusk.

Principles for Judging Associational Values

1. Some works of art, because of their suggestive use of easily recognizable symbols generally regarded as meaning terror, kindliness, reasonableness, or power, may be appropriately used in circumstances calling for a display of these qualities. The same symbols would be inappropriate if used in connection with effects other than those associated with their universal meaning. The words "dawn," "hush," "lullaby," "murmuring," "tranquil," "mist," "luminous," "chimes," "golden," "melody," were chosen by Wilfred J. Funk, the poet and publisher, not only for their melodious sound but also for their associative quality. If, for example, the word "lullaby" is written at the top of a piece of paper and all the words that come immediately to mind are written below it, the associative word list will be found to hold a preponderance of pleasant ideas.

2. The second principle, having to do with the power of a work of art to stimulate or, conversely, to soothe, arises from the unconscious associative processes of the mind, which lead most people to link objective effects with only half-remembered causes. A slight smell of wood smoke in a darkened theater, if the play is particularly tense, can be easily associated with the word "fire," and the audience, panic-stricken, will rush for an exit. During a gay musical comedy, a bit of smoke and the cry "Fire!" will not act so quickly. Any feeling of enjoyment makes people unwilling to take hasty action. When the propagandist influences people to violence, he first makes them uncomfortable by playing upon their fears. A brilliant color flaunted before a bull rouses him to anger. Similar effects of unconscious associations with color, sounds, or smells may be observed in human beings.

3. The principle of enlightenment or edification may be found in art when passages of sentiment have been presented realistically and with appropriate associated colors and words. The war posters for the Red Cross stimulated us to give for the benefit of wounded soldiers. During culture periods when organized groups, such as the church or the state, definitely tried to use art to further their purposes, the resulting creations displayed this principle in its purest form (Fig. 471, Chap. XV).

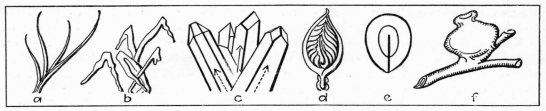

FIG. 10.—Line and shape in nature. *a*, living organic line; *b*, disintegrated line; *c*, inorganic crystalline; *d*, *e*, organic plant; *f*, wasp urn.

The Application of Principles in the Study of Art

The principles for judging useful and associational values in art may be viewed by the student in two ways: (1) as intellectual exercises and (2) as means to original creation. There exists no fundamental conflict between these two methods of study. The complete man needs both. As intellectual exercises, the principles may be memorized and used in the analysis of works of art; as means to original creation, they may be experienced through actual use in the laboratory in experimental attempts to recapitulate the efforts of earlier artists.

The Formal Elements of Design in Nature

The formal principles of art manifest themselves in the material or structural elements proper to each art. A knowledge of these elements in their simplest form, as they occur in nature, may help the student to recognize them in a more complicated structure, as they appear throughout the history of man's arts. The student may also use the simple natural forms as a point of departure in his own artistic creation.

Line in Nature

The dynamic power underlying all the phenomena of growth manifests itself in lines of force, or in those curvilinear contours proper to all living things in nature. These include the lines of growth in the grass (Fig. 10*a*), the flowers, and the trees, as well as the outlines of the animal body. Such unbroken lines contrast with the straight lines and angles of crystals found in minerals or other inorganic substances. The broken fragmentary lines of the wilting flower (Fig. 10*b*) or the disintegrated animal body strongly suggest death; conversely, an elastic, curved line suggests life.

Shape in Nature

By boiling down the rocks and by evaporating the salt-saturated waters of the earth, Nature continually creates shapes of angular crystals with polished plane surfaces (Fig. 10*c*).

Adding cell to cell in plant structure, she builds the satisfying shapes of stems, buds, flowers, and seeds (Fig. 10*d*) according to the principles of balance and proportion. Almost all the fundamental shapes employed by the potter arose first as seeds, fruit, or crystals in Nature's great craft shop. In western Pennsylvania and eastern Ohio, where potter wasps, or "jugmakers," are found, the prehistoric Indian Mound Builders made pottery which, in many instances, duplicates the shape of the wasp urns (Fig. 10*f*).

Color in Nature

The earth yields all the pigments necessary for preparation of the most exacting canvas. Even the blue of the ethereal sky may be found crystallized in the precious turquoise and lapis lazuli. Dependent upon Nature, man uses her gifts so unconsciously and so liberally that often his works are easily identifiable by the regional quality of the materials employed. In southern Tyrol, for example, one of the most successful painters of the 20th century, Egger-Lienz, like the cave man, made all his pigments from the earth of his native land. Again, Nature provides for seasonal changes in the coloring of animals, in response to protective and reproductive needs. Human creatures, likewise, make use of color to gain protection or attention.

Pattern in Nature

Following intricate laws capable of mathematical analysis, Nature arranges the elements of line, shape, and color in interesting patterns or designs. The lines of the snowflake, examined once in demonstrating the principle of symmetry, and the spiral snail shell, showing radiation, form the fundamental basis for many patterns in Nature's scheme.

Later, man adopted many of Nature's patterns directly, to express his artistic ideas. But before man learned to use the natural elements from which his art was constructed, the plants and animals used them instinctively in the process of living.

Elements of Sculptural Organization

Closely allied to that perfecting of shape which constitutes the art of the potter is the more complicated organization of forms in the art of the sculptor. The sculptor not only builds shapes from clay but carves them from wood and stone or casts them in bronze. All sculptural design, however, may be reduced to two fundamental patterns, both of which occur in nature. In the first of these, elements such as the cube and cylinder stand at right angles to each other within a cubical or rectangular form (Fig. 11a). Within the realm of crystalline nature many shapes follow this type of sculptural arrangement, which produces an effect of stability. In the second pattern, shapes spiral about a central axis in a design suggestive of growth (Fig.

11b). The seed pods arranged around a stem of milkweed, the buttressing roots of an elm tree, and the shell of a conch, all illustrate the growth pattern in natural life.

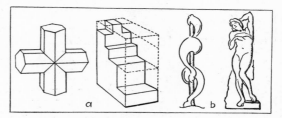

Fig. 11.—Elements of structural organization. *a*, crystalline; *b*, dynamic.

Elements of Architectural Organization

Architecture, the art of arranging areas in space for use as dwellings, communal meeting places, or memorials, may be studied from two different points of view. The purely useful or functional character of architecture is related to the space to be enclosed. The arrangement of masses of colored or uncolored material as viewed from the outside constitutes its more decorative or symbolic aspect. The elements of architectural form in nature seem more commonly of a purely functional type, taking on a decorative aspect in only a few rare instances.

Arch and Vault. The first and most commonly found architectural element—the arch or the vault—may be seen in the building activities of wasps. Many species of wasps build one-celled tubular houses for their young. Such a house on the side of a wall forms a primitive vault whose sides are braced by buttressing ridges of clay. As a structural element, this vault provides a maximum of strength, because the tensions are equalized on all sides as pressure applied from the top spreads out into the broad base (Fig. 12a). If this vault were cut transversely at any point, the resulting section could be called an arch (Fig. 12b). Nature has produced examples of the arch on a magnificent scale in many natural bridges.

Lintel and Corbeled Arch. The earliest form of memorial architecture built by man copies two common architectural elements appearing in nature more by accident than by design. Where frost and glacier have split and carried great rocks over terminal moraines and, melting, have

age. These masses arrange themselves so that the heavy weight of branches and leaves on one side of a stem counterbalance an unequal mass placed farther out on the opposite side (Fig.

Fig. 12.—Elements of architectural organization. *a*, vault in nature; *b*, the arch; *c*, *d*, post and lintel; *e*, *f*, corbeled arch.

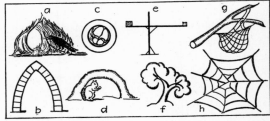

Fig. 13.—Elements of architectural organization. *a*, the pointed arch in nature; *b*, Gothic arch; *c*, *d*, the dome in nature; *e*, *f*, the cantilever; *g*, *h*, suspension.

left these rocks piled upon one another, two elementary patterns of construction result. The principle of the post and lintel structure is illustrated (Fig. 12*d*) when one stone rests upon two others. The corbeled arch needs five or more stones placed so that they form an opening (Fig. 12*f*).

The Pointed Arch. The runways of animals through a field of grass and the lines of growth in the branching trees of the forest, suggest the form of opening known as the pointed arch. A species of bird called the bowerbird ties upright twigs whose lower ends are anchored at the base, so that their tips are pulled together (Fig. 13*a*). The bird thus constructs a true pointed arch. When translated into the stone of the Gothic cathedral (Fig. 13*b*), such an arch suggests organic lines of growth.

The Dome. The dome, a hemisphere covering a square or a round space, may be derived by cutting through the earthen jar of the potter wasp or the spherical mud ball that in similar fashion serves the scarab beetle (Fig. 13*c*). Nature's builders go far toward the construction of the dome in the case of the beaver (Fig. 13*d*).

The Cantilever Principle. Trees and plants furnish the best examples of the cantilever principle of construction (Fig. 13*e*) as it is found in nature. Only by availing themselves of the principle of occult balance can thin-stemmed trees support huge overhanging masses of foli-

13*f*). An examination of the elements of construction in growing plants contrasted with those in mud or rock forms demonstrates that there exist in nature two general principles of construction, one relying upon inorganic weight, the other upon the organic cantilever. Classical and Byzantine vaulted, domed, and lintel buildings rely in the main upon the former; Gothic and Oriental wooden buildings, as well as our modern skyscrapers, employ the latter.

Suspension. The suspension principle of building may be traced in nature to the activities of wasps and nest-hanging birds, and to tendriled vines (Fig. 13*g*). Such nest builders as the oriole and the weaverbird of South Africa tie their homes to branches with bits of grass or thread. The spider, using a natural rayon, spins her net, attaching it to grass-blades or stems, and setting before man a diagram of the suspension element of building in its purest form.

Elements of Nonstructural or Decorative Design

Each work of architecture may be seen in its functional engineering or, as it is sometimes called, its architectonic aspect. The term "architectonic," applied throughout the arts, suggests that any given work shows the strong lines of its structure. A work of architecture, like a work of sculpture, may also be considered for its formal effect as a decorative arrangement of masses. Considered in this way, all architecture

FIG. 14.—Elements of nonstructural or decorative design. *a*, *b*, prism; *c*, cylinder (equisetum stalk); *d*, *e*, the pointed dome; *f*, *g*, the tent.

uses four elementary shapes: the prism, the cone and cylinder, the hemisphere, and the tent.

The Prism. Straight-sided elements in architecture originating in crystalline shapes include the cube, the pyramid, and the prism, which may be rectangular or many-sided. A picture of two of these crystals (Fig. 14*a*, *b*) suggests that many of the medieval and modern architectural shapes in churches and skyscrapers derive from these elements.

Cylinder and Cone. The cylinder occurs universally as a structural element in plant and tree growth. The cone usually terminates the cylindrical stem. These elements, frequently used in Saracenic and medieval Romanesque architecture, are so common in nature (Fig. 14*c*) that we seldom think of them as elements of structural design.

The Hemisphere. The dome, created functionally to roof a building, appears on the outside as a hemisphere. The top of the acorn (Fig. 14*d*), the shape of a seed, the spherical egg, as well as the breast of the mother, present to man the outer aspect of the dome (Fig. 14*e*), one of the most satisfying elements for use in ceremonial building.

The Tent. A final element of construction having distinctly ceremonial value arises from the outer aspect of the suspension constructive element in nature (Fig. 14*f*). Early adopted by primitive peoples, this tent shape, with its curvilinear pyramidal contours, finds use in so many cultures that it should be recognized as an elementary architectural form (Fig. 14*g*).

FIG. 15.—Elements of pictorial organization. I, surface pattern: *a*, repetition; *b*, allover design; *c*, space relationship.

The Close Union of Formal and Use Values in Architecture

The great architects of the past, building as though impelled by nature, unconsciously used both useful and formal aesthetic elements together. In our day the architect's office divides the work of creation between two men, one to consider the structural elements in the building, the other, the exterior, decorative elements.

Elements of Pictorial Organization

Nature continually passes in review before the eye of man a kaleidoscope of interesting pictures. Some of these may seem to him to be on a flat surface, whereas others call his attention into the distance. When primitive man examines the surfaces of stones and trees or the markings of animals near by, his shortsighted vision sees life in the flat.

Flat Surface Pattern or Design. The elements of design fall into three categories: (1) linear pattern repeated along an object as, for example, the diamonds on a snakeskin (Fig. 15*a*); (2) over-all design, as, for example, the dots on the feathers of the guinea fowl (Fig. 15*b*); and (3) placement of a given motif upon a flat plane with relation to a given space (Fig. 15*c*), as, for example, the design produced by the seed pods of an apple when the apple is cut in half. Within these designs the motifs, which may be dots, scales, or lines, can be arranged so that they

suggest either movement or a static over-all quality. As far as is known, primitive man remained unconscious of any other elements of pictorial arrangement or organization. Only

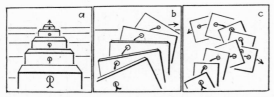

Fig. 16.—Elements of pictorial organization. II, movement of planes: *a*, straightforward progression; *b*, movement in two directions; *c*, movement toward innumerable points.

after thousands of years of drawing, during the Graeco-Roman development of painting, did a deeply cultured type of individual strive to create an effect of distance on a flat surface.

Movement of Planes away from the Picture Plane. The commonest type of movement into a picture is one in which all the planes shown appear to recede from the eye toward some one point on a distant horizon—a straightforward progression (Fig. 16*a*). A second type of movement arranges the planes within a picture so that they appear to carry the eye to distant horizon points, first on one side and then on the other (Fig. 16*b*). As a result, the viewer unconsciously wavers between the two directions. The final arrangement of planes within a picture is made around some vortex, so that they appear to recede from the eye toward innumerable points in infinity (Fig. 16*c*). All these movements within the picture can be and are experienced by man in nature, depending on the position of the sun and clouds.

To summarize, nature confronts man with six fundamental elements of pictorial arrangement. The first deals with continuous, allover, flat-surface patterns in absolute or occult balance; the second, with discontinuous linear patterns; the third, with the arrangement of an area within a given space. The fourth carries the attention out into the world picture directly toward one central object; the fifth, toward two

areas; and the sixth, toward innumerable spaces.

Elements of Musical Organization

The elements underlying all experience in music include the timbre or tone quality of instruments and the relative height and depth of tone. These organizations of atmospheric pulsation occurring in nature appear in animal voices as expressive of moods.

Timbre, or Tone Quality. The timbre, or tone quality, of an instrument may be defined superficially as its limpid or muffled effect. When the wind blows strongly across a hollow in a rock, or the broken end of a tubular reed sets up a series of pulsations, one notices an essential difference in the sound, depending on its origin.

The vocal cords of different birds and animals vary in length and produce characteristically differing sounds. The timbre of the animal's call, further modified in some cases by exciting or restful emotional states, causes instinctive reactions in other members of the animal kingdom. A mating call differs from a warning cry.

Height and Depth of Tone. Nature alters tones by increasing the pressure of the wind which produces them. Manipulation of the size of the opening across which wind tones are produced also causes high or low tones. In animal nature the greater air pressure developed under emotional stress adds shrillness to sound, while the controlled narrowing of the orifice adds sweetness. The fascinating subject of the physical production of sound will be developed in later chapters in connection with poetry, drama, and music.

Unison of Tones. The naturalist, Savage, reported that a number of black chimpanzees (*Troglodytes niger*) gathered at times into groups for the purpose of beating with sticks upon hollow logs, trees, and branches. They thus created an effect of unison. A final organization of the elements of music arises thus when two or more objects of different timbres and tone quality sound together. The wind, driving raindrops against the windowpane or whistling over a bed of rushes and through the pines, produces a harmony of sound which some human composer may later transpose into a symphony.

Elements of Dramatic Organization

The animals present many elements of the drama in their intuitive actions. Human drama consists of an essentially ceremonial, condensed, and symbolic presentation of everyday actions. The elements of drama found in nature include preparation, symbolic or condensed action, and conclusion. The following examples of two complicated dramatic actions in nature should clarify this definition.

In Africa, an observer, whose home was separated by a ravine from a plateau on which dwelt a band of apes, saw them huddled together each morning facing the eastern horizon. As the first light of dawn illumined the sky, the members of the band rushed to the edge of the plateau, each waving his arms while chattering joyfully and dancing about. Toward evening, as the sun approached the western horizon, the members of the band seemed subdued. Whimpering and crying, they cowered toward the sunset. This simple dramatic sequence includes the three elements mentioned. The lightening of dawn constituted a preparation; the rushing of the apes to greet the sun was a ceremonious or symbolic action opening the life of the day; the evening ceremony led to a quiet or restful conclusion. The Australian bowerbird (*Ptilonorhynchus holosereicus*), earlier mentioned as the builder of the pointed arch, designs its own stage for a dramatic action. The male of the species builds a little dance hall of reeds and branches, wherein it courts its mate.[1]

Plants open and close with the rising and setting of the sun. This action toward warmth and light, called "heliotropism," leads to those elements in dramatic presentation later to be known as the "Apollonian." Another aspect of the drama, concerning itself with the darkness out of which comes the recuperative element of sleep, will later be called the "Dionysiac," after the god Dionysus, who was worshiped at night.

Art and Meaning

Need art have meaning? This question, much debated by the students of aesthetics in our day, seems to be answered in the affirmative by our review of the formal elements of art occurring in nature. If the processes of nature have meaning, as the religious man must believe, then the formal elements occurring in nature must have meaning. If one cannot conceive that natural phenomena have meaning other than that contributed by the intellect of man—the agnostic or atheistic point of view—then, of course, the formal elements need have no meaning. For the agnostic, however, the formal elements, as has been seen, would not alone suffice to make a work of art. For him they must be used and given associational or symbolic values before they may be considered.

An example should make this clear. In the ruins of the Mesa Verde cliff dwellings one building has been identified as a temple to the sun. Great sunflowers of natural stone appear in the floor of this temple as the chief objects of veneration. The Indians, finding these flowers centuries ago, noticed their similarity to the face of the sun-god. Marveling that he had imprinted his image in the rock, they decided to worship the symbols and built a temple around them. Recently a geologist demonstrated that the flowers of stone were caused by a peculiar softening and rehardening of a crystalline deposit under dripping water—a process as wonderful and complicated as the mental processes by which the Indian, recognizing the

[1] In 1939 the American Museum of Natural History made motion pictures showing the elaborate dance of the New Guinea bird of paradise. After the flock has arranged and cleaned the choral area, adult males pose and pirouette with a continual movement of their multicolored feathers, displaying a remarkable feeling for the spectacle and rhythmical elements in an intricate ceremonial dance.

beneficent effect of the sun, decided to worship the stones as a symbol of goodness.

The scientist is compelled by his philosophy of life to approach art as such a natural phenomenon; the religious believer, as somewhat of a miracle. Both points of view seem necessary for a full enjoyment of any work of art. The student will benefit by first trying to recognize his own fundamental approach and, if it be one-sided, then determining to strive for an understanding of the other.

Summary

When the quality of imagination working with the elements of formal aesthetic value found in nature rearranges them, endows them with meaning, and strives to present them in connection with some human needs, we see that there is a differentiation between the unconscious art of nature and the conscious arts of man. When a clear-thinking individual with normal social desires and deep human sympathy abandons himself to an inspired moment of rearranging the formal elements of art, he finds expression in some new-created work that combines the formal and associational aspects in fine balance.

Whether one considers art as a necessary value for its own sake or whether, unsatisfied with this point of view, one would examine art in terms of its useful and associational values, he must acknowledge the fact that art has been produced by man creating under both views. Having examined in this chapter the formal elements with which artistic creation deals, we may now proceed to a study of the fortunes of these elements under the contrasting philosophies of art.

Bibliography

Spearman, Charles E.: *Creative Mind*, D. Appleton-Century Company, Inc., New York, 1931.
Gordon, Kate: *Aesthetics*, Henry Holt & Company, Inc., New York, 1909.
Gardiner, William: *The Music of Nature*, Wilkins, Rice & Kendall, Boston, 1852.

Recordings

Bird Songs, Sears, Roebuck record, 9134.
The Grand Canyon Suite, Ferde Grofé, Victor, VM-C18.

CHAPTER II

Arts in the Hunting Age

Art arises from two sources; from technical pursuits and from the expressions of emotions and thought as soon as these take fixed forms. The more energetic the control of form over uncoordinated movement, the more aesthetic the result. . . . [1]

DEEP understanding of art arises from an examination of its origins in the race or the individual. Research in the racial origins of art by students of anthropology during the past fifty years has made available a great mass of objective data. Scientific museums are full of specimens of early art—weapons, implements, figurines—discovered in geological strata that place them at remote periods in the history of mankind.

The fact that artistic productions can be found associated with human remains in Europe, Asia, and Africa as far back as 25,000 B.C., in the Paleolithic or Old Stone Age, would seem to put these artifacts far enough in antiquity to warrant our drawing completely objective conclusions from them. Unfortunately, although anthropologists in the main agree as to the dating and purposes of these earliest art works, the students of aesthetics disagree as to the interpretation of them and the reasons why man created them. A figure, for example, discovered at Brassempouy, France, in Magdalenian culture levels, may have been intended for a doll or for a fetish to insure fecundity (Fig. 25d). If the figure was a fetish, it might be taken as evidence that art had arisen as part of magic; if it was a doll, one might argue that art arose in connection with the play instinct.

In this chapter we shall examine not only the generally accepted facts concerning the art of early man but also a number of theories growing out of widely varying interpretations of these facts. The chief purpose of this exploration is to determine whether there is evidence to support the view that art arose as a separate impulse or whether art grew out of various aspects of universal desires, such as the desire for recognition, security, response, or adventure. Until an examination has been made of these two major premises, all attempts to construct an objective theory of artistic values must remain futile.

The final choice between the two theories cannot, of course, depend solely upon an examination of art activities in primitive societies. The choice becomes for each individual a matter of personal conviction and must arise from his own observations of the role played by art in the life of the developing child. Such observation can be made in retrospect through the student's laboratory experiments or, more objectively, by studying the psychology of the actions and creative efforts of children.

Much of the disagreement among aestheticians has arisen because scholars in the field unconsciously favor different points of view. In the absence of definitive data, their personal bias causes them to read into the artistic productions of early man evidence upon which they may construct either classical (intellectual) or romantic (emotional) theories concerning

---

[1] FRANZ BOAS, *Primitive Art*, Harvard University Press, Cambridge, Mass., 1927.

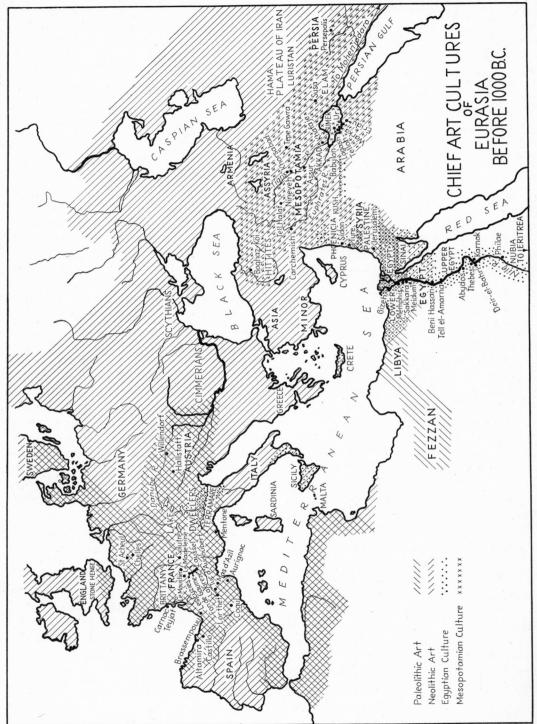

CHIEF ART CULTURES
OF
EURASIA
BEFORE 1000 B.C.

Paleolithic Art ///////
Neolithic Art
Egyptian Culture ········
Mesopotamian Culture ×××××××

FIG. 17.

artistic origins. If the student is to escape falling a prey to one or another of these unconsciously held beliefs, he must understand how they arose in what might be called the anthropological mythology concerning human origins.

Poetic Conceptions of the Origin of Primitive Man

The Perfectionist Conception

One of the earliest known conceptions of the origin of man describes his first condition as extremely happy. Man is pictured as living in a garden, abundantly supplied with fruits. At peace with nature, he feared neither animal creation nor destructive forces. This idyllic state continued until a spirit of discord or evil caused him to eat of the fruit of the tree of knowledge. Thereupon, overwhelmed with shame and sorrow, man and his partner, woman, were forced from this ideal garden world into a harsh world of toil and suffering.

This well-known conception of man's origin, which seems to have arisen in Mesopotamia or Palestine, underwent some modification at the hands of the early Greek poet, Hesiod. In the poem *Works and Days*, Hesiod held—in the 8th century B.C.—that the first age of man, which lasted for thousands of years, was an age of gold. In the Golden Age, man, freed from labor, was able to make only pleasant things and think only pleasant thoughts. This notion gave rise to the pleasurable, or hedonistic, philosophy of art which insists that art of the highest type, the Beautiful, exists only to bring pleasure to man. In time, Hesiod lamented, man degenerated, and descending through successive stages reached, during the poet's own lifetime, the age of iron. To Hesiod, the age of iron, full of cruelty and bloodshed, seemed to presage a complete destruction for mankind.

The above notion of man's origin has exerted far-reaching influence. Many art critics have held unconsciously to the belief that the perfection of the first man, born in innocence to an ideal existence, reappears in any perfect work of art. The idea that art is a separate instinct, arising perhaps from man's memory of a perfect past or from some spiritual, God-given idea, is noted in this philosophy.

The Evolutionary Conception

Another conception of man's origin necessarily influences our thoughts concerning the origin of art. Very early in the history of civilization poetic minds cherished the conviction that all mankind must have arisen from lower, more imperfect forms. The Egyptians likened man to the scarabaeus, a large beetle that was born into new life out of a ball of mud, or to the lotus which, rising from the slime, lifted its perfumed petals to the sun. In Greece, the spirit of man was compared to the butterfly, Psyche—capable of changing from an ugly, crawling caterpillar to a brilliant, aerial form. The Roman poet, Lucretius, a follower of the Greek philosopher, Epicurus, also conceived man to be a progressive being. His point of view, indeed, suggests the modern evolutionary interpretation of man's origin and progression through ever-changing forms.

Lucretius wrote that from the beginning each created thing must develop, true to its own appropriate form, though governed by nature's immutable general laws. Nor could man escape this circumstance.

But stronger far than we, by earth produced,
Were early types of men, with rugged frames.
They'd stouter hearts and nerves
To summer heat and frost alike superior.
They were to sickness and strange foods immune,
Roaming like wild beasts 'neath the circling stars,
And knew not how to guide the curved plow
Nor how with spade to till the fertile field,
Or yet to plant young saplings, making orchards grow
By pruning fruit-trees of their useless boughs.
These, hiding in the woods, all clothed themselves
With furs and skins, and fed upon
The nuts and berries which were growing there
Nought else had they save that which nature gave.[1]

---

[1] T. LUCRETI. CARI, *De rerum natura*, Liber V, 919–935, Teubner, Leipzig, 1852.

The Realistic Conception

A great dramatic poet often comes closer to truth than either the scientists or the students of aesthetics. Shakespeare sometimes combined the two conceptions just discussed. In *The Tempest*, Shakespeare created both the half-animal Caliban, as a symbol of man's connection with the lower forms, and Prospero, a man who might have come from the realm of perfection. In Shakespeare's mind, the human race partook of the two extremes.[1]

These three theories of the origin of man run through all modern thinking about man and about art. The task of the student today lies in understanding both the perfectionist and the evolutionary versions of man's origin and in being able to see that both partake of the truth. As far as the flesh is concerned, man must still arise from the clay; as far as the spirit is concerned, man is "a little lower than the angels." This means, in brief, that the student should properly be a realist in his approach to the origin of art.

Though art may seem to have developed as man has developed, some men of advanced culture consider art to be a special part of man's divine inheritance. Such a position, however, leads inevitably to a separation of art from daily living. This separation, in turn, makes one query: If art is a special, mystical expression, how may it be described in objective terms? Those who believe in art only as a divine impulse insist that there can be no description in scientific terms of art's unique values. They may be felt and appreciated but never intellectually understood. To one holding such a mystical view, all efforts to study art by any other means than experiment, or through personal experience, seem useless.

The greatest paradox of man's search for truth, however, lies in the fact that he is compelled, by the very limitations of his understanding, to clarify the meaning of the elements of his spiritual life—the True, the Good, the Sublime, the Beautiful—in terms of intellectual symbols. To the philosopher, this striving constitutes man's chief glory. His attempt to translate the elements of his spiritual life into conscious intellectual knowledge seems to many thinkers to be the essential difference between man and the lower animals.

Leaving, therefore, the realm of aesthetic mythology and mysticism, and with this warrant for intellectual research, let us consider the past creations of man as they can be studied in the caves of France.

The Origins of Art

The Spatial Arts

Implements. During the late 19th century scientists discovered, first in France and then in other parts of the world, skeletal remains of hitherto unknown forms of mankind, under many layers of terrestrial debris. These earlier races had nothing but rude caverns to protect them from the elements, nothing more than a few pieces of cracked flint as weapons against wild beasts.

The earliest remains of these primitive races are often found associated with handstones, rocks chipped into the rough shape of axheads. Though the stones found in the earliest cultural levels were without definite shape, with

[1] Anthropologists in general agree that around 200,000 years ago there existed at least three distinct types or races of man in the Caliban stage of development. One, *Homo erectus javanensis* (*Pithecanthropus erectus*) appeared in the East Indian area; a second, *Sinanthropus pekinensis*, dwelt near what is now Peiping, China; and the third, *Homo neanderthalensis*, moved over Northern Europe, Africa, and Palestine. Since each of these types had different cranial characteristics, it is proper to assume that they probably had different mental attitudes. This would account in part for the varying cultural attitudes categorically named in this book: Oriental, Gothic, and Classical. Obviously the human family has within the last 2,000 years become so intermingled that it is useless now to try to discover these characteristics in their pure form. As categories they are useful in helping to create an understanding of one aspect of aesthetic difference. For example, a quick review of the human types shown in the large illustrations of sculpture following in this book indicate differences of facial structure partly due to racial characteristics.

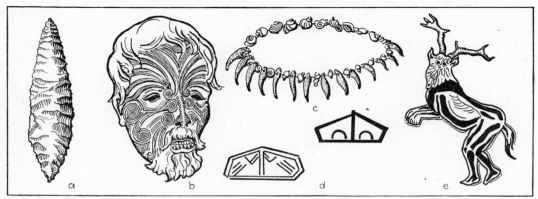

FIG. 18.—*a*, Solutrean spearhead; *b*, Maori tattooing (University of Pennsylvania Museum); *c*, Cro-Magnon necklace; *d*, tectiforms or hut drawings, Font de Gaume (Breuil); *e*, the sorcerer, Trois Frères (de Begouen).

the passing of millennia they assumed the bilateral symmetry we find in Solutrean spearheads (Fig. 18*a*). In nature there is little that is absolutely symmetrical, and early man may have derived some satisfaction in perfecting the shape of his weapons as a demonstration of his superiority over nature.

Certain it is that bilateral symmetry probably gave to man his first aesthetic experience in the realm of handicraft. Since a nicely balanced spear point finds its way to the mark more accurately than one poorly shaped, earliest man probably placed a high value on the symmetrical weapon for purely utilitarian reasons. As there is no evidence that the most primitive man had many higher thoughts than those connected with self-preservation and defense, one can only conjecture that for him the most perfect arrowhead, one which the aesthetic-minded anthropologist would today call the most beautiful, was that which was the most efficient.

A step in advance of the purely functional beauty of the earliest arrowheads was made in the Magdalenian period when the flint shaping became minute and regular. Then, tiny, ineffective models of spearheads were made, for use either as toys or as symbols in connection with burial or religious rites. Along with the spearheads we find knives, scrapers, and other tools. Observations of primitive tribes in Tierra del Fuego and Australia show that weapons of

this type are still fashioned and appreciated for their perfection.

Body Painting and Decoration. Among the arts practiced by primitive men one finds body painting and tattooing. Colored earth may be daubed in rings around the eyes or in great geometric zigzags across the chest. Ernst Grosse has collected the various reasons given by members of modern primitive tribes for body painting. Burial places of the earliest European cave men disclose bones and skulls decorated with red ocherous earth color. American Indians also used this convention in connection with interment. Body painting may also carry with it the idea of protection or insulation against evil. According to Grosse, a Duku man from the South Sea Andaman Islands, having decorated his body with designs (Fig. 18*b*), leaped around in a primitive dance, singing, "You can't kill me now—I am tattooed, I am tattooed."

The Swiss scholar, William Worringer, has suggested in *Form Problems of the Gothic* that all primitive art arises from the emotion of fear. The instinct for self-preservation, says Worringer, caused man to ornament himself like the Duku or at times to capture in geometric, expressionless lines the moving objects of the outer world that he feared. Unfortunately for this one-sided theory, which probably does explain certain phenomena in art, primitive man not only created geometric lines but also, as will be seen, made many things of a very realistic order. In other words, the primitive had other impulses than that of self-preserva-

FIG. 19.—*a*, Aurignacian mammoth Pindal; *b*, bison, 'La Grèze (Capitan, Breuil, Ampoulange); *c*, rhinoceros, Font de Gaume (Breuil); *d*, cave bear, Font de Gaume (Breuil).

tion, other emotions than fear, and other instincts than those of conquest.

Drawing. In the Aurignacian age of human development, when the glaciers were moving down from the mountains for the last time, the Europe of 20,000 years ago experienced a great migratory movement. The cave men proper, of the Neanderthal race, were overcome by the Cro-Magnons, a tall, finely developed folk, probably not unlike our Indians. It is not known whence these invaders came, but shortly after their arrival, perhaps with the fusion of the two stocks, man began to create a representative art. This art shows the beginnings of conventional and foliated ornament, animal and human representation, and the manufacture of clothes and jewelry (Fig. 18c). For 10,000 years these people ruled Europe, hunting, fishing, building wooden huts—of which they left drawings (Fig. 18d)—and repairing to the recesses of their caves to paint and model the animal life about them.

The Cro-Magnons were the first to bury their dead, and along with the skulls of the departed, one may still find traces of ocherous face paint, together with personal adornments in the shape of beads and other artifacts. Some anthropologists, as well as many theologians, see art as a necessary adjunct to religious observance. Such thinkers call attention to the nature dance of the primitive in which he at-

tempts to approach his creator by imitating some animal, which he endows with human attributes. The picture of the sorcerer from Trois Frères, clothed in his deerskin,

FIG. 20.—*a*, Aurignacian engraving tool, Hodenc; *b*, brush paint tubes, Mesa Verde; *c*, Magdalenian flint knife made with one blow; *d*, bone whistle, Laugerie Basse (Lartet and Christy).

illustrates this theory of the origin of art (Fig. 18e).

It should be noted in passing that the sorcerer of Trois Frères is an example of X-ray drawing. This artistic phenomenon may be seen in drawings by children, and, incidentally, in the work of many present-day Primitives. In his desire to communicate knowledge or to instruct, the child sometimes takes pains to draw not only the external appearance of the object but also its interior. A house, for example, may be shown with transparent walls, so that not only the outside bricks will be seen but the furniture within, as well. In the drawing of the sorcerer from Trois Frères, the legs and feet of the sorcerer, as well as the human face behind the deer mask, have all been portrayed. If art on the primitive level had been undertaken only as a means of free, joyous expression, one questions whether the figure would have been so clear an exposition of a religious rite.

Painting. The first wall paintings were outline drawings in colored chalk (Fig. 19a), such as children draw in their third or fourth year. One of the earliest representations of an animal may be found in the cavern of La Grèze in France (Fig. 19b). The silhouette outline shows only enough character to identify the animal as a bison.

The Aurignacians not only painted animals but engraved them on the cavern walls. By enlarging and rounding the lines of the engravings they achieved a suggestion of sculptured relief. The rhinoceros (Fig. 19c) from the late Aurignacian or Solutrean level of Font de Gaume in France illustrates the next development in graphic art. Here we find four legs

FIG. 21.—Magdalenian reindeer, Font de Gaume (Breuil and Perony).

shown instead of two, the body drawn in red crayon, and lines added to suggest modeling. This presage of shading ushers in the polychromic work of the Magdalenian period.

In the Font de Gaume cavern (Fig. 19d), Magdalenian artists of successive ages drew and painted on the same wall spaces, the lime water having deposited layers of protective glasslike stone over the earlier work. Thus the Cro-Magnon man of the thirteenth or fourteenth millennium profited by the experience of his predecessors. Also, through the discovery of new color materials, he was able to make his figures appear more and more lifelike.

The painter's technical apparatus in this period included engraving tools for working the walls (Fig. 20a), a palette of bone or stone, and probably brushes made of bundled split reeds, such as one finds today among the ruins of the Colorado cliff dwellers (Fig. 20b). He ground ocherous earths for his reds and yellows, and used bone or soot-black for his dark shading, along with a greenish tone made of manganese oxide. These colors were probably mixed with fatty oils and applied with the brush.

Development of skill in delineation kept pace with technical advancement, as the reindeer from Font de Gaume show (Fig. 21). Figures were now brought into relation with one another. The animals at Font de Gaume represent the artist's concept of both male and female reindeer. The wish of the artist is less important to us than the fact that the antlers, the curves of the bodies, and the position of the masses,

FIG. 22.—Deer and fish, Lorthet (after cast).

form a very interesting and pleasing rhythmical pattern, which gives a feeling of inner unity to the whole. This is one of the earliest examples of what is known as composition in picture making.

During the Magdalenian period appear the beginnings of several types of painting. In addition to the rhythmical pattern exemplified in the Font de Gaume reindeer, the narrative picture makes its appearance. The deer and fish engraving from Lorthet (Fig. 22) illustrates this storytelling type of art. The two dart heads shown may indicate that the deer were killed; the fish may symbolize the location of a stream. It seems possible that this story, like many an Indian record on a buffalo robe, was a bit of boasting on the part of the artist, whose skill in drawing the head of the first elk is to be noted.

That Cro-Magnon man did not always have the sense to choose a design appropriate to the material at hand is evident when we realize that this illustration was taken from the cylindrical face of a piece of bone, unrolled in a glue mold, so that what appears to us as a picture executed upon a plane surface was, at the time, seen only bit by bit as the bone was turned.

The Lorthet example gains particular importance as evidence that the cave painter must have created his realistic representations with the help of eideticism—a peculiar faculty now lost by most members of the race. The word "eidetic," taken from the Greek *eidos*, meaning image, was first used by the psychologist Jaensch, who discovered the phenomenon in a

FIG. 23.—*a*, decorative bison, Altamira (Cartailhac and Breuil); *b*, boar, Altamira (Cartailhac and Breuil).

number of German school children. Briefly described, eideticism means the ability to retain an image upon the retina of the eye long after the original outside stimulation has been withdrawn. Everyone has a very slight degree of eideticism. After looking fixedly at a bright window, for example, on closing the eyes one will see light bars where the mullions crossed the glass and dark spaces where there was light, the whole appearing somewhat like a photographic negative. The person who still retains full eidetic vision, however, will see not only this simple crossbarred arrangement but an accurate picture, as well, of the view outside the window. Tests in an American classroom show that from 1 to 3 per cent of the students still retain their youthful eideticism. The faculty has even been brought back to a noneidetic under hypnosis. It seems highly probable that some Oriental peoples have the ability to induce eidetic images at will when they wish to create realistic representations.

The deer and fish engraving, like the cave drawings, most probably came from an eidetic who could see the outline of the animal on the bone as he turned it. The picture forms no rhythmical pattern. The eidetic powers of the primitive, youthful mind dominated in this instance the sense of decorative balance.

In contrast to the pictorial representation from Lorthet, the bison from Altamira (Fig. 23*a*) has been folded together so that it just covers a projecting boss on the ceiling of the

cave. As may be seen in the illustrations of carved work (Fig. 27), some of the artists had a sense of fitness that made it possible for them to change the naturalistic form to fill a space

FIG. 24.—*a*, herd of deer, Teyjat, Spain (Capitan and Breuil); *b*, paintings, Cogul (American Museum of Natural History); *c*, drawing of deer, Adam Garh (*from Earliest Indian Rock Painting* by *Hellmut de Terra, Asia Magazine, March*, 1939, *New York*).

or decorate a limited surface. The skill required for such adaptations is allied to mental attitudes that make the individual receptive to outside influences. Freestanding composition, on the other hand, springs from egocentric ideals (Fig. 23*b*).

One more artistic type is represented in the Magdalenian deposits. The herd of reindeer (Fig. 24*a*) engraved on an eagle bone, from Teyjat in Spain, makes its appeal by stressing a few significant lines, which create in the imagination a whole herd of animals. The antlers and legs of several of the deer are well drawn; the rest are represented by a few skillful strokes. This form of art may be called impressionism. All the Magdalenian paintings emphasize essential details of anatomy, such as hoofs, horns, noses, tails, and outlines. Colors either create the illusion of form or indicate surface markings. There are groups in which one may detect rhythmical pattern; there are storytelling pictures, decorative designs, and impressionistic renderings. The types of painting discussed here will be traced in their development through the entire history of mankind's aesthetic evolution.

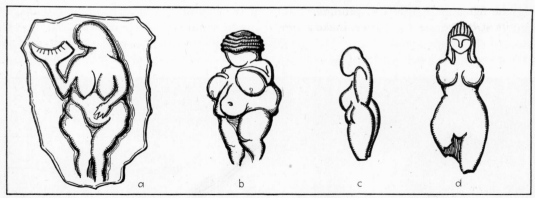

FIG. 25.—*a*, Aurignacian woman, Laussel; *b*, Venus of Willendorf; *c*, Aurignacian figure, Mentone; *d*, Magdalenian figure, Brassempouy.

The research carried on between 1910 and 1935 by **Dr. Leo Frobenius** and his Institute of Prehistoric Art has made clear that the paintings of the rock shelters at Cogul in southern Spain (Fig. 24*b*), like the paintings in the Fezzan District of North Africa and the works of some present-day tribes, were made by a people who lived contemporaneously with the Cro-Magnons but who belonged to another—probably the Grimaldi Negroid—stock. The paintings at Cogul show a very distinct difference from the cave paintings. In the first place, the group of skirted women around the small figure of a male would seem to indicate that these people had definite ceremonial rites. Human figures do not appear frequently in cave paintings. In the second place, some of the figures carry bows and arrows; one man is shooting at a stylized deer. The narrative element in this type of painting almost completely dominates the realistic formal element. Pleasure, if any, was derived from making clear the meaning of the ceremony or the methods of hunting, rather than from creating a representation as nearly as possible like the real thing. This painting, and others like it in these widely separated districts,[1] marks the first stage in the direction of abstract or ideoplastic art. The tendency will continue until man has developed a set of crude signs and, eventually, writing.

Sculpture. There seems to be no strict dividing line between painting and sculpture in the Aurignacian period. We have already called attention to the fact that, by rounding the inner surface of the engraved outline of his drawing, the early artist achieved the effect of very flat relief sculpture. The figure of a corpulent woman holding a drinking horn, from the grotto of Laussel in Dordogne (Fig. 25*a*), represents a transitional stage between the etched drawing and the full-relief model, or figure in the round.

A study of three freestanding figures from the same period teaches us that, in sculpture, abstraction or idealization of the form usually means the omission of naturalistic detail. The so-called Venus of Willendorf (Fig. 25*b*) from Austria has the same characteristics as the lady from Laussel. The features of the Venus's face have been entirely eliminated, and hands and feet are subordinated to the breasts and the rounded abdomen. Probably this figure is an idealization of the wish for an increase in family.

The figure from Mentone (Fig. 25*c*), also Aurignacian, goes still further toward abstraction of form. The long curves of the various parts of the body, flowing one into another, produce the feeling of compositional unity noted in the case of the Magdalenian deer (Fig. 21). Con-

[1] The most recent discoveries of Cro-Magnon art have been in India (Fig. 24*c*).

trast the Mentone figure with the figure and head (Fig. 25*d*) from the deposits at Brassempouy. In the Brassempouy example the parts of the body are no longer exaggerated, and the more primitive American communities will, for a price, make a figure to be destroyed through incantation and mutilation as a symbol of the overthrow of an enemy.[1]

Fig. 26.—Clay bison, Tuc d'Audoubert. (*Courtesy of de Begouen.*)

artist was at some pains to carve the features, which usually indicate the psychical characteristics of the individual.

As one might expect from the development of painting, the development in sculpture from figures of primitive mass to forms expressive of character continues through the Magdalenian period with growing freedom of technique. Groups in sculpture replace the single figures. The clay figures of Tuc d'Audoubert (Fig. 26) represent the male and female bison. Probably the wish for greater herds and relatively more food had something to do with the creation of this little group. In another cave of the time a model of a bear has been found. It had evidently been used as a target for spear thrusts and was probably the center of a semireligious dance. The primitive mind often delights in making figures to be used as instruments of destruction, much as the witch doctors in our

Sculpture as a decorative art was the most frequent type of carved work in the Magdalenian period. There are many carvings of horses' heads, reindeer, bison, and other animals, on scepters and dart throwers. The illustration of a throwing stick, or *atlatl* (Fig. 27), now in the museum at Saint-Germain-en-Laye near Paris, shows how cleverly an animal might be made to fit the natural conformation of the bone. Such commonplace ornament plays a great part in later Gothic architecture, in which elaborately twined animals decorate capitals, choir stalls, stained glass, and cathedral pinnacles. In the first attempts of students who enjoy carving and whittling, particularly if the mass of the object ornamented is not changed to the naturalistic form of the animal, one may often detect the characteristics of this early style, which led to the architectural sculpture of Northern Europe. We shall later contrast

[1] M. de Begouen, the French archaeologist, has written an interesting novel, *Bison in Clay*, stressing the idea that these works resulted from superstition and a belief in sorcery.

Fig. 27.—Magdalenian *atlatl*, or throwstick (from cast) (Saint-Germain-en Laye Museum).

the Northern European sculpture with that of the Mediterranean peoples.

Architecture and Ornamental Design. Our knowledge of the architecture of earliest man is limited to recurring drawings (Fig. 18*d*) that seem to portray the elevated section of a round hut. The Cro-Magnons probably lived in tepees or huts similar to those of our present Pima Indians. We know that they used bone scrapers and needles, probably to clean and sew the skins for these dwellings. Anthropologists now consider it likely that in Solutrean times some of the Cro-Magnons wandered with their skin

Fig. 28.—*a*, *a′*, bone implements with technomorphic design; *b*, *b′*, *b″*, Magdalenian phylomorphic designs; *c*, zoomorphic designs. (*Courtesy of Verworn.*)

tents across the northern ice fields to the shores of America.

In the field of ornamental design, early man evolved three kinds of geometric pattern. One type is illustrated by the markings on bone implements (Fig. 28*a*) and by the flint-chipped rhythmical indentations in Solutrean weapons (Fig. 18*a*). Such ornamentation, which is governed by the technique of manufacture, is called technomorphic. The zigzag design produced by the crisscrossed thongs binding the flints to the shafts of the weapons furnishes an even more obvious example. We shall find technomorphic ornament playing an important part in the pottery manufacture of the age of polished stone, discussed in the following chapter. This type of design is likely to be straight-lined, angular, and geometric.

A second type of ornament employed by early man is the plant, or phylomorphic, design created by copying and stylizing the spirals and growth lines of plants. In such ornament the lines are usually long and flowing, with a pattern of alternating strokes springing from a central staff (Fig. 28*b*).

A third type we call zoomorphic, or animal, design (Fig. 28*c*). The impressionistic quality of such design may be due to haste or the desire to communicate an idea with the fewest possible strokes. Useful in ideographic representation, zoomorphic design leads to the formation

Fig. 29.—*a*, mezolithic painted pebbles, Mas d'Azil. *b*, pictographs: 1, Bohuslan; Sweden; 2, Taos, New Mexico; 3, Mesa Verde, Colorado.

of alphabetic symbols, which begin to appear on the European culture horizon in the late Azilian period between 10,000 and 5000 B.C.

In these three types of primitive ornament we find the bases for all systems of decorative design. Students who use them have a tendency toward ideoplastic art creation, which should be encouraged and, when possible, refined by the study of natural objects.

With the decline of Cro-Magnon art, Negroid and Celtic peoples migrated into Europe. The transitional ages between chipped- and polished-stone implements witnessed a birth of ceremonial representation (Fig. 29). Symbolic art triumphed over storytelling or naturalistic art, and we may suppose that during this period much attention was paid to ceremonial dancing and music.

The Temporal Arts

The same quality of imagination that helped earliest man design a more efficient stone hatchet or construct a better home for himself led him in leisure moments toward activities that were not, in themselves, directly efficient. The end result of these activities, however, was to increase his effectiveness by, so to speak, improving his morale. By going ceremoniously through the actions of killing the antelope, pygmies prepared themselves mentally to be better hunters. Repeating again and again certain magical formulae, man convinced himself of his own importance.

Such ceremonies were not only tonic but pleasurable. When man repeated his magic formulae in varying tones, perhaps going through measured rhythmical exercises in shooting the arrow into the picture of the antelope, he not only made himself more effective but secured enjoyment. Thus, with the discovery of a musical pattern of expression which was applied to the arts of painting and the dance, one can see that earliest man really succeeded in uniting the physically useful and the pleasurable. It is impossible to decide how much of his pleasure came from retrospection, how much from the anticipation of success, and how much from heightened muscular tonus gained by rhythmical repetition of motions. Probably all contributed to his feeling of satisfaction.

The Dance. Instances of the ceremonial dramatic action have already been cited in connection with the wall paintings at Cogul. Boas, in his *Primitive Art*, points to the utilitarian origin of songs created by working groups. Sailors' chanteys furnish modern examples of utilitarian work songs. The Kwakiutl, an Indian tribe of the northwest American coast, has a canoe song in which every syllable is sung with a single stroke of the paddle.

In the case of the most primitive hunting man we lack evidence that there was much group activity. We can only imagine that the rhythmical feeling expressed in song or chant came from within the singer and, as such, would have to be almost pure expression of his pulse, his breathing, or his muscular action. Words repeated in rhythm with one's own pulse can cast an almost hypnotic spell. Having set some goal of achievement by repeating a formula for its attainment over and over, man can build up within himself a belief in his own powers to attain. Coué demonstrated this with a formula: "Every day, in every way, I am getting better and better."

Music. Investigations of the aboriginal tribes in South America, Africa, and Australia offer an opportunity to reconstruct in some measure the musical life of very early peoples. Records, for example, of the songs of Australian bushmen still living on early Stone Age levels have been made by the professors of the University of Adelaide. The examples reproduced by Sir Walter Davies, in his book *The Pursuit of Music*, show the prime characteristics of all primitive song. A phrase of words, starting high, moves downward through a primitive scale of five notes. This downward movement is natural to all human speech. The voice at the beginning of a sentence has greater strength than at the end and its diminution in volume leads to a descent in pitch. The bushman, so Davies tells us, repeated his song over and over again, always using the same sequence of notes, raising his voice at the beginning, lowering it at the end.

Just as races and individuals differ in their natural likes and dislikes for physioplastic and ideoplastic representation, so primitive races tend to develop either the rhythm of the drums or the harmony inherent in the whistle or flute. Bone whistles used thousands of years ago have been found in the French caves (Fig. 20*d*). Bundles of cut reeds that give forth pipe tunes made up the earliest organ, and human voices singing together produced, fortuitously at first, the elements of harmony. The dance stimulates the rhythmical faculties. Music and dancing are united in the ceremonial play of primitive man, as we may judge from listening to phonographic recording of American Indian rhythms.

Poetry. All primitive ceremonious action consists of closely interwoven dance, music, and poetry. His primary purpose being pure expression, the primitive being does not feel the need for differentiation. An example will illustrate the point. An Eskimo hunter, cast adrift on a floating cake of ice, was lost for many days. When finally rescued, he gave to his people the following song:

Aya, I am joyful; this is good!
Aya, there is nothing but ice around me, that is good!
Aya, I am joyful; that is good!
My country is nothing but slush, that is good!
Aya, I am joyful; this is good!
Aya, when, indeed, will this end? this is good!
I am tired of watching and waking, this is good![1]

Here is a record of man's gallant protest against the forces of death. The Eskimo doubtless composed and sang the song to himself as he jumped up and down and flapped his arms to keep warm, thus opposing himself to fate with a constant repetition of his belief in his own vitality. Little wonder that the entire village, so Boas tells us, took up the song. Its courage was inspiring.

Art, in its essence, is an expression of man's inner faith in his own ability to overcome life's vicissitudes. As such, art must have been born with man. If we were to try to consider it as a thing apart from his other activities, we should have to call art simply man's instinct for self-affirmation.

Anthropological Theories

Thus far in this chapter we have discussed the poetic theories concerning the origin of man and we have reviewed numerous examples of the art of primitive man. We should now turn to the theories that the anthropologists have evolved to explain in scientific terms these artistic expressions.

Theories Expressing Religion and Magic

George Grant MacCurdy, in his book *Human Origins*, takes the view held by most students of

anthropology that the origins of art are probably religious and magical. In regard to art's magical significance, MacCurdy points to the fact that an inventory of cave art reveals that the great majority of examples represent animals that were difficult to capture or beasts of prey that were feared by earliest man. In many cases these animals are portrayed as wounded or as having been struck by darts, while the dart throwers are practically always carved to resemble the animals being hunted. MacCurdy also points to the fact that there is much evidence of sex worship in Paleolithic times, so that the little figures of the women probably had something to do with a magic to achieve fecundity.

Theories Stressing Technique and Imagination

Not all anthropologists take the same point of view as MacCurdy. Boas and De Morgan furnish noticeable exceptions. In his book *Prehistoric Art*, De Morgan writes that his study of early artistic productions has led him to believe that art had two distinct origins: (1) delight in technical skill and (2) interest in the imaginative conception. He points out that weapons that have symmetry and earliest pottery that has form must both have been simply utilitarian objects. From the creation of these useful objects, De Morgan maintains, the artist would derive a secondary delight, which would have somewhat the effect of an aesthetic impulse.

Franz Boas in *Primitive Art* sums up the anthropological evidence in the words used at the head of this chapter and in the following paragraph:

The aesthetic effect of artistic work developing from the control of technique alone is based on the joy engendered by the mastery of technique and also by the pleasure produced by the perfection of form. The enjoyment of form may have an elevating effect upon the mind but this is not its primary effect. Its source is in particular the pleasure of the virtuoso

[1] See *Journal of American Folk Lore*, Vol. 7, p. 50.

who overcomes technical difficulties that baffle his cleverness. As long as any deeper meaning is felt in the significance of form, its effect is for most individuals pleasurable, not elevating.[1]

Social Theories

In the opinions of MacCurdy, De Morgan, and Boas, one may see a progression of thought away from the natural, useful, or functional aspects of art toward the point of view that aesthetic activity may exist for its own sake. Ernst Grosse, in *The Beginnings of Art*, has called attention to the fact that artistic activity is in many ways similar to play. Nevertheless, he finds in men's desire for decoration a possible evidence for a separate aesthetic instinct. Body painting, for example, although in greater part carried on as a ceremonial aspect of life by primitive people, is now and then practiced by some savage for the mere joy of painting himself. Grosse also noticed that ornament at some time was used as protection but, like Professors Baldwin Brown and Herbert Read of the University of Edinburgh, he points to the fact that there are times when primitive art cannot be traced to any of the above social impulses.

The Utilitarian Theory

It is a far cry from the evidence presented by these anthropologists to the modern specialized theory that art exists for its own sake. Our task through the remaining chapters of the book consists in tracing the development of this idea. One way to bridge the gap between the thoughts of the man in the cave and the cultured man of today would be to consider that everything which man represented in his art was a wish created by his imagination for well-being or better circumstance. Today everyone has desires that are not easily achieved in material terms. The work of art can serve as a unified symbol of the goals to which we would attain. Professor De Witt Parker of the University of

Illinois, in his book *The Analysis of Art*, has called attention to this idea in the words:

In life aesthetic expression is casual and transient —in art it is made permanent for all who can understand its language. Hence in art and in art only do we find an enduring record of the dreams of the race. Furthermore, through artistic expression the dream is not only preserved, it is transformed. There is given to it inevitably a coherence, a clarity, an intelligibility which otherwise it could not possess. . . . Art is the clarification, the communicable value of a dream.[2]

In a later book Professor Parker has stressed this idea of permanence and concludes that art's peculiar value probably lies in making permanent the flux of the world. Parker's theory thus seems very much like that of the Swiss art historian, Worringer, who held that the chief attribute of primitive art was its desire to reduce life to a condition of permanence.

Summary

Cro-Magnon art presents all the elements of aesthetic invention in their simplest form, as well as most of the techniques manifest in the arts of later people. Studying this, one observes that art arises from no single fundamental urge but accompanies the instincts of self-preservation, procreation, and the developing religious and social senses, aiding all the better to express themselves, so that their values are apparent to the primitive social group.

Bibliography

BROWN, GERALD BALDWIN: *Art of the Cave Dweller*, National Book Buyers Service, R. V. Coleman, New York, 1928.

MacCURDY, GEORGE G.: *Human Origins*, D. Appleton-Century Company, Inc., New York, 1924.

COMTE DE BEGOUEN: *Bison in Clay* (novel), translated by R. L. Duffus, Longmans, Green & Company, New York, 1926.

Recording

Dog Dance and Medicine Song—Blackfoot Indians, Victor, 17 611 a, b.

[1] FRANZ BOAS, *Primitive Art*, Harvard University Press, Cambridge, Mass., 1927.
[2] DE WITT PARKER, *The Analysis of Art*, pp. 26–28. Yale University Press, New Haven, Conn., 1926.

CHAPTER III

The Arts of Agricultural Man

Wind now commences to sing;
Wind now commences to sing;
Wind now commences to sing;
The land stretches before me,
Before me it stretches away.
"Song of the Pima Indians"[1]

ART ORIGINATED among the most primitive hunting men in connection with three fundamental desires: (1) a wish on the part of man to conquer the intangible elements of his environment through magic, (2) a desire for pleasurable ornamentation, and (3) a need to express himself as an entity opposed to natural forces. Although some of his geometric ornamental designs may have been symbolic (Fig. 29a), the greater part of man's art was an expression through lifelike representations of animals painted upon the cavern walls or engraved upon his implements.

The cave painter and hunter disappeared from Europe at the close of the Ice Age, almost 12,000 years ago. New races from Asia and Africa mingled with the older Cro-Magnon peoples and the resulting mixture forsook the ways of the hunter, to till the soil. Today, although a few tribes in Australia and Tierra del Fuego still live on the hunting levels, for the most part the cave man as an active artist has become a thing of the past.

Students of social development speak of the changed culture of the Mediterranean basin between the 10th and 3rd millennia as the Mother Age, or the matriarchal state of society. They point to the fact that, since life in the hunting age depends upon the strength and skill of the male, social power there is pre-dominantly masculine. In the second stage, when both men and women are able to till the soil, social life comes to revolve more around the home, which is dominated by the mother. Anthropologists and archaeologists, with their eyes upon tangible evidence, call this the age of polished stone, or the Neolithic age.

Changing Mental Characteristics of Agricultural Man

Shakespeare, as we have seen, found somewhere in the racial consciousness, or perhaps in the backward districts of England, either a memory or a living example of Caliban, the man from the caves. In the second part of *Faust*, Goethe, the German poet-philosopher, carries us back to the matriarchal state through which all advanced phases of human society have passed. When Faust asks Mephistopheles to produce the ghosts of Helen and Paris, the most perfectly formed human beings, Mephistopheles replies that there is but one way to re-create them—for the key to perfect form he must go to "The Mothers." Here, again, through the lines of a modern poetic genius we are linked with the mysterious past of the race.

The psychologist G. Stanley Hall suggested that all developing children grow through, first,

[1] Translation by Frank Russell, from *Twenty-sixth Annual Report of the Bureau of American Ethnology*, Smithsonian Institution, Washington, D. C.

FIG. 30.—*a*, African kraal; *b*, lake dwelling, Switzerland.

the hunting, then the matriarchal, stage. To judge from his works of art, a subtle change must have taken place in the psyche of man as he passed from the hunting to the domestic stage. Certainly the character of his art work changed. Expression for its own sake and the propitiation of spirits seem no longer to have sufficed. The impulse to decorate himself and to make ornamental clothing apparently increased greatly. Above all, as we shall see, the art of agricultural man was characterized by a great desire for completion. For him the end of art appears to have been technical finish or perfection.

Desire for Perfection in Implements. This desire for perfection appears first of all in the realm of the most practical objects. The spearheads and stone axes, no longer necessary in hunting —for there was little hunting—became practical as hoes, axes, knives, and corn pounders, or as aids in building. The stone implements of man from that time on are streamlined. All the rough but rhythmical chipping was ground down and polished so that the ax or the spearhead became smooth and pleasant to the touch. This change in surface indicates that man's sense of touch had become so refined, he could no longer enjoy handling a rough stone. A refined sense of touch, associated with a refined sense of sight, has a great deal to do with the appreciation of sculpture.

Desire for Orderly Design in Domestic and Feminine Crafts. The second difference in the mind of man as demonstrated by his changing art interest can be seen in the increasing number of domestic arts or crafts that arose in connection with the home-building desires of the women. Settled on his farm, which produced food for the long winter months, man was no longer forced continually to seek for game. He then had the leisure necessary to perfect his art work.

Desire for More Stable Organization of Society. Finally, the greater organization of the family around the farm acre and the fire led to a new, more stable organization of the tribe on the domestic model. Around the shores of the Mediterranean and in Southern Asia between 10,000 B.C. and 5000 B.C., one could have found tribes living in villages and towns as do the Pueblo Indians, the Africans (Fig. 30*a*), and the pile dwellers of Molucca today (Fig. 30*b*). This social organization took place around two chiefs: one, a war chief, symbolic of the masculine hunting or fighting functions; the other, a medicine man, symbolic of the feminine domestic element. At the direction of these leaders, ceremonies were elaborated and performed as complicated religious dramas. The women constructed great communal buildings, some of which still exist in the Indian pueblos or African kraals. In their spare time they made pottery utensils or wove the cultivated cotton and flax.

The two new arts of weaving and pottery making, unknown to the hunting man, rose to a dominant position, replacing the desire for realistic painting and sculpture.

FIG. 31.—Cherokee Indian basket.

The Rise of Technomorphic Design

Basket and Textile Weaving. The technique of weaving creates a design of alternate echeloned markings. The impressions made by the earliest textiles have in some cases been preserved for us in neolithic pile dwellings, as well as on some of the prehistoric American pottery. Whether used in basket or cloth weaving, the technique in its simplest form is the running of one set of threads or grasses over and under another set (Fig. 31). By alternating black grass or raffia with white, one may make the earliest, the checkerboard, design. By modifying this further with various colored threads sewn through the meshes of the woven cloth, almost any design can be built up of squares lapping one over the other, like the scales of a fish. This last technique is known as imbrication.

Today in watching Navajo weaving (Fig. 32), one may see the design work out in checkerboard, twill, or echelon pattern. It is apparent that design and technique grow simultaneously, one influencing the other. Since no two blankets look exactly alike, the weavers apparently do not have a clear memory image of old designs but are continually forced to create anew, making very slight innovations as they go. The voiced appreciation of the tribe causes them

to modify their designs still further or to retain certain elements. Thus, on very primitive levels it may be said that a design is the product and property of the group mind. The same holds

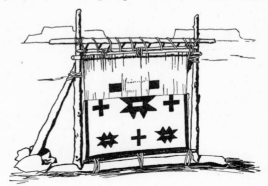

FIG. 32.—Navajo loom.

true, though less obviously, for artistic composition in more advanced culture stages.

Since the weaving of baskets and cloth leads to a technomorphic design which changes all motifs to quasi-geometrical or checkerboard effects, naturalistic design must be simplified, and curved lines must be created as zigzags (Fig. 33). The resultant conventionalization

FIG. 33.—Geometrization of nature forms in weaving. (*After Mead, Bull. Amer. Mus. of Natural History.*)

achieves an aesthetic effect through its rhythm rather than through its natural quality. The surface of the fabric, furthermore, demands a rather flat treatment. We have come to associate fabric with flatness to such an extent that

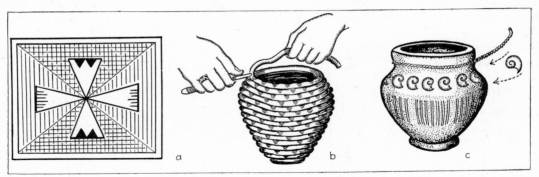

FIG. 34.—*a*, Sioux leather design; *b*, clay coiled pot; *c*, pot with snail shell and rope design, lake dwellers.

a carpet or wallpaper design which happens to be physioplastic and highly contrasted in light and shade gives us a disagreeable sensation, because it seems unsuitable to the medium of expression. In such subtle, yet normal, social ways as this has taste been formed.

Bark and Leather Design. The work in bark and leather in the agricultural age provides another source of technomorphic design that has left its traces in present-day art. Some of the American Plains Indians and the tribes of British Columbia decorate their leather-covered rectangular boxes with designs that indicate where the corners of the sides are located (Fig. 34*a*). Persians, the origin of whose pottery designs can be directly traced to agricultural Stone Age sites, still create fine tiles ornamented in designs many of which originally evolved from leatherwork.

Ceramic Design. The origins of abstract and geometric design in ceramics may be found in the crudest forms of pottery manufacture. Two possible explanations have been given to account for the invention of this new art. The child playing with clay soon learns to think of the accidental impressions from its fingers as cups. When allowed to harden in the sun, the crude form would naturally suggest itself as a counterpart of a primitive gourd or coconut-shell cup. It is possible that the baked-clay bowl owes its origin in part to the daubing of primitive baskets with clay in order that they might hold grain. Such baskets, with the clay

inside, have been found in ruined cliff dwellings. One may imagine a basket so daubed as burning by accident and then being discovered to have hardened into a bowl bearing a latticed design.

The potters in the pueblos, who work without wheels, take a roll of clay and coil it around as a spiral upon a flat stone, thus forming a base. They then press the clay down with their fingers or a stick (Fig. 34*b*) so that one coil adheres to the next, keeping the surfaces moist and tight, meanwhile, to prevent the formation of air bubbles. As the finger or the stick travels over the surface, pressing the coils together, it leaves a series of indentations and these, with the lines of the coils, form a technomorphic pattern. Today, some Indian women begin coiling their pots in low baskets, the design of the mold remaining on the finished pot.

The Central European lake dwellers made a very simple pottery upon which shells and weaving or plant stems were impressed before firing (Fig. 34*c*). The impression of a single stem or shell does not constitute a design, but if the motif is repeated around the pot, the element of repetition assures one that a willed intelligence desiring rhythmic expression has been at work. Design or composition has been defined as the arrangement of two or more objects or motifs to achieve unity.

Later in the development of pottery making, as the primitive cultures grew older, the surface of the pot was smoothed and then painted

FIG. 36.—*a*, pitcher, Mondsee; *b*, goblet, Crete; *c*, cup, Mesa Verde; *d*, burial urn, Troy.

upon with other colored clays. Such is the power of tradition, however, that the painted patterns often duplicated the older technomorphic patterns. When a design thus shows the influence of its earlier origin, it is still known by the original name but is spoken of as secondary or derived ornament. Thus a piece of pottery might bear a painted secondary ornament derived from technomorphic designs.

Fundamental Pottery Shapes. The pottery shapes that we have today may be traced back to a few original forms. The first of these, the universal bowl type, originated perhaps as a copy of basketware (Fig. 35*a*). The bowl pictured here (Fig. 35*b*) comes from north Germany, and the basket from the Moqui Indian pueblos of Arizona. The influence of the basket technique, evident in the lines on the bowl as well as its shape, is unmistakable.

FIG. 35.—*a*, Indian basket, Moqui; *b*, bowl, Hanover, Germany; *c*, hanging bowl (Usude), Japan.

The second or hanging-basket type (Fig. 35*c*) shows a piece of Japanese *Usude* ware, perhaps 2,000 years old. The nubbins left on the sides represent the old modified handles or places where drawstrings might have been inserted in

a skin basket. Similar hanging pots, some of which may be seen in the museum at Rochester, New York, were made by the Iroquois Indians.

The third type is an attenuated bowl to which, in some cases, a handle or handles may be attached, turning it into a pitcher or an urn (Fig. 36*a*). Engraved lines decorate the surface of this pile-dwelling pottery, or, as was noted in some instances, spiral shells, pressed into the sides, may produce the desired decorative effect. Another style of ornament that sometimes occurs in early pottery is an inlay of clay in a contrasting color inserted into the engraved lines and baked, so that the design shows white, or red, or black. The prehistoric inhabitants of Asia Minor used the inlay method to a great extent, and it was still further developed by the Peruvian Indians.

With the addition of a base to a bowl, patterned perhaps after an egg or a coconut shell and supported by a wooden foot, the potter discovered the chalice, or goblet, form. The earliest examples of this type of pottery come from Crete and date from the 4th millennium before Christ (Fig. 36*b*). The chalice, or goblet, one of the last shapes to develop, is found in its earliest form, covered with a slip of clay painted in another color and fired onto the surface.

The final type, the drinking cup or ladle, is found among the cliff dwellers of our Southwest (Fig. 36*c*). The Indian cup probably had wooden prototypes, for similar forms in wood have been discovered in the Swiss pile dwellings.

FIG. 37.—Pueblo Indian pottery. *a, b, e,* Zuñi; *c,* Santo Domingo; *d,* Laguna. (*Courtesy of Santa Fe Research Institute.*)

From such simple shapes, governed for the greater part by use, the finest Greek, Chinese, and Mohammedan pottery evolves. To bring the crude primitive forms to the most nearly perfect creations of the potter's art, however, required thousands of years of refinement (Fig. 37).

In discussing the aesthetic criteria by which to judge the excellence of pottery, we must bear in mind that the potter is continually trying to refine the shapes of his pots toward forms which are stable. Pottery, originating in use, should never appear unstable, and a piece that transgresses this law cannot have lasting appeal.

In the late Neolithic age one finds the pitcher type, or urn, molded into the shape of a torso with cap and human features, to serve as a burial urn for cremations (Fig. 36d). The bowl, too, suffered modification. Placed on three legs forming a tripod, it became a symbolic ceremonial dish of great importance to the metalworkers (Figs. 38a, and b). As pottery shapes were taken over by metalworking tribes in the bronze stage of culture, they became sharp-edged and angular. The influence of the metalworking technique in aesthetic production tends toward the precise and the angular. As pottery, these examples do not seem particularly pleasant.

After the age of metal there appears appliqué ornament; ornament, that is, molded and pressed on the surface so that it stands out in relief. Small molds have been found in France and South America for use in making indented and applied ornaments. Such excrescences upon pottery, not being proper to the original art, usually appear unpleasant (Fig. 38c). In art, that only is satisfying which is true to the nature of the material with which it has usually been associated. This constitutes the principle of the suitability of material. The man of the agricultural age felt this "sacredness" of natural materials to such an extent that in the representational art of sculpture he retained, unmodified, the natural forms of rock and tree.

Carved Symbolism. The sculpture of the neolithic culture, like the painting on the pottery, is stylized, but stylized in such a way that the block of carved stone or wood retains as nearly

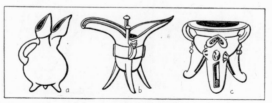

FIG. 38.—Tripods. *a*, Troy, tripod pitcher, 1100 B.C. (*after Schliemann*); *b*, China, *tsio*, or drinking vessel, Shang Dynasty, about 1800–1500 B.C. (*after de Morant*); *c*, Costa Rica (*after Franz Boas, Primitive Art, by permission of the Harvard University Press*).

as possible its original shape. A particular stone becomes powerful through religious belief—it must be given a face, hands, breasts—but it must not lose its stony quality. These characteristics are noticeable in the illustration of the piece from the grotto of Croizard in France (Fig. 39a). Here the features are merely suggested, but the suggestion alone is enough to stir the imagination.

From the mountains of Kentucky comes the little stone statue which may be compared with the Croizard piece (Fig. 39b). The face of this piece shows a flattening of the features. This fault in technique is characteristic of almost all the efforts of beginners when they carve a figure to be viewed from one angle only. Children in the early grades of school usually make the face flat and draw arms on the sides of the body.

The decorative effect, which seems to have been increasingly desired as neolithic culture advanced, appears at its best in the work of Central and South American sculptors. The human figure of green stone from Mexico (Fig. 39c), now in the United States National Museum, illustrates another stage in the trend away from the naturalistic. The eyes, mouth, nose, and headdress are reduced to geometric lines, while the body retains a rectangular shape. The European statuette from the Cyclades Is-

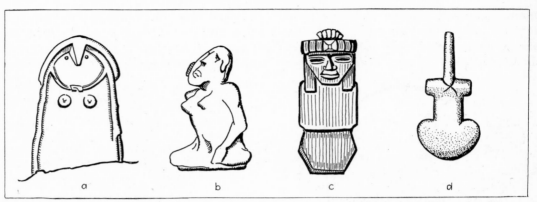

FIG. 39.—Neolithic stone figures. *a*, Croizard, France; *b*, Kentucky (Louisville Public Library); *c*, Mexico; *d*, Cyclades Islands.

lands in the Königsberg Museum (Fig. 39*d*) exhibits the violin form, which continued in Northern European sculpture until Christian times, when the musical instrument itself inherited the shape.

The greater part of the sculpture coming from the late Stone Age culture is in baked clay and has been modeled rather than carved. Wood and stone carving allow of no replacement if an error in technique produces the wrong effect. Hence, to achieve a naturalistic result the worker must have considerable skill. With clay, however, it is always possible to patch and repair. Thus it is that most novices like to work in clay.

From the prehistoric temples of Malta and Crete come many examples like the little figure of the woman lying on her couch (Fig. 40). She seems to be a direct descendant of the Venus of Willendorf, but differs in that she is dressed in underskirt and overskirt, with surface designs. The rounded heavy form and the construction of the couch suggest that the model in stone really was copied from something conceived in clay. We feel the influence of the one material on the other, which brings us to the point that one of the chief duties of our developing sense of taste lies in determining appropriate materials.

As the worth of the group became manifest, the personal human element in art seems to have declined. Even body painting and tattooing, transferred to clothing and afterward to clay sculptures (Fig. 41), show that certain of the designs, derived perhaps from sewing or weaving, gradually came to be desired because of their magical significance or through linkage with certain universal signs, such as the sun, the moon, or lightning.

Wood Carving and Wall Decoration. The art of the wood carver also contributes to the technical side of design development. As one may easily discover by experimenting with an ordinary angled wood-carving chisel or a penknife, a great variety of geometric designs composed of simple cuts can be made with but one tool. They will all have a rather blocky appearance, and the regular character of the line displays a sharpness that gives an aesthetic effect of power rather than of beauty. Most primitive decorative wood carving relies for its effect upon strong contrasts of light and shade (Fig. 42).

The use of color adds interest to the wood carvings of the Polynesians and Alaskans. In Alaskan work the surfaces of boxes, totem poles, and wooden canoes are ornamented with designs so rounded and polished that the wood loses some of its original carved character and resembles stone. Areas of color are outlined with black, so that they appear flat (Fig. 43*a*). This flatness gives a decorative quality that is appropriate to wall painting on a large scale. In South and Central America, as will be shown in a later chapter, late neolithic painted wall carving comes to highest development, the

Fig. 40.—Clay figure, Hal Saflieni, Malta.

motifs uniting physioplastic and ideoplastic elements in a monumental style strangely like our comic-paper art.

Sand Painting. In the preceding chapter, the paintings from the rock shelter of Cogul in Spain (Fig. 24b), made on Old Stone Age culture levels, served to demonstrate the first steps toward the abstract art of the Neolithic age. In the traditional ceremonies of the South African and Western American Indian tribes of our own day, we may trace a further step in this development. Accurate observations of the Navajo ritual connected with the construction of sand paintings make clear the psychology of the primitive artist and the aesthetic and social significance of his work.

The Navajo's sand paintings are by no means a simple aesthetic exercise carried on for the love of art or the creation of beauty, but are part of an elaborate ritual connected with the healing of the sick. The complete treatment of a desperate illness includes not only the use of such therapeutic measures as sweat baths and herbs, but also, as a more effective agent, the singing of chants and the painting of a sacred picture to propitiate the powerful wind-gods, who are thought to have brought the plague. From agricultural levels, therefore, comes the belief stressed in modern medical literature that art has some sort of therapeutic value.

The painting, which usually shows animals and plants, the wind-gods, and perhaps the colorful rainbow-god, instructs the sick man as to his proper place in the world of super-

Fig. 41.—Painted clay figure, Klicevac, Jugoslavia.

human forces. In this work of art appear the first signs of a later, more advanced, cultural philosophy which regards the completed work as a symbol of superhuman unity. The chant or prayer sung when the painting is finished clarifies the relation of the painter to the divinity symbolized.

> Where the dark rain veils the doorway,
> To which the path runs o'er the rainbow,
> Where the zigzag lightning is high on top,
> Where the he-rain stays high on top,
> O male-god
> With your crown of dark clouds
>   Come to us. . . .

After the medicine chanter has invoked the deity and asked him to bring many good gifts to mankind, for which man will greet him with pleasure, he ends:

> Pleasantly may I walk about (live),
> Before me it will be pleasant
> Behind me it will be pleasant
> With all my surroundings pleasant
> I will walk about

Pleasant again it has come to be
Pleasant again it has come to be.[1]

The gaps between painting and sculpture and between carved, appliqué, and stamped

FIG. 42.—Carved door, Maori Hall of Judgment. (*Courtesy of Auckland Museum, New Zealand.*)

work were not known to the Central American Indians. In their painted-stucco wall reliefs they combined all the styles. Mixing clay and lime with colors, they applied the compound to the carved wall surface, choosing a design that harmonized with the technomorphic architectural decoration so as to produce a consistent architectural whole. The surface was then repainted.

After observing the technomorphic designs gradually expanding until they ornament not only the implements but the walls surrounding agricultural man, one is led to inquire as to the status of architecture on neolithic levels.

Architecture in the Agricultural Age

Residential Architecture. Home life demands the building of permanent dwellings. In the age of

hunting man, the houses were impermanent skin tents, brush shelters, or caves. The agriculturists built in wood, brick, or stone. Wherever neolithic man has lived, the records of his

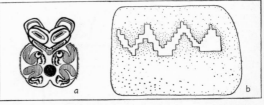

FIG. 43.—*a*, painting from house front, Tsimshian (*from Franz Boas, Primitive Art, Harvard University Press, Cambridge, Mass.*); *b*, wall painting, cavate dwelling, Rito de los Frijoles.

village life may be studied in the round and rectangular pits left where his houses stood. The earliest house form discovered in Europe, a Hallstatt dwelling in Grossgartach, Württemberg, had a rectangular shape, with low walls. Still clinging to the ancient walls were found remnants of yellow plaster painted with white and red zigzag lines similar to those from the ruined cliff dwellings at Rito de los Frijoles in New Mexico (Fig. 43*b*). Houses like the Grossgartach example were roofed with poles and earth. The villages of the period were walled or palisaded and often moated (Fig. 30*b*).

The hut urns (Figs. 44*a, b*) represent two still earlier types of house, built in both round and rectangular styles, with thatched roofs. These little models were made as repositories for the cremated bodies of the dead. It may be that the concept of the human body as a house for the spirit grew up at that time, for some of the hut urns gradually came to assume human shape, and were decorated with nose and eyes (Fig. 44*c*). Until a few years ago, there were Indian villages in northern New York, with houses like the ones shown in the hut urns. The Navajo hogan is constructed practically the same as the house of the beaver (Fig. 44*d*).

[1] Translation by Father Hailes, O.F.M. Dr. Washington Matthews's widely quoted translation of this medicine ceremony has the last lines read, "In beauty I walk, With beauty before me, etc." The Navajo words mean the pleasant condition which comes with regained health. As far as we know, our modern term "beauty" with all its complex overtones does not occur to the primitive.

FIG. 44.—*a, b*, hut urns, Etruria; *c*, hut urn, Troy; *d*, Navajo hogan.

For the student interested in the civic arts or in community planning, the development of the great pueblos and cliff dwellings holds the greatest interest. Such communal dwellings usually center around two structures: the great underground rooms or kivas in which the males congregate under the leadership of the war priest and the smaller, cell-like apartments built by the women under the supervision of the medicine man.

The picture of the kiva from the prehistoric pueblo at Aztec, New Mexico (Fig. 45), restored and photographed by Earl Morris, shows the probable origin of all domed architecture in the beaver-hut prototypes. Around the circular wall, sunk in a pit in the ground, the Indians placed pilasters at regular intervals. Upon these they laid a row of logs cut at the ends so as to fit snugly against one another. Another row was placed upon the first, a little nearer to the center, and still another above that, until finally, at the top, only a small opening remained. As the logs were laid, moist earth or clay was tamped around the outside, until the final layers of logs emerged above the ground. A circular stone wall filled with earth protected the upper part of the structure. The hole left in the top became the entrance. In the center of this underground lodge was a great council fire supplied with a draft of air by a duct, which crossed the floor and ran up inside the wall. The ceremonies connected with the kiva are accurately described in the novel *The Delight Makers* by the archaeologist, Bandelier.

Contrasted with this kiva building for the males were the communal houses or pueblos for the women and children (Fig. 46). The picture shows, to the left of the foremost ladder, the platform of the medicine man who supervised the feminine activities of the tribe, surrounded by the well-built, straight-walled rooms of a cliff dweller's pueblo, the so-called Spruce-tree House at Mesa Verde in southern Colorado. In pueblos such as this the rooms were built around a court or in a semicircle, forming an outer defensive wall. The illustration shows clearly the careful building methods and the angular step-back construction, which developed naturally from the character of the building materials and the necessity for a compact community. The appearance of this section of one of the earliest North American towns is not unlike that of our latest skyscraper cities. In meeting the need for light and air, for storage room, and for defense, the builders arrived at a similar, almost crystalline, aesthetic form.

The lake dwellings (Fig. 30*b*) built by the Swiss Alpine people more than 7,000 years ago were constructed over the water, with tamped earthen floors. The walls of the huts were wattled, that is, woven like basketwork, and plastered with mud. Some huts were built on sunken rafts, others on piles. Each had a causeway connecting it with the land.

Two Fundamental City Plans. In studying these early dwellings, the student should note the growth of two types of city plan, each with its particular aesthetic significance. The round pueblo type of village, with its underground, domed council rooms or kivas, like South African kraals (Fig. 30*a*), developed about the central plaza (Fig. 47a). In time, this arrangement came to be adopted as the circular city plan, much as we find it today in Washington, D. C. In such a city, the observer at the intersection

few and fundamental. They rise from the desire to express strength, dignity, and greatness through sheer mass. These fundamental characteristics will be observed as we follow

Fig. 45.—Interior underground kiva, Aztec, New Mexico. (*Photograph by Morris, courtesy of Amer. Mus. of Natural History.*)

of any two streets can always see the central building.

The square city plan resembles that of the Swiss lake dwellings or of the Terra Mare village built by late lake-dwelling people in northern Italy (Fig. 47b). This plan is rectangular, and in a city so constructed the dweller can see the center of the city only on the axial lines.

Funerary and Memorial Architecture. Funerary and memorial architecture duplicate in permanent form the dwellings of the living. The development of such architecture is, of necessity, delayed until the tribes are settled in fixed abodes. While possessing characteristics indigenous both geographically and historically to their creators, the structural designs are

around the world the attempts of primitive peoples to glorify their leaders and their gods. From the memorial building to the religious edifice is but a short step.

As a protection against predatory beasts, prehistoric man sometimes elevated the grave of the departed one on stilts. At other times the body was interred and covered with heavy stones. In Northern Europe, between the close of the early Stone Age and the beginning of the age of polished stone, a race of builders thrived who seem to have specialized in funerary architecture. The first stone-chest grave is in this locality. It is no more than its name implies—a chest of flat stone. In time, these builders varied their forms and constructed the stone chest aboveground, with a covered passage of stone leading up to it. The whole, covered with earth, formed a domical pile or tumulus. In their present state these chest

the most part, devoid of ornament, their weight alone suggesting their function. Many of the memorials of the late war take the shape of a heavy column. Styles in funerary art, inciden-

Fig. 46.—Spruce-tree House, Mesa Verde, Colorado.

graves, aboveground and denuded of the covering of earth, are known to us as dolmens. The dolmens were decorated with carvings, which may have been colored. The ornament, in most cases representing some part of the human body, probably indicated a particular quality of the person buried. The best known examples of modern tumulus tombs in Europe are those of Hadrian in Rome and of Napoleon in Paris. The tombs of Lincoln and Grant in the United States are also of the tumulus type.

The menhirs, monumental perpendicular shafts erected in commemoration of the brute strength of individuals or groups, are almost universal in their distribution. They are, for

tally, have changed less than those in connection with any other element of man's life. In Carnac, Brittany, the massive menhirs stand in long parallel rows that suggest the columns of a large open-air temple. The circular arrangement is best exemplified in the famous Stonehenge on Salisbury Plain in southwestern England (Fig. 48). Here the great stones, placed in a ring 106 feet in diameter, are joined by lintels. Five great sets of three stones each in post-and-lintel construction stand within the ring, and stones of lesser dimensions are so placed as to suggest that this was an open-air meeting ground, with the star-studded dome of the sky as its covering.

In Sardinia and Ireland round towers seem to mark the next step in prehistoric stone construction. These towers, called "nuraghi," at times rise two stories in height, with domed

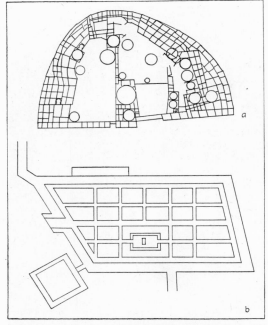

FIG. 47.—*a*, round city plan, Pueblo Bonito; *b*, square city plan, Terra Mare Castellazzo di Pavoletta.

chambers and passageways spiraling upward inside them. Their construction, as well as the shape of the high inner rooms, seems to link them with certain underground structures on the Island of Malta. At three points on that Island—Hagiar Kim, Gozo, and Hal Saflieni —great complexes of rooms forming underground temples have been discovered.

Possessing both circular and quadrate rooms, these labyrinths give us roofs constructed of superimposed stones (Fig. 12*f*). Wishing to roof a space too large for a low dome or a single flat rock, the builders invented what is known as the false or corbeled arch. A small stone was placed in the center of one of the round rooms. Upon this a slightly larger stone was placed, and this in turn was covered by another still

larger. The size of the upper rocks was increased gradually until the resulting column, tapering toward the base, joined the side walls (Fig. 49*a*). Some of the underground rooms in

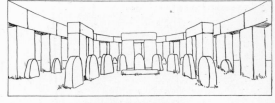

FIG. 48.—Stonehenge.

Malta, like the hypogeum, or Holy of Holies, in the temple, although carved out of solid rock, retain this corbeling, which now becomes an architectural[1] ornament (Fig. 49*b*). The effect is surprisingly modern. The corbeled column plays a very definite part in the architecture of the Palace of Knossos on Crete, while in Cretan art it appears frequently as an object of veneration. The reversed column is unstable and serves no architectonic purpose. As an aesthetic phenomenon, however, it persists throughout the history of European building. When man wishes to stress his mastery over materials, its very unsteadiness lends it an aesthetic significance.

The primitive types of funerary and memorial architecture earlier discussed will be found distributed throughout the globe. In Egypt the primitive chest grave was underground and covered with a structure of baked brick. The structure held a room to be used for the ancestral cult worship. In India, a building of similar origin in tumulus shape and fenced by a circular wall of ornamental megalithic blocks is known as the "stupa" (Fig. 415, Chap. XIV). Counterparts of the great inner portals of the prehistoric British Stonehenge serve as entrances to the stupa enclosures and also as the *torii* (ceremonial gateways) of the Japanese temples. This particular type of ornamental portal, covered with intricate decoration (Fig. 42), appears again as one of the chief elements

[1] The term "architectural" is used to signify ornament in building after its primary or architectonic significance has been lost.

a   b

Fig. 49.—*a*, reversed column, Hagiar Kim, Malta; *b*, Holy of Holies, in Hypogeum, Hal Saflieni, Malta. (*Courtesy of the National Geographic Society and Mr. W. A. Griffiths.*)

in the buildings of the races living on the shores of the Pacific. The erect pillar, too, is not wanting, for the elaborately carved totem poles of the American Northwest, the tribal poles of Turkestan, and the menhirs of Brittany, all have the same significance.

In South America, the engraved steles of the Maya and the monolithic doors of the Peruvian Incas complete the list of structures of monumental nature. In practically all neolithic carving of a ceremonial nature the entire surface is filled (Fig. 42), as though primitive man had a horror vacui—a fear of empty spaces in which evil spirits might lurk. This would seem to support the fear theory of early artistic origins, were it not for the fact that in European artifacts we find great simplicity at most neolithic levels.

This short review of the primitive building types serves to show that from the earliest times the spiritual significance of the building, as expressed in ornamental surfaces, has been closely united with its material function. From the tangible arts of pottery and weaving, with their effect upon architecture and the representational arts, let us now move to a consideration of music, drama, and poetry.

Music and Poetry in the Agricultural Age

Music

The musical instruments of the agricultural age may be divided into three classes: (1) percussion instruments, which include drums, rattles, and the marimba, or xylophone (Fig. 50*a*, *b*); (2) wind instruments, which include whistles, flutes, and horns (Fig. 50*c*, *d*); and (3) stringed instruments, including lyres and bowed fiddles (Fig. 50*f*, *g*).

Percussion Instruments. Percussion instruments, such as drums or tom-toms, achieve necessarily the finest rhythmic effects. This is probably owing to the fact that the drumhead, giving under the stroke of the stick, causes a rebound. The drum sounds one note, which may be repeated at rapid or slow intervals. As the rhythm is accelerated, the senses respond in terms of a more feverish pulse beat, with accompanying emotions of excitement, anger, fear, or the like. The effect of a slow rhythm, on the other hand, is calming. A heavy beat suggests power; a light beat, grace and movement.

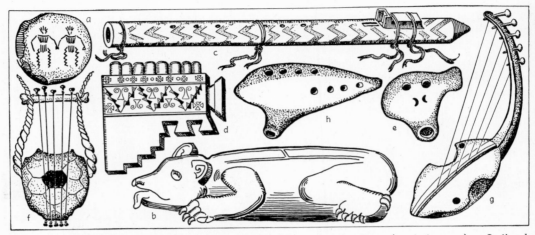

FIG. 50.—Musical instruments. *a*, Sioux Indian drum; *b*, Mayan wooden drum (marimba type); *c*, Indian love flute; *d*, Peruvian syrinx; *e*, Peruvian whistle; *f*, primitive African lyre; *g*, African harp; *h*, ocarina.

Wind Instruments. The reed, or whistle, may be made to give a succession of notes at different levels, which often form a pattern, or melody. Two or more reeds blown together produce a pleasing effect of harmony if the vibrations are regularly spaced; if, however, the vibrations are irregular, the combination of sounds is dissonant and imparts a feeling of unrest. Inharmonious combinations usually demand resolution into consonance.

Figure 50 shows an aboriginal pottery whistle (*e*) and its derivative, the ocarina (*h*), which has almost exactly the same range of notes as the ancient Peruvian syrinx (*d*). Figure 51*a* presents the notes which can be played upon these primitive Panpipes. Sometimes the whistles had five notes, sometimes more. One of the primitive scales used by the Indians, the Chinese, and the Celtic Scotch can be duplicated by playing upon the black keys of a piano. Using this scale and counting the group of three black notes with the numerals 1, 2, 3, and the group of two as 4 and 5 (See Fig. 51*b*), one can play a simple melody (probably derived as much from Indian as from Negro sources), recognizable as a theme in Dvořák's *New World Symphony*.

Stringed Instruments. The stringed instrument in its earliest form was probably a bowstring. When it was twanged, the string gave forth a note; when it was held with the fingers of one hand and twanged again, another note resulted. If the string had another bowstring drawn across it, particularly if the second string was resinated so that it gripped the first, the note could be sustained and made loud or soft at will. By varying the length of the first string, the player could produce a melody.

Instruments such as the lyre (Fig. 50*f*) were early made with strings of fixed length, to be plucked. Bowed instruments, however, remained in their primitive state in the Occident until the Middle Ages, when they were changed by the Celts into the ancestors of the violin. Just as the drum seems to create rhythm, stringed instruments create melody, almost of themselves. A little experience will make it possible to play a simple tune on one string of a violin. Each type of violin has a tonal quality, or timbre, of its own, depending upon the material of which it is made. Different varnishes and the grain of different pieces of wood affect the quality of the tone. The charm of the violin section in the great symphony orchestra arises from the collective effect of many differing voices uniting to express a common theme.

Poetry

With the introduction of musical instruments, the dramatic forms of art in dance and poetry can be recognized as separate and distinct creative exercises. The American Indian or the African native today delights in telling long, childish stories, endowing animals, trees, and inanimate objects with personalities. These tales contain much repetition of familiar words and imitation of animal cries. There may be action as well, mimicking the activity of the animals.

The following song of the Pima Indians, cited by Frank Russell, was probably part of a religious ceremony.

> Wind now commences to sing;
> Wind now commences to sing;
> Wind now commences to sing;
> The land stretches before me,
> Before me it stretches away.
>
> Wind's house now is thundering;
> Wind's house now is thundering;
> Came the myriad-legged wind,
> The wind came running hither.
>
> The Black Snake Wind came to me;
> The Black Snake Wind came to me.
> Came and wrapped itself about,
> Came here running with its song.[1]

It will be observed that even the English version of this song, when recited aloud, achieves a distinct emotional effect. In recitation the word "wind" can be made onomatopoetic, so that the wind seems identified with the reader's own breath. Thus the wind takes on personality. In like manner, the sibilants in the first lines by repetition become a hiss, and this sound, associated with the undulating movement and swirl of the wind, conjures up the image of the Black Snake in the third stanza. To further the personification of the wind, the singer envisions the land stretching ahead of him as the plain on which the wind will run. Running requires locomotion, the legs of a man. The storm cloud becomes the wind's home. Thunder means lightning as well, and with lightning the singer imagines torn tresses of clouds. Tresses in turn are associated with the Black Snake which wraps itself around an object. The singer now imagines himself as enfolded by the long strands of the wind-whipped black clouds, and the excitation of his fantasy seems complete. He has reached a pantheistic state of mind wherein his life, animal life, and

a

Fig. 51*a*.—Scale of Peruvian syrinx.

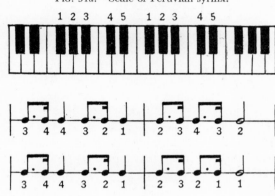

b

Fig. 51*b*.—Primitive type of melody in five-note scale.

natural phenomena have been woven into one fabric. Through his song the singer has become one with the energy and movement of the universe.

As the primitive singer tells the story of the Black Snake, he will probably rise from his place in the group and demonstrate in pantomime how the snake moves. If he is a natural leader, he will encourage other members of the tribe to follow him, until at last a long serpent of tribesmen is undulating around the campfire like a black snake. Thus the primitive dance drama begins along with poetry and song. Not content with their temporal veneration of the Black Snake, the group may bring together a long mound of earth, such as the Ohio serpent mound (Fig. 52). The circle of the arts is then complete; the ceremony has become a monumental religious edifice.

Much of primitive poetry, as Boas has pointed out, resembles the verse below, which has no end. One mental picture calls up another; and

---

[1] "Song of the Pima Indians," from *Twenty-sixth Annual Report of the Bureau of American Ethnology*, Smithsonian Institution, Washington, D. C.

with modern man, as with the Indian, such a poem would grow into epic proportions.

> The stem bends as the leaves shoot up,
> The leaf-stems sway to and fro.

FIG. 52. Serpent mound, Ohio. (*Photograph by Albert W. Stevens, courtesy of the National Geographic Society.*)

> To and fro they sway in diverse ways.
> We rub them and they lose their stiffness
> On Mount Inas they are blown about.
> On Mount Inas which is our home.
> Blown about by the light breeze.
> Blown about is the fog (?).
> Blown about is the haze.
> Blown about are the young shoots.
> Blown about is the haze of the hills,
> Blown about by the light breeze, etc.

This is the primitive mythological forerunner of the historical narrative. Its very monotony produces a certain rhythm which the primitive appreciates for its aesthetic value.

From the great body of undifferentiated primitive mythology handed down from generation to generation by the storytellers and medicine men emerge three distinct poetic themes. Among the tribes that eventually became the Greeks and the Hindus, the idea grew that the world dominated by man was controlled by anthropomorphic, or manlike, gods.

The great Homeric epics, *The Iliad* and *The Odyssey*, as we shall see, deal almost exclusively with the struggles of men among themselves. The northern Germanic epics, on the other hand, which arose from the people whose original homes were in the lake dwellings of Switzerland, are concerned with the struggles between the forces of good and evil. In poems such as *Beowulf*, the *Volsunga Saga*, and the *Nibelungenlied*, men are often shown as opposed to the powers of nature. A third type, the American epic, *Quetzalcoatl*, produced in the quasi-Oriental Mayan culture of Central America, deals with the hero-god who is almost completely identifiable with the never-ending charm of nature. In later chapters, the development of these three themes in literature, with their corresponding philosophies and psychology, will be used to explain the evolution of the other arts.

The Indian poem on page 68 is a purely eidetic representation in words. This effect is now known as "naturalism" in literature. Naturalistic literature is usually physioplastic. The first poem, the song of the wind, goes much further, in that it takes eidetic images and builds from them a mental abstraction, the personification of the wind—a personification which we know to be a nonnatural phenomenon. In such primitive abstractions one finds the beginning of later ideoplastic literature. These two currents of imaginative and naturalistic verbal expression persist throughout the entire development of literature.

Summary

In this chapter we have observed the changing styles of art that developed when the nomadic hunter shifted to a more sedentary agricultural life. The increased importance of the woman's function in society conditions the mind of agricultural man to an awakening appreciation of her influence upon life. Accompanying this change there goes a trend away from naturalism in the representational arts.

Decline of Naturalism. As has been already discovered, the causes for the decay of naturalism may have been threefold. (1) The predominance of technomorphic design, calling for geometric angular figures, probably influenced man's skill in painting and drawing. (2) A more organized religion came into being. In well-organized religions, as we shall discover in later chapters, the priestcraft tries to focus the imagination of the worshipers upon a few abstract symbols. These replace the need for an actual representation, such as one would find in the hunter's religion of magic, or fetishism. (3) Perhaps most important, the newly recognized universal powers of earth, sun, wind, and rain could not easily be represented naturalistically in terms of graphic and plastic arts.

Accompanying the decline of naturalism, greater emphasis was placed upon the arts of poetry, drama, and music, which were capable of more completely expressing abstract, involved ideas. Abstract ideas accompany cultivation, culture, or civilization. In the long history of culture, new thought groupings, along with new social and emotional needs, always call forth new combinations of these two early modes of expression—naturalistic and abstract art—in new art forms.

Painting vs. Writing. As man comes more and more to depend upon complicated thought groupings that cannot be expressed in simple pictures or in pictographic symbols (Figs. 22, 29), he invents a method of combining symbols to stand for the new spoken words that have grown up. These combinations replace the early picture language, for the symbols, once they are recognizable as writing, make the pictures unnecessary. Thus, writing comes to replace painting.

In Egyptian art, as we shall see, man was reluctant to leave his picture writing and used word-sound symbols and pictures together to record past events and future desires. Egyptian writing, therefore, remained in the pictographic stage, and Egyptian painting retained a certain amount of realism.

Bibliography

HARRISON, JANE: *Ancient Art and Ritual*, Henry Holt & Company, Inc., New York, 1913.

REINACH, SALOMON: *Orpheus*, Liveright Publishing Corporation, New York, 1935.

SPEARING, HERBERT GREEN: *The Childhood of Art*, Henry Holt & Company, Inc., New York.

BOAS, FRANZ: *Primitive Art*, Harvard University Press, Cambridge, Mass., 1927.

BANDELIER, A. F. A: *The Delight Makers* (novel), Dodd, Mead & Company, Inc., New York, 1916.

Recordings

Snake Dance (Hopi Chanters), V 20043.
Sunrise and *Blanket* songs, V 20983 a.
Lover's Wooing, V 20983 b.

CHAPTER IV

The Religious Art of Egypt

The waters of life that are in the sky come;
The waters of life that are in the earth come.
The sky burns for thee,
The earth trembles for thee,
Before the divine birth.
The two mountains divide,
The god becomes,
The god takes possession of his body,
The two mountains divide,
This king Neferkere becomes,
This king Neferkere takes possession of his body.
"HYMN TO OSIRIS"[1]

THUS FAR we have discussed the art of the human race as a whole. We have found that art is universal. We have discovered, too, that as long as the human race is fundamentally the same in all parts of the globe, so too will aesthetic production be fundamentally similar. As man advances beyond the two primitive culture stages of hunting and agriculture, however, his art is influenced by the ever-increasing complexity of human personality. With the innovation of recorded history, such changes as have occurred are further emphasized by the individual and complex personality of each separate people. The definition of racial styles is complete when each group has created its own criteria for aesthetic effectiveness—beauty, power of expression, or whatever it may be called. From a grouping of racial contributions one develops an unprejudiced understanding of the past, a sympathetic appreciation of what may be found in the art of the present, and perhaps a basis for predicting the art of the future.

Our first case study of racial style should be, logically, the aesthetic experience of the oldest people recorded in history. Which is the oldest culture? A Hindu or a Chinese might with some justice claim the distinction for his people. Influenced by Western thought habit, we are prone to award the palm to Egypt.

Despite evidence of Egypt's great antiquity, however, many archaeologists doubt whether Egyptian culture was, in point of time, the first. Recent discoveries in Mesopotamia and India lead many thinkers to believe that man grew into advanced states of culture in several places simultaneously. When we recall how widespread were the primitive cultures discussed in the preceding chapter, we see the logic of this conclusion.

Nevertheless, though future discoveries may bring to light ancient civilizations coeval with or even slightly older than Egypt, we shall somewhat arbitrarily deal first with Egyptian culture, chiefly because it has greatly influenced the classical, or humanistic, trend of Western thought.

[1] J. H. BREASTED, *Development of Religion and Thought in Ancient Egypt*, p. 145, Charles Scribner's Sons, New York, 1912.

Factors in the Evolution of Egyptian Art

The Will to Transcend Environment. Since the appearance of Hippolyte Taine's masterful *History of English Literature*, many art critics and aestheticians have attempted, not without some justice, to explain the arts primarily in terms of geophysical environment. This explanation is good as far as it goes. Certainly the civilization of Egypt was greatly influenced by the Nile, which regularly deposited its rich mud along the narrow strip of land between desert and cliffs. The lives of the inhabitants moved in a yearly rhythm governed by the ebb and flow of that mighty river.

Throughout that whole extent of river, desert, and cliffs, however, there were few media for aesthetic expression. The river yielded little more than materials for the mud huts in domestic architecture. There was some alabaster and limestone, which is fairly soft, but the basaltic cliffs along the banks of the upper Nile offered a very refractory material for stone carving—a material not to be compared with the easily cut marble of Greece. Although the flora and fauna —papyrus, lotus, crocodile, serpent, and hippopotamus—contributed to the totem-making propensities of the primitive Nile dwellers, there was little wood for firing pottery; there were no ready-made cave walls, such as the Cro-Magnons possessed, for painting, and few easily worked metals. Almost none of the materials and few of the art forms that make up the deathless power and mystical beauty of Egyptian art were indigenous to the Nile Valley proper. Ivory, lapis, bronze, copper, iron, precious woods, incense—all were introduced from other localities, some of which, like the land of Punt, have not been definitely placed, even in our day of archaeological exploration.

Were Egyptian art, then, governed entirely by local physical, geographic, or climatic conditions, it would no doubt have resembled that of the Pueblo culture in the Southwest of the United States. The fact, however, that the Egyptians went beyond their environment to find the materials necessary for self-expression points toward a more logical explanation of their aesthetic development. That explanation lies in the character of the Egyptians themselves, rather than in the character of their physical environment.

The Complex Character of the Egyptian. Before the dawn of history, when much of the desert was still forested, a racial mixture, perhaps of Grimaldi and Cro-Magnon men, must have taken place in the Nile Valley. The finely chipped flint knives associated with the hunting man persist as ceremonial objects throughout Egyptian history, alongside neolithic polished-stone instruments. The result of the mixture of the two cultures was a small, rather thin-boned individual, rarely exceeding five feet four inches in height. The physioplastic representative art proper to the hunting man and the ideoplastic abstract art of the agricultural man were both possible for him. During his 3,000 years of historical development, first representative and then abstract art prevailed, but with the abstract on the whole predominant. Having wider horizons and more diverse background, the mind of the early Egyptian soon outstripped that of the primitive savage.

The Importance of Organized Religion. The growth of a social structure is analogous to the development of a living organism: all its components do not mature with equal speed. Consequently, the favored factor in the social organism often becomes not only an influence upon all the other constituents of the social complex but a dominant impulse in the psychological mind-set of the race. In Egypt this dominant factor was religion, a social force which, as we have seen in earlier chapters, first led man's thoughts beyond his everyday material needs to a less physical view of life. The prestige exercised by the highly refined and intricate religious ritual of Egypt affected government, commerce, domestic and social life, education and science, war and art. Egyptian art, indeed, was entirely subordinated to Egyptian religion and became the most important means by which its grip upon the racial mind was retained.

This religious complex of Egyptian art had great influence upon the development of human thought, particularly in classical antiquity. In fact, it is by many considered the *sine qua non* for the study of all Western humanistic religions and arts. Many of the Greeks looked to Egypt as the spiritual mother of their civilization. Plato, when recounting the tale of Atlantis, points to Egypt as the source of his information concerning that lost civilization. Hence, in examining Egyptian art before all others, we enter upon a sequence of allied art movements from which evolves our own modern conception that the purpose of art is to make man's dreams and religious aspirations or ideals permanent. This thought is the center of the humanistic, or classical, art complex.

The Influence of Political History. History as yet presents no clear picture of the years of precultural development in the Nile Valley between 6000 and 3400 B.C. It is known that the people who lived in the fertile delta of the Nile near the shores of the Mediterranean came from many places—from Asia, from the coast of Northern Africa, and from the general direction of the southern deserts beyond which lay Eritrea and Somaliland.

Among the invaders who reached the delta around the year 5000 B.C. was one particularly dynamic group headed by a great war chief called "Horus." In later dynastic times his name became identified with that of the sky-god whose symbol was the eagle or the hawk. By 4241 B.C. the people of the delta had invented a calendar that allowed 365 days for the year. This invention shows that they had reached a relatively advanced stage in astronomical investigation and had begun to record history. By 3400 B.C. several of the strong monarchs of southern Egypt, who considered Horus their ancestor, succeeded in uniting that terri-

tory with the delta. Among these kings occur the names of Ip (the scorpion king), Narmer, and AhaMen, or Menes. The signs, or totems, of these kings appear on a number of ceremonial palettes or spearheads, one of which —the palette of Narmer—we shall discuss later.

The important thing to remember concerning these half-legendary war chiefs who became the Pharaohs is that they must have been accompanied in their work by medicine men who became the priests. During the early dynasties between 3400 and 2980 B.C., the Pharaohs were dominant. During the dynasties between the Third (2980 B.C.) and the end of the Middle Kingdom (1580 B.C.), the priests ruled. Then for a time in the early part of the New Kingdom (dynasties of 1580 to 1205 B.C.) came a line of strong Pharaohs, followed by a return of the priests until Roman times. When the Pharaohs dominated, great memorial tombs and pyramids were built. When the priests dominated, enormous temples for communal worship were constructed. Both priests and Pharaohs had as their chief interest the exploitation, feeding, and protection of the people, who constituted part of their inheritance.

Pre-dynastic Artifacts

In studying the art of the various cultures a general law of development may be observed at work: The most advanced or complete compositions in the finest days of a culture are but refinements and enlargements upon the simple, geometric forms conceived in the prehistoric days of the culture. The law operates as follows. As a culture grows, the most talented craftsmen produce the monumental, publicly acclaimed works. To appeal to a wide public, however, these works must be based upon the broadly accepted folk art. Their composition schemes of color, line, and form are, therefore, similar to the composition schemes of the most primitive art of the culture. Only by the fineness of his work, by the appropriate use of

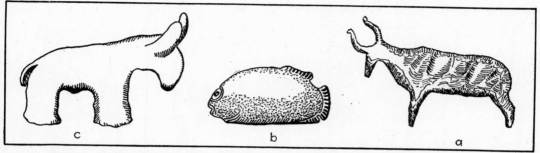

FIG. 53.—Prehistoric sculpture. *a*, flint, Abydos; *b*, polished stone, Nakkad; *c*, clay Abydos.

themes, or the introduction now and then of some new spiritual concept, may the individual artist raise his work above the folk-art level. In our own day, the large numbers of murals created in the United States between 1910 and 1935 by Cornwall, Benton, Rivera, Orozco, and others show the composition and color schemes to be found in the folk art of the colored comic strips to which, over the last forty years, American children have been conditioned.

Egyptian art never loses the following primitive elements inherited from its early designs: Human figures are used as geometric space-filling areas. Usually the shoulders are turned to face out, so that the form more completely fills the space. The more important figures, such as the Pharaoh, occupy more space, impressing by their size. The eye is usually shown from the front, even in a profile face, probably because to the primitive the eye has more power to charm if seen from that angle. The pose of the figures, dominated by the geometric composition form, always appears stiff and angular. For the greater part, true perspective is unknown, figures being shown one above another when depth is to be indicated. When figures are sculptured in the round, they present a continual reminder of the blocks from which they were hewn.

Sculpture in Flint and Clay. Pre-dynastic Egyptian sculpture grows naturally, by easy stages, out of paleolithic and neolithic techniques. The three forms shown in Fig. 53 will make this clear. In (*a*), the art of flint chipping, as finally developed in the highest Magdalenian levels, was applied to the problem of rendering the animal form. In shape, this and many other animals are similar to those found in the line drawings of the rock shelter at Cogul and elsewhere in Northern Africa.

With a desire for greater finish came animal sculptures in polished stone (Fig. 53*b*). These are particularly noteworthy as demonstrating the tendency to simplification and abstraction of form peculiar to the work of neolithic, or agricultural, man. Instead of carving fragile, easily broken legs or horns, the artist now brings the extremities of the animal into the mass, or selects as his subject matter animals, like this fish, which suggest the mass.

As the art of working in clay developed and it was discovered that the clay could be hardened in the fire, heavy, seminaturalistic figures (Fig. 53*c*) were made in the new medium and painted in color. Pre-dynastic sculptors acknowledged two possible ways of rendering a form: naturalistically and abstractly. As time went on, the abstract was to develop in preference to the naturalistic, particularly in the monumental works.

Our immediate mental image when Egyptian sculpture is mentioned is the seated or standing form of the Pharaoh. The seated and standing types of Egyptian sculpture originated and became fixed during the pre-dynastic times (Fig. 54*a*). Usually the figure stands stiffly, with one foot advanced slightly in front of the other and with the arms held close to the sides.

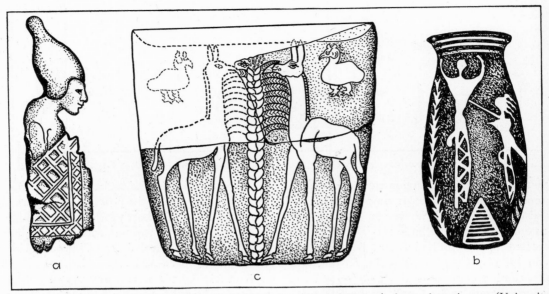

FIG. 54.—*a*, ivory figure, Abydos, height about 3⅓ inches (British Museum); *b*, pre-dynastic vase (University College, London); *c*, reconstructed palette, Thinite dynasty, 11 by 13 inches (Ashmolean Museum, Oxford).

Architecture. In prehistoric times agricultural man in Egypt buried his dead in great pottery urns, the body being flexed into a crouching position. He also built tumulus tombs, of which the dolmens or stone remains still appear. In pre-dynastic graves one can study the development of both the corbeled and the true arch and of the post-and-lintel construction. The graves of the early pre-dynastic kings are crudely arched structures. Significantly enough, this arched or vaulted grave form later disappears, for the most part, in Egyptian architecture, giving place to the stone post and lintel. In other words, a static rather than an organic form of architecture, with but few notable exceptions, becomes the rule in dynastic times.

There is a great difference between the aesthetic possibilities of the two types of structure. In the post-and-lintel construction the horizontal lines of the lintel hold one's attention to the ground. One can almost feel the tremendous weight of the material. The springing arch or dome, on the other hand, carries the eye upward and has less feeling of heaviness. Holding the eye along the horizontal line of the ground,

the post-and-lintel construction suggests that Egyptian concept of religion which made the final destination of the soul a shadowy realm under the earth.

Early Spatial Design on Pottery and in Relief Carving. The pottery of pre-dynastic Egypt developed through all the forms found in the previous neolithic culture. Somewhere about the sixth millennium B.C., however, Egyptian potters discovered the possibility of painting a layer of white clay over the ordinary red fired pot or vase. Most pre-dynastic vases similar to the one pictured in Fig. 54*b* combined the geometric designs of agricultural man with human figures. The bodies, perhaps under the influence of a weaving technique, were represented by a series of straight lines. The heads and torsos, like those in the neolithic pictographs, appear as triangles. In the new development these geometric figures were so arranged that they made a well-defined pattern, with interesting intervening spaces in darker values. This space-filling refinement of early Egyptian pictorial composition appears in the finest of later dynastic work, although lacking in the great mass of Egyptian pictures. It is closely related to the occult balance later to be found in the best of Oriental painting.

Like the bit of pottery, the stone palettes or the gazelle, on the other hand, are in correct perspective, one infers that by this time the Egyptian artist could create at will either physioplastic (naturalistic) or ideoplastic (abstract)

Fig. 55.—Palette of Narmer (Boudjaou), pre-dynastic or First dynasty, 3400-3060 B.C. *a*, obverse; *b*, reverse. Height about 20 inches (Cairo Egyptian Museum). (*Courtesy of Lesch-Carnegie.*)

ceremonial spearheads often seen in the graves of late pre-dynastic or early dynastic times present some of the finest examples of balance. On the palette from the Oxford University Museum one sees two gazelles, one on each side of a palm tree (Fig. 54*c*). So realistic are they that they might well have been the work of a physioplastic Magdalenian artist. Geometrical forms, however, were already strong in this artist's mind. The two legs of the bird, one behind the other, suggest that he had the will to create a space-filling design. Since the legs of

art. In Fig. 54*c* he chose to put both types on one artistic object. Though the primitive experimenter does not mind this, the aesthetically refined individual finds such attempts unpleasant.

The opposite side of the little palette from the Oxford Museum has a scene like that found on the famous palette of Narmer, one of the legendary founders of the First Egyptian or Thinite dynasty. As this palette unites all the characteristics of Egyptian art so far discussed, it may be regarded as a connecting link between pre-dynastic and dynastic art.

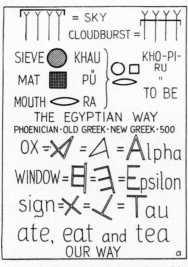

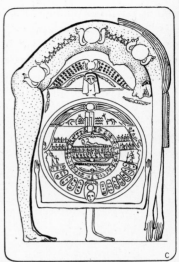

Fig. 56.—*a*, Egyptian pictographs or hieroglyphs (Maspero); *b*, goddess Thoueris, Twenty-sixth dynasty, Karnak, height about 3½ feet (Cairo Museum); *c*. sky-goddess Nut, relief from coffin, Sakkareh, Thirtieth dynasty, c. 35 B.C. (cast in Metropolitan Museum of Art).

The Palette of Narmer. Archaeologists believe that such slate palettes as this served not only the useful function of holders for war paint, but had also ceremonial significance as insignia. Similar large ceremonial spearheads have been found in the mounds of the American Indians.

At the top of the palette of Narmer, two heads decorate the nubbins by which the spear was fastened to the shaft. These great-eyed cows, symbolizing the mother goddess Hathor, appear later at the top of Egyptian columns. Below the nubbins, a pictorial band shows the king wearing the crown of Lower, or northern, Egypt. He appears again on the other side of the palette with the crown of Upper Egypt (Fig. 55). Observe that the king is characteristically much larger than his subjects, who carry banners. The staves from which the banners fly are topped with the hawk symbol and other totemistic signs, comparable to the ceremonial eagles on our flagstaffs today. The decapitated victims of the king's military conquests appear alongside in neat rows, each with his head tucked between his legs. All this detail betokens the desire of the artist to fill the surface completely with design—a reminder of his

primitivism. In the band below the king and his subjects, slaves restrain two long-necked, catlike animals from fighting each other. This symbolic scene, which appears many times in the art of Egypt, refers to the power of the Pharaoh who pacified Upper and Lower Egypt. The last band shows the monarch as a bull breaking down the walls of a city and trampling upon its "people," here personified by one man.

The bands of decoration distributed over the surface of the palette bear little relation to its shape. They, therefore, detract from the decorative quality of the object itself. We shall have to wait for the Greeks to take over this type of ornament in their early vases and refine it to a more perfect unity with the shape to which it is applied. The Egyptians, like the wood carvers of the South Sea Islands, used their decoration rather indiscriminately, choosing for the most part to leave no surface unadorned. This characteristic may be regarded as an aesthetic primitivism.

The Rise of Writing. The ceremonial palette of Narmer furnishes what is perhaps the first historical record. Here art has obviously been used as a means of narration. To make the narrative clearer, pictographic signs have been developed and the name of the king appears on the palette as such a sign between the two cow heads.

In Egypt the pictographs from prehistoric times always retained their naturalistic outlines. Although some of the phrases in time developed a shortened, cursive script—the demotic (Fig. 82)—it seems as though the scribes were reluctant to leave the finely drawn pictures of utensils, animals, insects, and people which stood for their word sounds and ideas (56*a*). The sun, for example, was always represented by the sign ☉, a centered disk, the moon by ☽, a crescent and a man by ⚹ a squatting figure. As the spoken language became complicated and abstract, the old signs were variously combined to stand for new words and new concepts, though they kept as far as possible their naturalistic forms. Compound words were represented somewhat as follows. The Egyptians always pictured the heavens as upheld by four tree trunks, rather like the legs which held up the body of the sacred cow. The sign for the heavens, 𝍬, dropped down over the upper part of the sign for the pillars of the sky, 𝍬, meant a "cloudburst." Again, signs for different words were added together to make another word with the combined sound values. For example, the word "sieve," ◉, was called "khau"; the word "mat" ▦, "pu" or "pi"; and the word "mouth," ⬭, "ra" or "ru." The three together sounded khau-pi-ru. This was like the word "khopiru," which meant the verb "to be," so this verb was written with the three signs combined, as in Fig. 56*a*.

Obviously, so clumsy a system of pictographic writing made it difficult to coin new words for new thoughts. The emphasis of the Egyptian's spiritual life, accordingly, was upon the retention of the old magical charms and prayers, rather than on the creation of new values. This is not to say that during 3,000 years the Egyptian religion remained the same. Change was inevitable over so long a period. The rate of change, however, was distinctly retarded by the Egyptian method of writing.

Egyptian Religion and Literature

The Totemistic Gods. The lowest level of Egyptian religious experience, symbolized by the worship of wild-animal totems, was an inheritance from the Old Stone Age. The earliest tribes of the Nile Valley, like modern Indian clans, were known by their totems. These included the hawk, the ibis, the jackal, the crocodile, and the hippopotamus. As religious concepts developed and manlike or anthropomorphic gods were conceived, the more savage of these wild animals were given a place as demons of the underworld. Amenit, the god with the head of a crocodile, became the devourer of souls, like the horned dragon or devil of Christian times. Anubis, the jackal-headed god, weighed the soul in the last judgment; and the ibis-headed god, Thoth, like Christianity's recording angel, reported to the sky-gods the result of the weighing. One of these deities, Thoueris, the hippopotamus goddess, associated with the fertile, life-giving Nile, is represented in Fig. 56*b*.

The Agricultural Maternal Deities. The deities of the agricultural level included goddesses of tree, field, and stream, as well as such domestic animals as the cow and the cat. Nut, the sky-goddess (Fig. 56*c*), was represented as a female figure whose breasts were the milky way or as a great cow giving milk to the thirsty.

The illustration of the goddess Nut, taken from a late sarcophagus, makes clear the fact that in Egypt the religious idea usually dominated the physical, pleasure-giving appearance of an object. If we were to attempt to frame a definition of art based on what we find in Egypt, we should have recourse to the old formula: Art is the handmaiden of religion. The attenuated figure of the goddess, stretched above another figure made up of circles, with two sets of arms and two heads, appears more as a diagram than as a human being. To the Egyptian the associational value of the object as a symbol was higher than its physical ap-

Fig. 57.—Bronze statues of Isis and Osiris, height about 8 inches. (*Courtesy of University Museum, University of Pennsylvania.*)

pearance. The abstract artists and expressionists of today take the same point of view. Figure 56c might easily be the work of some 20th-century artist inclined toward surrealism. But there is an important underlying difference. For the Egyptian artist the symbols employed had the universal sanction of the society in which he moved. The modern abstract artist is often forced to invent his symbols. As they are by no means readily accepted, he too often works as a nonsocial being in a world of his own.

The Personification of the Nile and of Upper and Lower Egypt. From the agricultural level come the earliest attempts to personify the Nile River as a source of life. At times the river was identified with a mother deity or her consort. Since the Egyptians could not conceive of life in the other world without such a river, they invented a lower or dark Nile which flowed through the underworld.

The lands of Upper and Lower Egypt were also personified, sometimes as long-necked cats (see the palette of Narmer), again as two women who wore different types of crowns. The Egyptian idea that the land which bears the life-giving grain should be personified as a woman has come down through the entire development of Occidental thought. The people of Attica thought of their city, Athens, as a woman; the English speak of Britannia; and from France we have taken our conception of the goddess Liberty, whose face appears on our coins and whose great statue stands in New York harbor.

The maternal ideal led to the development of a powerful cult which became a dominant factor in the Egyptian religion. This was the Osirian cult of Isis, Osiris, and Horus. In this religion, the goddess Isis, the great mother of a hawk-headed sun-god and the devoted wife of Osiris, took a leading role (Fig. 57).

The Fatalistic Religions of Isis, Osiris, and Horus. The northern people who were the second invaders in pre-dynastic times probably brought the worship of Osiris from Libya. This god was the son of Nut, the sky-goddess, and was regarded as the creative principle in vegetable life. His consort, Isis, was represented with the head of a cow or with a serpent crown, and his son, Horus, with the head of a hawk to denote that he was a sky deity. This family had its enemy, Set, a god of evil, who eventually murdered Osiris and distributed his body in twenty-two places throughout Egypt. Isis, however, brought together the fragments and buried them. Then from the god's reunited body grew the ripe grain.

After death, Osiris became king of the dark Nile in the underworld, and his death, dismemberment, and resurrection became a symbol of the destruction and resurrection of the human body. As rulers over the realm of death, Osiris, Isis, and Horus received the prayers for afterlife. The most glorious hymn to Osiris in the Book of the Dead runs as follows:

Glory to Osiris, the Prince of Everlastingness,
Who traveleth through all the million years into Eternity,
Crowned with the North and South, the Lord of gods and men,
Bearing the crook and whip of mercy and of power.

O King of Kings, O Prince of Princes, Lord of Lords,
Through thee the world is green again by virtue of thy Passion;
Thou leadest in thy train what has been and what shall be,
My heart shall rest content upon the hidden Mountain.
Thy body is of shining metal, and thy head is azure;
The color of the turquoise plays about thee where thou goest.
All-pervading is thy body, radiant thy countenance,
As the fields and river valleys of the world hereafter.[1]

The Progressive Religion of Amon-Ra. By the Fifth dynasty, Semitic migrations, which started in prehistoric times and came down across the Isthmus of Suez, brought with them their deity, Ra, Re, or Amon-Ra, the sun-god, who flew with the wings of an eagle or sailed as a boat across the sky. It must be stressed that in contrast with the Osirian religion, which was on the whole a matriarchal cult, the religion of Amon-Ra was masculine, centering the thoughts upon the father rather than upon the functions of the mother. Just as the hymns in honor of Osiris emphasized the life of the underworld and a resurrection into the realms of the dead, so the hymns in honor of Amon-Ra stressed the action of everyday life on earth. There was about the religion of Osiris an inevitable, closed quality; the priestcraft encouraged the idea of predestination. In the fields of the graphic and plastic arts, as we shall see, this emphasis resulted in a static effect. Amon-Ra, the sun-god, on the other hand, was dynamic. When the Pharaoh identified himself with Ra, as several of the Eighteenth-dynasty rulers did, their poetry, like the selection following, was associated with the idea of progress.

I am the Lord of Light, the self-begotten Youth,
First-born of life primeval, first Name from nameless matter.
I am the Prince of years; my body is Eternity;
My form is Everlastingness that trampleth down the darkness.

Call me by name: the Master who dwelleth in the Vineyard,
The Boy who roameth through the town, the Young Man in the plain.
Call me by name: the Child who traveleth toward his Father,
The child of Light who findeth his Father in the Evening.[1]

The Book of the Dead. The Egyptian gradually created an epic story of the delights of the underworld lying along the banks of the lower or black Nile, as, for twelve dynasties the priests of the Osirian cult encouraged the artists to record all the charms that might possibly help the soul to discover its place in this immortal existence. By the Thirteenth dynasty the collection, and its attendant pictures, had reached a state of equilibrium which allowed of codification. Called the Book of the Dead, this code of laws for the spiritual life, this guidebook for the soul in eternity, came to play the part that the Bible was later to play in the Christian Church. The work was in no sense a book as we conceive a book today, but simply the body of material usually presented on the tomb walls, on the mummy cases, or on the wrappings around the corpse. The Osirian priests, who were the sole interpreters of this powerful set of charms had tickets for entrance into the hereafter printed in quantities with blank spaces left where the names of buyers could be inserted. Whenever a group of individuals such as this comes to believe itself the unique guardian of all the rules for living, it becomes a highly conservative factor in society.

During the Middle Kingdom, also, grew up the idea of rewards and punishments. In a

[1] Mark van Doren, *An Anthology of World Poetry*, Albert and Charles Boni, New York, 1928.

poem of the period, "The Song of the Harper," the poet advises that, since none can fly the grave, one must try to live an honest life in order that Isis may eventually give her blessing —eternal life. This sentiment represents a certain further advance along the road of man's spiritual development which grew out of his relationship to the Book of the Dead.

Mind thee of the day, when thou too shalt start for the
    land,
to which one goeth to return not thence.
Good for thee then will have been (an honest life,)
therefore be just and hate transgressions,
for he who loveth justice (will be blessed).
The coward and the bold, neither can fly (the grave,)
the friendless and proud are alike. . . .
Then let thy bounty give abundantly, as is fit,
(love) truth, and Isis shall bless the good,
(and thou shalt attain a happy) old age.[1]

The Monotheism of the Eighteenth Dynasty. In the Eighteenth dynasty of the New Kingdom, Egypt established new contacts with Asia. There occurred also an infusion of new blood from the north. These broadening influences resulted in a reorientation of the Egyptian religion which was to have far-reaching effects on the development of the human mind as a whole. The new thoughts arising from the religious revolution of the Eighteenth dynasty culminated in the monotheism of the so-called heretic king, Akhenaten, son of Amenhotep III.

Contrary to opinion, the movement did not originate with Akhenaten, but began as early as the time of Queen Hatshepsut (1501 B.C.). Following Hatshepsut, two great Pharaohs, Amenhotep II and III, who as warriors also stressed the cult of the masculine sun-god, encouraged the new tendency in religion. Although hymns to the sun took precedence, the idea that the highest deity was not only masculine but also feminine, continued to seek expression. One of the architects of Amenhotep III wrote of God as both mother and father.

Hail to thee, beautiful god of every day!
Rising in the morning without ceasing,

(Not) wearied in labor.
When thy rays are visible,
Gold is not considered,
It is not like thy brilliance.
Thou art a craftsman shaping thine own limbs;
Fashioner without being fashioned;
. . . .
Taking possession of the Two Lands (Egypt), from
    great to small,
A mother, profitable to gods and men,
A craftsman of experience, . . .
Valiant herdsman who drives his cattle, . . . [2]

Akhenaten united the worship of all solar deities into one, the spiritualized Aton. The mind of this remarkable man was such that he could, probably for the first time in human history, conceive of a union of love and power in the personality of one god. The concepts of beauty and love in religion and poetry come into use at the same time, and one may ask whether love has not beauty as its necessary counterpart in the human mind.

Thy dawning is beautiful in the horizon of the sky,
O living Aton, Beginning of life!
When thou risest in the eastern horizon,
Thou fillest every land with thy beauty.
Thou art beautiful, great, glittering, high above every
    land,
Thy rays, they encompass the lands, even all that thou
    hast made.
Thou art Re, and thou carriest them all away captive;
Thou bindest them by thy love.
Though thou art far away, thy rays are upon earth;
Though thou art on high, thy footprints are the day.[2]

In this great hymn to Aton the elements of both Osirian and Ra worship have been united. Note the similarity between the following verse and the Hebrew psalms. Many of the ideas of Akhenaten found their way into the monotheistic religion of the Hebrews and thence into Christianity.

How manifold are thy works!
They are hidden from before (us),
O sole God, whose powers no other possesseth.
Thou didst create the earth according to thy heart
While thou wast alone:
Men, all cattle large and small,
All that are upon the earth,
That go about upon their feet;

[1] "The Song of the Harper" from the volume on Egyptian Literature, *The World's Great Classics*, translated by Ludwig Stern, Colonial Press, New York, 1901.
[2] J. H. BREASTED, *Development of Religion and Thought in Ancient Egypt*, Charles Scribner's Sons, New York, 1912.

(All) that are on high,
That fly with their wings.
The foreign countries, Syria and Kush,
The land of Egypt;
Thou settest every man into his place,
Thou suppliest their necessities.[1]

Before the time of Akhenaten, poetry was either outspokenly physioplastic or ideoplastic. We may now observe in a little poem of the period a creation that closely unites both types, so that the words are expressive and impressive in equal quantity. This fragment is differentiated from prose by its depth of symbolic value and its regular form.

> I am the pure lotus,
> Springing up in splendor
> Fed by the breath of Ra.
>
> Rising into sunlight,
> Out of soil and darkness,
> I blossom in the Field.[2]

The relation of the head rising from the lotus (Fig. 58), associated with the name of Akhenaten's son-in-law, Tutankhamen, is obvious here. Poem and picture explain each other. To such poetry is given the name "lyric." In aesthetic terms it has both formal value and associational content and in a harmonious balance of both elements attains a universal quality that gives it lasting appeal.

Although the organized priestcraft brought back the worship of Osiris and Amon-Ra, erasing from the monuments all mention of the heretic king and his sun-god, Aton, nevertheless, the people could never wholly forget his words. Long after the fall of the dynasty of Akhenaten, the elements that he had fused persisted in Egyptian religion, though the qualities of Aton were transferred to Amon-Ra. In this final peak of Egyptian religious experience, we find God revealed to man as a humane, cosmic deity. He "supplieth the needs of the mice in their holes, sustaineth alive the birds in every tree." In the words of a scribe of Thebes,

he "cometh to the silent, . . . saveth the poor, . . . giveth breath to every one he loveth."[3] This is great art. It is man, making himself over by making his gods over.

Fig. 58.—Young Tutankhamen as lotus, Eighteenth dynasty. Height about 8 inches (Cairo Museum).

Music and Drama

When he has studied the great treasures of literature left upon the walls of the temples and in the mummy wrappings of the Egyptian, it seems hard for modern man to realize at first that they were all written in metrical or verse form. Still harder is it to grasp the fact that these verses, intoned at times by the priests or sung as lyrics, were an essential part of Egyptian music. In Egypt, as in the agricultural society from which she grew, anything deemed worthy of record was part of the ceremonial aspect of living. As a ceremony dramatic in form it had rhythm, beat, and melody. The verses previously studied, it must be stressed again, were a vital part of Egyptian music.

Recognition of Separate Musical Arts. Although Egyptian ceremonies were accompanied by music, no records remain that indicate the rise and fall of the voice. Upon the walls of some

[1] J. H. BREASTED, *Development of Religion and Thought in Ancient Egypt*, Charles Scribner's Sons, New York, 1912.
[2] MARK VAN DOREN, *An Anthology of World Poetry*, Albert and Charles Boni, New York, 1928.
[3] BREASTED, *op. cit.* pp. 347, 349.

of the temples, particularly in connection with certain work songs, the signs ☽☉ indicate that the phrase is to be repeated. These signs furnish the first example of musical notation.

FIG. 59.—*a*, dancers with tambourines and castanets from grave in Sakkareh, Nineteenth dynasty (Cairo Museum); *b*, musicians, wall painting in grave of Nakht, Thebes, Eighteenth dynasty.

By studying many pictures of musical instruments, however, one gains some idea of the scales used. These instruments show that Egyptian music must have advanced from the primitive three-toned scale to a five- or seven-note scale, though the intervals were probably different from ours. Tradition has it that the music of the Hebrew song, *Kol Nidre*, which is sung with a five-note, or pentatonic, scale, came, perhaps, from Egypt. Most Egyptian music must have been religious in character and controlled by the priests who, like the cantor in the synagogue or the Catholic priest at the Mass today, probably created a service of great charm. Under the leadership of the priests most of the folk music was in time appropriated to the service of some deity.

Types of Songs. Chief in point of volume and number, we find the hymns to the gods, psalms of praise and thanksgiving usually called the *Maneros*, which means "Let us be glad." These psalms, which have come to us through the Hebrew psalms in the Bible, correspond roughly to the great mass of hymns sung in our churches today.

The elegy, or lament, of which "The Song of the Harper" furnished an example, arose particularly during dynasties of the Middle Kingdom, forming a second class of song, half religious, half philosophical.

As we shall observe in the other arts of Egypt, the sacerdotal or religious approach to life did not constitute the entire creative expression of the Egyptian. He was on the whole of a happy, sunny disposition. When his crops were growing and the land was at peace, or when he was at play with his family, the Egyptian could be as carefree as the next—perhaps even more so, because of the many assurances that, provided he live justly, he need never fear death.

From agricultural levels the Egyptian brought the work song, sung to the accompaniment of his reaping and sowing. Such a work song has come down to us from the Nineteenth dynasty:

Thresh, oxen, thresh for your master,
The grain you are threshing is also for yourselves.

These lines were followed by the sign showing that they should be repeated.

Love and drinking songs are frequently found upon the walls of the temples, particularly those of the Eighteenth dynasty. The lyric of the young lotus illustrates this type of composition. The Egyptian believed that such songs were destined to be sung again in the afterlife, for paradise included many happy moments.

Instruments. As might be expected, a people of such diverse origins as the Egyptians had many types of instruments. Both men and women accompanied the dancing at parties and folk festivals with rhythmical handclapping. Rattles, or sistra, of bronze, and castanets such as those illustrated in Fig. 59*a*, were used to accentuate the beat.

The Egyptians plucked instruments, including large ceremonial harps, each with twenty strings, a smaller type of shoulder harp, the kennuar, with seven strings, and a sort of mandolin or lute (Fig. 59*b*). They had a species of lyre, as well—the kissar—introduced from the Semitic countries of Palestine and Mesopotamia. Among the wind instruments were trumpets and flutes, some of which were matched in pairs and blown together, probably giving a harmonious effect. Figure 59*b* shows that the instruments were apparently played simultaneously. There are records of ensemble groups employing as many as 300 harpists and 600 singers. Although we have no examples of Egyptian music, it must have filled an important place in the development of music in Europe, particularly as there were colonies of Egyptians in Italy and France and, perhaps, even so far away as England.

Drama. It is but natural for a people motivated by such fundamental urges as those shown in records of Egyptian poetry and music to attempt to dramatize their desires upon a truly magnificent scale. The story of the rising and setting of the sun; the planting, growing, and reaping of the grain; the rise and fall of the Nile; and the birth and death of a man—all these were the stuff of which Egyptian religious drama was made, coming to a focus in the festival presentation of the life of Osiris. Fragmentary remains of a book roll from the Eighteenth dynasty show stage directions, pictures, and dialogue of such a dramatic presentation.

An old inscription in one temple reads: "Veil after veil have I lifted, and ever becomes thy countenance more wonderful." This furnishes the clue to one of the oldest dramatic plots of history. One approaches the shrine, obstacles real or fancied are overcome, and some aspect of a mystery is disclosed. The Egyptian temple, as we see it, is arranged upon this plan.

Through entrance into a cult one may identify oneself with the god at its head. In the secular drama of our own day the heroes and heroines are people like ourselves magnified many times and endowed with almost superhuman powers upon the stage and screen. The priests led the Egyptian to believe that the Pharaoh was god incarnate in man. He appeared as the highest symbol of contact between man's everyday life and the happiness of the future beyond the grave.

Egypt contributed two elements to the aesthetics of the drama: (1) the orderly unfolding of a plot, with a general building up of tensions; (2) the development of a hero who is more than the primitive animal totem or fetish —a superhuman incorporation of an idea. The priestcraft added new elements to the drama, from time to time, but through the centuries the changes were few. The stone carvers and painters, who were in the slave class, had little opportunity for experimenting beyond the set forms.

With the Egyptian group mind preoccupied by a traditional hope for the eternal security of the human spirit, emphasis in the Egyptian aesthetics fell naturally upon the point of juncture between the known and the unknown. Since the soul was immortal only as long as the human form of its appearance persisted, funerary art took precedence over the arts of everyday life as a means of ensuring the survival of the soul in memory. Permanence was the element chiefly sought, an expression of unchanging certainty that would defy time and the forces of space and motion. Hence, the arts most allied to permanence—sculpture and architecture—dominated the Egyptian "form-will."

It is well to have this in mind before turning to the poetic musical drama made permanent, the temple and funeral architecture of the Egyptian.

Architecture

Early Tombs. The magnificent temple structure of the Egyptians can be shown to have evolved from earlier buildings connected with the tombs of the great kings. Up to the time of the Pharaoh Khasekhemui (2980 B.C.), funerary architecture had evolved slowly from the dolmen or tumulus type of grave to a form of tomb known as the mastaba (Fig. 60). The word "mastaba" is the Arab name for a bench. This mastaba or "bench" grave became the prototype of all Egyptian tombs and temples and, as we shall see, for many modern ceremonial buildings.

In the mastaba the burial chamber, which had been the center of the tumulus, was lowered into the ground. The shaft connecting this chamber with the upper room was carefully filled and hidden, so that the body with all its equipment for the journey into the other world might be protected from robbers. It must never

FIG. 60.—Mastaba.

be forgotten in this connection that the Egyptian, like many of us today, believed in the resurrection of the body and could not conceive of a happy afterlife without a complete body to accompany him. From this belief arose the practice of embalming the body and supplying food for it.

In the tomb the mummy case, or innermost coffin, of papier-mâché (mixed paper and glue) was molded to the form of the deceased after this had been embalmed and wrapped with cloth. The mummy case was then deposited in a wooden or stone sarcophagus (Fig. 61). The carving on the granite sarcophagus of King Haremhab, from Thebes, depicts two winged figures protecting the dead, who was accompanied in the underworld by the jackal-headed god, Anubis. The shape of this sarcophagus is that of the mastaba, with its crown molding at the top. The balance of the composition, with the long, rocking line of the wings, gives one a feeling of rest and peace, singularly appropriate to the subject of death.

The Decoration of the Tomb. In order that relatives of the deceased might not forget him, a portrait statue was carved and put into the

upper room, which was called the "serdab." A false or spirit door (Fig. 62) was usually carved in the serdab, often guarded by figures of servants or of deities, who could attend the

FIG. 61.—Red granite sarcophagus of King Haremhab from Thebes, Nineteenth dynasty (Cairo Museum).

soul on its journey. The symbolism of the door or gateway as an entrance into a new life was to play a great part in the development of ecclesiastical architecture the world over.

The design of the false door of Neferseshemptah, from his mastaba at Sakkareh, is both typical and instructive. The outside frame of the door consists of a fillet, a half-round molding with a geometric pattern simulating a binding. This fillet is itself a technomorphic design derived from the building materials out of which the earliest mastabas were made. The ruins of a few of these, as well as clay models of early houses, show that practically all the earliest Egyptian building was of mud or unbaked bricks. To protect these perishable structures from being carried away by rains, they were faced on the outside with wattling, like the walls of the lake-dweller houses. At the corners of the buildings this wattling was tied into large palm trees, the tops of which, curving out, naturally suggested a type of molding. This was known as the "gorge, crown," or "cavetto" molding. When the bordering trees or twigs were tied together, they made up a fillet or half-round molding such as is employed on doors even in our own day. It is important to remember that throughout the entire history of building most architectural ornament in stone is secondary and derived from architectonic, or functional ornament, arising out of techniques of building in clay, wood, or metal.

When in the course of time perishable building material in Egypt gave way to stone, these details of construction were, of course, no longer actually necessary. Moldings carved of stone were still used, however, and were decorated with painted palm fronds. In this way they retained their associational significance. Nine-tenths of art has this associational significance. Its importance cannot be overemphasized.

Within the borders made by the fillet molding, the names and titles of Neferseshemptah rise above the relief carvings of his servants. In some tombs, relief carvings are replaced by freestanding statues in the round. The proportions of this particular spirit door indicate that the Egyptians of that early time had discovered the geometric figure of the square. The main part of the door measures two squares high and the top also is developed into spaces derived from the square. The use of this fundamental geometric figure creates an altogether static feeling, which will be found typical of most Egyptian architectural design.

Around the interiors of the mastabas, wall paintings recorded incidents from the life of the deceased, such as his hunting and fishing, the story of the preparation of his body in embalming, and his last journey into the underworld for judgment. During the Middle Kingdom—that is, after 2430 B.C.—such accounts were organized into the set ritualistic Book of the Dead. Supplementing the wall paintings were models of the servants of the deceased engaged in the work they would do for him in the Land of the Dark Nile or "Happy Hunting Ground." Examples of both models and wall paintings will be discussed more thoroughly under painting and sculpture.

The complicated Egyptian tomb was actually a house in which the living might meet the dead. Anyone who visits the tomb of Abraham Lincoln at Springfield or of General Grant in New York, or the cenotaph of the Unknown

Soldier in Washington, may experience somewhat the feeling of the Egyptian when he stood before the statue of his ancestor in the mastaba. All portrait sculpture has brought with it from

Fig. 62.—Spirit door of Neferseshemptah in mastaba, Sakkareh, c. Sixth dynasty. (*Courtesy of University Prints.*)

the tomb the associational values—the spirit values. Try as hard as he may, who can ever completely dissociate these values from great works of art? An analysis of a work of art on the ground of formal values alone robs it of some of its emotional quality.

Functionalism in Dynastic Architecture. Khasekhemui, the first Pharaoh of the Old Kingdom, had a master builder who placed inside his mastaba the first complete chamber of hewn stone. This Pharaoh had already identified himself with Horus, the hawk-headed god, and thus inaugurated the idea that the ruler was divine: that church and state were one. This union of powers, which gave the Pharaoh control not only over the bodies but also over the imaginations of his subjects, was necessary for the great civic building enterprise that followed. Khasekhemui understood what every capable administrator knows, that no great

Fig. 63.—Pyramid of Zoser, proto-Doric columns in front of mastaba, Sakkareh. (*Courtesy of Hall.*)

cathedrals or public buildings can be constructed unless people are willing to support the undertaking with surplus earnings in taxes and surplus spiritual creative energies.

Khasekhemui's master builder, Kanofer by name, had a son, Imhotep, who, stepping upon his father's shoulders, completed for Zoser, the son of Khasekhemui, the first great city plan, that complex of temples and tombs around the pyramid at Sakkareh. This ceremonial city for the dead was paralleled by plans for the beautification of Memphis, the city of the living.

Imhotep, whose name means "Who comes in peace," was not only an architect but the court astronomer and the "chief lector priest," or ritualist, of his country. A great medicine man and labor organizer as well, he became the secretary of the treasury and prime minister, or

vizier, to the Pharaoh. With these powers concentrated in his hands, he was able to organize all classes—merchants, soldiers, farmers, and laborers—as well as the total wealth of the

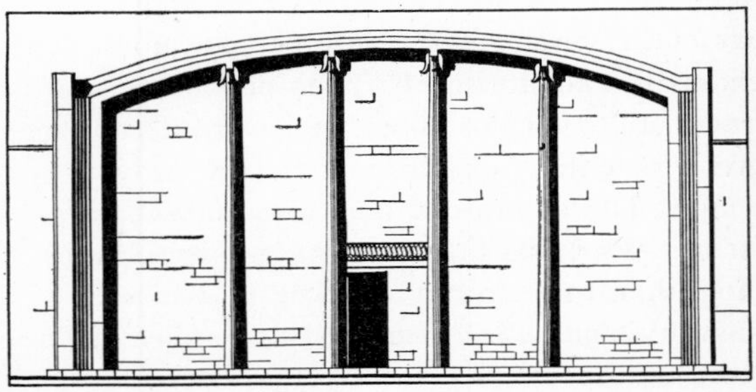

Fig. 64.—Chapel of Princess Hetep-hementi (Fig. 136, left, Chap. VI). Reconstruction of Fig. 63. Compare with Fig. 146, Chap. VI, (*Courtesy of Egypt Exploration Society.*)

state, to build the first pyramid with its temples and surrounding mastabas. Beloved in his lifetime as a great physician, after his death Imhotep was offered sacrifices as a god. In our own day, similarly, we find figures like Washington and Lincoln gradually coming to be worshiped as benefactors of civilization.

Imhotep conceived the idea of designing a supermastaba by erecting six mastabas, one upon the other, making six great steps each of a slightly different proportion. He then faced the entire structure with finely cut white limestone (Fig. 63). In this way he made the low tomb form take on somewhat the aspect of the menhir, so that it became visible from a great distance. Beneath this pyramid the architect built a burial chamber for the sarcophagus and lined it with blue and green glazed tiles of the finest color and technique. Two points are noteworthy here: (1) Only a few hundred years after man had left the neolithic stage he had learned so much about pottery and practical chemistry that he could make glass or glaze. (2) He had come so far in civil organization that he could build this great monument to the god who was to rule in a happy afterlife.

Imhotep designed two tombs for Inthas and Hetep-hementi, the daughters of Zoser. The façades of these pyramid tombs (Fig. 64) are remarkable architecturally, in that their white limestone facing displays slender, tapering, engaged columns, which support a fine crown molding or cornice carved in the form of an arc of the circle. The columns have concave channels, called "flutes," running their length from base to cornice. These perpendicular lines give the entire structure a feeling of added height. The capitals of the columns, with leaf forms folded back, resemble Persian designs more than they do the usual Egyptian lotus or palm capitals. The façades of the pyramid tombs reappear later on early Greek vases and contribute to the design of the Doric temple. Inherited over the centuries, the same architectural pattern may be recognized in the porches of New England churches.

The most interesting thing about these structures of Imhotep, which in a way rivaled the Greek temples, is that they had no known antecedents. So much more refined were they than the architecture of the next fourteen hundred years that it seems almost as though all Egyptian building degenerated from this point on. Actually, the pyramid tombs and the later structures were of two distinct types. The tombs that are almost purely functional in line and decoration represent the abstract style of architecture, called "architectonic." In later tombs and temples the columns were copied from plant forms, which while inappropriate to building construction were perhaps of greater interest from a dramatic or literary point of view. To the priestcraft these later structures were more valuable because better adapted for teaching. Their lotus columns, symbolic pylons, and dim cult rooms all contributed to the elaborate ceremonies of the Egyptian religion.

In periods when the emphasis on distinctively human interests was strong and the power of the priestcraft correspondingly weak —under Hatshepsut and Akhenaten in Egypt and in the later culture of Greece—the abstract, architectonic style returned. We may say in general that the functional predominates,

on the whole, when a great architect builds for a definite personality such as a Pharaoh. When, however, the priest controls architecture, associational values dominate. Interestingly enough

Fig. 65.—Hall in gateway temple to pyramid of King Khafre, Gizeh, Fourth dynasty. (*Courtesy of Hall.*)

this law of architecture seems to hold throughout Occidental history. The humanistic development of the mind tends to use the functional style. Under strong religious influence, architecture becomes more associational, and the functional disappears in a dramatic façade or a decorated wall surface.

Dramatic Temple Architecture. As the Pharaohs in the early dynasties grew powerful, they were able to raise supermastabas, or pyramids. These structures evolved from the simple mastaba form through a stepped-pyramid stage to the splendid limestone-faced pyramids of Gizeh in the Fourth dynasty (2900 B.C.). As the mastaba proper grew into the pyramid, the temple facilities connected with it increased. The pyramid of Khafre at Gizeh, for example, had an ad-

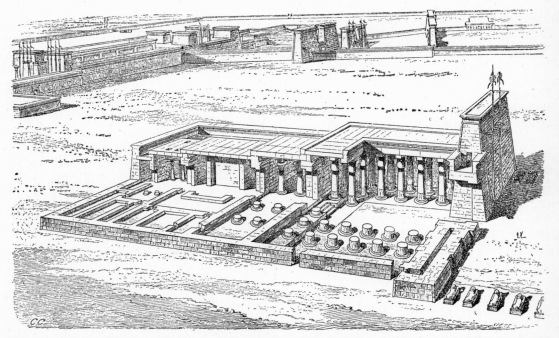

Fig. 66.—Temple of Khons at Karnak, c. 1200 B.C. (*From L'Histoire de l'art dans l'antiquité, by Perrot and Chipiez; courtesy of Libraire Hachette, Paris.*)

joining temple consisting of a closed hall surrounded by heavy square columns (Fig. 65).

Later monarchs, not content to be worshiped only after death, built great free-standing temples to the deities from whom they thought they were descended. As one approaches such a temple (Fig. 66), its logical growth from the neolithic buildings of earlier ages becomes apparent. The first approach is between rows of statues personifying the Pharaoh as lion or ram and calculated to make the beholder stand in awe of him. Next, one passes between the mighty obelisks which are the Pharaoh's totem signs; and ahead rises the pylon, or gateway, flanked by towers. Figures of gods many times life size carved on the towers intensify the feeling of power and seem ready to challenge entrance. The corners of the pylon carry the crown or cavetto molding, which recalls early mud-wattle construction, although the building is no longer of perishable clay but eternal stone. Over the lintel of the doorway appears the sign of the sun, with its outstretched wings and serpent headdress, for sun-god and serpent are now united in Egypt. The door itself is relatively small; a man feels humbled as he passes through.

Inside, one finds himself in an inner court open to the sky, like the court in the temple of Horus (Fig. 67). If he belongs to the inner group of the cult, the worshiper proceeds through another doorway into the forest of columns that support the roof of the hypostyle, or cross hall (Fig. 68). This hall is dark on each side, the main aisle lighted dimly by windows above the centermost columns. These windows are known as the "clerestory" or light story, a word derived from the French, because this architectural feature was first named in France. The size of the hall is awe-inspiring. The hypostyle hall of the temple of Amon at Karnak, the greatest of its kind, measures 170 feet deep and 332 feet wide (Fig. 69).

In the temple hall one must look far up to examine the capitals of the columns. The great hall at Karnak furnishes superlative examples of the spreading type of capital whose form derives from the crown of a palm tree. So enormous are they that, authorities estimate, seventy men could stand on one of them. Their tremendous spread hides from the worshiper below the blocks on which the crossbeams rest, so that the ceiling appears to float high overhead. Painted with stars, it must have seemed like a mysterious night sky.

In spite of their colossal size, these columns do not have structural quality or appear to exert any upward thrust against the weight of the roof. This inertness is due to the fact that they are ringed about with bands of figures and writing. In avoiding the implications of the structure, the builders of the great hall at Karnak proved themselves transcendentalists, interested more in the story than in the building. It is possible that they had no choice in the matter and were under orders to simulate the interior of an immense tomb, in which case associational values would dominate.

The spreading capital is not the only type used in temple architecture of the period. Other rows of columns in Karnak are of the closed lotus-bud type. Still others, around the outer courts, have bell capitals. In another part there are complex columns with long flutings running perpendicularly, the so-called proto-Doric columns, because they suggest the later Greek Doric order. The variation at Karnak is easily understood when one considers that the temple was in process of building for over 500 years. Side courts were constantly being added by different Pharaohs until the whole building covered a vast area.

In the later dynasties the different types of column were often combined to form composite styles, and the head of the goddess Hathor was introduced into the capitals. Great figures of the Pharaohs were sometimes carved as though connected with the pillars supporting the roof, so that the power of the king appeared to be part of the strength of the building. Such supporting figures are called "atlantes" or "caryatids," depending upon whether they represent men or women. They are wholly un-

Fig. 67.—Entrance court from temple of Horus at Edfu, c. 237 B.C. (*Courtesy of Egypt Exploration Society.*)

architectonic and stand at the opposite pole from Imhotep's fluted columns.

From front to rear in the Egyptian temple, the rooms become progressively smaller, so that imperceptibly one feels the greater constriction. The dimly lighted shrine or innermost room of the Egyptian temple, corresponding to the earlier serdab of the mastaba, held a statue of the god or some object peculiar to him (Fig. 70). Sometimes this was a boat, as in the temple of Khons, or an "Ark of the Covenant" wherein were enclosed sacred writings, as in the Hebrew Temple.

It must be stressed that the temple architecture of the Egyptians was chosen for its dramatic effect. Though the ceremonial music, motion, color, and incense are now lacking, if all these could be added, one might get some notion of the total effect on the minds of the lower-class Egyptians, who were just emerging from the primitive state. In our day, the great cathedral services of the Old World and theatrical spectacles such as Max Reinhardt's production of *The Miracle* achieve somewhat the same effect.

The Functional Architecture of Queen Hatshepsut. During the feudal age of Egyptian history, that is, after the first pyramid-building kings had disappeared and when the nobility held the greater power, many tombs were carved in the cliffs bordering the Nile. Some of these were simple and primitive; others, like the tomb temple of Queen Hatshepsut at Deir-el-Bahri (Fig. 71) are among the noblest works of world

Hatshepsut employed a builder named Senmut who, with the finest appreciation of the natural surroundings, planned three terraced courts, the upper two with colonnades, simple

Fig. 68.—Model of hypostyle hall at Karnak, c. 1340 B.C. (*Courtesy of Metropolitan Museum of Art.*)

architecture. The purity of its architectonic style harks back to the structures built by Imhotep in the Third dynasty. Already attention has been called to the fact that the movement toward monotheism, which culminated in the reign of Akhenaten, originated many years earlier. In the twenty-year rule of Queen Hatshepsut a balance was achieved between the matriarchal, underworld cults and the sky-gods, with a resultant weakening of the power of the Osirian priestcraft. As a woman, the queen favored the worship of Hathor, the cow goddess, but her temple tomb was dedicated to Amon-Ra, signifying a reconciliation of the masculine and feminine religions. Under Hatshepsut, Egypt enjoyed not only religious unity, but peace and prosperity.

and architectonic, which by their very structure not only suggest the perpendicular masses of the cliffs but seem to modify them toward a human scale. From the practically level river bottom, one approaches the temple along an avenue flanked by sphinxes. These animals, each of which had the head of the queen, are significant as the first of the feminine sphinxes —a style later adopted by the Greeks. A delicate pylon, before which stood two trees instead of obelisks, opened upon the first court, which was filled with palm trees and grapevines. A gentle inclined ramp at the rear led to the first terrace, which was fronted by a cool arcade of columns. This terrace was bounded on the right side by a columnar arcade that connected it with the cliff (Fig. 72). The arcade also ran

FIG. 69.—Columns, interior of hypostyle hall at Karnak, c. 1340 B.C. (*Courtesy of G. E. Kidder-Smith.*)

around the rear of the court and terminated at the left in a small temple.

From the first terrace a second ramp led to the uppermost level, with another arcade mak-

Fig. 70.—Small painted tabernacle of wood from tomb of Kasa, Nineteenth dynasty, Thebes (Museum of Turin) (Maspero).

ing an enclosed court holding an altar to the sun-god. Space was provided on each side of this court for the ancestral worship of the queen. Beyond, deep in the cliff, an arched room held a statue of Hathor, the ultimate divinity, sign of the matriarchal powers of the queen.

Inside the enclosed court, wall paintings set forth the story of the queen's peaceful exploits. Here her ships were shown returning from Punt (Fig. 73). The queen appeared in communion with her gods, especially Hathor, while through her mother, Aahmes, her relationship with the god Amon-Ra was also established and her birth recorded.

Almost more than any other structure, this temple seems to lure the worshiper into its inmost shrine until he is at last made one with the cult and the cliffs of which it is a part. Here the architect sought to blend his building with nature and thus to derive stability and grace from her forms. Later, the same architectural

aesthetic qualities developed in the tombs of the Chinese Ming emperors. The motif of the wide arcades appears, too, in the great open colonnade of St. Peter's Church in Rome. It is significant that, like the Egyptian matriarchal cults, the Roman church attempts to embrace all religious philosophies so that the worshiper will feel all his emotions at rest within the cult.

Unfortunately, Hatshepsut and Senmut were not themselves destined to lie at peace in their sanctuary. Not long after burial, the bodies of the architect and the queen were removed from the temple by Thothmes III, Hatshepsut's jealous husband, and secreted in a miserable hole in the cliffs outside.[1] The queen's sphinxes were overthrown, her statues shattered, and her name erased wherever it was found and that of Thothmes substituted. Enough fragments have been found, however, to show what manner of woman Hatshepsut was (Fig. 89).

Nonfunctional Architecture of the Priestly Pharaohs. The most overpowering and awe-inspiring of the Egyptian rock-cut tomb temples is the work of Ramses II near Abu-Simbel (Fig. 74). Here in front of the pylonlike doorway to an entire building carved out of solid rock deep in the hillside rise four colossal statues of the king seated with his hands upon his knees. The figure of Horus, the hawk-headed sun-god, stands above the door and the serpent, many times repeated, forms a molding above the crown. In point of view of formal values, the statues are not to be compared with the best Egyptian work. They lack everything except absolute balance and geometric form. Their stiff, lifeless bodies, essentially parts of the architecture, suggest inert stone rather than human structure. They must be judged as examples of primitive art on its most magnificent scale.

Great size impresses, however, because it must always be associated in the mind with some strong underlying social organization. To

---

[1] An expedition from the Metropolitan Museum of New York discovered the grave wrappings in this hiding place. It is interesting to note, also, that the obelisk of Thothmes III now stands in Central Park, New York.

erect colossal statues like these requires an immense amount of man power. Social organization implies a spiritual organization of the type that raised the great menhirs or the Stonehenge

The rock-cut temples illustrate the type of architecture that results when the forces of church and state, of religious and political rule, unite in one individual. Similar architecture will ap-

FIG. 71.—Model of temple of Hatshepsut, Deir-el-Bahri, Eighteenth dynasty (Metropolitan Museum of Art). *(Courtesy of Metropolitan Museum of Art.)*

circle. Spiritual organization, in turn, usually means that a belief in some idea was so strong that it unified the culture. Thus, insofar as unity is an essential of a work of art, these statues fulfill at least one aesthetic purpose.

In the interior of the tomb the first great room, corresponding to the outer court of the freestanding temple, is decorated with huge figures of the Pharaoh as Osiris, the god of resurrection (Fig. 75). We may imagine that those who toiled for Ramses must have done so in the expectation of a reward in the next world from the Pharaoh, who was a god. Here was a motive sufficiently powerful to persuade an army of workers to unite in a common task.

pear again in Assyria, in Rome, and in baroque Europe.

The Small Freestanding Temple. The remaining type of temple built by the Egyptians was freestanding (Fig. 76). In style the freestanding temple resembled the naos, the shrine, greatly enlarged and brought out of the dim mysterious depths of the tomb-temple, making the god accessible to all. There were a number of temples of this type, most of which have been destroyed. The best-known example of those that remain is the kiosk at Philae, now covered by the dammed-up waters of the Nile.

In Mesopotamia, where the cult of the sun-god was indigenous, this type of structure is the rule. In Egypt, however, where the worship of the sun-god was less common than that of the Osirian deities, the low, horizontal temple predominated. But, whereas the low temple

Fig. 72.—Colonnade at Deir-el-Bahri. (*Courtesy of Egypt Exploration Society.*)

with its series of rooms each smaller than the preceding suggested the mysterious underworld, and the rock-cut tomb, with its statue-guarded entrance, a gateway to that underworld, the freestanding sun temple, with its erect open colonnade (usually elevated slightly upon platforms and approached by steps or ramps), symbolized a flight of the spirit upward.

Though he saw no great difference between life on earth and in the hereafter, the Egyptian insisted that the afterlife was the more valuable and built permanent temples to substantiate his belief. His earthly homes, palaces, and huts, hastily constructed, have disappeared. Many paintings and models, however, show what his houses must have looked like.

Residences. The common folk lived in mud huts, one or two stories in height. Figure 77

illustrates the home of a lower middle-class person. The model has two flights of stairs leading up on each side of the court to a second story, which is supported by a column. This

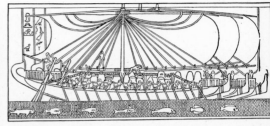

Fig. 73.—Relief in temple of Hatshepsut, Deir-el Bahri. Differing remarkably from most Egyptian reliefs, this one shows the ships behind each other, giving somewhat the effect of perspective. The quality of design and execution suggests the later skill of the Amarna Age.

type of house was furnished with the simplest cane furniture and grass mats. A wall from the mastaba of Hesire at Sakkareh reproduces the decoration on matting, such as hung on the wall of an Egyptian dwelling (Fig. 77b).

The houses of the nobles were sometimes three stories high, the several floors being connected by flights of stairs (Fig. 77c). They were probably made of mud-wattling construction, palm trunks serving for columns to support the roof. Paintings and plans from tomb walls show that the upper-class houses were surrounded by gardens with walls, orchards, and pools. They were decorated inside and out with brightly colored borders, and all architectural detail were colored. There probably were courtyard with columns around three sides and a porch across the fourth. A series of models in the Metropolitan Museum, taken from a tomb shows the various small houses enclosed by the walls of such a villa. The floors were often made of painted plaster and the wall decorations were probably like those of the tombs.

Painting

The arts of primitive man do not appear to have been influenced by preconceived ideas of what painting, sculpture, or architecture, a separate arts, should be. Not until the Hellenic cultures shall we find intellectual judgments separating and evaluating the arts. In Egypt, accordingly, there is no distinct boundary be-

FIG. 74.—Entrance, temple-tomb of Ramses II, Abu-Simbel, c. 1330 B.C. Seated figures over 65 feet high. (*Courtesy of Egypt Exploration Society.*)

tween the fields of architecture, sculpture, and painting.

Most of the painting in Egypt is a surface decoration on the tomb walls, more valuable as an indication of the cultural life and environment of the Egyptian home than for its purely formal, aesthetic appeal. Wherever possible, painting gives way to painted sculpture, which was felt to be more real. We may infer that color decoration was used only when a man lacked the money to pay for the more arduous and expensive relief carving. On the

whole, the sculptor's craft takes precedence over the painter's because of its greater permanence.

The Painter's Methods. Most Egyptian wall painting was carried out by artisans, who copied

FIG. 75.—Interior of rock-cut temple at Abu-Simbel showing Ramses II as Osiris, Nineteenth dynasty. (*Courtesy of Egypt Exploration Society.*)

little sketches on clay or stone which served as models for the monumenta work. These small sketches, drawn by the master artists, were squared off, the squares were then enlarged upon the walls, and the figures drawn in. As always happens in monumental work of this kind, the copyists were not so skilled in rendering anatomy as were the master artists. Hence the figures became stiff and often lost much of the fine balance of areas created by the talented master. Some of the models, as well as sections of walls with the guidelines for the painting still in place, have been found in the tombs.

Despite the businesslike factory production necessary to turn out the enormous mass of Egyptian painting, one finds here and there charming intimate passages which reveal a fine

Fig. 76.—Kiosk at Philae erected under the Roman Emperors Augustus and Trajan. (*Courtesy of Egypt Exploration Society.*)

sense of occult balance, a knowledge of anatomy, and figures whose postures indicate some insight into emotional feeling. All the figures, however, even in the most realistic of Egyptian art, display a geometricity and a primitive color quality that appeal more to children than to adults (Fig. 78).

Decorative Use of Color. In the art of the earliest dynasties, particularly in connection with the mastabas of Sakkareh, one finds some of the most naturalistic painting. The famous Geese of Meidum were originally part of the wall decoration in a tomb. As these geese are usually reproduced in black and white (Fig. 79), they illustrate the almost perfect symmetrical balance usually found in most Egyptian monumental art. When they are studied in color, the asymmetry of color patterns on the two sides makes the entire composition much more interesting. The whole is unified by the strong geometric quality of the design and the balance of equal areas bounded by heavy lines.

In this place it is proper to point out a law that should be remembered in connection with the aesthetics of painting: The ultimate unity of any painting depends on more than its lines or arrangement of areas; often when these are unbalanced, a judicious placing of colors will bring the entire composition into balance. In the case of the Geese of Meidum, just the opposite is true. The monotonous effect of balance has been somewhat overcome and made interesting by the unbalance of color areas.

The Egyptian strove to represent the colors in actual life, and his failure to accomplish this, which we sometimes assume to have been premeditated, was probably due to his lack of proper color materials. He obtained charming decorative effects from blacks, reds, and yellows which, like the paleolithic man, he derived from ocherous or manganous earths. To these colors the Egyptian added a blue, made by grinding cuprous semiprecious stones, such as malachite or turquoise. All these earth colors commonly seen together in nature give harmony to painting. The Egyptians also used black and white, which are of great decorative value, and, like neolithic painters, heavily outlined their figures. This made them appear flat on the surface of the wall.

Occult Balance in Pictorial Design. The painted flat-relief carving from the grave of Ti near Sakkareh (Fig. 80), which was executed in the Fifth dynasty, demonstrates the remarkable combination of useful, associational, and formal values reached by the Egyptian artist at his best. This little panel, useful as instruction for the soul of Ti in its life in the underworld, shows a fine feeling for texture, an excellent occult balance, and a clear narrative value. The long, parallel, perpendicular stems of the lotus stalks suggest a woven tapestry or matting background on which the figures of the noble and his attendants stand out by contrast. In order that the importance of Ti may be stressed, the area of grayed lines around him is greater than that around his smaller servants. The bending stalks of the plants are so arranged that one's eye must follow them until it is subtly led to the figure of the noble. Where the plants blossom, in the upper part of the picture, birds

FIG. 77.—*a*, clay model of Egyptian house; *b*, wall painting showing matting from Egyptian tomb; *c*, reconstruction of Egyptian house.

are flying and animals walking about among the stalks. Below the level of the boats, an area carved with zigzag lines symbolizes the water, in which are seen many kinds of fish and several hippopotami. This much is characteristic of all Egyptian painting. Depth is usually indicated by placing objects one above the other; here the conventional way of representing perspective has another, more logical ground, for the water naturally should be below and the flowers and birds above. We see how different this painted relief is from most Egyptian mural representations by comparing it with the painting from the Book of the Dead that follows.

Associational and Formal Values in Egyptian Painting. The painting from the Book of the Dead (Fig. 81), from a papyrus in the British Museum, shows how the hieroglyphic writing, which was still highly pictorial, was combined with representations of the human form without any great feeling for aesthetic spacing. The entire painting represents a cursive style of art, in reality little more than picture writing.

Remembering the place that religious poetic charms had in the life of the Egyptian, however, one must realize that to him this painting probably had an aesthetic unity that it lacks for us. We have pointed out that the painter uses color to bring an otherwise unbalanced linear design

into harmony with the entire concept of a picture. So a religious painter or a modern advertising artist might use a combination of words, lines, and colors to achieve a unified effect that

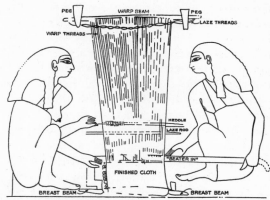

FIG. 78.—Wall painting from the tomb of Khnumhotep, Beni-Hasan, Twelfth dynasty, c. 2000 B.C. Formal aesthetic appeal is sacrificed to narrative clarity in most Egyptian painting. The weaver at the left inserts a heddle with one hand to separate the warp for passage of a shuttle bearing the woof. With the other hand she helps her companion push down the woof with the beater-in. This is similar to the loom of the Navajo. See Chap. III, Fig. 32. (*Courtesy of Metropolitan Museum of Art.*)

would be lost to one unfamiliar with the language.

Many times in the history of the arts the student will be called upon to judge effects similar to those in Egyptian religious painting. Medieval manuscript illumination, some Chinese painting, modern advertising, all call for an intricate balance of words, colors, and pat-

touches the mummy. Here the associational values of the story, which make it desirable that the soul appear to belong to the body, outweigh the purely formal desire for balance.

FIG. 79.—Geese of Meidum, Third dynasty. Height about 18 inches (Cairo Museum). (*Courtesy of Lesch-Carnegie.*)

terns. Modern man is forced to judge aesthetic effects even more complicated than these, for the motion picture and grand opera include music and dancing. He needs for this task an aesthetic philosophy which allows him to weigh formal values against associational values.

Painting developed away from the priestly art in the Book of the Dead toward realism in the drawing from the temple of Queen Hatshepsut at Deir-el-Bahri (Fig. 73). Here three boats appear side by side, moving over the sea, their sails outstretched to the winds, their rowers pulling at the oars. The design element and the naturalistic representational element are equally balanced. There is a rhythmical movement implied in the placing of the fish in the zigzag waves. The long curved lines of spars and the straight lines of hawsers and masts form an intricate, though pleasing, pattern. The picture writing, however, obtrudes from each side, for even in this, one of the finest of Egyptian line drawings, we know that the subject matter was of more value than the aesthetic appeal.

The peak of pure pictorial design, considered simply from the point of view of formal aesthetic values, is reached in another picture from the papyrus narrating the journey of the soul of Ani (Fig. 82). Observe that the artist placed the two tapers at each end of the bier so that their flames fill the space above and around the soul, represented as a human-headed hawk. It is true that the bier is placed too near the right and the hawk a little far down, so that one wing

The writing, however, which appears in the cursive script, a kind of shorthand hieroglyph, has not been allowed to run over into the picture space, which is distinctly separated from the figures by a frame. Hence, because of its inner unity and the varied placing of the areas of color, the aesthetic effect of this painting seems good. The balance—no longer simple, obvious, and absolute—attracts the modern as well as the ancient. Such occult balance seems to indicate an advance away from the primitive, for it suggests that life has movement as well as permanence.

Fragments of limestone slabs from painters' studios in Thebes show what realistic work the Egyptian draftsman could produce when in a playful mood, unhampered by priestly formulae (Fig. 83). The rendering of the bow of the rider and the legs, mane, and tail of the horse are such that we are sure the Egyptian could, when he wished, compose as realistically as men of any later culture. This example is the exception and not the rule.

In his purely decorative designs, created to ornament his house furnishings, the Egyptian attempted to stylize the natural objects that were around him. The lotus bud in flower, the papyrus reed, the palm fronds, and the waves of the river gave him an opportunity to express his feelings through circles, spirals, and geometric zigzags. The stars were depicted sometimes, and the sun always. The scarab, or beetle, rolling his larva in a round mud ball became the symbol of everlasting life, and the form of the beetle, with its shiny wings, was imitated as a good-luck charm.

Sculpture

An examination of the world's finest sculpture should convince anyone that it always contains a unity of geometric or abstract qualities and enough realistic form to make it seem plausible and natural. The idea or mood to be expressed, usually symbolized by the geometric composition scheme, is clothed, so to speak, with planes and forms so arranged that the result, although it may not be entirely natural, still is not improbable. In the head of Nofretete (Fig. 84) first appears such an example of superlative art. It may be that some deeply intuitive or sculpturally talented reader after looking at the illustration will understand at once why this is so. For most of the world, however, some further explanation is needed to make clear the means by which the sculptor achieved his result, for the excellence of this piece is not easy to analyze.

In studying examples of great art, as was demonstrated in the Introduction, it is futile to hope for a simple explanation of what may be a complicated combination of attributes. To approach the portrait of Nofretete intelligently one must consider it in relation to lesser works. Since the attributes more easily recognized in these simpler examples unite in the portrait of the queen, an examination of eight such sculptural pieces will not only explain the portrait but will also give a brief survey of the evolution of the sculptor's art in Egypt. Only so can one visualize the fact that the Nofretete head is the climax of a long period of growth.

Realism and Conventionalism in Egyptian Sculpture. The Egyptian inherited from Early Stone Age man a desire for realism in his sculpture as great as that of the Romans or Renaissance Italians. His desire for realism was surpassed only by his desire for permanence, which, as we have seen in the case of architecture, was associated in his mind with an almost religious belief in his duty to his ancestors.

Completeness of Form. The protection of the

FIG. 80.—Painted relief carving showing Ti hunting in papyrus from his tomb in Sakkareh, Fifth dynasty. Height about 4 feet. (*Courtesy of Egypt Exploration Society.*)

body started with the construction of a case for the mummy. This case was made of paper, linen strips, and glue. The paper, an Egyptian invention, consisted of the soaked beaten reeds of the papyrus plant. It was laid, while still moist, over the wrapped mummy. This covering was then cemented together with glue and strips of linen. The whole mass, when hardened, became stiff. Here the idea of bodily immortality connects itself with a certain contained quality and roundness of form in the mummy case. The shape of the encased mummy, with its closely bound arms and its

FIG. 81.—Section from painted scroll called Papyrus of Ani, Eighteenth dynasty. This part of the Book of the Dead shows the weighing or judgment of Ani's soul. Painting in tempera, writing in ink. (*Courtesy of British Museum.*)

FIG. 82.—Detail showing flight of soul, Papyrus of Ani. Hieroglyphs in ink becoming cursive. Now changing to demotic style of Egyptian writing. (*Courtesy of British Museum.*)

lack of projecting ornament, predetermines the shape of almost all Egyptian standing sculpture. To the Egyptian, sculpture in the round was simply the human body made permanent and protected by its wrappings and decorative shell.

The mummy case was enclosed in one or more other cases, also elaborately decorated, particularly if the deceased were wealthy. All the cases were then enclosed in sarcophagi of wood or stone, the outermost being in the form of a house, with false doors and eyes so that the soul might see out. This outer sarcophagus was usually placed in a room containing food and models of servants, so that life in the other world should be well provided for. Statues of retainers in relief or in the round guarded the false doors outside the mortuary chamber.[1]

Realism and the Geometric Pose. The familiar Sheik-el-Beled, or Kaaper (Fig. 85), a guardian statue of this type, was found by Arab workmen in a tomb of one of the earliest dynasties. This figure, which probably represents one of the overseers of the noble buried in the mastaba, supports the view that the Egyptian could, when he wanted, carve a realistic representation of a human being. The face of Kaaper seems so alive and full of character that one is almost able to recognize his blood brother today on the streets of Cairo or in the fields beside the Nile. The eyes of the statue are startlingly real. The quartz inlay that produces this lifelike effect is further evidence that the Egyptian really wanted to make a counterpart of a human being. The pose of the body, however, though the walking attitude suggests life, is geometric.

It has come to be recognized that the sculpture of the first three dynasties, which was produced for the nobles rather than for the organized priestcraft, was on the whole more realistic than later work. During the times of Hatshepsut and Akhenaten in the Eighteenth

dynasty and again after the Twenty-fourth dynasty, however, the Egyptian's desire for realism again breaks through the conventions. In general, throughout all the dynasties, figures of

FIG. 83.—Artist's sketch of Amazon on limestone slab from Thebes, Nineteenth dynasty. Height about 3.7 inches. (*Courtesy of Berlin Museum.*)

the nobles, particularly the smaller wooden tomb figures, are realistic in style. Only the statues of the great were carved in the stylized conventional forms.

Influence of the Architectonic Prism. In contrast with the statue of the commoner Kaaper from the early dynasties is the colossal statue of the Pharaoh, Ramses II, and his queen at Luxor (Fig. 86). This figure, though it takes the geometric pose of Kaaper, reminds us of the architectonic prism of stone from which it was carved and is faintly suggestive of the mummy case. No extraneous parts project which could easily be broken away. Beard, arms, and headdress connect closely with the central mass and, although one foot is advanced as though the king would move forward, the leg remains attached to the block.

Since wisdom and strength were the attributes most desired in a Pharaoh who wished to

---

[1] In some instances the actual bodies of servants have been discovered entombed with the sarcophagus. The practice of killing the servants of the Pharaoh at his death so that they might attend him in the underworld persisted until the Middle Kingdom.

Fig. 84.—Head of Nofretete, Eighteenth dynasty, c. 1375 B.C. Painted limestone, eyes of rock crystal, life size (Berlin Museum). (*Courtesy of Lesch-Carnegie.*)

FIG. 85.—The scribe Kaaper (Sheikh-el-Beled), Fourth dynasty, c. 2800 B.C. Statue in wood with inlaid eyes of white quartz crystal and ebony, height about 3 feet 7½ inches (Cairo Museum). (*Courtesy of Lesch-Carnegie.*)

be considered as a god, the monarch was always shown at the height of his physical development. Nevertheless, the archaeologist Capart, in showing that no two of the statues of the Pharaoh Mycerinus look exactly alike, proved

FIG. 86.—Ramses II and queen in temple, Luxor, Nineteenth dynasty. Height about 20 feet. (*Courtesy of Egypt Exploration Society.*)

that, despite all his restrictions, the Egyptian artist had at least a modicum of freedom.

Other conventions usually associated with the statue of the Pharaoh are these: No Pharaoh was ever shown absolutely nude, as were the slaves; parts of the body such as the chin and lower torso were covered with a ceremonial beard and sheath. At times, as an inheritance from central African forebears, the Pharaoh was given a tail. When he wished to appear in his full strength, he was given the body of a lion, most powerful of beasts, and

FIG. 87.—Head of Khafre (Chephren) with protective hawk, Fourth dynasty, c. 2800 B.C. Height of detail about 16 inches. (Cairo Museum). (*Courtesy of Lesch-Carnegie.*)

the resulting creation was called a sphinx. He was usually shown so that the worshiper approaching him would see him from the front and thus be awed by his direct stare and massive shoulders. In this way by a cumulative process, the symbols of power connected with the office of the Pharaoh were added one to another until the effect on the mind of the worshiper became overpowering.

With the statue of Ramses it can be seen that, to the rear of the Pharaoh, his queen has been depicted, her hand resting upon the calf of his leg. In addition to being relatively much smaller, the figure of the queen appears also to be more delicately carved. Since the queen is represented as about a quarter the size of her lord and master, we may judge of her relative importance in Egypt at the time. On the whole the Egyptian showed his womenfolk as only

slightly smaller than himself. Servants and prisoners of war were still smaller in size. During the periods of enlightenment, such as the Amarna Age, one sometimes finds the queen of equal size with the Pharaoh. In all his art, the Egyptian uses this primitive method of showing the relative importance of individuals. Those who are important are large; those who are less important are small.

Symbolism and Idealism. A work in sculpture that exemplifies a balance of firmness and power comes from the Fourth dynasty and is the well-known head of the pyramid builder Khafre, or Chephren (Fig. 87), found in his pyramid temple. The entire figure of this monarch, although seated, is not unlike that of Ramses. The head of Khafre, however, is less heavy than that of Ramses. Such was the Egyptian's knowledge of anatomy that he succeeded in suggesting the muscles beneath the broad planes of the face. At the same time, enough detail was omitted so that we feel the work to have been an idealization rather than a portrait. Plaster masks, as well as studies for the statue of Khafre, show that the Egyptians carefully copied the faces of the living; but the finished work, carved from stone, was an idealized memory image and in no sense a realistic copy. The associational idea, so necessary in Egyptian art, is to be found in the hawk behind the headdress. This bird, the symbol of the sun-deity, represents the Ka, or the protecting soul, of the Pharaoh.

The Element of Charm. Small sculptures made of clay, wood, or bone, serving often as handles to utensils, show a new combination of the geometric composition scheme and the charming figure. Here the artists represented the human form more realistically, but the geometric pattern was more complex and not necessarily suggestive of the primary prism. In these works, associated with the feminine side of Egyptian life, the desire to make the object delicate for its particular use dominated the associational symbolic quality, which almost disappears, leaving only the formal value and a certain

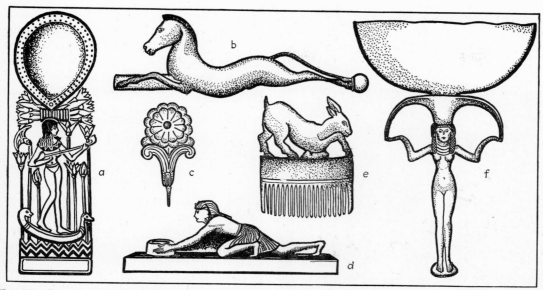

Fig. 88.—Delicacy of Egyptian design in objects for everyday use. *a.* incense spoon (University College, London); *b*, ivory whip handle (Metropolitan Museum of Art); *c*, detail from handle of spoon (Berlin Museum); *d*, slate figurine, Ramses II presenting offering to gods; *e*, comb (Museum, Brussels); *f*, bronze mirror (Berlin Museum).

playful realism. Nevertheless, a small degree of geometric stiffness, still symbolic of the permanence of life, is always retained.

The further we go from the Pharaoh and the nearer to the common man, the more convincing is the proof that the Egyptian was well able to portray the pleasures of life in realistic art, particularly noticeable in the drawing of the Amazon from Thebes (Fig. 83). The maiden lute player on the incense spoon (Fig. 88*a*), although enmeshed in a geometric papyrus thicket and riding in a boat upon geometric waves, yet carries herself with a verve which is not today outmoded. The wooden comb from the museum at Brussels is also an astonishingly modern bit of genre (Fig. 88*e*).

A seated figure of Queen Hatshepsut found in her temple at Deir-el-Bahri (Fig. 89), although observing the canons of taste that require its being carved within the blocky mass, shows the greater delicacy of form usually associated with women. The arms are still closely bound to the sides and the legs are stiff, but the upper part of the body, which has been left nude, has a more subtle rendering of natural forms than any found in earlier sculpture outside the realistic creations of the Third dynasty. The tendency toward greater delicacy and realism, which can be observed not only here but in other creations during Hatshepsut's reign, grew under her successors, Amenophis II and Amenophis III, until it flowered into the realistic art of Akhenaten (Amenophis IV), the heretic king.

The Union of Associational and Formal Values. Akhenaten built himself a city with fine gardens and an open sun temple at Tell el-Amarna. From this town is taken the name of the Amarna Age. The many objects of art found there differ from the rest of Egyptian sculpture. The naturalistic forms of sculpture previously allowed only to inconsequential things, now came to dominate, so that realistic portraiture, a certain *joie de vivre*, and a quality of delicate fragility characterized the work of the period.

Finest among extant examples of the work of the Amarna Age is the well-known head of Queen Nofretete (The-Beautiful-One-Has-Come), wife of Akhenaten (Fig. 84). This head shows refined features and a long, graceful neck that would be admired in our day by the apostles of slenderness in Hollywood. The poise of the head and the slight tension on the muscles of the neck are nicely balanced by the weight

FIG. 89.—Slate statue of Queen Hatshepsut, life size (Metropolitan Museum of Art). (*Courtesy of Metropolitan Museum of Art.*)

of the geometric mass of the headdress. So delicate is this balance that were the head tipped ever so slightly forward or back the beholder would feel its instability. The painted lips and eyebrows of the queen give her face a some-

what doll-like or conventional character which, departing from the purely naturalistic, focuses attention unconsciously upon its geometric quality. This quality of geometric design con-

FIG. 90.—Relief carving of Akhenaten and his family worshiping the sun's rays from Tell el-Amarna. About 1 foot 9 inches (Cairo Museum). (*Courtesy of Egypt Exploration Society.*)

nects the face with the design of the headdress and the painted necklace about the lower part of the neck.

In this remarkable work one feels, moving within the naturalism of the outer forms, a series of angular geometric lines. These seem to grow out of the base in a geometric progression, gaining weight as they ascend.

The Amarna Age represents a stage in the development of Egyptian thought when the soul of man conceived as a growing plant had more weight than the thought of the permanence of the body. This interpretation of the inner meaning of the remarkable portrait of queen Nofretete seems justified when a relationship is recalled between the portrait and the bust of the queen's son-in-law, Tutankhamen, in which the head of the young man actually grows out of the lotus.

Thus, in the sculptured head of Nofretete, for the first time in the history of the sculptor's art, is shown the expression of a literary idea—here, the thought of a human being as a grow-

inner intention and outer form has rightly been considered one of the earliest objects of beauty in the development of art. Such creations as this are very rare. The use of the adjective

Fig. 91.—Low relief (bas-relief) showing Seti, Osiris, and Horus, temple of Seti I, Abydos, c. 1350 B.C. (*Courtesy of Metropolitan Museum of Art.*)

ing lotus—in perfect balance with a refinement of planes and curves, all contributing to the idea without being dominated by it. Hence this portrait bust has the universal quality of great art. It speaks to the thinking mind as well as to the feeling senses. Since universal quality appeals to all ages, the bust seems quite modern. In contrast, the head of Khafre, with its protecting hawk showing a slight dominance of the idea or associational qualities over the formal qualities, is more specifically Egyptian.

The Birth of the Concept of Beauty. The head of Nofretete, because of the nice balance of its

"beautiful" reserved for just such a work calls for a definition. Probably the most successful tentative definition, which may be derived from an examination of this work and its relationship to the poetry of Akhenaten, would be: "Beauty is the most perfect harmony or unity of the inner thought and the outward parts of a work of art."

The term "beauty" should not be used lightly. The statue of Khafre, for example, with its guardian hawk, heavy static forms, and massive construction, could not be called beautiful. It might be called powerful or awe-inspiring.

The temple of Hatshepsut, on the other hand, with its regular ordering of courts and its human approachableness, could be called beautiful in contrast to the great, complex, columnar

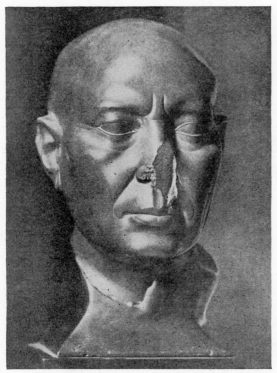

Fig. 92.—Portrait head in green stone from Memphis, c. 400 B.C. Height about 8¼ inches (Berlin Museum). (*Courtesy of Egypt Exploration Society.*)

temple of Karnak. This is to suggest that there is about the concept of beauty an element of human kindliness and pleasure-giving charm. Many of the small household objects of the Egyptians, such as the incense spoon (Fig. 88*a*) or the furniture illustrated in this chapter (Fig. 95), could be called charming with a tendency toward beauty, because there is about them not only meaning but a fine balance of formal values.

Contrasting Styles of Relief Sculpture. Although no better example than the Nofretete head could be cited to illustrate the fine balance of the conventional and naturalistic elements during this flowering of Egyptian art, a low relief

of Akhenaten followed by his wife and daughter (Fig. 90) serves to illustrate the combination of sculpture and painting which decorated the tomb walls. On the flat wall surface the outline of the figure was engraved much as it was in paleolithic times. Then, within the outlines, the body was carved into a slightly rounded relief, with lines of clothing upon its surface. It still seems very flat unless viewed under a glancing light from above or off to one side. In the example chosen, the Pharaoh, wearing the great crown of Upper Egypt, holds two offerings in his outstretched hands. It is noteworthy that, even in this time of great freedom, the sculptor cannot see the figure in true perspective but continues to show the shoulders turned out toward us. From the higher right side of the relief the sun sends down rays in the shape of beneficent hands, endowing the Pharaoh and his wife with the key of life. The entire composition, including the hieroglyphs, is consistent, unified, and clear in its storytelling intent.

In contrast with the spirit and treatment of this relief, a second (Fig. 91) showing Seti I, a harsh, militant king of the succeeding dynasty, in the act of making offerings to Osiris and Horus illustrates the swing back to hieratic art after the fall of Akhenaten's house. When, as in this case, the stone was cut away from the form, the relief was undoubtedly much harder to make and is correspondingly more impressive, as finished and laborious stone carving on a large scale always impresses one—however falsely—with the sanctity and value of the object represented. The Pharaoh, nevertheless, is much more stiff in his position and unnatural in his movements. The shoulders still face us. Horus has two left hands. Osiris, swathed as a mummy and wearing the crown of Upper Egypt, sits on the throne of judgment, holding the symbols of his power over slaves and herds. Behind him Horus, the hawk-headed, appears in the body of a man.

When, as appears obvious from these details, the Egyptians could create such excellent abstract design, it seems strange that the entire

FIG. 93.—The falcon of Horus with King Nectanebos I in basalt, Thirtieth dynasty, 370 B.C. Height about 18 inches. (*Courtesy of Metropolitan Museum of Art.*)

relief should not be balanced. The explanation probably lies in the fact that the taskmaster who controlled the work was more of a labor organizer than an artist, and that individual

FIG. 94.—Portrait of Cleopatra in high relief on temple at Denderah, Ptolemaic period. (*Courtesy of Egypt Exploration Society.*)

stone carvers varied greatly. As a number of them were employed on a huge relief such as this, with figures over life size, the work on different parts of the wall surface varied in quality. The study of these sculpture reliefs affords the finest possible contrast between the two systems of religion and the types of art they engendered.

The Eclectic Character of the Late Egyptian Sculpture. When the people of a culture have lived through and enjoyed several artistic styles and when the culture is no longer dominated by a single religious idea, men's characters show a greater degree of variation. Some desire physioplastic art; others, ideoplastic. Those individuals who are born in the later days of a culture inherit not only the ideas that accompanied the many kinds of art still to be seen in their temples but also the emotional states and mental attitudes that they symbolize.

Egyptians in the late dynasties assimilated ideas from Assyria, Greece, and Rome. During the 8th century, invasions from Ethiopia brought in fresh blood and a revival of old attitudes from hunting-age cultures. The portraits (Fig. 92) indicate that there was intermarriage with Negroes. The sculpture of the period shows a strong tendency toward realism, while religion in many of its expressions seems to have gone back to totemistic levels.

In its remarkably fine carving, the hawk of the sun-god, Horus, as guardian of the Pharaoh Nectanebos, now in the Metropolitan Museum, is one of the most significant works in the history of Egyptian art (Fig. 93). It proclaims that in the Thirtieth dynasty (*c.* 370 B.C.) the power of the god, who now wears the double crown of Upper and Lower Egypt, completely overshadows that of the Pharaoh. Compare this statue with the statue of the early Pharaoh, Khafre. In formal qualities the two are similar, in that all the forms are space-excluding and completely bound to the block. On the other hand, the lines on the wing of the bird sweep upward and blend at the shoulders into the hood. Soft, rounded areas change into sharp edges at such significant points as the bill and the front of the wings. Sculptural planes contrasting with rounded surfaces give an effect of great interest and variety. From the associational side, this great totem completely dominates the tiny figure of the Pharaoh.

In the late religious art, one finds not only a highly spiritual conception such as this, in which even a king resides in the shadows of the wings of the Almighty, but many fantastic combinations of ideas. The goddess Thoueris is such a late Egyptian creation (Fig. 56*b*), combining

is called eclecticism, or the combination of many styles. When motifs that do not belong together are united thus into an almost plausible whole, the result stimulates a large number

FIG. 95.—Egyptian furniture (Metropolitan Museum of Art). (*Courtesy of Metropolitan Museum of Art.*)

parts from the lion, the woman, the hippopotamus, and the eagle, with the headdress of a sphinx to top all. Although the separate parts are realistic, the general appearance of the figure is geometric. There is a certain plausibility about the figure, which is fascinating though grotesque.

Greek influence, with the importation of the archaic smile from Cyprus, decrees that Cleopatra (Fig. 94) should appear with the first change of expression that Egyptian sculpture was to know—the attempt at a smile, in which the corners of the mouth were turned up but the eyes remained unsmiling.

Through all these vicissitudes of fashion, Egyptian sculpture remains compact, adamant, and eternal, and if it seems to lose its sense of permanence in Alexandrian times, that is because it is no longer Egyptian—it has become cosmopolitan.

In studying these late examples the student may recognize for the first time a phenomenon that will occur again in the history of art. This

of associated ideas without suggesting that they have been completely thought through and combined. This phenomenon will become most apparent in the period following the Italian Renaissance, called the "baroque."

Household Arts

In Egyptian, as in every succeeding culture, one can see the interdependence of the monumental and the household arts. The forms invented in building the great temples and in carving the statues of the Pharaohs were copied in the furniture of the Egyptians. Ornament in Egypt employed the human form and the flora and fauna of the Nile on both large and small creations.

Furniture. In the group of Egyptian furniture from the Metropolitan Museum (Fig. 95), one can see that the table copies the lines of the temple pylon. The legs slant inward slightly and the top is joined to them with a crown or cavetto molding. The lines of the chair, on the

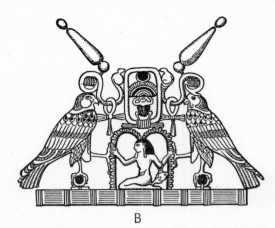

A   B   C

FIG. 96.—Pottery and jewelry. *a*, lotiform cup in blue faïence with scenes in low relief, Nineteenth dynasty, c. 1350 B.C.; *b*, pectoral or pendant in cloisonné, daughter of Sesostris II, height 1¾ inches; *c*, ointment vase with lotus flowers in faïence, Eighteenth dynasty, c. 1400 B.C. (*Courtesy of Metropolitan Museum of Art.*)

other hand, suggest the rounded contours of the seated Pharaohs. Its legs have been copied from a lion's legs. The table, then, copies architectural design; the chair, monumental sculpture. In contrast to these two pieces, the great basket and the folding campstool, on whose practicality no improvement has been made even in our own day, are purely functional articles of use and have no decorative lines other than those dictated by the necessities of their structure.

The refinement of the Egyptian and his dependence upon religious associations are nowhere better illustrated than in this temple table and chair. They serve their function as useful household articles but they go beyond this, suggesting the architectural and sculptural quality of the culture by which they were made. In much the same way, many of our household articles are now streamlined, suggesting the lines of the newer automobiles and airplanes.

Pottery and Jewelry. In his pottery the Egyptian copied natural floral forms. The primitive shapes—the gourd, the egg, and the basket—were early enriched by a new creation of refinement and great suggestive power. This was the lily-bud design. Both open and closed forms of this bud were copied for the drinking chalice and the incense bottle (Fig. 96*a*, *c*).

In the earliest dynasties the Egyptians discovered a method for combining sand, lead, and ferruginous or cuprous earths to make green and blue glass. They not only covered the smaller pottery with this glaze but in a few cases made tiles with which they lined the walls of the tombs. They learned to fuse the glass and blow it into animal shapes, combining the colors in interesting mosaic patterns. Finally, they learned to make imitation precious stones of the glass and fused it within small strips of gold that had been soldered to a surface of the precious metal (Fig. 96*b*). The resulting jewelry of glass and metal is called "cloisonné." The tiny metallic strips are the *cloisons*.

When he invented this new technique for making his colors more permanent than any paints could be, the Egyptian followed his natural desire to change all appearance into some imperishable material, but his designs remained the same as those monumental designs on the walls of tomb and temple. The inlaid pectoral pendant of a princess, daughter of Sesostris II, in the Metropolitan Museum shows the common Egyptian religious motif of the two hawks, one on each side of the sun. It charms through its fine craftsmanship and even more by the glittering effect so appealing to the heart of a child or a bowerbird.

Summary

The Egyptians' Contribution to Our Concept of Art. The Egyptian used both ideoplastic and physioplastic art on the earliest culture horizons. As the power of his organized religious cults grew strong, the concept of art as a means to record his dreams of immortality became so strong that ideoplastic creations drove out physioplastic.

In the Eighteenth dynasty, which allowed great freedom of expression on the part of the artists, one man left on the walls of his workshop the first recorded art criticism: "All art is a combination of cubes, squares, and cones." Such a concept of art would seem to indicate that the free Egyptian could reach a purely formal aesthetic judgment, one which excluded the associational values.

During the same dynasties much of the poetry gives a word sign called "the inner organs," which is usually translated as the word "beauty." This association of the idea of beauty with the old ideograph for the viscera seems to indicate that at that time the Egyptian concept of beauty, like that of the Navajo medicine chanter, meant simply "a healthy pleasant condition inside the body."

Probably at that level of culture the most intelligent concept of art was associated with pleasure, either the pleasure of knowing that one's appearance, and therefore one's soul, had been made permanent for eternity or else that playlike satisfaction which the sculptor may have had in arranging his cubes, squares, and cones.

It seems significant from a psychological angle that the art which best combined physioplastic and ideoplastic attributes was created for those rulers, such as Hatshepsut and Akhenaten, whose religions united the solar and matriarchal cults. Finally, the concept of beauty as we understand it today appears in poetry by Akhenaten, which has an ethical level higher than that of the other monarchs. This observation, based upon a historic fact, may give a clue to the fortunes of art in succeeding cultures. Those cultures, particularly in Greece and Renaissance Florence, that encouraged individual freedom and intellectual inquiry, produced arts that resemble those of the Amarna Age.

In summarizing, to the Egyptian, art was on the whole a method for making his wish for immortality permanent and a charm to assure him a place in the afterworld.

Bibliography

BREASTED, JAMES HENRY: *The Dawn of Conscience*, Charles Scribner's Sons, New York, 1933.

BREASTED, JAMES HENRY: *Development of Religion and Thought in Ancient Egypt*, Charles Scribner's Sons, New York, 1912.

QUIBELL, A. A.: *Egyptian History and Art*, The Macmillan Company, New York, 1923.

MURRAY, MARGARET: *Egyptian Sculpture*, Charles Scribner's Sons, New York, 1930.

COOK, F. C.: translation of "Hymn to the Nile" in *World's Classics*, *Egyptian Literature*, Colonial Press, New York.

EBERS, GEORGE M.: *An Egyptian Princess* (novel) Harcourt, Brace & Company, Inc., New York, 1913.

Recordings

Kol Nidre, Eili, Eili, Victor, 35830, a & b.

CHAPTER V

The Art of Power in Western Asia

My neck which had been twisted and bent low,
He made erect and like a cedar raised up.
He made my stature like one of perfect strength,
Like one released from a demon, he polished my nails.
. . . .
My entire body he restored,
He wiped away the blemish,
Making it resplendent,
The oppressed stature regained its splendor,
On the banks of the stream where judgment is held over men
The brand of slavery was removed, the fetters taken off.[1]

TWO GREAT streams of thought have contributed to the development of the arts in modern life. The source of one of these may be traced to Egypt, that of the other to Mesopotamia. While the religious art of Egypt stressed permanence and the form of the human body, the arts of Mesopotamia emphasized the more dynamic aspects of being shown in linear design. To understand the difference between the arts of the two cultures, one must first consider both the geographic differences between the two lands and the contrasting racial mixtures.

The Land of Two Rivers. While civilization emerged from prehistoric culture levels in Egypt around 4000 B.C., three distinct peoples —the Semites, the Sumerians, and a highland group, perhaps Aryan in origin—were outgrowing the primitive culture stages in Mesopotamia. The land they occupied differed greatly from that of the Egyptians. The broad river valleys of the Tigris and the Euphrates, stretching toward the east from the mountains of Armenia and Asia Minor, ended at the Persian Gulf. Beyond the headwaters to the west of the Euphrates lay the lands of Syria and Palestine, that is, ancient Canaan; north of the mountain passes of Armenia extended the great steppes of Asia; to the south were the barren deserts of Arabia. From the mouth of the river, along the coast of the gulf or over the seas, stretched an open route to India. Compared with Egypt, a land relatively sheltered, Mesopotamia stood open to invasion from all sides. Significant above all else in comparing the arts of Egypt and Mesopotamia is the fact that the former stressed completeness; the latter, contrast. The geographic dissimilarities of the two lands accounted in part for these differences in their artistic concepts.

The swiftly changing dynasties of Mesopotamian rulers and the ever expanding and contracting boundaries of the successive cultures of the region make the historical and geographical study of the arts of Mesopotamia very confusing. This confusion is increased by the various names given to the cultures and localities by different schools of archaeologists. In general, however, the lower or eastern part of the dual river valley between present-day Bagdad and the Persian Gulf is usually known as Babylonia. This region was settled in prehis-

[1] MORRIS JASTROW, *The Civilization of Babylonia and Assyria*, Chap. VIII, J. B. Lippincott Company, Philadelphia, 1915.

toric times by the Sumerians (Fig. 97b), a people of unknown origin, although on the basis of linguistic features, scholars have connected them with the Dravidians of southern India. The upper or western part of the valleys, next to Armenia and Syria, supported a composite group of Semites (Fig. 97a) and mountaineers. This section was known as Assyria.

The somewhat simplified story which follows, together with a study of the map in Chap. II, will make clear the general cultural trends in Mesopotamian history.

The Historical Development of the Two Lands. Before the 5th millennium the mountainous country called "Elam," to the northeast of Babylonia, was inhabited in all likelihood by people in the neolithic stage of development. About the turn of the fifth millennium, at what is now the town of Susa, located just where the mountains meet the plains, the Elamites had reached the agricultural stage of development and were beginning to make pottery.

Although from the beginning of settlement the population in southern Mesopotamia was mixed, the principal cultural factor came from the Sumerians, whose remains at Ur, Uruk, and Lagash mark the transition into the historic period. As the natural resources of Babylonia were limited, it was necessary for the inhabitants to travel afar to secure metals, precious stones, and wood. The late neolithic cultures could not remain isolated, therefore, and commercial activities brought numerous foreign contacts. Evidence of connections between the early Sumerian cultures and the town of Mohenjo-Daro in the Indus River valley of northeastern India, has been found (Fig. 98b).

The Sumerian kings of Ur and Mari ruled Sumer around 3000 B.C. as the early Pharaohs ruled Egypt. Sumer gradually extended her influence to the west and eventually encroached upon Semitic territory at Kish, a town near modern Bagdad. In the next phase of development, the land from Kish to Assur was called "Akkad." The two cultures, the

Sumerian and the Semitic, were united about 2650 B.C. by the first Sargon, who brought all the land as far as the Mediterranean under one rule. If the reader will imagine the balance of

a   *b*

Fig. 97.—*a*, alabaster Semitic head of man, height 3½ inches; *b*, sandstone Sumerian head of woman from Bismaya (?), height 2½ inches. (*Courtesy of the Oriental Institute, University of Chicago.*)

power swinging back and forth through the centuries between the Sumerians inhabiting the lower valley and the Semites in the upper part around Assur, he will have a sketchy picture of the entire history of Mesopotamia.

Between 1955 and 1913 B.C., Hammurabi, the first great lawgiver of history, ruled the two countries with Babylon as his capital. The period from 2057 to 1758 B.C. comprises the first Babylonian dynasty. Semitic Assyrian kings following Shalmanesar ruled from their capital at Assur between 1300 and 1100 B.C., in what is known as the First Assyrian dynasty. Babylonian monarchs rule again between 1169 and 1039 B.C. The Assyrians are in the ascendant between 900 and 600 B.C., and the Babylonians between 600 and 500 B.C. Finally, in what is known as the Persian Empire, a virile race took possession of the lands, ruling between 558 and 330 B.C. The capital of Persia, at Persepolis, was not far from the ancient town of Susa.

The mental attitudes resulting from the continual upheavals in Mesopotamia called for a different type of religion and art from that of Egypt. These differences, as we shall see, may be recognized even in the prehistoric aesthetic productions of the people.

Aesthetic Desires of the Mesopotamian Peoples. We have seen that the man of the hunting age produced physioplastic representations of animal life, most of which, apparently, grew out of memory pictures suggested by inanimate natural objects; whereas, agricultural man constructed or wove his art. From his manufactured technomorphic patterns he achieved a sense of rhythmical design, which eventually produced a number of abstract composition schemes.

The Mesopotamian, possessing a background obtained from both hunting and agricultural men, produced paintings and figures that stressed the life forces within the bodies of men and beasts. In his monumental wall decorations, and by the use of cylinder seals, he achieved a linear continuity that was lacking in the work of the Egyptians, who used stamp seals. Similar differences between other phases of Egyptian and Mesopotamian cultures will be shown later.

These differences between the aesthetic expression of the two civilizations spring from two great contrasting methods of thinking about life and art which have come down to us today. Without our being conscious of them, they still influence most of our aesthetic judgment. The pictures in our churches and art galleries represent, on the whole, our attempts—like those of Egypt—to make life permanent; our billboards and advertisements, also works of art, represent, in contrast, our attempts—like those of Mesopotamia—to produce action, to make people eat some special brand of food, perhaps, or to drive a supercharged automobile. Striving for different effects, the two forms of graphic art use different means, and we must judge them in relation to their goals.

We shall analyze the formal means by which the Mesopotamian achieved his aesthetic purposes when we consider the primitive origins of Mesopotamian design. For evidence of the dynamic quality of the Mesopotamian mind, we now turn to a study of Mesopotamian literature and mythology.

The Origins of Mesopotamian Thought

The importance of two contrasting conceptions of God must be understood if we are to determine accurately the influence of associative factors in art. The one conception is that of a god of love, conferring immortality on man in the afterworld; the other, that of a god of power, conferring health, strength, and prestige upon man in his life on earth. The mental attitudes of love or fear generated by the dominance of one or the other of these two concepts profoundly influence the individual in his approach to and appreciation of a work of art.

Mesopotamian literature is of the highest importance as the first world literature to stress the story of the creation of man by a god of power. The earliest agricultural inhabitants of Mesopotamia, as well as the mountain dwellers, had their totems and fetishes, as did the pre-dynastic Egyptians. In Egypt during the early dynasties the humanized trinity of Isis, Osiris, and Horus gradually came to the fore. In this system of deities, the passive feminine element was at least as great as the masculine, or active, element. In Mesopotamia the case was otherwise. Perhaps because of the predominance of the Semitic, patriarchal, herding people and the continuous incursions of warlike mountain folk, the totems that grew into deities were on the whole dynamic and masculine.

All the active components of nature were thought of as masculine, warrior, or hunter gods. True, a feminine religious element was always recognized by the agricultural people in Sumer and appeared later in Babylon. The Babylonian goddess Ishtar was worshiped first in the shape of a date palm tree, later, in that of a woman. Too realistic to ignore wholly the feminine aspect in nature, the Mesopotamian also allowed each warrior god a child-bearing wife, but her position was distinctly subordinate to that of the male deity.

The Mesopotamian created four great stories, all of which left their impress on the development of European literature. Two of them, the creation story and the tale of the flood, were incorporated in the Bible. Another, the story of Gilgamesh, is of special significance as the prototype of the Perseus and Herakles stories in Greek legendry. That of Ishtar and her two lovers, Tammuz and Izdubar, appears later as an essential element in medieval romances.

The Story of the Creation and the Epic of the Hero God. Man, according to the Mesopotamian story of creation, was created because the gods were lonely and wanted someone to worship them. This situation came about as follows:

In the beginning was Tiamat or Chaos, a wicked she-monster, goddess of the rains and winds of winter. Apsu, the ocean, and Tiamat, mingled their waters from the sea and the sky. Out of this union came life. First appeared two gods, Lakhmu and Lakhmanu. From this pair arose two more, Anshar and Kishar, who became the progenitors of three great male gods.

The first of these, Anu, god of the daytime sky, became king; Ea, the second member, ruled the seas; the third, Enlil, was god of thunder and of the moving air. Like the Egyptian goddess, Isis, Ea exerted a beneficent influence. As the god of the arts, he protected humanity and taught man how to build, to cast metal, and to carve precious stones. Enlil, gradually absorbing many of the attributes of various local solar deities, usurped the power of Anu and became, in time, the symbol of fertility, which resided in the sun. Like the Hebrew god, Jehovah, Enlil was worshiped as the god of light and strength. His hymn sounds like many of the psalms.

So far the creation story emphasized the masculine rule. Now enters the feminine element. The old god Apsu and the goddess Tiamat feared the new masculine trinity and decided that it must be destroyed. To aid in the task of destruction, Tiamat gave birth to a host of nightmarish monsters.

With these powers at her disposal, the goddess besought the help of Anshar and Kishar and marched upon the trinity. In the meantime, Ea, the beneficent god, had conceived a heroic son, variously called Gilgamesh in early Sumerian days, Marduk in Assyrian times, and Izdubar in the late Babylonian period. Gilgamesh created four wind gods, later to become the four horsemen of the Apocalypse. With the wind of pestilence he attacked Tiamat, driving a blast into her mouth until she choked; then he killed her with his spear. Her body he divided and had the north wind take one half to make up the heavens, the other half, the earth. He then formed the stars, arranged the constellations, and made houses for the gods of the trinity.

When at last all was at peace, Tiamat (Chaos) had vanished from the earth to return only in war or perhaps in the dreams of men. Everything was then so well ordered that the world seemed lonely. So Gilgamesh, as the story runs, created man out of his own "bones and blood," that the gods might be worshiped.

Psychologically this story is of the greatest importance, in that it represents an almost purely masculine concept of the creative processes. In this concept the feminine components of the mind are thought of as chaotic, untamed forces. Only by overcoming this chaos and putting all the internal forces in order can peace be achieved. In Mesopotamia, it is Gilgamesh, a masculine lord, who distributes the body of the woman, Tiamat; in Egypt, it is Isis, the mother goddess, who reunites the dismembered parts of Osiris's body. The Mesopotamian concept of creation is an ordering of forces; the Egyptian, a bringing together of fragments. The one has to do essentially with energy, the other with masses.

The Story of the Flood. The literature of Egypt at no place suggests anything so destructive as a world cataclysm in which all mankind was destroyed. The regular flow of the Nile, bringing its rich black soil from the interior of Africa, made beneficence seem inevitable. The Tigris and Euphrates, on the other hand, rising in a myriad of mountain streams, overflowed their banks at irregular intervals and brought floods as destructive as those of the Mississippi.

The oldest Sumerian account of the flood forms part of a cycle of hero tales, the first great epic story in history, concerning the hero god Gilgamesh. This story, imprinted on twelve clay tablets, consisted of episodes corresponding to the monthly activities of the god and, allegorically, to those of mankind. Like the late medieval morality play *Everyman*, the epic has one of the oldest of dramatic plots. Significantly enough, the deluge story occurs on the eleventh tablet, which corresponds to the winter season, when the storms produced the greatest damage. We may judge, then, that the account was inspired by the flood, an annual disaster, if not by the memory of some one great cataclysm. The hero of the Sumerian story, Utna Pishtim, corresponding to the Biblical Noah, lived in the city of Shuruppak on the Euphrates. The site has been identified in the mound of Fara, a real place where actual traces of a great flood have been found. Gilgamesh, meeting Utna Pishtim in the underworld, learned that the great male gods, Anu and Enlil, at the behest of the local gods of Shuruppak, had decided to destroy the city, much as Jehovah later destroyed Sodom and Gomorrah. Ea, the beneficent god, hearing of the plot decided to save at least one man. Appearing in a dream to Utna Pishtim, Ea told him to destroy his primitive reed hut and to build an ark. The details of the construction of the ark are very similar to those in the Biblical tale, which was recorded a thousand years later.

Having built the ship, Utna Pishtim brought into it his family, all his cattle, the beasts of the field, and even his workmen. The account of the storm that follows is the prototype of most of the great descriptive battle scenes in the world's great epics. The passage describes how the black clouds rose high in the heavens, while three wind gods, Adad, Nabu, and Lugal, rushed thundering to the fray, and Ira, the god of pestilence, tore out the mast of the ship. Even the gods in heaven, terrified, fled to the highest levels.

After six days the tumult departed, and the great ship came to rest on Mt. Nicere, a name which in Sumerian meant "Mount of Salvation." Like Noah, Utna Pishtim sent out birds, first a dove, then a swallow, and finally a raven, to tell him whether the waters had subsided. When the last of these did not return, Utna Pishtim opened the ship and let his people go into the four regions of the earth.

In this story, the harassed Mesopotamians, groping toward some reason for existence, sought to demonstrate how man through inventive power might thwart the will of the highest gods. The strategy of Utna Pishtim thus inaugurates the plot of the later epics of Prometheus, Siegfried, and Beowulf. Stories of revolt such as these accompany all ideas of social improvement throughout the history of European thought.

The Ishtar Story. Our meager knowledge of the Mesopotamian beliefs concerning a possible life after death come for the most part from the various versions of the story of Ishtar, the nature goddess. In this tale we learn that the abode of departed spirits was thought to be a great indefinite plain filled with dust. To this dark, gloomy level, called Aralu, descended the just and the unjust. There, as winged beings clothed with feathers, they lived in complete passivity unless released to haunt the living.

In the fall of every year Ishtar, goddess of life was compelled to go down to the underworld, governed by her cruel sister, Eresh-Kigal. As she passed through the seven gates, at the command of the jealous queen, Ishtar's garments and jewels were one by one stripped from her, until at last she reached Eresh-Kigal naked, to be imprisoned with the demons of pestilence in the palace of the dead.

When Ishtar departed from the earth, all vegetation died, the beasts no longer desired to create their kind, and love left the hearts of lover and beloved. Soon the gods mourned the loss of one who had made life pleasant. Then Ea, the wise god, formed a man whose name, Asu-Shu-Namir, means "the resplendent rising sun." This man was sent as a messenger to bring back the goddess after she had been baptized with "the water of life." As she was led out through the seven gates, Ishtar gradually resumed the clothing that had been stripped from her at her entrance and at last, with the coming of spring, reappeared on earth to gladden men with her beauty.

This important legend traveled to Greece, where the goddess, sometimes called "Astarte," took on three separate personalities: Aphrodite, the goddess of love; Demeter, the goddess of nature; and Persephone, who represents Nature in her generative aspect. Other tales grew from the story. Orpheus (man) seeks his lost love Eurydice in the underworld; Christ, hung on the cross—another symbol of the mother goddess—descended into the underworld to free the souls of the righteous. Thus the story of a necessary death and an inevitable rebirth became a great factor in the development of religious literature.

The Beginnings of Romanticism in the Izdubar Legend. The creation and flood stories bring out the fact that most Mesopotamian literature took as its subject the self-discovery of man in the fullness of his powers. The Ishtar story shows that, despite the dominance of the masculine concept of life, the feminine element, although subordinate, was also present. As the agricultural Sumerian stock became preponderant, the worship of the mother goddess filled a greater place in Mesopotamian life (Fig. 99e).

In the epic of Izdubar we find united for the first time the masculine hero and the mother goddess as the goddess of love. Izdubar, who is in reality none other than Gilgamesh or Marduk, was born the son of an earthly king, Ourouk. When Ourouk was overthrown by the Elamites, Izdubar fled to the wilderness, where he distinguished himself, as had Gilgamesh and Marduk, by killing many demons. Reconquering his father's kingdom with the help of the jinn (a half-human demon), Izdubar became king. Then Ishtar fell in love with the hero, followed him to his palace and appeared to him in his dreams, adopting sometimes a beautiful, sometimes a terrifying, aspect. Under her protection Izdubar defeated his enemies; but when Ishtar asked his hand, he spurned the goddess. Ishtar then descended into the underworld, where she tried to breathe life into her former lover, Tammuz (Adonis), whom she had destroyed. Tammuz was restored to life, and the two flew away from the gates of death toward the clouds. There Tammuz again died. While Ishtar mourned over his body, Tammuz returned to Aralu to be crowned king of the underworld. Ishtar renewed her pursuit of Izdubar, who eventually had also to journey to the underworld before he could finally marry a beautiful princess, Mua, daughter of the wise magician, Khasisadra, ruler of the Elysian fields, a kind of heavenly paradise. Mua who corresponds to a sort of heavenly beauty becomes the true love of Izdubar. He was granted immortality, but, as an earthly king, must depart from paradise. He told Mua that her love was sweeter than all earthly things and that he would return to her soon, when his task as king was over on earth.

The great significance of this story lies in the fact that it marks the beginning of a type of poetry, the romantic epic, which persisted in Mesopotamia through the early years of the Christian Era and was carried back to Europe by the Western crusaders. The tales of Parsifal, Launcelot, Gawain, and Ewain in the Arthurian cycles, as well as Tasso's *Jerusalem Delivered* and other romantic epics of the Renaissance, all follow the general plot of the Mesopotamian legend.

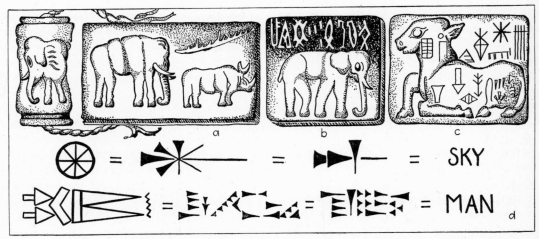

FIG. 98.—*a*, seal and impression from Tell Asmar about 2600 B.C.; *b*, elephant seal from Mohenjo-Daro (*after Marshall*); *c*, seal of Ur-Nina, Lagash; *d*, writing (*after Maspero*).

Many passages in the poem describe the life of the people of Babylon. One tells of the annual sale of maidens which takes place on the day sacred to Ishtar. The poet also sings of the attributes of the perfect wife. In this discussion the word "beauty" appears, connected with the idea of feminine charm and purity. The beautiful woman was one who did not try to tempt man, had caresses only for her husband, and was physically attractive. The ideal woman is, of course, Mua, the heavenly beauty, who represents man's hope for happiness in spiritual love. Although the true man can never be at peace with the forces of the goddess of love, yet her heavenly aspect inspires him with hope of a perfect union.

The Rise of an Ethical Concept. In Egypt, religious literature gradually freed itself from the primitive charms that stood for permanence, until it reached an expression of the high ethical thought that all mankind were brothers under a god of love and beauty. In Mesopotamia, a somewhat parallel development took place, but with two important differences: (1) rewards were desired on this earth in terms of renewed vitality; (2) beauty seemed less desirable than health and splendor. Meso-

potamian ethical poetry rose more from a fear of punishment by the powerful gods than from a desire to attain perfection. Nebuchadnezzar, a king in the Late Babylonian Empire, prayed to Marduk, the counterpart of Gilgamesh, saying:

I love thy sublime appearance as my own precious life—since I love the fear of thy divinity and I am zealous for thy rule, be gracious to my prayer for I am the king who adorns thy temple—the thoughtful governor who beautifies all thy settlements. At thy command, O merciful Marduk, may the house that I have built endure forever. May I be satiated with its splendor, attain old age therein with abundant offspring and receive therein tribute of the kings of all regions from all mankind.[1]

This prayer, typical of the desires of the ordinary Mesopotamian, introduces the words "sublime" and "splendor." The verb "to beautify" meant apparently "to arrange and put in order." In still other prayers these kings used the term "brilliant" to describe the temples. This adjective, as we shall see, was applicable because of the custom of facing the buildings with shining enameled tiles.

Many of the prayers of the Mesopotamians

[1] MORRIS JASTROW, *The Civilization of Babylonia and Assyria*, p. 466, J. B. Lippincott Company, Philadelphia.

besought strength and vitality. Apparently the greatest misfortune that could come to man in their fierce civilization was to lose bodily vigor. In a lamentation quoted at the beginning of this chapter, which is a worthy predecessor of the Book of Job, an inhabitant of Babylon named Tabi-utul-Enlil recites the evils that have fallen upon him and tells how, with the help of Marduk, he was healed.

Here, for the Mesopotamian, is the happy ending—a man restored to the fullness of vigor and bearing about him an aura of power. Thus in Mesopotamian literature one finds the psychological origins of the aesthetics that considers a palace or a great sky temple glistening in the sun, a king hunting lions, or a sun-god overcoming the chaotic powers of death to have the highest associational value.

The Art of Writing in Mesopotamia. The literature of Mesopotamia, stressing as it did the active elements in man's character, demanded a system of writing that allowed for the rapid transmission of thought. The desire for a hasty record early led the people to invent a printing tool that could impress upon tablets a series of signs standing for word sounds. Like the Egyptian, the Mesopotamian script started with fairly naturalistic pictures. The sky was shown as a circle with six spokes, perhaps reminiscent of the wheel of the sun wagon. Very early, this symbol changed to a star and later to a cross with a little extra protuberance. The earliest sign for man, which was naturalistic, became a hieroglyph with which it is not easy to trace the connection (Fig. 98). In the Late Babylonian Empire the scribes, interested in the origin of their writing, tried to indicate on a series of tablets the derivation of the signs. This fact shows not only that these people were what we should today call progressive and inventive, but that they also had a scientific interest in historical origins. However, we are still ignorant as to where this type of writing, which is called "cuneiform," originated.

Writing in Egypt and writing in Mesopotamia present many contrasts. The Egyptians separated their pictures from the smaller pictures, or hieroglyphs, which stood for words. The Mesopotamians, in contrast, had so little reverence for the human form that in many cases they ran their inscriptions over the pictured bodies of the people concerned (Fig. 112). They made pictures and writing look wholly unlike and often made the words the dominant motive. The great mass of Egyptian writing had to do with the ceremonies of the Book of the Dead. The Mesopotamian was interested particularly in laws and business transactions. His early development of the seal, for signing legal documents, may be taken as a cue to the inner practicality that underlay his art throughout its development.

The Origins of Mesopotamian Design

Before the Mesopotamians recorded the myths that formed the bases for their literature, they developed a number of fundamental design patterns.[1] These patterns resulted from the desire to express in graphic and plastic media the same ideas as those later recorded in the myths. Their aesthetic values are especially appealing to us because they seem close to American Indian designs, which have come to take a significant place in the development of American patterns. Most of the Mesopotamian designs come from the Elamite town of Susa, from Tepe Gawra, and Persepolis—all prehistoric sites on the border between the mountain country and the plain. They demonstrate that in the third millennium before Christ the Mesopotamians were carrying on a lively commerce in articles of design with northwestern India, the neolithic cultures north of the Caucasus, the Dniestro-Danubian basin, and the steppes beyond the Caspian Sea.

[1] Discovered, for the greater part, in the excavations of the Oriental Institute of the University of Chicago and of the University of Pennsylvania Museum since 1910.

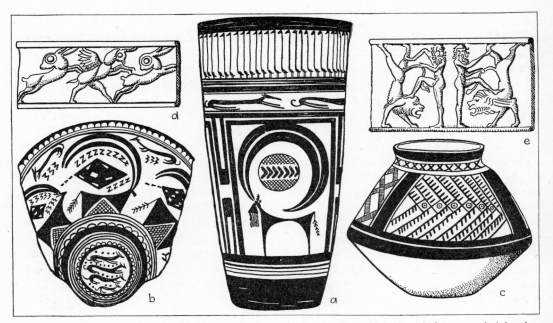

Fig. 99.—*a, b,* and *c,* early Stone Age pottery from Susa (*a,* height about 11 inches; *b,* fragment, height about 3 inches; *c,* height about 3⅛ inches); *d* and *e,* impressions from early Babylonian seals, showing (*d*) pursuit motif and (*e*) Gilgamesh with the lion of Ishtar (Louvre Museum).

The Dynamic Quality of Mesopotamian Design

The Egyptians decorated their pottery, for the most part, with geometricized figures of human beings. These figures, statically arranged in flat areas with little regard for the structure of the pottery, suggest that the artist was interested in some story. Mesopotamian pottery from Susa, Tepe Gawra, and Tell Billa, on the other hand, shows distinct bands of animal ornament, so arranged in zigzag or circular repeated lines that the eye is carried from one element of the pattern to the next. Such design, characterized by a repetition of motifs leading one to another, we may call dynamic, in contrast to the more static Egyptian decoration.

On the Susian pottery illustrated (Fig. 99), the figures of elongated curvilinear greyhounds running around the vase suggest action. Even at the bottom of the vase (Fig. 99*b*), where the circle is necessary to fill the inside of the base,

the greyhounds have been fitted to the area in such a way that the eye moves in restless motion from one line to the other. Contrast this with the pre-dynastic Egyptian vase (Fig. 54*b,* Chap. IV).

The tall center vase from Susa (Fig. 99*a*) has a dynamic border at the top which possesses both refinement and interest. It far surpasses similar decorations on contemporaneous Egyptian vases. Between the horns of the geometricized animal we see a copy of an Azilian painted pebble, possibly having some religious significance. Here is a good example in early vase painting of a design at once static and dynamic, interesting and appropriate.

The little bowl at the lower right (Fig. 99*c*) shows conventionalized birds, all pointing in one direction so as to make a border. The action of this border is stopped by vertical lines between which the static triangle, repeated, makes for a dynamic perpendicular motion, which is stopped again by bottom and top borders. Interesting pottery design carries

Fig. 100.—*a* and *b*, bowls, Stone Age village at Persepolis (*courtesy of the Oriental Institute, University of Chicago*); *c* and *d*, bowls from Tepe Gawra, about 3000 B.C. (*courtesy of the University Museum, University of Pennsylvania*).

the eye over the surface of the object, so that unconsciously the feelings are stimulated by the form of the object. In this way, the design enhances rather than destroys the form.

The remarkable feeling for pottery design that we find at Susa runs through all the Mesopotamian cultures and, when combined with the colored glaze work of the Late Babylonian Empire, eventually flowers into the justly celebrated Persian and Mohammedan pottery of the Christian Era.

Plant and Animal Motifs

The elements of design discussed above appear in more abstract form on vases from the Stone Age village at Persepolis. In decoration, these vases stand among the world's finest primitive pottery, ranking with the American Pueblo Indian pots for excellent balance in abstract design.

The first example is a bowl circled with a broad band of abstract decoration (Fig. 100*a*).

This decoration still holds a faint suggestion of technomorphic origins, as though the design had started with a basket weave. The shape of the individual stripes, however, and the angle at which they are placed on the surface of the bowl so well repeat the exterior shape that a well-developed unity results between surface design and shape. The band also has a slight motion from left to right, for the alternate stripes are free from the zigzag band and, being placed on alternate diagonals of the zigzag, help the eye to move around the form. The addition of three small horizontal bands at the top and bottom, marking the base and the lip, hold the design on the base.

The second piece, a large bowl about 16 inches across at the top (Fig. 100*b*), incorporates the animal style with a checkerboard motif probably derived from basketry. The inlays, made up of various-sized circles above the horns of the animal and in the checkerboard areas, create an occult balance that we shall see again and again in Oriental painting. Since these pieces point to possible origins of early

Chinese pottery design in Turkestan, their discovery has been of great significance. The animal vase, particularly, furnishes a schematic basis for occult design patterns in Oriental art.

On the tiny bowl from the Mound of Tepe Gawra, northern Mesopotamia (Figs. 100c, d), can be traced the development of the brush stroke with which the areas of decoration were painted. The skillful use of any tool, such as a brush or a chisel, adds a dynamic element of suggestion to the total effect of the art object. Taken by itself, virtuosity, or skill in the manipulation of material, cannot be considered highly in a well-rounded scheme of aesthetic values; but when coupled with excellent design and ideational content, virtuosity lends an element of authority to any work. The Mesopotamian made geometric figures, triangles, and parallelograms with great sureness, each apparently with one stroke of the brush. Hence the development of techniques of design may be studied in Mesopotamian art with particular reference to skill in painting with a free brush stroke.

The Eye Motif

An element of design that demonstrates the contrasting mentalities of the Egyptians and Mesopotamians appears on the early Babylonian seal (Fig. 101a) and on early Sumerian figures of gods. Conspicuous in such examples are great round dots, one on each side of a single stroke, which distinctly suggest staring eyes. Primitives the world over use the large eyes as a means of denoting fright (Fig. 101b), for the physical reaction to fright is to open the eyes wide. If the large, circular eye spots could be combined with the dynamic lines of force, we should have a design with a maximum of aesthetic power. This may in some measure explain the striking effect of the animal vase with the round spots (Fig. 100b).

The conventional use of large eyes is lacking in Egyptian art until the 8th century, when it

was introduced by Persian invaders. We must explain this difference in the two arts either on the ground that the Mesopotamian peoples, with their worship of masculine virility, derived aesthetic enjoyment from a picturization of the fear elements, or on the ground that even in the centuries of their prehistoric culture a fear complex had grown up as a dominant factor in Mesopotamian statecraft and religion. In general, the effect of Egyptian art may be said to be quieting; that of Mesopotamian art, exciting.

The Development of Symbols

In Egypt, most pictorial and sculptural design was arranged inside squares, rectangles, and cubes—all static figures. In Mesopotamia, the fundamental symbols were the sun wheel or swastika, vitalized lines of animal bodies, and a zigzag ∧∧∧/ arrangement of lines and areas to suggest tension (Fig. 101c). When the Mesopotamian allowed himself to think about Ishtar, the mother goddess, he was confronted with a number of feminine symbols (Fig. 101d). The earliest of these was the tree of life, later modified to a cross; this symbol became the sign for the planet Venus, sacred to Ishtar. The loin cloth worn by the goddess makes the figure of a triangle, considered feminine when the apex is down. In contrast, the ceremonial spear or dart of the masculine sun-god was also a triangle with the apex pointing upward. In later cultures these two triangles played significant roles as representations of the human soul, the masculine soul coming down from the heavens, the feminine emerging from the ground.

Four Directions in Design

It is significant that between the arts of Egypt and the arts of Mesopotamia practically all the fundamental means of expression through design were discovered and used, to be later appropriated and refined by the Greeks. The design elements that we have just studied as they arose beyond the prehistoric horizons of Mesopotamian art developed in four distinct directions. Three of these lines of development suggest power, each in its own way. Hence, they found favor in Mesopotamia. The fourth

Fig. 101.—*a*, early Babylonian seal, Tello (Collection Le Clerc, Louvre Museum); *b*, face of God (?), Tell Asmar; *c*, early Susian pottery design; *d*, clay figure of a goddess, Tell Asmar. (*b* and *d*, *courtesy of the Oriental Institute, University of Chicago*.)

—a tendency to generate naturalistic pictures out of fortuitous designs in nature—was dropped in that country, although it became of great significance in Indian and Chinese art. The four directions of design are these:

1. The design of active pattern; that is, design suggesting action over the surface of an object.

2. Abstract design in shapes that suggest growth.

3. Design from symbols of power; that is, design following sculptural masses in the human figure to suggest dynamic energy.

4. Fortuitous design arising from natural effects; that is, naturalistic design stimulated by irregular striations in rocks, clouds, and the like.

The Design of Active Pattern. A seal from the prehistoric town of Tell Asmar (Fig. 102*a*) shows what may well be the earliest expression of the Gilgamesh story. The hero, represented as a bundle of angular limbs, has a torpedo-shaped horned head, poised so as to lead the eye toward a second object. This object, a technomorphic pattern of lines suggestive of the feminine art of weaving, represents the dragon form of Tiamat. In contrast to early Egyptian design, such as that on the palette of Narmer, the line of the rear leg of the hero, coupled

with the angle of the face and some of the other lines of the composition, connects with the interweave of the dragon. The development of this pattern of dynamic interweave can be

b

Fig. 102.—*a*, impression from cylinder seal, Tell Asmar; *b*, stamp seal of shell carved to represent couchant bull, actual size (compare with Fig. 435 Chap. XIV). (*Courtesy of the Oriental Institute, University of Chicago*.)

traced not only throughout Mesopotamian art but into the Scythian art beyond the Caucasus River and the Celto-Germanic art of Europe. Its fullest expression is found in the architecture of the Gothic cathedral and the baroque paintings of the 16th century.

Abstract Design in Shapes That Suggest Growth. In Egypt, the lotus flower suggested the shape of a cup, and the cup always copied the lotus. The analysis of the head of Nofretete (Fig. 84, Chap. IV) showed that the lines of growth, although geometricized and abstract, still formed the internal composition lines around which the masses were placed. Similarly, the cup of gold from the grave of Shub-ad in Sumer (Fig. 103) has been molded into a shape suggested not directly by a flower but by abstract lines derived from a flower-vase decoration similar to that in Fig. 100. This gold cup appears to be a product of pure imagination. So far abstracted is it from the original source in nature that the source can no longer be recognized. In the field of useful arts such abstract design seems highly appropriate, because it symbolizes man's inventive power in its purest form. Designs of that kind have become common in the 20th

Fig. 103.—Gold receptacles from grave of Shub-ad, early Sumerian. The fluted cup has delicate chevrons and herringbone engraving near the lips and base. On the bottom is an eight-petaled rosette. Height about 8 inches. (*Courtesy of the University Museum, University of Pennsylvania.*)

century. The columns of the great temple of Hatshepsut and some of the ornament of Romanesque and Gothic cathedrals also display the same type of design, the use of which is called "functionalism."

Design from Symbols of Power. The third direction in Mesopotamian design leads to the application of the first and second—a combination of surface lines of force, plus functional design in shape—to the human figure. The earliest statue of Enlil (?) (Fig. 104), found at Tell Asmar, exhibits this combination with the added attribute of enlarged eyes, the whole producing an aesthetic effect of great force. This heavy columnar figure, with its obvious "feet of clay," terminates in an arrangement of arms, shoulders, and chest so carved that they create an impression similar to that produced by the active lines found on the seal. Functionalism like that of the cup (Fig. 103) shows itself in the strong carving of hair and arms, nose and brows. This angular massing of details, as dynamic as though generated by an electric force within, prepares the spectator for the hypnotizing impact of the terrific eyes.

Fortuitous Design Arising from Natural Effects. The markings in a striated stone or on the surface of a shell, like the fortuitous impressions received from floating clouds, seem sometimes

Fig. 104.—Alabaster figure from Tell Asmar, height about 2 feet. (*Courtesy of the Oriental Institute, University of Chicago.*)

to suggest figures from the animal world. The tiny amulet from Khafaje, used as a stamp seal

Fig. 105.—*a*, tile walls, Warka, about 3000 B.C. (after Loftus); *b*, relief showing domed houses, palace of Sanherib, about 705–681 B.C. (British Museum after Layard); *c*, drainage vaults, Khorsabad. (*From L'Histoire de l'art dans l'antiquité, by Perrot and Chipiez, courtesy of Libraire Hachette, Paris.*)

(Fig. 102*b*), demonstrates this quality of design. The striations of the shell material evidently suggested to the carver the figure of a bullock whose legs were twisted back over the flank from right to left, so that the head with its horns came in the center. Here holes were bored so that the object could be suspended from the neck of its owner. To the Egyptian interested in preserving actual appearance, or to the mass of Mesopotamians interested in expressing power, this type of art would not have been considered art at all. It is this type of design, however, that particularly underlies Indian and Chinese painting and sculpture. The greatest artists of the Western world have often been inspired by such indistinct markings as water-spots upon the walls of rooms or the shapes of curling clouds.

Architecture

The greater part of Egyptian architecture had to do with the cult of the dead and the gods

of the underworld. Mesopotamian architecture was associated with the needs of the living and the gods of the sky. However, evidence found in the great mounds of earth that cover the sites of ancient Ur, Assur, Babylon, and Khorsabad has enabled careful excavators to piece together a picture of what the Tower of Babel and the Hanging Gardens of Queen Semiramis must have been like. Some of the ancient palaces, dwelling houses, fortifications, and temples, furthermore, still existed in Greco-Roman times, and were described by early historians from the West.

Prehistoric Building Forms. Utna Pishtim, the Noah of the Mesopotamian deluge story, lived, we are told, in a typical hut of wattling, daubed with clay. From its plastered walls with their basket-weave pattern came technomorphic designs of zigzag and interweave decoration later found on the tile-covered walls of the Red Temple at Warka in the fourth millennium B.C. (Fig. 105*a*). When hung with woolen rugs or tapestries, the dwellings probably had a

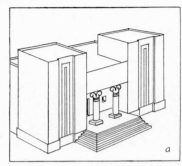 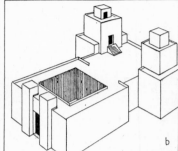 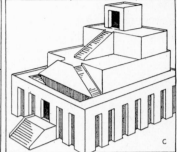

Fɪɢ. 106.—*a*, hilani at Khorsabad; *b*, Anu-Adad temple; *c*, ziggurat temple.

modicum of comfort in a climate not too strenuous.

It has been conjectured that two significant types of building construction started with these wattled huts. When the large branches of the wattling were bent over at the top and tied together, the hut must have assumed an arched or a vaulted form. Striving to retain this form with walls built of adobe brick, the Mesopotamian invented the true arch around 3500 B.C. When the houses were built upon a circular plan and the branches came together at the top, the structural form of the dome must have been suggested. Both the arch and the dome are usually considered to have been inventions of early Mesopotamian people. A relief from the palace of Sanherib at Kujundschik (Fig. 105*b*), now in the British Museum, shows that the houses of the Assyrians in historic times were roofed with domes, some high and pointed, others low and semicircular.

Another origin of the vault is possible. Like the early Egyptians, the Mesopotamians who buried their dead in dolmen tombs developed crude vaults, first of corbeled stone, later of brick. Early grave vaults found in ancient Ur, at Warka, Tello, and Nippur, average five feet in height, three and a half in breadth, and seven in length. Some of the vaults have pointed, others round, arches. In the lower foundations of the later palaces the drainage canals were covered with pointed vaults. Archaeologists suppose that the passageways were also vaulted (Fig. 105*c*).

The Judgment Hall, or Hilani. In ancient Mesopotamian society the king, as head of the state, was the supreme judge and the earthly representative of the god Enlil or Shamash. His judgments were given in a ceremonial council chamber, or *hilani*, associated with his palace. The idea of this temple of judgment seems to have been taken from those westerners called "Hurrians." Among the Hittite peoples, as well as the Elamites, the house of the chief usually consisted of a square building with a porch in front supported by two columns. In the late Hittite cities of Carchemish and Sendschirli, the chief's house was raised to a platform (previously reserved for sacred menhirs) and statues of the gods were placed inside. Among the Mesopotamians such a ceremonial structure appears as a hall with an audience chamber, in which the statue of the god could be set up (Fig. 106*a*). The building was approached by a broad stairway, on which accused and accuser could stand. The best-known example of such a judgment hall was found in the great palace of Sargon at Khorsabad (Fig. 107*c*).

The plan of the Hilani was that of a rectangle, with the entrance on one side rather than at the end. In time it came to be raised upon an elevated mound platform and is found as a sky temple on top of the ziggurat (Fig. 106*c*). From this structure eventually arose the idea of the Roman basilica as a judgment hall, and of the broad hall of Huns and Vikings in Europe. Carried by the seafaring folk of the lower Mesopotamian lands, this plan of building appeared in India at Mohenjo-Daro and, later, wherever the Hindu cults penetrated. In far-off Ceylon, Java, and Sumatra, in Turkestan and China, the judgment-hall temple became the most im-

with glazed bricks, which protected the heavy inner mass of sun-dried brick masonry from the rain.

Towers of Tile. Associated at times with the

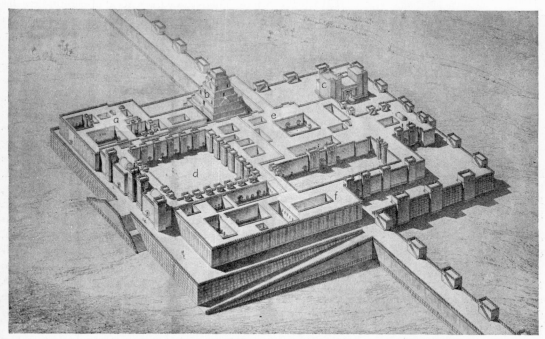

FIG. 107.—Palace of Sargon II at Khorsabad, 722 B.C., reconstructed according to Perrot and Chipiez, Place, and others. This reconstruction takes into consideration the newest discoveries by Andrae and Koldewey concerning the structure of ziggurats and hilanis. *a*, group of small temples after the Egyptian style; *b*, ziggurat; *c*, hilani, this is detached from palace proper although upon the same raised platform; *d*, entrance court; *e*, living quarters; *f*, stables.

portant type of religious edifice. From the Malayan peninsula, the idea of the platform, with either the menhirs or the building, spread over the islands of the South Seas (see map, Fig. 401, Chap. XIV).

The Earth Temple. Besides the judgment hall, the Mesopotamian cities held many examples of temples similar to those of the Egyptians (Fig. 106*b*). These buildings had large outer courts in which the congregation could worship under the open sky, inner courts for the priests, and a low-roofed room for the statue of the god. Unlike the Egyptian structures, these had no pretentious pylons guarding the entrance. The outer walls, like those of the palaces, were faced

low temples were great towers, or *ziggurats*, of glazed brick. The Greek historian Herodotus, describing such a ziggurat at Ekbatanu, a town in Persia, said that it had seven stories, the first of white glazed bricks; the second, of black; the third, of red; the fourth, of blue; the fifth, of orange-red; the sixth, of silver-gray; and the last of shining gold. In the palace of King Sargon at Khorsabad (Fig. 107*b*), the first four stages of the ziggurat still show traces of the white, black, red, and light blue.

Ziggurats differed in construction and had various means of ascent. The purpose was to elevate the performance of the rites in honor of the sky-gods, so that they could be seen from all parts of the city and so that the priests might be nearer their deities. Since the Mesopotamians were a practical people, the towers probably also served as means for signaling from

Fig. 108.—Southeast gateway, palace of Sargon II, Khorsabad, 722 B.C., showing ceremonial stairway and the Lamassu. (*After Thomas.*)

one town to another on the approach of an enemy.

When the ziggurats were united with the temple, as in the case of the Anu-Adad temple at Assur (Fig. 106*b*), the resulting structure formed the prototype for the Christian churches built in Mesopotamia after the 5th century. This type of church with its two towers found its way, eventually, into Northern Europe, where it became peculiar to Romanesque and Gothic construction.

Palace Architecture. In Mesopotamia the palaces of the dynasts served as the chief repositories of artistic creation. Of those that have been discovered perhaps the most widely known and significant is the palace of Sargon II at Khorsabad (Fig. 107), built during the second great Assyrian ascendancy in the 8th century B.C. This palace, set into a part of the city wall, stood on a high, raised platform, so that it dominated the town. It was approached from the front by a double stairway (Fig. 108) and on the side by a ramp for chariots. Confronted by a double stairway, one must choose between right and left approaches. The resulting feeling of confusion must have created disturbing inner tensions which tended to suggest fear in the

face of a great power. In the later Persian palaces, the effect of power was heightened by the use of relief scenes, in either glazed tile or stone, placed along the wall and bordering the steps. These show the arrival of tribute-bearing ambassadors or scenes in the life of the monarch as conqueror.

The palace walls at Khorsabad were built of unbaked brick, fronted with water-shedding glazed tiles. These tiles not only protected the surface but also had a distinct formal value as they glittered in the sun. The palace was the most heavily fortified part of the city. Its walls were reveted; that is, built with protecting buttresses and deeper indented surfaces. At the top, the wall was crowned with especially hard, baked bricks laid so that there were protective, upstanding barriers (merlons) behind which archers might stand and repel attacks. This system of wall-capping, known as crenelation, used by the Romans and throughout the Middle Ages, still appears as a decorative feature in many modern buildings. It, too, has its formal, aesthetic effect, for the alternate low and high sections break the horizontal lines of the roof and increase the feeling of height.

Two towers, one on each side of the arched entrance to the court, stood upon heavy stone bases carved to represent great human-headed bulls, or Lamassus. These will be described in greater detail in the section on sculpture.

The Arch. Above the Lamassus rose a true arch, chief glory of the Mesopotamian builders. The arch appearing in the portal at Khorsabad was made by building up a semicircular form of wood—the centering—on which the bricks were laid, each brick having been previously formed in a wedge shape. When the building was completed, the wooden forms were removed. Since all the thrust came from the sides and downward, the brick wedges were pressed together by the weight of the load above. The heavier the load, the firmer the arch. Such arch building of course, requires tremendous stretches of wall on each side to support the lateral pressure; but at Khorsabad there was no difficulty of this kind, for the side walls of the palace were several yards thick and very long.

Residential Architecture. The reconstruction of the palace at Khorsabad shows a significant of this man who united the functions of church and state. In Khorsabad we have the prototypes of the palaces of the god-Caesars of Rome and of the Sun King of France.

FIG. 109.—Apadana of Xerxes, Persepolis, 485–465 B.C. (*From L'Histoire de l'art dans l'antiquité, by Perrot and Chipiez; courtesy of Libraire Hachette, Paris.*)

union of the three types of temple earlier discussed. Back of the palace, on a level with the top of the city wall, appears the hilani, or judgment hall; the great ziggurat with its winding ramp in seven colorful stories rises to the left; and within the palace walls, at the upper left-hand corner of the picture, stands a ground temple on the Egyptian model. The part of the palace to the right of the great center court contained the stables and the harem of the monarch.

The central court formed a ceremonial approach to the king's apartment and to an audience hall, both of which lay toward the rear of the palace. The dramatic arrangement of the court in relation to the audience hall suggests the Egyptian temple structure. Aesthetically, the palace seems to have been planned to magnify the importance of the monarch. The front staircase, the glittering façade, the great monolithic carved bulls, the walls of the court with the frieze showing the hunting exploits of the king, the temple of judgment, and the ziggurat—all served to convince the Mesopotamian of the omnipotence

Persian Palaces. In early Mesopotamian buildings, such as the palace at Khorsabad, relatively small vaulted passages and domed square spaces were the only parts roofed. The precious hewn stone was used only for doorsills or in thin slabs to cover the inside walls of the palace. Great gates consisting of wood covered with plates of bronze were set in bronze sockets, some of which have recently been found. As the river valleys afforded no great abundance of wood, large court areas could not be covered, but small rooms in palaces and dwelling houses were roofed with wooden beams laid over with wattled mats and covered with tamped mud —a technique still used by the Pueblo Indians.

The later palaces built by the Persians near the wooded mountain country at Susa and Persepolis greatly developed the judgment-hall temple, which was united with the audience hall of the king to form the *apadana*.

The apadana was a columned hall, supporting a great wooden roof made of heavy timbers and wattling. A picture of the apadana of Xerxes at Persepolis (Fig. 109) shows a structure similar in many respects to the hypostyle hall of the Egyptian temple. As the Persians had previously conquered Egypt, it is possible that some of their ideas came from that country. In place of the heavy Egyptian columns, how-

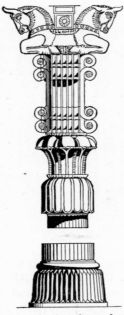

Fig. 110.—Persian eclectic column from the apadana of Xerxes at Persepolis. (*After Flandin and Coste.*)

ever, the Persians invented a curious eclectic column (Fig. 110) uniting details from Egyptian and earlier Mesopotamian sources. The fluted base suggested growth; the long slender shaft lent height. Above an arrangement of the volutes, or spiraled members, placed back to back to form the capital, two protruding bulls supported the crossbeams. The aesthetic appearance of this column is as unarchitectonic as possible. The parts do not hold together. But the effect of the room as a whole, with its forest of columns, must have been at least dramatic, in a purely theatrical manner.

The Sassanian Palace. Many of the architectonic forms from Assyrian and Persian palaces unite in the more consistent structures built by Sassanian monarchs who lived between A.D. 212 and 600. After the legions of Alexander and the Roman Caesars had overrun Mesopotamia,

a race of Persian monarchs succeeded in uniting the country for 400 years. During this last and final development of the Mesopotamian culture, the great palaces at Sarvistan and Ctesiphon were built. The pictures of these palaces (Fig. 111) show arched vaults and domes in their final development, rising in magnificent spans over great central audience halls. On each side of these spans lay the rooms of the palace proper. A great wall around the entire building enclosed a lovely garden. The arch, earlier used simply as an architectonic structure in the Assyrian empire, here functioned as an element of architectural decoration, for the entire façade of the building was covered with a blind or decorative arcade. This, the final point in the development of Mesopotamian architecture, was taken over both by the Mohammedans, who made it familiar from India to Spain, and by the Christians, who used it in Constantinople and Europe.

Chief Characteristics of Mesopotamian Architecture. Conspicuous throughout the entire history of Mesopotamian architecture is the attempt to build imposing structures for the use of the monarch. The dome and the arch were used to a great extent. From Mesopotamia came the tile-decorated towers, or minarets, which served throughout the Middle Ages and in Mohammedan lands as places from which the people could be called to worship. The Mesopotamians were the first great people to recognize the fact that buildings may be constructed of perishable materials, provided their outer surfaces are coated with a veneer of some permanent glazed or vitrified material. Thus to them may be given credit for having solved some, at least, of the problems involved in the building of modern skyscrapers. In decoration they found that tile-covered buildings lent themselves to colorful geometric designs and to an application of modeled sculpture, so designed as to suggest a strength sufficient to support the perpendicular lines of the building. The common houses of the Mesopotamians, however,

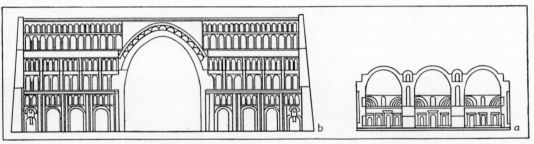

Fig. 111.—*a*, transverse view, palace, Sarvistan, showing dome on squinch arches, about A.D. 350; *b*, the palace of Ctesiphon with open throne room and elliptical arch, about A.D. 550, height 112 feet. (*After Flandin and Coste.*)

had no particular aesthetic significance. It should be mentioned in passing that Mesopotamia, with its elaborate system of irrigation, designed excellent gardens. One group of these gardens was arranged on a great ziggurat at Babylon. By some means unknown to us water was elevated to the top of the structure and allowed to run down into plots along the side, so that the entire ascent seemed a great palace or hill of flowers and foliage—the famous Hanging Gardens of Babylon associated with the name of a great queen, Semiramis.

Sculpture and Painting

In none of the early cultures were boundary lines drawn between painting and sculpture. The carved image was thought to gain interest and verisimilitude if painted; the wall painting, to gain force and character if engraved or carved in low relief. The Mesopotamians seem to have felt the difference between the two arts even less than did the Egyptians. According to archaeological remains, most of their sculpture must have been colored and most of their graphic art, today studied as pictorial design, was in the form of low-relief carvings or glazed modeled tiles. In a few instances, it is true, palace walls show traces of fresco painting in blue, black, and yellow, a color scheme quite different from that of the Egyptians. The compositions, subject matter, and coloring of these works, however, do not differ from those of the relief carvings that, today, fall logically under the head of sculpture.

In Mesopotamian art, the primitive geometric composition schemes gradually merged with strongly physioplastic figures. Such figures, it may be noticed, differ from those carved by the Egyptians in that the muscular masses are strongly defined by deeply cut lines, themselves suggestive of animal energy.

Throughout the development of Mesopotamian sculpture and painting two general types of composition appear—one, using the absolute balance of parts, suggesting stability; the other, more common, suggesting motion and activity through the use of an occult spacing of lines and masses.

The Block Stele as Boundary Stone. The statue of a *patesi*, or priest-king, from the ancient Sumerian town of Lagash (Fig. 112) is one of the earliest datable monuments of Mesopotamian sculpture. A number of similar figures of this king, Gudea by name, have been placed at about the year 2400 B.C. They were probably used as boundary stones marking the limit of that ruler's kingdom.

The diminutive figure in green diorite, along with the others of its kind, stands only about two feet high. Unlike the Egyptian statues, this one makes no attempt to awe through size. Like the Egyptian statues, however, it has been left frankly in the shape of a menhir, solid and blocky with no projecting points to be easily broken off. In contrast with the figures of the Pharaohs, the following peculiarities are to be noticed: the eyes are oversize, the arms are strongly muscular in appearance, the ceremonial cap is covered with tiny spirals. Each of these attributes, taken by itself, might mean little or nothing but, concentrated as they are within a small space, they have a definite symbolic significance. We have seen that the

The folded hands of Gudea, geometrical and carved in the shape of a cube, suggest symbolically the inner power and satisfaction of an individual completely at peace with himself.

FIG. 112.—Gudea of Lagash, green diorite, height 17¾ inches, about 2400 B.C. (Louvre Museum). (*Courtesy of Lesch-Carnegie-Giraudon.*)

FIG. 113.—Winged bull or Lamassu from palace at Khorsabad. Height about 16 feet. This shows a remarkable concretion of aesthetic symbols from the various Mesopotamian cultures (Oriental Institute, Chicago). (*Courtesy of the Oriental Institute, University of Chicago.*)

oversize eyes had to do with the powers of the lightning god, Enlil. The muscular arms, although more realistically carved on Enlil's statues, still remind us of such representations. The woolen cap might easily have had spiral curls. In Mesopotamian art, however, spirals mean more than naturally kinky hair. They are symbols of movement through infinity, for they start at a point and end in space. They came also to be associated with the natural virility of the curly-haired Semitic and Sumerian stocks that made up the inhabitants of the valley.

The herringbone pattern of the eyebrows, meeting far down on the nose, lend to the face an abstract air of impersonality. The unsmiling mouth adds to this impression. The arms and feet have been modeled physioplastically. Thus the statue resembles in many ways that of the Egyptian Khafre with which it is contemporaneous. In it ideoplastic and physioplastic attributes have been skillfully combined, the ideoplastic slightly predominant. In the case of Khafre's statue realistic forms had greater weight than inner meaning or purpose. Here the inner idea dominates the realistic form. In order that no one should doubt the meaning of this statue, the monarch had engraved upon its skirt and arm his name and the purpose for which it was to serve.

the portals (Fig. 113). These human-headed bulls of stone, called "Lamassus," had a definite architectonic function. Being carved out of great blocks of stone, they served as protection

Fig. 114.—Kings and winged genii pollinating a sacred tree. Alabaster frieze in low relief (bas-relief) from the palace of Assurnasirpal III, Nimroud-Calach, near Nineveh, 884–859 B.C. (*Courtesy of British Museum.*)

The study of the statue of Gudea leads one to wonder whether it represented the Mesopotamians' idea of great art. To those matter-of-fact people, this statue must certainly have represented a most satisfactory use for art. Indeed, if usefulness were the sole basis of their aesthetic judgment, such a monument must have been as satisfying to Gudea as a well-spaced advertising page is to the advertiser. To Gudea's friends and party it probably symbolized the king's function as the source of the law; to the people enslaved in Gudea's dominion it must have stood as a symbol of their fetters. Nevertheless, it is hard to understand today how this monument could have appealed to all equally. It represents, then, a little less than the greatest in Mesopotamian art.

Architectural Sculpture. [WHEN In describing the Assyrian palace at Khorsabad, attention was HAS TO] called to the great winged figures that guarded

for the ends of the brick walls. The feeling of height desired in the towers, furthermore, is aided by the composition of each of the figures, whose forelegs, chest decoration, decorative beard, and high, feathered hat together make a strong, upthrusting mass.[3] This mass connects with the rest of the wall through the mass of the body and the wing. The feathers in the wing and the spiraled patterns of hair under the belly and on the haunches of the animal draw the attention over to the front, whence it is directed upward to the face. All that has been noticed in the case of the statue of Gudea may be found in this representation of the king as a superhuman being endowed with the attributes of sky and earth deities. The head has been so conventionalized as to appear impersonal. The heavy beard is well barbered and full of vital spiral curls, as is also the heavy hair behind. Each part of the face has been carved with such sharp angles that the features are overaccentuated. This is particularly apparent in the mouth, the curve of the nostrils, and the carving of eyes and brows. The heavy, accentuated combining symbolic and representational scenes. The example from the palace of Assurnasirpal III (Fig. 114), showing the kings guarded by winged beings in the act of fertiliz-

FIG. 115.—Lion hunt of Assurnasirpal III. Alabaster frieze in low relief. (*Courtesy of British Museum.*)

carving makes the face stand out more than any other part of the figure.

The king wears the triple tiara crown, with its three rows of bulls' horns, symbolic of his *mana*, or life-giving power. His feet are the feet of the bull, but his wings show that he had the swiftness of the eagle. For the greatest dramatic effect, the figure was so carved that it was provided with five legs—two seen from the front, and four seen from the side. In this way the artist kept the mass of the stone which was necessary to hold up the tower and at the same time preserved the realistic appearance of the animal. In the technique of carving, as in the case of the Gudea statue, some details have been geometricized and made formal, others are strikingly realistic. The legs, for example, show great knowledge of anatomy. Even the veins were represented, because the Assyrians had observed that through them coursed the life-giving blood. The Egyptian looked upon the body superficially, the Mesopotamian, anatomically.

Decorative Sculpture. A visitor exploring an Assyrian palace such as that of Khorsabad would have found within the courts great friezes ing the sacred tree is decorative and symbolic in intent. The scene was a common one. At times the tree was flanked by the kings alone, each bearing in his hand a palm cone. At other times eagle-headed genii were shown fertilizing the tree. The intent was always the same. The tree, representing the fertility of the earth goddess and later of Ishtar, could bear fruit only after it had been pollinated.

The tree in Fig. 114 deserves special study. Its leaves show it to be a date palm, but its branches are woven together and tied at the ends as though they were part of a rug. The zigzag lines upon the middle of the trunk all point heavenward, and the branches seem to flow out of the center. Just as Gudea and the Lamassu united all the Assyrian masculine symbols, so this tree unites the feminine.

Above the tree a winged disk shows the figure of a sky-god, his horns turning into spirals as they leave his forehead. This sky-god, known as Shamash to the Assyrian, was later to become Ahura-Mazda, the Persian god of light. The winged genii behind the king probably represented Gilgamesh, the hero god, whose powers descended through the king. The moral of this sculpture is obvious. The dynast with his supernatural helper fructifies the land, and if he is peaceful, good crops result. If he should be the warlike leader of a state, the mothers would bear many soldiers to fight his battles.

Realistic Sculpture. Assurnasirpal III, being above all a practical person, suffered no qualms of aesthetic conscience when he directed his slave artists to decorate the palace walls with a mixture of symbolic and realistic sculpture. He wished to appear both in his godlike function of ruling and fertilizing the land and in his function as a mighty hunter ridding the land of wild beasts. The first symbolic representations brought forth the decorative abilities of the sculptor; the second (Fig. 116) called for a realism transcending that of the Egyptians. Both the realistic and the symbolic appear side by side—as they might on some poorly designed news page or poster today.

The lion hunt of Assurnasirpal III (Fig. 115) furnishes an excellent example for comparison with Egyptian wall carving. The first point of contrast lies in the fact that the entire composition has been made on one level and that where people are represented as behind one another, there is an illusion of depth, desirable because it allowed for a greater play of forces. So the arms and legs of the two soldiers at the left of the panel, although not in perfect depth relationship to one another, nevertheless create the effect of activity. Another point arises in connection with the composition: many of the spaces around the animals have been left quite free of decoration—a further step away from the primitive, agricultural technique of filling all spaces.

The entire narration shows a unity of dramatic purpose, which is helped by having all the action of the minor characters read toward the right. Only the chief character, the king, faces in the opposite direction. The action thus centers on his relationship to the attacking lion. The muscles on both man and beast have been carefully studied and deeply carved, so that we feel their vigorous strain. The lively, fighting lion is represented in sweeping, vital lines; the dying lion under the horses, by broken straight lines.

In these two animals, for the first time in the development of man's art, one may notice the effect called "empathy." Empathy is that feeling of participation inspired by a work of art when its arrangement of parts makes the beholder feel himself actually drawn into it. The swing of the lines in the live animal and the strength of its tense limbs make us feel that all the muscles are well coordinated and working together. In the case of the second lion, one feels the disintegrated, broken-down effect that is naturally associated with sickness and death. No one with a fighting spirit could help being drawn into the action of this relief.

Turning to the other figures, one sees that the horses, pulling at the lines, stretch their legs out as far as possible. This gives a particular impression of speed, because the eyes are pulled from one extremity of the animal to the other. If the legs were brought together or shown as in a gallop, one would not have so much of an emphatic reaction. Despite the fact that the relief has many realistic details, it must be stressed that the whole is a masterpiece of arrangement rather than pure realism. Notice that the king is certainly not taking very good aim at the lion. If his aim were lower, however, his bow would not fill the space so well. Let the skeptical reader strive to rearrange any of the component parts of this composition. Its skillful design will then be evident to him.

The primary strength of the composition derives from the fact that the figures are arranged in an interweave—that fundamental composition form discovered in the prehistoric art of Mesopotamia. This is most apparent in the case of the right arm of the king, which is drawn back behind his head and twisted out of the natural plane. It is as though the artist had taken the elementary, primitive interweave from the Gilgamesh seal and disposed his fig-

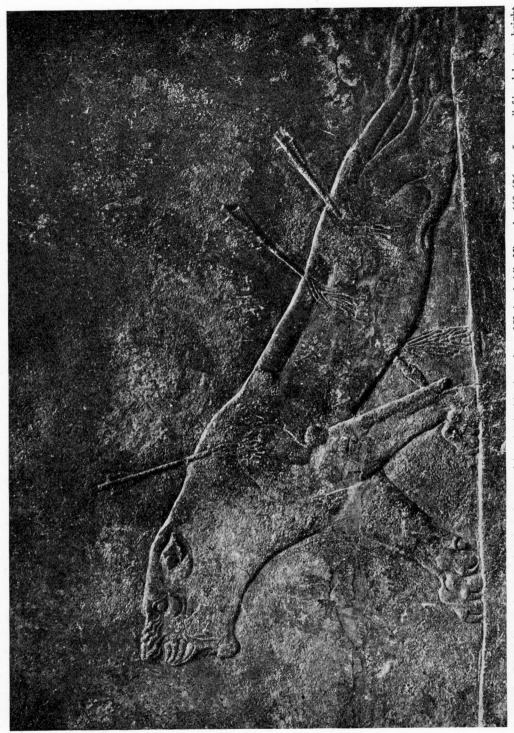

Fig. 116.—Dying lioness from the hunting pictures of Assurbanipal in the palace of Kujundschik, Nineveh, 668–626 B.C. Low relief in alabaster, height about 4 feet (British Museum). (*Courtesy of Lesch-Carnegie.*)

ures along its lines. Also, the king's figure recalled the hero king, Gilgamesh, who fought with the dragon of Chaos, or Tiamat; and the tree (Fig. 114), the tree-goddess, Ishtar, a logical descendant of Tiamat. The two works of art thus belong together after all, not only because their formal, aesthetic quality is consistent, but also because they are part of one associational pattern.

The Wounded Lioness. Comparable in its superb combination of the physioplastic and ideoplastic, of formal and ideational elements, to the Egyptian head of Nofretete is the wounded lioness in the British Museum (Fig. 116). This —perhaps the finest example of the sculptor's art in Mesopotamia—forms part of a hunting relief similar to that of Assurnasirpal. The wounded lioness is represented in a relief so low that it seems little more than a drawing. The artist has shown the animal half dead and half alive. This last moment of defiance, between life and death, holds within itself great emotional power. The arrangement of the limbs and neck have that architectural quality earlier noticed in the case of the Lamassu. On the other hand, where death overtakes the beast, we feel the utter powerlessness of the wounded animal dragging the helpless limbs behind her. As no one part of the lioness has been unduly exaggerated, one might almost say that this is a wholly physioplastic work of art. A careful examination will show, however, that the muscles and the hair pattern have been slightly formalized. The blood streams oozing from the wounds have also been conventionalized. The arrows entering the body at different angles cut the great free spaces above the animal in such a way as to make a very intricate occult balance. This can in no way be improved upon by changing the positions of the arrows. Like the head of Nofretete in Egypt, this fragment appeals because of universal qualities that transcend the purely Mesopotamian styles. It has long been considered one of the masterpieces of the sculptor's art.

The Development of the Grotesque

The word "grotesque," by which one characterizes art that stimulates in the spectator feelings of pain, disgust, or horror, comes from the Italian word meaning a dark, shady place or cavern—in short, a grotto. In Egypt, the art connected with the cult of the underworld, the Book of the Dead, and the tombs was by no means all grotesque. Only that which had to do with the fetishistic figures of Amemit, Thoueris, and the dwarf god Bes, all more or less connected with the more painful aspects of the Last-Judgment story, may be said to be typically grotesque. Late Mesopotamian art evidences more clearly the origins of some of the grotesque art forms of later cultures.

The Origins of the Gorgon-Medusa Fantasy. One tendency toward the grotesque can be noticed throughout 3,000 years of Mesopotamian art: whenever the masculine, Semitic peoples dominated, they depicted their conquering hero-gods as overcoming repulsive or dangerous beings connected in some way with the monster Tiamat, or Chaos, whom they associated with the fundamentally indestructible matriarchal stocks of the dual river valley. Gilgamesh in a few instances, most pertinent to the development of the Gorgon type, was pictured in the act of slaying a demon, Humbaba, whose great apotropaic or hypnotic eyes, fanged grinning mouth, and long grisly hair made him a fearsome sight. In the Ishtar legend Humbaba appears as the fierce, shrieking demon guarding the Sacred Grove of Ishtar, by many thought to have been the famous cedars of Lebanon in Palestine. This monster had the attributes both of the cyclonic sky-gods and of a feminine underworld demon.[1]

In Syria, Humbaba fused with representations of the god Bes and eventually was seated upon the shoulders of a feminine deity, perhaps Ishtar herself. The resultant hermaphroditic form shows the breasts of the goddess and the grinning head of the Bes-Humbaba. This night-

[1] CLARK HOPKINS, "Assyrian Elements in the Perseus and Gorgon Story," *American Journal of Archaeology*, 1934.

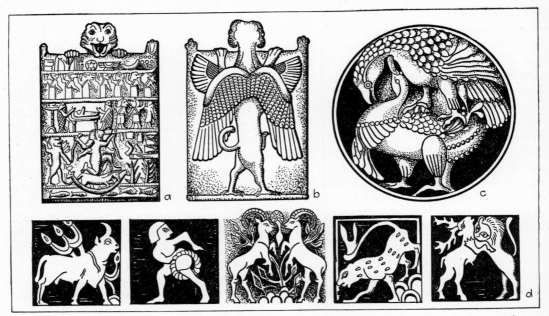

Fig. 117.—*a*, bronze plaque from Hama, northern Syria. Allat (Eresh-Kigal, Queen of the Underworld) passes through Hades on her boat. Nergal, the sun in drought, spirit of war and pestilence, who is the husband of Allat and King of Hades, peers over the top. *b*, reverse of the Hama bronze, the Destruction God, combines the attributes of the eagle, lion, and poisonous serpent. His chief function is to kill men in order to provide subjects for his wife (Collection LeClerc, Louvre Museum). *c*, stucco plaque showing heraldic sign of eagle attacking goose from Rayy in northern Persia, about A.D. 500. The artists of this area repeat the motifs invented by Sumerians 3,000 years earlier (see *d*, below) (Boston Museum). *d*, ancient Sumerian shell plaques from Ur, about 3500 B.C. (*From The Development of Sumerian Art, by C. Leonard Woolley, Charles Scribner's Sons.*)

marish creation became a guardian deity of the underworld, perhaps standing for the cruel queen Eresh-Kigal. A bronze plaque (Fig. 117*a*, *b*), found at Hama in northern Syria, shows all the elements later taken over by the Greeks in their representation of the Gorgon story.

On the back of the plaque (now in the Louvre) can be seen a figure with the body of a lion and the legs of an eagle. The body is protected by four wings and has a serpent growing from the lower part of its torso. On the front of the plaque this monster, probably Humbaba himself, has the hands of a man and a conventionalized lion's head, with open mouth, lolling tongue, and staring, apotropaic eyes. The beast peers over upon a scene divided into five levels, representing the highest heavens, the lower air, the earth, the underworld, and the primeval sea that underlies all substance.

The most important space has been given over to the underworld. Here, kneeling upon a horse—an animal sacred to Ishtar—is the Humbaba-Gorgon, her breasts suckling two lions, her outstretched arms carrying two serpents. Behind her is shown the masculine form of Humbaba; before her, two trees representing the Sacred Grove. This important grotesque figure was taken over and beautified by the Greeks. In the West, the figure reached the cities of the Etruscans and, carried by Scythian traders and Persian soldiers, followed the Danube River into Northern Europe, where the Vikings kept the idea in the personification of Hel as the dread goddess of the underworld.

What is the ultimate cause and significance of the grotesque in art? All the evidence, both archaeological and psychological, tends to show that the grotesque arises when the artist labors under the impulse of fear. In Egypt, for example, where thoughts of the afterlife and the underworld were accompanied by feelings of pleasure, and where Isis, the beneficent goddess, was conceived as one who could literally put together and make whole the body of the male Osiris, art on the whole was pleasant. In Mesopotamia, on the other hand, where men not only looked upon life as a fierce struggle but dreaded the afterlife and their contact with Ishtar, the grotesque held a relatively higher place. It is important to remember, however, that in both cases, *art existed by virtue of its power to make man more effective for the type of life his environment forced him to live.*

The Dragon of Ishtar. A second form of grotesque of great significance in the development of Asiatic art was the concept of the dragon. The glittering gates of Babylon, dedicated to Ishtar, the patron goddess of the city, were guarded by glazed lions and dragons in relief (Fig. 118). Fundamental to the concept of the dragon was the serpent of Tiamat, to the head of which was added the spiral curve symbolizing infinite vitality. A single horn also affixed to the head, perhaps suggested by the horn of the rhinoceros, later gave rise to the medieval concept of the fabulous unicorn. The serpent neck was attached to the lion's body, which had rear legs like those of the fierce, hunting falcon. Studied thus in terms of its symbolic origin, even a dragon has some sort of false logic. So all grotesquerie in art has some connected analyzable *raison d'être*, only the reason is an illogical one, such as always arises when a concept or an idea is born in a state of fear.

As the dragon traveled eastward to China, where the fear of Nature was sublimated to a sense of awe and joy in her phenomena, it took on the form of the cloud and was considered beneficent. All the various animal forms were subordinated to the flowing cloud lines, which were much more abstract than the realistic body parts. As we shall see in a later chapter, this resulted in greater aesthetic unity. In Northwestern Europe, where it became synonymous with the devil, the dragon had a less beneficent aspect.

The Animal Interweave. The interwoven struc-

FIG. 118.—The dragon of Ishtar from the city gates of Babylon, about 550 B.C. Yellow and blue on green, height about 5 feet (Detroit Museum). (*Courtesy of Detroit Museum.*)

ture of the earliest dragon form became the basis of a type of composition particularly expressive of the barbarian tribes who lived to the north of Mesopotamia. During the thousand years before the birth of Christ and in the thousand years after, the fierce nomadic Scythians, who roamed the steppes of Russia from the Danube to the mountains of India, continually absorbed and transformed certain of the fundamental Mesopotamian designs into a style that was to exert great influence upon Saracenic, Chinese, and Gothic art. The hunting scenes of the Assyrian dynasts, which were thus absorbed and transmitted, had taken on a certain symbolic significance and a more decorative appearance in late Persian times and under the Sassanian monarchs. The hare, the duck, the gazelle, and the deer—all animals sacred to Ishtar—were shown being attacked by the lion or the hawk, animals more closely associated with the sky-gods. The stucco plaque from Rayy in Persia, of Sassanian date or earlier, furnishes an excellent example of this final phase in the development of Mesopotamian design (Fig. 117c). The entire composition is based upon a series of spiraling lines, interwoven so as to suggest the abstract idea of struggle. This suggestion is heightened by the way in which rounded forms alternate with sharply cut angular surfaces, producing heavy shadows that contrast with strong high lights.

Music and Drama

Out of this idea of conflict, essentially unsculptural and unarchitectonic, one could hardly expect more than interwoven linear and light-and-shade effects in the spatial arts. The sense of inner conflict finds a more appropriate means of expression in the arts of music, drama, and the dance, all of which we know to have been engaged in by the Mesopotamian peoples.

The Instruments. The Mesopotamians not only inherited the Egyptian musical instruments, but also invented many types of their own, including the psaltery—ancestor of the modern piano—and the bagpipe, which is related to the organ. Canon Galpin in *The Music of the Sumerians* explains that these instruments consisted of the horn (either of bronze or animal horn), the flute (either a whistle or double-reed flute like the oboe), the cithara (a large lyre or shoulder harp), a seven-stringed lyre (from which the Welsh crowth may have derived later), and a zither or dulcimer (a box covered with gut strings, to be plucked or played with hammers). These instruments later take a most significant part in the development of the orchestra.

Harp and Lyre. From the earliest levels of Sumerian culture, in the time of King Gudea, the first archaeologists working in southern Mesopotamia found sculptured representations of great harps, each with eleven strings. Scientists from the University of Pennsylvania and the British Museum discovered and restored an original harp of that type (Fig. 119). This harp, from the grave of the unknown husband of Queen Shub-ad of Ur, is probably the first instrument known in that long progression of harps, lyres, and dulcimers which led eventually to the invention of the piano. It is inter-esting not only for the knowledge it gives us of the notes of the Sumerian scale, but also because of its decoration.

The Flutes of Ishtar. From the great temples of Babylon a particular type of musical religious ceremony was broadcast over the ancient world. The worship of the nature goddess in her cruel aspect, as the slayer of her lover, Tammuz-Adonis, called for processions and dancing. Women wailed their grief and the men whipped themselves until the blood came or cut themselves with knives to the accompaniment of shrill-sounding instruments—flutes in their higher register—and cymbals.

At the feast that marked the change from spring to the hot desert summer—corresponding to our autumn—the flute was used to accompany autumnal lyric or Linos songs, which derive their name from the mournful refrain "*ai Linon,*" which was wailed with them. In time, this feast in honor of Tammuz and many of the orgiastic rites were taken over by the Greeks in the worship of Dionysus, who became the god of the theater. A "wailing flute" or whistle of baked clay found at Birs Nimrod has the three notes of the C minor chord.

Lute and Psaltery. Besides taking the flute and the harp from Egypt, the Mesopotamians probably invented two other instruments. The first, a crescent-shaped harp, called by the Sumerians the "pan-tur," or little bow, has already been discussed in connection with Egyptian music. In the centuries just preceding or shortly after the coming of Christ, this harp, shaped like a bow, was stroked with a second bow of horse hair. Thus arose the violin.

The second instrument invented in Mesopotamia was the psaltery. Records exist of psalteries with eighteen or twenty strings. This instrument, which allows accurate tuning, must have filled an even greater part in the development of set scales than did the harp. The Mesopotamians, according to Galpin, were the first to leave a recorded hymn with notes to be played as a harp accompaniment.

The Mesopotamian Scales. The earliest Mesopotamian and Chinese scales were seven-toned, the fourth and seventh notes being slightly raised. There are indications that the Mesopotamians strove to find theoretical connections

double-reed flute; that is, a pipe blown through a double-beating reed, the ancestor of the oboe. Throughout the long range of Mesopotamian literature, music is spoken of as an art asso-

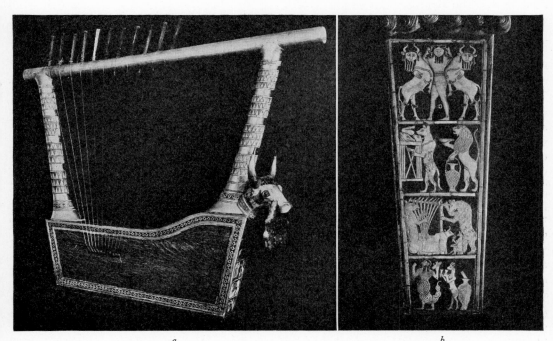

a   *b*

FIG. 119.—*a*, harp from grave of unknown king. The bull's head hammered of thin gold over a wooden core has a beard of carved lapis lazuli. *b*, the engraved shell plaque set in the front of the sounding board has great mythological significance. Gilgamesh in the top of the panel holds two human-headed bulls symbolizing the conquest of civilization over the wilder tribes. The animals and the scorpion man in the lower scenes may have to do with the underworld. The ass playing on the harp symbolizes Allat (Eresh-Kigal), goddess of the Shades. These figures illustrate the stories sung to the accompaniment of this instrument. (University Museum.) (*Courtesy of the University Museum, University of Pennsylvania.*)

between the movements of the seven planets and the seven notes of the scale. Such a scale, composed of the notes G, A, B, C#, D, E, F#, may be played not only upon the ancient Sumerian pipes but also on the oldest Scotch bagpipes. Galpin conjectures that the Sumerian harp, on which this scale was first played, may have found its way north during the time of the early folk migrations, reaching Scotland by way of Finland and Scandinavia.

The Uses of Music in Mesopotamian Life. The early Sumerians considered music as a gift of the hero god Gilgamesh, who first used the

ciated with the temple. As the temple for the Mesopotamian was the center of life, music was regarded as a health- and life-giving art. The sound of the copper kettledrum, used together with the great bells in the temple, was called the "living sound."

Musical Dramatic Poetry. The musical dramatic poetry of the Assyrians and Babylonians, but recently deciphered from the cuneiform tablets by the archaeologists, is practically the same in all points as the psalms and prayers in the Bible. It is therefore apparent that its influence has been very great in the formation of the European thought complex in both Catholic and Protestant countries. The Thirtieth Psalm as it stands today in the Bible, furnishes an excellent example of a dramatic poem that, long before the development of the Greek drama, was danced and sung by two choral groups. The performance of this Hebrew song was similar in most respects to the performances of the American Indians earlier discussed.

At times the Psalms were sung in what is called the antiphonal style; at others, a cantor sang the verses and the congregation replied with "Hallelujah," or, as in the case of the One Hundred and Thirty-sixth Psalm, with a phrase such as "His mercy endureth forever." This dramatic technique of making the listeners part of the ceremony by assigning a response to them plays an important part in all religious drama.

Mesopotamian Contributions to the Drama. In the above discussion of music it can be seen that dramatic expression was used wherever action was required; that is, in all forms but the singing of the epic. Much of the later Greek drama owes its power to elements derived from Mesopotamia through Syria and Cyprus, where there was a temple to Ishtar-Astarte. The worship of Dionysus, associated as it was with the rite of Tammuz-Adonis in Ionian Greece (Phrygia and Lydia), brought into the drama the chorus, which under Aeschylus actually became a chorus of Gorgonlike furies at war with the sky-gods of Greece. Euripides presents in his *Bacchae* the Corybantes, or chorus of dancing women with their flutes and castanets.

Summary

The art of the Mesopotamian peoples, insofar as it presents a unified creation, strove to express power rather than permanence. When the artist is forced to create under an excess of fear-stimulating power, his productions express no simple unity but a grotesque combination of symbolic forms associated with his fear fantasies. The Mesopotamian artist achieved unity by making one object or line larger and subordinating all other parts of the creation to it. Mesopotamian art gave to the world the linear composition form known as the "interweave"; to architecture, the glazed, arched building; to music and poetry, a dramatic story of natural forces conquered by man and a story of the struggle between the male and female principles in society. Out of this last arose the dramatic chorus, later perfected by the Greeks. To the development of medieval European art Mesopotamia bequeathed composition forms —particularly the interweave—and the building methods that made possible the Gothic cathedral.

Bibliography

JASTROW, MORRIS: *Civilization of Babylonia and Assyria*, J. B. Lippincott Company, Philadelphia, 1915.

WOOLLEY, C. L.: *Development of Sumerian Art*, Charles Scribner's Sons, New York, 1935.

WOOLLEY, C. L.: *Ur of the Chaldees*, Charles Scribner's Sons, New York, 1930.

ALBRIGHT, W. F.: *Archaeology of Palestine and the Bible*, Fleming H. Revell Company, New York, 1935.

BEDDOES, CAPT. W.: *A Son of Ashur* (novel). Sonnenschein, Swan and Co., London, 1905.

Recordings

Hebrew Music-Decca 38174.

CHAPTER VI

The Formative Influences in Greek Art

Fine linen the maidens had on, and the youths well-woven doublets, faintly glistening with oil. Fair wreaths had the maidens and the youths daggers of gold hanging from silver baldrics. And now would they run round with deft feet exceeding lightly, as when a potter sitting by his wheel that fitted between his hands maketh trial of it whether it runs; and now anon they would run in lines to meet each other and a great company stood round the lovely dance in joy; and through the midst of them leading the measure two tumblers whirled. Also he set therein the great might of the River of Ocean around the uttermost rim of the cunningly fashioned shield.

"THE ILIAD OF HOMER"[1]

IN EGYPT the greatest force for inspiring and limiting art emanated from the cult of the dead; in Mesopotamia, from totemism or worship of power. In the first country, artistic merit was judged in terms of permanence; in the second, in terms of vitalism. In both cases the arts that resulted were relatively simple and easy to understand in sociopsychological terms. The art of the Hellenic peoples, on the other hand—classical art, as it has come to be called —is relatively more complex, because it was built upon forms borrowed for the most part from preceding styles.

The influence of the older cultures, furthermore, inevitably determined the type of design considered best by the Greeks. While the Egyptians showed a predilection for massive forms arranged in geometric relationships and the Assyrians for dynamic lines bounding active muscle forms, the Greeks developed a design in which rhythmical pattern blended with a realistic portrayal of man—the whole arranged upon hidden geometric schemata in an almost playful spirit. They may be said to have devised a nearly perfect interrelationship between formal, associational, and useful values, eventually reaching a position in which it is impossible to separate categorically ideoplastic and physioplastic elements. This art, in which outer form harmonizes with inner will or idea, the world has come to call beautiful.

Cultural Influences in the Formation of the Greek Style. The Greek love of freedom, distrust of superstition, penchant for sharp trading, and ready wit—qualities that led them to the discovery of the scientific method, which the Greeks called "philosophy"—probably derived from a racial background so diverse that the Greek mind was kept in a continual state of ferment.

A study of the map (Fig. 120) and the end paper will make clear the diverse origins and the various phases in the development of the classical or Greek style. Influences from all corners of the ancient world converged on the coasts and islands of the Aegean Sea in six culture periods, each distinguished by a different style of art and each contributing its style to the following period. These styles are most easily studied in the pottery decoration and in

[1] From the translation by Lang, Leaf and Myers, p. 345, by permission of The Macmillan Company, New York.

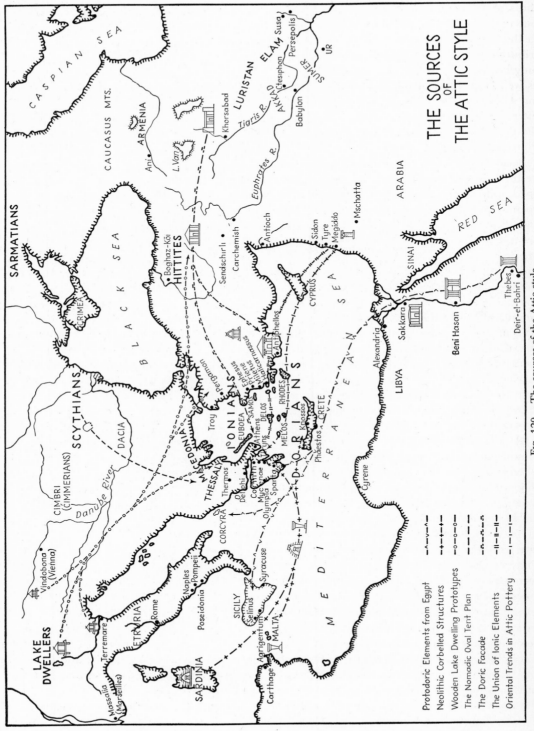

Fig. 120.—The sources of the Attic style.

the sculptural treatment of the human form, but they can also be followed to some extent in the literature and music. Each of the contributing cultural influences, passing on not only its designs but their associated symbolism as well, had to be assimilated by the developing Greek mind before it could achieve the interest and unity of the sculpture of Phidias, the drama of Aeschylus, or the philosophy of Plato and Aristotle.

Beneath the early Greek mentality lay the freshness of the cave man's cultures as developed around the shore of the Aegean. The opening period, which flourished between 7000 and 2000 B.C., contemporaneously with the pre-dynastic period in Egypt and the Susian in Mesopotamia, was called the Cycladic or island culture. This development was that of an agricultural people, who left behind them simple black pottery (Fig. 36, Chap. III), great underground labyrinthine temples (Fig. 49, Chap. III), and little alabaster figurines of the goddess of fertility, not unlike the Venus of Willendorf (Fig. 40, Chap. III). There is good reason to believe that, for the most part, these people were the same as those Grimaldi Negroid folk who lived in Southern Europe during the last days of the Old Stone Age.

By 2000 B.C., influences from Egypt and Mesopotamia, following trade routes established first by the Egyptians and later by the Phoenicians, were filtering into the Aegean region and continued to invade the peninsula and islands at intermittent periods until as late as 700. Along the trade routes came also designs from the Danube River valley. This mixture of influences early culminated in the Creto-Minoan culture, which reached its height between 2000 and 1500 B.C. In that period developed the peculiarly Minoan art style, remarkable for its natural physioplastic basis. Here the Mesopotamian and Egyptian styles at their best were appreciated and fused.

Following the Cretan development, from 1500 to 1000 B.C., northern invaders of the Celto-Germanic races penetrated the Greek peninsula and Asia Minor, bringing about a culture known in its early part as the Mycenaean Age. Its latter part, the Homeric Age, saw the struggles against Troy—last surviving remnant of the Minoan civilization.

During the centuries following, from 1000 to 600 B.C., sometimes called the Age of Anarchy or the Age of Tyrants, the various tribes of northern invaders, mingling with the ancient Cycladic and Minoan folk, came to be known as the Dorian and Ionian Greeks. The Dorians occupied the territory in the peninsula of the Peloponnesus, Crete, and eventually southern Italy and Sicily. The Ionians occupied most of the Aegean Islands and Asia Minor. The influences from Mesopotamia carried by the Phoenicians from Palestine, grew particularly strong in the Ionian culture, while Egyptian influences, brought up from the South, prevailed in the Doric.

The Backgrounds of Graphic Design

Of the several sources from which Greek art derived its character, perhaps the most fruitful was the Cretan. Many passages in Homer's *Iliad* attest the excellence of *objets d'art*, thought to have been made in some previous golden age, which today we know were the productions of artists who worked in the Minoan palaces. In the eighth book of the *Iliad* occurs a remarkable description of a shield made by Hephaestus (Vulcan), the blacksmith god, for the Grecian hero, Achilles. On the shield many concentric bands of decoration displayed pictures like the following:

Also the glorious lame god wrought therein a pasture in a fair glen, a great pasture of white sheep, and a steading, and roofed huts and folds. Also did the glorious lame god devise a dancing place, like unto that which once in wide Knossos Daidalos wrought for Ariadne of the lovely tresses. There were youths dancing and maidens, of costly wooing, their hands upon one another's wrists.[1]

[1] *The Iliad of Homer*, translated by Lang, Leaf and Myers, p. 345, The Macmillan Company, New York, 1929.

In another place on the same shield Homer described the dancers singing a Linos song at autumn in the vineyards, to the accompaniment of a musical instrument. Today several

Fig. 121.—Four examples of Pre-Minoan *bucchero* ware.

museums in America and in Europe possess fragments of just such shields, some of which were found in Asia Minor, others in tombs upon the Aegean Islands.

From the descriptions of Homer, as well as from countless wall and vase paintings, gems, and sculptures, it is possible now to reconstruct to a considerable extent the life of the Cretans who lived between 2000 and 1200 B.C. These remarkable people brought art to a degree of perfection that became traditional in the mythology of the classical Greeks. The sculptors and painters of the 5th century B.C. strove to emulate the mythical Cretan artist Daedalus, whose statues were said to be so perfect that they came to life and walked about. This tradition of naturalism was further reinforced by contacts with Egypt and Mesopotamia in the 7th and 6th centuries B.C. In the Egyptian tombs and in Mesopotamian palace wall carvings there survived a realistic style allied to the best of the Cretan work. When the fear of the grave or the power of the tyrant dominated man's mind, art clung either to geometric static forms or to the use of sharp angles and vitalized lines. The Cretans, free from these culture patterns, bequeathed to Greece a tradition of an aesthetic lyric quality and a realistic way of looking at life, similar to that of paleolithic man. Seeking the discrete quality of Greek design, therefore, we may proceed to chart its development in vase painting, considering in detail a number of early examples.

Abstract Spiraled Formal Design in Kamares Ware.

By 3000 B.C. the Cretans had developed a pottery with a distinctive form of design and had invented many shapes afterward used in Greek art. The earliest black pottery, decorated with geometric forms suggestive of technical origins in basketry and leather flasks, was *bucchero* ware. The oldest specimens, like the huts of pile dwellers in Northern Europe, have incised surface decoration filled with a clay which when fired turned white to make an interesting pattern (Fig. 121).

The first development away from the *bucchero* ware took place when the Cretans came into contact with the Danubian and Susian pottery. Then the spiral meander or wave motif—probably inspired by their love of the sea—was painted in broad bands of stylized leaves, flowers, and marine plants, in white, yellow, orange, and cherry-red slip on a black, varnished surface. Most of this type of pottery has been found in the town of Kamares, from which it takes its name. Three vases best illustrate this development. The small cup from Phaistos (Fig. 122a), on which a collar of diagonal lines separates the painted zigzag bands, shows that the usual straight strokes have given way to slightly curved lines that differentiate it from the true neolithic ware. This use of the curved line in drawing adds aesthetic value, for it symbolizes growth. In many details this pottery shows connections with Susian pottery (Fig. 99, Chap. V).

The painted jar from Knossos (Fig. 122b)—a prototype of the later classical amphora—in purple, brown, and white, shows the Danubian spiral pattern applied to some form of algae or seaweed. The outer band, of three circles connected by four double leaves, appears to move around the inner five-leafed swastika form. At each side of the vase two lilies with spirals grow out of the bottom band, the top petals resting under the banded handles. Careful examination of this pot will show that the central motifs on the sides connect with the top or lip decoration and that out of this lip, opposite the handles, another floral form hangs downward, as

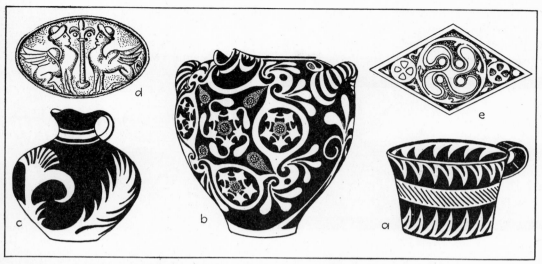

Fig. 122.—*a*, cup, Phaistos, height about 2½ inches; *b*, jar, Knossos, height about 8½ inches; *c*, pitcher, Candia, height about 5 inches (*a*, *b*, and *c*, Kamares style, Middle Minoan, 1800–1700 B.C.); *d*, signet ring, Mycenae; *e*, gold plaque, Mycenae (*d* and *e*, Late Minoan, 1580–1200 B.C.).

though to receive the upthrust lily petal from the lower border. All this natural design, which seems so well to fit the shape of the vase, may have a simple symbolic significance—that of the tree of life.

The third vase, a pitcher (*oenochoë*) from Candia (Fig. 122*c*), shows two stylized white lilies with red anthers and white leafy stalks, arranged in a very refined occult balance against a lustrous black ground. This vase merits comparison with the early Susian vases and with examples of Chinese pottery. Abstract floral design in this type of occult balance passes out of the European art complex, not to return again until its 18th-century importation from China.

The Kamares Scheme of Design in Wall Painting. While the Kamares ware marks the chief aesthetic production of the Middle Minoan period, the very end of this period (1580 B.C.), contemporaneous with the Thirteenth dynasty in Egypt, found a new development in wall painting. To the paintings in the palace at Knossos, which already featured spiral designs similar to those used on the pottery, were added human figures. Sketches were made on the

moist plaster and then covered with colors mixed with water, so that the lime fixed them on the wall without the use of any further binding medium. This is the true fresco technique. Sometimes, as in the case of paleolithic paintings, the outlines were incised and a heavy black contour line was drawn around the various forms, making them appear quite flat. The subjects were rendered with the same freedom as in the Altamira paintings. Many realistic frescoes showed plant and animal life or life under the sea. One of them pictures flying fish.

Figure 123, like the pitcher from Candia, shows what fine balance of spaces could be achieved in making a design for a border around a room. Although only a small section remains, it is possible to reconstruct the rest of the design. The fish are of blue, with white-and-yellow wings. The long curves of their bodies move in counterposition against one another through the water, which is suggested by green and white forms of coral and algae. The motion follows a continuous line, but the placing of wings and fins, of algae and coral reefs, suggests gliding or swimming. Here we see the crude beginning of a composition form which later developed into the Vaphio cups and which, after a thousand years, eventuated in the perfect composition of the Ionic frieze—the procession under the portico of the Parthenon.

FIG. 123.—Fresco, Phylakopi, height about 9 inches, Middle Minoan III, c. 1700–1550 B.C.

The Rise of Naturalism in the Later Palace Styles. The products of the Late Minoan period, which runs from 1580 to 1200 B.C. contemporaneously with the reigns of Hatshepsut and Akhenaten in Egypt, belong to the so-called Palace Style. The octopus vase from Gournia (Fig. 124a) shows the way in which a combination of the Kamares spirals and the naturalistic fresco painting produced a kind of conventionalized naturalism. Here the animal form is interspersed with the sea-snail shells of the murex, from which the famous Tyrian purple dye was made. The spirals of the octopus, the rosettes of tiny sea gastropods, as well as sprigs of seaweed, unite with the suction cups on the tentacles of the octopus to form a design that makes anyone looking at it want to turn the vase round and round. Such an art has a pleasure-giving effect, without much distinct symbolic significance.

Conventionalization began to come into the painting as the Late Minoan period advanced. The lily vase illustrated (Fig. 124b), however, represents the product of a happy moment between realism and conventionalization. This perfect example of the potter's art embodies one of the most complete combinations of form and meaning ever produced. The vase follows the shape of a very slightly opened lily bud; the

base just large enough to give the feeling that the clay form rests securely. A band around the foot and two lighter double bands around the top frame pictures of three lily stems with open-

FIG. 124.—*a*, octopus vase, Gournia, height about 7 inches, Late Minoan I, 1580–1500 B.C.; *b*, lily vase, Knossos, height about 10 inches, Middle Minoan III, 1700–1550 B.C.; *c*, amphora, palace style, Knossos, height about 2 feet, Late Minoan II, 1550–1400 B.C.; *d*, oenochoë or pitcher of hammered gold, shaft-grave, Mycenae, about 1700 B.C.

ing flowers in yellow and white against a purple background. The whole intent is to suggest living form emerging from the ground.

The Realism of Late Palace Figure Paintings. A number of the palace frescoes, during the earlier part of the Late Minoan development, show scenes connected with the various cults or the bull-leaping sports, which was apparently half ceremonial in nature. The picture of a woman carrying a carved casket or ointment box (Fig. 125) comes from the palace of Tiryns. From a similar representation in Crete we know that the woman is probably a priestess taking some offering to the shrine of the mother goddess. This work is most significant, not only for the light it throws upon the decoration around the wall of the palace room—it forms one of a long series of figures in procession—but also in its color rendering of the costume of the time. The colored border above the figure shows a repeated rosette and conventionalized lily design. The woman walks upon a huge timber supported by blocks of blue and red stone. The background is also of blue. The Cretans at that period must have reveled in bright colors. Here, too, the art is more playful than was the Egyptian or the Mesopotamian.

Realism in Cretan Religious Painting. The art of the Cretan palaces reveals shrines and symbols associated with both the solar cult of the bull and the underground cult of the mother goddess. The latter was worshiped under the sign of the cross or the double ax, symbols of the phenomenon of birth which separated the child from its mother.

On two sides of the casket discovered at Hagia Triada, two very interesting scenes demonstrate not only the quality of Cretan design but also the dual elements of this worship. On one side appears a procession of women, preceded by a man playing a double flute, or aulos (Fig. 126). The women present a bull as a sacrifice to a shrine enclosing a sacred tree and guarded by a double ax or cross, topped by a dove. The building of the shrine is surmounted by erect symbols representing sets of bull's horns and bears a painted decoration composed of connected spirals and round plaques, which may represent the beam ends at the top of the room. Since the shrine pictured on the sarcophagus is connected with the tree and the double ax, signifying that it had to do with the mother rite, and since, further, the procession of women follows a man playing a flute, we may be sure that this is an early representation of the Linos song. The other side of the sarcophagus shows a double ceremonial procession.

On each end of the sarcophagus, figures in chariots are drawn by horses and griffins. Two bands, similar to the border above the head of the woman of Tiryns, encompass the sarcophagus above and below. Here, too, are the same gaudy colors, the same postures of the figures, and the same arrangement of top, bottom, and central bands.

The great aesthetic significance of this work lies in the fact that, although obviously religious, it shows neither a dominance of a stiff Egyptian geometric quality nor the dynamic quality of the Assyrian palace art. It seems to occupy a position midway between the two and is closely related to the representation on

the harp of Shub-ad (Fig. 119, Chap V), which, it will be remembered, was associated with a similar religion. The human figures seem to be shown not merely for their decorative effect

Fig. 125.—Tiryns fresco, woman with ivory chest, height about 8½ feet. (*Courtesy of Metropolitan Museum of Art.*)

but for their own value, if not as a contribution to the narrative. There is, besides, a faint attempt to get a feeling of depth, in contrast with the flat design of most Egyptian wall painting. This work serves as a fitting introduction to the lyric narrative quality of later Greek and Roman painting.

a technique called *repoussé* work. Aesthetically, the two bands of decoration, which show the capturing of the bull and part of the ceremony of the bull-leaping sport, have a freedom never

FIG. 126.—Painted sarcophagus, Hagia Triada, Crete, length about 4½ feet, c.1400 B.C. Note the lyre and aulos, musical instruments used in later Greek culture. Bottom, frieze from other side of chest. (*Courtesy of Metropolitan Museum of Art.*)

The Balanced Quality of the Harvester Vase and the Vaphio Cups. Three remarkable objects, two cups found at Vaphio, near Sparta, and the Harvester vase from Crete, stand among the finest creations of the engraver's art. We might discuss them equally well under the head of drawing, as they compare in a way to the later vase painting of the Greek masters, Douris and Polygnotus, or under the head of relief sculpture as comparing with the Parthenon frieze by Phidias. They are the spiritual progenitors of the best in Athenian 5th-century graphic design.

The cup from Vaphio (Fig. 127b), now in the museum at Athens, was hammered out of thin sheets of gold over terra cotta or stone forms,

before reached in ancient art. Nor was it to be reached again until Hellenistic times. The drawing is more Asiatic than Greek, in that landscape, denoted by the trees, appears as an integral part of the composition. The forms are in correct perspective, which is natural in all cases except the one where the twisted animal is caught in a net.

Allied to engraved or *repoussé* articles in gold are vases and cups of gold leaf laid upon stone. The Harvester vase (Fig. 127c), in the Museum of Candia, a black steatite ointment jar, now reconstructed as an aryballus, belongs to this class. The shape can be traced, probably, to the Cretan and Egyptian custom of decorating an ostrich egg with painting, gold inlay, and a

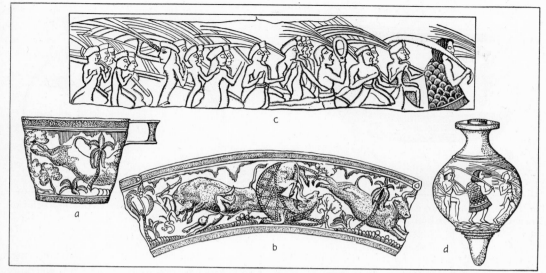

FIG. 127.—*a* and *b*, gold cup from Vaphio, height about 3 inches, 1700–1550 B.C. (Athens Museum); *c* and *d*, harvester vase, Hagia Triada, steatite, height about 6 inches, 1550 B.C. (Candia Museum).

neck. Although the gold leaf has disappeared, the splendid linear design still remains. The carving shows lithe-limbed young harvesters, led by a priest, singing on their way to the fields. The flails and pitchforks held across their shoulders make a braided band of decoration around the upper part of the vase. The heavier bodies move around the central part and the lightly tripping feet around the base. One priest, who has a bell-shaped robe similar to those found in the old Babylonian cultures, smiles happily. The other leads the singing, holding aloft a sistrum—a kind of Egyptian musical rattle. Influences from both Mesopotamia and Egypt are apparent here. The artist has been bold enough to try true perspective, and the figures are carved in rows, to simulate depth. A similar harvest procession carved on the shield of Achilles was described by Homer.

Conventionalization in Mycenaean Art. In Mycenae, after the Minoan period, between the 12th and 7th centuries, naturalistic art became greatly conventionalized and geometricized. The Mycenaean vase from Cyprus (Fig. 128*a*) shows this process of stylistic change. On each side of a tree of life, two figures representing a

winged sphinx and a harpy are so drawn that wings and legs appear as detached flat areas. In the chariot drawn by the sphinx two heads stand for the occupants. The tree shows a form of conventionalization.

A cylix from Ialysos, now in the Louvre, shows an octopus united with two glaring eyes rising above a banded base (Fig. 128*b*). The form is here as good as that of any earlier work, but a comparison of this piece with the earlier octopus vase of Candia shows how a balanced geometric decoration has grown from an occult naturalistic representation.

Asiatic Influences in the Cypriote Vases. The oenochoë, or pitcher, from the island of Cyprus (Fig. 128*c*), manufactured in the 7th century B.C., during the Age of Anarchy, unites elements of design from Mesopotamia and the Scythian countries north of the Caucasus Mountains. It should be compared with the stucco plaque from Rayy described in the preceding chapter (Fig. 117*c*, Chap. V). The body of the vase, covered with a white slip, carries the painted figure of a bird in red and black. This figure is arranged in remarkable occult balance, furnishing a new and satisfying motive

FIG. 128.—*a*, Mycenaean vase, Cyprus (British Museum); *b*, Mycenaean chalice, Ialysos, height about 3⅓ inches; *c*, oenochoe or pitcher from Cyprus, height about 6 inches (Metropolitan Museum of Art). All about 1200*v*700 B.C.

to be incorporated later in the development of Greek vases.

The way in which abstract lines and areas of color combine to make up the body of the bird is an aesthetic phenomenon of the greatest importance. The various sections, each of which is interesting for its own sake, have been fitted together so that the whole appears like a natural bird's body. To the Scythians and Mesopotamians more importance would have attached to the abstract curving lines. Such lines were to play a great part in the later development of Gothic styles of decoration. To that element in the Greek nature which desired realism, the total aspect of the bird was more appealing. The type of design that resulted from the primitive combination of abstraction and representation stimulated one part of the imagination to think in terms of serpentine lines, the other part to see the bird realistically. This complicated mental exercise, with its resulting emotional repercussions, was not only favored in Gothic and Oriental art but has also had a rebirth in the most modern of 20th-century art expression—surrealism.

An art so paradoxical, however, could not appeal to the Hellenic nature. One or the other of the styles had to be absorbed. The abstract elements were accordingly subordinated to the realistic, without, however, losing the fine oc-

cult balance characteristic of the Cypriote vases. The Greek potters, at their best, furthermore, always succeeded in getting into the spaces between the figures the abstract quality of the curvilinear areas that went to make up the body of the Cypriote bird design. The vitalistic quality of the line, also, can be felt in the figure composition.

The Artemis Vase and the Absorption of the Cypriote Style. A representation of the famous Artemis vase from the island of Melos (Fig. 129) will make clear the next step in the union of the Creto-Mycenaean realistic and Cypriote-Asiatic vitalistic elements in Greek vase design. This painting from the second half of the 7th century revived an old Cretan motif—namely, the two-wheeled chariot drawn by winged horses. The figures are painted in red and black upon a white slip ground. Artemis, the goddess of the moon, in her aspect as a huntress brings into the picture from the right a deer that she is about to present to the lyre-playing Apollo. Behind him in the chariot stand two women, supposedly representing nymphs. The animals and people are all divided into flat spaces of colors. Among the wealth of symbols represented in all the spaces, particular notice is due the conventionalized papyrus design, which may here stand for a tree of life in which the tendrils have become spiral volutes. This form

Fig. 129.—Detail of an amphora from Melos: Artemis, Apollo, and two nymphs, second half of 7th century B.C. (Athens Museum).

of decoration was used as the capital of the developing Ionic column.

Aesthetically, the effect of this vase is one of baroque restlessness. We seem to be almost back to the Egyptian wall painting. But there is one great difference: here we have no writing. With the invention of the alphabet, script and painting had now become two completely dissociated methods of communication. This dissociation of pictures from words is symbolic of the movement away from the primitive that characterized all the products of Greek culture.

The Geometric Quality of the Greek Vase. Greek pictorial design at its best incorporates a fine balance of formal elements, which makes for a satisfying unity. We have seen how the realistic static and dynamic design elements from earlier Mediterranean cultures form a background for Greek pictorial composition. There lacks only a cement to bind them together and this cement—the peculiar quality of the Greek mind, associated in literature particularly with the products of the Achaean and Dorian folk from Thessaly—first shows itself in the Dipylon

pottery. Through all later forms of pictorial composition, whether in the medium of paint or sculptured marble, the logical geometric quality of this early Attic vase design makes itself felt.

The earliest examples of the Dipylon pottery are found outside the city gate of Athens from whose two pylons the name "Dipylon" is derived. Here on each side of the road to sacred Eleusis lay the potters' quarter called the Ceramicus. From this word comes the term "ceramics" to describe all pottery. Here were the oldest of the Athenian tombs—stone-chest graves in which were placed food and utensils for the journey into the underworld. Some of the occupants of these graves were buried in great funereal urns. These were the coffins of the city fathers.

The importance of funerary and memorial urns should not be underestimated. They became the chief articles of export for the city of Athens. In the matter-of-fact, prosaic civilization of the 20th century, which follows the Mesopotamian rather than the Egyptian model, it is hard to believe that the greatness of Athens and Corinth, centers of the ancient world, was due in great part to their superior manufacture of an article of beauty that com-

in the Metropolitan Museum of Art, shows a form, obviously derived from Cretan prototypes, which combines the cylix and an egg-shaped bowl. Above the zigzag ornament on

Fig. 130.—Dipylon grave vase in geometric style, 8th century B.C., height about 4 feet. (*Courtesy of Athens Museum.*)

Fig. 131.—So-called François vase. Attic combination hydria and crater painted by Clitias in the workshop of Ergotimos. Height about 2 feet, about the middle of the 6th century B.C. (Florence Archaeological Museum). (*Courtesy of Lesch.*)

bined the purposes of our athletic trophies, loving cups, and tombstones. Egyptian priests and Phoenician traders had efficiently built up a market for these funeral commodities. Most of the Mediterranean world valued an art that suggested the phenomenon of life after death. That art was neatly combined in the ovoid form, the narrative subject matter, and the symbolic decoration of the Grecian urn.

The Fundamental Rhythm Change to Measure in Early Design. The famous Dipylon crater (Fig. 130) of the Athens Museum, similar to one now

its foot rises a heavy black band followed in turn by another zigzag and other bands, each so composed that they all lead to the main bands of figures that encircle the upper part of the bowl. The lower of these figured bands shows a procession with three-horse chariots driven by one-eyed men whose bodies are composed of triangles. After them come other one-eyed men, whose bodies consist of great ax-shaped Boeotian shields.

Anyone walking around this vase, which stands four feet high, can see that charioteers and shieldsmen form a pattern of measured beats—first, a long beat and then two shorter ones, duplicating the beat of elegiac, or funereal, poetry. This accords with the scene on the largest band, which shows the deceased arranged upon his bier, attended by mourning women, wife, and children. The pattern at the very top of the vase also suggests a movement around in slow, intricate measure. It consists of a peculiar mixture of something both static and dynamic, a right-angled rendition of the spiraling, progressive motion studied earlier in connection with Susian pottery. This type of design is called, variously, the "fret," the "running dog," and in later times, the "Vitruvian scroll."

As a forerunner and formal scheme of everything the Attic artists were later to complete, this Dipylon vase has the greatest significance. It represents a plan or design for the complete vase and temple decoration which developed over the next 200 years. Already in this stage appears a nicety of arrangement unfelt by the primitive Egyptians or Susians, though their pottery several thousand years earlier had looked vaguely like this. The upper band, with its funeral scene, in reality forms a complete picture, with a definite beginning, a middle point, and an end, terminating at each side in three vertical bands next to the handles.

A network of vertical lines, which runs through all the sections like the weft of a woven pattern, contributes a certain architectonic strength that keeps the bowl from appearing to sag. The small band of zigzags on the base, the legs of the horses on the first pictorial band, and the verticals of the bodies in the second pictorial band together form the construction lines that brace the horizontals. How well planned and logical this construction, like the building of a Doric temple! Each part of the structure frames a picture. It may appear that all is static and geometric on this primitive tomb, but its logic helps the later vase painters to construct the rhythmical, moving compositions of the 5th century.

The Archaic Period and the François Vase. To the early military funereal vases, with their Doric sternness, were added during the 7th century B.C. the technique and the more realistic forms of the still conventionalized Ionic

island pots. The geometric scheme remains the same, but the usual chariot and horses driven by Apollo together made a more active pattern. The result of this combination of static and active styles produced the famous historical vase named after its discoverer, the archaeologist François, who repaired it after it had been found in an Etruscan tomb not far from Florence in Italy.

In the middle of the 6th century B.C., the potter Ergotimos turned out this great mixing crater (Fig. 131) and covered it with a layer of pinkish white slip on which the painter Clitias drew in red and black a number of the best loved Attic myths. Like the earlier Dipylon vase and like most of the vases that have come to us from ancient Greece, this example was associated with funeral rites.

In the form of the vase, Ergotimos combined two previous shapes. The large neck makes of it a crater, or mixing bowl, while the belly remains that of an amphora. These two parts are united by composite handles whose lower sections belong to the amphora. The upper sections turned into Ionic volutes, framing little pictures, and belong to the crater form. The vase lacks the unity of the earlier Dipylon pot.

When analyzed simply in terms of the arrangement and size, each band of the vase, starting with the lowest and working up, appears to increase slightly in size. The base, with its stylized leaf ornament, suggests the bases of Persian columns. It frames a delicate band of tiny, fighting pygmies and cranes. This lowest band shows no regular rhythm, but consists of a primitive network of zigzag lines making an active, all-over pattern without definite direction. It needed a strong transition to the other parts. This was accomplished by painting the opening petals of a stylized lotus or sun's rays which, turned upward, support the bowl. These rays touch another band composed of ancient coats of arms—the lion and the deer brought by the Achaeans from the Scythian north, the womanly sphinx, and the tree of life, symbol of ancient mother cults. In size, this band is larger than the lower one, but relatively more static.

The next section is still larger and shows a poorly arranged historical scene: the story of

Fig. 132.—Detail of black figured vase by Lydos, c. 560 B.C., showing archaic decorative style of drawing and use of apotropaic eyes (drawing by Hall). (*Courtesy of Metropolitan Museum of Art.*)

Hephaestos, the blacksmith god, and Troilos, a Trojan hero. On this section appears the picture of an early Doric megaron or tomb, a statue of Athena, and other gods and goddesses. This particular band is as lacking in pictorial unity as the first section of the Papyrus of Ani. It forms a complete contrast with the rhythmic band next higher, on which there is a procession of Olympian deities following the Chthonian Dionysus, whose face reminds one of a Gorgon. He carries his wine jar with him. This frieze, the largest of the group, has a definite motion from left to right.

Above the frieze, on the neck, the artist depicted a chariot race in which the horses and the wheels of the chariots form a regular series of beats, like those in the band of the Dipylon vase. See how this contrasts with the unregulated scene below. The artist set the neck apart from the rest by a fine border, which repeats the border of the base in gentler, echoing tones. Then he capped the entire structure with two scenes: one side, which can be seen in the illustration, shows the hunt of the Calydonian boar by the Greek hero Meleager; the other tells of the arrival of Theseus' ship at Delos on his return from killing the Minotaur. It makes a balanced composition such as that of the Dipylon vase.

In this progressive development of the bands there is a distinct movement from the small, formless base up through ever weightier subjects to the procession of the gods, then down in a more moderate tone, through smaller bands with rhythmical arrangement, to a balanced composition. From warfare, remote and almost forgotten, between dwarfs and animals, one is led to a final conquest of the animal by his superior, man. Out of a primitive chaos of tribal conflicts, the artist arrived at a conscious unity, with struggle sublimated to sport and art.

The progress here seen later became the plot of the classic drama. First came the conflict, then the high middle point or climax, and finally the unified conclusion. Centuries later, under the hands of Gothic musicians, along the River Danube, in old Vienna and throughout the northern nations, the same scheme was used for the development, in music, of the symphony; in philosophy, of Hegel's law of *thesis*, *antithesis*, and *synthesis*. Here, then, appears the first instance of a definite aesthetic law applicable to any work of art that needs a time element for complete comprehension. Unity with power is achieved by showing a conflict, suggesting a union in some law, and then rearranging the conflict in terms of a simple unifying scheme that is both rhythmical and geometric.

The Technique of Vase Painting in the Archaic Style. A closer study of the technique used by Clitias in painting can be made by examining a section (Fig. 132) from a similar crater by the contemporaneous painter, Lydos, from the Metropolitan Museum. With this example it is easy to demonstrate the finest of the style, which is called the early archaic style of vase painting.

The first pinkish white slip served as a background on which the face of Hephaestos was colored red. The woman, however, has a pure white face and limbs, as was conventional in

Egyptian and Cretan painting. In this fragment, the horse is in black, although on the François vase some of the horses were painted white. The colors were applied with a brush and the fine lines on the clothes, which denote pattern, were then scratched on or engraved through the color to the base of light-reddish clay beneath. Some of the blacks have a decidedly purple tone. The painting resembles Egyptian wall painting, but lacks the brighter colors, the greens and blues.

The Origins of Greek Sculptural Design

The Cycladic Style. Paralleling the development of painting, Greek sculpture incorporated elements from diverse localities. The little figures of the harper and the flute player (Fig. 133), from the island of Keros, typify the work of the Cycladic, or island, sculptors working on a neolithic level at several places around the Aegean. They were found in conjunction with violin-shaped idols of the mother goddess, similar to those of ancient Sumer and others, like the Venus of Willendorf. The geometric character of these figures, found not only in stone and metal but also in clay, points to possible influences from Egypt. The entire body of the harper, for example, has been so stylized as to preclude any possibility of thinking of it naturalistically. The tilted head, with its sharp, geometric nose, and the angular position of arms and harp serve to increase the pleasure derived from the geometrical counterposition of the limbs. The statues, though primitive and unrealistic, seem to issue from playful activity, like the work of some child untouched by the power complex of the Mesopotamians or the religious superstition of the Egyptians. No fitter introduction could be given to the meaning of classical sculpture than these little figures, most certainly created with pleasure.

The Realism of Minoan Sculpture. Certain developments in sculptural form took place in the Late Minoan style. Bronze casting reached a higher stage of perfection than that attained in Egypt, though it had been approximated early in Mesopotamia. Bronze figures of men and women show a liveliness that could have

Fig. 133.—*a*, marble harper from Keros, height about 8⅓ inches. Early Cyclades culture, 4000–2000 B.C. (Athens Museum); *b*, marble flute player from Keros, height about 7½ inches. Early Cyclades culture, 4000–2000 B.C. (Athens Museum); *c*, dog and young, clay, from Argos, height about 5½ inches, about 1000 B.C. (Robinson Collection, Johns-Hopkins University.)

been attained only by modeling directly in wax. The wax figure was covered with a mold of clay or plaster, bound together with dung or some fibrous, rocklike asbestos. This mold was then heated so that the wax flowed out, whereupon bronze was poured into the hollow form. The little figure of the priestess with the snakes around her waist and in her hair (Fig. 134) shows this technique very clearly, first because the surface of the bronze shows no chiseling, second because of the natural curve of the figure.

The Inner Vitality of the Snake Goddess. The same feeling of inner vitality noticed in the bronzes characterizes the chryselephantine statue about seven inches high of the priestess, now in the Museum of Fine Arts in Boston (Fig. 135). Carved from a tusk of ivory, the main body and head of the figure bend slightly, as the tusk curves. The arms, which are held out, tense, as though to protect the face from the two hooded snakes, form a sort of counterpost against the forward bend of the body. The head is held erect, but the attention is pulled downward by the mass of the breasts, which are inlaid with gold. The carving of the crown indicates that the locks of hair that originally came from the little holes around the face were probably serpentine in character. Other holes around the abdomen and below the golden belt show that

because of the contrast between the curve of the body and the straight line of the arms; as jewelry, because of the delicacy of the goldsmithing and the ivory carving. The color com-

Fig. 134.—Bronze priestess with serpents, Crete, height about 7½ inches, Late Minoan 1580–1200 B.C. (*Courtesy of the National Museum, Berlin.*)

Fig. 135.—Ivory and gold priestess, Late Minoan palace style, 1500 B.C., height about 6½ inches (Boston Museum of Fine Arts). (*Courtesy of Boston Museum of Fine Arts.*)

there must have been some short of ceremonial apron over the flounced skirt, also decorated with gold bands. The face is so naturalistically carved and has a profile so much like the profiles of Swedish and Midwestern American girls in our own day and culture that we may reasonably conclude that this Cretan civilization belonged to people like ourselves. This is the first example of what we might call European or Occidental art, contrasting with the Asiatic art of Mesopotamia and the African art of Egypt.

As sculpture the statue has aesthetic interest

bination of gold and ivory is also pleasing, and to this must be added the fact that in our day the rarity of gold and ivory lends a feeling of richness or value which plays its part in our emotional reaction to the work.

The Transitional Forms. The development in Greek sculpture of the realistic human form arranged on rhythmical and geometric patterns of motion unfolds parallel to the development in painting. The following illustrations from the evolution of Hellenic sculpture during what is called the geometric and archaic periods from 800 through 600 B.C. demonstrate the way in which separate memory images eventually coalesce in the mind of the artist as some new idea comes to birth.

With the disappearance of Cretan realism, the old geometric style of the Cycladic island sculpture again became dominant from 1000 through 800 B.C. Figurines in terra cotta and stone, like the little group of the bitch and her young (Fig. 138c), have an almost playful appearance, although they were not necessarily toys but usually votive offerings left at the shrines of the many semitotemistic gods associated with fields and spring.

The Recognition of Doric and Ionic Elements in Style. After the 7th century B.C. two general tendencies became prominent in the growth of Greek sculpture—the Ionic and the Doric. The works found on the Aegean Islands and in Asia Minor, created by people speaking Ionian dialects, show many characteristics of the Mesopotamian style. The figures associated with the Dorian Greeks residing in the Peloponnesus, southern Italy, Sicily, and Crete seem angular, stocky, and close to Egyptian models. Gradually during the 6th century, as the sculptors were drawn to Athens, the two styles united, and from the union arose the well-balanced Attic style of the 5th century.

The Ionic Hera of Samos. The statue of Hera (Fig. 136), queen of the gods, from the Island of Samos, was found in a temple dedicated to that deity which had been built around 550 B.C. The stiff columnar form, refined and made graceful by the developing Hellenic will to humanize, still suggests the carving of Gudea, particularly with respect to the arms and feet. The drapery follows Mesopotamian models of dress, but the long, sweeping line of the silhouette and the delicate carving of the folds have the quality of gracefulness found in the gold

cup of Shub-ad, the head of Nofretete, and the columns from the mastabas at Sakkareh. One wonders why this singular refinement, so alike in these cases, should appear in works so far

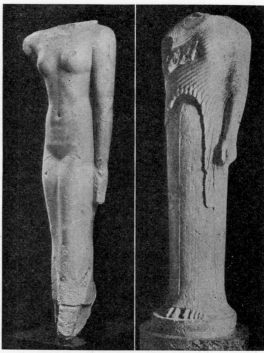

FIG. 136.—Right, Hera from Samos, c. 350 B.C., white marble, height about 6 feet (Louvre Museum); left, figure of Princess from Sakkareh (Worcester Museum). (See Fig. 64, Chap. IV.) (*Courtesy of Lesch-Carnegie.*)

separated in point of time? It would be difficult to prove direct relationship, but we must remember that the Greeks of the 6th century B.C. were the busiest commercial people of the Mediterranean world. It is by no means impossible that Greek artists, coming upon the rich storehouses of Egypt and Mesopotamia, found there forms that inspired them to greater perfection. In the case of the Hera of Samos, the fine formal balance struck between the visual pattern of the light lines of the skirt and the heavier lines of the cloak, combined with the suggestive underlying form of breasts and hips to introduce new possibilities in sculptural treatment. This combination, which enables the artist to retain absolute sculptural form while bringing in enough of the human element

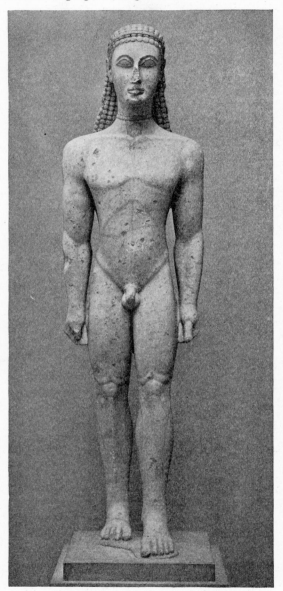

Fig. 137.—Archaic Greek Apollo, c. 600 B.C., height 6 feet 4 inches (Metropolitan Museum of Art). (*Courtesy of Metropolitan Museum of Art.*)

to make it appeal, is the *sine qua non* of the classical spirit of art.

The Doric Apollo from Attica. Contemporaneous with the carving of the Ionic Hera and representative of the Doric style of sculpture are a number of nude masculine figures usually called the Apollos, after Helios-Apollo, the sun-god who was patron of the arts. The Apollo in the Metropolitan Museum (Fig. 137) possesses the Egyptian characteristics common to all of the type. His frontal striding position with hands clasped tightly at his side has become familiar through our study of Egyptian temple and tomb sculpture. The position of the left leg, the broad shoulders, and narrow waist present further evidence of the close connections with the Egyptian. Other Doric figurines in terra cotta recently discovered in Sicily seem to be copies of mummy cases. The Egyptian connection can further be demonstrated in a study of the growth of the Doric column and temple structures. This figure differs from the Egyptian, however, as radically as the Ionic figure of Hera differed from the Mesopotamian. It lacks the heavy supporting block which would suggest a relationship with architecture. It is completely nude, a circumstance pointing to the Hellenic pride in the structure of the human body for its own sake. Finally—and this is most important—the head, that part of the figure usually associated with the human personality, is relatively much larger than the heads of Egyptian figures—this although the locks of hair around the neck have been retained as a mass, perhaps to prevent breakage.

The entire body has been carved in a pattern, like the Assyrian palace figures of Khorsabad, which were contemporaneous with this statue. The Greek pattern differs from the Assyrian, however, in that, like Egyptian patterns, it is angular and geometric while the Assyrian is vitalistic. In this sculpture there is an early evidence of the lighthearted spirit with which the Greek approached the work of art. In Egypt and Assyria, as we have seen, art had a serious religious purpose for the culture itself. The Greeks, on the other hand, were the first people who made a business of selling their art prod-

Fig. 138.—Head of archaic Apollo, limestone, height about 8 inches (Athens Museum). (*Courtesy of Clarence Kennedy.*)

ucts to others. In this archaic sculpture the formal aspects of the older civilizations still dominate, but the spirit of free artistic invention continually breaks through, so that it seems the best Greek pottery, but their arrangement corresponds to the rhythmical pattern of a Greek dance. If the reader will try drawing them, starting with the brows, he will find a

Fig. 139.—Archaic relief, c. 600 b.c., marble, width about 2 feet (Museum of Athens). (*Courtesy of Clarence Kennedy.*)

interesting, particularly in the 20th century— another day of great artistic innovation.

The Head of an Archaic Figure. The emergent vitalistic qualities of archaic art, its directness and naïveté, which make it most appealing to young vigorous peoples such as the Americans, find complete expression in the head of an archaic figure (Fig. 138). This head, of an Apollo type, carved in porous limestone, displays those qualities at their best.

Despite the headdress, which suggests early Mesopotamian work, the Greek quality is apparent. The aliveness of the head is not due to any one attribute, such as a realistic portrayal, vitalized line, or juxtaposition of sculpturesque forms, but results from a combination of them all. At first glance the line of brow and nose appears straight and unbroken, contrasting with the pleasing curves of lips and chin. Closer examination, however, reveals that the seemingly straight line is composed of delicate curves, which can be seen at the brow and at the bridge of the nose. The eye thus prepared then meets the fuller curves below, dances over the line of the lips, swings round the semicircle of the chin and back to the long straight line of the throat. All these curves repeat the curves of

high degree of sense pleasure in following this profile line. Here is a clue to one of the chief attributes of all Greek sculpture, one taken from the line drawings of Greek vases.

In keeping with this youthful delicacy, the very slight curvature on the planes of the face and the slight beginning of a smile seen in the upraised corners of the lips suggest a certain freshness in the sculptor's approach to his work. The eye, superficially carved on the surface, strikes a definitely primitive note.

The delicate treatment of the face contrasts strongly with the deep, bold carving of the conventionalized hair with its tiny crown spirals and heavy locks at the nape of the neck. All these component parts frame an exquisitely modeled ear, correctly drawn and completely realistic. This face, then, unites realistic elements found in Minoan art with more formal elements from the Egyptian Doric and the Mesopotamian Ionic styles. The charm in the piece arises from the fact that its formal qualities just reveal and balance its human qualities without allowing the human to dominate.

The Athenian Archaic Relief. The same youthful qualities seen in the head above appear in a tiny relief from the base of a statue now in the museum at Athens (Fig. 139). A study of this work not only serves to capture for us archaic relief sculpture in its happiest moment but also introduces monumental sculpture as associated with architecture and grave monuments. Here a free composition of a number of figures arranged in a rectangle stands for that aspect of Greek art which was complete in itself. The metopes, friezes, and pediments—all, parts of temple structures—differ from this in making greater conventional demands upon the artist. These two forces—art as an issue of experimental or playful activity and art as an appropriate enhancement of existing social institutions—were both at work in Greek society.

The exquisite relief of the wrestlers displays in even greater degree that quality of inner unity found in the figures on the hunting reliefs of the Assyrian monarchs. In the discussion of the wounded lioness, attention was called to the way in which the unknown sculptor had succeeded in making us feel the pain of the dying beast. In the Greek relief the figures actually seem to be interested in one another. The artist has so managed the postures and so arranged the muscles that they suggest tensions from side to side. Obviously, the two figures in the center wrestling with each other stand in a state of balance just before the one is pushed over or the other jerked off his feet. The muscles are so carved that they have less of the geometric pattern noticeable in the archaic Apollo. They appear by no means realistic, however, and still suggest the treatment of the muscles in Assyrian reliefs. It is the two figures at the sides of the central group that actually contribute most to the feeling of tension. The one at the left, whose left leg is partly drawn up, suggests in his posture that the left wrestler will fall in just a moment, while the standing man at the right, so delicately balanced with his weight on his left leg and running down through the right arm and the staff to the ground, suggests that the right wrestler has the more stable position.

What meaning outside the pure joy of expressive movement can this little relief have

had? In Greece, warfare between the tribes became sublimated to rhythmical athletic exercise carried on as a duty to state and gods. This was not the commercial athleticism of the

Fig. 140.—Metope from Selinus: Athena, Perseus, and Gorgon; early 6th century B.C., brown tufa, height about 4 feet 10 inches (Palermo Museum). (*Courtesy of Lesch-Carnegie.*)

modern day but a ceremonial observance gradually freeing itself from the more primitive combats. Hence the artist who portrayed this struggle did not, like some modern artist, work simply for himself but as a paid gravestone carver commissioned to make a base for a memorial statue.

The playful spirit in Attica was strong, however. Turning to the contemporaneous religious metopal relief from the Doric temple at Selinus on the island of Sicily, one may study the contrasting mood.

The Metope from Selinus. The figures carved in high relief as part of the architectural decoration of the early Doric temple at Selinus (Fig. 140) show an obvious, somewhat Egyptian, geometric scheme of construction. The lower part of each figure appears in profile; the upper, in full face. The faces of Perseus and Athena, at the left, are small and rather natural, although the eyes stare blankly and the ears protrude from the sides of the head. The two faces balance the much larger head of the Medusa, who kneels so that she will fit into the

FIG. 141.—The Acropolis maidens. Left, Doric type by Antenor, Island marble, c. 510–500 B.C.; right, Ionic type (Acropolis Museum, Athens). (*Courtesy of Lesch-Carnegie.*)

space. If she were standing, her superior physical power, denoted by her greater size, would make her protrude above the top border of the relief. Her kneeling position brings her head nearer the level of the other two. This arrangement of figures so that all heads, regardless of body size, may appear to be on the same level, is called isocephaly. The Greeks employed it regularly to obtain a fine decorative pattern. Since the problem in designing a metope or a continuous frieze of architectural sculpture or painting is to integrate the human figures with the design of the architecture, all the chief accents will repeat the total design of the frieze. Thus the free forms appear as strong verticals repeating the lines of the triglyphs on each side of the metopes, and the lines of the arms, running almost horizontal, serve to bind the composition transversely with the line of the frieze as a whole. The Doric frieze, although discontinuous, has a rhythmical sweep, interspersed with the three strong beats of the triglyphs. The arrangement exactly parallels the arrangement of narrative bits on the black-figured vases of the time. The subject matter has anthropological significance, as it shows a story like that of the Mesopotamian sun-god slaying the demon Humbaba, who had been associated with the matriarchal deities of the underworld.

Contrasting this relief with the Ionic relief of the wrestlers, one sees that here all is regularity imposed from without, while the wrestlers seem to be animated from within. In the group of the wrestlers the artist is revealed to be working for the effect of feeling; in the Perseus metope, to be working for the telling of an intellectual story. Later, in the works of Phidias, there appeared an art in which emotional and intellectual elements came into a nice state of balance, each individual figure partaking of the architectonic structure of the whole, while the whole retained the inner expressive vitality of the individual figure. Two further steps on the way to the sculpture of Phidias will be discussed in the following chapter, in connection with the pediments of Aegina and Olympia.

The two modes of thinking were very definitely part of the developing Greek mind. Whence did they arise? Everything points to the fact that Doric and Ionic Greeks had differing emotional temperaments, contrasting, let us say, as much as those of the average Scandinavian and the Latin. Since emotional tone bears a relation to the bodily characteristics of a people, we may seek confirmatory evidence in portraits of the two types. Fortunately, during the century preceding the destruction of Athens by the Persians, selected maidens from the best Athenian families posed for statues that were set up on the Acropolis. (Fig. 141.) In these portrait figures, one easily recognizes the two types, Doric and Ionic—the one, short and heavy; the other, tall and delicate. Polyclitus, a sculptor from a Dorian town, held that the most beautiful human being stood seven heads high, while an Attic sculptor, Lysippus, coming later, insisted that the best-proportioned person measured eight heads in height. A conclusive answer lay not in the extreme but in the mean, and as we shall see in the next chapter the greatest artists united characteristics from both styles.

The Acropolis Maidens. The Acropolis Maidens display advances in technique over the Hera of Samos and the archaic Apollo. All the figures retain the erect columnar posture, for its monumental quality and permanence were recognized as valuable. The arms of all the figures have been raised and freed from the sides. In the case of the tall figure, the left arm raises the dress slightly, while the right arm in each case was outstretched, perhaps to hold some offering. The hair, carved in delicate geometric pattern, still lends to the figure a certain conventional dignity. The Doric types all have short, oval faces nearly square in proportion, although, since each was a recognizable portrait, no two are exactly alike. In each case the Doric ladies show little or no emotion, while the Ionic girls have the corners of their mouths lifted as though in a smile. The Ionic faces are thin and the eyes set at oblique angles with the center line of the nose, so that their outer ends point upward. The eyes are also smaller in proportion to the whole face than are those of the Doric maidens. Another difference is in the headdress, the Doric being arranged so that the head appears short, the Ionic so that the head appears still taller.

All the figures of Acropolis maidens show traces of colored decoration painted to simulate embroidery on the clothing. Since the embroidery was geometric, the painted decoration, like the permanent waves of the hair, has a tendency to nullify naturalistic form. Nevertheless, although geometric qualities persist, these figures are recognizably human. They are only fragmentary, however, and since the base of but one exists, we know only that one of them was made by the sculptor Antenor. Their broken condition is due to the fact that they were thrown down and partly destroyed by the Persians and then used later, when Pericles reconstructed the Acropolis, to fill the space behind the new walls. What an unhappy fate for last year's beauty contest winners!

The Bases of the Doric and Ionic Styles in Greek Architecture

The fine simplicity of the Parthenon and the Erechtheum, which are epitomes of the Doric and Ionic styles, respectively, can be fully appreciated only if one recognizes the complexity of motifs from which they arose. Our respect for them and the unifying power of the Greek mind grows as we come to understand their diverse origins. The map (Fig. 120) is an attempt to explain graphically the various component influences in the development of the Attic style.

The Diverse Forms of Cycladic Architecture. On the islands of Amorgos and Melos archaeologists have found terra-cotta urns, perhaps for cinerary use, in the form of round huts (Fig. 44, Chap. III), associated with the Cycladic culture. Some of these urns represent houses built upon piles or stilts. From them we must assume that the people on the shores of the prehistoric Mediterranean lakes were pile dwellers, like the pile dwellers of the terramara culture and the lake dwellers in Switzerland. Building forms inherited from the wooden architecture of these people can be found translated into the stone façades of tombs in Asia Minor, particularly those around Antiphellos. Their discovery gave rise to the much disputed theory that all Greek architecture has immediate antecedents in wooden buildings. The Melian urn (Fig. 142a) shows a group of seven round huts placed about a central court. The entrance gateway is protected by a gabled porch, and the outer surface is covered with a design of connected spirals, a design worked in mud on the original houses.

At Chamaizi on the island of Crete and at Tepe Gawra in Mesopotamia are ruins of similar sets of rooms, forming great oval dwellings (Fig. 142b,c). Hypogea, like those of Malta (Fig.

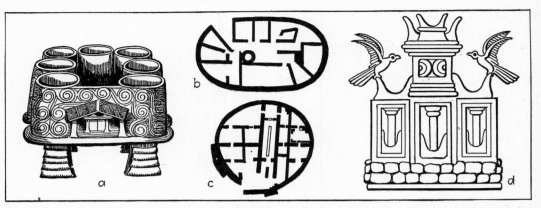

Fig. 142.—*a*, urn carved from slate showing seven huts around a central court on piles with gabled porch from Melos Early Cyclades culture, 4000–2000 B.C., height about 4 inches (Museum for Ancient Minor Arts, Munich); *b*, plan of communal house, Chamaizi, Crete, Early Cyclades culture, 4000–2000 B.C.; *c*, plan of round house, Tepe Gawra, about 3500 B.C. (University of Pennsylvania Museum); *d*, gold model of temple, Late Middle Minoan, 1700–1550 B.C., height 2½ inches, shaft-graves at Mycenae (National Museum, Athens).

49*b*, Chap. III), lie beneath the Cretan palace at Knossos. Most significant of all, the corbeled dolmen structure of neolithic graves in Crete gradually grew into the corbeled tomb. From the Maltese temples, with their oval rooms and center pillars, the corbeled pillar with expanded top and small base produced in time the reversed column of the Cretans. It will be found again on Cretan gems (Fig. 142*d*). From this column was derived the capital structure of the Greek Doric style.

The Cretan-Minoan Palace. The palace at Knossos, like the Mesopotamian palaces, consisted of an ordered group of rooms, three stories high, built around a great central court. Included were storage rooms for olive oil, grain, and precious metals; at least two distinct cult rooms; and apartments for the ruler, his courtiers, women, servants, and artists. The walls displayed frescoes and raised reliefs in plaster. The floors were well laid and drained by an elaborate system of sewers. Streams of running water for bathing and drinking purposes were conducted by aqueducts and clay pipes from distant mountain rivulets to the necessary outlets in the palace. Life in this building must have approached very closely to our modern ideas of sanitary living, so that if like environments breed like habits and minds, these Cretans must have been in most respects like ourselves.

The Architecture of the Mycenaean Culture. In architecture the Mycenaeans copied from Crete and Asia Minor. Their fortress cities resembled those of the Hittites. They learned to build long passages or galleries, roofed with monoliths in corbeled triangular arches. Infiltrations of Celtic races from the Danube, as well as possible connections with the Hittite stock, point to the fact that these were essentially dolmen-building people. Their grave dolmens, of which the Treasury of Atreus is one (Fig. 143*a*), represent modified forms of late neolithic cruciform structures such as the one at New Grange in Ireland. The shape of this particular tomb resembles that of the old Maltese and Cretan hypogea.

The gate of the lionesses at Mycenae (Fig. 143*b*) closes the end of a long fortified passage. Its heavy lintel structure would have been destroyed by the weight of stone above the doorway, had the Mycenaeans not built the heavier wall as a corbel arch. The triangular space then left was filled with a thinner relief panel on which was carved, as a center, the fundamental architectural order of the Cretan palaces—that is, a column upon a heavy base with a well-developed capital, abacus, and four rosettes.

FIG. 143.—*a*, so-called Treasury of Atreus, domed grave at Mycenae, about 1400 B.C., length about 60 yards, height about 26 feet; *b*, gate of the lionesses at Mycenae, width about 10 feet, height about 26 feet.

On each side of this column, which stands for whatever religious power the Mycenaeans inherited from their Cretan forebears, pose two well-modeled lions, which at one time had heads of bronze in *repoussé*. This coat of arms unites the column or tree worship with the cult of force.

The Domestic Buildings of the Aegean Peoples. The rooms of the palace at Knossos were rectangular and square, like those in the Egyptian and Mesopotamian palaces. They opened upon large central courts and in some cases were fronted by colonnades. During the last half of the second millennium two distinct departures from this complex type of dwelling seem to have arisen in the Aegean area. The first variation may be traced to nomadic peoples from the steppes of Asia who wandered south through Thessaly, probably before the Dorian migrations. Their tents, when set out with a row of rocks around the base, left a plan that shows a semicircular rear wall (Fig. 144*a*). In time, this apsidal building was made into a permanent shrine. At Olympia (Fig. 144*b*) two of these buildings still stand, each about 60 feet long; they have been given the name *bouleuterion*. In far-off India, with the coming of Scythian peoples, similar tent plans moved down into the most ancient levels and were taken over to become the chaityas, or apsidal temples, of the Hindu builders.

The second variant, which became in time the most typical of Greek structures, was a rectangular wooden building with a gabled roof and a porch supported by two front columns (Fig. 145). This building design seems to have come from the direction of the Danube River valley and the Swiss lakes, where ruins have been found that antedate the Aegean cultures. During the last part of the second millennium, it also appears among the terramara dwellings and the Hallstatt cultures of Austria. The structure is associated with a zigzag, or chevron, type of decoration. In its simplest form it consists of a rectangular room with four central columns supporting a sort of clerestory, which gives an opening above a central hearth fire. Through this opening the smoke of the fire escaped. In the citadels of Troy, Tiryns, and Mycenae, this type of building, often modified so that it had two rooms behind the porch, served as the central dwelling house of the chief. These houses, now called the "megara," always faced a central court and were separated from each other by narrow passageways through which the rain water might run off. In the remains discovered, the largest building always shows evidence of having been the hall of the king, and as such must have been similar in function to the Mesopotamian hilani, which was studied in the palace at Khorsabad (Fig. 144*e*) and was found in most

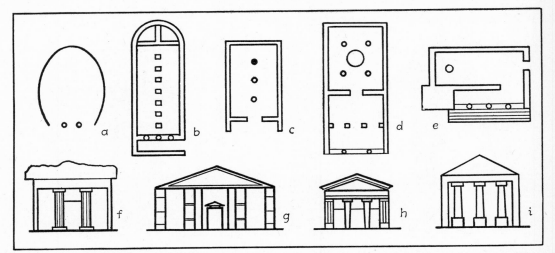

FIG. 144.—*a*, semicircular tent plan, Thessaly; *b*, *bouleuterion*, Olympia; *c*, megaron, Troy; *d*, megaron, Tiryns; *e*, ceremonial entrance to palace at Sendschirli; *f*, proto-Doric tomb, Beni Hasan, Egypt; *g*, Armenian gabled temple from an Assyrian relief in the Louvre Museum; *h*, façade, megaron, Tiryns; *i*, rock-cut tomb, Hambarkaia, Phrygia.

of the Hittite towns of Asia Minor (Fig. 144*g*). The megaron is the most direct progenitor of the Greek temple *in antis*—the temple with the

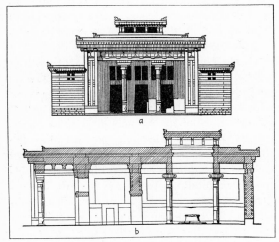

FIG. 145.—Mycenaean megaron about 1400 B.C. *a*, façade; *b*, longitudinal section. (*From L'Histoire de l'art dans l'antiquité, by Perrot and Chipiez; courtesy of Librairie Hachette, Paris.*)

front porch. Relatives of the Aegean peoples who lived in Etruria also built this type of temple, and it carried over into Roman religious usage.

The earliest megaron at Mycenae (Fig. 146*b*), as restored by Charles Chipiez, shows the above type. Here each shaft is capped by a circular member called the "echinus," which grew logically out of the Maltese corbeled column. This member makes a satisfactory aesthetic transition from the shaft to the square or abacus on which rests the long crossbeam of the front of the porch. The roof was made of round poles probably covered with smaller twigs and tamped clay. These poles rested upon the front beam and their ends made a pattern of circles, which persisted as purely architectural decoration late in the development of classical building. The shafts of the columns rested upon bases. When the shafts in this type of building were made of wood, some such base was necessary to prevent rotting near the ground.

The fragments that enabled Charles Chipiez to restore the megaron of the second period denote a distinct change in the type of column employed and the ornament under the porch (Fig. 145). When the northern invaders first came down into the Aegean area, the Minoans probably used them as mercenaries or allies for various raids on cities around the Mediterranean. As is usually the case, these allies came

FIG. 146.—Evolution of the Doric column. *a*, Knossos, about 2000 B.C.; *b*, early megaron, Mycenae, about 1500 B.C.; *c*, late megaron, Mycenae, about 1250 B.C.; *d*, tomb of Atreus, about 1000 B.C.; *e*, building on François vase, about 700 B.C.

to dominate the men who employed them. They eventually destroyed the palace of Knossos itself, looting it and taking back with them to Mycenae and Tiryns, on the mainland, tremendous treasures of gold. They then built at Mycenae a second megaron, decorating it much more richly, and giving the shafts the zigzag ornament of the northern peoples, instead of the purely Minoan columns with Egyptian fluted shafts. This same zigzag was spread along the lower courses of the house. It appears not only in the megara, but also upon the shafts of the tomb of Atreus (Fig. 146*d*). Then, with the coming of the northern peoples, they were covered with zigzags. In Mycenae, long afterward, between the 8th and 7th centuries B.C., a Doric temple was built upon the citadel, cutting across the areas previously covered by the megaron. Possibly, the descendants of Agamemnon and the family of Atreus, coming upon the cast-down shafts of the early or Egyptian columns, set them up again, only this time, having no interest whatever in the religion of the reversed column, they used the shaft as we find it in Greek buildings of the classical period. They set it up, in other words, with the heavy part down—without a

base—and fitted a capital to the top, but the capital, being the capital of the old reversed column, looked curiously out of place (Fig. 146*e*). Through the 200 years that followed, the Greeks refined this column until it became the perfectly balanced architectonic member of the Parthenon.

Doric and Ionic Art in Asia Minor during the Age of Anarchy. During the Trojan War, while this building was in progress at Mycenae and Tiryns, other branches of the invading Achaeans, relatives of the Dorians, conquered Phrygia and Lydia in Asia Minor, pushing their outposts through the Hittite cities to Armenia, the borders of Assyria, and southward into Palestine where they met the Egyptians. Between the 10th and 8th centuries B.C. they carved into the rocks of the hill country many tombs whose façades furnish accurate copies of their gabled wooden buildings. The tombs at Antiphellos in Lydia (Fig. 147) indicate the careful joining of the wooden beams, the use of the round pole ends as decoration, and the gabled construction, without, however, the addition of the front columns. In other cases one finds the columns attached to the front, and in still others, instead of the straight-line gabled roof,

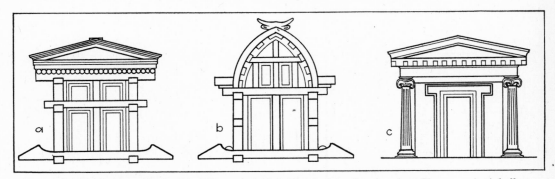

FIG. 147.—Rock-cut tombs in Asia Minor. *a*, Antiphellos; *b*, the pointed arch at Pinara; *c*, Antiphellos.

a roof with a pointed arch surmounted by the horns of a bull.

Southward, where the invading northerners met the Egyptian culture in Syria and Phoenicia or on the Island of Cyprus, a modification of the palmetto capital was affixed to the shaft of the column (Fig. 148). This capital had two spiral members coming out, instead of the echinus, under the square abacus. The spirals give a feeling of resiliency to the construction. From this Asiatic direction, then, following the path of the Phoenicians selling vases of the Cypriote style, comes the Ionic column (Fig. 148*f*) which is essentially the slender column from the Persian apadana, surmounted by the volute capital.

The Discrete Quality of Attic Architecture. It has been shown that the peculiar quality underlying all Greek pictorial design was the logical architectonic structure of the Greek vase. In like manner, the fine balance of decorative and functional parts typical of the fully developed Attic column is comparable to the elegant simplicity of the highly functional spoon or ladle in clay, found in the town of Zygouries in Corinth (Fig. 149). It was probably manufactured between 1400 and 1150 B.C. A similar refined functionalism characterized the earliest Mesopotamian pottery, culminating in the gold vase from the grave of Shub-ad. This ladle, an object of use, displays in the fine combination of its balance of parts with refined curves the factor that unified the various elements in Greek temple building. It seems almost to fit the hand. It was made for man. If the reader can appreciate its remarkable qualities, he will be able to understand the excellence of its counterpart, the Greek temple.

The Origins of Greek Literature

The Rhythmic Quality of Greek Literature

Greek literature carried much richer philosophic and social implications than did that of Egypt and Mesopotamia, and these implications were bound up with a far greater degree of lyric quality. Greek poetry has all the intimate charm and freshness of the human soul at that happy moment when it first began to substitute science and morality for superstition and dogma. Hence the consummation of Greek poetry in the Greek drama produced one of the richest social arts the world has known, comparable only to the Gothic cathedral and the romantic symphony in its inclusive grandeur. The Greek drama may be found, on analysis, to consist of the epic folk songs and lyric dances of the various Greek tribes. The great tragedies of Aeschylus combine soliloquies, half religious, half philosophical, with a rich background of martial, ceremonial, or purely rhapsodic action and the rhythm of the folk soul, incorporated in the various choral dances, each of which suggests in its movement some distinct emotional tone (Figs. 131 and 150).

Rhythm and Meter as Aids to Expression in Music and Verse. In preceding chapters it has been

FIG. 148.—Asiatic origins of the Ionic column. *a*, entrance to shrine of mother goddess, Old Babylonian, about 2000 B.C.; *b*, Hathor pillar, Egyptian, about 900 B.C. (*after Gail Habaud*); *c*, gold ornament on silver hairpin, shaft-grave, Mycenae, about 1550 B.C.; *d*, Egyptian colonnette, about 1000 B.C. (*after Prisse d'Avennes*); *e*, termination tree of life, Late Assyrian, about 1000 B.C.; *f*, capital, Megiddo, Palestine, 955 B.C.; *g*, stele in palace, Khorsabad, about 650 B.C. (*after Place*).

seen that the rhythms of work and war played their part in the development of man's first poetic and musical utterance. Not content with a primitive indulgence in poetry and song, the Greeks arranged these utterances in consistent sequences and so built up the form now known as the drama. In this process they were forced to define categorically the effects and uses of poetic and musical expression. The first stage in the eventual scientific definition was a classi-

FIG. 150.—*a*, detail, black-figured amphora showing dance with lyre (Louvre Museum); *b*, detail, François vase showing rhythm of circle dance, Theseus and Ariadne on Delos.

FIG. 149.—Clay ladle, Zygouries, Corinth, c. 1150 B.C., length about 8 inches. (*Courtesy of the Metropolitan Museum of Art.*)

fication of the varied steps used in the dances. These steps reproduced the metrical beat of the songs sung with these dances.

The Greeks noticed for the first time that, in

order to produce a rhythm, some force must intervene to divide the uninterrupted flow of time into portions. When such a force operated strongly, they called it "ictus," or "beat." The energy necessary to lift the foot in the dance they called the "arsis," and the lowering of the foot with energy, the "thesis." Sometimes the foot was lifted slowly and brought down rapidly;

at other times, the reverse. The definition of time in terms of length of beat the Greeks called "measure," in Greek, *metron*, from which we derive our word "meter." Long and short ing time, the reader must remember, were not invented until the Middle Ages, when their need was felt by a people even more musical than the Greeks.

PRINCIPAL CLASSIC FEET[1]

Names of feet	Values	Values, notes	Characteristics
Pyrrhic	short short	♪ ♪	Associated with a war dance, as in our Indian war dances
Spondee	long long	♩ ♩	Measured and slow; used for religious hymns
Iamb	short long	♪ ♩	Named after a young girl, Iambe, who poked fun at her neighbors; used for satires
Trochee (or Choree)	long short	♩ ♪	Less vivacious than the iambus, but also used to express individual feeling. The name "choree" referred to its use in choral dancing
Tribrach	short short short	♪ ♪ ♪	A laughing meter used in comedy, suggesting the jolly ha-ha-ha at the end of a good joke
Molussus	long long long	♩ ♩ ♩	Used in solemn religious melodies
Anapaest	short short long	♪ ♪ ♩	A marching foot derived from Spartan military songs; used particularly in theatrical performances as the chorus entered or left the orchestra
Dactyl	long short short	♩ ♪ ♪	"Winged-footed"; the heroic measure of the great epic poems
Amphibrach	short long short	♪ ♩ ♪	From the island of Crete
Amphimacer	long short long	♩ ♪ ♩	Also Cretan. This and the amphibrach suggest origins in animal cries, perhaps the bellowing of bulls
Bacchius	short long long	♪ ♩ ♩	Associated with the worship of Dionysus in his more solemn moments; used in the dithyrambic chorus
Antibacchius	long long short	♩ ♩ ♪	The reverse of the Bacchius, and similarly used

[1] From T. S. ORMOND, *A Study of Metre*, De La More Press, Alexander Moring, Ltd., London, England, 1903.

measures parallel, in a way, the stresses of rhythm, that is, arsis—lesser stress in raising the foot—and thesis—greater stress in putting it down (Fig. 150a).

The Kinds of Meter. The Greeks seem to have differentiated between the various measures by giving the short time a value of one, and the longer time a value twice as long, so that the long was measured by the short. Meter, a definite succession of longs and shorts, served to measure the steps of a dance or, equally, the syllables in a poem. Each combination of both long and short measures the Greeks called a *podes*, or a "foot." They recognized twelve principal types of foot, as well as innumerable subordinate ones. In the brief table, these feet have been listed, along with their values in terms of long and short marks and of quarter and eighth notes, though musical notes denot-

Greek Lyric Verse

In general, the more pronounced metrical accents arose either in marching songs or in songs having to do with the worship of the mother goddess and her associate, Dionysus. Purely lyric meter probably had its origin in animal and human cries. In the chapter on Egyptian art the term "lyric" signified a poetic utterance that embodied the poet's own personal thoughts and feelings. Such emotional expression contrasts with epic poetry, which narrates the experience of others, and descriptive poetry, which attempts to capture the movement of nature. The term "lyric" was not used by the Greeks, however, but invented during the Renaissance and applied to the poetry that the Greeks were thought to have sung to the accompaniment of the lyre. The

Greeks themselves divided this type of poetry into three classes, which they called the "elegiac," the "iambic," and the "melic," depending on the arrangement, number, and quality of the different feet in a line.

Probable Origin of the Greek Lyric in the Linos Song. All primitive people have the tendency to create lyric or self-expressive poetry accompanied by the dance, in connection with the formal ceremonies of life. The phenomenon of birth, the rite of initiation into manhood, the wedding ceremony, and the death or departure for the land of the shades, all inspire to special poetic utterance that is neither epic nor simply descriptive. The Greeks called this type of verse the "Linos song." The term "Linos," arose from a personification of the departing summer as a youth who left his friends with sadness for whom the refrain "Ai Linon" was sung.[1] This sadness was not the same as the grief of the final departure at death, but rather a kind of preparation for that greater sorrow. In the description of the shield of Achilles a vineyard is depicted in which maidens and others gathered grapes while "in the midst of them a boy made pleasant music on a clear-toned viol, and sang thereto a sweet Linos-song with delicate voice; while the rest with feet falling together kept time with the music and song."[2] Such songs early furnished the basis for Chinese as well as Greek lyric poetry. In our own cultural existence something like the Linos song finds expression in the work songs of the Western cowhands and the Negroes.

Elegiac Verse. Since we have spoken of the Linos song as one with slight accents of sorrow, let us turn next to the elegy. To the Greeks the name did not necessarily mean a poem of death but was applied to any verse composed in an elegiac couplet; that is, with a line of dactylic hexameter—six-footed—followed by the so-called pentameter, or five-footed, line. It usually took as its subject matter a celebration of warlike exploits, an expression of personal philosophy, or a description of the simple pleasures of life, and was recited to the accompaniment of the flute, an instrument said to be of Phrygian or Asiatic origin. There is a wide range of these subjects. One of the earliest of the elegies, written by an Ionian Greek, Calinus of Ephesus (700 B.C.), was obviously a bardic exhortation to his fellow citizens to battle against the invading Persians.

Symonds's translation of an elegy by Mimnermus of Smyrna, an Ionian Greek who lived near the end of the 7th century B.C., voices a mourning for departed joys. The spirit of youth and love has deserted an old man, now too feeble to appreciate the embraces of his beloved Nanno, to whom the poem is addressed.

What's life of pleasure wanting Aphrodite?
    When to the gold-haired goddess cold am I,
When love and love's soft gifts no more delight me,
    Nor stolen dalliance, then I fain would die!
Ah! fair and lovely bloom the flowers of youth;
    On men and maids they beautifully smile:
But soon comes doleful eld, who, void of ruth,
    Indifferently afflicts the fair and vile;
Then cares wear out the heart; old eyes forlorn
    Scarce reck the very sunshine to behold—
Unloved by youths, of every maid the scorn—
    So hard a lot God lays upon the old.[3]

The Elegiac Epigram. Our modern conception of the elegy has arisen from the fact that many of the later Greek poets and philosophers used elegiac verse for brief inscriptions of a dedicatory nature, or for expressions of love such as today we find on birthday cards and valentines. Thus this style is particularly fitting for monuments in honor of the dead. In the 10th century of the Christian Era the late Greeks of the Byzantine Empire collected many of the elegiac epigrams in an anthology, *The Garland of Flowers*, and it is from this source that we have the famous epitaph of Simonides, written at Thermopylae:

---

[1] See discussion Chap. V, p. 142.
[2] *The Iliad of Homer*, translated by Lang, Leaf and Myers, pp. 344–345, The Macmillan Company, New York, 1929.
[3] Translated by J. A. Symonds, Sr.

Go, passers-by, and Sparta tell
Obedient to her laws we fell.

Iambic Verse. This form, which usually consisted of six iambic feet, was used for biting satiric verse by Archilochus, a poet living in the 7th century B.C. From this association, iambic meter during the later development of the drama came to suggest a satirical passage. In most of the verse of Archilochus, a forerunner of the Cynic philosophers, one finds this bitterness, caused, it is said, by a disappointment in youthful love, which the poet never outgrew. Only in the following poem does Archilochus rise to lyric heights.

Tossed on a sea of troubles, Soul, my Soul,
Thyself do thou control
And to the weapons of advancing foes
A stubborn breast oppose;
Undaunted 'mid the hostile might
Of squadrons burning for the fight.

Thine be no boasting when the victor's crown
Wins the deserved renown;
Thine no dejected sorrow when defeat
Would urge a base retreat:
Rejoice in joyous things—nor overmuch
Let grief thy bosom touch
'Midst evil, and still bear in mind,
How changeful are the ways of humankind.[1]

Melic Verse. What we today know as lyric poetry was further divided into two other kinds: the melic, which was individualistic and which probably led, in the drama, to the desire for the individual performances of an actor; and the choral, which was developed by the Dorians of Sparta.

In the melic verse as recited, the rise and fall of the voice, accompanied by the music of the lyre, created what has ever since been called the "melody." A melic verse is today known as a song; the melic poet was a ballad singer. According to legend, his instrument, the lyre, was invented by Hermes, the messenger of the gods, but such a lyre had only four strings. The ancients believed that the seven-stringed lyre was invented by Terpander, a poet of Lesbos who lived around 660 B.C.

Two poets of Lesbos merit particular attention. The first, Alcaeus, inventor of the Alcaic stanza, was a wanderer exiled to Egypt. Most of his life, if we may judge from the fragments of poems surviving, was employed in praising Dionysus as the god of wine and forgetfulness. Of all the poets of Lesbos, however, by far the most famous was Sappho, a citizen of the town of Mytilene and a lady of noble birth. All direct contemporary evidence tends to show that she was a kindly wife and loving mother, but like Alcaeus she was driven into exile and fled to Dorian Sicily.

The particular form of verse that Sappho is said to have invented appears in the translation by Symonds of her "Prayer to Aphrodite" —Aphrodite, the goddess of love and marriage.

Glittering-throned, undying Aphrodite,
Wile-weaving daughter of high Zeus, I pray thee
Tame not my soul with heavy woe, dread mistress,
   Nay, nor with Anguish!
But hither come, if ever erst of old time
Thou didst incline and listenedst to my crying
And from thy father's palace down descending
   Camest with golden
Chariot yoked: thee fair swift-flying sparrows
Over dark earth with multitudinous fluttering
Pinion on pinion, through middle ether
   Down from heaven hurried.[2]

Sappho's poems have served as lamps to kindle similar lyric fires in the lives of Western poets since the Middle Ages, and their beautiful combinations of melody and peace appear again and again throughout the entire history of dramatic poetry.

A GIRL IN LOVE

Oh, my sweet mother, 'tis in vain,
   I cannot weave as once I wove,
So wildered is my heart and brain
   With thinking of that youth I love.[3]

This theme appears again, greatly elaborated, as Margarete's song in Goethe's *Faust*.

The Dorian Choral Lyric. Dorian Sparta, renowned for her powers in war and for her increasingly narrow conception of patriotism,

---

[1] Translated by William Hay.　　[2] Translated by J. A. Symonds, Sr.　　[3] Translated by Thomas Moore.

celebrated in her poetry the Olympian gods, local heroes, and her victories in games or in war. Alcman, one of the earliest Dorian poets, danced and sang his poetry with the help of a chorus and arranged his odes so that the first stanza, called the "strophe," was accompanied by a movement of dancers toward the right. The second stanza, with a movement to the left, was called "antistrophe," a form of verse already discussed in connection with Mesopotamian music and poetry. This formulation of dance movements in terms of poetic stanzas corresponds to the placing of bands of metrical decoration on the Greek vase. Stesichorus, another Dorian, from Sicily, added to each strophe a third stanza, called the "epode." This was sung while the dancers stood at rest.

The form of the ode is made clear in the famous "First Pythian Ode" by Pindar, greatest of the Dorian poets, who created most of his poems in honor of victors at the games.

Strophe

O golden lyre,
Apollo's, dark-haired Muses' joint heirloom,
    Alert for whom
The dancer's footstep listens, and the choir
    Of singers wait the sound,
    Beginning of the round
    Of festal joy, whene'er thy quivering strings
    Strike up a prelude to their carolings.
Thou slakest the lanced bolt of quenchless fire;
Yea, drooped each wing that through the aether
    sweeps,
    Upon his sceptre Zeus's eagle sleeps.

Antistrophe

    The bird-king crowned!
The while thou sheddest o'er his beaked head bowed
    A darkling cloud,
Sweet seal of the eyelids—and in dreamful swound
    His rippling back and sides
    Heave with thy music's tides;
    Thou bidst impetuous Ares lay apart
His keen-edged spear, and soothe with sleep his heart;
Thou launchest at the breasts of gods, and bound
    As by a spell, they own thy lulling power,
    Latiodes and the deep-zoned Muses' dower.[1]

The music for this ode, which still exists, will be discussed under the subject of Greek music.

[1] Translated by Newcomer.

The Poetic Development of the Greek Drama

Arion and the Dithyrambic Chorus. The final stage, the union of the Dorian choral music and the individualistic Dionysiac inspiration, was attained in the lyrics of Arion. He combined the two in a hymn to Dionysus; the dithyramb. His chorus, which included as many as fifty people, called for particular ballet training. It is not known exactly what changes Arion brought about in the patterns of the dance, but they were significant enough so that antiquity accorded to him the honor of being called the inventor of the movement that made possible the tragedy.

The Epic Hero Tales. Of the many component parts of the rich Greek drama, the heroic epic narratives held an inherent dramatic kernel in that their subject matter dealt with human character acting under the stress of external circumstances. These circumstances were created by two warring groups of deities, each more or less symbolic of the matriarchal and patriarchal folk components gradually fusing during the Age of Anarchy to form the Hellenic, or Greek, mind. Although only two epics, the *Iliad* and the *Odyssey*, are generally known, actually there were many cycles of heroic narrative poems in that dancing meter, the dactylic hexameter, which has one long beat followed by two short beats. These cycles were sung by wandering bards to the accompaniment of the harp or the lyre, instruments imported with the pattern of the epic from Mesopotamia or the Hittite cities of Asia Minor. The stories arose between the time of the destruction of the Cretan palace and the fall of Troy—that is, between the early part of the 12th century and the 8th century B.C. The *Iliad* and the *Odyssey* are known to have been either revised or first written down in the 6th century under the rule of the tyrant Pisistratus in Athens. It was at that time and under the same beneficent despot that the various component parts of the drama were brought together. These two epics and their less-known rivals gave rise to the plots used by Aeschylus and the later Greek dramatic poets.

One of the stories had to do with the wars of Thebes, a city that long retained its matriarchal worship. This probably gave rise to Aeschylus's drama *The Seven against Thebes*. Another story had for its theme the fateful judgment of the Trojan prince, Paris, which led to his abduction of Helen, wife of the king of Sparta, and indirectly to the destruction of Troy. This tale, the *Cypria*, came from the bard Stasinus of Cyprus.

Another story, in four parts, which links the contest for the arms of Achilles to the taking of Troy, is said to have been written down by Lesches of Mytilene and was known as the "Little Iliad." The *Nostoi*, or home-coming of the Greek chieftains, was sung by Aegias of Troezen, and the *Sack of Ilium*, by Arctinus from the town of Miletus in Ionia. A story about the Amazon queen Penthesilea, also by Arctinus, was called the *Aethiopis*, and tells what happened from the end of the *Iliad* to the death of Achilles. In all these, the battles between invading Dorian tribes and the followers of matriarchial cults contributed a favorite subject for the earliest Greek poets. Probably back of each cycle of poems lay some real historic event, so that the destruction of Troy, called in Greek the "Iliupersis," which forms the body of the *Iliad*, probably accumulated elements from the final destruction of the Cretan palace by northern wanderers and the expedition of Agamemnon and his fellow Achaeans against the small town of Troy. The *Odyssey* probably narrated the travels of a real man; the home-comings of the Greek chieftains have given us such a story as the *Agamemnon* of Aeschylus.

The Social Significance of the Iliad and the Odyssey. It is assumed that one man, the blind Homer, who lived around 800 B.C., collected the fragments of these hero tales and swept them together from his lyre in the music of

two mighty masterworks. In them he tells how Paris, the son of Priam, King of Troy, carried off Helen, wife of Menelaus, King of Sparta. Besought by Menelaus, Agamemnon, Lord of Tiryns and Mycenae, with many other princes of Greece, among them Odysseus of Ithaca, besieged Troy for ten years. Having finally captured the city through the stratagem of Odysseus, the Greeks flashed the news from mountain top to mountain top until it at last reached Mycenae. Then Odysseus, sailing homeward, circumnavigated the Mediterranean, presaging the colonial glory of the Greek city-states.

Great-hearted men were Greek warriors who fought and spoke with the fury of the tempest.

. . . but Hector shining with fire on all sides, leaped on the throng and fell upon them, as when beneath the storm-clouds a fleet wave reared of the winds falls on a swift ship, and she is all hidden with foam, and the dread blast of the wind roars against the sail, and the sailors fear, and tremble in their hearts, . . . even so the spirit was torn in the breasts of the Achaians.[1]

Such word pictures as the above not only added their element of richness to the dramatic performance, but passages that depict objects from the Golden Age of the lost Utopian Atlantis also challenged the vase painters, goldsmiths, and sculptors to surpass these masterpieces. The description of the dancing groups on the shield of Achilles has the same lyric quality as the Parthenon frieze by Phidias; in like manner, the story of the Iliupersis has the restrained, monumental qualities of the later paintings by masters like Douris and Polygnotus.

Furthermore, the character sketches of heroes such as Nestor, Agamemnon, Achilles, and Odysseus portrayed real people rather than supernatural beings like Gilgamesh. Even the Greek counterpart of Gilgamesh, the demigod Herakles, appealed to the Greeks because of his human qualities. These characterizations gave strength to the drama of Aeschylus.

The Cultural Origins of Greek Drama. The Greek epic, like the Egyptian Book of the Dead,

[1] *The Iliad of Homer*, translated by Lang, Leaf, and Myers, p. 378, The Macmillan Company, New York, 1929.

was a voyage of the soul, even in the case of Odysseus, into the very realm of the shades. Like the Mesopotamian Gilgamesh epic, it tells of the earthly trials of an ennobled being embattled by fate, and of the fickle goddess of love. And yet the Greek epic differs from and rises above the others, in that it presents the stories of living men who are in some respects better than the very gods they are forced to serve.

In the discussion of the Egyptian religion it has been pointed out that the ritual symbolizing the death, partition, and resurrection of Osiris offered an opportunity for a religious dramatic representation, such as was later to grow into the Christian office of the Mass. In the Mesopotamian religious rites, two stories, one dealing with the underworld sojourn of Ishtar and the other with the death and bewailing of the young beloved, Tammuz-Adonis, became the Linos song, half sung, half danced, and acted by the votaries of Ishtar. In the union of all these discrete elements into one well-rounded performance lies the great contribution of the Greek dramatists.

The Scholarly Theories as to the Origin of Greek Drama. The many scholars who have attempted to show that the Greek drama developed from one or another of a number of folk customs have performed invaluable service in laying bare all the origins. Early scholars were led astray by Aristotle, who in his otherwise valuable analysis of the drama in the fragmentary *Poetics* tried to derive all dramatic poetry from one source—the dithyrambic satyr choruses of the Peloponnesus. Aristotle also did later critics a real disservice in contrasting what he calls "dramatic" poetry with epic poetry. Actually, as we shall see, the dramatic includes epic verse as well as lyric, iambic, choral, and a host of other forms.

Pickard-Cambridge, in his *Dithyramb, Tragedy and Comedy*, has made a valuable contribution by showing that Greek drama did not arise from purely ritual observance at the tombs of the civic heroes or from the fertility rites. Analyzing the comedies of Aristophanes, Pickard-Cambridge shows that each has about ten different types of poetic utterance. As will be seen in the study of a play by Aeschylus, each type of poetry with its own peculiar rhythm must have produced in the audience a different emotional tone. This observation in turn leads to the discovery of some general laws concerning dramatic values which will aid in judging the excellence of such a modern technique as that of the motion picture. More than any other dramatic form since the time of the Greeks, the motion picture depends for its effectiveness on rhythmical patterns.

The Origin of Tragedy. The meaning of tragedy seems to be inextricably bound up with the idea of struggle, defeat, death, and resurrection. Great tragedy in the course of its development usually shows the body overcome but the spirit rewarded and triumphant. The dramatist may picture rewards as achieved upon earth or as achieved in a spiritual realm. The Greeks pictured both types of rewards, but Greek tragedy differs essentially from the more primitive religious forms in placing vastly more emphasis on the psychological aspect of the struggle than on a contemplation of the goal.

Greek tragedy found its inspiration in the god Dionysus, who with his wine changed men into strange shapes and brought out the inner truth of their being. He it was who, because of his intimate knowledge of their innermost secrets, enchanted the women and made them run after him in choral procession. The very son of the mother goddess, he partook of the womanly wisdom of Ishtar. On the ancient harp of Shub-ad from Sumerian Ur (Fig. 119, Chap. V) we saw the first Dionysiac procession, perhaps an ancient drama. In the panel above, the hero Gilgamesh strangles two lions. During the desperate moment when the human soul thus overcomes the animal forces in its own nature bringing out of the disordered mind some new vision of social unity—some new truth—a great drama is brought to birth. Out of Mesopotamia and Palestine, then, through the half-Greek, half-Hittite country of Phrygia, came the idea of inward struggle essential to the worship of Dionysus. To the accompaniment of the shrill-voiced flute, his votaries, the cory-bantes, danced and sang the joy of the spring, the autumn Linos song of sorrow, and the all-revealing magic of the wine.

During the Age of Anarchy, the satyric choral dance with strophe and antistrophe, like the song of David, was danced by people dressed as were those on the harp of Shub-ad—the satyrs with horses' ears and tails, the fauns with goats' hoofs and horns, and the sileni like the scorpion man with the apotropaic face. This choral dance was also used by Arion, who developed it in the northern Peloponnesus un-til one, Pratinas, created a true dramatic form by adding a speaking part for the leader, who was called the "choryphaeus." Pratinas brought this new creation from the town of Phlius to Athens, where during the latter part of the 6th century B.C. it developed into the satyr play or satire.

Union of the Linos Song and the Hero Tale. In the meantime, probably in the village of Icaria, the more solemn Linos songs that dealt with death and sorrow became linked with the stories of Dionysus and gradually expanded to tell of the fate of some of the local heroes, in tales such as were being sung by the Homeric bards. Epigones of Sicyon, the first tragic poet, linked a tragic chorus with such a recital at the behest of the tyrant Cleisthenes. From hero stories, which were called dramas, Thespis created something corresponding to the satyr play with its choryphaeus by adding an actor who could take the part of the hero. Then the tragic choruses and the satyr plays were put together on one bill and played for the spring festival at Athens in honor of Dionysus.

Thus at last the two sides of the nature of Dionysus—the solemn, godlike aspect and the animal, grotesque element—expressed in the choral lyrics of Arion and the Linos-song hero tales with their epic backgrounds, made pos-sible the supremely noble dramatic perform-ance found in the works of Aeschylus and Sophocles. Early in the 5th century B.C. the literary form was improved, first by the intro-duction of a prologue of set speeches delivered by a chorus leader, who became a separate actor, next by the introduction of a second actor and a stage under Aeschylus, and finally by the introduction of a third actor and scenery by Sophocles.

The Origins of Comedy. The origins of comedy were as diverse as those of tragedy. Many of the elementary comic situations were first devised and played in the Dorian lands of Sicily and southern Italy. The comic or grotesque spirit in dramatic literature bears the same relation-ship to the more unified tragedy and satire as does the Gorgon grotesque to the figure of a Greek goddess. The intent of the ancient com-edy at first seems to have less of the aspect of clownishness and in the hands of Aristophanes developed definite social goals. It then took on the unified form of the already developed trag-edy and left buffoonery to the satyr play.

The Place of Music in Greek Life

The diversity of rhythms and scales used by the many highly individualistic Greek tribes was so great that the theorists of Greco-Roman times listed fifteen elaborate scales, or modes, each of which had eighteen notes. To make the matter a bit more complicated, one ancient writer, Alypius, recognized forty-five different scales of eighteen notes. Only one known race of people today has a more complicated formal system of music—the Hindus. Since authorities by no means agree on what constituted the Greek scales, one can only surmise a few general principles, based upon historic evidence, which give a general notion of Greek music—a notion at least compatible with what is known of the development of the other arts.

The Archaic or Formative Period. Music in the primitive sense of the term—that is, without notation—accompanied every activity of Greek life during the formative period. Work in the field and on shipboard, the various festival

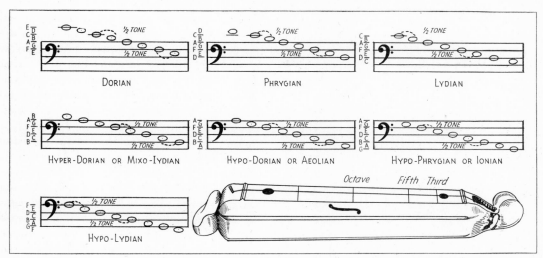

FIG. 151.—Table of Greek modes. Below, right, monochord from mountains of Kentucky.

dances, the epic narrative of Homer, the philosophy of Hesiod and Heraclitus, all were performed to music. Each of the poems discussed not only had its distinctive rhythmical measure but its musical accompaniment on the flute or lyre in separate scales associated with the homeland of its composer. The Olympic games, instituted in 776 B.C., opened with blasts on a war trumpet called the "phormynx." Such instruments were used also for signaling from place to place. Women played upon the lyre or the flute for a household diversion; the old men of the family handed down ballads, connecting them with their ancestors who led Achaean tribes from the north; and the shepherd boys in the hills played upon the syrinx, a set of reed pipes dedicated to Pan, the spirit of vitality in nature (see Fig. 50d, Chap. III).

The Instruments. The philosophic poetry and first exercises in mathematics were sung to the accompaniment of the lyre. The early Greek philosopher-mathematician, Pythagoras, made music the very spiritual center of his philosophy. He invented the monochord (Fig. 151, right), which was essentially a one-string lyre—that is, a string stretched over a sounding board with a movable bridge. When the bridge stood under the center of the string, the note sounded

was what we today call eight tones above the note that sounded when the string was open. If the bridge was placed two-thirds of the way along the string, the note sounded five tones above the original; if three-quarters of the way, four tones from the original. Now, if four monochords with these different bridges were all struck at once, the resulting sound made a perfect chord, the effect of which was pleasing. It is said that Pythagoras invented a lyre embodying this principle. Whether that is true or not, the Greeks of the 6th century B.C. had begun to devise a means for measuring the distance between tones in mathematical terms. Since the students learned the beginnings of mathematics along with the dance and the declamation of poetry, no schoolroom, as shown in vase painting, is without a pair of flutes, a lyre, or even cymbals hanging upon the wall alongside trophies and a birch rod. From these vases, from one or two actual instruments found in manuscripts and upon stone walls, as well as from the work of early artistic critics, one can picture with some degree of accuracy the development of Greek music. During the formative period, there were at least three instruments—the lyre, the cithara, and the double flute or aulos (Figs. 126 and 133). The lyre (Fig. 150), as shown in the hands of Alcaeus and Sappho, had seven strings—enough to play an octave.

The Dorian Lyre. The legendary, earliest Greek scale is thought to have been a simple downward sequence of four notes, called the "Dorian tetrachord." These notes were probably the same as those from E above middle C, down to B below. Olympus, a flute player of the 6th century B.C., supposedly added four notes—the so-called tetrachord of Olympus—which moved down the scale from A to F. The entire sequence of eight notes was called the "Doric heptachord" or "Dorian mode," the type of music to which Homer's *Iliad* or the great philosophic hymns of Hesiod were sung.

As each locality had its own native instruments and as no two city-states seem to have had the same scale, one can see that there must have been many types of music for the art critics to extol or criticize. Plato thought that the Lydian mode, a little lower than the Dorian and probably coinciding with our major scale of C, was highly sensuous, perhaps because it was usually associated with the worship of the mother goddess and played upon the flute.[1]

The Double Flute, or Aulos. The double flute, or aulos (Fig. 133), is thought to have been introduced by Olympus, who came from Phrygia. This instrument probably used a movable reed, like that of the clarinet or oboe, fastened inside the two bulbs near the mouthpiece. The higher of the two pipes, a fixed tone, blew continuously as the aulode (aulos player) played a melody down the scale on the other pipe. This instrument, the primitive ancestor of the bagpipes, usually accompanied the violent dances of the worshipers of Dionysus, as well as the iambics and elegies.

The Scales of the Cithara. The cithara (Fig. 126), a larger, more completely developed form of the lyre, was an instrument capable of being tuned in several modes. It is possible that the handle of the crossbar on which the strings were

fastened could be turned slightly, tightening all of them, so that with one simple action the player could change from the lower, Lydian mode to the higher, Dorian. The poetic passages of the Greek drama called for different rhythms and therefore for differing modes. By the time of Plato, nine scales or modes were recognized, of which the Dorian, Lydian, and Phrygian, with perhaps the mixolydian and Aeolian or hypodorian, were considered fundamental. The hyper-Phrygian, a mode from Asia Minor also called the "Ionian," accompanied certain types of poetry. Two other modes, the hyper-Lydian and hypolydian were also recognized. The brief table (Fig. 151) shows how to play these modes upon the piano by using the white keys. When a simple melody such as "My Country, 'tis of Thee" is played in the Lydian mode (our scale of C), it sounds natural to us. When it is played in any of the other modes, it sounds Greek.

Summary

The diverse origins of Greek art traced in this chapter account for those rich associational values that constitute a perennial appeal to a wide variety of people. Three chief cultural influences united to create (1) the style of the Minoan palaces, (2) the Doric and Ionic aspects of Greek art, and (3) the Attic style. These influences came from prehistoric European and West Mediterranean areas where people lived on a paleolithic and neolithic level, from Egypt, and from Mesopotamia.

The European prehistoric cultures contributed a fresh physioplastic outlook and technomorphic designs, particularly the spiral band. From the Egyptians came a geometricized formal style. The Mesopotamian people transmitted compositions in which natural forms—plant, animal, and human—were rendered in curvilinear designs of great vitality. In Crete,

[1] The mixolydian mode, a whole-toned scale reaching from E to E, was sacred to the sun-god Helios-Apollo; the Phrygian, to Zeus; and the Dorian, to Ares, the god of war. As each god was represented by a planet, the Pythagoreans appropriately spoke of "the music of the spheres."

the European and Mesopotamian motifs combined in the remarkably fine Kamares and palace pottery. All three styles united in the colored mural compositions as well as in the sculpture. All were slightly dominated by a playful physioplastic tendency.

Following the dispersion of the Minoan style, as the northern Celto-Germanic invaders occupied the Aegean area, the prevailing artistic influence in the southwestern Dorian territory gradually became that of the Egyptians. The Mesopotamian influence dominated in the northeastern Ionian towns. During the 8th and 7th centuries B.C., Athenian potters and sculptors arranged the human figure with a strict geometric plan as a basis for composition. Gradually they brought more and more life into their portrayal of action, illustrating the eternal struggle between heroes associated with the old underworld deities and those descended from the new Olympian sky-gods. Eventually, in the 6th century B.C., Dorian and Ionian elements united in pictorial and sculptural compositions which surpassed, in richness and strength, the work of the Minoan artists.

Accompanying this development in the graphic and plastic arts went a similar development in poetry and music. The delight of the Greeks in the dance rhythms of their poetry combined with the ever-present tendency to better their creations in contests of artistic skill. The fresh, human, psychological interest of the Greek stories made their productions more interesting than those of either the Egyptians or the Mesopotamians. Of primary importance in the development of poetry and music was the manner in which the Greeks dramatically expressed their emotions in different types of meters, each meter being particularly appropriate to the feeling it strove to express. A knowledge of the various types of Greek poetry, with their characteristic meters, is advisable for an understanding of European verse and dance.

Starting with Doric hero songs and Ionian Linos songs, the Greek poets created the Greek drama which eventually became associated with the worship of Dionysus. Music contributed to this development. Instruments, scales, and melodies, accompanying all the discrete styles, retained their individual characteristics, so that each type of scale or mode symbolized the qualities of the deity or folk with which it had been connected.

The remarkable unifying creative power of the Greek mind becomes apparent only after a study of the diversity of formative influences underlying the magnificent creations of the Attic style during and just after the Golden Age of Pericles. The universally admired dramas of Aeschylus and Sophocles, the Parthenon, the sculptures of Phidias grew from the rough ground, just replowed here. In them the idea of beauty as a significant factor in art reached its fullest visible definition.

Bibliography

BAIKIE, J.: *Sea Kings of Crete*, A. & C. Black, Ltd., London, 1920.

MYRES, J. L.: *Who Were the Greeks?* University of California Press, Berkeley, Calif., 1930.

SWINDLER, M. H.: *Ancient Painting*, Yale University Press, New Haven, Conn., 1929.

WEIGALL, ARTHUR: *Sappho of Lesbos* (novel), Garden City Publishing Co., Inc., Garden City, N. Y., 1932.

Recordings

Greek Dance, Columbia 56015 F, 56031 F.

Greek Rhapsody, Greek Record Co., A 512.

CHAPTER VII

Greek Art—Social, Political, and Philosophical Backgrounds

They told me, Heracleitus, they told me you were
    dead:
They brought me bitter news to hear and bitter tears
    to shed.
I wept, as I remembered, how often you and I
Had tired the sun with talking and sent him down
    the sky.
And now that thou art lying, my dear old Carian
    guest,
A handful of gray ashes, long, long ago at rest,
Still are thy pleasant voices, thy nightingales, awake,
For Death, he taketh all away, but them he cannot
    take.

"Elegiac Epigram"[1]

THE PREVIOUS chapter showed the diverse origins of Hellenic art. In the 6th century B.C., two opposing tendencies, usually called the Doric and the Ionic, united to form one of the two great original art styles of the Western world. The beginnings of scientific inquiry and free artistic invention already discernible in the 8th century grew rapidly, bringing a freedom from the Egyptian superstitious belief in permanence and the Mesopotamian reliance upon force and power. The primitive fetishistic religions gave way to an aesthetic anthropomorphism and eventually led to the ethical concept of a spiritualized deity, who united the attributes of revealed truth, man-like reason, and beauty. To understand this significant change in the human mind, one must study the social and political backgrounds of Attic thought and the beginnings of that mental exercise which the athletic Greeks called *philosophia*.

Social and Political Backgrounds of Attic Art

Historically, the Age of the Thalassocrats, or seafolk, which was one of anarchy, gradually gave way to an era in which a number of city-states, including the Dorian cities of Sparta, Corinth, and Thebes, and Ionian Athens, capital of Attica, began to approximate more or less democratic forms of government. These city-states were at first ruled by feudal lords who acted in council—a form of government called an "oligarchy." Athens was the first to outgrow oligarchy and to reach a condition where every citizen had an equal voice in electing or banning state officials. Her lawgivers, such as Draco and Solon, first codified, then equalized the laws, thus giving the lower classes, including craftsmen and merchants but excepting the lowest stratum, which was made up of slaves, civic rights approximating those of the

---

[1] This epigram by Callimachus dates from c. 260 B.C. The translation is by W. J. Cory.

warrior knights who claimed descent from the old half-mythical heroes. This new freedom of opportunity for all brought with it an art that seems more realistic than the best of the Cretan palace styles or the works of artists under Akhenaten in Egypt.

The Artistic Supremacy of Athens. Two cities, Corinth and Athens, early became rivals in trade and sent their long ships, laden with pottery, oils, and wine, to colonies and cities in every part of the Mediterranean. In the quality of their artistic wares they surpassed their Syrian competitor, Phoenicia. In time, the Athenians, combining astute business ability with sharp political practice, brought Athens to the headship of the Ionic states, making her a bulwark against Asiatic conquerors from Persia on one side and the military despotism of Sparta on the other. The art goods of Corinth were then put out of the market to remain eclipsed until Athens and Sparta had worn themselves out in useless wars, and until Alexander—Macedonian dictator—had overcome all three. Before this denouement, Athens stood as the center of the Hellenic world and for a short space of time during the 5th century B.C. supported a score of artists whose names have become synonymous with the idea of beauty and the classical style. This brief period was the so-called Golden Age of Pericles (Fig. 152).

The Athenian, or Attic, style achieved its great unity between 448 and 429 B.C., at the time of Pericles, the first great democratic statesman of history. Attic art runs through two stages of development, which must be understood if one is to grasp the remarkable unity it achieved in the hands of the sculptor Phidias, the architects Ictinus and Callicrates, the painters Brygos and Polygnotus, and the dramatic poet Aeschylus.

The Democratic Backgrounds of Periclean Art. The condition of freedom or servitude under which the artist works, by emphasizing his propensity to conservatism or experimental invention, inevitably influences his style. The artists of the time of Akhenaten and of the Late

Minoan period created with a *joie d'esprit* unknown to the dynastic artists of Egypt and Mesopotamia. In Athens, religious, political, and aesthetic discussion reached a degree of

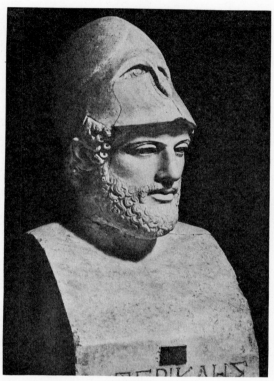

Fig. 152.—Pericles, after Cresilas, c. 440–430 B.C. Larger than life size, Vatican Rome. (*Courtesy of Lesch-Carnegie.*)

freedom never before known and from this spirit of free inquiry rose the great art of the Periclean Age. With this in mind, let us examine briefly some of the institutions that made such democracy possible.

It can be said with justice that, during the last days of Pericles, Athens was the most democratic city in the world. At that time the city had 120,000 inhabitants. Although democratic privileges did not extend to all classes, the free inhabitants—excepting women, children, and resident farmers—were for the most part eligible to vote. About 30,000 of the men above the age of eighteen were entitled to meet in the *ecclesia*, or Athenian assembly, and could partake in discussion while casting their votes upon the questions of the hour. The most important selection the assembly was required to make was that of the ten *strategoi*, or generals, who

League, which paid her a large annual tribute for the protection her fleet afforded against piracy. She also held certain state properties, such as the silver mines at Laurium, which

Fig. 153.—The Acropolis, Athens. Chief buildings erected by Pericles with public funds (restoration by Lambert, 1877). Lower right, circular Odeon; upper right-center, the Parthenon; upper left, Erectheum and monumental statue of Athena; below Athena, ceremonial gateway of Propylaeum; left of Propylaeum, library and picture gallery; right of Propylaeum, small Temple of Victory (Nike Apteros). Other buildings and monuments erected by leading citizens. (*Courtesy of Institute of France, from Monuments antiques, by d'Espouy.*)

not only served as commanders of the united forces of army and navy but also had charge of foreign diplomacy and the reception of ambassadors from neighboring states. Besides the assembly, another representative body, the *boule*, or council, was selected by lot from the ten Attic tribes. Its fifty members were called elders. Since citizens became eligible for membership at the age of thirty, it would seem that the ancient Greeks reached maturity sooner than do 20th-century Americans. The chief functions of the council were the framing of laws to be passed upon by the assembly and the disbursement of public funds.

Governmental Control of Finances and the Effect on Art. The public funds controlled by the council were derived from various sources. Athens numbered many allied cities in the Delian

produced a steady revenue. Finally, she imposed tariff duties and sales taxes, as well as a residence tax on foreigners.

Just as the government was a communal affair, so artistic undertakings exacted contributions from all. The chief citizens of patriotic mind were forced by custom to pay for many of the games, festivals, and religious processions, and to subscribe to public-works projects. The theatrical festivals particularly were supported by citizens called "choragi," each of whom paid some dramatist to train his chorus for a performance.

The Athenian Use of Leisure in the Development of Philosophy and Art. If the Athenian government expected much of its citizens, it accorded them numerous benefits in return. Civil and military services were paid from public funds.

From government coffers, also, came bonuses and pensions, which were granted to the poor as well as to orphans of soldiers killed in the wars. In addition to enjoying financial security,

power between revolutionary democratic forces and the conservative oligarchical party, stands as a work of governmental art, and as such it has been studied by all succeeding democratic

Fig. 154.—The Acropolis today. Right, civic theater of Dionysus; lower left, Roman theater of Herodes Atticus on site of Odeon; upper left, Propylaeum; upper center, Parthenon and Erectheum; between Parthenon and Erectheum, foundations of Hekatompedon, a council hall or temple built on the site of ancient megaron of the Mycenaean kings of Athens. (*Courtesy of Victor Allen.*)

the Athenians employed an abundance of slave labor.

As a result of these financial and social advantages, the citizens of the Golden Age had leisure—leisure to enjoy art and the argumentative mental exercise that eventually created a philosophy of artistic living—and excess energy for building the Parthenon. In the Roman era, as in our own, that energy might have been used to create ostentatious dwellings, great private estates, and still larger fortunes. The Greeks, apparently, looked upon such self-glorification as dangerous and abnormal. Usually, citizens who showed any sign of it were banished to other countries (Fig. 153).

The political construction of Athens during the Golden Age of Pericles, with its balance of

governments. The qualities of political leadership displayed by the art-loving Pericles should not be minimized, however. In the troubled years following his death, Athens found to her sorrow that more than anything else she needed his intelligent guidance (Fig. 154).

The Weaknesses of Athenian Democracy. A paucity of competent leaders, coupled with the forces of reaction within the Athenian state eventually caused the downfall of the great city. The men who succeeded Pericles lacked the foresight necessary to pursue a balanced international policy. The art of politics depended too much upon dialectic and not enough upon a sound program. Eventually, Athens was embroiled in a series of wars with Sparta, which so weakened all the Greek city-states that they fell easy prey to the half-barbarian dictators, Philip and Alexander of Macedon. It is as though today democratic countries such as the United States, Great Britain, and Canada— should decide to fight one another for colonies in the Orient. As a result, they would soon be mastered by some dictatorial or undemocratic nation.

Despite the loss of Athenian freedom in the late 5th century B.C. and despite successive generations of tyrannical governors, both Greek and Roman, Athens long remained the center of world culture. The Athenians, conquered politically, became, as slaves, the schoolteachers of the ancient world. In the 4th century, however, their civic building lost its fine, simple unity, their sculpture lost its inner power. As slaves, the Greeks then lived in fear and fantasy. They could dream and act, but they could no longer create in the free style of free men.

The Poetic Beginnings of Philosophy

In the preceding chapters we traced the religious background of folklore and myth from whose rich associational patterns the subject matter of the arts arose. In Athens at the time of Pericles the mass of common people still believed in two great groups of deities—the Olympians, ruled by Zeus, and the earth-goddesses, led by Demeter. These deities, however, had become so humanized and familiar that they were only half believed in and were taken seriously only in times of trouble. In their stead, to supply an explanation of human action and natural appearance, the Greeks began to substitute the art of philosophy. As this pursuit influenced the entire pattern of the Greek mind for the three centuries following and as its chief concepts had an important place in the development of medieval and Renaissance arts, it warrants study as forming part of the social background out of which the artist created.

The Philosopher as Poet. Plato, who with Akhenaten holds a place in history as one of the first really civilized men, said with reason that all philosophers could be called poets. He described his master Socrates as a poet who set the fables of Aesop in verse and composed a hymn to Apollo just before he was sent to death. The term "philosophy"—*philosophia*, in Greek —means by derivation love of wisdom. Philosophy consists of two elements—the inspirational or psychological-religious and the observational or scientific. The inspirational element, of great importance in understanding art, will be considered first. Hesiod, an epic poet associated in Greek tradition with Homer, founded this branch of philosophy, about the year 800 B.C.

Hesiod's Explanation of Creation and the Problem of Strife. In his poem *The Theogony*, Hesiod explained the origin of the universe and the gods, telling how they evolved from a mixture of chaos, earth, hell, love, and night. In most details Hesiod's poem follows the Mesopotamian creation myth. It differs in taking on a more personal tone as Hesiod begins to explain the relationship between the gods and man. For example, he tells how Prometheus, an earth giant, in his determination to help man, like the beneficent Ea of the Sumerians, stole from Zeus the secret of fire. Zeus, in retaliation, not only chained Prometheus to a rock but, to punish man, commissioned Hephaestus, the blacksmith god, to create Pandora, the first woman.

The story has two points of philosophy beyond the grasp of more primitive people. (1) The name "Prometheus" means forethought, the very quality that distinguishes man from the animals. (2) The story attempts to explain the very real mental difficulties that arise between the sexes as soon as they abandon the strict taboos that keep them contented in primitive societies.

Another of Hesiod's poems, the *Works and Days*, consists of a collection of moral maxims, descriptions of farm life, and a calendar of days lucky or unlucky for doing particular things. In considering the actions of mankind, as the following lines show, Hesiod recognized the problems raised by competition.

So, after all, there was not one kind of Strife alone, but all over the earth there are two. As for the one, a man would praise her when he came to understand her; but the other is blameworthy; and they are wholly different in nature. For one fosters evil war and battle, being cruel; her no man loves; but perforce, through the will of the deathless gods, men pay harsh Strife her honor due. But the other is the elder daughter of dark Night, and the son of Kronos who sits above and dwells in the aether, set her in the roots of the earth; and she is far kinder to men. She stirs up even the shiftless to toil; for a man grows eager to work when he considers his neighbor, a rich man who hastens to plow and plant and put his house in good order; and neighbor vies with his neighbor as he hurries after wealth. This Strife is wholesome for men. And potter is angry with potter, and craftsman with craftsman, and beggar is jealous of beggar, and minstrel of minstrel.[1]

The problem of strife, with its tensions between opposites, led to an investigation of the phenomenon of change. Hesiod was the first philosopher to attempt an explanation of the evolution of mankind. True, he saw this as a degenerative process. In his *Works*, Hesiod described the descent of man from an age of gold down through successive periods of silver, copper, bronze, and iron, each more warlike and ruinous than the last. By Hesiod's day, man had come a long way from the Golden Minoan Age. In his writings one recognizes a number of maxims that became leading Greek proverbs. One of these, "The half is greater than the whole," seems paradoxical. The meaning of another, "The immortal gods placed sweat before virtue," is more apparent. In these maxims of Hesiod we recognize the beginnings of ethical philosophy, the reasoning about relative good and evil.

Individual thinkers between the 8th and 6th centuries B.C. accepted these half-religious maxims of Hesiod's along with others, from Egypt and Mesopotamia, and in a spirit of friendly argument began to discover in them two general principles descriptive of all phenomena—stability and change. Playing with these two concepts as a sculptor plays with the clay, they finally created the primary question from which all philosophy grows: What is the original ground of things which outlasts all temporal change, and how does it change itself into these things or these things back into itself?

The Ionian Philosophers and the Concept of Monism. The Ionian thinkers who lived in Miletus taught that there was an underlying, indestructible "world matter." Their philosophy, which persists today, is called Monism. One of them, Thales, who lived to see the invasion of the Persians in the middle of the 6th century, held that this world matter was water. Anaximenes picked air, rather than water, as the primary substance, because it seemed to have Infinity. He ended by calling it "the Infinite" or "the Divine." Both of these early thinkers were obliged to admit that the great mass of matter did have movement within itself. The attempt to give this mass a name or a property parallels the work of Homer and Hesiod, who would call Zeus, "the Just," and Aphrodite or Apollo, "the Beautiful"; and of Phidias, who would strive to make a figure which might symbolize the Perfect, the Absolute, or the Changeless. At that time artistic concepts were born.

Xenophanes and the Problem of Permanence. Xenophanes, born in Ionia at the town of Colophon in 570 B.C., fled, before the Persian invasion, to Elea in southern Italy. This poet wrote that there was but one universal nature underlying all deistic appearance. Intuitively he put his thought into the sentence: "Wherever I look, all is continually flowing together into one nature." It must be remembered that Xenophanes lived just before Phidias created his superb anthropomorphic picturizations of the gods, and contemporaneously with Aeschylus's expression, in *Prometheus Bound*, of the idea that there was a power to which even Zeus must bow—a truly Egyptian idea.

Heraclitus and the Idea of Movement. Following

[1] HESIOD, *Works and Days*, translation by Evelyn White, in the Loeb Classical Library, Harvard University Press, Cambridge, Mass.

Xenophanes, Heraclitus, whose thoughts were more active, demanded that all the world matter be moving in ceaseless revolution. Now the deity was no longer seen to be matter in a state of being, but matter in a state of becoming— or Becoming, itself. Seeking a universal element to symbolize this Becoming, Heraclitus chose fire, a substance worshiped even then by ancient Persians.

Parmenides and the Affirmation of Reality. To understand fully the great extent to which this early philosophy was art, one must examine the great monistic poems of Parmenides, a follower of Xenophanes, who had absorbed some of the teachings of the Milesians and who lived in Elea, writing around 470 B.C. One such poem, *Error*, is divided into three parts, the first of which begins

> Steeds who carry me far,
> So far as my longing may drive you.
> This time seek to pursue,
> Along the pathway of Godhood,
> Change; for intelligent man,
> In all of his parts bears the world.
> And so I was driven along
> By highly intelligent horses,
> Who sought out the way anew,
> And Her maidens showed us the roadway.

The second part of the poem is called "Truth" and reveals that "nonexistence is impossible." Existence, or being, is something that may be observed. Being enfolds all, like a sphere in which all points on the surface are equidistant from the center. The third part of Parmenides's poem is called "Illusion." Only the goddess of love, who holds together all illusions, has reality. Out of her come night and day, earth, sun, moon, the Milky Way, the glow of the stars, the very life that grows out of the earth under the warming rays of a sungoddess. For Parmenides there were no Olympian deities. He apparently grew up under the influence of religions in which the mother goddess was very strong. Emerging from this type of religion, his philosophy ended in defining reality as a sphere—a completely sculpturesque concept of being.

Empedocles and Ethical Judgments. Empedocles of Agrigentum, Sicily (490–430 B.C.), was prophet, physician, statesman, mystic, and poet. Following Heraclitus and the other Ionians, Empedocles, of necessity, recognized the part that Becoming as well as Being plays in life. His great contribution to thought was his belief in the need for order or definition. He defined four elements—earth, water, air, and fire—all of which he thought of as fundamental substances or principles. These elements were continually kept in motion by the opposing forces of love and hate, which he dimly thought of as being good and evil. Empedocles thus prepared men to make judgments of worth, that is, ethical judgments. He maintained that the forces of love and hate must be judged in relation to their action upon men. It was necessary that this ethical point of view should come into philosophy before anyone could define beauty, which, as will be seen, was soon considered the highest measure of artistic effectiveness relative to man.

The Pythagoreans and the Philosophy of Music. While the two opposing schools of philosophy —the inspirational and the observational—endeavored to paint in poetic terms a picture of being, a third school had grown up under Pythagoras, who was born on the island of Samos around 580 B.C. This scholar, according to the Roman philosopher Boethius, contributed to philosophy what is today known as the scientific method. He encouraged his students to agree with him only until such time as they could gather enough observational evidence to prove he was wrong. In this attitude science departs from the method of religion, which demands complete belief, or the method of art, which demands emotional acquiescence, with some possible mental reservations.

Pythagoras acknowledged both change and stability as phenomena worthy of study. He defined philosophy as that mental activity concerned with the investigation of the relationship between changing forms, which he called "the Many," and the changeless, which he called "the Mass." He saw a continual movement from the tiny unified mass to infinite number.

The followers of Pythagoras declared that the earth, like a square, a triangle, or a circle, was static, but that the universe, which moved, was dynamic. Mathematics as a tool for recording ordered relationships is one of the two fundamentals of science, the other being experiment. Art may grow through experiment, much as does science, but mathematics, by a nonsensuous recording of material, moves in a direction opposed to that taken by art.

The most scientific gift of Pythagoras to philosophy, if we are to believe Boethius, was his careful observation of tonal phenomena. It is said that the philosopher, hearing the musical sound of a blacksmith's hammer, noticed that a small-sized hammer gave a different tone from that of a large one. Weighing the two, he found that the one that was half the size of the other produced a tone similar to the first but much higher. In this way he discovered what we call musical consonance. That is to say, the vibrations of the air caused by the smaller hammer were twice as quick as those from the large, and the resulting sounds harmonized, although each had a different character. Carrying his experiment further, Pythagoras discovered eventually the tones that bear a relation to each other of one to two—the octave; two to three—the fifth; and three to four—the fourth. Still unsatisfied, Pythagoras next devised a one-stringed lyre, the monochord, by which he could demonstrate the same phenomenon with a sounding string. As was noted in the preceding chapter, when the strings on a number of these monochords were struck together, the resultant pleasurable effect came to be called "harmony."

Just as the efforts of the poetic philosophers influenced the later explanation of the psychological approach to the associational values of the arts, so these mathematical discoveries of Pythagoras helped to define the formal values of art. Neither approach alone quite reached

what is needed for our complete definition of an aesthetic judgment. The task of bringing them together remained for that original genius, Socrates, the sculptor and poet who lived contemporaneously with Aeschylus and Phidias at the close of the Periclean Age.

This brief review of early Greek thought during the transitional age shows that reason in its first strivings to create a philosophy explaining existence relied upon the same poetic inspiration—a religious background—out of which grew the works of art. In their philosophy, as in their art, the Greeks recognized the forces of change, but continually tried to define or limit all phenomena in terms of sculpturesque masses built one upon another like the various stones of a temple. Because of this sculpturesque tangible quality, a study of Greek philosophy in the formative stage is particularly valuable as an introduction to all philosophy. It has the particular value of showing how a number of terms, such as "form," "change," "permanence," and "matter"—all of which must be used in describing aesthetic phenomena—were first defined. Most apropos to our knowledge of the minds of the artists creating in Greece contemporaneously with the development of the philosophy is the fact that this philosophy explains the ideals the artists were striving to express.

The Philosophical Backgrounds of Late Greek Art

To understand clearly the philosophy and psychology underlying late Greek artistic production, as well as most pre-Christian Greco-Roman art, one must consider briefly three great philosophies developed between 429 and 338—Materialism, Idealism, and a combination of the two called "Development." The first of these was linked with the names of Protagoras the Sophist and Democritus; the second, with Socrates and Plato; and the third, with Aristotle.

The Sophists and the Philosophy of Materialism.

Early philosophers like Pythagoras and Heraclitus, who considered change the essence of life, gave rise to a school of thinkers called the "Sophists." This group, who maintained that they and they alone possessed *sophia* (wisdom), practiced the art of dialectic, or active argument for the sake of convincing in court and the government. The chief of this school, Protagoras, believed that only the outward appearance of things could be observed. For the Sophists, therefore, the entire psychical life consisted in experiencing sensations. Such a theory of knowledge is called "sensualism." In art, sensualism corresponds with what we have come to know as the physioplastic approach.

Protagoras maintained, further, that all perception depended upon motion, whether the motion of sound waves bringing tones to the ear or the movements of bodies in space. Motion, therefore, must be the only reality. Since the perceiving sense could not know the object or the subject which perceived the object, it could know only the interrelationship or motion between object and subject. This interrelationship differs from both. Thus Protagoras came to the belief that his own thought process in perceiving the relationship between subject and object constituted the only reality. But, he observed, no two people perceive this relationship in exactly the same way. Hence every man's perception seems as good as the next one's. Such a belief eliminated any lasting common ground for agreement. This discovery of Protagoras is called the "subjectivity of sense perception." For the Sophists all knowledge was simply relative to a given individual at a given time. Protagoras celebrated his position as the center of his own one-man universe in that famous proposition, "A man is the measure of all things." Here we have a warrant for complete individualism.

In this connection it must be remembered that the Sophists became the chief teachers of the Athenian youth during the Golden Age of Pericles. Since, in the Sophistical scheme, regard for the common good stood second to personal advancement, Athens's political misfortune could probably be traced to the popularity of this philosophy. In the realm of art, the philosophy of sensualism explains in part the desire for photographic realism which appears throughout the succeeding 500 years of Greco-Roman activity.

Among the followers of Protagoras, one, Democritus, while accepting the theory of perception, maintained that there existed another reality, a world of invisible atoms in continual motion, from which arose all phenomena. Democritus attempted to explain all feeling and knowing in terms of such atomic quantities. Such a system of thought is called "materialism."

Socrates and the Philosophy of Idealism. Socrates and his follower Plato also started with the theory that sensation gives the first opinion about things. Unlike Democritus, however, Socrates held the belief that reality consists not of an invisible world of atoms moving in space but of an idea toward which all thoughts growing out of feeling would inevitably lead the inquiring mind. This idea, which Socrates and his pupil Plato held to culminate in Truth, or True Being, was one with beauty and goodness. Such a point of view is called "idealism."

The philosophy of the Sophists led to endless scientific analysis and discussion for its own sake. That of Socrates and Plato, acknowledging the method of poetic insight and revelation, focused on an artistic synthesis of the personality. By nature the Sophists were better equipped to record artistic, formal qualities. The idealists, on the other hand, sought to explore the associative aspects of the artist's mind.

Socrates and the Definition of the Term "Concept." Striving to discover a reasonable element behind all phenomena, Socrates developed the maieutic method of obtaining information. This method consisted in leading group discussions so as to get a consensus of opinion about a given subject. This consensus of opinion, or general notion, Socrates called a "concept." He limited his concepts to ethical ideas, however; that is, to ideas having to do with the relationship of man to the state. In the last analysis, furthermore, he relied, like a poet, upon oracles and inspirations from the gods. He held that he had an individual genius or demon who warned him when he was doing wrong; and as the advice of this demon seems always to have been for his spiritual good, we may infer that Socrates was probably the first man to possess a conscience, in the modern sense of the term.

Plato and Man as an Image of the Ideal State. Plato, the follower of Socrates, held that the general concepts of Socrates, gained by reasoning with others, formed part of a still higher reality. Dimly Plato perceived that all desire, all changing opinion, and all phenomena, must unite at last in one eternal concept. For him, the ultimate truth existed in a world apart, like the world of atoms of Democritus, though paralleled by appearances in this corporeal world.

Throughout Plato's writings one discovers the discrepancy in this dualistic position, for he never found a way to bring together the two worlds—material and spiritual. In trying to unite the two, Plato created a fictitious Socrates, who in many discourses, called "Dialogues," speaks with leading Sophists, statesmen, physicians, and artists, striving to connect their various occupations with a central idea. Finally, in a general treatise, the *Republic*, Plato tried to bring all his thoughts into sequential order. Here he examined the mental processes of the individual as a miniature of an ideal state or republic. Such was the inspired quality of Plato's mind that in his treatise he presented most of the progressive ideas in government and education by which the Western world has advanced since his time.

Many of Plato's ideas seem contradictory, although they become logical if studied in terms of his development. Educated under both the individualistic Sophists and the social-minded Socrates, Plato partook of views of both schools. During his life, for example, he described two ideal cities—the mythical Atlantis, home of the arts, and a republic built on the Spartan model. From the republic Plato at first wished to ban all artists. In the end he relented, saying that the poets might remain if they could compose lyric poems giving good reasons why they should stay.

Platonic Concepts as Associational Patterns in European Art. Of particular value to the mental pattern of European thought and to the artists of the Middle Ages and the Renaissance were Plato's concepts of the ideal City of God and of the structure of the soul. Plato pictured the soul as a triangle whose apex represented the God-given element, or reason. Its two base angles, desire and ambition, stood for the procreative and self-preservative impulses, respectively. With profound psychological insight, Plato perceived that when the apex ruled, a "complete" man resulted. When one of the lower angles ruled, the individual became a tyrant, risking all for love or power. In his picture of the soul, Plato gives a clue to the psychology of those great artists of genius who create contrasting types of art under first one and then another of these drives. Plato seems to have been a man trying to reconcile within his soul the forces of conservatism and radicalism. Like most of his fellow Athenians and many modern intellectuals, he possessed what might be called a "split personality." This constitutes one of his greatest appeals to modern intelligence. Always groping toward a unified life, Plato never quite succeeded in coordinating his conceptions so that he could arrange a logical pyramid with the most pure, or least material, at the top and the most material at the bottom. That task remained for his student and follower, Aristotle.

The Developmental Philosophy of Aristotle. Aristotle, by many considered the greatest mind of all time, was born in 384 and died in 322 B.C. This son of a physician from Macedon, a semi-barbarous province north of Attica, early showed inclinations toward materialism in his studies of natural science and medicine. Going to Athens, he entered the Academy of Plato at the age of eighteen. He believed in the doctrine of idealism, but saw the need of connecting this doctrine with the phenomenal world. Knowledge, he concluded, was of two kinds: (1) that of *revelation*, consisting of knowledge proceeding down from truth or God; (2) that of *empiricism*, consisting of knowledge on the way up, or knowledge derived from a consensus of opinion on perceived phenomena.

The Return to Individualism and the Humanism of Aristotle. Plato held the idea that the best man was the individualist who understood and developed his own capabilities; Aristotle maintained that true reality lay in the individual being whose character was determined by his own essence, which had evolved out of the primordial substance of life. The individual knowing himself in terms of his own inner state of being, like Socrates, received light from above; that is, he gained knowledge *on the way down.* The individual knowing himself in terms of his relation to other beings or phenomena followed the path of knowledge *on the way up.* The first represents essentially the process of the ideoplastic artist inspired to create pure form; the second, the process of the physioplastic artist or scientific observer, recording phenomena so that eventually an idea might be discovered. Over the centuries two parallel patterns of reasoning in aesthetics can be followed —one interested in recording the formal values, which can be easily charted; the other concerned with explaining psychologically the associational values which add particular weight to the quality of inspiration. The first process epitomizes what is called "classicism," the second, what is known as "romanticism."

The Psychology of Aristotle. Not content with Plato's more or less static definition of the soul, Aristotle undertook to describe it as a growing organism, developing through the vegetative to the animal and thence, through a transitional stage, which may be called the imaginative, to the reasonable. The vegetative soul possessed simply the vital forces of life; the animal soul possessed the capability of spontaneous motion in space and of sensation and desire, with feelings of pleasure and pain. Through common-sense reasoning the animal soul on a human level can unite individual perceptions and thus grasp the relationship of number, situation, and motion. Out of these commonly held perceptions arises memory, which is a sort of involuntary recollection, and imagination, a voluntary bringing together of thought—both factors of great importance in understanding art. In one part of his *Poetics,* Aristotle observes that the earliest poets were simply imitators but that succeeding generations of poets imitated the imitations, changing them until in time there eventuated an original creation that had never existed in nature. This definition of imagination marks a momentous step forward in the study of aesthetic phenomena.

In man the vegetative and animal souls contribute elements out of which grows the "form" peculiar to man—that is, the power of reasoning. Under reason, impulses become will power, while imagination helps to assemble the perceptions of phenomena so that they become knowledge. Reason, Aristotle divided into two parts—active reason (*nous poietekos*) and passive reason (*nous pathetikos*). Active reason needs imagination in order to function. Passive reason, built upon the material of perception, tends toward what we have called the physioplastic in art. Active reason has ethos; passive reason, pathos. To achieve the ethical in art, the artist requires a trained will; to achieve the pathetic, he must concentrate on the elements of sense and action. The perfected character, which sees itself in relation to the whole, has both ethos and pathos.[1]

The Beginnings of Aesthetics

From the above brief discussion of the systems of thought which unconsciously influenced

[1] *For potential philosophers:* As Greek culture ages, character changes of the human figure in the spatial arts accompany the evolution of thought patterns. The ideal concepts of Socrates and Plato find parallels in the relatively

the late Greek artists, turn now to the writings of the philosophers themselves on the art of their contemporaries. Only in this way can a just appraisal of Greek art be reached.

Socrates and the Three Primary Artistic Values. Xenophon, in his *Memorabilia*, relates that Socrates asked Cleiton, the sculptor, how he could so clearly distinguish between wrestlers and boxers in his statuary. Cleiton explained that he tried to make his figures expressive of the difference by a suitable facial expression and by imitating in the muscles the various strains put upon the body. Socrates was pleased with this reply for, as he said, "expression helps the sculptor to represent in bodily forms the energies of the spirit." Socrates, who was brought up in a sculptor's workshop, here asked for activity and a more naturalistic representation than that given in the lifeless archaic statues of ancient gods and athletes.

Socrates next went to the armorer's workshop, where he asked for a definition of a beautiful breastplate. From this conversation it became apparent that a breastplate was beautiful only if it were heavy enough to ward off the spears of the enemy, light enough to allow its owner to run, and fitted so well under the arms that its wearer could wield his own javelin. In other words, Socrates held that "for whatever purpose anything may be useful, for that purpose it is beautiful." In brief, the beautiful is the suitable. Here Socrates the craftsman appears.

Socrates then asked the question: "Do you think that people look with more pleasure on paintings in which beautiful, good, and loving characters are exhibited, or on those in which the deformed and evil are represented?" He suggested that the sculptor or painter must put together parts of the body that express the most perfect souls, so that, through the expression of the face and the attitudes of the body, manliness, temperance, and wisdom will shine forth. In conclusion, it seems that beauty for Socrates was "that element in art which was expressive, or suitable, or which would make men appear as virtuous gods."

Plato's Dual Approach to Art. The essence of Plato's twofold position on art seems summarized in the following three statements:

There is a kind of madness, a possession by the muses, which inspires a frenzy in the virgin soul so that there awaken the lyric and all other kinds of creation. But if the creator is not inspired and has no touch of madness in his soul, but thinks that he will get into the temple by the help of art alone, he will find that he and his poetry are not admitted.[1]

Beauty of style and harmony and grace and good rhythm depend upon simplicity in the art of the painter as in any other creative or constructive art such as weaving, embroidery, architecture and music.[2]

Every discourse ought to be a living creature, having its own body, head, and feet—a middle, beginning, and an end, arranged in a manner agreeable to one another and to the whole.[3]

The paradox of Plato's thought as illustrated by these three quotations never resolved itself in any closed system of aesthetics. The cause of this inconclusiveness lies in the equal weight Plato unconsciously gave to the two systems of thought under which he was educated, the Sophistic and the Socratic.

Plato in His Dorian Mode. Borrowing terms

---

abstract appearance of sculptures by Phidias (Fig. 190, Chap. VIII) and Polyclitus (Fig. 191a, Chap. VIII). In these figures ethos is suggested by an inner symbolic construction and simplified planes. Beginning with Praxiteles, a contemporary of Aristotle, pathos replaces sublime detachment in the beautiful figures as the will to particularize appears (Figs. 215, 216, Chap. IX). In the final phase, photographic realism dominates as there is a widespread acceptance of the Sophists' sensate materialism (Fig. 220, Chap. IX). At this same time other artists who probably accepted the individualistic philosophies of Stoicism, Cynicism, or Epicureanism indulged in passionate, overdramatic display (Fig. 219, Chap. IX). Further apparent relationships between the philosophers' thought-symbolism and the symbolic structure underlying Greek graphic and plastic composition will appear in the following chapters.

[1] *Phaedrus*, translation by Jowett.   [2] *The Republic*, translation by Jowett, Book II.

[3] *The Republic*, translation by Jowett.

from music, it may be said that when Plato writes in his Dorian mode—planning, measuring, and building step by step, the structure of his perfect state—he creates a hierarchy of artistic values. "Grace or its absence," he says, "is the effect of good or bad rhythm." Good rhythm leads to good style, this in turn to harmony (unity), this to good words, and good words to a good soul. Plato makes music the highest of the arts, because "musical training is a more potent instrument than any other, since rhythm and harmony find their way into the inward places of the soul." He concludes, finally, that the inspired philosopher who knows truth is the greatest artist. Next to him comes the musician, below the musician the weaver and the embroiderer, and after them the architect. Actor, painter, and sculptor stand furthest away from the truth. In this judgment of Plato, one first discovers a line of reasoning common to many modern critics who consider abstract art and functional design of greater worth than the more representative arts.

Plato in His Lydian Mode. In the *Critias*, Plato told the story of lost Atlantis, the perfect home of the arts. In the last book of the *Republic*, Plato projected his concept of Atlantis into the future, describing it as an artistic Utopia above the clouds. In his discussion of this ideal state, Plato recognized the value of inspiration and imagination, telling us that "poetry can narrate events in the past, the present, or to come" and that "a painter could not be considered bad if after having delineated with consummate skill an ideal of a perfectly beautiful man, he was unable to show that any such man could ever have existed."[1] Here his entire line of reasoning contradicts Plato's other idea that music is the highest of the arts because it is the least tangible and therefore more spiritual.

Endeavoring to coordinate the two points of view, Plato acknowledges that even the painter may be inspired, though he values painting below what seems the more highly inspired art

of the musician. Since music, which needs motion to gain expression, presupposes change, or becoming, while the spatial arts presuppose permanence, or being, we see that the old arguments of the pre-Socratic philosophers have been transposed by Plato to the field of aesthetics. Because of Plato's bias for the nonspatial arts, modern critics after the Renaissance who based their theories of aesthetics on the formal analysis of the spatial arts have undervalued him. Actually, he did not neglect to analyze even the formal values, though he perceived them less clearly than did his follower Aristotle.

Plato's Discussion of Formal Values. Though Plato nowhere gives a complete discussion of formal value, he contributes to our knowledge in various fields. He analyzed to some extent the measure, or beat, of the different types of poetry. In the same way, he partially analyzed the effect of different types of musical scale. In one or two places he described the effect of diminution or perspective, saying that "while we are severe critics of figure painters, we are not so critical of painters of landscape because they are indefinite and we know little of rivers, woods and mountains."[2] Beauty of form Plato defined as a relationship of part to part. Throughout all his formal judgment runs the thought that form is inseparable from spiritual content. In other words, Plato was too much of a philosopher to conceive of a work of art in purely formal, analytic terms.

Plato and Harmony. The idea of harmony for Plato does not necessarily refer to the formal idea of a harmony of tones or colors but to a more general principle, such as the unity of the idea and the form. Yet in the *Symposium*, Plato tells us that a harmony is composed of different notes sounding together. This was that formal harmony discovered by the Pythagoreans. "Rhythm is made up of elements short and long, united now in concord. Music like medicine makes love and unison grow up."[3] Here,

---

[1] *The Republic*, translation by Jowett, 210.   [2] *Critias*, translation by Jowett, 379.
[3] *Symposium*, translation by Jowett, 311.

FIG. 155.—Outside of chalice by Douris, showing instruction in music and grammar. The student recites from a scroll, now lost, of the *Ethiopian Lay* by Arctinus. This story, dealing with the expedition of the Amazons to Troy, begins with the lines "Oh, my muse, I begin to sing about the fair-flowing Scamander." (Translation by Lucas-Robinson.)

in passing, we notice the recurrence of the primitive idea that music may have a therapeutic effect. "Every good physician and skilled artist does all things for the sake of the whole."[1]

Plato on Art Education. In the *Republic* Plato holds that music should be taught to every youth for three years, in order that he may have an inner harmony; but he advises against training youth in music as a profession (Fig. 155). Himself poetic and sensitive, he declares that in the usual education the child was "straightened by threats and blows like a piece of warped wood." In his ideal education, he observed that to be a good builder when grown, the child should play at building houses. Thus he would gain beforehand knowledge required for his art. A good teacher strives to incline the children to those pleasures in their play which would contribute to their final goal in life. The young will more quickly follow the example of a teacher skilled in some art. Thus Plato discovered for all time the principle of true education. In the arts, as well as in every other branch of human endeavor, no subject can be taught by a teacher who has not mastered it.

Summary of Aesthetic Ideas Inherited from Plato.
[1] *The Republic*, translation by Jowett, Book V, 463.

The following ideas inherited from Plato have played a tremendous part in the formation of European art criticism: (1) The idea of mansions in heaven from which the unspoiled child or artist's soul descends to the world with a fresh vision of beauty. This poetic notion has been taken as a warrant by poets and painters since William Blake. In their use of art forms that have high associational value and low formal value, the philosophy of Wordsworth, the poetry of Coleridge, and the expression of other writers have followed this thought pattern. (2) The idea formulated in the *Republic* that art is of greatest value when serving some ideal end. This idea has had particular appeal to the propagandists for church, state, and organized business. (3) The idea that art, descending from the divine light, casts its shadows upon the walls of the cavern called the world. This concept has served to give the modern artist a feeling of validity as the intermediary for revelation. (4) The idea of a hierarchy of artistic values, with music at the top and realistic sculpture at the bottom. This scale of values has placed abstract art using geometric forms relatively high. Twentieth-century artists of the cubist and abstractionist schools use Platonic quotations along this line to support their point of view. (5) The fact that, on the whole, Plato gives very little definite analysis of formal values makes him an invaluable source of inspiration for most romantic artists and critics. An analysis of formal values such as appears in the aesthetics of Aristotle, on the other hand, leads to what is known as the classicist's position.

The Aesthetics of Aristotle. In contrast to the inspired manner in which Plato handled the arts stands Aristotle's scholarly attempt to place them in relation to an observable social phenomenon. In his *Poetics*, which examines the art of poetry with particular reference to the construction and effects of the drama, Aristotle furnished the first great consistent work on art criticism. Here he hints that at some time or other he had given thought to criteria for the formal judgment of sculpture and painting. Although Aristotle, like Plato, called painting and sculpture the "mimetic" (imitative) arts, he did not condemn them for their naturalistic qualities but maintained that they should imitate the ideal in nature. He developed the theme that imitation is not enough and that the finest work combines a number of ideal qualities, each in its appropriate place. He was the first to notice that portrait painters or sculptors, while reproducing the forms that particularize an individual, often add to the likeness something finer than the original. He came thus to the conclusion that "imitation is itself a creative act."

Essentials of the Drama. The essential difference between the points of view of Plato and Aristotle arises from the fact that Plato undertook to criticize particular or separate arts while Aristotle dealt with a synthetic art—the drama. Greek drama, as we have seen, consisted of the union of epic, narrative, musical, and poetic passages, with accompanying dance movements and the personal soliloquies of decorative living statues—the actors—who moved in relation to scenery that was essentially architecture. To put this complex art in order, Aristotle selected as the most important element an action-plot invented by the poet as creator. Below this plot in hierarchical (descending) order, beginning with narrative actions, he eventually came to the display of character.

In defining comedy and tragedy, Aristotle says that the epic poets became the tragedians and the iambic poets the comedians. Actually, there were tragic poets in our sense of the term among the iambists and there was plenty of comedy in the epic *Odyssey*. What Aristotle was really trying to say, understood in the light of what is now known about the origins of the Greek drama, was that the Dionysiac elements allied to drunkenness, which accompanied the Linos song, made for a weaker structural character than the more Apollonian rhythms of the marching epic plot.

The Phenomenon of Catharsis. The practical, common-sense Aristotle observed that while epic poetry might create a desire to emulate the heroes it described, dramatic poetry seemed even more effective in moving people to noble action. Hence he came to the conclusion that of all types of poetry the dramatic was the noblest. The contrast Aristotle draws between epic and dramatic poetry confuses the modern mind, because we usually think of the epic in terms of the formally defined hexameter verse. To Aristotle, however, the term "epic" really meant something like the modern literary term "novel." Actually, in Aristotle's time, both epic hexameter verse and plot elements were included in the drama. There is, thus, no real contrast between dramatic and epic poetry, though there is a definite contrast today between the methods and effects of the novel and the drama.

At the Dionysiac festivals Aristotle observed that as he lost himself in the characters of the actors all the latent fear and pity in his mind rose to the surface until, at the end of a perfect play, he left the theater purged of his baser nature and lifted to a higher plane. This doctrine of release of the emotions through a dramatic presentation was called "catharsis," or purgation. Aristotle believed that catharsis was brought about for the noble man through the performance of a tragedy only. He dismissed comedy with the statement that it merely imitated men worse than the average. Ignoring possible cathartic effects of laughter, he only noticed that in the tragedies the idealized characters were so noble that the meanest of them performed heroic actions, while the comedies of Aristophanes portrayed slaves and ignoble types (Fig. 156).

Aristotle's Definition of the Tragedy. As defined by Aristotle, a tragedy is

an imitation of an action that is serious, complete and of a certain magnitude, . . . in the form of action, not of narrative; through pity and fear effecting the proper purgation of these emotions. By "language embellished" I mean language into which rhythm, "harmony" and song enter. By the "several kinds" "in separate parts" I mean, that some parts are rendered through the medium of verse alone, others again with the aid of song.[1]

Tragedy, further defined in terms of its formal values, consists of six elements. The three internal (ideological) elements, in order of importance, are the plot (*pathos*), the character (*ethos*), and the thought (*dianoia*). The three external (sensible) elements are the diction, the lyrical song, and the spectacle or the spectacular presentment. Aristotle is here creating a new hierarchy of values based not, in Platonic style, on the element of ethos, but on the element of pathos. Pathos, or the plot, for Aristotle lies in the structure of the dramatic incidents, for tragedy consists of an imitation "not of men but of an action." "Life consists in action, and its end is a mode of action, not a quality."[2] Since character (ethos) determines men's quality but through their actions they seem happy or sorrowful, it is by their actions

that we must judge of the drama. Character, then, is subsidiary to action. Aristotle held that without action there can be no tragedy, though there may be tragedy without character, and

Fig. 156.—Theater of Dionysus, a civic enterprise, c.340 B.C. Radius, 165 feet. Here Aristotle observed the drama. (*Courtesy of Lesch-Carnegie.*)

explained this by saying that the tragedies by his contemporaries fail in rendering character. He explained further by saying that Polygnotus drew character well, while Zeuxis, a later artist, was devoid of this ethical quality. He likened a dramatic plot to an outline drawing such as Polygnotus might have made and character to beautiful colors laid on in confused areas. The colors, he pointed out, do not give so much pleasure as does the drawing (significant in terms of the red-figured vase drawing in Fig. 179, Chap. VIII).

The last of the internal elements is an idea or thought pertinent to explain a certain given circumstance. Of the three external elements, the first—diction—refers to the use of the proper words for expressing the meaning of the

[1] *The Poetics of Aristotle,* translated by Butcher, Book VI, p. 23, Macmillan & Company, New York and London, 1895.
[2] *The Poetics of Aristotle,* translated by Butcher, Book VI, p. 27, Macmillan & Company, New York and London, 1895.

plot. Among the less valuable decorative elements, lyrical song carries greater weight than the spectacle, which Aristotle, following the example of Plato, considered less worthy than the art of poetry.

As any tragedy must imitate an action complete in itself Aristotle believed that it should have a very logical beginning, work up to a middle action, and finally reach a definite conclusion. On the whole, he believed that a play ending in bad fortune had greater value than one ending happily, although he admitted, perhaps with Aeschylus in mind, that a happy ending was not necessarily undesirable. This idea of a unified action within very definite time limits differs distinctly from the romantic conception of art, which relies for its effect upon suggestive power. In addition to these general principles of proportion, Aristotle maintained that all plays should follow certain formal elements of order or sequence. Each tragedy should have a prologue preceding the entrance, or *parados*, of the chorus. The episode was that part of a tragedy between the first choric song (the *parados*) and the *exodos*, the choric song on which the chorus retired.

Late Greek Philosophies of Art Based upon Formal Values. Socrates, Plato, and Aristotle examined, particularly, useful and associational values in art in an effort to define beauty. Later philosophers attempted to describe the effect of formal values in a theory of art for art's sake. Many of these late critics were Hellenistic artists, themselves practicing the effects they described. Throughout the entire history of art criticism one may discern this difference between metaphysician and artist-critics. Artists judging the excellence of art tend to base their judgments on purely formal values, except in the case of a few great geniuses like Leonardo da Vinci and Albrecht Dürer, who strove to bring the system of formal values under a more inclusive definition of beauty. Among the late Greek artist-critics, Lysippus and Xenocrates of Sicyon were sculptors, while Apelles won renown as a painter.

The pages of Pliny's *Natural History* contain much of the criticism of Xenocrates, which was based on his study of Greek art in the 5th and 4th centuries B.C. The criticism of Xenocrates differs from that of his predecessors in the degree to which he tried to relate his own artistic principles, discovered through his own use of artistic media, to the effects gained by other artistic personalities. It must be remembered that if Socrates had not been the son of a sculptor, Plato a poet, and Aristotle perhaps to some extent a playwright, these philosophers would probably have lacked much of their insight into the nature of art. Xenocrates, like his master Lysippus, was what might be called a professional artist, at a time when professional artists were coming to be highly respected.

Appearing late in the development of Greek art, Xenocrates was more interested in methods of achieving realism than in the underlying geometric bases of composition. He was the first man to attempt to write a history of art founded upon what we have called the physioplastic or sensate point of view. Naturally, for such a critic, sculpture began with Polyclitus (Fig. 191, Chap. VIII), chiefly because that artist had made his figures look more lifelike than those of his predecessors. Xenocrates was the first to write about the curving line and chiasmatic pose of the figure, with its weight resting upon one foot (Fig. 189, Chap. VIII). He blamed Polyclitus, however, because his figures did not show enough variety. Myron (Fig. 192, Chap. VIII) he complimented, because his figures showed not only variety but an interesting grouping, as well. This type of criticism parallels that of Aristotle's *Poetics*, where the statement may be found that a play is more effective if it shows variety in plot and actions. The criticism of Xenocrates remains essentially dramatic and literary criticism applied to the static art of sculpture.

Like all the other late critics, with the exception of the painter Pamphilus, Xenocrates considered formal values only as contributing to a more perfect mimesis, or imitation. Pamphilus, perhaps a Pythagorean, like Plato and Aristotle believed that arithmetic and geometry were necessary to the creation of art. This type of criticism corresponds to what the 20th-century art critic means when he speaks of "significant form"—that is, some inner, non-substantial scheme of composition probably based on geometric figures leading to abstract art.

Xenocrates and Painting. Xenocrates's judgments on painting comprise a résumé of the historical steps through which the earliest geometric forms were clothed with the appearance of reality. He believed that painting started with a simple outline drawing to which the artist first added only one flat color. He thought that Cimon of Kleonai had invented foreshortening and introduced anatomical details of rendering. Polygnotus (Fig. 179, Chap. VIII), he wrote, first depicted female bodies through transparent drapery. To this artist he also attributed the addition of facial expression. Zeuxis he criticized for having painted heads and limbs too long. Parrhasius first used light and shade in painting, a discovery that greatly influenced Roman art.

Apelles, the peer of all, was renowned for the grace and ease in action of his figures. In discussing his work, Xenocrates mentioned a number of formal values that, taken together, made a perfect picture. (1) There must be a perfect distribution of figures or a well-related composition. (2) There must be a good perspective or indication of depth. (3) The outline of each figure, like the profile line to be discussed in connection with Praxiteles's Hermes (Fig. 215, Chap. IX), must have a significant grace of its own. (4) Each individual figure must have correct proportions, probably the Ionic canon, as that dominated the idea of physical beauty when Xenocrates wrote. (5) The colors must be toned harmoniously. (6) Each face must express the inner emotion of the figure. (7) Every body must possess an indefinable something called "grace," *xaris.* (8) Last comes the element in Xenocrates's criticism which makes it universal—he suggested that the great secret of Apelles lay in the fact that he knew enough to leave a picture unfinished in parts so that there would be room for the imagination of the beholder to enlarge upon it. This constitutes the power of suggestiveness, a factor highly valued by great masters like Rembrandt and by the finest Chinese painters. Adolfo Venturi, in *The History of Art Criticism*, has suggested that the insight of Xenocrates's criticism may have been due to the fact that it was actually taken from a lost treatise by Apelles. If so, Apelles and Zeuxis at their best must have created paintings in many respects like the works of some of the early Renaissance masters. That such painting did not exceed the capabilities of these Greek masters will become apparent in a later chapter through a study of Pompeiian wall paintings.

Summary

From an inheritance of superstitious notions concerning the causes of life, the earliest Greek poetic philosophers discovered by a combination of logical reasoning and scientific observation, that the concepts of change and stability rested upon the basic concepts of matter and idea, substance and spirit.

The Pythagoreans were the first to observe that both the static and the dynamic aspects of existence could be measured or defined with the help of geometrical symbols and arithmetical linear formulae. Socrates and his pupil Plato further differentiated an entire world of thought content (associated pattern) from the world of sensible or tangible object, postulating that the abstract idea, like the geometric composition on which a vase painting or a pedimental sculpture was built, could be separated from its physical appearance. Aristotle, taking a common-sense point of view, refused to recognize a contradistinction between the worlds of flesh and spirit. As a dramatic critic he pointed out that no sensible object (physioplastic art) was without some inherent idea (ideology).

This idea, often seeming to spring from the action (pathos), could move the entire object over toward the purely ideal abstraction (ethos), which might be likened to ideoplastic art. For Aristotle, thought moved in a circle, and the work of art, like his philosophy, constituted a complete system in which the spatial and the temporal united. Thus all the world of sense continually moved toward the spirit and the spirit continually sought to manifest itself in the world of sense. In other words, the actor, creating his part correctly, was potentially the dramatist and the director conceiving the whole. Such a conclusive philosophy of relativity prepares the way for a study of the effects found in many Oriental works of art.

On the other hand, to the superficial student of Hellenistic or Roman times this one element of individual character may satisfactorily explain the highly individualistic philosophy of late Greek dramatic virtuosos and operatic singers who put more emphasis on scenic effects than on the spiritual content of the plot. Individualistic philosophy led to the formulation of an aesthetics glorifying pathos, rather than ethos. It also led to the growth of a number of quasi-religious philosophies of salvation, including Cynicism, Skepticism, Stoicism, and Epicureanism. These, as we shall see, had a great influence in forming the Roman, Renaissance, and modern Protestant minds. From this aspect of Aristotle's philosophy, combined with certain transcendental elements in Platonism, grew the aesthetic doctrines of art for art's sake, pure sensualism, and eventually pure abstractionism. There resulted a split in the artist's character, so that during Roman times and in the early 20th century there was no one style but as great a diversity of styles as there were individual artists.

Bibliography

MYRES, J. L.: *Who Were the Greeks?* University of California Press, Berkeley, Calif., 1930.

ARISTOTLE: *Poetics*, edited by Charles Sears Baldwin, The Macmillan Company, New York, 1930.

LONGINUS: *On the Sublime*, edited by Charles Sears Baldwin, The Macmillan Company, New York, 1930.

CAPPS, EDWARD: *From Homer to Theocritus*, Charles Scribner's Sons, New York, 1901.

XENOPHON: *Memorabilia of Socrates*, introduction by R. D. C. Robbins, D. Appleton-Century Company, Inc., New York, 1853.

THUCYDIDES: *History of the Peloponnesian War*, translated by Jowett, Oxford University Press, New York, 1900.

GARDNER, PERCY: *Principles of Greek Art*, The Macmillan Company, New York, 1914.

PLATO: *Dialogues*, translated by Jowett, Clarendon Press, London, 1875.

PLATO: *Republic*, translated by Jowett, Clarendon Press, London, 1888.

DAVIS, W. STERNS: *A Victor of Salamis* (novel), The Macmillan Company, New York, 1907.

DICKINSON, G. LOWES: *The Greek View of Life*, Doubleday, Doran & Company, Inc., New York, 1916.

CHAPTER VIII

The Triumph of the Attic Style, I

We enjoy a form of government which does not copy the laws of our neighbors; but we are rather a pattern to others than imitators of them. From its not being administered for the benefit of the few, but of the many, our state is called a democracy; but with regard to its laws, all enjoy equality. . . .

For we study taste with economy, and philosophy without effeminacy; and employ wealth rather for opportunity of action than for boastfulness; poverty is nothing disgraceful for a man to confess; but not to escape it by exertion is considered shameful.

In short, I say that the whole city is a school for Greece, and, in my opinion, any individual amongst us would prove himself qualified for the most varied kinds of action, and with the most graceful versatility.

"FUNERAL ORATION" BY PERICLES[1]

THE TWO preceding chapters demonstrate the fusion of many artistic styles, with their symbolic association, and the emergence of a new philosophical approach to life. During the Golden Age of Pericles and immediately following, for a short space of time, all the arts reached a state of equilibrium, no one surpassing the others in importance. The Athenian mind, influenced by its optimistic ideals of empire, appears unified. Its unity was aptly symbolized by its architecture, in which structures were designed with direct reference to human proportions.

Arising definitely out of the useful, architecture is the least representational, the most abstract, of all the visual arts. The aesthetics of architecture, having to deal with this combination of utility and abstraction, is less simple than that of painting or sculpture. Architecture presents two problems. One, that of construction, may be solved by the engineer; the other, that of appearance, by the artist designer. The good architect combines the functions of both artist and engineer.

The Perfection of the Doric and Ionic Styles in Architecture

The Greeks made no new significant advances in engineering over the Egyptians. In some ways they lagged behind the Mesopotamian peoples with their domes and vaults, though during the late part of the 6th century B.C. they probably used the pulley and crane for raising the marble blocks of their temples. Before that time there seems to be some evidence that the larger structures were built, as were the Egyptian temples, by means of mounds of earth, inclined planes, and rollers for moving the stones into place.

In limiting themselves to post-and-lintel construction, the Greeks set very definite boundaries to the type of architecture they could develop. The greatest distance between two columns which a block of marble would cover was 20 feet. We have seen that the limits set by the shape of the vase and the placing of bands of decoration made the Greek potter work toward greater perfection. The same holds

[1] THUCYDIDES, *History of the Peloponnesian War*, 471–400 B.C., Book II, ll. 37*ff*.

true for the architect. Because he could build only temples and civic porticoes around his city square, and because he felt himself restricted to the traditional forms inherited from

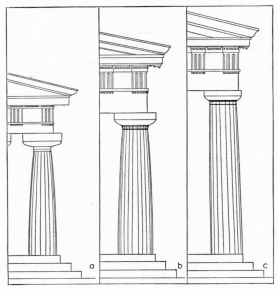

FIG. 157.—Growing refinement of the Doric order. *a*, basilica at Paestum, 550 B.C., height of column 25 feet; *b*, temple of Poseidon at Paestum, 500 B.C., height of column 28 feet 8 inches; *c*, Parthenon, 454–438 B.C., height of column 34 feet 3 inches.

earliest times, the Greek reached a perfection in columnar architecture that has not since been surpassed.

The Growth of the Doric Temple Structure. The temple, which offers the finest example of civic monumental architecture, reached its most perfect proportions in the Parthenon, the Erechtheum, and the Tholos at Epidaurus in the 5th and 4th centuries B.C. The two former developed from the Mycenaean megaron and Egyptian tomb plans; the latter, probably from the hypogeum.

The megaron, as seen in Chap. VI (see Fig. 120 for complete development), came to have first three and then four columns in front. Next, the gable took shape on the flat façade and, as a final step, columns like those from Hatshepsut's colonnades replaced the reversed Cretan col-

umns. Soon the number of columns in front changed to six, then eight, and even more. As the ancestral home of the sacred hero, the megaron became the naos, or cella, of the temple, wherein was housed the statue of the god who had protected that hero and his descendants. Some inventive architect, who probably saw the Egyptian proto-Doric models at Deir-el-Bahri, Beni Hasan, Karnak, or Sakkareh, then put the colonnade around the naos directly by extending the front porch down both sides and across the rear. Then the naos was divided into two sections; the forepart became the shrine for the god, and the rear was sometimes used as a repository for gifts to the god.

The Temple of Hera at Olympia. In the 8th century B.C. the Dorian Greeks erected at Olympia a temple to Hera, wife of Zeus, who was king of the gods. This was a megaron with a porch at both ends—that is, an amphiprostyle temple. The entire structure—cella and colonnade—rested on a platform, called a "stereobate," made up of three high steps. The top level of the three, known as the "stylobate," formed the base from which rose the Doric columns without any intermediate parts. The ruins of the temple show that the structure was originally built of dried brick and fashioned with wooden planks, very much as the megaron had been built. The columns around the outside furnish an interesting record of the evolution of the Doric form (Fig. 157a). Some of them have a very pronounced bulge in the center, called the "entasis." The capitals under the square abacus take the form of a wide cushion (the echinus), like that found on Cretan columns. Later columns in the colonnade, however, show a less pronounced entasis and a smaller, more refined echinus.

Pausanias, a Greco-Roman traveler of the 2nd century after Christ, related that two of the columns in the porch of the cella of this Heraeum were made of oak. Scholars have therefore conjectured that at one time all the columns may have been of wood. The temple was roofed

FIG. 158.—Ornaments from Doric buildings. *a*, acroterium; *b*, lower acroterium; *c*, antefix at end of eave tile; *d*, downspout, with profile of cymatium.

with wooden beams and had a gable of low pitch covered with terra-cotta tiles. Unfortunately, not enough fragments remain to show us what sculpture adorned the pediment. At each end of the roof ridge stood ornaments of glazed terra cotta in brown, white, and black (Fig. 158*a*). Such an ornament is called an "acroterium." Similar ornaments at the lower ends of the roof suggested the power of visiting spirits. There is evidence that most parts of the building were painted and all the architectural details above the columns picked out in colors, so that the temple did not appear to be too heavy. The columns themselves were decorative and gay. As in the case of the purely functional type of Egyptian column, the shafts were unpainted, although their abaci and echini were colored, as in the floral Egyptian column.

The Temple of Poseidon at Paestum. In the town of Poseidonia, or Paestum, in southern Italy, in the 5th and 6th centuries B.C., the Dorian Greeks built three temples that show all the transitional stages between the early Heraeum and the Parthenon. Figure 157*b*, showing the development of the column, will make clear the process of refinement then going on. The first column, belonging to the so-called basil-

ica, carries a wide-spreading echinus, to which the shaft is joined by a collar (the neck), suggestive of the Egyptian palm capital. The sides of the shaft rise straight for two-thirds of the way up and then suddenly bend in. The effect is unpleasant.

The second temple (Fig. 159), dedicated to Poseidon, the sea-god, has columns that grow consistently smaller from base to capital. The heavy echinus is little larger than the largest diameter of the shaft. The individual columns seem rather chunky and do not carry the maximum span of the architrave, or lintel beam.

This building, because of its excellent state of preservation, offers a good opportunity for studying the interior construction of a Greek temple (Fig. 160). Two rows of Doric columns, one above the other, supported the heavy roof inside the cella. These columns were so designed that the contour of the uppermost shafts continued the lines of the low shafts, carrying them upward toward some hypothetical point. This in itself would make the interior of the building appear somewhat lighter. It differs considerably from the interiors of Egyptian buildings, which exhibited a definite attempt to achieve a feeling of massive weight.[1]

[1] A study of the chart (Fig. 161) showing the gradual development of proportions in the Doric temple, paralleling a similar development of the proportions of the automobile, suggests that there exists some general law in the

The Aesthetics of the Parthenon. The Greeks achieved the most suitable balance between stereobate, shafts, entablature, and pediments in the construction of the Parthenon in Athens

FIG. 159.—Temple of Poseidon and so-called basilica at Paestum, 6th century B.C. (*Courtesy of Hall.*)

(Fig. 163). This temple was built on the Acropolis and dedicated to the civic goddess, Athena, between the years 447 and 432 B.C.

The builders used eight columns on the façade and seventeen on each side. The columns lean in very slightly, so that unconsciously one extends their line toward the unseen apex of a pyramid in the sky. The four corner columns lean toward the corners of the cella. The entasis for each column is so subtle that it can be measured only by the most intricate mathematical formulae—formulae that were far beyond the powers of the Greek geometricians at the time. On an unfinished temple at Segesta, Sicily, the marks of the masons remain in the stones, showing that the measurements were given by some master mason, who probably

worked them out by rule of thumb on a model, observing from structure to structure the effect of various contours.

The relations of echinus to abacus and of

FIG. 160.—Interior, temple of Poseidon, Paestum, showing construction of cella with two stories of interior columns to support slab roof. Materials, travertine originally covered with stucco, c. 500 B.C. (*Courtesy of Carnegie-Lesch.*)

both to the architrave, which is lighter than the frieze, are also very subtle. Some general principle of design governed the Greek builder. The principle was one of a rhythmical growth curve or line, very abstract in character, in which the Greek architect believed but which

evolution of artistic forms. Fechner, the psychologist, was able to demonstrate that when the outer contour of an object approximated a rectangle, most people chose one particular rectangle as the most pleasing. This figure, called the "golden-mean rectangle," can be made by dropping the diagonal of a square to form the long side of the rectangle and retaining the side of the square for the short side of the rectangle (Fig. 162*a*). When this process is repeated with other diagonals (Fig. 162*b*), and the points *a*, *b*, *c*, and *d* are connected with curved lines, a logarithmic spiral of pleasing design results. This type of spiral, found on most snail shells, as well as in the unfolding tendrils of a plant, was approximated by the Greek designers who perfected the Ionic volute. The Greeks may have drawn this spiral by means of a piece of chalk on the end of a string unwound from a conch shell (Fig. 162*c*). No evidence exists to show that complicated geometric formulae, such as those proposed by the late J. Hambidge, were known and used by the Greeks in building their temples or forming their vases.

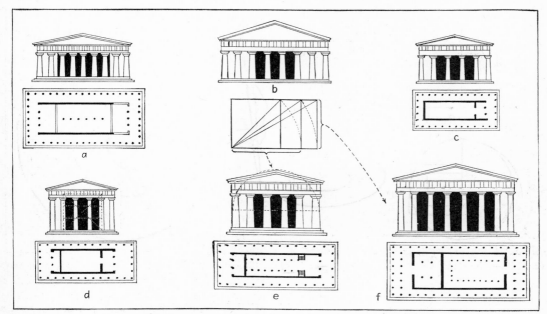

FIG. 161.—Development of the Doric façade and plan. *a*, basilica, Paestum; *b*, Gorgon temple, Korfu (*after Dörp-feld*); *c*, temple at Assos; *d*, temple at Nemea; *e*, temple of Poseidon, Paestum; *f*, Parthenon, Athens.

he could never measure. As we saw in the discussion of Plato's philosophy of art, there prevailed at this time a rather mystical belief in certain canons of beauty. The Greeks also recognized an *eidos*, or "correct image." From this term come the words "idea" and "ideal." This *eidos*, held to be a gift of the gods, probably was considered the sacred property of the master architect.[1]

In the case of the Parthenon, an abstract, generative ratio possibly controlled the entire Doric exterior. This ratio compares to the time relations within a musical sequence. If the colonnade of Doric columns (Fig. 164) were taken to represent such a sequence, the shafts might stand for whole notes and the entablature, with its triglyphs and metopes, half and quarter notes. The discontinuous frieze, with its alter-nate long and two short beats, suggests the anapaestic foot used for Spartan marching songs and for the choral processions of the theater—a rhythm which coincides with the character of the continuous frieze around the cella. As both the Doric exterior frieze and the cella frieze must, of necessity, be viewed together, one feels the presence of a superior type of design particularly appropriate to the character of the building. However, a temple like that of Zeus at Olympia seems relatively lifeless when placed beside the Parthenon. The reason for this is that the architects of the Parthenon, Ictinus and Callicrates, along with their sculptor, Phidias, designed a building in which they *deviated slightly from these exact measurements* in order to get a more pleasing effect. Nature's spiral shell curve is more interesting than the

[1] Pennethorne, Dinsmore, Goodyear, Penrose, and others, following Vitruvius, have shown that the master architects must have possessed a few secret formulae for constructing simple measuring blocks, used in laying out the entasis of the columns and the horizontal lines of the temples so that they would look right. It seems significant that, according to Penrose, the Egyptian architects also used entasis in designing their temple courts. Further, the Greek Doric buildings improved vastly in style during the 6th century B.C., which was the very century in which the Greeks had their greatest contacts with Egypt and when traveling Greek architects must have had the greatest opportunity to study the Egyptian temples.

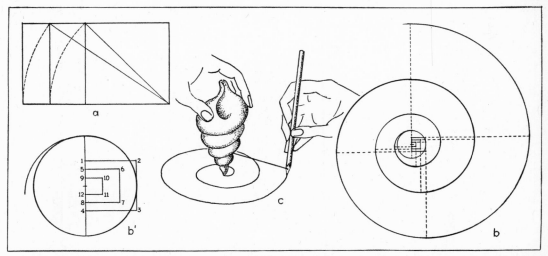

FIG. 162.—The elementary geometry underlying Greek architecture. *a*, the golden-mean rectangle; *b*, Goldman's method for drawing an Ionic volute; *c*, a natural construction of the Ionic volute.

curve laid out by the mathematician, because of the very slight deviations that keep it from being a purely mechanical abstraction. So it is with architectural design.

The Parthenon, the supreme example of Doric structure, parallels the best Greek vases in many particulars. The broad stylobate (Fig. 165) leads to the slender columns, that unite in support of the continuous band of the lower architrave, above which rises the discontinuous metrical band of the frieze. Above the frieze is the gable, with its sculptured pediment (Fig. 166), sculpture which, as we shall see, follows the composition of the top band on most vases. The continuous band of the frieze from the vase, furthermore, was actually paralleled on Ionic temples and on the earliest Doric temple at Assos, although on the Parthenon it was moved inside under the portico and used to decorate the cella wall.

These observations lead us to conclude that the entire Greek temple, like the Greek vase, was but a fitting abstract frame for the pictorial story of the god who dwelled within. There was no fixed separation between Greek vase design and the design of architecture. They developed from the same source: *that refined sense of rhyth-mical design which grew over two centuries toward a pictorial realization in the sculptured human form.* Nor can one hope to understand this refinement by any shorter road than a careful study of the steps through which it evolved.

The Subtle Refinements of the Mature Doric. Architects of the 4th century B.C. built Doric temples, as did the Romans later, by purely geometric rules. The vital appeal of the Parthenon, however, is lacking in the later temples. The echinus of a Parthenon column, contoured with a long ogival curve, seems to have inner life. The later Doric column, in contrast, has this same echinus cut off in a straight line, or quarter round, and the effect, which has less streamlining, lacks organic vitality. We have no proof, nevertheless, that the Greek temple arose by any other means than through a long evolutionary process in which the trained eyes of sculptors and engineers at last found a design that expressed the balance between the abstract idea and the living form.

Measurement of the façade of the Parthenon to check the refinements reveals not only that the column shafts slant inward and that all moldings are set off by subtle curves, but also that the metopes above the architrave are not

Fig. 163.—The Parthenon, Temple of Athena and Treasury, 454-438 B.C., by Phidias, Ictinus, and Callicrates, Acropolis, Athens. (*Courtesy of the Metropolitan Museum of Art.*)

all of the same width. Those near the center columns are broader than those toward the outside; so, too, the spaces between the columns differ, getting a bit longer toward the

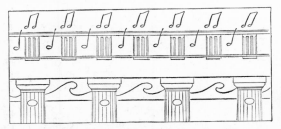

FIG. 164.—Rhythm and measure in Greek architecture.

center. Finally, all the horizontal lines of the building have something corresponding to the entasis of the columns. This subtle curving is not noticeable to the eye unless one stands at the corner of the stylobate and sights along the top across the length of the temple toward the opposite corner. Then a hat placed at the opposite corner will be hidden by the curvature at the center, which amounts to about eight inches. This entasis of the horizontal lines tends to correct a certain appearance of sagging which would result if all the lines were parallel.

By this distortion of parallel lines the Greeks compensated for optical illusions due to the structure of the lens of the eye. In the 20th century many artists, taking note of this visual peculiarity, overcompensate for it and create distorted pictures to call attention to it. The Greeks were satisfied to make the compensation subtly, to trick the eye into feeling that the building abided by some mathematical law of simple numbers, while actually it approximated a much more complex law of growth. By refinements such as this the Greek created that unity of emotion, form, and intellectual idea which has been called "beauty."

The Ionic Style of Architecture. Vitruvius, the Roman architect, early pointed out that the Doric style was strong and masculine. Its columns seem to march with an almost military beat. The Ionic, wrote Vitruvius, resembles a tall, slender maiden, her head crowned with

a delicate, twin-spiraling, cushioned member called a volute, on which the weight of the architrave rests lightly.

The development of the Ionic column is even

FIG. 165.—Construction of Parthenon, height about 60 feet. *a,* stylobate; *b,* shaft; *c,* echinus; *d,* abacus; *e,* architrave; *f,* guttae; *g,* discontinuous frieze with alternate triglyphs and metopes; *h,* mutules; *i,* pediment; *j,* cornice; *k,* Ionic frieze.

more exciting from an aesthetic point of view than that of the Doric, chiefly because it unites two very different forms of column and makes of them an abstract creation. Just as behind the Doric lay the inverted Cretan column and the Egyptian chamfered shaft, both already abstract and functional, so behind the Ionic lay papyrus and palm-leaf columns, both decorative and realistic, suggestive of Ishtar.

The Ionic Column. Probably some of the earliest Ionian experiments in building were in wood. A capital from a temple of the 7th century B.C. on the island of Delos (Fig. 167a) indicates in its blocky ends and heavy, square plan a definitely wooden origin. Two spirals and a papyrus design are painted on the surface of the capital.

A second capital (Fig. 167b), from an Attic temple built much later at Delphi, serves to illustrate the other element that went into Ionic building—the palm form. The two elements—palm and spirals—were brought together, though very loosely, in the capital from Neandria (Fig. 167c). This partakes of the Oriental tendency noticed in the Persian column from the Apadana of Xerxes (Fig. 110, Chap. V). In this third example, two bands of drooping leaves appear below the volutes. All the forms show careful carving, with very delicate lines. Both volutes and leaves are quite naturalistic; there is no attempt to make them abstract.

In Athens, however, the tendency was toward abstraction. Among the archaic Athenian temples of the 6th century B.C., one (Fig. 167e) exemplifies the early efforts to combine the two elements. The shaft was fluted, not like the Doric with shallow flutes and pointed arrises, but with deep, half-round cuttings and squared arrises. The lights and shadows created by this carving combined to lend greater height and delicacy to the already slender shaft.

Omitting other stages, we come to the finest of the Ionic columns (Fig. 167f)—those of the Propylaea, or entrance to the Acropolis, and those on the north porch of the Erechtheum (Fig. 169), a temple also on the Acropolis, at Athens. Here, the Attic base, divided in two parts, displays an ornament made up of a basket weave. This is called a "guilloche." Inevitably the eye follows the finely carved shaft to the volutes, carved with a multitude of spiral lines. Most of the traces of the naturalistic origin have disappeared; the leaves have become an egg-and-dart molding. An extra collar with a modified form of papyrus or lotus design has been placed below the echinus, and a faint suggestion of an abacus remains above the cushioning volutes.

The Erechtheum. The earliest Ionic temples, like the Doric temples, probably went back in plan to a modified form of megaron used in

Asia Minor. From judgment halls and ancient Phoenician temples come modified forms of the Ionic capital, such as the one found at Megiddo (Fig. 148f, Chap. VI). The Ionic tem-

FIG. 166.—The Parthenon reconstructed (Nashville, Tenn.). (*Photograph by Axel.*)

ples for the most part retain the cella form with a porch in front and omit the peripteral colonnade. This style lends itself more easily to uneven ground elevations than does the Doric.

The Erechtheum (Fig. 168), best-known temple in the Ionic style, was planned in part before the destruction of the buildings on the Acropolis by the Persians, and finished contemporaneously with the Parthenon. The German archaeologist, Dörpfeld, holds that originally the temple must have been a larger building with the famous Porch of the Maidens exactly opposite the north porch and a wing stretching down toward the west, exactly equal to the present eastern section. This plan would give a broad temple like the various hilanis in Asia Minor and Mesopotamia. The Erechtheum and the Parthenon would, then, recall two of the origins of Attic culture—the Mesopotamian and the Egyptian.

The North Porch of the Erechtheum. The north porch of the Erechtheum has columns taller than those of the east porch, for this entrance is down on the side of the hill so that the porch itself must be higher. The columns measure nine and one-tenth diameters high, while the

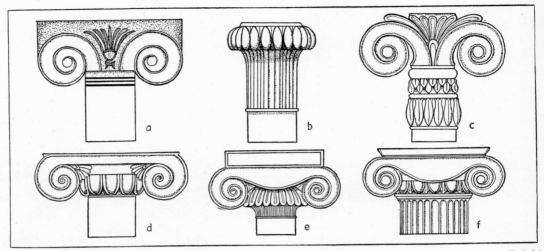

FIG. 167.—Refinement of the Ionic capitals. *a*, Delos; *b*, Delphi; *c*, Neandria; *d*, temple of the Naxians, Delphi; *e*, archaic temple, Athens; *f*, Propylaeum, Athens.

height of those on the east porch is nine and one-third diameters. The marble ceiling of the north porch is constructed with beams 20 feet long that support a coffering of light marble slabs, having the center of each decorated with a gilded rosette. The doorway sheltered by the porch also shows the Oriental rosettes. It has lines more refined than has any other doorway in Greek building.

The distance from the peak of the gable of the porch to the stereobate equals the distance between the outsides of the columnar bases, making an exact square. It is significant that in the case of the Parthenon and the Erechtheum porch, whether the Greeks started with a rectangle or a square, they reached pleasing results. Which is the more pleasing is impossible to say. What counts is the relationship of the parts within the shapes. Perhaps even more significant is the fact that the Parthenon, a static building, has the dynamic rectangle; and the Erechtheum, a dynamic, irregular building, has the static square—as though the Greeks really desired an equilibrium.

The Significance of the Porch of the Caryatids. In the Porch of the Maidens, or the Caryatids (Fig. 170), on the opposite side of the temple from the north porch, and so facing the Par-

thenon and the great central area of the Acropolis, the Ionic builders created by a tour de force something entirely unstructural. Nevertheless, it seems entirely appropriate. Why is this? As already has been explained, it was customary for the best Greek families to select each year for the service of Athena the most beautiful of their daughters. These beauty contest winners then became priestesses at the shrine of the virgin goddess, and the proud families erected portrait statues of them. In archaic times these statues were all strictly columnar and may have suggested the use of the human figure as a column. The architect of this porch, undoubtedly a sculptor, depicted, accordingly, a group of six maidens carrying the entire architrave forward in a slow, stately procession. There exists nothing like it in the entire realm of architecture. The Greeks, having created the abstract style from naturalistic origins, were here so sure of their own ability as to bring back the naturalistic origin in its most realistic form and make it part of the building.

Secular Buildings

The Greek Dwelling. The Greek dwelling house (Fig. 171), as discovered and reconstructed by

Robinson at Olynthus, seems to have taken over the plan of the Hallstatt Danubian farmstead. It was composed of three parts arranged around an open court, which faced the south. and a front courtyard, which in the next century became the atrium. This latter type of house grew into the great establishments found in Greco-Roman Pompeii.

Fig. 168.—Erechtheum seen from the east, 420–393 B.C., height 33 feet. Restoration by Tetaz, 1848. (*Courtesy of Institute of France, from Monuments antiques, by d'Espouy.*)

On one side was a part probably for slaves or domestic animals; on the other, a stable for horses. The rear part had a long, two-storied porch, which formed the front of the dwelling. Kitchen and living rooms opened below and sleeping quarters above. A stairway at the right ascended to the upper balcony. This house was as simple as the daily life of the Greeks. Remains of similar houses have been found in Athens, among them one probably occupied by Pericles. It did not differ from the rest. Like the Egyptians, the Athenians seem to have saved their aesthetic energies for the communal buildings.

In cities in which the tyrants were more powerful, more ornate house forms can be found. In plan they show a combination of the megaron with its colonnaded room and porch

Theaters and Stadia. Structures that we today know as "buildings" were for the Greeks of Pericles's time but little more than arrangements of seats upon the hillsides. The Theater of Dionysus, to be discussed further in the section on the drama, consisted of seats for twenty thousand people on the western end of the southern slope of the Acropolis, with a dancing floor or orchestra and a low stage, on which wooden scenery could be constructed. Pericles, who especially favored the dithyrambic contests, built to the west a much smaller circular covered building called the "Odeon." This was later replaced by the Roman Theater of Herodes Atticus, which united the greater seating capacity of the Theater of Dionysus with a triple-storied covered stage.

The stadia developed for the games at Olym-

Fig. 169.—North porch of Erechtheum looking toward Propylaeum and the sea. Height 36 feet. (*Courtesy of Lesch-Carnegie-Alinari.*)

pia, Delphi, and Athens consisted of rows of seats on each side of a rectangular running track, usually about 200 yards long.

The Stoa. The city market place, or agora (Fig. 172), with its booths for peddlers and money changers, was bounded by a portico in the Doric style raised above the ground level on a low stereobate. This portico was called the "stoa." The stoa served the same function as the arcaded street with its sidewalk cafés in present-day Latin cities.

The Greeks, who seem to have had a great deal of leisure time for bargaining and arguing, sought a pleasant decoration for the walls of these semipublic buildings. Consider, then, what Socrates and his friends saw about them as they walked along the stoa.

Painting in the Golden Age

The city of Socrates, Pericles, and Aeschylus was decorated with many paintings and free-standing sculptures. The stoa displayed a mural showing the military victories of the Athenians over the Persians. This remarkable painting by the great Polygnotus, described by Pausanias as one of the greatest of the ancient world, has disappeared. To reconstruct it in imagination, one must turn to its antecedents in the Athenian vase painting of the time (Fig. 173). Such a collection of the finest examples of the potter's art was kept in the public museum to the left of the Propylaeum in ancient times.

The Dionysus Vase by Exekias. The unity toward which the archaic painters had been striving (Fig. 174a) was attained in the second half of the 6th century B.C. The cylix, a type of drinking cup, by Exekias (Fig. 174b), now in Munich, shows the god Dionysus surrounded by dolphins. In the legend, piratical mariners were said to have kidnaped Dionysus. In playful revenge, he turned the mast of their boat into a grape-bearing vine, made them all

drunk, and changed them into dolphins. The refined, delicate contour of the vase contrasts strongly with the earlier Cretan and Mycenaean chalices.

Fig. 170.—Porch of the Caryatids, Erechtheum. Height 18 feet. (*Courtesy of Clarence Kennedy.*)

The Exekias vase stands unsurpassed for its intricate combination of occult and absolute balance. From a purely formal, aesthetic standpoint, it is important that the dolphins are so placed around the relatively stable vine and boat that no one of them can be moved without upsetting this balance.[1] The Greeks gave time to their art, and time is required to produce the most perfect aesthetic effect.

[1] If a slide of this vase is reversed, it appears unbalanced, as the prow of the boat suggests too great a movement toward the right. Unconsciously our eyes compensate for a tendency to stop at the right side of a page, a peculiarity of Occidental design which started when writing first began to move regularly from left to right. Before the time of Exekias, Greek writing, like Etruscan, went both ways or from right to left.

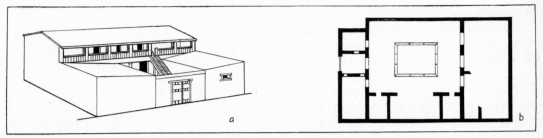

Fig. 171.—*a*, dwelling house at Olynthus (*after Robinson*); *b*, house at Delos (*Borrmann, Geschichte der Baukunst*, I, Fig. 136).

The Painter Brygos and the Red-figured Vase Style. The next step in the development of vase manufacture was taken in the last quarter of the 6th century B.C. and the first part of the 5th. Instead of painting a dark figure on a ground covered with white, the potter cut down on his labor by letting the bright-colored clay stand for the flesh tones. The more freely drawn outlines were no longer incised, the painting could be erased and redrawn if not properly arranged. When the figure areas were perfect, the spaces were filled in with a lustrous black coat by some apprentice. The manufacture of vases had advanced to such a degree that the workshops of the masters had a number of helpers. The painting of a hydria from Ruvo in the Naples Museum (Fig. 175) shows several artists, among them apprentices and a woman, who were employed to help the master designer. Many an Athenian grew wealthy in the business of vase painting. The cult of the dead still flourished around the Mediterranean, and any man of consequence wished the best possible Athenian vases for his grave.

The figured cylix (Fig. 176), by the master painter, Brygos, who lived in the first quarter of the 5th century B.C., shows the earlier victory by the Greeks over the Asiatic city of the Trojans. This representation, among the most common of the time, is called the *Iliupersis* (the destruction of Ilium). Probably the best example of the early red-figured style, the cylix also represents the last of the archaic styles in vase painting. As can be seen, the drapery is not painted realistically and often defies the laws

of gravity. The eyes of the combatants, for the most part, are still represented as if seen full face, but the center figure, that of the Greek hero, has eyes that almost seem to be drawn correctly in profile for the first time.

On one side of the cylix a Greek hero fights with a wounded Trojan. He is attacked by a Trojan woman, who uses a club, while another woman tries to flee. A second hero, this time a Trojan—for his shield carries the serpent—attacks a fallen Greek. Where there is a need for some slight relief of the black space, a few letters have been painted in to name one or the other of the heroes. Those letters, as well as the figures, are seemingly arranged in haphazard fashion, but a little study will show that, like the dolphins of Exekias, they fall in exactly the right places.

In composition, this cylix surpasses all the previous vases. Its movement, suggested by a rhythmical pattern, does not exclude an occult balance formed by the stresses and strains seen within the figures. The lower parts of the bodies form an interweave very much like that of the lowest band on the foot of the François vase. Tracing one thread of connecting limbs will make this clear. Let us start with the upraised arm of the standing Trojan at the left and see what happens to the arms of the uppermost figures. The first arm bends back with the sword. Its action is repeated in the arm of the woman next it, whose left arm seems to push out toward the arm of the Greek, the hand silhouetted against the black space. The two arms of the Greek warrior extend as long

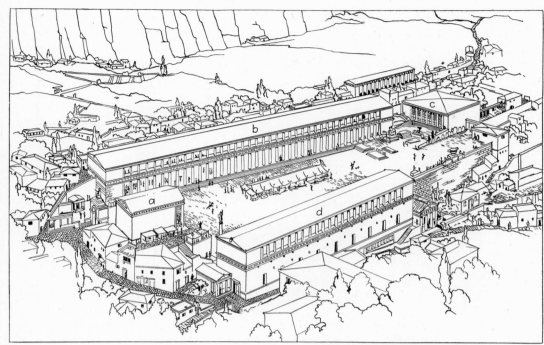

Fig. 172.—Agora or civic center at Assos. *a*, temple and entrance gate; *b*, stoa; *c*, *bouleuterion* or council house; *d*, stoa above civic baths. Note ingenuity with which the Greeks adapted this market place to the side of the hill. (*Courtesy of Archaeological Institute of America; after Bacon, Investigations at Assos.*)

"S" curves through his body and past the shield, to be carried over into the motion of the two arms of the woman with the club. Thus the action which starts with the sword at the left ends with the club at the right. This club and the back-thrust leg of the woman continue down through the leg of the fleeing boy and send the eye around to the other side of the vase. Contrast the vigorous moving line which runs through the arms with the sagging, broken character of the limbs of the two fallen heroes. In summary, it here appears that almost monumental human figures have been completely fitted to the shape of the cup.

The Individualism of Makron. The cylix modeled by Hieron and painted by Makron (Fig. 177), which shows a group of dancing maenads (woman votaries of Dionysus), contrasts with the clear-cut work of Brygos. The drawing is softer and the flowing curves of the drapery seem equal. The figures move in reckless abandon about the circle of the cup, but how they differ from the figures of Brygos! The concentrated vigor of the former master is lacking, nor are the figures so well connected in point of composition. Although Makron shows a more realistic drapery, he has given the faces eyes that are in full face, not profile. His archaism is not in the figure but in the face drawing.

The Geometric Composition Scheme of Douris. A third contemporaneous painter is the artist, Douris, whose red-figured cylix (Fig. 178) shows the voting between Ajax and Odysseus, another scene from the story of the Trojan War. The work of Douris displays careful, selective draftsmanship. The whole composition has the rigid "academic" scaffold of the geometric vase dominating the rhythmical movement and the bodily form. It seems inferior aesthetically to the others studied, but no one of these masters has as yet reached the excellence of design appropriate to his inheritance of technique, form, and idea.

The great point to be made in studying the forerunners of the Polygnotan style worked as free citizens, each following his own lights. From their studios was to come the master painter of the age.

FIG. 173.—Greek black-figured vases of the early 5th century with names recorded by Athenaeus. *a*, skyphos; when small, used for a cup; when large, for a washing basin; *b* and *c*, early form of cylix, drinking cup used at banquets; *d*, oenochoë, wine pitcher; *e*, alabastron, perfume flask; *f*, stamnos, storage jar for oil or wine; *g*, lekythos, ceremonial oil flask; *h*, olpe, pitcher; *i*, amphora, a storage jar; *j*, hydria, used for carrying water, has three handles; *k*, crater with column-handles, a mixing or punch bowl often placed upon a special stand, sometimes reaching a capacity of four gallons. (*Courtesy of the Metropolitan Museum of Art.*)

work of all these men who lived during the disrupting years of the Persian Wars and who ushered in the Golden Age of Pericles is that by their very definite personal characteristics and style they suggest what one should expect when any great art is coming to birth. These

The Climax of Painting in the Polygnotan Style. A little-known workshop of the early 5th century B.C. was managed by the potter Aglaephon. He probably employed his two sons, Aristophon and Polygnotus, as apprentices. After the buildings on the Acropolis had been

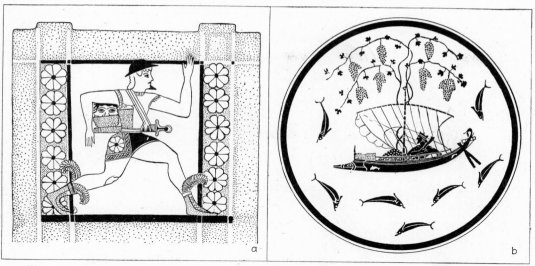

Fig. 174.—*a*, metope in painted terra cotta, Perseus with Gorgon Head, about 550 B.C. Height about 2½ feet, colors black, red, and white, with orange-yellow, Temple of Apollo, Thermos (National Museum, Athens). *b*, inside of black-figured cylix, Dionysus in Boat, by Exekias, about 525 B.C. Diameter about 12 inches (Alte Pinakothek, Munich).

Fig. 175.—Workshop of a potter on a hydria from Ruvo. Three painters at work with brushes upon vases. How many types can you identify? A woman painter is at work on the right; Athena and two Victories bring wreaths for the men (Naples Museum). (*After Blümner, Technologie und Terminologie der Gewerbe und Künste.*)

razed by the Persians in 480 B.C., Cimon, the head of the Athenian state, invited Polygnotus to help in the rebuilding of the city. The young artist accordingly moved to Athens from his home in Thasos and painted many scenes on the various public buildings, giving his service free, as we are told by the Roman Pausanius. For this service he was made a citizen of Athens.

Although Polygnotus is not known through any signed work, many scholars have tried to define his style. It is said that he won many prizes for his mural compositions, which pos-

Fig. 176.—Red-figured cylix by Brygos, showing sack of Troy (Iliupersis), c. 480 B.C.

Fig. 177.—Cylix by Hieron and Makron, showing dancing maenads, c. 480 B.C. Width about 12 inches (Berlin, Old Museum).

sessed "grandeur and completeness of style." His painting is held to have been like a play by Aeschylus, with a definite beginning, middle, and end—that is, his compositions had a distinct measure. He is supposed to have made advances in perspective, showing limbs as though foreshortened. His color scheme, for wall paintings, is said to have been sober, for he used only red, black, white, and yellow, which is very much the scheme of the François vase.

The Aeneas Vase. A vase found many years

Fig. 178.—Outside of red-figured cylix, Voting of Ajax and Odysseus, by Douris, c. 460 B.C. (Austrian Museum of Art and Industry, Vienna). (*After Pottière, Le Peinture industrielle chez les grecs.*)

ago in the little town of Ruvo, a Greek city in southern Italy, tentatively assigned to the man called the "Kleophrades painter," may have been the work of the young Polygnotus, as he could have been employed by his father at about the time indicated by its style. At least it shows a similarity to descriptions of his later mural paintings.

This vase (Fig. 179), named after Aeneas, who appears on it in the act of fleeing from the destruction of Troy, unites the qualities of Brygos, Makron and Douris. The feet and hands are drawn in perspective and every line shows a mastery of the human form. The figures in the center of the scene, the Greek hero who attacks the ancient Priam, and the tree, which appears to be weeping, form a group built upon a triangle. The line of the trunk of the tree meets a line which continues from the right leg of the warrior's body to a point on the upper-most spiraling band. The figures in this group are slightly larger in size than the figures at each side, but the difference is so slight as to be at first imperceptible. The composition of this vase follows very definitely the monumental composition of the pedimental art, as one would

expect of the young mural painter Polygnotus, who grew up when sculptures for the pediments were being made.

The entire composition representing Greeks and Trojans in the various scenes divides into five distinct parts. It is arranged so that the large central scene occupies the outside of the hydria. The smaller figures come at the rear near the pitcher handle. When the scene is stretched out, as in this illustration, it is apparent that it could easily form the subject for a great pedimental sculpture to be used, perhaps, on some temple. The rhythmical movement, however, is not so simple as that on previous works. There seems to be a spiraling, active motion from right to left which weaves back and forth from a front plane to what might be considered a rear plane of the painting. Is this, perhaps, what was meant when people spoke of the perspective of Polygnotus? The eyes, it will be seen, are no longer all archaic; some appear in profile, although not quite a complete profile. Finally, the bodies of women show through the drapery.

The remainder of the decoration frames without being obtrusive. At the bottom runs a fairly heavy band of lotus leaves and spirals, above that a tongue ornament, and at the top the spiral which gives the rhythmical meaning of the whole. This spiral connects with the picture

in a relatively primitive, fortuitous fashion while the free-standing human figure was usually conceived as a bit of architecture. In Greece, on the other hand, as already seen in the case of

FIG. 179.—Red-figured hydria, showing Iliupersis, called the Aeneas vase, by young Polygnotus(?), Ruvo, c. 450 B.C. Height about 16 inches (Naples Museum).

through the sword of the Greek hero. It is as though the painter would assure us of our tempo by introducing the upper band as a leitmotiv.

Color in Painting of the Fifth Century. Very few examples of colored painting as a separate art have been left to us. The fresco (Fig. 180) from a tomb at Ruvo, a Dorian town on the southeastern coast of Italy, is one of these examples, perhaps as early as the 5th century B.C. The design of the figures shown dancing the ratta, the Greek national dance, is that of a combination Vitruvian scroll and guilloche. The interwoven pattern of the colored garments was laid on in broad areas of yellow, red, blue, and black. The color scheme remains as primitive as that used by Egyptian tomb painters. The effect has harmony, insofar as the Greeks used ground earth colors. They did not attempt anything like the more intricate color schemes of Roman times.

Sculpture in the Golden Age

Throughout Egypt and Mesopotamia the narrative wall sculptures covered large surfaces

vase painting, narrative elements were strictly circumscribed or framed by the architectonic structure of the vase. These limitations also controlled the narrative sculpture on the temples. The free-standing sculpture, meanwhile, strove to suggest complete freedom of movement in infinity. Thus dignity and strength of composition first appeared in connection with the narrative elements, while the free-standing sculpture gained a natural rhythm of an almost lyric quality.

At one period in the development of Greek sculpture, called the "transitional age," just before or during the Persian Wars, one may observe the very moment in which the freestanding sculpture loses its archaic stiffness, while the narrative sculpture, becoming dramatic, still retains a strong feeling of underlying geometric composition. Four monuments from this period serve to make clear the problems of form and composition with which the highly inventive masters occupied themselves.

The Charioteer of Delphi. The Charioteer of Delphi (Fig. 181) was part of a group in bronze which included four horses, a chariot, and perhaps a second figure standing for Victory. Remains of these other parts of the group have

FIG. 180.—Dancing maidens from tomb, Ruvo, southern Italy, unknown 5th-century painter. Height 22 inches, colors black, dark red, red, blue, yellow-ocher, pink, and white (Naples Museum).

been found, including the chariot reins of thin bronze.

The base of the group showed that the charioteer was dedicated at Delphi by Polyzalus, a brother of the tyrant, Hiero of Syracuse, as a gift to the god who brought in the winning chariot for the tyrant. Dated approximately between 480 and 450 B.C., the statue may have come from the studio of the famous Calamis, who is said to have made figures of horses and chariots for Hiero. It represents better than any other single piece the excellence of Greek bronze technique just after the time of the Persian invasion and merits close study because of a number of peculiarities.

The statue may not be taken as a literal portrait, but rather as an idealized version of the type of man who could drive a chariot. The Charioteer is a strongly columnar figure. The greater area of his garment hangs in folds that repeat the fluting on the Ionic column. His feet, which the chariot concealed, are natural and anticipate the general movement toward realism in Greek sculpture. They could have been made only by someone who knew they were to be hidden so that the conservative art

critics of the day would not call them too revolutionary. The upper part of the figure is in much stricter conventionalized form, the out-

FIG. 181.—Charioteer in bronze with enamel and silver inlay, c. 475 B.C. Height about 5 feet 11 inches (Delphi, Museum). (*Courtesy of Lesch-Carnegie.*)

stretched arm and hand are modeled strongly, with minor details eliminated. The same may be said for the head and neck (Fig. 182).

The carefully cut line of the brows points to the drawing tradition of the time as illustrated on the contemporaneous vases. The head has the proportion of most heads on early Attic red-figured vases, with a characteristically heavy chin. The hair, cut in tiny ringlets, is bound by a flat fillet, which once had a fret pattern inlaid in silver. The eyes are inlaid with reddish-brown iris and black pupil, the eye-

FIG. 182.—Detail, Charioteer of Delphi. (*Courtesy of Clarence Kennedy.*)

lashes each separately cut in bronze. There are three distinct types of drapery folds: the heavy folds that hold the figure erect, the lighter folds of the chiton above the girdle, and the light

position of sculpture in the triangle. The west pediment shows the hero of the island, Telamon, supported by Herakles, overcoming the Trojan hero, King Laomedon; the east pedi-

FIG. 183.—Marble archer called Herakles, from gable of the Athena (Aphaia) temple, Aegina, by Onatas·or Kalliteles, c. 470 B.C. Height about 3 feet (Glyptothek, Munich). (*Courtesy of Clarence Kennedy.*)

folds over the shoulders, which seem to suggest that the arms could move. When they are seen together, their contrast implies both rest and the possibility of movement.

The Archer from the East Pediment of the Temple at Aegina. An early school of sculpture developed on Aegina, a small island in the Aegean Sea just slightly southeast of Athens, coming to its height between the years 485 and 455 B.C., at which time the Athenians conquered the island. The archer Herakles, from the east pediment of the Doric temple of Aphaia, is from this period (Fig. 183).

Standing, aesthetically, between the pediments of the Gorgon temple of Corfu (Fig. 184*a*) and those of the later Temple of Zeus at Olympia, the two pedimental groups of the temple of Aphaia form an interesting step in the com-

ment (Fig. 184*b*) shows a band of Greek heroes battling against the Trojans. Both groups seem very disjointed and parallel the designs in the lower bands on the François vase (Fig. 131, Chap. VI) or the red-figured vase of Douris (Fig. 178), which is contemporaneous. Aesthetically, each figure resembles that of the archer, who at first glance seems to have been posed like some poorly made wax dummy in a store window. While each limb of this figure is in its proper place (an evidence that the artist knew the principles of anatomy), its linear composition is so lacking that as a whole it does not suggest life.

From the time of the Aegina pediment on, Greek sculptors began to recognize what the Oriental painter Hsieh-Ho called the "principle of rhythmical vitality." Comparing the

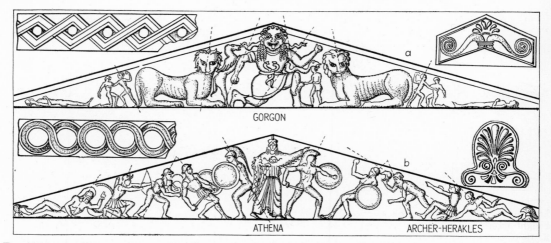

FIG. 184.—*a*, pediment reconstruction, Gorgon temple, Corfu (*after Dörpfeld*); *b*, east pediment, temple of Aphaia, Aegina (*after Furtwängler*).

archer with the figure of Theseus from the Parthenon pediment (Fig. 196), one can see at once the importance of this principle. The figure of Theseus, though in repose, seems actually a part of the rhythm of its entire group.

The pedimental group (Fig. 184*b*) at Aegina lacks the principle of inner vitality, although it does have what might be called the element of underlying geometric composition. In contrast, the pedimental groups of the temple of Zeus at Olympia seem much more unified in composition.

The West Pediment at Olympia. The sculpture in the western pediment of the Doric temple of Zeus at Olympia (Fig. 185*a*) marks a further advance toward a unity of the three fundamental values of use, form, and association, discussed in the introduction. The work has associational value in that it tells a story symbolizing the superiority of the Greeks over their enemies. It has useful value because the arrangement of the figures forms a more complete decorative unit on the temple façade. Its formal values are almost perfect, in that rhythmical vitality and geometric composition closely unite with a more natural sculptural form to tell a dramatic story. According to the Roman traveler Pausanias, the sculpture was planned by Alcamenes, a Doric sculptor active in the

early part of the 5th century B.C. As the temple was complete in 457 B.C. the sculpture must have been carved before this time, probably around 470 B.C.

The narrative story, a mythical battle between Greeks and centaurs, was singularly appropriate, as the temple was dedicated to the deity worshiped by all the Hellenic people, who had just become conscious of the need for unity against the invading hosts of barbarians. These barbarians, represented as half animal and half man, may have stood for northern Scythian hosts of horsemen employed by the Persians. In the center of the group, erect and columnar, reminding one of the ancient Gilgamesh, stands the Greek sun-god, Helios (Apollo), flanked by two Greek heroes, Pirithoüs and Theseus. The god directs the triumph of the Greek arms. The centaurs are shown vainly striving to capture the Greek women. All the action seems to proceed naturally out of the firmly set stable figure of Apollo through the horizontal bodies of the centaurs, and the rhythmical vitality of the entire group appears in the flow of the drapery and the natural curves of the limbs, which contribute to this action.

One detail of the group, a struggling centaur and a Greek woman (Fig. 186), shows clearly

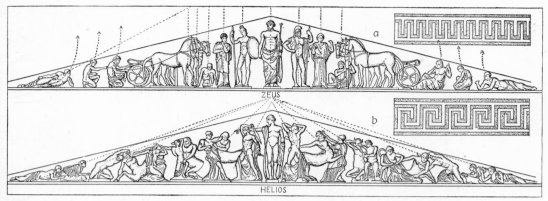

Fɪɢ. 185.—Pedimental sculpture, Temple of Zeus, Olympia, by unknown masters (or Alcamenes), c. 470 ʙ.c. Height about 10 feet. *a*, east pediment, Preparations for Race between Oinomaos and Pelops; *b*, west pediment, Battle of Greeks and Centaurs.

the advance in form made by Alcamenes over the unknown sculptor of the Aegina pediment. The pose of this woman, repeating the pose of the hero in a line exactly perpendicular to the line of the cornice, gives her a natural superiority over the weaker flowing lines of the centaur. This contrast in pose is intensified by the dramatic treatment of the faces, hers calm, almost we may imagine oblivious, his frustrated. All that was written to explain the excellence of the composition by Polygnotus serves to explain the unity of this pedimental group.

In detail, as can be seen by a close study of the carving, although the figures of the pediment indicate advance in realism, the drapery still seems to be engraved or drawn rather than carved deeply. It offers little contrast with the white areas in the brilliant sunlight. Alcamenes, like the archaic sculptors, still relied on pigments to give an interesting effect of detail, and the entire group was made to appear more alive by being painted. Imagine what the pediment would look like with the background painted a dark purple, the flesh parts left the delicate pinkish-white of Parian and Pentelic marble, the hair and eyes tinted, and the draperies painted red, green, or blue. The weapons used by the Greeks were probably in bronze. In the bright sun of Greece, how fitting this decoration set high above men's heads must have seemed, particularly as the cornices, mold-

ings, and various architectural parts, were also picked out in colors, and as the athletes and maidens below were clad in varicolored garments!

A Metope from Olympia. The great unity of the Olympian pedimental sculpture is due to the coordination of a number of aesthetic principles. These principles appear most clearly in some of the metopes placed over the internal columns forming the entrances to the cella. They presented the labors of that athletic hero, Herakles, a favorite of the Dorian Greeks.

The metopal composition showing Herakles and the Cretan bull, found under the western portico (Fig. 187), is the finest of twelve in vigor and balance of composition. The bull, springing to the right with all its strength, has been pulled back violently by the hero, who twists its neck toward the left. The great masses of the two bodies thus form a cross, constructed roughly on the diagonals of the field. The long curving line of the bull's spine is snapped around with the neck, thus holding the attention within the picture, while the direction of the animal's head sends the gaze to the powerful torso of the hero.

Herakle's muscles are not carved separately but have been rendered in broad, sculptural forms, detail being rather severely eliminated. These forms, however, are correctly placed, so that they show clearly and naturally the tensions of the figure. Three long, curving contour lines here dominate the realistic representation of muscular forms.

When this metope is placed beside the pic-

FIG. 186.—Centaur and Greek (Lapith) maiden, west pediment, Temple of Zeus (Olympia Museum). (*Courtesy of Lesch.*)

ture of the maiden and the centaur (Fig. 186), it can be seen that they deal with essentially the same subject: both convey the message that superiority of intellect can conquer brute force. Maiden and centaur are rendered in terms of linear surface drawing, running into sculptural mass. They form part of a long, rhythmical linear design, while Herakles and the bull, intended to fill a square, concentrate their energy within the four sides, so that attention is held to the center. Both these compositions fit the space for which they were designed, and the space in turn fits the need of the temple.

These bits of sculpture have usefulness, for they tell a story proper to the occasion, and the means employed to tell the story are so

fitting that they seem almost completely convincing. In other words, as Socrates would say, they are almost perfect representations of what the Greek meant by the beautiful. If they lack conviction for 20th-century minds, it may be assumed that there lingers a bit of archaism or professional clumsiness, or else that, since they cannot be seen in the proper light and in their original colors, something that the artist originally put into them has been lost.

The Mourning Athena. The mourning Athena in the Acropolis Museum at Athens (Fig. 188) is a small relief found built into a wall not far from the Parthenon. Scholars unite in affirming that the style of this little piece determines that it must have been made near the middle of the 5th century B.C., at about the time when the greatest Greek sculptor, Phidias, was starting his greatest work at Athens. As Phidias, who was born early in the century, left the city while in the fullness of his powers, in 438 B.C., only a slight stretch of imagination, along with a deeper study of this relief, gives reason for believing that the work dates from the end of the first quarter of the century and may be looked upon as the first work of the young genius who, with Aeschylus and Socrates, returned to the city after the Greek victory at Salamis and the departure of the destroying Persians.

The carving, which shows the goddess Athena leaning on her spear while gazing down at a grave stele on which may have been inscribed the names of her fallen heroes, demonstrates very distinctly that element of refined measure, "sweet reasonableness"—to the Greeks, *sophrosyne.* Here one sees the full pause in the stately, rhythmical movement of the funeral dance. This element of rest, like the central group of the Aeneas vase or the Olympian pediments, depends upon a triangle whose apex rises above the upper band of the relief.

Here is static balance. Motion is also suggested by the fact that, although the figure has just leaned over, the folds of the chiton have not yet come to rest, for at the front they have

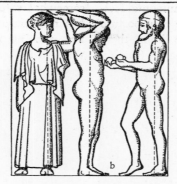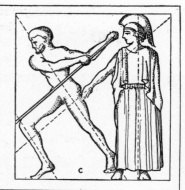

FIG. 187.—Metopes from Temple of Zeus, Olympia, about 470 B.C. *a*, Herakles and the Cretan Bull (Louvre Museum); *b*, Herakles Holding the World (Olympia Museum); *c*, Herakles Cleaning the Augean Stables (Olympia Museum). Height about 5 feet.

not fallen to a perpendicular position. At first glance it may seem as though the folds belong to an archaic statue that leans as a whole, but a more careful study shows that this cannot be so, for the folds hang more nearly perpendicular toward the center than at the left.

There is probably no more touching war memorial than this in the history of the human race. The relief should be studied in comparison with the Aeneas vase (Fig. 179). We have noticed, as a principle of figure composition on the mid-5th-century vases, that the lower part of the figured band formed a closely woven mass out of which the individual figures grew more personal and active as they reached the lip. The upper part of the figures had more distinct lines and in every case were connected, by some limb or sword, with a top border. Obviously the sculptor who carved this relief understood this painter's principle. The lower part of the figure of the goddess, like the lower part of the Charioteer of Delphi, is carved in a mass, while the upper part above the girdle breaks into a series of curved lines that bring it to life. The most obvious lines to attract attention are those formed by the two arms. Throughout the work of Phidias we shall see that he, as a religious thinker, was reluctant to leave the old symbols, although as a progressive, forward-looking contemporary of Socrates, he invented new sculptural techniques. What

a subtle relation of lines, masses, and symbols appears in this tiny relief and how well they have been combined to convey the feeling of that most inexpressible thing, grief!

The student who has not followed carefully each step in the evolution of Greek design will be tempted to ask at this point whether the writer is not simply reading all these things into the composition. The answer lies (1) in the reader's own experiments with creative work, where he has proved to himself that artists actually create in this way, although unconscious of the fact at the moment of creation; and (2) in the preceding review of the productions of other cultures, in which it became apparent that primitive, lifeless, geometrical symbols assume lifelike, curvilinear forms and an appearance of reality as the culture achieves mental freedom from superstition.

Athena Lemnia. If there is any work on which more than two classical scholars would agree as to its being a very close copy of an original by Phidias himself, it would be the famous Athena from Lemnos, of which the original body is in Dresden and the head in Bologna (Fig. 189).

The drapery of the lower part of the figure falls easily in long folds, here rendered with more variety than those of the chiton on the Charioteer. Some of these folds have been cut deep, others are shallow. Further, although they have not lost their columnar, monumental feeling, they continually suggest the easy posture of the limbs beneath them. The limbs, then, arrange themselves on the pelvic apex (the hip

somewhat external in the Mourning Athena, has now become the central line of the figure, moving not only on one surface, but through the mass from front to back.

Fig. 188.—Mourning Athena, c. 450 B.C. Marble, height about 18 inches (Acropolis Museum, Athens).

line) of the body, so that the right shoulder falls slightly and the left comes up. Such an effect is called "counterposition" when used with respect to the masses of the human figure; when this balance of parts is found in literature it is called "*chiasmic*[1] *structure*": "Do not live to eat, but eat to live," for example. The chiasmic structure is somewhat helped in this statue by the fact that Athena's left arm is raised, held out perhaps by a spear, while her right arm must have extended some gift or symbol. In this statue the long, spiraling flame curve,

Fig. 189.—Athena Lemnia, by Phidias, c. 440 B.C. Marble, height about 7 feet (body, Albertinum, Dresden; head, Museo Civico, Bologna). (*Photograph by Hanauer; courtesy of Dayton Art Institute.*)

A close study of the head (Fig. 190) makes clear the further advance in the combination of sculptural form and line, as well as the fine union of the masculine and feminine types of

[1] From the Greek word *chiazein*, which means to mark with a cross.

FIG. 190.—Marble head, Athena Lemnia (Museo Civico, Bologna). (*Courtesy of Clarence Kennedy.*)

beauty. From the head itself, one would have difficulty in saying whether it belonged to a man or a woman; only the headdress determines the sex. This is, then, before all else, an

a   b

Fig. 191.—Doric and Ionic canons of proportion. *a*, Doryphorus, by Polyclitus, c. 440 B.C., marble Roman copy after original bronze, height 7 feet (National Museum, Naples); *b*, Apoxyomenus, by Lysippus, Roman copy, height 6 feet 8½ inches (Vatican). (*Courtesy of Lesch-Carnegie.*)

idealized human face, neither masculine nor feminine.

The brow line of the goddess has been cut sharply, but it blends in the center with the form of the nose and, at the end, with the temples. The nose itself is shorter and more delicate than that of the Apollo from Olympia, and the chin is less heavy than that of the Charioteer. The lips, on the other hand, have become fuller and more rounded. They no longer break into the archaic smile, nor are they depressed and saddening, as in later works. With the quiet control of the other features, they bespeak perfect calm and give one a sense of restfulness. The hair, bound by a fillet, is no longer merely drawn on the surface, as it was in the case of the Charioteer. The deep-cut single locks fall in large, inclusive masses. No lines are broken, but their sharpness in places

reveals or contrasts with the placid rendering of the greater muscle forms. This precise drawing of eyes and brows balances in an occult fashion the mass of the broad, unbroken cheek.

Fig. 192.—Discobolus, after Myron, c. 450 B.C. Roman copy in marble from original bronze, height 5½ feet (Vatican).

Probably among the Greeks this face stood for a superior form of beauty, displaying, as Plato and Socrates expressed it, a harmony of the outer and the inner man.

The Doryphorus of Polyclitus. Something of this harmony finds expression in the free-standing figure of an athlete, called the "Doryphorus," or spear bearer (Fig. 191*a*). Its creator, Polyclitus, was a Dorian sculptor from Argos. As the second known sculptor to attempt to explain his art, Polyclitus holds particular interest for the student of formal aesthetics. The first, the reader will remember, was the Egyptian who wrote that all art is a combination of cones, squares, and cubes. In his book, *The Canon*, or rule, Polyclitus stressed the importance of measure or proportion and held that the perfect figure must be seven heads high. Most of the Ionic archaic figures studied measure between eight and ten heads in height; the Dorian, about seven. Polyclitus, then, gave a measure of the style most agreeable to his fellow Dorians. From what we know of them, the Dorians were on the whole short and solidly built. The figure favored by Phidias, as we may see by comparing the Athena Lemnia with the Doryphorus, comes nearer being eight heads high, which was the Ionic standard later set by the sculptor Lysippus in his canon of proportion (Fig. 191*b*).

The chief aesthetic significance of the Doryphorus lies not in its being seven heads high, but in the skillful arrangement of the limbs and broad muscle masses so that the entire figure suggests potential power at a moment of repose. Although it is hardly proper to infer too much of Polyclitus' style from this Roman copy, nevertheless, it is probable that the artist actually made those advances toward realism suggested by the modeling of the knees and the muscles of the region around the ribs. The head shows a nice balance between realism and formal sculpturesque quality. Tilted slightly and turned, it forms the natural termination of a long, graceful S curve running up through the body. The shoulders and hips poise on this curve so as to form chiasmic structure like that in the figure of the Mourning Athena. As Polyclitus was both a contemporary and to some extent a rival of Phidias, one marks with interest the presence of this same line of vitality in the work of both men. As it appears also in the work of one other contemporary sculptor, Myron, we may safely infer that the line expresses some commonly held idea. Seeking such an idea, we remember that Heraclitus, the philosopher, suggested that the spiritual substance from which all life derived was fire. This vital line follows the curve of flame.

Its presence will lend to any figure a dynamic quality. In the development of Greek sculpture it becomes more and more the dominating motif until late Hellenistic times. It appears again in the sculpture of Michelangelo, who defined the flame in his poetry, and finds its latest expression in the works of the modern sculptor, Carl Milles.

In measuring his creations, Polyclitus used the same laws of mathematics that Pythagoras used to measure the tonal intervals on a vibrating string. The exact proportion of seven units of measure is necessary to make the perfect consonance of an octave. The sculptor-scientist measured every part of the body in terms of a fixed unit, the length of a finger. With him began that effort, occurring again and again among artists of a scientific turn of mind, to arrive at some universal physical law that would explain aesthetic effects.

What Polyclitus, Lysippus, Vitruvius, Leonardo da Vinci, Albrecht Dürer, the French Academicians of the 18th century, and the late Jay Hambidge measured, then, was not some absolute beauty but the images created by their own personal or contemporary styles. Such exercise has some value, however, as it aids the artist in making a careful objective study of art forms. Its futility as a complete explanation for the artistic phenomenon becomes at once apparent when an artist of lesser ability tries to create a new work of art using the old formula.

The Discobolus of Myron. The Dorian sculptor Myron specialized in athletes. He is best known for his bronze Discus Thrower (Fig. 192). A marble copy found in Rome demonstrates the way a sculptor may at the same time hold to conventions and reach out toward new forms. The Discus Thrower is really designed to be seen only from the front. Anyone who moves around to the side of this piece can see that it is all on a flat plane, though the treatment of individual muscles is more natural than in the archer from Aegina. The general line of the figure, which starts with the left foot and runs up through the arms, ending in the discus, suggests somewhat the tension of an opened spring, which will snap shut and propel the wheel into space. The muscles appear about as natural as

FIG. 193.—Pedimental sculpture, Parthenon, height about 10 feet. *a*, east pediment, Birth of Athena, showing position of Theseus, Fates, and horse of Helios (*after Rhys Carpenter, Hesperia*, 1933); *b*, west pediment showing Strife of Athena and Poseidon (*after drawing by Carrey*). The remaining drawings show decorative details from the temple. Notice that the inner geometric structure of the pediments repeats that of the ornaments. Compare with Fig. 185.

those in the contemporary Olympian pediment sculpture, and yet this is a single figure. Up to that time, single figures had always some religious significance and therefore remained columnar or geometric. This one is frankly realistic and may have been made pretty much for its own sake.

Phidias and the Sculpture of the Parthenon. When in 461 B.C. Pericles decided to build upon the Acropolis the finest public buildings in the world, he had his sculptor friend, Phidias, placed in charge of all the work. This fact is significant: a sculptor had charge of the building of the Parthenon and directed the work of the architects Ictinus and Callicrates. The temple treasury, under the master design of Phidias, became a perfect frame for the sculpture it was built to enshrine.

Phidias, who, it is said, had at one time been a vase painter, devised the sculptural decoration of pediments, metopes, and the continuous Ionic frieze within the portico with all the skill in line and unity of composition characteristic of the finest work of Brygos and Polygnotus.

Since the sculpture of the Parthenon was probably finished between 447 and 443 B.C., it was physically impossible for Phidias to carve all the figures. Indeed, one may detect the presence of many hands at work upon the various parts of the sculpture. There can be little doubt, however, that the designs were drawn

and perhaps made into small terra-cotta models by the master artist, and it is in the magnificent designs as well as in certain fragments that we seem to feel the master's personal touch.

The Composition of the Parthenon Pediments. The two pediments, one at each end of the building (Fig. 193), can be reconstructed from a few fragments, from designs on some contemporary jewelry, and from drawings made by the Frenchman Carrey in the 17th century of the Christian Era. In the east pediment the central figure was apparently Zeus enthroned. Possibly by this time Phidias had made just such a figure for the temple at Olympia. Zeus was represented as looking toward his newborn daughter Pallas Athena, who had moved toward the left, preceded by a figure of Victory. On the other side of Zeus stood either Hephaestus or Prometheus, holding a great ax with which he had cloven the god's aching head so that Athena might be born. The figures on each side of this central group represented either the Olympian gods or the city's heroes. Some scholars see in them local nature deities, or personifications of streams and mountains. In the outermost corner of the eastern pediment, to the left, Helios, the sun-god, was seen urging his horses up out of the sea, while to the right, Selene, goddess of the night, was driving her weary horses down. These two touches lend to the composition a literary quality similar to the opening and closing chorus of a Greek tragedy. Among the figures on the right side of Zeus sit three usually called the "Fates," perhaps personifications of three nymphs. At the left re-

the draped figures of the eastern pediment are the three magnificent women usually, though without full evidence, called the "Three Fates" (Fig. 194). Whether these really are fates—

Fig. 194.—The Fates, east gable, Parthenon, 447–432 B.C. Pentelic marble, height about 4 feet 2 inches (originals in British Museum). (*Photograph by Hanauer, from cast in Dayton Art Institute.*)

clines the magnificent figure variously named "Theseus," "Dionysus," or "Mount Olympus."

The western gable took as its central subject the strife between Athena and Poseidon for the supremacy of Athens. The sacred olive tree of Athena and the spring of Poseidon probably occupied the central position, between the two human figures. Various figures on each side of the central group are usually thought to have been personifications of local earth deities, Ilissus, the river-god, being particularly noteworthy because of the way the sculptor suggested in his recumbent figure the flowing movement of a stream. Even from the fragments it is possible to see that these two pediments represented the ultimate in the designer's art. In them, associational and formal values, anatomical correctness, and the monumental effect of each single figure have been brought into complete unity with the underlying rhythmical and geometric composition lines of the whole.

The Three Fates. Chief in excellence among

Clotho, who spins the thread of human destiny; Lachesis, who measures it; and Atropos, who cuts it short—or three nymphs may be left to the scholars. The excellence of these figures as examples of monumental decorative sculpture lies in the fact that every line, form, and plane in which the two great blocks of marble have been carved contributes to, or derives from, the flowing, rhythmical line of the composition as a whole, without detracting from the individual dignity of the figures themselves. The linear drapery both conceals and suggests the elemental form of the underlying bodies. At first, this drapery appears to be simply realistic, but closer study reveals that it was designed with the sole object of aiding the eye to follow the flowing motion from the central group out toward the vanishing horses.

Although the first figure of the group must originally have had her head turned slightly to the left, the position of her legs, and the deep-cut folds of their drapery carry the eye toward the right, where it is caught and carried by the folds of the second figure toward those hurrying spirals that flow like a mountain torrent down the body and limbs of the reclining one. Perhaps, as in the figure of Ilissus on the

Fig. 195.—Horse, east gable, Parthenon, 447–432 B.C. (original in British Museum). (*Photograph by Hanauer, from cast in Dayton Art Institute.*)

western pediment, the sculptor intended here to indicate that these were the personifications of three mountain streams. Not only do the folds carry a motion through the group as a whole, but each figure has its individual pattern of drapery so disposed that the smooth rounded forms of the breasts and knees act as broad static centers that balance the dynamic flow of the line.

The fundamental planes in which the marble was first hewn produce great areas of dark and light. These planes follow the natural disposition of the limbs. They constitute a third factor in the sculptural composition, lending a massive dynamic movement to each individual form, while suggesting motion back into the depth of the composition and out again.

Contrasting these figures with those of the woman and the centaur from Olympia, one feels that the Three Fates require no color, to be understood from a distance. With his deeply carved drapery, Phidias was able to give an effect that at a distance carried the impression of linear flow without distracting the attention from the subject. Although the folds are intricate, they do not dominate the greater masses,

chiefly because the sculptor made the action of the drapery harmonious with the body forms, and because he designed each separate part of the drapery so that every fold contributed to the motion from left to right. Aristotle, the critic, looking at these folds, might have likened them to the separate lines and words sung by an actor in a great tragedy, which, he said, "should so lend themselves to the plot as to be appropriate and to advance its action by heightening its emotional effect."

The Horse from the Parthenon. The Greeks of the 5th century B.C., like many 19th-century Americans, valued highly not only their women but their horses. Phidias depicted the horse many times in the friezes, metopes, and pediments of the Parthenon. This head of the horse from the east gable (Fig. 195), probably carved about 439–432 B.C., demonstrates in more obvious fashion the subtle balance of modeling earlier studied in the head of the Athena Lemnia, as well as the contrast of lines and planes in the Three Fates. The steed, harnessed to the chariot of Helios, is alive with the action of the race he must run. Yet he seems somehow to be permanent and monumental—not realistic alone, but idealized and abstract. The sculptor gained this effect by making the long sweep of the neck muscle in one piece and the cheek in one great form, and then carving in detail all the muscles around the nostrils, with their veins, sinews, and wrinkles. The lips and eyelids are also rendered in a realistic fashion. Here again appears a contrast between small, exciting forms that move our senses rapidly and large, placid areas that rest the eye. Thus balance is achieved between the sense exciting and the sense subduing.

The Theseus or the Dionysus. Of all the Parthenon sculpture, the figure of ultimate perfection, probably one of the most satisfying pieces of sculpture the world has known, is the Theseus (or Dionysus) from the eastern pediment (Fig. 196). This godlike being, superb in his arrangement of broad muscular forms, well-proportioned limbs, and contained silhouette, half

FIG. 196.—Theseus or Dionysus, east gable, Parthenon, c. 447–432 B.C. Pentelic marble, height about 3 feet 10 inches. (*Courtesy of British Museum.*)

reclines in dreamy, detached contemplation of some far-off event. He appears as one awakening from a dream, and the forces that are about

The Metopes. The sculpture of the Parthenon was all finished within eight years. Since it was physically impossible for one man to carve all

Fig. 197.—Metopes, south side of Parthenon, Lapiths and centaurs, c. 447–441 B.C. Height 3 feet 4 inches (originals in British Museum).

to inspire him can be seen active in the folds of the drapery beneath him. Within the figure itself we sense the capability of a more personal unfolding movement. The latent power is suggested by the counterposition of the limbs around the torso, whose great muscle bands have been carved in the form of a spiraling, swelling shell. The lowest and smallest coil of such a shell forms the muscle of the hip, the next convolution the muscle above it. After that each muscle form grows progressively larger until, when the eye reaches the upper chest, the two broadest bands blend in a restful shape out of which rise the monumental neck and head.

Although the marble surface has been badly weathered, enough of the features remain to show us that the face had the same calm as that of the Athena Lemnia. Theseus, the greatest hero of the city, was a demigod, in a way related to the virgin goddess, and in him brain and brawn were equally combined.

the figures on the building and at the same time complete the statue on the inside, various parts were left to assistants. As a result, not all the Parthenon sculpture is of equal excellence in either composition or rendering.

Two metopes forming part of the story of the Lapiths and centaurs make this clear (Fig. 197). In the one at the left, which shows a horseman trampling upon a Greek, the rendering of details is clumsy and without conviction. The lion skin at the right is too regular and static, the tail at the left unnatural and over-detailed in carving. The metope could never have been well composed, furthermore, even when the head and the upraised arm hurling its vase were in place. The vacant space at the left does not produce good occult balance, and the broken body of the Greek lies too far toward the right. The group has no center of interest and seems to be flying apart. In the metope at the right the horizontal, twisting figure of the centaur is balanced by the force within the figure of the

Greek, and although the group has less vigor than the similar metope from Olympia, the heavy folds of the drapery unite the various entire relief tilted inward at the bottom. There are other refinements. The contour lines are heavy, and shadows are cast from below. This

FIG. 198.   FIG. 199.

FIGS. 198 and 199.—Portion of Parthenon frieze showing correct lighting and rolling rhythm, 447–441 B.C. Pentelic marble, height 3 feet 4 inches, entire length 525 feet (originals in British Museum). (*Photograph by Lorado Taft.*)

parts so that the eye sweeps in great curves through the forms of the combatants.

The Frieze of the Parthenon. Inside the portico of the temple, running around the cella wall, Phidias designed in low relief a continuous Ionic frieze about three feet four inches high (Figs. 198 and 199). The frieze had for its subject the Panathenaic procession in which every year the sacred peplos, or robe of the goddess, was borne by selected Athenian women to the temple. In this procession could march only the finest of the Athenian aristocracy, priests and judges, maidens chosen for their beauty and virtue, and youths distinguished by their noble bearing.

Aesthetically, one cannot help being interested in the way Phidias held the procession together, although it moves in a number of diverse rhythms, some slow and stately, others, like the company of horsemen, rapid. The band was planned so that the slow movement came to a stop at the corners and seemed to accelerate near the center of each side, and ended above the entrance portal, in a number of seated figures of the deities (Figs. 200 and 201).

When this relief was in place, people walking around the temple could best view it at the lower edge of the stereobate. To help the illusion of proper perspective, Phidias had the

gives the relief a great feeling of depth when it is properly lighted (Fig. 199). These optical illusions compare to the entasis of the building as a whole and the varying sizes of the metopes.

The effect of movement was gained not only by the rhythmical lines and the repetition of perpendicular beats, but also by the fact that the columns continually interrupted the view of the spectator as he walked about the building, so that the frieze became a sort of motion picture with intermittent scenes, each showing some progress in motion. All the principles discovered in linear vase painting serve to heighten the illusion of movement.

In the frieze, too, it is possible to differentiate between the work of one carver and another. Some of the horses have been rendered in broad masses that carry well from a distance, others with fine, jewellike carving, archaic in character, which does not carry. Despite individual discrepancies, the entire effect is one of harmony and shows the part that a democratic group can play in art production when under a competent master.

The Athena Parthenos. Today it comes as a shock to find that the work of art for which Phidias was most noted by his contemporaries was not any one of the finely unified marbles in the pediments of the Parthenon but a great, columnar statue of Athena built of ivory and gold upon a wooden core, which stood within the cella (Fig. 202). The few copies of this Athena Parthenos which have survived, to-

plate, or aegis, made of glittering gold scales, with the head of the Gorgon hanging in its center as we saw it on the aegis of the Athena Lemnia. Her great shield, which rested on the

FIG. 200.   FIG. 201.

FIGS. 200 and 201.—East frieze of vase bearers, musicians, and elders from Parthenon, showing correct lighting and stately movement of procession. (*Photograph by Lorado Taft.*)

gether with representations of the statue on coins and gems, show it to have been a great, symbolic figure tricked out with all the barbaric ornament and intricate detail that would delight the mind of a primitive. The details of the goddess's armor were of gold, probably in-

FIG. 202.—Restored interior of Parthenon, with Athena Parthenos, of chryselephantine (ivory, gold, and gems) by Phidias; after model. (*Courtesy of Metropolitan Museum of Art.*)

laid with precious stones and marble; she stood fully equipped with a spear and a helmet on which a three-horse chariot seemed poised, ready to leap off into space. She wore a breast-

ground by her left side, was faced with a remarkable *repoussé* decoration showing a battle of the Greeks and Amazons. Among the figures in this relief Phidias is supposed to have portrayed himself and his friend Pericles. Soon, these representations caused Phidias a great deal of trouble, for the enemies of Pericles pointed to them as an instance of sacrilege for which the artist should be banished.

Inside the shield was painted the story of the battle of the gods and giants, and next to this was a great serpent, the Erichthonius snake of the underworld. Even the thick-soled sandals of Athena bore a representation of the contest between the Greeks and the centaurs. The pedestal on which the statue stood measured four or five feet in height. It, too, was carved, bearing a representation of the old story from Hesiod which told of the birth of Pandora, the first woman, who learned all woman's chief accomplishments from the goddess herself. As the socket in which the pedestal rested was about ten feet wide and only three or four feet deep, the statue was probably carved to be seen only from the front. It was essentially a great ikon, a work more of the jeweler's craft than of the sculptor's. Significant it is that Pericles seems to have valued it chiefly for the gold it contained. He said on one occasion that, if need be, the plates could be melted down to supply the city with money for a war.

FIG. 203.—Hegeso stele, grave monument, late 5th century. Pentelic marble, height 4 feet 10½ inches (Athens, Dipylon Cemetery). (*Courtesy of Lesch-Carnegie; Alinari.*)

Summary

In this chapter the study of the evolution of the Doric and Ionic styles of Greek architecture has demonstrated the great refinement and state of balanced equilibrium reached during the so-called Golden Age of Pericles. The early Doric temples at Paestum and Olympia showed contours and many details of columnar construction traceable to Egypt and Crete. The Ionic temples indicated connections with Asia Minor. The former stressed the element of sturdiness and stability; the latter, gracefulness. The Doric temple developed a grave, dignified, measured decoration in its discontinuous frieze; the Ionic, a more dynamic decoration in the continuous frieze. Characteristics of both Doric and Ionic styles united in the Parthenon, which played the dual role of a civic treasury and a temple to the goddess Athena. This building is considered the finest of all classical architecture.

The Ionic Erechtheum on the Acropolis stands as the apogee of the Ionic style. It has a less orderly, though interesting, plan. Its details, perfect and refined in themselves, show great variety, and the sum total of its effect indicates a certain romanticizing tendency even in the Greek mind.

In all Greek building, an interest in great refinement of material and the effort to symbolize a human control of mass replaced the primitive desire for overpowering size or glittering effect. Greek building, hence, establishes suitable relationships between the human size and the size of the structure. Valuing their civic buildings more highly than their homes, the Athenians made no significant contributions to private architecture. They developed the market place, however, whose stoa served as a civic meeting ground.

In Attic painting, the Oriental influence of the Ionic style united with the stately Dorian compositions. Unity and balance were first achieved by the fine spacing of areas in the black-figured style of Exekias. To this, Brygos, an early painter in the red-figured style, added greater realism and a more unified interwoven composition based upon the geometric structure of the prehistoric Danubian and Mesopotamian guilloche. Meidias, another red-figure painter, interested himself in the Dionysian element of individual expression for his figures. Douris began the combination of all these elements, but stressed the strong architectonic structure earlier indicated in the geometric Dipylon style. The climax of Greek pictorial composition arrived in what, for the sake of simplicity, has been called the "early Polygnotan style." Further developments in the last part of the 5th century B.C. included foreshortening and the beginnings of perspective, together with effects of light and shade suggested by lines.

The development of sculpture parallels that of painting. First, there appeared a movement away from angular geometric composition and the columnar or block form. Polyclitus and Myron gave particular attention to the individual figures and to action, as did Brygos and Meidias in painting. Phidias, like Polygnotus, finally combined a natural refined sense of the dramatic with strong architectonic composition and the interweaving flow of the guilloche. His figures served as models for all later anthropomorphic conceptions of the gods. The Theseus and the Three Fates from the Parthenon, combining well-developed sculptured form with inner life, reach a final state of equilibrium, where the values of use, form, and association rest in perfect balance (Fig. 203).

Bibliography

GARDNER, E. A.: *Handbook of Greek Sculpture*, The Macmillan Company, New York, 1915.

POTTIER, EDMOND: *Douris and the Painters of Greek Vases*, E. P. Dutton & Company, Inc., New York, 1909.

ROBERTSON, D. S.: *Handbook of Greek and Roman Architecture*, The Macmillan Company, New York, 1929.

CARPENTER, RHYS: *The Aesthetic Basis of Greek Art*, Longmans, Green & Company, New York, 1921.

LANDOR, W. S.: *Pericles and Aspasia* (novel), Saunders & Otely, London, 1836.

CHAPTER IX

The Triumph of the Attic Style, II

"And when you would represent beautiful figures, do you, since it is not easy to find one person with every part perfect, select, out of many, the most beautiful parts of each, and thus represent figures beautiful in every part?"

"We do so," said Parrhasius the painter. "And do you also," said Socrates, "give imitations of the disposition of the mind, as it may be most persuasive, most agreeable, most friendly, most full of regret, or most amiable?"

"MEMORABILIA OF SOCRATES"[1]

"Superficial beauty is not enough—witty discourse, playfulness, tender words and humor surpass the too-simple nature, for the devices of art season beauty."

"FRAGMENTS NUMBER 89"[2]

THE PARADOX of Plato's thought epitomizes that of the Athenian mind after the Golden Age of Pericles. Pericles is said to have called Athens "the school of Hellas." To her came the finest artistic genius from Doric and Ionic lands. Nevertheless, the mental quality of the average citizen seems to have been justly characterized by the historian Thucydides, who wrote of the Athenians as "revolutionary, quick at conceiving new plans and putting them into execution, bolder than their strength, running risks which a prudent man would condemn—always hoping for the best, always thinking up new schemes for advancement when the old ones failed, and if by chance they did gain some good things, never enjoying them because greedy for more." He ends by telling us that the Athenians "were born neither to have peace themselves nor to let anyone else have it."[3]

While Athenian commerce was expanding, this philosophy of living sufficed. Soon, however, the Mediterranean world proved too small for the rival city-states. In the inevitable trade wars that followed, Athens, at last, suffered defeat. All the energy of the Athenian mind then turned inward, and there followed a period of subjective, soul-searching analysis, with an art correspondingly emotional. This later art stands in sharp contrast to the detached archaic art of the pre-Periclean Age (*Cf.* Figs. 138 and 141 Chap. VI). Influenced unconsciously by the abruptly changing political alignments, the minds of the late artists vacillated between two concepts of being. On one side lay the pattern of democracy inherited from the days of Pericles; on the other, the patterns of tyranny set by Cleon, the proletarian, and Alcibiades, the Fascist, whose picture and philosophy as a typical despot are described in Plato's *Republic*.

The Drama

The tensions of the artists resolved themselves in dramatic presentations. Within the drama itself these tensions played themselves out between the action and the music, the staging and the poetry, thus greatly intensifying its emotional appeal. The strongly ethical art of the Aeschylean drama gave way to a style full of pathos and emotional action. This

[1] XENOPHON, *Memorabilia*, Book III, Chap. X, translated by J. S. Watson.
[2] By Caius Petronius, *c.* 50 A.D.
[3] THUCYDIDES, *History of the Peloponnesian War*, translated by Jowett, I. 70.

alteration in tone had a corresponding effect upon the graphic and plastic arts of Greco-Roman times. To understand the dramatic development and to apply the judgments of

Fig. 204.—Early Italian wooden stages from Pompeian wall paintings. (*After A. M. G. Little, "Scaenographia," College Art Bulletin, vol. XVIII, No. 3.*)

Aristotle, one must return to the theater of pre-Periclean times.

The Development of the Theatral Area and the Mechanics of the Stage in Greece. Early in the 6th century B.C., Athenians who had an interest in the dance and in the recital of patriotic dramatic poems met by custom at the market place just north of the Acropolis. Here wooden seats were erected and a dancing space or orchestra laid out on the ground, the earth tamped firmly as it still is in the Pueblo dancing places. This open-air meeting place without a definite stage, called a "theatron," probably differed little from a similar place in the Minoan palace of Knossos.

By 534 B.C., under the rule of the benevolent tyrant Pisistratus, the yearly festival at the Dionysia had attracted all the leaders of dramatic pageantry—the dithyrambic, satyric, and tragic choruses, and those Dorian mimes from Megara who brought the comedy. The Dionysian performances then moved to the southeastern slope of the Acropolis, at that time on the outskirts of the city, where a precinct with a temple had been dedicated to the Dionysus of Eleutheria. There on an open floor, assisted by his chorus, the first well-known actor, Thespis, recited several parts of a drama, perhaps mounting to a table or to the steps of the central altar to deliver his chief lines, then dancing back into the chorus as one of the group or retiring to some small tent to change his costume.

Early in the 5th century B.C., probably a low wooden or earthen stage was built and a large canvas or sail strung between posts to form a *skene*, or scene. This form of setting had possibly become customary by the time of Aeschylus, although it may be imagined that then, as today, the inventive dramatist devised new types of backgrounds and stages for the performances in different years (see Fig. 204).

In his early tragedies, Aeschylus needed only a minimum of scenery. In the *Supplices*, an altar to the gods in the center of the stage would have been sufficient. The *Persae* called for a "tomb of Darius," the Persian dynast. Such simple effects might easily have been arranged on a wooden platform slightly raised, in the rear of the orchestra.

When Aeschylus's great trilogy, *The House of Atreus*, was performed, the first two plays, *Agamemnon* and *The Libation Bearers*, called for several doors in the background and for some sort of apparatus to announce the deeds performed inside the palace. The last of the trilogy, *The Furies*, had even a change of locale from Delphi to Athens. At this point and very possibly for this very play, the stage must have been enlarged and its mechanics greatly improved. Perhaps the inventive playwright actually did this himself, as Vitruvius the Roman architect later suggested.

The Stage during the Performance. Remains exist of many theaters contemporaneous with the earliest Athenian drama. From these remains, from stage directions, and from the writings of several ancient authorities, as well as from recently published pictures of early Italian stages,

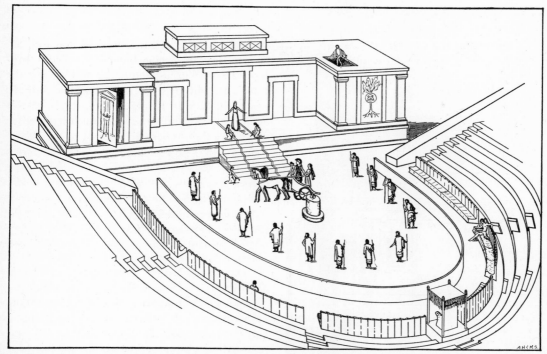

FIG. 205.—Reconstruction of Theater of Dionysus, Athens, with stage set for performance of *House of Atreus*. Compare with Figs. 154 and 156, Chap. VII.

archaeologists have collected enough data to reconstruct such a stage as the *The House of Atreus* would have required (Fig. 205).

While looking at the diagram one must imagine himself part of the great audience of about 17,000 people arranged on the hillside above the dancing place. These people, the entire population of Athens, have gathered to hear a number of old stories resung and danced in the most dramatic fashion. Every citizen enjoyed a free seat in this theater. The audience by its applause picked the winner among the dancing and ballad-singing teams and expressed disapproval by hissing, stamping, or throwing ripe fruit. The festival, which lasted for two or three days, each of which saw a number of plays produced, figured more as a patriotic and religious rite than as a simple form of amusement. The public-spirited citizen, called a "choragus," who paid for the production of a play, considered himself highly privi-

leged. If the performance so sponsored won first place, the donor was honored with a monument (Fig. 206). Thus the ancient aristocracy of Athens gained recognition by supporting contemporaneous art.

Judging from a few foundation walls of the theater at Athens, the stage was as much as 15 feet deep in the center (adjoining the orchestra) and between 60 and 70 feet long. The *Agamemnon* opens with the appearance, on the top of a tower, of a watchman, who may have ascended by ladder or who was perhaps hoisted up from below by some sort of elevator. Aristotle actually described such an elevator, or *mechane*.

When, in the course of the play, Agamemnon's murder took place in the interior of the palace, the audience could hear his cries offstage. After this event, a platform on wheels was pushed out through the doorway, showing the hero's dead body. Conventionally, the Greeks did not actually show the moment of killing. In this they resembled 20th-century motion-picture censors who allow a close-up of a revolver and a close-up of the man receiving

Fig. 206.—Choragic monument of Lysicrates, c. 334 B.C. Pentelic marble on Piraeic stone base, total height 34½ feet. (*Courtesy of Lesch-Carnegie.*)

the bullet but may not allow both victim and revolver to appear at the moment of the discharge.

The actors usually entered the scene through the *parodoi*, that is, from the sides of the orchestra, along with the chorus, although on some occasions both actors and chorus came in through the central stage entrances. This again required steps or a ramp from stage to orchestra. In the 4th and 3rd centuries B.C., when the

works of Aeschylus and Aristophanes gave way to the more personal dramas of Sophocles and Euripides, there was less need for a close connection between chorus and actors. The theaters were then greatly enlarged and in some the *proskenion*, with its stage, was raised eight or ten feet high. Late in Roman times, the stage was again lowered and steps were built leading up to it from the orchestra.

As Greek plays took place under the open skies, the actors had to have voices that would carry well, especially when performing before large audiences. The acoustics of the theater at Athens were remarkable. Today, providing the theater is unoccupied, lines spoken from a place at the front of the orchestra carry to the rear seats.

Aeschylus

The poet Aeschylus (525–454 B.C.) brought to the performance we shall witness a mind that had grown consistently for sixty-nine years. A native of Eleusis, home of the ancient mysteries associated with the worship of Demeter and Persephone, Aeschylus fought through the Persian Wars and served with courage in the first battle, at Marathon, and the last, at Salamis. When forty-one years of age, in 484 B.C., he won his first dramatic prize at the Dionysia. Throughout twenty-eight years of active writing, during which he wrote seventy tragedies, he is said to have won twenty-eight victories in various theatrical contests. Thus he may justly be called the founder of Attic tragedy, particularly because of his introduction of a second actor, in addition to the leader of the chorus. These two, by changing costumes, could take the parts of seven or eight characters. In addition to this innovation, Aeschylus greatly developed the dramatic plot and appears now to have exerted great influence in the realms of morality and religion.

From what is known of the dramatist's life, demonstrated by the seven tragedies remaining to us, it is apparent that he began as merely a patriotic Athenian who appealed to the people's pride in their overthrow of the Persians and their superior position in Hellenic culture. Toward the close of his life, however, and particularly in the writing of *Prometheus Bound*, a play shortly preceding the one studied, Aeschylus became convinced that the forces of superstition, symbolized by the powerful Olympian deities, were at war with a people endowed with some superior wisdom through their contact with the old earth deities. The implications of this drama of rebellion were so far-reaching that Aeschylus dared not let it stand, but wrote another in which Prometheus and Zeus at last became reconciled. It cannot be known exactly what effect this suggestion of revolt had upon the powerful followers of the old gods; it is perhaps significant that Aeschylus died an exile in Sicily.

The House of Atreus, or the Oresteia. The trilogy, *The House of Atreus*, better than any other drama of Aeschylus, united the elements of historical plot; an inner psychological, or moral, plot; and continuous, rhythmical, poetic utterance. It became the greatest dramatic heritage of the Athenian people. The year after it was played (458 B.C.) Aeschylus left for Sicily. A few years later, in 454 B.C., he died.

Imagine that you, with all the people of Athens, are seated on the slope of the Acropolis, in the great auditorium of the Dionysian theater for the festival, in March of the year 458 B.C. In the lower rows sit the magistrates, priests, and nobles; above them, the merchants, the soldiers and sailors, the farmers, the freedmen, and their families. As the dawn breaks in the eastern horizon out toward Salamis and the sea, we spy, on the tower at the right side of the stage below, a man lying asleep. The priest of Dionysus, descending from his seat, goes to the central altar, kindles the fire, says a brief prayer to the god, and returns to his seat. Then slowly the watchman, for he it is on the tower, looks out toward the morning light, raises himself upon one arm, and begins to sing his tale.

The play embodies a story that everyone in the audience knows by heart. Atreus, whose beehive tomb still stands below the town of Mycenae, was the son of Pelops, head of the Dorians. In a moment of savage cruelty this primitive Spartan monarch had cooked the flesh of his brother Thyestes' innocent children and then persuaded that prince to eat them; thus was Thyestes to be cursed. But the curse was redundant, for Thyestes asked the underworld goddesses who protect little children to bring ruin upon Atreus and his children's children to the third generation.

Menelaus of Sparta and Agamemnon of Mycenae, the sons of Atreus, impelled by fate, married two women destined to cause great woe. Menelaus took Helen, the most beautiful woman in the world, to wife; and Agamemnon, her sister Clytemnestra, a proud princess with a desire for dominance. When Paris, Prince of Troy, stole Helen, Agamemnon, in duty bound to his brother, enlisted in the war for her recapture. He left the city of Mycenae in care of his wife, Clytemnestra, by whom he had had a son, Orestes, and three daughters, Iphigenia, Chrysothemis, and Electra. The fate that pursued him predestined that Iphigenia, the daughter best loved by Clytemnestra, must be sacrificed if the Greeks were to win the war. Although the goddess who demanded this sacrifice hated the family of Atreus and the Greeks, she did not harm the girl but carried her away in a cloud. Clytemnestra, supposing Iphigenia had been killed, vowed vengeance upon her husband and in this was encouraged by Aegisthus, a son of Thyestes, who had already been foresworn by his father to murder Agamemnon. Together these two plotters, now in love with each other, sent Orestes away to Phocis and Electra to the kitchen as a serving maid.

So much is background. The action of the trilogy begins with the murder of Agamemnon on his return from Troy. His vengeful son, Orestes, then kills the guilty Clytemnestra and Aegisthus. Orestes, in turn, is afterward pursued by the Furies, and, although protected by Apollo, who had throughout the feud taken the part of Agamemnon, flees for his life to Athens. His case there comes to trial, and the play ends with the verdict.

The audience knew this story very much as most of us today know the plots of Shakespeare's plays or the general tenor of some musical show we go to see. In judging the drama, emphasis was laid on the means by which the poet and his chorus interpreted the plot, rather than on the novelty of the story.

Poet and People. The dramatic tension of the audience on that morning in 458 B.C. must have been very great, for it was known that Aeschylus was not completely in sympathy with many of the old ideas concerning the gods. The younger dramatist, Sophocles, was to present a play later in the program, and the old titan of the stage was now to be put to the test. Would he produce another great patriotic drama, a further defense of the earth-goddesses who always warred with the Olympian gods, or some story that would touch the heart of every Athenian? The political parties of the city ranged themselves unconsciously on the side of one or the other set of deities. This was no mere afternoon or evening's entertainment, but a day in which all the opposing tendencies in the Athenian state made themselves vocal through the poetic arguments of Aeschylus. He could win only if both the form of his drama and its ethical political content bespoke the heart of the majority.

The Prologue of Agamemnon. The watchman on the tower has only a brief prologue, forty-seven lines of poetry. How long and wearily has he looked for the beacon fire that will signal the end of the Trojan War! Glad will he be when his watch is over and he can shout to all the good news; at this he pauses and wonders if this will really be good news to all. From his point of vantage overlooking the palace, he has seen many things happen in this kingly house, and he has noted that it is no longer guided by honor but by treachery.

The beacon flame rises. The watchman descends from the tower and runs out through the door into the right, crying joyfully in a voice that will wake the queen, while he dances around the orchestra. Then again he pauses. He closes his prologue with the lines:

> Had it voice,
> The home itself might soothliest tell its tale;
> I, of set will, speak words the wise may learn,
> To others, nought remember nor discern.[1]

In these few lines of poetry Aeschylus creates a complete psychological setting calculated to stir in the mind of everyone in the audience a thousand memories of folklore, which weave into the story as it develops. On Greek vases, as observed earlier, one sees a geometric or decorative motif that points to the composition form underlying the main picture. This prologue of the watchman parallels the decoration around the base of the Greek vase; it suggests clearly what will follow.

The Part of the Chorus. Aristotle, who stressed the limiting form of drama, also called attention to the rhythmical development of the action. The next movement of the drama comes from the left. Twelve old men move slowly forward into the orchestra, chanting of the Trojan expedition.

So far the tone has been that of the epic. Soon, however, the old men of this chorus soliloquize among themselves, using the elegiac type of verse associated with the 7th-century poets, Mimnermus and Anacreon—a regret for the joys of youth which are past.

> And ah! when flower and fruit are o'er,
>   And on life's tree the leaves are sere,
>   Age wendeth propped its journey drear,
> As forceless as a child, as light
> And fleeting as a dream of night
> Lost in the garish day![2]

As the chorus moves around, Queen Clytemnestra comes out of the palace door, holding in her hands an unlighted torch. She goes down the steps, kindles the torch at the central altar,

---

[1] AESCHYLUS, *The House of Atreus*, translated by E. D. A. Morshead, p. 4, The Macmillan Company, New York, 1928.   [2] *Ibid.*, p. 6.

and returns to the altars placed along the palace wall—altars to all the other gods. Thus Aeschylus united the ceremonial occasion with his story, upholding Socrates' dictum that art is greatest when appropriate to the occasion. The members of the chorus recite the causes of the queen's grief and anger. At the same time they advance reasons why she should forgive her husband, who was forced by blood ties to leave his home, and by fate to sacrifice his daughter.

So it appears that the chorus performs a double function. Not only does it describe the epic background and link this past historical material with what must be going on in the minds of the actors, but it also vocalizes the various questions raised in the minds of the audience. These questions the actors answer by their actions, but their actions do not arise from within, as in modern drama; they are compelled from without.

The Inner Plot. The inner plot of the trilogy conveys the idea that vengeance should be superseded by a reign of law, that mercy and forgiveness must conquer hatred. In her first two long speeches, Clytemnestra identifies herself with the love of the Greeks for their native land. She recognizes every woodland, mountain, and shrine in Greece. No one can wholly hate the person who knows so well the places he loves. Later, when Clytemnestra tells of the conduct of the marauding Greeks who are sacking Troy, she shows her hatred for warfare. When her anger rises against those who slaughter children, everyone knows that she is thinking of her daughter, Iphigenia, the first to be sacrificed at the altar of war. We know, however, that her hatred holds no true solution of the problem.

Aeschylus later proposed a fit ending to the cursed feud, in the words of Cassandra, the prophetess daughter of Priam, who, captured by Agamemnon, was destined to be consumed in the vengeance of the queen.

Sun! thou whose beam I shall not see again,
To thee I cry, Let those whom vengeance calls
To slay their kindred's slayers, quit withal
The death of me, the slave, the fenceless prey.[1]

After having made us conscious of the depth of Clytemnestra's guilt and the horror of the dual murder, the chorus ends with this dirge, calculated to hold the interest over to the next play:

Lo! sin by sin and sorrow dogg'd by sorrow—
And who the end can know?
The slayer of today shall die tomorrow—
The wage of wrong is woe.[2]

The Libation Bearers, or Choephoroi. In the second play of the trilogy, *The Libation Bearers,* Aeschylus discloses the family of Atreus still driven by fate. Orestes has killed his mother and her lover and has been assured by Apollo that with him the curse of the house will pass away. Despite this promise, the gods who impelled his mother to avenge the death of Iphigenia now come to him as Gorgonlike Furies—conscience, if you will. Their ghastly faces pursue him to the very shrine of Apollo.

The Furies, or Eumenides. In the last play of the trilogy, *The Furies,* Aeschylus describes the way the gods act toward one another. Apollo, the sun-god, rules not through justice but by superior power. The Furies, representing Artemis and the dead, act not as beneficent earth-goddesses but fiends aroused by the ghost of Clytemnestra. Orestes, flying before them, reaches Athens where Athena, like a good judge, puts the case up to a jury of Athenian citizens, reserving for herself the right to cast a deciding vote in case the jury cannot agree. Since there is a certain amount of justice on both sides, a hung jury results. Athena then casts the deciding vote for mercy, making essentially the same plea as that Portia used later in Shakespeare's *Merchant of Venice.*

The chorus of Furies, metamorphosed into a group of beneficent deities, becomes almost

[1] AESCHYLUS, *The House of Atreus,* translated by E. D. A. Morshead, p. 61, The Macmillan Company, New York, 1928.   [2] *Ibid.,* p. 72.

sublime in its foresight, singing that all broil and vengeance shall cease, and

> . . . man with man and state with state
> Shall vow *The pledge of common hate*
> *And common friendship, that for man*
> *Hath oft made blessing out of ban,*
>   *Be ours unto all time.*[1]

Epilogue. Athena tells them that this type of justice shall make their country famous for eternity. A band of women and children, carrying flowers and dressed as for the Panathenaic procession of the Parthenon frieze, then escort the Fates, for such they have become, to their home in a cave under the Aeropagus, the whole group chanting together the final epilogue.

> With loyalty we lead you; proudly go,
> Night's childless children to your home below!
>   (*O citizens, awhile from words forbear!*)
> . . . .
> Behind them, as they downward fare,
> Let holy hands libations bear,
>   And torches' sacred flame.
> All-seeing Zeus and Fate come down
> To battle fair for Pallas' town!
> (*Ring out your chant, ring out your joy's acclaim!*)[2]

Aesthetically, as many conceive the aesthetic in the 20th century—something apart from social values—this drama may seem to move slowly. But in the original melodious Greek words, with all the added pageantry of colorful costume and intricate dance steps, it must have completely satisfied its audience. It has a distinct measure; the plot moves forward, helped at every stage by appropriate gestures and rhetoric. The stage setting, to Aristotle the least important element in the drama, was probably simpler than we would consider appropriate, but folk drama of this sort sets its own stage in the heart and imagination of the beholder. Some of the feeling that the Greeks would have felt for this play was paralleled in the 20th century when sophisticated audiences were held spellbound by *Green Pastures*, a play in which Bible legends, by many only partially believed, took on new meaning under the magic of dramatic art.

Sophocles

The gigantic figure of Aeschylus represented the beginning of the Periclean Age and the literary source of the heroic conceptions of Phidias and Polygnotus. Sophocles, the second of the great Greek tragedians, was born about 495 B.C. in the charming village of Colonus near Athens and died about 405 B.C. In the sixty years of his productive life Sophocles composed over a hundred plays, eighteen of which won the choral crown of victory in Athens and six in other towns. His first dramatic award, gained over Aeschylus in the Dionysia, came in 468 B.C., when he was twenty-seven.

In his earlier work, Sophocles kept much of the irresistible epic sweep of Aeschylus, as well as his monumental plot construction and heroic characterization. Unlike Aeschylus, he laid emphasis on the personality of the individual characters and the human motives that guided them. Sophocles also differs from Aeschylus in giving more attention to action, a dramatic quality that Aristotle called "pathos." In graphic terms, the heroic figures of Aeschylus's resemble the detached demigods of the Parthenon pediments (Fig. 196, Chap. VIII). They possess what might almost be termed a universal or sublime quality, while the characters of Sophocles suggest the youths and maidens on the Parthenon frieze or even such a statue as the Hermes by Praxiteles or the Scopaic head (Figs. 215 and 216).

Of Sophocles's plays seven exist in larger part: *Ajax* (produced before 440 B.C.), *Electra* (produced at some indefinite date), *Antigone* (441 B.C.), *Oedipus the King* (430 B.C.), *Women of Trachis* (420 B.C.), *Philoctetes* (409 B.C.), and *Oedipus at Colonus* (406 B.C.).

Ajax. The *Ajax* tells the story of the madness and suicide of a Greek hero before the walls of Troy. Perhaps the earliest of the known plays by Sophocles, this work, dealing with an epic tale from the *Iliad*, stands very close to the

[1] AESCHYLUS, *The House of Atreus,* translated by E. D. A. Morshead, p. 180, The Macmillan Company, New York, 1928.   [2] *Ibid.,* p. 182.

work of Aeschylus. As Ajax came from Salamis, the play gave Sophocles an opportunity to compose a charming choral ode to that island. This ode served to thrill the hearts of the patriotic audience, for Salamis was the island where many of them took refuge during the Persian invasion.

Electra and Tragic Irony. Sophocles' *Electra* deals with the same subject matter as *The Libation Bearers*, second in the Aeschylean trilogy of *The House of Atreus*. The plot of *The Libation Bearers*, the reader will remember, concerned the way in which Orestes and his sister Electra avenged their father's death on their mother, Clytemnestra, and her paramour, Aegisthus. The character interest in that play was rather general. In the *Electra*, on the other hand, the interest focuses upon the courageous character of Electra as contrasted with that of her vacillating sister, Chrysothemis. The brother, Orestes, arrives unrecognized, with a friend, Pylades, to slay the murderers. Only after he has killed Clytemnestra does Orestes reveal himself. The corpse of Clytemnestra having been covered, the brother and sister call Aegisthus, with the news that Orestes lies dead. Aegisthus, expecting to see the body of the man he had feared, pulls away the shroud only to discover his slain wife.

Here appears one of the finest examples of tragic irony. In such a situation all the spectators are called upon to witness the discomfiture of one who goes to his doom before their eyes. Insofar as they sympathize with the actor, their horror is so much the greater. Something in all of us makes it impossible for us to see even the most hardened criminal going unwittingly to his death without wishing to warn him of his danger.

Antigone and the Idea of Duty. The heroine of the play *Antigone* has been called by Symonds "the most perfect female character in Greek poetry." As portrayed by Sophocles, Antigone, like an Aeschylean character, remains nobly detached from human interest. She approximates the figure of the maiden repulsing the

centaur on the Olympian pediment. The story is as follows. Creon, king of Thebes, has a son Haemon, who loves Antigone, daughter of the former king, Oedipus. The two brothers of Antigone, Eteocles and Polynices, have slain each other in a battle for the possession of Thebes. Since Eteocles defended Thebes against the seven Argive chieftains led by Polynices, he was given burial, while Polynices was left unburied. Creon ruled that any who should bury Polynices should be stoned to death. Antigone, obeying the divine law that no kin be left unburied, buries her brother and is condemned to death. His pleas for her life refused, Haemon slays himself over the dead body of Antigone. Hearing of this, the queen also kills herself after cursing her husband. Creon, his family lost through his inhuman, unjust actions, begs the gods for death. Twenty years later, in his *Women of Trachis*, Sophocles pictured Deianira as a much more feminine woman than either Electra or Antigone. Throughout the plays of Sophocles, human love occasions strife.

Oedipus the King and the Development of Character. The greatest of the tragedies of Sophocles, written in the prime of his life—*Oedipus the King*—tells the story of every one of ourselves, for like Oedipus we all carry a sense of inner guilt, or conscience. The play centers about a man who unwittingly, through the perverse operation of fate, committed a series of crimes which afterward revealed themselves to him, destroying all his pride in what he had believed was a blameless life.

On the road to Thebes, the young Oedipus had slain an unknown man. Growing into a valued citizen of Thebes, the city of his adoption, he eventually married the queen, Jocasta, and reigned as a just king beloved by all. When a pestilence suddenly struck the city, Oedipus dispatched his brother-in-law Creon to Delphi for some oracle to allay the plague. Through the oracle Oedipus learned that the former king, Laius, had been murdered and that not until the murderer was found could Thebes be saved. Anxious for the welfare of his city,

Oedipus proclaimed that the murderer, once found, should be cursed and denied intercourse with men and gods. The rest of the play unfolds a series of ironic situations, each more deadly than the last, by which Oedipus discovers that it was he who killed King Laius, he who married the queen, and, most horrible of all, that he was actually their own son. Jocasta, who sees the truth before Oedipus, tries in vain to halt his relentless search for the murderer, but finally, recognizing his strength of inner character, takes her own life. Oedipus, seeing the dead body of his beloved wife and mother, tears out his eyes and sorrowfully takes farewell of his daughters.

Throughout the play Oedipus retains our sympathy. We see him as the upright judge who, discovering in himself the criminal, abides by his own decrees. Any great tragedy captures in its characters various aspects of guilt sense, as this one does. Magnifying them many times, it lends to them an element of objectivity so that, losing ourselves in the fears of the actors, we gain release from our own. This process constitutes what Aristotle meant by purgation, or catharsis.

The thinking Greek who identified himself with Oedipus, like those who earlier identified themselves with Prometheus or Orestes, could not fail to rebel against the needless cruelty of the old gods who would thus cause a just man to suffer. Hence these tragedies must have stimulated Plato and Aristotle in their search for a higher concept of God, a God who was true and good, even at times tender, like the God later to be proclaimed by Christ.

The Development of Romanticism in the Last Plays of Sophocles. In the last extant plays by Sophocles, all the fineness of human character comes to the fore and the gods take a minor place. In the *Women of Trachis* Sophocles tells the story of the unhappy fate of Herakles, the great demigod. Here appears for the first time in Greek drama what the 20th-century motion-picture scenarist calls "love interest."

Deianira has a love charm given her by the centaur Nessus to use in case she should lose the love of her husband. She does not know that Nessus, in reality an enemy of her husband, has actually given her a poisonous substance that will burn into his flesh. Discovering on Herakles's return from a long absence that he loves one of the maidens he has captured, Deianira anoints a rich robe with the magic charm and sends it to her husband. When she hears that he has been poisoned by it, she kills herself. The action of the drama then centers on the sufferings of Herakles as he recognizes that his unfaithfulness has caused not only his own pain but the death of his wife.

The character of Deianira displays far more human qualities than does that of Antigone. The same naturalness, this time in a masculine character, appears in Neoptolemus, the son of Achilles, in the play *Philoctetes*. This story tells of the sufferings of a wounded Greek hero, Philoctetes, deserted by his comrades on the island of Lemnos. After a series of trials, he is saved and promised healing. This play, like *The Furies* of Aeschylus, has a happy ending. These favorable solutions, employed at the end of the lives of both great dramatists, lead one to think that by nature these greathearted spirits of Greece, all 19th-century criticisms to the contrary, must have been optimists. In the last of Sophocles's tragedies, *Oedipus at Colonus*, this optimism sounded its final triumphant note.

In this play, Oedipus and Antigone, having been driven from Thebes by Creon and his two sons, wander to a grove at Colonus sacred to the Furies. Here, Oedipus remembers, an oracle had predicted his death. His daughter Ismene arrives to tell him that his two sons, Eteocles and Polynices, are fighting for possession of the city. Creon and then Polynices, representing the different parties of Thebes, both try to lure him from the grove, where he is protected by Theseus, the king of Athens. Finally, in a scene of tremendous power, Oedipus walks into the sacred grove to meet his death, only to be carried off by the gods to a triumphant life hereafter. We are reminded of the words of

Agamemnon: "Call no man blest 'til happy death hath crowned a life of woe."

In *Oedipus at Colonus*, one finds the entire meaning of the life of Sophocles. In the choral ode to Colonus, where as a happy youth he had led his first chorus, the aged Sophocles wrote of the tender earth soon to receive him. These lines, dedicated to Dionysus, who was related to the old mother goddess Ishtar in another incarnation, uses the same enchanted pastoral words earlier found in the first romantic epic of Ishtar and Izdubar.

Of all the land far famed for goodly steeds,
Thou com'st, O stranger, to the noblest spot,
    Colonus, glistening bright,
Where evermore, in thickets freshly green,
    The clear-voiced nightingale
    Still haunts, and pours her song,
    By purpling ivy hid,
And the thick leafage sacred to the god,
    With all its myriad fruits,
    By mortal's foot untouched,
    By sun's hot ray unscathed,
    Sheltered from every blast;
There wanders Dionysos evermore,
    In full, wild revelry,
And waits upon the Nymphs who nursed his youth.[1]

Euripides

Euripides, the third of the great tragedians, created plays which more nearly approximate the 20th-century idea of drama than do those of his predecessors. Living at the end of the Periclean Age, Euripides experienced the disillusion of one who sees a once great nation disintegrating under the rule of demagogues and dictators. The capacity of this artist for suffering, heightened by the tragic character of his time and perhaps by his own life, imparted itself to his characters. Their actions, overcast with pathos, breathed a humanity that anticipated all the art of the late Greeks.

The Personality of Euripides. Euripides had a romantic nature endowed with great fertility of invention, in the grip of inner tensions set up by the warfare of masculine and feminine elements. In justice to the dramatist, it must be

[1] Translation by E. H. Plumptre.

made clear that he depicted with deep insight not only weaknesses in woman's nature but also sources of strength—affection, self-sacrifice, and innate tenderness. Sophocles once said of his younger rival that, although his own creations painted man as he should be, Euripides showed him as he was.

How much of Euripides' emotional realism was due to his own character and how much to the desire of the audience can never be known, for in the theater more than in any other art the artist must seem to give the audience what it desires. Despite the efforts of philosophers such as Socrates and Plato to create an ideal world, the tenor of Athenian thought as a whole was that of the Sophists. We should say today that Euripides' audiences were "sophisticated." Men no longer went to the theater as to a sacred or patriotic festival but to appease their appetites for novelty and wit. A clever play on words or a breath-taking situation meant more to them than the dignified stories of the old gods, the deep philosophical questioning of Aeschylus, or a résumé of the ideals of a just government. With this growing desire for action and tragic irony there also went a greater appreciation of individual professional talent. In place of stately choral odes, the audience expected the operatic trills and cadenzas of professional singers. Euripides even employed professional song writers to compose his choruses. The music of one of these still exists in part (Fig. 207).

Though Euripides knew all the stage tricks necessary to gain him first place with his audience, he received only fifteen prizes for the ninety dramas he produced. Many of his plays were thinly veiled satires, and outspoken criticisms of the Athenian government. In 415 B.C., for example, at just the time when the Athenian war spirit reached its height, Euripides produced *The Trojan Women*, as telling an indictment of war as has ever been written. Shortly after this he was banished. The dramatist's life throughout seems to have followed the tragic pattern of his own creation. This very fateful quality made him popular with the Hellenistic Greeks, the Romans, and the great playwrights of the 18th and 19th centuries. The latter considered him a classic Greek, while actually he was the romantic forerunner of their own desires.

Medea as the First Melodrama. In *Medea*, produced in 431 B.C., Euripides used the tragic inner plot of the Agamemnon story. Jason, leader of the Argonauts, like Agamemnon, is the unfaithful lover; Medea, his jealous mistress, like Clytemnestra, is willing to sacrifice all for vengeance. In *Medea* we confront naked human emotions, packed together in quick action. The guilty sin, and are punished before our eyes. Everyone in the audience is made to feel that the burden of his own sin and punishment rests within himself.

The problem is that of the eternal triangle. According to the old legends, Medea, a sorceress-princess of Colchis, the island on which the Golden Fleece was guarded by a dragon, betrayed her own kindred for the sake of Jason, leader of the Argonauts, who desired to steal

nauts had made their escape. Blind to her vices, Jason took Medea to Corinth, only to forsake her in order to marry the daughter of the Corinthian king, Creon.

FIG. 207.—*a*, fragment of a score of the *Orestes* by Euripides, c. 408 B.C. (*after A. Thierfelder, Altgriechische Musik*); *b*, English translation (*by C. F. A. Williams, Musical Times, May* 1, 1894). This may be considered as a kind of linos song.

the fleece. The princess revealed her not-too-gentle nature when, after murdering her brother Absyrtos, she cut his body into small pieces, which she threw into the sea one by one so that her pursuing father, stopping to retrieve the fragments, would be delayed until the Argo-

The action of the play began with a dialogue between an old nurse and a tutor who enter with the children of Jason and Medea. Before one's eyes young children (unusual in Greek art), innocent victims of the crime about to be committed, appear on the stage. After the nurse and the chorus have described Medea's state of mind, Medea herself enters, a striking figure in a crimson embroidered robe. She resolves to kill her husband's betrothed on her wedding day by sending to her a poisoned robe and crown, a dramatic device later borrowed by the older dramatist Sophocles for his *Women of Trachis*. The description of the horrible death of the princess, sung by a messenger, is terrifying in its power. Her old father, the king, embraces his daughter in an effort to save her, only to be himself consumed by the fatal robe, a nice touch of tragic irony.

After the chorus has told her that her horrible deed will drive her to the very gates of Hades, Medea, realizing that her children may be blamed and punished, decides to kill them. From inside the house come the screams of the children imploring their mother not to kill them, as the chorus, like a group of tortured Furies, pantomimes its horror. We then hear the sound of blows and furniture thrown about and finally—silence. Jason comes rushing in, only to see his witch of a wife with their two murdered children ride out through the roof in a chariot of fire drawn by dragons. She goes free and he is left to suffer.

The word "melodrama" meant originally "drama with melody." In the dramas of Aeschylus and Sophocles, the music formed part of the whole. In the works of Euripides, the melody stands apart as a separate thing. In the 20th century the term "melodrama" came to indicate a type of drama in which the action was obvious and somewhat overdone. In this sense, also, the tragedies of Euripides are more melodramatic than those of his predecessors. We must not forget that in all Greek drama the highly descriptive parts were sung.

Hippolytus and the Romantic Tortures of Love. The chief interest of the *Hippolytus*, which was awarded the first prize in 428 B.C., lies in its splendid construction and its analysis of the emotion of love. As the play antedates by eight years Sophocles's *Women of Trachis*, it is apparent that Euripides used not only the poisonous-robe story but also the love plot ahead of his older rival. Here again, as in *Medea*, Euripides created a type of romantic fantasy that became a favorite plot throughout two thousand years of Western playwriting.

The Plays of the Trojan Heroes. Following the tradition set by Aeschylus and Sophocles, Euripides also wrote a number of plays about the House of Atreus and the heroes of the Trojan War. *Iphigenia among the Taurians, Iphigenia in Aulis, Orestes,* and *Electra,* all deal with the fortunes of the House of Atreus. These works contrast markedly with the plays of the earlier dramatists. As in his *Medea*, Euripides transforms and humanizes the monumental figures of Aeschylus and Sophocles.

Electra and the Appeal to the Crowd. Aeschylus in his *Libation Bearers* stressed the divine decrees that impelled Orestes to kill his mother. Sophocles in *Electra* emphasized the role of Orestes' sister and represented Orestes as impelled by an earthly interest in his sister's fate, rather than by divine guidance. Euripides made of this same story a still more human drama, in which brother and sister together plot their mother's death.

Euripides's story is as follows. Aegisthus and Clytemnestra marry off Electra to a peasant, so that her children will have no claim to the throne. Here the dramatist provides an additional motive for the murder of the mother. Orestes, finding his sister in the mean hut of the peasant, plots with her the murder of Clytemnestra. Again we have melodrama, as the queen in all her regal finery drives up to the poor hut. The very change of scene from the palace to the pasture must have carried an appeal to the democratic audience. After the murder of Agamemnon has been avenged in the death of Clytemnestra, the heavenly twins Castor and Pollux, acting as a sort of double *deus ex machina*,[1] see to it that Electra marries the noble Pylades.

---

[1] *Deus ex machina.* To bring about a happy ending or cause other events to happen, in a play, the Greek dramatists used a convention which consisted of the introduction of some god who could make even implau-

Even the peasant is compensated for the loss of his wife. As an afterthought, Orestes learns that the Furies are still unappeased and that he must face trial at Athens. Here, certainly, we have a drama that any 20th-century motion-picture director would call "box-office" material.

The Trojan Women as Propaganda against War. The sympathies of Euripides included even the enemies of the Athenian state. In 415 B.C. the Athenian imperialists had captured the island of Melos, killing all the men and enslaving the women and children. Emboldened by this success, the Athenian war party, under the leadership of the young Fascist, Alcibiades, decided to outfit a great expedition against Syracuse. While the war spirit was at its highest, Euripides brought out his drama, *The Trojan Women.* In this play, with the greatest attention to realistic detail, Euripides elaborated upon the theme announced by Clytemnestra in *Agamemnon*—the curse that falls upon warlike men who destroy helpless women and children. Euripides tells of the capture of Troy and of mothers whose sons and daughters were destroyed by the Greeks. In a later play, *Hecuba*, Euripides carried the story further, allowing one Trojan mother to take her vengeance upon the Greek hero, Polymnestor, who had murdered her son Polydorus.

These plays stand as man's first gallant protest against the horrors of war. In them, realism, in the best sense of the term, awoke the people of Athens to the results of their ambition in the sorrow and suffering of others.

The Bacchanals and the Dionysiac Origins of Tragedy. The play, the *Bacchae*, produced after Euripides's death, probes the lowest depths of the romantic soul. The story relates the conflict of an unwitting sinner, an earthly king, with the divinely inspired god of the drama, Dionysus. The play may have been a thinly veiled allegory, a warning to Athens that she should listen to her dramatists or be destroyed. Pen-

theus, king of Thebes, failed to recognize Dionysus, who is being worshiped in his town by a band of Corybantes, or Bacchanalian women. The women of Thebes, caught up by the chorus of these Dionysiac votaries, worship with them. Pentheus puts Dionysus in jail. The god, freeing himself, departs with all the women for the mountains, where they celebrate those rites for which the island of Delos had become famous —rites which no man could see and live.

Pentheus, on his way to see the rites, is discovered by the women and torn limb from limb, his mother and sisters taking part. This description of the fate of a man falling into the hands of women when they are inspired by the god of the theater has haunted romantics ever since. As the witches' Sabbath, it appears in Goethe's *Faust.*

The Satyr Play. In the Greek dramatic festivals, the finished series of three dramas were frequently interrupted by a short intermediate satyr play, relic of the oldest Dionysiac worship. The only example of a satyr play that has come down to us from antiquity is *The Cyclops* by Euripides. This work relates the story of the combat between Odysseus and the one-eyed giant Polyphemus. Polyphemus is the counterpart of the medieval giant in *Jack and the Beanstalk*, of the Renaissance Morgante of Pulci, and the Gargantua of Rabelais. This grotesque destroyer was first cousin to the creatures of pure comedy.

Comedy

The philosophies of Cynicism, Stoicism, and Epicureanism particularly appealed to the masses in the 5th century B.C. and after. All three individualistic philosophies centered more or less upon the desire of the individual to retreat from the responsibility of social intercourse into his own world of fantasy.

The philosophy of the Cynics approximated the comic approach to life heralded by the

sible things come true. This convention of the "god from the machine" did not affect the aesthetic sensibilities of the audience, as it took the place of what we should call "the element of fate."

dramas of Aristophanes. When one suffers under persecution or stands thwarted by some irrevocable evil, it is customary to seek refuge in an attitude of scorn. The grotesque elements in a situation, if not too tragic, induce no tears but the emotional effects of laughter. Comedy rarely constructs a new ideal. As slaves, we may laugh at our dictators and their grotesque posturings, while we secretly worship their power. Only when, as free men, we face the tragedy of their persecutions, do we take active measures to overthrow them.

Hence comedy, as an artistic form, must always follow tragedy. A sense of the comic derives its force from postures and actions that seem disconnected—movements, that is, which are unrhythmical and allied to destructive or disintegrating moments. Comedy often appeals more readily to the uneducated than to the educated classes.

Origins and Development of Comedy. Among the Ionians, the Dionysiac worship led to that form of rebirth which produced the great aesthetic tragedies. To them, the pitiful god wandering alone became the prototype of all human suffering. In Sparta, the sacred drink seems to have worked in the opposite way. The rustic revelers abandoned themselves to the Comus ode—the humorous song, or comedy, which almost, but never completely, approximated the unified effects of the tragic. Susarion of Megara occupies a position in the growth of this comic form similar to that of Arion in the tragic. He composed balladlike verses in which he added to the animal delight in grotesque situations a satirical strain directed toward the dignified citizens who were especially active in public affairs.

A chorus for the comedy developed during the early part of the 5th century B.C., and in Dorian Sicily, Epicharmus, who was contemporary with Aeschylus, wove all these elements around a distinct plot. In the time of Pericles, the developed comedy moved to Athens and was used to lampoon those opposed to the popular point of view. The tragic poets were parodied, people were likened to animals, and in the later part of the 5th century even heroes and gods had their share of ridicule. The first great comic poet, Cratinus, took as the special object of his choruses the policies of Pericles, calling him "the onion-headed," while Aristophanes, whose appeal was much broader and less personal, poked fun at Socrates.

The Comedies of Aristophanes. The first well-known master of the comic form, Aristophanes, produced his earliest play, *The Acharnians*, in 425 B.C. This comedy, which dealt with the Athenians' desire for peace with Sparta, satirized the policies of Pericles, who had died four years earlier. At the same time it parodied the tragic style then being developed by Euripides. Aristophanes's *Peace*, produced in 421 B.C., further satirized the conduct of the Peloponnesian War. This was followed in 414 B.C. by *The Birds*, which is probably the most valued work of the poet.

The Birds. The Birds tells of the escape of two citizens, Plausible and Hopeful, from the troublous life of Athens. These two wanderers found their home among the birds, with whom they proceeded to build a new state called "cloud cuckoo town," a settlement inaccessible not only to other men but also to the plaguing gods. The action of the play revolves about the difficulties of the two adventurers in repelling the efforts of men and gods to break in upon their paradise. The two wits were finally allowed to keep their "cloud cuckoo" land, in other words, to be slightly insane, and so the comedy ends. Today this seems to be the most successful of Aristophanes's comedies. The work did not, however, fill first place with the Athenians, who at that time probably wanted something much more drastic.

The Late Plays and the Rise of Theatrical Institutionalism. Aristophanes followed *The Birds*, in 411 B.C., with the comedy *Lysistrata*. This play suggested a way in which the women might lead the state to victory in the long-drawn-out war. After *Lysistrata* came another well-balanced comedy, *The Frogs*, in 405 B.C. Here the playwright commented on the place occupied by organized theatrical production in Athenian life. The play deals almost exclusively with the theater and criticizes satirically the works of Euripides and other dramatists.

Aristophanes's final suggestions for remedying the unhappy political plight of the Athenians appeared in his two plays, *The Parliament of Women*, produced just three years before his death, and *Plutus*, during his last year. In the first of these he concluded that the women might as well take over the state, and in the second that the wealth should be wrested from the wicked rich and given to the worthy poor—a suggestion perennially popular with demagogues.

Music in the Periclean Age

After the middle of the 6th century B.C., instruction in music, which during the Age of Anarchy under the ancient Dorian supremacy had been only for the nobles, became part of the general education of the Hellenic people. The popular Dionysiac festivals, then evolving into the theatrical performance, used various types of music. Athens drew to her the greatest musicians of all Hellas, and as part of his gigantic public works project Pericles built a great concert hall called the "Odeon." Here the choral dithyrambs were sung.

The Choral Odes of Pindar. The first musician to write a theoretical work in music, a man named Iasos, led the earliest dithyrambic choruses. Both Pindar of Thebes, whose odes at the Olympian games had won him recognition, and Simonides of Chios were invited to be guests of Athens. A bronze statue of Pindar was erected by the city fathers. Simonides made noteworthy additions to the choral art by unifying his dance numbers, so that melody, words, movements of the body, and accompaniment, all contributed to the total effect. Pindar, on the other hand, concerned himself with the quieter types of hymns. The first musician, in our modern sense of the term, he was interested

simply in fineness of tone and the singing word. The first Pythian ode of Pindar, with its original music, came to light in the monastery at Messina, Sicily, in the 17th century (Fig. 208).

Music and the Drama. A fragment of the score of *Orestes* by Euripides (Fig. 207), originally sung in 408 B.C., preserves both the manner of recording melodies and the connection between the music and the choral lines. The lines illustrated come from the passage invoking pity for one who has murdered his mother. The continuous lines of letters represent the words, and the letters and marks above, called "neumes," stand for musical notes. Each note was named according to its position on the lyre or aulos rather than in relation to a number of lines showing its position in the scale. Written in the letters of our descending scale, the Doric mode would be E, D, C, B, A, G, F, E.

Both Aeschylus and Sophocles composed their own music and choreutics. They regarded their choruses as a group of spectators whose lyric folk melodies explained the dramatic situation. Euripides, further in point of time from the folk soul, thought of the individuals in his chorus as solo singers and employed the musicians, Cephisophon and Timocrates, to compose duets and arias for them. The final stage in this development toward the use of musical effects for their own sake came with Euripides's follower, the lesser dramatist Agathon, who converted the drama into something like the present-day opera. The chorus in the works of Agathon acted as a mass to produce a musical, almost orchestral, background of tone. He even wrote parts for the flute, to accompany the various speakers.

This movement away from the old folk art attracted the attention of two writers in particular, Aristophanes and Aristotle. Aristophanes, poking fun at the new tendency, wrote the chorus of his *Frogs* so that their croakings would set off the speeches of Aeschylus and Euripides arguing in Hades. He definitely considered the older performances of Aeschylus, with their bolder epic sweep and magnificent associational

Fig. 208.—Ode of Pindar with music copied from the Messina Manuscript. For another less literal translation of this ode, see Chap. VI, page 177. (*After Fleischer, Reste Altgriechische Musik.*)

passages, superior to the individualistic grand-opera manner of Euripides's singers. Aristotle merely commented on the fact that during Euripides's time the folk-story background was no longer known to the mass of people, so that an explanation was necessary.

The Separation of Poetry and Music in Hellenistic Times. Music and poetry were separated completely during the time of Alexander the Great. Despite the preachments of Plato, who asked for a return to the noble Doric modes and the music of Apollo's lyre, the flutes of Ishtar and Dionysus with their possibilities for more individualistic expression became the dominant style. The lyre, or cithara, was less often used as a solo instrument. New instruments such as the *epigonion* with forty strings, and the water organ, a magnified kind of Panpipes blown by compressed air, made their appearance. At this time in Egypt great concerts were given, one of which required an orchestra of 600 musicians. Out of this milieu grew a number of musical treatises. A follower of Aristotle, Aristoxenos, wrote on both the melody and the rhythm of Greek music and, using the monochord, tried to derive a mathematically correct or tempered scale.

The Hymn to Apollo and the First Classical Re-

I will sing in praise of thee glo-rious son of Zeus! Who dwell-est on the snow-y peak of the hill, Where in sac-red or-a-cles to mor-tal men, Thou dost pro-claim tid-ings pro-phet-ic from the di-vine tri-pod-ic seat. Thou_ hast driv'n forth from his place the dra-gon who watched o-ver the shrine And, with thy darts, hast forced him to hide far in the dark un-der-wood.

FIG. 209.—Hymn to Apollo with melody taken from inscription, Delphi, 3rd century B.C. (*After C. F. A. Williams, Musical Times, June 1, 1894.*)

vival. The Hymn to Apollo (Fig. 209)[1] carved on the walls of the Treasury of the Athenians at Delphi represents one attempt to record a paean in the old Doric manner. Although set down at a later date, this hymn probably stands much nearer the finest choruses of Aeschylus in style than does the fragment by Euripides. This song gives one a fairly accurate idea of the noblest Greek music. Being in modal form, it sounds minor and plaintive.

The Greek Dance. From wall paintings, a few relief sculptures, and the meters of the various Greek verses, it has been possible to reconstruct the Greek folk dance. The dancers seem to have used the same steps and musical accompaniment that we find at modern Greek folk festivals in American cities. This community dance, illustrated in the fresco of the Ruvo Maidens (Fig. 180, Chap. VIII), is called the "Ratta."

The dance lends itself to an interpretation of all the forms of choral poetry found in ancient verse, and we may infer that the musical rhythm followed that of the poetry.[2] It is customary for a leader, the *choryphaeus*, to step out in front of the group and perform a highly individualistic step, at the conclusion of which

[1] *Hymn to Apollo*, translated by C. F. A. Williams, courtesy of Novello and Co., London, and H. W. Gray & Co., New York.
[2] Dancing the Ratta provides a fitting introduction to any study of Greek design. The rhythm of the music can easily be obtained on a gramophone record such as *The Syrtos* (Columbia).

FIG. 210.—Tholos of Epidaurus, by the younger Polyclitus, end of 4th century B.C. Height about 40 feet. *a*, exterior; *b*, cross section. (*After Defrasse, from Monuments antiques, by d'Espouy, Institute of France.*)

he again falls into line. The dance thus symbolizes the idea of democracy, for, though any participant may lead, he remains part of the group. The Ratta has many steps, each peculiar to some province or deme of Greece.

The Exaggerated Pathos in Late Greek Art

In Hellenic life, with the passing of the old cults, a worship of the healer god Aesculapius grew in power. In the town of Epidaurus, the priests of Aesculapius built up a remarkable sanitarium around a great open court bounded by a colonnaded stoa. In the center of this court stood the Tholos, one of the earliest of circular temples, erected by Polyclitus the younger.

The Tholos of Epidaurus and the Corinthian Style. On the outside of the Tholos of Epidaurus (Fig. 210), one finds the usual Doric portico with twenty-six columns. Inside the temple, however, appears a new style of architecture, one which became most important in later building. This was the so-called Corinthian style.

The Corinthian column (Fig. 211*b*) is more delicate and ornate than either the Doric or the Ionic. The shaft measures longer in proportion to width than does the Ionic shaft and seems to grow naturally into the leaves of the acanthus plant that form the capital. Authori-

ties derive the Corinthian capital from a union of Ionic volutes and the old Egyptian palmette form. The column usually rises from a light, decorative base constructed of two or more parts, sometimes, in Hellenic building, mounted upon a plinth or circular drum carved with human figures. The Corinthian style depends for its effect upon a lacy, jewellike play of light and shade in the upper part of the structure.

The chief significance of the temple at Epidaurus is that it seems to be a new architectural creation. In function the structure differs from both the old Doric temple, which was either an open commemorative shrine or a treasury, and from the Egyptian temple, which was arranged so that the worshiper approached the mysterious shrine through various degrees. The circular temple, especially when it includes the pit, resembles, to some extent, the ancient tomb temple, such as the Hypogeum of Malta. It is psychologically the prototype of the circular baptisteries used in conjunction with the earliest Christian churches. The element, water, through which the soul is reborn, is one of the original four elements. In Rome the round temple was used as the repository for another element, the fire, which symbolized the sacred hearth and was guarded by the vestal virgins.

The Corinthian column appears in other circular buildings, such as the Choragic Monument of Lysicrates and a temple, built by Philip of Macedon, at Olympia. The style spread quickly to Asia Minor and harmonized particularly with the later styles of Roman architecture.

The Choragic Monument of Lysicrates. Through

taller. The device of placing the shafts of the engaged columns so that they rest upon a stylobate above a podium increases the illusion of height.

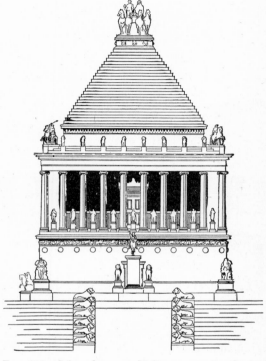

FIG. 212.—Mausoleum at Halicarnassus, by Satyros and Pythias, with sculpture by Scopas, 353 B.C. Height 142 feet. The standing portrait of Mausolus (Fig. 218) was on the top of this structure. (*After Bernier*, 1878.)

FIG. 211.—*a*, Ionic column from north porch of Erechtheum (see Fig. 169, Chap. VIII); *b*, Corinthian column (engaged) from Choragic Monument of Lysicrates (see Fig. 206).

Greek hands the Corinthian style flowered in a monument of purely decorative significance erected in honor of a dramatic victory won by the troupe of actors employed by Lysicrates in 335 B.C. (Figs. 206 and 211*b*). This structure, when compared with the buildings in Doric and Ionic style, is found to be relatively much

In terms of human measurements, the enormous infiltration of Celto-Germanic peoples from the north to the Mediterranean basin had by this time become so great that the entire racial stock was growing noticeably taller. With that change came a corresponding modification in the proportions of the sculptured human figure. The form considered beautiful became one in which the body was longer in relation to the head. It is possible that along with this physical alteration came a shift in philosophic outlook. Then, what the architect desired to build, what the painter painted, what the sculptor carved, all changed with this changing racial mixture. In architecture the dramatic elements supplanted the architectonic, in painting color was used for its own sake rather than as extraneous decoration, and in sculpture the by a broad flight of steps. Around the upper story ran a colonnade of Ionic columns supporting a roof like a stepped pyramid of about twenty-four rises. On the broad top was a four-

Fig. 213.—Porch, Altar of Zeus at Pergamum, 197–159 B.C. (*Courtesy of Berlin Pergamum Museum.*)

quality of pathos replaced the more restrained ethos. These differences can best be understood by studying two monuments of the 3rd century B.C. in which sculpture and architecture were remarkably combined.

The Mausoleum at Halicarnassus. The tomb of the tyrant Mausolus (Fig. 212) was built in 351 B.C. by the architects Pythios and Satyros. This structure, the best-known example of funerary architecture in the Hellenic world, justly ranked as one of the seven wonders of the world, along with the hanging gardens of Babylon, the Colossus at Rhodes, the pyramids, the lighthouse or Pharos at Alexandria, the Temple of Diana at Ephesus, and the Altar of Zeus at Pergamum. The corbeled hypogeum of the Mausoleum stood upon a high base approached

horse chariot in which stood the figures of Mausolus and his queen.

The Altar of Zeus at Pergamum and the Development of a Romantic Style. Eumenes, the second tyrant of Pergamum, who ruled between 197 and 159 B.C., built another famous monument of the ancient world—the great Altar of Zeus (Fig. 213). The ruins of this altar have recently been moved, stone by stone, with all the remaining sculpture, to a special museum in Berlin. As the monument now stands, the lower course of the stereobate measures about 100 feet in front. Monumental steps once led through two side wings to a central doorway in a long colonnade. This door opened on a court in which stood a small altar. The wings were decorated with a great frieze in high re-

Fig. 214.—Hydria, by Meidias, Dioscuri Stealing the Daughters of Leucippus, c. 410 B.C. (British Museum). Compare with Figs. 176, 177, and 178, Chap. VIII, and notice how drawing of profile has changed.

lief, showing the battle of the gods and the giants.

Architecturally, the significant thing to notice is that, although this relief rests upon a base and is crowned with a terminating cornice, above it rises an Ionic colonnade that bounds the entire structure. Aesthetically, the dramatic frieze running below the colonnade detracts from the value of the architectural elements, obviously used merely for effect. Therefore, this monument is studied as an example of Hellenistic sculpture rather than as architecture. In the Altar of Zeus, the battling figures with their strenuous lines, moving almost without design, form a base so unstable that the colonnade above seems ready to topple over. The sense of the melodramatic, so strong in the artist who conceived this monument, demanded that he reverse the functions of sculpture and architecture, placing the former below and the latter above—a striking contrast to the ordered restraint of the Parthenon.

Perhaps the designer's quality of mind can better be understood if he is thought of as a painter rather than an architect. The final phase in the development of Greek vase painting shows that the animated human figure rendered realistically had become the ideal.

The Meidias Vase and the Rise of Illusionism. After the work of Polygnotus, a new influence began to dominate Greek vase painting. When once perspective had been discovered and the effects of light and shade had been suggested in lines other than contour lines, the draftsmen paid more attention to depth. Forsaking formal, flat, linear decoration, they began definitely to try modeling and in so doing must have studied the relief sculptures by Phidias for the Parthenon.

The British Museum's red-figured hydria by Meidias (Fig. 214) makes clear the final development in the 5th-century Greek vase style. This shows a definite attempt to depict grass and trees, as well as various levels of staging.

Such a development of landscape leads inevitably to Greco-Roman illusionistic wall painting. It is most significant that there is no longer one connecting rhythm uniting the composition. The carefully drawn drapery lines bring out the individual beauty of each figure, as in the case of the Maenad vase (Fig. 177, Chap. VIII); but the fine balance between the function of the vase, the dignified narrative, and the rhythmical dramatic treatment of the whole, has now passed. In its place has come a desire to create a panel picture as a miniature dramatic episode for its own sake.

The Rise of Pathos in Late Greek Sculpture. After Phidias, the desire to express in sculpture greater pathos or dramatic action, rather than ethos or inner moral character, shows itself in three general tendencies. The first of these, apparent in the work of Praxiteles and the unknown sculptor of the head of Aphrodite (Figs. 215 and 216), led toward a kind of introspective illusionism—that is, an attempt on the part of the sculptor to make the spectator feel that he saw before him a real person lost in his own thought.

The second tendency led toward a highly magnified, outward, dramatic action. This propensity has a beginning in the work of Lysippus, the court sculptor of Alexander; continues in the figures of Scopas, who worked for Mausolus, the tyrant of Pergamum; and culminates in the dramatic relief sculptures of the Altar of Zeus at Pergamum (Fig. 219).

The third tendency led toward an outright, literal realism, such as that demonstrated in the Dying Gaul, from Pergamum. Such small figures (genre) as the Boy and Goose by Boethos and the Spinario illustrate the desire for realism, which was to become the dominating force in Roman sculpture. The sculptors who joined in this movement were influenced in many cases by late Greek painters who had discovered depth perspective, foreshortening, and a way to model in light and shade. A magnificent figure like the Nike of Samothrace (Fig. 224) unites the best qualities of all these realistic

works with something of the monumental style of Phidias.

The Hermes of Praxiteles. Praxiteles, who was born in Boeotia and may have studied under

FIG. 215.—Hermes and Dionysus, by Praxiteles, c. 350 B.C. Parian marble, height 6 feet 11 inches (Olympia Museum). (*Courtesy of Lesch-Carnegie.*)

the Dorian sculptor Ageladas of Argos, was known in antiquity particularly for his rendition of the nude female figure in his statues of Aphrodite. The soft, tender sensualism of the lovely goddess dominates even the masculine figure of Hermes, who here acts as nurse to the infant Dionysus (Fig. 215). This kindly deity

FIG. 216.—Aphrodite, so-called Bartlett head, c. 350 B.C. Parian marble, height 11½ inches (Museum of Fine Arts, Boston). (*Courtesy of Clarence Kennedy.*)

seems more human than the rugged, masculine Theseus of Phidias.

The statue of Hermes has particular interest for the archaeologist because it was found lying, face down, in the muddy ruins of the temple of Hera at Olympia in exactly the spot where the Roman traveler Pausanias had last seen it, in the 2nd century after Christ. Probably this is the only statue that practically all archaeologists agree is the original work of a known Greek sculptor of superior ability. It shows us, as nothing else can, the marvelous craftsmanship of a great Greek sculptor.

The god rests easily on one foot, his hips swung in counterposition, his weight distributed between his right leg and the tall tree trunk on which he leans. The dominant composition form of the Hermes is a long, upward-spiraling S curve, which lends to the statue a three-dimensional quality lacking in the Spear Bearer (Fig. 191a, Chap. VIII). To appreciate the work, one must walk around it, following the line indicated by the spiral. He then discovers that this so-called "curve of Praxiteles" or "Praxitelean line of beauty" runs through all the great masses of the figure, so that the changing curves along the various parts of the profile suggest a multitude of long spirals, each running into another. The profiles caused by the muscle forms of the legs spiral gently, breaking into still smaller spirals in the muscles of the hips and the abdomen. The spirals of the arm muscles lead into the smaller curves of the face, which alternate with the broad but broken planes of nose and brow. Seeking a reason why critics consider this one of the world's finest statues, we suggest that it almost exactly parallels the development of a thesis by Aristotle. The lines and forms of the lower limbs suggest the vegetable or plant soul growing from the earth. Becoming more forceful, the muscle forms of the abdomen and chest symbolize the animal soul, above which the dreamy face recalls the imaginative element decorated by the delightful contrasts of the mind in the ideal brow and nebulous hair.

The strokes of the chisel have been completely eradicated in a finishing process which included sanding, polishing, and rubbing with the wax of honey-carrying bees. Although the infant Dionysus has begun to reach for the bunch of grapes held above his head, Hermes pays no attention to the child. As though he were lost in his own thoughts, his deep-set eyes, with projecting upper lids, gaze abstractedly past the little Dionysus on his arm. The essence of pathos, or dramatic action, in sculpture lies in its ability to hold our attention within the object. It will appear that, from this point on, one measure of a great work of art lies in its power to hold our attention over a relatively long period of time.

The purely formal values of measure and proportion here unite so subtly with the associational that one is scarcely conscious of their presence. Unlike the earlier statues of athletes, this figure does not have a heavy, Dorian appearance. Because of its grace it gives the impression of being Ionic, although actually it comes near the Doric canon of proportions.

The most significant thing about the entire creation is the fact that so much of the monumental character and the ideal ethical quality of the earlier sculpture has been retained by a man who knew and could practice realism (note the drapery and the tree trunk), a man who was interested in detail but who, like some truly great dramatist, preferred to subordinate this to the effect of the whole.

The Head of Aphrodite. The little marble head of Aphrodite (Fig. 216) called the Bartlett head, now in the Boston Museum of Fine Arts, represents the work of some unknown follower of Praxiteles living in the 4th century B.C. It displays all the qualities for which Praxiteles was justly famous and advances one step further along the path of introspective illusionism.

Analyzing the charm of this piece, one perceives that here is no proud, jealous goddess of the Homeric tales nor yet one of the regal, matronly women created by Praxiteles. Instead, there appears a girlish, delectable child, appealing because of her freshness and youth. The light masses of her hair, suggesting wind-blown clouds, are ornamental and feminine. In treatment they strike a balance between the formal style of Phidias seen in the Athena Lemnia (Fig. 190, Chap. VIII) and the illu-sionistic style of Praxiteles (Fig. 215). Seen from the front, the hair mass occupies the up-per quarter of the head, below and contrasting with it the broad, placid, unbroken form of the forehead—symbol of the mind—takes up the next quarter.

The lids of the deep-set eyes resemble those of the Hermes, while the fully modeled brow forms suggest the work of a contemporary sculptor, Scopas. The subtle treatment of the region around the eyes gives them an illusion of mystery or depth, suggesting confidence and trust. The eyes and the rather strict columnar, Doric nose form connected directly with the upper brows seem to carry the intellectual ele-ment into the lower, more sensate part of the face. There the dainty, delicate Cupid's bow of the upper lip rests lightly upon the broader form of the sensuous lower lip, which nicely balances the small chin. Throughout the entire head one feels planned contrasts between broad planes of modeling and refined decorative fea-tures. It may seem at first glance that these planes are oversimplified, but a close study of the head turned slowly in the light discloses under the planes a great variety of subtle forms.

In the Bartlett head appears at last what by the sum total of definitions of Plato and Aris-totle might be considered a beautiful work of art, a universal being in which outward form harmonizes with inward soul. This ideal girl seems to breathe inner contentment, and is fitting for her own sake. Here we have the quality of pathos in its highest sense. The head of Theseus by Phidias must have been similar to this, when first carved. That statue, how-ever, formed a part of a more inclusive, uni-versal ideal. From what we know of these two works of art, we may imagine that Socrates, Plato, and Aristotle would have chosen the

Theseus as the more significant or beautiful creation. All three philosophers valued most highly the associational, ethical qualities. Many 20th-century artists or aestheticians who, as specialists, admire a work of art for its own sake would probably choose the Aphrodite.

The Apoxyomenos, the Canon of Lysippus. The second tendency in late Greek sculpture—that which led to the creation of an overdramatic realism—first appears in the work of the sculp-tor Lysippus, a man from the island of Sicyon. This artist rose to the position of court sculptor to Alexander the Great. In the opinion of the Roman critics neither Phidias nor Praxiteles rivaled Lysippus, who in a busy lifetime turned out almost fifteen hundred figures of athletes and rulers, so that in time by the very weight of numbers, if for no other reason, he became known as a great sculptor. Despite his prolific output, however, not one figure remains that can with confidence be ascribed to the master. A Roman copy of an athlete scraping his arm with a strigil after leaving the baths probably comes fairly close to the original (Fig. 191*b*, Chap. VIII). This figure is known as the "Apoxyomenos," which means simply the Scraper. As in the Hermes of Praxiteles, the body follows a spiral curve and should be seen from all sides. The great significance of the work lies not in any superb aesthetic quality, for it is at the most but an inferior example of all we found in the work of Praxiteles, but in the fact that it demonstrates a new canon of proportion for the human body formulated by the sculptor. The figure stands eight instead of seven heads high.

Lysippus and his brother, Lysistratus, en-deavored to create more realistic figures than any of their predecessors. Possibly for this reason more than any other the Romans ad-mired their work.

The Boxer from Olympia. Lysistratus, the brother of Lysippus, rediscovered the ancient Egyptian reproduction technique of making casts in plaster. He was the first known sculp-tor to use this technique for making studies of

FIG. 217.—Head of boxer, by Lysistratus, c. 320 B.C. Bronze, height about 11 inches. (*Courtesy of Clarence Kennedy.*)

FIG. 218.—Portrait of Mausolus, by Scopas, from mausoleum at Halicarnassus, c. 350 B.C. Marble, height 9 feet 10½ inches (British Museum). See Fig. 212. Observe the deeply carved drapery and "Scopaic" eyes, both of which make the figure carry from its high position on top of the monument.

hands and arms. Naturally, any desires in this direction led inevitably to the creation of a very realistic type of sculpture. The bronze boxer found at Olympia (Fig. 217) not only shows this realism in the quality of the bronze casting, but also indicates that the late Hellenes had not lost their sense of design. The curls of the hair, the counterposition of the two eyebrows, the modeling of the lips, all make the surfaces appear more violent and thus emphasize the energy of the man.

For the student of modern sculpture who wishes to combine realism with inner expression, this illustration may well serve as a model. He should notice particularly the effect gained by the sharply cut eyes and the abrupt angle of the brow contrasting with the broad forms of the cheek and the curves of the nose. This element—contrast of light and shade—which accompanied the development of the Hellenistic style, grew more pronounced in the works of the northern Scythians during the early centuries of the Christian Era, and developed through the Gothic into the baroque style of the late Renaissance.

Dramatic Realism in the Sculpture of Scopas. Another great sculptor of the early part of the 4th century B.C. who worked for a tyrant was the Ionian, Scopas. Leaving his home in Asia Minor as a youth, Scopas probably studied in Dorian territory under followers of Polyclitus. Next he is said to have been in Athens, where he must have met the followers of Phidias and where, on the Aeropagus, he left two monumental statues of the Fates. He executed many monumental works also in Sicyon, Tegea, Megara, and Elis. More than any other sculptor of the 4th century B.C., Scopas shows signs of being a true heir to the style of Phidias.

Antiquity valued Scopas for the same qualities that predominated in the dramas of Euripides. Scopas understood the construction of the ideal figure but preferred to use new inventions and technical tricks to stress dramatic elements. He found the spiral curve of composition the best medium of expression but compressed it so that his figures for the most part show greater inner springs of action. He handled draperies and limbs as though he were a Romantic painter, giving his figures an effect

Mausolus stands in an easy pose, with his weight resting upon his right leg. The folds of the drapery, carved in great detail, deserve special study. They display much the same

FIG. 219.—Sculpture from Pergamum altar, Athens Fighting the Giant Alcyoneus, c. 180 B.C. Height 7 feet 6½ inches (Pergamum Museum, Berlin). (*Courtesy of Lesch-Carnegie.*)

of ecstatic movement. In the ancient world, Scopas was celebrated for his ability to depict such fine differences as the variant expressions of love, longing, and desire.

Among the greatest works of Scopas stand two figures that reveal him in his quietest moments: the statues of Mausolus and his wife standing in their chariot on top of the great Mausoleum at Halicarnassus. The fragments of this sculpture, now in the British Museum, although not accepted by all scholars as the work of Scopas himself, show such qualities of greatness that we may well credit them to him. In the figure of Mausolus (Fig. 218), Scopas created an ideal that so stirred the imagination of the ancients that they attached its attributes to all the more kindly tyrants of antiquity.

character as the draperies on the Parthenon figures. All the lines of the clothing lead upward, and several bands of light, broadly carved folds contrast with the broken dark bands of finely carved folds. Above his massive chest a square Dorian head rises upon a heavy, columnar neck protected by a great mass of hair. The deep-set eyes are modeled much more realistically than those of Hermes. Instead of dreaminess and mystery, their expression is, rather, one of power—an expression achieved particularly by means of the detailed modeling of the folds of flesh over the brows and of the upper and lower eyelids. This figure of a great actor who was also a dictator first shows the beginnings of a dramatic realism that was to develop in two directions through the efforts of the various sculptors in the city of Pergamum.

The Altar Frieze at Pergamum. The gigantic struggling forms of the Pergamum frieze (Fig. 219) epitomize the pathetic in its ultimate expression. This overdramatic but technically

hordes of Gauls from the North, Attalus II distinguished himself by defeating the barbarians and became the founder of a ruling house so strong that it vied with Athens and Alexandria.

FIG. 220.—The Dying Gaul, Asia Minor, c. 220 B.C. Marble, height 3 feet.

superb carving shows the obvious influence of the art of the late painters and dramatists. Perhaps the strife between the father and the mother deities, the earth and the sky, had become so intense in the minds of these people that only a composition approaching the chaotic could express it. From the dramatic angle, the group lacks the element of measure or proportion. The plot does not build up to a climax. These same characteristics appear in late European art as the so-called "painterly" or "baroque" style.

Literal Realism in the Sculpture of Pergamum. From the many fruitful schools of sculpture of the 3rd century B.C., such as those of Rhodes, Alexandria, Orontes, and Antioch, one—the school of Pergamum—can be chosen as a typical example of the final tendency in Greek sculpture toward literal realism. During the battles between Pergamum and the invading

Pausanias reports that Attalus gave Athens a number of votive offerings in the form of small groups of sculpture, many of which can still be found in the museums of Europe. These groups commemorated the various victories of the Greeks over not only the Gauls and Persians but also the mythical Amazons and giants. All these groups were supposedly copied from bronze originals in Pergamum. They have one thing in common—a completely unidealized realism and a portrayal of deeply pathetic actions.

The Dying Gaul. The most famous of many figures from this source is the so-called Dying Gaul (Fig. 220), today in the Capitoline Museum at Rome. A careful study of this piece, carved in fine island marble with the greatest attention to detail, will reveal all the qualities that appeal to the realist in sculpture. To the art historian, the style of the hair and mustache and the bronze Celtic torque around the neck indicate definitely that this man is a Gaul. The anthropologist finds confirmatory evidence in the thickness of the leg joints and the angularity

FIG. 221.—Late Greek genre sculpture. *a*, Boy and Goose, by Boethos of Chalcedon; *b*, the Spinario (bronze).

of the face. The fatal, bleeding wound, the expression of pain, and the recognition of approaching death in the face, compel the attention, especially of anyone who is interested in the details of tragedy. Nor has the sculptor neglected the internal lines of composition. The triangles are breaking down and the vital spiral disintegrates in heavy masses of flesh. Much about the figure suggests the Wounded Lioness from Nineveh (Fig. 116, Chap. V), but with certain essential differences. In the case of the lioness, the effect is wholly exterior; here the sculptor has succeeded in making us identify ourselves with the dying man. He was able to do this because he had at his disposal all the inheritance of the Greek advance in composition, knowledge of significant sculptural form, and deeper understanding of human emotions. This Dying Gaul, therefore, arouses a correspondingly greater feeling of empathy than the Wounded Lioness can.

Rise of Genre in the Hellenistic Age. The wide dispersion of Greek sculptural styles and the growing versatility of many second-rate creators led to the carving of innumerable small

sculptural groups dealing with subjects of everyday life. The Boy and the Goose (Fig. 221*a*) by Boethos of Chalcedon was copied many times, as was another famous piece, the Spinario (Fig.

FIG. 222.—Terra-cotta pyxis or ointment box with painting in white-figured style. Height 6½ inches. (*Courtesy of Metropolitan Museum of Art.*)

221*b*). This last, which shows a young boy pulling a thorn from his foot, was one of the first pieces studied as an antique by the Renaissance masters. Figures of men fishing, slaves grinding tools, and similar objects fall under the head of genre. This term covers a type of art dealing realistically with scenes from everyday life. It is particularly noteworthy that at this time the sculptors began to carve the figures of children in proper proportion and to picture domestic animals for their own sake.

Along with the smallest objects—tiny earrings, mirror handles, and dainty ointment boxes (Fig. 222)—men strove to create the colossal, also. On the island of Rhodes a towering bronze figure of a man guarded the entrance to the harbor. According to ancient pictures, this colossus, by the sculptor Chares, was a much more daring work of sculpture than the Statue of Liberty inside New York harbor.

Fig. 223.—Late Greek white-figured vase with brilliant blue, red, and yellow decoration, Southern Italy, c. 100 B.C. Height 40 inches. (*Courtesy of Metropolitan Museum of Art.*)

It stood with legs astride, so that ships entering the port could sail between them. Size is no substitute for grace (Fig. 223), however, and one inclines to agree with Socrates that true beauty arises only when the inner soul har-monizes with outward form—with Plato that the inner soul must harmonize in all its parts—and with Aristotle that outer form must harmonize in every part with inner soul.

Summary

This chapter has demonstrated how the ceremonial use of folk dances, mimic action, poetry, and music culminated in the civic function of the yearly Athenian festival in honor of Dionysus.

All Greek drama, based on widely understood folk stories, stressed cleverness of presentation and harmonious relation of part to part rather than originality of idea. The study of Greek drama gives one a fine sense of appropriateness or measure. In the dramas of Aeschylus, the measured Dorian or Apollonian elements of the epic and dithyrambic verse, the religious-hymn character, and the ethos or reasonable action, dominated the more Dionysiac, pathetic elements of individual character analysis. In the hands of Euripides, melodramatic incidents, making a direct, emotional appeal to audience reaction, replaced the dignified measure and refinement of the earlier works. Contemporaneous with this development, the comedy, growing in part out of natural buffoonery, in part, perhaps, from the satyr plays, rose to a position of greater importance. As the Athenians lost their patriotic sense of heroic idealism and became sophisticated, the audiences turned to wit and satire, although the finest comedy of Aristophanes partakes of the high ethical character of the dramas of Aeschylus and Sophocles.

At this time music gradually detached itself from the drama and poetry. Dramatic poets wrote virtuoso parts and professional musicians composed music for them. An aesthetic attitude in musical criticism took the place of the earlier folk participation.

After the 5th century B.C., the plastic and graphic arts seem to be dominated by a more rapid Dionysiac dance rhythm. The individual figures of the gods become humanized and take on more personal characteristics, indicative of a deeper psychological analysis on the part of their creators. The architecture of the time grew in the direction of greater delicacy, the column becoming thinner and taller, with deeply cut foliated ornamental capitals. The structure of the building façade, following the movement in the theater and the other arts, became melodramatic, as the simple architectonic character of the Doric and the refined delicacy of the Ionic gave way to the ornate Corinthian at Ephesus, Halicarnassus, and Pergamum (Fig. 224).

These changes in the aspect of the arts paralleled the changes in politics and philosophy, as individualism came to have greater value than social conscience. The individual correspondingly broadened his own mental horizon. The universal soul of Aristotle, benefiting by the conquests of Alexander, encompassed the world in an encyclopedic system of knowledge that united the best points in Sophistry with the ideals of Plato, the Monistic view of Parmenides with the Atomism of Democritus. This philosophical background prepared man for his place in the world citizenship of the Greco-Roman civilization that followed.

Bibliography

Harvard Classics, *Nine Greek Dramas*, P. F. Collier & Son Corp., New York, 1909.

MURRAY, GILBERT, translator: *Ten Greek Plays*, Oxford University Press, London, 1929.

FLICKINGER, R. C.: *The Greek Theatre and Its Drama*, University of Chicago Press, Chicago, 1922.

NICOLL, ALLARDYCE: *Masks, Mimes and Miracles*, Harcourt, Brace & Company, Inc., New York, 1931.

CHURCH, A. J.: *Calias: The Fall of Athens* (novel), The G. W. Jacobs Co., Philadelphia, 1906.

FIG. 224.—Victory (Nike) of Samothrace, by a follower of Lysippus, c. 300 B.C. Marble, height about 12 feet (Louvre Museum). (*Courtesy of Lesch.*)

CHAPTER X

Art under the Romans

We ought to observe also that even the things which follow after the things which are produced according to nature contain something pleasing and attractive. For instance, when bread is baked some parts split open at the surface and these parts which are thus open, and have a certain fashion contrary to the baker's art, are beautiful in a manner, and in a peculiar way excite a desire for eating. . . . If a man have a deep insight with respect to the things which are produced in the universe, he will see even the real gaping jaws of the wild beasts with no less pleasure than those which painters and sculptors show by imitation; and in an old woman and an old man he will be able to see a certain maturity and comeliness; and the attractive loveliness of young persons, he will be able to look upon with chaste eyes; and many such things will present themselves not pleasing to every man, but to him only who has become truly familiar with nature and her works.

"The Thoughts of the Emperor Marcus Aurelius Antoninus"[1]

Since no one but a skilled painter or sculptor can judge rightly of excellence in these arts, so a man should have formed advanced opinions in philosophy before he essays to judge the worth of any philosopher.

"Letters to Atrius Clemens"[2]

THESE words of the Stoic emperor Marcus Aurelius and of the younger Pliny denote the changed attitude toward art which came about during the Roman ascendancy. The idea expressed by Marcus Aurelius derived from Aristotle, whose careful analysis of the component parts of the drama allowed attention to center on the particular, thus encouraging realism in art. Pliny's idea stemmed from Plato, who conceived the philosopher as an artist knowing his own medium. During the period of Roman domination this seemed to warrant the artist's acting as the primary judge of his own work.

So much of Western life and education, in the humanist tradition, goes back to Greek origins seen through Roman eyes that a brief summary of the social, political, and aesthetic psychology of the Roman citizen seems essential in order that his most significant artistic contributions may be surveyed satisfactorily.

The Historical Backgrounds of Roman Art

Ramnes, Latins, and Tities. In central Italy at some time during the 6th century B.C., a small settlement on the southeastern bank of the River Tiber about 18 miles inland from the sea drew into one locality three related groups of people. The first of these, the Ramnes, were a race of neolithic farmers similar to the pre-Mycenaean inhabitants of ancient Greece. They had a small fortified settlement on the Palatine Hill, which rose on the northernmost border of an area inhabited by a second group, a tribe who called themselves Latins. The third group, another neolithic people called the Tities, represented an outpost of a nation known as the Sabines, who lived to the northeast of the Ramnes on the Quirinal Hill.

After some warfare, the three groups decided to merge their interests around a common mar-

---

[1] Translation by George Long, Book III, No. II, Henry Altemus Company, Inc., Philadelphia, 1864.
[2] Plinius Caecilius Secundus.

ket place, or agora, which they called the "Forum," a low spot lying between the two hills. Here they set up a statue to a god, Janus, whose head had two faces, one looking toward each settlement. Thus, at the outset, we find the future Rome dedicated to a deity who acknowledged that there were always two sides to an argument. Such a balanced point of view, leading to the intellectualization of emotional drives, does not conduce to the production of art. Art develops slowly from mythological backgrounds and emerges into the intellectual only through the critic's pen. Janus became the god of codification, a creator of categories. These two racial predilections—intellectualization of emotion and codification of laws—tended to make of the future Romans an unemotional people.

The Coming of the Etruscans. Into this balanced group of neolithic races early came a fourth racial element by no means so stable. The strong kings of Etruria, the country to the northwest, lived as feudal lords in their mountain fortresses, as had their kindred in Mycenae and the Hittite states of Asia Minor. Much as pirates, they forced themselves into the young Roman state bringing with them the royal insignia of the crown, the scepter, and the bundles of rods bound around ceremonial axes called the *fasces*. By the year 510 B.C., these Etruscan kings had settled upon a third Roman hill, the Caelian, and had bound to themselves by force the Latins and the peoples of the first two hills. They built a good drainage system—a great arched sewer, the Cloaca Maxima—and installed their principal deities upon a fourth hill, the Capitoline. From the name of this hill we have taken our term "capitol" for the center of government.

Much of the aggressive aspect of Roman life can be ascribed to these Etruscan overlords, whose fleets ranged the broad seas, harassing the Greek and Phoenician merchantmen who voyaged northward toward Marseilles. The artistic productions of the Etruscans suggest a moody disposition. Though their religion included a cruel concept of the Last Judgment, much of their attention focused on a blessed hereafter of feasting.

The Political History of the Roman Empire. The 5th and 4th centuries B.C. saw the fusion of these four racial elements, and by 295 B.C., most of central Italy had become a well-regulated extension of the city of Rome. By 201 B.C., Rome had destroyed Carthage and subdued Spain, lower Gaul or France, Northern Africa, and the shores of the Adriatic opposite the Italian peninsula. In 168 B.C., conquest enabled her to consolidate Greece and Macedonia. In 146 B.C., her general, Mummius, destroyed the Greek city of Corinth and removed all its art treasures to Rome. In 138 B.C., the kingdom of Pergamum was willed to Rome by Attalus III, the last of the tyrants, thus adding to Roman territory a rich province in Asia Minor.

During the century immediately preceding the birth of Christ, Roman traditions began to decline, but under the leadership of one of Rome's aristocratic families, this heterogeneous group of provinces gradually became a great empire. The Romans early had before them the example of Alexander with his conquering Greeks and his short-lived kingdom, which, created overnight, collapsed with the death of its creator. The Roman state, in contrast, evolved slowly and methodically. Conquered peoples were made economically dependent and incorporated into the empire; Roman citizenship was given to their leaders. In artistic terms, we might compare Alexander's empire to a painting hastily executed, and the Roman Empire to an architectonic structure erected on a solid foundation. Such an empire could not have existed earlier in history. It became an actuality only because the territories it incorporated were already well organized and connected through Greek commercial activities.

The Religion of the Roman. The religious backgrounds of Roman art lacked the warmth and imagination of a mythology. Unlike the Greeks, the earliest Romans created no half-human

Olympian deities. They lacked also the civic heroes elevated to the condition of demigods and the personification of natural forces in the nymphs and fauns, satyrs and centaurs. Instead, the Roman religious ceremony, brief and formal, was based upon allegories growing out of the daily occupations of men. The act of sowing the grain, for example, became the god Saturnus; faithfulness, the god Fides; boundary, Terminus.

These abstract, often ethical concepts, arising directly from human relationships, carried no wealth of associational religious meaning upon which artists might draw for inspiration. By nature the Roman was more or less of an agnostic, incapable of creating ideal religious figures.

During the early years of expansion the Romans took from the Etruscans the belief in auguries. These consisted of oracles or advice read by the *haruspices*, or diviners, from the entrails of sacrificed animals. The Roman never abandoned the primitive superstition that in the long run his actions were guided by Fortuna, the goddess of chance. In brief, the Roman was at heart an opportunist in philosophy and religion. After coming into contact with the Greek civilization, for example, the Romans transformed the Etruscan deities Jupiter, Minerva, and Diana into Latinized forms of the Greek deities Zeus, Athena, and Artemis. In similar fashion, the Greek Demeter became Ceres, goddess of the harvest, the earth-goddess Rhea became Tellus, and Dionysus became Liber or Bacchus, the god of wine. Deeply underlying all these new deities, however, stood an ancient Etruscan version of the mother goddess, known as Matuta. As a neolithic farming people, the Romans were always cognizant of this old underworld deity, who was represented with a child in her lap. In the last part of the development of Roman life, Matuta was adopted by the Christians as the Madonna.

As a practical folk, the Romans valued highly the life of the home, with its megaron hearth fire. Although the father, pater familias, had complete control of the hearth fire, the goddess of the hearth, Vesta, held a significant place in the late Roman pantheon, or congregation of the gods. Many circular temples were built for her worship. In the Forum one of the earliest of these housed a sacred flame from which all the cities' hearth fires were kindled anew every year. The six vestal virgins who tended the fire stood in high esteem, and in the early days of the Republic, particularly, this same respect was accorded to Roman mothers, on whom rested the responsibility for the early training of men who in later life were to rule the world. Of all gods, however, the Romans revered most highly Roma, the personification of their city.

The Philosophy of the Roman. In the Roman mind, a number of quasi-religious beliefs gradually took the place of the well-reasoned philosophies of Plato and Aristotle. A few of the leading thinkers of the Empire, men trained in the Academy of Plato or the School of Aristotle, who lived for the most part in Athens or Alexandria, still understood the ideal plans for the development of the human mind. Most of the higher class Romans, however, followed the philosophic Cynicism, Stoicism, or Epicureanism. The middle-class people accepted these as semireligious beliefs, while the great masses remained in a primitive superstitious condition, preyed upon by fortunetellers and astrologers, who followed the various gods of old Egypt, Phoenicia, and Mesopotamia. During the last days of the Empire followers of Plato, called "Neo-Platonists," invented a more or less superstitious religion based on idealism. The followers of Pythagoras, under the name "Neo-Pythagoreans," similarly made a religion of their science.

All these systems of thought helped to formulate the ideals expressed by artists in various parts of the Empire.

The Growth of Cynicism. The philosophy known as Cynicism grew contemporaneously with the tragedies of Euripides and the birth of the late Greek pathetic movement in sculpture. Like the magnificent creations of Plato and Aristotle, Cynicism may be said to have stemmed from the thought of Socrates. Antisthenes, the founder of the system, like Plato, a pupil of Socrates, observed the decline of the Athenian morale. Confronting the abuses to which he was subjected by the degeneration of the democracy, Antisthenes strove to perfect a system of personal conduct that would correct them.

Although Antisthenes was an honored citizen, it seems that his mother was a freed slave and, as one who was not wholly an Athenian, he made his later friends among the slaves of Athens. From the gymnasium for slaves, the Cynosarges, where he conducted a class in philosophy, Antisthenes took the name "Cynic," which was applied to his philosophy. Among his disciples was the son of a forger—a young man whose name was Diogenes.

Antisthenes and Diogenes came to the conclusion that the only thing of worth in life was the idea of virtue (*erete*) and that all worldly goods were a delusion. This is similar, of course, to the ideas of Plato. Plato had evolved a philosophy in which a tyrant after 10,000 years might move upward toward the sublime state of the philosopher, going through the various mental attitudes of artisans, painters, and brave men. Antisthenes seems to have made repentance a necessary prerequisite for this movement. Perhaps for this reason he stood psychologically a step in advance of Plato.

Like St. John the Evangelist, the young Diogenes preached a return to nature, a negation of all that man called valuable—wealth, fame, family, and bodily comfort. Casting off all social conventions, he slept in a great coffin (like a Dipylon vase) near the temple of Demeter and lived what he himself characterized as the best life—"a dog's life." We today should probably call him a "hobo." He considered himself a sort of second Socrates, sent on a mission to prove to all Athenians the delusion of pleasurable activity, and gave to himself the titles, "Healer of Passions" and "Saviour of Mankind."

In Diogenes there appeared the first known example of a personality influenced by the art of its time. Up to this point in the book we have discussed only the effect of culture upon art. Oscar Wilde, in his *Decay of Lying*, first called attention to an important fact demonstrated here. The artists who create types and styles eventually influence men to live and act like these types. Diogenes represents the dramatic picture of the comic philosopher created by Aristophanes. Some of the stories about Diogenes, the best-known Cynic, are enlightening, for they show the characteristics of a perennial type. This one-man comedy went around the streets of Athens in the daytime with his lantern, "looking," so he said, "for an honest man"—thus the son of a forger!

In the life of Diogenes there is little of balance or of the refined sense of measure, which the Greeks called *sophrosyne*. He represents the severe ascetic mood that seeks a kingdom of heaven not of this earth. Unlike Cassandra in the tragedy by Aeschylus, Diogenes hoped for something that was not merely death and a cessation of the human tragedy; he really wanted a definite salvation for his countrymen and took this abrupt manner, as evangelists often do, to attract attention to his gospel. Unlike Plato, Diogenes made no attempt to formulate a scheme for a better society. Cynics like Diogenes usually remain constant to some ideal, and the pursuit of an idea becomes a duty, in the end more satisfactory than no philosophy at all.

The Stoic Ideal. Zeno, another disciple of Antisthenes, came as a merchant to Athens from Oriental Cyprus. He devised a more positive statement of belief than that of the Cynics. Zeno held his discourses in the great stoa, or porch, which ran around the agora. From this locality his school took its name "The Stoic," or "The Porch." Briefly, he attempted in his philosophy to reconcile the belief in salvation through pursuing virtue with the more relative values of human life which attempt to beautify it.

Zeno was greatly influenced by the new astronomical discoveries of his time. These tended to show that the stars move in set paths, perhaps around the earth. The concept of a fixed principle or purpose which seemed to have scientific weight he identified with the Good. Once he had accepted the belief that the divine purpose was the Good, it became his duty to find his part in helping that purpose to function. Under the terms of such a philosophy, the artist gifted in the production of beautiful objects constituted a microcosm, a tiny growing world formed in the image of the macrocosm, the greater world—which was God or Creative Reason (*logos spermatikos*). Through Stoicism the artist received a definite objective sanction for his necessary production as long as he did not consider his productions to be ends in themselves, but simply necessary shadow forms projected by the Great Purpose.

The position of the Stoics appears in its most concrete literary form in the following passage by Marcus Aurelius, a late Roman emperor:

Every one has the power to withdraw into himself where the well-ordered mind may find peace. Never forget to return to this little domain of your own, avoiding all distraction, nor straining to achieve anything else but freedom. Look at life as a man, as a good citizen, as one who is but human. Be assured that nothing material can harm the spirit, that all mental struggle arises in opinion which at the worst is but relative. Remembering how often you have seen things change, comfort yourself with the thought that soon all things will change again, for the Universal is an endless Becoming, and human life but an opinion about it.[1]

This type of philosophy, which approached the Oriental point of view, assisted the later growth of Christianity, particularly that expressed in the Gospel of St. John. Out of it grew an understanding of the part played by friendship, forbearance, and low estate in life. As long as the virtuous soul envisaged the ultimate triumph of the Good, earthly pain might be endured as mere illusion.

[1] Marcus Aurelius, *Meditations*, Book IV, #3.

Stoicism even allowed man to recognize his lesser desires as necessary parts of the greater, without losing faith in his ultimate good intentions. It also allowed aesthetic values to function as part of active life, without denying the ultimate victory of the nonsensuous or hypothetical Good.

Epicurus and the School of the Garden. The third great popular school of philosophy centered about Epicurus, an Athenian citizen born on the island of Samos in 341 B.C. The philosophy of Epicurus was definitely religious but antiecclesiastic. He not only conceived of God as the Good Purpose, but, anticipating Christianity, denied that any evil could come from this good source. All that was harmful, therefore, was illusory. The only genuine evil arose from useless fears. Pain was always worse in anticipation than in actuality, and death was nothing but a painless sleep.

The wellspring of Epicurus's own faith lay in his affection for his family, who had been driven from their home in Samos during a war. He showed the people around him that the humble lot of this group of exiles, tilling the soil on a tiny farm while caring for one another, was of greater value than anything else in the world. Out of this grew his idea of the Beloved Community as a center of all values.

The thoughts of Epicurus soon gathered many adherents, and some friends insisted on buying him a house and garden in Athens, where he might expand his ideas. The "School of the Garden," as it was called, soon became known as a center of social welfare and a spiritual retreat. Despite popular accusations against its principles, there is no real evidence of other than simple, friendly living without ostentation during the life of Epicurus. Certainly, this life was far from the commonly held notions associated with Epicureanism, such as "Eat, drink, and be merry, for tomorrow we die."

The Evolutionary Theory of Lucretius. The philosophical poetic writings of Lucretius, born about 95 B.C. presents a further development of the early Greek Democritean point of view. It includes suggestions of Aristotle's idea of the ascent of knowledge, seen through the eyes of Epicurus. Lucretius, trained in both physical science and poetry, neglected the inspired, or religious, aspect of existence and strove to unite atomism with a high ethical tone. In the philosophical poetry of Empedocles and the drama of Aeschylus, Lucretius found his warrant for the new interest in nature, at this time showing itself in Roman landscape painting.

Eventually, the questions of Lucretius led him to the Garden of Epicurus. The Epicureans, believing completely in atomism, held that with the death of the body the soul also must die. Thus, a refined earthly existence became their chief concern. Lucretius progressed beyond Epicureanism by finding in his scientific nature study a principle of evolution. This he characterized as a progression from atoms and voids toward a pure spirit or whole. In this he followed that part of the program of Aristotle which acknowledged that the particular detail could progress toward the universal truth. The evolutionary ethical poetry of Lucretius, which represents the philosophy of the Roman scientists, may be perceived in a few lines from his great poem, *De rerum natura*.

When Man's life upon earth in base dismay,
Crushed by the burthen of Religion, lay,
Whose face, from all the regions of the sky,
Hung, glaring hate upon mortality,
First one Greek man against her dared to raise
His eyes, against her strive through all his days;
Him noise of Gods nor lightnings nor the roar
Of raging heaven subdued, but pricked the more
His spirit's valiance, till he longed the Gate
To burst of this low prison of man's fate.

And thus the living ardour of his mind
Conquered, and clove its way; he passed behind
The world's last flaming wall, and through the whole
Of space uncharted ranged his mind and soul.
Whence, conquering, he returned to make Man see
At last what can, what cannot, come to be;
By what law to each Thing its power hath been

Assigned, and what deep boundary set between;
Till underfoot is tamed Religion trod,
And, by his victory, Man ascends to God.[1]

The last line of the quotation makes clear the psychological mind-set of the Greco-Roman individualist. After casting out desire, then fear, man might finally consider himself *en rapport* with the source of inspiration. He would then be willing to break through conventions in both religion and art.

The Roman Mind as Exemplified by Cicero. The Roman was a man with a mission, who felt called upon to put the world in order. His proudest boast was *Civis Romanus sum* (I am a citizen of Rome). Naturally, with such strong patriotic feelings, the Romans looked at art from the political angle. The beautiful, in the long run, became that which best advanced the purposes of the state.

The Greek ideal of measure Romans transformed into the more ceremonial ideal of decorum. For a man like Cicero, decorum became a wellspring of beauty and manliness. The Greeks chose as an aesthetic ideal the pursuit of reason for its own sake. From Plato's *Republic*, the practical Romans took as their highest ideal the service of the state.

In many of his letters and addresses, Cicero has given us a picture of the ideal seen through the eyes of a Roman lawyer. From the best Stoic thought he derived as his noblest ideal four cardinal virtues: justice, wisdom, courage, and temperance, which in their total effect made man's character truly beautiful. In his book on Duty he wrote: "As beauty and saneness of the body are inseparable from its healthy condition, so is the highest ability to be traced to an inner morality from which it can be separated only in theory." This psychological observation sprang from Plato's earlier use of the term "art" to mean effectiveness, or ability to control. Carried further, in the Renaissance, this type of aesthetics, misinterpreted, led to the practice of virtuosity, which means that

[1] Reprinted from G. Murray, *Five Stages of Greek Religion*, by permission of Columbia University Press, New York City, 1925.

that is truly beautiful which best displays a proper control of some medium of expression. The Roman as an actor upon the world's stage had to control himself to control others.

FIG. 225.—The theater, Orange, France, 2nd century A.D. Width of stage 203 feet, depth of stage 45 feet, capacity about 7,000 spectators. (*After d'Espouy.*)

Cicero, also, in his speech to Brutus, held that Phidias did not need a model for the statue of Zeus, but carried in his mind an image of the ultimate beauty, which he called *species pulchritudinis eximia quaedam.* By identifying this image of beauty with Roman law, Cicero gains a measure of consistency for his philosophy. Cicero held to the belief not only that ideas were permanent, but that individual man could create new ideas or artistic fantasies—a point necessary for the development of mixed art or eclecticism.

Drama and Poetry

In their literature, the Romans rarely reached the height of emotional expressiveness and the richness of invention attained by the Greeks. Lacking a background of deep religious mythology, they failed to express great truths in dramatic form. This is not to overlook the excellence of style and passages of lyric beauty in the poems of Horace and Vergil; nor is it to deny that these two writers, along with Lu-

cretius, had some real insight into that natural grandeur which Longinus was to call "the Sublime." The orations and essays of Cicero, furthermore, as well as the letters of Caesar and Seneca, developed a concise and pointed style that holds great appeal for prose writers. On the whole, however, Roman literature did not contribute a great deal to the development of the other arts, although it contributed greatly to all literary art criticism of associational values throughout the history of Western art.

The Roman attitude toward the drama is epitomized in the structure of the Roman theaters (Fig. 225). The Greek theater, built around a circular orchestra, served for great folk festivals, whose aim was to unite the elements of action, spectacle, music, and folklore. The actors and poets were held in high honor by their fellow citizens. The Roman theater, on the other hand, surrounded a semicircular orchestra with an imposing stage. The orchestra was occupied not by a dancing chorus that would have connected the audience with the play, but by the favored chief magistrates, senators, and guests of honor who might be visiting the city. The audience in no way participated in the performance, but simply "went to the show," very much as the 20th-century audience goes, to be amused. Playwrights and actors (*histriones*) were usually slaves and outcasts.

Five Types of Dramatic Performance. Several significant elements for the development of later European drama go back to five types of dramatic presentation practiced by the Romans. Some of these seem to have arisen from native Etruscan origins, others to have been borrowed from the Greeks.

These five types of dramatic performance, in order of their appearance over the first 400 years of Roman life, comprised the *Fescenninae,* the *saturae,* the *Atellanae,* the *mimes,* and the *pantomimes.*

The first of these, the *Fescennina,* was a comic presentation growing out of the rude banter of the rustics in the harvest fields. The *Fescenninae* arose in the Etruscan town of Fescennia, where such presentations were first formalized and produced to accompany the wedding ceremony, which usually gave opportunity for witty repartee.

Performances of the second type, the *saturae*, according to the historian Livy, seem to have corresponded to the Greek satyr dramas. They were performed by one or more actors, accompanied by the music of the flute. Like the satyr dramas, the *saturae* usually followed some more serious presentation, particularly after Roman tragedy had developed.

The third type of dramatic form, the *Atellanae*, named after the town of Atella in Campagna (lower Italy), was the most typically Latin. This form persisted throughout the Middle Ages and eventually became the well-recognized *commedia dell' arte* shortly after the Renaissance. Originally the *Atellanae*, a type of burlesque of rustic life, was performed by young nobles who wore masks and improvised their lines. The masks became a number of stock characters who still appear in the lower forms of present-day comedy, such as the burlesque. Particularly familiar is Maccus, a clown and harlequin with a large head, who although always getting into trouble eventually triumphs over all obstacles. Pappus, another character, became Pantaleone in the *commedia dell' arte;* he is the typical yes man, or "stooge," who is the butt of all the jokes.

In connection with the *Atellanae*, a certain Roman type of trochaic meter, the Saturnian, was invented to serve for all the passages corresponding to Greek choral parts. As Macaulay suggests, the line, "The queen was in the parlor eating bread and honey," comes closest to the rhythm. The Latins failed to develop in their drama the fine rhythmical feeling that gave form to the ceremonious Greek drama. Put in graphic terms, the Saturnian meter looks something like the Etruscan design illustrated in Fig. 227.

The mimes and pantomimes grew up during the Empire, after Greek influence had become strong in Roman literary life. Their plots followed the stories of the late Greek comedies of Menander, although the character of the dramatic action went back to the earlier Latin forms. In the mimes the players acted without masks, and for the first time women were allowed to take part in the performances. As liberties were taken with these actresses, rough humor soon degenerated into indecency. The mimes served as interludes between acts of tragedies, furnishing a lighter element of music, dancing, and jesting built around a plot that never varied. The story disclosed how an unfaithful wife might outwit her jealous but stupid husband and have adventures with innumerable lovers.

As the Roman taste for the spectacular developed, the directors of these mimes introduced into them freaks and savages taken captive in the wars, boxing matches, dancing bears, and processions of wild animals similar to those in a circus parade. One experiment that had some elements of charm was the invention of the pantomime. While a reader recited the words of the play, a group of dancers somewhat like the ballet tried to show emotions of love and terror through gestures alone. Thus was reached the final stage of theatrical virtuosity.

The Comedies of Plautus and Terence. Two early comic writers, Plautus and Terence, who lived in the 3rd century B.C., show in what directions Roman drama might have gone had the Roman legalistic mind permitted. Of twenty comedies by Plautus, one, *Amphitruo*, inspired later writers such as Molière, Dryden, and Giraudoux. Copied from the old comedy by the Greek Archippus, *Amphitruo* tells the story of the visit of Jupiter to Thebes, where he fell in love with Amphitruo's wife, Alcmena. Most of Plautus's comedies derived from the late Greek plays of Menander, which had the cosmopolitan character of Alexandrian Greek life rather than the strong ethos of the Attic comedy. The most humorous, *Menaechmi*, furnished the plot for Shakespeare's *Comedy of Errors* (*The Boys from Syracuse*). It poses the comic situation of two pairs of twin brothers who are continually mistaken for one another.

Plautus dressed his actors in Greek clothing and supplied his plays with a Greek background, thus giving his Roman audience a feeling of superiority over a race whose higher culture they envied. We might draw an interesting parallel between the way in which the Roman comedian handled the Greeks and the way in which, at different times in the development of the American theater, first the English, then the Irish, Germans, Jews, and finally Greeks, have been made the comic elements. Plautus was the only truly inventive writer in the development of the Roman drama. He introduced many new words into the language, as well as some new elements of action.

His successor, Terence, a Carthaginian by birth, adapted the plays of Menander so as to make them teach moral lessons. Lacking ready wit and insight into human character, Terence's work seems tedious chiefly because the main purpose of art is not moral instruction, although moral instruction may be present incidentally. Yet Terence pointed the way in which Roman drama might have gone if it had developed into something as great as the Greek. In Greek drama, where patriotism and an underlying religious spirit were always present, great social and spiritual problems could work themselves out naturally within the characters. The Romans might similarly have developed a real dramatic interest out of the conflict between personal desire and a feeling of duty to the state. The senatorial oligarchy, however, set up a board of dramatic censors, which effectively killed that democratic give-and-take necessary to the development of the art.

The Tragedies of Ennius and the Statement of the Humanist Ideal. The greatest of the Roman tragedians, Ennius (209–167 B.C.), who was called the father of Roman poetry, interested himself in Greek philosophy. As a member of the mystical sect of the Neo-Pythagoreans, he believed in the doctrine of the transmigration of souls. He became convinced that in another incarnation he had been Homer, whose soul reached

him through a peacock. As a follower of Epicurus, also, he felt it his mission to teach virtue through the drama. He wished the whole Roman people to gain the broad concept of civilization expressed in the word *humanitas*. In one of his plays the line *Homo sum; humani nihil a me alienum puto* ("I am a man; nothing human should be foreign to me") brought his republican audience to its feet with cheers. Here we glimpse the last spark of the Roman drama. The late tragedies, written by Julius Caesar, Cicero, and Seneca, were merely literary exercises undertaken to help them perfect their prose style.

Vergil's Aeneid and the First Classical Literary Revival. The *Aeneid* of Vergil (Publius Vergilius Maro) furnishes the first example of the classic revival in literature. In his poem, Vergil incorporated some of the best thought of Roman and Greek writers. It possessed a distinct antiquarian interest for any learned Roman who could find in it evidence of the old Roman virtues, laws, manners, and religious ceremonies. For some it served as an epic introduction to the triumph of the Caesars, with Augustus, the first god-emperor, seen dimly in the form of Aeneas. Throughout, the poem celebrates the triumph of law and civilization, personified by the Roman state, over the savage instincts of man. Its subject, in the last analysis, is the divine destiny of Rome. Both in the *Aeneid* and in his shorter poems, the *Georgics*, Vergil pictures with a sort of sentimental regard local scenes around Naples, where he had his villa. Like Horace, Vergil reveals an interest in grottoes, lakes, and shady vales. In a quiet, countryman's fashion, he was a Romantic, and his sense of the beautiful in nature exerted a distinct influence on Dante.

Horace and the Roman Ideal of Effectiveness. Quintus Horatius Flaccus, in his *Ars Poetica*, left a compendium of critical ideas on the development of literary style, garnered from his predecessors in the ancient world. This work, together with the writings of Longinus, underlies nearly all our systems of teaching the art of writing today. To write well, says Horace, one must have unity, consistency, truthfulness, and sanity. He cautions against giving too great weight to the Platonic fiction of poetic madness and suggests that the real sources of successful unity lie in careful observation and experience. As a judicious Roman, however, he admits that some writers undoubtedly possess inspired genius.

Following Aristotle, Horace specified that all incidental action should be subordinate to the main plot, and that characters should be drawn consistently. He also stressed measure, which meant the attainment of clarity through necessary descriptive matter rather than wordiness. Proof of the validity of his criticism lies in his verse, which is so polished that in translation its full flavor is lost. For those who do not read Latin, however, Grant Showerman's rendition of "The Bandusian Spring" will serve to illustrate the "Romantic" interest in nature that runs through Roman art. The reading of the poem should be accompanied by contemplation of the painted landscape from the Villa Albani (Fig. 252).

> O crystal-bright Bandusian Spring,
>   Worthy thou of the mellow wine
> And flowers I give to thy pure depths:
>   A kid the morrow shall be thine.
>
> The day of lustful strife draws on,
>   The starting horn begins to gleam;
> In vain! His red blood soon shall tinge
>   The waters of thy clear, cold stream.
>
> The dog-star's fiercely blazing hour
>   Ne'er with its heat doth change thy pool;
> To wandering flock and ploughworn steer
>   Thou givest waters fresh and cool.
>
> Thee, too, 'mong storied founts I'll place,
>   Singing the oak that slants the steep,
> Above the hollowed home of rock
>   From which thy prattling streamlets leap.[1]

Etruscan Origins of Roman Spatial Arts

Etruscan art emerging from its subterranean tombs provides a shadowy curtain background for the Roman mind. Etruscan bronzes, terra cottas, and even the painted walls of the tombs have about them the damp smell of death. Unlike the dry, bright-colored death depicted by Egyptian art, they are dreary gray things—the essence of what we describe as the macabre. This effect is perhaps heightened by the fact that the Etruscan lacked that sense of rhythmical unity which seems essential for taste.

The origins of the Etruscan people may perhaps reveal the reason. According to their own legends, they came from a country north of Palestine in the Hittite territory. Not far from this region lived the Phoenicians, who practiced the cult of Baal and had as one of their chief symbols the grotesque mask of the Gorgon's head. This unpleasant symbol occurs more frequently in the tombs of the Etruscans than any other and partly accounts for the repulsiveness of Etruscan art. Another possible explanation is that death shown realistically is always unpleasant. Lines of the human figure displayed as broken and sagging remind one of the process of disintegration.

Etruscan Sculpture and the Expression of Death. An antefix, or roof ornament, from an Etruscan temple will clarify the reference to the art of the Etruscans as an "art of disintegration." When we compare this work with the figures from the Parthenon or the Temple of Zeus at Olympia, the distinction at once becomes clear. The figures of a Silenus and a Maenad here shown (Fig. 226) combine a realistic quality of detail in some parts with archaistic abstract design in others. The feet and knees of the Silenus show a genuine knowledge of anatomy, but being heavy and dropsical, suggest that they are returning to the condition of unformed clay. A complete disregard for proper human proportions, combined with the lack of coordinating rhythm or interweave, makes the beholder who has any empathy for the group feel slightly befuddled. The same quality appears in the futuristic and surrealistic sculpture and painting of the 20th century. The Hegeso relief (Fig. 203, Chap. VIII) also shows a figure whose proportions are not altogether correct, but the

[1] Grant Showerman, *Horace and His Influence*, Marshall Jones Co., Boston, 1922.

strength of the composition lines tricks the attention away from the parts in question. Here it seems almost as though the artist wished to give expression to something which should be

Fig. 226.—Silenus and Maenad from Etruscan temple, c. 300 B.C. (Etruscan Museum, Rome.) (*Photograph by Alinari.*)

the reverse of beauty, like the grotesque, yet more somber than ludicrous. The effect has been achieved because one associates archaism, seen in the faces, with strength of design in planes and forms, and realism with weakness of design but correct rendition of anatomical details. Here neither archaism nor realism dominates, nor is either well done within its own sphere. Hence, it seems as though a desire for realistic expression on the part of a sophisticated people had developed before the artists could devise a design composition or knowledge of form strong enough to sustain that life.

Geometric Sources of Etruscan Composition. The same lack of taste and barbaric quality already remarked in sculpture appear in the few existing remains of painted terra-cotta tiles and sections of walls of Etruscan temples (Fig. 227). These require more than a superficial analysis. Observe that the central circles of this ornamental architectural design resemble the grave ornaments from Mycenae with the rounding spiral within the circle tending to denote action. There is also a suggestion of the Greek

guilloche. Here, however, the continuous rhythmical movement of the guilloche disappears in the dizzying movement of the circles. The tortuous motion leads inward, but seems to move

Fig. 227.—Painted terra cotta from Etruscan temple, c. 300 B.C. (Ny-Carlsberg Museum, Copenhagen). (*After Wiegand.*)

merely for its own sake. This design, which is typical of Etruscan terra cottas, is the dominating movement in the dancing figures from the wall of the Tomb of the Triclinium at Corneto (Fig. 228).

As an exercise in aesthetics, it is interesting to compare the relatively simple guilloche which eventuates in the Dance of the Maidens from Ruvo (Fig. 180, Chap. VIII) with the more animated reliefs of the Etruscan design and tomb painting. The motions implied by the Greek design are slow and regular, while those in the Etruscan are jumpy. The Mediterranean world absorbed this motion, much as the Cretan and pre-Greek peoples had absorbed the spiral designs of the Danubian potters. Roman art as it eventually developed shows a less refined rhythm than the finest Greek and stands nearer to the Etruscan with its jerky design and its penchant for realism.

The Architecture of the Romans

The significant advances made by the Romans in the art of building lay in the mechanics of construction rather than in the realm of style. A visit to the ruins of any Roman basilica or bath will make this clear. In such practical business structures the Roman builder stood supreme. In a chronological study of Roman architecture, however, we must begin with the temple, which developed first, growing out of or upon Etruscan styles.

demonstrates at a glance that in architecture, as in painting, the Hellenic mind developed a new form that gradually dominated Etrusco-Roman building.

Fɪɢ. 228.—Dancers, Tomb of the Triclinium at Corneto, c. 400 ʙ.c. Colors, cinnabar-red, yellow, and green.

The Roman Temple and Its Etruscan Antecedents. Most of the Etruscan models used by the Roman architects relate to the Greek temple *in antis,* which was a cella with a porch. The cella of the Etruscan plan usually included three parts, one for each member of a trinity of gods. The old temple of Jupiter Capitolinus in Rome, for example, built by Etruscan architects, reserved a place not only for Jupiter, but for Juno and Minerva as well. In the temple called the Maison Carrée at Nîmes (Fig. 229), erected in the 1st century ᴀ.ᴅ. by the princes Caius and Nicius, may still be seen the triple cella. Here the porch, three columns deep and six columns across, stands on a high stereobate, approached by a long flight of steps. Structurally, the porch is connected with the cella by the engaged columns on the sides, which give the appearance of a portico around the entire building. The shafts, with their slight entasis, the Corinthian capitals supporting the finely designed architrave, the delicate frieze and moldings, lend a certain gemlike quality similar to that of a piece of Roman silversmithing. The austere elegance of the building makes it quite unlike the earlier, less formal Greek temple. As a whole, its design is one of the most satisfactory among the Roman temples standing today. A comparison of this building with the reconstruction of an earlier Etruscan temple (Fig. 230)

The Pantheon and Roman Concrete Construction. The subterranean round tomb and the circular fire temple of the Etruscans served as the plan for the great circular hall of the Pantheon, erected under Hadrian's rule on the site of a different building, called a "nymphaeum," that dated from the time of Agrippa. The approach is through a gabled porch (Fig. 231). This form in architecture is distinctly new. The great structure extends about 340 feet from the front of the porch to the rear of the hall; the central rotunda itself measures 142 feet in diameter and 140 feet in height. This was built of bricks backed by concrete, laid or set up on a huge wooden frame, which was later removed. A lining of black, white, and yellow marble embellished the interior.

The method of construction was simple and entailed mainly a good organization of labor. The dome, like that of the beehive tomb, was built upon the corbel principle, its lower story consisting simply of a circular drum (Fig. 232). The one touch of constructive genius appears in the great opening in the ceiling, admitting a light which diffuses perfectly over the coffered ceiling and the niches in the wall, thus removing some of the feeling of weight. Aesthetically, this building represents a logical development of Stonehenge, with the dome of the sky further enclosed by the temple walls.

The portico consists of four rows of columns, which form three aisles. The two side aisles end in niches for colossal statues of Augustus and Agrippa; the center aisle leads to the door-

contain the tombs of great modern Italian statesmen. The Pantheon is said to have been the first building in the Western world designed for interior rather than for exterior

FIG. 229.—Maison Carrée, Nîmes, from the southwest, early 1st century A.D. (*Courtesy of Lesch-Carnegie.*)

way, which expands into the sky circle. Upon entering, one sees around the wall the eight

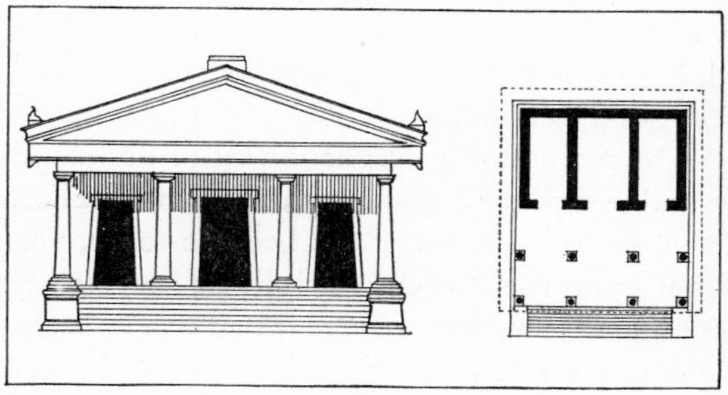

FIG. 230.—Etruscan temple.

altars originally dedicated to the chief Roman deities, for the Pantheon is the house of all the gods. Three semicircular niches alternate with four rectangular granite niches bounded by Corinthian columns. Today these niches

effect. We must not forget, however, that centuries before, the Egyptians had designed their

FIG. 231.—Model of Pantheon, Rome, showing rotunda and portico, A.D. 120–124. Height about 145 feet. (*Courtesy of Metropolitan Museum of Art.*)

temple courts with a view to the temple interiors.

The Baths and the Roman Art of Vaulting. Without the invention of a new building technique, the great span of the Pantheon dome would not have been possible. Roman architects in the ancient East had early come in contact with that two long barrel vaults crossing each other formed at their intersection a square groined space (Fig. 233). He next observed that by using a concrete roof laid in a solid mass he might

FIG. 232.—The Pantheon, interior of rotunda. (*Courtesy of Lesch-Carnegie.*)

the Syrian method of backing a hard layer of facing brick with a tamped layer of cement mixed with broken brick or loose stone. This building method was readily adopted in Italy, because the materials were available there in large deposits of a sandy earth called "pozzuolana," which forms a cement of great strength when mixed with lime and flint, and in deposits of clay suitable for making bricks. These materials made possible the Pantheon dome, as well as other notable structures.

From Persia and Babylonia—perhaps, too, from the Etruscan stone masons—came a second important building method: the true arch. Probably some Roman architect first noticed

cut away the side vaults so that with strong corner piers the groined vault would stand with a minimum of outside bracing. This new system of roof construction, with the newly discovered concrete and groined vault, made possible the great halls of the Roman baths, some of which are still in use today.

Figure 234 shows the hall of the *tepidarium*, once part of the great Baths of Diocletian, the last great municipal bath to be built in Rome. Today this hall, which formed only a small part of the original structure, is the Church of St. Mary of the Angels. The addition of an altar at the end and the placing of some Renaissance paintings are the only changes that

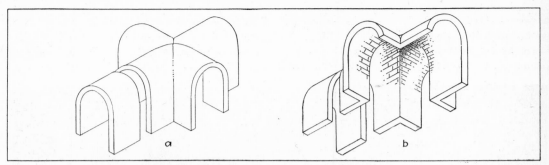

FIG. 233.—Construction of barrel and groin vaults.

have been made since old Roman days. The hall has a familiar look to Americans who have been in the great railway terminal stations of our country built during the early part of the 20th century, for these were modeled on the Roman baths. Aesthetically, this type of construction gives one a feeling of expansiveness and power.

The Roman baths consisted of huge groups of rooms (Fig. 235) devoted not only to bathing but to gymnastic contests as well. They were also art museums, libraries, and meeting places for the clubs of the city. So many functions naturally required many rooms, which were always laid out logically along a central axis, as the plan of the Baths of Diocletian shows. Anyone entering the front gate of such an establishment might wander through groves of trees past the many exercise rooms (Fig. 236). In the rear, on the plan, one can see part of a stadium and a semicircular theater. The central building consisted of three parts. Under the rotunda lay the *caldarium*, or hot-water bath; in front of this, occupying the main part of the building, was the *tepidarium*, where warm and cooler water mixed, and next to it the *frigidarium*, or cold bath. Outside, under the sky, stretched a great open-air swimming pool. The rooms on each side of the indoor pools were for dressing, or held smaller private baths. The heating system was ingenious. In the basement, slaves brought wood to great furnaces from which the hot air was conducted into hypocausts, or chambers within the floor, and from them distributed by means of tiled flues inside the walls.

The halls were paneled with many-colored marbles (Fig. 234). False columns suggesting the great monolithic Oriental granite columns added to the effect of richness. Their purpose was more than decorative, for they actually supported the weight of the groined roof. An extra cornice block called the "impost block" also helped to distribute this weight effectively. In the tepidarium these impost blocks bind the column to the wall. They also distribute some of the weight horizontally, preventing the arch of the roof from bearing too heavily upon the light Corinthian capitals. The contribution of the impost block, for use as well as for decoration, was considered very valuable by Renaissance architects.

The Basilica as a Communal Meeting Place. The cities of the Roman world, like the towns of the Greeks, focused around a square or rectangular market place, or agora, which in Rome was called the *forum*. A temple to the titulary deity and a basilica always stood among the buildings on this market place. The basilica consisted simply of a long hall serving as a protected center for the banking industry and the small jewelry shops. It was used also as a stock exchange and for the imperial law courts. Usually rectangular in plan, it possessed an *exedra*, or apse—a small circular recess with a bench— somewhere on the side or at the end. This apse contained a statue of the emperor before which litigants took oath. In the early days of Rome, long timbers roofed over the large span of the basilica; in later times—the 3rd and 4th centuries of the Christian Era—great vaults such as were used in the construction of the baths superseded these timbers.

In the Julian basilica, the columns are connected by an arcade, or row of arches, rather

a porch at one end and a door at the side, with an extra exedra opposite the side door.

One common aesthetic motive, arising from a practical need, dominates the Roman civic

FIG. 234.—Interior of tepidarium, Baths of Diocletian (now St. Mary of the Angels), A.D. 302. Height 90 feet. (*Courtesy of Lesch.*)

than by an architrave. This double-storied colonnade separates a central aisle with a clerestory from two side aisles, the whole being roofed with wood covered with lead. Such interiors resemble those of Greek temples with a wider main aisle (Fig. 237).

The basilica first built by Maxentius and dedicated by his successor Constantine, offers an excellent plan and elevation of the later vaulted type (Fig. 238). It divides into three sections: a main aisle and two side aisles. The central aisle had three coffered groined vaults, the side aisles, at right angles to this central vault, being strong enough to withstand its lateral pressure. The basilica here shown had

structures such as the baths and basilicas. All their builders strove to create interesting, expansive interiors, well lighted and ornate. Thus they stand as the first buildings specifically designed to please the large groups of people who daily frequented them. They form the necessary link between the more ancient structures and the Christian church.

The Arch of Titus. The idea of a ceremonial portal or gateway originated as far back as the Neolithic age. The Romans seem to have taken the idea from the Greeks, who built such portals in Hellenic times. Like the primitive people of the north, the Romans erected colossal memorial columns also, such as the column of

Trajan, still standing in that ruler's Forum. Between the Forum and the Colosseum, on the Sacred Way, stands an arch erected by the Roman Senate and the people, A.D. 81, to com-

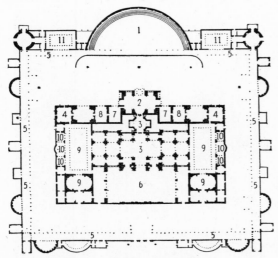

FIG. 235.—Plan of the Baths of Diocletian. 1, theater; 2, caldarium; 3, tepidarium; 4, frigidarium; 5, peristyle; 6, cold swimming pool; 7, sudatorium or laconicum (steam bath); 8, warm bath; 9, tablinum (open salon); 10, ephebeum (salon); 11, library.

memorate the victory of the Emperor Titus over the Jews in Palestine (Fig. 239).

In the Arch of Titus the capitals and ornamented cornicelike architrave act as base for an Ionic frieze. Above this a still richer projecting cornice emphasizes the division between the lower part of the arch and its high attic story. This attic section holds an inscription, the beautifully designed letters of which are among the best devised by the Roman architects.

The façade of the Arch of Titus became a classic of Roman architecture and was copied many times in antiquity, as well as in the Renaissance period and in the 19th century. Its proportions and aesthetic intent deserve particular study. Never again did triumphal portals achieve so fine a balance of parts, or sculptural decoration appear so well fitted to architectural design (Fig. 265).

The lower story of the arch is designed in a square; diagonals thrown across this square

give a center point at their intersection upon which the semicircle of the arch may be constructed with a diameter equal to one-third the length of the base, which also equals the width of the side. The attic, which at one time supported an equestrian statue of the emperor, measures about one-half the height of the lower square. This very simple geometrical formula gives the structure a stability and dignity appropriately symbolizing the power of the emperor and of the state and the citizens who built it.

Under the coffered vault the reliefs (Fig. 261) showing the procession of the emperor are noteworthy for their contrasts of light and shade. Though illusionistic, they lack true perspective. The figures on the forward planes bear no relation to those on the rear wall of the relief. The movement of the procession, however, is carried out with liveliness and we find here more rhythm than is usual in Roman relief sculpture.

The Greco-Roman City Plan. Following the example set by Alexander, who is said to have planned the city of Alexandria, the various Greek tyrants and colonizers of the Roman world laid out several cities. Most of these followed the plan of the prehistoric Terra Mare town (Fig. 47, Chap. III). An architect, Hippodamus, first suggested that a city should be laid out around a rectangular agora or market place with a system of right-angled cross streets. Many cities, including Priene (Fig. 240). Magnesia, Ephesus, and Miletus followed the system of Hippodamus and centered around a market place bounded by a two-story structure like the stoa of Athens. The Romans adopted this arrangement, making the entrances to the market place in the form of monumental structures or gates approached by arcades. In Rome the portico around the market was joined to the basilica and other civic buildings. The streets terminated at the forum and vehicular traffic could not come into the square. Thus the forum had somewhat the same meaning for a city that the Roman peristyle and the Renaissance courtyard had for the Mediterranean house. Many of the Mediterranean cities of the Middle Ages retained these civic centers and, in the late Renaissance, rearranged them ac-

tals, formed by uniting Ionic and Corinthian details. Above these capitals the architrave in three parts supports a jewellike frieze with moldings so decorated that they lose structural

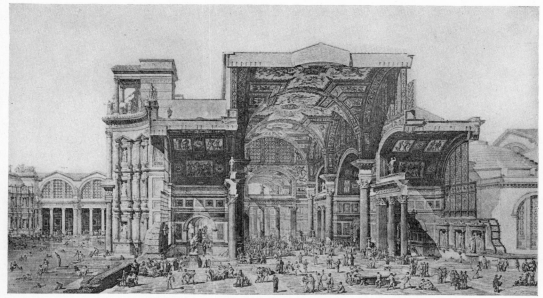

FIG. 236.—Baths of Diocletian. Left, swimming pool, and right, tepidarium, showing use in construction of side barrel vaults buttressing central groin vaults (Paulin).

cording to the Roman model. The finest example today may be seen in the square of St. Mark's in Venice.

The Market Gate at Miletus and the Design of a Façade. The gate built by the Romans at the entrance to the forum at Miletus (Fig. 241) is one of the most interesting and significant examples of a Roman façade. From the strongly functional building of the Greeks the Romans removed details, which were then attached according to a new scheme of construction to heavy, solid, arched walls. Engaged columns, such as one may see on buildings like the Colosseum, became engaged decorative porches, without functional significance. The intent was to create an interesting wall surface over which the eye might weave in and out. This effect can be observed in the smallest details.

The columns set upon high pedestals, called "plinths," terminate in lacy Composite capi-

FIG. 237.—Wooden basilica of Fano. (*After Vitruvius, The Ten Books of Architecture, translated by Morgan, Harvard University Press, Cambridge, Mass.*)

significance. How unstructural the entire system is, can best be shown by a study of the broken pediment over the center niche. To throw full light upon the enshrined statues of the emperor in the second story, the line of the cornice has been broken in three places. Like the altar at Pergamum, this highly decorative architecture, completely alien to the ancient Greek spirit, shows the influence of the painter's

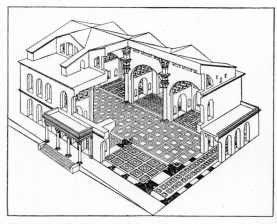

FIG. 238.—Basilica of Maxentius and Constantine, A.D. 306–312.

art—in this case, the art of the scene painter. This style, dormant throughout the Middle Ages, was revived in European architecture after the 16th century and called the "baroque." One characteristic of the baroque building is that its skyline seen from several positions offers a succession of interesting picturesque effects.

Roman Painting

The Roman House and Its Decoration. Roman painting may best be studied in the houses of wealthy citizens on the Palatine or in the buried cities around the Bay of Naples. The old saying, "a man's house is his castle," might well have been invented by the Romans, with the addition that the Roman's house was also the place of his business and his leisure occupation. The Roman house formed the center of a trade area covering a small city block. The landlord lived inside the block and rented the small stores or booths around the outside. Such a house usually had balconies on the second story, and often a roof garden, whose plants

might be seen from the street. In the center of the block, the entrance way, or *prothyrum*, with its *fauces*, or jaws, was guarded by a concierge, who kept out unwanted beggars.

FIG. 239.—The Arch of Titus, Rome, A.D. 81, seen from the northeast.

The interior of the house enclosed two or more courts. In the house illustrated here (Fig. 242), imagine yourself already admitted to an *atrium*, or vestibule, waiting for the master. He sits at a table in the *tablinum*, or small reception room directly ahead, which serves as his library and office. This particular house, one of the oldest in Pompeii, is called the House of the Faun in honor of the little statue of the dancing satyr found in the *impluvium*, or central pool. The opening in the roof of the atrium gives light to the rooms. Below this aperture the rain water is caught in the impluvium, whence it is conducted to a subterranean cistern. This architectural scheme is suitable for a climate offering little rain and much sunlight. Notice in passing toward the tablinum that the walls, which from a distance looked like marble, consist of painted blocks of *gesso* or plaster of Paris. This decoration, the earliest ("incrustation"). Pompeian style of wall treatment, was made by the Greek artists, who also built the house.

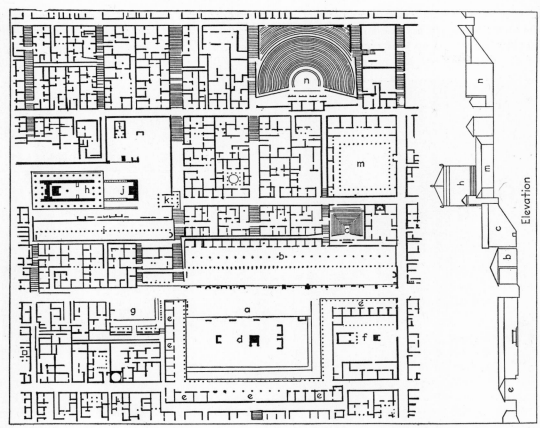

Fig. 240.—Plan of civic center, Priene, c. 300 B.C. *a*, agora (forum); *b*, consecrated stoa with civic bureaus; *c*, bouleuterion (curia, meeting place of town council); *d*, civic altar with commemorative statues; *e*, covered market stands; *f*, Temple of Aesculapius with hospital; *g*, slaughterhouse; *h*, civic temple of Athena; *i*, portico; *j*, great altar; *k*, propylaeum; *l*, treasury; *m*, gymnasium; *n*, theater. Arranged on the side of a hill; see elevation. This plan shows the great ingenuity of Greek designers, inherited only in part by Romans. All streets unmarked by steps were free for wheeled traffic. (*After Bonnet.*)

After greeting the master of the house, notice on the pedestal behind him a portrait figure, modeled in terra cotta, which resembles him closely and looks not unlike some prominent American. This noble Roman says that the atrium was built by his ancestors over 200 years ago. Among other Greek artists they employed a craftsman to reproduce in the *opus musivum*, or mosaic, one of the great paintings of the ancient world. After passing through the portico of the *peristylum*, or second atrium (Fig. 243), you will see a great mosaic decoration set in the floor (Fig. 244). It depicts the victory of Alexander over Darius in the battle of the Issus. A copy of an older painting by the Greek master Philoxenus, of the 4th century B.C., it furnishes the best extant example of the style of painting connected with the name of Polygnotus.

The *tesserae*, or small cubes of varicolored marble that form the mosaic, are arranged so as to produce a tonal harmony. Against the background of sky, represented in white marble, the spears of the warriors form an interesting pattern of brown and black. The skillful portrayal of Alexander advancing with his

Greeks from the left emphasizes the vigor of the thrusting spears, and the anxiety of Darius, looking back with troubled eyes as he turns to flee in his great chariot, is convincingly de-

such as columns, porticoes, windows, and vistas, arranged with perspective, cast shadows, and almost naturalistic coloring.

Our illustration (Fig. 245), from the Villa of

Fig. 241.—Market gateway from Miletus. (*Courtesy of Berlin Deutsches Museum; Lesch.*)

picted. The bodies of horses and men are ably foreshortened, although the scene does not suggest depth because of the flatness of the background. This mosaic differs from later Roman work and from our own in lacking depth expressed through color. It is interesting to note that the Romans thought such a representation suitable for a floor.

The Second Pompeian Style and the Development of Perspective. After the austere first mural style of wall decoration, a second style was invented, or perhaps imported from Alexandria, in the 1st century B.C. This the Romans deemed especially fitting for smaller rooms. It was called the "architectural" or "second Pompeian" style. This scheme attempted to give an illusion of spaciousness by using architectural members,

Fannius Sinistor at Boscoreale, a small town near Pompeii, shows a part of a wall in the second style. At first glance, all the lines of buildings, which retreat from the picture plane, or front of the wall, appear to converge at some common vanishing point. Here for the first time we can study that artistic trick known as "linear perspective." The lower lines of the niche and the lines of the walls on each side of the altar seem most of them to converge in the altar. So far, the perspective is correct; but the receding lines of the canopy above the statue that stands in the shrine beyond the altar do not converge as they should at a vanishing point on an imaginary line behind the altar. The illusion of perspective fails in this detail.

It may be difficult at first to see exactly

where the error lies, since most of us are not familiar with the laws of perspective drawing. Discrepancies will be felt, however, though they may not be noticed. The composition of

FIG. 242.—Atrium, House of the Faun, Pompeii, with wall painting in first style, 2nd century B.C. Beyond, looking through the tablinum, appear two colonnaded courts, the peristyles. (*Courtesy of Hammerton, Wonders of the Past, G. P. Putnam's Sons.*)

the entire wall holds together because of the fact that the two side parts stand in absolute balance with relation to the third—the larger center area. Our attention is more attracted to the strong vertical lines of the two rounded Corinthian columns of the niche, which are in correct perspective, than to the small houses in the rear, whose perspective is incorrect. The long receding lines of the porticoes in the upper part of the side panel within this strong vertical framework also help to nullify the effect of the small discrepant lines. The large design of the panel thus dominates the smaller details. Actually, the small, irregular details lend a certain contrasting element of interest to the whole, an effect heightened by the gay color scheme. In addition to this, the 20th-century mind has become accustomed to incorrect perspective from seeing pictures by Picasso and other latter-day painters.

A study of the diagrammatic sketches of a tiny vignette from a house in Pompeii (Fig. 246) will make clear the laws of linear perspec-

tive. The sketch on the left is the original; the one on the right shows this same sketch corrected according to the laws developed by the late-15th-century Florentine masters. The first

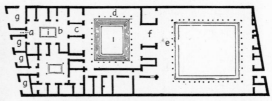

FIG. 243.—Plan, House of the Faun. *a*, prothyrum; *b*, atrium with impluvium (*i*); *c*, tablinum; *d*, first peristyle with impluvium (*i*); *e*, second peristyle with garden; *f*, exedra or reception room with Alexander mosaic; *g*, shop. Other rooms shown include bedrooms, kitchens, and dining and service rooms.

law states that all horizontal retreating lines must converge in a common point on the horizon line, known as the vanishing point. The Greek painter Agatharcus probably had knowledge of this law. It is cited by the Roman architect Vitruvius, but did not reach the majority of Roman painters, and there is no indication that it was in general use before the Renaissance in the Western world.[1] In the Pompeian vignette, the objects in the distance are smaller than those near by, but not all the horizontal lines converge at that high point indicated by the lines of the mole in the distance.

The Romans developed their architectural style of painting almost to the point of perfection, and then proceeded in another direction. They began to work out the law of *color perspective*—that is, the illusion of distance in a picture brought about through color rather than line. They carefully observed the colors of distant sea and sky and painted the heavens near the zenith dark blue, grading down to pink or orange tones near the horizon. Shadows cast by objects were studied and used to increase the illusion of spaciousness. In this way there developed the style of painting known as illusionism.

The Third and Fourth Pompeian Styles. Late

[1] In China, however, as early as the 12th century the artists of the Sung dynasty had mastered the problems of perspective.

FIG. 244.—Alexander mosaic, Battle of Issus, House of the Faun, Pompeii, 2nd century B.C. (*Courtesy of Lesch-Carnegie.*)

FIG. 245.—Pompeian wall decoration, second style, Villa of Fannius Sinistor, Boscoreale, 280–230 B.C. (*Courtesy of Metropolitan Museum of Art.*)

in the 1st century of the Christian Era, just before the destruction of Pompeii, two other styles of painting seem either to have grown from the second architectural style or to have

FIG. 246.—Left, vignette from house in Pompeii with incorrect perspective; right, same sketch corrected according to laws of true perspective.

been imported from Asia Minor or Egypt. The third, or "ornate," style (Fig. 247), which may have come from Pergamum, created flat designs on the surface of the walls. Columns were blended with the wall plane and shadows cast by projections discarded; the linear-perspective effects in many cases were reversed. Mythological subject matter was frequently used. Much of this work shows the greatest aesthetic refinement.

From the second style developed also the fourth, or "intricate," style. This strove for an aesthetic effect without architectonic structure. The columns, large and heavy in the beginning, have become jewellike candelabra, and fantastic houses display delicate balconies hung with garlands of flowers. The small panel pictures are held in place by tiny chains, painted on the wall. The pictures vary in type; the illusionistic represent space and atmosphere, others show purely decorative flat scenes. Flying cupids, or *putti*, nymphs, and satyrs are painted with hasty, short brush strokes between jeweled borders on black backgrounds. The walls were sometimes polished with wax so that they appeared to have a porphyry surface.

Realistic Panel Painting and the Development of

Light and Shade. A painting of the 1st century after Christ, from a house in Herculaneum, a town near Pompeii, offers a fine example of the realistic style (Fig. 248). It depicts Hercules

FIG. 247.—Third or ornate style of wall decoration, House of Mesor, Pompeii, 30 B.C.–A.D. 60. Elements from fourth or intricate style in border above.

finding his son Telephos in the mountains of Arcadia. The little scene of Telephos with Hercules and the hind appears on the coins of Pergamum. Hercules, as represented here, also can be found on the sculpture of the Altar of Zeus. The reader will remember that this sculpture was called "painterly," or "baroque." It was suggested that the whole altar represented a painter's conception rather than that of an architect or a sculptor. In this panel painting the sculpture of Pergamum has come into its own as colored light and shadow upon a flat wall. Unfortunately, we must study the composition without its original color, which was so toned that it blended all the parts, as Zeuxis' color is said to have done. All pictures in color reproduced in black and white are essentially falsifications of the truth, for pictorial ture directs our attention from one rich detail to another. The Roman, as we have seen from the philosophy of Marcus Aurelius at the head of the chapter, enjoyed contemplating the

FIG. 248.—Left, Hercules and Telephos, wall painting, Herculaneum, about A.D. 50 (Naples Museum). (*Courtesy of Lesch.*) Right, chiasmic composition scheme later employed by baroque masters.

unity depends not only upon rhythm and decorative quality, but also upon the tonal unity of colors. This color scheme was not unlike that of the boy in Fig. 251.

Notice the geometrical scheme of composition on which the painting is based. This consists of two diagonal lines, one extending from the lower right front toward the left background, the other from the right background toward the left foreground. This chiasmatic scheme resembles that of the metope from Olympia that shows Hercules cleaning the Augean stables (Fig. 187, Chap. VIII). In the metope, however, the diagonals lie simply on the flat surface instead of retreating into the painting, as they do in this Roman work.

All the forms have a very definite plastic quality that is due to their being modeled in light and shade. The linear design of the pic-

particular. Soon he would paint the little, intimate details of fruit and drapery for their own sakes. Nor has the artist been content to give us a mere surface rendition. Rather, he has tried deliberately to force our attention into the depth of the picture. The more one studies the superb details, the more will he become convinced of the picture's dramatic richness. Such work comes close to the baroque style of the late Renaissance.

Eastern and Western Styles in Roman Painting. No clear, straightforward picture of general tendencies during the 1st and 2nd centuries after Christ is possible, for by this time travel between the various parts of the Empire had become greatly facilitated, and local schools contributed their artistic psychologies but lost their own particular individuality. Although the picture of Hercules shows peculiarities connecting it with the town of Pergamum, for example, it was actually painted near Pompeii and its distinctly sculptural style suggests definite Hellenic origins. At the time of its painting, a journey to the Roman border town of Dura in Syria would have disclosed artists portraying the human figure in a flat manner not unlike that of the ancient Egyptians; while most contemporaneous Egyptian painting, influenced by Greek ideals, had grown to resemble that of Pergamum.

Thus, although we cannot speak of an East and a West in Roman art, in almost every Roman town there lived some painters who saw in terms of substance or rounded form, and others who thought in terms of flat design. Since these two ways of seeing never completely fused into one style, we cannot speak of a Roman style as we do of a Gothic or Chinese. Still, these fresco paintings of Dura (Fig. 249) might be studied as the beginnings of Oriental painting. The paintings depict a group of priests and the family of Conon, the wealthy man who commissioned the work. A pattern of flat color areas, arranged rhythmically as in the earliest Greek painting, is here used without cast shadows or surface modeling.

The picture depends for its effectiveness upon the way in which the purplish-pink color of the architecture in the background connects with the same color in some of the dresses of the figures in the foreground. These figures appear as part of the color pattern, rather than as individuals. Here we see the beginning of that movement in art which sees the human being as part of an integrated, colorful, but flat, pattern of existence. Egyptian art stood one step nearer a primitive conception of life, which sees objects next to each other but rarely combined. It shows the human figure either as part of a system of writing or as a free-standing object definitely separated from the background and isolated from other figures.

The rhythmical composition of the Dura fresco differs significantly from that of the Ruvo maidens (Fig. 180, Chap. VIII) with its distinct movement from left to right. In the fresco a much more subtle movement is only slightly suggested by the position of the feet and the gentle sway of the figures toward the right.

Fig. 249.—Fresco painting, Dura, 2nd century A.D. (?) (*Courtesy of Oriental Institute, University of Chicago.*)

Here we have the prototype of the rhythmical arrangement found in many of the Byzantine mosaics three or four centuries later. The emphasis on the outline drawing of the details, to the detriment of substantial form, reminds us of the Egyptian wall paintings.

While this art was evolving in Roman Syria, the West was working out from similar Egyptian origins the style and philosophy that made man the center of the universe. Hellenism took an interest in pointing out cause-and-effect relationships and delighted in dramatic arrangements of human figures with allegorical meanings.

Cities of the Roman Empire, such as Antioch and Alexandria, which stood near the borders of the East, possessed many artists who fluctuated between the two philosophies—the practi-

FIG. 250.—Egyptian girl portrayed on mummy case, 2nd century A.D. (Detroit Museum). (*Courtesy of Detroit Museum.*)

cal Hellenistic and the mystical Eastern. The result was an individualistic art development, and the same diversity of styles that we find today in the modern world.

The Illusionistic Technique in Roman Portraits. Two painted heads in wax or encaustic taken from mummy cases of 2nd-century Alexandria will help to clarify this fact. The portrait of the woman (Fig. 250), although showing a person of obviously Eastern origin, represents the work of a master who held certain of the Hellenic ideals. The modeling of the face makes it stand out from the background; the raised torque with the locket, around the neck, adds to the illusion of depth. Around the hair and under

the jaws, on the other hand, the shadows blend with the background, as the flesh does also, and the robe at the right is definitely lost in gray. The intent is toward substantiality, although the color pattern resembles the Oriental. Here, then, the two styles have fused.

The portrait of the Greek boy, Eutyches (Fig. 251), reveals a different combination of Oriental and Hellenic elements. The artist seems to have gone out of his way to make the face and the robe appear flat by the very heavy outlines with which he has cut up the surface into a series of flat spaces. The right ear of the boy is shown as from front view, the better to fill the space at the left. This combination of several points of visual view typifies Oriental design. On the Hellenic side, the modeling of the eyes, nose, and mouth is stronger even than in the picture of the woman, and the face does not blend with the background.

Actually, it is possible that the same man might have painted these two pictures, either at different stages of his development or, if he were a truly eclectic artist, with only a week between the two. Metropolitan life, with the vast amount of activity it offers, tends to stimulate experimentation with the different styles at hand. This experimental habit of mind led to the production of a few great masterpieces during the Renaissance. However experimentation without adherence to some ideal results in shallow virtuosity. We have seen how all styles fuse, approximating complete unity in such a great genius as Phidias. The Romans attained no great aesthetic vision; Roman life was not conducive to the creation of prophetic original work.

The Development of Landscape Painting. The first landscape painting in the modern sense of the term came from Alexandrian Greek masters of the 2nd century B.C. Examples of this Alexandrian landscape work appear in wall paintings of the second Pompeian style. Several houses in Rome, also, from as early as 80 B.C. preserve evidence of such painting. It is in Rome, rather than Alexandria or Pompeii,

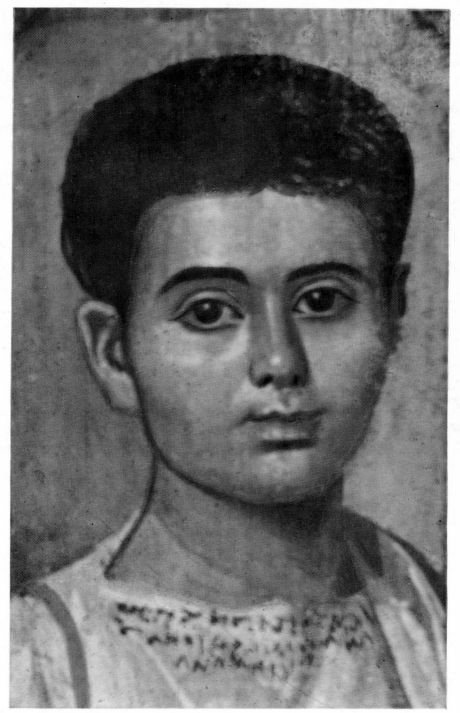

FIG. 251.—Portrait of the Freedman Eutyches, 2d century A. D., painted in encaustic pigment mixed in wax. (*Metropolitan Museum of Art.*) (*Courtesy of Metropolitan Museum of Art; Hanauer.*)

that the art of landscape painting came into full bloom with the famous frescoes called the "Odyssey" landscapes, found in a house on the Esquiline, and the frescoes from the Villa

ing toward an expression in plastic form of the grandeur of nature, could never completely lose the idea of the greatness of man. The great Greek Colossus of Rhodes, one of the seven

FIG. 252.—Wall painting, Villa Albani, Rome, c. 20 B.C. (*Courtesy of Lesch.*)

Albani, executed during the reign of Augustus (Fig. 252).

The Roman, much more than the Greek, interested himself in nature for its own sake. With Vergil, Horace, and Pliny, he learned to perceive such beauty in natural scenes that Longinus, the Greco-Roman philosopher, devised an aesthetics around the idea of natural beauty, which he called "the Sublime."

In the landscape of the Villa Albani the human elements form but a small part of the whole. Distant objects appear slightly smaller than those near by. Yet, in the rendering of values, no perspective depth has been given. Instead, the entire picture forms a pattern of colors, composed of separate elements appearing against a gray background. Certain weaknesses occur in the rendition of single objects. The large sacred tree with its attendant worshipers in the foreground seems less substantial than the bridge and the arch in the middle ground. The cow on the bridge stands out as sharply as the cows in the foreground. Everything, including distant hills and temples, appears to float in space. The Greek mind, groping toward an expression in plastic form of the

wonders of the ancient world, could not suggest the sublime quality of nature as well as a tiny landscape painting could do.

Although antedating them by 400 years, these Roman landscapes parallel and to some degree explain the works of the Sung dynasty in China. Possibly the Chinese developed their landscape rolls from contacts with this very style taken from Alexandrian landscapes. The Roman landscapes differ from the Chinese in that they lack rhythmical sweep, which is to say that the Chinese, working on the problem several hundred years more, developed a composition form that the Romans probably would have reached had their culture not been destroyed.

The Roman Interest in Still Life and Genre. Among the many wall paintings of Pompeii and Rome appear examples of genre—idyllic bits of landscape with little children or *amorini* engaged in various occupations—and groupings of fruit and flowers. The latter are known as "still life." Figure 253 shows an example of such still life composed of several peaches and a glass bowl of water. One can find no reason for such a painting other than the sensate joy in beholding the ripe fruit or the sparkle of the water in its crystal container. The composition, haphazard as it seems, contrasts strongly with

Belated Archaism in the Artemis from Pompeii. This statue was found in the house of a wealthy Roman, who probably prized it highly because it suggested both the Greek culture and more

FIG. 253.—Pompeian wall painting, 1st century A.D. This copies the wooden panel painting called the Xenion given as a banquet favor (Naples Museum).

the works of still-life painters in the 19th and 20th centuries, whose productions attempt significant arrangement of the objects. For the Roman artist there could have been little more than primitive joy in the recognition of the objects, in the rendering of surfaces, or in presenting a harmony of color. Hence, although this picture shows the same aesthetic faults as the Roman landscape, still it points the way to a type of work which was to become popular after the Renaissance.

Roman Sculpture

Roman artists who desired to copy the old Greek sculpture produced figures in the so-called Neo-Attic style. The poses invented by Polyclitus and Lysippus were used for statues of Roman athletes with heavy, over-developed muscles. Within this Neo-Attic style there developed an archaistic tendency, evidenced in figures such as the Artemis from Pompeii (Fig. 254).

FIG. 254.—Archaistic Artemis (Diana) from Pompeii, 25 B.C. (*Courtesy of Lesch.*)

realistic Etruscan origins. As a further development in the spirit of the Etruscan sculpture, it furnishes a remarkable example of the aesthetic effect that occurs when two artistic styles have not become completely fused. Details, such as the arms, the feet, and the flesh of the face, are realistic, showing a relatively complete knowledge of sculptural form. The position of the fingers on the hands likewise possesses the delicacy associated with late Hellenic work. Contrasted with these details, the folds of the draperies have been made to appear archaic, with a rather stiff geometrical quality in their design. At one place, however, where the folds of the chiton break over the advancing foot, the sculptor betrayed his knowledge of realistic drapery.

This figure bears a likeness to a number of works done by a goldsmith, one Pasiteles, who had turned sculptor. This man perfected an invention in technique copied from Lysistratus (Fig. 217, Chap. IX), which enabled him to achieve the greatest realism. He modeled his figures in clay, first building up the mass upon an armature, or wooden cross, shaped so as to get the most lifelike posture of the limbs. After completing the model in clay, he covered it with a plaster-of-Paris mold, probably made in sections. Into this mold he poured more plaster, making a model, which was then reproduced in stone by a process called "pointing," from a Roman term *puntelli* (nails). The most prominent parts of the figure were marked with nails on a block of marble, and the excess marble was chiseled away or cut with a stone drill.

Late Attic Realism. The archaistic element in the Neo-Attic school headed by Pasiteles, like all such attempts in art to copy an outmoded style, was destined to prove unfruitful. Roman sculpture advanced by concentrating on the literary element in late Greek art until it discovered that realism praised by Marcus Aurelius. A figure like the Old Market Woman from Miletus (Fig. 255), probably late Greek in origin, shows that a love of the genre with a quality of pathos suggested by Aristotle could lead to a production that has power to stir one emotionally without being overdramatic. The old woman, bent over by the weight of her basket, reaches out as though to offer some of her wares for sale. All the drapery lines contribute to the feeling of age and weariness in the ancient body. Despite this, her form is not infirm nor has the realism been driven to the point of making her look decrepit. The strong lines in her face and the modeling of its forms

give her a touch of youthful energy which vanquishes the effect of the wrinkles. This union of vitality and age calls to mind feelings

Fig. 255.—Old Market Woman, 2nd century B.C. (?) Height about 4 feet (Metropolitan Museum of Art). (*Courtesy of Metropolitan Museum of Art.*)

of contentment without sadness, for such is the effect of robust old age.

The superb torso of a nymph found in the Tiber (Fig. 256) is one of the most completely satisfying sculptures of antiquity that have come to light. The long lines of the drapery reveal and yet conceal the human form, which seems to grow as though part of some natural plantlike beauty. The heavy folds of drapery around the feet lend to the lower part of the figure a columnar quality akin to that of the most ancient Attic style. Yet there is no trace

Fig. 256.—Nymph of the Tiber, School of Arcesilaus, c. 50 B.C. (Therme Museum, Rome).

of archaism in the carving. Out of this base, which is met later in Gothic art, the folds hold-

ing up the lower part of the figure grow naturally into a human form.

Here is a mature conception without sophistication. It will stand comparison with the best of Oriental and Gothic sculpture and seems to present a union of qualities that will be noted again in both of those styles. Like certain elements in Roman landscape painting, it points to the fact that Neo-Attic sculpture, if it had not been terminated by the decay of Roman civilization, might have reached something like the most mature Renaissance work. This figure stands midway between the Gothic Nuremberg Madonna (Fig. 376, Chap. XIII) and the Athena Lemnia (Fig. 189, Chap. VIII), and is not unlike the Oriental Kwan-Yin (Fig. 434, Chap. XIV).

The Realism of Portrait Sculpture. In studying the 400 years of the development of Roman sculpture, one gains a lasting impression that form, design, and composition were all subordinated to a single central purpose—the portrayal of character. The Roman artist was not interested in character in the ideal, however, nor in any one idea of character. He sought to portray the actual appearance of men whose personalities had taken on individual traits, whether high or low, good or bad, strong or weak.

The realism of the Roman sculptor has been unjustly called photographic; but the photograph lacks the form and completeness of characterization that are possible to sculpture. It sees only the outer man, unless the photographer has turned painter and erased or added certain lines. The eye of the sculptor, on the other hand, has the assistance of his whole thinking mind, which consciously or unconsciously evaluates the sitter. The Roman sculptor, as we know from art critics of the time, followed Aristotle in holding that his work was never purely natural but a reinterpretation of nature.

The head of the old man, sometimes called "Cicero" (Fig. 257), in the Boston Museum, might well have been a sculptor's terra-cotta

FIG. 257.—Portrait of Roman, 1st century B.C. Terra cotta (Museum of Fine Arts, Boston). (*Courtesy of Museum of Fine Arts, Boston.*)

model for reproduction in marble.[1] If the portrait is not actually that of Cicero, it ought to be. The corners of the lips, pulled down as though by a certain sophistication, perhaps

FIG. 258.—Portrait of Augustus from Prima Porta, c. 13 B.C. Height 6 feet 8¼ inches (Vatican Museum). (*Courtesy of Lesch-Carnegie.*)

pessimism, reveal the type of man we know Cicero to have been. The set of the jaws, also, seems to indicate the qualities found in his letters.

From a technical point of view, the sculptor arrived at his effects by keeping the big mass intact with good sculptural form, while drawing a certain number of wrinkles upon the surface. The hair he hastily indicated with a few strokes in clay attached to the crown of the head. Modeling in terra cotta must be all of a piece to be successful; that is, the mass of clay

must be kept moist until all the parts are added with clay of the same consistency. Then, with quick strokes of the knifelike modeling tool, the sculptor may undertake careful surface draw-

FIG. 259.—Relief from Ara Pacis Augusti, 13–9 B.C. Height about 5 feet (Uffizi, Florence). (*Courtesy of Lesch-Carnegie.*)

ing. These strokes show here in the wrinkles on the brow, and particularly in the eyelids, whose sharp edges stand out against the softer flesh forms. There is no better way of rendering flesh realistically than in the warm pink terra cotta, on which can be laid a delicate tint of color mixed with oil or wax.

As the Romans, like the Etruscans before them, used tomb effigies, there grew up a great demand for portraits. So general and so strong was the pride in ancestry that no house was complete without ancestor portraits.

The Combination of Greek and Roman Sculptural Ideals in the Statue of Augustus. The sturdy, manly body of Augustus from Prima Porta (Fig. 258) carries a strong head, endowed with the genius of the statesman. The portrait is idealized somewhat in the posture of the body, copied perhaps from some earlier work of the school of Polyclitus or Scopas. The pose shows a balance of strength and vitality. The decorative ceremonial character of the breastplate associates the personality of the emperor with his position as the deified head of the state. An earthly repre-

[1] The terra-cotta models of Arcesilaus were held more valuable than the finished work of his contemporaries. In an age when virtuosity is prized above craftsmanship the unfinished sketch, with all its suggestive power, receives a high valuation.

sentative of his patron, the sun-god Apollo, Augustus Imperator stands resplendent in shining armor, his right arm raised as though commanding his army. His face, showing a little of

members of the Julian family, led by allegorical figures, moves forward to worship the goddess of peace. It includes several idealized portraits of the Julians. At the west stands a section

Fig. 260.—Dionysus Relief, c. 100 B.C. (*Courtesy of British Museum.*)

the cares of age, has become ennobled by his exalted office and he seems above the vicissitudes of mortal fate. History, of which he is already a part, is portrayed in the reliefs on his cuirass, whose figures are for the most part recognizable as personifications of events pertaining to the glory of the Empire.[1]

The Last Influences of the Neo-Attic Style in the Ara Pacis Reliefs. Roman relief sculpture culminated in the great altar erected by Augustus on the Campus Martius after he had brought a measure of peace to the newly founded empire. This monumental sculpture on a wall enclosing the altar, called the *Ara Pacis Augusti*, was completed in 13 B.C. The panels both inside and outside show the various services that the imperial house of the Julians had rendered to the state. A procession of Roman statesmen and

devoted to Tellus (Fig. 259), the great earth mother, who appears with two attendants. She is not unlike the mountain goddess Arcadia in the painting from Herculaneum. In her lap lie the fruits of her abundance; behind her stand the wheat blossoms, the flowers of the earth. In the addition of these details from nature the Romans show their difference from the early Greeks.

Roman Sculpture without Greek Influences. Scholars particularly interested in pointing to the continuance of Greek ideals in Roman art insist that the Augustan reliefs are still too Greek in style to be considered Roman. Even the Dionysus relief in the British Museum (Fig. 260), despite its landscape and architecture which link it with the second Pompeian style, appears Greek to their eyes. For these scholars,

[1] The German scholar Amelung, in *The Museums of Rome*, has given an excellent description of this statue.

the truly Roman work adorns the Arch of Titus (Fig. 261), the columns of Trajan and Marcus Aurelius, and the Arch of Constantine. To this author, these final works of the Roman develop-

cellence that the cameo technique, as in the case of the Portland vase (Fig. 262), could be applied to a cheaper material. Hence we find these ideal figures, copied perhaps from old

Fig. 261.—Relief from Arch of Titus, The Spoils of Jerusalem, A.D. 81. (*Courtesy of Lesch-Carnegie.*)

ment appear to differ not in kind, but simply in quality, from the works of the Augustan age. Hence, we shall select the cameolike Portland vase, the sarcophagus of Constantine, and the portrait bust of Commodus, as examples of the final stage in sculptural development.

The Portland Vase. During the Augustan age the art of cameo carving reached its highest degree of excellence. The desire for a colorful contrast in relief sculpture that would make it approach more closely the condition of painting found its medium in striated agates and conch shells, whose various levels could be carved so that a layer of white would show against a layer of dark. Almost priceless, such cameos could belong to only a few favored individuals. The art of glassmaking, however, had by this time reached such a degree of ex-

Greek vases, seated in a landscape composed of rocks and trees. The refined spacing of the white bodies against the dark background almost transcends anything devised by the Greeks. The rendition of the tree with its fronded foliage bespeaks the painter's rather than the carver's technique, but the drapery lacks the rhythm found on Greek vases. The illusion of advancing and retreating planes, of darkness and light in the structure of the rocks, is the most significant feature of all Roman relief carving. While the Greeks in their relief sculpture always kept their planes separate from one another, the Romans endeavored to unite them, thus producing the effect of well-modeled painting rather than of well-designed sculpture.

The Constantine Sarcophagus and the Baroque Ef-

fect. The Constantine sarcophagus (Fig. 263) demonstrates the effect of relief carving without definite planes as carried to its final degree of development. The design lacks all inner continuity. The total effect of the struggling mass of Romans and Gauls is that of a rich jewelry pattern, interweaving not only on the surface but back into space. For the classical scholar, the Constantine sarcophagus stands as the degenerate Roman ending to the Greek relief style. We shall later find that the Renaissance artists used it, or similar pieces, as a model for their compositions.

The Bust of Commodus and the Degeneration of Classical Ideals. The dominating literary temper of ancient classical art criticism judged the formal values of an art work in terms of its spirit. We have seen that associational and formal values appear to be inseparable. The bust of Commodus (Fig. 264) may be taken to illustrate this. The man represented was the insane, degenerate son of the Emperor Marcus Aurelius. The artist has balanced the bust of this emperor, who fancied himself a reincarnation of Hercules, upon a tiny, fragile base, which makes us tremble for the stability of the piece. The jewellike decorative effects of hair, lion's skin, club, and pedestal so dominate the whole that the attention is drawn from a face which, studied closely, reveals no trace of nobility. All character lines have been erased until the features are as nearly expressionless as possible. A portrait must be built around a character. Lacking a character, the artist can only suggest the fanciful appendages of office. This artist has done more. Without knowing it, he has suggested the fickle quality of the man and the resulting instability of an empire about to be destroyed.

Music in Rome

The Romans played the same part in the development of classical music as in that of sculpture and painting. They adopted and enriched with new instrumental effects the music of the Greeks, while their philosophers, interested for the most part in returning to the simple melodies of the earlier Greeks, condemned what they considered a decline in the art. Save

Fig. 262.—Portland vase, 1st century A.D. Height about 10 inches. (*Courtesy of British Museum.*)

for the historian Pliny, no critic had a good word to say for the colorful effects produced by the Roman virtuosi. With the exception of the water organ—a magnified set of Panpipes attached to a chest of air filled by hydraulic means—the Romans developed no new instruments. They used pipes and trumpets, the harp, and the lyre. Music from these instruments accompanied theatrical performances, the organ being played during a pantomimic dance rather like our ballet.

The only development over early Greek music took place in the 2nd century after Christ, when the Emperor Hadrian endeavored to revise the earlier forms. At this time two Greeks, Mesomedes and Dionysius, composed several hymns with more interesting melodic patterns

critics. He defined at length the function of each, but held that the last class included the greatest musicians. The pattern of thought set by Boethius in his *Critique of Musical Types*

Fig. 263.—Constantine Sarcophagus, Battle of Romans and Gauls, about A.D. 300. Marble (Therme Museum, Rome). (*Courtesy of Lesch.*)

than those of earlier compositions. Another attempt to revive the old Greek music, which was by the Emperor Julian in the 4th century, brought forward no new development. During Roman times many treatises appeared on the art of music. Plutarch, Alypius, and Dionysius of Halicarnassus, all wrote theoretical discussions.

The Place of Boethius in the History of Music. A study of the writings of the late philosopher Boethius reveals a richness and depth of musical understanding astonishing to those who believe that the ancients had little notion of the aesthetics of music. His works indicate considerable knowledge of the essentials of harmony and include as well a tremendous mass of theoretical material covering the interrelationship of emotional states. For Boethius, whose thought followed patterns set by Pythagoras, Plato, and Aristotle, three classes of musicians exist—performers, composers, and

seems to have influenced the great Romantic composers, such as Wagner, Berlioz, and Schumann, all of whom strove to unite performance, composition, and critical analysis. The greatest service of Boethius to posterity, however, lay in his careful recording of the Greek modes. His manuscripts, available to medieval scholars, served as a source of continual inspiration in the early development of European music.

Aesthetic Philosophies in Roman Times

During the 500 years' development in aesthetic philosophy which elapsed between the writings of Vitruvius in the 1st century and those of Boethius in the 5th, we may perceive a formulation and summarization of all previously discovered principles. The early Romans stressed the pragmatically useful and formal values of art, while later men interested themselves in a quasi-psychological examination of associational values. Take a brief survey of the contributions of Vitruvius, Pliny, Dionysius, Plutarch, Longinus, and Plotinus.

are also formulae for other arts, some philosophical discussion, and notes on city plans. The third and fourth books describe the building of temples and the four orders of archi-

FIG. 264.—Bust of Commodus, about A.D. 190 (Palazzo dei Conservatori, Rome). (*Courtesy of Lesch.*)

FIG. 265.—Composite order of the Arch of Titus, A.D. 91. (*Drawing from Institute of France; courtesy of Harvard University College of Architecture.*)

Vitruvius and the Ideals of Architecture. Vitruvius Pollio, the architect, was born in 64 B.C. Although he was a mediocre writer, his collection of the aesthetic formulae of Greek architects played an important part in the development of architectural theory, not only through the Middle Ages but in Renaissance and modern times. Of his ten books, eight have to do with the materials and principles of building, including city planning, and two with war and time-measuring machines.

In the first two books, the education of the architect and a list of materials to be used in building occupy most of the space, but there

tecture, listed as Doric, Ionic, Corinthian, and Composite (Fig. 265). The fifth and sixth have to do with plans and arrangements of civic buildings and private houses. The seventh concerns wall painting, which held a position of great importance in Roman life. The eighth supplies an essay on the water supply. From the matter-of-fact pragmatic formulae of Vitruvius come most of our ideas on the aesthetics of architecture. These formulae may be summed up in the ancient dictum of Socrates that a good house is a useful one.

Four Critics on the Value of Color in Painting. With the rise of illusionistic painting came an increasing consciousness of the importance of color as an aesthetic factor. Of the Roman critics, however, only Plutarch dared suggest that color had great value. He wrote that drawing was inferior to coloring, which stimulated the mind, creating a greater sense of illusion. The judgment of Plutarch arose from no joy in color phenomena as such, but from the simple aesthetic formula of giving pleasure through recognition. Vitruvius and Pliny suggested that only the common people could be emotionally stirred by bright colors, such as purple. Dionysius of Halicarnassus, writing in the 1st century, described the manner in which light and shade with rich coloring lent emotional power to the works of contemporaneous painters.

Classical aesthetic theory, on the whole, demanded of the painter simple color schemes, composed of four primaries, such as we have seen in Egyptian painting, and perhaps modified by some neutral covering tone. These colors were to be applied so as to enhance, rather than detract from, the delicate line drawing and the significant silhouette.

Philostratus and the Aesthetics of Inspired Composition. A Greek philosopher, Philostratus, living in the 3rd century B.C., connects a little-noticed passage from Aristotle with the profound critical system of Longinus. Philostratus first suggested that the imitation of the ideal need no longer be the sole end of art. Art might function by stimulating the imagination. This doctrine, like the Stoic doctrine of regeneration, shifted the emphasis from the purpose of a work of art to its innate power to stimulate action or thought without regard to ends. From 300 B.C. on, as we have seen, artists tended to self-expression rather than to the expression of generally accepted social ideals.

Philostratus, who belonged to the semimystical cult of the Neo-Pythagoreans, prepared the way for Longinus and Plotinus. Longinus, as a follower of Aristotle, strove to unite the formal and the inspired associational values of art. Plotinus, as a Neo-Platonist, strove to derive all art from a mystical vision of an ideal beauty.

Longinus on the Sublime. Although Longinus interested himself particularly in the literary arts, his system may be applied to the critical analysis of all other art forms. His five sources of a lofty literary style serve equally as the sources for a lofty pictorial or sculptural creation. The seeing eye, the well-coordinated hand, the mind gifted with psychological insight, all lend tone not only to the words of an orator but also to the inspired brush of a Rembrandt and the chisel of a Michelangelo.

The first point of the treatise of Longinus, that the artist of genius is born and not made, also holds true for all the arts. In the last analysis the great conception in any art can be explained only in superrational terms. Given this genius, however, one may improve upon it by properly handling not only figures of thought and diction, but also planes of color and light and shade. The aesthetic aims of Socrates, Plato, and Aristotle stopped with beauty. Longinus asked for more. But the Sublime of Longinus is one with the "superbeautiful" Beauty of Plotinus, who came after him.

The Sources of the Sublime. The sources of the Sublime, says Longinus, are five, the first two of which are indespensable and are gifts of nature or inherited traits, resembling Plato's "inspiration," without which the poet can never enter the gates of the temple of art. The first lies in the ability to create an atmosphere of magnificence or grandeur; the second, in an inherent dramatic power that enables the artist to arouse the enthusiasm of his audience. On further analysis one can see that they have to do essentially with associational values.

The three other sources of the Sublime correspond to formal values. The first of these, which Longinus calls "amplification," requires that the artist master the use of figures of speech, or the "metaphors" of Aristotle. Next, he must express himself gracefully, that is, with appropriate rhythms, so that his style will be elegant and decorative. Then, he must know how to construct each sentence so that it has value in and of itself. Last of all, the artist must be able to combine harmoniously all these elements. As these five points have great significance in the judgment of any art, whether literary or spatial, we shall follow Longinus' analysis more closely.

Grandeur, according to Longinus, arises from the union of Plato's ideal of the ultimate good with a conception of the tremendous scope of nature. He cites a number of passages in Homer's *Iliad* to illustrate its epic sweep and to show that the poet conceived both his gods and his heroes in heroic proportions.

The inherent dramatic power of a great artist to sway his audience arises in his ability to find the proper actions or circumstances to fit a given subject and then to combine them skillfully in one production. Some people have such clear, fresh vision, coupled with unified powers of expression, that they bring out in a flash what the less gifted may take hours to express. Longinus quotes a dramatic poem of Sappho's to show how the poetess makes us feel both the grandeur and the horrors of love. From our vantage point of time we may cite appropriate passages in Dante, Milton, or Shakespeare.

Amplifying Factors in the Work of Art. The first of Longinus' formal values, amplification, consists in building up a number of figures of speech, one upon another, until they reach a climax. The great artist, one who inherits the sublime, will instill a quality of grandeur even in the figures he uses. Longinus contrasts sublimity with amplification in a comparison of Demosthenes and Cicero. Demosthenes, the Greek orator, had a way of uttering every sentence with such force and strength that it seemed to strike whatever lay before it like a thunderbolt. Cicero's oratory, on the other hand, resembled a conflagration in which many little fires breaking out in different places build up to one great flame.

Longinus saw very significantly that, although a great artist engaged on a work of epic proportions may make mistakes here and there, he has a grandeur of stroke or sweep of imagination big enough to outweigh his mistakes. The "charming" writer, on the other hand, may have a number of what Longinus calls "beauties," which arise from understanding all the rules, but he will never reach the Sublime, for he lacks quality of thought.

Factors of Grace, Elegance, and Decoration. The second of Longinus' formal values consist of qualities that he characterizes as elegance, grace, or decoration, all of which have to do essentially with balance and rhythm. Longinus noticed that, while human statuary might have fine proportion and measure, which lend it elegance and grace, it could not simulate natural grandeur. The nonspatial literary and dramatic arts which, like landscape, could depict the infinite stretches of nature, need an aesthetics of the Sublime. Where grace, charm, and elegance are to be considered, an aesthetics of beauty, with formal values, would suffice. Under an aesthetics of the Sublime, the principles of beauty need not always hold, for Nature creates defects and appeals through her contrasts. Longinus noticed that, since we are all human, we value the simple unity of formal values which constitutes beauty. We may, however, impute to Nature a more complex unity, like that of a harmonious musical composition. This thought led him to a consideration of the phenomenon of rhythm in speech.

The last source of sublimity derives from harmonious sentence composition. Hearing fine notes in music, we feel almost as though something moved within our minds, and we want to dance. A note by itself has no significance, but the changes of melody, the harmony of chords, and the symphonic arrangement of parts can greatly please. Longinus speaks of the cadence of language and attempts to analyze the way in which the word sounds in one of Demosthenes's orations gained effectiveness by arrangement in proper rhythmical sequence.

His final plea is for a greater harmony of

formal parts, suggesting proper associational images. This means that for Longinus, as for Aristotle and Socrates, the quality of appropriateness constitutes the criterion for excellence in art.

Alexandria and Oriental Influences in Roman Aesthetics. The greatest single influence upon Roman artistic creation and aesthetic thought came from the fertile minds of the Egyptian artists and critics in the centuries following the birth of Christ. In Alexandria, where African, Asiatic, Greek, and Roman thought combined, aesthetic criticism reached a refinement similar to that later achieved in the systems of Hindu and Chinese philosophers. History presents some evidence that Alexandrian thought could even have had an influence on the development of Chinese and Indian philosophy.

Many late Greek scholars taught in the great Library school founded by Ptolemy Soter, around 285 B.C. Its 532,802 volumes were distributed between a building called the "Museum" ("home of the muses") and the temple of Serapis, a late Egyptian teacher-god. The chief librarian was a priest of one of the gods Isis, Osiris, or Serapis. Under his direction, the great learning from Greece and the ancient Orient, later transmitted to the Romans, became a function of the priestcraft. This tradition was inherited by the Roman Catholic Church. In Alexandria, Euclid and Archimedes worked in mathematics and Aristarchus revised many of the ancient Greek texts. There, also, Plotinus, one of the greatest followers of Plato, living around A.D. 200, developed the Neo-Platonic school of philosophy.

In the philosophy of Plotinus, the idealistic fruits of Greek culture and the ancient Oriental religions gradually united to form a complex of thought influencing the development of the Christian religion. This thought pattern, which underlies Christian mysticism as well as the Hindu aesthetic philosophy, demands a slight appraisal at this point, for it came to play a great part in European aesthetics during the Middle Ages. Since the thought of Plotinus presents great difficulty for the beginner, it must be presented in a schematic form.

Plotinus' Definition of Beauty. In his essay on beauty, which occupies the eighth book of his fifth *Ennead*, Plotinus unites most of the thoughts on the nature of art discovered by Plato and Aristotle when they were in their most Ionian or Dionysiac moods. As a religious follower of Plato, he conceived beauty and truth as synonymous. For him, as for Keats,

"Beauty is truth, truth beauty"—that is all
Ye know on earth, and all ye need to know.

Plotinus was practical enough to recognize, however, that unless beauty or truth, presented through man's representational art, could affect our senses, most ordinary mortals could gain no vision of it. He formulated an ideoplastic position by maintaining that the arts do not limit themselves to the simulation of objects seen, but may be "derived from that ideal reason in which the character of all objects is born."[1]

Plotinus' Explanation of Artistic Creation. Following the above line of reasoning, probably suggested by Aristotle, Plotinus concluded that the artist could create new things by perfecting or changing the appearance of the old. He reasoned that, just as Phidias represented the god Zeus without having any physical likeness of the god before him, so all the great creations of beauty—whether the beauty of Helen or of Aphrodite herself—must arise in some ideal image or quality from the divine Creator. Accepted by the Christian Church Father, Augustine, this was to become the dominant aesthetic philosophy for the medieval artist until the Renaissance.

Like Plato, Plotinus placed the artist-philosopher in a favored position as a primary recipient or high priest of the divine vision. This "superbeautiful Beauty" was something like "the Sublime" of Longinus. Plotinus observes

---

[1] PLOTINUS, *Eighth Book of Fifth Ennead*, translated by Kenneth Sylvan Guthrie, courtesy of George Bell & Sons, Ltd., London, 1918.

that something happens to the artist as he is creating a work of art. He apparently starts with material under his hands; this takes form, and gradually a human appearance—a portrait, a character, a soul—stands where before was only disorganized material. Further, Plotinus observed that this creative exercise worked better if one put himself *en rapport* with the concepts of goodness and beauty. He wrote that "for the reception of the divine illumination, silence and a cessation of all mental energy are requisite, then the soul goes out alone to meet the alone"—a most significant psychological observation, for no one while awake is more completely detached from his surroundings than the artist in the moment of creation.

Although Plotinus left no writings on formal aesthetic values and little on associational and use values, he did discover a new value or point of view from which art could be studied and appreciated, one which has come to be widely recognized in the 20th century. This fourth value we might call the "expressive" value of art. It may be defined as that value which emphasizes the degree of release or self-objectification gained by the artist as he creates. This approach to art may be called the "introspective psychology" of art. Aristotle with his theory of catharsis, as we have seen, noticed the effect of art upon the spectator. Plotinus first noticed the effect of creation upon the artist. This constitutes his own great contribution to the study of art. He recognized artistic talent as derived not from an aberration, as some 20th-century psychiatrists think, but from the inherent reasonableness of the divine Creator, who has endowed man with artistic creative gifts along with his physical creative power.

Plotinus' Idea of Ecstasy. According to Plotinus, the artist must seek to lose himself in contemplation of the divinity. He wrote: "If the soul's gaze is piercing enough she finds the object she contemplates within herself; thus a man possessed by a divinity, whether Phoebus or some muse, may contemplate this divinity within himself." In the Middle Ages, when artists were completely educated and embraced by the ideology of the church and the formal aesthetics of their separate art guilds, this mystical philosophy led to superb creations. But in the late Roman Empire, when artists were slaves; or during and after the Renaissance, when each artist became a law unto himself; and in the 20th century, when artists may be afflicted by war psychoses, the Neo-Platonic aesthetics could be taken not only as a philosophic warrant for antisocial Bohemianism, but also for the creation of childish, primitive, and often neurotic fantasies.

For Plotinus, suicide was an antisocial escape from life; art, a more social escape. From this aspect of Plotinus' thought has arisen that modern idea of art which many egotistic artists use as a warrant for a complete rejection of other social duties. The aesthetic philosophy of Plotinus, although it may lead through an unintelligent romanticism to a complete egotistic disregard of others, in the hands of a social and formally trained person can lead to the creation of works of art that not only please but inspire. The writings of Leonardo, Michelangelo, and Goethe abound with sentences from the thought of Plotinus. The Chinese artists and the artists of the Western world all recognized within themselves this aspect of Neo-Platonic philosophy.

Oriental Influences on the Aesthetics of Music. The writings of the Neo-Platonists and Neo-Pythagoreans indicate the Orientalizing Alexandrian influence on Roman music. The two mystical schools suggested that good music consists of a divine harmony, defying all formal analysis. Following Plato, they considered music the most spiritual, because the least tangible, and therefore the most worthy of the arts. They named music, along with religion, philosophy, and rhetoric, as the free arts, while painting and sculpture were considered servile, a division which persisted throughout the Middle Ages.

The final stage in the mystical development of the aesthetics of music was reached by a

Syrian, Gamblichus, who lived around A.D. 330. This writer associated specific melodies with the various gods, like the leitmotivs of a Wagnerian opera. Gamblichus assumed that on hearing a given melody the worshiper became conscious of the presence of the deity. This Oriental concept of the use and power of music rests upon a firm psychological basis, for distinct melodies, associated in our minds with patriotic, religious, and recreative occasions we have experienced, have the power to excite, comfort, or quiet us. If we had been educated to associate *The Star-Spangled Banner* with Zeus, instead of with his eagle, and *America* with Athena, rather than with the Goddess of Liberty, the melodies would actually have the power to bring to mind pictures of those deities.

Summary

The Romans in the days of the early Republic showed some capacity for original artistic creation, particularly in sculpture and the drama, insofar as these had Etruscan and Latin origins. First absorbing and then absorbed by Greek art, the Roman aristocracy used its artists as slaves and their productions as a veneer of culture. Its great civic structures, the triumphal arches, baths, basilicas, and aqueducts, united this veneer of the Greek styles with great vaulted halls and arches built of concrete.

Painting, under the Romans, advanced beyond that of the Greeks, with a greater knowledge of perspective and the use of the landscape vista—a symbol derived from nature. The Roman's interest in detail led to his depiction of still life and genre. Seeking an aesthetic philosophy to justify his secondhand artistic taste, the Roman adopted the thoughts of Plato and Aristotle as seen through the eyes of their mystical followers. The Romans codified aesthetic formulae or else developed a highly individualistic aesthetic mysticism. The most enlightened Roman, at his best, had an enclyclopedic mind, stored with data about art and a miscellaneous collection of aesthetic formulae only

partly understood and digested. These formulae, the ultimate aesthetic position possible to ancient man, may be thus summarized:

The Aesthetic Inheritance from Antiquity. The social philosopher Oswald Spengler differentiated among three philosophies of life, which he called Apollonian, Faustian, and Magian. These correspond to three of our four aesthetic types—the Classical, the Gothic, and the Oriental. The fourth, or primitive, consists of the undifferentiated energy of a new race before it has created a definite philosophy of life during that period of time when its art, although rich and exuberant, remains strong only in use and formal values, without rich associational pattern, such as grows up with the development of culture. By the end of the period of expansion in the Roman Empire, ancient man had discovered all these types, and from them, as we have seen, there had grown a number of ways for judging the excellence of art.

To the primitive, the chief values of art were either physically useful, as in the case of the technomorphic patterns growing out of manufacture, or else quasi-religious. That is, he conceived the work of art as totemistic or fetishistic. In his playful moments, when he had any leisure time, the primitive artist undoubtedly enjoyed the manipulation of material for its own sake and the resulting discovery of pleasurable formal values.

In Egypt, where the forces of a religion allied to the cults of the underworld strongly influenced the development of a style, the chief emphasis was placed upon permanence. Abstract forms, lines, cones, and planes became the formal values appearing most desirable; and in the graphic arts, particularly, flat areas of color limited by heavy black lines seemed the most pleasing decorative effect.

In contrast to Egyptian culture, which developed the idea of permanence as the highest aesthetic value, stood the culture of the Mesopotamians, who sought an expression of force and vitality as most enjoyable. The Mesopotamian culture also gave rise in its palace architecture to the beginnings of a structural aesthetics or functionalism built around the arch and dome as space-enclosing patterns, with an arrangement of exterior building forms expressive of interior arrangement. This development was on a most elementary or primitive scale, however, and far from the eventual development into the Faustian Gothic, on one hand, and the Magian Byzantine and Persian domed architecture, on the other.

The Greeks, inheriting primitive Egyptian and Mesopotamian habits of thought, valued above all else the character of man as a thinking individual capable of creating form from material. Their architecture, sculpture, and painting wrought patterns associated with the underlying thought that the Egyptian and Mesopotamian patterns of thought could be brought into a state of equilibrium within the individual. Hence, Greek art achieved an almost perfect triangular balance between formal, associational, and useful values. This balance accounts for what is called the "beauty" of the classical style. In achieving beauty, the Greeks unconsciously, at first, and then consciously, through their philosophers, gave expression to a number of artistic formulae, which have become centers for the various moods of aesthetic thinking used by the critics of the 20th century. Briefly, these are as follows:

Socrates held that anything appropriately useful, anything expressing emotion through action, or anything which inculcated virtue, was beautiful.

His pupil, Plato, inheriting all these thoughts, added to them the idea that genius and a vision of the ideal beauty were necessary to achieve the beautiful.

Summarization of all Formulae. From the unknown Egyptian sculptor came the formula that anything was beautiful that consisted of a pattern or arrangement of planes, cones, and cubes.

Stressing the Socratic and Platonic dogmas that beauty must produce desirable social effects, Aristotle modified their definitions of character by pointing out that the portrayal of base actions might effect a catharsis, or purging, of the emotions through empathy. Further, Aristotle considered that there must be an orderly pattern or arrangement of actions around some central theme, with a proper relationship and proportion of the parts to the whole. Aristotle also noted the elements of musical interweave or rhythm as necessary for unifying the emotions after they had been aroused. This last constitutes the theory of specific form.

By pointing to the significance of the particular or characteristic, Aristotle opened the way for the Roman philosophers to stress realism. Both Aristotle and Plato at times held that art could be an imitation of nature, but both maintained that only the representation of the ideal could be beautiful.

Not contented with achieving a balance of values in the realm of spatial arts, Pythagoras, Plato, and Aristotle strove to define beauty and harmony in the temporal arts of drama and music. Dominated by the ethical ideal of education for perfect citizenship, all these thinkers stressed the value of art as an effective medium for education toward inner harmony and outer conformity with the ideals of a perfect city-state.

Longinus, striving to unite various aspects of the theories of Aristotle and Plato, discovered a new need in the creation of his philosophy of the Sublime. The representation of Nature outside of man, uniting with the aesthetics of specific form from Aristotle, and the idea of imaginative genius, discovered by Plato, formed the basis of Longinus' philosophy of the Sublime.

Carried forward by Stoic philosophers, who stressed the characteristic, and eventually explained by Plotinus in terms of the complete loss of self-consciousness as the artist created, there developed the Oriental concept of artistic ecstasy.

It might well seem as though the ancients, having discovered practically all possible moods for aesthetic thinking, would suffice for an

FIG. 266.—Head of Satyr, the Agora, Athens, 3rd century A.D. (*Courtesy of T. Leslie Shear and the American School at Athens.*)

analysis of modern art styles. This is true to some extent if we consider making only an elementary analysis; but it is well to notice that all the arts, with the exception perhaps of music and the drama, were visualized and on a static plane. In other words, the Egyptian idea of permanence dominated the ancient world of art insofar as it came under the Roman ideal of stability and order. A few outlying districts, such as Scythia, the European borders of the Empire, and northern Syria, had in them the germs of an artistic style—the Gothic— which was to value the element of motion in the arts over the element of permanence (Fig. 266). This style eventually reached its highest expression in the northern art of Gothic building, the world dramas of Shakespeare and Goethe, the music of Bach, Beethoven, and Wagner, and the 20th-century art of the motion picture. New combinations and inventions of aesthetic thought arose with new formulae for explaining not only the Beautiful but the Sublime, as this other style developed.

The final development in art took place after the 19th century, when the Classical and Gothic conceptions of the highest aesthetic values united in a world art that approximated closely the Magian aesthetic formulae. These formulae, as we shall see, developed out of the late Greco-Roman philosophies of Longinus and Plotinus, at the hands of the Indian thinkers, whose transcendental philosophy closely approached the condition of Plato's thought, and the matter-of-fact Chinese, whose philosophy is essentially Aristotelian. Projecting our thought into the future, we need an analysis of the Gothic, Indian, and Chinese contributions to art in order that the creative minds of the future may develop a suitable world style and the philosophers, a final formula in which the Beautiful and the Sublime, the static and the dynamic elements may unite.

Bibliography

ANDERSON, W. S., R. P. SPIERS, THOMAS ASHBY: *Architecture of Ancient Rome*, Charles Scribner's Sons, New York, 1927.

VITRUVIUS: *Ten Books on Architecture*, translated by Maurice H. Morgan, Harvard University Press, Cambridge, Mass., 1926.

WALTERS, H. B.: *Art of the Romans*, The Macmillan Company, New York, 1911.

LUCRETIUS: *On the Nature of Things*, translated by W. E. Leonard, E. P. Dutton & Company, Inc., New York, 1916.

ANTONINUS, MARCUS AURELIUS: *The Thoughts of the Emperor Marcus Aurelius Antoninus*, translated by George Long, Henry Altemus Company, Inc., Philadelphia, 1864.

HORACE: *Satires, Epistles and Ars Poetica*, translated by H. Rushton Furclough, G. P. Putnam's Sons, New York, 1929.

LONGINUS: *Essay on the Sublime*, translated by William Smith, London, 1843.

PLOTINUS: *Ennead, Eighth Book of Fifth Ennead*, translated by Kenneth Sylvan Guthrie, George Bell & Sons, Ltd., London, 1918.

GRAVES, ROBERT: *I, Claudius* (novel), Harrison Smith & Robert Haas, Inc., New York, 1934.

Recordings

Hymn to the Sun, by Mesomedes, Decca 20156 A.

CHAPTER XI

Early Christian and Byzantine Art

These things I then knew not, and I loved these lower beauties, and I was sinking to the very depths, and to my friends I said, "Do we love anything but the beautiful? What then is the beautiful? and what is beauty? What is it that attracts and wins us to the things we love? for unless there were in them a grace and beauty, they could by no means draw us unto them." And I marked and perceived that in bodies themselves, there was a beauty, from their forming a sort of whole, and again, another from apt and mutual correspondence, as of a part of the body with its whole, or a shoe with a foot, and the like. And this consideration sprang up in my mind, out of my inmost heart, and I wrote "on the fair and fit," I think, two or three books.

"Confessions of St. Augustine"

THIS PASSAGE from the *Confessions of St. Augustine* shows better than almost anything else the attitude of the early Christians on matters of aesthetic interest. Augustine, like Plotinus, believed that "he who achieves union with the ultimate beauty is from himself set free." The "ultimate beauty" was, of course, the "highest good" of Plato—intangible thought so universal that it could not be depicted. Such mystical goals could be best described, perhaps, in some realm of ecstasy or through the speaking in strange tongues at Pentecost. Although the Christian acknowledged that God as a spirit was the highest good, he could also accept the lesser spiritual beauty of the body of God, manifest first in the Son, then in the church. The human being, as part of the church, which the theologian calls the body of Christ, had his fitting and proper place, so that every individual might be said to have a beauty in kind, relative to his effectiveness in the church.

Historical Backgrounds

The history of the rise and development of the early Christian spirit in art should be a fascinating one for the student because it is still incomplete. Each year brings fresh archaeological discoveries from the treasures of the Vatican and the ruined monasteries of Egypt, Syria, and Turkestan. Naturally these fresh discoveries raise many questions, and scholars do not agree on all the details.

The chief question still raised in discussing the origins of Christian art is that of the relative importance of Rome, Alexandria, Antioch, and Jerusalem as centers for the dispersion of definitely Christian art objects. Whichever city was preeminent, we know it is possible for Christian art to have sprung up in many places simultaneously. The disciples of Christ carried his teachings over a wide area. Paul and Barnabas were sent to Antioch, which had been the home of the physician-disciple Luke. Legend

[1] From Edward B. Pusey's translation of the *Confessions of St. Augustine*, P. F. Collier & Son Corp., New York, 1909.

322

says that St. Peter, accompanied by his secretary St. Mark, who is said to have founded the church at Alexandria, went to Rome. St. John the Evangelist lived at Ephesus, while Philip is said to have gone to Persia, and Thomas through Persia to India.

The early history of Christianity in Rome is one of persecution and suppression. In Persia and Syria, however, the new sect was tolerated and by the 2nd century the gospel had been sufficiently accepted as a state religion to allow the building of churches in the town of Adiabene beyond the Tigris River. By the 3rd century the Christians had a state church, with Edessa as its center, and had founded a school of theology at Nisibis on the southern border of Armenia. There is a record of a baptistery's having been built there in A.D. 359 in honor of St. James. The structure had a domed roof raised upon a square, after the fashion of the old Assyrian and Persian palace buildings.

Though the Roman persecution under the Emperor Decius, which ran from A.D. 250 to 258, made martyrs of the bishops of Jerusalem, Antioch, Rome, and Carthage, the message of Christianity had by that date so gripped the minds of the masses in the Empire that most of the succeeding rulers followed a policy of compromise, which culminated at Milan in A.D. 313 with Constantine's Edict of Toleration. During the next hundred years the Christians unconsciously incorporated some of the religion of the Empire (Fig. 267). That was the time of the great councils and the definition of dogma.

The Council of Nicaea, A.D. 325, promulgated the creed that declared Jesus to be "the Son of God, of the Substance of the Father, and Cosubstantial with Him, begotten not born, eternal like the Father, and immutable by nature." The Council of Constantinople, in 381, proclaimed that the Holy Spirit, symbolized by the dove, was the third member of a trinity. This suggests Plato's idea of the soul as a triangle, the beliefs of the Cretans and, as the dove was the pagan symbol of the mother-goddess, a normal family relationship. In 431,

FIG. 267.—Archangel Michael (?), leaf of ivory diptych, 4th century (?). Height 16¼ inches (British Museum). (*Courtesy of Lesch-Carnegie.*)

FIG. 268.—Coptic Christian designs, *a*, stone frieze with sharp carving from Ahnas, 5th century (Egyptian Museum, Cairo); *b*, detail of woolen woven tapestry showing saint killing dragon, 6th century (Metropolitan Museum of Art); *c*, wooden door showing Last Supper, 12th century; note rhythmical interweave or arabesque of human figures due to Turkish influence (Coptic Museum, Cairo).

the Council of Ephesus declared that since the Virgin Mary was herself divine and was the mother of Christ, who was by earlier definition God, she was the Mother of God, therefore divine. The Greeks came to worship her as *Hagia Sophia*, or Holy Wisdom. In this way the feminine member, which is by nature social and institutional, came to dominate gradually the masculine element in the Christian religion.[1]

Nestorius, a patriarch of Constantinople and a follower of Arius, disagreed with the Council of Ephesus, holding that Mary was only the earthly mother of Christ. He was deposed, but his followers were accepted in Persia and Armenia and had much to do with the Christianization of the Goths. They then moved eastward, founding monasteries in Turkestan, and even-

tually reached China, where by the 7th century they had persuaded the emperor to build churches for them.

In Egypt, which was filled with religious lore, the Christians, who were later called "Copts," founded monastic communities in the desert (Fig. 268*a*, *b*). These formed productive centers of religious philosophy, which the developing legalistic Roman Church had to combat. In the thesis called "Monophysitism," the Copts held that Christ had only one nature and that in it were blended the human and the divine. The Council of Ephesus, on the other hand, declared that Christ was wholly divine. A monk by the name of Pelagius, who is supposed to have been born in Britain and who had probably come into contact with the Monophysites

---

[1] St. Augustine at one time suggested in his *Liber de vera religione*, Vol. X, that the true Christian religion had existed from the very beginning of the human race until after the coming of Christ in the flesh, when it began to be called by his name. This belief, accepted by the medieval church, made possible the use of elements not only from the Old Testament narrative but also many of the symbols from other Oriental cults. It may account in part for the appearance of the Manichaean battle of the virtues and vices as the Psychomachia of Prudentius. In the Eastern Christian Church even Buddha was accepted as a saint.

in the Christian community in Carthage, held that the human race as a whole would not have to be condemned for the original sin of Adam. His followers were active in Christianizing England and Ireland before the coming of St. Patrick, who represented the Roman rule.

By the 5th century, Christianity in some form had been accepted by great numbers of people from Ireland to Chinese Turkestan, from Ethiopia to the steppes of Russia. Meantime, the Eastern Rome—Constantinople, or Byzantium —had become its most influential artistic center. Into this city came all the stylistic creations of the ancient world. There they developed as the Byzantine style, unbroken by outside influences until the 14th century. During almost ten centuries Byzantium sent out to the troubled countries of Western Europe her version of the art of antiquity, until finally the Empire was broken up by the Turks. With the ultimate triumph of the Roman Church in the European Renaissance, the humanistic art of antiquity, Christianized, became the dominant style for Southern Europe.

Philosophical Backgrounds

Christianity combines the democratic ideals of the Greeks and the piety of the Hebrews with the world citizenship of the Romans as unified in the personality of Christ, who lifted men toward his own position by saying, "You are my brothers; we are all children of one Father." Such a message was easily put into written form by a number of Church Fathers, the most significant of whom was St. Augustine.

St. Augustine was born at Tagaste, a town near Carthage in North Africa, in A.D. 354. Educated at the University of Carthage, he served his religious apprenticeship as a follower of Mani, an Oriental mystic prophet who founded the cult of the Manichaeans. St. Augustine lived a full life on the pagan model until he went as a teacher of rhetoric in the law school to the university in Milan. Here he was baptized as a Christian by St. Ambrose in 387.

Eight years later he became the Bishop of Hippo in North Africa and there, greatly loved and respected, he spent the remaining thirty-five years of his life. Out of this long, fruitful period of existence Augustine left a number of theological definitions that helped make Roman Christianity the victor in its struggle over the differing schismatic versions. It was Augustine who formulated the doctrine of predestination, which meant, in short, that God controlled all action, that all effect was preceded by a predetermined cause. In his kindliness, he suggested the doctrine of "irresistible Grace," which meant an eventual salvation for all mankind, and the doctrine of "final perseverance," which meant that God's will would finally prevail. Though they allowed little room for free will and for personal predilections, these doctrines gave to the orthodox an underlying feeling of security in unstable times. The followers of Mani and Pelagius could not have the same certainty.

The later Roman concept of a universal law, written by Augustine into his famous treatise, *The City of God*, enabled the church to function as an arbiter over the destiny of nations. After the 10th century, first the Catholic Church and then the Holy Roman Empire, because of the political philosophy of Augustine, were to play decisive roles in the history of European thought.

The Genius of Augustine

Augustine inherited the artistic flair of a Plato, the revealing self-analysis of a Socrates, and the scholarly, methodical, and scientific mind of an Aristotle. He takes his place as perhaps the first world citizen, the first man with a Christian vision of the unity of nations. This breadth of view was by no means due to a simple, mystical attitude such as is usually ascribed to the earliest Christians. In his *Confessions*, which is the first known example of a psychological autobiography, Augustine led himself back to the roots of his own personal

FIG. 269.—Symbols on early Christian sarcophagi. *a*, Livia Primitiva, 3rd century (?) (Louvre); *b*, central panel from the Passion Sarcophagus, 4th century (Lateran Museum); *c*, representation of the Baptism of Christ, Ravenna, 6th century.

desires. He discussed his early education as described to him by his mother and his nurse, and weighed those elements that had helped or hindered his development of character. He spoke of his love for one who was not his wife and of his companionship with the young blades of the town while he was sowing his wild oats. Finally, he discussed his religious experiences with the Manichaeans. As a teacher of rhetoric, he had become acquainted with the philosophy of Aristotle and in his arguments with the Manichaean priests discovered that the latter were neither logical nor scientific—a fact which led him to look toward Christianity. In the life of Augustine there is evidence that Plato's idea of the "ultimate good"—a trinity of the spirit, mind, and body—placed at the service of some great ideal, made him an effective, happy man. There is a solid core of the philosophy of Augustine in the educational ideals of our Christian democracy, where his teachings should have their greatest scope.

The City of God. Because Augustine was a mature man who could visualize the City of God, his writings were to the development of Christian art what the Homeric stories of the gods were to the Greeks. In his celestial city, God was the ruler; below him as intermediaries were first Christ, then the Virgin, then the angels, the saints, the body of Christian worshipers, the unsaved, the animals, and finally the Spirit of Darkness himself, who was obedient in the end to the law of God. The city was like the ideal of a world-wide Rome, with God as emperor and Christ and the Virgin as intermediaries in a final judgment (Fig. 471, Chap. XV).

St. Augustine's analysis of beauty, with which this chapter began, shows, as do other quotations from the *Confessions* and the *City of God*, that he considered the highest beauty to be one with the highest goodness. Within the plan of Grace descending from the source of all goodness, there were various stages of beauty; there was even beauty in bodies by themselves, though this was not of as much value as the beauty that made the body part of the whole. In other words, individualistic beauty, such as one might find in late Greek times, was of less value than the beauty that was part of a balanced structure. This aesthetics dominated Christian art until the Renaissance.

Symbolism

When the early Christian tried to symbolize these abstract thoughts, his purposes were best served by a few mystical symbols. The monogram of Christ, the Chi Rho (Fig. 269*b*, *c*), is such a symbol. Later on, in the baroque painting of the Counter Reformation, it appears as the central composition line upon which artistic creation was based.

Another symbol was the fish (Fig. 269*a*), which stood for the mystical words *Iesous CHristos THeous HYios Soter* ("Jesus Christ, of God the

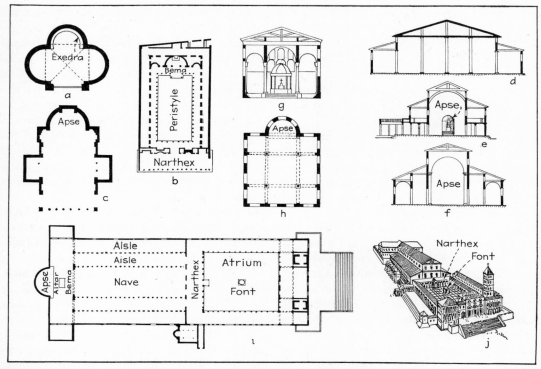

Fig. 270.—Elements contributing to the Christian basilica. *a*, cruciform tomb with exedra, Sidi-Mohammed-el-Guebioni; *b*, atrium or peristyle with bema and narthex, House of Eumachia, Pompeii; *c*, apse and transept in Temple of the Public Lares, Pompeii; *d*, Greek basilica, Delos; *e*, Basilica of Trajan, Rome; *f*, section, St. Paul's-outside-the-Walls; *g* and *h*, plan and section of pagan-Christian basilica at Treves; *i*, plan of old St. Peter's; *j*, restoration of old St. Peter's.

Son, the Saviour"). The first letters of the words, taken together, form the Greek word for fish, *ichthys*. The cross as a symbol of birth was also used (Fig. 269*c*). Christianity, which had a new central thought proclaiming the highest type of religion yet reached in the Western world, borrowed from the strongest of the old cults the buildings, thought-forms, and symbols that had been most effective in enlightening mankind (Fig. 269*c*).

Architecture

Scholars heartily disagree over the origins of the Christian church. As early as the persecution of Diocletian in A.D. 303, Christians in Africa wrote of their meeting place as a "basilica." Undoubtedly the old Greco-Roman building known by that name, which functioned as banking house and law court, presented as a model for early Christian architects a structure spacious enough to accommodate the large congregations. Constantine's Edict of Milan in A.D. 327, which made possible the public assembly of Christians, ushered in an age of great building activity in all parts of the Roman Empire. From Persia to the Limes Germanicus, most of the buildings erected took the basilican form. In Treves, a town on the German border, eventually the Roman imperial basilica was made over into a church, which is still in use today.

The illustration (Fig. 270) suggests some of the elements from pagan antiquity that eventually found their way into that Christian basilica whose finished plan appears above.

Obviously, this structure has origins more complex than those of the Greek Doric temple. Curiously, many scholars still seek to derive it from some single building. Its very power as a symbolic structure probably arises from the fact that to a Roman it could suggest his home or his law court; to a Greek, the *bouleuterion*, or democratic meeting place, if not the hall of the Eleusinian mysteries or the sacred healing precinct of Epidaurus; while to the Egyptian, the arrangement of the basilica would appeal as a variation of the ancient temple plan, and to the Hebrew its crypt would suggest his meetings for family worship in the tomb.

Early Christians throughout the Empire, like the Egyptians, congregated sometimes in tombs, to be near the spirits of their loved ones, and sometimes in private dwellings. One ancient rite—the agape, or love feast, symbolic of the celestial banquet—was not unlike the old banquets represented in Etruscan tombs and certain of the Hebrew feasts. Several tombs of cruciform shape, with exedrae or semicircular apses, have been found in Rome and Africa (Fig. 270*a*). The exedra has also been found in Roman houses at Pompeii and Ostia, placed at the rear of the atrium (Fig. 270*b*). Many of the Roman basilicas used the exedra as a law court where litigants brought their cases before a statue of the emperor, who, after the time of Augustus, was considered divine. Something of the associational overtones of all these buildings carried over to the exedra of the Christian church (Fig. 270*c*).

The elevation of the Roman basilica, with its clerestory copied from Greek and Egyptian predecessors and its triforium gallery offering increased floor space, is exactly that of the Christian basilica (Fig. 270*d*, *e*, *f*, *g*).[1] Three other parts remain to be accounted for—the transept (bema), or cross arm between the exedra (apse) and the nave proper; the atrium, with its peristyle, before the nave; and the

baptistery, a circular building occasionally found in place of the atrium, but more regularly at one side of the church. The symbol of salvation through water and the primary rite of rebirth through baptism are still retained in the baptismal font and the holy-water basin found near the entrance to the church. In the earliest Christian churches the lustral basin was in the center of the atrium. The transept first appears in Egypt, where the early rise of monasticism swelled the ranks of the clergy who were accommodated in this part of the church. Such transept areas are usually found behind the hypostyle hall adjacent to the cella in Egyptian temples. The atrium may have been suggested by the forum in front of the basilica, but more probably by the peristyle court in the Egyptian temple or by the forecourt of Solomon's Temple in Jerusalem. It offered a place of worship for the partly initiated and the women, in the earliest buildings, and was retained long into the Middle Ages as the Galilee chapel of English cathedrals. The baptistery has both the plan and the function of the tholos at Epidaurus.

Symbolism and Aesthetics of the Basilican Church

In summary, the parts and function of the Christian basilica which may be studied today in their original form in a few remaining examples are as presented in Fig. 270*j*. The atrium shows the original portico, later, in monastic churches, to become the cloister. In the center one might have found the baptismal font, or baptistery. At the farther side of the atrium a covered porch, called the "narthex," ran along the front of the building proper. Anyone entering the nave, although he might notice the treatment of wall spaces (Fig. 286) later described in detail, would be particularly impressed by the triumphal arch separating the

[1] An excellent résumé of the theories concerning the origins of the Christian basilica may be found in Kingsley Porter's *Medieval Architecture*, Vol. I, pp. 49–71. Porter inclines to regard the Greek basilica, modified in the Eastern cities of the Roman Empire, as the most logical ancestor of the Christian basilica.

nave from transept and apse (Fig. 285). The altar, erected over the crypt where repose the bones of saints and bishops, stands on the chord, or diameter, of the apse. Directly behind it is the raised seat (*cathedra*) of the bishop, from which the name "cathedral" was taken to designate the type of church in which that dignitary presided. The cathedral at Torcello (Fig. 271) offers one of the rare examples of this arrangement still existing in the original condition. On each side of the bishop's throne were the seats of the presbyters, or chief priests. Above them one sees the great apse mosaics, usually representing Christ and His disciples or, in many later cases, the Virgin. The chief difference between the Christian church and the Egyptian temple now becomes clear; the temple ended in a shrine, while the Christian church, like the democratic Greek *bouleuterion* or the Roman basilica, had behind the altar a public organization of human beings to which any man in the congregation might eventually be elected. Early Christianity was essentially a communal religion and, although it retained many elements from the cult of the dead, it was oriented toward the living.

As Christianity grew in power, the simple democracy of the earliest congregation gave way to a well-organized priesthood, and the apses with the altar were separated from the congregation by *cancelli*, or railings. That is to say, a chancel, or sacred place, was created, like the old Egyptian shrine. The altar was raised and covered with a canopy, or *ciborium*. Finally, a low wall or screen was thrown across the nave; and the clergy, who had gradually increased in number, were seated behind this, separated from the congregation. Two *ambones*, or pulpits, were placed on the left and right sides of the nave, outside the choir screen. From them the Gospels and the Epistles were read.

Eastern Church Building. Although Rome was the center of the basilican building form, Italian churches until the late Middle Ages remained merely great halls planned without thought to

external appearances. One must turn to the East for some of the most original church construction and for most of the elements of the

FIG. 271.—Apse of the cathedral at Torcello, Apostle mosaics, c. 1008. Madonna, 12th century. From model by author. (*Photograph by Cosman.*)

new decorative style peculiar to early Christian architecture.

In Syria the cross with an apse early became a set church form. The Hauran, an area around Damascus rich in ruins of distinctive Christian churches, furnishes several examples whose structure and decoration were to play a significant part in Eastern church building from the

6th through the 12th century. Here and in Syria Sassanian dynasts built the palaces of Ctesiphon, Sarvistan, and Firuzabad during the early centuries. Details of the decoration as

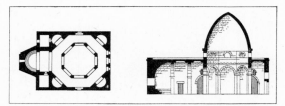

Fig. 272.—Plan and elevation, Church of St. George at Ezra, Syria, A.D. 515. (*After De Vogüé.*)

well as the domed construction from these palaces influenced not only the Byzantine but also Moslem architecture. The Persians knew how to construct domes of brick over square rooms. The technique called for much more ingenuity than that exercised by the Romans who built the circular Pantheon. The first attempts were made in wood perhaps and were rather like the kivas of the Indians (Fig. 45, Chap. III). In the palace of Sarvistan (Fig. 111, Chap. V), which was probably built in the 4th century, one may see that the transition from the square to the dome was made by throwing arches across the corners. These arches were arranged at the angles of the square so that each arch projected beyond the other. When the eleventh arch was reached, its inner surface coincided with the plan of an octagon. Upon this octagon the dome could be raised by placing slabs over the angles, making a sixteen-sided figure. The thrust of the dome was not entirely outward toward the sides because, as will be seen, the dome was higher than it was wide. Such a dome is said to be raised on squinches. At Sarvistan the squinch is a trumpet squinch.

The early Syrian churches adopted this method of covering their large central square halls. In the case of the Church of St. George, at Ezra (Fig. 272), built in A.D. 515, the square plan was made to include an octagonal central section raised upon piers. The corners of the square were niches with relatively heavy ma-

sonry. Finally, above the octagon there was a raised clerestory with windows, called a drum. The angles of the octagon may have made use of flat beam squinches. Both of these makeshifts were unaesthetic, because the transition from the lower to the upper parts of the dome was clumsy.

In Syria or Transjordania, by the 2nd century after Christ, architects had begun to construct a type of compound dome, called the dome upon pendentives, which is found with pendentives of cut stone in the baths at Gerash as early as the end of the 1st century.

Morey has justly remarked that there have existed in the Western world only three great architectural styles—the classical, the Byzantine, and the Gothic. The classical depends for its effect upon relationship of the column to the architrave. The Byzantine has as its prime constructive principle the dome on pendentives, which makes a pleasing transition from the square to the spherical space.

The diagrams (Fig. 273) show the way in which the dome on pendentives may be set up. In (*a*) the square gives the area to be covered, and the circle inscribed in it is the circumference of the dome. First let another and larger circle then be circumscribed about the square. Let that stand for a large dome that can be constructed directly over the square. This dome would not be complete, however. First, the places arising perpendicularly from the square would be made to cut off four sides of it, and this would make four arches; then we would start building it at a point just above the top of these arches. Each one of the sections that now appears is called a pendentive. To make this stand up, barrel vaults or half domes must then be thrown up on all sides to buttress the first dome, which would hold together when the circle was complete at the top. Upon this circle a drum was usually erected and this could be pierced by many windows, if extra buttressing were provided outside. Finally, the dome (*b*) would be erected upon the circular drum. Seen from the inside, this dome would

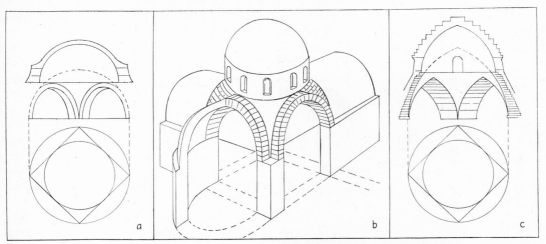

Fig. 273.—Construction of dome on pendentives. *a*, early type; *b*, late Byzantine type raised on drum; *c*, Romanesque pointed type, St. Front, Périgueux, A.D. 1120.

Fig. 274*a*.—Exterior, Hagia Sophia, Constantinople, by Anthemius and Isidorus, A.D. 532–537. (*Courtesy of Lesch-Carnegie.*)

appear to float above the windows and the four segments of the lower dome thus would seem to be depending from it. Finally, if pendentives and the upper dome were covered with a layer

FIG. 274*b*.—Interior, Hagia Sophia. Width of nave 108 feet, height of central dome 180 feet. (*Courtesy of K. Conant.*)

of gold mosaic, as at Hagia Sophia, one can easily imagine the magnificent effect (Fig. 274*b*).

The Exterior of the Eastern Christian Church. The creativeness of the Asiatic architects is shown not only by their invention of the dome on pendentives, but also in their perfection of an exterior church design and decoration fitting to the interior. In Rome and the West, the church exterior went without proper decoration until the Romanesque building, after the 11th century. The building of the Armenian church at Mastara (Fig. 275*a*) shows the splendid composition of masses for which the Eastern architects were justly famed. This church has a dome like the one in the palace of Sarvistan, built upon squinches and buttressed by four apsidal niches.

The Syrian Basilica. The palace at Chaqqa, built in the 2nd century, has several interesting large halls, which yielded new contributions

to the basilican type of building. As the Hauran possessed no wood and as cement was not used as it was in Rome, the Syrians in the Djebel Druse often covered their basilicas with great

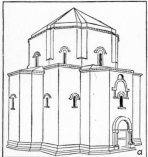

FIG. 275.—*a*, exterior, church at Mastara, A.D. 650 (*after Strzygowski*); *b*, basilica at Chaqqa, showing perspective of construction (*after De Vogüé*).

arches of stone. The central hall at Chaqqa has eight arches (Fig. 275*b*) set in walls running out to the side walls of the building. Their thrust is braced against the side walls, and buttresses give still further support. The side aisles are covered with small arches and each has an upper story, or triforium gallery, with windows through the outside walls. Along the walls, cross stones are set so that they corbel out and partly cover the ceiling area. Upon these cross stones other flat slabs are laid to form the ceiling. All these stones were so well cut and the thrust of the arches is so well balanced by the buttresses that the whole building was set together without mortar. This shows a skill on the part of the Syrian builders equal, if not superior, to that of the builders of the Parthenon.

On the outside of some of the southern Syrian churches appear elements of decoration taken from such Syrian palaces as the hall at Chaqqa (Fig. 276*a*). The niche with the scallop shell, the engaged pilasters, and the corbel table were transported to Cappadocia and Ravenna, later to be widely adopted in European Romanesque architecture. The church of Tourmanin, built in A.D. 540, had another original detail of construction which, added to the triforium gallery, the buttresses, and the corbel tables, was to

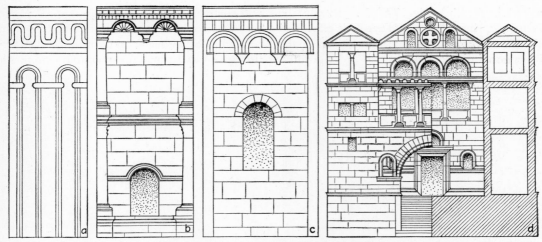

FIG. 276.—Details of Syrian churches, 6th century. *a*, wall decoration, Sassanian palace (*after Sarre*); *b*, exterior apse, St. Simeon Stylites, Kal' at Sim'ân (*after De Vogüê*); *c*, apse, St. Clement, Tahull, Spain; *d*, façade, Tourmanin.

reappear in the Romanesque churches of a later time. This was the addition on the façade of two triple-storied towers that formed a companion part of the structure (Fig. 276*d*), like the ziggurats on the ancient temple of Anu-Adad. Here in Syria during the first centuries of the Christian Era a unique style of Christian architecture was perfected, with a more consistent exterior than the Roman church.

The Union of Eastern and Western Styles of Church Building in Hagia Sophia. In Greece, where architectural tradition demanded a high degree of aesthetic unity, the rulers of the new Christian empire needed a unified church structure —a type of building symbolizing the communality of all Christians sects. The Emperor Justinian, who ascended the throne in 527, summoned two architects—Anthemius of Tralles and Isidorus of Miletus—to build a church that should replace the old basilica of Hagia Sophia, destroyed in a fire during the rioting between two opposing circus factions.

Although the pagan Roman architects had used domical construction in combination with the trabeated Greek style, they rarely employed pendentives. Further, their domes arose directly from the circular plan and always suggested strongly the lintel principle (Fig. 232, Chap.

X). On the other hand, Roman engineers contributed a real knowledge of concrete vault construction, which was to be used by the Byzantine architects. These builders also had in Greece and Syria domed basilicas and structures, like the Church of Sts. Sergius and Bacchus, which had a dome mounted on pendentives above the square.

The culmination of Greek, Roman, and Syrian building genius appeared in the fabric of the new Hagia Sophia, constructed by Anthemius and Isidorus between 532 and 537 in Constantinople. The dome, which rose 180 feet above the floor of the church, was 107 feet in diameter. In it all lintel construction was abandoned. The old Greco-Roman orders were superseded by a new Oriental type of column and the pendentives, many times larger than any previously built, were designed to rise so naturally from the square plan that the whole structure seemed like a living organism whose arches, vaults and dome satisfactorily unite this plan and elevation. The structure is so buttressed that each necessary functional part contributes to a unified aesthetic effect, which is further enhanced by an appropriate decoration of precious stones, inlaid marbles, decorative carving, cast metals, and gold glittering mosaics. The drawing (Fig. 277a) demonstrates the former, intrinsic, functional aesthetic effect and the photograph of the interior (Fig. 274), the latter, extrinsic decoration.

and colors. But there is also a temporal aspect to the work of the architect, for no building can be studied at a glance; and the transition from the outside to the inside, from member to mem-

FIG. 277a.—Hagia Sophia, arrangement of masses. (*After Choisy.*)

The principle composition factor in the plan of Hagia Sophia is a longitudinal axis, which dominates by its size the total effect of the square. Although in effect the building is a cross, the plan has no cross arms. In their place are two very broad longitudinal side aisles, above which second-story galleries connect with a similar transverse gallery on the west end. Light comes from clerestory windows in the domes and semidomes, as well as from the north and south arch lunettes. These last are elements taken from the cross-vault lunettes in the Roman baths; while the former were derived from Syrian church building.

No better example than Hagia Sophia can be cited to demonstrate that the architect who conceives in space and mass combines the mind of the sculptor, using bodily forms and lines, with that of the painter, who manipulates lines

ber, from detail to vista, is similar to the structure of a dramatic or a musical masterpiece. In order really to understand such a building as Hagia Sophia, one must follow the evolution of its various decorative parts, its colorful mosaic surfaces, its Oriental sculptural patterns from prototypes in Rome, Egypt, Ravenna, and the East.

Early Christian Painting

The Catacombs

In the catacombs, or underground burial cities of the Roman world, there are to be found many decorated tombs, some for the pagan members of Roman society, others for the Christians. The wealthier citizens of Rome were able to employ the best of craftsmen to beautify the walls of their family burial vaults with designs in stucco and with painted scenes similar to those found in the Roman houses. The Christians, at first recruited from the poorer classes, marked their earliest tombs with only a few

by partaking of His body and blood. Studied from age to age, its many pictorial versions reveal the ability of the artist to deal with the subject in as many changing styles.

FIG. 277b.—Hagia Sophia, section. (*After Prost, courtesy of Institute of France.*)

meager symbols. To the few such symbols already given may be added the anchor as a symbol of hope, and the wreath, which stood for Christian victory in the other world (Fig. 269a, b).

In the 2nd or 3rd century, the Christian tombs were for the first time decorated with scenes that are much more representational— stories from the Old and the New Testament. One of these, the miracle of the loaves and fishes (Fig. 278), was found on the walls of the catacomb of St. Calixtus in Rome. Here are represented the Eucharistic fish and bread, and seven diners, who are eating after the customary fashion of the Romans. The posture of the man at the right, who is shown reclining toward the meal, serves to indicate that the other six, whose shoulders and heads appear, are also reclining.

This extremely schematic representation of a ceremonial meal, particularly fitting to a tomb, was to become one of the most frequently used symbols of the Christian faith, the love feast (agape), and in the 4th century, the Last Supper, which stood for the mystical office of the Mass—the union of the celebrant with God

In the case of the catacomb painting, the artist made the scene flat, without attention to light and shade and with the minimum of modeling. When we compare the painting with the picture of Hercules from Herculaneum (Fig. 248, Chap. X), our first conclusion is that the miraculous meal shows a definite degeneration in style. If we look at it through the eyes of St.

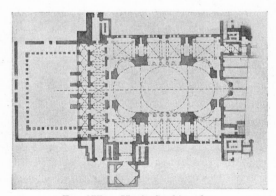

FIG. 277c.—Hagia Sophia, plan.

Augustine, however, we see that the artist intended to focus attention on the fact of the divine miracle rather than upon the corporeality of the disciples or the earthly reality of fish, bread, and wine. The fact that the group is semicircular allows us to imagine ourselves seated opposite, looking toward the diners. We are thus made to feel that we belong to the

shadows, the delineation and perfection, of the realistic Roman portrait style, such as appeared on the mummy cases. We have noted how early Christianity was torn by dissenting views con-

FIG. 278.—Miracle of Loaves and Fishes, Catacomb of St. Calixtus, Rome. (*After Wilpert.*)

picture, which symbolizes the church. Christ is not seen but is symbolized in the bread and fish of which the individuals partake. It is well to remember this pertinent example of a minimum of body and a maximum of idea, which is typical not only of most early Christian art but also of the modern movement called "expressionism." In Buddhistic art, also, we shall find that the intent of the artist is to display the idea with the minimum of physical appearance. The distinctly ideoplastic art resulting depends for its effect upon abstract lines rather than upon naturalistic forms.

Third-century Glass Painting

By the 3rd or 4th century, in the many Christian centers, amulets such as that in Fig. 279 were made as charms for the faithful. Among many examples of this style, those coming from the studios of Alexandria display the highest excellence. The picture of St. Mark, now in the Toledo Museum, shows a definite tendency in the 4th and 5th centuries to display the Christian apostle realistically. Here are the lights and

cerning the nature of Christ. It is but natural to find paralleling the various early Christian sects dissimilar views concerning the nature of art. This and the preceding figure are contemporaneous; they probably appealed to different types of Christians.

The little medal shows the addition in late Roman art of a new aesthetic element, which became particularly strong during the Byzantine development. This might be called the associational aesthetic value of the artistic material used. We noticed in connection with the gold-and-faïence inlay of Egypt and the chryselephantine figures of the Greeks, that precious materials such as gold and ivory, which have a pleasing luster, purity, and fineness, suggest because of their rarity a certain extra value that is added to the abstract aesthetic qualities of the work of art. As scientists, we may try to separate this associational element from the other values, but we find that, like the element of symbolism, it is so firmly wedded to the work as a whole that without it the work suffers somewhat. The human mind is so constituted that unconsciously it associates worth with rarity. Among the primitives, the reader will remember, precious stones and gold were valued for their own sakes. As man became more cultured, a thin layer of gold leaf or a white gesso ground that looked like ivory could suggest the precious quality, and this suggestion carried a higher aesthetic value than the intrinsic worth of the material. People who insist upon the actuality are thus likely to be interested in monetary rather than spiritual values.

This little plaque with the portrait of St. Mark looks precious, and its craftsmanship is superb. According to St. Augustine, its highest value would not have been its inherent beauty but its decorative importance as part of the apparatus to convince the Christian worshiper that St. Mark, a very real person, had lived and was now enshrined in an indestructible material. In time, by contemplating this object the worshiper might easily achieve a sense of permanence in feeling at one with the saint, who had his proper beauty in the structure of the Christian community. So this little plaque is one of the earliest of a long line of icons, or holy pictures of Christ and the saints, which, done in glass, decorated the covers of holy books. As greatly enlarged wall decorations, such portraits became the Byzantine mosaics and, with painted gold backgrounds, the Byzantine and Russian icons.

The Joshua Rotulus and the Landscape Style

The Christian settlement in Alexandria, being a direct outgrowth of the Jewish religious groups in that city, inherited the long, rolled books with stories of the Old Testament that accompanied all Hebrew followers. As early as the 5th century, one of these books was composed to tell the story of the conquest of Palestine (Fig. 280). Later, between the 7th and the 10th century, the earlier manuscript was copied directly and now forms one of the treasures of the Vatican Library.

The Joshua Rotulus, as it is called, is neither purely realistic nor abstract, but unites these two qualities with a rhythmical sweep of composition that carries the attention of the reader from episode to episode as the book is unrolled,

Fig. 279.—Glass plaque with portrait of St. Mark, 4th century. Actual size. (*Courtesy of Toledo Museum of Art.*)

until its entire 30 feet have been viewed. The section of the Joshua Roll that shows the hero both standing and kneeling before the angel outside the city of Jericho demonstrates a tendency that arises perennially in hieratic art. The hero is shown twice, to indicate the progress of an action.

Observe how the artist attempts to lead the eye from one part to another. To the left there is a tree with a few rocks, which stand for landscape much as did those in the painting from the Villa Albani (Fig. 252, Chap. X). The tree, which has a light-and-shade effect in its leaves but a modeled trunk, leans toward the right. Where our eyes are captured in the foliage, the tree joins with the roofs of houses in a distant town. These roofs are not done in correct perspective but are similar to those found in Pompeian painting.

The tip of the angel's wing carries the attention to his haloed head, then down the scabbard of his sword to the groveling figure of Joshua. This figure, being horizontal, leads the eye over and up the vertical figure of Joshua, whose arm stretched out toward the left helps to send the attention back toward the angel, enclosing in a circular area part of the passage describing the event. Once having read the passage, the reader's eye naturally moves toward the right, where the spear of the standing figure parallels the lines of the second tree, which also leans toward the right. Joshua's toga, which is slightly geometricized, helps to

to the fact that this roll is like the long, continuous frieze of relief sculpture winding around the columns of Trajan and Marcus Aurelius.

The Joshua Rotulus and similar rolls were

FIG. 280.—Joshua Roll, Joshua Meeting the Angel before Jericho, 7th to 8th century (Vatican Library). (*Courtesy of Index of Christian Art, Princeton University.*)

move the eye toward the seated figure of a crowned local mountain goddess, the personification of Jericho similar to the Arcadia in the Herculaneum picture. Anyone who compares these two compositions, finds that the Greco-Roman painting moved the eye about within a rectangular area, whereas, following the gaze of Arcadia sent the thought outward toward the revealing light. In the Joshua Roll, the eye is invited to move backward and forward in space, braiding together two kinds of subject matter—landscape and action figures. This may be seen as a revival of a suggested movement in late Greek vase painting and relief sculpture.

The roofs of the houses, thrust backward by the trees, continue their movement down into the marching host of Israelites, who come forward from the rear toward the front of the picture at the right. Morey has called attention

carried by Christian traders to many places in the Roman world. The pictures from this famous manuscript were copied during the Middle Ages by Byzantine ivory carvers and manuscript illuminators, as well as by the designers of mosaics. Of all the works produced in the Western world, the Joshua Roll most closely approximates the aesthetic interest of the Chinese scroll painting, which depends for its effect upon a rhythmical movement between interrelated forces in the actions of man and the act of nature.

Syrian and Armenian Gospels

While the Alexandrian versions of the Old Testament stories were standardized in rolls of the Joshua type, the New Testament subjects that grew up in the many churches of

Syria, Ephesus, Gaul, and Italy, as well as in Egypt, each developed its own pictorial style.

Two important codices in the Syrian style were called the Gospel of Rabula and the

FIG. 281*a*.—Gospel of Rabula, canon page showing Christ paying the tribute money and two prophets, Syrian, late 6th century. On vellum, height 13¼ inches (Laurentian Library, Florence). (*Courtesy of Lesch-Carnegie*.)

Etchmiadzin Gospel. The first of these (Fig. 281*a*) was illuminated by a monk named Rabula in A.D. 586 at the Monastery of Zagba in northern Mesopotamia. The miniatures of the Etchmiadzin Gospel (Fig. 281*b*) are believed to come from the 10th century, representing a late development of the tradition with Byzantine influence. Their author is unknown.

Obviously, both the Syrian and the Armenian examples are connected with the monumental wall paintings from Dura, which form a coloristic basis for fresco and mosaic wall decoration in all the Byzantine churches. The architecture in the manuscripts, as may be seen, is almost as fantastic as that of the ornate

style of Roman wall painting. The human figures are flat color areas heavily outlined. The same is true of the columns, which show no trace of modeling but rather a pattern, indi-

FIG. 281*b*.—Gospel of Etchmiadzin, Christ between two saints, Armenian, 10th century. (*After Macler*.)

cating that they are of precious marble. The arches are intangible rainbows instead of structures. The birds and flowers are likewise brilliantly colored with rich purples, greens, and reds. The cross takes a dominating place in both compositions, between the elements of floral decoration.

The aesthetic effect of this Oriental style, like the picture from Dura (Fig. 249, Chap. X), is not one of motion like that of the Joshua Rotulus, but of static forms and color harmony. The reader was held by the color areas and his thoughts were focused to move neither toward the right nor toward the left but ever inward toward self-exploration.

The Goths, who settled for a time near Armenia and then built their Arian churches in Ravenna during the 6th century, used architecture and symbols like the above, but, desiring more realism, they sometimes carved the acanthus leaves of the capitals in churches, where such scenes were shown, in a way to make them appear to be blown back, as though by a gentle breeze from the sanctuary (Fig.

FIG. 282.—Wind-blown capital from Salonika, 6th century.

282). Such subtlety, coupled with much fine suggestive power, characterizes most of the Byzantine art. Aesthetically, these mystical refinements make their greatest appeal to those versed in early Christian symbolism, but the same element is always present in any great universal work of art. Here they must be examined and understood in order that there may be a clear understanding of what the Oriental particularly looks for in art.

The influence of these manuscript illuminators of Syria lay behind all the later miniature painting in precious manuscripts. The art was also carried by Egyptian and Syrian traders, as well as the Goths, to France. There in the hands of Carolingian painters and enamelers its like culminates in colorful stained glass.

The Development of Monumental Mural Art

The principles of mural decoration can nowhere be studied to better advantage than in the early Christian and Byzantine church decorations executed between the 4th and the 12th century. These draw upon all the resources of Egyptian, Greek, and Roman techniques, as well as their composition types. The mosaic

workers, who were given special privileges by Constantine in the 4th century, turned from their commissions in the imperial palaces and the houses of the wealthy to adorn the new communal temples dedicated to the new God, to Christ, and to the Virgin Mary. A more appropriate taste in mural decoration grew with the more appropriate religion. No longer were realistic pictures, like the Alexander mosaic, set in the floor for people to walk upon. One may walk with impunity upon the pictured face of an earthly emperor or a dictator, but no one will walk upon an image of the Deity.

The Technique of Mosaic Work. The art of the mosaic worker—the *opus musivum* of antiquity—was closely associated with the Egyptians, who in their earlier dynasties had experimented with a glass of many colors fused together. As the Egyptian jeweler's art progressed, he used small cubes of glass paste or precious stones, set in gold cloisonné framework. This work because of its preciosity, like that used in delineating the head of St. Mark, suggests wealth. A simple recital of the names of stone tesserae found by Sir Arthur Evans in the small palace at Knossos on levels of the first Minoan style—all prepared for some forgotten mosaic worker—will stimulate the mind of any colorist. There were crystal, amethyst, beryl, and lapis lazuli! Robinson's discoveries of pebble mosaics at Olynthus indicate that the early Greeks favored colored stones.

By the 1st century, craftsmen had learned to take a mass of glass of any required tint, apply to it a thin sheet of gold foil, subject it to a temperature that would cause the foil to adhere, and over the gold layer pour a fused glass in a dark color to act as a backing. The whole was then further flattened by rolling while in the molten state, fired once more, and cooled slowly. From this golden mirror of plate glass the small tesserae were cut and set in a thin layer of cement applied over a brick or stone surface. No two plates had exactly the same tint, and when the tesserae were mingled they gave the golden wall an interesting texture further heightened by the slight unevenness of the early wall surfaces. Consequently, when the sun, reflecting up from the marble pavements, moved over the surface of such mosaic walls, it was again reflected from many tiny mirrors, changing continuously because of the varying angles of reflection. When human figures in richly embroidered robes of colored glass and with faces carefully modeled in colored marble were part of the entire design, the effect was indescribably rich.

In the rear of the peristyles of several Pompeian houses and at Ostia, niches with fountains are to be found and in them also are mosaics. This suggests that the later principle of adorning the apses of Christian churches may have come from mosaicists who ornamented similar niches in Roman houses. In Rome mosaics were used in the Golden House of Nero, and it has been suggested that the building may have gained its title because of some gold mosaic work under the portico. In a few of the Christian catacombs there are 4th- and 5th-century mosaics with simple subjects like the dove and the crown.

The Mosaics of Santa Costanza. The first known mosaics in a Western Christian building are those to be found in the circular church of Santa Costanza in Rome, primarily erected as a mausoleum for Constantia, the sister of the Emperor Constantine. The interior of this domed structure, with its ringed vault, was at one time completely decorated with marble paneling and mosaics (Fig. 283). Those now remaining in the vault are definitely pagan, being composed of scenes that show little cupids, or *amorini*, Psyches, birds, and flowers. Some of the scenes that suggested to early archaeologists that this might have been a temple dedicated to the wine-god Bacchus show the process of making the vintage. One, in very poor taste, reproduces the remains of a Roman banquet as they would have been seen strewn about the floor. In some places the composi-

tions are more appropriate to a ceiling and show squares, hexagons, and crosses set in a continuous geometrical latticework. According to Dalton, these sections, which are the most

Fig. 283.—Santa Costanza, mosaic-covered vault of annular aisle, first half of 4th century A.D. Width of aisle 19 feet. (*Courtesy of Lesch-Carnegie.*)

successful as decoration, are probably of Syrian design. Figures similar to theirs appear on the works of Persian tilemakers, as well as in some contemporaneous palace buildings from Amida.

Hunting Mosaic from Antioch. The character of the work in Santa Costanza, as well as its very color schemes, occurs again in the 5th-century hunting mosaic from the city of Antioch (Fig. 284).[1] The subject matter is wholly pagan: a hunt such as delighted the Achaemenian monarchs and Roman residents of Syria. The picture has much the same scheme of design as a Persian rug, the central figure of the victorious huntsman with the animals about him taking the place of the tree of life. He

[1] This is one of many significant mosaics brought back to the Worcester Museum. It forms the climax to a remarkable series that shows the development of mosaics during the first five centuries of the Christian Era.

reminds us of Gilgamesh, the hunter demigod. On each of the four sides are distinctive scenes. Most significant for the development of Christian mosaic art is the combination of the ab-

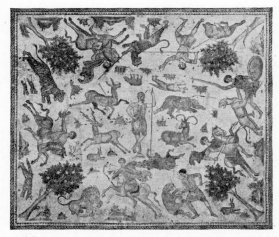

Fig. 284.—Pavement mosaic from villa at Antioch, early 6th century. Length 20 feet 5 inches, width 23 feet. This combination of Hellenistic tradition with Asiatic art shows as its central figure either a Byzantine ruler or a mythological personage surrounded by hunting scenes. (*Courtesy of Worcester Art Museum.*)

stract trees and tiny rocky hillsides with bushes, to symbolize landscape. These are similar in style to like objects in the Joshua Roll.

This informing archaeological treasure is particularly valuable to the aesthetician because of certain primitive and aesthetically negative aspects. In this work is displayed better than in any other production of antiquity the lack of unity that occurs when a monumental art is without a significant ideal. Each separate part of the mosaic scene taken by itself has a unified quality, but as a whole it is disorganized. When seen in a museum, on the floor, its flat harmonious marble tones make it quite unobjectionable and it is definitely interesting as one walks around looking at the various episodes: Constantia had this type of mosaic put on the ceiling of her tomb!

The Mosaic Decoration of Basilican Churches. As the Christian faith gained power in the 4th and 5th centuries, wealthy Christian families and emperors vied with one another in decorating the churches. The stories used on the walls were copied from manuscripts, most of which were of Eastern origin. In Jerusalem, a donation by Constantine made it possible to decorate the atrium of the Church of the Holy Sepulcher with mosaics. The Church of the Nativity at Bethlehem had a façade on which very rich mosaics told, among other things, of the adoration of the Magi. As Jerusalem was the pilgrimage center of the Roman world, its mosaics—now, alas, long since destroyed—must have had a great influence upon the art throughout the Empire.

In the city of Rome, the apse of the Church of Santa Pudenziana is thought to have been decorated by mosaicists working from Eastern models. Here the Christ, enthroned and surrounded by the heavenly city, sits in the midst of His disciples and others, who may be members of the family of the Senator Pudens. This wealthy Roman gave his palace to the church as a place for meetings. Many of the remaining mosaics in the Church of Santa Maria Maggiore show obvious connection with early manuscripts from which their scenes were copied.

The best known and perhaps the best planned of the 5th-century mosaic decorations was laid on the triumphal arch in the Church of St. Paul's-outside-the-Walls (Fig. 285). The scene represents a story from the apocalyptic Last Judgment. In the great central medallion is the head of Christ with a long beard and overlarge eyes, while rays of Divine sunlight issue from His head. Four and twenty elders, half bowing, approach from each side, preceded by two angels who adore the Saviour. The four Evangelists are represented by winged beings floating in the clouds. The bull at the left stands for St. Luke, the winged man for St. Matthew, the lion for St. Mark, and the eagle for that Gospel which comes nearest to the sky-born mystical version of Christ's purpose, St. John. Below this upper heavenly band are the figures of St. Paul and St. Peter, one with his arm reaching downward as though to claim our attention, the other with his arm pointing up to the scene above. These two saints were to become the earthly representatives of the Deity. In time, the Church of Rome was to claim its unique power to raise man most useful for institutional religion. The associational overtones, it will be remembered, were originally the hero-god flanked by animals or the tree of life with attendant genii.

FIG. 285.—Triumphal arch, St. Paul's-outside-the-Walls, Rome, 6th century. Nave rebuilt, 19th century. (*Courtesy of Metropolitan Museum of Art.*)

was to claim its unique power to raise man toward God through a primacy inherited from its first bishop, Peter.

Behind this triumphal arch one can see in the apse of the church the Christ seated in glory with four saints, placed above a row of twelve Apostles interspersed with trees. Such a representation is called a *Majestas*.

The entire rear portion of this church is symbolic of the earthly triumph of the Christian Church. Its compositional scheme suggests certitude and direction. In both cases Christ is the center around which the disciples are placed. It is only through them and particularly through the spandrel figures of St. Peter and St. Paul that one may approach the Divinity. Pictures in absolute balance always have a tendency to make one feel stability and are

The Mural Decoration of the Basilica. The arrangement of figures and pictorial designs on the wall of St. Apollinare Nuovo at Ravenna furnishes one of the finest examples of the early Christian mural style. This structure was built by Theodoric, the Ostrogothic king, between A.D. 500 and 523. The upper part of the right wall (Fig. 286), on which saints appear between the clerestory windows and the scenes in the frieze above, was decorated at that time. The lower frieze of saints was put in place by the Bishop Agnellus, who died in 566. Theodoric was an Arian Christian, and Agnellus took over the church for the Catholics. Perhaps it is significant that the upper pictures and the frontal views of the saints represent narrative scenes in the life of Christ and single personalities, while the mosaics designed for the Catholic

Church form a long, connected band leading up to an Adoration scene on each side. Interesting it is that for these two branches of Christianity the artists should have perfected a wall

Fig. 286.—Mosaic decoration on wall in St. Apollinare Nuovo, Ravenna, 6th century. (*Courtesy of Alinari.*)

that shows no clash, although the two branches were incompatible and the Arian faith was termed a heresy.

The surface of this wall reaches a consistency similar to that of the sculptural arrangement on the Parthenon. The floor, which is laid in slabs of pink and white marble, reflects a warm tone up over the grayish marble columns supporting lacy capitals. These capitals have decorated impost blocks connecting the various arches in the arcade. Above the arcade the figures of saints in brilliant robes, each with his

crown of martyrdom, seem to move slowly over a tissue of gold toward the front of the church, their bodies forming a stately, connected series, very much like the figures from the wall painting at Dura. Their motion forward toward the Madonna, who is greeted by four angels and who is represented as being seated in glory, is checked by the palm trees that appear between them. Near the entrance of the church one sees that the saints progress from a palace like those represented in silversmithing of the period, the curtains of which are drawn back as they were in the circular structure of the Etchmiadzin Gospel.

On the opposite wall, at the left side of the church, a procession of female saints appears to move out of a group of buildings labeled "Classe," which represents the seaport town near by. The women are led by the Three Wise Men, who bend above a representation of the Virgin and the Child near the apse. The design of this procession is much finer than that of the men at the right, chiefly because the folds in the women's costumes always point forward, while the folds in the robes of the men have many lines counteracting the forward motion. Then, too, the dark-colored robes of the women, heavily embroidered with gold, appear to blend with the background, while the white robes of the men stand out in relief. The textile designer can go to no better place for his studies than to the mosaics from the 6th century through the 12th.

The next highest zone in St. Apollinare is made up of representations of Old and New Testament authors, placed between the windows in a paneled arrangement like that of the statues on the Sidamara sarcophagus, to be studied later (Fig. 293). The realistic figures, each in a separate niche, seem to be a final echo in mosaic of the Neo-Attic style. Designed in perspective, the niches carry scalloped arches that give an illusion of space. The upper parts of these niches repeat the curves of the tops of the windows running into the band next to the border of the wall. Scenes representing the Life

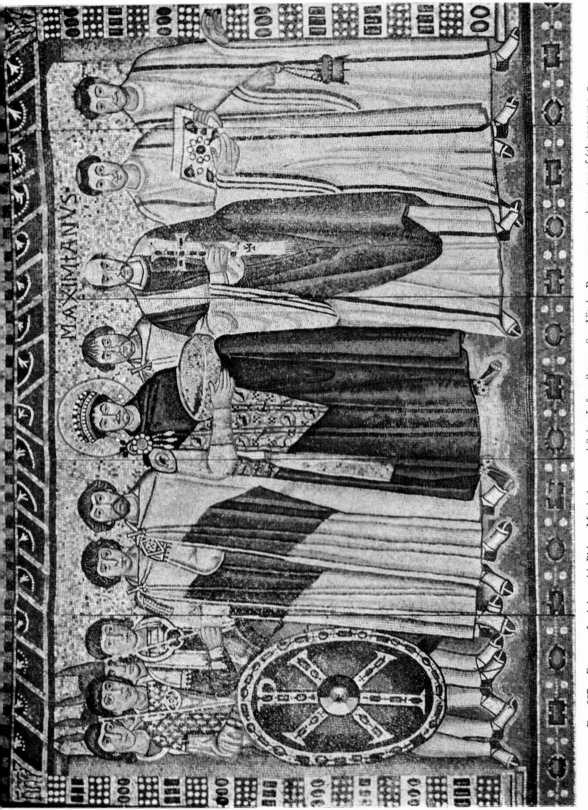

Fig. 287.—Emperor Justinian with Bishop Maximianus and Suite. Left wall apse, San Vitale, Ravenna, second quarter of 6th century A. D. Figures slightly above life size. (*Courtesy of Metropolitan Museum of Art.*)

and Passion of Christ fill the paneled spaces above the windows, the subjects from the Life being on the left, those from the Passion on the right. Except for the color, all these scenes are very similar to 3rd-century catacomb paintings or to bits from manuscripts like the Joshua Roll. The colors used are the rich blues, purples, and reds, like those in Syrian and Armenian manuscripts, with a very vivid emerald green. Here we see a greater union of styles— Neo-Attic, Alexandrian, and Syriac.

In the scenes on the left wall, the Christ is represented in Greco-Roman fashion as a beardless youth, but on the right he is shown with blond beard and hair. It should be stressed again as we observe this developing artistic phenomenon, which occurs when racial intermixture creates an emotional conflict, that the artist unifies society through his work. The feeling of unity in a work of art comes from the ability of the artist to assimilate opposing thought patterns and combine them in terms of emotional expression. These mosaic panels, then, denote a distinct step in the formation of a new type of painting and with it the creation of a new symbol of Christ—a symbol that would not have emerged if the Ostrogoths had not emigrated from Russia and lived in contact with the Eastern version of Christianity.

The Justinian Panel in San Vitale. In the circular Church of San Vitale at Ravenna are two large mosaic panels, one showing the Emperor Justinian with his courtiers, the other showing his empress, Theodora, with her ladies in waiting. At first glance, each panel seems to be a richly embroidered tapestry. In these panels, the composition in color and line unites all the aesthetic advances made by the Christian artists up to the 6th century. They epitomize what has justly been called the Golden Age of church decoration.

In one panel the emperor forms the obvious center of the composition (Fig. 287). From this point of view, the panel would seem to have been arranged in absolute balance. Balance, however, is not the chief impression made upon the spectator. This mosaic panel demonstrates a union of what Augustine called "the properties of fairness and fitness in beauty." Like the Dura figures, the work is decorative; its lines lead our eyes toward the altar, which is part of the religious function of the church; it lends a feeling of stability to the worshiper. In addition to all these merits, it includes the individualization of every character represented.

So the mosaicists had, by the 6th century, brought together all the splendor of the Roman Empire in a type of design that symbolized stability, and this design was used by the church to perpetuate its own leaders. We must acknowledge that the panel is propaganda. If Maximianus had left his name out of the picture, its universal qualities alone would make it one of the finest mural designs ever created. Design and realism have been united, color supplementing linear interweave. In the case of the drawing on the Aeneas vase of the 5th century B.C., there was a rhythmical movement around a center, a lack of color, and a much stronger suggestion of body outlines. A comparison of these two pictures should make clear the essential difference between the finest Greek and the finest early Christian art.

The Growth of the Icon. In looking at the portrait of Justinian (Fig. 287), one becomes aware that the eyes are rather large, that the position is frontal and, therefore, most impressive, and that the emperor has a halo behind his head, which suggests the emanation of power from his personality. In the same way, the reader will remember, King Gudea of Lagash was represented with large eyes. In most Eastern religions, the figure of God as a king was enlarged to include other pictures that had a power significance. These pictures or representations were called "icons"; they did not function as narration of events, but rather as amulets or charms. The history of Byzantine mosaic, from the time of Justinian forward, became ever more the history of icons. Finally, these were transposed to painted panels and became the central altar images in Russian churches.

St. Peter of Hosios Lucas. During the Macedonian period of Byzantine history—that is, from the 9th to the 12th century, while the Eastern Empire was ruled by members of the

Fig. 288.—Mosaic of St. Peter from Church of Hosios Lucas in Stiris, Phocis, Greece, c. 1050. (*After Diez and Demus, Byzantine Mosaics in Greece, Harvard University Press, Cambridge, Mass.*)

Macedonian and Comnenian houses—there was a second Golden Age of painting, following the period of iconoclastic controversy. It will be remembered that for a time the human figure was not considered a correct subject for church decoration in the Eastern Church, and that the Western Church, centered in Rome, differed from the Eastern in this particular. The great monasteries of the Macedonian period, particularly the two at Daphni and Phocis, were centers of mosaic work. The monks not only designed mosaics but also illuminated manuscripts, many of which found their way to Europe, in particular to Venice, southern

Italy, Sicily, and central Germany. These Byzantine monasteries were the chief inspirational centers for much European art of the 9th and 10th centuries.

From the Monastery of St. Luke at Stiris comes the head of St. Peter shown in Fig. 288. This work demonstrates the quality for which the mosaics of Byzantium were famous and also the color scheme out of which grew the mosaics of Torcello and Venice. The Venetian painters of the late 14th century who ushered in the Renaissance, as well as Cimabue in Florence and Simone Martini in Siena, used the color schemes and types of figures seen here; nor was this influence lost in the 15th-century art of Fra Angelico. This reproduction makes clear, therefore, one of the most significant types of composition in the history of European painting.

It can be seen that the face still shows traces of the old illusionistic technique of Alexandria. Although the features seem partly realistic, still the curving designs of beard and hair make the portrait definitely an icon. The modeling of the facial forms in distinct planes of color would naturally be emphasized by being done in stone. Here, however, the emphasis is intentional; circumstance has been changed to a style and the various parts of the face have become a regular design. The arrangement of the folds, which also suggests at first glance a naturalistic treatment, is broken up into geometrical design like the drapery in the Justinian mosaic. The design is so arranged that the eye must travel over one part of the figure after another, ricocheting as a billiard ball does against the sides of a table.

As the pupils of the eyes are very large and without high lights, they appear to be occupied with some distant, other world and seem unreal. By thus drawing attention to the eyes, the artist has given the face an appearance of great spirituality. A further development of this technique may be seen in Russian church icons (Fig. 289). The famous panel showing St. Gregory Thaumaturgus (the Wonder-worker), now in the National Museum at Leningrad, must be compared with this picture of St. Peter.

The color scheme of the St. Peter is very refined: delicate shades of green, lavender, and brown, with bits of pink and red, are bordered by single fine lines of black. One is compelled to admire the juxtaposition of the tones simply for their pleasure-giving effect. An admirer of the works of a modern painter such as Picasso or some of the abstractionists would find that a small section of the robe of St. Peter would give him the highest conceivable aesthetic pleasure. To the Byzantine artist such an aesthetic judgment would be one-sided; he would insist that we cannot dissociate from the abstract folds of drapery all the symbolic values and associational social values noted above in the rendering of the face. He would finally point out that St. Augustine would deem this drapery "fair" in itself, but that it would lack value if it were not "fit." The color and design of this figure are such that today we can remove it from its context in the story of the Christian Church and get what we call purely aesthetic pleasure from it. This comes about because today our lives too often lack union with some whole in which such a subject could be a part.

We might say that, like the late Romans, we are a race of museum-minded folk. The museums as educational institutions have noted this disintegrative tendency in aesthetics and are installing entire rooms, monastery cloisters, and aesthetic wholes, in which an object may be seen in its proper cultural setting. There is a tendency in all 20th-century education to strive for unity, and this comes about because the human soul lacks unity. It is a question, of course, how far unified pictures of other cultures can help us to attain a unified aesthetic drive in our own time, but this book attempts to show how we may study old cultures in order to perfect our own.

In the realm of painting, the figure of St. Peter has those qualities of universality earlier found in the Theseus from the pediment of the

Parthenon. The icon of St. Gregory Thaumaturgus, on the other hand, is a work of magic, and aesthetic tricks have been used by the priests in this latter picture to impress the wor-

Fig. 289.—St. Gregory, the Wonder-worker, Byzantine icon, Leningrad, 10th century A.D. (*After Diez and Demus, Byzantine Mosaics in Greece, Harvard University Press, Cambridge, Mass.*)

shiper so that he will be mystified. The lines of drapery are much more complicated than those of St. Peter, and the face has been made more regular, with hypnotic eyes and a high brow, again connoting supernatural powers. Can such a picture ever be stripped of this magic-making effect, or must it not always be unconsciously associated with our most superstitious thoughts? The Middle Ages, following Plato's aesthetics, held that a work had its chief value as part of the whole. The development of Christian painting so far studied has given the companion parts. In conclusion, let us examine the decoration of one church as a whole.

The Mosaics at Torcello. One of the most consistent and simple schemes of mosaic decoration in a Western cathedral is to be found on Torcello, an island in the lagoons not far north of Venice.[1] These mosaics were laid in the 11th or 12th century by Byzantine artists who probably did the mosaics in St. Mark's, Venice. The technique, color scheme, and composition of the figures in the apse at Torcello (Fig. 271) are similar to those in St. Luke's in Stiris.

The magnificent figure of the Virgin with the Christ Child (the Hodegitria, or Guide) dominates the golden apse (Fig. 290). The head is very small, so that the figure is given a monumental appearance; her fingers are long and delicate; the body swaying gently to the right does not exist as a corporeal thing. Here is the highest ideal of womanhood as represented in the Western world throughout the late Middle Ages. It should be compared with the Athena Lemnia of Phidias, on the one hand, and with the Nuremberg Madonna of Peter Vischer, on the other; its flat Byzantine form can then be seen to be more allied in spirit to Buddhistic figures in China and Japan than to the other two.

Below the Madonna is a band of twelve disciples, whose faces are designed like that of St. Peter of Hosios Lucas. No two of these faces have the same design. Thus they give the impression that each figure is a separate personality. The drapery is composed as a band that forms a geometric pattern around the apse. Although the figures do not touch, the design connects them. This zigzag design repeats a similar motif in the marble paneling that forms the last band in the apse above the seats. A close examination of this paneling, which is of gray-and-white striated Istrian marble, makes clear the technique by which it was formed. A slab of marble was sawed in two and the two halves were laid open side by side; the striations thus formed a zigzag pattern.

Below the marble were ten rows of seats arranged in a semicircle, with the central seat in the top row for the bishop. In front of these seats stood a marble altar on which reposed the Sacred Book. The Book itself became an icon, to be translated and read only by the priest. The attention of the worshiper was led through the back to the seated row of clergy in their rich robes, up past the bishop, through a picture of St. Heliodorus, which was in the center of the marble band, then through the iconic representations of the disciples to the Virgin. Here was an impression of complete ecclesiastical order. For those who could not feel this order aesthetically, there was a band of writing, which separated the disciples from the Virgin. Freely translated from the Latin it reads: "I am the Star of the Sea leading the sailor to the harbor of Salvation. I am Mary who by giving birth to the Christ atoned for the sin of the original Eve." Stella Maris, the Star of the Sea, had a church whose tower outside, like similar towers in Classe and Portogruaro, served as a lighthouse to welcome the sailors of Torcello home from their journeyings.

The worship of the Madonna, which expanded in Byzantine art after the 6th century, may some day be traced to a church in Athens. That church was the made-over Parthenon, rich in its associations with the virgin Athena. The worship of the Mother of God—"Mariolatry," as it is called—became so strong after the 12th century that the greatest Gothic cathedrals in France were dedicated to this cult. Woman's influence upon the arts always seems to be strongest in a period in which design means more than the individualistic depiction of the human forms. Under her influence religion becomes more of a home, less of a journeying.

The opposing masculine element, however,

[1] The mosaics in the Church of St. Mark in Venice are far too complicated to describe in an elementary book. Ruskin's *St. Mark's Rest*, which is in greater part written about them, will give an adequate description for those who desire to study more deeply.

Fig. 290.—The Hodegitria, apse, Torcello, 12th century. Height about 25 feet. (*Photograph by Alinari.*)

is shown in Torcello. It had a terrifying effect in the background of the medieval mind. If we had entered the church by the west door and remained entranced in adoration of the Madonna, we might have been told by the priest in a sermon, as people still are, that if we were to look behind us we should see the fate from which the Madonna could save us. The mosaic on the west wall is a picture of the Last Judgment, or Doom (Fig. 291). At the very top of the wall, which is over 70 feet high, is a Crucifixion with the Virgin and St. John the Baptist; below this scene are five bands of mosaic, gradually diminishing in width as they approach the bottom. In the center of the first zone is a representation of the Resurrection. Here a figure of Christ almost 15 feet high leaps out of a black pit, in which one sees bits of locks, bolts, and broken doors. In this way, the mosaicist has represented a passage of the Bible that says: "The Gates of Hell were burst asunder."

On one side of the Christ, St. Thomas rushes up, reaching forward to touch the Saviour and make sure that He is alive. The presence of Thomas is calculated to remove all doubt in the mind of the worshiper. On the other side of the Christ, St. John the Baptist testifies that this is indeed the Son of God. Thomas and John are only half as large as the Christ; next in size to them are the Virgin and the two kings, David and Solomon, who prophesied that Christ would be the Messiah. Still smaller in size are a number of prophets, and finally hundreds of the dead, who witness from purgatory the entire scene. It is well to recall that in Egyptian hieratical art the king was represented as large, his subjects smaller. Here, also, importance is indicated throughout by relative size. On each side of the panel loom the two great archangels, Michael and Gabriel, trampling upon dragons; they are as large as the Christ.

What is the aesthetic value of this scene? Today in terms of modern art we should characterize it as expressionism, which means that the artist has striven to represent through line,

shape, and color arrangement an emotional state rather than a narrative or an event. In the Torcello mosaic there is still a narrative element, but it has no unity of time. The Christ is not like representations of Egyptian gods, for the folds of his drapery indicate great dramatic tension. A Byzantine Christ of this type is called the "demiurgos"—the underlying force of creation. It is because of inner power rather than by pure accident that such a Christ could burst the bonds of hell. In his Moses (Fig. 488, Chap. XV), Michelangelo later captured the same spirit. The scattered designs on the robes of the two archangels, as well as the disposal of color areas against the black pit, all lend energy to this expression of primal force.

The next lower zone of the mosaic is smaller and much quieter. It centers around the figure of Christ in an egg-shaped *mandorla*. The Virgin and St. John the Baptist, one on each side of the seated Christ, together constitute what is called the *deësis*, or the Christ Enthroned in Judgment. Seated apostles and standing saints on each side of them represent the highest order in heaven. The *mandorla* rests on two wheels, so that it resembles the chariot of Triptolemus, an ancient Greek savior god who was the son of Ceres, the earth mother. Two cherubim with quadruple wings guard the chariot. These wings, like the wings of the peacock Argus, are covered with many eyes, the inference being that the cherubim can see everything. From this central chariot a stream of fire, representing hell, flows out toward the right.

In the third zone, below the *deësis*, stands a cushioned throne on which rests the Book of the Passion: the crown of thorns, the spear, the cross, and the sponge. Two kneeling figures bow before the group of sacred symbols. On each side of this central composition great angels rush out, blowing upon carved hunting horns such as we know were actually used by the Germanic invaders of the Roman world. Beyond the angels, on the outermost part of the band, sea monsters, lions, tigers, and elephants spew forth the fragments of bodies, while one

FIG. 291.—Descent into Hell and Last Judgment, West Wall, Torcello, 11th century. Height about 70 feet. *(Courtesy of Lesch.)*

angel at the right plucks stars from a scroll in his hand and strews them about the universe. The whole scene is one mad dream of violent action.

In the center of the next band below, an angel holds the scales of judgment, taking the place of Anubis in the Egyptian papyrus drawing (Fig. 81, Chap. IV). Flying devils with spears try to depress the scales so that the soul being weighed will be their portion. In this way a man's evil deeds will come to plague him at the final judgment of his soul. At the right, two angels with pikes push the damned into a river of fire that flows into a lake of brimstone. In the middle of the lake sits Satan, looking exactly like the figure of Hades, or Pluto, as the god was depicted in countless Etruscan tombs. Below Satan, in blackest hell, languish those whose eyes have seen too much of evil and sin. From their sightless skulls come writhing serpents. The slothful are found caught in a bog. Most delightful of all to the people of Torcello must have been the scene in the lowest right-hand corner. Here are the heads of Saracens, recognizable by their great earrings. The Saracens were the piratical enemies of the seafaring Torcellanese and, of course, as enemies of Christendom, deserved what they received.

To the left of the door, the saints are shown grouped together in Paradise. This side of the mosaic is unified and very restful. St. Peter stands near a marble gate, which is guarded by seraphim. In the Garden of Eden, recognizable by its palm tree, Father Abraham (or St. Nicholas?) sits with the Christ Child on his lap, attended by the Virgin and a host of little children. The contrast in color scheme between hell and paradise is most significant. Hell, with its browns, black, red, and sulphur yellow, produces a most unpleasant effect; while paradise gleams in gold, green, purple, and blue, with touches of ruby here and there. In other words, expressionism is used in this mosaic in the color composition, as well as in the linear effect. Obviously the artist was striving not for beauty but for contrast and tension.

This Last Judgment scene, which came from Greek monasteries, is one of the most dramatic representations of the Middle Ages. The subject spread to the portals of Gothic cathedrals far to the north. It was to be found in countless manuscripts and became the inspiration for miracle plays. The English found it particularly desirable as fresco painting on the walls of their churches, and it is said that Dante, passing through Torcello, took this particular scene as a starting point for his description of the Inferno, although the contemporaneous Doom of his home town of Florence would be a more plausible influence.

The essence of this highly dramatic art lies in its contrasting passages. The reds oppose blues in color; gentle lines oppose rough angular lines and jagged edges, in terms of color areas. There is a balanced scheme to the whole, but with many elements of unbalance in particulars. This Last Judgment is not essentially classical, and as an example of purely Byzantine art it suffers by falling into elements that are perhaps Etruscan and Celto-Germanic. The ultimate energetic goals of the style may be better understood after studying the two following chapters.

Most significant about the work at Torcello is the dramatic way in which the Judgment contrasts with the apse mosaic. In their sermons the priests of the church still make this contrast between the restful aesthetic effect of the mother goddess and the restless disintegrative effect of the Last Judgment dominated by the fearsome Pantocrator, Christ, who having conquered death, will judge the living. The two conceptions are inseparable aesthetic parts of a dramatic sermon or homily; both were to be fused and assimilated by the soul of medieval man during the development of Romanesque and Gothic art in the next five centuries.

Sculpture

The earliest examples of Christian sculpture derive, like the mosaics of Santa Costanza, from made-over Neo-Attic Roman models. There are today two figures of the Christ. One in the Lateran Museum shows him as a young shep-

FIG. 292.—The Good Shepherd, 3rd century (?). Greek marble, height 3 feet 1½ inches (Lateran Museum, Rome). (*Courtesy of Lesch-Carnegie.*)

herd (Fig. 292) wearing a Syrian cap suggestive of his Eastern origin. The other figure, in the Terme Museum, shows Christ as a young philosopher. On the base of the statue there are traces of a name that was erased before that of Christ was placed there. The earlier name is that of Serapis, a youthful Egyptian teacher god, who was worshiped during Roman times. There is really nothing to show definitely that either of these two figures was intended to stand for Christ when it was first made. They are both significant as demonstrations that the Christian religion strove to fit itself into eastern Hellenic art forms before new, definitely Christian, types were created. In technique there is

little to distinguish such figures from those on the pagan Constantine sarcophagus (Fig. 263, Chap. X). What little there is may best be

FIG. 293.—End of a Sidamara sarcophagus. Young Christ between two Apostles (?), 4th century (Berlin Museum). (*Courtesy of Lesch.*)

studied upon a monument by many scholars considered Christian.

Sarcophagi of Sidamara. During the 3rd and 4th centuries there flourished in some as yet unidentified center in Asia Minor a school of sculptors who made a specialty of a type of sarcophagus which combined in its decoration, its treatment of human figures, and the technique of its stone carving all those elements of sculptural style earlier used by the Greco-Romans (Fig. 293). More of the sarcophagi carved by this school have been found in Asia Minor than elsewhere; but apparently some were shipped to Rome, others to Constantinople and Athens. They were of an Asiatic marble, which may have come from some quarry in Anatolia. Some authorities think they were carved at ancient Antioch; others, in Cyzicus or Proconnesus. Aesthetically they are very similar to the painted figures from Dura, and so are of the highest importance as indicating a union of taste derived from Eastern and Western sources. On the one hand, the statuesque figures that stand before arched

FIG. 294.—Mschatta façade, Arabia, 7th or 8th century. (*Courtesy of Metropolitan Museum of Art.*)

niches and in the unarched interspaces are the last phase of the Neo-Attic style, which at its best produced the Augustus from Prima Porta.

The architectural background against which the figures are placed has been shown to have been connected with the *scena* of the Roman theater with its triple portals. The details of the architecture suggest interposed impost blocks between capitals and pediments, but the spirally fluted columns, on bases of Hellenistic type, bespeak the triumph of transcendentalism in Roman art. To the same aesthetic note one may trace the employment of the drill in carving the ornament. The use of the drill produces color contrast, with high lights set off by deep shadow, giving a lacy

effect. This style was particularly desirable to Oriental peoples, and was developed first by the Copts and, in succeeding centuries, more fully by the Saracens. It is a distinctly coloristic effect in sculpture.

The treatment of the drapery in the figures became progressively more flat as the art developed until in the 4th century, when the sarcophagus now in the Berlin Museum was carved, it lost all plasticity. The central figure under the pediment blends into the rinceau, capital, columnar and imposed decoration. Here is an aesthetic consistency that may well signify the new unity that had entered the Roman mind as Christianity came to the fore. While this style was being perfected in Asia Minor, in far-off Gandhara, India, the followers of Buddha, inspired probably by the same late Neo-Attic figures, created similar relief carvings. The scholar Graeven has indicated the affinity between the central figure of the Berlin sarcophagus and the Buddhistic types of India. Many details of attitude and drapery are alike in the two widely separated places.

The Mschatta Façade. The façade of the palace of Mschatta (Fig. 294) in the Arabian Desert, southeast of Jerusalem, was carved during the Neo-Persian or Sassanian period probably in the 8th century. This type of decoration was applied to the exterior of domed palaces like that of Firuzabad or that of Sarvistan. The floral origins of the style seem to be indigenous to Mesopotamia and can be traced back to some of the earliest pottery of Susa.

The vine forms the center of the panel; the sun above it, here borrowed perhaps from Greco-Roman coffered ceilings, as the rosette, appears in a zigzag geometric ornament that likewise stems from neolithic pottery. These three elements of decoration—the vine, the sun, and the zigzag ornament—and the technique employed in rendering them had the greatest effect upon not only Byzantine but also Saracenic, Carolingian, and Romanesque art.

As Dalton has pointed out, the vine as an element of decoration was not native to either

Fig. 295.—The Fruitful Vine. *a*, Leptis Magna, stone portal, 2nd century A.D.; *b*, Greco-Roman woolen tapestry, 4th century (Victoria and Albert Museum); *c*, detail, throne of Maximianus, ivory, 6th century, Ravenna; *d*, portal sculpture, Torcello, 6th century; *e*, Neo-Persian palace, 7th century; *f*, Manichaean miniature, East Turkestan, 9th century (Berlin Sociological Museum).

Greek or Roman art; it arose in Mesopotamia and reached the Mediterranean only after the 4th century B.C. At the same time, it moved eastward toward Iran, where the Chinese found it in the 2nd century B.C. and used it to decorate the backs of their bronze mirrors. In the cities of Northern Africa, such as Leptis Magna, one finds the human figure set in the vine, and early Christian sculptors carved a multitude of animals among its interwoven tendrils (Fig. 295).

By this time, also, the decorative element had grown strong in tapestry and rug weaving, arts for which the Persians were early noted. When this development is remembered, it becomes apparent that the façade at Mschatta resembles a Persian rug. The lowest border shows a deeply cut acanthus decoration with the vine as a continuous scroll. Between the large angles of the zigzag molding are rosettes of acanthus—the ancient symbol of the sun. Below each central rosette is a bowl, with the

animals customarily attendant in Assyrian reliefs—the lion and the griffin. The abstract pattern of light and dark, with its probably technomorphic origins, so dominates this composition that we have a flat, decorative unity. A geometric plan runs through the entire decoration and there is absolute balance in every triangle. This is Oriental art at its best. What may be observed here will later help to explain the painting of the Chinese and the sculpture of India.

As one can trace the creations of the classical style in Europe back to an inevitable source in the Parthenon, so we shall be able to trace the great pictorial compositions of the Renaissance and the baroque to the Byzantine mosaics and the Gothic cathedral windows. So also the Oriental spirit, wherever it is found in Western art, may some day be traced back to this façade.

What is the religious meaning of the symbolism here so closely interwoven? Simply that the sun and the stream of water that wells up from the earth—phenomena that constitute the whole of creation to the desert dwellers—unite in the vine, the source of life. One should remember, too, that this art grew up in the land

Fig. 296.—Madonna and Child, ivory, Syria or Egypt, Coptic, 6th or 7th century. (*Courtesy of Walters Art Gallery.*)

where Christ had lived. He had said: "I am the true vine; ye are the branches." The Psalmist had sung of the waters of life and the fountains in a thirsty land; he had spoken of the soul as the hart panting after the water brooks. In the Persian religions this particular scene was called the *Havarenah* (landscape).

Madonna and Child. Turning from the Mschatta façade to the fast-developing Christian art, we study a small ivory carving (Fig. 296), probably from Egypt. The piece, which is a little over 10 inches h gh, still reveals the shape of the elephant's tusk from which it was carved. It has the same abstract quality and the same treatment of the human form that we found in the earlier catacomb paintings. In time, this figure was to lead to the development of the Gothic Madonna, which reached its finest expression in the figure by Peter Vischer in Nu-

remberg (Fig. 376, Chap. XIII). One must remember how the Greek figure of Athena gradually evolved from the old, stiff, postlike Hera of Samos.

Fig. 297.—Chair of Maximianus, 6th century, Cathedral of Ravenna. Ivory plaques on wood, height of back 4 feet. (*Courtesy of Lesch-Carnegie.*)

As in the Byzantine icons, the drapery of the figure is so arranged that the folds shift the eye of the beholder from one section of the surface to another. Various parts of the robe lead to observation of the legs of the Christ Child or the arms of the Madonna. These, in turn, carry the attention around the shoulder drapery up into the egg shape of the head, which bears the same relation to the shoulders as did the head of the Venus of Mentone. The face of the child blends with that of his mother and the two are part of the same elemental force that runs up through growing bone.

The Throne of Maximianus. Perhaps the best example of Byzantine ivory carving that is still preserved for us is the episcopal throne of Maximianus, a chair belonging to a 6th-century bishop of Ravenna (Fig. 297). The chair, as we have it today, is a masterpiece of archaeological reconstruction, for fifty years ago its dismembered parts were distributed in museums all over Italy. Its restoration has revealed that some of the workmen who carved the piece were probably members of the artist group in Alexandria. The side posts are practically the same in design as the Coptic tapestries (Figs. 268 and 295).

The carving on the chair represents a mixture of several styles. The vine-and-vase design, which appears below on the front, resembles the Arabic carving from Mschatta, and the figures, each in its little niche, are like the Byzantine diptychs (Fig. 267) given away by the consuls, or the Sidamara sarcophagus figures. Since we are more interested in the sum total of aesthetic effects than in archaeological details, it must be acknowledged that the chair as a work of art impresses more because of its precious character, delicate appearance, and the subject matter of its panels, than by reason of its aesthetic unity. If it is to be studied at all, it must be regarded rather in the same way as a bit of jewelry, which should always impress because of its value and delicacy. Any panel taken by itself may have more appeal than the chair as a whole.

The aesthetic disunity is due mainly to the fact that the single front panels do not tie in well with the plant designs. This inconsistency explains why such a tour de force in carving is not so impressive as the section of the Mschatta façade. In the latter, although there are animal figures, they are so much a part of the plant decoration that they do not stand out as single large spaces. The various moldings, also, are carved each with a different degree of intricacy, so that a light molding is differentiated from a heavy one. Finally, the carved zigzag that runs across the façade, alternating with rosettes, is all very consistent.

Not every part of the chair of Maximianus

is inconsistent. The small side panels showing the story of Joseph and his brethren and the miracles of Christ are so fine as to connect with the purely decorative carving. Only the front is

Fig. 298.—Bust of Byzantine ruler, 8th century. Height about 3 feet (Egyptian Museum). (*Courtesy of Egyptian Exploration Society.*)

somehow or other out of keeping, but this, of course, may be the fault of the restorer.

Head of a Byzantine Ruler in Cairo. The Mschatta façade, as the reader has doubtless noticed, was without representations of the human figure. The religion of the Arabs, who came to the position of supremacy in Mesopotamia, was somewhat like that of the earlier Hebrews. They were unfriendly to depicting the human figure. The same tendency grew in the Christian Church at the time of the Emperor Leo, the Isaurian, who rebelled against the superstitions that had grown up within the church around certain wonder-working icons. In 726, he forbade the worship of images and had most of them destroyed, keeping only the cross as a symbol, without the image of Christ. At that time, the cross was united with the vine, becoming in this way the tree of life. The Pope in Rome and most of the clergy fought this move, and the iconoclastic controversy that arose was carried on with great bitterness until, in 787, the Empress Irene summoned the Council of Nicaea and reversed the decree of Leo.

bia, Spain, and Europe. The casket from the Cathedral of Veroli in Italy (Fig. 299) offers the finest example of this type of Byzantine article.

FIG. 299.—Side panels of ivory casket from Cathedral of Veroli, 9th or 10th century (Victoria and Albert Museum). (*Courtesy of Metropolitan Museum of Art.*)

The head of the Byzantine ruler from Cairo (Fig. 298) probably dates from about the time of Irene. Notice that the Roman style of head-dress is still adhered to, as well as the toga; but notice, too, what a difference there is in aesthetic form between this and the Neo-Attic style. The Byzantine head shows an almost complete return to the ancient Sumerian formula for the representation of a ruler. Here are large, staring eyes with stylized brows. The face, completely depersonalized, is a fear-creating icon. Two such figures, found by the crusaders in the 12th century, were brought back to St. Mark's Church in Venice. They and others of similar character in metal greatly influenced the development of European Romanesque sculpture.

The Veroli Casket. When worship of images was forbidden, Byzantine sculpture took a new direction. Since church decorations were limited to representations of the tree of life or the cross, secular art remained free for a revival of classical motifs. Into these were introduced many Oriental designs, such as the lines and curves from the Mschatta façade. Richly carved jewel caskets were greatly desired not only by the Christians but by the Saracens. Many of these objects found their way to North Africa, Ara-

The casket consists of a number of panels carved with figures derived from classical mythology. The outer borders of the scenes have fine patterns similar to those in the Mschatta frieze. On the lid there is another border made up of rows of heads in medallions interspersed with rosettes. These heads may have been copied from Roman coins. The meaning of the scene on the lid is unknown, or perhaps it had no meaning. At the left it seems to be part of the ancient story of Europa and the bull. These details do not matter so much as the fact that the artist has given to the scenes an expression of freshness and insouciance. They have a quality of charm as playful as the paintings of *amorini* on Pompeian walls. The delicate carving and the fineness of the drapery, as well as the postures of the figures, suggest that they are particularly appropriate to the object they adorn. The figures are so carved that they seem to stand out and almost to float in front of the surface of the casket. Figures of the same type were later used by Donatello on his Singing Gallery in Florence.

The casket serves to illustrate better than any other object the fact that artistic style is not a matter of history alone, but of the existence through several cultures of a mode of thinking

Fig. 300.—*a*, linen cloth, with representation of Annunciation, printed by reserve (batik), Egypt, 5th century (Victoria and Albert Museum); *b*, enamel, Samson and the Gates of Gaza, 10th century (British Museum).

about life. Byzantine craftsmen, making such caskets for Moorish princes in Spain, helped to carry the Neo-Attic style through the so-called Dark Ages to the beginnings of the Renaissance.

Byzantine Textiles

The distinction between what are called "applied" and "fine" arts is part of a fiction indulged in by Europeans since the Renaissance. The Orient today knows no such distinction. There is no better place to study the interrelationship of the applied and the fine arts than in connection with East Christian development in Byzantium. Here we see that monumental forms which were used as decoration for wall surfaces have within them composition patterns used by the designers for cloisonné and tapestries. It may be said that all through the development of great art cultures the minor craftsmen, or the more primitive levels of a people, will prefer the monumental composition forms and will render them with less skill, perhaps, but with more elemental vigor.

In America of the 20th century art developed in much the same way. This folk art has within it elements from the aboriginal Indian designs. Our murals are uniting with patterns found in our comic-paper art, which approximates in a way the manuscript illumination in the Middle Ages. The stream of design does not move in one direction alone, that is, from the monumental to the trivial, but in the hands of an artistic genius moves from the trivial to the monumental. Byzantine tapestries and enamels (Fig. 300) show the breakdown of a naturalistic figure art to a flat Oriental design at the other extreme. These objects held the compositions out of which Gothic designers made their windows and, later, Renaissance masters were to perfect their great canvases.

Early Christian Church Music

The music of the early Christians, like their graphic and plastic arts, held elements drawn from all parts of the ancient world. The first recorded collection of early Christian songs, the Antiphonarium, said to have been compiled by Pope Gregory the Great between 589 and 604, presumably displayed Greek, Jewish, and Syrian, as well as Latin, elements. This treasure of early songs, probably melodically enriched by the monks who set them down, was, according to legend, fastened to the altar of St. Peter's by a golden chain. In it Gregory, celebrating the Mass, could no doubt find the early Psalms of the Christians as they were sung in Palestine, Egyptian elements from Alexandria, or hymns that had their ultimate origins in the early Greek mysteries.

Music in Byzantium

The earliest and longest continuous development of early Christian music was not in Rome

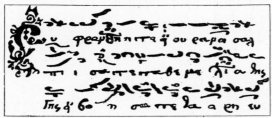

Fig. 301*a*.—Lines from early Byzantine choir book with note signs.

but in Byzantium. During the time of the great church councils after the edict of the Emperor Constantine in 312, all the elements above mentioned united in Byzantine music. The old Greek melodies received Christian meaning and were sung with a lusty accompaniment of handclapping and bell ringing. Great choirs were assembled and performed these hymns to the accompaniment of organs and, according to an ancient relief on the sarcophagus of the Emperor Theodosius, even to the accompaniment of the double aulos. Naturally, this almost pagan celebration of Christian rites disturbed many of the early Church Fathers; and St. Augustine, among the others, inveighed against it. Finally, however, it was decided that this music could not be wrong, since the Bible said that the angels sang and that sweet music was helpful in casting out devils.

The words of these very early songs were recorded in carefully written choir books (Fig. 301). These manuscripts are just beginning to be translated by Western scholars, although they may have been used by the chanters of the Greek Orthodox and Russian churches. In such books, as the example shows, the music was written down as neume marks above the line, some of the characters in red ink. In the oldest of them only the accents are recorded.

The Byzantine Instruments. The organ, invented by an Alexandrian Greek, from the first played a decisive part in the early Byzantine church service. The aulos, with its one set note functioning in the treble as a drone, was a favorite instrument in classical antiquity. The organ made possible the use of a similar drone

Fig. 301*b*.—The Te Deum of St. Ambrose, about A.D. 380.

accompaniment, which the Christians transferred from treble to bass. Thus, by holding down one low note while the melody was played above, the Christian musicians laid the beginnings of modern harmony. Besides the organ, the Christians retained the cithara and the aulos, also adopting the Syrian or Egyptian instrument, the harp, in place of the Greek lyre. Trumpets, horns, and cymbals, too, were introduced, particularly in the procession of the emperor to the church. Throughout the Middle Ages, the instruments and new musical inventions of the Byzantines continued to be introduced into the courts of the European kings and into the monasteries.

The Transmission of the Sequences. In the 5th to the 6th century, Romanos-Melodos, a Syrian living in Byzantium, arranged the Christmas story in the form of a dramatic song; that is, with response and chorus. This was the first "sequence."

Other sequences, arranged to be acted and sung in the celebration of Christmas and Easter Masses, were perfected between the 8th and the 12th century. During the first centuries of the Christian era, Byzantine and Eastern influences were very strong in Roman music. A number of Syrian colonists, led by Bishop Hilarius of Poitiers, brought with them hymns from Asia Minor. These were translated into Latin. Many of the hymns of Bishop Ambrose of Milan can be traced to Byzantine origins.

While the Byzantine Church was thus transmitting to the Europe of the Middle Ages Greek dramatic musical elements, the Roman Church, building in its own way, developed melodic singing and a more specific system of notation, which made possible the more accurate transmission of the melody necessary for the performance of the Mass. It will be remembered that the normal, primitive way of speaking or singing is to allow the voice to move downward. The Western Christians, however, seemed to wish to project their hymns upward, as though in a desire to reach the heavenly Deity. While the voices of the congregation as a whole retained a lower tone, like the drone bass, the voice of the chanter carried the words upward in a shrill tenor. Finally, the Latin genius for codification was a decisive factor in bringing about a set system for recording the music.

The Beginnings of European Music

St. Ambrose, who was close to the Greek origins, built up a liturgy for his church in which he used several melodies that have come down through the centuries. The *Te Deum Laudamus* is one of the best known of these (Fig. 301*b*). The dramatic character of his liturgy, with the antiphonal responses, has the testimony of St. Augustine, who was converted from Manichaeism. In his *Confessions*, St. Augustine writes: "With lovely songs the word of God penetrates the heart so that the soul is lifted up to experience truth and new life."[1]

Pope Gregory carried the development of liturgical music still further, perfecting its dramatic and musical form. The texts from the Psalms were sung in antiphonal manner, those from Old Testament prophecy in uninterrupted arias. The tone and color of voice were changed during the various parts of the service, which were the entrance, or *Introit*, the gradual, the communion, and the offertory.

One of the popes named Gregory, coming before the 9th century, employed a system of neumes to mark changes in pitch. The earliest manuscripts describing the complicated process of the Gregorian Mass did not reach the condition of exact notation, however, until after the 10th century.

With a simple system of neumes, or signs showing ascending or descending tones, a line or verse could be fairly well indicated melodically, at least, well enough to help the musician remember the tune. The Gregorian chants set down in the later Middle Ages and still sung in the Roman Church were originally transmitted in this unsatisfactory, ambiguous fashion. The next step toward our precise notation was made by monks in the 10th century and will be considered in the following chapter.

Drama

The theater continued its activities through the Byzantine Empire, alternately threatened by and escaping from the rule of the ecclesiastics until finally most of its techniques had been taken over by the church. The mimes were severely criticized by the Church Fathers, Cyprian, Tertullian, and Chrysostom, whose preachments go far to indicate how strong the theater really was. There was much licentiousness in connection with the late Roman drama, and most of the comic performances had degenerated below the level of our lowest burlesque houses. There is evidence to be adduced from the sermons that large numbers of Christians attended the theater and that it was hard to keep them from going even on Sunday. The god Dionysus, who ruled the classical theater, was after all a pagan deity and, until his worship could be absorbed, he necessarily remained in the hostile camp. Since Homer and Aeschylus are mentioned by the actor Choricius in his dissertation on the theater, it is logical to assume that classical tragedies were still being produced in the 4th century, much as they had been performed in Greece.

The emperors alternately condemned or sup-

[1] *Confessions of St. Augustine*, translated by Edward B. Pusey, P. F. Collier & Son Corp., New York, 1909.

ported the theater according to their various predilections. Theodoric, the Goth, who was an Arian, had Cassiodorus, his prime minister, reconstruct one of the old theaters in Rome. Justinian created laws that had to do with the stage, and his wife, it will be remembered, was an actress. Theodosius later defined the position of actors in society, and although their position was a lowly one, this gave some prestige to the profession.

The Drama of the Mass

The followers of Arius were among the first to notice the dramatic possibilities of the Mass. It is probable that the introduction of dramatic action, music, and inflections of the voice, which have become so much a part of the Catholic service, were actually introduced in the first place as a means of competing with the older worship of Dionysus, although the use of dramatic action for religious expression is fundamental to human nature.

The central action and oldest part of the drama of the Mass comprises a ceremonial feast, in which the worshipers, led by a priest, partake of the bread and wine that are miraculously changed into the person of God. At first started as a simple love feast, the agape, later a memory of Christ's Last Supper with his disciples, the ceremony was probably first held in a tomb. In this stage of the Mass development, there arose not only the idea of a communion with the resurrected God but also of intercession with and for the departed spirits of the loved ones. After almost 2,000 years of evolution out of those simple beginnings, the Mass has become a remarkable spiritual drama, providing complete catharsis for the faithful who take part in its music and symbolic action. Around it and for it the great churches of the Western world were built. To understand Christian art one must understand the dramatic pageantry of the Mass.

The Mass of the Catechumens. The first part of the Mass, particularly designed for the un-baptized, or catechumens, commences with the ceremonial entry of a priest carrying the chalice. He is accompanied by an acolyte who carries the censer with its smoking incense. Passages from the Scriptures are read to suggest the meaning of the particular feast day celebrated. This part is known as the "Introit." It is followed by the Greek prayer, *Kyrie eleison,* which calls upon God for mercy. Next, the Gloria, said or sung, heralds the birth of Christ, in that message which the angels sang to the shepherds. The Collects, a series of prayers, make petition to the God of the Cross.

A section of the Epistles, called the "lesson," is read and followed by the sequences—folk tunes added to the old Gregorian plain chant in Europe about the 10th and 11th centuries. Following the sequences, the priest crosses to the other side of the altar, and reads the Gospel, which reaches the congregation as a message directly from the Godhead present on the altar. The dogma of the Real Presence affirms that the bread and wine used in the second part of the Mass miraculously become the real body and blood of Christ. Following the Gospel-reading, the people profess their faith through the *Credo,* or Creed, and the catechumens are dismissed.

The Mass of the Faithful. The second part of the Mass, which follows, is called the "Mass of the Faithful" or "High Mass." It includes the opening of the shrine, bringing forth the Host, or God, and distributing Him in the Communion to the people. The first part of this Mass, called the "offertory," has changed its purpose considerably since the earliest days of the church. The central moment has become, since 1100, that part in which the priest says, "For this is My Body." Earlier, in the agape, the ecstatic moment came when the priest gave the bread to the people saying, "Take and eat ye all of this." In the earlier form, the people had the ecstasy on receiving the Host; in the later, the priest has the supreme moment when the power to work the miracle possesses him. This change in emphasis from the moment of communion to the performance of a miracle accompanies an increasing power in the centralized authority of the church. About the year 1100, the Host, or the body and blood of God, were first elevated so that all the congregation might see the miracle which had taken place. This Elevation of the Host is accompanied by the ringing of a bell three times.

In the next part of the Mass, after the Host has been blessed with the sign of the cross, the saintly dead are called to mind in a prayer, the "Memento of the Dead." Christ is implored to give them help and light in the other world. After other prayers have been said, including the *Pater Noster*, or "Our Father," and the *Agnus Dei*, or "Lamb of God," the faithful approach the altar and receive the wafer of the Host, while the priest drinks from the chalice, after that, in turn, has been elevated. The conclusion of the Mass comes when the priest gives the dismissal, *Ite, missa est*, "Go, the Mass is ended," after which the people hear a part of the mystical Gospel of St. John and depart with the blessing. Accompanying every part of the Mass, priests and acolytes, people and choir sing and perform actions which become highly expressive and dramatic when entered into with complete faith and feeling. All the fineness in Christian character displays itself in this action at the Mass. When the priest, a trained singer and actor, as well as a true spiritual leader of the flock, conducts the Mass in perfect time with the natural rhythm of his congregation, the experience for the believer is completely refreshing and sustaining.

Character of Religious Dramatic Performances Other than the Mass

By the end of the 8th century, at the time when Charlemagne was ruling Western Europe, a Greek monk by the name of Stephanos the Sabbaite had composed in Byzantium a sacred play called *The Death of Christ*. Another cleric, the Deacon Ignatius of Constantinople, wrote *The Passion of Christ*. It is significant that this interest in the drama as a means for spreading the faith came just after the close of the iconoclastic controversy. In the same century, farther west in Europe, a very primitive form of dialogue play—the *estrif*, or *débat*—was being sung by the bards for their noble patrons. None of the *estrifs* remain, but it is known that one was called *The Pride of Life*, another, *The Harrowing of Hell*. In these bardic songs were probably laid the foundations of that plot, half Christian, half pagan, which later became the basis for the morality play *Everyman* and the story *Pilgrim's Progress*.

Bishop Liutprand of Cremona reported, in 968, that the church of Hagia Sophia had been turned into a theater and that a play about Elijah was being given when he visited there. Liutprand refers to the dramatic sermons, or homilies, which had to do with the stories of the Annunciation, the Nativity, and the Descent into Hell. In these, there were still to be found elements of the Old Roman comic plot. Joseph was accused by Mary of being a jealous husband; the Devil was seen as the boastful captain (*miles gloriosus*); and the clown Orcus was the Etruscan figure taken from the old tombs, here seen as guardian of the portals of hell.

Allardyce Nicoll has performed a service of great historical worth in pointing to the fact that part of one of these Byzantine plays, or something closely akin to it, was used in the 9th-century Anglo-Saxon poem *Christ*. It contains thirty lines of purely dramatic dialogue much further advanced toward what we know as modern drama than was the 10th-century liturgical play, or trope, called the *Quem Quaeritis*, which will be discussed in the following chapter.

Summary

During the declining years of the Roman Empire, two new artistic styles, significant of the rapidly growing interest in the new Christian religion, evolved from a mixture of local Greco-Roman, African, and Syrian prototypes. The first of these, called "Early Christian" art, can be categorized as little more than a degeneration of ancient classical art. The second, however—the Byzantine—bears the aspect of a new creation.

From the workshops of glass painters, house decorators and mosaicists of the ancient world there grew, first in the catacombs, and later in the basilican churches, a new monumental mural style, the glass mosaic. This is characterized by a geometric interwoven composition of rich, lustrous colors and by the construction of human forms with drapery arranged in stiff hierarchical patterns reminiscent of archaic Greek and Egyptian painting. In this new decorative mural style precious marbles and glittering surfaces enhanced a subject matter that suggested the mystical character of the new religion, now become strong, as a perquisite of empire.

In the realm of architecture, talented Greco-Syrian builders wrought the new Byzantine style on firm Roman engineering foundations out of many diverse building types which they found in all parts of the Empire or beyond its borders in Persia. The result is typified by the Church of Hagia Sophia at Constantinople. This new domical building had both a satisfying monumental exterior and an imposing, spacious, decorative interior, capable of holding great congregations. Its structure presented dramatically the meaning of the new imperial church, which also symbolized a heavenly kingdom.

In the field of sculpture, nonspatial patterns of carving, in strongly contrasting light and shade, replaced the old Greek concept of nicely balanced mass and line within the human form. The more purely decorative arts of wrought metal, enameling, and textile design, because of a certain iconoclastic tendency in the Christian religion, came for a time to replace monumental mural sculpture. Precious ivory carving furnishes the chief means for the study of Byzantine sculptural form.

Classical dramas were still played by professional troupes of actors, but comedy and burlesque, the satire and the mime held the center of the stage. The most serious dramatic presentation of the era arose in connection with Christian worship where the performance of the Mass replaced older religious forms, borrowing much from the dramatic character of the Orphic, Mithraic, Eleusinian and Dionysiac mysteries.

Ancient folk melodies grew into the Christian hymns played upon organs, sung by priests and congregations. The organizing genius of such early Christian bishops as Ambrose and Gregory was responsible for the first steps toward modern musical notation.

From the 3rd through the 14th century, Byzantium, or Constantinople, a central meeting place for influences from the East and the West, kept alive much of the philosophy and enlightened mental attitudes of the ancient Greeks, while formulating the new, transcendental Christian religion.

Bibliography

DALTON, O. M.: *Byzantine Art and Archaeology*, Oxford, at the Clarendon Press, 1911.

MOREY, C. R.: *Christian Art*, Longmans, Green & Company, New York, 1935.

JACKSON, T. G.: *Byzantine and Romanesque Architecture*, Vol. I, Cambridge University Press, 1920.

DIEZ, ERNST, and OTTO DEMUS: *Byzantine Mosaics in Greece*, Harvard University Press, Cambridge Mass., 1931.

ANTHONY, E. W.: *History of Mosaic*, Sargent Press, Boston, 1935.

DAWSON, E. B.: *Enamels*, Methuen & Company, Ltd. London, 1911.

AUGUSTINE: *Confessions*, translated by E. B. Pusey, Everyman's Library, 1909.

NICOLL, ALLARDYCE: *Masks, Mimes and Miracles*, Harcourt, Brace & Company, Inc., New York 1931.

GRAVES, ROBERT: *Count Belisarius* (novel), Random House, 1938.

Recordings

Gregorian Chants—St. Ambrose Plain Chant, Victor V 20896, V 20897a.

Decca 20157.

Byzantine Easter Service, V 28954.

CHAPTER XII

The Art of Crusading Peoples

> ·Away with you, walls of hewn stone! Much fairer
>   It seems to me a masterful work, here the timbered hall.
>
> Wood-paneled rooms protect us from weather and wind,
>   Nor will the carpenter's hand allow any cracks to remain.
>
> In other lands, stone and cement give man a shelter from storm;
>   Here, better still, in our own native woods friendly protection is found.
>
> Around each side of the house embracing, stately arcades
>   Come rich from the master's hand, playfully, artfully carved.[1]

R EDUCED to simplest terms, the history of man's arts in Europe between the 5th and the 20th century becomes a struggle for dominance between two modes of thought and expression: the Classical and the Gothic. Both styles show traces of Oriental influence, transmitted directly through the markets of Byzantium or Alexandria, or indirectly through recurring invasions of Hun and Avar, of Mongol and Turk.

Up to this point detailed consideration has been given to the origin and development of classical art, which constitutes half of our European art inheritance. The other half derives from the exuberant, colorful fancy of Celto-Germanic design. How this art pattern, characterizing pictorially the restless soul of Gothic or Faustian man, has affected the world of today can be seen only by studying, in turn, its origin and evolution.

The Backgrounds of the Celto-Germanic, or Gothic, Style

Throughout the background of Greek art we recognized a unifying linear interweave of design, partly Mesopotamian and partly Danu-bian in origin. This interweave stood in sharp contrast to the geometricized human form from Egypt and the eidetic imagery from the caves. The art of the Celto-Germans shows even closer affinity to the serpentine patterns of the old Sumerian seals, the designs of the wandering Scythian hordes, and the painted Cimmerian pottery of the Danubian plains. From these sources come the earliest traces of the vitalized Celtic line, with its recurrent spirals, sometimes of plant, sometimes of animal origin.

Historical and Ethnic Factors

To the Greeks, the Celts were a blond-haired race living in France. The Greek Hecataeus of Miletus, who lived about 450 B.C., described a land called Keltike, which lay opposite the Island Albion (England): that is, in northern France or along the southern coast of the North Sea. Earlier Greek voyagers, about 900 B.C., spoke of the tin land (southern England), which must also have been inhabited by Celts, since the Greek name for the metal, *kassiteros* —a term used by Homer—is of Celtic origin. As these people had blue eyes much like our present-day Scandinavians, we should

[1] By the Gothic Bishop Venantius Fortunatus of Poitiers, c. 650, in translation by the author.

365

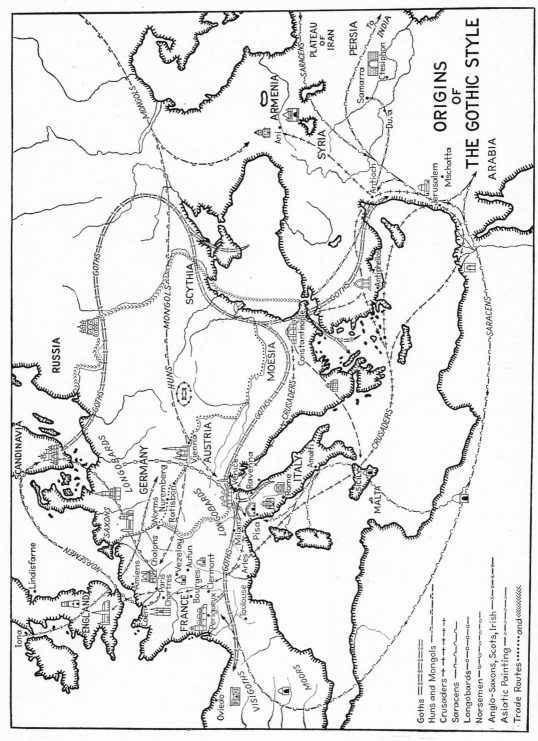

FIG. 302.

ORIGINS
OF
THE GOTHIC STYLE

Goths
Huns and Mongols
Crusaders
Saracens
Longobards
Norsemen
Anglo-Saxons, Scots, Irish
Asiatic Painting
Trade Routes

probably speak of them as Germanic. From these two associations comes the adjective "Celto-Germanic."

Primary Importance of the Celto-Germans as Culture Bearers

Along the northern borders of the Roman Empire, Celto-Germanic peoples continually filtered down into the older Mediterranean stock—first as slaves or mercenaries in the legions, next as accepted citizens in colonial towns, and finally as governors and even emperors. In the last thousand years before Christ, relatives of the Celto-Germans had moved down into India, Persia, Asia Minor, Greece, and Italy. Wherever they traveled, the eager-minded northerners adopted the designs of the cultures with which they came in contact and distributed them over their new territory.

For example, one group of the northerners, the Goths, whose earliest home was in Scandinavia, moved eastward through Russia at about the time of the birth of Christ. The Goths were divided into two groups: the Visigoths, or West Goths, and the Ostrogoths, or East Goths. By the 4th century after Christ, both groups had allied themselves with the Roman emperor, and in A.D. 488, the Ostrogoths, under their great king, Theodoric, took all of Italy as their kingdom (Fig. 302).

Other Germanic peoples that exerted influence upon the art of the early Middle Ages were the Lombards, the Franks, the Burgundians, the Angles and Saxons, and the Normans. The Lombards migrated from north central Germany into northern Italy between Verona and Milan in the province now called Lombardy. The Franks and Burgundians settled in the northern part of Gaul, occupying what we now call northern France. The Angles and Saxons moved to England. The Normans, a group of Scandinavian sea rovers, first known as "Norsemen," settled in northwestern France in the 10th century. In 1066 they took England, which had been settled by Angles and Saxons. Quickly converted to Christianity, they imported ecclesiastics from Italy to build churches. Wherever the Normans settled, tremendous building activity sprang up; they have been called the Romans of the Middle Ages.

In 1095, under the guidance of the church, the Normans, along with the leaders of the other restless northern people, marched to take Palestine away from the Turks. For almost 200 years, until 1270, led by nobility and priests, the hardier members of the Germanic nations fought for the land oversea—"outremer," as they called it. In their ceaseless roving, they occupied Armenia and the Hauran. They captured Byzantium and looted it, sending its treasures, its reliquaries, and its icons, to grace their home churches.[1] In Europe, their wives, stimulated by the clergy, formulated codes of chivalry and built costly shrines to house the spoils from the East.

These 700 years of marching, seafaring, and migrations—usually called the Dark Ages, the Carolingian, and the Romanesque epochs—paralleled that period in classical development which we know as the "Greek Age of Anarchy." As the earlier age culminated in the structures on the Acropolis, this later age brought into being the Gothic cathedral. As the earlier age led to the sculpture of Phidias and Praxiteles, the art of the Dark Ages led to the portals of

---

[1] Theophilus, a German monk, tells how mosaic tesserae can be melted down for their glass, and another chronicler of the time speaks of "bushels of precious stones brought home by crusaders to be melted into stained-glass." The passage in Theophilus reads: "In the ancient edifices of the Pagans, different kinds of glass are found in mosaic work, namely, white, black, green, yellow, sapphire, red, and purple; it is not clear, but opaque, like marble, and they are like square stones; from which coloured gems are made in gold, silver, and brass work, of which we speak fully in their proper place. Divers small vases are also found, of the same colours, which the French, most intelligent in this work, collect, and some melt the sapphire in their furnaces, adding to it a little clear and white glass, and make costly plates of sapphire, and very useful in windows. They work also from the purple and green in a similar manner." From Book II, Chap. XII of the *Essay on Various Arts* by Theophilus (Roger of Helmershausen), translated by Robert Hendrie, John Murray, London, 1847.

Chartres, Amiens, Reims, and Bourges, and eventually to the magnificent stained-glass windows. Classic drama arose from Homeric poems, dithyrambs, and lyric songs; modern drama stems from the sagas of Beowulf, Siegfried, and Dietrich. Even our music today is derived from the minstrels and troubadours of the Middle Ages; our concept of the gentleman, from the story of Arthur and his knights; and our idea of love, from such tales as that of Tristan and Isolde.

Religious and Literary Influences

The Cults of Celts and Germans

The beginnings of the Celto-Germanic religious belief lie deep in the Stone Age. At first the Celtic tribes of France and Britain must have had a worship like that indicated in paleolithic art. Fetishism and magic later combined to give birth to the well-organized priestcraft of Druids. The Druids, uniting the worship of totemic animals and trees with a belief in the life after death, built a religion that is still strong in the legends of the Irish, Welsh, and Bretons. Druidic worship early flourished in the Black Forest of Germany and the Ardennes of France. During the Roman domination, the Druids moved to England and Ireland. As an organized group they prevailed in Ireland until Tara, the last seat of the Irish kings, was abandoned in 560.

The German Pantheon in the Eddas. When the Germanic, or Nordic, part of the Celto-Germanic mixture became dominant in Europe, its religious folklore found expression in writing. The Germans, like the Celts, passed through an animistic stage of religious development. At first, they associated themselves with trees and considered the forests the cradle of their race. Into Germanic lore filtered not only the Celtic myths, but also many stories that seem to have come from the Greeks or the Romans.

The Germans worshiped a trinity of male deities very much like the earlier Sumerian

trinity of Anu, Enlil, and Ea. Stories of these gods come to us from a number of sources, of which the most original is a collection of poems from Iceland, called the "Eddas." These poems, probably sung by Norse poets in the British Isles, were carried northward as the isles became Christianized. The most famous of the Eddas, the *Voluspa* ("Prediction of the Norns"), bears a strong resemblance to the old Sumerian creation myth. In the beginning, so it runs, there was only Chaos, which hung between fire (Muspellsheim) and darkness (Niflheim). From these two principles was created Ymir, the father of a race of evil giants. A divine cow, like the goddess Nut of the Egyptians, discovered under the snow a god, Burl, who had three grown children—Odin, Vili, and Ve.

Odin killed Ymir, the giant, as Gilgamesh had killed Tiamat, and made the world from his body, the earth being his flesh and the rocks his bones. The gods then created man and woman out of the ash and alder trees and afterwards built a celestial city called Asgard. In this city Odin, his wife Freya, and Thor (the thunder-god) sit ruling over a race of gods.

The Twilight of the Gods and the Destruction by Fire, or Doom. The giant sons of Ymir, who had sworn revenge against the race of Odin, persuaded an evil, traitorous god, Loki, to help them in their work of destruction. Among Odin's sons, the Ases, is one Baldur, the most beautiful god of the bright, sunlight day— virtuous, mild, and friendly to all mankind. Like the Mesopotamian Ea, Baldur fostered the arts. Loki killed Baldur and sent his soul to Hel, a half-black giantess who ruled the underworld. As in the Ishtar and Tammuz story, all Nature wept for Baldur. When at last the giants overcame the gods, destroying Asgard with fire, the gates of Hel swung open, and the damned fought until the world burst into flames.

In most details this story of the Last Judgment, or Doom, follows closely the Gilgamesh, Tiamat, Adonis, and Ishtar legends, which the Goths in their long sojourn on the Black Sea must have taken from the Scythians and Persians and carried all over Europe. The stories from the Eddas, particularly that just above, which was called "The Twilight of the Gods," had tremendous influence upon Northern European literature. Another saga, that of Beowulf, lies at the base of English literature.

The Beowulf Saga and the Strife between Good and Evil. The Danish saga of Beowulf was brought into English literature by the Germanic peoples when they migrated to Britain. First recited shortly after the 7th century, the poem relates the story of a hero who fights with the dragons emerging from Chaos. Chief among his adversaries was Grendel, a monster whose wicked mother lived in the sea. Grendel begrudges the clansmen their revels.

> In the darkness dwelt a demon-sprite,
> Whose heart was filled with fury and hate,
> When he heard each night the noise of revel
> Loud in the hall, laughter and song.
> To the sound of the harp the singer chanted
> Lays he had learned, of long ago;
> How the Almighty had made the earth.
> Wonder-bright lands, washed by the ocean;
> How he set triumphant, sun and moon
> To lighten all men that live on the earth.
> He brightened the land with leaves and branches;
> Life he created for every being,
> Each in its kind, that moves upon earth.[1]

In these very few lines we may find the key to nearly everything the Celto-German tried to express throughout the development of his art up to the modern romantic movements and the motion picture. There is present, for example, the element of struggle between two opposing forces—the good, represented by light, and the evil, represented by the powers of darkness. We note, also, the call for harpers in the great hall, presaging the great place music was to play in European art. Again, the Almighty creates a remarkable landscape, adorned with foliage—the beloved forests. This figure of speech succinctly characterizes the fundamental quality of Celto-Germanic pattern. It reminds

the reader of the Mesopotamian hero tale, Gilgamesh, and of Tiamat.

The particular quality of all the early Celto-Germanic epics that distinguishes them from the Egyptian Book of the Dead and the Greco-Roman hero tales, arises from the fact that they sprang from a harsh life, circumscribed by an unending struggle with the elements and other natural enemies. Throughout his life conflict, however, Gothic man—Christian-Faust, as we might call him—was always conscious of a beautiful helper—Christ, Baldur, or Gilgamesh, as you will. Against this ally were ranged the dragon, the wolf, and the god who was one with falsehood—the spirit of denial, or the devil. But "the vision of the City of God at the other end of the road" toward which Christian-Faust made his laborious way holds the greatest meaning in life. The Homeric epic chose as its plot a contest to rescue earthly beauty, in the guise of Helen. The northern epic envisioned the redemption of the world in terms of a perfectly ordered society. The northern mind, striving toward that ideal of art which Longinus called the Sublime, expressed itself in music, architecture, a drama of struggle, and a type of painting that attempted to capture infinity. Yet even in the concept of the Sublime, the idea of perfection and wholeness came into its own as Augustine's picture of the City of God became, in the hands of the church, the ideal of the Christianized northerners. Thus in one version of the Twilight of the Gods, perhaps recorded by a Christian, two gods survive to build a wonderful city, portioning out the body of Baldur to a new and perfect race of men.

The Advance of Christianity

Early missionaries among the Roman soldiers inhabiting Gaul and Britain made slight impression upon the people. In Wales and Ireland, in the first part of the 5th century, a type

---

[1] *Beowulf*, Part I, P. 4, translated by J. Duncan Spaeth, in Old English Poetry, Princeton University Press, Princeton, 1922.

of Christianity that probably used Alexandrian, or Eastern, church rites led to the foundation of an Irish monastery at Clonfert by the half-mythical St. Brendan. In 596, Pope Gregory sent a mission under Augustine direct to England, from the Roman Church.

For some time the Eastern and Western types of Christianity both existed in the British Isles, the old Eastern Church rites persisting in the Irish monasteries for several centuries after they had been declared heretical in England. Despite continuous raids by the northern peoples, the monasteries grew and the two orders eventually united. A consciousness of some unity of purpose underlying all Christian activity steadily grew among the people of Europe. The monasteries, increasing in age during the 9th and 10th centuries, inherited vast wealth, and their abbots, powerful princes in many cases, built great monastic churches throughout Europe. By the 10th century, the monasteries had become both the chief centers of culture and the schools for the education of the young Germanic nobles. As vassals of the church, the tribal chiefs of Burgundians, Goths, and Lombards became the warrior bishops, as powerful in their way as the princes of the Holy Roman Empire.

The historic periods under discussion in this chapter are usually referred to as the period of folk migrations, the Dark Ages (500–750), the Carolingian period (750–850), the Pre-Romanesque period (850–1000), and the Romanesque period (1000–1175). The term "Carolingian" has its derivation from the dynasty of the Karlings, that is, Charlemagne and his descendants; the term "Romanesque," from the word "Roman."

The Origins of Gothic Design

Earliest Celtic Designs

Celtic ornaments upon the dolmens and menhirs first appear around 1200 B.C. at New Grange, Ireland. These comprise two types of design: the first, a modified form of spiral looking like a greatly enlarged series of whorls on a human thumb; the second, a trumpet pattern similar to that used on Kamares vases. The trumpet pattern in the Celtic manuscripts and jewelry consists of two winding lines diverging to a trumpet form whose open end is closed by a curved line (Fig. 303a). From the points of the curved line springs a new spiral made up of two more lines that diverge until they make another trumpet, or converge until they make a complete spiral. The total geographic distribution of this type of ornament reaches from Malta north to Germany, and from Ireland east through China. Its center of distribution is thought to have been the Cimmerians, a Celtic people living along the banks of the Danube. In the Halstatt and La Tène cultures, between 1500 and 500 B.C., both trumpet and spiral patterns were cast in bronze.

Where the Celt came in contact with the Mesopotamian or the Greco-Roman culture, he modified both plant and animal ornaments with his trumpet pattern. Two coins from France illustrate this blending of styles. The first (Fig. 303b) shows a Greek tetradrachme of Philip of Macedon, probably paid to some Celtic mercenary. The second (Fig. 303c), minted by the Celts, shows the naturalistic design changed to one of abstract linear character. Here the beard, face, and wreath have been transformed into a series of spiraling, flamelike locks. Similarly, a bronze ornament from Poledon Hill, Somerset, England, which shows a further, balanced development of the trumpet pattern, may have been derived from the Greek palmette (Fig. 303d). Finally, from St. Goar, in Germany, comes a stone on which is a human face that seems to grow out of the whirlpool of spiraling lines (Fig. 303e).

Germanic Interweaves

The richest ornament of the Celto-Germanic peoples was first produced after the 2nd century of the Christian Era, when the Goths, having left their home in Scandinavia, had

FIG. 303.—Early examples of Celtic ornament. *a*, stone from Turoe, County Galway, Ireland, La Tène period; *b*, Greek tetradrachme with head of Zeus; *c*, Celtic copy of (*b*), Hungary; *d*, bronze inlaid with red enamel, Poledon Hill, Somerset, England, 100 B.C. (?) (British Museum); *e*, stone from St. Goar, West Germany, La Tène period, about 200 B.C.; *f*, late Babylonian form of palmette; *g*, Greek leaf and dart ornament; *h*, Germanic modification of (*g*), Verona; *i*, Ostrogothic modification of (*g*), Tomb of Theodoric, Ravenna.

wandered down the Russian river valleys toward the Black Sea. At that time, the plant and animal interweave, arising perhaps from a union of the ancient Mesopotamian guilloche and Celtic trumpet motives with late Greek animal designs, began to dominate. In Viking design, this motive came to be known as a symbol of endless struggle. As such, it probably derived through Scythia from the ancient Mesopotamian seal showing Gilgamesh fighting with the dragon Tiamat (Fig. 102, Chap. V). The final development of Celto-Germanic ornament came about when the struggling dragon united with plant forms and spirals, as in the initial page from the Irish manuscript, the Book of Kells (Fig. 306).

The aesthetic effect of both the spiral and the animal interweave is to carry the eye back and forth across the surface of the object. From these rhythms one gains a sensation of either excitement or bewilderment. Where the Greeks desired the beauty of balanced unity, the northerners desired an expression of energetic, dynamic unbalance for its own sake.

Queen Ase's Ship Carvings. The greatest single source of our knowledge of purely Germanic

designs is the burial ship of Ase, the early 9th-century Viking queen. On this ship were buried wagons, sleds, and household utensils ornamented with finely carved designs. Parts of the ship itself also bear carvings of intricate dragon interweaves. In these decorations appear five general types of design. The first (Fig. 304*a*) consists of variations of geometric checkerboard or diaper patterns, with red and blue dots at the intersection of the cross bands. This type occurs in many places, the example here having been taken from one of the sleds. This technomorphic design probably originated in basket or rug weaving.

The second type includes many variations of a regular interweave like braided rope (Fig. 304*b*). This may have originated in the Greek or Mesopotamian guilloche or more directly from the rope braiding of the sailors themselves.

The third class of ornament furnishes many examples of animal designs, woven in circles so as to suggest the Persian plant and vine ornaments (Fig. 304*c*). The arrangement of these animals in curves like those of the trumpet pattern indicates close connection with the Scythian and Siberian ornaments of the time.

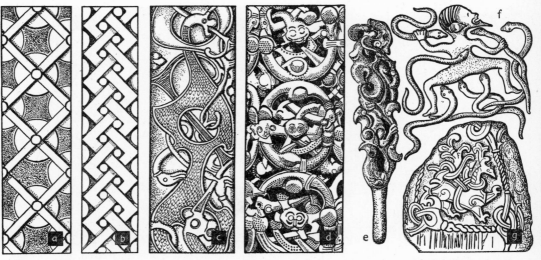

Fig. 304.—*a*, diaper pattern, Viking ship of Ase; *b*, braided interweave, same source; *c*, animal designs, same source; *d*, interwoven serpents, same source; *e*, Chinese bronze, Ordos Territory; *f*, man and serpents from Viking sled, ship of Ase; *g*, runic stone, Norway.

A fourth class of ornament consists entirely of serpents with great heads and staring eyes, arranged in circles twined into one another. Deeply cut in the wood, these circles make of the entire object a solid writhing mass, in whose shadows seem to lurk horrifying dragons (Fig. 304*d*). This type of sculptural composition in terms of facets of light and shade, also to be found in Siberian gold and bronze work (Fig. 304*e*), becomes the aesthetic pattern for later Romanesque and Gothic sculpture.

The fifth element of decoration, most significant from a literary point of view, appears on one of the wagons (Fig. 304*f*). A man is shown struggling with two serpents. Around him move rings of serpents, twisting dragons, and hounds accompanied by a sea animal like a mermaid, recognizable as the mother of Grendel. Here we see, probably, the earliest representation of Beowulf's fight to overcome the evil one. Arising in ancient Mesopotamia, this design of the man battling in the toils of the serpent may have traveled through Persian and Scythian art up the rivers of Russia to Scandinavia, if it was not carried first to England, Ireland, and central France by Copts from Egypt. It fur-

nished the prototype for medieval representations of Christ and St. George overcoming the dragon of the evil one.

Two portals on the church at Urnäs and at Syllestad (Fig. 305) show the connection not only with preceding Scythian and Persian designs but also with the portal carvings of Romanesque and Gothic cathedrals. Significant of the ornament at Syllestad is the fact that it covers altogether the column, capital, and side posts, completely obscuring the architectonic structure. The intent is exactly that of the Maori wood carving (Fig. 42, Chap. III). This decorative portal acts as a spell through which one enters the safety of the church, freed from the interweave of monsters, which must stay on the outside.

Irish Manuscript Decoration

All the resources of prehistoric design later used to decorate the mature Gothic appear in the Irish manuscripts and jewelry of the early 9th century. The illuminations in the great books of Kells and Lindisfarne mark the culmination of a movement in design that must

Fig. 305.—Origins of Romanesque portal sculpture. *a*, animal interweave on wooden doorway, church at Urnäs, Norway, 9th to 11th century (?); *b*, Neo-Persian motifs, stone portal, St. Peter at Moissac, early 12th century; *c*, Archivolt with grotesques and Mithraic symbols, Kilpeck Church, England, about 1140; *d*, chimeras on trumeau of stone portal, Notre Dame, Souillac, 12th century; *e*, wooden doorway, church at Syllestad, Norway, showing story of Siegfried, about 1200 (Oslo University Museum); *f*, details of portal, west façade, Chartres, stone, middle 12th century.

have begun in the Irish monasteries of the 6th century. From the 6th through the 9th century, the Vikings had invaded Ireland, becoming established there by 800. In the meantime, Irish monks, having founded monasteries in Scotland, Iona, and Lindisfarne, began their work in Germany. Through this interchange, the Germanic designs of the rope, plant, and animal interweave came to unite with the Celtic trumpet and spirals. In one page of the Book of Kells—a manuscript written in the 8th or the 9th century—appear all the ornaments we have discussed, firmly united around the

cross (Fig. 306). To appreciate this design, the reader must understand that it formed the monogram page of the Gospel, or God's Spell. It thus embodies the most powerful charms known against all the forces of the evil one. The two monks who drew the pages of the manuscript inserted all the signs from the old pagan religions, indicating in this way that the new religion had overcome them. In the *Quoniam* page, for example, a group of men, probably the saved, are seen protected, in a part of the Q, from a great serpent that struggles in vain to break through the charm and devour them.

In our illustration, all the various elements that at first seem to be in a state of restless, meaningless motion actually bear a significant relationship to the lozenge, or diamond, that

Fig. 306.—Monogram page, the Book of Kells, 8th century (Trinity College Library, Dublin). (*Courtesy of Metropolitan Museum of Art.*)

forms the center of the cross. Allowing the eye to glance over the page, gradually one becomes aware of three great letters, X, P, I, standing for the word Christ. Below, in finely ordered script, the abbreviation K stands for *Autem*, followed by the word *Generatio*, the opening words of the Gospel according to St. Matthew. The fine, clear-cut character of the letters below written in the uncial style, a precursor of our longhand writing, denotes that they came from a cultured people, not from one indulging in barbaric primitivism for its own sake, as some classical scholars have contended, when confronted with these illuminations. The farthest spaces in the three upper arms of the X show the wildest, least-contained patterns. The end of the lower arm terminates in a combination

of plant and animal interweaves, outside which, between two circles filled with spirals, lies a great area of animal interweave.

The extremities of the letter terminate in three groups of circles, each holding many smaller circles made up of spirals. Such a circle containing three groups of spirals is called a triquetra. As this ornament appears very frequently throughout the Gothic, the term should be fixed in mind. Around the nine sets of circles smaller spirals and trumpet patterns break into the myriad wheels used by the prophet to describe the universe.

Human and realistic animal figures appear at several points in the initial, the first instance being above the cross. This head, like the face on the St. Goar stone, arises from the midst of a group of spirals. Its position above the cross may signify that the head is that of Christ. Below, on the left, three angels carry symbols.

The monks of Kells, possibly acquainted with Aristotle's description of the various types of soul, seem to have used in this manuscript all the symbols necessary to denote the vegetable, animal, and imaginative elements which, when put in order, might lead to the ideal Christian. In the later development of the Christian cathedral these types of ornament actually appear to stand for the different aspects of creation. The monogram plate of the Book of Kells shows for the first time the scheme of knowledge around which the greatest Gothic works of art were later constructed.

The Celto-Germanic Color Scheme

As the design patterns of the Book of Kells underlie all Gothic art until the Renaissance, so its color scheme displays the characteristics associated with stained glass, tapestry, mural and panel painting. This color scheme has a threefold origin, stemming (1) from Coptic embroidery and painting; (2) from examples of Byzantine illumination which probably reached Ireland by the 6th century; (3) from Gallic jewelry, whose rich reds, blues, and greens

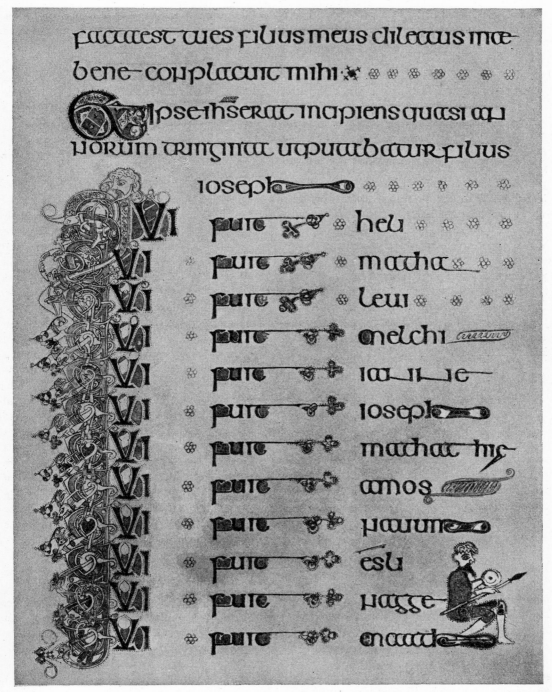

Fig. 307.—Page from Book of Kells with genealogy. (*Courtesy of Sir Edward Sullivan, The Book of Kells, The Studio Publications, New York, 1933.*)

were reproduced in the spots of color on Viking wood carvings (Fig. 307).

The pigments used—malachite green, chrysocolla blue, hematite red, chrome and ocher yellow, and perhaps an oyster-shell white—were all found in Ireland. The black pigment came from lamps or fishbones; the light yellow (orpiment) was a native trisulphide of arsenic; the bright red (realgar) an arsenic disulphide; and the purple, perhaps finely ground glass tesserae. This last must have been imported, probably from Constantinople. Pale blues and lilacs, made by mixing the above, together with a deep lapis-lazuli blue, added greatly to the effect of many of the pages, no two of which show the same color scheme. As was usual for most medieval manuscripts, all the pigments were ground in gum, glue, or gelatin, if not egg white. That this love of color seen in the Book of Kells bespoke a peculiar quality of the Celtic mind we know from many descriptions of color in early manuscripts, such as the Book of Lismore.

Painting

During the five centuries between the Book of Kells and the culmination of the Romanesque style in the monumental stained-glass windows, the northerners developed many types of manuscript and mural design. Monks from the Irish and English schools, founding monasteries in Germany or teaching in the palace school of Charlemagne, carried with them manuscripts like the one we have studied. At Reims, where they came in contact with Benedictine monks from the monastery of Monte Cassino in southern Italy, they eagerly seized upon works like the Alexandrian Joshua Roll and copied them. The result of such copying accounts in part for the lyrical expressionistic style of the Utrecht Psalter (Fig. 308).

West Frankish Lyricism in the Psalter of Utrecht. In this manuscript, now in the library of the University of Utrecht in Holland, small pen drawings, each complete in itself, illustrate the accompanying text. Contrast this work with the limiting, contour-line drawing of the Greeks. In the Greek drawing, the line traces the curves of the figure and suggests only by its subtle changes in direction that the figure has solidity. Here the line, varying in character, suggests not so much the solidity of the figure as the vital force of the muscles. This feeling of activity is particularly apparent in the composition of the draperies, which seem animated as though by a life of their own. Quick, short, triangular strokes indicate the eyes, whose shape was copied from eyes in some southern illusionistic original. The character of the stroke changes for the hair, the wings, or the plants. This use of line as an instrument of expression animates the entire drawing. The classical origin of the composition appears in the balanced position of the figures on each side of a central axis formed by the figure of Christ and that earthly symbol of the harmony of sound, the organ.

Flanked by attendant angels, the Christ in his *mandorla* rises from the clouds, which are blown across the heavens by the four winds. The head of the Christ marks the apex of an equilateral triangle whose base lies along the base of the organ. Two lines of landscape weave across the triangle, binding to it four groups of musicians. The lower groups play upon the great hunting horns, the *olifants;* the upper ones carry harp, lyre, cymbal, rebec, and psaltery. Each of these groups, itself held together by a linear interweave, seems tied to the center of the composition by the dramatic, upturned gaze of its members. Only the two organists and the four boys who pump the organ are too busy to heed the heavenly vision. One of the organists gestures as though to urge them to greater effort. Every part of this composition sings the words of the psalm above: "Let them all praise His name in chorus with tympanum and psaltery and sounding cymbals."

The drawings in the Psalter of Utrecht demonstrate the first step in the taming of the northern spirit by the classical southern ideals of form. The composition we have analyzed appears again in Romanesque portal sculptures and in the monumental paintings of Leonardo and Raphael.

LAUDINTINOMINIIUSIN CHORO INTYMPANO IIPSALTERIOPSALLANTII QUIABINIPLACITUMIST

EXSULTATIONESDIINGUT TURIIORUM IIGLADII ANCIPITESINMANIB:EOR ADIACIENDAMUINDICIA

UTIACIANTINIISIUDICIU CONSCRIPTUM GLORIA HAICISTOMNIBUSSCIS IIUS

FIG. 308.—Page from Psalter of Utrecht, showing medieval musical instruments, Carolingian, c. 800 (University Library, Utrecht). (*Courtesy of Index of Christian Art, Princeton University.*)

The style of the Psalter developed further in England. Anglo-Saxon artists, returning it to Europe in the 11th and early 12th centuries, made it the dominant style in the territory of the West Franks, that is, in the part of France west of the Saône and the Rhone. It inspired the sculptors of Burgundy and Languedoc in the 12th century. The prophet from the church at Souillac (Fig. 335) and the portal of the church at Moissac (Fig. 334) exemplify the monumental development of this manuscript style.

East Frankish Color Areas in the Ada Manuscript. In the territory of the East Franks, which included what is now southern Germany and the valley of the Rhine, the primitive northern style came in contact directly with manuscripts brought from Asia Minor and Byzantium. The page from a manuscript painted for Ada (Fig. 309), the sister of Charlemagne, typifies the more colorful, mosaiclike illumination that resulted from this encounter. In this manuscript,

the drapery still shows the active force of the native drawing. The figure, which occupies a niche framed by columns and a rainbow arch probably copied from some Armenian or Byzantine prototype, is heavy and solid, although the painting of the drapery lends it a flat, Oriental appearance. The large, clumsy hands and feet, animated still by an inner light, grew larger and more clumsy as this school developed through the time of the crusades. Most significant, as expressing the Oriental tendencies of the East Frankish school, is the arrangement of large flat areas of color, negating any possible perspective effect. As the Utrecht Psalter style formed a basis for the sculpture of Burgundy, so this Germanic style, moving southward with the Lombards, influenced the sculptors and mural painters of northern Italy.

Latinizing Tendencies in the Bayeux Tapestry. Whenever the East or West Frankish styles encountered the strong Latinizing missionaries of the Benedictine order, bringing with them from Italy and Provence the last traces of late Roman figure painting, such as that found in the catacombs of the 4th and 5th centuries, a figure style resulted in which the individual forms, characterized by infantile faces and a profile pose, lost much of their vigor. In this third style (Fig. 310), the expressionism of the Eng-

Fig. 309.—East Frankish illumination. Page from the manuscript of Ada, 9th century (Staatsbibliothek, Trier). (*Courtesy of Swarzenski.*)

lish manuscript and the monumental, Oriental character of the East Frankish works gave way to pure narration. The single figures lacked articulation, however, and the episodes illustrated lacked a sense of composition. The Bayeux tapestry characterizes this style, which became the official method of representation for the powerful forces of church and state. This tapestry, created at the end of the 11th century, measures 100 feet long and shows, motion-picture fashion, the incidents relative to the Norman conquest of England by Wil-

liam the Conqueror. It represents the type of decoration found in fresco on the walls of castle rooms, a few fragments of which remain. All the elements from the unified manuscript compositions here appear separate and side by side. It constitutes an object of historical record rather than a work conducive to aesthetic enjoyment.

The Revival of Panel Painting in the Altar of Soest. One monument, an altarpiece in the church of the Wiesen at the town of Soest, in Westphalia, Germany (Fig. 311), unites all the characteristics of the various Celto-Germanic styles discernible in the manuscripts. Romanesque murals having for the greater part disappeared, one must seek the best of the color compositions in such works. This little arcaded panel, now in the Berlin Museum, takes as its central composition the figure of the Eternal Father holding the crucified Saviour, above whose cross rests the dove of the Spirit. To right and left of this representation of the mystery of the Trinity stand the Virgin and St. John. The great brightness and vitality of the central group, coursing through the angular draperies, both dominates the outer figures and lends force to them.

The composition scheme of the center panel betrays a peculiarity which becomes more noticeable in later times; that is, the panel is designed on a geometric plan, as were the earlier classical paintings. The arm of the cross forms the upper side of a square whose base lies along the bottom of the frame. The head of God the Father centers on the apex of an equilateral triangle which has as its base the top of a square. Despite this classical composition, the figures are reduced to flat areas of color, like the figures in Byzantine mosaics.

The Methods of the Medieval Painter. The medieval painter during Carolingian and Romanesque times inherited from the past the methods of painting in fresco and tempera. The art of manuscript illumination had also taught him Byzantine methods of applying thin layers of gold upon parchment, using egg white as a binding medium. In the 12th century a monk, Theophilus, wrote a book on the crafts, which he called *The List of Diverse Arts*. An entire chapter on the precepts and technical secrets

ing through the glaze, lent a harmonious tone to the entire composition.

The Origins of Stained-glass Painting. The original genius of the Celto-Germanic designers

Fig. 310.—Harold sees the comet and arms to resist William the Conqueror, Bayeux tapestry by Queen Mathilda, about A.D. 1080 (Museum, Bayeux).

of panel painting makes clear the techniques used in creating the Soest panel.

A seasoned wooden panel, carefully braced with crosspieces to prevent warping, was first covered with a very thin coat of leather glue mixed with water. Upon this was laid a mixture of lead white, whiting, and more glue water. When dry, this coat was either burnished with a smooth agate or covered with further smooth coats. Upon this "ground," as it was called, a drawing copied from a cartoon, or large sketch, furnished the basis for the finished design. Next came a thin layer of gold leaf, attached with egg white beaten in water or oil for binding. At times, the gold leaf covered the entire panel; at others, it reached only to the borders of the figures. Finally the pigments, mixed with egg-white size or various gums, such as gum arabic, were applied either thick, as in tempera, or in thin glazes. The warm gold background, shin-

early led them to turn from the imitation of Byzantine and Roman methods of wall decoration to the creation of a new technique. As the Romanesque churches of the north became higher and lighter with the improvements in masonic techniques and the use of the flying buttress, the wall areas for fresco painting and mosaic became smaller, as the light areas expanded. This made possible the development of painted glass as a mural art. The invention of this new craft, like all other inventions, consisted in an adaptation of techniques derived from a number of sources. From Copts and Saracens, from Byzantine mosaic workers, and from their own workers in enamel and jewelry, the Romanesque craftsmen borrowed not only the techniques but also the designs of their new art.

The first stage in the development of stained glass was the Celto-Germanic art of jewelry

FIG. 311.—Altar panel of Soest, c. 1250 (Berlin Museum). (*Courtesy of Amsler and Ruthardt.*)

FIG. 312.—The origins of stained-glass design. *a*, Visigothic fibula, A.D. 500–520 (Walters Art Gallery); *b*, medallion, bust of Christ, Frankish, 8th century, cloisonné enamel, 1⁹⁄₁₀ inches diameter (Cleveland Museum of Art); *c*, initial S, Book of Kells, 8th century; *d*, pierced stone window, Pola, Italy, 9th century; *e*, inlaid marble plaque, Church of Saint Agatha, Constantinople, 9th century (?); *f*, King David, stained glass, Augsburg, c. 1000.

Fig. 313.—*a*, Celto-Germanic frame-house construction from Michelsberg, Siebenbürgen, Germany (*after Haupt, Baukunst der Germanen*); *b*, exterior, mast church at Borgund, Norway, 10th to 12th century.

making, in which precious stones were set between *cloisons*, or partitions, of gold and bronze. Little amulets like the Visigoth fibula in the Walters Art Gallery (Fig. 312*a*) can be found wherever the Celto-Germans traveled, from Ireland to the banks of the Ordos River in China.

The next step in the development of both design and technique came with the Frankish enamels of the Carolingian period. A rare enamel showing the influence of Irish design, now in the Cleveland Museum of Art, illustrates this second stage (Fig. 312*b*). In the meantime, both East and West Goths, Lombards, and Anglo-Saxons, who had come in contact with the Saracens, learned to fill their windows with stone or stucco plaques pierced with geometric designs holding small pieces of colored glass, so as to modify the light. By the end of the 9th century, some ingenious craftsman in northern France or Germany had combined the two techniques. Substituting small strips of lead for the *cloisons* and painting with enamels upon bits of colored glass, he constructed the first stained-glass window. Theophilus, writing in the 11th century, already speaks of the art as an ancient one.

The figures in the earliest glass more closely approximate those in Byzantine enamels and designs on Coptic wooden panels, such as Fig. 268*c*, Chap. XI, than they do the earlier Celtic figures. During the long periods of truce between the Christians and the Turks, such panels in wood and ivory became articles of import from Byzantium to Germany and from Alexandria to southern France and the west coast of Italy. The earliest French stained-glass windows in St. Denis and Chartres show patterns resembling the Greco-Roman design which suggests a tree of life with figures placed in the branches (Fig. 295*a*, Chap. XI). The German windows often copy the style of Byzantine enamels. The two types of design unite in the 13th-century glass of Chartres Cathedral, which we shall consider in the next chapter (Fig. 382, Chap. XIII).

Earliest Windows in the Archaic Manner. The earliest large windows known were made for the Cathedral of Augsburg about 1000. They include figures of Moses, David, Jonah, Daniel, and Hosea. The figure of David (Fig. 312*f*) indicates a close connection with the late East Frankish, or Ottonian, manuscript style and with Byzantine mosaics. The king stands stiffly, lacking almost all vitality and interweave. Only the spiral on his cloak and the way in which the folds of his sleeves arrange themselves over his arm, indicate some of the possibilities for

FIG. 314.—Mast church at Borgund, interior construction.

Celtic design as yet undeveloped in the new medium. The window consists of large areas of light glass fitted with colored patches. The design of the leading received little attention, nor was there any attempt to arrange the colored areas of the figure so that they blended in the gaze of the spectator, with the vibrating effect of later windows. This figure represents the archaic stage of stained-glass designs (Fig. 312*f*).

Architecture

The architecture of the Celto-Germans in localities outside Roman influence grew from the beloved forests of the northern folk. Remains of log huts found in old Gothic settlements prove them to have been of a form of construction still in use wherever wood abounds. The house from Michelsberg, in Germany (Fig. 313*a*), shows the details of this construction, which is familiar to everyone. It differs from Roman and Greek building in one aesthetic particular: the house is conceived first as a frame, mortised together, to which the walls are literally hung. Sometimes the walls, as in the illustration, consist of flat slabs covered with stucco, today called lath-and-plaster construction; at other times, a filling of brick and rubble was placed between the beams.

Wherever the Germans wandered, they built their huts and castles, their judgment halls and temples, of wood. When wood failed them, they built in stone, retaining as ornaments the technomorphic designs derived from the earlier wooden structures. A poem by the Bishop Venantius Fortunatus, a Goth who lived under Theodoric, in central France, during the 6th century, expresses the pride of the Germans in their wooden houses (see page 365).

The hall of the Hun king, Attila, the mead hall of Beowulf, a house described in the Book of Lismore, and many of the council halls in old Saxon castles aptly fit this description by the Gothic bishop. So also do the Viking churches of Norway (Fig. 313*b*).

The Mast Churches of Norway. The earliest mast churches of Norway were constructed on a simple rectangular plan around four perpendicular masts, similar to the wooden churches of Rumania today. The masts rose through the gable roof to support a tall tower with a clerestory over the center. In the later churches, such as the ones at Borgund and Gol (Fig. 314), the four masts were replaced by four groups of three columns each, which supported the high gabled roof held together by transverse beams. Around this central skeleton, the walls, built of panels hung on a frame, were braced by ship-ribbing construction. All the joints were mortised and pinned together by the shipwright's technique. This method of wooden bracing is particularly apparent in the curved beams of the roof and in the ship-railing decoration that separates the lower from the

FIG. 315*a*.—Tower, Earls Barton, England, early 11th century. Height about 110 feet. (*Courtesy of Lesch-Carnegie.*)

upper part of the church in the place where later we find the triforium gallery.

Most details of construction in these churches can be explained in terms of shipbuilding and early Byzantine or Saracenic structures, without reference to the Roman basilican style. The outside decoration of the mast churches (Fig. 305*a,e*) likewise is derived from Viking ship carving or Saracenic and Persian design. The great dragon heads acting as finials at the ends of the ridgepoles, the carving around the doors, the grotesques and gargoyles, which appear in some cases even inside the building, all seem more allied to the decorations on the

wooden pagodas of China and the cult houses of some tribes in Indo-China and the Malay Archipelago than to elements in early Christian architecture. There is a possible connection

FIG. 315*b*.—Tower Portoguaro, Italy, early 10th century. Height about 150 feet. (*Courtesy of John Shapley.*)

between these widely separated places, through the relatives of the Celto-Germanic people— Danubian Cimmerians—who invaded China and influenced even Indo-China, probably in the 8th century B.C.

The general appearance of most of the finished Gothic churches built in the 13th and 14th centuries around the Île de France, where the Vikings settled in the 10th and 11th centuries, more closely approximates the appearance of these wooden churches than that of the low basilican churches of Lombardy, from which all the Romanesque styles are said to derive.

The Tower Churches of England and Germany. In the early Saxon castles of England, the watch-

towers were at first built of perpendicular wooden beams interlaced with struts, the spaces filled with stones and mortar. The long, thin pilasters, accentuating the perpendicular ap-

Fɪɢ. 317.—Interior, Santa Maria de Naranco, Oviedo, Spain. c. 850. (*Courtesy of Lesch-Carnegie.*)

pearance of the tower, were joined at times by a zigzag of beams and at times by false arches. When these castle towers were converted into stone structures, during the 6th and 7th centuries, they retained the characteristics of the wood construction (Fig. 315a). The mysterious towers of Ireland, some of them probably associated with long-vanished monasteries, developed from round towers, such as that in the town of Portoguaro, Italy (Fig. 315b). In Saxon churches, the square tower predominated; but in later German and French Romanesque buildings, round and square types were used simultaneously, or the round tower was built above the square one, with an intermediate octagon.

Fɪɢ. 316.—Double church, Schwarzrheindorf, Germany, 1149–1151. Length 112 feet, length of transept 53 feet. This skyscraper church, which closely approximates the Viking mast-church elevation, is one of the earliest instances of the great central tower later used in English Gothic. (*Courtesy of Lesch-Carnegie.*)

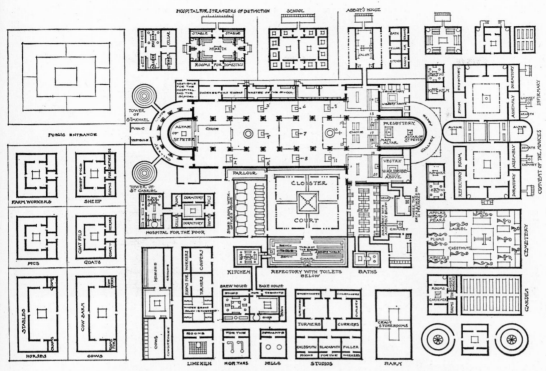

Fig. 318.—Plan of the Monastery of St. Gall, redrawn after 9th-century manuscript. (*Courtesy of Mrs. A. Kingsley Porter, Medieval Architecture, Yale University Press.*)

The chief meaning of the Romanesque church, insofar as it is a Celto-Germanic or an Oriental structure, lies first of all in its tower. At Earls Barton, England, the Anglo-Saxon church has a central tower almost larger than the rest of the building. At Deerhurst on the Severn, in England, the nave of the 9th-century church, which is very short, is actually a tower, with a second, slightly taller tower placed in front of it, like the two parts of the church at Borgund. The intent here seems clear. The worshipers in this early pre-Romanesque church wanted a building that would give them a feeling of great height. The effect of such a building is always to make the worshiper feel his own insignificance, while it leads his thoughts upward toward infinity.

This *will to height* we shall see develop as the Southern Romanesque basilicas give way to the high Northern Romanesque churches, many

of which, particularly the German and the English, seem to be built around great towers. The church at Schwarzrheindorf (Fig. 316) demonstrates the ultimate development of this typically northern form in the finished Romanesque style about 1150. Such a church could have been built by Armenian or Byzantine masons under northern inspiration without any help from the Latin builders of Italy. Similarly, the pre-Romanesque buildings in the period just studied, including the Chapel of Charlemagne at Aix-la-Chapelle, the halls of the Visigothic kings, and many others, were only partly related to ancient classical building. They inherited many elements from Syrian, Mohammedan, Byzantine, and northern wood building styles. As an example of this mixture of motives turn to the hall at Naranco.

The Visigothic King's Hall of Naranco. In Spain, at the town of Naranco, once the capital of the

Fig. 319.—Cathedral group, Pisa. Cathedral, 1063–1100; length 312 feet. Campanile, 1174–1350, height 179 feet. (*Courtesy of Lesch-Carnegie.*)

Fig. 320.—Apse, Cathedral of Murano, 12th century. (*Courtesy of Alinari.*)

Visigothic kings, there still remains an ancient church, later dedicated to Santa Maria (Fig. 317). At one time the council hall of a Gothic king, it still retains the old arrangement of doors placed in the middle of the long axis instead of at one end. One must, accordingly, approach the church from the side and, ascending one of a double flight of steps, enter on the side opposite the king's seat, now replaced by an altar. Most of the early Germanic tribes used such a structure for the king's hall, and its remains may be found in early Romanesque palaces like the one at Goslar in Germany. Later, to this transverse hall was added the long nave, but in some Romanesque buildings, such as those in Germany, the side doors were retained and an apse was built at each end. The plan of the early abbey church at St. Gall in Germany, shows such a double apse (Fig. 318).

The Horizontalism of Tuscan Basilican Churches. In contrast to the northern buildings with their penchant for verticality, the pre-Romanesque and early Romanesque churches of Italy follow consistently the ancient Christian basilican models, with their strong feeling for classical horizontality.

At the town of Pisa, near the famous marble quarries of Carrara in the province of Tuscany, an architect by the name of Busketus planned a church in which the two types of structure, the broad and the long, lay athwart each other (Fig. 319). As Busketus was Greek, it was natural that a domed church should suggest itself to him, but as the location was near the Roman center, the basilican plan dominated. Hence, he built a Latin cross with deep transepts, almost like the later Northern Gothic cathedrals, but with a great dome over the crossing. The building, lined inside and out with precious marbles, shows a façade built up of four rows of true arcades placed above a false arcade in the lower story. These arcades lend to the building a horizontal feeling, as though several classical temples were piled one upon another. The western façade combines symmetry with interesting variety, and slight refinements which

produce an almost imperceptible effect upon the beholder.

The Cathedral of Murano, behind the city of Venice, possesses an apse in which super-

Fig. 321.—Baptistery, Florence, c. 1200. (*Courtesy of Lesch-Carnegie.*)

imposed columns give an effect of delicate beauty (Fig. 320). In the Church of San Michele at Pavia, the arcade used as a decorative motif combines with the tall façade pilasters to lend interest to an otherwise barnlike structure. The Cathedral of Pisa, with its relatively high roof, has, however, a basilican, flat, coffered ceiling. Saracenic arches adorn the crossing, as in the Sicilian Romanesque churches. The connections here are of the greatest interest, for the Pisans were trade rivals of the Saracens, who were building up at this time in Palermo a remarkable architecture that used the pointed arch. In 1063 the Pisans had destroyed the Saracenic fleet off Palermo and captured a huge amount of booty that served in part to build their cathedral. Later, the Normans took Palermo from the Saracens and again united Saracenic and Romanesque styles.

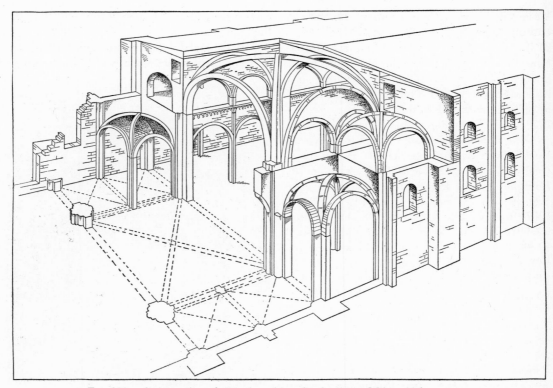

Fig. 322.—Construction of ribbed vaulting, St. Ambrose, Milan, 11th century.

The Octagonal Baptistery at Florence. Another feature that the Tuscan builders took from the Saracens was the use of varicolored marbles laid in geometric patterns on the walls. The Baptistery in Florence (Fig. 321) illustrates this type of ornamentation. This structure, built, like earlier baptisteries, on an octagon, shows several stories of superimposed pilasters and arches enclosing a dome. Like the cathedral church at Torcello, it is of special interest in that it houses a great mosaic of the Last Judgment (showing the Doom). This work, among others, probably inspired Dante, who called the Baptistery "mio bel San Giovanni" ("my beautiful St. John"). If we seek the sources of these buildings in the East, we discover their prototype in the Church of the Holy Sepulcher in Jerusalem. In the West, the Pantheon and the Roman baths may have furnished models.

The Invention of the Ribbed Vault in Lombard Churches. Between the 9th and the 11th century, the stone masons of Lombardy, who were called the "Comacini" after their home on Lake Como, made an experiment in roofing that led to one of the most significant inventions of the builder's art—the ribbed vault.

The Romans had observed the particularly strong intersection formed where two barrel vaults came together. From this type of construction arose the cross vault, which they used in their baths and basilicas to give greater height. The method of building such cross vaults seems to have been lost later. It was not until the 10th century that the Comacini, building the Church of St. Eustorgio in Milan, experimented in throwing transverse arches across the side aisles from the heavy square piers to the side walls, perhaps to steady the walls of the clerestory above. These arches created a difficulty in the piers, for the old square piers that had replaced the columns were monopolized by the main arcade and so offered no support for this new arch. The builders, accordingly, added a spur on the inside of the pier to carry the transverse arch. The spur they later replaced by engaged columns as decorative details, along both the side aisle and the nave.

The next step was to consider the small squares formed by the transverse arches of the aisles very much as though each one were the point of intersection of two barrel vaults. It was discovered that diagonal arches could be thrown across these square bays and that a system of corbeling could be built upon them so as to produce in the side aisles a series of low groined vaults built upon ribs. Next it was found feasible, because of the heavy bracing in the side aisles, to construct ribbed vaults over the great center bays (Fig. 322). The windows of the clerestory now appeared under a second story of arches which rose above the aisle arcade. The effect was not one of a continuous barrel vault, but of a series of domes, rather gloomy and dark at their crowns, culminating in the opening of the higher, lighter dome above the ciborium. With many modifications, this constituted the plan and construction of all Romanesque buildings.

Two elements of decoration should be noted: (1) the pilaster strip that ran up the outside of the building or up the piers; (2) the arched corbel table built upon projecting nubbins in the wall as a sort of border on top of which ran a molding separating the upper from the lower story on the inside of the building and acting as a cornice under the roof on the outside. This last is a remnant of the colonnades that served as architectural decoration in Roman buildings and on the great Persian palace at Ctesiphon.

St. Ambrose at Milan—A Typical Lombard Church. In plan, St. Ambrose differs little from the early Christian basilicas. The alternate large and small piers, however, with their engaged columns and pilasters, indicate the

Romanesque, as do the alternate layers of marble and brick in the arches and the architectonic ornament of the corbeled tables along the border of the triforium gallery.

Fig. 323a.—St. Ambrose, atrium façade. (*Courtesy of Lesch-Carnegie.*)

Entering the church, one passes through an atrium (Fig. 323a), behind which follow the narthex, the main aisle or nave (Fig. 323b), with its two low side aisles, and a choir raised above the crypt, with a canopied altar placed before it under the high opening over the crossing. Above the crypt lies the apse, with an exedra for the clergy. Two characteristics seem significant in connection with this building. (1) Outside, two square towers, forming an integral part of the narthex façade, are placed as were those in the Syrian church at Tourmanin. The towers appear again in Northern Romanesque styles wherever the Comacini aided in the building. (2) Inside the church, the light above the crossing indicates an ill-fated attempt to raise a dome on squinch arches. The aesthetic significance of this lantern is to suggest the heavens above the altar, so that the eye, leaving the gloomy nave, may wander upward toward the regions of the sky.

The Domed Churches of Venice and Their Eastern Decoration. The Eastern influence is most easily seen in the Church of St. Mark at

Venice (Fig. 324). This church, built in the 10th century in the form of a Greek cross, with domes over the arms and the center, follows the plan of the earlier Church of the Apostles (now destroyed), which was constructed under Justinian in Constantinople. The Venetians, through their great merchant marine, had kept in touch with Constantinople during the 8th and 9th centuries. Their spiritual allegiance clung to the Eastern Roman Empire rather than to the Western Empire and the Pope. After a ruinous trade war, which culminated when the crusaders took Constantinople, the Venetians imported architects and mosaicists from the conquered city. Columns, marble carvings, and the precious sacred vessels of the church were also moved over to the city of the lagoons, where they were used with parts of ruined Roman temples to clothe the walls of St. Mark's. Spoils came also from Palestine,

Istria, and earlier Christian churches that had been destroyed by the Huns in towns and cities north of Venice. This wealth, tastefully displayed and regarded as the common property

Fig. 323*b*.—St. Ambrose, interior looking toward apse. Note lantern on squinches. Apse, A.D. 789–824. Ciborium or altar canopy, 12th century. Width of middle aisle 38 feet, length 238 feet. (*Courtesy of Lesch-Carnegie.*)

of every citizen of the Republic of Venice, loses vulgarity and ostentation, particularly as the gold background glows richly varied and sparkling in the direct rays of the sun, lies softly warm and brown in the shadows, or is flushed delicately pink and purple where the reflected rays from the marble floor glance off the tesserae. To this brilliance must be added the richness of the embroidered, jeweled robes in which the mosaic figures are garbed.

Dispersion of the Domed Style in Aquitaine. At the end of the 10th century, the Venetians and the Syrians had established a trading colony in Lyons, France. From this point the domed architecture of the East spread into the Romanesque church building of Aquitaine. St. Front, in Perigueux, and the Cathedral of Angoulême furnish the two best examples of the combination of styles. In St. Front we have a cruciform church, obviously built upon the model of St.

each set between smaller colonnaded spires. In the interior of the Cathedral of Angoulême (Fig. 326) one notices the presence of pointed arches, again probably Saracenic or Armenian

Fig. 324.—Interior, St. Mark's, Venice, looking east. Largely 1063–1094. Width of middle aisle 38 feet, height of central dome 92 feet. (*Courtesy of Lesch-Carnegie.*)

Mark's in Venice. In the case of Angoulême, the long basilican plan dominates. A number of domes rise over the bays of the nave, however, though only the central one shows on the exterior (Fig. 325).

In the west façade of Angoulême we see one of the finest examples of Romanesque sculptural and architectural composition. The lower story consists of an arcade in five parts, built so as to frame a series of sculptured lunettes. The arches are repeated at the top, each enclosing some Biblical or heroic scene. Eastern connections are suggested by the arcades and the towers topped with tiled, conelike spires,

in origin. Here in central France, then, Eastern and Western building details united to produce the domed Romanesque style.

The Revival of the Pointed Arch and the Invention of the Flying Buttress. In southern France and Spain, wherever the Visigothic builders had been at work, the long, continuous barrel vault, like that at Naranco, was the earliest vault used for roofing. In the Church of Notre Dame du Port, at Clermont-Ferrand (Fig. 327a), as well as in the church at Issoire, and the Church of St. Sernin in Toulouse, heavy transverse arches, like those in contemporary Armenian churches, were used to support the central vault. The aisles, roofed with quadripartite vaults, such as those at St. Ambrose, often rose two stories in height, so that the upper roof, being half a barrel vault, buttressed the central

FIG. 325.—Cathedral of Angoulême, Aquitaine, largely first half of 12th century. Width about 60 feet, length about 250 feet. (*Courtesy of Lesch-Carnegie.*)

vault a little above the point at which it sprang from the wall. At Autun, where the same method was used, the entire central vault was pointed (Fig. 327*b*), assuming the shape of the pointed arch first found on the façade of the early Greek tomb near Pinara (Fig. 147*b*, Chap. VI). This pointed vault, carried by the Saracens to Cairo and used in Moorish building, traveled over into Spain and France.

In most of the early Romanesque churches of central France, although the central aisle is roofed with the barrel vault, either round or pointed, the lower side aisles are covered by clumsy ribbed or groin vaults. Thus the two styles of vaulting existed side by side until some ingenious individual discovered that the side buttressing in the upper story of the aisles needed strength only at the place where it met the interior ribs. One of the earliest examples

of this more effective method of vaulting appears on the exterior at Vézelay; another, the earlier perhaps, in the Abbaye aux Dames at Caen, built for Mathilda, the wife of William

FIG. 326.—Interior, Cathedral of Angoulême. Height of nave piers about 30 feet. For section of this type see Fig. 273*c*, Chap. XI. (*Courtesy of Lesch-Carnegie.*)

the Conqueror. Although at Vézelay the external buttresses, which brace the transverse ribs, lie hidden beneath the upper aisle roof, they function as true exterior or flying buttresses. Their existence makes possible the later development of the Gothic cathedral with its high, well-lighted nave.

The German Churches. The plans of German Romanesque churches show interesting variations from other contemporaneous church plans. Many of them, including those of the abbey churches at St. Gall, Laach, and Hildesheim, and of the cathedrals at Mainz and Worms, show apses at both ends. The chief entrances, as in the halls of the ancient Visigothic kings, stand at the side. The aesthetic effect of the two apses is one of the greatest tension, for the feelings of the worshipers are drawn between two possible extremes (Fig. 328).

The great cathedral at Mainz, although planned under Bishop Willigis in 996, was

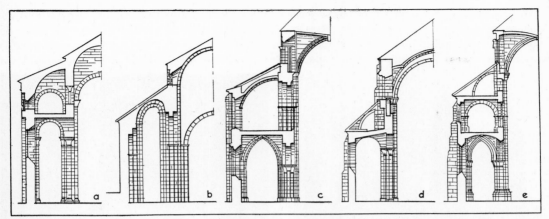

FIG. 327.—Romanesque constructive principles; development of the flying buttress. *a*, Notre Dame du Port, Clermont-Ferrand, Auvergne, 11 to 12th century; *b*, Cathedral of Vaison, Vaucluse, Provence, 12th century (type of Autun); *c*, St. Etienne (L'Abbaye aux Hommes), Caen, 1066 to 13th century; *d*, La Trinité (L'Abbaye aux Dames), Caen, 11th and 12th centuries; length 279 feet, length of transept 110 feet, width of façade 79 feet, width of middle aisle 26 feet, height about 50 feet; *e*, St. Germer de Fly, 1130–1160.

built, for the most part, by 1050. The exterior view shows an apse at each end, with great towers rising over the transept and the eastern apse flanked by smaller round towers. The towers have arcaded galleries like the one at Portoguaro, and similar galleries form decorative elements around the apses.

The Norman Church of William the Conqueror. In 11th-century Normandy, the Romanesque style reached its fullest development. The well-proportioned churches of this section unite all the typical details of Romanesque construction. The view of the interior of the Church of St. Étienne at Caen (Fig. 329), built about 1066 for William the Conqueror, demonstrates the logical severity and refinement of the Romanesque at its best.

Because of the presence in Normandy of leaders of the great monastic orders, many of whom had come from Italy, the Norman churches show great affinity for the constructive features of the Lombard churches. At St. Étienne, the piers and vaulting shafts, the nave arcade and triforium galleries copy models set by Lombard churches, but the clerestory and nave vaulting soar far beyond the aspirations of Lombard masters.

The illusion of height is aided by the vaulting shafts rising unbroken from the floor and terminating in capitals from which spring the ribs of the vault. As the central rib of a bay is a true arch, the diagonal ribs must form flat arches. Fearing to trust such a low vault, the builders strengthened it by the introduction of transverse ribs springing from intermediate vaulting shafts. Thus the ceiling compartment became sexpartite, or six-parted. This final development in vaulting, when coupled with the practice of using the pointed arches inherited from the central French churches, served to introduce the true Gothic, for with the high central arch the entire vault could be pointed.

At Caen, the interesting lights and shadows of the ceiling are brought out by the row of clerestory windows, which open upon a narrow gallery. The spacious triforium gallery, also lighted by windows, can accommodate large masses of the congregation. The decorative moldings, confined to the clerestory windows and gallery border, like many of the capitals, consist of simple fret carvings and interweave, such as one might have found upon the ships of William the Conqueror. The entire structure breathes an almost military air.

The Decorative Forms of the Romanesque Churches. The architectural decoration of the Romanesque churches originated in four different ways. Some was obviously derived from de-

Fig. 328.—Cathedral of Worms, 12th century. Width about 90 feet, length of transept 120 feet. (*Courtesy of Lesch-Carnegie.*)

generate, geometricized, classical rinceaux and egg-and-dart borders. Much of it, however, was truly technomorphic and architectonic in origin. The design formed by retaining the pattern of the diagonal beams on Saxon towers furnishes an example of this second type. A third origin lay in the backgrounds of Persian and Saracenic buildings. The church at Sahagùn in Spain, for example, used pilasters and false arcades copied from similar ornaments on the outside of ancient Sassanian and Persian palaces. In some cases, when the engaged arcades had degenerated and lost their meaning, the arches alone were retained under the eaves, as corbeled tables. The roof then appears to rest upon a floating arcade instead of upon something connected with the ground. Seeing this,

the later Scholastic philosophers could have said that the upper part of the church represented the Heavenly City of God.

Architectonic ornament that originated in

Fig. 329.—Interior, St. Étienne (L'Abbaye aux Hommes), Caen, c. 1066 to 13th century. Length about 350 feet. Sexpartite vaults, c. 1135. (*Courtesy of Clarence Ward.*)

Persia, Armenia, or Byzantium was usually accompanied by plant designs (Fig. 330). Wherever obvious wooden origins predetermine the ornament, however, we find instances of human or animal interweave, such as will be discussed later in connection with the portal sculptures at Moissac. The decorations of Lombard and Spanish porches, with their crouching lions, seem direct derivatives of ancient Syrian palace architecture. Many of the symbols, such as the signs of the zodiac, were probably derived from gravestones of the followers of the Persian god Mithras. A common subject, the *psychomachia*, or battle of the virtues and vices, shows iconography of Eastern origin.[1]

[1] Originally, the *psychomachia* was described by the Roman bishop, Prudentius, but most of the legendry that accompanies the story seems to derive from Manichaean Persian sources. In Manichaeism the primal man gave his five sons to the Sons of Darkness to be eaten, but the evil spirits were slain by Adamas, a belligerent hero aided by another king of Light, called the "King of Glory," who was helped by the King of Honor. Here three

The Picturesque Forms of Romanesque in the Russian Churches. At the end of every period of artistic development, we have found appearing a certain picturesque style that used all the origi-

Fig. 330.—Detail, western portal, Blazemont, showing foliate design of Neo-Persian origins and psychomachia. (*Courtesy of A. Kingsley-Porter, Romanesque Sculpture of the Pilgrimage Roads.*)

nal fundamental designs, seemingly without comprehension of their meaning. This phenomenon has come to be called the "baroque" movement in a style. Romanesque-Byzantine domed churches, so plentiful in Eastern Europe during the 12th century, were paralleled in the newly Christianized Russia of the 14th and 15th

centuries. St. Basil's Church in Moscow (Fig. 331), built in the 15th century, furnishes a late example of the Russian domed style. Around a central tower cluster a number of domes

Fig. 331.—St. Basil's Church, Moscow, 15th century. (*Courtesy of Lesch.*)

whose ornament shows Byzantine, Slavic, and Persian motifs. With their engaged arcades, corbel tables, and zigzag ornaments thrown out of normal Romanesque proportion, they furnish a museum of all possible types of Viking, Byzantine, and Mongol design. In the midst of this heterogeneous decoration, the church re-

light gods overcame spirits of darkness. These light gods called into existence twelve virtues: Sovereignty, Wisdom, Victory, Reconciliation, Purity, Truth, Faith, Long-suffering, Rectitude, Beneficence, Justice, and Light. Next, Adamas, like Gilgamesh and Beowulf, conquered an evil she-demon, and pierced her heart with his spear. This feminine demon, called "Az," personified greed, personal craving, avarice, concupiscence, and lust. She is called in the Manichaean prayer Tarhish "the insatiable shameless envy." The Manichaeans conceived God as consisting of three spirits, (1) the friend of light, (2) the great architect, and (3) the *spiritus vivens* or living spirit, coming as a "pure marvelous wind which is a white dove." This living spirit had five sons, the first Pity, the envoy of light; the second Good Faith, who was the king of ten heavens; the third Contentment, called Adamas, who overthrows demons; the fourth Patience, who, like Atlas, holds up the sky; and the fifth Wisdom, who creates brightness. It remained for the Christians, who fought Manichaeism, to place the virtues or sometimes knights above the vices, in the act of conquering them, upon the cathedral portals. With this change, however, there must have gone into the Christian mind much of the old Manichaean associational values that animate virtuous characters in the later Protestant morality plays.

Fig. 332.—Bronze plate from door, St. Zeno, Verona, second quarter of 11th century. (*Courtesy of Mrs. A. Kingsley-Porter and Clarence Kennedy.*)

mains a central tower church, on the old Norwegian model. The builders—half-Viking, half-Mongol—here constructed a fantastic parody distantly related to the earlier Romanesque styles.

Romanesque Sculpture

The characteristic wood carvings from Viking ships and Norwegian churches, with the addition of realistic figures transposed into bronze and stone, constitute Romanesque sculpture. A detail from the bronze plates bolted to the door of the Church of St. Zeno in Verona displays the barbaric, almost savage nature of this style (Fig. 332). The nearest face in the illustration shows the same angular carving with the same sharp contrast between light and shade as the Scythian and Siberian bronzes. Since at the time of Charlemagne Verona was inhabited by the Avars, a Mongoloid people, it seems plausible to find there such an expression of the more barbaric nature of the Asiatic plainsman.

Bishop Bernward's Bronze Doors. In south-German sculpture a similar primitivism appears in the bronze doors and candlestick cast for Bishop Bernward of Hildesheim. This powerful cleric, having visited Rome in the year 1001, decided to emulate the ancients. Bringing together a group of bronze founders, he sought to have the wooden doors of a Roman church rivaled by doors of bronze, and one of the Imperial victory columns cast into a monumental paschal candlestick.

One panel from the doors (Fig. 333) displays in its pictorial composition the quality of interweave that later dominated Gothic figure sculpture. The pointing figure of God directs the gaze beyond the figure of Adam to that of Eve who, having plucked the apple of Paradise, points to the serpent. This dramatic suggestion of the transmission of a thought follows the model set by the Psalter of Utrecht and repeats the motif of the interwoven trees.

Lyric Expressionism and the School of Languedoc.

In the West Frankish territory of Languedoc a more monumental type of sculpture came into existence toward the end of the 11th century. Here characteristics of northern and Saracenic

FIG. 333.—Bronze doors of Bernward at Hildesheim, panel showing Adam and Eve in the garden, A.D. 1007–1015. (*Courtesy of Lesch.*)

cenic styles united with the lyric quality of the Utrecht Psalter. This is shown in the sculpture of the south portal of St. Pierre of Moissac, particularly on the *trumeau*, the central pillar that supports the arch above the double door (Fig. 334). The face of the *trumeau*, with its interwoven lions and vine, protects an elongated figure of one of the prophets.

The prophet musicians seated above the lintel display a lively curiosity in the *Majestas Domini*, or Christ in Glory, which forms the center lunette composition. The little animals and the figure of St. Peter attached at the side of the door bear no direct connection with the lines of the architecture. These appliquéd figures, characteristic of some north-Italian churches, also suggest possible connections with similar figures on the faraway Christian churches of Armenia.

The figure of the prophet Isaiah on the portal of the church at Souillac (Fig. 335) is the most expressive piece in the entire school of Languedoc. This figure, designed upon a geometric plan, has a vigor that seems about to send him leaping from his place.

The Massive Character of the East Frankish, or German, School. The East Franks, who in their manuscript painting had developed more solid

Fig. 334.—South portal and trumeau, St. Pierre of Moissac, first half of 12th century. (*Courtesy of Clarence Ward.*)

figures than those in the Utrecht Psalter, displayed a corresponding sculptural style. Solidity of form, quieter pose, and a more naturalistic drapery replace the animation of

FIG. 335.—Isaiah, detail of portal, Notre Dame, Souillac, 12th century. (*Courtesy of Lesch-Carnegie.*)

the Languedoc school. The 13th-century figure of the Archangel Michael from the cathedral in Bamberg epitomizes this German style (Fig.

336). Here the patron of the crusaders has at last taken the place of Beowulf destroying the dragon. His heavy limbs and features show a matter-of-factness that completely dominates

FIG. 336.—Archangel Michael from choir, cathedral in Bamberg, 13th century. (*Courtesy of Metropolitan Museum of Art.*)

the interweave of the draperies, which now cease to show true vigor and dynamic continuity. The upper robe, carved in naturalistic fashion, is not in unity with the lower part, which keeps to the northern style.

The Climax of the Romanesque Style in the Western Portal at Chartres. The cathedral portal, as we have already seen in the development of the Romanesque style, developed in Provence and Burgundy, where it was definitely a modification of the narthex. It took ever a more important part in Gothic building, expanding its function until it absorbed the entire lower story of the façade. We have seen how the arcaded façade of the Cathedral of Angoulême served as a show place for sculpture (Fig. 325). As the Gothic developed, the sculpture became more an integral part of the architecture until the human form blended with the decorated surface. At this point the Gothic stands nearer to the Oriental than to the Greek, for Oriental figure sculpture on temples is lost in the deco-

FIG. 337.—Central portal sculpture, west façade, Chartres Cathedral, Glorification of the Saviour, A.D. 1145. (*Courtesy of Clarence Ward.*)

rative effect. In the Greek temple the sculpture was always framed, and its function as human form was enhanced.

The climax of Romanesque sculpture appears in the magnificently ordered arrangement and advanced form of the figures on the west portal of Chartres Cathedral (Fig. 337). This composition, completed in 1145, drew upon the services of stone carvers from both East and West Frankish schools. Not only does the late Romanesque style find place on this façade, but, in details of the ornament, many elements of Viking and Oriental designs also appear. Here we have a complete demonstration of the final triumph of Christianity over the less civilized northern spirit.

The central portal contains a *Majestas Domini*

—Christ seated in the *mandorla*—surrounded by the signs of the four Evangelists. Above him and on each side in the reveals of the arch rest the figures of angels and prophets. At a distance where small details cannot be perceived, these little figures seem part of a leafy foliage arising from the trunks of the lower portal branching overhead.

Each reveal above the doorway rests upon what at first glance appears to be a Corinthian capital. Close study shows that these seeming plant forms actually include many little figures under canopies. Each engaged column of the portal, carved with a strong technomorphic pattern, carries the statue of some abbot or abbess, king or queen, who had contributed to the building of the church. These statues have realistic portraitlike faces, although they may actually be symbolic. Lacking the massiveness of the East Frankish style and the vigor of the West Frankish, the figures, though well composed, stand closer to the style of the Bayeux tapestry. Every detail contributes to the regularizing, unified effect of the whole.

The face of the Christ shows that something like the process of idealization observed in the growth of Greek sculpture has taken place in the north. If all the faces of the men on the columns below could be fused in one, the composite head would express the ideal displayed in the face of the Master. In its calm dignity and reserve of force, it compares favorably with the Apollo of Olympia and the Athena Lemnia. All the lines of the composition have been so arranged that they subtly draw attention to the majestic features.

Although the entire composition of all three portals balances formally upon the figure of Christ, another more linear motive seems to animate the whole. This does not consist of a battle around a central figure, as is the case in Greek pedimental sculpture, but the exposition of a life story—the episodes in the journey of Christ. The figures of the right bay, dedicated to the Virgin, represent the descent of Christ into the world; those of the left, His ascension.

On the right bay, the upper part of the lunette given over to the Madonna and angels has a complete balance (Fig. 338*a*). Below, the figures of the presentation of Christ display

FIG. 338*b*.—Portal of the Ascension, Chartres. (*Courtesy of Clarence Ward.*)

FIG. 338*a*.—West front, Chartres, Portal of the Virgin. (*Courtesy of Clarence Ward.*)

little action. One step lower, the action of the Annunciation and the scene of the birth of Christ has more vitality, but the total effect of this portal is one of calm. In contrast, the figures of angels and disciples witnessing the Ascension on the left portal (Fig. 338*b*) have an animation befitting such a scene of supernatural power. The figures filling the reveals of the portal of the Virgin impersonate the seven liberal arts necessary for the complete education of the mind. The outdoor labors of the months alternate with the changing signs of the zodiac on the opposite, more dynamic portal. Thus the two portals in their arrangement and association suggest that quality of appropriateness considered by Aristotle the *sine qua non* of the finest art.

In summary, the Romanesque sculpture presented by the west portal of Chartres demonstrates that there resulted from the union of Celtic expression in the vitalized line with the southern, more Classical rules of composition, based upon the human figure accompanied by a tendency toward the Oriental in the use of light and shade, a distinctive, essentially architectonic style. Contrasted with Classical sculpture, this, the precursor of the Gothic style, appears not as the sole reason for the building but as a component, though decorative, part of its structure. Modified by the necessity for dignity, and channeled by the magnificent vision of the City of God, the transcendental Celtic imagination has here created a monument that ranks with the finest of Greek transitional sculpture. However, it expresses energy, and a power approaching the Sublime, rather than human beauty.

FIG. 339.—Musical instruments, central portal, Cathedral Santiago de Compostela, Spain, 12th century. *a*, viol; *b*, zither; *c*, vielle or hurdy-gurdy; *d*, Irish harp; *e*, lute. (*Courtesy of A. Kingsley-Porter, Romanesque Sculpture of the Pilgrimage Roads.*)

Music

The Melodic Interweave of Northern Music. The Celto-Germanic peoples, like the early Greeks, conceived their natural folk music in combination with dancing and poetry of a strongly rhythmic character. From earliest times, however, Latin records of the Celtic peoples indicate that their musical design, like the pattern of their graphic arts, differed from the music of the Mediterranean folk in one particular. European music expresses an interweave of melodies and geometric dance patterns, in contrast to the simple, clear melodic line rising above single chords, and the single-line dance in the two-dimensional pictorial composition of the southerners. The musical term used to describe this new phenomenon is "polyphony," or the movement of several voices. Regulated and recorded in a graphic scheme using the staff and notes indicative of time duration and so placed as to record the rise and fall of two opposed voices, sounding alternately contrasting harmonic and dissonant tones, this art is called counterpoint, or contrapuntal music. The development of a great variety of instruments (over thirty types) had taken place by the beginning of the 13th century (Fig. 339). This rich musical equipment, added to new refinements in the use of loud and soft tones, lent to the music produced by the Celto-Ger-

mans between the 4th and the 20th century powerful, new formal values analogous to the enriched color, depth, and atmospheric effects in contemporaneous European painting. The fundamentals of this fresh artistic revelation were laid down in the period under discussion.

The Basis of Modern Music in Folk Music and Ecclesiastical Modes. Two distinct elements unite in the development of European music. The first—a great body of folk music, including epic ceremonial marches, ballads, dances, and philosophical or religious poems—constitutes the raw material. The second derives from the power of the Christian Church, which continually strove to mold the folk music into patterns useful for enriching that dramatic presentation of Christian belief, the Mass. The Celto-Germans thought in terms of natural music dissociated from verse. The church always maintained that the measured melody was good; the unmeasured, inspired folk melodies, evil. To the modern mind, both elements carry equal weight.

It is of the greatest importance for us to remember that the great epic poems and ballads, as well as many of the other forms of verse, today studied as literature, arose as songs. Nor should we forget that the various movements of sonatas and symphonies first developed as dances. For this reason the appreciation of modern symphonic music and poetic or dramatic literature remains incomplete without some knowledge of their early forms in folk songs and dances. Significant improvements in musical instruments made during the period under discussion also account in large part for the greatest of European musical contributions —the development of new tonalities uniting in harmonic sequences with a truly Celto-Germanic interweave of contrapuntal melodies.

Instruments of Crusading Times. Celto-Germanic instruments arose from forms used by the Egyptians, Mesopotamians, Greeks, and Romans, with the possible exception of one—the viol, an ancestor of the violin—which may have been either a Celtic invention or an instrument of Eastern-Asiatic origin.

In the viol, a combination lute and lyre sound box, with measured lyric quality and singing tone, as well as organ associations of sustained harmonic chords, may be found the single instrument that more than any other expresses the spirit of Celto-Germanic music. A viol, or violin, in its power to suggest the sounds of laughing or crying, marching, dancing, and singing, compasses the greatest range of expression of all instruments. Not only this, but a quartet or chest of viols, as it is called, can suggest all the other instruments of the orchestra. The bass viol can be strummed to simulate the beat of a drum or the booming of a gong; the cello may be made to sound like a lyre or a cithara; the viola can imitate low flutes and recorders; the violins can pipe and whistle. Even the many tones in a chorus of human voices are not beyond the powers of these instruments.

The most important of the ancestors of the viol, the lute, arose in Egypt or Mesopotamia, perhaps from a primitive hand harp with curved neck and gourd sounding box. Early introduced into India and China, the lute was played in the first centuries of the Christian Era, with a cord of horsehair strung upon the bow. The Saracenic peoples of southern Russia and the Arabs of Syria and Africa used this two-stringed, bowed instrument, which they called the "re-

bec," as early as the 4th century. By the 6th century, the Welsh bards had combined with the rebec, a form of the Greek lyre, to make an instrument called the *crwth* (krooth), or "chrotta."

Although a clumsy instrument, the *crwth* added a system of six strings to the small thin-voiced rebec. It was so tuned that the two lowest strings sounded five notes apart in a sustained fifth that underlay the melodies played on the four upper strings. In Celtic music, the low masculine tones form a heavy drone bass underlying the upper, more feminine voices, which sing as though they would soar into the sky. Eventually, the *crwth* gave way to two other instruments—the fidel and the viol, in which the chief melodies might be played on either the upper or the lower strings. The fidel, a name taken from the Latin *fidelus* (faithful), became the constant companion of the jongleurs. The viol, possibly a later development of the *crwth* and the fidel, had six strings. The sound box, now shaped like a human torso, permitted the player to bring his bow down on either side, thus allowing greater freedom in melodic playing. With a range like that of the present viola, extending from bass C to high A above the upper, or treble, clef, this instrument combined bass and soprano voices.

The bagpipe, a form of mouth organ made by uniting the Greek aulos with an air reservoir in a skin bag, may have been invented in ancient Syria or the Grecian islands. Carried northward by Greek traders, Roman soldiers, or returning Gothic sea rovers, the bagpipes were perfected in Ireland and Scotland by the 10th century. The *crwth* and the bagpipe, like the church organ, make it possible to hold a sustained chord while developing the melody, or to play two melodies simultaneously. From the 5th through the 10th century, records show that organs made by Greek builders in Byzantium were given to various northern kings and emperors, including Charlemagne. One of these organs appears in the 9th-century manuscript, the Psalter of Utrecht (Fig. 308). Such instruments usually had two octaves of pipes with the following tuning—C D E F G A B C (middle) D′ E′ F′ G′ A′ B′ C′. The *crwths* and lyres of the time were tuned in the same way.

The harp, developed in Egypt and Mesopotamia, passed northward into Russia and into the British Isles, probably during the time of the folk migrations, between the 6th and the 8th century. Harps were tuned at first in the old Mesopotamian seven-toned scale, using the notes G A B C♯ D E F♯. Such a scale is also found on the oldest Scottish bagpipes. Between the measured scale the church developed on the organ and the remnants of the old modes that traveled with the Gothic folk music from Russia to Ireland, the church scale took precedence. Nevertheless, some of the old folk melodies still persist in Ireland, Scotland, and Finland.

The psaltery, an instrument carried by the Moors from Mesopotamia to Spain, figures in Europe after the 10th century. A triangular box crossed by strings of different length, this instrument developed into the Italian and English dulcimers and, eventually, into the piano. It differs from the harp in being played with little hammers, although as the zither, a combination of psaltery and cithara, it is shown being plucked.

The most complicated of all instruments developed in the crusading times was the vielle (*organistrum*), or hurdy-gurdy, the ancestor of the player piano. This combination of the viol and the lute is first pictured at the beginning of the 12th century. The vielle was played by means of a little crank at one end, which turned a resonating spindle operating against the six strings. The two lowest strings, sounding continuously as the spindle revolved, gave out a drone bass, while the upper strings, stopped by an ingenious keyboard arrangement copied from the organ, played the melody. The vielle, an instrument easy to play, is still used in Provence, the home of the troubadours.

Besides those described, numerous other instruments were in use by the end of the period under discussion. One 13th-century manuscript alone shows twenty stringed instruments played with or without the bow, besides a dozen wind instruments in metal, horn, and wood and many types of drums. In other sources there are allusions to double- and single-reed flutes, hornpipes and whistles, bells and drums, great hunting horns—oliphants—made from elephant's tusks, and bronze *luren*—fine-toned Viking trumpets sounding like large trombones. While at no time were all these instruments used together, they actually include representatives of all the instruments of the modern symphony orchestra.

Epic Songs and Ballads. The great epic poems, such as *Beowulf*, the *Kalevala* and the *Volsunga Saga*, were originally sung by comrades of the dead northern heroes as they rode and marched around the tumulus tombs or funeral pyres. In these early songs, the East Germans who had come in contact with the old Greek epic used a four-line strophe with a refrain. This sequence, when danced, later received the old French name, "*ballade*." An excellent example of the ballade style, although a very late one, is the song *Malbrough s'en va t-en guerre* (*To War Hath Gone Duke Marlborough*), to which Americans usually sing the words *We Won't Go Home until Morning.* The air of this lusty song probably has its source in Viking music. The Anglo-Saxon scops and gleemen used just such songs to lead the bands of sea rovers into battle. Similar songs were heard also in the great mead halls on winter nights when the warriors boasted of their conquests.

Strolling Players—The Jongleurs and Jongleuses. The home of the jongleurs and troubadours lay in the kingdom of Aragon—a remainder of the old Gothic Christian kingdom in northern Spain—and in Provence, that part of France which lies next to Spain and borders on the shores of the Mediterranean. Here, as has been suggested, Romanesque sculpture was most richly endowed with patterns from Oriental and classical sources. In Provence and northern Spain, the ancient Roman theatrical performances persisted until late in the 9th century. After the actors (*joculatores*) were banned by the church they wandered, as jongleurs and *jongleuses*, to the courts of the Germanic nobles, singing and acting the stories of the old Greek and Roman heroes—Hector of Troy, Alexander, or Julius Caesar. In the 10th and 11th centuries these strolling players revived bits of the old Roman comedies for the people of the towns, using music only incidentally or where a dance might enliven the action.

The Tenzone and the Chanson. In the 12th century, when the church succeeded in diverting all the martial energies of Gothic man into the warfare of the crusades, the singers, many of them now in the class of the nobility, accompanied the armies to the Orient, where they acquired numerous Oriental ideas of love. One of the types of musical debate (*estrif* or *débat*), called the *tenzone*, then came into being. In this, two or more singers vied with each other, each describing the charms of the woman whom he loved. During this period, man first noticed the principle of all musical composition; namely, that a melodic phrase to appear complete seems always to ask a question and give an answer.

Perhaps the best known of the jongleurs was Bernard de Ventadorn, who lived in the 12th century. This musician rose from the low rank of jongleur to the noble condition of troubadour. The church employed him to translate its miracle and passion plays, the tropes, into the common speech with appropriate musical accompaniments. The fact that the church should employ a man who had belonged to an almost outcast group is significant of the temper of the institution and explains, as well, the development of the Mass as an efficient drama.

The Troubadours and Troubars in Southern France and Italy. The singers of Aragon and Provence from the 11th through the 13th century were known as the troubadours and troubars. The troubadour called his art, which elevated music and poetry to a place above the action of the jongleurs, the *Gai Saber* or *Gaie Science*. In it, wit and a certain nobility of meaning replaced the

rougher humor of the jongleurs. During the 12th century, when the Church and the women formulated the codes of chivalry, it became customary for the nobles to compose music. The mottoes of these noble troubadours—"Love and Religion protect all virtues" or "My soul to God, my life for the King, my heart for my lady, my honor for myself"—denote clearly the civilizing influence of the church.

The chief contribution of the troubadours to European music lay in their union of three elements: the ancient Greek folk melodies; Arabic vocal ornamentation, called the "grace notes" of a melody; and the beginnings of harmony inherent in the old Gregorian church music. Even more significant, perhaps, the troubadours wove into their songs new, associational, instrumental effects that called to mind the songs of the birds and the sounds of woods and fields. These natural suggestions, along with poetic allusions to the sights, sounds, and odors of spring, partly interpreted in terms of musical effects, became the forerunners of the romantic art songs of the 19th century and the tone poems of the 20th.

Composition, or the science of music, troubadours considered of higher importance than excellence of performance. That science included a knowledge of the chief rhythms of speech, the rhythms of action, and the rhythms of melodic music. Among the troubadours themselves, however, the musician who could not only compose but accompany and sing his own compositions held highest rank. Many of the knightly troubadours employed jongleurs to accompany them on instruments; some hired singers, called *cantadors* or *musars*, as soloists.

Musical Forms of the Troubadours. The jongleurs who served as instrumentalists for the troubadours taught them a number of dance movements to use when entertaining. The first of these, a slow stately march around a circle hands joined, was called the "pavan," or "peacock." Next on the program came the galliard, a dance in three-quarter time. The German *May Song* (Fig. 340) probably comes the closest

Gen - tle May sends a - way jeal - ous - y and its pain. Re-
On the plain you will find glow-ing bright fra-grant flow - ers.

turn - ing now sweet joy will bring with love a - gain
There they blow with ev - 'ry wind in gold em'- rald bowers

Through green fields these gems so gay ap - pear - ing.

While in wak - en - ing woods spring's glad tones ring - ing.

One could ne'er know bet - ter theme for sing - ing.

Fig. 340.—*May Song* by Neidhardt von Reuenthal, c. 1200.

to the rhythm of this step. From the galliard are derived our minuet and, eventually, the two-step waltz.

After a galliard, the company might be induced to dance a ballade, like the *Duke Marlborough*, with everyone joining in the singing chorus. The ring then broke up into smaller circles of two or four couples, who danced a carol, or ring-around. The modern folk dances of Europe and America all arose out of these different dance forms, which combined the stately figures of the classical dance with the intricate, lively, geometric figures originating in the north. These dance forms later developed into the different movements of the sonata, the carol, or ballade, corresponding approximately to the allegro; the pavan, to the adagio; the *allemande* or the *sarabande*, to the rondo; and the galliard, to the minuet or the scherzo. Since they also correspond to the measures of the earlier Greek verse, we see the significant part played by the troubadours in transmitting to the Middle Ages the legacy of antiquity. The troubadours also perfected melodic, rhythmical songs called "canzonets" (lit-

tle *chansons* or short epic pieces), "serenades," and *aubades*, songs about the happenings of the day. Besides love songs, the troubadours sang rounds, pastorales, tenzones, and a proverb song of a single strophe.

The Trouvères and Minstrels in Northern France. In northern France and England, the singers who corresponded to the Provençal troubadours were known as trouvères and minstrels. Their creations differed from those of the southerners in two ways: (1) their songs remained nearer the crude folk level than did the artificial creations of the troubadours; (2) they cultivated the northern epic and lyric poetry, such as the Germanic lays and Bretonic romances. The trouvères and minstrels sang the Celtic stories of Arthur's Round Table and of the Welsh knight, Peredur, who became the Anglo-Saxon Percivale. They also sang of the fateful love of Tristan and Isolde—a medieval version of the Mesopotamian legend of Izdubar and Ishtar, which reached them perhaps through their Eastern contacts in Palestine. In the tale of Aucassin and Nicolette, more than in any other medieval romance, we find a fine appreciation of nature and a love so deep that Aucassin prefers Hell, where his lady may go, to Heaven, which is inhabited by monks. From the trouvères also came the *Song of Roland*.

The quality of the hardy chansons of the trouvères appears, as well, in the *War Song of the Normans*, which asks of each "gentle Norman" that he emulate the bravery of Roland.

> On, gentle Normans, think of Roland.
> Fair is his guerdon who died on the field.
> Left dead and honored here and hereafter,
> Leading in death the man who scorns to yield.
> Never in danger wail at our fathers.
> Free and undaunted, they thought of renown.
> Let us then prove ourselves worthy of Roland.
> On, gentle Normans, we strike for a crown.[1]

The Minnesingers in Germany. The German nobles employed singers who traveled to southern Italy and Sicily, as well as to the country of the trouvères in northern France. These minnesingers not only recorded the old German sagas but enlarged upon the Arthurian legends. Wolfram von Eschenbach, for example, developed the Percivale story into the epic romance of Parsifal, incorporating many elements from the Izdubar legends. Gottfried von Strassburg did the same for the story of Tristan and Isolde, while Kuerenberger von Aist sang the Nibelungen songs. The measures of the verses of Walther von der Vogelweide come to us in such a song as *Du Bist Mein, Ich Bin Dein*. His *A Song from Palestine*, written on the crusade, is in the ecclesiastical Doric mode, ending with the phrase, DCDEFED.

The Church and Musical Measure. Until the 13th century, the folk songs of the crusading northern folk were transmitted from musician to musician by ear. The great service of the church to medieval and modern music lay in its gradual development of the means for recording music in written form so that it would not be lost. The church, of course, had no interest in recording the folk music we have just studied, except, perhaps, in such a case as that of Bernard de Ventadorn, the jongleur who was invited to help popularize the mass

so that its ancient power would not diminish through constant innovation.

St. Ambrose, no longer contented with natural rhythmical patterns and needing, perhaps, to send his hymns to distant missions, used a type of verse in which the accents were strongly marked. His hymns called *cantus planus*, or "plain song," were written in iambic meter, with four accents so arranged that they created a perfectly alternating pattern between the arsis and the thesis within the bounds of eight syllables. He thus achieved a complete musical symmetry, beginning what came to be called "musical form."

The Greeks, it will be remembered, used letters of the alphabet (neumes) arranged in various positions over the text lines to indicate the rise and fall of the voice. The Byzantine musicians revised these letters into a series of cursive signs to indicate the melodic flow. By the 8th century, several systems of neumes were in use in Europe, some very close to Byzantine forms, such as those in the manuscripts of Lombard and German monasteries (Fig. 341a, b). One set of neumes used almost universally included eight signs. These signs in different combinations directed the singing master, who followed their movement with his hand as he led the singers, indicating by the gestures when the voices should rise or fall. This practice of directing by sign is called chironomy (Fig. 341b).

The next step in the development of present-day notation came from an abbott of the great monastery of Cluny—Odo, by name. Odo rediscovered the ancient Greek idea of placing letters above the words to be sung, and recorded a song using the letters, A, B, C, D, E, F, G, corresponding exactly to the same notes in our modern scale (Fig. 341a). An early 10th-century manuscript, in the Bodleian Library at Oxford, was written in Cornwall and used these letters to denote the keys on an organ that accompanied the voices.

In the 10th century, some unknown genius living in a Lombard monastery recognized the

[1] From *The Modern Music Series*, Book IV, by permission of Silver, Burdett & Company, New York.

FIG. 341.—Origins of modern musical notation (1000–1300). *a*, neume letters in manuscript written by Count Henry the Lame of Reichenau, about 1020, Vienna (Codex 2500); *b*, section of Easter trope, neumes suggesting chironomy or hand direction up and down the scale, about 1200, Cloister Neuberg, Austria (Ms 574); *c*, page from Guido d'Arezzo's *Treatise micrologus de disciplina artis musiche*, showing early attempt to record the flow of melody with neume letters above and below the F line, about 1200, Vienna (Codex 51); *d*, hymn in honor of St. John the Baptist as written in the 13th-century manuscript; note manuscript guide lines becoming useful as guide for placing neume notes, Vienna (Codex 2503); *e*, origin of syllable names of notes in Hymn to St. John, final stage, after 1700. (*Taken from A History of Music in Pictures by George Knisky, E. P. Dutton & Company, Inc., New York.*)

lack of definiteness in neume notation. Drawing a red line above the text to be sung, he gave it the value of Odo's note F, the fourth line in our bass clef. The old Gothic letter F eventually became the sign Ⅎ or Ɔ standing for the F, or bass, clef (Fig. 341*c*). From that time on, the neumes were written in relation to the red line, which stood for the low voices. Soon another musician, or perhaps the same man, added a yellow line above the verse with the letter C, which became in time 𝕭. This stood for the middle C, below the upper clef of our music, and was sung by the tenor. This second clef accommodated the range of tone used by the *crwth* and viol players and today is used for the viola part of the orchestra. The

soprana, or G, clef Ɠ = 𝄞 was a later development.

The Invention of the Staff by Guido d'Arezzo. It remained for a monk, Guido of Arezzo, to complete the invention of the staff (prototypes of clefs having been devised before) by uniting a four-lined staff, standing for four notes, with neumes changed into square notes, indicative still of the rise and fall of voice. With this staff, which sufficed for the octave of notes used in the plain song, the singer, without further instruction, could read directly from the sacred songbooks, or psalteries. Pope John IX, struck with the practicality of Guido's idea, insisted on its being used in all the monasteries.

Guido then composed a hymn in honor of

St. John the Baptist (Fig. 341*d*), patron of music, in the sixth, or Ionian, church mode. This mode, synonymous with our modern scale of C, was made up of the leading notes of the other five authentic modes. Guido used the syllables "ut, re, mi, fa, sol, la" (Fig. 341*e*). His pupils, singing the hymn over and over, fixed the tones so firmly in mind that they could locate any of the church modes accurately. The Italians of the 17th century finally used the term "do" for "ut," because it could be sounded more easily. In the 16th century, a fifth line added to the staff gave it the form in use today.

The Recording of Time in Music. After Guido's invention of the staff in 1050, the old neumic notes, whose different shapes indicated movement up or down, no longer seemed necessary. In the 12th century, Franco of Paris used these notes to indicate duration of time: the virga became the long note, or *longa;* the porectus, half as long, became the *brevis;* and the *currus* took half the value of the brevis, eventually corresponding to a measure of time a little over our quarter note. Finally, a double longa, or *maxima*, joined the group.

At that time, six types of verse employed by the troubadours were recognized as the trochaic, the iambic, the dactylic, the anapaestic, the spondaic, and the modus. The singers also recognized that all rhythm moved in two kinds of time—one, called the "double time," using two beats; the other, called "triple time," using three. The bars, lines drawn across the staff by the troubadours, added to the notes of different time value, thus came to indicate measures of time. The circle, perhaps taken from the triple beat of the round dance (called "perfect time"), and the half circle, standing for two beats (called "imperfect time"), then appeared at the beginning of the staff to indicate the rhythm employed. We still retain the half circle, or C, for two-two or four-four, common time. Black notes gave way to a combination of white and black, leading to the approximate note values used today.

The Development of Harmony. The great service of the church to the art of music lay in its perfecting a method by which the Celto-Germanic folk melodies might be recorded. Isidore, archbishop of Seville, about 600, wrote that harmonious music consisted "not only of a modulation of the voice but also of a union of sounds." He described two types of harmony, which he called "symphony" and "diaphony." Symphony, in the old Greek sense, meant a harmony produced by two notes sounding together in consonance; diaphony signified two notes sounding together in dissonance.

As Pythagoras had shown, consonance, or agreeableness of sound, arises when the vibrations produced by two tones in unison stand in the simple proportions of one to two, two to three, three to four, or four to five; that is, when the notes played are an octave, a fifth, a fourth, or a third apart. Dissonance arises from the use of other intervals. The first set gives rise to pleasant sounds, the second to unpleasant. Modern composers realize, however, that the dissonant intervals have the special value of suggesting motion, while the consonant intervals suggest rest. Insofar as life consists of both rest and motion, musical expression needs both consonance and dissonance. The rough war hymns and folk songs of the Celto-Germans contained natural dissonant combinations of sound. During the first centuries of written music, however, the church refused to record any but the consonant intervals. The earliest church music, furthermore, the *planus*, or plain song of St. Ambrose, was written in notes of the greatest possible time value. Thus in the history of music, as in the history of medieval architecture, we see the church striving to retard, regularize, and make stable, the wild northern character.

The Sequence and the "Dies Irae." The monk Notker Balbulus, who lived in the monastery of St. Gall about the year 900, in order to unite some of the folk melodies and the Greek ideas of music with the early Ambrosian hymns, developed a little melodic response by the congregation, using the Greek words "kyrie eleison," or the Hebrew "alleluia." These melodies, which were called "sequences," were derived from folk tunes. They were accompanied, after the Greek manner, upon the organ. Later writers

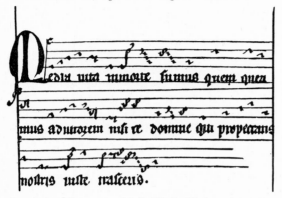

FIG. 342a.—Sequence, *Media Vita* by Notker, about A.D. 900. (From manuscript in Prague.)

made complete hymns of the interpolations. Six of these hymns, recognized by the church, are now sung on special occasions. They include the *Veni Sancte Spiritus*, by King Robert of France; *Victimae Paschali Laudes*, by Wipo; *Lauda Sion* and *Pange Lingua*, by Thomas Aquinas; *Stabat Mater*, by Jacob of Todi; and *Dies Irae*, by Thomas of Celano (Fig. 342). A final stage in the development of the sequences came when they were united with the old Greek and Hebrew practice of antiphonal singing.

The measured plain song having been connected with the melodic sequence so that one followed the other, the next step in harmonic development led toward a closer union of the two. Organum, or diaphony, where two voices move forward at regular intervals five notes apart, led eventually to descant, or counterpoint. This came about as the voices imitated the drone bass of the bagpipes and the *crwth*.

Descant and Counterpoint. In descant and counterpoint, both tenor and bass voices had equal value. Both carried distinct melodies, which moved forward simultaneously, producing varying degrees of consonance and dissonance. The church considered the octave the most consonant interval, the fifth next, and the

fourth next. Two notes a third apart were at first thought completely dissonant, although to modern ears the third seems a very pleasing interval.

Day of wrath, O　day of burn-ing,
Oh, what fear　shall it　en-gen-der,

Seer　and Sib-yl speak con-cern - ing
When the Judge shall come in splen-dor,

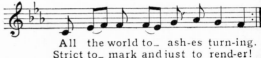

All　the world to_　ash-es turn-ing.
Strict to_　mark and just to　rend-er!

FIG. 342b.—Sequence, *Dies Irae* by Thomas of Celano, 11th century.

The earliest descant, as written in the 11th century, arose when the composer took the melody, called the *cantus firmus*, and by exactly reversing its direction produced a second melody, which he then combined with the first. Beginning with two notes an octave apart, he would move the upper one down and the lower one up, bringing them to a distance a fifth apart, and then to a fourth. He might even have the tenors and the basses sing the same note in unison, and then move them out again till they reached a fourth or an octave. The melody thus written, to contrast with the *cantus firmus* received the name "descant," from the French *déchanter*, meaning to sing apart. This movement of the melodies, note against note, came to be called "counterpoint." The principle, once discovered during the 13th century, led the musicians to unite three, four, and sometimes five parts, very much as we today combine the different instrumental voices in an orchestra. An example of descant from a 13th-century hymn illustrates what is meant by counterpoint in its simplest form (Fig. 343).

The Round, or Canon. Once the principle of counterpoint had been recognized by the church, it became apparent that an old form

Ver - bum_ bo - num et su - a - ve   Per - so - ne - mus il - lud A   ve.

FIG. 343.—*Verbum Bonum*, example of descant, the principle of counterpoint, 12th century.

of folk singing underlay the entire development of harmony. Just as the democracy of old Athens expressed itself in the polyrhythmic movements of the *ratta*, so the democracy of the northern folk emerged in the form of a round, danced and sung by three or more voices. The round *Three Blind Mice* illustrates this principle.

In a round, one voice sings the first line alone; a second voice then joins in, recommencing the same melody, and starting the first line just as the first voice has reached the second. When the first voice reaches the third line, a third voice begins the melody. Now the three voices move forward and, as each is singing a different section of the melody, the chords resulting produce an interweave of melodic lines.

The practice of arranging a little motif with separate words and melody in the drone bass was followed by many of the early troubadours. When a dissimilar melody is repeated in the bass below a set of other melodies in the upper voices, the piece is called a "motet."

Defects in Early Harmony. The early church writers lacked a sense of contrast in the progression of their melodies. In their attempt to keep all the parts moving they neglected to allow for the periods of rest. On the other hand, this music was part of the drama of the Mass, and the periods of rest came during the moments of significant action. Again, as far as the records inform us, there seems to have been no allowance for contrast in volume. We cannot be sure that the good musicians actually sang recorded intervals as written. Scotus Erigina, an English monk, in 880 explained that good organum called for prudence in rendering. All the defects frequently cited by music historians may be creatures of our own ignorance, for in

the last analysis, no one knows exactly how any of the songs were actually sung. One thing, however, is certain: many of the notes, if sung simultaneously as written, would produce discords. There is no evidence that the discords were other than accidental. There existed no idea of using chords of varying degrees of dissonance for musical dramatic effect.

Briefly summarizing, the northern monks of St. Gall, using modes and musical inventions of the ancient Greeks, reformed the folk melodies of the northern people into Roman Church modes and recorded them by means of a process that grew out of the Greek neume writing, or chironomy. The staff and notes standing for different time values also arose as part of the civilizing process of the church. Into the ancient church hymn forms, such as the Ambrosian hymns and plain songs, came the melodic sequences of the Greek Church and the folk music of the troubadours. From the union of all these elements arose modern European music. The connected groupings of dances led to the orchestral forms of the sonata and the symphony; the sequences to chorales and oratorios, while the verse, both ecclesiastical and secular, contributed to the development of European drama.

Drama

The drama persisted throughout the Dark Ages, connected with worship in the Eastern Christian Church as well as under the patronage of Celto-Germanic leaders.

Drama during the Germanic Invasions. Theodoric the Ostrogoth encouraged the mimes at Rome and had his vizier Cassiodorus reconstruct the old playhouses in the ancient capital city. The Emperor Theodosius also patronized the stage and, in Constantinople, Justinian, who married an actress, gave much attention in his code of laws to the treatment of the theatrical profession.

In the Visigothic kingdom of Spain, Seville had theatrical performances as late as the 7th century. These were quite unlike the old classical drama. The *skene* became a house on a platform with an orchestra around it. On this platform the comic and tragic actors chanted, while the mimes, perhaps pantomimes, danced the action below in the orchestra. One writer of the time gave to these choral dancers the name *histriones*, from which comes our word "histrionic."

Charlemagne, endeavoring to revive the customs of the old Roman Empire, had dramas given at his court in Aix-la-Chapelle. Devil masks, called *larves demonorum*, figured in such performances. These masks either originated in some of the grotesque Etruscan underworld figures or were brought into Europe by invading Mongols. Most of those today in the museums of Tyrol resemble in many details the Tibetan devil masks. The concept of the devil as a dragon, which came into European poetry at this time, called for the use of such masks.

By the time of Charlemagne, the European monasteries had recognized and used the remnants of the old Roman theatrical troupes known as the *gestoures* and jongleurs. The kings of the time had not only their own private *gestoures* and mimes but those in Germany employed men called "spelars," the equivalent of the modern German word meaning player. Some of these sang dramatic songs, such as *The Pride of Life* and the *Harrowing of Hell*, essentially religious *estrifs* or *débats* (cf. p. 405). Poems of this nature revolved around a dramatic debate between the forces of good and evil.

Byzantine Influences in 9th-century English Drama. That some of the dramatic poems were actually produced in the churches is highly probable. A Lombard bishop, Liudprand, from Cremona, who visited Byzantium between 949 and 969, wrote that a play-sermon (homily) about Elijah was then being produced in the Church of Hagia Sophia, which had been turned into a theater. In these dramatic sermons, which on occasion could be expanded into active performances, the scenes of the Annunciation, the Nativity, and the Descent into Hell were distinctly influenced by earlier character types from the secular theater. Joseph becomes the type of the jealous husband; the devil is the boasting soldier, *miles gloriosus;* and the clown of the late Roman mimes can be recognized in Orcus, the guardian of Limbo. Scholars now believe that some of the Western mystery plays were inspired by these earlier Byzantine sermons. An Anglo-Saxon poem, *The Christ*, tells the story of the birth of Jesus in the style of the Teutonic epic.

Similar poems, in the hands of Tutilo and Wipo, the monks of St. Gall and Hildesheim, became the dramatic tropes which played an important part in the Christmas and Easter services. The mimes may also have borrowed copies of these plays from the monasteries, very much as the troubadours and trouvères used church music as a basis for some of their creations.

The Tropes. In the 10th century, monasteries, including St. Gall, Einsiedeln, Limoges, Rouen, Beauvais, and some of the English establishments, produced extra dramatic parts in the Christmas and Easter Mass. The *Concordia Regularis*, a book of monastic exercises, calls such action a "trope." The first of these was a Christmas trope written by Tutilo in 1024. This included a bit of action showing the coming of the three wise kings, garbed in regal style followed by servants bringing gifts. Christmas also had another trope, called *Pastores* (Shepherds). Priests and choirboys played the chief parts. Following these Christmas tropes, Wipo, another monk, created an Easter trope known as the *Quem Quaeritis* (Whom Seek Ye?). This consisted of a song alternating between three women who approach the tomb of Christ and an angel waiting there. The angel sang: *Quem quaeritis in sepulchro, O Christicole?* (Whom do you seek in the tomb, O Christians?). To which the women answered: *Jesum Nazarenum crucifixum, O Coelicola!* (Jesus of Nazareth, who was crucified, O celestial One!). The rest of the Easter story follows.

At the time the tropes were first sung, Irish monks attempting to Christianize the barbarian Germanic tribes, used this drama to present Christianity in an interesting way. The simple action took place in front of the spectators. Here we notice the first great difference between medieval and ancient drama. In the Middle Ages nothing was suggested. The classical writer, in contrast, relied upon literary implication.

The Staging of the Play. Curious mistakes in the interpretations of old classical manuscripts led to interesting developments in the staging of plays. It was thought, for example, that the comedies of Terence called for a house, or *domus*, in which the chief protagonist, seated, recited the play, while the actors below interpreted in pantomime. This separation of idea and execution returns the drama to its very earliest beginnings. In time, the *domus*, put on wheels, became the traveling stage of the medieval miracle plays.

The trope, on the other hand, had the various parts of the cathedral as stage sets, the main action taking place directly before the altar. Herod and Pilate, representing the forces of evil, stationed themselves beside the pulpit at the right, in the position that the present-day actor calls "stage left." Later on, in the outdoor mystery plays, this side became the location of the entrance to Hell, usually symbolized by a great, gaping dragon's head.

Stage costumes of the period show the persistence of the traditional ideas of the *phylax*, or fool, with the ass's ears and the coxcomb, later to become Shakespeare's character, Bottom. Other evidence indicates the retention of the traditional costumes of the ancient mimes.

Summary

Medieval Europe, north and south, developed a number of highly individualistic styles of art between the fall of the Roman Empire in 450 and the rise of the modern spirit of scientific inquiry in the late 15th century. These styles are dominated by two general form tendencies, which vie with each other for precedence. In southern Europe, where, because of easy access to remains of ancient architecture and sculpture, the influence of classic art predominated, the classical style appeared again and again, as various artists were commissioned by church or state to build monuments on the imperial models. Charlemagne, who dreamed of uniting the Eastern and Western churches of the Roman Empire, brought building details from the Ravennate churches, particularly San Vitale, in order to erect at Aix-la-Chapelle what he considered a truly Roman building. This happened in the 9th century. Two hundred years later, Bishop Bernward of Hildesheim tried to bring Roman art to southern Germany, and planned a triumphal column and bronze doors similar to models he had seen in Rome. Under the Hohenstaufen emperor, Frederick II, in the 12th century, there came in Sicily and southern Italy a rebirth of classical form, in both sculpture and architecture. Romanesque sculpture in Provence and Germany felt strongly the influence of classical and Byzantine prototypes.

On the other hand, from earliest prehistoric times the folk art of Northern Europe had produced a style of ornament that was unclassical in being nonhumanistic, unbalanced, and more or less uncontrolled. This ornament emphasized abstract lines of force, using intricate patterns rather than human representation. It appears to some extent in Minoan times on vases of Danubian origin, in 5th-century Greek sculpture here and there, and then to a greater degree in Hellenistic times, as the Celto-Germanic northern nations moved into the area occupied by the old Mediterranean stock.

Throughout the times of the folk wandering,

these patterns appear in Viking ships and wooden church building. In the Romanesque architecture of the 10th and 12th centuries, northern art retreats to a purely ornamental position before the superior building methods of the Comacini, guilds of stone masons from the south who were skilled in late Roman and Byzantine methods of construction. As, with the help of the Saracenic pointed arch, the northern builders mastered the art of stone building, they transformed it, along with any last vestiges of the Roman architectural decoration, into a new style—the Gothic, predicated on models from wooden ship and church building. This northern, or Gothic, style carries with it new advances in painting, first in stained glass, with its interest in chroma, then in panel painting.

The greater tension of the northern spirit, striving to find itself in terms of universals, broke the bonds of plausible graphic representation and, expanding beyond architecture, created out of a union of melodic phrase and harmonious chords the art of counterpoint. This new form, with the development of orchestral instruments and the organ, made possible the later symphonies. The new rhythmical tensions, in turn, created a new form of drama —the miracle and mystery plays—and these, with the music and colorful stained glass, were to make of the community cathedral a home for all the arts. Finally, out of the union of the two artistic styles, the Classical and the Gothic, arose a new concept of aesthetics, which ex-

panded upon the classical models of Aristotle and Plato, as the Christian religion added its mystical philosophy, giving to them a distinctly transcendental flavor.

Bibliography

STRZYGOWSKI, J.: *Origins of Christian Art*, Clarendon Press, Oxford, 1923.

SULLIVAN, SIR EDWARD: The Book of Kells, The Studio Publications, Inc., New York, 1933.

HAMMETT, RALPH W.: *Romanesque Architecture of Western Europe*, Architectural Book Publishing Company, Inc., New York, 1927.

JACKSON, T. G.: *Byzantine and Romanesque Architecture*, Vol. II, Cambridge University Press, 1920.

RUSKIN, JOHN: *St. Mark's Rest*, Home Book Co., New York.

ADAMS, HENRY: *Mont St. Michel and Chartres*, Houghton Mifflin Co., Boston, 1913.

Beowulf, translated by J. Duncan Spaeth, Old English Poetry, Princeton University Press, Princeton, 1922.

The Song of Roland, translated by M. Sherwood, Longmans, Green & Co., New York, 1938.

ALLEN, PHILIP SCHUYLER: *Romanesque Lyric*, University of North Carolina, Chapel Hill, 1928.

13th Century Romances, translated by William A. Morris, Charles Scribner's Sons, New York, 1914.

BROWN, G. B.: *Arts and Crafts of Our Teutonic Forefathers* G. T. Foulis & Co., Ltd., London, 1910.

VON SCHEFFEL, VIKTOR: *Ekkehard* (novel), edited by W. H. Carruth, Henry Holt & Company, Inc., New York, 1895.

Recordings

Ballads and *War Songs* of the Normans, V 20152 a & b.

Troubadour Songs, V 20227 Decca 20158 a.

Minnesingers, Decca 20158 b.

Beginnings of sacred polyphonic music, V 20897 b Decca 20157 b.

Sequences—including *Dies Irae*, V 21621.

CHAPTER XIII

The Gothic Style in North and South

Animated, dearest son, by these covenants with the virtues, thou hast confidently approached the house of God, hast decorated with the utmost beauty ceilings or walls with various work, and, showing forth with different colours a likeness of the paradise of God, glowing with various flowers, and verdant with herbs and leaves, and cherishing the lives of the saints with crowns of various merit, thou hast, after a fashion, shown to beholders everything in creation praising God, its Creator, and hast caused them to proclaim him admirable in all his works. Nor is the eye of man even able to decide upon which work it may first fix its glance; if it beholds the ceilings, they glow like draperies; if it regards the walls, there is the appearance of paradise; if it marks the abundance of light from the windows, it admires the inestimable beauty of the glass and the variety of the most costly work. But if perchance a faithful mind should behold a representation of our Lord's passion expressed in drawing, it is penetrated with compunction; if it beholds how many sufferings the saints have bodily supported, and how many rewards of eternal life they have received, it quickly induces the observance of a better life; if it regards how much rejoicing is in heaven, and how much suffering in the flames of hell, it is animated by hope for its good actions, and is struck with fear by the consideration of its sins.[1]

THE ABOVE words of the monk Theophilus express better than do any others written in the Middle Ages the meaning and purpose of the Gothic cathedral. Consideration of the questions how closely the artist approximated this ideal and with what means he achieved his effect, constitutes the substance of this chapter.

Gothic construction symbolizes man's gallant attempt to encompass nature and conquer the forces in space through communal activity. The art of crusading times resulted, in greater part, from the efforts of cloistered monks or knightly singers. The mature Gothic style of the cathedrals arose from the townsfolk under the leadership of the guildsmen, architects, and clergy who had grown from the ranks of Celto-Germanic tribesmen. The rise of the Gothic cathedral parallels the development in late medieval European history of new consciousness of the importance of the individual. Under great individual leaders, the church structure became a highly decorated symbol of spiritual life in rising trade cities. Thus the Gothic cathedral may be said to have resulted from the united energies of bishops, guilds, and architects.

The very richness of the result would suggest that much of the action was carried on not under the goad of fear but through the union of veneration and love with a joy in detailed craftsmanship. The luxuriance and variety of the cathedral ornament became the dominating element in all the other Gothic arts between the 13th and the 16th century. The paintings and tapestries on castle walls copied its windows; the jewelry, its crockets and finials; the civic architecture, its pointed arches and spires. Hence, of all structures to be studied in Gothic architecture, the cathedral stands first.

---

[1] From *Essay on Various Arts*, Book III, Preface, by Theophilus (Roger of Helmershausen), translated by Robert Hendrie, John Murray, London, 1847.

A careful examination of its detail will make clear the essential features of all other medieval artistic creations.

Social and Political Backgrounds

The Three Estates: Nobles, Clergy, and Bourgeoisie. Three political groups battled for power in the late Middle Ages. The first group, an aristocracy, was composed of kings and nobles, descended for the most part from Germanic chieftains. The second, the church, represented the body of ancient spiritual knowledge which, uniting with the religious elements of classical humanism and Roman legalism, made itself the strongest single factor for controlling the emotions of the people. The third group, the townsfolk, or *bourgeoisie*, composed of shopkeepers, craftsmen, and petty officials, gained increasing importance after the 14th century, when first the church and then the nobility gradually lost prestige.

The great days of the church in crusading times came after the rule of Pope Gregory VII. Elevated to its maximum power by this spiritual monarch, the church under Pope Urban organized the first crusade in 1095. The end of the crusades in 1204 saw the church under Pope Innocent III, pitted equally against the Hohenstaufen emperor, Frederick II. The fourth crusade, which destroyed Byzantium, opened the way for new commercial and cultural exchange between the towns of Europe and the Orient. The consequent rise of the great trading centers in the 13th century, fostered the development of a new class, the *bourgeoisie*, who, siding at times with the nobility, at times with the church, eventually outmaneuvered its two rivals.

The church suffered its greatest humiliation after 1309, in a period called the "Babylonish Captivity," inaugurated when Pope Clement was forced to retire to Avignon, France. There, for 70 years, the popes lived under the domination of the French kings until, in the Great Schism of 1378, two popes were elected—one, Urban VI, residing in Rome, the other, Clement VII, in France. The schism lasted until 1418.

While the tremendous forces of the time struggled for equilibrium, Gothic art flowered in the cathedrals. The universities grew, and the intellectual revival emanating from the cathedral cities of the north awakened an almost scientific interest in realism which, combining with the Italian revival of classical ideas, was to culminate in the Renaissance. The three and a half centuries of cathedral building, between 1150 and 1492, mark the fullest development of the Gothic style.

Towns and Guilds. As early as the 11th century, the *bourgeoisie*, seeking exemption from the unreasonable taxation of the feudal lords, formed trade guilds or mutual protective associations. By the 13th century, the Florentine *arti*, or guilds, joining together, succeeded in obtaining a charter for their city. In England, France, and Germany, similar incorporated towns, whose government represented the guilds, bought the privilege of exemption from feudal taxation and achieved industrial monopoly for their products. Thus the roots of modern capitalism may be said to have got a start in the guild system established in the Middle Ages.

Pragmatic and astute, although still superstitiously religious, the townsmen partially freed themselves from the domination of the church, represented by the prince bishops. Imbued with civic pride, they usually united with the bishops in building the great cathedrals, which not only were dedicated to the service of the Deity but also to some extent served to advertise the town. In Italy, where an anticivic class of dispossessed nobles existed as late as the 15th century, the struggle to retain the old aristocratic privileges led to innumerable clashes between townsmen and nobles, which persisted in all bitterness late into the Renaissance. In the northern cities, such as Bourges, the *bourgeoisie* often besieged their bishop in his castle. In many of the English and German cities, however, as in the French town of Chartres, the relation between townsmen, nobles, and clergy was all that could be desired.

The many guilds that came into being fall into two divisions: traders' guilds and craft guilds. The traders' guilds regulated the commercial monopolies in a given town. These organizations soon attempted to control all the industries of the town in which they held power. The man of the Middle Ages knew no other form of industrial labor than that of the collective guild privilege, which gave the guild that most quickly won control—a complete monopoly in labor.

The craft guilds probably grew up around the houses of the nobles. At Chartres, for example, both the count and the bishop employed artisans who, through particular skill in their craft, gradually freed themselves and organized guilds. Each trade lived in its own quarter of the city and had a guild hall or lodge where the masters met to decide upon matters of policy. Strongest among the northern guilds were the stonemasons, shipwrights, and butchers. In the southern cities jewelers, armorers, carpenters, saddlers, and painters wielded little less power. Here, then, we find practitioners of the servile arts, or handicrafts, receiving equal privileges with other solid citizens—butchers, bakers, and candlestick makers. All aspired to good workmanship and integrity of production on a handicraft level, rather than to lofty artistic creation.

The craft guilds functioned under the leadership of master workmen who had achieved their position through a combination of superior ability and political acumen. The masters employed apprentices, each of whom served from five to ten years before he was allowed to produce some masterwork that should entitle him to the privileges of a master's position. In Germany the custom of the *Wanderjahr*, or year's journey, gave the apprentice an opportunity to visit the workshops of other cities before completing his masterpiece. Naturally, the masters vied with one another to hold the best apprentices. In this feature of the guild system lay the beginnings of the idea of free

trade. By the end of the 13th century, the towns of England, Germany, and France had become completely organized around regional industries controlled by the guilds.

The Effect of the Guilds on Art. With security of position and leisure time, the guildsmen began to patronize the arts. In the 15th century, the Meistersinger Hans Sachs, a member of the cobbler's guild in Nuremberg, collected hundreds of the ancient minnesongs into a number of operas. The guildsmen of Chartres paid for and created many of the storied windows of the cathedral. The guildsmen of Coventry and Norwich formed mystery cycles of plays.

Art, as a skillful craft arising from this industrial guild training, contributed much to the decorative character of cathedral and town hall. While the creative inspiration of Gothic building came, in part, from the cloisters, and the symbolic meaning of the scenes represented was supplied by ecclesiastics and nobles, the honesty of craftsmanship which has kept the cathedrals standing and which has endowed Gothic panel painting with unfading colors is the product of the guild system.

The Emerging Importance of the Master Builder—Villard de Honnecourt. The planning of the Gothic cathedral was essentially the product of two men—the bishop, representing the church, and the architect, or master builder, representing the guilds. Whatever ecclesiastical teaching was to be embodied in the building depended upon the bishop; whatever aesthetic value it possessed came from the master builder.

Contrary to popular belief, the names of scores of medieval architects have come down to us. The Cathedral of Amiens was built, in part, by Robert de Luzarches; that of Reims, by Jean le Loup. Peter Parler was one of the two architects of Prague's cathedral and is also mentioned in connection with the Cathedral of Milan. One of the best known of these master builders, Villard de Honnecourt, left a notebook (Fig. 374), whose sketches and comments show the tools and theories at the disposal of the medieval builder.

FIG. 344.—Notebook of Villard de Honnecourt. *a,* Tower of Laon; *b,* human figures constructed geometrically with words "Here begins the material of portraiture"; *c,* the vegetative man, and studies of plants with architectural design; compare with Fig. 305*f,* Chap. XII.

Villard, who lived during the first years of the 13th century in a town of Picardy near Cambrai, was the head of a Gothic *chantier,* or stonemason's workshop. Included in his notebook are drawings for the use of the shop over which he presided. Nothing is known of Villard's building except that he probably received his training in the Cistercian Abbey of Vaucelles near Honnecourt and constructed churches for the Cistercian monks. One of his drawings, made in collaboration with another architect, Pierre de Corbie, shows the presbyterium, or *chevet,* of a church. The plan exactly follows the enlargement of the double ambulatory at Vaucelles, which may have been built by these two. Villard also shows designs of details from Cambrai, Laon (Fig. 344*a*), Meaux, Chartres, Reims, and Lausanne, which he probably intended to use on structures of his own.

The notebook gives invaluable evidence of the mental processes of the medieval artist and may be taken as an introduction to the formal and associational values of Gothic aesthetics. Villard, for example, endeavored to explain the geometry of the human figure in terms of radiating lines which centered, in the drawing, in the crotch. It is also significant that while

Villard constructed many figures on geometric schemes (Fig. 374*b*), at no time did he try to evolve a geometric formula from observed phenomena. Here we see a fundamental difference between the Gothic and the Classical point of view. Again, Villard's rendering of the tower at Laon shows definitely that the medieval building was thought of as a sequence of parts constructed one upon the other, rather than as a whole. His drawings of the inside and the outside of Reims Cathedral, being in reverse perspective, indicate that the medieval architect thought in terms of decorative elements, intended to express many aspects of a single idea, rather than in terms of a plastic image contemplated from without.

The architect's notebook became an illustrated history of his craft. In many cases these records were handed down from father to son, or from master to apprentice, for generations. As Villard's sketches show, the notes included not only aesthetic ideas (Fig. 344*c*) but also practical mechanical formulae for constructing engines to raise stones into place. The architect of the Middle Ages was not only sculptor, designer, and engineer, but in many cases an active participant in the work of his fellow

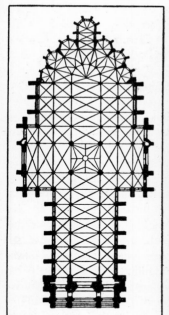

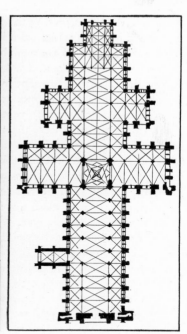

FIG. 345a.—Plan of A m i e n s, France, c. 1220–1288.　FIG. 345b.—Early Gothic glass with Abbot Suger, St. Denis, 1132–1144.　FIG. 345c.—Plan of Salisbury, England, 1220–1258.

guildsmen. William of Sens, a French master builder, went to England in 1174 to apply for work in rebuilding the cathedral at Canterbury, which had been almost completely destroyed by fire. The records of his stay reveal that he worked as carpenter in erecting centering for arches. In 1507, an architect, Jean Texier, built the Gothic tower of Chartres Cathedral; in 1514, he appears again on the records as the sculptor who carved the choir screen. Craftsman and artist, designer, traveler, and journeyman, the medieval architect, like his creations, became a repository of all the artistic impulses of his time. Yet, in the end, he did no more than carry out the bidding of another man, who, ignorant as he may have been as to the architectural practicability of his ideas, knew what he wanted ecclesiastically.

The Bishop as Aesthetic Arbiter in Cathedral Building. It was the bishop who commissioned the architect to draw the plans and build the models from which the cathedral was to be constructed. In some few cases, bishop and

architect may have been one and the same person. The Abbot Suger of St. Denis (Fig. 345b) wrote so well and so copiously on the construction of his cathedral that some think he had charge of the building. From the illustration it is apparent that he prided himself on his stained glass—some of the earliest Gothic glass in France. In any case, the architect was directly responsible to the cleric, who supplied the pictorial ideas that the architect tried to make structurally possible. The cleric, moreover, had the power of appointment and removal. The architect Ingebram, commissioned to build the façade of Notre Dame at Rouen, was replaced after a year and a half by Walter of Melun, because the bishop did not approve of Ingebram's work. So powerful was the bishop's influence that many towns passed laws forbidding the erection of any building that would reach above the height of the cathedral eaves—thus assuring that the church would tower above the town.

As a competent administrator, the bishop's

chief interest lay in getting the largest possible gathering place in which to address his flock. The nave of his cathedral must be large enough to hold the townsfolk, and if he were also an abbot, the choir and transepts must accommodate the members of his monastery. Once the physical accommodations were secured, the bishop desired to express the mystical significance of the church in the statuary and stained glass of the cathedral. This effort was directed chiefly at the clergy, the townsmen at that time probably being too ignorant to grasp the involved symbolism of medieval art. They were readily impressed, however, by the magnificence and splendor of the building, which was really its aesthetic intent.

To understand this aesthetic purpose, we must examine (1) the mind and philosophy of the bishop, (2) the mind and ability of the architect, and (3) the folk art of the masses, as revealed in the decoration of the cathedral.

Philosophical Backgrounds

The philosophy of the Greeks concerned itself, for the greater part, with the interrelationship of objects, individuals, and societies. Medieval philosophy strove to explain the emergence of will and idea as dynamic factors in human conduct. The feeling of strife and tension between opposites, which appeared as a predestined tendency underlying all Celto-Germanic literature, came into the light of reason as the philosophy of the scholastics during the formative period of the Gothic style. Paralleling the development of Greek philosophy, scholasticism left the realm of fantasy and gradually achieved a logical structure.

The Importance of Scholasticism. The great importance of Scholastic philosophy lies in the fact that from it stemmed the modern Catholic codes of morality and the Protestant philosophies of individualism. The rise of medieval Scholasticism, chiefly in the schools of Paris during the 12th century, differed in one important particular from the development of Greek philosophy. The latter grew step by step, like a Doric temple; the former proceeded from the given revelations of Plato's *Timaeus* and from many works by Aristotle as interpreted from Arabian sources.

The early Christian Church Father, Porphyry, wrote an introduction to the categories of Aristotle in which he recapitulated many of the ideas of both Plato and Aristotle, thus formulating the chief topics of Scholastic discussion. Celto-Germanic man, lacking the background of the Greek—natural, scientific knowledge— inherited as catchwords the most profound Greek ideas. These he strove to explain and connect with the facts of his warlike everyday existence. The northerner felt, also, that the human personality, if deemed worthy of Christian salvation, demanded a reason for its existence. He also enjoyed with almost primitive curiosity the aspect of the particular thing or *res* ("nominalism"), which he saw as an expression of the greater reality ("realism").

The realists accepted as an a priori hypothesis the idea that the original reality was the primary class concept, proceeding from itself like the Being of Parmenides and containing within itself the particular, which included both the species and the individual. To the realist, the idea that was most nearly universal was most real. Out of this universal being, or God, by a process of unfolding (*egressus*) reality became manifest in the individual parts of the world. The universal thing nearest the realm of sense perception, having least of the universal being, was naturally furthest from God. All generation and change, the realist believed, arose through the process of logical thought, and God as the Universal, which neither creates nor is created, becomes essentially the same as the Ultimate Being of Parmenides. This Ultimate Being, having more of reality than all other beings, had also a greater degree of perfection. Bernard of Chartres and other Scholastics, following Plato, conceived of a second or higher transcendental world of pure ideas. To some extent the medieval cathedral, with its pendentive ribs, could be thought of as an earthly prototype of that heavenly city.

Nominalists vs. Realists. The realists, whose philosophy agreed with the ideals of Plato, found worthy rivals in the nominalists. For these latter Scholastics, the universals were nothing but collective names, *nomina*. In this belief we have the beginnings of the modern philosophy of individualism, which maintains that only things are actual. Roscellinus maintained that reality existed rather in the individual thing that could be felt and seen. Here, again, the Middle Ages, without knowing it, returned to the primitive philosophy of sensualism propounded by the pre-Socratic Sophists.

In general, the Scholastic arguments followed the ancient question as to which came first, the hen or the egg. The great medieval mystics, such as Eckhardt and Bernard of Clairvaux, resolved the argument in words similar to those that Goethe placed in the mouth of his medieval scholar, Faust: "Within us also lies the universe." Realism, during the Middle Ages, corresponded on the whole to what today we should call Platonic idealism, and nominalism to what we might call Aristotelian materialism. The church needed both philosophies—realism for its spiritual meaning and nominalism for the details of its moral code.

The Angelic Doctor and the Aristotelian Philosophy. The 12th-century mystic, Adam of St. Victor, condemned the nominalistic point of view, because it turned man's attention from contemplation of the Divine reality to the intriguing variety of phenomenal existence. It remained for St. Thomas Aquinas, "the angelic doctor," as the Roman Church still calls him, to demonstrate that no fundamental conflict existed between the realist and the nominalist and that a deeper study of Aristotle would disclose a way out of the dilemma. The resultant scheme of philosophy, called the "Aristotelian Thomism," of St. Thomas, which typifies the most enlightened medieval point of view, rested on the incontrovertible proof of absolute logic. His aim was not a painstaking scientific research, such as that of the philosophers after Spinoza; but his logical method, deriving the particular from a universal concept, constitutes essentially the method of the religious and ethical teacher.[1]

Although the method of St. Thomas did not lead directly to modern science, it played a great part in determining the attitude of the church toward art. Through it the churchmen came to regard the purposes of life as simple and rigid. All of life became informed by an ethical, or moral, ideal. This conception exerted its influence upon medieval art. The sculptural and painted decoration of the Greek temple contributed to a total effect that told the story of some civic deity. The ornament of the medieval cathedral, in contrast, attempted to express the highest conceivable purpose: man's aspiration to achieve unity with the Divine. Greek ornament in human form seems unified, concrete, and attached; the ornament of the Gothic cathedral appears ready to detach itself from the building and fly out toward the heavens. The medieval explanation of this phenomenon is set forth in the writings of St. Thomas, Witelo, Ulrich Engelbert, and Vincent of Beauvais.

Aesthetic Backgrounds

The fundamental difference between classical and medieval aesthetics is this. Classical critics, on the whole, strove to base their aesthetics on observed material phenomena, while the Christian aesthetician started with a preconceived idea of what art should portray.

The Christian Church Fathers and the Aesthetics of Light. St. Augustine expressed his entire theory of art in the words: "All beauty is one with the divine light." His introduction here of the term "light" for God, was an inheritance

---

[1] THOMAS AQUINAS, *Summa Contra Gentiles*, Book I, Chap. 37, in the translation by Rickaby entitled *On God and His Creatures*, furnishes an excellent example.

from those passionate boyhood days when, as a follower of the Persian religious leader, Mani, he looked upon Ahura-Mazda, the Persian sun-god, as the ultimate divinity. This change from a concept of the highest good as simply Truth or Beauty to that of Light was to influence the development of formal aesthetics after the 13th century and during the Italian Renaissance. A recognition of light rather than musical harmony as the highest aesthetic value meant, essentially, that the sense of sight, disclosing the material aspect of existence, would give increasing importance to the graphic arts.

Pseudo Dionysius the Areopagite, an early Christian monk of Athens who lived in the latter part of the 3rd century, like Plotinus, held the doctrine that the Good, which is one with Beauty, was indivisible from the divine whole. He wrote: "There is a super-substantial or absolute beauty which causes all things (to act) in harmony (*consonantia*) and which has the power of illumination (*claritas*)."[1] He inferred that this divine illumination could not only draw all things into itself, but could send forth its rays so that all things became visible. From this superbeautiful Beauty continually emanated a stream of individual beauties that became proper to individual artistic objects. Augustine, less of a mystic than Dionysius, strove to explain this indefinite formula by separating the useful and associational values of a work of art in the following manner: "An iron stylus or pen is made useful that we may write with it, and this is its proper or individual beauty, but in so far as we get an aesthetic pleasure from it, it is part of the divine beauty."[2] Thus for Augustine there existed two types of beauty, one based upon material or use values, the other upon spiritual or associational values. The latter lay in the decorative effect of the object, closely allied to the symbols that may have graced it. This idea led to the theory of ornamentation held by later writers, such as Vincent of Beauvais.

The Threefold Beauty of St. Thomas. In his *Summa Theologica*, St. Thomas discloses a threefold conception of beauty. First, the beautiful thing must have wholeness or perfection, which makes it a miniature counterpart of the heavenly Beauty. By contrast, the Ugly is that which appears incomplete. The second attribute of beauty has to do with the proportion of parts which constitute any work of art. This is in a way a formal value. Finally, a mystical correspondence must exist between the object and the divine light, or *claritas*. The physical symbol of the heavenly, inspired illumination, or *claritas*, is color, which makes life seem more significant.

Ulrich Engelbert and the Problems of Color, Form, and Mass. Ulrich Engelbert, a fellow pupil of St. Thomas living in the second half of the 13th century, observed that beauty required a proper proportioning of material to form. That is, the material must suit the type of form to be portrayed in it. The figure of an active, rugged man, for example, should be cast in bronze, while that of a tender, soft woman might well be carved in ivory or marble (Fig. 346). This new aesthetic element, first recognized in the Middle Ages, might be called the "significance of material."

Ulrich also stated that an appropriate quantity of masses existed for a given form. This suggests a recognition of the expression of activity through the position of masses, a principle superbly illustrated in the sculpture of Michelangelo (Fig. 487, Chap. XV).

Ulrich and the Value of Contrast. Ulrich recognized the presence in the world of the Grotesque and the Ugly. These he explained in terms of lack of the complete properties of the Beautiful. He concluded that their purpose was to induce a clearer perception of the value of beauty through the element of contrast. Contrast, then, allows for the inclusion of the humorous or the distorted in an aesthetic creation to make more apparent the completeness of the Good and the Beautiful, whose universality includes the Nonbeautiful.

[1] COOMARASWAMY, "A Medieval Aesthetic," *The Art Bulletin*, March, 1935.   [2] COOMARASWAMY, *op. cit.*

The Aesthetics of Witelo. Witelo, a friend of St. Thomas Aquinas, carried idealistic aesthetics a step further toward realism by stating that the artificial seemed more beautiful than the natural. In other words, the human artist could concentrate in his production a more significant idea and a more harmonious arrangement than any afforded by nature. This position, which elevated man above all other works of the Heavenly Creator, became a warrant for Renaissance individualism. The element of individualism appears at other places in the writings of Witelo. He discussed matters of taste, for example, writing that almond-shaped eyes were more beautiful than round ones.

Vincent of Beauvais and the Theory of Ornamentation. A curious, almost primitive aspect of the idealistic theory of the Middle Ages arose first in the writings of Isidore of Seville as they were transformed by the pen of Vincent of Beauvais. In contrast with Ulrich and St. Thomas, who found beauty inherent in the object, this cleric held that beauty was something that could be used to add richness and ornament. Beauty for him seems to have been synonymous with the particular substance added, such as pigments, varicolored marbles, and bright, gilded roofs, all of which ornamented the churches.

Thus, in the Middle Ages there gradually arose a consciousness of the fact that men dealt with two different types of aesthetic ideas: one, an idea of goodness, synonymous with beauty, which shone through every connected particular of the universe; the other, an idea of an artistic object that in itself possessed integrity.

The "Mirrors" of Durandus (Guillaume Durand) and Vincent of Beauvais. As Scholasticism reached its culmination in the 13th century, all medieval knowledge, a strange mixture of fact and fancy, was organized by the scholars into a series of encyclopedias of symbolism, called the *Specula,* or "Mirrors." Durandus of Mende in his *Rationale divinorum officiorum* and Vincent of Beauvais in the *Speculum majus* produced the most famous of these compendiums.

Fig. 346.—Virgin and Child, ivory, Île de France, 14th century. (*Courtesy of Taft Museum, Cincinnati.*)

Durandus attempted to explain in symbolic terms all parts of the church and of the Mass, which had become very involved. Vincent listed the allegories portrayed in the sculpture, glass,

Fig. 347.—Figure of Music, portal, Chartres. (*Courtesy of Metropolitan Museum of Art.*)

and painting of the cathedrals. The writings of Durandus inform us that the cathedral represents the body of Christ; those of Vincent, that it forms in a way a book of instruction. These Scholastic philosophers—one a realist, the other a nominalist—stressed two functions of the church, that of inspiration and that of instruction. Both functions have to do with the useful and associational values of art; neither philosopher had much to say about formal values.

The four *Mirrors* of Vincent deal with nature, science and instruction, morals, and history. The *Mirror of Nature* comprised scenes of the creation and their allegorical significance. It explained the symbolic meaning of each type of animal and vegetable ornament, the mon-

sters, the grotesque—in short, the various aspects of Aristotle's vegetative soul. A picture of the vegetative man appears in the notebook of Villard de Honnecourt (Fig. 344*c*).

The *Mirror of Science and Instruction* explained the representations of all forms of human labor, the handicrafts, and the seven arts—theology, philosophy, rhetoric, logic, astronomy, geometry, and music. These fields of endeavor fell within Aristotle's idea of the functions of the imaginative soul. The figure of Music, from Chartres, illustrates a subject later described by this Mirror (Fig. 347).

The *Mirror of Morals*, characterizing the reasonable soul of man, included the seven virtues —faith, hope, charity, temperance, fortitude, prudence, and justice—and the corresponding vices, also seven in number—idolatry, despair, avarice, intemperance, cowardice, folly, and injustice. Each of the seven virtues was divided into seven subvirtues, so that the entire scheme was most complete.

Leaving the realm of Aristotelian philosophy, in the *Mirror of History*, Vincent described the use of Old and New Testament stories, the lives of the saints, and the vision of the Apocalypse, or Last Judgment, which constitutes the Christian-Platonic revelation. History was shown as stemming from a central thought— the creation of God—which led to salvation for the just and damnation for the unjust. Every kingly character and prophet of the Old Testament stood for some disciple or parable in the New Testament. By the 13th century, the various portals of the cathedral had been allocated to aspects of this history. At Chartres, for example, the 12th-century west façade depicted the Last Judgment and the story of Christ, with a tale of the Virgin on His left hand, that of the Ascension on His right. Even more characteristic are the façades of Paris, Amiens and Laon.

It has been assumed that these *Mirrors* helped in the planning and decoration of the cathedral. However, as can be seen, the cathedrals had been built before the *Mirrors* were written. Some clergy did use the scenes as a means of visual instruction. The Abbot Suger of St. Denis wrote that the sole purpose of the windows in his cathedral was to show the unlettered people who could not read the Holy Scriptures what they should believe. Nevertheless, much of Gothic cathedral art, like our comic sheets and motion pictures, represented not a pedantic purpose but a true attempt to make the cathedral more interesting and enjoyable.

The Cathedral

The Nave

The Engineering Construction of the Cathedral. We have seen how the pointed vault with its buttressing over the side aisles (Fig. 349*a* and *b*) originated in early Gothic architecture as Romanesque architects of the 11th and 12th centuries brought the old Lombard system up to northern requirements of height and light space. In the Île de France the Saracenic pointed arch (Fig. 349*c*) was either taken directly from the East or evolved perhaps from long vaults such as Notre Dame du Port or Autun. The architects had found that this higher arch relieved the thrust at the springing point (Fig. 349*d*) and enabled them to build wider structures. They next pointed the sides of the square bays (Fig. 349*e*) so that they reached the same height as the diagonal ribs over each square vault.

In several of the Romanesque churches the builders discovered that the aesthetic effect of height was enhanced if the engaged columns on the inner side of the piers (Fig. 349*f*) ran up through all the courses toward the ceiling in an unbroken line. In Normandy, the space above the lower nave arcade was broken by another arcade, the triforium (Fig. 349*g* and *h*), much as in some of the late Byzantine constructions. This gallery, which in St. Ambrogio seemed so low, was further modified so that its columns and arches appeared as a row of vertical lines leading toward the higher vaults.

Eventually, the buttresses holding the nave

ribs were moved up outside the aisle roof and definitely connected to piers on the outermost walls, where they came to have a certain decorative significance for the outside of the church. An arch exerts force at several points in its span; the top, where it springs from its piers, and the haunches. Finally, in the mature Gothic, a free "flying buttress" (Fig. 349*b*) braced the outer pier. Then builders could support the arch against the pier at two places; in other words, they built two arches, one above the other, connected in some cases, such as at Chartres and Bourges, by a row of colonnettes. In later cathedrals even these were broken away, and a single colonnette just outside the clerestory window of the nave wall supported the upper arch. Eventually, the outer piers were surmounted with pinnacles and lacy crockets or finials (Fig. 349*i* and *k*). Their decorative character as tall spires seems to deny the very weight by which they exert force downward.

The Verticality of the Nave at Amiens. Let us study the nave at Amiens (Fig. 348), observing how its great height and fine proportion of parts lead logically upward along the slender piers, past the foliate-decorated triforium gallery, to the celestial realm of the roof, where the physical light from God is made manifest through the high expanse of stained-glass clerestory windows. The cathedral at Amiens has a nave considered by most critics the finest in all France. Its consistency arises in part from the fact that it was built by three architects working in harmony. The first of these three, Robert de Luzarches, started in 1220. His successor, Thomas de Corment, bequeathed the work to his son, Regnauld de Corment, who completed the monumental task in 1288.

Inevitably, the lines of the nave in any fine Gothic interior carry us forward to the choir, where the gallery itself—now part of the upper wall—lies within the realm of light made by its own clerestory windows. The low, fortress-like character of the Romanesque has given way to walls of colored light, in which the func-

Fig. 348.—Nave at Amiens. (*Courtesy of Clarence Ward.*)

FIG. 349.—Mature Gothic construction in the nave at Amiens, Robert de Luzarches, 1220–1288. Height of vault 140 feet, width 150 feet, length 450 feet, peak of wooden roof about 200 feet. *a*, central pointed vault; *b*, flying buttresses; *c*, pointed arch; *d*, springline of arch; *e*, clerestory arch; *f*, engaged columns; *g* and *h*, triforium galleries; *i*, exterior piers; *j*, bracing colonnettes; *k*, crockets and finials; *l*, chapel; *m*, Peter Parler, architect, Cathedral of Prague, about 1250; *n*, Anthony Pilgram, architect, Cathedral of Vienna, about 1450. A subtle entasis occurs in many cathedrals including Amiens. The engaged columns (*f*) bow outward in the middle of the nave at the triforium so that the space is shaped like a boat. This can be seen at the transept in Fig. 348.

tional arrangement of the stones achieves a balanced unity of lines that embody all the previous structural advantages.

The diagrammatic perspective drawing show-

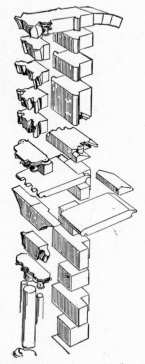

FIG. 350.—Arrangement of stones in section of Notre Dame at Dijon. (*After Viollet-le-Duc.*)

ing two bays of the nave at Amiens with one section of the side aisles (Fig. 349) should make clear every architectural element that went into the creation of this aesthetic effect, as well as the method used in building. First, each clustered pier of the entire section, including the nave bay and the side aisles, was built up to a height of 40 feet above the floor level and topped with a carved capital. Above these piers the builders erected two arches over a wooden form of centering, and across the side-aisle bays threw arched ribs. These being light did not disturb the central piers. Outside the aisles, along the line of the walls, they erected heavier piers, which became the bases of the flying buttresses. Between the piers they eventually placed little

vaulted chapels, each lighted by a window. Above the side aisles sprang the arches of the triforium gallery, which was built up along with the outside wall until the clerestory level was reached. Cross timbers were probably thrown over the nave so that the lower flying buttresses, built in from the outer piers to the clerestory, would balance their forces against one another. The walls were then built up to the haunch of the nave arches, which were braced inside with timbers until the outside buttresses could be constructed. Finally, the thin ribs met at a point 141 feet above the pavement, and the pinnacles were set on the outer piers. The panels of each vault were then laid in place between the ribs. With a complete structural unity thus achieved for the section, and equilibrium established, the builders lowered the great bracing timbers and began work on another section.

The planning and execution of the stonework, particularly in the upper and ribbed courses, required phenomenal skill. The section of the cathedral wall from Dijon (Fig. 350), reproduced here after drawings by Viollet-le-Duc, will make this clear. Although the master architect supervised the stonework, three different classes, or degrees, of masons carried out his directions—the freemason, the layer, and the hardhewer. Each of these had his appointed work, and large groups of them were responsible for certain sections of the wall.

The builders of the Parthenon achieved so fine a balance in the exterior disposition of architectural parts that any rearrangement would destroy the effect of the whole, much as the removal of a leg or an arm would affect a statue. The architects of the Gothic cathedral, however, had to incorporate in their structure a system of knowledge and feeling far more complex than any that the Greeks dreamed of. The longest span of marble used by the Greeks at Athens, between two columns on the porch of the Erechtheum, measured about 20 feet. The Gothic builders also knew limits, not, however, the limits of the lintel or the aesthetic

Fig. 351.—Nave of Exeter Cathedral, Decorated Period, 1307–1377. Note lierne vaulting. (*Courtesy of Travel and Industrial Development Association of Great Britain and Ireland.*)

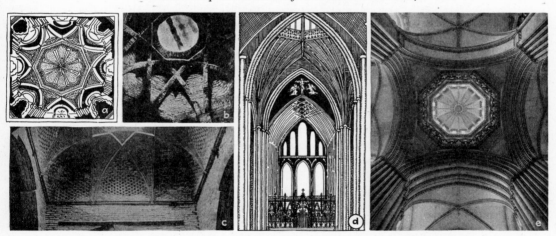

Fig. 352.—Saracenic and Gothic construction of the lantern. *a,* vault over mihrab with arched ribs, Mosque of Cordova, Spain, 10th century; *b,* ribbed cupola, Church at Hospice of St. Blaise, Oloron, France, 11th century, copied directly from type *a* or from the Pilgrimage Church of St. James at Jerusalem (*after M. Aubert, Bulletin monumental de France, Vol. 93, 1934, p. 39*); *c,* Masdjid-i-Djum'a, Isfahan, Iran (Persia), 13th century; Saracenic derivation of *a* (*courtesy of M. B. Smith*); *d,* central octagon, Ely Cathedral, 14th century, false conoid vaulting covering wooden ribbed vault like *a* and *c*; *e,* lantern at Coutances on modified beam squinches, 13th century. (*Courtesy of C. Ward.*)

The interrelationship between Moslem and Gothic architecture suggested by these constructions finds parallels in the science, literary art, and graphic design of the Middle Ages. Productive centers in Spain and North Africa exchanged ideas through the commercial life of the Mediterranean. See Fig. 302, Chap. XII.

limits of the sculptured façade, but the material limits set by the fragility of their attenuated stone columns and piers. Unconsciously, the Gothic builders strove for an aesthetic effect

Fig. 353.—Pendant vaults, Chapel of Henry VII, Westminster Abbey, c. 1500. (*Courtesy of Metropolitan Museum of Art.*)

in stone which was particularly appropriate to wood or, centuries later, to modern steel construction.

The Distant Vistas of the English Naves. The great feeling of verticality developed in the French cathedrals contrasts with the desire for depth, combined with intricate patterns of light and shade in the vaultings, peculiar to the English churches. The nave of the cathedral at Exeter (Fig. 351), begun in the latter part of the 13th century, illustrates the ways in which the English Gothic style differs from the French.

The piers of the English cathedral seem heavy, massive, almost Romanesque in character, although composed of clusters of colonnettes. No single colonnette runs up to connect the lower pier with the triforium level; instead, other engaged columns seem to depend from the ribs of the ceiling vaults like the medallions in Santa Maria of Naranco (Fig. 317, Chap.

XII). This trend toward a transcendental decorative element, almost Oriental in character, the English developed still further in their vaults and lanterns (Fig. 352).

The narrow triforium gallery serves as a decorative feature rather than as a true functional member. Above it the clerestory windows, low and broad, are so arranged that their light becomes lost in the mazes of the roof. The vista of interwoven branches that composes the nave vaulting seems interminable. The great length of the English cathedrals is due to the fact that most of them were connected with monastic establishments, whose numerous clergy necessitated a large choir space. This requirement often led to the use of a double transept. In the case of Exeter, the feeling of length has been accentuated in the vaulting by the introduction of a ridge rib, which guides the eye down toward the crossing.

The tendency to increase the number of ribs led eventually, in Gloucester and other English cathedrals built in the so-called perpendicular style, to the adoption of an entirely new principle of vaulting. Instead of building the free-standing ribs first, as was done in the early French Gothic, the masons laid solid, conoid masses that intersected each other in the ceiling, replacing the functional ribs by an applied latticework of purely decorative significance. The final development of this design came when the centers of the vaults, following the pendentive tendencies already noted, dropped in stalactite formations patterned on Saracenic models (Fig. 353). Such pendant vaults characterize 15th- and 16th-century English and French flamboyant Gothic. Rich, lacy, and ornamental, they follow the aesthetic criteria enunciated by Vincent of Beauvais, which call for purely decorative additions to an otherwise functional structure. Most late Gothic architecture has this highly decorative appearance, which relates to the Romanesque and early Gothic as the Corinthian style relates to the early Greek Doric. Here we see demonstrated the means by which decorative richness reaches a style after functional problems have been solved. In any culture, art itself can arise only after the early struggles of that culture to establish its position have abated.

forium gallery. The only Gothic church in Rome, Santa Maria sopra Minerva, built in 1280, when German influence was strongest in Italian political and religious life, stands

FIG. 354.—Interior, Santa Croce, Florence, Arnolfo di Cambio and others, 1294–1442. Length 361 feet, width 123 feet, height of nave 56 feet. (*Courtesy of Lesch-Carnegie.*)

The Horizontality of the Italian Gothic. Carried southward by the great monastic orders, the Gothic style spread over northern Italy as its decorative features were adapted to basilican churches and to many civic buildings. With the exception of a few cathedrals, such as Siena, Pisa, Milan, and Florence, the majority of Italian churches, like Santa Croce in Florence (Fig. 354), retained their low, basilican appearance. The decoration, as can be seen in Pisa and Siena, was usually horizontal in its effect.

In many churches the arches of the nave arcade rest on columns still classical in intent, and the roofs are flat and beamed. Practically all the vaulting was closer to the Romanesque than to the true Gothic. With the exception of Milan, the flying buttress was not used. Most Italian Gothic buildings also lacked the tri-

nearer to Sant' Ambrogio in construction than to the Gothic of the Île de France.

The Choir of Beauvais. The choir of the Cathedral of Beauvais (Fig. 355) shows the maximum height attained in Gothic interior construction. Here is a complete union of structural possibilities and aesthetic form. Like the first dome of Hagia Sophia in Constantinople, however, the first choir at Beauvais fell. It had to be rebuilt—by rule of thumb, for unlike the modern architect, the Gothic mason possessed no means of computing the stress and weight of stone.

As it now stands, the choir of Beauvais measures 157 feet in height to the top of the vaults, a structure considerably higher than the nave of Amiens. A careful study of the plan and drawing by Viollet-le-Duc (Fig. 356*a, b*) in comparison with the view of the exterior (Fig.

Fig. 355.—Sexpartite vaulting, choir, Cathedral of Beauvais, 1225–1568. Height 157 feet. (*Courtesy of Clarence Ward.*)

357) will make clear how in this supreme achievement of the Gothic mason all the interior aesthetic effects were subordinated to the desire to gain the greatest possible window space for the stained glass.

There are two distinct heights to be considered. The first, in the center, is marked by the nave vault, which rests on ribs springing from thin engaged colonnettes. These colonnettes run up the surface of the bottom row of columns, built of a particularly resistant stone. From the capitals of these columns the colonnettes again continue up past the high, stilted arches of the lower side aisles and the triforium gallery, to the tall clerestory windows. The final vault is braced on the outside by boldly flung buttresses, reaching out toward tall, thin piers. These piers rise from the supports between the outer and inner choir aisles. Since the piers are not heavy enough in themselves to take up all the thrust of the buttresses, they are in turn braced with other, lighter buttresses to heavier, outside piers, which rise from the walls of the radiating chapels below.

To make sure that this double buttressing transferred its weight downward against the ground, the builders added pinnacles, terminating in flowerlike finials. Runnels, carved down some of the buttresses, carry the rain and snow away from the high, peaked roof out through grotesque spouts, known as "gargoyles," throwing it clear of the building. Every decorative part of this building has some structural use. Nothing is superfluous. Even the statues add weight where weight is needed to help hold the vaults.

Contrasted with such a structure, a Greek temple appears full of needless details—metopes, pedimental sculptures, acroteria—which have no structural meaning. In the 13th-century Gothic temple, the architectural engineer might justly claim that use, symbolism, and ornamental quality were one. The medieval scholar writing of his cathedral must have gloried in observing that in God's house everything had purpose.

The Function of the Façade

The decoration of the front, or façade, of the church proper developed in connection with the Romanesque style. The façade decora-

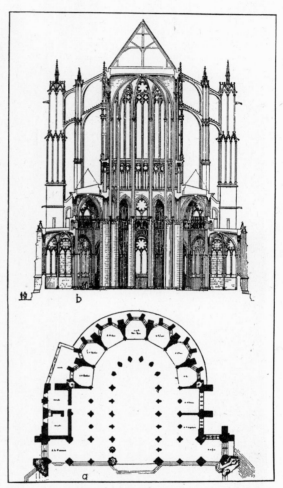

Fig. 356.—Cathedral of Beauvais. *a*, plan; *b*, transverse section showing double triforium gallery and flying buttresses. (*After Viollet-le-Duc.*)

tion devised at St. Trophîme of Arles and Notre Dame of Poitiers is duplicated to some extent in the later Gothic buildings. In the wooden church buildings of the north, as in the Visigothic hall at Naranco, emphasis fell on the side entrance or porch. In some late Gothic

Fig. 357.—Exterior, Cathedral of Beauvais. (*Courtesy of Clarence Ward.*)

FIG. 358.—Façade arrangement of French and English Gothic. *a*, Laon, 1160–1205; *b*, Notre Dame at Paris 1163–1325; *c*, Lincoln, 1185–1200; *d*, Peterborough, 1170–1190.

churches the decoration of this side porch takes precedence over the frontal decoration.

Verticality at Laon. Comparing the Gothic façade of the Cathedral of Laon (Fig. 358*a*) with the earlier Romanesque façade of the Cathedral of Angoulême (Fig. 325, Chap. XII), one finds in the Gothic building the first attempt to attain a consistent perpendicular effect. Above a cavernous opening, the towers rise in definite stories. Although each square story plan has four corner towers, there is no intent to use these in making a transition to an octagon. A sort of restless movement surges upward through the whole façade, retarded only by the heaviness of the applied decoration. The builder combined the towers skillfully with the level courses of the façade, however, chiefly by breaking the horizontals with gables, even in the ground floor.

The Geometric Disposition of Notre Dame at Paris. The architect of the Cathedral of Notre Dame in Paris (Fig. 358*b*) achieved an admirable unity of parts by building the central section of the façade within a square. The verticals of the piers cutting the horizontals serve to connect the upper towers and produce a flatter but more consistent surface. Two arcaded galleries ornament the façade, the lower, less delicate one acting as a frame for statues of the kings of Judah. There is a general movement upward in this structure, with its ordered

regularity and restraint. To many, the finest of Gothic fronts, it reaches something similar to the classic balance of the Parthenon, although a careful study of details will show that the decoration of the two sides is by no means alike. Ordered space has been given to the sculpture, which not only fills all the reveals in the first portals, but also breaks the heavy buttresses. The purely decorative crockets and foliated finials (invented about 1200) concentrate along the tops of the towers and the façade. The heavier carvings and relief wall spaces fall below. In point of total space given to decorated and to flat surfaces, the façade shows better balance, perhaps, than any other in France. Here is the structural consistency shown in the lower part of St. Étienne, with an intelligent use of the upper story. Further, the use of the wheel window and the trefoils as elements in the decoration, as well as the lacy shadow effects of the upper gallery, help to make the transition from the lower stories to the towers.

These two examples, the cathedrals of Laon and Paris, illustrate two tendencies in the advanced development of the Gothic façade in France. At Laon the architect attempted to make the whole front express a consistent, dynamic, upward movement; at Paris he held back the upward movement by the use of static horizontal courses within the square.

The Architectonic Horizontality of the English

Fig. 359.—Façade arrangement of Italian Gothic. *a*, cathedral and campanile, Florence, 1206–1387; *b*, Cathedral of Orvieto, 1290–1310; *c*, Cathedral of Milan, 1385–1485.

Façades. In contrast to the French architects, who laid their greatest emphasis upon the façades and the side portals, the English often subordinated the façade to the central tower. The diagrammatic drawing of the front of Lincoln illustrates the way in which this massing toward the central tower took place in the finest of English cathedrals (Fig. 358*c*).

In the Lincoln façade the great, pointed, central portal is flanked by two smaller ones with round arches. These, in turn, are flanked by still smaller niches. This exterior arrangement of parts bespeaks the inner vaulting. The rest of the façade, with its lower side towers, is classical in its regularity. Above it two larger towers mount from hidden bases, and above them the third reaches highest of all, although the finished façade is partly accidental, having been destroyed in 1185 and rebuilt. The resulting arrangement represents a very complete and orderly version of the City of God. The sculptural decoration is negligible. This English building inspires a feeling of confidence, security, and repose, which many have come to associate with the English character.

The front of Peterborough Cathedral (Fig. 358*d*) exhibits even better the horizontality of English façades. No one part seems to mount skyward faster than any other, but all move upward in long, perpendicular lines that make ascension inevitable. The threefold gable ends give the effect of three Gothic churches set side by side.

The Contrast between Southern and Northern Use of the Gothic. The Italian churches in the Gothic style built during the 13th and 14th centuries show many decorative details invented in the more active Gothic north, applied to buildings of an essentially pre-Romanesque, basilican type. The façades of Orvieto and Florence cathedrals (Fig. 359) accentuate the use of fundamental geometrical symbols—square, circle, and triangle. The architects never learned, however, to link these forms with one another or with architectonic sculpture, as did the builders of the Île de France. Nor did they succeed in making their symbols move skyward. In the cathedrals of Milan and Siena the tiny spires are but the termination of thin piers. In Florence, also, as in most Italian churches, the campanile remains detached. The flèche, or tiborium, in Milan, was planned first from mod-

Fig. 360.—Façade, metropolitan Church of Our Lady at Reims, 1211–1290. (*Courtesy of Clarence Ward.*)

els by Bramante and Leonardo, who worked on it unsuccessfully, and was finally given its definitely Gothic form by German architects. The effect of this Gothic form is negated, however,

Fig. 361.—Façade, Vendôme, 15th century. (*Courtesy of Clarence Ward.*)

by the classical details later placed over the surface of the façade. The Gothic buildings of the south retained from the Romanesque their exterior covering of varicolored marbles which, with delicate crockets and inlaid mosaics or relief sculpture, gives them the appearance of delightful picture frames rather than of architectonic structures. Such decoration is static rather than dynamic, applied rather than functional in character.

The Complete Union of Pictorial and Geometric Elements at Reims. As the choir of Beauvais climaxes choir buildings, so the façade of the Cathedral of the Virgin at Reims (Fig. 360) represents the finest achievement in façade construction. This cathedral front exhibits complete unity in sculpture and architectonic feeling. The regular plan and fine arrangement

of flying buttresses in nave and choir show such symmetry that the structure occupies a place in relation to the development of Gothic architecture parallel to that of the Parthenon in relation to Greek building.

The three front portals are flanked on each side by small turret gables, so that a regular progression of gables extends from the two sides up to the central point in the first story. The masses of the two towers rise naturally out of the two side gables, their corner buttresses having been broken into small canopied turrets at the second story. Between these towers the rose window rests in a pointed frame suggesting the interior height and pointed character of the nave. Above this window, the row of kings, each in his separate canopied niche forms a crown, out of which the lightly built upper stories of the towers bring the finest of the stonework into relief against the sky. The motif of the highest gable over the central portal is repeated in the roof gable, projecting above the rows of kings. The entire ensemble thus produces a complete balance of rhythmical architectural forms, enshrining the sculpture, which celebrates Our Lady, to whom the church is dedicated. A statue of her as queen appears on the central portal, and it is her coronation that constitutes the delicate central gable sculpture. On each side of her, in the lesser gables, appear representations of the Crucifixion and the Last Judgment. Considering it from a formal point of view alone, one feels that here is a complete façade, except for the missing spires, which were not completed simply because funds were lacking.

How did the architect finally achieve this unity? It should be pointed out that consonant with medieval writings on aesthetics, the cathedral was conceived to be a place where the formal light from Heaven, symbolized by the pyramidal lines from the spires, revealed all aspects of God's creation. Underneath the whole system of Gothic building lay a mystical belief in the power of numbers, inherited from partly understood Neo-Pythagorean treatises.

FIG. 362.—Development of the Northern Gothic tower. *a*, Chartres, right tower, 1044–1080; *b*, St. Étienne, Caen, about 1077; *c*, St. Pierre, Caen, about 1300; *d*, St. Stephen's, Vienna, 1300–1510; *e*, Chartres, left tower, 1134–1506; *f*, Freiburg Cathedral, about 1300.

St. Augustine wrote: "A divine wisdom is recognized in the numbers imprinted on everything." During the Middle Ages the planets were supposed to revolve about the earth in seven mystical spheres, thus making sublime music. The number seven was made up of the number three and the number four. Three was the number of the Trinity. The number four stood for the square and for the four Evangelists, while its multiple, twelve, was the number of the disciples. On the façade of Reims, one finds five gables on the first story, two small and three large. Out of these arise three parts of the front, in three stories, with two towers enclosing the circle—sign of unity—in the pointed arch of virility and aspiration. At the top of the central part stand seven statues, flanked, in each side of the side towers, by four more. Thus the fundamental geometric symbols—square, triangle, and circle—appear together with a certain primitive harmony of number. To a scientific age such an arrangement seems quite inevitable, but to the ignorant masses of the Middle Ages, it must have appeared miraculous. To the priests, this geometrical arrangement was a diagram that symbolized the many parts of a remarkable story.

The English Decorative Styles and the Flamboyant Façade. Two monkish architects, Alan of Walsingham and Brother John of Wisbeach, were employed at Ely, where they built a lady chapel slightly apart from the main cathedral. Desiring to panel the walls, they copied a type of curvilinear decoration that had been developed by some unknown carver on the rood screen at Southwell. This new style, which has been called the "English flowing decoration," spread through later English cathedrals and thence to France.

The French made of this decorated mode an exuberant flamboyant, or flaming, style, whose deep-cut, sharp moldings created dark shadows and a strong contrast of light and shade. The façade of the church at Vendôme (Fig. 361) demonstrates better than any other the lacy delicacy of the late Gothic.

This flamboyant style caught the enthusiastic spirit of the French and spread on to Rouen, to the transept of Beauvais, and to the dwelling houses and civic buildings, ending finally in

Jean Texier's northern tower and choir screen of Chartres, built about 1504. It persisted for another hundred years in Germany and became the essential composition scheme of the

the right tower of that cathedral (Fig. 362a). At first, this tower stood apart from the façade, like the ancient bell tower of Portoguaro. Throughout its building, it achieved a consist-

Fig. 363.—Abbey and town, Mont St. Michel, 12th and 13th centuries. (*Courtesy of Dayton Art Institute, Metcalf.*)

German baroque style of decoration, later absorbing many classical details.

The Function of the Tower

The pre-Romanesque tower at Portoguaro on the northeastern coast of Italy (Fig. 315, Chap. XII) had a structural peculiarity of great significance. The upper part of the tower, separated from the lower by very slender columns, appeared to float from the clouds. Examination of the towers on the façade of St. Étienne at Caen (Fig. 362b), reveals this same characteristic. The towers do not connect organically with the lower part of the church, but in their final story branch out into a number of tiny spires set on baldachins.

The South Tower at Chartres. Contemporaneously with the erection of St. Étienne, or slightly earlier, the builders at Chartres began to erect

ency that the rest of the cathedral did not have. The gradations of the large arches on the bottom story lead the eye gradually toward similar secondary arches on the next story, with four arches placed on colonnettes above them. There results a pleasant progression upward toward the point where four pinnacled towers placed at the angles, break the line of the square base into an octagonal plan. This gives a further basis for the development of the octagonal spire. To draw attention from the transition from base to spire, four gable structures, each made up of three perpendicular arches different in shape and size, rise flush with the square faces of the towers. These have higher pinnacles than the smaller, attached corner towers. Thus the spire seems to grow from a group of eight pinnacles. Comparing this arrangement with the plan of the spires on St. Étienne, one observes that the architect of Chartres has made it easier for the attention to move upward toward heaven.

St. Stephen's at Vienna. The final development of this tendency to make the single tower a complete work of beauty within itself appears in the spire of the Church of St. Stephen at Vienna (Fig. 362*d*). This structure serves as the chief entrance to the church through the transept. At the bottom, the entrance portal projects into the street like a miniature façade. Above this, between buttresses, appear four crotched gables constructed with lacy filigree carving. Out of these gables arise the four piers of the main part of the tower, covered with a false latticework similar to the pre-Romanesque decoration on the tower of Earls Barton (Fig. 315, Chap. XII). The decoration thus definitely reminds one of wooden origins. Between the piers the tall belfry window appears as a mullioned space four stories in height. Above it crosses a negligible horizontal molding with eight gables rising two on a side. Out of this square section next rises the octagon, the transition being made, as at Chartres, by using small corner spires and pinnacles. The central gables on this level almost disappear in the general hazy effect of the myriad points. Finally, the pointed spire proper, crowned with a cruciform flower or finial, rises from an open fretwork of stone. A line drawn from the top of this spire and following the contour of the fretwork would be included just inside the square plan of the base. Every structural story unit falls between the four lines of the pyramid so formed. The tower was definitely planned as a pyramidal structure rather than as a square tower with a spire.

Giotto's Campanile at Florence. In contrast with the northern spires, the campaniles, or bell towers, of the south retain their feeling of horizontality. Giotto's companile (Fig. 359*a*), beside the cathedral at Florence, has the general sturdy shape of a Romanesque watch tower, using the pointed arch and mullioned window in tall stories broken by marble paneling. By means of this arrangement of panels

and rather high stories, Arnolfo di Cambio succeeded in giving this tower some upward movement. The very heavy crown at the top, however, effectively stops any perpendicular

Fig. 364.—Medieval street La Petite France, Strasbourg, 14th century. (*Courtesy of David Edwards.*)

intent. The tower remains simply a tall pile of rich-colored marble.

Civic Buildings

The construction of civic and domestic buildings during the Middle Ages was dictated by the close quarters of the highly communal city life. Every member of a medieval town felt himself part of a small, contained family, guarded by a secure, high wall to keep out the rival warring parties of nobles, king, and often bishops, as well as bands of mercenaries that roamed the countryside. The medieval town (Fig. 363), usually built on the side of a hill overtopped by the castle of some powerful protecting feudal lord, grew in time into the city. Its distinctive skyline differed from that of the classical city by including many of the tall watch towers dominated by the spires of the cathedral. From the 12th to the 15th century, as the government of the cities came under the influence of elected boards of citizens composed of the heads of various guilds, each burgher had his own home, individual in taste and appearance.

times three or four stories in height, topped the whole structure.

The narrow streets, following the contours of the hill on which the town was located, usually

Fig. 365.—House of Jacques Coeur, Bourges, c. 1440. (*Courtesy of Lesch.*)

This he usually built above his workshop, which in the south fronted on some narrow, often arcaded street. In Northern Europe, the lower house stories were usually built of stone; the upper ones, of timber frames filled in with a rubble construction, or with brick and plaster (Fig. 364). The tenement alleys in the poor quarters of the American cities give somewhat the effect of those closely packed dwellings.

The upper stories of the buildings projected over the arcading, each story being built a little farther out than the one below, probably to provide maximum interior space. The beams showing on the exterior were often elaborately carved and painted. A high peak roof, some-

terminated in a town square, around which were set the cathedral, the guild hall and the city hall. In the great guild cities of the north and in Belgium and France, as well as in Italian cities such as Venice and Siena, the public buildings, decorated in the Gothic style, often reached the greatest magnificence.

Town Houses, North and South. Two houses of wealthy burghers, one in France and the other in Italy, serve as interesting examples of the 15th-century residential style. The house of Jacques Coeur, treasurer of Emperor Charles VII, in Bourges, demonstrates the manner in which the castle became transformed into a palace (Fig. 365).

In the center of the façade a large tower mounts above a great entrance gateway, flanked by a smaller, postern door. Both are decorated with moldings in the flamboyant style. Cano-

Fig. 366.—Courtyard with summerhouse, Castle Runkelstein, c. 1400.

pied niches for statues embellish the walls above the gateway and the postern. From false windows on each side of the niches peer portrait busts of ladies of the house. On this small second-story level, the highly decorated rectangular windows form pleasing areas of light and shade, mullioned with strongly molded uprights and crosspieces.

A chapel in the upper story of the tower is flanked by a smaller octagonal tower that rises high above the building like a church spire. High roofs, ornamental chimneys, bordered eaves, and waterspouts with gargoyles, all copy the conventional church decoration of the time. Through the entrance gateway one reaches a square courtyard bounded by loggias.

The courtyard of Castle Runkelstein, built near Bozen in the southern Tyrol for Nicholas Vintler in 1400, demonstrates the mode of mural decorations common to most of the wealthy houses and rarely preserved (Fig. 366). Above an arcaded loggia forming an outdoor drinking hall, a wooden balcony leads to the

great guest rooms of the second story. The frescoes below portray the kings of Austria; those above, more legendary figures from the epic tales of the minnesingers.

Fig. 367.—Ca d'Oro, Venice, 1424–1437. (*Courtesy of Lesch.*)

Great is the contrast between the architectural character of the house of Jacques Coeur and one of the typical Gothic palaces of Venice, the famous Ca d'Oro, or House of Gold (Fig. 367). The northern house displays an irregular structure, picturesque in plan and façade, showing the French delight in occult balance and diversity of design. The Italians, in contrast, regularly built within the square or the rectangle. In Venice, however, enough of the true Gothic spirit prevailed so that the architects of the Ca d'Oro, Giovanni and Bartolemeo Buon (1424–1437), designed the wide entrance portico far to the left, making necessary a rich asymmetrical arrangement for the other parts.

On the first story, the lower porch combines Romanesque and Gothic or Saracenic arches. Above appears the peculiarly Venetian type of flamboyant Gothic. The cusped tracery rises upon Romanesque columns; the ogival window arches mount to a flamelike point; all the arches other than those of the entrance group are cusped, so that their delicacy seems the more apparent. The most significant difference between the Venetian and the northern residential Gothic is the distinct framing that rises up

As in the case of the house of Jacques Coeur, the central tower rises above a great entranceway flanked by arcades. To get the necessary Gothic asymmetry, the architect planned seven

a   *b*

FIG. 368.—*a*, Bruges, Town Hall to left (1377), Halles and Belfry in center (1280), height 352 feet; *b*, Brussels Town Hall (1402–1454), height of tower 370 feet, guild houses at the right. (*Courtesy of Metropolitan Museum of Art.*)

both sides and along the cornice. The fine moldings make of the façade, which is covered with white Istrian marble inlaid with early Christian floral designs, a sort of tapestry rather than an architectural structure.

Town Halls and Guild Houses. In Belgium, particularly where the commercial power of the burghers had grown so strong that they overcame their feudal overlords, the civic buildings came to be as imposing as the churches. The symbols of the rising commercial power are represented by the magnificent market hall of Bruges (Fig. 368*a*), the cloth hall of Ypres, and the great town hall of Brussels. This last, contemporaneous with the house of Jacques Coeur, along with the row of guild houses fronting the city square, constitutes one of the most typical examples of medieval civic planning (Fig. 368*b*).

arches on one side of the gate and eleven on the other. The two upper stories have square and arched windows, interspersed with canopied statues. The late Gothic spire, built in the English manner with a relatively strict arrangement of stories, rises as high again as the entire lower building. Within this structure are the great council chambers, where the heads of the guilds met to discuss all the civic functions, including the regulation of their products.

Architectural Design in Jewelry and Furniture. The products of the armorers', goldsmiths', and carpenters' guilds all show the use of ornament directly derived from cathedral styles. Furniture, jewelry, and house furnishings in general, such as hinges and light fixtures, were richly ornamented whenever possible with scroll and interweave.

The table fountain in silver gilt and enamel

(Fig. 369) shows the fineness of the medieval goldsmiths' craft. From a molded vase with pierced ornaments rise slender colonnettes set around a heavy shaft, through which water or wine flowed to the basin above. The ribs stemming from these colonnettes support a crenelated wall with turrets and water spouts. Tiny shields and colorful enamel plaques riveted to this wall furnish relieving spots of color against the gold. From the center of a basin formed by the wall, a delicate tower with a balcony and Gothic arcade carries a row of tiny metal mill wheels fastened to bells. The liquid running from openings in the uppermost story causes the wheels to revolve and the bells to tinkle. Dropping another story it sets going another row of wheels in the lower basin. In this way there was a continuous movement as long as the fountain flowed.

All the details of a Gothic building, the cusped arches, pinnacles, towers, and even stained glass, are represented in this skillfully executed little machine. Comparing it with a piece of Egyptian or Greek furniture, we see at once how different were the stylistic ideas that inspired the Classical and the Gothic peoples. Yet each is perfect in its own way, the first approximating the canons of beauty, the second giving expression to energy.

Sculpture

Many of the origins of Gothic sculpture, as of the Gothic structures, are to be found in the Romanesque styles of Italy and Provence. Romanesque sculpture developed as an architectonic style characterized by stiff wooden forms suggestive of the upward movement in the architecture of which it was a part. Sometimes, as in the case of Burgundian sculpture, an angular geometric movement ran through the composition, or, as in Provençal sculpture, a classical or Byzantine reminiscence appears in the treatment of figures or drapery. These distinctions disappeared after the 12th century as the sculpture became Gothic and a variety

of local styles coalesced. This fusion resulted in the 14th century in a style that produced realistic figures with a minimum of movement at times copying antique drapery. Following this,

Fig. 369.—Table fountain, Burgundian (?), late 14th century. (*Courtesy of Cleveland Museum of Art.*)

there came a trend to the flamboyant, with heavy, animated draperies so arranged that the figures appeared to be part of a mounting flame.

The Architectonic Sculpture in the South Porch at Chartres. The south porch of the cathedral at Chartres (Fig. 370) furnishes a good example of the arrangement and technique of 13th-century architectural sculpture. Here more than anywhere else, each individual figure forms part of a great functional movement. This doorway, dedicated to the Last Judgment, centers around the figure of Christ, as does the front portal. The effect of light and shadows moving through the large recess makes the sculpture, seen from a distance, what appears to be a mass of natural stalactites. The aesthetic effect is indescribably rich. Every piece of carving seems part of the perpendicular movement of the cathedral. The lines of drapery continue the twisted lines of the supporting columns.

hand upraised to bless. He appears beneath a representation of the heavenly city, which looks quite like the many spires and windows of the cathedral.

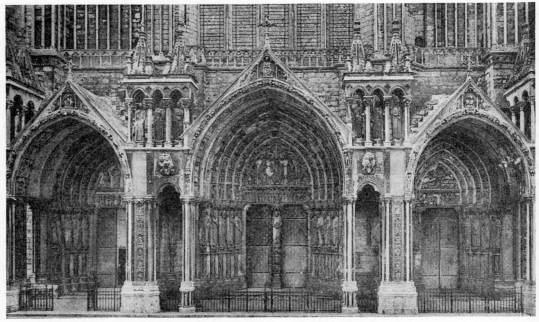

FIG. 370.—South porch, Chartres. (*Courtesy of E. Houvet.*)

These start a spiraling motion that moves up the reveals. At the top of the gable this movement is resolved in the Adoration.

The Meaning of the Trumeau. The central prop, or *trumeau*, of the doorway holds a magnificent figure of the Christ, similar in style to the famous Beau Dieu of Amiens (Fig. 371). At Chartres the Christ is represented above kneeling figures of the two donors of the porch—Pierre Mauclerc, Count of Dreux, and his wife, Anne of Brittany. As at Amiens, He stands with His feet on two animals, a lion and a peculiar dragon, called a basilisk, which has the head of a rooster. Below this group the sculptor placed a vine motif, for Christ is thought of as the true vine, from which the whole church branches. Above the vine runs a wall with crenelations and clouds, on which stands the majestic figure with His holy book and His

The figures on each side of the Christ represent the twelve apostles, each holding some symbolic attribute (such as the keys for St. Peter) or the instruments of his martyrdom. Above the disciples, the reveals of the arch display scenes connected with the Last Judgment. Those nearest the top show the choir of angels and archangels, representing the heavenly court of Christ. Moving down the reveals one sees the angels awakening the dead, who clamber out of their tombs. Thus every part of the architecture contributes to the central theme of the Last Judgment, which follows the description in the Gospel of St. Matthew.

The Doom, or Last Judgment. The central scene, a Doom, on the tympanum is divided into three levels. The upper shows Christ seated, holding out his hands so as to display his wounds. To his left one sees the damned, to his right the saved. The outermost reveal of the porch proper holds the kings and queens of the Old Testament and the major prophets. Next come the major blessings, which, for the body, are beauty, swiftness, strength, liberty, health, pleasure, and long life. For the soul they are wisdom, friendship, concord, honor, power, security and joy. Here the classical, or pagan, virtues mingle with the Christian.

The square pillars at the right and left of the portal show the four and twenty elders of Israel, also the virtues and the vices. Two lions appear as waterspouts, one on each side of the central arch. They have been moved upward to this position from their old place on southern Romanesque portals, where they bore the columns on which the porch rested. The great richness of detail and monumental composition of this bears witness to the fact that Northern Europe was definitely the productive artistic center in the 13th century. No work produced in the same period among the southern churches of Italy equals this porch in consistency of plan and execution.

The Golden Age of Cathedral Sculpture. Thirteenth-century sculpture introduces a careful, detailed study of foliate forms, as well as of human features. The human figures received distinctive lineaments intended to express the various mental states through which the characters were supposed to be going. This study of human features took place a century before the sculpture of Giotto in the south. The faces of his figures, on the whole, know but one means of expression—the turned-up corners of the mouth.

On the façade of the cathedral at Reims stands a statue, representing the Virgin (Fig. 372*a*), whose face might have been carved by some Roman sculptor. Here the sculptor wished to produce an effect of calm. Another figure, St. Joseph (Fig. 372*b*), stands near by. His face, with its quizzical expression, is as animated as the Virgin's is restful. In many details the Virgin's figure resembles a Greek statue, and her drapery would seem to indicate classical

origins. Villard de Honnecourt included in his notes drawings of several figures from antique models that were known in his time. Other evidence indicates that the people of Reims

Fig. 371.—Trumeau figure, the Beau Dieu, Amiens.

knew not only the Roman arch in their city wall, but examples of antique sculpture. However, as the head of St. Joseph shows, the northern artist was more interested in the expression of inner force and tension than in classical unity and repose. This force he expressed by means of sculptural forms made linear rather than in terms of sculptural forms as mass.

Expression in the Doom at Bourges. The sense of the dramatic, which is allied to the development of the mystery and miracle plays, is best shown in the representation of the Last Judg-

FIG. 372*a*.—Virgin from Reims. (*Courtesy of Metropolitan Museum of Art.*)

ment at Bourges (Fig. 373). As in Chartres and Amiens, this entire scene has been placed in the tympanum above the figure of Christ. The problem of properly arranging the figures in the high space was first approached by dividing that space into three separate bands, with the representation of the heavenly city making a zigzag line behind the throned figure of the Christ. The position of His arms, like the wings and arms of the angels behind the gables, helps to accentuate this zigzag motion. Below, on each side, the angels, who hold the instruments of the Passion, stand in easy posture, draped like antique statues.

In the band beneath the feet of the Christ, the angel Michael holds the scales. The soul, represented by a little child, rests on the heavy side, while a tiny demon climbs on the light side, trying to weight the balance down. The smiling angel has his left hand around a naked

child, representing the pure soul, as though to protect it from a demon who comes in from the right. Farther to the right, the damned fall into the gaping mouth of a great dragon, Leviathan,

FIG. 372*b*.—St. Joseph from Reims. (*Courtesy of Metropolitan Museum of Art.*)

from which come the hot flames of hell. This frequently figures in the medieval mystery plays.

This entire section of the scene, with the representation of the resurrection of bodies below, has been given a restless motion through the use of haphazard diagonals, which contrast with the tall, gently moving figures in the Paradise at the left. By thus opposing rhythmical and unrhythmical linear design the sculptor shows the peaceful mental state of the saved and the anguish of the damned. This mental anguish, or aesthetic unrest, is further associated with the grotesque. The demons have faces resembling masks. One has a tail that terminates in a stinging serpent; this comes up under his legs to torment a fleeing soul which he is pushing toward the flames. Several of the demons here, as at Chartres, have grotesque faces peering out from beneath their legs. Bands

FIG. 373.—The Doom at Bourges, 13th century. (*Courtesy of Clarence Ward.*)

of plastic floral decoration, and interlaced twigs and vines, which again carry the attention back to the original Gothic interweave motif, bind together this rich composition.

Fig. 374.—Assumption of the Virgin, Paris, 14th century. (*Courtesy of Lesch.*)

The Assumption of the Virgin at Paris. The 14th-century relief showing the Assumption of the Virgin, from Notre Dame in Paris, will demonstrate to what lengths the Gothic sculptor went in achieving realism (Fig. 374). In the stained glass of the time, the Virgin was pictured rising in an aureole of color. The sculptor tried to translate into stone the luminous effect of the glass and, to simulate the irradiation of the glorious figure, invented the peculiar sinuous, ribbonlike planes that move back into the surface of the relief. In so doing, whether he knew it or not, he was working in a good traditional manner, for his Gothic forebears, as shown in the section on Romanesque sculpture, used this very means of composition before adopting the human form. The wings and drapery of the angels and the vibrating leaves around the quatrefoil, remind us of the Moorish and Gothic pre-Romanesque wood carving from which this whole movement developed. Here at Paris, sculpture returns, in almost flamboyant style, to the dramatic sense that seeks contrast of light and shade rather than well-proportioned body representation.

The Burgundian Realism of Claus Sluter. In contrast to this restless style, the Burgundian sculp-

Fig. 375.—Fountain of Moses at Dijon, Claus Sluter, early 15th century. (*Courtesy of Metropolitan Museum of Art.*)

tors of France developed during the second half of the 14th century a realistic mode of portraying the human figure. That school, centered in the ducal court at Dijon, included many sculptors from the Low Countries and Germany. Claus Sluter, the best known member of this group, working early in the 15th century, carved simple, natural figures, swathed in heavy drapery. His Moses from the Fountain of Moses at Dijon (Fig. 375) characterizes the works of this precursor of later Renaissance sculptors in Italy.

The figures made by Sluter show a new form of expression that depends upon dramatic arrangement in the folds of the drapery, the lines of the face, and the realistic pose. His work lacks the inner, vitalizing, energetic line of the earlier Gothic. With it begins the realistic tendency in French sculpture that was to culminate in the 19th-century works of Rodin.

The Nuremberg Madonna and the Athena Lemnia. The final step in the development of Gothic

FIG. 376.—Nuremberg Madonna, Vischer atelier (?), early 16th century. Painted wood, height 5 feet (Nuremberg Germanic Museum). (*Courtesy of Lesch-Carnegie.*)

sculpture brings the realistic human being and the linear composition to a point of entire equi-

librium. The statue of the Madonna of Nuremberg (Fig. 376) by Peter Vischer unites all the attributes of the Gothic. The work stands to the Gothic movement as does the Athena

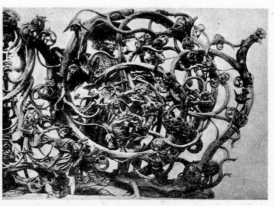

FIG. 377.—Wood carving by Henry Douvermann, on altar of Collegiate Church, Xanten, Germany, 16th century. (*Courtesy of Lesch.*)

Lemnia to Greek sculpture. A comparison of the two figures will make clear the aesthetic will of the Greek and the Gothic artist.

The Athena stands, a well-proportioned human goddess, proudly self-possessed, well armed, yet completely at rest. The Madonna is not a body but a spirit looking within and projecting her prayers towards something above and outside herself. The columnar drapery of the Athena unites her with the ground. Upon her breastplate she carries many decorative symbols, among them, the gorgoneion indicating her superior position as a woman. The Madonna of Nuremberg wears no ornament; her eyes from under her wimple are half-shaded with modesty. The Madonna needs no protection, for she has brought new life to the earth. Athena is the child of Zeus, the sky-god; the Madonna, the chosen wife of the All Highest. The lines of the Athena are graceful but muscular and stalwart; they reveal the human form. The lines of the Madonna conceal the human form. More than merely graceful, they seem to live.

Late Gothic German Sculpture. With the coming

of the flamboyant style, Gothic sculpture showed a more violent movement. During the 15th century, in Germany, where the art of wood carving had been greatly developed in

Fig. 378.—Tree of Judgment, façade at Orvieto, Lorenzo Maitani (?), 1330. (*Courtesy of Lesch.*)

connection with the making of altarpieces and cathedral furniture, one sees the plant completely ensnare the human being, who struggles in its coils as though to escape some demoniac power (Fig. 377). All was confusion in the mind that conceived this. For contrast, this carving should be compared on one hand with the nicely ordered Tree of Doom from Orvieto (Fig. 378), and on the other with the figure of the Yakshini in the tree on the Indian stupa at Sañchi (Fig. 415). Here are three conceptions of life, three variant symbolizations of the rela-

tionship of man to nature: in the Classical piece, man uses nature as a frame; in the Gothic, man struggles with nature; in the Oriental, man seems to be an integral part of nature.

Comparison of Northern and Southern Gothic Sculpture. In the cathedral sculpture of 12th- and 13th-century Italy, nothing approaches either the mastery of composition or the individual knowledge of form displayed in contemporaneous Gothic carvings. This can be seen by comparing the supreme achievement of Chartres with the Italian Gothic cathedral of Orvieto, built in 1310. The sculpture of the latter was carved almost 100 years later than that of Chartres. The façade at Orvieto conventionally serves as a frame to hold not sculpture as such, but carved pictorial compositions. Among these, Maitani's low-relief representation of the Last Judgment repeats a theme frequently used on northern façades (Fig. 378).

In southern sculpture, while every human form stands out clear and well proportioned, each form is part of a mass of human beings or a crowd. In the northern Gothic, each figure has within itself as much unity as the southern figures. Its unity, however, partakes of the effect of the whole, serving as part of the architecture.

Painting

Gothic painting, like Gothic sculpture, derived from the workshop, or *chantier*, of monastery and cathedral. As the guilds grew and the lay artists emerged, a new style of painting and tapestry weaving arose. This was intimately connected with the development of the monumental mural art of stained-glass designing, whose technique became so strong that it dominated all other graphic arts. To understand fully Gothic painting, both manuscript and mural, one must understand the stained-glass composition.

Wolfram von Eschenbach, the 12th-century minnesinger, characterized the stained-glass window thus:

Adamite and amethyst
. . . .
Topaz and garnet fine
Chrysolite and rubies twine
With sardonyx and emeralds
Thus these precious windows shine.

In the writings of both Theophilus and Wolfram, the emphasis rests upon the precious quality of the materials, with a mere suggestion of the aesthetic value in variety of color. No mention is made of the design element in the leading, which today strikes us as being remarkable. All the colors have associational values which, combined with the associational values of precious stones, suggested other, more mystical values. The ruby, for instance, might stand for the rich blood of the Saviour; the emerald, for the green sea ruled over by the Virgin. The purple, which was the color of royalty, was blended of the heaven's blue and the ruby wine.

The Development of Mullions in Rose and Lancet Windows. With the perfecting of the Gothic cathedral structure in the 12th and 13th centuries, the work of the stained-glass painter was enormously expanded. The lancet windows became 20 or 30 feet high. The mullions, or stone divisions, which in the Italian Romanesque churches had appeared as spokes of a wheel, gradually assumed cusped forms, the spaces terminating in pointed arches. In the late Gothic this tracery became greatly elaborated and interwoven, both in the circular and the tall lancet windows. The rose windows in the façade and transepts—greatly enlarged wheel windows—could accommodate more scenes. Thus the design had to be composed in two areas—one tall and pointed, the other circular. The design of the rose window was to the interior of the cathedral what the façade was to the exterior. Villard de Honnecourt shows, among other sketches in his notebook, a copy of the wheel window at Chartres.

The Tree of Jesse and the Tree of Life. The close linkage of parts characteristic of the finest window design is well illustrated by a small section of glass from the Tree-of-Jesse window,

at St. Denis (Fig. 379), considered by many to be the earliest church in Gothic style. Here a study of one of the kings set in the branches of the tree will show how the human form almost

Fig. 379.—Tree-of-Jesse window, St. Denis, c. 1150. *(After Lassus.)*

seems to grow out of the main trunk, so that it is difficult to see where the feet of the king terminate and the trunk of the tree begins. To understand this interwoven composition of the finest French glass, it must be compared not only with the Book of Kells but also with the sculptured columns and pilasters from Moissac and Souillac; and further, with the style of ornament developed by the Saracenic culture in contact with Christianity around the shores of the Mediterranean. The composition of two wooden doors of a 12th-century church in ancient Cairo, where the Christian subject matter is used in the definitely Oriental and Gothic style (Fig. 268c, Chap. XI) invites such a comparison. The same subject—the human figure seated in a tree and appearing to grow out of the tree—occurs in contemporaneous Buddhistic art, where it was conventional to show the Buddha as part of either the lotus or the Bo Tree.

The Passion Window at Le Mans. This same interlaced composition unites the famous Passion window at Le Mans (Fig. 380), where the style changes to a simpler, more pictorial, or

Fig. 380.—Passion Window, Le Mans, 12th century.
(*After Lassus.*)

classical representation. The parts of the window do not so completely intertwine, and yet the main bars which hold up the leading seem to partake of the character of a tree. The subject of the window, one of the many versions of the *Mirrors* of Vincent of Beauvais, illustrates the way Old and New Testament symbolism was woven together. The trunk of the tree displays four episodes in the Passion of Christ. The first of these, in the lowest central light, one of the most remarkable compositions in window design, focuses around the cross, which binds together the two sides of the quatrefoil. The scene shows the moment at which the Christ has fallen under the weight of the cross and St. Simon of Cyrene comes to his assistance. On the left side, the patriarch Jacob blesses the sons of Joseph—Ephraim and Manasseh, who stand for the Gentiles and the Jews. Contrasting with this relatively peaceful composition, the scene at the right shows the murder of Abel. Since the subject is one of passionate crime, the artist has given expression to the violent explosion of the moment by making the various parts of his composition as disparate as possible. The second quatrefoil shows the Crucifixion in almost absolute balance. The sun and moon appear on each side of the cross, with a door, standing for the city, at the left, and two trees, for the country, at the right. Preaching salvation through this cross, the artist placed around it four scenes of redemptive nature. At the left, Moses appears in the act of striking the rock in the wilderness. By thus quenching the thirst of the Jewish people, who are represented with their tall caps, Moses saved Israel. Opposite this, Moses is again shown, suggesting that the Israelites look upon the brazen serpent in the wilderness. As he points upward, we notice that his hand continues the movement of the drapery. Above this scene play young lions, and at the left King David sees the eagle feeding its young. These two representations stand for the Resurrection and the Ascension.

The third quatrefoil brings Christ, as the central figure, out of the horizontal tomb,

FIG. 381.—Detail of Fig. 382, Chartres. (*Courtesy of Dayton Art Institute; photograph by Metcalf.*)

which cuts across the panel. The angels stand on each side and the sleeping soldiers lie in the lowest part of the field. The scene to the lower left shows the prophet Elias healing the daughter of the widow. At the lower right, Jonah escapes from the mouth of a monstrous fish. At the upper left, Elisha, like Christ rejected by his Jewish compatriots, seeks refuge with the widow of Sarepta in Sidon. She holds two branches in the form of a cross, so that the holy sign appears here again. At the upper right, Elias gives his rod to the servant, who was unable to make it function in healing the widow's daughter because of his lack of faith. This entire section presents a sermon on the need for belief in the Resurrection.

The fourth and final quatrefoil of the lancet shows Christ seated in his majesty (the *Majestas*). From each side come the angels with their trumpets, calling the dead from their tombs. Here Christ very definitely marks the center of the composition. Each stage of the story is clear. No scene lacks the presence of the cross. The glory of the risen Christ shines down from the top, illuminating every part of the sermon.

The Color Composition and the Leading at Chartres. The section of a window from Chartres makes clear the method of composition used by the 12th-century painters (Fig. 381) (Fig. 382). The scene shows Christ washing the feet of his disciples. The head of the Saviour, usually marking the center of the composition, has here been placed at one side of the panel, for the artist wished to set up a tension between the groups of people. Hence, through the folds of his robe, the figure of the Christ connects with a group of disciples at the left, whose heads are suggested and bound together by segments of halos. The foot of the Christ, which runs over into the circular border, binds this group to the border, a trick used, the reader will remember, on the best Greek vase painting. On the other side, the group at the right connects with Peter, at their head. Now the point of interest becomes the place where Christ washes the feet

of Peter. Since the two groups divide our interest, one may ask what holds the entire composition together. Peter's foot also overlaps the border, and the eye runs up the border of the

Fig. 382.—Section of 12th-century window, Chartres, showing leading. (*After Lassus.*)

circle to the top, where this blends with a group of buildings standing for the city of Jerusalem. The border as a whole overlaps the still greater border of the side of the window, and ties into other compositions on the left through small bits of floral design. In this way there is a suggestion of that greater theme, the Tree of Jesse, whose movement underlies the construction of the whole cathedral. Studying the lines of the leading alone, giving no attention to details of drapery, one marks an advance in design over earlier German work. The final aesthetic touch in this superior design is that the lines of the halos are repeated in the circular segments of the base of the buildings—the City of Jerusalem.

Late Gothic Glass. The final stage in the aesthetic development of the glass window is illustrated by one of the products of the workshop connected with St. Stephen's Church in Vienna. This shop was supported not alone by the church but by commissions from the ducal

Fig. 383.—Late Gothic glass, St. Stephen's, Vienna, c. 1400. (*After Kieslinger.*)

house of the Hapsburgs. The section of the window with six lights comes from the chapel of St. Eligius (patron of the goldsmiths) in the cathedral (Fig. 383). The figures form each one a part of a framed panel, and are set off by themselves yet interwoven more than ever as the folds of their drapery blend with a background composed entirely of vine scrolls.

A study of their composition in connection with this fantastic architecture shows the tendency in flamboyant times to lose the human body in a jungle, not of linear interweave, but of architectural forms. The greater amount of brushwork on the glass indicates the influence of the panel painter. The faces display more realistic character; a close examination reveals their similarity to the head of St. Joseph from the front of Reims (Fig. 372). The twisted, flowing hair, as well as the contorted forms of the face, show the dramatic tension of the artist's mind.

The Murals of Runkelstein. Some of the stained-glass cartoons from the workshop of St. Stephen's were used to decorate the walls of Castle Runkelstein near Bozen in southern Tyrol (Fig. 366). The various rooms of this castle give us a good insight into the secular painting of the time. The subject matter, which illustrates the medieval idea of history from the point of view of the nobles, differs considerably from the ecclesiastical topics. Here, along the line of the outer balcony, ancient heroes—Alexander the Great, Julius Caesar, and Hector of Troy—sit beside King Arthur, Godfrey of Bouillon, and the knights Parsifal, Gawaine, and Iwaine, or half-legendary figures, such as Theodoric, Dietlieb of Steiermark, and Siegfried. Various painters from Austria and Flanders decorated the rooms inside the balcony with the stories of Tristan and Isolde and Sir Garel of the Flowering Vale.

The walls depicting the history of Sir Garel were painted by the artist who did the pictures on the balcony. This man came apparently from the ducal stained-glass school in Vienna, for we find here the same drawing, color scheme

FIG. 384.—Diagram of wall painting in Garel Hall, Castle Runkelstein, Austrian style, c. 1400.

and composition that enriched the chapel of St. Eligius. A diagrammatic drawing of the composition of the end wall, with three connected pictures and a detail from another part shows how the artist adapted the composition of the windows to his monumental wall painting (Fig. 384). Against the expanse of the blue background, he placed smaller areas, bounded by lines similar to the leading lines of the windows,

general lines of his composition, using a true fresco technique, with water color upon wet plaster. The red lines of his original drawing still show where the rain has washed away the overpainting. He then retraced these lines with tempera colors; that is, with colors mixed in casein glue or egg white, in what is called *fresco secco*, or "dry fresco."

In another room of the castle, whose walls

FIG. 385.—Dance fresco from the Tournament Hall, Castle Runkelstein, style of Avignon, c. 1350.

which interweave from picture to picture. Just so must the bardic singer have interwoven the episodes of the narrative to the music of harp or lute. First upon the wall the artist painted the

depict sports and tournaments, appears a picture of a medieval dance (Fig. 385). The style here differs considerably from that of the Garel room. The colors of the first fresco were rich blues, red, and a deep green. The colors in the dance fresco are light, inclined to pinks, greens, and yellows. Just as the first type of painting stems directly from the stained-glass workshop,

FIG. 386.—Madonna Enthroned, Cimabue, c. 1285. Tempera on wood, height 127½ inches (Florence, Uffizi). Note static composition gained by placing figures on diagonals and horizontal lines. (*Courtesy of Lesch-Carnegie.*)

the second derives from the art of tapestry weaving, carried up from Avignon, in France. It resembles the Romanesque wall decorations in castles of Provence and the miniatures in French manuscripts showing the joys of the hunt. The famous connected series of tapestries, "The Hunting of the Unicorn," now in The Cloisters, New York, unites the attributes of both styles.

These two styles of painting might be likened to two types of music then in vogue. From Provence came the songs of the troubadours and trouvères, with short melodic line, definitely rhythmical beat, and set stanzas; from the north, the songs of the minnesingers, with longer and more involved melodic line, less set beat, and a tendency toward counterpoint. The one represents the style of the south, measured and relatively simple; the other, the "infinite melody of northern line," interwoven and obscure.

Gothic Influences in Southern Painting. The composition styles that developed in the stained-glass painting of the north found their way to the south and were eagerly adopted by the Italian painters of the 13th century. In their hands the new discovery of realism in art became the influence that helped them break away from the hierarchical Byzantine style of the church.

The discovery of reality in Italian painting began with Cimabue in the late 13th century. This artist first attempted to put individual character into his figures and to make men more substantial. His Madonna Enthroned shows this first innovation (Fig. 386). The composition is still the strictly hierarchical one with the woman in the center and the attendant angels on each side. The artist attempted correct perspective in the throne, thus freeing himself from the Byzantine formulae of reverse perspective and flat representation.

The second innovation in this picture is the introduction of faces that seem almost portrait-like in character, though those of the Madonna, the child, and the angels are still stylized. The folds on the drapery, also, are more naturalistic than in most Byzantine work. The Byzantine influence persists in the technique, however, for the entire picture is held together by being painted on a gold-sized panel so that the warm yellow shines through the glazelike paint. The technique on the whole remains that of the medieval artist in enamel. A careful study of the robes of the Madonna will show the many fine lines of gold gleaming like metal *cloisons.*

Simone Martini, of Siena, shortly after the time of Cimabue, displays even more influence of the northern style. The Virgin and the angel in his Annunciation (Fig. 387), show greater through the whole center panel, make this one of the most significant of Gothic compositions. Martini's realism exceeds even that of Cimabue, as may be seen in the figures of the two

Fig. 387.—The Annunciation with SS. Ansanus and Juliet, by Simone Martini and Lippo Memmi, 1333. Tempera on wood, height 5 feet 11¼ inches (Florence, Uffizi). (*Courtesy of Lesch-Carnegie.*)

vitality than Cimabue's figures, both in their dramatic action and in the rendering of the folds of drapery. A magnificent sweep of line coming down through the pointed wings and wind-blown robe of the angel, crosses to the figure of the Virgin, to be picked up again by the folds of her robe and the position of her right hand. The drawing of the Virgin suggests contemporaneous Chinese painting.

The spacing of the silhouette of the Virgin's body under the right arch, the position of the lily stems and flowers under the dove in the central arch, and the interweave of lines

saints in the side panels. The city of Siena, with its Gothic cathedral, retained the northern style in painting along with traces of the Byzantine long after its neighbor, Florence, had rediscovered and used classical art forms and ushered in the Renaissance.

Giotto's Classical Mood—the Death of St. Francis. To understand the part played in the development of Italian art by the Gothic style, the reader need only compare the many compositions in Giovanni Pisano's Florentine Baptistery doors with the portal quatrefoils of Paris and Reims, or with the stained-glass panels in

Chartres and Le Mans. The paintings of Giotto illustrate even better the effect of this union of aesthetic styles. Students of art usually approach Giotto as the first of the great masters of

vital symbolic point. This fact may be taken simply as evidence of Giotto's desire for realism, albeit a very dramatic realism.

Giotto has further attempted to depict the

FIG. 388.—Death of St. Francis, by Giotto, c. 1325, Bardi Chapel, Santa Croce, Florence. Fresco, figures about life size. (*Courtesy of Lesch-Carnegie.*)

the Renaissance. It is also possible to study him as one of the Gothic masters working in Italy. Observe, first, his Classical Death of St. Francis (Fig. 388) in the Bardi chapel of Santa Croce.

The figures in this work are all quite solid. Giotto's perspective, much more realistic than Martini's, gives a feeling of depth. A dark blue, which lends a feeling of distance, replaces the conventional gold background. The red on the gown of the prelate who kneels before the bier of St. Francis brings the front plane of the picture far forward from the blue plane in the rear. This bit of practical color psychology also contributes to the feeling of depth. The only medieval touch remaining in the symbolism is the use of halos for the saint and the group of angels who carry his soul away into the sky. The perspective lines do not end in any one

feelings of the various monks present at the death of the saint. Like the early Greek sculptors, however, he seems to have known only two ways to indicate emotion. He either turns up the corners of the lips, which makes some faces appear to be laughing when they should be crying, or he makes his figures gesticulate. The bodies remain puppetlike or, if they move at all, as in Giotto's other works, the motion is violent.

This picture may be taken as an interesting organization of dramatic medieval stage material. Five groups of figures surround the horizontal body of the saint, which connects the whole composition. The eye is directed to the head of the saint by the gaze of every one in the five groups, so that the head and face of the saint vie with the departing soul to claim our attention. Thus, the two possible centers of interest in this painting set up tension. In its realism and its desire to portray depth, the work is somewhat Gothic. On the other hand,

the figure of Drusiana. The attention is held back somewhat by the figure of the man with his hands raised.

On the other side of the scene, behind John,

Fig. 389.—Raising of Drusiana, by Giotto, Peruzzi Chapel, Santa Croce, Florence. Fresco, figures about life size.
(*Courtesy of Lesch.*)

it remains relatively static because of the fact that the more peaceful horizontal lines are, on the whole, dominant.

Giotto's Gothic Mood—the Raising of Drusiana. Giotto's most Gothic style appears in the fresco, the Raising of Drusiana (Fig. 389), in the Peruzzi Chapel of Santa Croce. No one obvious center of interest controls this picture. Its composition resembles that of the circular window from Chartres, which showed Christ washing the feet of Peter (Fig. 381). The groups form two large masses out of which project the body and hands of Drusiana and St. John. Close inspection of the group at the right shows a restless motion of the drapery folds, starting at the lower right and working over toward the center, finally running out into the bending form of the man who carries the stretcher. His figure suggests the motion which culminates in

stand a number of his followers, most of whom follow his action with their eyes, or look at his wonder-working hand. Only one man, whose arm and drapery carry upward, catches the eye. We suddenly find it very easy to look upward and now we realize that, unconsciously, again and again, our eyes have been leaving these interesting groups in the foreground, drawn upward by a forest of verticals in the back of the picture. Exactly opposite the left upward-gazing man, stands another similar figure in the right of the picture. If one were to draw a line following their gaze to the place in the blue at which they look, these lines would cross on the vertical line that rises between the hand of Drusiana and the hand of John. This, the most decided and longest straight line in the entire painting, points in the direction from which the healing power comes.

To help get his effect, Giotto used the two architectural masses at the right and left of the picture with their twenty-odd vertical lines, not only to direct attention toward the sky but

Fig. 390.—Page from Windmill Psalter, English, Canterbury, 13th century. Judgment of Solomon above with initial of first Psalm. Height about 12 inches, width about 8 inches (Morgan Library). (*Courtesy of Morgan Library.*)

to make one feel the movement of the procession from right to left. Further, the wall consists of a number of planes that move the eyes backward and forward from the front to the rear of the picture. This gives the same type of depth composition that appears in Gothic relief sculpture. Modern critics associate this very quality in painting with the works of Cézanne, although Cézanne rarely achieves it as well as Giotto has here.

The general intent of the mass of domed buildings to the right ends in the angle of the

wall, which marks the line just beyond Drusiana's hand. The buildings to the left seem to move forward and to form part of the throng behind John. This directs the eyes from the front right toward the rear left, meeting a countermotion from the rear left toward the front right. Both groups connect definitely with the architecture, and as the architecture stands for landscape, one may say that figures and landscape here unite, all moving around the line which points into heaven.

Another and more subtle effect of the masses calls for attention. The towers at the left reach down from the outside of the picture plane. Their movement, helped by the leg and crutches of the man at the left of the picture, as well as by the folds, in the group, left, all concentrate in the hand. Thus the power of the hand seems actually to derive from the sky. The mass of the stretcher carries this power over into the vortex formed by the folds of the clothing of the right stretcherbearer. He and the two men behind him form the base for a taper held in the hands of the monk, and this rises, carrying the implications of power, up into the domed building, which symbolizes the feminine element. Thus with a vital spirit coming from the sky at the left down through John to quicken and revive the mass of the church at the right, the sermon becomes complete. Both the obvious and the occult symbolism used here were later adopted by Michelangelo as the composition motif of the Birth of Adam, and by Leonardo, in his Last Supper.

The control of space by the use of planes moving back into the picture developed later by baroque masters was revived by late 19th-century artists, particularly the followers of Cézanne. Here it serves a social purpose, that of making a religious story effective. In the 20th century, the technique alone was enjoyed aesthetically, purely for the sake of its formal values.

Realism in Gothic Painting—The Windmill Psalter. The same care that Giotto gave to details and to the dramatic action of his figures, the

FIG. 391.—The Madonna of Chancellor Rollin, attributed to Jan or Hubert Van Eyck, c. 1432 (*Louvre Museum*). (*Courtesy of Lesch.*)

northern artist accorded to all the minutest details of nature. In the 14th-century English Windmill Psalter (Fig. 390), which shows the influence of the English, flowing, decorated, or flamboyant style, one sees human figures, more dramatic and lifelike than those of Giotto, walking among the floral branches of an initial letter with a rather haphazard or naturalistic composition. Out of the mass of foliage, vines sprout and grow among the letters of the page, accompanied by an entire menagerie of Gothic animals. This page approaches closely the Oriental idea of the illustrated poem, containing a few written thoughts set in an area of design. It differs from the Oriental in that the human figures here have an almost equal place with nature. The page is not simply composed on a flat plane, however, as one may see by studying the figure of the angel that flies out of the mass of foliage. The rendering of the foliage, too, is such that certain planes retreat while others come forward. This work should be compared with the stained glass from the late 14th-century workshop, as well as with examples of contemporaneous tapestry, many of which show Persian influences.

Realism in Northern Panel Painting—the Van Eycks. The desire to compose *into the picture* rather than on the surface grew stronger in the north during the 15th century, along with the desire for still greater realism in portraiture. Landscape came to play an even greater part in the picture, as may be seen in the panel by Van Eyck (Fig. 391). The Flemish painters of the north, far distant from the ecclesiastical center at Rome, found in medieval aesthetics a warrant for the study of the effects of the physical light not only on every part of their cathedral but through all the passages of an ideal world. Here one of the brothers Van Eyck succeeded in uniting the outer world, with its river, cities, and snow-clad mountains, and the inner world, where the good believer might worship alone the Madonna and her Child. Both worlds are full of color, the outer because of a sunset sky, the inner because of the

stained-glass windows, which appear at the top of the picture. The formal light coming through the open arcade blends with the physical light in bringing out the details of the sculptured

Fig. 392.—Head of Christ, drawing by Albrecht Dürer. (*Courtesy of British Museum.*)

capitals. The floor is covered with warm-toned tiles, and the wings of the angel carry all the hues of the rainbow. Here can be found mastery of atmospheric and linear perspective far in advance of that in Italy at the time. No evidence exists that the northern painters understood perspective mathematically, as the Italians later attempted to do. They reached perspective, not by rule of thumb, but by careful objective observation. This method became the underlying spirit in the developing field of northern empirical science by the 16th century.

The same care evident in drawing and coloring was encouraged by the northern guilds,

FIG. 393.—The Knight, Death, and the Devil, engraving by Albrecht Dürer. (*Courtesy of Lesch-Carnegie.*)

whose members learned to mix pigments and prepare their panels with the greatest pains. The brothers Van Eyck, in their attempt to create panels that in chromatic quality would approximate stained-glass windows, used a method of painting in which the pigment was ground at times into varnish, to make a thick glaze, and later, in oil. In the Virgin and Donor, by uniting these two methods of painting with the tempera technique, they achieved delicacy in the light flesh parts and richness in the cloth. This richness is particularly apparent in the blue and red robes and the brocaded coat, with its fur collar, worn by the donor. The Gothic composition of the painting appears in the way the bold pattern on the gown of the donor attracts the eye to his person and his characterful face. His gaze leads us to the Mother and Child, with their attendant angel and crown. These foreground figures vie for our attention with the two on the outside wall and with the distant landscapes. The Gothic world has become ordered and complete. It is —shall we say?—a vision of the world as a perfect home.

Retention of Gothic Elements in the 16th-Century Germanic Countries

The Emergence of the Individual Artist in the Late Gothic. The last part of the 15th century and the first part of the 16th call for a study of three northern painters of the greatest genius. The first of these, Albrecht Dürer, composed naturally in the Gothic style. In Dürer's Head of Christ (Fig. 392) can be seen the quality of linear interweave that this artist achieved when he composed freely. His sketchbooks contain many studies of plants and animals in which he attempted to get the utmost possible realism. Even in those the love for linear pattern, although subordinated, is readily apparent.

Dürer's etching of "Knight, Death, and the Devil" (Fig. 393) unites all the characteristics of the Gothic style. Superficially, one marks at first a man riding on a horse—a man with but first a man riding on a horse—a man with but

nose and mouth and a part of one eye visible. The chin is interwoven and lost in the helmet; the helmet forms part of a carapace of armor that conceals more of the human form than it clarifies; the body of the horse consists of a series of forms curving one into the other. Around this unsubstantial center twines an interweave of sword and lance, of jagged rock and grotesque demon, of tangled branches, harness, and hair, that makes of the knight a symbol of one tangible idea in a world of changing forms. A dog runs along on the other side of the horse. The head of the dog is engraved so lightly that it comes out as a white spot in the foremost part of the picture plane and in front of the horse, behind which he is supposed to be running. Death, in the left background, has a lighter value than the knight, and the face of his horse comes forward into the front part of the picture plane. As we know from the many watercolors that he painted, Dürer could use correct perspective. He also understood the human form. However, in most of his work, an innate desire to express himself through an interwoven pattern connects him definitely with the cathedral builders.

The Crucifixion, by Grünewald. In the early development of Gothic culture, archaic Romanesque and Byzantine figures, with their geometrical motion, became humanized. Later, with the introduction of flamboyant architecture, the individual sculptured figures began to be swayed in mass, as though by some inner force. Their natural rhythm lost, they became expressionistic. The same phenomenon may be observed in the development of Gothic painting. Mathias Grünewald, who lived in the early part of the 16th century, reveals this tendency in his Isenheim altar (Fig. 394). Here the motion of the figures escapes the bounds of the plausible as the energy of their grief bends and twists them. The great central form of the dead Christ, with ghastly, thorn-bitten flesh, seems to be struggling to escape from the cross. St. John of the Wilderness, at the right, points with a finger electric in its intensity, while the figures at the left—John the Disciple, Mary the mother, and Mary Magdalene—are bent backward under the power of their emotion. Nature, bathed with a green light, is in a state

individual elements of the drapery all seem animated by their own life. Such a scene of torment is hard to escape. Here pain seems to be worshiped for its own sake, as the awful

Fig. 394.—Isenheim altar by Mathias Grünewald. Oil and varnish on wood, c. 1509–1511 (Museum, Colmar). *(Courtesy of Lesch-Carnegie.)*

of flux behind the cross. The tension of the scene has driven all the blood from the face and hands of the Madonna, and she seems about to swoon. The lines of the arms of the Christ, the upper right arm of John the Baptist, and the contour of John the Disciple together form a parallel zigzag that reaches down from the dark heavens and terminates, after moving past the bloody feet of Christ, in the cup into which drains the blood from the Lamb. The

agony of the Crucifixion is shown without any relief or thought of resurrection. Force, which usually causes pain, is the ultimate meaning of this composition. Behind force lies power, the power that built the cathedrals, the power that hopes to make the world over, the power that is in its essence the absolute negation of beauty, but which is a necessary phenomenon for aesthetic consideration in the art of the northern peoples.

The Humorous Realism of Pieter Breughel. The unrelieved contemplation of the various aspects of force in nature lends to the Gothic personality not only his vigor but also a nervous a Flemish farmer who lived between 1520 and 1569, saw the tragic world in which he lived, a world of cruelest persecution and religious warfare, through eyes relieved by the spectacles

Fig. 395.—Scharaffenland (In the Big Rock Candy Mountains!), by Pieter Breughel the Elder, c. 1568 (Alten Pinakothek Museum, Munich). (*Courtesy of Lesch.*)

compulsion that eventually seeks outlet in the dynamics of humor. The Gothic cathedral was not all a sublime adoration of supreme purpose. It had its light moments in grotesques and gargoyles. Hardly a medieval manuscript lacks a few demons tucked, grinning, among psalms and proverbs. Hence, some of the finest Gothic painters give most of their attention to those aspects of nature and man which are not beautiful and unified, but unexpected, and therefore humorous. Humor grows out of simple overstatement or the presence of the unexpected in the center of an otherwise complete composition. A Neapolitan poet, San Nazzaro, living at the end of the 15th century, created a beautiful dream poem about the ideal artist's land, called Arcadia. Pieter Breughel the Elder,

of humor (Frontispiece). To such an artist, the idea of a beautiful Arcadia was simply humorous. In his *Scharaffenland* (Fig. 395), now in the Alten Pinakothek in Munich, Breughel tried to picture his idea of Arcadia. The land lay somewhere in the south, as the cactus at the right, made up of pies, will testify. Around a central tree lie a soldier, a farmer, and a merchant. The tree holds a circular table, from which all kinds of delicacies fall into the mouths of those below. An egg runs along the ground, with a spoon in it, just begging for consumption; a roast chicken walks up and lays itself out upon a plate; and a pig turning into sausages comes from one side. The house at the left has a roof made up of pies, and the knight below lies openmouthed, as though waiting for a pie to drop in. The whole painting depicts a fantastic dream which, by its very overstatement, makes Arcadia an impossibility. The Breughel picture which is used as frontispiece to this volume contrasts the lifeless, pedantic critic with the vital Gothic artist. These pictures, when judged by laws of Oriental and Gothic art, rather than by Classical standards of beauty, will be found to have emotional appeal, occult balance, energy, and meaning.

Poetic Literature

Three great literary figures enliven the medieval scene with their wisdom and wit. The first was a saint, the second a politician, and the third an English diplomat.

St. Francis of Assisi. The first of these, Francesco di Bernardone, later called St. Francis of Assisi, was born in September, 1182, from the marriage of a Tuscan burgher and a Provençal noblewoman. Growing up as a skillful businessman in his father's shop, Francesco enjoyed a lively companionship with youthful troubadours and nobles. The reckless leader of a large circle of friends, he was careless of his money, lighthearted, and adventurous. In one respect he differed from his companions. Sensitive by nature, he felt the greatest compassion for the poor. He inherited, perhaps through his Provençal mother, a love for the lesser animals and a joy in the beauties of nature.

Francesco early became intimate with the *chansons de geste*, which included the stories of King Arthur and the Round Table as well as of the Holy Grail. Inspired by tales of knightly valor, the young man enlisted as a soldier in the armies of Pope Innocent III to fight against an Imperial general, Markwald, in southern Italy. Forced by a fever to return home before the earliest battles, Francesco received the command of God to lay aside his earthly armor. At a banquet in 1205, again advised by divine command, he forsook the world and went as a penitent hermit to live in poverty and to pray

in the caves outside the city walls. He gave all his clothes to the poor; his gold went to supply poor priests and churches with the means to further their ministry. After making a pilgrimage to Rome as a penitent beggar, Francesco received a command to minister to the lepers, whom he most loathed. Having performed this penance, he embarked upon a life of preaching and organizing.

Though at first feared by the church as a heretic, St. Francis was allowed to preach and to found three monastic orders. The first of these, the Friars Minor, also called the Gray Friars, soon had its counterpart in the Poor Clares, an organization composed of noblewomen of saintly disposition. These are two of the three Franciscan orders. Preaching to the birds, the fishes, the wolves, the crickets, and the poor, St. Francis brought an almost Oriental doctrine of redemptive love to a world weary of bloody persecution and the turmoil of crusades. As a poet, St. Francis wrote many hymns and songs, among which the best known are *The Hymn to the Sun, Love Sets My Heart Aflame*, and the *Song of the Creatures*. In the *Little Flowers of St. Francis*, the followers of the saint collected some of his most beautiful sermons, in themselves gems of poetic prose. These represent the essential part of Christian doctrine more closely than does any other literature of the Middle Ages.

Dante Alighieri. The writings of Dante Alighieri unite all the intellectual subtleties of the Scholastic philosophers, the spiritual wisdom of the mystics, and the chivalrous poetry of the troubadours. Fused by the imagination of this master poet, the strife between elements of church and state, between the powers of light and the powers of darkness, come to rest in one comprehensive literary scheme.

Dante was born in Florence, probably in May, 1265. His father, Alighiero di Alighieri, belonged to an ancient, impoverished family among the lowest ranks of the *grandi*, or dispossessed nobility, who were allowed no part in the city government by the democratic burghers. In 1283, when eighteen years of age, Dante wrote his first sonnet in honor of love, and within a few years he fell in love with Beatrice, who died in 1290. Between 1292 and 1294 Dante gathered the lyrics he had written in honor of Beatrice into a connected prose narrative, which he called the *Vita Nuova*. In the *Vita Nuova* Dante turned to follow his earthly love through the gates of heaven. His memory of Beatrice became the symbol of the queenly science, Theology, and gradually her image fused with that of the Virgin. In his songs to Beatrice, Dante unites all the love of a troubadour for his lady and all the religious allegory of Scholasticism. For a few years after the death of Beatrice, Dante became involved in the politics of Florence and served briefly as one of the chief magistrates of the republic. Eventually he was banished.

Throughout all his life, this poet, like all the other great medieval artists, turned away from the reality of the senses to find true meaning in symbolic allegory. All the currents of medieval life flowed together in the life of Dante. He stood to his time as Akhenaten to Egyptian thought; Plato to that of Athens. Having mastered all medieval knowledge, having explored Greco-Arabian astronomy, he united these with the cosmic dream of Plato and the Scholastic reasoning of the Aristotelian Thomist philosophy.

In a medieval way, that is, more for their content than their form, Dante studied the ancient Latin classics, showing an almost superstitious reverence for the myths of imperial Rome. Consorting with the troubadours, he invented a new form of verse, the stanza of the *terza rima*. This was composed of three-line stanzas closed by an extra rhyming line. Every ten lines rhymed as follows: the first and third; the second, fourth, and sixth; the fifth, seventh, and ninth; the eighth and tenth.

Prepared by his political experience to pass judgment upon his time, he tells us in his essay *De Monarchia* that Roman history contains the key to all further political developments. To him the ancient Roman Empire had been divinely ordained to civilize the world and to formulate its laws.

In exile, about the year 1304, Dante wrote his *De Vulgari Eloquentia*, or *On Vernacular Eloquence*. Here, starting as a realist, he observed the many dialects of the Romance languages in Europe and, finding one common to most of the towns in Italy, suggested that with some refinement it might become the universal Italian language. Having written the *Convivio*, or *Banquet*, and the *Canzoni*, a collection of amatory, philosophic, and didactic poems, he turned in his last years after 1313 to his great work, the *Divina Commedia*.

This poem, like some great Gothic cathedral, includes in its three parts—the *Inferno*, *Purgatorio*, and *Paradiso*—all the elements of medieval thought. In its stanzas the medieval quality of contrast appears at its best. Here the loveliest expressions of the Beautiful stand beside the bitterest expressions of the Loathsome. Heaven and hell are set beside each other with all the sweetness of reward contrasted with the despair of eventual punishment. Here are love and hate, pleasure and pain. Throughout the pages of his *Inferno* Dante rid himself of his worst hates and fears; in his *Paradiso*, he pictured a heaven possible only to the most refined Christian mind. The great polarity of the medieval soul is shown in this contrast.

The *Commedia* also has a detailed structural plan, completely decorated with all the realism necessary to make clear its meaning as a way to salvation. Paralleling the *Summa* of St. Thomas Aquinas, it presents in poetic form the entire medieval drama of salvation. The accompanying chart (Fig. 396) shows Dante's conception of the universe.

The *Inferno* preaches the doctrine of divine vengeance for the differing sins. Since the church had not laid out an explicit plan of hell, as it had the way to salvation, Dante invented his own, basing it upon the writings of Vergil, St. Bernard, Thomas Aquinas, Aristotle, and Cicero as well as many inherited Tuscan super-

stitions stemming from Egyptian and Mesopotamian thought. Among all the punishments
meted out to sinners, the lightest are for in-
continents, the heaviest for traitors. Hence,

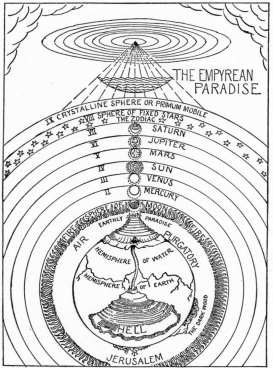

Fig. 396.—The medieval conception of the universe
based upon the poems of Dante. (*After Hearnshaw,
Medieval Contributions to Modern Civilization, Harrap & Co.
London.*)

Brutus, Judas, and Cassius are seen cruelly
mangled by the dripping jaws of Lucifer in the
lowest pit.

In Dante's *Purgatorio*, the soul that seeks freedom from sin can, by a series of disciplines,
gradually attain the salvation of paradise. Love
of the Good, the belief in free will, and the
astrological effect of the planetary spheres upon
human desires, as taught by St. Thomas, help
the Christian to approach salvation.

The *Paradiso* suggests the final solution of
the chief problems of human life, in the knowledge that the soul in paradise desires nothing
more than what it has. To live in Dante's

paradise is to know the entire meaning of the
spirit of St. Francis. Paradise delights in the
vision of the Virgin herself—the perfect rose
whose earthly prototype, Beatrice, had led
Dante through his adoration of the ideal
woman to the mystic vision of the Trinity,
which includes all existence. Here the psychomachia of Prudentius, which, at the beginning
of the Gothic culture, posed the problem of the
strife between the virtues and the vices, finds
its answer in the profound comprehensive psychology of the mature Gothic mind.

*Sir Geoffrey Chaucer—English Trouvère and Poet
of Men.* Chaucer, the third outstanding literary
genius of the Middle Ages, was born about
1340, the son of a London vintner. The youth
Geoffrey served as a court page. By his twentieth year he had fought in the French wars
with Prince Lionel and had been taken prisoner
near Reims. Since he was considered valuable,
his large ransom was paid by King Edward
himself, and Chaucer returned to England
where he was prepared for a life of public
service at the Inner Temple.

His marriage to Philippa, daughter of Sir
Payne Roet, eventually brought relationship
with the powerful Prince John of Gaunt, who
became his brother-in-law. After his thirtieth
year, Chaucer was sent on several important
diplomatic missions to France and Italy, where
he probably met Petrarch and, possibly, Boccaccio. He carried home with him the works of
these men as well as those of Dante. In the
meantime, he performed a great variety of
yeoman services for the king and held various
official posts, including that of Collector of
Customs for the Port of London.

This soldier, businessman, diplomat, and
justice of the peace, was above all, as he tells us,
a lover of books. His whole life, so it seems,
was a matter of interested self-education, and
his dominating philosophy was that of the
nominalist. Although widely read in the French
and Italian literature of his time, versed in
legal Latin and obliged to carry on his daily
intercourse in French, the language of the

Plantagenet court, Chaucer preferred to write in English, the language of the common people. He popularized this as a literary language very much as Dante had Italian, and his works were among the first printed in English by Caxton.

Chaucer's many ballades and rondels, as well as his longer poems, suggest that he might be appropriately called an English trouvère, or better a troubadour, for he was knighted. Among his friends or correspondents he seems to have had the trouvères, Guillaume de Machaut and Eustache Deschamps, and the chronicler Jean Froissart. Early in his literary career, Chaucer translated two serious works, which were to introduce the best of medieval philosophy and courtesy to the English burghers. The first of these, the *Consolations of Philosophy*, was by Boethius, widely studied as a popular ancient philosopher in the Middle Ages; the other was the *Roman de la rose*.

Started by the trouvère Guillaume de Lorris in 1225, the *Roman* presented a sort of lovers' guidebook, helping the courteous man to enter the castle of love, there to achieve the mystical rose. The second and larger part of the tale, written by Jean de Meun after 1270, furnished a philosophical discussion of the "pains" (or penalties) of love, in more satirical vein. This part included a popular compendium of all medieval knowledge matching, as a secular speculum, the encyclopedic Scholasticism of Vincent and Durandus.

Both aspects of life were deftly joined by Chaucer in his more original dramatic chanson, *Troilus and Criseyde*. Here the plot was derived from another great chanson, the *Roman de Troie*. In Chaucer's work the Stoic philosophy of Boethius combines with truly medieval religious feeling, for he concludes that earthly love is folly; that only the desire for salvation and the love of Christ are good.

In a number of other early works, including *The Death of Blanche the Duchess*, the *Parlement of Foules*, and *The Legende of Good Women*, Chaucer shows his debt to the trouvères. In *The House of Fame* he employs the love *débat*,

lays, and motets very much as they may be found in Guillaume de Machaut's *Le Jugement dou Roy de Navarre*.

After a creative life of interesting contact with all conditions of people, almost as an afterthought it might seem, Chaucer brought together, in his epic-length *Canterbury Tales*, a series of *novelle* rivaling those of Boccaccio. At the Tabard Inn of Southwark he gathered nine and twenty pilgrims who were on their way to the shrine of St. Thomas à Becket. As they traveled the pilgrimage road from Winchester to Canterbury, the characters regaled one another with their tales—each appropriate in style and content to its narrator.

Out of his busy life as Collector of Customs, Clerk of the King's Works, his country posts in Somerset and Surrey, and out of his omnivorous reading, Chaucer wove the most complete literary tapestry of the Middle Ages. The long rhythmical sweep of his procession is like a graceful medieval dance combined with the episodic journey of a castle wall painting. It reveals better than any other work of his period the individuals of the time: the Monk and the Friar, the Miller and the Franklyn, the Plowman, the Merchant, and the Good Wife of Bath. With the exception, perhaps, of Shakespeare, no one of the English writers has shown so complete a knowledge of human motives, for Chaucer was above all a student of moral characteristics, actions, and dreams—including within himself the entire meaning of a human being—a very poet of men.

The Drama in the Late Middle Ages

Previous study of the development of the drama up to the Middle Ages has demonstrated certain facts concerning the staging of the plays and the movement of the actors. In the primitive dance the spectator himself occupied the stage and moved as one of the actors. In the ancient Egyptian temple processions, dancing, singing, and mourning groups moved before him toward the shrine. In the primitive Greek theater, the spectators themselves danced, but in the great days of the drama a semiprofessional chorus developed which served to represent the feelings of the audience, connecting

Fig. 397a.—Wagon stage in English cycle play. (*After Thomas Sharp, A Dissertation on the Pageants; courtesy of Yale School of Drama.*)

them with the two or three actors who moved back and forth in one plane upon a raised, shallow stage. In Rome the actors, moving without a chorus to connect them with the audience, also performed upon a shallow, almost two-dimensional stage.

In the early Middle Ages, in association with the rise of new culture patterns, the processional movement again dominated the drama, accompanied at times by circular or square dances in which spatial patterns were made on the ground. A movement from various parts of the great cathedral audience toward the central shrine also took place. When the drama was performed in the open air, during the later Middle Ages, moving stage wagons often passed from one part of the town to another along a processional way that led to the cathedral. At first glance, this type of performance seems a return to the fundamental religious drama of the Egyptians; but with all the richness of Greek

and Celto-Germanic folk drama added to the original processional idea, it is apparent that here appears a new form. We shall now consider briefly the various types of play presentation common to the period between the 12th and the 16th century.

The Miracles and Mysteries. Besides the tropes, discussed in the previous chapter, the monasteries gave to the world many plays called "miracles" and "mysteries." In Gandersheim, Germany, the scholars of the Abbess Hrotsvitha performed the comedies of Terence, though not for the general public. The medieval mimes or jongleurs, many of whom frequented the monasteries, adopted these comedies for popular presentation in the streets of the city. Their interpretation of the Roman stage may seem strange to us who know the actuality, but this adaptation is highly significant of the change in dramatic movement that came about during the Middle Ages. A late-14th-century manuscript of Terence carries an illustration showing the medieval performance. Around the circle of the amphitheater sit the spectators. In the center, a tall curtained canopy, like a Punch and Judy show, houses the poet, who reads the play. Below him dance the mimes with masks and trumpets.

At Dunstable, England, in 1110, the scholars of Geoffrey the Norman dramatized the miracles of the saints, particularly those of St. Catherine of Alexandria and of St. Nicholas of Bari, the children's saint, better known as Santa Claus. The miracles and mysteries dealing with the life of Christ, first performed in the church at the two great festivals of Christmas and Easter, were elaborated into long cycles later in the 12th century. As towns and guilds came to fill a greater part in English life, the performances were introduced into the streets. In the town of Norwich, at Whitsuntide, the various guilds developed a cycle of plays which began with the creation of Eve and led up through the stories of Christ. Each guild was responsible for a wagon on which was played one episode of a cycle. This arrangement gave

FIG. 397b.—Medieval masks of various origins used in mystery plays. *a*, Roman comic character for slave; *b*, Roman comic Senex who later becomes Pantaleone; *c*, Roman soldier *miles gloriosus*, later becomes the Captain; *d*, Tibetan devil mask as the Christian devil. (*From Allardyce Nicoll, Masks, Mimes and Miracles.*)

every craft an opportunity to advertise its wares. The guild of shipwrights built Noah's ark; the guild of the goldsmiths equipped the Three Kings with their rich gifts. The wagons also carried noise-making machines, masks, and all the other properties necessary to make the presentation interesting (Fig. 397a).

The plays show much ready-made humor. The situations, often only loosely connected with the Biblical story, offered many opportunities for lively slapstick comedy. Such by-play occurs when Eve presents Adam with the apple. In another episode, Noah is obliged to use force to save his wife, who does not wish to leave her gossipy companions, preferring to sing one last song and drink a pot of ale with them. Cain appears as a man who refuses to pay tithes to the church, a not-too-subtle reminder for many in the audience.

The Pageants. Many of the old pagan festival days, survivals of Druidical worship, were celebrated throughout the Middle Ages by means of pageants. On May Day, for example, the people danced around the Maypole, an emblem of the tree of life. Hock Tuesday, which came after the second Sunday following Easter, was given over to the women as a sort of Dionysiac revel. Usually, some man dressed in woman's clothes was chased by the women, much as Falstaff in Shakespeare's play was pursued by the Merry Wives. A fool dressed in an animal skin, taken from this pageant, probably accounts for the character Bottom.

The Oxfordshire play, in honor of St. George, brought together characters from both Christian and pagan mythology. Here Father Christmas, St. George, King Alfred, and the Giant Blunderbore acted along with Litte Jack ("Jack be nimble, Jack be quick"), Old King Cole, and the Old Dragon—now quite harmless (Fig. 397b, part *d*).

The Dances. Most of the pageants were built upon characteristic dance forms. The Morris men, with leg bells, danced to the tune *Gathering Peascods* or *Sellinger's Round*. Each of these square dances had a sort of ballad of its own. From these the American country dances and, eventually, the Big Apple have descended. In the Scandinavian countries many of the dance forms included face slapping and kicking. Characteristic of Scotland were sword dances and the Highland fling. The northern dance strove to express with much foot stamping and arm waving, or by intricate geometric patterns, those same tensions which we have seen in set geometric form in the cathedral vaulting (Fig. 355).

The Morality Dramas and the Rising Protestant Spirit. With the growth of the bourgeois class and the rise of the universities, the church gradually lost its hold upon the imagination of the people. The vision of the City of God began to fade into infinity, and a new religious mood, growing partly out of nominalism and partly

Fig. 398.—"Sumer is Icumen in," round for six voices composed at Reading Abbey, England, c. 1240, with notation like that described in "Musica et ars cantus mensurabilis" by Franco of Cologne, c. 1220.

from survivals of the Manichaean heresies, appeared among the northern peoples. This was a mood of revolt or protest. During the time of this Protestant Gothic mental development, there came a revival of the *esprit*, or argument between the soul and body, which gave rise to a number of plays, such as *Mankind*, *Mundus et Infans*, *Everyman*, and *Dr. Faustus*.

The morality plays *Mankind* and *Everyman* picture man moving toward his goal of perfection, the celestial kingdom, from which he can be barred only by his evil deeds and toward which he may be helped by the good. In the early medieval church plays, man appears to be either predestined or damned. In these later

two, as the nominalist element of free will becomes strong, the significant dramatic tensions revolve about man's good actions in conflict with the forces of the Evil One.

In the play *Hykse-Skorner* may be found the truly nominalist characters of Imagination and Free Will, accompanied by Perseverance, Pity, and Contemplation. Here begin those psychological types that today play so great a part upon stage and screen, where actors are cast as distinct vices or virtues. Shakespeare, drawing heavily upon his Gothic inheritance, adopted Caliban to stand for brutality and Prospero to typify imagination or free will. Thus in modern drama both the plot elements of conflict and the type characters derive in great part from the Middle Ages.

The Rise of the Faust Story. In the later Middle Ages there gradually grew the half-superstitious, half-profound belief that the great intellectual explorers Roger Bacon, Albertus Magnus, and others possessed some occult wisdom. Since that wisdom brought new inventions and fresh discoveries that had no place in the Scholastic *specula*, it was thought to proceed from the Evil One. So arose the Faust legend, telling of a scholar who sold his soul to the devil in return for a mastery of the powers of darkness. This Faust story made a profound impression upon the untamable elements in the northern soul, which eventually broke forth in the individualism of Protestant Christianity. Faust became a prototype of the Germanic soul freed from the restraints of morality, religion, and the church. As Goethe rendered the story, Faust could be defeated only if he found some moment so complete that he was content to remain with it. Satisfied with this lesser ideal, he would lose his soul. But Goethe's Faust, with the mind of a Celto-German, must ever be discontented with any goal he attains with the devil's help. Always seeking a greater degree of perfection, he must eventually reach God. Thus in the end the devil, the spirit of denial, suffers defeat through the superior power of affirmation, or God.

Fig. 399a.—Manuscript showing music from the medieval opera *Robin and Marion*, c. 1280.

Rob - ins m'aime, Rob - ins m'a;

Rob - ins m'a de - man - dé - e, si m'ara.

Rob - ins m'a - ca - ta co - tè - le D'escar -

la - te bone et bè - le, Souskan-ie et

chaintu-rèle, A leur i - va. Robins m'aime, Robins m'a;

Rob-ins m'a de - man - dé - e, si m'ara.

Fig. 399b.—*Robins m'aime* in notation used by Adam.

Music

The Gothic period from the 13th through the 15th century marked significant advances in the development of contrapuntal music and the recording of time. In abbeys, castles, and cathedrals, folk melodies, sequences, and the plain chant were sung or arranged by professional choirmasters and secular musicians alike.

Development of Counterpoint—the Round "Sumer is Icumen in." A canon written at Reading Abbey (Fig. 398) has four equal voices repeating the melody, note for note, each new voice beginning as the preceding voice reaches the bar line. Two lower voices, indicated by the word "Pes" on the manuscript, sing a drone descant in the bass. The note values and signs below the canon are those first recorded by Franco of Cologne about 1220, in his treatise *Musica et Ars Cantus Mensurabilis.* This notation remains essentially the same throughout the period until the invention of movable musical type in 1498.

Adam de la Halle—a Secular Professional Composer. The most famous of the trouvères, Adam de la Halle, who was educated in the Abbey of Vaucelles and possibly the University of Paris,

mastered all the forms of music then known. He composed countless chansons, rondos, and motets, as well as two plays—*Adam the Fool* and *A Pilgrim.* In his ballad opera, *Robin and Marion,* produced at the court of Naples, Adam used rounds like *Sumer is Icumen in* (Fig. 399a).

This earliest recorded music drama had ten characters and is significant as indicating an advanced use of singers and instrumentalists. It includes most of the medieval forms mentioned in the preceding chapter. The chief characters are Robin, a true-hearted rustic lover; the shepherdess Marion; and Sir Hubert, a knight. Through six scenes the rustic lover performs deeds of valor for the lass, who rejects the unworthy attentions of the knight. In the first scene one finds the famous song, *Robins m'aime* (Fig. 399b). There follow bits of dialogue and dance, with a part at the end (the ensemble) in which all the actors sing together. The plot of this musical drama later inspired the romantic poem *Arcadia* of San Nazzaro, furnishing a stock situation for the *commedia dell' arte,* the theater of Molière, and many later operas. Adam created the type of the poor-but-honest hero who rescues his love from the devices of the wealthy villain. Musically, the opera is

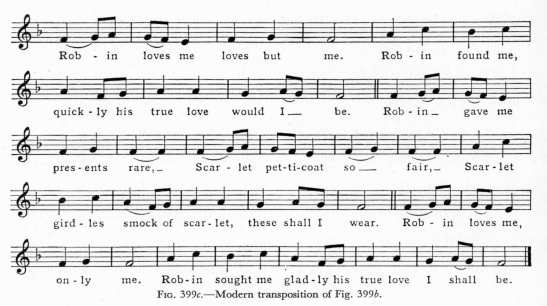

Rob - in loves me loves but me. Rob - in found me,
quick - ly his true love would I __ be. Rob - in __ gave me
pres - ents rare, __ Scar - let pet-ti-coat so __ fair, __ Scar - let
gird - les smock of scar - let, these shall I wear. Rob - in loves me,
on - ly me. Rob - in sought me glad - ly his true love I shall be.

Fig. 399c.—Modern transposition of Fig. 399b.

even more significant for the light it throws on the parallel developments in church music. Another trouvère, Guillaume de Machaut, was engaged by churches in Prague and Reims to make their music more interesting.

Secular Music in the Ars Nova. During the 14th and 15th centuries the most important centers musically were the Netherlands and Burgundy. Here Guillaume Dufay, Jan Ockeghem, Josquin des Prés and John Dunstable brought together in the Mass the folk melodies of the bards and trouvères in a style called the *Ars Nova* to differentiate it from the older plain song. These composers wove intricate canonic passages around the *tenor,* or "holding voice," which either followed the melodic sequences of the Gregorian plain chant or folk melodies such as the popular *L'homme armé*—"The Armed Man." Ockeghem and des Prés, particularly, developed the art of contrapuntal writing by making the groups of dissonant notes in their canons fall upon unaccented parts of the measure or upon passing notes. Thus they achieved a smoother melodic flow of the many-voiced chorus. These men also developed instrumental music so that it harmonized with the voices of the singers. Their sequences, when sung in unison by the entire congregation, came to be known as the "chorales." In Germany, at the end of the period, Heinrich Finck constructed a five-part chorale, *Christ is Risen,* about the sequences in the Easter chant. Thus secular and ecclesiastical music united in the service of God.

Summary

The cathedral, representing in visible form the magnificent structure of the mature Gothic medieval mind, can be understood only in terms of a philosophy based upon the interrelations between the general and the particular, the dynamic and the static. Such a philosophy was clearly formulated by Aristotle. The Aristotelian world view, however, with its splendid logical structure, appears here as misinterpreted by the transcendentalizing Celto-Germans. Instead of striving to comprehend the structure as a whole, in Classical fashion, the medieval Scholastic philosophers, freed from that necessity by the belief that God alone could know the entire pattern, turned to a fascinated preoccupation with the particular. This interest for all of the possible elements in the particular—all

Fig. 400.—Abraham, stone sculpture, north portal, Chartres Cathedral, 13th century. (*Courtesy of Dayton Art Institute; photograph by Metcalf.*)

the veins of a leaf, all the lines in the face of a man—which, conceivably, might lead eventually to the static unified ideal, is known as realism. Naturally, since nature holds a countless variety of pleasant instances, the mind that built the Gothic cathedral often lost itself in the intricacies of ever-unfolding phenomena, and this preoccupation with particulars aroused its greatest feelings of pleasure; for, through them, life took on the guise of a journey between birth and the grave. At any stage on the journey, happily, by thinking on any particular aspect of God, man could lend himself to a mystical contemplation of the entire fabric of creation (Fig. 400).

The cathedral, a tangible evidence of the meaning of life and the significance of God, planned in the shape of a cross, stood for the body of the Crucified One. Each part of the structure testified to the all-pervading presence of the Deity. In the cathedral, the Celto-Germanic mind, with its Druidic beliefs in the transmigration of the soul, found an art form diverse yet reasonable, apparently infinite in variety, yet ordered according to symbolic laws of associational pattern, structural laws of stresses and strains pragmatically understood, and formal laws derived from a mixture of Celto-German, Oriental, and some Classical elements. In this magnificent setting, the ancient drama of the Mass found its complete consummation, accompanied by the changing colors of the glass and the melodic interweave of choral and earthly instrumental music. Here the earthly Christian community found a visible counterpart of the Celestial City.

In this chapter appears a demonstration of the aesthetic meanings used to create the art of the cathedral. Here it can be seen that Gothic art brought forth an aesthetic formula more inclusive than any achieved earlier—a formula that united Plato's and Aristotle's concepts of the Beautiful with an unconscious vision of that Sublimity recorded by Longinus.

Bibliography

BROWNE, E. K.: *Gothic Architecture*, The Macmillan Company, New York, 1928.

ACKERMAN, PHYLLIS: *Tapestry, The Mirror of Civilization*, Oxford University Press, New York, 1933.

AUBERT, MARCEL: *Stained Glass of the XII and XIII Centuries from French Cathedrals*, B. T. Batsford, Ltd., London, 1937.

THOMPSON, D. B.: *Materials of Medieval Painting*, Yale University Press, New Haven, 1936.

HEARNSHAW, F. J. C.: *Medieval Contributions to Modern Civilizations*, George G. Harrap & Company, Ltd., London, 1923.

COULTON, C. G.: *Art and the Reformation*, Alfred A. Knopf, Inc., New York, 1928.

AQUINAS, THOMAS: *Summa Contra Gentiles*, Book I, Chap. 37, translated by Joseph Rickaby, as *Studies on God and His Creatures*, Longmans, Green & Company, New York, 1924.

MARCHANT, G.: *The Kalendar and Compost of Shepherds*. English Edition, Peter Davies, London, 1931.

VORAGINE, JACOBUS DE: *The Golden Legend*, translated by W. Caxton, E. P. Dutton & Company, Inc., New York, 1910.

CHAUCER, GEOFFREY: *Canterbury Tales*, Modern Library, Inc., New York, 1937.

DANTE ALIGHIERI: *De monarchia*, edited by E. Moore, Oxford, Clarendon Press, New York, 1916.

DANTE ALIGHIERI: *La Divina commedia*, translated by Carlyle-Wickstead, Modern Library, Inc., New York, 1932.

The Little Flowers of St. Francis of Assisi, translated by Abby L'Alger, Little, Brown & Co., Boston, 1892.

READE, CHARLES: *The Cloister and the Hearth* (novel), E. P. Dutton & Company, Inc., New York, 1907.

The Play of Robin and Marion (musical play), by Adam de la Halle, harmonized by Jean Beck, G. Schirmer, Inc., New York, 1939.

Recordings

ADAM DE LA HALLE: V 20227 B.

DANCES, V 20445 V 20641.

GUILLAUME DUFAY and JOSQUIN DES PRÉS: Decca 20159 A.

CHAPTER XIV

The Arts of Asia—East and West

After a ceremonial purification the image maker
must pray before beginning his work, "O thou lord
of all the gods, teach me in dreams how to carry out
all the work I have in mind."

FROM THE AGNI PURANA[1]

In writing, first sit silently, quiet your mind and
let yourself be free. Do not speak, do not breathe
fully; rest reverently, feeling as if you were before a
most respected person. Then all will be well.

TSAI YUNG, DESCRIBED BY CH'EN SSU[2]

FOR PRIMITIVE man, art represented a way of decorating himself or his surroundings so that he might gain either the satisfactions of sense or a feeling of superiority over his own fears. The Classical man, freed in part from ancient taboos and religious superstition, sought in art an intellectualization of his emotions by using his ability to reproduce human forms so that they appeared to narrate events. The Celto-German of the Middle Ages felt within himself tremendous dynamic tensions, which he strove to subordinate to a scheme of salvation, using his art as a means of saving his soul.

The Chief Characteristic of the Oriental Mind. Both the Indians and the Chinese have more direct approaches to the joyful creative urge from which grow life and art than had either the intellectual Greek or the energetic, militant Celto-German. Peace-loving and fatalistic by nature, their art mirrors their fundamental passivity coupled with an alert awareness of spiritual values. Too ripe in culture to remain in a state of fear, too wise to assume a primacy of humanity in the scheme of creation, and possessed of too much self-knowledge to believe in the idea of salvation through energetic physical progress, the man of the Orient retains the primitive poetic and pictorial outlook on life.

He develops his art as an aid in the conquest of his own emotions.

Hence, Indian philosophy always remained poetry, while Greek philosophy early left its poetic form to become a prosaic mental exercise. Chinese philosophy is presented in word pictures, or characters, which carry from the elemental soil and the caves of prehistoric man much of their original pictographic significance. Both poetry and pictures retain their rich emotional overtones. Naturally, without the classical intellectualization, the qualities of formal, aesthetic values do not hold first place. Nor do use values hold highest place as in much of Gothic art. Oriental man always subordinates the capture of energy expressed in functional form to a certain decorative quality. For him the formal and useful values of art remain secondary to the associational. In the main, the arts of all Oriental cultures carry with them a strong literary flavor. Employing symbols for both the static and the dynamic moments of his existence, the Chinese painter-poet, more than any other artist, with the exception, perhaps, of the Western musician, recognizes the fundamental dualism of all phenomena.

The Fundamental Acceptance of a Dualistic Belief. The dualism of the Indian differs from that of

[1] Translated by A. K. Coomaraswamy in *The Dance of Siva*, The Sunwise Turn, Inc., New York, 1924.
[2] Translated by Lucy Driscoll and Kanji Toda in *Chinese Calligraphy*, University of Chicago Press, Chicago, 1935.

479

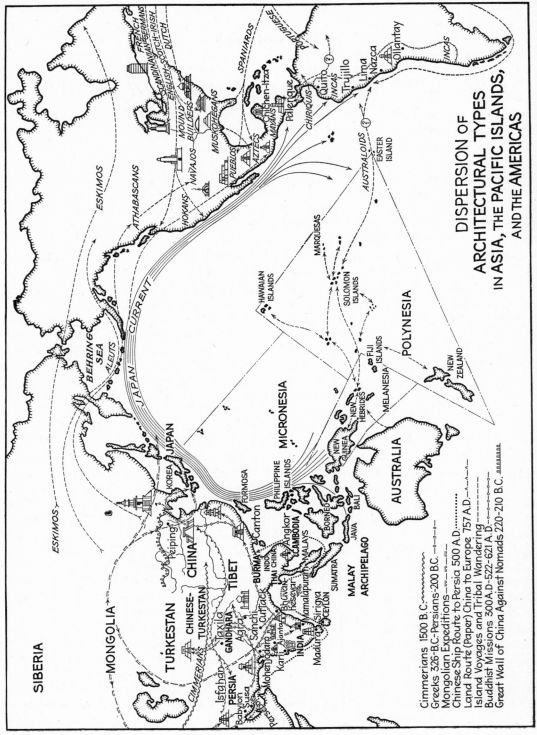

DISPERSION OF ARCHITECTURAL TYPES IN ASIA, THE PACIFIC ISLANDS, AND THE AMERICAS

Cimmerians 1500 B.C.
Greeks 326-B.C.-Persians-200 B.C.
Mongolian Expeditions
Chinese Ship Route to Persia 500 A.D.
Land Route (Paper) China to Europe 757 A.D.
Island Voyages and Tribal Wandering
Buddhist Missions 300 A.D-522-621 A.D.
Great Wall of China Against Nomads 220-210 B.C.

Fig. 401.

the Chinese in its humanism. The dualism of the Chinese is naturalistic and appears to be an outgrowth of his agricultural pursuits. For the Indian, the force of Siva (the symbol of change) continually opposes that of Vishnu (symbol of permanence). Within the one concept of Brahma—endless being—Siva and Vishnu achieve unity. The Indian conceives all three states of being anthropomorphically. To the Chinese all the observable phenomena of heaven and earth derive from positive and negative principles, the *yang* and the *yin*, symbolized by the two signs — (positive) and – – (negative). These signs also characterize the dynamic and the static, the forces of change and stability in nature, the masculine and the feminine, and the strong and the tender aspects of human character, or, as the Indians idealized them, the Siva and the Vishnu aspects of the eternal deity, Brahma.

Through introspection, the Indian seeks a synthesis of the fundamental dualism within himself. The Chinese lose themselves in an interested examination of external natural phenomena. Their greatest teacher, Confucius, led to a naturalistic point of view and cultivated an interest in the particular. Unlike most Western thinkers in the Classical or Gothic modes, both Indians and Chinese experience no difficulty in taking both sides of any argument. It is said that when Confucius gave his word of his own free will, he never broke it. When forced by superior power to agree to this or that measure, he felt under no necessity to keep his word. Such a point of view recognizes both an inner adherence to truth and an ability to escape the external pressure of circumstance. This story explains much of the so-called mystery of Oriental character.

Historical and Ethnical Backgrounds

To understand the growth and common characteristics of the many diverse Oriental arts in the East and the West, one must study the geographic distribution of the various Oriental cultures (Fig. 401) and their aesthetic, ethnical, and religious backgrounds. Asiatic styles of art at one time or another spread from the highlands of Persia and the plains of China westward across Mesopotamia and northern Africa to Spain and eastward, possibly as far as Central America. Beginning with the earliest Chinese culture at about 3000 B.C. and the Indian cultures of Mohenjo-Daro around 2800 B.C., one may study the art complexes of at least eight different groups. These comprise the earliest inhabitants of India, the most ancient Chinese, the Scythians, the Persians, the Mongols, the Aryan invaders of India, the inhabitants of Southeast Asia and the Pacific Islands, and the Mohammedans.

The Static Character of Prehistoric Indians and Chinese. The first of the two great fundamental racial groups of Asia were non-Aryan inhabitants of India. This pacific agricultural folk who inhabited India were invaded at different times, not only by Mongols from Tibet and Melanesians from Indo-China, but also, around the 10th century B.C., by Aryans similar to the Persians, and in the 5th century by the armies of Alexander the Great.

The character of the people may be inferred from a statue of a yaksha, or fertility god, from the 3rd century B.C. (Fig. 402). This massive stone, little more than a menhir, may have been conceived originally as a funerary statue connected with ancestor worship. Comparing it with similar Egyptian works, one notices a significant difference. The geometric Egyptian piece seems animated by an intellectual formula. The Indian statue, standing with legs apart and with heavy drapery lines holding it to the ground, seems to partake more of the character of earth than of any vitalizing mental influence.

The Cultural History of India. Remains of paleolithic culture have been found in the great Indian river valleys, south of the Himalaya and east of the Indus. At Adam Garh in the Narbada valley of central India, Hellmut de Terra and Dr. Teilhard Chardin have found painted rock shelters where animals are represented similar to those in the mesolithic site of Pindal, Spain. Other evidence proves conclusively that

FIG. 402.—Yaksha from Parkham, India, stone, Mauryan dynasty (322–185 B.C.). Compare with early Mayan figures (Fig. 598, Chap. XIX). (*Courtesy of Dr. Rowland, Fogg Museum, Harvard University.*)

India was inhabited through the Paleolithic era, at least as early as in Europe.

The earliest Indian culture, at Mohenjo-Daro and Harappa in the northwest of India, dates from 2800 B.C. Aryan invaders entered India between 1200 and 1000 B.C. By 618 B.C. a dynasty of rulers, the Saisunaga, had arisen. Since we know that the army of Xerxes included levies of troops from India, connections with Persia must have been established by 550 B.C. At about that time, an Indian prince, Gautama Buddha, forsook the world to meditate and preach the gospel of inner enlightenment and Mahavira founded Jainism.

Alexander the Great, marching through Turkestan with his Grecian legionaries, crossed into the Punjab in 326 B.C., sending a fleet under his general Nearchus down the Indus River. An Indian monarch, Chandragupta I, expelled the Macedonians in 322 B.C. and founded the great Mauryan dynasty, whose enlightened emperor, Asoka, embraced Buddhism in 250 B.C. Before he died, in 232 B.C., Asoka had sent Buddhist missionaries to Ceylon. This peaceful monarch not only ruled his own country well but also exchanged amenities with the Greek Seleucid monarchs, Antiochus I and II, and established commercial relationships with the Ptolemies in Egypt. This period saw the development of the first great monumental sculpture and architecture of India. The dynasty terminated within 50 years of Asoka's death, however, and centuries passed before another great revival of art and learning took place in the Gupta empire, founded in A.D. 320 by Chandragupta II. The second Gupta empire, founded in 413, inaugurated a great literary era, during which was written the *Sakuntala* of Kalidasa. In 606, in the reign of Harsha, Arabs and the Asiatic Mohammedans of Persia invaded the country. Between 1526 and 1530, the Persian Baber, a descendant of the Mohammedan Tamerlane, conquered India and, importing Persian artists, established the Mughal school of painting. In addition to this group, several native Indian schools were attached to the courts of Rajput monarchs in northern India.

Connections between the Indian and the Island Cultures. As the history of India unfolds, it becomes clear that about the time of Christ, a period of folk wandering began during which Indian tribes moved across India down into the Malay Archipelago. In the Indian epic tale, *Ramayana*, Sita, the wife of Rama, was carried off by the king of the demons, Ravana, to the island of Ceylon, whence she was rescued in a war. This legend thus connects the Indian culture with that of other powerful seafaring peoples who lived in the eastern Malay Archipelago. From Cambodia come other tales that seem to connect the states of western India with invasions of that country, also during the first years of the Christian centuries. The motif of the gorgoneion mask, or Tao-Tieh, furthermore, is widely distributed, not only in India, but throughout the Melanesian Island culture. It also has its parallels in South and Central American art.

The Cultural History of the Chinese. History begins in China with the Shang dynasty after 1766 B.C. By that time the Chinese had achieved a state of social equilibrium which, despite numerous invasions, has persisted with but little change until the present day. Most of the invasions came from north and west, wherefore Mongols and Scythians left some impress on Chinese art. Because of favorable environmental conditions in the vast fertile plains of northern China, a contented people developed in the area around present-day Peiping, Tientsin, and Tsinanfu.

The great distance of the Chinese center of culture from the leading cultures of Mesopotamia and the Mediterranean world led to the formation of an art style relatively unaffected by foreign influences. Some Western patterns were taken over, however, and a spiral type of pottery, resembling some of the late Cretan vases, developed. By the end of the Chou dynasty, c. 250 B.C., the Danubian interweave became common, presumably brought to the Orient by an invasion of red-haired, blue-eyed people whose faces, as shown on fresco paintings in Chinese Turkestan, were of European type. These newcomers left evidence of their workmanship in the Scythian grave mounds of southern Russia, along the Celestial Mountains to the west of China, and in the depths of Mongolia. They were probably related to the Cimmerians.

During the 6th century B.C., when the Chou dynasty was at its height, two great original thinkers, Confucius (Kung-fu-tse) and Lao-tze, greatly influenced the culture. The arts of writing and bronze casting flourished. In 221 B.C. the Emperor Shih Huang Ti, founder of the Ch'in dynasty, united all the small kingdoms and duchies of feudal China. A strong dictator, he banned all independent inquiry and destroyed the rich literature. From the time of Shih Huang Ti into the T'ang dynasty, until A.D. 907, Buddhistic influences had an enlightening effect. The Chinese Buddhists translated many of the Indian canons and Sanskrit texts. During the Sung dynasty (960–1279), a fusion of the teachings of Confucius and Mahayana Buddhism brought about a renaissance of thought. The emperor Hui Tsung of this dynasty founded the first academy of painting.

A Mongolian invasion ushered in the Yuan dynasty (1280–1368). Producing little of intellectual or aesthetic value, this dynasty prepared the way for the cultured Ming dynasty (1368–1644).

The Movement of the Perso-Mohammedan Cultures. In 622 Mohammed made his hegira, or flight, from Mecca to Medina, inaugurating a religious movement whose leaders eventually conquered India in the 16th century. Shortly after the death of Mohammed in 633, the Arabian armies of his followers conquered all of Mesopotamia, Palestine, Persia, Egypt, North Africa, and Spain. Wherever they went, these intelligent Hamitic people embraced the arts, using Christian workmen in Syria, Mesopotamia, and Egypt, to build their mosques and to paint their palace walls. In Persia they copied the motifs of the late Sassanian renaissance (226–637). These designs persisted in Arabic pottery, painting, and metalwork until the 14th century.

The first great artistic development of the Mohammedans, called the "Abbasid," centered around Samarra, a city north of Bagdad, whose mosques and palaces were decorated with stuccos and frescoes between 838 and 883. The Fatimid period in Egypt and Sicily, named after the descendants of Fatima, daughter of Mohammed, ran from 909 to 1171. In the 11th century the Seljuks, a Turkish tribe from Central Asia, moved across the Mohammedan world under the leadership of Seljuk and soon conquered Persia. The Seljuk period, extending over the 12th and 13th centuries, left many great monuments in Bagdad and Mosul, as well as a school of painting called the "Mesopotamian" school, with its center at Bagdad. During this period, also, through their occupation of the rich architectural area of the Armenians and their wars with the crusaders in Palestine, the Turks experienced their closest contact with Christianity. In Persia, or Iran, at the same time, the fine Rhages pottery, decorated with hunting scenes, made its appearance.

Throughout the 13th and 14th centuries the Mongols, under Genghis Khan and his followers, built their great empire from China to European Russia. Invading Persia, they there embraced Mohammedanism. Hulagu, a Mongol ruler, introduced Chinese culture to Persia and founded the Il Khan dynasty. This conquest inaugurated a long period of magnificent manuscript painting in which influences from Mesopotamia, China, and India united. Followers of the Mongol Tamerlane, called the "Timurids," moved westward toward India between 1369 and 1404, shifting the Mohammedan art center to Herhe in eastern Persia. A school of painting and poetry grew up, headed by the painter Bihzad, born around 1440. The paintings of this school excel almost all others in Persian art. The Mughal school established by Baber after his conquest of India, between 1526 and 1530, combined Indian and Persian styles. Akbar, a follower of Baber, built many great palaces at Fatehpur Sikri in 1569, founding an academy of painting frequented by Indian and Persian artists, who developed wall paintings as well as a manuscript style.

Religious and Literary Backgrounds

Indian

The Literary Backgrounds of the Vedic Religion. The early prehistoric Indians worshiped a serpent-god of the underworld, Naga, while the Aryan invaders worshiped fire- and sun-gods. Out of this background, between the 10th century and the dawn of the Christian Era, emerged a number of religious works. These early writings significantly contrast Indian culture with that developing among the peoples in Asia Minor and in Northern Africa. The Indians did not focus their religion upon the passage of the soul from life on earth to life in another world. On the contrary, they seem to have been incapable of imagining death.

The earliest of the Indian sacred books—the *Rig-Veda*, a collection of hymns—so closely parallels the ancient Mesopotamian legendry that we may infer a relation between the Indian gods and the gods of the Sumerians during the years when Mohenjo-Daro and Sumer were connected. Like the Mesopotamian hymns, the *Rig-Veda* praised natural forces, particularly the wind, the rain, and the fire, all of which are distinctly active elements. The gods of the *Rig-Veda*, however, are less anthropomorphic than are those of Mesopotamia. The world inhabited by the gods of India consisted of the sky dome —the atmosphere or region between earth and sky—and the earth, each continually altering with the endless round of nature's seasons. Change and activity inspired the Vedic poets. They sang of the primal fires, and deified the wind, particularly because it had no definite form. Among the host of cosmic forces beneficent and maleficent, a god, Varuna, at last took form. Like the Persian God Ahura-Mazda, Varuna controlled light and probably was a descendent of Ouranus (Father Time), the ancestor of the Greek Zeus. Approached through the priestly fire-god, Agni, Varuna lived in the altar flame or in the homes of the Vedic Indians, as the sacred hearth fire. Like Gilgamesh in Mesopotamia, Varuna personified ethical law.

Of his gifts to mankind, the *soma* has special significance. The concept of soma as a vital force running through all human life—the *élan vital*, as the French philosopher Bergson called it—emphasizes the part played by the generative instinct in carrying forward all invention. Associated with Agni and Varuna stood Indra, the third member of the Indian triad of gods. The god of justice, Indra slew the wicked with his shafts of lightning and particularly directed his ire against those prehistoric Indians who worshiped the serpent. Gradually the three came to be thought of as one god, Brahma, the eternal principle which includes all else —Vishnu, the god of stability, and Siva, the god of change. More important than the development of this unifying principle, however, was the rise, in the *Rig-Veda*, of the concept of Purusa—a man endowed with the vitalizing quality of all his gods, the "greater man, who has a thousand heads, a thousand eyes, and a thousand feet." The *Rig-Veda* relates that Indra, the lightning-god, befriended Purusa, whose potentialities were so great that he could eat 300 buffalo and drink three lakes of the vital somatic fluid in preparation for his fight with the evil one, Vritra.

A further development of the superman legend took place in the evolution of Chinese thought, in which the "greater man," Pan-Ku, hewed out a place for himself, thus creating the world. This inversion of the relationship between god and man made the Oriental artist consider himself in his creative moments a microtype of the divine creator. The creative act, hence, became a religious ceremony and a mystical union with the greatest forces of the universe.

In the *Sama-Veda*, a book of ritual written later than the *Rig-Veda*, the idea of sacrifice came into prominence; and in the *Yajur-Veda*, another ritual book, a record is set down of various ceremonies that were then becoming well-established religious usages. Here the influence of the prehistoric religion made itself felt, with its worship of the serpent associated with the mother cults.

The Philosophy of the Hindu Religion. At about the 6th century B.C., there appeared a collection of theological treatises, the *Brahmanas*, indicating the formation of the caste system and the rise of a group of priests called the Brahmans. In the Brahman caste, the highest of all, the Eternal concept of life became personalized. This priesthood gathered the essential wisdom of the prehistoric mother cults and the Vedic religions into a system called Hinduism. Two centuries later, the Brahmans offered their solution to the riddle of existence in a series of writings composed by ascetic members of the caste who had retreated into the wilderness. One group of these ascetics, following Mahavira, founded the religion of Jain. Another group questioned the ascetic's right to withdraw from the world for personal salvation. To this latter group belonged Gautama Buddha (563–483 B.C.), the founder of Buddhism.

The Buddhistic Philosophy of the Way of Life and the Lord's Lay. The Brahmans, like the Greek philosophers, included skeptics who believed in a purely mechanistic concept of mental life. Other Brahmanic philosophers, comparable to Plato and Socrates, sought to show that there exists a "true knowledge" or "Way" which reveals the connection between the human and the divine. Their followers worked out various methods for achieving this unity. Some, like Gautama Buddha, sought first a retreat into the forest, whence, after a period of introspection, they returned to help mankind. These were known as Bodhisattvas. Hindus still believe that the spirits of these virtuous Bodhisattvas wander through the world, guiding men toward the good life. They also believe that the soul itself, which never dies, lives in the bodies of animals. Even plants may have souls that strive for rebirth in the soul of man, hoping eventually to attain complete union with the Deity in a state of nonconsciousness, or Nirvana. This doctrine is called the transmigration of souls.

The final flowering of this Hindu thought system, essentially introspective and subjective, resulted in the *Upanishads*, a series of essays by the forest priests. Among these, the one known as the *Bhagavad-Gita* is the most important, chiefly because it links the highest ethical ideals with instruction for attaining a state of inner harmony with the universe. This *Bhagavad-Gita*, or the *Lord's Lay*, is described by modern Brahmans as a book of divine union, being a colloquy between Krishna and Arjuna, two semigods, which is supposed to have taken place somewhere around 3000 B.C. In this holy book the state of death is considered not in material terms, as in the Egyptian religion, nor in terms of a shadowy land of fear, as in Mesopotamian. Like the Christian, the Hindu accepts death as a happy broadening of life.

The Importance of Yoga in Artistic Creation. In the twenty-sixth to the twenty-ninth verses of the fifth chapter of the *Bhagavad-Gita*, the reader learns how to obtain complete identification with the Supreme Deity, who is the great spirit of the ancient universe, as well as the spirit that dwells in all human hearts. The process described is a simple one and can be actually practiced, although most of us are too young and too active to achieve instant success with it. If one will lie quietly, stretched out, preferably in the woods or some lonely place, with hands crossed upon one's breast and with eyelids half-closed and will focus one's mind completely upon some such thought as "Eternal life" or "God is truth and friendship," it is possible actually to experience a complete cessation of bodily awareness. Such a state is similar in a way to the unconsciousness of the hypnotic state; but there is a fundamental difference. In the exercise of the Hindu rite, the barrier between the conscious and unconscious mind is broken down without the interposition of a second person. Also, the worshiper may, if he wishes, recall himself from the state of Nirvana.

Ananda Coomaraswamy, in his book *The Dance of Siva*, has made clear that every Oriental artist prepares himself for creating a work of art by undergoing a process similar to the one just described. The *Agni Purana*, another *Upanishad*, points out that craftsmanship, or the process of creating a work of the hands, causes a similar loss of self-consciousness. The Hindus were the first to make a psychological analysis of the phenomenon of craftsmanship. They discovered that the very action of allowing the hands to work upon some material often frees the mind to such an extent that it can no longer control the production of fantasy, and one thought develops quickly upon another without definite boundaries.

The Hindu does not rest in these fantasy images, however, but develops a more definite figure of some deity (Fig. 419). In order to portray a concrete image there must be a unity of consciousness about some definite thought, and this unity must be so intense that the artist identifies himself closely with the object. When a Japanese artist wished to compose a very fine representation of the crane, a bird of good omen, he is said to have stood all one night on one leg with the other pulled up, thus imitating the bird, so that the next morning he could truly represent the animal's inner feelings. This state of mental concentration, which is necessary if the artist is to lose himself completely in something other than himself, is called "yoga."

In the *Agni Purana*, the obvious connection between the subconscious, or dream, life and the creation of artistic fantasy, is recognized in the following passage: "After a ceremonial purification, the image maker must pray before beginning his work, 'Oh, thou lord of all the gods, teach me in dreams how to carry out all the work I have in mind.'" The Hindu assumes that the image maker has a well-ordered subconscious mind filled with unified pictures of the Deity, which express themselves in socially useful and natural forms. Modern psychologists teach that there exists a type of mental phenomenon observable in Occidental minds that has heretofore gone unnoticed, or has been regarded with superstition. Under the general term "subconsciousness," or "unconsciousness," they have placed the large amount of any individual's sum total of recorded mental impressions not usually accessible to one's memory. Briefly, every one of us is able to remember a certain amount of knowledge which is useful and directly connected with everyday needs. Actually, every one of us has experienced many times as much as he can easily remember. This is the subconscious.

The Oriental Artist's Control of the Eidetic Faculties. The Hindu apparently early recognized and overcame the phenomenon of the subconscious in his aesthetic creation and, contemporaneous with Aristotle, developed a formula for creating art.

The artist must after ceremonial purification proceed to a solitary place. There he is to perform the sevenfold office. First, he must invoke the hosts of Buddhas and Bodhisattvas (Buddhas who returned to help mankind), and offer to them real or imaginary flowers. Secondly, he must realize in thought four infinite moods; friendliness, compassion, sympathy, and impartiality. The third point for the artist is to meditate upon the emptiness or non-existence of all things, for "by the fire or the idea of the abyss, it is said, there are destroyed beyond recovery the five factors of egoconsciousness."[1]

As a fourth step in his procedure, the artist must invoke an image of the desired aspect of God by uttering a seed-word, or *bija*—a word that describes the particular virtue for which this aspect of the Deity is noted. Next, the artist should completely immerse himself in this idea of the divinity. He will then feel impelled to pronounce a formula, the *Dhyana Mantram*, which will define the attributes of the divinity. As the final step, an image of the divinity will become visible, "like a reflection" or "as in a dream." And this brilliant image is a model from which the artist can draw.

Leonardo da Vinci observed that when he focused his eyes upon an irregular spot on a gray wall or on the ceiling, images of battles or events of history would often appear and that he could copy them. We have noted in earlier chapters that apparently many primitives and some moderns can reproduce very natural images by means of the phenomenon known as eideticism. It has been observed that many children can see such images. Probably the Oriental artist has simply perfected a technique for inducing eidetic images. Experiments have

shown that related effects may be produced with the help of hypnosis.

Chinese

The Ethicoreligious Aspects of Chinese Art. A study of Chinese culture demonstrates qualities vastly different from the religious expressions underlying Western thought. Although the origins of religion in China appear essentially the same as those in other primitive societies on the agricultural level, a philosophical attitude developed which early made man, rather than anthropomorphic gods, the center of ethical life. The simple fetishism associated with the propitiation of maleficent and benign spirits is, however, still retained in the Chinese religion as a kind of ceremonial observance.

The Chinese conceived no great supernatural creator particularly interested in man. Instead, reversing the order, the Chinese held that Pan-Ku, the first man, created the world out of chaos with his adze. Chinese humanism thus early proved itself practical and pragmatic. Essentially, each Chinese thought of himself as a sculptor, carving his own destiny from the ever-changing material of nature. The Chinese considered heaven, or T'ien, as a beneficent power. The idea of heaven is also associated with the idea of greatness and with the character Jen, which meant humanity. The characters for all three ideas derived from the pictograph, 木 standing for man on Shang-dynasty oracle bones.

The Chinese (Fig. 433) pictured God as a quiet, deliberate, ethical person, exercising his function as a highly moral ruler raised from the people because of his goodness. The most ancient Chinese book, the *Shu King*, advises that "whoever is able to govern the people must be a man of moral perfection; whoever is perfect in goodness is entitled to rulership." The great reverence of the Chinese for the written word of wisdom appears in the *Yih King*, or *Book of Changes*, whose very origin is mythological. Con-

[1] ANANDA COOMARASWAMY, *The Dance of Siva*, The Sunwise Turn, Inc., New York, 1924.

fucius (551–479) attempted to derive from this collection of odes its chief philosophic import. Since the book concerns itself with change and since change exists in all forms of life, we find the Chinese at the beginnings of their philosophy paralleling the thought patterns of the contemporaneous pre-Socratic philosophers. The Chinese, however, differed from the Greeks in accepting the phenomena of change as primary and almost unanimously rejecting the Parmenidean concept of a static being.

The Pragmatic Dualism of Chinese Philosophy. Since change is caused by the interplay of the male, or positive, heavenly principle yang, and the female, or negative, principle yin, we may detect a fundamental dualism in all Chinese thought. From the first, the Chinese acknowledged the dual aspect of existence in all they conceived, and sought a balance between the two, their whole philosophy being that of propriety.

From the signs for the two fundamental principles, an early emperor, Fu Hsi, who is said to have lived about 1766 B.C., derived eight combinations symbolizing comprehensive natural phenomena or elements. By this time in the Shang dynasty many pictographs descriptive of real objects were in use. From a union of the signs representing the intangible forces and those representing tangible forms, eventually arose Chinese calligraphy. The logical-minded Fu Hsi arranged his combinations of the original two symbols in the following manner: ☰ Heaven (solely positive); ☷ earth (solely negative). Water ☵ is heaven enclosed by earth; fire ☲, earth enclosed by heaven. The river (vapor) is two parts heaven below earth ☱; the mountain ☶ two parts earth under heaven; the wind ☴, two parts heaven above earth; the thunder ☳, two parts earth above heaven.

The interaction of these eight principles symbolizes the strength and tenderness in all the phenomena of existence. The strong, masculine principle generates life; the weaker, feminine principle brings it to completion. With a passion for explanation and order, the practical Chinese soon devised sixty-four signs, or trigrams, compounded from these eight. These symbols, the *kua*, served as oracles to explain all human affairs. From the sixty-four trigrams Confucius drew his analects, or moral judgments. A practical ethical philosopher, Confucius had little interest in the transcendental elements and none in a possible life hereafter. "How can we know death," he queried, "when life is not yet understood?" It remained for another philosopher, Lao-tze, to find in the same source a monistic interpretation of life.

The Ethical Teachings of Confucius. The mind of Confucius, clear and sane, epitomizes the Chinese mentality. Confucius tells of his own education: "At fifteen I made up my mind to consecrate my life to study. At thirty I stood firm in my consecration. At forty I no longer doubted I was right. At fifty I began to understand the divine laws. At sixty I never committed any known wrong, and by seventy I was sure that I could follow my own desires and never do a wrong thing."

Confucius by no means avoided the imaginative side of life, however. Of teaching he wrote: "Memorizing without thought is labor lost; thought without a body of memorized material is perilous." He said further: "If I have presented one corner of the subject and the pupil by himself cannot derive the other three, I shall not repeat my lesson." And again: "All life is poetry in the beginning, manners in the center, and music at the end." Seeking practical guidance for life, the followers of Confucius stressed two great ethical doctrines profoundly significant not only for an understanding of Chinese thought but also for a better understanding of all human relationships. These two doctrines, the *Jen* and the *Cheng*, have particular significance in their relationship to our understanding of the greatest art.

The first doctrine, that of Jen or fundamental human virtue, is part of the *Tao* or way of life. According to Confucius, the right way lay in sympathy, or a feeling of human fellowship—

that particular characteristic which differentiates man from the animals. Wrote Confucius, "A man with Jen, wishing to be happy, would have others happy, wishing to succeed, would have others succeed." To this philosopher every mature human heart possessed Jen. The second principle, that of Cheng or sincerity, seems more egocentric. It arises from the ability of every person to be absolutely sincere with himself in his thinking. Tze-shi, a disciple of Confucius, wrote: "The superior man watches always over the self in his moments of solitude. . . . One who possesses *Cheng* makes perfect not only himself but others. That which makes the self perfect is humanity. That which makes others perfect is intelligence." From the feeling of sincerity arises an awareness not only of one's own moral integrity but also of the integrity and fitness of all other things. Integrity demands appropriateness within the self. In understanding any great work of art, one cannot help being impressed by its sincerity, its integration, and the appropriateness of all its parts.

Taoism and the Philosophy of Lao-Tze. The philosophy of Lao-tze stresses the static element in the doctrine of yang and yin. Lao-tze held that a monistic world starts with nameless matter. The Chinese concept of the Tao, or Way, though it has no demonstrable connection with the Buddhist Way, is essentially the same. It is a losing of oneself in this primordial life. By contemplation and by the cessation of all activity one may withdraw into eternal being. Chuang-tse, a follower of Lao-tze, derived a phenomenal world from this matter, but insisted on giving every person his innate freedom and his right to act and think as he might feel. This doctrine of individualism led eventually to an idealistic mysticism. "The Tao can be handed down by the teacher but may not be received by the student—when you want to express it and communicate it to an-

other it is lost." Taoism had only a subtle, indirect effect upon the development of Chinese art.

Chinese Buddhism. A second fruitful philosophy for aesthetic development came with the introduction of Buddhism into China between 206 B.C. and A.D. 23, during the Han dynasty. The doctrines of Mahayana Buddhism originate in the book of *Kwan-yin-tze.* The Contemplative Buddhistic life led to the foundation of monasteries which, like the European monasteries of the Middle Ages, came to be centers of culture. The Buddhist missionaries wrote:

One essential substance becomes the cold in Heaven, the water on earth, and the soul in man. One spirit becomes the heat in Heaven, fire upon earth, and the heart of man.

Let my essence be merged in the essence of all things, my spirit merged in the spirit of Heaven and earth. Let my soul be joined with the communal soul as one tree might be grafted on another and become a part of it. To the wise there is one mind, one substance, one reason (Tao) and all three are conceived in oneness. All things change but their nature remains the same. The wise know this unity nor are they disturbed by outward signs.[1]

The Importance of Ideographic Characters in the Development of Chinese Thought. Chinese writing carries with it pleasant, suggestive visual patterns which call to mind ideas and pictures without any interpolation of sound. Western man cannot think of the letters of the alphabet without sound associations. Chinese writing has a twofold origin: (1) its physioplastic, pictographic form, older than the beginnings of the Shang dynasty; (2) the ideoplastic arrangement of the trigrams developed during the Shang dynasty. These two unite to form the modern Chinese characters (Fig. 403).[2]

The construction of Chinese literary signs indicates the innate aestheticism of the people. Each of these signs is drawn with a flowing

[1] D. T. SUZUKI: *A Brief History of Chinese Philosophy*, Arthur Probsthain, London, 1914.
[2] An instructive chapter on Chinese writing in *The Birth of China*, by Herrlee Glessner Creel, clarifies the thoroughly logical construction of Chinese characters and their relations to the prehistoric pictograph.

brush stroke, which can become hasty if the writer is simply interested in a matter-of-fact record, or can be elaborated into what in the West is known as "naturalistic" painting.

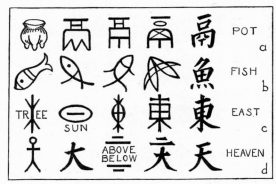

FIG. 403.—Evolution of Chinese characters. (*Brush work by Dr. C. J. Ho.*)

Perso-Mohammedan

The religions of Persians and Mohammedans, developed for the greater part between the 2nd and 12th centuries of the Christian Era, had distinct influence upon the subject matter of the decorative styles carried from Asia Minor to India, Africa, and the shores of Spain. Since the older Persian forms underlie the later Mohammedan religion, we may consider them as definitive.

Ahura-Mazda, Mithra, and the Gods of Light and Darkness. Zoroaster, the almost mythical religious lawgiver of Persia, who lived around 700 B.C., may have gathered the collection of exorcisms and sacrificial hymns that constitute the *Zend-Avesta*, the sacred book of Persia. This book, compiled about A.D. 230 from many documents during the Sassanian revival of Persian art, tells the story of a battle between Ahura-Mazda, a beneficent solar deity, and Ahriman, a destroying spirit of evil. With the final victory of Mazda, the Zoroastrians believed that a virgin would conceive a Messiah by the spirit of the prophet Zoroaster. Through the Messiah the dead would be brought to life, the good blessed, and after a purifying destruc-

tion of the world by fire, all souls would eventually be redeemed.

In the *Zend-Avesta*, another and older light god, Mithra, also appears. This deity inherits most of the attributes of Gilgamesh and Ea. He is shown slaying the bull from whose blood all living creatures are born. Like Christianity, Mithraism had its baptismal rites and its communion, with consecrated bread and wine. It enjoined celibacy upon its votaries, both male and female. The symbols connected with Mithraism—the serpent of earth, the vase of water, and particularly the lion, symbolic of the sacred fire—supply motives for much of Iranian and Mohammedan art. The Havarenah landscape, which usually includes the vine, the vase, and the lion, as on the Mschatta façade (Fig. 294, Chap. XI), furnishes a symbol of paradise, and appears many times in Persian decoration. Significant is the fact that most of the decorative sculpture and the arrangement of architectural details in building stress the element of contrast between the dark and the light, probably symbolic of the fundamental struggle between the two forces underlying Zoroastrianism and Mohammedanism.

The Prehistoric Origins of Asiatic Design

The same original three sources of design studied in connection with the primitive beginnings of the Occidental cultures underlie all the designs of India and China. Technomorphic patterns arise with the earliest pottery and basket weaving. Physioplastic, zoomorphic, and phylomorphic motives abound. All are stylized into abstract curvilinear design wherever the influence of the Scytho-Cimmerian invaders dominates.

The Beginnings of Abstraction. The earliest Indian carvings on seals at Mohenjo-Daro in northeastern India include very realistic representations of elephants and rhinoceri. The earliest Chinese clay figures of animals are likewise strictly physioplastic (Fig. 404*a*).

FIG. 404.—*a*, Seal, Mohenjo-Daro, with three-faced god, seated on low Asiatic throne; note naturalistic animals; this deity probably a prototype of Brahma; *b*, engraved figure of elephant, Kalsi; *c*, elephant seal, Shang dynasty (collection of T. C. Liu); *d*, cloud design or interwoven dragons, Chou dynasty (British Museum); compare with *c*, Fig. 596*b*, Chap. XIX; *e*, T'ao-T'ieh mask with feathered headdress, human and animal crest and fleur-de-lis, late Chou dynasty (collection of C. L. Rutherston); *f*, T'ao-T'ieh mask, bronze pot, Chou dynasty (Freer Collection); compare with Fig. 596*b*, Chap. XIX; *g*, jade dragon, Chou or Shang dynasty (Museum of Natural History, New York).

In one of the sacred caves of Kalsi, India, an elephant (Fig. 404*b*), symbol of the merciful Buddha, accompanied by the words "the most perfect white elephant," shows the first significant advance away from a purely physioplastic conception such as might have been found on the paleolithic cavern walls of Altamira (Fig. 23, Chap. II) and the seals of Mohenjo-Daro (Fig. 98, Chap. V). This difference appears in superior arrangement of the lines in tusks, tail, ear, and head. Cursorily examined, they seem purely representational; on closer inspection, they give evidence of a quality of line that permeates all mature Asiatic art. The vitality of the elephant has been represented not by a movement of the limbs particularly, but by flowing lines that seem to work together in a less dynamic interweave.

The same tendency toward abstract linear representation appears in a Shang-dynasty seal. This seal, shaped like an elephant's head, has had the various bodily attributes removed from their proper positions and used as parts of a decorative design arranged on the head. The head, for example, lacks the trunk, but the lines of the trunk appear in the drawing of the ear. Story content or idea, as well as use values, have here been subordinated to formal aesthetic values. The facility with which the Oriental can abstract decorative lines from any physical appearance and make them appear plausible in some new, unrealistic arrangement connotes a high degree of aesthetic ability. This skill arises in an eagerness to play with areas, lines, and forms for the pure joy of arrangement.

Scytho-Cimmerian Patterns. A third element, directly traceable to the Scytho-Cimmerian migrations during the Shang and Chou dynasties from 1766 to 255 B.C., unites physioplastic art forms with abstract, playful design. With the introduction of bronze casting by the lost wax method appeared fortuitous cloud patterns, such as those earlier developed in the most ancient Mesopotamian art, combined with Cretan spirals and the animal interweave. A comparison of the Chinese examples with those

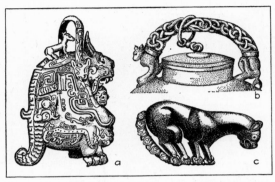

Fig. 405.—*a*, bronze vessel of *yu* type, Chou dynasty, uniting designs of Scythian and Indo-Chinese origin, height about 1 foot (Cernuschi Museum, Paris); *b*, handle from bronze kettle of Ho type, Chou dynasty; note similarity to Viking ship carvings; *c*, gold beast of Kalermes. (*After Strzygowski, Der Bildende Kunst der Gegenwart.*)

of earlier cultures will make clear this development (Fig. 404*d*).

The childlike intricacy of animal forms often creates the illusion of restless motion, as can be seen in the little sword pommel. This design includes four masks, one rising above another, with a suggestion of a feathered headdress on each side. At four places on this simple axis appear grotesque faces, each in combination with dismembered parts of animal heads. The complicated headdress of a ceremonial mask probably inspired this creation. The same design, greatly enlarged, appears over the portals of Indo-Chinese, Malayan, and Central American temples, as well as on the stelae in ancient Mayan cities (Fig. 404*e*).

An all-over pattern of this type, made slightly more realistic, can be studied on a pre-Han vessel called a *yu* (Fig. 405). This bronze pot has the head and limbs of a jaguar or a lion, collapsed into one body and combined at the rear with an elephant mask, whose stylized trunk serves as the third foot. The surface of the body carries a multitude of small dragons, lizards,

and other animal heads. All the spaces between have been filled with spirals representing clouds and thunder symbols. One of these designs, particularly interesting to students of American Indian lore, bears an elephant's head with a plumed headdress. Similar feathered serpents, as they are called, form the chief motifs in Mayan architectural decoration.

The rich demoniac fantasy of the primitive Scytho-Chinese workmen here presents something comparable to the Egyptian Palette of Narmer. In the Occidental piece the human representation dominated. Here the human element is present, but in a not easily discernible form. The open mouth of the great front jaguar encircles a frightened human face that seems to peer out of the jaws of the monster. Significant is the fact that here the natural animal world has engulfed man without destroying him.

The mature arts of all Asia grow from the three types studied here—the realistic, the abstract, and the cloud interweave, which we have called the "energetic." Regardless of the type of pattern used, the Oriental arranges it in occult balance. In mature Oriental art primitive space filling becomes an intricate arrangement of parts refined to a point at which it is intellectually provocative.

The abstraction and fineness seen in the earliest pottery of the Shang period develop further in connection with other utensils in bronze, ivory, and wood. The gold beasts of Kalermes, which figure in the discussion of the Celtic arts (Fig. 405*c*), and the bronzes from the Ordos territory in China (Fig. 405*b*) show similarities between pre-Romanesque European art and that of China. In the Ordos bronzes the degree of abstraction is so great that the animal form has completely disappeared, although it is still suggested by the vigor of the lines and the strong contrast of light and shade made by the sharply cut intersections of planes and curved surfaces. From these bronzes to the work of 20th-century futurist and cubist sculptors is but a step.

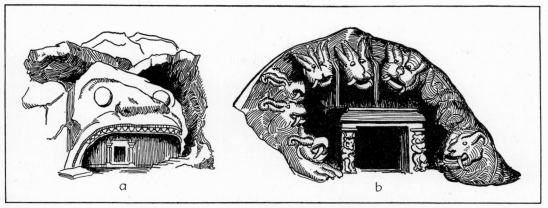

FIG. 406.—*a*, entrance of tiger cave temple, Cuttack, southern India, prehistoric; *b*, entrance of cave temple, Saluvan Kuppan, southern India, prehistoric (*after Fergusson, History of Indian Architecture, Vol.* I); compare with Fig. 598, Chap. XIX.

Indian Architecture

Within the dim coolness of his cavelike temples, the Indian loses himself in contemplation of the Deity, gaining that inner stability so desired by the mystical mind. One branch of the temple architecture of India derives from the cave; another, from the memorial tumulus and the Neolithic stone circle; but many of the constructive features must have come from long experience in wooden building.

From massive stone mountain walls the Indian carves his building, so that it remains always part of the earth. Even in the freestanding temple structures carved down into the stone, in which appear traces of various types of wooden architecture introduced into India by successive invasions, the spectator can never entirely drop the feeling that this structure was not fabricated but grew as an expression of the Creator carving his own dwelling through the hands of man.

The Prehistoric Rock-cut Temples of Southern India. The definitive quality of Oriental thought that differentiates it from that of the humanistic Occident lies, as we have seen, in its emphasis on the persistence of the spirit through many transformations, a belief crystallized in the doctrine of the transmigration of souls. All Indian building represents an attempt to create a structure in which the soul may change from one form to another.

Among the earliest and most obvious examples of this conception of the temple as the entrance to another life, we may observe the two cave temples of Cuttack and Saluvan Kuppan found not far from Madras in southern India (Fig. 406a and b). At the cave temple of Cuttack the worshiper must enter the subterranean animal world of the spirit through two monstrous jaws. In the case of the temple at Saluvan Kuppan, the introduction of carved pillars with figures suggestive of totemistic wooden origins modifies the original opening, here surrounded by a row of dragon heads. Comparing this temple entrance with the Romanesque portal of Moissac with its many grotesque heads and beasts, or with the lion porches of various Romanesque churches, one may see the probable origin of that Oriental influence which traveled westward with the doctrines of Mani to influence artists in Europe a thousand years later. In the Saluvan Kuppan temple the association with forbidding jaws and demons was not altogether unpleasant to the primitive mind, since the totemistic figures of the central portal suggested man's control over the terrifying forms of animal existence.

The Primitive Tumulus Graves and the Buddhistic Stupas. The second basic element contributing to the formation of Indian architectural style was the retention in the stupa, or shrine grave, of the original tumulus and stone circle. King Asoka opened the tumulus of Gautama Buddha

In the course of a thousand years the simple plan of the ceremonial stupa with its surrounding walls developed into the great temple complexes of Angkor Wat and Angkor Thom in

FIG. 407.—Temple at Angkor Wat, French Indo-China, 12th century. (*Courtesy of Lesch-Carnegie.*)

and distributed parts of the body and personal belongings of the sage over India and Ceylon. These fragments were enshrined in a large number of ceremonial tumuli. The stupas at Barhut and Sanchi, perhaps the two best known early examples (Fig. 415), look like great inverted bowls or American Indian mounds. The stupas as they enlarged, absorbed some of the attributes of Mesopotamian pyramid temples. Soon ramps were so arranged that priests might ascend to the summits for purposes of worship. Great carved ceremonial stone fences around them retained some of the attributes of the neolithic ceremonial stone circle, particularly the great trilithons, or gateways. As we shall see, the portals at Sanchi developed an unarchitectonic, highly decorative character.

Java (Fig. 407). These edifices mark the culmination of the stupa style. With the growth of the pyramid came a further development of the gateway, which absorbed its high comb from northern Indian origins. Corner towers, perhaps of Chinese origin, were added also.

The Buddhistic Vestibule Temples at Karli. At the close of the 1st century B.C., the tomb temple had developed into a set form, with an interior suggestive of buildings arising among the wandering Scythian and Celto-Germanic peoples. The interior of the Chaitya, or vestibule temple, at Karli, illustrates this type. Passing through a porch with a rose window not unlike those of later Gothic cathedrals, one enters a long nave terminated by an apse, which encloses a small shrine. Side aisles, continuing behind this apse, form an ambulatory like those of later Gothic buildings. No simple structural pillars adorn the nave. Instead, heavy polygonal columns, like the freestanding columns erected in honor of Buddha by Asoka, line the

serve to decorate the two pillars of the porch. While the entrance thus retains the general appearance of the cave, in the temple as a whole we recognize many details brought by

Fig. 408.—Karli cave temple, general view of interior. Length 125 feet, width 46 feet, height 46 feet. The dagoba is surmounted by a wooden umbrella, about 200 B.C. (*Ewing Galloway.*)

sides. These columns terminate in the heavy, unfunctional bell capitals suggested by the earliest Jain phallic capitals. Above the capitals sacred elephants appear driven by yakshas and yakshis, in the guise of mahouts. The false wooden ceiling depending from the top of the cave bears no relation to the columns, appearing to float in the air. The origins of such a ceiling probably lie in the structure of Scythian tents (Fig. 408).

Mesopotamian Influence and the Development of the Combed Temple. At Mamallapuram near Madras in southern India, a number of temples were built in the 7th century of the Christian Era. One of these, the Ganesa Ratha, cut from a single rock, marks a step away from the subterranean cave form (Fig. 409). The animals retained as guardian genii at the entrance

the Scythian invaders to India from the West. The general shape of the structure is a pyramid, resembling the ziggurat. A long hall, similar to the halls of the Scythian and Celto-Germanic folk or the Huns, described in Chap. XII, crowns the top level of the pyramid. The shape of this hall, with its pointed, arched roof, is reminiscent of the cave tomb near Pinara (Fig. 147, Chap. VI). In the history of Indian architecture one may find this pyramidal form taking on an ever-increasing number of stories, the sides becoming steeper, until a domed temple form eventually results.

The Development of the Pyramid Temple. In northwestern India, at Gandhara, where the Greek influence dominated in the first three centuries of the Christian Era, many of the temples followed the plan of the Greek temple *in antis*, with columns and sculpture of distinctly classical origin.

In Turkestan the broad temple of the hilani type was placed on top of a pyramid and ap-

Fig. 409.—The Ganesa Ratha, Mamallapuram, near Madras, southern India, A.D. 750–950. Note lion columns in this audience-hall temple, cut from a single rock; also high combed roof. (*Courtesy of Fogg Museum.*)

proached by a ceremonial stairway (Fig. 410). This combination of temple and pyramid had great significance in Indian architecture. It added to the ceremonial importance of the stupa building and led to the creation of the great complex pyramid temples at Angkor Wat and in Indo-China.

At Anuradhapura, in Ceylon, between 161 and 137 B.C., the inhabitants erected the Ruanwalli Dagoba, a stupa in pyramidal form mounted upon three stepped platforms. The first of these platforms rests upon a frieze of elephants, whose trunks project at the corners. The end pillars on each side of the flight of steps leading to the altar on top have side railings in the shape of the great serpent, Naga. In Cambodia this many-headed serpent eventually came to have a head terminating in an ele-

phant's trunk (Fig. 411), after which it was known as the Makhara. The Makhara united with the winged dragons later seen under the feet of the yakshina at Barhut. This subject appears in most of the great temples built in pyramidal shape, along with portals decorated with the open mouth from the ancient caves.

In the Malayan Islands, the pyramidal stupa, with its ceremonial steps, developed further between the 1st and 7th centuries. Eventually, the type of building found at Mamallapuram was placed on top of a ziggurat. This structure became the center of a cruciform plan with four ceremonial gateways, a great outer wall, and many smaller stupas. Thus, in Indian architecture, one may see the cave temple modified into the hilani type, which eventually was placed upon the pyramid. The most primitive forms of this structure, dated about 2500 B.C., appear in Mohenjo-Daro.

The final stage in the development of the great pyramidal temples took place in Cambodia, Ceylon, and Indo-China between the 9th and the 12th century. At Angkor, Cambodia, the temple called the Baksei Chamkrong is a four-storied, stepped pyramid approached by a balustraded flight of steps. It has a high-combed roof above a single quadrate cell. The steps of the pyramid are so delicately designed that each higher step is not only smaller in width than the one below it but also in height. This gives the illusion of perspective that makes the temple appear higher than it actually is. Such refinement shows a high degree of aesthetic sensibility. The temples at Angkor Wat and at Boro Budur in Java combine all the peculiarities noticed in the previous structures. In each case the entire structure is planned as a square pyramid, with steps, ceremonial gateways, and, in the case of Boro Budur, with a number of stupas around the two top sets of steps (Figs. 407 and 410*c*).

The dispersion of these temples from their center on the Malay Peninsula may be traced far out into the Pacific Ocean. The similarities between them and the Central American pyra-

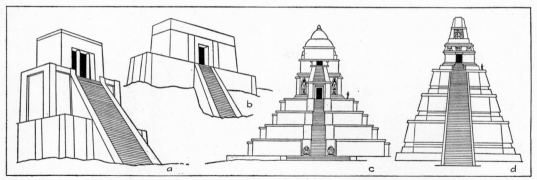

Fig. 410.—*a*, Assyrian ziggurat; *b*, Buddhist pyramid temple with ramp, Ara Tam, near Komul, Chinese Turkestan, 3rd century B.C. to 3rd century A.D. (*after A. von le Coq*); *c*, pyramid temple, Baksei Chamkrong, Angkor, early Khmer, 9th to 12th century A.D. (?) (*after Parmentier*); *d*, great temple 2, Tikal, Guatemala, early Mayan, about A.D. 300 (*after Totten, Mayan Architecture*).

mid temples are so striking that one is tempted to suggest direct influences.[1]

The Aesthetic Significance of the Tower-temple Form. The great ceremonial gateways of the pyramid temples gradually evolved into steep towers covered with a rich tracery of sculpture, like the gopuram at Madura (Fig. 412). Another freestanding form, the sikhara, like the Lingaraja Bhuvanesvara (Fig. 413), probably built about 1150, shows the final development of the tower. Here the compactness of grouping on the individual parts denotes a keen awareness of architectonic functional form combined with fine decorative feeling. The dominant motif of the central mass derives from a bud form. Unlike the Gothic building, this does not express sky-flung, tense, dynamic forces, but a natural, persistent floral growth from the soil. The deep-cut vertical lines strengthen the composition, and the supernumerary side masses lend to the feeling of perpendicularity. These fuse with the central mass because of the lightly

cut horizontal lines that bind the composition together.

The sculpture has been confined to the lower story. Each group, displayed in a separate frame or niche, seems enshrined. Contrasting this sikhara with the gopuram at Madura, we find that the former building seems more barbaric because the sculpture has been distributed over the entire surface, without regard for position. Refinement always means appropriateness. Much of Indian art, because of the very profusion of its detail, gives the Westerner the impression of barbarity.

Indian Sculpture

In connection with our discussion of the underlying characteristics of Indian sculpture, we have already seen in the figure of the pre-Mauryan yaksha (Fig. 402) the obvious earthiness of the early physioplastic representations. Almost all Indian sculpture is associated in one

[1] The following attributes characterize both the Asiatic and the American temples. (1) The pyramid carried a temple of the hilani type with two columns *in antis*. (2) This crowning cella is usually roofed with a corbeled arch and has a high comb. (3) The ceremonial stairway leading to the top in most cases is flanked with balusters ending in circles, which, in both South America and Asia, come to have long, curved, elephantine trunks and in many cases feathered combs. (4) To enter such a temple, one must pass through the jaws of the grotesque head. (5) The supporting columns of the cella in many cases have been carved to represent serpents.

From such abundance of evidence one feels inclined to predict that thorough archaeological investigation may some day demonstrate connections between eastern India and Central America during the first four centuries of the Christian Era. The presence in Melanesia of ambitious migratory peoples and their possession of large, well-built sailing ships capable of crossing the Pacific point to the possibility of a long period of colonization, which may account for the many similarities between Central American and Indian art.

way or another with the memorial Buddhistic shrines, stupas, or with temples. It is architectural sculpture without being architectonic.

FIG. 411.—Many-headed serpent with elephant's trunks, the Makhara, Cambodian temple balustrade, Khmer, about A.D. 1000. Sandstone, height 50¾ inches, width 29 inches, length 41 inches. (*Courtesy of Toledo Museum of Art.*)

The Vitalism in the Yakshas and Yakshis. From the railing of the stupa at Barhut comes the figure of an aboriginal deity or nature spirit, the yaksha (Fig. 414). Here the prehistoric

phallic nature-god is shown trampling on a dwarf that has practically the same characteristics as the Phoenician dwarf god, Bes. Next

FIG. 412.—The south gopuram at Madura, 1623, Chola dynasty, height about 120 feet. (*Courtesy of Metropolitan Museum of Art.*)

to the yaksha on another side of the column stands his consort, the yakshi (Fig. 414), a dryad who dances around a tree upon a winged griffin. Both of these deities have turbans, and the yakshi wears her hair in long braids. Above the yaksha appears the open lotus, or sun stone (a rosette), next to an Egyptian form of lotus. The yaksha, as represented, seems restless and disconnected. The pose of the yakshi unites her with the static tree, whose branches seem to partake of the same quality as her limbs. Her flesh forms are full, and the outlines of her figure, like the lines of the tree, appear to flow into one another. Thus this column from Barhut, with its two representations, suggests a psychological and philosophical background essentially balanced. The yaksha, representing the active masculine principle in nature, dances upon the dwarf of the underworld. The yak-shi, representing the feminine vegetative cult,

FIG. 413.—The Lingaraja Bhuvanesvara temple, 9th to 13th century. (*Courtesy of Metropolitan Museum of Art.*)

dances upon a winged, goat-headed griffin, which represents the unregulated vital elements of masculine power. In this early production of the Indian sculptor's art, one finds the two chief life principles carrying equal weight.

A Sculptured Gateway at Sanchi. The sculptured portal of the great stupa at Sanchi (Fig. 415) was erected in its present form under the patronage of Andhra kings, probably between 70 and 50 B.C. The four portals of the stupa display reliefs showing animals, symbols, guardian yakshas and yakshis, and historical scenes from the Buddha's life. The dreamlike fantasy of the artist led him to unite the many parts of the portal in a rather haphazard and primitive way. The general character of the carving suggests prehistoric wooden prototypes. The lower pillars of the portal resemble those at Barhut (Fig. 414), but like other pillars set up by Asoka, these have capitals topped by four elephants. Above them the lintel structure rises in three pictorial stories, decorated with scenes of worship at the stupa and with episodes from

the life of Buddha. From the elephants on each side, trees, representing the sacred Bo Tree, grow up to make connection with the lintel.

FIG. 414.—Kubera yaksha, front, and Chanda yakshi, side, reliefs on pillar from stone fence of stupa, Barhut, c. 200 B.C. (*Courtesy of Fogg Museum.*)

Closer inspection discloses that the trees form a central plant motif connecting all the architectural scaffolding. In their branches appear exquisite figures of yakshis (Fig. 415*b*).

Greek Influences in Northern India. Between the latter half of the 1st century and the end of the

FIG. 415*a.*—Northern gateway, great stupa, Sañchi, middle of 1st century B.C. (*Courtesy of India Office.*)

3rd, the sculptors of the great monasteries of Taxila and the Gandhara provinces on the northwest frontier of India, produced many figures in which Greek influences are readily apparent. The tiny relief from the Cleveland Museum (Fig. 416*a*) shows clearly the influence of models brought from the West. The very obvious realistic posture of these little celebrants, with their wine skins, palms, cups, and drums, indicates a classical origin. Only the connective rhythm of the entire frieze, so different from the rhythm in a Greek frieze, shows we are here on Indian soil.

The first steps away from the purely Greek influence in Indian sculpture may be found in a number of stucco heads, many of which are now in various American museums. The little head from the Boston Museum (Fig. 417), carved several centuries later, seems astonishing. One is tempted to ask whether crusaders returning from the Far East may not have seen

these Indian figures. The sculptors of the Tarim Valley did not attempt to imitate nature. The lines and planes of the faces are stylized, and yet enough of the natural forms persist so that,

FIG. 415*b.*—Detail of Fig. 415*a.* Yakshini or dryad. (*Courtesy of Fogg Museum.*)

as in the case of the archaic Apollo head (Fig. 138), we feel ourselves in the presence of eternal youth. The sculptor achieved this crisp freshness by carving the eye sockets on a delicate line connecting the brows with the ridge of the nose. The conventionalized eyes, properly placed, do not bulge from their sockets as did the earlier, archaic Greek eyes. Consequently, there remains no impression of fear.

From heads of this type to the stucco heads of Buddha that later developed in Gandhara during the 4th and 5th centuries is but a step. Western scholars have delighted in pointing to the fact that this Hellenic influence was necessary before the Indians could create a significant, humane statue of the enlightened Buddha. It is true that the prehistoric Indian sculpture lacks the vitality of these pieces; but, as Coomaraswamy has pointed out, admitting that some Buddhist figures in Gandhara are adaptations of Western types, still the com-

FIG. 416a.—Buddha, Gandhara, stone, 1st to 2nd century. (*Courtesy of Seattle Art Museum.*)

pleted figure of the Buddha (Fig. 416a) shows attitudes and symbols foreign to Greek art. The Buddha regularly appears seated upon the lotus. His attitude, with his legs crossed, is not Greek. As a yogi, seated in contemplation, gazing upon the end of his nose, he has a certain inner vision, likewise not associated with Greek art. After Gandhara, whatever the causes, a new Indian Buddhistic art developed, which probably united attributes from both Indian and classic styles (Fig. 418).

The Buddhistic Relief of Deogerh. No direct representations of the Buddha were carved in India during the 1st century B.C. The Bo Tree,

symbol of the Buddha's place of enlightenment, the footprints of the sage, and his representation as an elephant, do appear upon the stupas. After the beginnings of the Gandhara style,

FIG. 416b.—Bacchanalian relief, Swat valley, India, Greco-Buddhist style of Gandhara, A.D. 100. Gray schist, width about 20 inches. Note modified Corinthian column and Greek vase forms. (*Courtesy of Cleveland Museum of Art.*)

during the 2nd century, one figure of the Buddha seated upon a throne with his hand upraised in blessing decorates a stupa at Amaravati. At the temple of Deogerh, built about 500, a representation of the Buddha as the elephant king rescued from his enemies by Vishnu affords another example, most significant for our knowledge of the Indian's artistic fantasy. This relief panel, framed by lintels of sweeping floral forms, shows the elephant king chained to the ground. Vishnu, as the dragon king, appears with the many-headed serpent, Naga, behind the Buddha. This image, in turn, resembles a smaller one in the lower right part of the panel, which arises from the ground near the growing lotus flower. The juxtaposition of these two figures seems to indicate that the smaller figure may expand in power. Above the two forms Vishnu appears a third time, his many arms holding the symbols of his sovereignty.

Dancing Siva and Brahmanical Art. The Indian mind thinks in caste levels. The highest religious concepts of Indian thought lay in the system known as Mahayana Buddhism. Brahmanism, a more practical religion, based upon an acceptance of the dualistic principle, while less humanistic in character, perhaps had equal intellectual appeal. The great mass of Indians, superstitiously worshiping the male principle,

Fig. 417.—Stucco head, Tash Kurgan, Turkestan, 4th century A.D. Height about 7 inches. (*Courtesy of Boston Museum of Fine Arts.*)

found in the temples of Siva two types of image: (1) a static, phallic menhir—the *dhruva*, or immovable icon; and (2) a manifestation of Siva as Nataraja. The 14th-century figure of

as a pattern of dancing limbs and exquisitely modeled body forms delicately balanced, it becomes an object of the greatest aesthetic enjoyment.

FIG. 418.—Buddha as the elephant king freed by Vishnu, stone relief, temple at Deogerh, c. 500 A.D. Height about 5 feet. (*After W. Cohn, Indische Plastik.*)

Nataraja (Fig. 420) represents cosmic activity (*Pancakrtya*), or the five actions of Siva, dancing upon the dwarf of indolence. Siva carries in his right hand a drum, indicating the rhythm of creation, and in his left, its fire. One of his forward hands expresses involution; the other, continuance of the dance. All the motions of the body, which once moved within a circle of flame, suggest the completely integrated personality, that superior being capable of overcoming all inertia. Here is a magnificent conception of the absolute in its active aspect.

Seen through Western eyes, this four-armed figure may at first appear grotesque, for the Westerner has become accustomed to think in terms of a physical body. Here is a thought expressed with the help of bodily symbols. Studied

FIG. 419.—Female figure of Kali, India, 14th century. Bronze, height 16¼ inches. (*Courtesy of William Rockhill Nelson Gallery of Art.*)

The Geometricism in the Figure of Kali. Any religion that has as one of its tenets the negation of the world eventually produces among its votaries exercises of penance and asceticism. Both Buddhism and Brahmanism, stressing the retreat from the difficulties of a physical human existence, produced men and women who, in their search for yoga, or the higher wisdom, mortified the flesh. The goddess Kali, repre-

FIG. 420.—Dancing Siva, India, 14th century. Bronze, height 33½ inches. (*Courtesy of William Rockhill Nelson Gallery of Art.*)

sented in Fig. 419, symbolizes this ideal of spirituality.

Seated upon the lotus throne of birth, the goddess dances with her hands alone. The posi-

Indian Painting

The Wall Paintings of Ajanta. Indian painting may best be studied in the cavern temple at

FIG. 421.—Padmapani and his wife, Ajanta, fresco, 6th to 7th century. (*Courtesy of Indian Railways.*)

tion of her legs suggests a gentle rocking motion generated in the lower torso. The archaic, primitive face, with its sharply cut features and the geometric frontality of the shoulders, contrasts with the gentler curved forms of the lower body. In this relationship of the upper, geometric, intellectual faculties to the lower, emotional responses, we have the meaning of the piece. Thought of as an abstraction, it may appeal as design. Looked upon through Western eyes oriented toward a humanistic point of view, it may call up feelings of disgust. Aesthetically, it ranks very high in formal and associational values. Many sculptors of the 20th century, such as Epstein and Brancusi, stand closer in point of view to the man who cast the figure of Kali than they do to Phidias.

Ajanta, where between the 1st and the 7th century the story of the Buddha was painted upon the walls for the priests of the monastery. These paintings, like Indian sculpture, give an impression of pervasive vitality, manifest in an astonishing variety of forms and postures. The inner faith in the unity of all life, which is the *sine qua non* of Hindu philosophy, here finds expression in graphic form. An exuberant jungle of many flowers, children, animals, and trees interweaves in a great, colorful tapestry. The limbs, as in Indian sculpture, are pliant and subtle like the plant forms. All nature seems to dance. The paintings depict the life of Buddha in his various incarnations—as a deer, an elephant, a goose, or a man. Every part of the composition sets forth the idea of his tenderness and charity (Fig. 421).

The center of this whole scheme of decoration is the 6th- or 7th-century figure of Padma-

Fig. 422.—Fresco, Serigya, Ceylon, A.D. 479–497.

pani, a Bodhisattva, who takes upon himself the earthly duties of Gautama until he returns again to earth as Maitreya. This figure shows the living Buddha as an earthly ruler, seated with his wife. On each side of him one can faintly discern elephants, servants, ceremonial pillars, and a coronation scene. All parts of the composition are flat, the color areas bounded by definite, though finely drawn, lines. A few high lights, however, give a faint indication of solidity. The colors form a pleasing pattern like that used today by Rivera.

The Purity of the Ceylonese Style. Similar paintings exist in the temples at Gandhara and Bagh. Since these were created under Greek influences, they show more plastic form. Moving farther south to the island of Ceylon, we find

the acme of Indian painting on the walls of the fortress of Serigya in seventeen over-life-size figures, painted between A.D. 479 and 497. The movement of these dancers is strong. One sees in the torso illustrated (Fig. 422) the geometrical quality that appears in Balinese and Javanese dancing today. Here the trinity, or *Trimurti*, of Brahma, Vishnu, and Siva, is represented over and over again by an infinite number of triangles. Such figures appear wherever the dragon king, or Naga, was worshiped.

Perso-Mohammedan Art

The secret of the art of the Perso-Mohammedan peoples lies bound up with the desert, the garden, and the rug. Nature gave to the invading Turks and Arabs the dusty ruins and dried-up irrigation ditches of ancient Mesopotamia, a land denuded of forests and slowly turning to desert. In these barren stretches the fountain and the green flowering oasis became that symbol of paradise, the Havarenah landscape, already studied in the carvings of the Mschatta palace façade. Inheriting from the ancient Mesopotamians their rug weaving, the Mohammedans enjoyed the geometric, technomorphic patterns that arose from this craft. These patterns display in countless varieties all possible aspects of the oasis ideal. Manuscripts, pottery, mosque walls, and fabrics all bear such intricate designs, into which are woven hunting scenes similar to those of ancient Syrian monarchs and cloud or mountain forms related to Chinese painting.

The Significance of the Rug. A Persian rug of the 16th century now at the Metropolitan Museum affords one of the finest examples of the decorative art of rug weaving. In the central compartment of an interwoven vine appear human figures in blue, green, and red costumes, holding animals or playing upon musical instruments. Richly colored trees on a yellow ground form the background for this section, the rest of the field being decorated with formal scrolls. It also bears palmettes interspersed with

Fig. 423.—Persian rug, Herat (?), 16th century, Tabriz medallion. About 7 feet 8 inches by 5 feet 8 inches. (*Courtesy of Metropolitan Museum of Art.*)

animals in many colors on a dark-red background. A dark-green border contains floral scrolls, palmettes, and birds. Among the realistically drawn animals one may distinguish

Fɪɢ. 424.—Entrance portal, shrine, Imam Riza, Meshed, Persia, 15th century, tile. (*Courtesy of American Institute for Iranian Art and Archaeology.*)

leopards pursuing deer, tigers fighting with dragons, and lions attacking demons, very much as one sees them on Chinese rugs.

Large palmettes with strongly serrated outlines in the interspaces, similar to those on the rug illustrated, characterize the rugs of Herat and indicate a possible Eastern origin. Other details suggest origins in northwestern Persia. This rug, like the paintings of Bihzad in the Safavid school, epitomizes Persian art at its richest when, under Shah Thmasp (1524–1576), the great painters, such as Bihzad, Mirak, and Sultan Mohammed, worked as designers with the craftsmen (Fig. 423).

The decoration and color scheme of the Tabriz rugs produced by these masters were borrowed from the illustrations on illuminated manuscripts (Fig. 429). Each rug was a work of art produced by craftsmen, who were directed by the greatest painters. Like the manuscript paintings, the various parts of the rug included a field and a border, the latter divided at times into smaller bands. The border served to accentuate the central design by means of contrast, but the contrast was never great enough to isolate it completely from the floor—a principle applicable to the picture frame, which came to play so important a part in connection with Western panel painting after the 16th century. Since the rugs were used as floor coverings, the favorite composition principle was symmetrical, allowing the spectator to see the rug design right side up from either end. In the rug shown this holds for all the scrollwork, arabesques, and plants, though not for the center panel.

The associational value, or symbolic meaning, of such royal floor coverings drew verses of praise from the Persian poets. One such lyric, inscribed on a Persian rug in the Poldi-Pozzoli Museum of Milan, informs us what the Persian thought of his rug.

O happy the carpet whose shadow at the banquet
So longed for lay under the footsteps of the king . . .
This is no carpet, but a wild white rose;
it is a veil for the sight of the lustrous eyes (houris).
It is a garden full of tulips and roses;
therefore has the nightingale made its abode there.
It has made plain the pucker of its lace-work;
streams of water flowing from every corner.
It shows the way to the fountain of life;
a picture of every wild beast has a place.
It is better than the cheeks of the ladies of Chegel;
a garden-plot is ashamed before its face.
Before its roses a rose-garden is but a thorn;
it is like the down, (beautiful) as the moon, on the cheek
    of the adored one.
. . . .
Its weft is woven from the threads of life;
for the Darius of the world is it woven.
Oh phoenix, lift up the hands in prayer
that with a gift the end of the work may be completed.
Yea, Lord, this new rose is free from blemish

which has come forth from the garden of hope.
Let this carpet be in the path of the Darius of the world
A (healing) flower of his garden be his safety.[1]

The Rug and the Portal of a Mohammedan Shrine. The excellence of Perso-Mohammedan decorative design on large building surfaces may be judged by the view of the entrance to the shrine of Imam Riza at Meshed (Fig. 424). This imposing portal to the sanctuary of Persia's greatest saint, who lived a thousand years ago, was built in the 15th century. It has a decorative architectonic quality based upon simple, refined lines and exact geometric areas, combined regularly with the bold upthrust of the great pointed arch.

The porch, both on the exterior and in the interior, is covered with mosaic tiles in brilliant hues and shows a pattern of mellow gold, pale emerald, turquoise, milk white, and mirror black. These combine in a multitude of interesting patterns based upon rug designs. Above the arch, a border, composed of finely executed Kufic script, binds the composition together. This script, like Chinese calligraphy, carries a high degree of decorative designing beyond its thought-carrying functions. The spandrels on each side of the upper arch also carry an intricate floral pattern. From a distance the entire façade seems like a great rug in whose central panel, the porch, may be seen the figures of philosophers and poets. Under the arch a similar scheme of decoration shows other rug patterns, the central panel carrying strict geometric designs similar to those found on primitive Chinese bronzes.

The formal values in all Mohammedan building lie particularly in their union of brilliant and delicate colors, boldness of conception and refinement of line, richness of detail and proper subordination of that detail to a finely balanced geometric scheme.

Stucco Decoration and the Contrast of Light and Shade. Richness of detail in building finds another means of expression than color in the deeply cut, intricate interweave of stucco designs. The south corner of the Hāmadān (Fig. 425), carved in the 12th century, shows a further development of classical motifs first recog-

FIG. 425.—Stucco arabesques, south corner, Hāmadān, Gunbaa-i-Alawiyan, 12th century. (*Courtesy of Myron B. Smith.*)

nizable in the Mschatta style. Of particular significance is the central design of the niche, which is called an arabesque. Around a swirling swastika, abstract floral forms, like the Celtic drawings of the Book of Kells, indicate a restless motion, which forces the eye not only over the surface but also into the depth of the pic-

[1] M. S. DIMAND, *A Guide to an Exhibition of Oriental Rugs and Textiles,* Metropolitan Museum of Art, New York, 1935.

ture panel. Its intent seems to be to intrigue by its regulated variety and to arrest by its sharp contrasts of light and shade. The incomparable richness of this decorative carving is

Fig. 426.—Court of the Lions, Alhambra, Granada, Spain, 1309–1354. Size 115 feet by 66 feet. (*Courtesy of Metropolitan Museum of Art.*)

not only a matter of depth but also the result of the definition of various patterns used so that the spectator may follow one motif after another. This type of stuccowork becomes the significant interior decoration for most Mohammedan architecture, vying only with mosaic tile.

The Court of the Lions in the Alhambra. Mohammedan building, moving westward after the 8th century, finally reached Spain, carrying with it elements derived from Mesopotamian and Coptic sources. In the magnificent Court of the Lions in the Alhambra, Granada, built during the early 14th century, richly decorated stucco ceilings with pendent stalactite vaulting rest upon slender colonnettes, too fragile to

hold a weight of stone. Moorish architecture such as this is rarely functional. The light wooden domes covered with glittering exterior tiles and faced on the interior with plaster, need no buttressing, because they are false. Here again we recognize that the chief value of the structure lies in its contrasts, its lacy pierced designs, and its colorful rug-patterned surfaces. By these the fancy is excited, the eye beguiled (Fig. 426).

Functionalism of the Bridge at Kaflan-Quh. In the bridge at Kaflan-Quh (Fig. 427), built, about 1400, over the Kizil-Uzen River, on the road between Tabriz and Mianeh, appear refinements and structural qualities that recommend it to the architectural designer of the 20th century. The bold central pointed span has been well buttressed by two side piers, built on the upstream side so as to brace the structure against torrential floods. Each of these piers is further buttressed by two smaller abutments, built in crystalline, polyhedral forms (Fig. 14). Here natural necessity, such as we shall eventually find at work in the construction of 20th-century bridges and skyscrapers, has created functional aesthetic forms. The final evidence for the practicality of the builders can be seen in the introduction of two small arches above the lower piers. In time of high floodwaters these arches accommodated a volume of water equal to that shut off by the narrowing span of the central arch.

The Taj Mahal at Agra. The Taj Mahal, that Indian building best known to the world as an architectural masterpiece, came into being as a result of the fusion of Indian and Perso-Mohammedan art during the most fertile period of late Indian development, the period of the Mughal emperors. This perfect structure, a memorial to Mumtaz-i-Mahal, the wife of Shah Jehan, was built between 1630 and 1648. Even a cursory glance convinces one that this marble mausoleum has high formal and associational values. It includes a forecourt, garden, and terrace, with two gateway buildings, corner towers, and minarets. The central portion includes the swelling dome set above deep niches bordered with marble-inlaid designs proper to Persian rugs. The entire garden measures 567 by 305 meters. The boundary wall, of red sandstone, encloses a water basin that reflects the of its imperial value, simple in its functionalism, and refined in its precious decoration of colored marbles, pierced window lights, and brilliant borders. No similar rich form exists

FIG. 427.—Bridge of Kaflan-Quh between Tabriz and Mianeh, over the Kizil-Uzen, Persia, 14th century. (*Courtesy of American Institute for Iranian Art and Archaeology.*)

central structure. The disposition of the garden, always particularly significant to the Oriental, constitutes a chief charm of the structure (Fig. 428).

The central mausoleum, covering the cenotaph of Mumtaz-i-Mahal and her husband, consists of an octagonal building with four entrances. In shape, the dome suggests a stupa or bud, rather than the true buttressed dome of the Byzantine type. Needing the suggestion of a buttress, the architects built four smaller domes raised as canopies, which rise at some distance from the central dome. In the same way, to give balance to the structure, the four corner minarets placed on the edge of the central platform seem to hold the composition together. The entire arrangement forms a masterpiece of architectural design, rich because

in the other mosques of the Persians found farther west. This structure could have grown only from the soil of India. To discover in the Orient another building of similar fineness, one must go to the circular temples and pagodas of China.

An Indo-Persian Painting of the Mughal School. The paintings of the early Mughal school in India during the period of Akbar (1556–1605) unite the chief definitive characteristics of Persian and Indian pictorial design and color. The Prince Riding an Elephant (Fig. 429) in the Metropolitan Museum, New York, offers one of the best examples of this school. On the center field the prince rides his magnificent ceremonial animal, which is decorated with gold tusk bands. Bells adorn its ankles and trappings. Red, green, and yellow streamers and colors in large areas make interesting spots against the black of the beast. The runner in front, with his black horsetail pennant, likewise appears in colorful raiment. The prince, simply

teristic of all Asiatic art. Truly remarkable is the fine balance achieved between the large flat-color areas on the elephant's back and the delicate outer borders. Such a combination of

FIG. 428.—Taj Mahal, Agra, India, by Shah Jehan, A.D. 1630. White marble, width and length of platform 313 feet, height of dome 200 feet. (*Courtesy of Lesch; photograph by Dr. Martin Hürlimann.*)

dressed in white, wears richly brocaded turban and scarf.

The color design, slightly more bold than that in earlier Persian manuscripts by Bihzad, is more Indian than Persian in character. The grouping of the figures, however, with its subtle occult balance, is more perfect than that in the Gandhara frescoes and is definitely Persian. The Indian artists allowed their objects to produce individual effects, without any idea of grouping. The deep-rose border, also, with its delicate gold design, has definite Persian origin. The other two abstract borders are charac-

delicacy and strength represents the Oriental ideal of beauty, for here energy has been completely absorbed in flat pattern.

Chinese and Japanese Art

Sculpture

During the Shang and Chou periods, the ceremonial bronze sculptures of China exhibited fantastic, primitive-design characteristics (Fig. 405). In the Ch'in and Han periods, Chinese sculpture approximated a realistic, physioplastic art. Throughout the Six Dynasties that centered about Nanking, after the fall of the Han, came a great infusion of Tartar blood in northern China. The fantastic elements in parallelism in development but by the superior qualities of aesthetic abstraction displayed by the Chinese animal. In the Mesopotamian work, the body form and a primitive geometricism

Fig. 429.—Indo-Persian painting, Mughal school, period of Akbar, India, 1556–1605. Water color, 12¼ by 18½ inches (Metropolitan Museum of Art). (*Courtesy of Lesch.*)

sculpture had by that time united with the physioplastic in the creation of a number of works that in quality suggest the influence of the painter's technique (Fig. 430).

The Dynamic Pattern of the Dragon Form. Two centuries after the earliest painterly influence, the monumental sculpture of China looked like the chimera (Fig. 431)—a combination of the cloud dragon and the lion. A number of similar figures, associated with the tombs of the emperors of the Six Dynasties, were carved in the 5th and 6th centuries. The energetic lines suggest swirling cloud forms melting into lion-bodied winged figures, which appear to move forward irresistibly. Contrasting this figure with the Mesopotamian griffins executed 12 centuries earlier, we are struck not only by the

dominated. Here, the energetic line, inspiring the action of the mass, creates a greater illusion of movement, and the whole figure has an integration lacking in the Mesopotamian creation. Further, the central composition outweighs the surface design of wings and muscles.

The Horse from the T'ang Dynasty and the Renaissance of Realism. During the first part of the T'ang dynasty (619–907), the tombs of the Emperor T'ai Tsung (649) were decorated with six monumental stone reliefs, of which one of the finest examples may now be seen in the University of Pennsylvania Museum. In the Han period, the horse had become a favorite subject of representation. Into such physioplastic representations of the horse went the vitality of the chimera, and this living quality, coupled with the occult spatial design typical of Chinese art, here results in a creation comparable in fineness to the horses of Phidias. How well all parts of this relief weave together without de-

(Fig. 440) and is echoed, curiously enough, in a saying by Diego Rivera, the American artist, who, confronted with the destruction of his masterpiece, said, "I am like a tree who must

Fɪɢ. 430.—Fight between man and tiger, from tomb near Sian Fu, Shen-si Province, China, Han dynasty, 206 ʙ.ᴄ.–ᴀ.ᴅ. 220. Terra-cotta bas-relief, length about 18 inches. Note perfect spacing of design areas and compare with Greek Exekias Cylix, Fig. 174*b*, Chap. VIII. (*Courtesy of Cleveland Museum of Art.*)

stroying that moment of relationship expressed in the faces of the general and the emperor's charger! Wherever the eye starts in the panel, it eventually leads back to the eye of the horse and the head of the man. The artist has subordinated all other detail to the two faces, so that the interest unconsciously moves from the larger vacant areas of the composition to its psychical center. A study of the paintings of the period, which show the relationship between men and horses, will give a further understanding of this relief and will demonstrate the accuracy of this interpretation.

The Floral Lines of the Fertility God. Studied closely, the head of the general in the T'ang relief (Fig. 432) reveals a personality as contained and dignified as the head of the old fertility god (Fig. 433). The Chinese conceives God as a magnified man, but man, as seen here, partakes of the lines of plant growth which root him to the soil. The greatest contrast possible may be remarked between this concept of fertility and the Greek idea of the youthful Pan, or the spirit of growth in nature. To the Chinese, fertility is something lasting, which blossoms even in old age. Something of that spirit appears in the portrait of the Ming gentleman

needs flower in its season." The natural powers of growth in a man or a nation deeply rooted in the soil do not diminish with age.

The Essence of Oriental Sculpture in the Statue of Kwan-Yin. During the T'ang dynasty (619–907), all the chief attributes of Indian and Chinese Buddhistic sculpture united in superb figures of Kwan-Yin, the Bodhisattva of mercy, or the Buddha as the merciful all-mother. In its earliest forms, Indian Buddhism was characterized by devotion to a personal god, an ideal which gradually gave way in the Mauryan, Sunga and Andhra periods of Indian culture to a more spiritual concept of the Buddha. The Buddha came to be the enlightened one who, after death, changed to the Mahayana, or the embodiment of a principle. This deified Buddha took to himself Hindu images of Brahma and of the yakshas, yakshis, and Nagas who were his protectors and assistants. Other holy Buddhas —the Dhyani of the Four Quarters—and their spiritual sons, the Bodhisattvas, incarnations of the respective virtues by which they were known, joined the Buddhist pantheon. Of these, the Dhyani and the Bodhisattvas particularly appealed to the Chinese.

The earliest Chinese representations of the

Buddha are similar in most details to the ancient statue of the fertility god, the chief differentiating characteristic being a younger, more distinctly Indian type of face. During the 6th

part of the figure to the ground. These two systems of folds form a contrast stressed by the *mudras*, or positions of the hands, one pointed downward, the other raised in blessing. Thus

Fig. 431.—Chimera, statue from imperial tomb near Nanking, 6th century A.D. Stone, length about 10 feet. (*Courtesy of University of Pennsylvania Museum.*)

Fig. 432.—Grave relief of general under Emperor T'ai Tsung, T'ang dynasty, c. 649. Stone, length about 5½ feet. (*Courtesy of University of Pennsylvania Museum.*)

century, the stiff, blocky figure gradually became animated with a gentle, spiraling motion similar to the so-called Praxitilean curve. Classical scholars point to this as a Greek influence coming from Sassanian Turkestan and Gandharan origins. It is not necessary, however, to postulate this origin, for over the centuries the Kwan-Yin, as we see it in the statue in the Boston Museum (Fig. 434), might have developed from a combination of Hindu and Chinese sculpture without the intervention of Greek models. Sculptors interested in the human form, with the background of a love for floral nature, must eventually arrive at this form as they study the human body and strive to express the gentle, compassionate elements in nature.

The all-mother is born from the double lotus, itself a symbol of birth, guarded by lions and animals arising from the lower world. The sweeping folds of her long drapery carry up from the lotus petals in a long, vital curve, which terminates naturally in the slightly inclined head. In contrast, the delicate folds of the *dhopi*, or lower garment, held by a belt around the hips, are heavy and tie the lower

the Bodhisattva partakes of both the heavenly and the earthly. The lower part of the body, which is of the earth, is clothed. The upper part is bare, except for the jeweled symbols. The headdress is a cross between the earlier crown and the later plaited turban, which became popular after the T'ang dynasty. The figure still retains much of the masculine attribute of the original worldly Buddha, but has almost an equal amount of the feminine thought element. Seldom has man embodied in sculptured form a more satisfactory conception of humane beneficence.

The Romanticism of Late Sung Sculpture. During the final development of Chinese sculpture in the Sung dynasty, as the artists sought relief from the evils of the world in an aesthetic escape from life, the figures of Bodhisattvas become more dreamlike and pictorial in quality. Siren has suggested that the creative energy which had in former times expressed itself in simple sculpturesque forms, turning to painting at this time, brought the influence of that painting into stone and wood. Thus late Sung, early Yuan, and much other Chinese sculpture, from this time on, came to include backgrounds treated like rocky landscapes with human figures massed so as to create broad effects of light and shade. Wood, which, softer in grain,

FIG. 433.—Fertility god, Chinese, T'ang dynasty (?) (Field Museum, Chicago). (*Courtesy of Field Museum.*)

stimulated the artist to pictorializing fantasy, replaced stone, and color was subtly applied. Scholars such as Coomaraswamy point to the ever-recurrent influence of Indian ideals in Chinese art and even assign to Indian origins such a magnificent bronze casting as the Screen of the Trinity of Tachibana Fujin at Horiuji. As Indo-China at this period was undergoing a renaissance of building and sculptural activity, it is possible that we shall eventually discover that its artists played an important role in the development of this pictorial sculpture, which spread over northern China during the 12th and 13th centuries to become an important factor in the plastic arts through the Yuan and Ming dynasties (Fig. 435).

Painting

An analysis of the Chinese art of painting discloses not only the principles of design used by

FIG. 434.—Kwan-Yin, Padmapani, China, Sui dynasty, late 6th or early 7th century. Limestone, height about 7 feet. (*Courtesy of Boston Museum of Fine Arts.*)

the greatest artists of the Western world but also the same underlying spirit. Painting in both Occident and Orient moved toward the same goal: the apprehension of eternal truths and their embodiment in forms comprehensible to the human mind. Despite this fact, most

Chinese painting looks strange to Western eyes, and until the 20th century, differed markedly from the mass of European painting. Somewhere very early in the evolution of their painting the Chinese played with an aesthetic symbol that stands for the idea that man is a permanent, substantial form emerging from the world of shadows. This symbol is called "chiaroscuro," or light and shade. We shall find that European artists lingered long and lovingly over canvases on which they modeled with paints the appearance of man emerging from the primal darkness. It was as though they would fix forever the moment in which man became of age. The Orientals early understood this symbol, but preferred to use it sparingly, as though they had already passed on to the mature realization that man represents only a small part of the changing pattern of existence. For this reason, most Chinese painting looks flat and unsubstantial to the realistic Western observer.

Chinese painting differs from European also in that it forms part of the development of Chinese poetry and writing. Because he does not believe in compartmentalized knowledge, the Oriental affirms in the unity of these three arts the continuity of a creative existence.

Poetic Literature as Subject Matter. Nearly a thousand years ago, during the Sung dynasty (960–1279), a Chinese artist, Kuo Hsi, whose writings show a fine union of the three great ethical and religious strains of Chinese thought, wrote an essay on landscape painting for his son. This essay defines the aesthetic essence of all Chinese painting, and is perhaps the most significant commentary on all painting to be had in a small compass. From Kuo Hsi alone the reader can gain all the background necessary for a comprehension of Chinese art.

Kuo Hsi tells us that the great painter Ku K'ai-chih (A.D. 350–412), being a man of vision and of noble mind, could not paint unless he first built a high pavilion for his studio. Greatness of spirit and singleness of purpose— qualities that the Hindu calls *chandomaya*, or

self-integration—are necessary for artistic creation. Kuo Hsi defined poetry as a picture without form, and painting as a poem with form. From the ancient poetry of the Ts'in and T'ang

Fig. 435.—Lin Chi in attitude of shouting. Wood sculpture, height 3 feet 5 inches, width 30 inches. (*Fuller Collection, Seattle Art Museum.*)

dynasties he culled pertinent lines, on which he pondered until they aroused in him a desire to paint. Among the poems recorded by the artist, two suggest classic themes repeatedly used by Sung-dynasty painters.

THOUGHTS ON MY BROTHER

When will my brother, sojourning in the south return:
I only know he is among the Three Rivers and the Five
  Ranges.
Alone I stand at the Heng Gate and gaze over the
  immensity of the autumn waters wide;
A lone raven starts away, and the sun steps behind the
  mountain.

Tou Fung

In the sixth month with a cane I come to a stony pass;
In the noontide shade, I hear a murmuring stream.

WANG CHIH-FU[1]

A third poem, translated by Arthur Waley, from a 4th-century poet, bears witness to the ceremonious, symbolic aspect of the poet painter's art.

Swiftly the years, beyond recall.
Solemn the stillness of this fair morning.
I will clothe myself in spring clothing
And visit the slopes of the Eastern Hill.
By the mountain-stream a mist hovers.
Hovers a moment, and then scatters.
There comes a wind blowing from the South
That brushes the fields of new corn.

T'AO CH'EN[2]

The natural grandeur or sublimity suggested by the poems in Kuo Hsi's essay denotes a peculiarity in his character and in the character of most Sung-dynasty painting. This can still be seen in a few remaining pictures attributed to Kuo Hsi, such as the Early Spring and Sitting in Contemplation by a Stream, hanging scrolls belonging to the Chinese Government (Fig. 436). Concerning such creations Oswald Siren has written that they are filled with an infinite number of varying structures and shapes rendered in finest detail. These are deftly interwoven with the dominant spiraling movement of the pictures so that the climactic peaks appear strong and serene. The work of Kuo Hsi presents the culminating moment of a school, none of whose earlier masters could fuse so many rich associational patterns into unifying rhythm while losing so little the fundamental expression of an idea.

The quality of the work of Kuo Hsi is also approximated in a remarkable scroll painting by one of his predecessors, Tung Yuan, now in the Boston Museum (Fig. 443). This scroll, painted in the Sung dynasty, might have been suggested by the first poem.

The subject matter of Chinese and Japanese painting frequently deals with the delicate and intimate aspects of nature—the gossamer wings of a dragonfly, fish swimming in a pool amid lily blossoms, a dog wandering in a field of flowers, bamboos and birds in the rain. We also find characterful human portraits, as well as portraits or still-life paintings of mellow fruit and more humble vegetables, each with its own poetry and place. One artist spent a lifetime studying cranes; another enjoyed fishing; a third, companionships with friends; a fourth, a retreat in the mountains.

Hsieh Ho and the Principles of Perfect Composition. Shortly after painting had reached its definitive form in the works of China's first great painter, Ku K'ai-chih, there lived a talented figure painter and art critic, Hsieh Ho, in the Ch'i dynasty (479–502). Hsieh Ho formulated six canons for perfect painting. These are as follows: rhythmic vitality, anatomical structure rendered through brushwork, accurate representations of recognizable forms, appropriate distribution of colors, careful composition with subordination of less important objects to some important center, and the transmission of classic literary models.

Here is an easily comprehended scheme by which anyone may judge a work of graphic or plastic art. One detects at once the polarity of the yin and the yang, rhythmic vitality at one extreme standing for the dynamic aspect of existence, and the set poetic formula at the other, representing the static. Between these two poles are ranged all those niceties of craftsmanship that enable the artist to make his painting interesting.

Early Paintings of Ku K'ai-chih and the Sense of Rhythmic Vitality. The earliest Chinese paintings, really engravings on the walls of the Wu tombs near Shantung, tell of memorable events in the life of the Wu family. Confucius apparently thought that the chief object of painting should be the preservation of the noble features of an illustrious ancestor. Thus painting in China arose from the most practical considerations. The innate sense of balance of

[1] Taken from *An Essay on Landscape Painting* by Kuo Hsi, published in the Wisdom of the East Series by E. P. Dutton & Co., Inc., New York, 1935. Translated by Shio Sakanishi.
[2] ARTHUR WALEY, *One Hundred and Seventy Chinese Poems*, Alfred A. Knopf, Inc., N. Y., 1919.

FIG. 436.—Hanging scroll or kakemono, Sitting in Contemplation by a Stream. Painting in ink on silk, about 5 feet 2 inches by 3 feet 6 inches. Although this is attributed to Fan K'uan (A.D. 990–1030), it is possibly a work by Kuo Hsi. (*Courtesy of the Chinese Government; photograph by Prof. Rowley, Princeton University.*)

the Chinese artist and his desire for pleasant spacing of objects early led to the creation of an art far beyond the comprehension of any contemporary European craftsman. Aesthet-

gestion of the mood of life in the environment of this pleasant lady. The dignity and gentleness of this movement contrast with the regular flow of the Greek dance, the strenuous convolu-

FIG. 437.—Admonitions of the Instructress, attributed to Ku K'ai-Chih, about A.D. 350–400. Ink on silk. (*Courtesy of British Museum.*)

ically, Chinese brush painting on manuscripts, dating from the 4th or the 5th century, begins where late Greco-Roman painting ended (Fig. 252). Possibly the introduction to China of scrolls similar to the Joshua Roll from Alexandria, as well as the lesser known Persian Manichaean manuscripts of the 3rd and 4th centuries, may have acted as a point of departure for the Chinese painters. The first great Chinese painter, Ku K'ai-chih left a series of unconnected scenes from a prose composition, *The Admonitions of the Instructress in the Palace,* by an author of the 3rd century. The scene tells of a lady, Feng, who saved the life of an emperor. A second scene tells of another lady, who, to save the emperor's honor, refused to ride with him in his palanquin. A symbolic landscape follows and, at the end of a number of scenes evidencing the influence of women upon Chinese life, one finds the instructress herself writing down her admonition (Fig. 437). The illustration makes clear the meaning of the term "rhythmic vitality," for, in the undulating scarf and the almost ceremonious dancing rhythm that moves the figure, one notes a sug-

tions of the medieval dance, and the staccato jazz primitivism of the wartime Western world. The order of the Oriental rhythm is much more complex than the Occidental, however, because it includes a recognition of change as the law of life.

Anatomical Rendering in the Dragons of Ch'en Jung. The second of Hsieh Ho's six principles, which has to do with the vitality and accuracy of the brush stroke, is best illustrated by a detail (Fig. 438) from the picture of nine dragons by Ch'en Jung of the southern Sung school, who lived in the 13th century. Kuo Hsi tells us that the great painter does not grasp his brush hurriedly, plan carelessly, and splash ink impulsively. The brush in many cases is thought to be inspired by some spirit; the ink, of greatest delicacy and capable of infinite nuances of color, is made in many varieties. Kuo Hsi gives in great detail the names of various brush manipulations, explaining that a repeated use of light ink in a circling motion is called the light-ink touch, while the use of a sharp-pointed brush horizontally, backward and forward, is called the smoothing of the wrinkles. Repeated rinsing of a drawing with water and ink will make the colors stand out in relief. The point of the brush dropped and held will draw figures and leaves, while a long, steady, backward *sentation of Recognizable Form.* The third canon of Hsieh Ho seems but a further extension of the second. Actually, it has less of the inspirational about it and stresses the necessity for a pains-

FIG. 438.—Detail of Nine Dragons Scroll, by Ch'en Jung, Sung dynasty, 1235–1255. Ink and tints on paper (Boston Museum of Fine Arts). (*Courtesy of Boston Museum of Fine Arts.*)

stroke may be used for drawing pine needles. Other essays on brush strokes by several masters tell in detail exactly how to suggest some accent of nature by a single mark.

A careful study of the dragon picture will disclose a number of brush strokes and treatments of wash. The greatest contrast in stroke comes between the long, wavy lines of the stream and the sharp, horny claws of the dragon. The next great contrast appears in the scales of the dragon compared with the flame lines of his wings. The artist achieved a third type of contrast by means of washes, the very dark background behind the dragon's head and neck rounding over into the lighter cloud forms. Through significant brush strokes, he suggests enough of the tail, protruding vertebrae, joints, and head of the dragon to lend him an air of verisimilitude. We see that the creature is compounded of serpent, eagle, wolf, and antelope. All needless detail is omitted, however.

The Fairy by Wu Wei and the Accurate Repre-

taking study of natural phenomena. The painter Wu Wei, in the fantasy figures of the fairy and the phoenix (Fig. 439), shows great knowledge of the peculiarities of bird life, the human features, and the action of drapery folds. The artist discovered in the phoenix three different kinds of feathers, each characterized by a peculiar brush stroke. These strokes contrast with the shorter, delicate, and heavy strokes of the fairy's drapery, with the heavy wash of her hair, and with the light drawing of her flowers.

A Gentleman of the Ming Dynasty and the Appropriate Use of Colors. An unknown artist of the late Ming dynasty (1368–1644) drew the portrait of a gentleman (Fig. 440). This simple, decorous panel, with its few lines and five tones, epitomizes all Chinese color distribution of the highest type. The largest area of the picture in a warm, greenish brown is broken by a secondary area, about one-third the size of the first, which forms the body of the sitter. The lightest tones of the flesh and the darkest tone of the hat, which together form the greatest point of contrast, are placed in such a position, slightly above and to the right of the center, that no matter how we turn the picture,

Fig. 439.—Fairy and Phoenix, by Wu Wei, 1458–1508, Ming dynasty. Ink lightly colored on silk, 58 by 37½ inches (British Museum).

the two spots always seem to be in good balance with the larger areas. This subtlety of occult balance cannot find its match in most Western painting. More intimate study discovers other subtle nuances of color. The inner vest of the man, slightly lighter than his cloak, forms a pattern leading up to the face, which, with its beard, seems to arise like a flower at the end of a stalk, growing from a point low down in the picture where many drapery lines converge. Within the face itself the eyes, sharply drawn, vie with the red of the lips for attention,

forming a balance around the nose. The stroke of genius that displays the master touch is the placing of the queue, which hangs over the right shoulder. Remove that one dark spot and how empty the entire picture would seem!

Composition as Subordination and the Album Painting by Yen Tz'ŭ-Yü. The matter of orderly composition as explained by Hsieh Ho and elaborated by Kuo Hsi has a dual significance. Pictures may center around some object to which lesser details are subordinate, or may be designed to suggest an allover pattern in which two unlike objects vie for attention. Each composition type has its particular value. The landscape painting by Yen Tz'ŭ-Yü furnishes an excellent example of subordination, a quality which Kuo Hsi describes in minutest detail in his rules for painting. Kuo Hsi tells us that in painting a landscape the artist must give attention first of all to a large mountain around which other mountains may be grouped. All perspective and proportion should be drawn in relation to the master peak, which will bear the same relationship to the other parts as an emperor to his subjects. Upon that master peak, or, for that matter, in any painting that includes stones and trees, the artist should depict a large pine or groups of pines. Pine trees set upon peaks are good omens. Around the great pine, called the aged master, may be grouped smaller trees. In the same way, rocks should be subordinated to some central mass. An inn or a hut should stand by a ravine, not too far from the water, for water is necessary. The mist should be shown rising out of the mountains.

Here in all its details our picture (Fig. 441) is described for us. Only one thing is lacking—its meaning. A careful examination of the roadway leading from the left in the lower part of the picture discloses a traveler seated upon a donkey, followed by a servant. They have crossed the bridge, whose presence suggests the consideration or culture of those whom they will soon visit. Following the road, before the evening mists obscure the mountaintops,

Fig. 440.—Portrait, Ming Dynasty, 1350–1650 (*British Museum*). (*Courtesy of Lesch.*)

the travelers will have entered the tiny village where, beneath the friendly pines, they may find friends. On the morrow they will pass out into the mist. Among his poems Kuo Hsi included one by Ch'ang-Sun Tso-fu—"A Visit to a Mountain Retreat."

Alone I set out to visit a mountain retreat, now stopping, now proceeding again.
Thatched cottages are linked behind the pine branches.
Though the host hears my voice, the gate is not yet open;
By the fence over the wild lettuce flutters a yellow butterfly.[1]

Balance and Harmony in the Narcissus by Chao Mêng-Chien. The second type of composition, one in which balance and harmony have been achieved through pattern rather than through subordination, is exemplified in the narcissus by Chao Mêng-Chien (Fig. 442). Here the intent was to reproduce the contrast between the long, sinuous, swordlike leaves of the three plants and their delicate fragile blooms. The design is that of the interweave, in the midst of which appear three handfuls of starlike blossoms. The artist achieved balance by placing his poem far to the right. It reads

> With no dust on feet, quietly dressed,
> Fanning sleeves induce the poetic mind,
> Worships God during night of clear dew
> Flesh of gold and jade forms the petals.
>   YI-CHAI.[2]

This composition affords an excellent example for the study of the brush strokes. The few darting quills of the grass form the greatest possible contrast with the gentle, rounded curves of the petals. Between these two the long strokes of the blades form a transitional border, and the pattern of the blades a fugal counterpoint, carrying such melody as might be suggested by the fragrance of the flowers.

The Aspect of the Sublime in the Landscape by Tung Yüan. In our previous studies of the evolution of classical art, we found two criteria—beauty and grandeur—for its judgment, stem-

ming from the thoughts of Plato and Longinus. Chinese and Japanese art, like Occidental art, achieves at times beauty, at times grandeur, and occasionally a perfect combination of the

FIG. 441.—Landscape, an album painting, by Yen Tz'ŭ-Yü. Ink and tint on silk, about 10 inches square. Note the difference in artist personality suggested by this and the other two Sung landscapes by Kuo Hsi and Tung Yüan. The vertical, horizontal, and square shapes each suggest a different outlook on life, with Sublimity, Energy, and, here, Beauty as end-goals. (*Courtesy of Freer Gallery of Art.*)

two. We shall here examine three works of art that illustrate these goals in Chinese painting.

The landscape by Tung Yüan (Fig. 443), painted in the early Sung dynasty, that is, the late 10th century, shows a masterful control of the brush, indicating fundamental knowledge of the greatest rhythm of existence. The folded mountain ridges at the right of the picture shelter in their deep, misty valleys monastic retreats to which the meditative soul may retire. Distilled from their mists a mountain torrent rushes out to add its limpid waters to the broadening sea. On the plain among the trees nestles a home, to which the traveler may come. By the shore, the boat indicates the possibility

---

[1] Taken from *An Essay on Landscape Painting* by Kuo Hsi, published in the Wisdom of the East Series by E. P. Dutton & Co., Inc., New York, 1935, translated by Shio Sakanishi.
[2] Translation by Dr. C. J. Ho.

of a voyage out past the promontory where fisherfolk ply their trade. On the broad expanse of the sea appear other boats. Beyond the opening waters, one perceives distant lands as the goddess of birth—painted by the 19th-century Japanese artist, Kano Hogai, and now placed in the Imperial Art School of Tokio, marks the culmination of Asiatic religious paint-

FIG. 442.—Horizontal scroll or makimono, Narcissus, by Chao Mêng-Chien, 13th century. Ink on paper, about 12 by 30 inches. (*Courtesy of Freer Gallery of Art.*)

and towering mountain ranges; but the vision, which has constantly moved from right to left across the scroll, turns and is carried back toward the center section, where one small, striking peak—a lonely mountain—contrasts with the misty space.

Each detail of this scroll forms a perfect picture. Although each can be enjoyed alone, each part receives added grandeur through its relationship to the whole. Without the few small human figures, the landscape would appear lonely. The Chinese rarely pictures the universe without some indication of man's humble place in it. His humility, however, springs from no abject servitude or fear. If the paintings of the Sung school indicate a fine balance between the Confucian philosophy of life and the Taoistic philosophy, which stresses man's journeying, the paintings of other schools—particularly the Ming—and the works of the Japanese Buddhistic artists emphasize the ideal elements of human character.

The Buddhist Kwan-Yin by Kano Hogai. The Kwan-Yin Hibo (in Japanese, Kwannon) (Fig. 444)—the merciful all-mother, or the Buddha

ing. Standing in the clouds high above the peaks of the earth, the beneficent deity, holding in one hand a flower, in the other the staff of life, sends floating gently down into the world a tiny babe. Thus the soul descends from its maker, gazing back with longing at the source of all goodness.

The gently animated folds of Kwan-Yin's drapery, her tender, unsmiling face, and the regal magnificence of her jeweled headdress lend to her an unearthly magnificence. Nothing of her body seems substantial; she is as ethereal as the clouds. The careful drawing of her feet, hands, and face, however, lends to her the aspect of reality necessary for belief. The literary touch in the picture comes with the manner in which the artist has shown the peaks as jagged rocks which must eventually burst the protective bubble around the child, leaving it to fend for itself amid the harsh battles of the world.

A Picture by Hui Tsung and the Formation of the Classical Ideal. The scroll paintings by Emperor Hui Tsung, simple, dignified, and deeply expressive, are among the great Chinese classics.

In these pictures the emperor sees himself as a free spirit at times exploring the universe or seated beneath a tree by the side of the road, pondering upon the infinite future. Presumably, the philosophy underlying his painting includes Taoistic and Buddhistic ideals united in the practical ethical point of view of Confucianism. Although realism was encouraged by Hui Tsung, simplicity and appropriateness in style were held to be of superior worth. In order that all court dignitaries might benefit by the rules of life manifest in painting, the emperor decreed that officials taking civil service examinations be able to illustrate a line or phrase from the Confucian classics or some well-known poem. Since the artists had at their disposal the rules of painting formulated by Hsieh Ho and Kuo Hsi, we may well understand how there could result pictures whose thought content and formal values unite in perfect proportion. Here at last we have the perfect ideal figure-and-landscape painting.

Into the emperor's painting went a wealth of human sympathy and an insight possessed by few artists. He was known for his delicate bird and flower paintings (Fig. 445). His style is characterized by fine, precise strokes, realistic scenes not overburdened with detail, and a high degree of selectivity.

Under Hui Tsung, two schools of landscape, the northern and the southern, grew up, the northern associated with fine, delicate brushwork, the southern, with heavier, bolder strokes. Of the northern school, Yüan alone used the bold type of stroke called the "ax-cut." This artist, following Hui Tsung, simplified and condensed the great landscapes by Tung Yüan of the southern school (Fig. 443) and, using a few powerful strokes, could paint a small pile of rocks and a few feet of stream which caught in a simplified composition the essence of the whole.

Seeking a reason for the inspirational impulses of the Sung school, we find that, during this dynasty, China had its most open relationships with Persia, India, Turkey, Japan, and Korea. At that time the king of Korea sent his artists to China for instruction in painting, and the Japanese copied the works of the great Chinese masters. The Sung dynasty ended with the coming of the Mongols, who took the emperor prisoner. The court officials fled to their mountain retreats, where they painted album paintings and joined the Zen sect of Buddhism, biding their time until their conquerors recalled them to the court as administrators of the great empire. To the artist-emperor and poet-painters of the Sung dynasty we owe a recognition of the fact that for the intelligent oppressed man art may mean a release for psychical energies which, uncontrolled, might destroy his soul.

Architecture

The Pailou, or Ceremonial Gateway. The spirit underlying all Chinese architectural construction appears most clearly in the ceremonial gateway, or pailou, erected by the Emperor Yung Lo in 1420 as the entrance to the Ming tomb area. Essentially, this gateway, although stemming in part from wooden architecture, remains the primitive trilithon. It escapes the primitive in two ways: (1) by its appropriate refined use of decorative detail; (2) in its exquisite relationship to the landscape behind it (Fig. 446).

Considering first the formal values of this spirit gateway to the other world, we observe a symmetrical structure almost 50 feet high and a little over 100 feet in length. Its profile suggests a mountain with gently rising slopes and a central peak. The ornamental roofs, with their colorful porcelain tiles, seem to float like a heavenly city above the tablets inscribed with cloud motifs. The entire superstructure is nicely balanced on six slender, tapering marble pillars, so intricately joined that they have withstood the shocks of earthquake and storm for centuries. The functional intricacy of the stone joining is matched by a decorative union of motifs deriving from wooden, stone, bronze, and ceramic origins. Thus, technomorphic patterns associating the observer with all phases of Chinese aesthetic creativity unite to act upon the mind.

The low, broad bases on which the super-

tangible world from that of the spirit world. Such a belief has its use in making the lot of man a happier one.

The Tower, or Pagoda. Contemporaneously

FIG. 443.—Scroll or makimono, Landscape, by Tung Yüan, early Sung dynasty, late

structure rests are carved with lotus petals, calling to mind Buddhistic thought. The square plinths, covered with intricate cloud dragons, suggest Taoism. These are capped with a molding of lotus petals, above which crouching lions and plant forms again suggest Buddhism. The upper six pillars connect functionally with the plinths and the superstructure by means of engaged pilasters that seem to rise from the backs of the animals. The pilasters flower into capitals, above which corbeled blocks carved with cloud patterns act as transitional braces for the simple lintels.

How pleasantly and with what sureness the eye moves from the simple, massive, functional elements to the paneled designs! The most refined aspect of the primitive monolithic structure here unites with the most reasonable aspect of the cultured design. As an architectural monument, this memorial arch ranks in excellence with the Parthenon and the façade of Reims Cathedral. It lacks the useful values of those Western structures, however, unless one can accept the Oriental belief that only such a decorative opening separates the life of the

with the development of the tower in India, the Chinese Buddhists elevated the tope, or stupa, into a high, towerlike building. The great Pagoda of the Wild Geese near Si-an, constructed in 652, and the Pagoda of Hsiang Chi Ssu near by, erected in 681, are essentially the same as the Indian gopuram (Fig. 447a). Both of these towers reveal obvious wooden origins in their stone decoration. For a complete understanding of these origins we must examine a type of wooden architecture similar to that employed in the Norwegian mast churches. Whether this structure developed first in China or in Celto-Germanic Europe remains a moot point. We must also consider the possibility of parallel origins or, more likely, a distribution from some central point, such as Persia or Turkestan. This last origin would be indicated by some of the decorative features.

Significantly enough, the pagoda as a wooden building, with its many wide-spreading tiled roofs (Fig. 447b), developed a form similar to that of the spreading pine tree. Just as the Celto-Germans at times considered the life of a man as one with the life of a tree, the Chinese in their earliest ideographs made the tree sign and the man sign practically synonymous. What was more natural than that the pagoda, a home for man made of wood, should retain its

pailou, as we have already seen, represents a decorative feature, pure and simple, crowning the structure rather than covering it.

The chief problem in constructing the roof

10th century (Boston Museum of Fine Arts). (*Courtesy of Boston Museum of Fine Arts.*)

primary symbolic and formal significance? The intricate construction of the mortised wooden posts connecting the stories with their balconies and galleries depends on an infinite skill in cantilever construction. These structures, being symbolic rather than useful, call for an abundance of ornament.

The Union of Architectural Design and Nature in Chinese Building. The spirit gateway and the pagoda supply the clues to the external form of Chinese building. Underlying this formal aspect remains the more practical, functional necessity of building a home for man. The earliest Chinese structures still in existence include temples, palaces, and her great protective walls. The primitive thatch-covered huts of the prehistoric Chinese probably had wide, projecting roofs of tentlike character. Later, the roofs were covered with tiles when the walls were built of brick. Once the Chinese had realized the pleasant effect of their deep-shadowed roofs, which seemed to float in the air, they developed them into decorative members. In the more elaborate types of Chinese building, the roof supplied the chief ornament. The roof of the Ming

we have already discussed in connection with the structure of the pagoda. The intricate system of bracketing may be seen, with all its colorful decoration, under the eaves of the porch of the Temple of Confucius at Chufou near Shantung (Fig. 448). This great hall building, with its magnificent colonnade, stands over the old family residence of the Kung family, where Confucius was born and lies buried. Since the cloud pattern supplies the most significant element of decoration in the brackets, the roof would seem to represent the tent of the heavens.

Many Chinese and Japanese temple and domestic structures have great entrance porches similar to the above, which serve as ceremonial entrance ways. In the Temple of Confucius the character of the building is particularly apparent in the intricate carving of the great stone columns with their cloud-dragon designs. Each column rises from a broad lotus base, above which the first pattern suggests the waters, rocks, and trees of the world. The next stage has a cloud scroll, out of which the dragon, with its flamelike wings, mounts toward the heavens. The cloud pattern of the dragon's head is carried over into the painting of the beams. The entire quality of the carving suggests the leafy foliage we see beyond, so that

Fig. 444.—The Bodhisattva (Hibo Kwannon) or compassionate mother, by Kano Hogai, Japan, 1828–1888. Colors on silk, about 65 by 35 inches. (*Courtesy of Institute of Art Research, Tokio.*)

the building as a whole unites with the landscape. How intimate can be this connection between building and landscape is shown by the picture of the dragon stairway at the Temple of Confucius in Peiping (Fig. 449).

In the discussion of the development of the Indian raised hall temple on the pyramid, the importance of the dragon balustrade in Asiatic architecture became apparent. The Chinese hall temples, like those of Mesopotamia, India, and Central America, stood on platforms approached by ceremonial staircases. In the Temple of Confucius the dragon forms a central ramp. The dragon shapes are retained also in the terminations of the side balustrades, but although we can recognize the spiral eye and the trunk of the *makhara*, the fine architectonic sense of the Chinese has changed the dragon into an abstraction. Details of the balustrade suggest bud and lotus forms, the upright posts serving to interrupt the long diagonal flow of the railing. The illustration also gives an excellent idea of the intricate joining and paneling of the side wall, as well as the construction of the roof. How closely Chinese architecture connects with nature is clear in the way the tree form seems to harmonize with the building. A finer combination has rarely been achieved in the entire history of the world's architecture.

The Temple of Prayer for the Year, at Peiping. The most refined and dignified form of pagoda construction to be found in Chinese architecture is the ceremonial Temple of Prayer for the Year, originally erected in A.D. 1421 by the Emperor Yung Lo and, after having been struck by lightning and burned down, in 1889 rebuilt by the Manchu emperor, Kuang Hsü. This great circular structure (Fig. 450), on a stepped platform of carved marble, lifts its triple roof of shining azure tile high toward the dome of the heaven it symbolizes. To this temple the emperor yearly came with offerings to the great god of heaven for an abundant harvest. Only the emperor might worship here. The balustrades resemble those of the Temple of

Confucius, and the dragon-spirit stairway forms the chief element in the ceremonial entrance.

The contour of this magnificent design seems little less impressive than that of the Taj Mahal.

rise in gradual progression, similar to the pyramid-temple steps in Indo-China.

Chinese temples lack any kind of façade in the Occidental sense, the building being con-

FIG. 445.—Five-colored parakeet, by Emperor Hui Tsung, 1082–1135. Ink with full color on silk. Sung dynasty, (Boston Museum of Fine Arts). (*Courtesy of Boston Museum of Fine Arts.*)

The wide-flung base of the pyramid forms a restful foundation for the superstructure, suggesting both the stupa and the pine-tree pagoda. Like most of the early temples, including the Temple of Confucius, which is a simple hall with refined lines, this circular temple shows Chinese architecture in its classic mood.

The later temples, in the Chinese baroque style, are not so effective. Their powerful curved roofs become fantastic at times and dominate the rest of the architecture. The steps leading up the terraces to the temple entrance usually

ceived as a whole. The entire system of upper roof stories, covered with glittering tiles or bricks, is usually handled as a decorative motif, lending dignity and meaning to the entire structure. On the roofs of the ornate temples the earliest decoration of figured terra cottas seems to arise from technomorphic survivals in the carved finials of the old wooden buildings, with their thatched roofs. These figures, corresponding to the Gothic gargoyles and to the acroteria on Greek temples, show their greatest development in the southern provinces.

Inside the temples and palaces, red-lacquered wooden posts support the roofs. They are adorned with ornamental plaster and colored with many bright paintings, particularly gests most ancient cooking vessels and the form of a lily bulb. The upper lip, developing through the lower form from the base, suggests the lines of growth that one might expect in the

Fig. 446.—Pailou, ceremonial gateway to Ming tomb area, Peiping, Emperor Yung Lo, c. 1420. Width about 100 feet. (*Courtesy of White Bros.*)

around the capitals. The lower parts of the room, those nearest the occupants, are left relatively simple, the ornament being appropriately confined to the heavenly regions.

Pottery

Early in the Han dynasty (206 B.C.–A.D. 220), the Chinese learned to use a pottery glaze made of lead, colored green with copper oxide. During the fifteen hundred years following, the Chinese developed the art of glazed pottery further than did any other people. Two illustrations indicate two tendencies in the development of Chinese pottery. The first—a flower jar, or *chun*, from the Sung dynasty—demonstrates the retention in the most refined Chinese culture of the prehistoric, neolithic pottery forms. The simple lower part of the bowl sug-

unfolding plant. The two portions stand in almost perfect relation to each other. This relationship is enhanced by a grayish-green glaze with slightly blue tones and the fortuitous crackle, which the Chinese prize highly because of its suggestive power (Fig. 451*a*).

The simple dignity of the Sung flower jar finds its more delicate decorative counterpart in a Korean wine pot (Fig. 451*b*) of the Korai period (936–1392). The central shape of the pot is that of a melon growing from a lotus pattern in the base. The fine handle seems like a tendril, nicely balancing a spout at the left. Against a bisque glaze, delicate flowers, drawn as though copied from some ancient Persian manuscript, add interest to the surface.

Various combinations of these two pottery forms, with the greatest variety of perfect glazes, afford a rich treasure linking the art of the

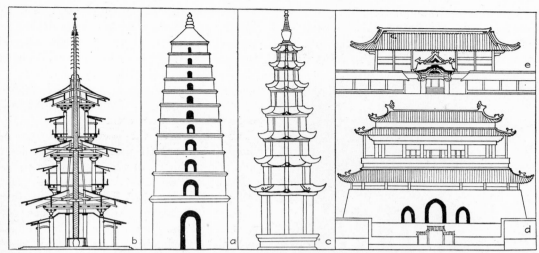

Fig. 447.—Chinese and Japanese buildings. *a*, great pagoda, Si-an, 7th to 10th century (*after Siren*); *b*, Yakushiji, Japan, 8th century (*after Baltzer*); *c*, jade fountain pagoda, China (*after White Bros.*); *d*, drum tower, Peiping, 1273; *e*, Japanese temple, Nikko, 15th century.

Chinese craftsman with the finest Chinese painting. Two types of pottery have particular significance. The celadon porcelain has a thick, translucent glaze in tones of bluish green and sea green, applied to an orange-red body that shows through the glaze in carved and incised designs or molded reliefs. Almost equally famous is the red-glazed ware, called *sang de boeuf*, made in the Kang Hsi period (1662–1722). The two glazes, associated with celadon and *sang de boeuf* vases, with the purples, reds, blues, and sea greens of the Sung-dynasty Chun ware, compose the color scheme of the finest Chinese pottery.

Japanese Art

The Aesthetic Refinement of the Japanese House. To the Japanese, a house serves not entirely as a protection against the hostile elements, but rather as an orderly corner of the world-garden. Originating in the prehistoric wattled hut, the Japanese house early took on the form of the old Celto-German frame house. The floor beams are usually raised about two feet above the ground on stones. Corner posts, ceiling, and roof beams are dovetailed or set together with mortise-and-tenon joints. The house has a ridgepole and a thatched roof. The walls consist of bamboo lath woven together with straw rope and plastered with mud bound with chopped rice straw. A smooth coating of clay and sand cemented with a gelatinous size made from seaweed is laid upon this, the final surface being painted with white lime.

Wooden boards on floor and ceiling finish the interior. The fine-grained woods of the ceiling, carefully dovetailed together, are attached to rafters in such a way that no nails show. The natural grain of the boarding, left unstained and unvarnished, furnishes a pleasant decorative feature. Window and wall openings leading to the garden are covered with sliding panels or screens (Fig. 452).

The plan of the house centers on a large communal room, distinguished by an alcove—the *tokonoma*—at one end. The tokonoma, usually about three feet deep and nine feet wide, serves as a study as well as a picture gallery for the display of family treasures. At one side of the tokonoma, a group of shelves and cupboards serves to hold necessary household equipment. These are called the *chigaidani*. The third feature of the house is the *genkan*, a decorative porch under which guests may alight from their carriages. This porch covers a large, flat entrance stone. At other openings from the house flat stones indicate the close relationship

FIG. 448.—Porch and dragon columns, Temple of Confucius, Chufou, Shantung, 14th century. (*Courtesy of White Bros.*)

of the house to the out-of-doors. When the sliding panels are pushed back, the guest seated within the house may feel that he is part of nature. The various service rooms take subordinate positions around this central ceremonial living hall.

Of particular aesthetic significance in studying the Japanese house is the fine balance between simple, flat wall space and the functional members that support the roof. Drawers sliding away, cupboards that do not project into the room, the simplest of furniture, the clean grass mats that serve as floor coverings, all act as a frame for one or two exquisite objects of art

—a scroll, an *ikebana* (flower group), or the vista out into the garden.

The Oriental Art of Gardening. In all Oriental countries the garden, as a symbol of man's relationship to external nature, becomes a ceremonial aspect of life. In the Orient every man is entitled to his garden, but of all Oriental peoples the Japanese excel in this art.

For the Japanese the house remains incomplete without its proper garden setting. Domestic architecture requires a garden as a vista beyond the room, visible when the side wall panels are pushed back, or silhouetting the paper sliding screens with patterns of swaying foliage. The Japanese leaves no ground space about the house, however small, without arrangement. Within his tiny plot he places a minute box garden, the *hako-niwa*, which is a landscape in miniature. In the window opening he sets a tray complete with moss and rocks, the *bonkei*. Other aspects of this Oriental desire to change nature subtly and with proper decorum may be seen in the painstaking culture of dwarf trees, the *bon-sai*, and the final, most refined, aesthetic sensibility required for the art of *ikebana*, or flower arrangement.

All garden and floral arrangements arise from canons of design such as those formulated by the Chinese landscape painter, Hsieh Ho. To understand these canons is to understand the formal values of most Japanese and Chinese gardens. The symbolical or associational values, far more detailed, can be studied only in the Japanese garden books. Briefly, the Japanese garden focuses around the symbolism inherent in the relationship between a hill, a plain, and a river. Two general types of garden prevail, one, the *tsuki-yama*, dominated by the hill; the other, *hira-niwa*, dominated by the plain. In these two styles we find certain common elements that may be studied in the illustration (Fig. 453a) borrowed from the *Tsuki-yama Teizo Den*, a famous book of gardens published around 1818 to serve as a mentor for Japanese gardeners. In the illustration one distinguishes the hill, the plain, and the river. At the lower left, leading from the well, flat stones form pathways through the landscape. Paths arranged so as to lead the visitor into the picture pass seven different ceremonial stones, each with its

fied contemplation from which to view the life well lived.

According to the *Tsuki-yama Teizo Den*, trees also have their peculiar significance. The prin-

Fig. 449.—The dragon stairway, Temple of Confucius, Peiping, Emperor Yung Lo, c. 1420. Marble stairs and balustrade, wooden walls, and tiled roof. (*Courtesy of White Bros.*)

special significance. The Guardian Stone (I) probably suggests an ancestral menhir; the Waiting Stone (II), possibly companionship or the marriage rite; and the Hill Stone (III), the tomb. The Worshiping Stone (IV) rests beside the water at a point from which one may view the entire garden world. The Evening Sun Stone (V) and the Moon Shadow Stone (VI) have to do with two heavenly orbs controlling the solar and lunar years, which influence the destinies of man. The Seat of Heaven Stone (VII), on the other side of the river from the Worshiping Stone, marks a place of dignified

cipal tree form, *A*, called the "Tree of the Upright Spirit," dominates the garden and serves as a central pivot on which the rest of the composition is based. *B*, the View-perfecting Tree, a lesser aspect of *A*, must be so placed as to provide a fine occult balance. Other tree forms in the more complex gardens include a Tree of Solitude, a Distancing Pine, suggestive of far-off forests, a Stretching Pine, whose branches reach out as though to embrace the water, and the Cascade Screen Tree, placed at one side of a waterfall. This last is so arranged as to break part of the line of the fall and to give it the appearance of emergent life. The tree, as a symbol of longevity, and the water, as a sign of virility, represent the dynamic aspects of the garden, the hill and the rocks being

the *Shin-No-Hana*, employed an absolute balance of three or five seasonable flowers, placed around a central pine or bamboo branch. As late as the 14th century this symmetrical ar-

Fig. 450.—Temple of Prayer for the Year, Peiping, Emperor Yung Lo, c. 1420. (*Courtesy of White Bros.*)

static. Despite the strictness of this formal scene, no two gardens are alike.

Ikebana—the Japanese Art of Flower Arrangement. No more refined instance of formal aesthetic arrangement can be found than the ceremonial art of ikebana. An old Buddhist poem reads

> Heaven and earth are flowers
> Gods as well as Buddha are flowers
> The heart of man is also the soul of flowers.[1]

Tradition relates that the early Buddhist priests, arranging the gifts of plants and flowers upon the altar, first invented the art in China, which later in Japan became a nonreligious art, pursued for its own sake.

The earliest religious arrangements, called

rangement can still be found in the Japanese religious pictures (Fig. 453*b*). In Shin-No-Hana, the large central tree symbolizes the distant woods; the blossoming plants, the middle distance; and the small plants, the foreground.

The second type of arrangement was invented by the celebrated painter Soami (1436–1490), who lived under the Shogun Yoshimashi, in the Ashikaga dynasty. Soami formulated the principle that the flower group should have three parts, one upright (the heaven element), a second pointing downward (the earth element), and a third (man), pointing upward between earth and heaven (Fig. 453*c*). Since all parts of the arrangement were highly symbolical, great knowledge was necessary in order to use the proper flowers and branches. Red

[1] Mary Averill, *The Flower Art of Japan*, Dodd, Mead & Company, Inc., New York, 1930.

flowers, for example, which suggested flames and were used for funerals, rarely appear in floral arrangements. Odd numbers of branches, leaves, and blossoms were considered lucky;

garden. For most of the many schools in Japan, occult balance has higher value than the old religious formal values. Interesting arrangement bears greater weight than stateliness.

a   *b*

FIG. 451.—*a*, flower jar or *chun*, Chinese, height about 10 inches (*courtesy of Freer Gallery of Art*); *b*, wine pot, Korea, height 8½ inches, Korai period, A.D. 936–1392 (*courtesy of Freer Gallery.*)

even numbers, unlucky. The former also gave the more dynamic form of occult balance.

The formal principles of ikebana, as listed by Miss Averill, are seven. (1) The arrangement must always suggest a living plant. (2) The appropriate season of the year must find its echo in the lines of the composition. Cold wintry winds, for example, would force the heaven branch downward. (3) Buds, open flowers, and bright or withered leaves must also suggest the condition of plant growth. (4) Unity must be achieved by having all parts stem from some central point. (5) Branches and leaves must not cross one another. (6) Under no condition should blossoms be stressed; they must always appear one of the necessary details in the arrangement. (7) The branches must be uneven in number. The selection of jars for various types of plant is considered very important.

In brief, the chief principles of ikebana are those discussed in connection with the composition of Chinese painting and the Japanese

Oriental Drama

The drama of the Orient partakes of the character of primitive religious ceremonials. In the Oriental drama, appropriate gesture, music, and words unite with the greatest emphasis on rhythmical pantomime. In this particular it differs from Occidental drama, which emphasizes thought content through words, and comes closer to the ideals of the opera and the talking motion picture.

In India the dramatic songs have to do with the deeds of Krishna and Vishnu and with the loves of the divine heroes for their heroines, with all their symbolic esoteric meaning. In China the drama is of two sorts, both historical: the one a drama of primitive religious and Buddhistic origins, the other a drama of morals connected from earliest times with the courts. The Chinese also show shadow and puppet plays, as do the Japanese and Ceylonese. The earliest shadow plays indigenous to China were

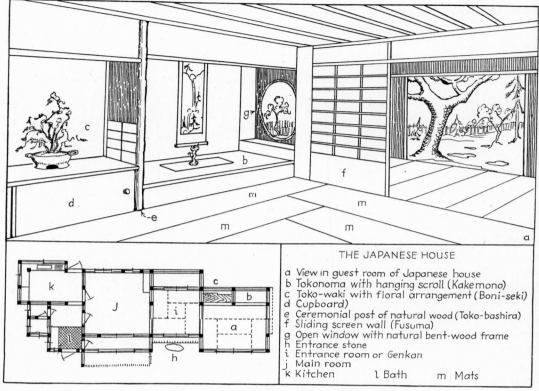

FIG. 452.—Plan and main room in Japanese house.

THE JAPANESE HOUSE

a View in guest room of Japanese house
b Tokonoma with hanging scroll (Kakemono)
c Toko-waki with floral arrangement (Boni-seki)
d Cupboard)
e Ceremonial post of natural wood (Toko-bashira)
f Sliding screen wall (Fusuma)
g Open window with natural bent-wood frame
h Entrance stone
i Entrance room or Genkan
j Main room
k Kitchen   l Bath   m Mats

first mentioned in 121 B.C.; the puppets apparently originated later in Byzantium. The Lamaistic mystery plays of Tibet, like those of the European Middle Ages, were first played in the 7th century, when Christian monks first missionized China.

In Japan, the *nō* drama developed after the 15th century, arising from song and dance. Two types of music—harvest folk songs (*den gaku*) and rice-field music—contributed the tragic elements, and monkey music (*saru gaku*) the comic. From these crude beginnings arose the refined aesthetic form of the *nō* drama, which has to do with the lives of the goblins, warriors and their ghosts, the chief deities, and with human failings.

In Java and Ceylon complex dance dramas developed against a background of primitive music around the most fundamental emotions of human existence. One of these, a Senegalese devil ballet, has the following plot. A mother, rocking her child, is beset by demons who steal the young one. After many vain attempts to rescue it, the frantic mother calls all the other mothers, who pursue the demons and wage war upon them. Eventually, mother love winning, the child is rescued.

Subject Matter of Chinese Drama. The beginnings of the Chinese drama before 2205 B.C. lay in a primitive nature worship with music and dancing similar to that described in the chapter on the arts of agricultural man. The primitive dance dramas dealt with sowing and reaping the grain, with love-making and home building; they represented, in short, a ceremonialization of all the occupations of war and peace. Throughout the Chou dynasty these dramas came to have a set ritualistic form,

Fig. 453.—*a*, abstract style, hill garden, Japan (*after Jiro Harada, The Gardens of Japan, Studio Publications*); *b*, ikebana, symmetrical balance; *c*, ikebana, occult balance.

culminating in a theater by the 8th century. In 550 B.C. the Emperor Shih Huang Ti banned the dramatic performances, together with all other forms of art expression.

A revival of the drama took place in the 8th century after Christ, when the Emperor Hsuan Tsung conducted a dramatic school in his palace garden. Thus began the imperial heroic drama. Present-day Chinese drama dates from 1280 when, with the coming of the Mongols in the Yuan dynasty, possible foreign influences from India and Byzantium may have stimulated rich creativity.

Chinese drama makes no distinction between comedy and tragedy, the finished play possessing elements of both, like the European drama of the Middle Ages. Three types of play deal with three types of social intercourse. (1) The *Vun Pan Shi* stresses political and filial devotion. (2) The *Jen Pan Shi* deals with the happenings of everyday life in the family. (3) The *Vun Min Shi* deals with civil and military conditions. The first two groups are distinctly ceremonial. Plays of the third group, called "modern plays" by the Chinese, although they are also historical, have the quality of genre.

Most Chinese plays stress the element of morals, and in the Western world would be called social or propaganda dramas. Some plots show the corruption of the public officials; others, the degeneracy of the priesthood. Still others exalt the benefits brought about by Confucian scholarship. Harvest plays and pageants, like those of ancient Greece and the European Middle Ages, are often paid for by the rich man of the village. Such plays, the most ancient form of Chinese drama, have persisted almost unchanged since the Chou dynasty.

One great point of difference between Chinese drama and that of the West calls for emphasis. Love motifs are noticeable by their absence. The Chinese, being a mature people, cannot conceive of a tyrannical, tormenting love, such as that dramatized by Euripides. Characters indulging in such passion are sometimes assigned to adolescents as comic roles. Chinese drama does not lack instances of mature wifely devotion, however, such as that shown in the splendid play, *Lady Precious Stream*.

The Staging of the Chinese Play. The two types of Chinese theaters, the fixed and the portable, have similar plans. In the portable theater the stage consists of a raised covered platform like the old Greek *skene* (Fig. 454*a*), surrounded by covered loges for the wealthy, the space below being left for the crowd. Traveling stock companies, whose actors are contracted for by the year, carry such theaters on showboats from village to village. Permanent theaters have the same stage arrangement, but with a gallery opposite and loges on a level with the stage. The imperial theater in Peiping possesses a triple stage. The highest, called the "heaven" stage, is reserved for the gods; the second shows the movements of mortals on the earth; the third and lowest, called the "water" stage, rep-

Fig. 454.—*a*, Chinese portable theater (*after Buss, Studies in the Chinese Drama, Peter Smith*); *b*, *nō* mask; *c*, Japanese theater of the Kabuki Drama with revolving stage and flowery way.

resents the lower regions. The stages have no screens or curtains, though at times smoke screens mask the entrance and disappearance of a god. The actors appear on the stage and introduce themselves to the audience telling something about the character each represents.

The Symbolism of Stage Characters. In Chinese drama, as in Roman comedy and many medieval plays, each character stands for some distinct type and wears a traditional dress and make-up. These include the Young Civilian or Young Hero; the Emperor, who regularly appears wearing a long beard; the Elderly General, also with a beard; and the villain, with a dark painted face. The clown regularly has a painted face, as does the spearman, or warrior.

In most Chinese dramas the women's parts are taken by men. The principal feminine characters include the Empress, the Youthful Heroine, the Servant Girl, the Young Married Woman, and the Woman Soldier. Most of the face—and costume—painting carries a distinct color symbolism. Clever dignity calls for white paint, nobility in a god or an emperor for red. The honest workman wears black, demons wear green, and the gods are often clad in gold. Postures and movements, as well as positions on the stage, also carry set, formal significance. The drama is usually accompanied by symbolic music.

The Development of Japanese Drama. Japanese drama, like the Chinese, arose in part from ceremonial dances; in part, from puppet plays. It first appeared during the reign of the Empress Suiko in the 7th century after Christ, and now includes three general forms, the *nō* and Kyōgen plays with their masks (Fig. 454*b*) and conventional heroic characters, approved by the noble or samurai class, and the Kabuki Drama of the masses.

The latter form, which probably grew out of the puppet play, is similar to the late Roman pantomime. In this performance a musician sits at one side of the stage singing epic stories to the accompaniment of the *samisen* (a stringed instrument like a banjo), while the actors gesture and dance without words. In the 17th century, a leading Kabuki dramatist—Shōzō Namiki, of Osaka—invented the revolving stage, a device later to prove very valuable to the 20th-century European theater. Shōzō mounted his sets upon a platform that turned in full view of the spectators, creating a continuity of scenic effects like that in a motion picture. The Kabuki Drama also makes use of a long ramped stage approach, called the "flowery way," over which the actors move in and out of the audience. At times this stands for a mountain road, at times for a veranda, or again for the street of a town (Fig. 454*c*). The movement of splendidly garbed actors over the flowery way lends intimate richness and decorative quality to the spectacle.

Oriental Music

Oriental music, though it arose from the same natural origins as the music of the Greeks and the Celts, followed such different paths of evolution that it now offers the greatest contrast to modern Occidental music. Like the primitive cultures of Europe and of the Mediterranean basin, the various Oriental cultures all employed both the pentatonic, or five-note, scale and the heptatonic, or seven-note, scale. The Persians and the Indians developed elaborate systems of modes. In the main, all Oriental music is highly melodic and, with the exception of some Javanese music, does not consider the effects of harmony. The Orientals, particularly the Chinese, early interested themselves in the idea of contrast in musical tone. A Chinese orchestra, despite opinions to the contrary, is not all noise but uses noise and peculiar instrumental qualities to suggest contrasts in feeling. Most Oriental music is thought of as incidental music, that is, as an accompaniment for literary and dramatic presentations.

The instruments of the various Oriental cultures include all the types known to the Occident up through the Middle Ages. Galpin has shown that the Sumerian flute, or *ti-gi*, became the Chinese flute *ti*, or *tih*, when the Chiang people from the western regions entered China around 1200 B.C. The scale on this early flute, which was heptatonic, consisted of the following notes: G A B C# D E F#. The augmented fourth note, which is slightly higher than a normal C, is called a "tritone." This scale not only reached China but eventually, with the introduction of the bagpipe, appeared in Scotland. The ritual flute of the Shang dynasty had a dragon's head and tail. Similar flutes of clay may be found in South American Peruvian cultures. Another Chinese instrument of Mesopotamian origin was a harp, now no longer used, although a very early Buddhist stele in the University of Pennsylvania Museum shows such an instrument.

The Chinese early developed an official musical tone register, the *king*, a rack holding a number of suspended stone plates, tuned to a twelve-tone chromatic scale. They had also the *kin* and *che* (zitherlike instruments), a long flute and a flute to be blown sideways, a syrinx or Panpipes, clay pipes, oboes, drums, gongs, rattles, and other noise-making instruments. The fact that they early devised a cylindrical Panpipes, using reeds of metal, which became a miniature reed organ to be blown by the mouth, testifies to the high degree of their musical culture. Music for four of these instruments, called the *Tchiengs*, was written to be played on ceremonial occasions. Their tones are soft and mellow. Japanese instruments follow the Chinese, with the addition of the *koto*, a combination string guitar and dulcimer with a long sound box, to be plucked and strummed. The Japanese instruments on the whole give a softer, more refined tone than do the Chinese.

Indian instruments include a number of forms of horns, lutes, and drums. The national instrument, the *vina*, is a kind of lute with a large gourd sound box attached to a tubular fret board over which run two or three strings. A type of oboe, the *nagassaran*, and a Bengal horn, the *nursing*, are like the Gothic hunting horn. The Hindus also have a kind of bagpipe, the *qurti*.

Chinese Ceremonial Music. The *Shi King* (between 1765 and 585 B.C.) includes many songs that must have been accompanied by musical instruments. At the time it was written the Chinese differentiated between a yang, or masculine, scale, composed of the notes F G A B C D, and a yin, or feminine, scale, F G A C D E. By 1300 B.C. another scale with the notes C D E G A was in use; and by 1122 B.C., in the Chou dynasty, a temple song used the notes F C G D A. All these set scales, like the Greek modes, had their appropriate uses. The temple song from the Chou dynasty, in honor of the ancestors, follows. The air is typical of the finest Chinese music (Fig. 455a).

The three songs, *Ambushes Everywhere*, *Dragons Crossing a River*, and *Moonlight on the River*,

FIG. 455a.—a, ancestral hymn, Chou dynasty.

FIG. 455b.—Indian raga, *Nada-Namakria*.

demonstrate the dramatic quality of classical Chinese music of nonceremonial character. The first of these seems to pull the attention first in one direction, then the other; the second has a sort of dignity, such as one would expect when the great cloud dragons sweep over the river; and the last has a tender, romantic feeling. Allowing for differences in scale and instrumental quality, these songs do not appear particularly strange, especially to those trained in music since the time of Debussy and Schönberg.

Music in Persia and India. Arabic and Persian scales, devised mathematically, are among the most comprehensive in the world. Musically far in advance of their European contemporaries, by the 10th century the Persians used a scale that included all the note intervals of modern European music. In the time of Tamerlane, Persian music recognized at least twelve different modes. The first three duplicated the Greek Ionic, Phrygian, and Myxolydian modes. These scales were sometimes tuned with such minute intervals as quarter tones, one having a note lying between Ab and A in our scale of C. In melodic systems of music, such quarter intervals when employed regularly, so as to constitute part of the musical form, give very pleasing effects. The Persians divided the octave into seventeen notes instead of twelve, all arranged systematically. Modern Persian music has octaves holding as many as twenty-four quarter tones.

In India, music developed still smaller intervals, as the vina allowed a certain latitude in tuning. Twelve Indian modes approximate European scales. Interested as they were in all the possible ceremonious observances of life, the Indians devised seventy-two formal modes, made more complex by the adoption of a number of set melodic sequences, or *ragas*, obligatory for the use of the players. A raga was a set melodic sequence of tones that could be modified by the addition of many grace notes and whole phrases of melody, as long as the player returned at the proper rhythmical intervals to the required scheme. This quality of Indian music corresponds to the use of prescribed artistic formulae in creating figures in sculpture and painting.

An idea of the complications of the system may be gained from the fact that some ragas could be played only at given times of the day or at set seasons of the year. Some of the ragas had one group of notes for use in an ascending scale and another group for a descending scale. The raga called *Nada-Namakria*, for example, used the ascending notes C Db F G Ab and C, and the descending notes C B Ab G F E Db C.[1] A line of music written in this raga makes the procedure clear (Fig. 455b).

The Gamelans of Java. The inhabitants of Java developed a complex orchestra, the *gamelan*, capable of a real symphonic quality. Melodies are often played in two different scales: one, a

[1] CAPTAIN DAY, *Music of Southern India.*

pentatonic scale of Chinese origin, called the *solendro;* the other, a heptatonic scale, called the *pelog.* The instruments of the gamelan orchestra consist of *gambangs* (wooden plates from which developed the South Sea Island marimbas), *genders* (metal rods hung on strings), *sarons* (bronze plates), three sets of *bonangs* (xylophones), and two gongs. All the instruments, with the exception of the gongs and one set of bonangs, play in the upper or treble clef.

A suite of music on the gamelan usually opens with a recitative theme played by the gambangs and the upper bonang. Variations follow on other instruments. At the end of each variation the gong sounds. A great variety of melodies weave in and out like a motet, constituting a true polyphonic style in gamelan music, which shows great rhythmical intricacy and a high degree of contrast.

All Oriental music has a much more complicated rhythmical structure than has European. Indian music, particularly, has five-four and seven-four time signatures, which appear difficult to most European musicians.

Summary

One may summarize all Oriental art by saying that it represents the utmost refinement of natural grace, leading man to associate himself with an outer nature beneficent and necessary for his spiritual development. To the understanding of Oriental art in its most subtle forms the observer must bring a well-balanced feeling and a complete knowledge of formal, associational, and use values. Particularly on the side of formal values, Chinese architecture and painting, Indian sculpture, and the plan of the Japanese garden have much to teach the Occidental.

The mind of the Oriental, never losing its contacts with man's infancy in the caves, places almost equal value upon the formal and ideational aspects of thought. Nor does thought for the Oriental ever lose its emotional overtones. Consequently, until the 19th century, the Ori-

ental regarded science, in the Western sense of the term, as of inferior value. After the 19th century, science having been forced into his unwilling hands, we find him using it with a ruthlessness and realistic lack of romanticism shocking to the Occidental mind. Knowing both his creative and his destructive powers, and being dominated by no ideal, romantic dream of a heavenly city, the Oriental makes war with but a single purpose—total annihilation of the enemy. Nor does he need such idealistic slogans as "Save the world for democracy" to stimulate his hatred. He seems incapable of true enmity or sentimentalism, and could be stopped in war only by some appeal to his own aesthetic sensibilities. The Western world needs more of the mature Oriental point of view if it would face squarely the issue of human life and death.

With the Oriental we might well consider the world a garden that man can plan despite the disintegrating forces of natural decay. When man eventually grows to the spiritual stature of the great Oriental religious leaders, Jesus Christ, Buddha, and Confucius, he will perceive that the aesthetic values inherent in the lilies of the field, the Chinese landscape painting, and the garden, can completely accommodate man's natural ambitious striving for adventure, today often misused in attempts to dominate society.

The art of the Orient, more than any other art, teaches that each has a right to his own creative outlet, to beautify his own home, and to arrange his own section of the world, in order that eventually the larger home of the globe, hung lonely in the universe of stars, shall become a well-ordered dwelling place for a happy race of men.

In order to comprehend the great art of the Orient, one must feel and understand that Siva and Vishnu, the yin and the yang, reach a balance. Every great artistic symbol displays this perfection. Anything less than this *synaeresis* creates an illusion of the superior worth of either the static or the dynamic point of view. In musical rhythm, where the time element dominates and contrast suggests progression, the static and dynamic instances follow one another, eventually achieving balance in what we call equilibrium. In painting, the elements rest beside each other; in sculpture, within each other. In architecture they appear in a relationship of a building to its surroundings. In every case, appropriateness must furnish the final measure of aesthetic value. A feeling for appropriateness can come only through the absorption of appropriate examples and continuous experimentation with the materials of art. Like the Oriental, we must conceive art in our dreams and practice it in our writing and in all our relationships with our fellow men.

Bibliography

Japanese Art, *Encyclopaedia Britannica*, 14th edition, New York, 1933.

COOMARASWAMY, A. K.: *The Dance of Siva*, The Sunwise Turn, Inc., New York, 1924.

Confucius, The Wisdom of, edited and translated by Lin Yu Tang, Modern Library, Inc., New York, 1938.

CONFUCIUS: *Book of Odes (Shĭ-King)*, edited by L. Cranmer-Byng, Wisdom of the East Series, E. P. Dutton & Co., New York, 1910.

BINYON, LAURENCE: *The Spirit of Man in Asian Art*, Harvard University Press, Cambridge, Mass., 1935.

ROSS, E. D. (Luzac): *Persian Art*, American Institute for Iranian Art and Archaeology, New York, 1930.

BINYON, LAURENCE: *The Flight of the Dragon*, John Murray, London, 1922.

GARRATT, G. T.: *The Legacy of India*, Oxford, Clarendon Press, New York, 1937.

YEE, CHIANG: *The Chinese Eye*, Methuen & Company, Ltd., London, 1935, and E. P. Dutton & Co. Inc., New York.

KUO HSI: *An Essay on Landscape Painting*, translated by *Shio Sakanishi*, John Murray, London, 1935.

CHATTERJI, M.: *Mahabharata, Bhagavadgita*, Houghton Mifflin Company, Boston, 1887.

OKAKURA, KAKUZO: *The Ideals of the East*, E. P. Dutton & Company, Inc., New York, 1921.

FITZGERALD, EDWARD: *The Rubáiyát of Omar Khayám*, Houghton Mifflin Company, Boston, 1886.

DRISCOLL, LUCY, and KANJI TODA: *Chinese Calligraphy*, University of Chicago Press, Chicago, 1935.

WANG PAO-CHUAN: *Lady Precious Stream*, translated by S. J. Hsuing, Liveright Publishing Corporation, New York, 1935.

AVERILL, MARY: *The Flower Art of Japan*, Dodd, Mead & Company, Inc. New York, 1930.

HARADA, JIRO: *The Gardens of Japan*, Studio Limited, London, 1928.

HARADA, JIRO: *The Lesson of Japanese Architecture*, Studio Limited, London, 1936.

BUSS, KATE: *The Chinese Drama*, Jonathan Cape, Ltd., New York, 1930.

SUZUKI, D. J.: *Brief History of Chinese Philosophy*, Arthur Probsthain, London, 1914.

GJELLERUP, KARL: *The Pilgrim Kamanita* (novel), translated by J. E. Logie, E. P. Dutton & Co., New York, 1912.

Recordings

Hindu Ragas—V 24548 a and b.
Chinese Instrumental Music—V 24549 a.
Javanese Gamelan Gong music—C-D30001/3
Japanese—V-4104
Persia—Rar Solos. G-k7000

CHAPTER XV

The Renaissance

How can that be, lady, which all men learn
  By long experience? Shapes that seem
    alive,
  Wrought in hard mountain marble, will
    survive
  Their maker, whom the years to dust
    return!
Thus to effect cause yields. Art hath her turn,
  And triumphs over Nature. I, who strive
  With Sculpture, know this well; her won-
    ders live
  In spite of time and death, those tyrants
    stern.
So I can give long life to both of us
  In either way, by colour or by stone,
  Making the semblance of thy face and
    mine.
Centuries hence when both are buried, thus
  Thy beauty and my sadness shall be
    shown,
  And men shall say, "For her 'twas wise
    to pine."
           "THE ARTIST AND HIS WORK"[1]

Oh, make me see Thee, Lord, where'er I go!
  If mortal beauty sets my soul on fire,
  That flame when near to Thine must
    needs expire,
  And I with love of only Thee shall glow.
Dear Lord, Thy help I seek against this woe,
  These torments that my spirit vex and
    tire;
  Thou only with new strength canst re-
    inspire
  My will, my sense, my courage faint and
    low.
Thou gavest me on earth this soul divine;
  And Thou within this body weak and
    frail
  Didst prison it—how sadly there to live!
How can I make its lot less vile than mine?
  Without Thee, Lord, all goodness seems
    to fail.
  To alter fate is God's prerogative.
           "A PRAYER FOR AID"[1]

DEEP INSIGHT into the meaning of the Renaissance comes only to one psychologically equipped to understand the paradox of Renaissance genius, which in many respects resembles the paradox of Plato. This paradox nowhere finds clearer expression than in the contrasting points of view of the two above sonnets by Michelangelo—one, the fruit of his love for sculptural form and a high-minded woman; the other, a penitential prayer to a god of fire. Michelangelo first fell in love with a woman at the age of sixty. Throughout the long adolescent period of his life, he lived in a state of mind typical of the Renaissance. In every stroke of his chisel and brush he struggled to synthesize his concepts of love and beauty, his classic and Gothic modes of expression, his pagan and Christian ideologies. These disparate tendencies found expression in his Classical sculptural forms, appealing sensually to the eye, and his melodious Gothic lines of drawing and verse, appealing primarily to the sense of rhythm or to the ears.

Our study of cultural art patterns should have made clear that styles in art, as well as modes of thinking, do not die. The complexes of emotion concentrated in the art works of a nation or a period carry over through centuries, starting to new life in the minds of a people prepared to comprehend them. The Gothic mode of thought, for example, mirrored in patterns of spatial and musical design will be found to persist through the Renaissance and late baroque art into romanticism and modern art long after the Middle Ages, as a historical actuality, ceased to exist. The Oriental mode of thought, spreading over the great reaches of Asia into the peninsula of Europe,

[1] *Sonnets of Michael Angelo Buonarroti*, translated by John Addington Symonds, London, 1877.

leavened man's mind from the time of St. Francis on. The Classical love of formal aesthetic values, latent always in Latin cultures, flowered again and again throughout the Middle Ages, forming a sort of archaeological centrum for much of the thought of the Renaissance after the 15th century.

The Meaning of the Term "Renaissance." The term "Renaissance," invented by 18th-century French writers of the Classical Academy, has unfortunately come to mean simply a rebirth of antiquity or a revival of learning. The 20th-century historian, trained in social psychology and with more facts concerning the Renaissance at his disposal, is prepared to show the inadequacy of both interpretations.

We must run the grave risk here of confusing the student by pointing out that the hard and fast categories used in defining man's cultural advances are, at the most, only superficial criteria invented by scholars to aid the beginner in memorizing a given body of knowledge. Life itself is all of a piece. The universal productions of Renaissance and modern man cannot be understood in terms of a narrow historic formula.

The difficulty of truthfully defining the term "Renaissance" in accurate historic nomenclature becomes apparent when we see that the historians of sculpture usually date it from the works produced by Nicola Pisano and his school, between 1240 and 1320; and historians of painting find its beginning in Giotto (c. 1266–1337). The architects, on the other hand, consider the Renaissance to have begun with the works of Brunelleschi in the early part of the 15th century. Many literary historians consider that the coming of Greek scholars to Florence in 1453 marked the beginning of the era. One can avoid this confusion only by considering the Renaissance not as a definite period but as a state of mind reached by some individuals, like the Pisani and Petrarch, in the 13th and 14th centuries, and by others as late as the 16th. It may touch any individual reader of this book as he leaves behind him medieval modes of thought and approaches a mature outlook on life. We may, hence, liken the Renaissance to that individual stage of late adolescence coming just before mature manhood and womanhood.

Nor can one forget that the style categorically declared by art historians to be the Renaissance, a style characterized by humanism and revived classical forms, comes to full fruition in people dominated by intense folk energies, using composition patterns that we have called Celto-Germanic, Gothic, or Faustian. Hence we may say that in many cases Renaissance pictorial compositions are Gothic creations with a veneer of classical decorations. In Giotto's compositions, for example, we have already studied the use of the interweave under the heading of medieval art. But Giotto's static figures are usually thought to mark the beginnings of Renaissance painting. The costumes worn during the whole of the Renaissance we should consider medieval. With but few exceptions, no one tried to copy Roman togas or Greek dresses as did the dress designers after the French Revolution. Renaissance houses were furnished with tapestries in the medieval manner, and the massive furniture had Gothic shapes, although classical decoration was applied to it after the 15th century. In literature, although the bourgeois aristocracy revived the classics, the mass of the people still enjoyed the medieval chansons, and as late as the 16th century Gothic literary forms dominated in the court of the family of Este at Ferrara.

Let us remember, too, that throughout the Middle Ages, in the graphic and plastic arts old classical forms had never completely died, and that, between the 14th and the 16th century, what we have called Celto-Germanic energies revitalized them in Italy, producing an art superficially classical and physioplastic, actually highly ideoplastic. Hence we must expect to find in the creations of men like Masaccio, Leonardo, Michelangelo, and Giorgione, both the Classical concept of static beauty and the Gothic concept of dynamic power.

Viewed broadly, the Renaissance stands for

that period of European cultural development characterized by an awakened interest in man's relationship to his fellow man, rather than to God through the church or to the state through the empire. The change did not come about simply because of a revival of interest in the classics. Rather, the study and interpretation of these works, which had been known and read as gospel truth throughout the early Middle Ages, was now undertaken for its psychological and historical value. Men suddenly realized that Vergil, Plato, Livy, Horace, and Cicero were not prophets speaking in allegorical terms, but human beings like themselves. This new interest resulted in the beginnings of objective scientific inquiry freed from the bonds of superstition, and in an art that differed from medieval art in stressing formal value in place of associational and symbolic aspects.

For us, then, the Renaissance, historically considered, begins in the 14th century with the efforts of the earliest humanists—Petrarch and Boccaccio—to discover in antique philosophy new moral codes. Geographically, the Renaissance belongs to the south and characterizes the art of the Italian cities, particularly Florence, in the 14th and 15th centuries, spreading in the 16th to France, Germany, and England.

Political, Religious, and Social Backgrounds of the Renaissance

The Rise of a Bourgeois Aristocracy of Wealth. The rivalry between the church and the state, active even in the early Middle Ages, grew in intensity after the 9th century. Within each town, the aristocratic parties of pope and emperor fought mercilessly to ally the *bourgeoisie* with one side or the other. The early Renaissance found the free cities of Florence, Assisi, Perugia, Genoa, Milan, Venice, and Pisa relying for their government upon the heads of their guilds. From time to time the business leaders of some guild who succeeded in elevating themselves to the positions of *principi* and *signori* or, functioning as *condottieri*—military

leaders with private armies of mercenary troops —took possession of the cities by force. In this way, the great families of the Este in Ferrara, the Scaliger in Verona, the Visconti in Milan, and the Medici in Florence came to power. Accepted at first by popular consent, the new leaders soon developed into tyrants. By the beginning of the 15th century, most of the cities, with the exception of Venice and Naples, were controlled by an aristocracy for the most part of commercial or military origin. Venice remained a republic governed by elected doges, while Naples was ruled by a king.

The Ideal of Virtù. The motives that impelled the most astute members of the bourgeois aristocracy, and eventually the popes who came from it during the 15th and 16th centuries, were those of the medieval emperors and of the *condottieri*. Landucci tells in his diary how Lorenzo de' Medici, having escaped assassination many times, deliberately put himself at the mercy of his worst enemy, the king of Naples, trusting to his wits to get back safely, with new benefits for the city of Florence. Such bravery and skill in achieving one's personal goals appears the dominating ideal of the Renaissance, symbolized by the word *virtù*. The meaning of this word comes close in some respects to that of the 20th-century term "rugged individualism," with this slight difference: The adjective "rugged" implies a bluff, hearty forthrightness; the idea of *virtù*, in contrast, includes the thought that all action should be undertaken with the greatest subtlety and finesse. The conscienceless pursuit of *virtù*, however, might lead a man to prestige and power at the cost of violating his most humane instincts.

In *The Prince*, Niccolo Machiavelli, a clerk of Florence with an interesting literary style and a remarkable insight into the purely practical side of politics, drew a picture of the accepted "man of power." The philosophy of the bully, which runs throughout this clever piece of writing, was as much inherent in the Renaissance as was the pattern of artistic achievement. The career of Pope Alexander Borgia and of his son,

Cesare; that of Machiavelli himself and of the art critic, Spinello Aretino; and in the realm of the graphic arts, the adventures of Castagno and of that genial braggart, though mediocre artist, Benvenuto Cellini, exemplify the ideal of *virtù* in all its innate ruthlessness. Certain elements of this nature are to be found, during his youth, in the character of even so cultured an individual as Leonardo da Vinci.

The Ideal of Cortesia and the Concept of the Gentleman. As the civic ideal of the urbane man displaced that of the medieval knight, Castiglione wrote his essay on *Il Cortigiano*, the perfect courtier—the first of a long line of books on etiquette, leading to the 20th-century efforts of Emily Post and Dale Carnegie. Castiglione defined the gentleman as one who had perfected himself in decorous behavior. He must be accomplished in sports and in the use of arms, must dance well and show skill in music, must have a knowledge of several languages, including Latin, and a familiarity with literature and the graphic arts. Above all, no one accomplishment should outweigh the others. This ideal may be traced back to Plato.

Such a man, the gentleman, enjoyed the stimulating company of equally accomplished gentlewomen. The Renaissance brought the chivalrous ideal of "Our Lady" down to earth and acknowledged for the first time that womanhood might have as high social value as manhood. Artists like Raphael and Del Sarto celebrated the women they admired, using them as models for images of the Madonna, and humanized the Mother of God by making her the real mother of earthly children.

The Aristocracy as Patrons of Art. In line with the ideal of *cortesia*, the new civic tyrants, though interested primarily in enlarging their revenues and dominions by means of commercial or political warfare, became in many cases the great patrons of Renaissance art. This aristocracy, like new aristocracies the world over, interested themselves in collecting antiquities. From them came the main support for a revival of classical learning. Nor was an interest

in antiquity their only service to the cause of culture. Unlike the *nouveaux riches* of the Victorian era, the vigorous *signori* seem to have valued not only the genius of the past but also the talents of their fellow citizens. They vied with one another and with the guilds in donating buildings and paintings to the churches and to the communes. Four families, in particular, deserve special mention for a long tradition of this artistic patronage.

The first and most distinguished of these great houses was that of the Medici, who for almost a hundred years guided with great wisdom the destiny of Florence. Three generations of this family employed the best artists of their time. They created a museum for the study of antique art and paid for the exploration of ancient Etruscan and Roman ruins. Bertoldo, Michelangelo, Leonardo da Vinci, and Verrocchio, as well as a host of other artists, less well known, were at various times invited to work in this museum. The family of Sforza at Milan, that of Este in Ferrara, and that of Gonzaga of Mantua also employed artists regularly. The employment, although at times undoubtedly for purposes of ostentation, did not always remain on the level of a vulgar desire to impress others. The *signori* were themselves highly creative, with a knowledge of music and poetry. Both Lorenzo de' Medici and his mother composed hymns and popular songs. Alfonso d'Este of Ferrara traveled extensively in France, England, and the Netherlands for purposes of study. In his leisure he practiced wood turning and bronze casting.

The Rise of the Academies. As the power of the guilds declined, the artists looked for commissions to the new aristocracy. The *bottega*, or guild workshop, of the 15th century gave way to the *atelier*, or studio, of the 16th-century artist. The cult of the individual artist and the idea of a Bohemian existence for the inspired, pampered darling of the wealthy connoisseur took the place of the bourgeois respect for the honest craftsman.

The aristocracy, on their side, desiring assurance that they would never be without artists uncontrolled by guild ethics, coupled the archaeological research of their humanist scholars with the education of young artists. During the late 15th and 16th centuries, the academic idea of art training, which brought literature and antique models into the curriculum of the young artist, grew strong in this way. Eventually even individual artists formed their own academies. The so-called servile arts of sculpture, painting, and architecture rose to the condition of the liberal art of music and discarded, much to their detriment, the ideals of craftsmanship held by the potters, wood carvers, and ironworkers. These last arts came to be known as "crafts," in contrast to the others, which were called the "fine arts."

When the so-called fine arts separated from craftsmanship, they became the particular property of the upper classes and correspondingly symbolic of commercial values. *Gusto*, or taste, as an aesthetic term, appeared first in the Renaissance and became a prerogative of the gentleman, particularly the Florentine gentleman. To Florence, city of humanistic culture, following the business connections made by the Medici and other great families, came all the culture seekers of the world. From Florence went the missionizing artists of the 16th century to educate the "barbarous Gothick" people of Germany, France, and England.

The Individualism of the Artist. With art recognized by both commercial and political leaders, the artist of great talent, his *bottega* full of students, came to occupy a position of leadership in the community such as he had not known before and has not known since. Partaking of both ideals—of *virtù* and *cortesia*—the Renaissance artist was a gentleman and a citizen of the world, at home in France or Constantinople as well as in Florence. At his best, he was supported by an inner ethical religion, whose core included the ancient Roman virtues of wisdom, justice, courage, and temperance, whose spirit moved outward in Christian well-doing. Leonardo da Vinci, born in the Middle Ages, maturing through the Renaissance, points the way to 20th-century ethics when he leaves in his notes such Platonic ideas as "The soul can never be infected by the corruption of the body, but acts in the body like the wind which causes the sound in the organ" and "Our body is subject to Heaven, and Heaven is subject to the spirit." Salvation through good works, a religious idea that was to permeate the northern Reformation, finds its counterpart in Leonardo's "As a day well spent brings happy sleep so a life well planned brings peaceful death."

The Renaissance, unlike 5th-century Athens and 13th-century France, cannot be said to have created a fundamental style. The Renaissance created great individuals whose strivings in the field of art united the opposing aspects of previous European styles into a few great unified expressions.

The Renaissance as the Beginning of Modern Times. Our feeling for the Italian Renaissance culture is particularly strong because our 20th-century American culture, in part, arises fresh from it. From Northern Europe, 17th-century American colonists brought a Biblical religious education, Gothic in type. Our 18th-century academic education derives, in greater part, from the ideals held by Renaissance humanists. Thus, from Sunday school and day school we inherit thought patterns and spiritual conflicts similar to those of the Renaissance. Like the men of the Renaissance, we lay great stress upon the development of the individual. We believe in the processes of democracy. We lack a feudal aristocracy but have an aristocracy of wealth, from which comes support for our great civic art academies, theaters, and musical enterprises.

The Renaissance city-state, furthermore, marks the beginning of a political development ending with the modern concept of the nation. The Americans, however, like the Florentines of the 15th century, find themselves at home the world over and are coming, like the men of the Renaissance, to conceive of themselves as internationalists. Twentieth-century science, in addition, brings to full fruition studies begun in the 15th and 16th centuries. Most of the mechanical principles underlying those inventions that brought about the industrial revolution of which we are a part were recognized and used by Leonardo da Vinci and published in the 16th century by Cardanus. The modernism of the Renaissance thinker concerning industrial development can be seen in the following note by the inventor, Leonardo, who wrote it while working upon a machine for making needles.

Early tomorrow, Jan. 2, 1496, I shall make the leather belt and proceed to a trial . . . One hundred times in each hour 400 needles will be finished, making 40,000 in an hour and 480,000 in 12 hours. Suppose we say 4,000 thousands (implying 10 machines) which at 5 solidi per thousand gives 20,000 solidi: 1,000 lira per working day, and if one works 20 days in the month 60,000 ducats the year.[1]

At the time when Leonardo wrote this, he was trying to earn some extra money, possibly to finish The Last Supper, for the state was unable to supply him with the funds for materials.

The Birth of Humanism and Classical Elements in Renaissance Literature

The term "humanism," narrower than the concept of the revival of learning, indicates a part in the development of that movement when a few technical scholars applied themselves exclusively to the task of teaching the methods of the classical authors, of translating from Greek into Latin many of the ancient philosophers, and of restoring the monuments of antiquity. The humanists gave to the world a new perception of man as a reasonable being, combined with the belief that in the literature of Greece and Rome, more than in any other place, human nature might find the means for freeing the intellect of superstitious fears and the theological control of morality.

In the realm of religion, these eager seekers after long-prohibited thought patterns joyfully abandoned medieval theology for the pagan mythology and ethics of the ancient world. In their new pantheistic religion, the humanists forsook both hell and purgatory as well as the joys of the heavenly kingdom. For hell they substituted the fear of defeat for their earthly desires, or a thwarting of that ambition to expand and perfect themselves in *virtù*. To purgatory they preferred a present membership in an Arcadian society, where wit and literary fellowship brought applause for their scholarly labors. As the movement aged, however, the goals for achievement came to lie more within the field of literary endeavors. Simple creativity, the energetic moment of art, gave way first to love of form and then to formalism, ending eventually in archaeological erudition and grammatical quibbling over the translation of and commentary on the classics.

The Importance of Petrarch as the Founder of Humanism. Petrarch, the founder of humanism, like his contemporary, Dante, was a lyrical poet and a troubadour at heart. His medieval sonnets to Laura, cast in the form devised by Lentini and perfected by Dante, remain for most students of romantic literature Petrarch's foremost productions. Today we speak of the fourteen-lined poem in five-foot iambic— rhymed A B B A, A B B A, for the first eight lines, and C D E, C D E, or some other similar combination for the last six lines—as the Petrarchan sonnet. The mastery of form necessary to perfect such a poem is part of our literary inheritance from the humanists. The example, number eleven in the series dedicated to Laura, illustrates the former.

No wearied mariner to port e'er fled
From the dark billow, when some tempest's nigh,
As from tumultous gloomy thoughts I fly—
Thoughts by the force of goading passion bred:

[1] ABBOTT PAYSON USHER, *A History of Mechanical Inventions*, McGraw-Hill Book Company, Inc., New York, 1929, translated from *Zeitschrift des Vereins Deutscher Ingenieure*, Bd. 50, 1906.

Nor wrathful glance of heaven so surely sped
Destruction to man's sight, as does that eye
Within whose bright black orb Love's Deity
Sharpens each dart, and tips with gold its head.
Enthroned in radiance there he sits, not blind,
Quiver'd, and naked, or by shame just veil'd,
A live, not fabled boy, with changeful wing;
Thence unto me he lends instruction kind,
And arts of verse from meaner bards conceal'd
Thus am I taught whate'er of love I write or sing.[1]

To the men of the Renaissance, Petrarch was particularly known for his passionate pursuit of classical learning. Unlike later, less creative humanists, Petrarch did not content himself with mere grammatical research; for him the classics merited study as much for their truth as for their style. His love of antiquity led him to collect ancient Greek and Roman manuscripts, which he eventually gave to the city of Venice as a nucleus for the first public library. Scientific historical research he furthered by assembling coins and inscriptions, as documentary evidence to be used in studying antiquity. He was the first to suggest the governmental preservation of ancient monuments. Following Cicero and Vergil, Petrarch chose supremacy in poetry and oratory as his personal ideal of *virtù*.

Despite his humanistic interests, Petrarch remained a Christian. In St. Augustine he found a kindred spirit, standing midway between the pagan culture and the Christian. The early Church Father he used as an introduction to the classical world, retracing the steps that Augustine had taken away from it. Within Petrarch, as within the early artists of the Renaissance, Christian and pagan ideals fought for supremacy. His inherent vanity caused him to praise himself for his accomplishment in the realm of letters; his Christian conscience punished him for his lack of humility.

While he left behind no single great scholarly work, Petrarch, by his example and zeal, inspired a group of disciples who carried on his tradition in Florence and Venice. Thus in the years between his death in 1374 and the destruction of the Greek empire in 1453, as the treasured manuscripts of the Greek classics became available, because of his labors, men arose equipped to translate and publish them.

The Humanism of Boccaccio. Best known among the disciples and friends of Petrarch was Giovanni Boccaccio. Born in 1313, the son of a Florentine merchant and a Frenchwoman, Boccaccio early went to Naples. There, in his twenty-eighth year, he decided that his life must express itself through literature and the pursuit of humanistic subjects. His conversion, as narrated by his fellow countryman, Villani, was very similar to that of St. Francis, his love for pagan antiquity replacing the saint's love of God. Unschooled in Latin and Greek, Boccaccio applied himself to mastering the Latin language. Worshiping Vergil from afar, he chose for his heroes among contemporary writers first Dante and then the scholarly Petrarch. In later life, Boccaccio translated the *Iliad* and the *Odyssey* into Latin, transcribed all the works of Terence, and gathered a dictionary of biographical and mythological material from antiquity. In his early work, the *Genealogia Deorum* (*Genealogy of God*), Boccaccio wrote the first of many Renaissance essays in defense of some art, here the art of poetry.

Boccaccio's Decameron and the Novellieri. Boccaccio is best known through his greatest work, the *Decameron*, which marks the beginning of modern Italian prose. As contrasted with Dante's *Divine Comedy*, the *Decameron* has been called the "human" comedy. Dante's comedy shows human life in relation to the life hereafter; Boccaccio's neglects all transcendental spiritual values for the life of this earth. To this extent, Boccaccio's work takes its place as the first realistic novel.

The story of the *Decameron* has for its setting a villa two miles outside the plague-stricken Florence of 1350. In this villa, seven ladies and three men, to pass the time, regale one another with a series of tales, or *novelle*, which reveal

---

[1] Sonnet XI, "He Is Led by Love to Reason," translated by Nott, from *Eighteen Sonnets of Francis Petrarch*, Kahoe & Co., Yellow Springs, Ohio, 1929.

most of the customs of the time. Through his characters, Boccaccio satirizes not only the concept of chivalry but also the ideals of marriage and the home and even the service of God.

In other writings—namely, the *Filostrato*, *Fiammetta*, and the *Amorosa Visione*—Boccaccio mingles pagan and Christian mythology. In the *Filostrato*, he celebrates episodes from the stories of the Neapolitan court, using Greek names taken from the *Iliad*. In his *Fiammetta*, Boccaccio analyzes the effect of passion upon women. His bitterest of satires upon women is given in the *Corbaccio*, which was written out of pique toward a lady who had repelled his advances. In all his works, Boccaccio, having been freed from medieval superstition by his humanist research, gives full attention to psychological analysis. Although his writings paint pictures of the surface of life, he suggests throughout them the sources of characterful action.

The traditions of Boccaccio passed on into the *novelle* of Cinthio, Firenzuola, Machiavelli, and Bandello. Most of the *novellieri*, following the precedent of Boccaccio, drew together a small group of people who told a number of tales, each tale having for its purpose the representation of the characteristic actions of some type of human being. The original *novelle*, to be found in the chansons of the Middle Ages, aimed to present anecdotes illustrative of some moral quality. The Renaissance *novelle*, in contrast, focused attention upon realistic action, preferably action that flouted the moral and social conventions of the Middle Ages. Bandello, for example, delights in pointing to the comic aspects of clerical hypocrisy, revealing the debauchery of monastery and convent as though such debauchery were common. One of his most humorous stories has to do with a village priest who persuades his parishioners that the town is haunted by a griffin. Bandello treated the story of Romeo and Juliet in his tale of *Gerardo and Elena*, and that of Twelfth Night in the tale of *Nicuola*. Far to the north of Florence, Geoffrey Chaucer grouped his *novelle* about the journey of the Canterbury pilgrims. Chaucer, unlike the *novellieri* of Italy, remained true, as did most of his countrymen, to the temper of the medieval church.

The Significance of the Later Humanists. Around the persons of Cosimo and Lorenzo de' Medici, both of whom were ardent collectors and humanists, there thronged a number of scholars less creative than Petrarch and Boccaccio, but far more prolific in the translation of ancient manuscripts. In 1438, Cosimo de' Medici encouraged Pope Eugenius IV to come to Florence for a conference with the Byzantine emperor and head of the Eastern Church, John Paleologus. The Eastern monarch brought with him many trained Greek theologians and scribes, among whom one, Gemistos Plethon, had some knowledge of the ancient philosophers. Plethon had absorbed Neo-Platonism, which he literally preached to the Florentines, considering himself a reincarnation of Plato. Cosimo de' Medici, converted to Platonic studies by his conversations with this mystical fountainhead of wisdom, founded the Florentine Academy. Other Greeks, such as Argyropoulos and Trapezuntios, together with the Florentines Poggio, Pico de Mirandola, and Poliziano, added their scholarly achievements to the forerunners of humanism, Marsilio Ficino and Leonardo Bruni joining with Alberti the architect in reviving the entire body of classical learning. From Florence, the stream of erudition flowed out in all directions—to Rome, to Venice, to Nuremberg, Paris, and far-off London—until by the 16th century this city of the Arno was acknowledged to be the intellectual mistress of the world.

The Birth of the Historic Point of View and the Growth of Arcadias. Two types of scholarship united in Florence to bring about the birth of the historic point of view. The first arose with the Aristotelians of the Middle Ages, who attempted to explain their superstitions in terms of some sort of evolution of spiritual values. People who habitually think in terms of evolutionary sequences usually seek historic backgrounds for their actions. The second belongs to humanists like Petrarch who, intent on re-discovering antiquity, stressed the necessity for charting man's development in terms of his monumental works and inscriptions. The attendant revival of interest in Pliny, Xenophon, and other Greek and Roman historians, gave to the humanists the objective method of history.

The Florentine, cradled among the ruins of ancient Tuscany, had history in his blood. Ghiberti tried to explain art historically; Bruni wrote the history of Florence in Latin. Of more lively interest is the diary of Luca Landucci, a Florentine apothecary who, between the years 1450 and 1516, took time from his drugs to set down an intimate account of the history of his city during its golden age. Shortly after, Niccolo Machiavelli wrote his history of Florence and his treatise of the development of the perfect Renaissance tyrant, *The Prince*. In the 16th century, the Florentine, Vasari, reviewing the artistic glories of his native city, was to write the first art history in the romantic vein. This he called *The Lives of the Most Excellent Sculptors, Painters, and Architects*.

Lacking a vision of heaven, and living in a world of violence and ruthlessness, the man of the Renaissance, who found no interest in history, when thwarted in his personal desires turned to Neo-Platonic fantasies and created the first modern Utopia, called "Arcadia." The poem, *Arcadia*, written by Jacopo Sannazaro, in Naples, around 1500, tells of a dream world of poetry, inhabited by shepherds and shepherdesses, unfolding the pastoral ideal of a golden age. From this source, came Sir Philip Sidney's longer pastoral poem. In *Arcadia* we find the triumph of the classical ideal in Renaissance thought, although the wood nymphs seem like the girls of Sorrento, the boys like Neapolitan sailors.

Painting

Italian Renaissance painting unites all previous artistic discoveries of the Western world, and at the hands of its greatest masters, Leonardo, Botticelli, and Giorgione, discloses passages of lyric beauty comparable only to the work of Chinese artists. The mature point of view of the greatest Renaissance painters results in part from a natural cultural inheritance, but is reached at rare moments by only a few individuals in whom *virtù*, or the desire for complete self-expression, led to a complete integration of the Gothic and Classic moods. The greatest works of a few masters stand far above the turbulent productions that constitute the large body of Renaissance art. To understand these works, one must examine the sources of their strength in the definitive inventions and discoveries of the innovators—products which often lack great aesthetic value but which have significance because of their novelty.

Benozzo Gozzoli's Journey of the Magi and the Gothic Mood. A number of painters, including Gentile da Fabriano, Filippo Lippi, and Benozzo Gozzoli, persisted in the Gothic mood of medieval tapestry design throughout the 15th century. Such artists supplied the demand for pictures that should suggest the romantic, chivalric concept of life set forth in the literary works of Pulci, Boiardo, and Ariosto, still fostered by the nobility. The Gothic method of composition, with its interweave of figures and landscape, appears in the frescoes painted about 1459 by Gozzoli (1420–1497), in the Medici chapel of the Riccardi Palace, Florence (Fig. 456). These frescoes, like beautiful tapestries, show the masters of the Medicean house with their followers and guests, all of whom were present at the Florentine conference of 1438, following the Three Magi through a Tuscan landscape. The composition is held together vertically by tall trees; horizontally, by the masses of rocks that lead from section to section. The richly dressed figures in Florentine cloth of gold present realistic portraits, but the motions of horses and men are stilted, a few stock positions serving as models for all the representations.

An attempt at perspective depth has been

gained by making the background figures smaller than those in the foreground, but without true regard for nature. The hunter, for example, dressed in Roman robes copied per-

Masaccio's Tribute Money and the Dawn of Realism. The picture called The Tribute Money (Fig. 457), painted by Masaccio (1401–1428), illustrates the retention of the medieval narra-

FIG. 456.—The Journey of the Magi, fresco by Benozzo Gozzoli, c. 1459. Riccardi Palace, Florence. (*Courtesy of Lesch-Carnegie.*)

haps from some classical figure on a Roman coin, rides a horse quite a bit smaller than the doe he pursues. To the medieval mind, such discrepancies seemed of little importance. The doe was necessary for a hunt; it could be stressed, therefore, by making it twice the natural size. Lacking all solidity, many of the figures appear like cutouts against the green foliage of the tapestry trees. The modeling of the bodies of horses and men, however, indicates a tendency toward realism and in this particular suggests the work of another Florentine artist, Tommaso Masaccio.

tive style of composition combined with the greatest degree of realism in figure painting and landscape perspective. The disciples grouped around the Christ are approached by the tax-gatherer, who is clothed in 15th-century Italian costume in contrast to the disciples, who appear in togas. With commanding gesture, the Christ tells St. Peter to fish in the pond for the money. Far to the left, in conventional narrative style, St. Peter is shown discovering a coin in the mouth of a fish, and at the right, St. Peter again appears paying the tax to the official.

Up to this time, the painters had not succeeded in rendering a well-proportioned human form. Masaccio's taxgatherer, however, might have been copied from life. The work also shows a perspective as accurate as that of

uted their geometric strength to later Greek compositions.

Uccello's Rout of San Romano and the Beginnings of Geometric Perspective. The great difference be-

FIG. 457.—The Tribute Money, by Masaccio, c. 1427. Fresco with life-size figures, Brancacci Chapel, Church of the Carmine, Florence. (*Courtesy of Lesch-Carnegie.*)

the Van Eycks, far to the north in Flanders. The horizontal, retreating lines of the house at the right converge in a vanishing point on the horizon, which would be in the lower levels of the mountains in the background. The vanishing point to which they converge, furthermore, lies directly behind the head of the Christ, who is thus indicated as the center of the picture. By this triangle of lines attention is further shifted to the left, where it is engaged by the miracle. At the right, the painter celebrates the triumph of his art, framing Peter by the archway of the house and the taxgatherer by the vertical rectangle of the wall. The vital point at which the old convention and the new realism meet, that is, the point at which the coin passes from hand to hand, is stressed by the vertical dark strip of the door opening. In place of the medieval interweave, here there is a more monumental, sculpturesque grouping of figures, based upon a geometric design. Hence this painting may be likened to those archaic Greek pedimental groups that contrib-

tween the northern Gothic study of perspective and the perspective of the southern masters lies in the fact that the southerners, about the middle of the 15th century, endeavored to discover the geometric secrets of the art, perhaps with the unconscious confidence that they could thus tame nature on some intellectual pattern, such as that noted in the picture by Masaccio. Paolo Uccello (1396–1475), a mathematician whose color schemes and conventions are completely medieval, took the leadership in attempting the boldest perspective effects.

Uccello tried to show that figures retreating in the distant picture plane lose size in direct proportion to their distance from the front. In The Rout of San Romano (Fig. 458) this law of perspective has been religiously observed. The foreground of the picture, ruled off by lines, forms a scaffold upon which a fallen knight, pieces of armor, and shattered lances have been carefully foreshortened. The rich reds, blues, and greens, furthermore, which appear in the background as well as the foreground, show that Uccello had no idea of color or atmospheric perspective. He remained a mathematician with a splendid sense of design, playing with a simple geometric formula. His ability in design may be judged by his disposi-

classical humanism. Thus, they may be taken to represent two further stages of the Renaissance; one growing from the Gothic mood, the other from the Classical concept of beautiful form.

Fig. 458.—The Rout of San Romano, by Paolo Uccello, c. 1435. Tempera on wood, height 6 feet (National Gallery, London). (*Courtesy of Lesch-Carnegie.*)

tion of the spears binding the various parts of the picture together; his preoccupation with his formula, by his rendition of the horses, whose flat bodies cast no shadows, and by the haphazard distribution of the objects in the foreground. The idea of suggesting form by reproducing the effects of shadow upon the bodies apparently had not occurred to him.

In the works of Gozzoli, Masaccio, and Uccello appear the component parts of great Renaissance painting. In two workshops (*botteghe*) of Florence, during the last half of the 15th century, all these artistic tricks united and fused into the perfect creations of Leonardo da Vinci and Michelangelo. These two workshops were directed by Andrea Verrocchio and Domenico Ghirlandaio. The first was governed by a spirit of scientific inquiry; the second, by a love of

Verrocchio's Workshop and the Culmination of Realism. Andrea del Verrocchio (1435–1488), whose name means "true eye," had all the component abilities necessary to a universal genius, save one: he lacked a sense of appropriateness and design. Talented as sculptor and painter, mechanic and bronze founder, he also had the sociability or political acumen necessary for securing a large number of commissions from both the city fathers and the nobility. His busy workshop, in which anatomy and mathematics were studied along with the grinding of colors and the making of plaster replicas, became a focal center for a number of artist friends, including Botticelli, the Della Robbias, and the brothers Sangallo. In this *bottega* studied Lorenzo di Credi, Perugino, and —greatest of all—Leonardo da Vinci.

The picture The Baptism of Christ (Fig. 459) shows all the merits and defects of Verrocchio's workshop. The Renaissance painter, intent on surpassing the legendary fame of the Greek masters, Apelles and Zeuxis, and influenced by a few paintings by Flemish artists of the school of the Van Eycks, set out to achieve a realism so graphic that man would appear as a substantial living thing in an environment of perfect naturalness. Such was Verrocchio's ideal when he asked Leonardo and Lorenzo di Credi, both just past twenty years of age, to help him construct this picture.

A closer study of the details of the picture indicates three ways in which Verrocchio's workshop advanced the cause of realism. To begin with, in an attempt to get an accurate rendition of muscles and a description of the characteristic folds of drapery, Verrocchio copied plaster casts. Attempting to get a proper model for natural rocks, he apparently piled a number of stones one upon another, suggesting a stratification which, to our superior geological knowledge, appears incorrect. In contrast with these unsuccessful attempts to reach a perfect illusion, the upper part of the figure of the Christ shows a careful study of anatomy, combined with a fine appreciation of the effects of light upon the flesh. This leads to a consideration of the second advance toward realism made in Verrocchio's studio—namely, tactile values. Tactile value is the ability to render an object in paint so that the observer feels as though touching it would give a sensation appropriate to the particular substance represented. Perfect tactile values could not be achieved with the old, comparatively harsh, tempera painting. The introduction of glazes of colors, mixed in oil after the manner of the Van Eycks, accounts in part for the more perfect tactile values in the upper part of the figure of the Christ, in the face and hair of the angel, said to have been painted by Leonardo, and, if the term may be applied to landscape, in the distant Alpine vista.

The third and most astonishing innovation of the picture is the depth of the landscape, with its distant towering peaks, its woods, and its meandering stream. Probably this landscape, which is similar to sketches by the young Leo-

Fig. 459.—The Baptism of Christ, by Andrea Verrocchio and Leonardo da Vinci, 1465–1470. Oil and tempera on wood, height 5 feet 9⅝ inches (Uffizi, Florence). (*Courtesy of Lesch-Carnegie.*)

nardo, was done by that genial apprentice. Here is an instance of the use of haze or "sfumato," as Leonardo called it, to give atmospheric perspective quality—a technique developed further by Perugino, another member of the *bottega*.

Although the picture lacks unity and charm, it is highly significant as affording an entire museum of the advances made toward greater realism in painting during the last half of the 15th century by other Florentines, such as the brothers Pollaiuolo and Fra Filippo Lippi, and the Umbrian Piero della Francesca.

Atmospheric Perspective in the Crucifixion by Perugino. Among the students in Verrocchio's workshop, Pietro Vannucci (1446–1523), commonly called Perugino, carried furthest the art of painting in perspective, through a number of religious pictures. Perugino, born in the mountains of Umbria, inherited from the painter Piero della Francesca a natural disposition to

more than a collection of entertaining anecdotes concerning the lives of the artists in and after the Renaissance. Although that approach to art is minimized here, it is necessary to

Fig. 460.—Crucifixion triptych, by Pietro Perugino, 1493–1496. Fresco with life-size figures, Santa Maria Maddalena de' Pazzi. Note figures: Magdalene with red robe in central panel; St. Bernard in white and Virgin in purple, left panel; St. John the Evangelist in red and lavender, St. Benedict in gray, right panel. Composition unified by great curves of landscape and architectural framing. (*Courtesy of Lesch-Carnegie.*)

represent great open spaces in his landscapes. His picture of the Crucifixion (Fig. 460), painted around 1496, shows this tendency, as well as his superior sense of mural design. Perugino discovered that distance affects color. Objects that appear warm, perhaps even red in the foreground tend to become gray, lavender, or blue as they retreat from the eye. He also noticed that the sky, brilliant blue overhead, tones gradually to a lighter blue, then to robin's-egg blue, next to green, and often to pink as it meets the lavender hills on the distant horizon. Verrocchio's color tones were all relatively brown, green, and gray, even the colorful garments being robbed of their brilliance; Perugino brought to Florentine painting a greater appreciation of rich color and a knowledge of the way in which color might contribute to the illusion of depth.

The Mind of Leonardo. To the 20th-century literary mind, the history of art is often little

depart somewhat from an impersonal study of the times during and after the Renaissance, precisely because man has put such emphasis on personal idiosyncrasies since the 16th century.

Few artists have been more misinterpreted than Leonardo da Vinci, who has been chosen for examination here as the epitome of the Renaissance. The clue to the character of Leonardo's life and works lies in the fact that he completely outgrew the medieval romantic point of view, without falling into the error of worshiping antiquity, as did the humanists. His notebooks yield many sketches of classic ornament as well as copies of heads on old Roman and Hellenistic coins, but these never appear in his finished painting. His notes show a deep knowledge of Pliny, Horace, Celsus, Ovid, and a host of other classic authors, from whom he derived a philosophy very close to that of the Stoic emperor, Marcus Aurelius.

The Biography of Leonardo. Born the illegitimate son of a notary in a tiny mountain village, Leonardo was taken at the age of five from his natural mother and raised by his father's first wife, a woman of quasi-noble birth. Early in life, the mountain lad showed an interest in nature, science, and art. When the family moved to Florence, after some grammar-school training, at the age of thirteen, the youth was bound as apprentice to Verrocchio. He grew to manhood with an instinct for noble living, while feeling deeply the stigma of his illegitimate birth.

Driven from Florence by his own fears or through the compulsion of the police—for he had been arrested, probably because of his presence at the meetings of a conspiracy against the Medici—Leonardo journeyed to Milan, an unknown Florentine. After ten years of labor and study, during which he painted the Virgin of the Rocks and the portrait of Cecilia Gallerani, Leonardo entered the court of Duke Sforza. Gradually he came to be accepted as the town's leading artist. Painting, modeling, designing new sanitary sections of the city and a great villa, devising machinery for the industry of the town, founding cannon, and teaching a rather large group of students in a *bottega*, which he called his academy, Leonardo employed every waking moment of his life in useful labor. In achieving this freedom for all his powers, he came upon the method for exploring his unconscious mind which we today know as psychoanalysis. His psychological observation, both introspective and objective, displays the greatest keenness. In the field of physiology and anatomy, Da Vinci began at this time those studies which placed him 300 years ahead of the contemporary medical men.

After living in various parts of Italy, Leonardo finally moved north to the Gothic lands, where he spent the last ten years of his life as the honored adviser of Francis I, king of France. His notes, toward the close of his life, show Leonardo's mind to have been freed of most medieval superstitions; to have achieved a philosophy as penetrating as that of some Oriental sage.

The Adoration of the Magi. After serving an overlong apprenticeship under Verrocchio,

Fig. 461.—Adoration of the Magi, by Leonardo da Vinci, 1481–1504, unfinished. Oil on wooden panel, 7 feet 3 inches (Uffizi, Florence). (*Courtesy of Lesch-Carnegie.*)

Leonardo appeared as a full-fledged guild artist in 1480, at which time he was asked by the monks of St. Donato of Scopeto, a monastery in the suburbs of Florence, to paint an altarpiece depicting the visit of the Magi to the Child at Bethlehem. One studies this picture not so much for its beauty or unity as for its revelation of Leonardo's growth (Fig. 461). He worked upon it over a 25-year period, much as Ghiberti had worked upon the doors for the Baptistery of Florence. The painting shows both medieval and modern characteristics. Comparing it with the work of Leonardo's contemporaries, one gains a true sense of his universal quality.

Among the sketches for Leonardo's Adoration of the Magi, one (Fig. 462b) brings forth a significant innovation in composition. Both Classic and Gothic pictures gain a certain amount of restfulness and simplicity by being composed in a plane directly frontal to the eye, so that any illusion of space is in direct, or one-point, perspective with a single vanishing point on the horizon line. This sketch of Leonardo's presents the Madonna in a room set at an

ceived the place of honor, with her head a little above the center of the picture. Around her kneel the three Magi, arranged so that their bodies form an equilateral triangle, its apex

FIG. 462a.—Sketch by Leonardo da Vinci, 1478–1504, one-point perspective (Uffizi Gallery).

angle to the observer's line of sight. Thus, the attention may wander either to the right and farther into the room, or it may turn to the left toward a second vanishing point in infinity. Leonardo used this type of composition in only a few of his later pictures, notably, the Madonna and St. Anne and the St. John-Bacchus, in the Louvre. In the hands of the later Venetian artists, Giorgione and Titian, this arrangement had a further development, until it became the usual form of composition in the baroque art of the 16th and 17th centuries. This diagonal composition, denoting a greater activity within the picture plane, developed simultaneously with an interest in chiaroscuro, or painting in light and dark.

As Leonardo eventually designed his picture of the Adoration upon the finely prepared wooden panel with its white chalk ground, he strove to suggest all three modes of expression. These include the absolute balance of Perugino, the Gothic interweave of Gozzoli, and this new spatial concept. The Madonna re-

pointing to the left. At the right of the picture, peering out of the darkness, are the heads of shepherds, old and young. A standing figure at the extreme right looks out at the observer, as was customary in paintings of the Venetian school, pointing with his hand toward a kneeling king. Scholars surmise that this represents the young Leonardo calling our attention to his conception.

Forced by his expulsion from Florence to leave the Adoration of the Magi unfinished, Leonardo integrated his life and strengthened his Gothic style by realistic study in Milan between 1481 and 1493. He returned to work upon the picture in 1498 and above the peering faces of the lower right, drew the man whose upheld hand leads our attention to the background, where we see architectonic details, battling groups, and processions (Figs. 462a, c).

When he returned to his Magi for the last time, after the disillusionment of a military campaign with Borgia, Leonardo painted in the upper right the struggling horsemen, the foot soldiers rolling in the dust, the fleeing women, and a snapping dog. The climax of the Magi panel was reserved for the detail at the lower left. In a sketch at present in Windsor

Fig. 462b.—Sketch by Leonardo da Vinci, 1478–1504, two-point perspective (Metropolitan Museum of Art.)

Castle, Leonardo drew himself as a philosopher, watching the swirling waters of a flood. The same face and the form of the mature Leonardo appear in the Adoration of the Magi. Next to him is the face of the other angel from the Baptism of Christ, with the same pessimistic mouth. Leonardo's face and the pose of his body express quietness and peace.

In richness of associational values, the Adoration of the Magi may be compared with Hui Tsung's pictures. In formal values it provides interesting material for study. Without the integrating effect of the color and *sfumato*, or haze, it remains disconnected and lacks the unity of Leonardo's mature style. Some literary-minded critics, however, consider it Leonardo's greatest work. Comparing Leonardo and Hui Tsung, we find two similar spirits, both of whom

achieved a high degree of self-mastery. The Oriental found himself by picturing his complete union with nature; Leonardo, as seen in this painting, by consciously orienting his life

Fig. 462c.—Sketch by Leonardo da Vinci, 1478–1504, battle scene (The Academy, Venice).

toward the polar star of the child within him.

The Virgin of the Rocks. From 1483 to 1493, during the first of his absences from the Adoration of the Magi, Leonardo painted the picture called the Virgin of the Rocks (Fig. 463). Here he mastered the art of chiaroscuro in the superb treatment of the draperies of the Madonna, learned to draw the human form, and succeeded in creating a perfect illusion of depth in a landscape of fantasy. Unlike Verrocchio's Baptism, this masterpiece is dominated by a strong sense of design. Again we observe the union of two modes of composition. The Madonna's head and body, like that of the Cimabue Madonna (Fig. 386, Chap. XIII), rest on the diagonal intersecting lines of the rectangular frame. Around this central pyramid, an interweave of sight lines carries attention from one person to another, starting with the face of the angel who looks out at the observer, and following the direction of the pointing hand across to St. John, who looks down at the infant

FIG. 463.—Virgin of the Rocks, by Leonardo da Vinci, 1483–1493. Oil on wooden panel, height about 6 feet (Louvre Museum). (*Courtesy of Lesch-Carnegie.*)

Christ. If, on the other hand, our eyes turn first to the head of the Madonna, her eyes and outstretched hand, as well as the composition in the folds of her drapery, also send the attention down to the Christ Child. A pool of water in whose depths may be seen the bodies of aquatic animals separates us from this peaceful group. We may imagine this pool to be part of a stream flowing from the tall rocks far back at the left of the picture. These rocks appear in perfect atmospheric perspective, running from faint gray-blue to the warmer browns. Although the color scheme appears dark to our

eyes, the picture is infused by a sunny golden light that modifies, but does not dim the blue and red robes, especially in the high-light portions.

The artist's relationship to women, during the time when he was working on the Virgin of the Rocks, is clarified in several poignant passages in his notebooks. These show a genuine reciprocated love for Cecilia Gallerani, whom he celebrated as the angel in his picture, and whose portrait has recently been recognized in the Woman with the Ermine in Cracow.

The Last Supper as the Culmination of the Christian Painter's Art. Leonardo's painting, The Last Supper (Fig. 464), unites all the leading threads of Christian thought with the most significant inventions of the Gothic and Classical art moods. It was commissioned by Duke Sforza in 1494, when Leonardo was forty-two years of age. He worked on it for three years, painting it upon the end wall of the refectory in the monastery of Santa Maria delle Grazie (St. Mary of the Graces), using the Italian type of dry fresco called *al secco*, which was really tempera painting, instead of oil, as Vasari states.

To the monastic dining hall Leonardo brought the greatest sermon of the New Testament, the spiritual essence of the Mass. Probably the great difference between his work and that of other artists who painted The Last Supper came from the fact that Leonardo studied his Bible directly and strove to reconstruct the plot of an actual occurrence so that its dramatic overtones would touch all conditions of men. As his central theme he chose the moment at which the Christ, having dipped the sop, presented it to Judas, saying, "He who takes the bread from me will this night betray me." The disciples' response to these awful words forms the subject matter of the painting.

Among the psychological types that the artist depicted with almost scientific accuracy, each monk could find his own soul. The gentle John, directly to the left of Christ, counterbalances, in the swooning pose of his figure, the fierce face and pointing hand of Peter, whose right hand clutches a knife almost at the back of the sinister Judas. Philip, a little less gentle than John, three figures to the right of Christ, points to his breast, as though saying, "Is it I, Lord?"

it a point of departure for the study of the formal values.

The picture consists of five groups, the center being the equilateral triangle, that Platonic

Fig. 464.—The Last Supper, by Leonardo da Vinci, 1495–1498. Tempera (*al secco*) on plaster, figures over life size, Santa Maria delle Grazie, Milan. (*Courtesy of Lesch-Carnegie.*)

And Andrew, second to the right from Christ, draws back, with a gesture of amazement, looking toward that hand which by its movement should indicate the traitor. Matthew, the legalist among the disciples, leans with penetrating gaze over the table farthest to the left, as though to detect the culprit. His face, significantly, has the profile of Leonardo's father, as it is revealed in the manuscripts. Judas, whose face has exactly the same profile as that of St. Peter, clutches the money bag with one hand as he stretches out to reach the bread with the other.

In the midst of this hurly-burly of human types, the central figure of the Christ reaches a balance, with a face refined and tender, strong and contained as that of a Buddha. Its position in the center of the composition, framed by the doorway in the rear, marked as the convergence of all retreating perspective lines, and pointed to by a great variety of hands, makes

emblem of the complete soul of man—reason, sense, and body in balanced form. The disciples are arranged in groups of three, one rather feminine character being placed with two masculine in each case. These groups are bound together by the long horizontal mass of the table and the arrangement in the folds of their drapery. They are also connected more subtly by their action, which all refers to the central quiet figure. The disposition of their arms and drapery together forms a Celtic interweave, so that here, as in the Parthenon pedimental composition, we find an interweave around a central figure.

It is impossible to discuss the coloring of The Last Supper, because the original painting suffered severely from neglect over 300 years. The dung of Napoleon's horses, stabled here during the campaign of 1800, probably did more than anything else to ruin it, through the

FIG. 465.—The Mona Lisa, probably a portrait of Isabella d'Este, by Leonardo da Vinci, 1503–1506. Oil on wooden panel, height 2 feet 6⅜ inches (Louvre Museum). (*Reproduced from a Medici Print by permission of the publishers, Hale, Cushman & Flint, Boston.*)

action of the fumes on the tempera emulsion. But even in its mutilated condition, as it appears today, the work holds much of its original impressiveness and compels attention because of its thought-inspiring quality.

Leonardo's Mastery of Form and the Picture Called the Mona Lisa. Vasari's legend, which has veiled this remarkable portrait, Mona Lisa (Fig. 465), with a nebulous atmosphere of mystery, has become almost more famous than the artist himself. Vasari never saw the picture about which he wrote and gives no sources for his allegations, although there was a legend in Florence of Leonardo's having painted a portrait of the husband of a woman called Mona Lisa.

Poor reproductions of the picture account in part for the varied misconceptions of its quality. Few colored reproductions show that the lady is not garbed in mourning, but actually wears a green dress with dark red sleeves. The subtle modeling of the face, particularly in the regions about the eyes and mouth, changes from one reproduction to another, no two versions looking alike. Much has been written about the Mona Lisa smile, detected in all Leonardo's women. Actually, in the portraits of Leonardo no two expressions are alike.

Leonardo's anatomical studies, coupled with his knowledge of psychology and his mastery of the painter's craft, put at his disposal by his fiftieth year, when he probably painted this picture, ability possessed by no other artist with the exception of Velázquez and Rembrandt. In the face of the Mona Lisa, Leonardo has given an accurate characterization of the very woman, Isabella d'Este, the Marchioness of Mantua, whose portrait he is said to have shown to one of her friends in Venice. While there is no absolute way to show that Isabella sat directly for the portrait now in the Louvre, details of it, such as the embroidery and the hands, as well as the general face type, can be connected with her. She had a sense of humor, at times a bit cruel, as befitted a Renaissance woman. She was pious, a good mother, probably the best educated woman of her times, a genuine lover of art, a musician of no mean ability, and a very competent administrator.

The above historical background for any study of the picture is necessary even in this elementary history of culture, so that the student may learn how even the best known works of art gain false notoriety because of their imputed associational values. For a long time this picture was quite neglected by the connoisseurs. Until the middle of the 18th century, its cool tones, subtle coloring, and careful drawing eluded critical instincts that then demanded baroque and colorful romantic fantasy. Stripped of its mystery, this picture remains a great portrait of one of the world's great women. The distant vistas of the Dolomite Alps, previsioned in Leonardo's youthful fantasy and physically explored shortly after Leonardo had drawn the cartoon of Isabella now in the Louvre, add the masculine touch to an otherwise completely feminine picture. The central seated form is monumental, attention being nicely balanced between the features of the face and the hands, whose careful drawing is now somewhat disturbed by overpainting. The painting of Isabella's favorite embroidery, which Leonardo had earlier designed for her in Milan, and the fineness of the satin sleeves show a care like that which the artist earlier lavished upon the portrait of Cecilia in the Virgin of the Rocks. The contained quality of his emotion is best expressed in the pains with which he modeled the face. The two eyes and the two sides of the lips display different aspects of a character as complex as that complete definition of womanhood by Vergil: "Varium et mutabile semper femina."

The Sketch Drawing as the Ideal of Renaissance Virtuosity and Leonardo's Battle of Anghiari. Cennino Cennini, at the end of the 14th century, wrote in his *Book of Art* that drawing from nature was the best guide for painting and that copying the drawings of some master was the true entrance to a knowledge of form. He insisted that something in the heart, akin to love and gentleness, perhaps called the "imagination," led the hand to express things unseen, but the true artist would so control his imagination that the results would seem reality.

water stains upon the walls or ceiling of his room. That Leonardo was fully aware of their high associational and literary value, we know

Fig. 466.—Battle of Anghiari, copy by Rubens of original paper cartoon by Leonardo da Vinci, 1605. Drawing in bister on paper, height about 11 inches (Louvre Museum). (*Courtesy of Lesch-Carnegie.*)

The Renaissance artists, consciously or unconsciously, took these words as their ideal, and a study of Renaissance sketches discloses immediately their superiority, from an imaginative point of view, to those of the Greek masters.

Either just before or during his campaign with Borgia, the Florentine city fathers commissioned Leonardo to paint a battle scene. Into this scene, as sketched here (Fig. 462c), the artist wove a suggestion of natural grandeur, the clouds of smoke and dust from the cannon blending with the whirling bodies of charging horsemen and fighting foot soldiers.

In his notebooks Leonardo wrote that such sketches originated many times in the vague

from other passages in his notes, which thus advised the student to represent a battle:

First let the air exhibit a confused mixture of smoke, arising from the discharge of artillery and musquetry, and the dust raised by the horses of the combatants . . . The victorious party will be running forward, their hair and other light parts flying in the wind, their eyebrows lowered, and the motion of every member properly contrasted; for instance, in moving the right foot forwards, the left arm must be brought forward also. . . . Some should be in the agonies of death; their teeth shut, their eyes wildly staring, their fists clenched, and their legs in distorted position—There may be also a straggling horse without a rider, running in wild disorder; his mane flying in the wind, beating down with his feet all before him, and doing a deal of damage.[1]

Having clarified his thoughts on the subject of the battle by word and sketch, Leonardo painted his picture over it, and wrote in his life of Leonardo that the battle scene had been poorly painted. Probably the world was not yet appreciative of so realistic a view of war-

FIG. 467.—Primavera or The Allegory of Spring, by Sandro Botticelli, 1478. Tempera on wood, height 6 feet 8 inches (Uffizi, Florence). (*Courtesy of Lesch-Carnegie.*)

made models in terra cotta (Fig. 486), on which he studied the emotion-stirring light-and-shade effects desired in the finished picture. He finally made a great, detailed cartoon. While the work progressed, his younger rival, Michelangelo, was asked to paint a companion picture, and a contest developed similar to the old contests of the Gothic minnesingers. Michelangelo showed a magnificent group of nude soldiers bathing; Leonardo depicted all the fury of war.

The central panel of Leonardo's battle scene remained upon the wall for forty years, one of the principal attractions to art students and tourists in Florence. Eventually, when the "modern" humanistic art party, composed of Michelangelo's followers, triumphed, Vasari

fare, the critics preferring the noble victories of the baroque painters. A copy made of Leonardo's cartoon (Fig. 466) by Peter Paul Rubens, the Flemish master, is an aid in reconstructing the original, so ruthlessly destroyed.

The drawings of the Renaissance masters, both the simple sketches from life and the imaginative compositions such as this, had particular value in the workshop, where they were studied by the apprentices. In succeeding ages, their value to the connoisseur has so risen that today a drawing like that by Leonardo would be valued at as much as $50,000. For the Victorian art critic, the ability to detect the fine qualities of such a sketch was taken as a

[1] LEONARDO DA VINCI, *A Treatise on Painting*, translated by John Francis Rigaud, pp. 77–80, S. Gosnell, London, 1802.

true indication of taste. Aesthetic discrimination could go no further.

Botticelli's Allegories and the Gothic Lyric Mood. For a contrast with the balanced realism and dramatic feeling in Leonardo's paintings, works which transcend the average of the Italian Renaissance, one may turn to the pictures of Sandro Botticelli, an artist who epitomizes the Renaissance in the fullest development of its Gothic mood. The Allegory of Spring (Fig. 467), painted by Botticelli for one of the Medici, between 1476 and 1478, is compounded of Gothic emotional overtones and a classical story taken from Ovid. It characterizes, perhaps more than any other one painting, the individuality of the artist.

Botticelli, a friend of Verrocchio and Leonardo, was trained in the workshop of Fra Filippo Lippi, known for his Madonnas. A thoroughly religious character, Botticelli drew superb illustrations for Dante's *Divine Comedy*, comparable to the line drawings of the Utrecht Psalter. All his work is characterized by an interweave of lines, particularly well represented in the charming dancing group of the three Graces at the left of the picture of springtime. Although these maidens are anatomically correct in drawing, the artist has so stressed the linear disposition of their limbs that, seen realistically, they appear false. Only when considered in the light of pure aesthetic form, that is, as a group expressing the motion of the dance simply in the action of the drapery, the lines of the hair, and the position of the arms, can these three figures be enjoyed. To one interested simply in formal linear aesthetic values, the painting stands as one of the greatest moments in art.

The Allegory of Spring glorifies as Venus the charm of a young woman, beloved of Giuliano de' Medici. Flora, the goddess of spring, moves in from the right, scattering blossoms from her flower-adorned robe. A wind-god, pursuing a nymph through the trees, stands for winter, now fast losing his hold. These figures of classical allegory, seen through Gothic eyes, have no trace of the antique about them. The entire composition of the picture and the treatment of the forms suggests a medieval tapestry. The colors, pale and cool, as though painted by a man who feared the warmth of his own spirit, have the smallest amount of sensual appeal. Through all of Botticelli's work there moves a certain feeling of sadness; the faces of his characters never come closer to a smile than that of the Flora. Studied closely, this face shows the most careful modeling, with tiny brush strokes building up layer upon layer of tone until the forms are overburdened with a nervous plastic quality and the individual locks of hair seem dynamic with a Gothic vitality.

Ghirlandaio's Workshop and the Return to Classicism. As the cult of humanism gained strength during the second half of the 15th century, the workshop of Ghirlandaio became the most popular in Florentine art circles, the studios of Verrocchio and Botticelli gradually coming to be looked upon as old-fashioned. Ghirlandaio, whose chief grievance was that he could not paint the entire city wall of Florence with historical narratives, gained fame as a rapid painter in a rapidly moving age, when speed and mass production replaced the older Gothic ideal of painstaking craftsmanship. Although Ghirlandaio was not a revolutionary, he discovered in the antique treatment of the human figure the meaning of sculptural form. This he transferred to the painted panel, and on gaining great proficiency in the technique of fresco painting, carried it out in the Sistine Chapel in pictures of the calling of the apostles Peter and Andrew.

Ghirlandaio's picture of the Nativity (Fig. 468), in the Church of the Holy Trinity in Florence, shows both the merits and the defects of his painting. Here is a picture as lacking in strong composition as is the Baptism by Verrocchio. In the foreground, the kneeling Madonna is in every way medieval. The shepherds at the right are realistic and in some respects copies of details from Flemish pictures then being introduced into Florence. The long procession winding out of the landscape at the left is likewise medieval in coloring, although it comes through a Roman arch. The cattle feed from a trough made of an antique sarcophagus, carefully copied from some original. The two pilasters supporting the roof of the stall are also definitely classical.

While Verrocchio was having his students copy plaster casts made from life, Ghirlandaio had his apprentices copy human figures from ancient Greek and Roman monuments. Thus one might expect to find in the workshop of Ghirlandaio such a man as Michelangelo, who quickly outgrew the copying of classical forms and created new human forms in the ancient manner, but with the added interest of anatomical knowledge, expressing a greatness of spirit comparable to that of Leonardo.

Michelangelo's Birth of Adam as the Perfect Renaissance Composition. To discover one painting which unites all the attributes characteristic of the Renaissance, search must be made among the works of some master, defined as a truly Renaissance spirit, for some moment in which he reached the fullness of his powers while dealing with a subject of both Christian and humanistic import. Such a painting is Michelangelo's Birth of Adam (Fig. 469), executed in fresco on the ceiling of the Sistine Chapel, between May, 1508, and October, 1512. To understand this painting in terms of Michelangelo's own development, one must turn to the workshop of Ghirlandaio, where the young artist studied classical marbles, executing them in the bold, drawing style for some of the paintings of his master. Michelangelo grew up in part as a guest of the Medici, sitting at the family table with the prominent humanists of his day. In the Medici garden he received training in sculpture from the aged Bertoldo, who had studied with the great Donatello. His earliest work in sculpture, The Battle of the Centaurs, now in the Casa Buonarroti in Florence, shows an understanding of the spirit of classical sculpture till then unknown by any of his contemporaries.

In Michelangelo was born a spirit as great as that of Phidias. Like the works of the Greek sculptor, his compositions show a grasp of the pictorial. Unlike those of most of his contempo-

Fig. 468.—The Adoration of the Shepherds, by Domenico Ghirlandaio, 1485 (The Academy, Florence). (*Courtesy of Metropolitan Museum of Art.*)

raries, the figures in his pictures show a monumental sculpturesque quality. The young Michelangelo studied anatomy, perhaps for a time with Leonardo, now past fifty. In an artists' brawl with the older man about the placing of his gigantic statue of David, Michelangelo, in 1504, broke with all the members of the conservative artists' guild group and, at the age of twenty-nine, became the leader of the revolutionaries.

Known particularly as a sculptor, Michelangelo engaged in a contest of skill with Leonardo in 1506, drawing a great cartoon, showing a group of bathing soldiers, which was to rival Leonardo's Battle of Anghiari. Having demonstrated in his cartoon that he could draw the nude perfectly, in a scene which lacked the Gothic dramatic quality of Leonardo's work, Michelangelo left Florence for Rome, where he intended to create a monument to Pope Julius, but was turned aside by that pontiff to decorate the ceiling of the Sistine Chapel. To this work he brought a complete knowledge

Fig. 469.—The Creation of Adam, by Michelangelo Buonarroti, portion of ceiling decoration fresco, Sistine Chapel, Rome, 1508–1512. Length of Adam 10 feet. (*Courtesy of Lesch-Carnegie.*)

of the human form seen from every possible position.

In the four great panels of the ceiling, he showed Jehovah's creation of sun and moon,

FIG. 470a.—Madonna of the Chair, by Raphael, c. 1514. Oil on wood, height 24 inches (Pitti Gallery, Florence). (*Courtesy of Lesch-Carnegie.*)

the birth of Adam, the expulsion from Paradise, and the story of Noah; in smaller panels, the creation of the world, the creation of land and sea, the creation of woman, the building of the ark, and the drunkenness of Noah. Around the panels, he created an architectural fantasy, composed of caryatids framing great niched figures of the pagan sibyls and the Christian prophets. In all its richness and profusion of forms (the ceiling shows almost 350 figures, covering a surface of 10,000 square feet), Michelangelo worked like the builder of some Gothic façade, ordering his sermon in a series of geometrical areas. The finest moment of the entire series is concentrated in that sublime creation of the perfect "first man," conceived without sin, touched into life by a generative spark from the hand of God.

The Almighty, swirling in a cloud, floats in from the right, carrying with him the unborn Eve and a host of children still half conceived. Adam rests at the left, perfectly formed, but listless and asleep. The sky vies with the earth for attention, and the hand of Adam droops, waiting to be inspired. The entire composition thus falls into two parts with almost equal

FIG. 470b.—Diagram of Madonna of the Chair.

tension, a truly Gothic conception. The interweave in the lines of the bodies and the folds of the drapery carries the eye from one part of the space to another. Background there is none; the human form dominates all. Here, stripped of all unessentials, appears the Renaissance composition at its most perfect moment.

Raphael's School of Athens and the Renaissance Ideal of Beauty. The school of Athens (Fig. 472), painted by Raphael—an Umbrian who had studied with Perugino—at a time when he was under the influence of Leonardo, shows the final development in the direction of greater spatiality. The young Raphael, a man of remarkable talent and pleasant personality, had a fine feeling for the tenderness of the Madonna (Fig. 470). After working in Florence, where he studied the cartoons of Leonardo and Michelangelo, his compositions gained in power. Appointed to posts of high honor in Rome as court architect, archaeologist, and painter to the pope, he received a particular commission in 1511 at the age of twenty-eight, to paint a number of the Vatican rooms. In the Stanza della Segnatura, or Chamber of the Signatures —so called because the indulgences were sealed here in the presence of the pope—Raphael

tion of the picture remains that of the medieval sketch in the Utrecht Psalter (Fig. 308, Chap. XII).

Opposite The Dispute, Raphael painted The

Fig. 471.—The Dispute concerning the Sacrament, by Raphael, fresco, Vatican 1509–1511. Figures about life size. (*Courtesy of Lesch-Carnegie.*)

painted four great scenes which showed in allegorical form the ideal realms recognized by the church.

In the picture called The Dispute (Fig. 471), all the religious leaders and heroes of faith combined to affirm the real presence of Christ in the Host placed upon the altar. Above it, the heavens open, showing Christ throned in the center, flanked by the Virgin and John the Baptist, and by saints of the Old Testament and the New. God the Father stands above the Christ, with the dove, symbol of the Holy Spirit, coming toward the Host, as an intermediary. Among the holy men around the altar below, one may recognize Dante and the painter Fra Angelico. Essentially the composi-

School of Athens (Fig. 472), where were united in a Platonic manner philosophy and science as taught by the great humanist Marsilius Ficinus. The subject of the picture was already an old one. Throughout the Middle Ages cathedral sculpture had shown the seven liberal arts as allegorical figures of the historical personages who were supposed to have excelled in each field. Mathematics, for example, was always represented by a figure of Pythagoras; dialectic, by Aristotle; music, usually by David; and so on. Raphael brought together the philosophers, scientists, and teachers in one dramatic moment, in an expansive, skillfully drawn temple hall suggestive of the new St. Peter's, then being built. He framed within the arch at the rear the two greatest philosophers, Plato and Aristotle. Plato stands with hand upraised, the forefinger pointing up the side of the arch, which in its curve encloses Aristotle, much as and so dramatically arranged that no inconsistency exists between the implied thought and the expressed action. Though all lines lead obviously to the two men in the center, even

Fig. 472.—The School of Athens, by Raphael, fresco, Vatican, 1509–1511. Figures about life size. Note similarity of sculptured Apollo in left niche to Michelangelo's Slave (Fig. 488). (*Courtesy of Lesch-Carnegie.*)

though the Platonic vision of unity surpassed the Aristotelian science. Socrates stands to the left of Plato, and the half-nude Diogenes lies upon the steps. In the foreground are grouped the exponents of the sciences based upon philosophy; on the right, the geometricians and astronomers; to the left, musicians, arithmeticians, and grammarians. In the far corner of the picture, at the right, Raphael depicted himself next to his friend Sodoma.

In this picture appears for the first time a mastery of realistic mural composition based upon and uniting all the discoveries of Leonardo and Michelangelo. Now, truly, we have left the Middle Ages and are in the high Renaissance. All parts are so appropriately spaced

the outermost parts of the picture have interest. The figures are garbed either in contemporary costumes or in ancient Roman togas, archaeologically correct. The vision of the great arched hall is that of the Pantheon, or one of the Roman baths, which Raphael, as an archaeologist, had explored. The very placing of the large statues suggests ancient Rome revived in the mind of the archaeologist painter.

Raphael's School of Athens has become the ideal example of mural painting followed by the academic tradition from the 16th century to our own day. It looks modern and correct to us, because it has the humanistic architecture and the classical costumes that we have come to associate with antiquity. How unlike it really is to the actuality of Athenian life can be seen by comparing it with the sculptures of Phidias or Greek vase paintings. The Greeks had no concept of spaciousness, and the Romans fum-

FIG. 473.—Madonna of the Harpies, by Andrea del Sarto, 1517. Oil on wood, height 6 feet 10 inches (Uffizi, Florence). (*Courtesy of Lesch-Carnegie.*)

bled the subject in their Pompeian paintings. Nor did the northerners succeed in giving a feeling of interior grandeur to buildings in their paintings. It remained for Raphael to bring the vast expanse of the Roman bath into proper relationship with men who dominated it by reason of their superior intelligence and mathematical reasoning. The sight lines of the perspective unite at a point exactly between the hands of Aristotle and Plato. Diogenes rests on one of these; the figure in the left foreground, on the other. The entire picture may be broken up into groups of mathematically designed areas. This geometrical regularity gives the composition strength and static unity.

Andrea del Sarto's Madonna of the Harpies and the Late Florentine Union of Color and Form. The difficulty in demonstrating by means of black-and-white reproductions the interrelationship

between color and form in Florentine painting has made it impossible up to this point to do more than call attention to a few of the peculiarities of the masters. In general, the painters of the Florentine school were not great colorists in the sense of the Flemish Van Eyck (Fig. 391, Chap. XIII) or the Venetian Giorgione. They sought first to gain verisimilitude by a careful study of the effects of light upon rounded surfaces. Few had the insight of Leonardo to determine that colors actually had a different chroma in high light and deep shadow. Shadows were black, and high lights were white; in between was a simple mass of red or blue. Botticelli affected pale greens, grays, blues, and yellows; Michelangelo used large-toned areas of red and blue without particular regard for the juxtaposition of unpleasant color combinations. These men were essentially sculptors and draftsmen, conceiving in terms of line and form.

The richer Gothic color schemes of Uccello and Leonardo unite in the work of Andrea del Sarto, a painter who lived between 1486 and 1531—Browning's "perfect painter." Andrea's color schemes closely approximate those of Giorgione, the Venetian master (Fig. 478). His fine balance of color areas is perceptible even in the colorless illustration. His work also shows excellent atmospheric perspective and knowledge of modeling. Andrea enjoyed simple, refined, closed compositions, such as that of the Madonna of the Harpies (Fig. 473), in which the central figure, the Madonna, standing upon a pedestal decorated with harpies, is upheld by two cherubim. Two saints, one on each side, by their devout attitudes and the appeal in their eyes subtly direct attention to the central figures. All seem natural in their motions, and the result is a sweet invitation to partake in the worship of this glorified woman, whose face is more nearly akin to that of the naturalistic Cecilia in Leonardo's Virgin of the Rocks than it is to the face of his idealized Madonna.

As the Renaissance advanced, the ideal creations of the Middle Ages were gradually replaced by a worship of a very human womanhood. The monumental quality in the works of Leonardo da Vinci and Michelangelo gave way to a genre quality similar to that which dominated at the end of the Greek development in sculpture. In every culture cycle the gods become first human and then, in time, all too human, the final phase of the development resulting in a completely naturalistic point of view.

The Development of Color in the School of Venice. The intense individuality of the various Italian city-states led to the formation of local schools of painting, each of which can be distinguished by positive characteristics. The hill towns of Umbria had a number of painters who specialized in atmospheric perspective, a phenomenon more easily studied amid vistas of mountains and hills. Lombardy, with its long purple plains and distant mountains, developed rich coloring; Florence, with its perpetual dusty haze and dark, cool, Romanesque interiors, a greenish-brown tone; and Siena, ecclesiastical to the end of the Renaissance, retained the gold Byzantine backgrounds of its medieval painters. Venice, the mistress of the seas, building her marble palaces along the shores of Adriatic lagoons, early took to sail painting, her gaily decorated galleons furnishing the first mural canvases on which Titian, Tintoretto, and a host of 16th-century painters in the sunset of her glory, were to compose with golden tones gigantic histories of her splendid past.

Other factors besides sail painting had to do with the Venetians' love of color. Next to stained glass, mosaic ranks as the most colorful of the mural arts. Fresco painting never weathers well in the salty air of the seaside. Venetian artists were steeped in a tradition of tiny, colorful tesserae, fusing with golden backgrounds to make a limpid, sparkling picture. Naturally, when from Flanders the art of painting with oil and varnishes was brought south to them, the Venetians strove to approximate in their painting the color schemes of their mosaics. These three components constitute the background of the Venetian technique: painting on canvas, mosaic color schemes, and an early acceptance of the invention of that other maritime people, the Flemings.

The Workshop of the Bellinis and a Portrait of

Fig. 474.—Portrait of Doge Leonardo Loredano, by Giovanni Bellini, c. 1505. Oil on wood, height 2 feet (National Gallery, London). (*Courtesy of Lesch-Carnegie.*)

Doge Loredano. At the beginning of the 15th century, there was born in Venice a magnificent character, Jacopo Bellini, who became the head of the most famous of the Venetian *botteghe.* This founder of a great artist family influenced the work of his son-in-law, the Paduan painter, Andrea Mantegna; his contemporary, Antonio Vivarini, the founder of another great artist family; and his two sons, Gentile and Giovanni. The products of these last must be considered as the flowering of a rich tree. Their paintings represent the mature result of a long tradition, developed in one homelike workshop.

The portrait of Doge Loredano (Fig. 474) by Giovanni Bellini, one of the most significant products of the painter's art, demonstrates the fine sense of composition, the mellow tone, and

FIG. 475.—St. James Led to Execution, by Andrea Mantegna, fresco, Church of the Eremitani, Padua, 1454–1459. Figures about life size. (*Courtesy of Lesch-Carnegie.*)

the mastery of tactile values characteristic of this school. The gold-green background of the picture suggests the emerald waters of Venice. Hence in this small panel, a character symbolic of the republic emerges, simple, yet magnificent. As in every great portrait, the significance lies in the relationship between the eyes and the mouth. The underlying form of the rich Venetian brocaded jacket leads the vision toward the head. Then, the curved line of the front of the cap, framing the brow, suggests an enclosure of the deep-set, almost hypnotic eyes. The left side of the doge's face appears firm; the right side seems to smile. The modeling of the muscle forms in the face, done with an infinite number of delicate brush strokes, brings the mass out of the darkness in the shadowy

right. Color grows in intensity as one approaches the place where the plane of any one form rounds over into the light. This effect is termed "modeling in color."

The Bellinis discovered that reflex lights cast by objects outside the picture might even throw color into the shadows. In the drapery of some of Giovanni's Madonnas, one even finds the technique known as "pointillism." This consists of placing tiny spots of color next to one another so that at some distance from the canvas they appear to blend, giving a third color. Red and blue, for example, at some distance give purple. This technique, discovered by 13th-century Gothic glass painters of France, contrary to opinion, never influenced mosaic makers to any great extent. The Bellinis seem to have rediscovered the technique. They used it sparingly, however, and unlike the 19th-century French Impressionists, did not make it the specialty of an entire school.

Throughout his life, Giovanni Bellini, like his father and brother, specialized in sacred pictures. As he grew older, his Madonnas lost their ecclesiastical framework, and became more human. In his old age, touched by the humanism of his contemporaries, Giovanni produced the pagan Bacchanal of the Gods, now in the Widener Collection in Philadelphia. With its deep expanse of romantic landscape and its happy company of picnicking deities, mostly dressed in contemporary Venetian costume, the Bacchanal represents the first of a long line of Arcadian pictures, best known of which is Giorgione's Concert in the Fields.

Mantegna's Classical Realism. Andrea Mantegna, the son-in-law of Jacopo Bellini, exemplifies a large number of Renaissance painters influenced by humanistic archaeological research. In Padua, where the scholars of the university delighted in allegories and the solution of mathematical problems, one finds a center for monumental mural painting glorifying antiquity in the most realistic fashion. In the chapel of the Church of the Hermits, Mantegna painted a series of frescoes showing the lives of St. James and St. Christopher (Fig. 475). Richly decorated, quasi-Roman architecture fills the background of these pictures, though many of the details are of Renaissance

tions of churches and rooms appear more spacious. Thus, it contributed much to the baroque style of painting, which followed.

We notice in the St. James picture the use of

FIG. 476.—The Battle of Tritons, etching by Mantegna, height about 12⅞ inches. Note the medieval figure of Envy, holding her sign over the fighting sea gods on their hippocampi, and the Roman statue of Neptune with his dolphin in the background. All these figures were used by the Paduan bronze sculptors of the late 15th century. (*Courtesy of Lesch-Carnegie.*)

invention. The frieze of human figures carved upon the cavetto molding, for example, is quite unclassical, as is the disposition in all free spaces of bits of ornament. The placement of the forms, however, and the correct foreshortening of the figures give a feeling of intense realism.

In these pictures appears for the first time a completely new means for achieving pictorial illusion. The scenes were painted from the angle of the observer as he looked up from below. This point of view became one of the most significant advances in monumental ceiling and wall decoration after the 16th century and played a great part in making the upper sec-

Roman armor. In a series of murals painted in 1492 for the house of the Gonzaga, Mantegna depicted one of Julius Caesar's triumphal processions. In nine compositions painted with tempera upon paper glued to linen, the artist showed warriors, trumpeters, standard-bearers with banner trophies, elephants laden with booty, singers, prisoners, dancers, and finally the victor himself, seated upon his triumphal wagon.

Not contented with his monumental work, which had a relatively limited audience, Mantegna experimented with the etcher's craft (Fig. 476). Discovering that he could bite a copper or steel plate with acid, fill with ink the lines left there, and then print from the plate, the artist made a series of copper etchings, which could be distributed among the humanists of

Fɪɢ. 477.—Fête Champêtre (The Concert in the Fields), by Giorgione, c. 1510? Oil on canvas, height 3 feet 7¼ inches (Louvre Museum). (*Courtesy of Lesch-Carnegie.*)

the city. Mantegna had the help of a Paduan scholar in collecting the material for this, the first modern history illustration. In his quest for realism, Mantegna made accurate studies of human models. Similarly, in his search for historic authenticity, he made painstaking, scholarly researches that would delight a modern motion-picture director.

Giorgione's Concert in the Fields and Composition in Space. Giorgione of Castelfranco (1478–1510), as the result of twelve years of painting and a life filled, so legend tells, with music and the poetry of fortunate love, left behind three or four of the most beautiful pictures painted in the Western world. Like the rare masterpieces of Leonardo da Vinci, these works seem to transcend the limit of the Renaissance, and to reach out into universal stretches of the human imagination.

Giorgione's Concert in the Fields (Fig. 477), now in the Louvre, simplifies and carries further the work of his master, Giovanni Bellini. Two musicians, accompanied by two women— perhaps allegorical figures of the Muses—oc-

cupy a landscape all of whose forms and colors breathe contentment. In a black-and-white illustration, these plump Venetian versions of classical characters may seem a bit too heavy for 20th-century taste, but as seen in the colored picture the bodies blend with their drapery and the skies' golden tones repeating the distant clouds. The eye quickly passes over the Muses and centers on the two faces of the friendly musicians; thence, wandering backward to the shepherd in the landscape, the gaze travels into the depth of the picture toward the left, past the houses, and out toward the sea. Though everything in the composition seems haphazard and natural, nothing can be moved from its position without destroying the subtle balance.

In the paintings of Giorgione, we see for the first time the composition in depth suggested by Leonardo's sketch (Fig. 462*b*). This new movement of the primitive zigzag into space was to become a chief characteristic of baroque pictorial compositions during and after the 16th century. To appreciate its effect more fully, one must turn to Giorgione's composition of The Three Philosophers (Fig. 478).

Giorgione's Three Philosophers as a Union of Spirit and Form. In the year 1504, shortly after Leonardo da Vinci had reached Venice, Giorgione painted the picture called The Three Philosophers. Like most of his paintings, the canvas has a geometric plan. A diagonal from the upper right to the lower left separates the human from the natural elements. The young philosopher, a man of Giorgione's own age, gazes intently into a cave. The old man, carrying a manuscript suggestive of pages from Leonardo's notebooks, seems of about the age of that older artist who was in Venice at the time. He too looks with penetrating gaze into the cave; but the Oriental, the Turk, with his richly embroidered robe and his turban, looks away from nature, perhaps in resignation because her secrets, although they may be mathematically demonstrated, can never be intimately known.

The details of the foreground are simple but

suggestive. The trees appear as a few trunks and leaves, only one tree being completely drawn. Beyond the silhouette of these trees, the landscape, too, is simple and symbolic: three

of the Bellini workshop, Titian Vecellio, came from the Alps of Pieve di Cadore north of Venice. Born about 1477, he lived on until 1576, painting magnificent canvases even after

FIG. 478.—The Three Philosophers, by Giorgione, c. 1504. Oil on canvas, height 4 feet (Kunsthistorisches Museum, Vienna). Here the symbolism of the landscape and of man appears in almost equal balance. The three philosophers at the right by the richness of their colors—red, green, gold, and blue—form an occult balance with the shadowy brown cavern and the opalescent distance. (*Courtesy of Lesch-Carnegie.*)

roofs, a few trees, a field, and distant hills; above, the setting sun, some lavender clouds, and a cerulean blue sky. So simple a work as this speaks for itself in such a way that there is no need to point out more than a few salient characteristics. This masterpiece has such power to stimulate the imagination that the associational patterns it generates would fill a volume.

The Development of Space Expression in Titian's Madonna Pesaro. The second great apprentice

the age of ninety. A pupil of Giovanni Bellini, during his youth Titian rivaled Giorgione, and he lived far into the time of the baroque masters Tintoretto and Paolo Veronese. In his long life, Titian grew through and mastered all the stages of painting discussed in this chapter so far. All unite in his picture (Fig. 479) painted for the Pesaro family in 1526.

In this picture, Titian abandoned the usual symmetrical composition inherited from Bellini and turned toward the composition in occult balance, using the geometric zigzag in space, which was to dominate the baroque. Following Mantegna, Titian, having mastered perspec-

Fig. 479.—Madonna of the Pesaro family, by Titian, Church of the Frari, Venice, 1519–1526. Oil on canvas, height 16 feet 1 inch. (*Courtesy of Lesch-Carnegie.*)

tive, experimented with various eye levels. In the Madonna Pesaro he discovered one relatively low, so that the spectator stands about on a level with the youth gazing out of the corner of the picture at the lower right. Hence, the Madonna, throned high above, seems still to be within earthly reach; and the monumental figure of St. Peter, with his billowing drapery, seems a true natural intercessor between the members of the Pesaro family, who kneel before the altar, and the heavenly regions above. Heaven, suggested by the cross carried off above the clouds, connects with earth through the massive columns of the temple

leading down to St. Peter and the Madonna. The figures of the family are all subservient to the massive sculptural group of the saints and the Madonna, the columns and the sky. Thus, designedly, the eye is asked to choose between the beautiful human elements and the sublime natural elements. The dual meaning of much later European painting lies in this— that man tries to suggest not only Beauty but the Sublime, and that one is asked to choose between them.

Sculpture

Like the master painters, the great sculptors of the Renaissance, in most cases men skilled in pictorial composition and the making of fine jewelry, display through their works characters divided in allegiance between Gothic and Classical ideals. Their discoveries in form parallel the discoveries in painting. They strove for the same realism, the same mastery of perspective, and even for the illusion of tactile values in their handling of flesh and draperies. The strong geometric basis of design inherited from classical antiquity, and the Celtic interweave of forms expressive of inner dynamic tensions, bind together the more superficial surface motifs.

Gothic and Classical Elements in the Competition Panels of Ghiberti and Brunelleschi. During the years 1401 and 1402, the art world of Florence seethed with excitement over a competition to determine the sculptor who should design the second door for the Baptistery. An earlier Gothic door had been made by Andrea Pisano. Lorenzo Ghiberti, Filippo Brunelleschi, and five other sculptors, the best of Florence and Siena, entered the competition, having been given a year to demonstrate their ability in a plaque showing the offering of Abraham. The two panels of the contestants who tied for first place hang today in the Bargello at Florence. Together they offer a lively demonstration of the Gothic and Classical modes in Florentine sculpture.

Brunelleschi's panel (Fig. 480a) is far richer in dramatic moments, better composed in space, and more lively than that of Ghiberti. The part to which all action lines inevitably lead cate rinceau design of the altar, show a greater interest in surface. Brunelleschi, throughout his life, displayed all the qualities of the Renaissance virtuoso, turning from this panel to

FIG. 480.—The competition panels, Sacrifice of Isaac, 1402. Bronze, height 18 inches (Bargello, Florence). a, Filippo Brunelleschi; b, Lorenzo Ghiberti. (*Courtesy of Lesch-Carnegie.*)

is that section where the hand of the angel and the hand of the father with his knife at the throat of the boy, form a spiraling whirlpool of action. Below the altar, with its relief scene of a Roman sacrifice, Brunelleschi, who was an archaeologist, placed a copy of the famous Greco-Roman Spinario (Fig. 221b, Chap. IX) and a servant feeding a donkey. The Spinario differs from the actual classical original in having the same dynamic quality as the figure of Abraham.

In contrast to Brunelleschi's panel, the one by Ghiberti (Fig. 480b) seems more sculpturesque in conception. The figures move in gentler classical fashion, in accordance with the concept of beauty. The pattern does not fill the spaces so well as that of Brunelleschi, but the details, such as the embroidery on the robes, the hair of man and beast, and the deli-

painting, from painting to architecture and humanistic archaeological studies. In sculpture, the 15th-century Florentines preferred a little less drama, a little more honest craftsmanship. In the 16th century, Brunelleschi, because of his more aggressive personality, might have procured the entire commission.

Between 1403 and 1424, Ghiberti worked upon the reliefs, eventually perfecting twenty panels showing the life of Christ, with eight single figures of evangelists and Church Fathers. Although these doors followed the earlier model made by Andrea Pisano, in size and in general design, the representations being set in Gothic frames, the single figures show the late classical Praxitelean curves, and the draperies fall in classical fashion. Ghiberti's reliefs are much higher than the fow Greco-Roman sarcophagi or triumphal arches, which were composed com-

FIG. 481.—Ghiberti's Old Testament doors, bronze, east side of Baptistery, Florence, 1425–1452. Height of door valve 16½ feet. (*Courtesy of Lesch-Carnegie.*)

pletely around the human figure. Here, as in the picture by Giorgione, landscape and human elements nicely balance each other.

Ghiberti's Paragon—The Gates of Paradise. Ghiberti's completion of his commission after twenty years of work so pleased the Florentine guilds that he was asked to design the third, or central, portal of the Baptistery—that one which faced the cathedral. The many letters of leading humanists and scholars, prescribing the subject matter of the final doors, and the care with which these critics insisted that the scenes should be easily understood and of great educational value, seem strange to the 20th-century mind, which somehow imagines that great works of art arise only in the inspired mind of the artist. In none of the letters is the name of the artist so much as mentioned.

The doors, called by Michelangelo the "Gates of Paradise" (Fig. 481), still covered with the original gold leaf beneath their layer of grime, are framed by a border of garlands and fruit clusters issuing from vases at the base, and populated by a host of birds and beasts. Thus, the tree of life, fruitful, mounts on each side to meet and culminate in an eagle, symbol of St. John. Ten rectangular relief panels, framed by niches, with portraits, graces, and saints, tell the story of the Old Testament, beginning with the creation of the original parents and ending with the visit of the Queen of Sheba to Solomon. The panels throughout leave the monumental compositional form in Ghiberti's original competition panel, and take instead the pictorial composition perfected by Masaccio. They are Gothic only in their repetition of certain figures. Adam and Eve, for example, appear four times in the first panel; Noah, three times in the second. In other words, the ideology of Ghiberti's doors is in every point similar to that of the great northern Gothic cathedral sculpture. The style alone differs, this Renaissance classical style coming to its full fruition in Florence fifty years before the Gothic architect, John Texier, perfected his

late Gothic ambulatory screen in Chartres Cathedral.

The advances in linear perspective made by Ghiberti antedate the geometric experiments

FIG. 482.—St. George, by Donatello, from niche in Or San Michele, 1416. Marble, about 7 feet (Bargello, Florence). (*Courtesy of Metropolitan Museum of Art.*)

FIG. 483.—St. John the Baptist, by Donatello, c. 1430? Terra-cotta bust, colored, height about 18 inches (Berlin Museum). (*Courtesy of Clarence Kennedy.*)

of Uccello and constitute a treatise on perspective which must have been studied by many generations of Florentine painters, including Leonardo and Michelangelo. Both of them copied figure motifs and compositional schemes from these panels. As late as the time of Benvenuto Cellini, in the 16th century, passages inspired by these doors appear in the work of minor Florentine sculptors. Ghiberti, more than any other man in the Renaissance, was the father of the entire Florentine School.

The Realism of Donatello in the Statue of St. George. The works of Donatello, an apprentice of Ghiberti and a friend of Brunelleschi, present clearly the qualities that characterize Renaissance monumental sculpture. Donatello's works combine the attributes of Ghiberti's and Brunelleschi's panels in single figures and faces. The movement of the spirit within the limbs, showing itself by the actions of the body or under the surface modeling of the face, differentiates Renaissance sculpture from its classical antecedents, which, at first glance, it most closely resembles.

Throughout his life, Donatello's works never lost a certain archaic, geometric stiffness, such as that to be seen in his statue of St. George (Fig. 482). It was carved to fill a niche on the church Or San Michele, but the original statue was later removed to the National Museum of the Bargello. St. George stands, a knight in medieval armor, poised as though just about to step out into the struggle against evil which his intense gaze discovers in the distance. The large, simple form, the closed silhouette of the robe, the position of the right arm fastened to the shield, and a powerful counterpoint of massive forms, all lend impressive dignity to the body, which is a realistic study of some Florentine butcher boy. The slightly naïve way in which this piece combines the powerful and fortuitous suggests that moment of fresh vigor when a new art movement is born.

The Mature Style of Donatello in the Head of the Youthful John the Baptist. Turning from the early style of the master to a terra cotta of John the Baptist in the Berlin Museum (Fig. 483), one finds intense realism animated by a nervous energy. The sculptor emphasized those muscles and sinews which show the greatest spiritual activity. Not contented with this careful study of underlying form, Donatello broke up the greater planes of the face into a number of small indentations. Here are repeated with much greater refinement the phenomena observed in the early works of the ancient Etruscan sculptors (Fig. 226, Chap. X). Contrasting with the realism of the facial modeling, the swirling, vigorous locks of hair seem animated by an inner life of their own. This nervous, sensitive, high-strung youth, just about to speak, prophesies the coming of a Michelangelo and a Leonardo. The painting of the bust, by no means realistic, heightens the effect of its other artistic forms. Art does not copy nature here but concentrates in one face the attributes that signify youthfulness.

The Place of Sculpture as Architectural Decoration in the Singing Gallery by Luca della Robbia. Florentine sculpture, dynamic or severe, had its more tender moments. Contemporaneous with Donatello and Ghiberti, the *bottega* of the Della Robbias produced many reliefs in glazed terra cotta and marble. These showed a gentle, friendly spirit, contrasting with the fiercer work of Donatello. Between 1431 and 1438, Luca was engaged to build a singing gallery for the sacristy of the cathedral. With much the spirit of the ancient Greeks, Luca carved eight reliefs set in a framework of classical borders. The result is one of the most refined monuments of the Renaissance.

Each panel (Fig. 484), given over to a type of music or dance, expresses one element in the psalm carved in a Renaissance version of Roman letters on the three chief horizontal members. The fine spacing of these letters, as well as their well-conceived design, finds an echo in the proportions and placement of the figures in each panel. Comparing these panels with the Parthenon metopes, one discerns in them an atmospheric depth unknown to the Greeks, and a correctness of relief perspective far beyond that of the Romans. Each relief stands by itself. The Parthenon metopes suggested a continuation from panel to panel; here there is

Baptism of Christ, the David probably resulted from the communal activities of a number of people. In its awkward, boyish counterpoise imbued with the Gothic spirit of realism, one

Fig. 484.—Cantoria or Singing Gallery, by Luca della Robbia, 1431–1438. Marble, height about 12½ feet (Museum of the Cathedral, Florence).

less of a communal spirit. Although the people shown are animated by one type of happy music, they do not sing together. Only the delicacy with which the individual parts are modeled makes this a consistent creation. We do not mind the display of virtuosity, because the panels are small enough to be bound together by their heavy framework. Thus, in the end, proportion must always be the measurement of beauty.

Verrocchio's David and the Refinement of Realism. No great work of sculpture had come from the workshop of Verrocchio before Leonardo da Vinci entered it as an apprentice. How much of Verrocchio's David (Fig. 485) stems from terra-cotta sketches by Leonardo and how much from the master, who was seventeen years his senior, we cannot know. Like Verrocchio's

finds a further development of the tendency started in Donatello's statue of St. George.

In all Renaissance sculpture, one feels that the figure stands for a moment at rest just before taking action. In this case, as the head of Goliath indicates below, the moment of action has just passed, but the youthful David looks around for more giants to conquer. The awkwardness of the arms, the left one akimbo, denotes a certain strain that sets the nerves on edge. The veins and sinews of the right arm, with the sword in hand, suggest inner strength. The face and the hair display those characteristics discussed in connection with Donatello's St. John.

The Sculptural Style of Leonardo da Vinci. Leonardo da Vinci, in his book on painting, gives very definite recipes for carrying on the sculptor's art. He preferred work in terra cotta or bronze to the more dusty profession of the marble carver. Starting timidly in his youth, with Madonnas so poorly rendered that American

drawn. This illustration shows a section of such a model, part of a group consisting of a mounted knight battling with four foot soldiers, probably made as a study for the Battle of Anghiari.

FIG. 485.—David, by Andrea Verrocchio, c. 1465. Bronze, height 4 feet (Bargello, Florence). (*Courtesy of Lesch-Carnegie.*)

FIG. 486.—Sketch model for Battle of Anghiari, by Leonardo da Vinci, c. 1504. Terra cotta painted to simulate bronze, height about 18 inches (Camondo Collection, Louvre Museum).

art-school students quickly surpass them, Leonardo slowly perfected his sculptural style in right medieval fashion, growing in it much as Ghiberti had grown during the forty years in which he worked on the Baptistery doors.

The mastery of form in terra cotta acquired by Leonardo before his fiftieth year is evident in Fig. 486. To this artist, sculpture seems to have served as a means for perfecting his painting. He writes of the practice invented by his master, Verrocchio, of making a model from which studies in light and shade could be

Notice particularly the armor on the legs, the veins and the line of drapery on the right arm, and the spiral of the helmet. The virtuosity of the master is shown by the skill with which, in a few quick strokes, he indicated the toes of the rider and the mane of the horse.

This sculpture differs significantly from the work of Donatello and from that of Michelangelo. In this piece pictorial content and linear interweave—the desire for an interesting pattern of light and shade—dominate surface form. Leonardo's knowledge of anatomy was so great that he had difficulty in eliminating details. Such sculpture as this was to become the style

FIG. 487.—Moses, by Michelangelo, 1512–1516. Marble, height about 7½ feet (San Pietro in Vincoli, Rome). (*Photograph by Alinari.*)

during the baroque period. To that extent, then, Leonardo contributed to the later Renaissance art.

Michelangelo's Moses as the Fullest Achievement

FIG. 488.—Bound Slave, by Michelangelo, from the unfinished tomb of Julius II. Marble, about 10 feet (Louvre Museum). (*Photograph by Alinari.*)

of Renaissance Form. In seeking one monument that will epitomize Renaissance sculpture, one cannot avoid a consideration of Michelangelo's figure of Moses in marble (Fig. 487). This idealized portrait of Pope Julius II, was to have been the spiritual center of his great grave monument, never completed. Into a mountain of marble, quarried at Carrara hundreds of miles away and carried to the banks of the Tiber, Michelangelo proposed to carve a two-storied tomb, with niches holding eight allegorical Victories, separated by sixteen pillars of Bound Slaves, or Prisoners. On the corners of the platform, over a cornice capping the

first story, were to be four colossal seated figures —Moses, Paul, and two women, representing active and contemplative life. An oval temple, girt with bronze reliefs, was to mount above

FIG. 489.—Mask from the Night, by Michelangelo, from the Tomb of Giuliano de' Medici, New Sacristy, San Lorenzo, Florence, 1523–1533. Marble, about 12 inches. (*Courtesy of Paul La Porte.*)

these, capped by a sarcophagus bearing the figure of the dead pope held by two forms symbolizing heaven and earth. Altogether, there were to have been forty statues in this enormous pile. The grandeur of the concept may be imagined from the one figure of Moses and from a number of figures of the slaves, now in Florence and the Louvre (Fig. 488).

The heroic Moses, in most respects like the fierce pope to be commemorated, seems ready to spring from his seat. The energy concentrated in the figure flows from the beard and infuses every vein of the powerful hand. The massive planes of the body, broken by the folds of the drapery, compel the attention to move restlessly from part to part. The position of the head, turned alertly toward the left, suggests a quality of distrust which, generating inner fires of hatred, darts forth its passion through fierce eyes that stare from under intense brows. The horns of power fairly spring from the head. Careful study of the details of surface modeling brings realization of the contrast between large forms, such as the powerful shoulder muscles, and the many broken, nervous forms of the lower arms and hands. This movement from comparatively restful surfaces to restless ones marks the entrance of a new dramatic power in sculpture.

Michelangelo combined the methods of Ghiberti and Brunelleschi. In him, the Gothic and the Classical unite. His tender Madonnas symbolize his love of beauty, while his restless figures of Day and Night, on the Medici tombs (Fig. 489), and his tragic Pietà and Entombment spring from the ascetic elements of his nature. These two forces struggling within him, as earlier demonstrated by his sonnets, generated the statue of Moses.

Architecture

The concept of the Renaissance as a rebirth of motifs from classical antiquity is more apparent in the architecture of the 14th and 15th centuries than in any other art of the period. With the growth of humanism, antiquarians encouraged the artists to copy details from the ruins of Rome. Gradually cornices, capitals, pilasters, and small bits of antique decoration crept into the Tuscan Romanesque style, or lightened the fortresslike exteriors of Florentine palaces, with their heavy rustication of massive stone blocks.[1]

Of no less importance than the gradual introduction of antique details during the 15th century was a growing recognition of the beauty of proportion and harmony of masses to be gained by studying Roman arches and temples. The feeling for rhythmical spacing of masses, demonstrated by the singing gallery of Della Robbia, combined with a refined use of details appropriately placed, accounts for much of the charm of Renaissance architecture.

The antique originals, in many cases, served only to stimulate the fertile masters toward the creation of new, less organic forms from the older Ionic and Corinthian capitals. Renaissance architects experimented much with moldings, arguing among themselves at great length as to whether a crown molding looked better, designed simply as the termination of the highest story, or as a harmonious part of the whole façade. The desire for a well-designed front ruled almost every other consideration, the basilican churches of Italy allowing for little interest in the treatment of side or rear. One weakness of Renaissance architecture, from a 20th-century point of view, is its very lack of functional character. Its interest is concentrated in the pictorial treatment of the façade or in the decoration of nave and apse.

The Rucellai Palace and Alberti's Revival of the Orders. Between 1446 and 1451, the scholar and architect Alberti designed a palace for Giovanni Rucellai. The façade of this palace (Fig. 490) demonstrates the new arrangement of the orders on the surface of a rusticated three-story building. The horizontal design of the rustication is broken by the vertical lines of three sets of pilasters, bound together by moldings, friezes, and a great ornamental cornice. This façade offers one of the most pleasing combinations of the antique and the Etruscan fortress style to be found. The great stone seats for men-at-arms outside the two entrance portals connect the façade with the ground, their heavy shadows balancing the upper cornice. The square windows of the lower story, high and barred of necessity, because of the feuds which at times converted this palace into a refuge, have heavy moldings. As the lower story was most likely

[1] The word "rustication" denotes simply that the great building stones were left rough on the outside, and their monolithic character stressed by showing heavy, cut joints.

to be damaged, all its details are kept simple. Details of the second story, in contrast, are lighter and more decorative. The continuation of the pilaster lines, strong enough to break

FIG. 490.—Rucellai Palace, by Leon Battista Alberti, Florence, 1446–1451. Stone façade, width 75 feet, height 69 feet. (*Courtesy of Lesch-Carnegie.*)

through the frieze moldings, helps to support the heavy cornice line. Thus, there is a suggestion of functionalism, which is repeated inside the palace, in the courtyard, with its triple row of delicate columns, one upon the other.

The disposition of rooms around the balconies of the central court is simple. Stables and servants' quarters occupy the ground floor; great rectangular dining and living rooms, the second; and bedrooms, the third. Above this, the roof has a loggia cooled by breezes and used as a pleasant porch on hot summer days. In general, the plan of the house follows that of the ancient city house studied at Pompeii.

San Lorenzo of Florence as a Typical Renaissance Church. Brunelleschi, turning from his misadventure in sculpture, completed the great dome

for the cathedral at Florence, which dominates the entire city. After studying not only the mechanics of antique building but also its proportions and details, Brunelleschi left behind

FIG. 491.—Interior, San Lorenzo, Florence, by Brunelleschi and Manetti, 1425–1461. Width 95 feet, height about 70 feet. (*Photograph by Alinari.*)

him, in the nave of the church of San Lorenzo, the most significant early Renaissance interior (Fig. 491). When the old basilican church was renovated through the generosity of Cosimo de' Medici, Brunelleschi redecorated the choir. This he planned to extend twice as high as its square ground plan. After his death in 1446, his sketches were followed carefully by his pupil Manetti in decorating the nave.

The tall, slender arches of the nave rest upon Corinthian columns with unbroken shafts. The introduction of a high impost block, consisting of the three members of architrave, frieze, and cornice from the antique Corinthian order, not only heightens the column but helps to make a satisfactory transition from the circular shaft to the square from which the arch springs. All surfaces of the impost blocks, arcade arches, and capitals are richly decorated with ornaments in the antique manner, not copied, however, from the antique, but designed directly from garlands and oak wreaths by the man who had once been a jeweler.

The dark chapels, beyond the side aisles, raised three steps, seem like so many extra entrances to the well-ordered aisles and nave. The thinness of the nave wall, the relative stability of the outer chapels, and the arching of the aisles, with their round clerestory windows,

copied entire Roman arches, as in the case of San Francesco in Rimini. His dome in the Church of St. Andrea in Mantua, seen from within, is likewise noted for its excellence. Bra-

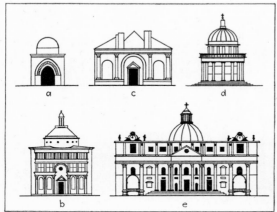

FIG. 492.—Experiments with the dome and façade. *a*, Saracenic dome, The Zisa, Sicily; *b*, Pazzi Chapel, by Brunelleschi, 1429, brick and marble, width 59 feet 9 inches, height about 90 feet; *c*, façade of San Francesco, Rimini, by Alberti, 1446–1455, marble over brick, length about 120 feet; *d*, Tempietto, San Pietro in Montorio, Rome, by Bramante, 1502, stone with granite columns, diameter 20 feet; *e*, St. Peter's as it appears today; *f*, St. Peter's, Michelangelo's conception, 1546–1564, height 450 feet (*reconstruction courtesy of K. Conant*). This effect is first fully achieved in the National Capitol at Washington.

all stand in such fine proportion to each other that one feels, in this church, a spirit of beauty as significant in quality as that of the Greeks and transcending any of the heavier, less refined work of the Romans. Only in one instance, that of the temple at Nîmes, did Roman architects reach this refinement, and never, as far as we know, in the interior of any building except the Pantheon, whose proportions and construction Brunelleschi carefully studied.

St. Peter's in Rome—the Problem of Dome and Façade. Two problems in particular interested the ambitious Renaissance architects—that of the façade and that of the dome. For Florence, Brunelleschi constructed, in a tour de force, a dome so large that it dwarfed the nave of the cathedral. In a small chapel of the Pazzi family, on the courtyard of Santa Croce in Florence, he designed a façade that dominated a poorly constructed dome. The two never quite came together. Alberti, noted for his façades, in his attempt to design an appropriate front, even

mante, copying Roman antecedents, built in his Tempietto in Rome—a circular building— an almost perfect exterior dome above a Doric porch, with a balustrade above its cornice. These attempts are shown in Fig. 492*b*, *c*, and *d*.

The attempt to unite dome and façade in a consistent building was made unsuccessfully on one of the greatest structures of the world, the Church of St. Peter in Rome. Its lack of consistency, as we see it today, is due to the conflicting ideas of its successive architects, of whom some believed in the dominance of the dome, others, in the primary importance of the façade.

In the middle of the 15th century, Pope Nicholas V decided to build a new St. Peter's in place of the old basilican church. The architect Bernardo Rossellino began with the restoration of the choir. By 1506, Bramante had drawn a number of plans for Pope Julius II (Fig. 493*a*), most of which indicated a central building crowned with a great dome, above a

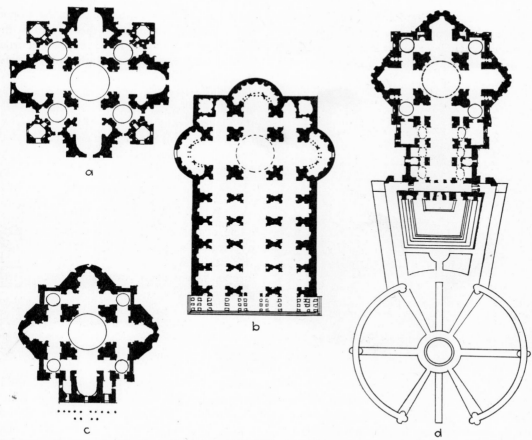

FIG. 493.—Plans for St. Peter's. *a*, Bramante, 1506–1513; *b*, Raphael, 1513–1520; *c*, Michelangelo, 1547–1564; *d*, finished, 1506–1667.

Greek cross with four smaller domes and semi-domes. Raphael, following Bramante, suggested a nave before the dome (Fig. 493*b*). Michelangelo, taking over the work in 1547, strove to finish the church in a form close to that suggested by Bramante (Fig. 493*c*). Still other architects following Michelangelo gave the church its present form, in which a mighty façade, placed at the front of the nave, obscures the magnificent dome completed by Michelangelo (Fig. 493*d*). The church as it would have looked if his intentions had been followed out can be seen in the drawing (Fig. 492*f*); the church as it looks today, in the small illustration (Fig. 492*e*).

A study of the splendid dome, which has become the basis for most great governmental buildings in the Western Hemisphere, can be made from the rear of the church (Fig. 494). From this point one sees the solid drum, surmounted by a clerestory of great windows separated by double columns, each holding a pedestal. On these pedestals Michelangelo planned to erect enormous statues. Each group of columns forms a heavy, bracing buttress. If the statues had been placed above, they would have filled much the same function as do the pinnacles on Gothic flying buttresses. From behind the pilasters, the functional ribs of the dome rise boldly to meet in a lantern far above. The structure of the lantern repeats in miniature the design of the clerestory. Panels with garlands and lions' heads, derived from antique downspouts, act as a frieze above the clerestory level. Jewellike windows open high on the dome between the ribs. Here, in titanic

Fig. 494.—Dome and details, apse, St. Peter's, by Michelangelo, view from the rear. (*Photograph by Alinari*.)

majesty, as though all were conceived by some superhuman mind, appears the same excellence in design and refinement of proportion as that observed earlier in the nave of San Lorenzo.

The Delicacy and Measure of Fra Giocondo's Loggia. The Loggia del Consiglio in Verona (Fig. 495), a civic law court designed by Fra Giocondo, an architect monk of the 15th century, stands as a monument to the civic pride of the Italian Renaissance city. It evidences also the artistic genius of a learned, well-traveled man, whose other buildings may be found scattered widely over Italy and France, far from his native town. The exterior of the loggia displays the same fine proportions as those of the interior of San Lorenzo. The low podium, approached by two flights of steps, forms the basis for a balustraded porch, whose refined arcade supports a lavishly decorated upper story. The decoration, while jewellike in quality, still seems appropriate because of its refine-

ment. The remains of paintings, on the upper walls, call our attention to the fact that the Renaissance architects loved color and that much of the sculptured decoration in the early Renaissance still made use of Gothic coloring. The pilasters of the two stories continue on through the cornice, terminating in pedestals on which stand figures of the chief legal heroes of antiquity. This use of statuary, inaugurated by Fra Giocondo, became very popular with later builders.

Drama

The drama of the Renaissance grew naturally from the mystery plays, miracles, and pageants of the Middle Ages. In the south of Europe, where the humanistic influence was strong, the pageants, with music and extensive scenery, held first place; in the north, emphasis was laid on action and grotesque humor. Since most people associate the Renaissance with Italy, turn first to the Italian origins of the drama.

The Italian Pageants or Sacre Rappresentazioni. In Italian cities, the mystery and miracle plays accompanying church festivals early took on a slightly different tone from those of the northern countries. Stress was laid particularly on the music and the elements of staging. The descent of the dove at Pentecost, for example, accompanied by fireworks, represented an exercise of theatrical ingenuity rather than a drama of psychological import. When the more religious lauds, or *divozione*, took place in the churches, a stage was erected in front of the choir screen, next to the pulpit. The connections with classical antiquity were evident in the disposition of the scenery, for the central part of the stage, comparable to the *scena* in the Roman drama, was flanked by two side rooms with galleries above.

In Florence, an archbishop, Antonino, encouraged the formation of a number of youth fraternities, or brotherhoods, each of which followed the banner of some saint. The boys in these brotherhoods, directed by a choral leader called the *Festajuolo*, staged the *sacre rappresentazioni*, or civic church pageants, each on the day peculiar to its saint. The chief action, contained

sance teemed with plots of dramatic import, many of which furnished northern writers, such as Shakespeare, with their most tragic stories. The novels of Boccaccio and Bandello could be

FIG. 495.—South façade, Loggia del Consiglio, by Fra Giocondo, Verona, 1476–1493. Marble, height about 52 feet. (*Courtesy of Lesch-Carnegie.*)

in a *libretto*, or book, was sung as a recitative with choral interludes by groups of voices, the whole accompanied by the music of viol and lute. The antecedents of this style must have lain in the works of the troubadours.

Among the *sacre rappresentazioni*, the greatest took place in connection with the midsummer feast of St. John in Florence. To announce the feast, twenty-two floats with tableaux were carried by guild members through the city. Not content with the representation of Christian subject matter, the Italians also drew upon classical myths and allegories, one pageant showing the tragedy of Iphigenia, another the story of the Minotaur.

Many explanations have been advanced as to why the Italians, an outspokenly dramatic people, never developed tragedy, in the northern sense. The actual life of the Italian Renais-

used today by motion-picture directors seeking fresh material, but the plot of Romeo and Juliet, narrated by Bandello, is actually too poignant for a stage presentation.

In the tomb scene, for example, Bandello has Romeo take a poison with delayed action, so that Juliet awakens in time to see him alive and then must watch him slowly die. This placing of the dagger in the wound and then twisting it to prolong the agony, so typical of real Italian Renaissance life, does not lend itself to stage presentation. The audience becomes so interested in the realistic detail of the action that it loses the greater emotional value of the play as a whole. In actuality, the Italian's life was too tragic; hence he turned again to comedy, reviving the old Roman theater in the *commedia dell' arte*.

The Birth of the Commedia dell' Arte. With a

world of wit about them, the Italians of the city of Lorenzo de' Medici might have produced great comedies had they not been so influenced by the plays of Plautus and Terence. The chief subject matter of the late Italian comedies derives mainly from these two authors. True, the stories were brought up to date by the mention of contemporaneous historic happenings, but the conventional characters of the Latin stage, furnished with new Italian masks, appeared again. The *miles gloriosus* became the professional captain of a band of mercenaries; the parasite, of the Latin comedy, appeared as the poor courtier dependent upon some prince. Eventually, the simple stories of the mistaken identity of two brothers or the discovery that some poor girl stolen in youth was the daughter of wealthy parents, ran their course, and in the 16th century excited the ridicule of the critics.

The Mandragola of Machiavelli as a Typical Comedy of Manners. From a number of late Latin comic plots and several stories by the *novellieri*, Machiavelli constructed his significant satire, the *Mandragola*. This play shows the complete degeneration of Christian society, and may be called the first modern realistic drama. Machiavelli gave such a clear, anatomical dissection of the morals of his time that the reforming pope, Leo X, who hated the dissolute monks, considered it worthy of his approbation. The Florentine audiences found in this penetrating analysis of their own failings a tremendously amusing spectacle. The play takes its name from a late medieval superstition, that the root of the mandrake, or mandragora, could give its owner power over other people.

The story is that of a young Florentine who desires to win the faithful wife of another. The plot displays a complete reversal of all moral values. The cleverness of a rogue who uses the mandragora to play upon the weaknesses of his fellow men forms the real subject of the comedy. Machiavelli built his comedy upon the false premise that cleverness in achieving one's ends is more important than moral scruples. Considering that his contemporaries included such high-minded men as Leonardo da Vinci, Botticelli, and Michelangelo, we point to the tale not as an accurate picture of the times but as an example of the modern temper of mind called naturalism, which persists in seeing life through splenetic eyes.

Avaricious confessors, wives in whom false pride dominates inner self-respect—to bring together such personality types and others of the sort for the sake of a plausible drama is the artist's privilege. When art becomes divorced from a deep human understanding, or when a love for artistic form or pure aesthetic values dominates use and associational values, there appears, as in the Renaissance, either the dreamlike fantasies of an Ariosto, bordering on the lunatic fringe, or the pessimistic naturalism of a Machiavelli, who seems to delight in his own affirmation that all social values are worthless. From this point of view, the Renaissance may be seen as the beginning of the end of the medieval Christian Era. As yet, no religious substitute has been found.

Music

While significant advances in music (in the 14th and 15th centuries) were coming about in Britain, the Netherlands, and Burgundy, the Italian Renaissance contributed as little to music as to the drama. Something in their nature, perhaps akin to that which made the southern art critics decide that the eye was more valuable than the ear, prevented the Italians from creating masterpieces in music that would attract the same interest as their painting and sculpture. In their church music they held to the Gregorian plain chant long after Northern Europe had accepted the *arsnova*. In connection with their circuslike pageants they used barbaric blaring trumpets and trombones with the drum and fife. In the 13th century the best instruments, as Dante mentions, were those imported from Ireland. The chief contribution of Italian music to later developments came through their secular melodies.

The Songs of the Canzonieri: Madrigals, Caccia, and Ballata. The *canzonieri* (songsters), descendants of the troubadours, brought to the Italian courts and free cities the northern ballads, hunting songs, rounds, and motets, which were danced and sung to the music of lute and viol.

Florence had three *canzonieri* of note—the blind Francesco Landino, who played on the small portable organ, or regal; Johannes de Florentia, famed for his *mandriales* (madrigals); and Ghirardello de Florentia, noted for his hunting songs, which were called *caccia* (catch or chase). The madrigal, a word originally derived from *mandra* (the herd) was a pastoral tune that gradually changed into the love song. Often it was dedicated, as in the case of a very famous two-voiced madrigal written in 1340 by Johannes to "The Sweet Science of Music." The *caccia*, or hunting song, as perfected by Ghirardello was a piece accompanied by the viol in which hunting calls and the barking of dogs can be distinguished. Such a modified catch can be found much later in Haydn's *Seasons*. The Florentines greatly enjoyed the realistic element in music and introduced various animal sounds, along with the calls of the peddlers and town criers. The third type of song, the *ballata*, was a danced *ballade* in three parts, often with prelude, interlude, and postlude. This form developed during the 16th century into the *balletti*—instrumental pieces without words.

The Importance of Venice in the Development of Choral Music. The most important musical centers of Italy during the early 16th century were Venice and Mantua. In the latter city, a printer, Petrucci, invented musical type, by 1498. His great collection of folk songs, printed in 1504, includes many melodies that had been brought to Venice by Netherland composers who had mastered the *arsnova* style, as well as the Italian types mentioned above. Petrucci printed villanelle (rustic songs), *morescas* (Moorish dances), and *frottolas* (carnival songs)—various Italian

forms in which one may recognize most of the dance and ballade types developed first by courtly troubadours and popularized during the Renaissance by the *bourgeoisie*. To these should be added such dances as the pavan, the Paduan, the saltarello, and the calata—the two former slow and stately, the latter, fast and leaping.

A powerful Venetian state church, operating independently of the Roman See, was able to engage the best of northern organists who had mastered the *ars-nova* style. Among them Arcadelt and Adrian Willaert, like the talented Mantuan Gastoldi, employed madrigals and instrumental balletti for choral and organ compositions. Under Willaert, who started teaching in Venice in 1527, there developed a style that carried forward the work of Dunstable with the chord, as will be explained in the following chapter. Zarlino, a native Venetian, the great theoretician of the school, in 1558 composed his treatise *Istituzioni Armoniche*. This incorporated the advances made by his fellow composers. These included a definition of the major and minor scales; the principles of counterpoint; the methods for creating fantasias, which were free fugues above a single theme; and *ricercari*, groups of themes linked in fugal form. Zarlino's textbook for counterpoint was not superseded until the great work of Johann Sebastian Bach. Most of the Venetian development, coming contemporaneously with the magnificent coloristic passages in baroque painting, should properly be considered in the next style period.

The Development of Printing

The most important single invention to arise late in the Middle Ages was the craft of printing. This technique contributed more than any other factor to the formation of the modern world point of view, chiefly because it aided in the dissemination of Italian Renaissance thought throughout Europe during the 16th and 17th centuries. Printing came from varied

libros diuisus e. Ariuus lector. Atq;
ita hut pier veteris legis libri viginti
duo: id e moysi quinq; et .pphar octo:
agio graphox noue. Quamq nonulli
ruth. z cinoch inter agiographa scrip
serut. z hos libros i suo putet numero
supputandos: ac p hoc esse prisce legis
libros vigintiquatuor quos sub nume
ro vigiti quatuor seniox. apocalipsis
iohis inducit. adorantes agnu. et co
ronas suas pstratis vultibz offerete:
stantibz cora quatuor aialibz ocularis
ante et retro id est in preteritu z in futur
respicietibz. et indefessa voce damati
bus. sanctus. scs. scs. dus deus omni
potens. qui erat. z qui est. z qui veturꝰ
est. Hic prologus scripturax quasi ga
leatu principiu. omibz libris quos de
hebreo vertim i latinu conuenire potest:
ut scire valeam quicquid extra hos est.
inter apocrapha ee ponendu. Igitur
sapia q vulgo salomois inscribit. et
iesu filii sirach lib. z iudith. z thobias.
z pastor non sut i canone. Machabeox
pmu libru hebraicu repei. Scds grecꝰ
e: qd ex ipsa phrasy pbari potest. Que
cu ita se habeat: obsecro te lector ne la
borem meu reprehensione estimes anti
quox. In templo dei offert vnusquisq;
qd potest. Alii aurꝰ et argentu et lapi
des pciosos: alii bissu et purpuram z
coccu offerut z iacindu. Nobiscu bene
agitur: si obrulerimꝰ pelles et caprax
pilos. Et tame apls ꝯtemptibiliora
nra magis necessaria iudicat. Unde
et tota illa tabernacli pulchritudo. et
p singlas species ecclie psentis. futureq;
distinctio pellibz tegit z ciliciis: ardore
q; solis. et iniuria ymbriu. ea q viliora
ra sut phibet. Lege ergo pmu samuel.

er malachim meu. Meu inqua meu.
Quicqd eni crebrius verrendo. z emen
dando sollicitius. z didicim z tenuꝰ:
nrim e. Et cu intellexis qd antea nescie
bas. ut interprem me estimato si grat
es: ut parafrasten si ingratus: quanq
michi omino ꝯscius non sim mutasse
me quippiam de hebraica veritate. Certe
si incredulus es. lege grecos codices et
latios. z ꝯfer cu hiis opusculis q nup
emedauimꝰ: z vbicuq; discrepare inter
se videris. interroga queliber hebreox
cui magis accomodare debeas fidem:
et si nostra firmauerit. puto qd eu non
estimes ꝯiectorem: ut i eode loco meu
simul diuinarit. Sed z vos famulas
xpi rogo q dni disputetis pciosissima
fidei mirra vngitis caput: q nequaq
saluatore queritis i sepulchro. quibz
iam ad prem xps ascedit: ut iuxta lacran
tes canes. qui aduersu me rabido ore
deseuiut. et circueut ciuitate. atq; in eo
se doctos arbitrant si aliis detrahat:
oracionum vrax clipeos opponatis.
Ego sciens humilitate mea. illiꝰ semp
sentencie recordabor. Dixi custodiam
vias meas: ut non delinqua i lingua
mea. Posui ori meo custodiam: cu con
sisteret peccator aduersu me. Obmutui
et humiliatꝰ su: z silui de bonis.

Incipit pmꝰ liber regu capitulu pmu

Fuit vir vnus de ra
machaim sophim
de mote ephraim:
et nome eiꝰ helcha
na. filius iheroboa
filii heliu. filii thau
filii suph. efrateus: z habuit duas vx
ores: nome vni anna: et nomen scde
fenenna. Fueruitq; fenenne filii: anne

FIG. 497.—*a*, runes from Frank's casket, 7th century (British Museum); *b*, Lindisfarne Gospels, about A.D. 700; *c*, stained glass, Augsburg, about 1075; *d*, tapestry, Alsace, about 1475 (French Collection, New York); *e*, St. Augustine, Speculum (Ashburnham), about A.D. 680; *f*, Pliny-Jenson, about A.D. 1475.

sources and its antecedents may be traced along the route taken by the technique of paper manufacture from China across Persia to Egypt and Spain, whence, by the 15th century, it reached France, Germany, and Italy.

The earliest printed objects found in Europe were playing cards introduced from Spain to Provence in the 14th century. Blocks with sets of such cards can still be found in some of the museums of southern Tyrol where they were printed contemporaneously with wood blocks showing religious subjects. One of these, a picture of St. Christopher carrying the Christ Child, printed in 1423, has two lines of carved letters at the bottom—perhaps the earliest example of European letter printing.

Whether a fully developed press with movable type was introduced directly from the Orient (such presses are known to have been used in China during the 13th century), invented by John Gutenberg of Mainz, or by some other printer between 1444 and 1450, is a question still unsolved. By 1454 Gutenberg had determined to print the Bible. For this he used type

FIG. 496.—Page from Gutenberg Bible, height 16½ inches. (*Courtesy of Library of Congress.*)

carved in relief from lead, which he copied from a hand-lettered manuscript of 1440, similar to the Windmill Psalter (Fig. 390, Chap. XIII).

The two-lined Bible published by Gutenberg, (with the help of Fust and Schoeffer) in Mainz, around 1456 (Fig. 496), is the earliest printed book. It consists of two columns with many inlaid letters printed in red or blue and large illuminated initials drawn in color by hand. The type, which is relatively narrow and distinctly Gothic in character, reminds one of the intricate crochets and finials of the medieval cathedral. Its perpendicular character is particularly suitable to the tall page. Such type was called by the Germans *textur* because the total effect of a page was that of a woven tapestry: the French called it *lettre de forme;* we call it "Old English." To understand the development of this kind of type, one must briefly review the manuscript letters from late Roman times until the 15th century.

During the early Middle Ages the round Roman letters called "uncials" (Fig. 308, Chap. XII) gradually changed their character. The Irish manuscripts (Fig. 307, Chap. XII) display this change along with some influence of Greek

Megaris diu ſtetit oleaſter in foro:cui uiri fortes affixerãt arma : quæ cortice ãbiente
ætas lõga occultauerat.Fuitq; arbor illa fatalis excidio urbis præmoñitæ oraculo : cũ
arbor arma peperiſſet.quod ſucciſæ accidit ocreis galeiſq; ĩtus repertis.Ferũt lapides
ita inuentos ad cõtinendos partus eſſe remedio.

DE Materiis. Ca.Lx.

DE Magnitudĩe arboȝ:& quæ carie & ruinã nõ ſĕtiũt.& de ppetuitate materiaȝ.
AMpliſſia arboȝ ad hoc æui exiſtimaͭ romæ uiſa:quã ppter miraculũ Tiberius
Cæſar in eodẽ põte naumachiario expoſuerat,aduectã cũ reliͦ materie.Dura,
uitq; ad Neronis principis ãphiteatȝ.Fuit aũt trabs è larice lõga pedes.cxx.bipedali
craſſitudine æͦlis.quo intelligebaͭ uix credibilis reliͦ altitudo,faſtigiũ ad cacumen
æſtimãtibus.Fuit & memoria noſtra in porticibus ſeptoȝ à.M.Agrippa relicta æque
miraculi cauſa:quæ delibaͭorio ſupfuerat.xx . pedibus breuior:ſeſqpedali craſſitu,
dine . Abies admirationis præcipuæ uiſa in naui:quæ ex ægypto Caii principis iuſſu
obeliſcũ in uaticano circo ſtatutum:quattuorq; trũcos lapidis eiuſdé ad ſuſtinendũ
eũ adduxit.Qua naue nil admirabilius uiſũ in mari certũ eſt . Cxx.modii tũc lentis
pro ſaburra ei fuere.Lõgitudo ſpatiũ obtinuit magna ex parte oſtienſis portus latere
leuo.ibi nãq; demerſa eſt à Claudio prĩcipe cũ tribus molibus turriũ altitudine in ea
exædificatis,obiter puteolano puluere aduectis.Quæ arboris craſſitudo ͦttuor hoĩũ
ulnas complectẽtiũ implebat.Vulgoq; audii.lxxx.nummoȝ & pluris malos ad eos
uenundari uſus.Rates uero cõnecti .xl.ſeſtertiis pleraſq;.At in ægypto ac ſyria reges
ĩnopia abietis cædro ad claſſes feruntur uſi.Maxima ea in cypro tradiͭ ad ũdeciremẽ
Demetrii ſucciſa.cxxx.pedũ lõgitudinis:craſſitudinis uero ad triũ hominũ cõplexũ.
Germaniæ prædones ſingulis arboribus cauatis nauigãt:ͦrũ quædã & triginta hoĩes
ferunt.Spiſſiſſima ex omni materie ideo & grauiſſima iudicatur hebenus & buxus:
graciles naͭa:neutra in aquis fluitat nec ſuber ſi demaͭ cortex : nec larix.Ex reliͦs
ſicciſſima lotos:quæ romæ ita appellatur.Deinde robur exalbunatum : et huic nigri,
cans color:magiſq; etiam cythiſo:quæ proxime accedere hebenum uidetur. Quanͦ
non deſint ͦ ſyriacas terebinthos nigriores affirment. Celebratur & Tericles nomine,
calices ex terebintho ſolitus facere torno.Per quã probatur materies:õniũ hæc ſola
ungi uult: meliorq; olea fit.Colos mire adulteratur iuglande,ac piro ſilueſtri tinctis
atq; in medicamine decoctis.Omnibus quæ diximus ſpiſſa firmitas.Ab his proxĩa
eſt cornus:ͦͦ non poteſt uideri materies ppter exilitatem:ſed lignum nõ alio peñe
ͦ ad radios rotarum utile:aut ſiͦd cuneadũ ſit in ligno clauiſue figendũ ceu ferreis.
Ilex item:& oleaſter:& olea:atq; caſtanea:carpinus : populus . Hæc omnia & criſpa
aceris mõ:ſi ulla materies idonea eſſet. Ramis ſæpe deputatis caſtraceo illis eſt:adi,
mitq; uires.De cætero plæriſq; eoȝ.ſed utiq; robori tanta duritia eſt:ut terebrari niſi
madefactũ nõ queat:& ne ſic ͦdé adactus auelli clauus . Ě diuerſo clauũ non tenet
cædrus . Molliſſima tilia : eadem uidetur & calidiſſimá.argumentum afferunt: ͦ
ćitiſſime aſcias retundat.Calidæ morus,laurus,hedera:& omnes quibus igniaria fiũt.
Exploratoȝ hoc uſus in caſtris paſtorumq; repperit:quoniam ad excuciendum igñe
non ſemper lapidis occaſio eſt. Teritur igiͭ lignum ligno.ignemq; concipit attritu :
excipĩente materia aridi fomitis fungi uel foliorum facillime conceptum . Sed nihil
hedera præſtantius : quæ teratur lauro:laurumq; terat.Probaͭ & uitis ſilueſtris alia
ͦ labruſca:& ipſa hederæ modo arborem ſcandens.Frigidiſſima quæcunq; aquatica.
Lentiſſima autè:& ideo ſcutis faciẽdis aptiſſima:quoȝ plaga contrahit ſe protinus:
clauditq; ſuũ uulnus:& ob id contumacius tranſmittit ferrum : in quo ſunt genere
fici:ut ſalix:tilia:betulla:ſambucus: populus utraq;. Leuiſſimæ ex his:ſicut & ſalix:
ideoq; utiliſſimæ.Omnes aũt etiam ad ciſtas quæcũq; flexibili crate conſtãt. Habét
& candorẽ rigoremq;:& ĩ ſculpturis facilitaté. Eſt lenticia platano:ſed madida ſicut
alno. Siccior eadem ulmo:fraxino:moro:ceraſo:ſed põderoſior.Rigorem fortiſſime

writing. The chief decisive factor in narrowing the letters and giving them Gothic character was the use of the Runic script, which may be found on many northern monuments, as well as in such documents as the *Domesday Book* (Fig. 497a). By the 13th century this Gothic letter style dominated in the manuscripts of France, Germany, and England (Fig. 390, Chap. XIII). While this type of letter composes into a very decorative page that might appeal to the nominalist northern mind intent upon details, it is not suitable for rapid reading, which tends to stress idea at the expense of the particular.

After the sack of Mainz in 1460 other printers, including Sweynheim, Pannartz, and perhaps Jenson, went to Italy, where they soon forsook the Gothic type, copying instead the Carolingian Roman cursive style of Italian manuscripts. This, having a more open face, proved suitable to the single-column manuscripts favored by the humanists. Jenson, the editor of Pliny's *Natural History*, printed in Venice around 1470 (Fig. 498), developed many excellent examples of this fundamental Roman form of type.

At Mainz, Fust and Schoeffer, after ousting Gutenberg from their establishment, prospered in their printing and with sails set to catch every breeze strove to perfect a type which should have characteristics of both the Gothic and the Roman. There resulted a mixed style called *bâtarde*. Most modern type faces used today can be traced to one of these three styles. The Roman, which became associated with the humanist culture, being very readable, dominates for most purposes. Old English is still used for church announcements and in German printing. This book is set in a modern adaptation of Baskerville, a type designed in England around 1700. It is a wide-spaced Roman with *bâtarde* characteristics. Another Roman type,

called "Garamond," in which these 13 lines are set, being a bit heavier, would probably have

Fig. 498.—Page from Jenson's edition of Pliny's *Natural History*, c. 1470. (*Courtesy of Library of Congress.*)

made a better looking page, but we should have sacrificed legibility in using it. The semiglossy paper on which these pages must be printed in order to get the best effect from our illustrations calls for the finer type. The arrangement of the large initials and the border at the beginning of each chapter are in the best printing tradition. Borders opening this and the next chapter actually have been taken directly from type designed by Renaissance and baroque printers.

Certain principles always hold in achieving good printing. (1) One must have legibility (a use value). (2) The decorative borders or initials and other illustrative material must carry the message of the text (an associational value). (3) Each page must be well woven together so that the eye is encouraged pleasantly to move from part to part (a formal value). Any distraction caused by the printing belies the purpose of the book. No better preparation can be gained for discussion of these principles than a study of late medieval manuscript layout.

Book designing declined in Italy after the 17th century, although a few great printers, such as Aldus Manutius of Venice, carried on the tradition there. Meanwhile the palm went to France where Granjon, Garamond, and Luce were at work. England produced Baskerville and finally William Morris, who, in the 19th century, strove to rediscover the earliest principles of book design (see Fig. 542, Chap. XVII).

Aesthetic Philosophies

Insofar as the man of the Renaissance inclined toward classical antiquity and a definition of the concept of beauty made visible in his art, he sought laws and mathematical formulae. Gothic realism he attempted to achieve through observed experiment. The writings of Alberti and Leonardo, throughout, illustrate both these tendencies. Other Renaissance writers, such as Ghiberti and Vasari, who were interested in an explanation of individual style, stressed history. In addition, there arose individuals, most significant of whom was Aretino, the first professional art critic, who combined both aesthetic and historic points of view with a penetrating analysis of the relationship of artists and their works to society. Thus, in the Renaissance, we may recognize three distinct critical approaches, corresponding roughly to our formal, associational, and useful values.

The Treatise of Ghiberti. Since the writings of Ghiberti show in primitive embryonic form the chief elements of all that Renaissance criticism which originated in the diaries of talented artists, one should begin with them, passing directly to the treatises of Alberti and Leonardo, which have to do, for the greater part, with the formal values in art.

Lorenzo Ghiberti, already considered as a sculptor, wrote a treatise on art, using many formulae that he had discovered in reading Vitruvius and Pliny. With Ghiberti begins the historic method of study. This critic endeavored to base an appreciation of art upon the discussion of a number of biographical details in the lives of the artists who had preceded him. He further tried to define the works of sculptors and painters in terms of their individual desires and in terms of the usefulness of these art works to society. Like Cennini and the Greeks, Ghiberti believed that good drawing (*bon disegno*) furnished the basis for the arts of painting and sculpture. In Giotto's many works he found true greatness, because they showed a combination of gentility, natural drawing, and measure or proportion in arrangement. Going beyond these values, Ghiberti, like some of the late Greek art critics, valued the element of suggestiveness in painting, telling how the painter Maso was able, through impressionistic rendering, to suggest, rather than to represent, shape.

The Classicism of Leon Battista Alberti. Leon Battista Alberti, architect, painter, and philosopher, found in the scholastic circles of Bologna the humanistic point of view for which his writings are famous. Educated as a noble into all the branches of *cortesia*, Alberti presents the first great example of *l'uomo universale* (the universal man), for whom the Renaissance became famous. So proficient in Latin composition that one of his comedies in that language was mistaken for an original work of Terence, Alberti could discover the essentials of Greco-Roman aesthetics in the writings of Vitruvius and Pliny. He sought to explain his contemporaries, Brunelleschi, Masaccio and Donatello, in terms of antique formulae, recognizing always the inherent Gothic religiosity and spirit in Florentine art.

Alberti's Treatise on Painting. On the side of Gothic nominalism, Alberti stressed the theory that the origins of the painter's style lay ultimately in nature. The idea to be expressed might become visible in art only as man, comprehending nature mathematically, learned to portray natural objects in correct perspective. To achieve the greatest naturalism and the ultimate degree of satisfaction in a painting, the painter must study most carefully the quality of line formed by the juncture of different planes. Thus the study of light and shade (chiaroscuro) seems to Alberti the most essential part of the painter's training. A further definition of formal values includes many items discovered in the pages of Pliny, Aristotle, and Cicero. Alberti writes, for example, that outlines in the drawing should be very delicate. He insists that the contour of the figure, or line at which the human substance ends and the natural space begins, deserves the greatest amount of study—a dictum that has descended to the art academies of the 20th century in the formula, "Study the contours." Each zone or plane of relief must also be so well joined to the next that no discord develops within the picture. The pictures by Verrocchio, Perugino, and Giorgione serve to demonstrate three successive steps in the achievement of this ideal.

Alberti seems to have been one of the first men of the Renaissance to appreciate the quality of a landscape. He was moved by the sight of trees and fields of grain and, according to legend, was cured of illness by contemplation of beautiful scenery. In his attempt to achieve complete naturalism in details, Alberti does not allow the physioplastic side of art to dominate his definition. With Plato, he insists on the retention of an ideal beauty, a position of Gothic realism.

Alberti's Treatise on Architecture. Studying Vitruvius, Alberti found a geometric definition of the old Roman orders, as well as mathematical canons for the rendition of the ideal human figure. He believed in the measured orders defined by Vitruvius and applied them with taste to the façades of churches and palaces, becoming the prototype of the modern office architect who can draw decorative exteriors, though he knows little of the builder's craft. Alberti's treatise on architecture, *De Re Aedificatoria*, written in 1452, consists in great part of his notes on Vitruvius. This work, together with a translation of Vitruvius, played a great part in determining the classicist idea that architecture was an art which could be pursued only by scholars skilled in archaeology and literature.

Although Alberti, unlike Leonardo, never made any psychological analysis of the moment of inspiration that underlies the conception of a work of art, his work abounds in terms that were to constitute a new vocabulary of the arts from that time forward. The classicist Alberti invented and used such terms as "unity," "harmony," "variety," "gracefulness," and "perfection," all of which have to do with formal aesthetic qualities, measurable in some degree by mathematical formulae. Terms such as these became the basis for that movement in modern European art called "classicism." In addition, something Gothic in Alberti introduced the words "invention," "imagination," "fantasy," and "caprice," which have to do with the less ordered elements of inspiration. Such terms underlay the movement toward romanticism. Thus the Classic and Romantic moods correspond roughly to what the Greeks might have called the Apollonian and the Dionysiac.

Renaissance critics also invented three other words of great significance. The first, *gusto* (taste), corresponds to Aristotle's appropriateness; the second, *ingegno* (ingenuity, cleverness, or wit), corresponds to the idea of virtuosity; and the third, a phrase, *la gran maniera* (the great style), characterizes a stately dramatic presentation of a noble human theme. Giorgione's painting, The Philosophers, exemplifies *gusto;* Leonardo's Virgin of the Rocks, *ingegno;* and Raphael's School of Athens, *la gran maniera.*

The Academic Architectural Treatises of Serlio, Vignola, Palladio, and Scamozzi. Following the treatise of Alberti, there appeared a number of similar attempts to explain or modify the works of Vitruvius by Fra Giocondo, Vignola, Serlio, Palladio, and Scamozzi, all architects of the 16th century. Vignola, a member of the Arcadian society founded in Rome by Cardinal Ippolito de' Medici, met with a group of scholars to read Vitruvius. Supported by this society, which was called *La Virtù*, Vignola made very careful measured drawings of Roman details. As the result of his archaeological research, he modified slightly the Vitruvian canons of proportions in relation to several of the orders and was rather harshly criticized. Andrea Palladio, an architect of Vicenza, published four books on architecture in 1470. Summing up the standard set by the other classical writers, these became the textbooks for academic architectural teaching during the following three centuries of the European and American development.

The Interest in Geometric Canons of Proportion. Accompanying the classicist preoccupation with architectural detail appears a lively interest in the canons of human proportion. Vitruvius had defined the proportions of the human figure, using a foot as a unit of measure, so that a perfect man must be six feet high. Alberti, studying antique statuary, also drew up tables of human proportions, using the head as a unit of measure, because, as he said, the head was a nobler part of the body. The head, in turn, was divided into degrees and minutes.

Alberti's head measurements were adopted and used by Leonardo da Vinci. He followed the Vitruvian rule for drawing the human figure, however, taking the navel as center and de-

ity for devising rational mathematical bases by which he hoped to explain his creative talent, the Renaissance theorist soon found himself lost in a mystical maze of mathematical for-

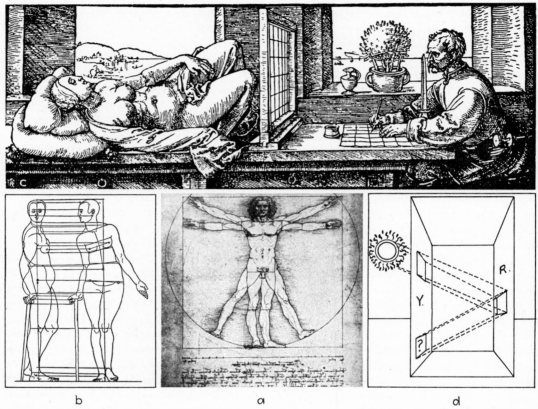

Fig. 499.—The canons of Renaissance artists. *a*, the human figure as constructed by Leonardo da Vinci, 1485–1490 (Venice Academy); *b*, details from Albrecht Dürer's *Vier Bücher von menschlicher Proportion*, Nuremberg, 1528, translated into Latin, 1532; *c*, plate from Dürer's *Underweysung der Messung*, Nuremberg, 1525; this shows a means of drawing mechanically or demonstrating perspective; *d*, diagram from Leonardo showing color mixtures in reflex light, *Treatise on Painting*, Chap. 237.

scribing a circle around it, which included the tips of the fingers and the soles of the feet on its circumference. The medieval architect, Villard de Honnecourt, in contrast, took the generative area as the center of his measurements. Practically all Florentine Renaissance writers on art introduce in their essays geometric measurements as a guide to the construction of figures and buildings (Fig. 499*a*).

Contemplating his own intellectual ingenu-

mulae. Michelangelo, it is said, believed in an occult figure, pyramidal in shape, revolving upon itself and multiplied by three. Albrecht Dürer, coming to Venice from Germany, bewailed the fact that certain of the Venetian artists knew secret proportions, derived from antiquity, which enabled them to make perfect figures and which they would not teach him. With Gothic scientific persistence, he turned to Nature herself, measuring many people to find an average that might be considered the ultimate in beauty. He succeeded in discovering sets of proportions for small, medium-sized, and tall men and women, which he carefully recorded in the many plates of his book, *De Symmetria Partium*, published in 1532 (Fig. 499*b*).

Leonardo's Treatise on Painting. To understand Leonardo's treatise on painting, one must recognize that this master, desiring to follow the model set by Alberti and, before him, Aristotle, intended to put the world of art in an order that should begin with a scientific observation of nature's details, and should reach up toward the divine moment of inspiration. Like the Platonists, he conceived the soul, also, as a triangle, and this figure rules most of his compositions. For Leonardo, however, the moment of supreme beauty lay in the border line between light and shade. Hence, he adjures the painter to take the utmost care to see that shadows and lights merge with one another "as smoke loses itself in the air." In his painting, in a technique which he called *sfumato*, he often throws a haze of glazed color over a contour so that his people and landscapes achieve an Oriental tone.

The aesthetic writings of Leonardo include two goals for the artist—one, the desire for dynamic expression; the other, for soothing beauty. To achieve a union of these goals in a perfect painting, Leonardo advised the young student to study art in the following order. (1) He must gain a knowledge of perspective with chiaroscuro. (2) He must copy details from nature under some able master. (3) He must study the relative proportions of the parts within the human figure. (4) He must study the composition schemes of the old masters. (5) He must study color. Leonardo's scheme ruled the Classical, academic training for the young artist in the Western world until the 20th century.

For Leonardo, however, all this formal preparation remained without purpose unless the painter had some inner dramatic story to tell.

He recognized that, although the story might be given in some classical subject such as a Madonna or The Last Supper, the imagination could achieve *ingegno* only through aesthetic play. For his own artistic invention or design, Leonardo recognized two origins: (1) geometric figures arising during his mathematical studies, (2) indistinct water spots or marking on old walls or the ceilings of a room. In his psychological examination of his own creative ability, Leonardo went far beyond the classical formulae of Alberti, penetrating deeply into the subject matter of romantic aesthetics—the unconscious mind. He also advanced beyond Alberti in his notes on color values, which he called *tono*.

Leonardo's Discoveries on Color. His so-called "elementary" colors Leonardo listed in their proper tone values from white through yellow, green, blue, red, and black. He noticed that a glaze of red light upon blue would create purple; yellow on blue, green; and red and yellow, a new color for which he had no name, but which we know as orange. Leonardo also discovered that red and yellow have their greatest luminosity in light, and that green and blue appear most pleasing in the shadow. Leonardo's method of color mixture may best be demonstrated by his own diagram and note (Fig. 499*d*), which proves that for him artistic effectiveness was synonymous with richness in color and new discovery.

Chap. CCXXXVII.—*What Part of a Colour is to be the most beautiful.* If *A* be the light, and *B* the object receiving it in a direct line, *E* cannot receive that light, but only the reflexion from *B*, which we shall suppose to be red. In that case, the light it produces being red it will tinge with red the object *E*; and if *E* happen to be also red before, you will see that colour increase in beauty, and appear redder than *B*; but if *E* were yellow, you will see a new colour, participating of the red and the yellow.[1]

Among his experiments, one picture, now

[1] LEONARDO DA VINCI, *A Treatise on Painting*, translated by John Francis Rigaud, pp. 123 and 124, S. Gosnell, London, 1802.

in Vienna, actually shows the use of points of color to give the effect of greater luminosity, much as they were employed by the Impressionists.

Leonardo observed the tonal and color effects in atmospheric perspective. He noticed that the outlines of opaque bodies appear proportionately less distinct as those bodies move farther from the eye. Many and ingenious were his inventions for achieving an exact naturalism, today proper to the camera. On the way, Leonardo invented the camera obscura, which captured upon a white screen in a dark room images reflected from the world outside. Throughout his writings and works one finds a tendency inherited from Plato to confuse the words "art" and "science," perhaps because *ingegno* (ingenuity) was common to both.

Vasari's "Lives" and the Birth of the Romantic Idea of the Artist Character. In the Renaissance, the medieval tendency to devise a historical background for all spiritual phenomena, uniting with the humanist tendency to celebrate the lives of great men, created a third style of writing. This strove to establish as the basis for a psychological analysis of an artist's style discussion of his personal history. Ghiberti's book on art comprised a series of lives of artists. Manetti, the biographer of Michelangelo, also wrote a life of Brunelleschi, attempting to explain the latter's productions in terms of a brief history of architecture, which praised the revival of the classical style while decrying "Gothic barbarism."

During the 16th century, after the Golden Age of Florentine painting had passed, the heroic artist figures were romantically depicted in a series of literary biographies. Best known of these is *The Lives of the Most Excellent Painters, Sculptors, and Architects,* written by Giorgio Vasari between 1550 and 1568. Vasari attempted, cleverly enough, to explain the artists in a series of interesting anecdotes, many of which, having a kernel of truth, developed as fictions. A mediocre Florentine painter following in the footsteps of Michelangelo, this Vasari shows in

his writing a tendency to praise his fellow countrymen at the expense of all others, and to stress the excellence of the works of Michelangelo and his followers in preference to the older 15th-century guild artists. With Vasari's contemporaries begins an unconscious tendency in historical criticism to condemn the Gothic and primitive arts because they do not coincide with the standards of taste formulated during the humanist period of the Classical art movement.

Purporting to be scientifically objective, most art history, like the writings of Vasari, can create a biased aesthetic attitude by ignoring or underrating the primitive origins of one or the other of the three great art styles we have discussed. The modern student must continually guard himself against the voluminous 19th-century Victorian art history, which drew heavily upon Vasari and was often inclined toward either classicism or romanticism, to the neglect of primitive, Gothic, and Oriental artistic productions.

The Venetian Critics and the Value of Color in Painting. Three Venetian critics—Pietro Aretino, Ludovico Dolce, and Paolo Pino—published dialogues on the arts during the 16th century. The writings of Aretino add little to our knowledge of formal aesthetic values beyond that contributed by Leonardo and Alberti. Aretino's significance rests upon his biting personal criticisms. Educated in Rome under the influence of Raphael and Michelangelo, he was an unlettered man in the humanist sense, for he lacked both Greek and Latin; but he had an intelligent insight into the struggles of his artist friends. He adopted a number of artists as his special protégés and insisted that his writings as an amateur art critic had contributed to their success. In a sense, he is the first art dealer or paid connoisseur of art, and thus wholly a product of the modern temper of life. Aretino, with Dolce and Pino, both of whom wrote dialogues on painting, praised particularly the qualities of color, movement, sensuousness, speed and sureness in execution, or virtuosity, along with the style of the free sketch, as the most important elements in painting. With these critics there arose a new, more romantic definition of perfection in painting. The finest painting, they averred, should have the freedom of Michelangelo's drawings, combined with the coloring of Titian. Here they laid the basis for most baroque criticism of the painter's art.

Summary

That state of mind necessary to produce the modern European artist, freed from the trammels of religious superstition and the domination of earthly power, is entitled the Renaissance. This French term, meaning a rebirth, is, however, a misnomer insofar as, in favoring the revival of interest in classical antiquity, it neglects the many elements of Gothic form and legendary content which proved the stimulus for much Italian Renaissance artistic creation.

The Renaissance epitomizes the birth of an interest in all fields of knowledge, including the natural sciences and mathematics, as well as the philosophies and histories of ancient man. It symbolizes a new spirit of exploration, which made itself felt in the individual expressions of those Italian artists who, leaving the guild workshops, from the 14th through the 16th century, set up studios of their own. Their efforts included an exploration into novel possibilities of formal aesthetic values, as well as intellectual exploration in the realm of associational values. Thus their painting and sculpture not only stressed the humanity of man, but did this in such a way as to gain the greatest amount of realism in human forms, which symbolized his dynamic and reflective qualities.

The artist came to be known by his *virtù*, that is, his ability to surpass others in the creation of new concepts in new forms. As the historical movement progressed, with a growing interest in scholarly research, the artists copied classical forms and tended to formulate concepts of beauty based upon ancient classical aesthetic theories. The artist's ability to surpass all others in the combined fields of invention, rendition, and the knowledge of classical formulae, came to be known as "virtuosity."

The essential virtuosity of an artist appeared primarily in his sketches, which showed the maximum quality of his conceptions with the minimum of form necessary to clarify that conception. Hence, the brush stroke, the expressive contour line, the tactile value, the *mot juste*, and the strong composition, as the measures of highest aesthetic values, or virtuosity, gradually replaced the decorative, dynamic, associational values of the Gothic, and the restful beauty and unity of the Classical. With this special interest in formal aesthetic values, man began to detach his pictures from their architectural setting and to consider the work of art as a separate thing, valuable for its own sake. Thus art came in some measure to replace religious values.

The Italian Renaissance aesthetic is dominated by the pictorial conception; the picture, in turn, by sculptural form, tactile values, and line drawing, rather than by color. The desire to represent man as a solid moving in space led to an almost mystical ecstatic study of the effects of light and shade (chiaroscuro), upon the human form, as it emerged from its natural background. This contrast symbolized Renaissance man's belief in a conflict between his intellectual desires, which he considered of classical origin, and his emotional drives, which he probably did not consider at all, but which, as we have seen, arose in great part from his medieval Gothic character.

Bibliography

VENTURI, ADOLFO: *A Short History of Italian Art*, The Macmillan Company, New York, 1926.

FREEMAN, L. T.: *Italian Sculpture of the Renaissance*, The Macmillan Company, New York, 1901.

MATHER, F. J.: *A History of Italian Painting*, Henry Holt & Company, Inc., New York, 1923.

ANDERSON, W. J., and A. STRATTON: *Architecture of the Renaissance in Italy*, Charles Scribner's Sons, New York, 1927.

BURCKHARDT, JACOB: *The Civilization of the Renaissance in Italy*, Albert & Charles Boni, New York, 1935.

SYMONDS, JOHN ADDINGTON: *The Renaissance in Italy*, 2 vols., Modern Library, Inc., New York, 1935.

KUHNS, OSCAR: *The Great Poets of Italy*, Houghton Mifflin Company, New York, 1913.

MACHIAVELLI, NICCOLO: *The Prince*, translated by Luigi Ricci, Oxford University Press, H. Milford, London, 1935.

CASTIGLIONE, BALDASSARE: *The Book of the Courtier*, translated by Leonard E. Opdycke, Liveright Publishing Corporation, New York, 1929.

BOCCACCIO: *The Decameron*, translated by John Payne, Blue Ribbon Books, New York, 1931.

LANDUCCI, LUCA: *A Florentine Diary*, translated by Alice de Rosen Jervis, J. M. Dent & Sons, Ltd., London, 1927.

Sonnets of Michael Angelo Buonarroti, translated by John Addington Symonds, London, 1877.

CELLINI, BENVENUTO: *Autobiography*, translated by Anne MacDonald, Everyman's Library, E. P. Dutton & Company, Inc., New York, 1919.

VASARI, GIORGIO: *Lives of the Painters*, Charles Scribner's Sons, New York, 1896.

Notebooks of Leonardo da Vinci, translated and edited by E. D. McCurdy, Reynal & Hitchcock, Inc., New York, 1938.

FINLAYSON, DONALD LORD: *Michelangelo the Man*, Tudor Publishing Co., New York, 1935.

Recordings

Madrigals by Arcadelt, Orlando di Lasso, Gesualdo da Venosa, V 20228 Decca 20162 a.

Penitential Psalm by Orlando di Lasso, Decca 20161 b

CHAPTER XVI

The Baroque Styles and the Rise of the Classical Academies

Know, then, thyself, presume not God to scan,
The proper study of mankind is man,
Placed on this isthmus of a middle state,
A being darkly wise, and rudely great;
With too much knowledge for the sceptic side,
With too much weakness for the stoic's pride,
He hangs between; in doubt to act, or rest;
In doubt to deem himself a god or beast;
Sole judge of truth, in endless error hurled;
The glory, jest, and riddle of the world!

THESE lines from Pope's *Essay on Man* aptly characterize the mind of the cultured northern European living in the 16th, 17th, or 18th century. That period, variously called the "northern Renaissance," the "Age of Enlightenment" or the "Age of Reason," simply marked a period of transition between medieval and modern times. French academic scholars of the 17th century coined the term "Renaissance" to describe the Italian rebirth of art; their own advanced age—the *Grand Siècle*—they considered to have a more enlightened culture, a faith less childlike, and knowledge based directly either upon a truer picture of antiquity or upon objective scientific research.

The man of the Age of Enlightenment differed from his Renaissance predecessor in the south chiefly in his much greater preoccupation with the critical examination of his own thoughts. This led eventually to a number of soul-searching analyses of beliefs; to the philosophical systems of Francis Bacon, René Descartes, and Immanuel Kant. Speaking generally, the northerner remained at heart the Gothic man, given to a somewhat moody dramatization of his soul struggles or to the

collection of encyclopedic descriptions of natural phenomena. Despite the efforts of those academicians who were paid by monarchs to arrange life simply, the northern philosopher never achieved the relatively clear spatial picture of the Greeks or his southern neighbors. Instead, he strove for a much more involved explanation, including the temporal aspects of existence. He revived and greatly elaborated upon sophisticated late Greco-Roman philosophies to heal his ailing soul, while pursuing something like the pre-Socratic quest for scientific certainty to satisfy his mind. Thus equipped to view his own shortcomings, the man of the north saw himself through the eyes of a Rabelais or a Molière with saving wit; more tragically, through those of Shakespeare and Rembrandt —"The glory, jest and riddle of the world."

Social and Political Backgrounds

Historical developments from the 16th through the 18th century brought to bear upon the individual more diverse social forces than had been felt at any time since the Alexandrian age of Greece. The artist left the safety and control of the church or the overlordship of

607

political feudalism for an adventurous voyage either into what was called the "Age of Reason," a French extension of the Renaissance, or into the emotionally charged political battles of the Reformation and Counter Reformation. After many revolutionary discoveries, he found himself at last, in the 19th century, a citizen of some industrial democracy with a maximum of individual freedom and a minimum of steady patronage.

Expanding Horizons of the European Mind. During this period of intellectual ferment the horizons of the European mind expanded to include primitive frontiers in the Americas and the ancient cultures of the Far East. The opening of India and China to European trade brought to the courts of Europe many examples of Oriental art in ceramics and woven designs, which added new patterns to rococo design. New physical boundaries to the universe were sought with the aid of the telescope and the microscope. Modern atomic chemistry and the phenomena of electricity startled the conservative mind almost as much as discoveries in geology. A nominalist attitude of mind uniting with new scientific discoveries helped the artist to escape the narrow bonds of an organized ecclesiastical formula to seek new meaning in the physical universe. The natural man, *l'homme naturel* of Rousseau, who sought a universal brotherhood even in the newly discovered primitive races, announced that all government should proceed from powers vested in it by the governed.

These significant historical moments had their effect upon the arts. New northern commercial nations came into existence accompanying the Reformation—two particularly, the English and Dutch, with a maximum of freedom for literary and pictorial arts. The growing power of the kings of France and England offered opposition to both the Roman Church and its supporting Holy Roman Empire on purely political grounds.

During this period of national development the great guild cities of the Netherlands, supported by local princes, revolted against the domination of the feudal Empire, seeking religious freedom and political independence from Spain and France. Although suppressed for a time by the Spanish emperor, Philip II, the Netherland *bourgeoisie* became wealthy enough to support a realistic regional art.

The Development of Nations. After 1609, the Netherlands made peace with Spain and eventually the Dutch republic became a sovereign state. Louis XIII, supported by his able minister Richelieu, built a strong French nation. Another cardinal, the Italian Mazarin, during the regency of Marie de Médicis further advanced the interests of this state. In England the Stuart kings were overthrown for a time by the Puritans and all the arts were reduced to the condition of literary moralizing; but, in 1660, Charles II, recalled to the throne, brought with him French artistic influences. In France during the same year, Louis XIV, then twenty-one years of age, was crowned with the heritage of power built for him by a long succession of peaceful ministers—Sully, Richelieu, Mazarin, and Colbert.

From 1660 to 1710 Louis XIV, who liked to be called the "Sun King," ruled France. Through the efforts of the able minister Colbert, new industries were founded and France set out on a period of maritime colonial expansion. In his unsuccessful attempt to dominate European politics, Louis was repulsed in England and Holland by William of Orange; in Austria and Poland, by John Sobieski. Consequently, at the close of his reign, walled about by enemies, France had only one outlet for her tremendous energies—creative intellectual and artistic life. At that time her courts and cities became the acknowledged cultural centers of the world. All Europe looked to her as an arbiter of taste, particularly the two new despotic nations Russia and Prussia, which emerged to take their places as world powers. Throughout Europe a new refined version of baroque art, the French rococo, became the dominating style.

In Germany, the Netherlands, and North

America, middle-class burghers wrested from the slowly declining aristocracy new prerogatives of government. The successful American Revolution, with its watchword "no taxation without representation," was soon followed by the French proletarian uprising, with its "Liberté, égalité et fraternité." Accompanying those revolutions arose the idea that church and state should be separated.

In some lands, such as Austria, clever monarchs like Joseph II, son of Maria Theresa, remained on their thrones. In Prussia and England kings ruled, supported by a strong landed aristocracy. Frederick the Great of Prussia adopted a Machiavellian view of political life but supported the arts, particularly music and architecture, adopting the French rococo style. In France, a foolish king living in a world of unreality lost his crown and his head. With the Revolution came a freedom from baroque and classical styles in art and a return to realism. The Revolution brought a dictator, Napoleon, who united all the released energies and set out to make the dreams of Louis XIV come true in a world conquest. Napoleon called for a return of the classical academy in art. In the less autocratic monarchies and newly founded democracies of the world, the control of the government finally came into the hands of a bourgeois commercial aristocracy, which used machinery for the production and distribution of agricultural and manufactured commodities. The power of organized wealth, or capital, took the place of the church or of monarchy in controlling the destinies and creative interests of the artist.

Religious Backgrounds

The Renaissance, inspiring man to joyful objective examination of all the aspects of life, humanized man's concepts of the Deity. Before the enlightenment brought by humanism and the experimental method, the medieval church, with its elaborate scholastic program for man's redemption and its ecclesiastical apparatus for achieving temporal power, inevitably lost ground where its hold was based upon superstitions. Sadly its greatest scholars, Erasmus and Melanchthon, admitted that a worldly political spirit displayed by such popes as the materialistic Spaniard, Alexander Borgia, had overshadowed the church's spiritual mission. Almost as sadly, the pious but stubborn German monk, Martin Luther, rebelled against the temporal authority of Rome. Seeking some new way to broadcast the Christian message, he translated the Bible into German so that the printers could make it available to the middle and lower classes. Inaugurated by Luther and supported by some German nobility, the Protestant Reformation was carried further by Calvin and Zwingli in Switzerland and France, by John Knox in England. Between 1517 and 1648 Protestantism, embraced by the growing bourgeois class, gradually displaced Romanism in the northern Teutonic countries.

The Reformation. The Reformation greatly influenced art, at first negatively, for the Protestants abandoned many of the rich liturgies and the visible appeal of sculpture and colorful glass decoration, along with the stories of the saints and their miracles. Deprived of the help of the priest, the Protestant had to carry his burdens of conscience alone. He became desperately aware of the old Manichaean struggle between the powers of light and of darkness for the possession of his soul. *The Pilgrim's Progress* by Bunyan graphically describes the Protestant Christians' predicament. Positively, the Protestant soul had a freedom to create new imagery and a new concept of man's worth as an individual capable of free will.

The Counter Reformation. To answer the rising forces of Protestantism, the Roman Church developed, in its Counter Reformation, a five-fold program which also had its influence upon the arts. First the church set out to reform itself through a series of councils held at Trent between 1540 and 1565. These councils not only attempted to regulate the arts, eliminating many of the pagan representations that had entered with classicism; but they also suggested appropriate subject matter for Christian contemplation. A college, called "the Propaganda," was founded in Rome for the propagation of faith. In 1557 the Council of Trent published the first of a long series of the *Indices of Prohibited Books* which have been continued to the present.

The order of the Jesuits, founded by the Spaniard Ignatius Loyola, began in 1540 to advance the cause of the Roman Church by means of a rational educational program based upon medieval Scholasticism, the study of Greek and Latin classics and of Euclidean geometry, and a revival of Aristotle's natural science. Along with these constructive measures went one more sinister—the revival of the Inquisition. This fearful tribunal, first founded to persecute only Moors and Jews, soon had a detrimental effect on all classes of society. Spain, the nation most dominated by inquisitors, produced least in the realm of the arts from the 17th century to modern times.

The Rise of Deism. The two greatest organized religious movements of the 17th and 18th centuries either advocated the furthering of the conservative, predestinarian medieval tradition or the Renaissance spirit of revolt stressing freedom of will and salvation by works. A third religious attitude, starting in realistic and scientific inquiry and ending in either nationalistic religions or complete religious anarchy, can also be observed. During the "Age of Enlightenment" (1700–1780) this attitude, which came to be known as Deism, flourished. Its influence upon art was less clear at first. It accompanied nominalism, encouraging creations that would stress "the brotherhood of man." Its full significance has only begun to be realized in the 20th century.

Avoiding both the excessive Protestant zeal for reform and the repressive measures of the Romanists, the Deists attempted to derive from their belief in the orderly activity of the universe, a God who would be like some law-abiding, progressive human being. For them God could be approached just as easily through the process of reasoning as through prayer. John Locke, the chief Deist philosopher, and Alexander Pope, the poet, agreed that both the life of reason and revelation seem necessary, but that faith should at all points give way to the latter as soon as the miraculous could be explained in terms of natural phenomena. So they encouraged the worship of God as a means to better understanding of the universe and of one's fellow men. This attempt to examine religion from the common-sense point of view accompanied the growth of realistic art and led eventually to the religious attitudes of the social revolution.

Foundations of a Religion of Science. In the 17th century, two great philosophers laid the foundations for that faith in physical science which almost approached a religious belief in the 18th and 19th centuries. The English statesman and philosopher, Francis Bacon, like Socrates before him, used common-sense methods in attacking the philosophical superstitions of his medieval predecessors. He proved that much Thomistic Aristotelianism was but a skillful play of words, more useful in gaining power over men's minds than in describing reality or in helping men to master nature for their own benefit. Next, Bacon suggested in his *Novum Organum* and other writings a program of experimental and logical examination of all the fields of science.

The Frenchman, René Descartes, also demonstrated the fallacies in most Scholastic reasoning, but suggested that in a program of experimentation all phenomena examined must be amenable to mathematical definition and proof. For Descartes that experience connected with what man called his emotional and religious life consisted of another substance, not amenable to reasonable examination. With Descartes, therefore, arose a mental habit which split man's mental life into two distinct parts. Eventually he characterized the real world as a machine, all of whose parts worked upon each other according to strict mathematical laws of cause and effect. He considered the fundamental reality to be spatial relationship and motion the source of all life.

A third thinker contributing to the creation of the scientific concept of God was the monk Giordano Bruno, finally burned for his heretical beliefs. Bruno, accepting the discoveries of Copernicus and Galileo concluded that the universe extended infinitely. Unwilling, because of his Christian faith, to conceive such a universe without order, Bruno held that God animated every part, manifesting Himself in the eternal rhythm of life, being essentially dynamic.

Isaac Newton united the thoughts of Bacon and Descartes with a knowledge of the astronomical theories of Bruno and Kepler. Accepting Kepler's discovery that the planets move in elliptical orbits, and Galileo's laws of falling bodies, Newton demonstrated that the law of gravitation must hold for the entire universe. It could then be assumed that all phenomena measurable on the earth would be similar in other parts of the universal machine. This, Newton believed, must be in perpetual motion.

The element of faith again entered the growing mechanistic conception of the universe with the philosophy of Baruch Spinoza. Accepting Descartes and Newton, Spinoza pointed to the dichotomy or separation caused by conceiving God and mental phenomena outside of the demonstrable Reality. Improving upon Bruno, he asserted that God must be the "meaning of the motion" or the mind in the machine, one in substance with logical mathematical law. With Spinoza there came to completion the scientific concept of a Deity guiding an orderly world predestined in all its motions and with no room for freedom of will, the exact counterpart of the academic point of view in art and the centrally controlled dictatorial nationalistic state in politics.

John Locke, a follower of Bacon, in his essay *Concerning Human Understanding*, dissented from Spinoza's absolute Deity. He suggested that principles must be derived from experience, which usually appears too complex for mathematical definition. He characterized the mathematical proofs as something nonexistent in reality. For Locke, all the knowledge of a Descartes or a Newton was subjective and detached from the world of everyday human action. Immanuel Kant, following Locke, even compared mathematical formulae to artistic creations. Kant also held that mathematics could not describe the true reality, but suggested that men should act as if what they discovered through scientific reasoning were that reality. In the field of ethics his categorical imperative, "Act as if your actions become laws of the universe," accompanies his revived Stoic philosophy. This philosophy modified by Nietzsche inspired most early 20th-century artistic activity.

Bacon's experimental method, called "empiricism," publicized by Diderot, contributed to the growth of natural science. It helped in the examination of geological, chemical, and physical phenomena. From it developed social psychology and anthropology—studies concerning the actions of men as individuals or in groups. Such realistic empirical descriptions of phenomena opened the way for a revival of religious Epicureanism, with its belief in God as a progressive or unfolding spirit.

In the 18th century these conflicts concerning the nature of God which arose in men's minds profoundly influenced the thinking artists. Those who believed in Descartes and Spinoza's mathematical God, could logically embrace the academic view of art. Those who followed Bacon, with his empiricism, could become realists or, if they elected to express the indefinable essence, baroque sensists. Those personalities who wavered between the two concepts, accepting now one, now the other, had to express some combination of the dynamic and the static.

The Skeptical Point of View in the Age of Revolution. The fourth stage in Western religious development was that of skepticism. The Frenchmen Montaigne and Voltaire, and such

English philosophers as Hobbes and Hume, introduced a strain of skeptical thought that grew from a realism made pessimistic by observation of injustices in the world about them. The skeptics concluded, as had the Stoics of old, that the entire burden of man's reconstruction rested with himself. Unconsciously they accepted semireligious philosophical beliefs like those of late antiquity. Montaigne, doubting the certainty of a future life, became an Epicurean and proclaimed that man's sole purpose in living was to live artistically. The Emperor Frederick the Great, leader of the German skeptics, occupied his time with wars and flute playing. Diderot consecrated his life to the ordering of all that the academies had discovered of art, science, philosophy, and religion in the *Encyclopédie.* The advance of skepticism accompanied the breakdown of the authoritarian ethics offered by the church. In its stead there grew among the rationalist philosophers a hedonistic ethics, that is, an ethical point of view which proposes that conduct shall be based upon enlightened self-interest. The hedonist usually acts so that his actions may give him the greatest pleasure for the longest period of time. The English third Earl of Shaftsbury and Immanuel Kant, the German philosopher, sometimes described as skeptics, go beyond hedonism by returning to the classical Greek belief that good conduct coincides with a sense of appropriateness, in short, that the True and the Beautiful are one.

Nationalistic and Individualistic Substitutes for Religion. The final stage in the disruption of organized religion accompanied the political revolutions during the late 18th and the 19th century. With the development of great commercial nations there arose many national, romantic, pseudoracial religions, which culminated in the 20th century with the almost fanatical Fascism and Nazism, extensions of the Napoleonic worship of *La Gloire.* In the democracies many worshiped wealth or the power to be gained therefrom. During these final years of the so-called "Age of Enlightenment" the artist, like his predecessor of Hellenistic times, became either the slave to economic or political tyrannies or else a man with individualistic, social, and religious vision.

Evolution of Structure and Form in Music from Palestrina to Mozart

Significance of Music as the Leading Baroque Art. During the period under discussion musicians accomplished more, in quantity and significance, toward perfecting the formal values of their art than did any other artists of the time. Composers, from Palestrina (1526–1594) to Mozart (1756–1791), discovered and solved nearly every structural problem necessary for conceiving music as we have it today. Historians or critics of the arts too often ignore this significant accomplishment in music, which influenced the static arts, perhaps because the terms that they use do not easily describe the evanescent effects of sound. One cannot capture in a brief visualizing sentence the complex, indefinite, associational patterns suggested by tonal phrases or by set musical forms. Nevertheless, these patterns are no less real than the patterns of painting and sculpture. Since music, the most richly creative art of the post-Renaissance period, profoundly influenced the temper of painters, architects, and sculptors, and since this influence is obvious and can be authenticated, even in the design of garden landscapes with musical fountain jets and water organs, one must make a special effort to understand the new inventions in the form and structure of music.

The Meaning of Form in Music. Great refinement of expression in music can arise only when movement, the spirit of music, is woven through some fixed structure limited by time, thus coming into form. By "form" we mean a limitation such as a sculptor puts upon his figure as he attempts to show its position in space.

In the spatial art of pottery, form is almost

synonymous with shape; in Greek architecture, it characterizes the method of building, or structure; and in the case of cathedral architecture, form is almost wholly dependent upon structure. So with the temporal arts, form may be defined in terms of structure. Musical form consists of the static chords awakening to life in melodies and even rhythms, so arranged that eventually certain shape boundaries or time limits become clear. The strength of the structure and the resultant perfection of the musical form, which is a dynamic thing in contrast to the sculptor's relatively static form, depends upon the number of suggestive associational patterns that can be compressed into a given time limit by means of a flow of sound. A comprehension of these elements of musical form in terms of the structure of the simpler spatial arts should help us understand the more dynamic art, which actually must be judged in terms of its ability to express energy, sublimity, and a synthesis of emotions, rather than upon grounds of its static unity of structure or its "beauty." In the baroque period, for the first time, man consciously tried to put the flow of sound into definite form amenable to strict academic laws based upon Aristotle's laws of the drama.

Briefly reviewing: the first element of musical form, found in connection with primitive and Greek art, appeared in the dance, where because of the alternation of heavy and light beats, the rhythmical element in music moved from static to dynamic position and back again. This principle was recognized in the Middle Ages as giving the music of the dance a certain figure or "form" corresponding to the linear or expanding-contracting patterns made by the dancers.

The second element governing the form of music was perceived in the relationship of the melody to the verse sung or to the length and figure of the dance tune played. The structure of the verse accompanying folk songs and early hymns determined the length, as well as the rise and fall of the voice in the lyric melodies.

Many of these, particularly the sequences constructed from northern folk songs, persisted in the chorales composed by the reformers, just as the troubadour songs became the melodies of the operas. Most of the ecclesiastical music of the Middle Ages, in the antiphonal singing and great polyphonic choruses, does not stress a single melody but exists with a certain indefiniteness both in the placing of the notes on the scale and in the termination. Like the Gothic cathedrals, these compositions appear superficially somewhat aimless and rambling in structure. A principle remained to be discovered by which the great, endless, polyphonic wanderings could be captured in a limited classical form. This principle appeared recognizably in the 15th century, when men came to understand the meaning of the harmonious chord in its relationship to the development of melody and eventually, in the 20th century, as influencing even rhythm.

The Chord as Active Determinant of Melodic Form. By 1450, it seems, a simple tonic chord as the basis of a melody was for the first time used consciously by the Englishman, John Dunstable. By "tonic chord" is meant a grouping of three tones such as C, E, G, built upon C, the first or tonic note of the scale or key of C (Fig. 500a). Such a chord, with its two upper notes sounding in the third and fifth steps of the scale, acts as a fundamental or static assertion, from which Dunstable drew a melody (Fig. 500c). Wishing an answer to his first melody, Dunstable devised a second chord built upon the fifth note of the scale, which in the old authentic church modes was called the dominant or chief note (Fig. 500b). This dominant chord, which included the notes G, B, and D, seems more dynamic than the tonic chord and therefore more suggestive of motion. In order to make his melody sound complete, Dunstable carried it back to the first or tonic chord (Fig. 500d). Thus, he achieved a balanced form for his phrase, which now had a definite beginning, middle, and end—like the action of the plot in Aristotle's poetic criticism.

FIG. 500.—*a*, tonic chord built on C, used by Dunstable; *b*, dominant chord; *c*, melody from tonic chord; *d*, cadence or return to first tonic chord; *e*, inversion of chord; *f*, dominant seventh chord of Monteverde; *g*, the ninth chord used by Bach.

In this way melody achieved a form that recognized a principle of harmonic development. Something akin to the first principle of rhythmical sequence and to the second poetic principle of question and answer had now been found in terms of the harmonic or tonal element in music. Progression in terms of relative feelings of rest and motion could be drawn from an alternation of tonic and dominant chords.

The Chord as a Passive Determinant of Melodic Form. A second method of melodic progression, more subtle in effect than the first, relating to the internal structure of a single chord, was recognized by Venetian masters around 1540. They found that a top-heavy inverted tonic chord (secondary two notes placed below tonic note) sought rest by resolving into the ordinary, or primary, tonic chord. Similarly, an inverted chord using the dominant note in the lowest position is more dynamic than one using the third note. Thus, in terms of relative weakness and strength, it may be said that chords seem to fall into position. The principle of inversion was first used in connection with the cadences or melodic fall at the end of a song or motet. Composers then had two new means for organizing the structure of music within a form literally bounded between two tonic chords. Soon a third chord, the dominant seventh, composed of the notes G, B, D, F—more restless, incomplete, and dynamic—was found. Phrases of melody rising from it were still further from the static, tonic chord. This was first consciously used by Monteverde about 1640. The ninth

chord, adding A to the G, B, D, F of the seventh, seems to have been first used by Bach (Fig. 500*f*, *g*).

Significance of the Keyboard Instruments in the Development of the Chord. Before surveying briefly the evolution of vocal and instrumental music in opera and oratorio, one must observe the influence of a new instrument on which, by means of a keyboard, a number of strings tuned to the different notes of the scale might be plucked simultaneously, to give sustained chords, or sequentially, to create melodies. From a number of early instruments—including the dulcimer or cymbalum, built upon the lyre principle, in which sets of strings were stretched across sound boxes—developed eventually the piano. From the organ, or perhaps the vielle, or hurdy-gurdy, came the keyboard, with levers actuating either quills, which plucked the strings in the case of the clavichord, or hammers, which struck them, in the harpsichord. The first instrument of this kind—the *chekker*, perfected in the 14th century—was described as "similar to an organ which sounds with strings,"[1] probably a form of dulcimer fitted with hammers and keys.

The Birth of the Opera. The most important field for experimentation with the chord in relation to homophonic, or single-voice, melodic music was in the development of the opera, during the 16th century. This art descended directly from the efforts of those Italian *canzonieri*, followers of the troubadour Adam de la Halle, creator of the music drama *Robin and*

[1] FRANCIS W. GALPIN, *A Textbook of European Musical Instruments*, pp. 103–108. Williams & Norgate, London, 1937.

Marion. In the courts of the Italian nobles, the art of recitation to music was encouraged throughout the 14th and 15th centuries. With the translation of ancient Greek and Roman plays, in the 16th century, it seemed natural for the recitation of them to be accompanied by the music of lute, flute, or lyre, interspersed with suites of dances played upon the viols.

In 1472, Angelo Poliziano, a humanist poet of Mantua produced a dramatic poem, *The Fable of Orpheus*, incorporating the melodies of the carnival songs called the *Frottola*, which were sung by the *canzonieri*, as well as the *Ballata* (ballets) or groups of old dance tunes. Not only did Poliziano have his actor singers accompany themselves upon the lute, but he also introduced two other instruments appropriate to the Greek setting—one, a shepherd's pipe or whistle, and the other, a lyre.

Other poets at the court of the Gonzaga princes at Mantua, particularly Niccolo da Corregio, produced plays in which instruments accompanied lyric solo melodies very much as they do in the modern opera. During the first half of the 16th century, the masters of northern Dutch schools, interested particularly in the polyphonic music of canons and madrigals, dominated the music of Europe. One of the best known Dutch masters, Willaert—active in Venice—who had discovered the principle of chord inversion, introduced madrigals into music drama in place of the instrumental accompaniment. For a time the homophonic, dramatically expressive troubadour melodies disappeared in polyphonic choruses. From 1500 to 1600 the two tendencies fought for precedence. A number of musicians, particularly Beccari, Lollio, and Agente produced operas in which the madrigals predominated, with an occasional melodic solo accompanied by an instrument.

The renaissance in painting had seen all influences united in the school of Florence during the late 15th century. In like manner, during the last quarter of the 16th century, the forms of opera and the oratorio came forth from the efforts of a number of Florentine amateur musicians, the *camerata* (Italian for group), whose universal tastes inspired them to essay both the homophonic music of the south and the polyphonic contrapuntal music of the Hollanders. One of the *camerata*, Jacopo Peri, produced the opera *Eurydice*, dramatically constructed according to the rules of Aristotle, with melodic solos and recitatives in which harmonic music accompanied melodies supporting the ideas in the words. To add an impressive volume of sound, Peri introduced as musical background a madrigal sung by a large chorus behind the scenes.

The second in the Florentine group of musicians, Emilio del Cavalieri, stressed the spectacular elements in the music drama. In 1589, in a pageant, *The Harmony of the Spheres*, he produced a processional dance, with actors dressed to represent the planets. For appropriate musical accompaniment, a number of instruments played while men danced a pantomime ballet. This short number between the acts of several longer plays was called an *intermezzo*.

Cavalieri and the Oratorio. Called to Rome, Cavalieri produced a musical morality play very much like *Everyman*, based upon the old *débat* between the mind and the body. In his play, *La Rappresentazione di anima e di corpo*, performed in the oratory of a church by actor singers in full costume, is found the ecclesiastical counterpart of the secular opera—that is, the oratorio. In this first oratorio, Cavalieri united a number of recitatives, solos, and choruses, combining the polyphonic style of the madrigal and the homophonic style of an opera with an intermezzo accompanied by instruments playing a suite of dances. His instruments included a large lute with twenty-four strings, called a *chitarrone*, and a double lyre, which must have had at least sixteen strings. Most important of all for developing chords was the *gravicembalo*, a large cymbalum. This had a keyboard actuating hammers, which either struck or plucked the strings. For purely melodic instruments the orchestra included two flutes and a violin. Since the dignity of the church demanded that the costumes be omitted, Carissimi, who wrote the next oratorios, dispensed with them, giving more attention to the form and structure of the music.

Although Peri and Cavalieri made many advances toward a complete union of the harmonic, chordal music and the polyphonic, contrapuntal style, another musician, Palestrina, who was their contemporary, finally brought the two together.

Palestrina and the Roman Church's Recognition of the New Styles. Giovanni Pierluigi, called Palestrina after his birthplace, a village near Rome, became the organist, choir leader, and composer of St. Peter's Church in 1551. During a long, active life he composed over ninety masses, hundreds of motets, madrigals, and smaller pieces. In his early works, Palestrina shows no evidence of having understood how to use chords to gain form and structure in his music, which at that time was composed of canons and motets. During the middle period of his development, he began to experiment with the chords and in the last years of his life he produced a number of masses in which the great polyphonic choruses of interwoven melodies progressed according to principles of chord development.

Between 1545 and 1563, the Council of Trent is said to have cited the early masses of Palestrina as canons of perfection. Secure in his position as papal composer, Palestrina, although never forsaking the old Gregorian melodies, adopted the inventions of the opera and oratorio composers, using them according to the rules of counterpoint employed by the Dutch musicians.

In the northern lands, the Dutch and German choirmasters, now members of the reformed church, wrote simple melodies derived from sequences of medieval folk songs, to be sung by the congregations in unison. These melodies, the chorales, moved to the accompaniment of great sustained chords played upon the organ. They developed through the oratorio into the cantata—a counterpart of the masses of Palestrina, in which a homophonic melody sequence dominated the polyphonic form.

Monteverde and the Opera in Mantua and Venice. Florentine composers early stressed the vocal accomplishments of the singers by lengthening the melodic trills developed from the chords. This display of virtuosity, like much of the purely decorative ornament on baroque churches, somewhat negated the structural form by stressing one element at the expense of others. It may be taken as a leading characteristic of Italian opera until the time of Rossini in the 19th century.

During the first half of the 17th century, Mantua and Venice led in the production of opera. In the latter city, opera scores were first printed. Claudio Monteverde produced his first opera, *Orpheus*, for the Duke of Mantua in 1607. In this and his *Ariadne*, produced in 1608, Monteverde disclosed a greater mastery of dramatic musical support for the spoken passages and more balanced formal melodies for the lyric songs than had his predecessors.

The Perfecting of the Violin and Monteverde's New Orchestra. The tone of the orchestra was greatly enhanced by the perfecting of the violin during the 17th century. In Cremona, Monteverde's birthplace, a family of instrument makers, the Amati, united the best features of the medieval bowed instruments, *crwths*, *liras*, rebecs, and viols, in the form that we today know as the violin. Following them, another family, the Stradivari, improved the acoustic properties of the Amati invention, and Joseph Guarnerius further strengthened the tone in the early part of the 18th century.

Monteverde, Gagliano, Cesti, and others of the Mantuan and Venetian schools soon recognized the great range of this new instrument. These masters added to their ensemble bass and tenor viols, the viola da gamba—ancestor of the cello—and two violins. Monteverde first achieved the pizzicato effect, simulating the lute or mandolin by plucking the strings. He discovered the tremolo gained by rolling the finger quickly on the string while the bow drew forth the melody. This latter effect added to the orchestra an almost human tone, so that the string section could be made to suggest a choral group contrasting with the band effects of horns and woodwinds. With these and many other means, Monteverde heightened the dramatic tone of the operatic music. His orchestra included sets of harpsichords, the double harp, the reed organ or regal, two small pipe organs, flutes, recorders, muted trumpets, and trombones. He devised certain combinations of instruments to accompany different characters of the opera, a suggestion in terms of harmony and instrumentation of the later melodic leitmotivs employed by Wagner.

Scarlatti and the Opera in Naples. Toward the end of the 17th century, Alessandro Scarlatti, a composer of church music in Naples, turned to the field of opera. He produced over a hundred operas, of which *La Griselda* and the *Prigionier Fortunato* are best known. Scarlatti, with his knowledge of contrapuntal church music and form, brought to the opera a richer instrumental accompaniment and more closely woven choruses. He invented the overture, a purely instrumental introduction consisting of three dance movements—the first and third, fast; the second, slow in character. He also built his individual melodies, which were called *arias*, upon this same balanced form. In the aria the first two sections contrast; the third, marked *da capo*, that is "from the head," repeats the first. So one observes in Scarlatti's song the triumph of Aristotle's dramatic scheme, with the definite beginning, middle, and end, applied to melody.

Rise of the Opera Buffa. During the 18th century, as the Italian opera became more sterile musically, something was needed to lighten the long series of arias, which at times reached the number of forty or fifty to a performance. Taking a cue from ancient drama, managers introduced, between the acts of the longer operas, short comic sketches built upon the intermezzo form invented by Cavalieri. The intermezzi included dances or ballets and rustic songs, or burlesques, with plots derived from the most ancient Italian folk comedies, the *Atellanae*, at that time being revived in the *commedia dell' arte*. This comic interlude, the *opera buffa*, first made use of the humorous qualities possible in the bass aria. Its composers adopted from German sources concerted choruses in which the voices of principal and minor characters united. From the French composers they took the *ensemble* in which the grand mass effect of orchestra and chorus supporting all the leading voices marked a crashing finale. Following Greek dramatic traditions, writers of the serious opera, like Pergolesi, created their own intermezzi or opera buffa. With the rise of opera, as with painting after the Renaissance, one may begin to speak of national characteristics. Italian, French, Austrian and German operas differed.

Lully and the Opera in France. The best known composer of opera in France was Jean Lully (1632–1687), a Florentine. He was brought to Paris as a youth and grew in the French tradition of the ballet or court dance, finally becoming the favorite composer of Louis XIV. As Italian opera had reached France by the middle of the 17th century, Lully brought the two forms of amusement together. He avoided the madrigal style of the Venetian opera and the *aria da capo* of the Neapolitans. Instead, he built his compositions around the ballets, designed to glorify the king, who usually danced the leading role.

Lully's operas opened with an overture, like that of Scarlatti, based upon stately court dance tunes. Then followed a pageantlike prologue similar to Cavalieri's intermezzo, with a ballet of dances and marching choruses. Following this, the music drama proper developed like Poliziano's *Orpheus* with a few arias and some recitative, accompanied by simple chords interspersed with suites of dances and concluded by a climactic ensemble, engaged in by all the performers of the first and second parts, that

FIG. 501a.—Melodies. *a, Ein Feste Burg ist unser Gott; b, Passion Chorale* by Hans Leo Hassler. These basic melodies derive from early church sequences.

is, by audience and actors alike. Here was completely communal drama in which Lully, the director, had everyone, including the king, take part. Like the French court painting of the time, Lully's opera, although completely satisfying to his little aristocratic world, seems quite boring from a musical standpoint, for the accompaniment was weak in counterpoint and monotonous in tone. Following Lully, Rameau and Gluck brought the classical opera form to its final stage of academic perfection.]

Henry Purcell and the Opera in England. Opera reached England relatively late, around 1660, developing from a kind of court pageant called a "masque." Charles II, during the Restoration, revived the masques, which the Puritans condemned. Henry Purcell, the most talented composer of incidental music for the masques, derived many of his ideas from Pelham Humfrey, who had studied with Lully. Purcell wrote over forty masques and operas, among which the best known are his *Dido and Aeneas, The Faery Queen,* and *King Arthur*—the last, set to words by the poet Dryden.

Purcell excelled in formal instrumental composition, which had expanded in Europe con-temporaneously with the development of the clavichord and the violin. In his orchestra, Purcell achieved well-balanced effects of keyboard and stringed instruments. His adoption of English folk melodies, combined with knowledge of counterpoint, which he used in the choruses and the orchestration, made his work more consistent musically than that of his Continental contemporaries. In his attempts to portray realistically effects of sorrow and joy through pauses or sighs in the melodies, he was not so successful, but he caught a vision of dramatic possibilities in melodic composition which were only fully recognized two centuries later by the Romantic composers of the German lieder. Purcell completely eliminated all spoken recitative from his operas, conceiving the entire performance as a complete musical drama. In this he was a forerunner of Gluck and Mozart. As these later men used many new resources of purely instrumental composition, advances in the oratorio and sonata forms must be considered before their work can be completely appreciated.

The Oratorio and the Cantata. The church's most dramatic musical form, the oratorio, begun by Cavalieri and perfected by Carissimi, found early acceptance in Germanic lands hostile to the opera. There a shorter form of oratorio, the cantata, was also developed, consisting of an instrumental prelude, solos, choruses in canon form, and a chorale, or hymn tune, at the end, with one persistent melody carried by strong harmonic connections becoming the dominant theme. The Protestant choirmasters, trained in contrapuntal and fugal music, adopted the idea of chord harmony slowly. Friends of Martin Luther, the reformer, early set his poetic hymns—for example, *Ein Feste Burg ist unser Gott*—in choral form. *The Passion Chorale* (1601) by Hans Leo Hassler (Fig. 501*a*, *b*), using words written by St. Bernard of Clairvaux (1090–1153), revised by Johann Sebastian Bach, the culminating figure in the school of oratorio writing, shows briefly the essential fugal style on which the oratorio form was based (Fig. 501*c*).

Instrumental Forms from the Overture to the Symphony. Closely related to the evolution of the opera and the oratorio was a rapid advance in pure instrumental music, whose form depended not upon the secular or church drama but upon local dances, upon the development of new melodies from chords, and particularly on new tonal effects possible with the clavichord, or piano, and the violin. The central principle animating all the many, involved, differing but related forms of purely instrumental music, is that of contrast. It may be a contrast between slow and fast dance rhythms, between melodies phrased in different scales, between loud and soft instrumental effects, or between phrases that are simple and those made complex by ornamentation.

Briefly one may follow the development of pure musical form from the overture of Scarlatti, which used a simple contrast of movements from fast to slow to fast again, through the "Choral" symphony of Beethoven with its many complex melodies, and a chorale of the oratorio type. As the violin came to take a more important place in the orchestra during the 18th century, instrumental compositions played in the style of the overture were expanded from three parts to four. These came to be known as "sonatas," to differentiate them from the vocal cantatas. The sonatas depended for their expression upon the development of melodic themes in the rhythms of the dance.

From the suites of ballet dances the composers of early sonatas took four: the allemande, a stately German folk dance in four-four time; the courante, a running step in triple time which was very fast; then a slow ceremonious saraband, in triple time; and at the end a *gigue*, a lively tune in six-eight time. These steps, which represented many local styles of folk dance, thus united in a sort of international form played chiefly upon a group of viols or violins, that is, by the viola da gamba, violas, and violins. During the 18th century other dances were added—particularly the gavotte, a syncopated step named after the inhabitants of the Pays de Gap, and the minuet, a graceful dance in three-quarter time.

In the most fundamental arrangement of the suite one generally finds first a fairly fast movement, the combination allemande-courante which, as the first movement of the sonata, was called the "allegro." The second part, or saraband, dreamy and most strongly melodic in character, appears as the "adagio" or "andante." The spirit of the lively gigue came to be called the "scherzo," meaning literally a jest. Each movement of the sonata—for example, the allegro—consists of an arrangement of phrases also built upon the same principle of contrasting melodies.

The words used to describe the forms and movements—in fact, most musical nomenclature—are simply Italian terms, such as fast, *presto;* slow, *andante;* rising, *crescendo;* diminishing, *diminuendo.*

The Final Structure of the Sonata Form. The modern sonata evolved (1) from the dance group called a *sonata da camera* (chamber sonata); (2) from the *sonata da chiesa* (church sonata), which was like the first only with the addition of a fugue incorporated in the old canzone form greatly elaborated; (3) from the concerto (a concerted effort) and from the operatic overtures, both of which were expansions of the *sonata da chiesa*. The overture, when played alone, came to be called the "sinfonia," from which arose the term "symphony," standing for an orchestral sonata.

The term "sonata" describes a piece of absolute music (complete without words) for a solo instrument with optional accompaniment. It is usually in three or four movements, at least one of which is technically in sonata allegro form. "Sonata allegro form" is a term used to designate the structural division of the movement (usually the first) of a sonata. This division arose from the *sonata da camera*, which had two sections divided by a cadence. From the overture and concerto came the three-movement order of the entire sonata—fast, slow, fast. In the early sonatas there appear in order (1) an intellectual fugal allegro, (2) a melodic adagio, (3) a rhythmic lively dance such as the gigue. Sometimes a slow dance form, preferably a minuet, added between the second and third movements constituted a fourth movement. Mozart's Sonata in C (Schirmer's Library, Vol. 1305, No. 3) serves as a good example of the simpler style; the final and most powerful finished sonata is Beethoven's *Pathétique*.

Johann Sebastian Bach. Two hundred years of European music culminated in the works of Johann Sebastian Bach, a member of the fifth generation of a great musical family. Trained by his brother on the organ and the clavichord, Bach pursued throughout a long life a steady, conscientious career as composer, or as he would say "an arranger of music." He filled consecutively the positions of organist or orchestra conductor in the towns of Annstadt, Mühlhausen, Weimar and Anhalt-Koethen, before he finally became the musical director of the Thomas School in Leipzig.

Living at a time when the court life about Leipzig demanded an almost Italian operatic treatment of the oratorio, and when the influence of the Italian style in German Protestant church music was at its height, Bach persisted in the pious task of coordinating in the great *Passion* oratorios and cantatas, all the inherited treasure of northern medieval religious melody that he found in the canons and chorales. Like Palestrina, Bach gathered into his great works the musical forms of his native land. He benefited, however, by the new harmonic development which had followed Palestrina. As Palestrina had taken for his subject matter the poetry of church ceremonials, Bach went for his inspiration directly to the Bible, dramatizing the Christian story in poignant, melodic passages, expanding the chorale from its simple, dignified chords to an instrumental fugue. Bach, like Martin Luther, adapted many of the hymns of the Roman Church. His *Passion* chorale *O Haupt voll Blut und Wunden* runs like a leitmotiv through the *St. Matthew Passion* (Fig. 501c).

Significance of Bach's Education. A brief study of Bach's growth and the principles by which he taught his students will serve to explain the essential education of almost every great European musician. In earliest youth, instructed by his father, Bach learned to play that instrument of personal expression par excellence, the violin. By the time he was fifteen, Bach passed from the study of the violin to the clavichord. Then he copied the music of the great German organists, Buxtehude and Pachlebel, renowned for excellence in counterpoint. His grammar schooling at this time included a study of the Bible in Greek and Latin and exercises in choral singing. At the age of fifteen, Bach left his brother and took his first paying position as a choirboy at Lüneburg. Here for the next three years, he not only sang but assisted in arranging the anthems and motets for the congregational singing in St. Michael's Church. Throughout these years Bach practiced each instrument creatively, thinking of it not simply as something on which to excel but as some new medium by which to express the melodies that continually sang within him.

Fɪɢ. 501c.—*O Haupt voll Blut und Wunden* (*O Sacred Head Surrounded*), third harmonization in *St. Matthew Passion*, by Johann Sebastian Bach. Words by St. Bernard of Clairvaux.

In later years, when preparing a course for his three composer sons, Bach advocated, first, simple melodies played on the clavichord, and then a series of rearrangements of the melodies, which he called "inventions." Thus we notice that Bach, like the medieval painters, thought of his art not as the creation of entirely new melodies but as the more perfect arrangement of old forms.

Bach's New Tuning of the Scales and The Well-tempered Clavichord. As the third element in the training of his students, Bach developed a series of preludes and fugues called *The Well-tempered Clavichord.* This collection of forty-eight creative exercises carried a series of themes through all the new equal-toned scales suggested by the French composer Rameau and perfected by Bach. To understand the significance of Bach's new tuning of the scales, one must realize that prior to his time the clavichord was tuned in the old modal scales, which had unequal intervals. The distance between C and D in the Lydian mode, for example, being different from that between C and D in the Phrygian, it was impossible to move easily from one scale to another without retuning the instrument—a lengthy procedure. Bach divided the octave into twelve equal half tones, so that all the scales could be played on the same instrument with but one tuning. Then, triumphantly proclaiming the advantage of his new note intervals, which freed the musician from the medieval formulae, Bach wrote his forty-eight studies (Fig. 501d).

With what inventive genius Bach teaches in *The Well-tempered Clavichord* one may hear in that *Fugue in C-sharp minor*, found in the first part of the series. Considered by many masters the most perfect, this has five voices discussing three themes. To some composers, the marvel of this fugue lies in the complete balance of these melodies within its complex structure; to others, its charm arises from the fine tone of the single voices, one of which sounds like a deep organ tone, another like a lyric violin, while the third is strongly rhythmical and pulsating.

Bach's St. Matthew Passion. Bach's *St. Matthew Passion*, produced in 1729, culminates all religious choral writing. Following the story of the Passion of Christ as chanted in the Good Friday Masses and in the medieval plays, the recitative was sung by a tenor voice. To the bass voices Bach gave the speeches of Christ,

Fig. 501d.—Original manuscript of Prelude in B minor for organ (Leipzig, c. 1740) by Johann Sebastian Bach. Note baroque curves of writing and compare with lines of Figs. 502 and 523c. (*Taken from A History of Music in Pictures by George Krisky, published by E. P. Dutton & Company, Inc., New York.*)

St. Peter, the High Priest, and Pilate, supported by a chorus representing the Jews. A second choir accompanying the Daughter of Zion stood for the ideal Christian congregation of Apostolic days. This choir, like the ancient Greek chorus, accompanied the more active voices with moralizing comments. The church congregation as a whole sang chorales and hymns between the major parts.

In this oratorio, Bach used the violins as an accompaniment for the lamentations preceding the Crucifixion and a string quartet to enrich the words of Christ. Only with the cry "Father, Father, why hast thou forsaken me?" comes the voice of the organ. So, in the most dramatic fashion possible, the sequences and tropes of the early German monks came to their final instrumental and choral development in the perfected oratorio.

The Masses of Bach. Bach wrote several masses; the *B minor Mass*, completed in 1738, was his most outstanding effort in this form. Bach, the Lutheran, conceived the Mass as an emotional and intellectual expression of the Christian doctrine, in contrast to the Roman musicians, who sought a simple accompaniment for colorful church pageantry. To express those elements

that were ecclesiastical, he chose the more formal music; for those that were poetic, his more emotional melodic passages. In no other art than this music of Bach could the platonic essence of the Christian doctrine have been more fittingly symbolized.

Gluck and the Renaissance of the Opera. From the time of Monteverde, the Italian operatic style, with its growing emphasis upon vocal virtuosity, dominated European music. Aristotle's classical dictum that music, action, and diction must be made to enhance the plot were forgotten on the operatic stage in deference to Italian-trained virtuosos advertised as are motion-picture stars today. Only in France, where the revival of the classical ideals of drama by Corneille, Racine and Molière united with a kind of patriotic preference for the works of Lully and Rameau, could a revolutionary musician hope to combat the influence of the Italian composers. Christoph Willibald Gluck, a native of Bohemia, went to Paris for just that purpose, in 1774. It was Gluck who for the first time advised that the overture should make the audience aware of the character and subject of the play; that the instrumental accompaniment throughout should be regulated by the needs of the action, filling all voids in the dialogue between recitative and arias. He proposed that the music should never break the sense or connection of the various periods, or weaken the action in any manner. Finally, he advocated simplicity throughout and closest attention to the character of the verse. To produce such an opera, Gluck said, a composer must be willing to break all the old laws of composition. When listening to an aria from his *Orfeo*, one finds it like the old Italian *aria da capo*. Its revolutionary quality consists of the fact that all the objectionable baroque decoration of useless trills has been stripped away, leaving a pure classical structure.

Handel, Haydn, and Mozart—The Development of Symphonic Form. The three composers, Handel, Haydn, and Mozart, perfected the modern symphonic orchestra, preparing the instrumental form for that titan, Beethoven, who was the last of the great classical composers and the first of the Romantic moderns. The symphony presents the culminating expansion of the sonata form into a majestic expression of pure orchestral music, unconnected with theatrical or church programs.

Georg Friedrich Handel (1685–1759), a contemporary of Bach, mastered all the chief instruments of his time—violin, harpsichord, oboe, and organ. In Italy Handel studied oratorio and opera. After visiting his home in Germany, he settled in England, where he produced several operas, including *Xerxes*. From this work the celebrated Largo best shows his dramatic power of expression. Handel, following most of the English and Italian dramatists of the time, favored plots taken from the great Romantic epics. His *Rinaldo* and *Almira* came from Italian sources. His greatest significance lies in his experiments with the orchestra, into which he introduced horns and early forms of the clarinet.

His great oratorios—particularly *The Messiah, Saul*, and *Joshua*—were modeled upon the Italian opera and lack Bach's purely musical form. That Handel had the feeling for the inevitable perfection of the symphonic style may be seen in the hastily written scores for his oratorios and *concerti grossi*, or small symphonies. Lacking time to write his works in full and having in his orchestra a number of skilled contrapuntal musicians, he merely indicated by a series of numbers below the bass clef what chords should be filled in above the melody. This figured bass consisted of a method of indicating chords by employing a number for each chord. Later composers, taking Handel's figured bass, were able to complete the instrumentations as full symphonies. *The Messiah*, as we have it today, was instrumentalized by Mozart.

Franz Joseph Haydn (1732–1809), when a boy, left his Croatian home for Vienna to sing in the choir of St. Stephen's Cathedral. Studying the works of K. P. E. Bach, son of Johann

Sebastian, Haydn brought the piano and violin sonatas to the form previously discussed, writing several hundred concertos, rondos, and fantasies, besides innumerable symphonies, oratorios, masses, and operas. To the orchestra he added kettledrums (tuned five notes apart) and several new woodwind and brass instruments, so that he had at his disposal not only a string section made up of first and second violins, violas, cellos, and bass viols, but also a complete band.

Through more than a hundred symphonies Haydn experimented with the sonata form, adding to the first movement a slow introduction and finally placing between the second and third movements a minuet. The *Symphony in E-flat major*, called the "Symphony with the drum roll," contains all the elements of complete form later used by Beethoven, without the later composer's Romantic fire. A study of one of Haydn's simpler symphonies and a comparison with the original suite of dances from which the sonata started will clarify the growth of symphonic form.

Wolfgang Amadeus Mozart (1756–1791), the last composer to be studied in this period, mastered operatic and instrumental form, excelling his predecessors in all branches of music. Born in Salzburg of musical parents, Mozart was taken at the age of six on a concert tour to Vienna, Berlin, and Paris. Four of his sonatas were published when he was seven. At twelve he composed his first opera. Traveling to Italy when twenty-four, Mozart produced two operas in Milan. His proficiency at that time brought him an order of knighthood from the Pope. Returning from these triumphs abroad, the young man retired to Salzburg to play in the orchestra of the archbishop. Because of the unfavorable circumstances under which he had lived, Mozart died at the early age of thirty-five. His most significant works began in 1786 with the production in Vienna of the *Marriage of Figaro*, followed in 1787 by *Don Giovanni*. These two, regularly performed today, may be considered the first of the modern operas. *Così fan tutti* and *Clemenza di Tito*, less well-known operas, intervened before *The Magic Flute*, the overture to which is considered one of the finest.

Beside many masses, cantatas, piano sonatas, string quartets, and other ensemble pieces, Mozart wrote fifty symphonies. In his greatest —called the "Jupiter Symphony," which is in C major, and the one in G minor, we have two of the most noble art works the world has ever known. By Mozart's time the symphony, an expanded sonata, had come to consist of four parts. At times, three of these followed a strict sonata allegro form, the fourth, a theme with variations. However, in many of his experiments, although the first part is the old sonata allegro, the second movement, the Andante, becomes an involved song in sonata form. The third, a minuet, is a suite of dances, and the finale, of no set form, is at times like a simple sonata; again, a rondo, like a ballade, a theme with variations, or a climax like the ensemble of an opera.

Mozart's *Symphony in G minor* shows an almost perfect balance achieved between this formal structure and a spirit seeking expression through melody, with contrasting rhythmical and strongly harmonic passages. Mozart gives in his Allegro a feeling of foreboding, introduced through a primary theme played by violins in great agitation. Then follows an Andante, with a singing, tender quality. For an introductory analysis to this symphony the student is recommended to the clear explanation with written examples of twenty-two themes in *Symphonic Masterpieces*.[1] Three or four of Mozart's operas and symphonies remain unsurpassed for unity and clarity of form. They stand in relation to the development of European music as do the works of Leonardo and Giorgione to painting.

Conclusion. Music, most significant of the arts between 1550 and 1800, grew out of humble folk origins and the melodies of the Mass to the Passion oratorios, symphonies, and fully developed operatic form. Great oratorios, cantatas, and symphonies proved the proper medium for expression of ethical-minded individuals, particularly the northern proponents of the Reformation. The southern Renaissance humanists, on the other hand, were chiefly responsible for the perfection of dramatic musical form in the opera.

To summarize: the consciousness of the value of chords underlying modern music came from three directions—(1) medieval experiments in counterpoint, (2) experiments with stringed instrumental accompaniment in opera and oratorio, and (3) from the congregational singing of the northern peoples. During the 16th and 17th centuries, nonliterary contrapuntal instrumental music from all these sources united in chordal, homophonic music with accompaniment, giving rise to a number of distinct forms, particularly the suites, rondos, sonatas, cantatas, and symphonies. There resulted an infinitely richer music and one more capable of sustaining the attention of the listener than any conceived in antiquity or the Middle Ages.

Most of the great inventive artists of Europe after the 16th century were either musicians or those painters whose work most closely approximates music—men like Rembrandt or Vermeer. In the paintings of these men one may detect a subtle balance of form against color, light and shade against depth, which together cause one to feel something akin to the greatest musical contrast and tension combined harmoniously. From the indefinite, rich, communal experience felt by the religious Gothic man in the infinite colorful reaches of the cathedral, blended with the antiphonal choral voices and organ tones, the ethical Protestant individual drew the spirit that expresses itself in formal tonal painting and the orchestral symphony. Thus the oratorio, the cantata, and the symphony, created by men whose characteristic qualities were caught in the portraits of Rembrandt, seem naturally to accompany our ideas of the aesthetic value of the cathedral.

[1] OLIN DOWNES, *Symphonic Masterpieces*, Dial Press (Lincoln MacVeagh), Inc., New York, 1935.

Painting

In no other comparable culture period has a greater volume of painting been produced. The reasons for this flood are threefold. (1) The Roman Church used baroque painters in Italy, France, Austria, and Spain, to advertise essential dogmas of the Counter Reformation. (2) The kings, heads of the newly founded nations, used entire schools or academies of painters to adorn their palaces and to advertise their victories. (3) The *bourgeoisie* in the great cities of the north, attempting to emulate the nobles and the earlier *bourgeoisie* of Italian cities, drew heavily upon local artists—the realist "Little Masters" of Holland, Flanders, England, and Germany. Money for this tremendous volume of artistic production came in great part from the gold mines of the newly discovered Americas.

The desire to own a painting, common to all upper middle-class homes, as well as to the nobility of church and state, is taken by some historians as a wider extension of the Renaissance spirit moving northward, through the 16th and 17th centuries. Instead of following schools in detail, this study selects a few of the advances in composition and color made by significant artists in this movement. These advances gave to baroque art its flash and expression; to Neo-Classicist art, its refinement; and to the bourgeois realistic art of the north, its color and pictorial unity. In the works of all the men usually listed under these different categories one observes the truly dramatic spirit, sometimes verging on the theatrical, and the musical overtones of color that add richness in all three branches.

The Last Supper by Tintoretto and the Composition of Volumes in Depth. Two followers of Titian in Venice, Paolo Veronese and Il Tintoretto, developed monumental mural painting to a point that made the city of the lagoons the 16th-century artistic center of Italy. In the days of her decline, the artists of Venice turned the treasures accumulated through commerce with the Orient during the Middle Ages into magnif-

icent mural canvases for the palaces of her bourgeois aristocracy and for her public buildings.

Titian's Madonna Pesaro (Fig. 479, Chap. XV) furnished a scheme of composition eagerly developed by his followers. They combined it with the perspective vistas of Mantegna and the resources of Florentine chiaroscuro, to create an illusion of motion into space symbolizing the expansiveness of Venetian character. It seems as though this sailor folk, thwarted in their desire to travel by the ascendancy of Spain and Portugal as maritime powers, turned to their artists, asking from them creations that would be nostalgic reminders of the old days of their city's glory.

Tintoretto (1518–1594) was well equipped by his restless character for creating countless new forms of composition suggestive of motion. His style was called the baroque, after the word *barocco*, a Spanish name for an irregular pearl, whose opalescent hues and contour often suggested elements of growth bursting into flame-like curves. Tintoretto painted with great, long-handled brushes and thinly mixed pigments in oil with quick-drying varnish. He produced, in great, swinging strokes at arm's length, superb enlarged sketches, which had the character of the tiny battle sketches of Leonardo (Fig. 462c, Chap. XV) and the masterful drawing of the human form by Michelangelo (Fig. 469, Chap. XV). In Tintoretto's pictures, rich reds and blues float with golden hues through the high lights and dark shadows. Unfortunately, in most cases Tintoretto's use of varnish and of ocherous earths combined with crimson lake resulted in a darkening of the tones, so that today only the drawing, the high lights, and the deep shadows remain. Tintoretto lived with this motto on the walls of his studio: "Paint with the colors of Titian and the drawing of Michelangelo" (Fig. 502).

Perhaps the strongest example of Tintoretto's introduction to the baroque style can be studied in his Last Supper, painted for the Venetian church of San Giorgio Maggiore. In this picture, the animated folds of the garments, picked out by intense high lights, send the gaze up and down a table whose forced perspective carries the attention deep into a vast, cavernous room. The main lines of the composition

section of the picture, the angels' wings tend to direct the eye around toward the Christ. After this much attention has been captured, one sees that the small head of the Master, sur-

Fig. 502.—Last Supper, by Jacopo Robusti, called Il Tintoretto, Church of St. Giorgio Maggiore, Venice, c. 1565–1587. Oil on canvas, foreground figures slightly larger than life size. (*Courtesy of Lesch.*)

do not at first revolve around the head of the Christ as one might naturally expect in a Christian religious picture. Instead, the first object to catch the eye is a hanging lamp around which floats a halo of ethereal angels. Caught by this bright spot in the upper left corner of the picture, the eye moves downward along the high lights on the robe of the servant at the lower left. Thence it swings along the leg of the disciple either traveling up the table toward the form of the Christ, distinguished by a halo larger than those of the disciples, or, more naturally following further right at the bottom of the picture, through the still-life group of the cat and the basket. From this point the postures of the servants send the gaze upward and toward the left. In the upper right

rounded by the greater aureole, is just about at the exact center of the upper part of the picture. In other words, the geometric composition scheme of the pedimental sculpture, with its central deity which persisted for all religious pictures throughout the Middle Ages, has now been almost lost in the dramatic flow of human forces. This picture inaugurates the style which the Roman Church, led by the militant Jesuit order, was to use in the Counter Reformation against the heresy of the Protestant northern people, as the medieval religion of contemplation gave way to a religion of action.

The composition, at first glance, parallels closely that in the Greco-Roman panel of Hercules and Telephos from Herculaneum (Fig. 248, Chap. X). It differs from the earlier example in its use of chiaroscuro. The former picture was composed of human forms in the light; the latter, of human forms almost lost in shadow. The Greek example was Apollonian; this, characterizing the dramatic struggle between light and darkness, almost Dionysiac. Here the Last Supper, the sacred rite portrayed, partakes of a Dionysiac ceremony; and within this cavern, one feels the presence of the spirits in ghostly angelic forms. This tremendous release of energy, generated by the impact of a reforming spirit upon the Christian Church, here not wholly controlled, was to run by stages through the works of El Greco and Caravaggio, until it reached the controlled compositions of the greatest baroque master, Peter Paul Rubens. After that, the style, fully developed, could be used to cover the walls and ceilings of the 17th-century Jesuit churches, whence it was taken to decorate the opera houses of the 19th century and the motion-picture palaces of the 20th.

El Greco, Painter of the Ecstatic. El Greco (the Greek)—Domenico Theotocopuli—early left his home on the Island of Crete. He studied in Venice under Titian, learned the secrets of light and shade in Rome, and eventually settled in Spain, where he found a haughty race in whose veins ran the blood of Oriental Moors and Latins. The Spaniards, who, until the 20th century, were to cling to medieval concepts in religion, enjoyed the ecstatic, mystical moments in the lives of their saints even more than they did the stories of the Bible.

When El Greco reached Toledo, about 1579, he had evolved a style that was unique and so universal in its power of expression that it looks "modern" in the 20th century. In a way, it may be called the first essay in an international style. Compounded of color schemes and figure proportions taken from Byzantine mosaics in the churches of Greece, the brush techniques of the Venetian masters, and a chiaroscuro studied with Correggio at Parma, El Greco's style has the power to stimulate the imagination of the 20th-century connoisseur as no other

baroque works have done. His elongated saints and angels partake of the elusive quality of those angular floating draperies of which they seem a part. His vital brush strokes create a

Fig. 503.—St. Francis in Ecstasy, by El Greco, c. 1585. Oil on canvas, 42½ by 32 inches (Detroit Institute of Art). (*Courtesy of Detroit Institute of Art.*)

fugal counterpoint of geometric forms in dull gold, green, black, blue, and crimson, which seem to appear and disappear from a spirit world in almost supernatural fashion. El Greco's pictures, in most cases, lie on the border line between a life of substantiality and the realm of the dream (Fig. 503)

The picture, St. Francis in Ecstasy, demonstrates completely the qualities for which El Greco's work is known. The entire purpose of this canvas, it would seem, is to express the feelings of St. Francis at the moment when he received the stigmata. The saint, in his monk's robe, seems part of a pattern of swirling, flame-like clouds torn by the winds of the spirit. His body lacks corporeality, and the folds of his garment all flow naturally toward the face. This is so completely modeled that its upcast eye, indicative of a trancelike condition, points up the entire picture. The pose of the hands,

FIG. 504.—The Entombment, by Michelangelo Caravaggio, c. 1596. Oil on canvas, figures above life size (Museum of the Vatican). (*Courtesy of Lesch-Carnegie.*)

indicated with a minimum of strokes, also suggests the inner willingness of the saint to receive his mental martyrdom. The hands do not impress at first, however, because the two light areas seem to be only natural, playful elements of the composition. The skull, set off by its dark background, in contrast, forces itself upon our attention, for, like the face, it has been completely modeled. The right angle formed by the belt of the saint and the depending cord lends geometric stability to the picture. This motif is repeated in the lines of cloud

framing the nose and lower part of the face of the saint. Once again it is repeated in the upper left part of the picture. The repetition of an angle from lower right, moving up and around toward the left, helps to carry the attention up the folds of the drapery and out, so that one follows the gaze of the saint toward the heaven from which he has received his inspiration. Almost all baroque painting of a religious nature employs this technique of actively forcing the attention toward heaven.

The picture of St. Francis lacks physical depth but suggests a movement from flat areas to solid objects. Here is a masterful bringing together of medieval decorative mural qualities, Celto-Germanic interweave, and Italian sculptural forms. Such a union of aesthetic formal values, symbolizing as it did those elements in the church which sought greater unity through the Counter Reformation, appealed particularly to the religious Spaniard. El Greco's technique was so simple and his painting so direct that we need not wonder at the great mass of works he left behind. Not all of these show the remarkable unity of design demonstrated in the St. Francis.

Eclecticism and Naturalism in the Schools of Rome. The late 16th and early 17th century found many local Italian schools outside the progressive baroque movement of Venice. Most Italian artists tried, as had Palestrina in music, to unite the discoveries of the Renaissance with dramatic Gothic composition schemes telling religious stories acceptable to the orthodox church. As they copied the efforts of Raphael, Michelangelo, or Leonardo, they came to be known as the "mannerist" painters. One artist family, the Carracci in Bologna, founded an academy on a definite eclectic program combining all the formal values sought by the mannerists. Ludovico Carracci (1555–1619) found in the art of antiquity perfection of drawing, in Raphael, finely balanced composition; in Titian, color; and in Michelangelo, an impressive grandeur. From Correggio, a Lombard master painting in the Leonardesque tradition, he appropriated *sfumato*, which lent an air of charm uniting all parts of the picture under a veil of color.

Annibale Carracci (1560–1609) carried the

ing, The Entombment (Fig. 504), earned for him such titles as "anti-Christ of painting" and the "painter of dirty feet." Probably no other work of the time showed a finer com-

Fig. 505.—Aurora, by Guido Reni, ceiling fresco, Casino Rospigliosi, Rome, 1615. (*Courtesy of Lesch-Carnegie.*)

teaching of his uncle Ludovico to Rome, where he decorated the walls of the Farnese Palace with a series of frescoes of theological subjects patterned after Michelangelo's Sistine designs. Annibale also painted pictures of the lower Roman classes. He avoided ecclesiastical criticism by confining his attempts at realism to the genre and idealizing his religious and mythological characters. Carracci devised noble vistas drawn with magnificent undulating lines and large masses of foliage clearly limited so that they had an almost sculpturesque quality, with golden color schemes suggestive of Titian and Giorgione. Carracci's formal type of landscape contrasts with the hazier, intricate picturesque landscapes of the northern people.

A contemporary of the Carracci—Caravaggio, a man who had risen from the trade of bricklayer to that of monumental fresco painter in Venice—brought a strongly realistic type of painting to Rome. He became the head of the school of the *tenebrosi*, painters of shadows. Caravaggio not only painted genre subjects, such as lute players and gamblers, gypsies and soldiers, but brought realism into his depiction of Biblical characters. His most powerful paint-

position of chiaroscuro and sculptural masses in space. Because they left the idealized, acceptable church painting of the mannerists and grandiose baroque conception and adopted a realism closer to the hearts of the people, Caravaggio and his follower Salvator Rosa were forced to live as outcasts.

Baroque Ceiling Decoration and the Aurora of Reni. A final development of the Roman schools came in the work of Guido Reni, an eclectic, who, starting as a realist in the tradition of Caravaggio, changed to the more acceptable academicism of the Carracci. In his well-known conception of Aurora (Fig. 505), painted for the ceiling of the Rospigliosi Palace, Reni left behind the full fruits of the eclectic program. His work is typical of the baroque ceiling decoration, which showed a floating vista breaking through into the clouds above the heads of the beholders. Here the charm of Correggio unites with Caravaggio's strength of composition, causing an equilibrium or balance acceptable to the classicist. The floating figures of Eros and Aurora suggest the element of transcendence. Beyond the clouds one sees an opening vista of landscape in the best Italian manner. From such paintings the later French academicians drew their inspiration. So, in the school of Rome one discovers baroque expressionism, realism, and the beginnings of an eclectic academic program.

The Art of Peter Paul Rubens. Peter Paul Rubens, a courtier, a happy family man, and the head of a large atelier, turned out gigantic decorative mural canvases for an appreciative clientele of nobles and churchmen who valued the effectiveness of his work as propaganda for the aristocratic idea and the Counter Reformation. Rubens completely expressed the baroque mood in painting at its height. Since he had no doubts and no mission, he was never thwarted; consequently, his art shows a unity of formal qualities. It remains on a plane a little lower than the greatest. The lack of intense struggle that inspirited Rembrandt, Leonardo, and Michelangelo kept Rubens from producing works of universal significance. If art could be said to exist for art's sake alone, or for the sake of propaganda, or even for a wholehearted joy in the virtuosity of the artists and a gratifying sense of accomplishment, the art of Rubens certainly might be considered with the highest. Presented here for contrast are two of his greatest compositions—the Descent from the Cross and the Birth of Marie de Médicis. Both, allegories for the elevation of the church and the state, show all the common baroque characteristics and two aspects of Rubens's work.

To understand the art of Rubens one must seek in his education those elements which built his character and style. His father, a bourgeois gentleman who had incurred the enmity of William of Orange, fled the Netherlands for Germany, where the young artist was born. After the death of the father, the family returned to Antwerp, where they embraced the Catholic faith. There the youth was apprenticed to Tobias Verhaegt, a Flemish landscape painter.

In his twenty-third year, Rubens made the usual journeyman's visit to Italy, where his talents brought him to the attention of the Duke of Mantua, at whose court great advances in the opera had been made. There the young man not only made realistic drawings of horses, hounds, and actors, but also studied music, alchemy, and astronomy. Above all, Rubens copied the compositions of the great Italian masters, pouring into his copies his own exuberant spirits. After eight years he returned to France, his sketchbooks filled with borrowed motifs for his own later designs. The tremendous vigor of the man protected him from mannerism and his works show very little of the love for the antique. With bold, dramatic strokes he wove realistic studies into a composition scheme based on the Venetian baroque, using the program of the Carracci for modeling and chiaroscuro. He combined these with gold, shimmering nude forms in landscapes traceable to his earliest Flemish teachers. The secret of Rubens's power lies in that lusty acceptance of life shown in The Farmer's Picnic in the Louvre, in The Drunken Silenus of the Munich galleries, and his self-portraits with his first wife Isabella Brant, or his second, Hélène Fourment. These are realistic, sensuous, full of the joy of life. This exuberance carried over into his religious and historical compositions (Fig. 506).

The Descent from the Cross by Rubens. Turning first to the religious aspect of Rubens's life, one may study The Descent from the Cross, painted in 1614 as the central panel of an altar triptych given by the armorers' guild to the cathedral in Antwerp. This picture, his deepest, stands closer to the realism of Caravaggio than does any other work of Rubens. Showing a mastery of composition rarely equaled for its monumental quality in other baroque paintings, The Descent gains its chief strength from the perpendicular and horizontal lines of the cross, around which are grouped the friends of Christ. The central element of action is the long, curving diagonal of the white cloth into which the two disciples above are lowering the body of their Saviour. The dead weight of the body, emphasized by the leaning figure of the lower right-hand disciple, suggests death not by rea-

Fig. 506.—Descent from the Cross, by Peter Paul Rubens, cathedral in Antwerp, 1611–1614. Oil on canvas, height about 14 feet, width about 10 feet. (*Courtesy of Lesch.*)

son of any emaciation or grotesque quality, but simply in the broken lines of the limbs. Contrast with this the three women and the five men, overflowing with energy. The figures in

FIG. 507.—Birth of Marie de Médicis, by Peter Paul Rubens, 1621–1625. Oil on canvas, height about 13 feet, width about 9 feet 8 inches (Louvre Museum). (*Courtesy of Lesch.*)

the foreground are most realistic, connecting the curved line of the Saviour's body with the earth. The upper left figure on the cross arm has a flying drapery and outstretched limb through which the central curved line flies off into the heavens. Thus, even in the scene of death, made so realistic in terms of bodies, the linear composition suggests life. The most dramatic element of the picture is the heaven-sent light pouring down from the upper right side, revealing figures that emerge from the background of sinister clouds.

The Birth of Marie de Médicis. Shortly after finishing The Descent from the Cross, Rubens was asked to paint a series of monumental canvases showing the miracles of St. Ignatius

Loyola and St. Francis Xavier, for the Jesuit church in Antwerp. Two of these may be seen in the museum at Vienna today. Following this commission came another, showing the life of Marie de Médicis. These twenty-one canvases, originally for the royal Luxembourg Palace in Paris, may now be studied in the Louvre. In this series, one showing the birth of the queen indicates the less religious side of the painter's life. Here as in the former picture, a great curving line of figures runs from the infant in the foreground up through the figure of Fame with a torch and out past Flora into the heavens. The old river-god with the lion in the foreground suggests that this is the Arno and that the infant was born in Florence. The rusticated masonry of a baroque palace at the left adds an element of stability to a scene which would otherwise lose all touch with reality. Here the same dramatic light descending from heaven reveals almost dancing forms that create a suggestion of joy, contrasting with the more somber mood in The Descent from the Cross. In the latter picture, the colors were dark and rich, like those in stained glass windows; in the Médicis canvas they are lighter and gay, with a predominance of pink, gold, and light blue. So this baroque master used color as an element for emotional expression instead of simply a tinting of figures. Into his shadows Rubens paints reflex greens and purples, such as no other master but Leonardo had conceived before him (Fig. 507).

The perspective of the picture seen from below suggests that all the happenings in the life of Marie de Médicis took place in a realm above that inhabited by ordinary mortals. In Rubens's other murals and in most wall painting of Jesuit churches, one finds this convention. It suggests that the spectator is present at some miraculous opening of the heavens, from which a supreme race of beings has come down to guide the destinies of lesser mortals. Many baroque painters allowed the figures simply to float above the earth. Rubens retained a sense of reality which led him to connect the pure fantasy with some intimate details in the foreground, an evidence of greater dramatic art.

Dutch Realism in Franz Hals. The homely wit and realism of the Gothic, Flemish, and Dutch painters, found in the works of Breughel and even Rubens, reaches its fullest development in the paintings of Franz Hals, Rembrandt, and Vermeer. These three, the greatest northern realists, stand almost opposed to the academic mannerist painters of 17th-century Italy. Starting with the genre paintings of the Breughels, one may trace this strain of realism in the works of Michel van Mierevelt, van Ravesteyn, de Keyser, and a number of other later men called the "Little Dutch Masters" (Fig. 508). A Low-Country background of farm and bourgeois city life, with emphasis on the humorous and pleasurable aspects of living, characterizes all this work. From such backgrounds the great Low-Country masters—Rubens, Hals, Rembrandt and Vermeer—always carried something of the flavor of the soil.

Hundreds of guild-hall pictures portray the Dutch—that hardy race of merchants and sailors who had founded the thriving colony of New Amsterdam and who enjoyed a lusty companionship—discussing their exploits in political meetings and communal banquets. In the council house of Haarlem, Franz Hals left eight portrait groups of guild officers. A study of these groups discloses his development from an early, gay, almost baroque manner to a subdued, masterful, realistic style. Beginning with nearly pure Gothic realism and a poorly knit composition scheme barely suggestive of activity, because of some inevitable law of artistic growth, Hals gradually reached such a condition of poise and equilibrium in his work that it has universal quality.

With that growth came a clearness and sureness of technique exemplified in his portrait of Hille Bobbe, a half-mad wench. This canvas sets forth a hearty acceptance of life in its most energetic, unbeautiful moments. The picture seems to exist simply for the joy the artist must have had in executing in a few snappy brush strokes a pattern that introduces us to a human soul on a simple, animal level. With penetrating insight Hals cut through the upper crust of culture to find the primeval strength of the

Fig. 508.—Hille Bobbe, by Franz Hals, 1635–1640. Oil on canvas, height about 2 feet 5 inches, width about 2 feet (Kaiser Friederich Museum, Berlin). (*Courtesy of Lesch.*)

recently civilized Gothic man. In the disposition of his brush strokes there is a crackling quality that makes it almost possible to hear the raucous laughter of this girl who consorts with a night owl. Here body does not exist; only a dynamic design of colorful strokes, like those patterns of contrast created by the Burgundian Romanesque sculptors (Fig. 335). More keen, however, than Hals's use of line is his spatial pattern. Notice that the ellipses on the stein at the left of the picture have been arranged so that the lower ellipse—which should, according to the laws of naturalistic perspective, be more round than the upper—has been reversed and flattened so that the color area of the stein will more completely fit the frame. Here neither subject matter nor pattern carries any associational values of beauty or sublimity, but presents a bold display of crude energy. Many would consider this pure virtuosity expressive of inner vitality the acme of art.

The Superior Realism of Rembrandt van Rijn. Rembrandt Harmensz van Rijn, "prince of the shadows," as a contemporary critic called him, found the means for uniting the Beautiful and the Sublime through a realistic approach to art. In subdued baroque composition schemes and Gothic color patterns under the revealing technique of chiaroscuro, he portrays with subtle psychological insight the essentially moral basis of human character. In the pictures of Rembrandt one finds affirmed with finality the ancient dictum of Leonardo and the Italian pioneers of the 15th century, that "all character is revealed at the point of union between light and shade." A brief biography discloses some of the elements of Rembrandt's education that gave him power to see character in others.

Born in Leyden in 1606, of fairly well-to-do parents, the youth studied Latin, exploring those humanist authors of antiquity whose spirit, uniting with the Christian ethic of the New Testament, guided his art throughout his life. At the age of fourteen he was apprenticed to Jacob von Swanenburch, a mediocre painter with whom he worked but a few years. Next he helped Peter Lastman, an eclectic who knew the recipes of the school of the Carracci. The decisive influence at the end of his educational period was a man by the name of Jacob Pynas, with whom he never studied. Pynas had created pictures of the life of Christ in the realistic manner of Caravaggio. Under the influence of these three masters Rembrandt's first paintings, executed in 1627, were clearly drawn with well-defined borders and realistic color like that of the Italians.

In 1631 the artist moved to Amsterdam and achieved success because of his ability to paint the realistic, almost photographic portraits desired by guild members. But from the start, his personal desires for more than naturalistic portrayal began to intrude in his work. His type of realism demanded that his group paintings

be connected within themselves by some subtle psychological bond between the sitters. Like Leonardo, he felt that he should paint not the superficial appearance of a man but the condition of his soul. Mere external academic rules for arranging planes and areas of dark and light or masses of bodies could not suffice. What Rembrandt sought was the same inner composition already discovered in the Virgin of the Rocks and The Last Supper by Leonardo, or in the paintings of Giorgione. Since Rembrandt never toured Italy but spent his time exploring his own mind in relationship to the people close to him, he was forced to reach his goal—as perhaps every great genius must—at home, without the benefit of these other masters.

Rembrandt's Study of Moral Character in Portraiture. By 1634, the successful painter had recognized the peculiar quality of his own genius in his group of the students in the Anatomical Clinic of Dr. Tulp. Subtly this composition combines the Gothic type of design, which caused the eye to travel around the picture area, with the Classical type, in which the interest was centered. Almost thirty years later, in 1661, Rembrandt brought the type of composition to its final degree of perfection in his group portrait of the *Staalmeesters*, or Syndics of the Cloth Guild (Fig. 509), by the addition of warm colors infusing the whole with the glow of life.

The Syndics of the Cloth Guild, perhaps the most successful group portrait ever painted, shows five guild masters accompanied by a servant, gathered to guarantee and seal the cloth manufactured locally. Although each sitter shows distinctive personality, each is necessary to the completely communal spirit of the group.

Rembrandt achieved this unity within diversity by capturing a moment in which one syndic has just finished speaking, while another, half rising from his chair, turns as though to address the observers. The two men farthest left and the pair at the right look directly at the beholder, creating a direct absolute balance of interest lines centering in the point at which one stands to look at the picture. The servant, standing behind, looks in the same direction as the central syndic, who has just finished expounding a point of law or describing a transaction, and seems to be gazing slightly to the left of the beholder as though addressing a second person, also outside the frame. With such magnificent invention Rembrandt suggests "we" instead of "I" to the observer. No more subtle tribute has ever been paid by an artist to the democratic ideal.

of the group. Finally, as in the picture of Dr. Tulp, the visual center of the composition—not obvious at first glance in the black-and-white reproduction—is the bright-red area caused

FIG. 509.—The Cloth Syndics, by Rembrandt van Rijn, 1661–1662. Oil on canvas, height 6 feet 2 inches (Rijks Museum, Amsterdam). (*Courtesy of Lesch-Carnegie.*)

The dignity and importance of the syndics is assured by placing them slightly above the eye level. The perspective lines of the table lead back toward the left of the picture and the lines of the chair lead toward the rear right so that one must assume that two intersecting retreating planes cross each other, linking the men and dividing our interest among members by sunlight striking the Oriental tablecloth. Slightly above the red spot, the hand of the man who has spoken seems to hold our attention to the Book, symbol of all the new Protestant dispensation. In true baroque fashion, the element of pleasure is suggested by the soft golden light falling over the scene from the windows at the left. This relieves the sobriety of the black-clothed individuals and the severe paneling of the room.

For the first ten years in Amsterdam, Rembrandt had a career as a successful portraitist, meanwhile illustrating many scenes from the Bible, for his own pleasure. He also began to experiment with landscapes and, after 1638, with the art of etching.

In 1642 there came a decisive turn in his fortunes. He was then engaged on his portrait group known as The Night Watch, which might also be named The Sortie of Captain Banning Cock's Sharpshooters. This is in some respects Rembrandt's greatest picture, because it unites all he had learned in his Biblical compositions and portraiture up to that time. The picture shows the members of the guild of riflemen at the precise moment when they were emerging from their lodge hall into full daylight for a practice shoot, or perhaps to man the walls against some enemy. Although seventeen members of the company are easily recognizable without destroying the effect of the whole, two might have felt slighted. At any rate, Rembrandt was thinking of pushing his artistic discoveries to their greatest limits in a composition completely unified. Unfortunately, his enthusiasm carried him so far that some of the commissioners protested it was no longer a portrait. His misfortunes began when the gunners each of whom wanted his face to appear as prominently as the others, refused to take the composition on which he had spent much time and money. After 1642, Rembrandt lost all desire to meet the outside world in a competitive way. During the next years he created his most remarkable pictures of the life of Christ, among which is The Supper at Emmaus (Fig. 510), painted in 1648. This provides an excellent example of Rembrandt's realism blending with baroque color and chiaroscuro in a strong geometric composition.

Rembrandt's Use of Color and The Supper at Emmaus. Scholars differentiate between four phases of Rembrandt's use of color. In the first period, before 1636, the artist used naturalistic local colors like those of the Italians in the school of the Carracci. Between 1636 and 1656, he subdued the brilliant local colors of objects by throwing over them a haze of gray or brown tones and developing the shadows of his pictures. In the third period, after 1656, he reached the greatest dramatic heights, pointing up great areas of brown or gray with some brilliant tone

caught in a ray of sunlight. In the final period, broken and scintillating color like that in the works of the 19th-century French Impressionists dominated his light and shade in such a way that it seems as though the master must have lost himself in a mystical adoration of light. It is highly probable that Rembrandt unconsciously accepted the medieval point of view of Eckhardt, which considered the highest beauty one of color as it emerged under the revealing rays of the Divine Light.

In respect to color, the mature Rembrandt was no naturalist. He distilled from the colors of nature their essence and chose the warm golden tones to suggest the good life. He does not move far from brown earth pigments, which form his backgrounds even in the sky, where a cool gray takes the place of the usual blue. In this gray-brown atmosphere brilliant flashes of red, yellow, purple, or green emerge to thrill the senses. The essential color scheme is that of the cathedral interior, with its stained-glass windows. The depth of the shadows arises in great part from the contrast afforded in the flashes of brilliant hues.

The picture of Christ dining with the two disciples—The Supper at Emmaus—reveals the great painter at his best. Here is no scene of ecclesiastical magnificence but the simple story of one of the greatest miracles—the survival of the spirit beyond the grave. The Christ appears both human and divine, certainly no ghostly apparition. Seated at a table set four-square in the lower corner of a huge room whose heavy stone walls and arch suggest antiquity, the returned Master breaks the bread with which He will give His two companions eternal life. The moment appears to be the one in which these two recognize their friend, who has returned from the realm of the shadows. One raises his hands in adoration, the other draws back almost as though in fear, and only the servant seems oblivious to the miracle taking place. With such profound psychological insight did Rembrandt bring the story to life.

The restfulness and majesty of the scene arise

FIG. 510.—Supper at Emmaus, by Rembrandt Harmensz van Rijn, 1648. Oil on canvas, 26½ by 25¼ inches (*Louvre Museum*). (*Courtesy of Lesch.*)

not only from the pleasurable effect of the warm golden tones flooding the canvas, but also from a few brilliant spots of red and purple on the sleeves of the disciple. In particular, it human Christ radiates a light of His own, with a brilliance equaling that of the Divine.

From its very simplicity and quietness, the picture gains power. In its presence one feels

Fig. 511.—The Three Trees, by Rembrandt van Rijn, 1643. Etching, 8⅜ by 11 inches. The artist has here transposed his rich chiaroscuro to a plate which, transcending most of his other etchings, contains not only his essential character but furnishes an epitome of Dutch landscape painting. (*Courtesy of Lesch-Carnegie.*)

arises from the subordination of a dramatic baroque composition scheme to the central, quieting influence of the Divine. Both disciples sit in chairs placed on a diagonal to the square of the floor and the table. Unlike the figures in the groups of the Cloth Syndics and the Anatomical Clinic of Dr. Tulp, none of these characters has the slightest interest outside the picture, so that the action is entirely contained within that hallowed spot where three friends have come together for a moment. Into this infinite room a shaft of light from the upper left signifies the Heavenly Source and still the very

the humane reality of the Divinity and is assured that Christ did visit His disciples in just this way, in the days following the Resurrection. After all the formal values of this composition have been examined, there still remains the inexplicable poignant sincerity which could have arisen only from the need of the artist for such an affirmation of faith.

Landscapes of Rembrandt and the Idea of the Sublime. In the final period of his life, like Franz Hals, Rembrandt used quick strokes of the brush full of pigment, laid upon the canvas like tesserae of a mosaic, so that the colors seem to scintillate. Then the outlines of his figures fade and forms are lost in an aureole of color like that around the Christ in The Supper at Emmaus. After his forty-seventh year, Rembrandt's rays of the sun and casting their shadows out over the foreground. Less obvious are two men who appear beside the stream which separates us from the trees and background, or the many

Fig. 512.—Shepherds of Arcadia, by Nicolas Poussin, 1638–1639. Oil on canvas, height 2 feet 9½ inches (Louvre Museum). (*Courtesy of Lesch-Carnegie.*)

etching and landscape painting, which had slowly been growing in power, reached their fullest development. Through a long life of laborious craftsmanship closely paralleling that of Bach, and through constant introspection and analysis of his own work, Rembrandt finally discovered the essential strength of his suggestive drawn line and his dramatic light and shade. These can be seen in his etchings Christ Healing the Sick, The Crucifixion, and The Resurrection.

Rembrandt's dramatic quality and suggestive power appear at their best in the landscape, The Three Trees (Fig. 511). Like three comrades these stand, just below the brow of a hill, catching in their lacy branches the low slanting farmers and cattle whose presence on the hills and in the fields seems to call us into the picture. Attention is called to the fisher because of his nearness to the seated figure silhouetted by a bright ray of light against the dark shadow cast by the hill. Beyond this shadow, the gaze wanders for miles toward the distant horizon with its windmills. Overhead, the sky divides into two parts. High cumulus clouds float on the upper right; on the left a shower seems to be sweeping the landscape clean. Here, as in The Supper at Emmaus, one slowly becomes conscious, as he studies the picture, of depths of genius beyond the power of easy analysis. All the associational values of this etching suggest that mankind may be at peace with the universe, that even storms have friendliness, and that all of space is ordered according to some intricate sublime laws. Here significant man dwells in the light between water and a shadow. In this tiny space Rembrandt has depicted universal qualities suggesting that which Longinus called the Sublime.

The Arcadia of Poussin as the Inspiration of the Academic Style. The art of the French Academy, a force in painting which dominated the official European mind for almost 300 years, arose from the joint efforts of two young painters, one a romantic soul who buried himself in the ruins of Italy, the other a political organizer of no small ability. The first, Nicolas Poussin, as a youth showed a touch of genius approaching that of Rembrandt, while the latter, Charles LeBrun, had less artistic talent than Rubens. The essentials of Poussin's activity can be studied in his Shepherds of Arcadia (Fig. 512), painted in 1638. LeBrun's influence accounts for the Apollo gallery in the Louvre (Fig. 513), most of the interior decoration of the palace of Versailles, innumerable badly organized mural canvases, but most of all for the foundation of the Academy of France.

To understand the place of these two figures in European art one must remember that during the 17th and 18th centuries two differing philosophies of instruction existed side by side in Europe. In the northern countries, the old guild ideals and apprenticeship still held. In the south, where the descendants of princely Renaissance families and the church patronized the artist, the *botteghe* had given way to academies, or art schools supported by the central authorities. There the academic method of instruction called for light and shade, study of Greco-Roman sculpture, a knowledge of the mathematical rules of perspective, a course in artistic anatomy, and a thorough grounding in the composition schemes of the old masters.

Poussin (1594–1665) received from his early Norman and Flemish teachers a color scheme and a realistic point of view like that of the van Eycks (Fig. 391). Inspired by engravings

of Raphael's pictures, and perhaps disliking the wearisome apprenticeship of the guild system, he went to Rome in 1624. There he completely lost himself in the absorbing study of ancient

Fig. 513.—The Apollo Gallery of the Louvre Palace, by Charles LeBrun, 1662. In this hall the baroque decoration of Venetians, such as Tiepolo, and Romans, such as the Caracci, Pozzo, and Reni reaches its greatest refinement at the hands of one who might be called the first "interior decorator." (*Courtesy of Metropolitan Museum of Art.*)

art. There the fires of his genius, separated from lively reality, gradually cooled.

The Shepherds in Arcadia, composed just before antiquity had completely claimed Poussin, illustrates the academic art at its best. It shows in all details his professed belief in a method which became the rule of the pedantic LeBrun. Poussin's creed held that "the sole object of painting is to give pleasure by means of an imitation in lines and colors on some plane surface of everything revealed by the light of the sun." Moreover, in this work he drew from both the antique and nature, uniting them with the warmth of rich Flemish color in describing a dramatic moment. There resulted a work with the same exalted style found in the tragedies of Poussin's contemporaries, Corneille and Racine. Usually, the eclectic program ends in a poorly integrated work of art, but this picture has integrity precisely because the artist actually believed in San Nazzaro's dream of Arcadia. Here he presents some shepherds of the Campagna gathered around a massive ancient tomb, on which they have discovered the words *et in Arcadia ego*. Gently the muse of history explains the meaning of the inscription: "I, too, once lived in Arcadia." So much for the purely literary, associational message, the *raison d'être* for the composition. Around this obvious center of the picture the arms and limbs of the shepherds suggest a gently swirling swastika, which leads the eye out into the bodies. The stately, robed figure, whose grace is accentuated by the gentle folds of her garment, seems to grow from the ground into the tree which passes out of the picture behind the tomb. In this way symbols of the past, the present, and the future unite with no sign of violence. All the baroque composition lines, planes, and masses center in the great block leading the attention slowly back toward the left. Even the landscape, which in a truly baroque picture would have been an encouragement to exploration, seems here to belong to the tomb. So one finds regularly, in Classical academic art, that a monumental group of human figures forms the center of interest and that movement is subordinated to a massive geometric scheme.

Since Poussin held painting to be a matter of imitation, it follows that the painter who would excel must choose some great universal dramatic theme for his subject. In such works, composition, of secondary importance, consists primarily of organizing the associational values as in a drama. After that, excellence depends upon the subordination of detail, so that all attention focuses in a plausible fashion upon the central idea. Formal values depend upon skill in presenting the action. Color, the emotional element—never a primary consideration —should be used simply to charm the eye into believing that the action is pleasant and acceptable. In Poussin's aesthetic theories one finds Aristotle's criterion for the judgment of the drama applied to painting. Even in the accompanying illustration, which lacks the charm of the color, one can see that Poussin reached a degree of plausibility comparable to that of Giorgione and Rembrandt. He could do this with perfect sincerity because, like many classical scholars and educators of the 20th century, he believed that antiquity alone held the secret of good living. With some justice the realistic critic may point out that Poussin, considered the foremost genius of the French Academy, might also be studied as the first of the Romantics. Inspired by Poussin's Arcadian existence, French artists who had visited him founded a branch of the Academy in Rome, after his death in 1665. In the 19th century other nations followed suit.

The Foundation of the Academy and a Print by LeClerc. Although the most genial painter of the French school, Poussin never belonged to the Academy. Because the typical academician is essentially a joiner, a politician, and a conservative, possibly no great genius can be an academician. Most creative artistic innovators since the Renaissance have been either the realists or romantic revolutionaries, who belonged to no school. Charles LeBrun, the idol of the minister Richelieu, after studying for four years in the Roman circle of Poussin, returned to France, where he gained the patronage of Colbert. In 1648, Louis XIV, persuaded by Colbert and LeBrun, founded the *Académie royale de peinture et de sculpture*, based on the model of the literary *Académie française* founded by Richelieu. LeBrun also had himself appointed director of the Gobelin tapestry and furniture factories, and was finally knighted. Backed by all the resources of the realm, LeBrun began to organize the art instruction on the models suggested by his friend Poussin. The significance of the many academic codes of painting and sculpture printed under his direction will be discussed at length in the section on aesthetic theories. That the efforts of LeBrun were but a small part of a general movement in all fields of education may be seen in the engraving by Sébastien LeClerc of the Foundation of the Academies (Fig. 514).

The central part of the typical academic composition below stresses the new advances in science, with geometry dominating every other form of activity. In the foreground one

here was that of Descartes. Correctly we assume that the Academy of Art is but an extension of the scientific method applied to man's emotions. The insight of LeClerc led him to evalu-

Fig. 514.—Foundation of the Academies of Arts and Sciences, by Sébastien LeClerc, drawing (British Museum). Compare this with the finished state of the print, illustrated opposite page 86 in *The History of Taste* by Chambers, Columbia University Press, 1932. (*Courtesy of British Museum.*)

sees the earliest chemical and electrical apparatus, along with the magic lantern, ancestor of the motion picture. Astronomical and geographical instruments symbolize new fields of exploration. Mechanics and physics are in the middle foreground. The useful arts of city planning and fortification building have a place in the center middle ground, accompanied by heraldry. Hardly recognizable, music, sculpture, and painting appear far in the distance, having scarcely more importance than theology, which had been relegated to a little-frequented library far back at the right. Architecture is everywhere present, but activity in this art is confined to the placing of a few statues on the colonnade, which is built in the style of the contemporary builder, Perrault. The philosophical program of the academies presented

ate highly those scientific activities that led to intellectual progress and the realistic point of view. From the movement recorded in the many activities of this picture there resulted in France the foundation of the *Encyclopédie* and, in the United States, the modern, progressive university. Strong in use and associational values, this print furnishes little more than a narrative for educational purposes. The composition scheme lacks forceful baroque movement into depth, although some movement appears guiding the attention by great planes of light and shadow arranged around the horizontal and vertical masses of the building.

The academic movement, inextricably bound to the royalist state, allowed a complete control of the arts similar to that exercised by Richelieu and Colbert in politics, by Malherbe and Boileau in literature. Anyone who would seek new artistic creation during the 17th century must turn to the realist brothers LeNain or to

Breda. Diego Velázquez (1599–1660) worked throughout his life in an environment that might have created an academician, had not his patron, King Philip IV of Spain, kept him

FIG. 515.—Surrender of Breda, by Diego Velázquez, 1634. Oil on canvas, height 10 feet 1 inch (Prado, Madrid).
(Courtesy of Lesch-Carnegie.)

the landscape painter Claude Lorrain. These artists did not subscribe to the chief purpose of the Academy, announced "to teach manners and measure." Working independently, they nearly starved to death. Following the history of the academic movement, one meets such painters as LeBrun and LeClerc, Hyacinthe Rigaud, Charles Coypel, LaTour, David, and last of the line, the "academic pope," Ingres.

The Realism of Velázquez and the Surrender of

so busy painting that he had no time to theorize about his art. This painter, brought to full fruition all that Leonardo da Vinci and the Florentines of the 15th century would have considered desirable. Behind Velázquez lay the dominating will and the realistic point of view which, combined with intense religious purpose, constitute the Spanish national character. The art of Velázquez demonstrates that side of the Spanish nature which had made Spain the greatest nation of soldiers and adventurers in the 17th century. From two masters of the school of Seville—one a genre painter, the other an aristocratic portraitist—Velázquez inherited a realism like that of Caravaggio and a mastery of light and color in the Venetian mode. Finally, he drew directly from nature a clarity and vitality almost unsurpassed elsewhere in the painter's art.

Velázquez, introduced to the court by his noble father-in-law, the painter Pacheco, found favor with a powerful prime minister, Duke of Olivares, and eventually gained the friendship of the king. Then he entered upon a thirty-eight years' commission, to paint the portraits of members of the royal family at all the most significant moments of their lives. Assured of his livelihood, Velázquez was able for his own amusement to compose a few of the most remarkable realistic genre pictures the world has known. The most significant are The Drinkers, The Tapestry Weavers, and Las Meniñas—the last a group portrait of the Infanta Margarita with her ladies in waiting as she was being painted by Velázquez himself. To make the subject more intriguing, Velázquez has framed the king and his wife in a mirror, as they appear to be looking at the picture from the vantage point of the observer. This canvas, more than any other ever painted, shows how close can be the connection between a great artist and an intelligent patron. Velázquez dared to subordinate royalty by painting himself larger than the king and queen, who nevertheless appreciated his consummate skill.

The painter's few pictures in the realm of mythology—Mercury and Argus, Menippus and Aesop, and The Forge of Vulcan—bring such realism to ancient legends that one feels their inherent plausibility. Unlike the pictures of Poussin, these lack properties suggesting antiquity, consequently Velázquez has labeled his characters so that all might know whom they represented. His religious pictures, including a Crucifixion and an Adoration of the Magi, have the same plausibility. These works by an intel-lectual, contained Spaniard, at heart an aristocrat, contrast powerfully with those by the emotional, tender, bourgeois Rembrandt.

Formal and Associational Values in The Surrender of Breda, by Velázquez. For the critic interested in purely formal values or almost academic realism, Velázquez seems one of the greatest painters, if not the greatest, who ever lived. On the one occasion when he painted a historical scene, he brought to it his great skill in portraiture, his happy mastery of genre, and a feeling of reality rarely surpassed in a narrative picture. This canvas, The Surrender of Breda (Fig. 515), shows that moment in which the Spanish general, Spinola, receives the keys of a conquered Dutch fortress. Here, clear drawing, natural disposition of the figures, and a remarkably fresh, delicate color effect have been united in a geometric composition scheme, such as usually typifies academic painting. The mass of Dutch troops at the left has a heavy character, which also rests upon its individual members. This group connects with the heavy horizontal line at the top of the fortress in the middle background. In contrast, the Spaniards —lighter more volatile—at the right, form a vertical mass, their spears carrying the attention up into the sky so that they seem to cast a shadow over the broad expanse of low Dutch landscape, with its canals and streams farther in the background. The faces of the men in the two groups tell the rest of the story.

Since refined color has such high value in the works of Velázquez, it is particularly unfortunate that this element is lacking in the reproduction. The artist recognized that usually nature has cool, clear colors with blue-grays, pink, dark-purple shadows, lemon-gold and silver lights, and only here and there, in the healthy flesh of a soldier or a laborer, those golden tones typical of the work of Rubens and Rembrandt. Since most of Velázquez's characters are from among the nobility—popes, courtiers, and indoor folk, whose skin is untouched by sunlight—he builds his color harmonies on the cool side of the scale, with a resultant intellectual flavor. His warm colors appear in the genre studies. A few pictures to be seen in American galleries—for example, the Man with the Wine Glass in Toledo and the St. John in

Fig. 516.—The Music Lesson, by Jan Vermeer van Delft. Oil on canvas, 29 by 25½ inches (Royal Gallery, Windsor).

the Chicago Art Institute—tend toward the warmer side of his palette. The finest and most typical of his portraits in the United States are probably the ones in the Detroit Institute of Art and the National Art Gallery at Washington. In these the painter has caught the essence of Spanish character as revealed by history.

The Music Lesson, by Jan Vermeer. The works of Jan Vermeer mark the culmination of the efforts of the "Little Masters"—those painters of Amsterdam, Haarlem, and Delft who chose as subject matter the landscapes and interiors associated with the Dutch national pride and love of home. This artist differs from the lesser figures—Terborch, Jan Steen, Peter de Hooch, Kasper Netscher, Ruisdael, and Hobbema, by giving greater attention to the human figures, which more nearly fill the room space of his

pictures and seem almost like part of the home furnishings. Vermeer, like others of the Little Masters, builds many of his compositions around the theme of music. The Music Lesson (Fig. 516) in the Royal Gallery, Windsor, indicates the fine degree of continuity typical of Vermeer. Across the top of the picture and down the left side, strong horizontal and vertical lines of shadow accentuate wall and ceiling planes, gently guiding the attention toward the right. In the lower right corner of the picture, the heavy form of a table covered with a splendid Persian rug sends the attention toward the left. The square marble tiles of the floor, set at an angle to the wall and picture plane, carry the attention back around the bass viol to the horizontal line of the harpsichord against the rear wall. This picture holds the same fine character interweave as The Three Philosophers and The Musicians by Giorgione or The Cloth Syndics by Rembrandt. If the purpose of the artist be to portray in so crude a material as paint the subtlest ties of human feeling created by music, Vermeer has come closer to this ideal than any other artist.

The harmonies of mellow, silvery gold light generated by the windows at the left blend the entire picture. Here Vermeer has caught for all eternity a vision of that happy home in which the art of music has a place. In his work one finds an affirmation of the essential aristocracy in the free human mind, whether it be in cottage or castle. He demonstrates that, with freedom to develop oneself in a free land, every man can reach an equilibrium in which emotional baroque composition schemes order themselves intellectually and academic geometricism comes to life. In this way the primitive joy at recognition of objects which is the basis of realism becomes inspired by associational thought passages suggested through ordered patterns. Studying the paintings of Vermeer, one concludes that in them, useful, associational, and formal balance have reached equilibrium, so that all of life appears to have been designed.

Antoine Watteau and the Diverse Origins of the Rococo. The three types of painting studied as separate cultural attitudes in the 17th century became the common property of the lesser

sure of his source of income. With Hyacinthe Rigaud, a successful academic portrait painter of the court, Watteau may be considered one of the inventors of the delicate rococo style of

FIG. 517.—Embarkation for Cythera, by Antoine Watteau, 1717. Oil on canvas, height 4 feet 3¼ inches (Royal Palace, Berlin). (*Courtesy of Lesch-Carnegie.*)

artists in the 18th. The Academy absorbed baroque composition schemes; the baroque painters relied less upon color, and the realists benefited by the methods of the other two. As an accompaniment to this change, painters lost their primitive vigor, the baroque became the rococo, the Academy turned from monumental mural canvases to smaller portraits, and the realists like Chardin perfected still-life groups approximating photographic objectivity.

Jean Antoine Watteau, the son of a tilemaker, appears as the first modern artist in the "Bohemian," or gypsy, tradition. Throughout his short, unfortunate life he worked in one style after another without ever being quite

painting. The term "rococo" comes from the word *rocaille*, meaning a spiral seashell. Motifs derived from these shells were used in decorating walls of 18th-century French palaces. Watteau kept a realistic vision for the depiction of the strolling players, peasants, and soldiers, despite the partial success attained in the last years of his life by his discovery of a type of painting appropriate to the aristocratic rococo environment. When finally his popular Fêtes Galantes led to his acceptance by the Academy, he still remembered his companions of the stage, who were not quite acceptable in the best society.

Watteau's earliest apprenticeship in Paris started with a belated guild artist, Metayer, in whose "Factory of Saints" religious pictures were turned out wholesale. After selling two small pictures of his own, Watteau left this sign-painting business for more academic study

Fig. 518.—Cupid a Captive, by François Boucher, c. 1752 (Wallace Collection, London). (*Courtesy of Lesch.*)

with Gillot, an artist interested in the world of the theater. Through Gillot he met Audran, a scenic painter, who initiated him in the art of drawing arabesques—great scroll-like curves of baroque decoration characterizing the pseudo-

Oriental sets called for by the operas of the time. Audran, who was also the concierge or gatekeeper of the Luxembourg Palace, introduced his young friend to the great galleries, where he was able to study the works of Rubens. With such a fanciful art schooling, Watteau finally received a commission to decorate the house of a wealthy bourgeois, the financier Pierre Crozat, whose collections of Italian and Dutch masters were renowned.

Watteau lived for some years in Crozat's home, recording the life of the Parisian society lavishly entertained there. Inspired by the charming picnics held in Crozat's gardens, Watteau created one or two superb paintings in a new style, to which he brought all the romance of the operatic stories he saw performed in the theater. The famous Embarkation for Cythera (Fig. 517), which shows the beginning of the voyage of lovers to an island paradise, is the best-known example of this, the genial beginning of the rococo. Here are the origins of the Romantic attitude and the hazy Impressionistic landscape found after the painting of Corot during the 19th century. The delightful plausibility with which Watteau wove together the silks and satins of aristocratic life under the Regency and the operatic mythology is made more acceptable because the action takes place in a most charming landscape. Here the soft, rosy glow cast over all misty distances suggests the music of Gluck and, later, of Debussy. This style, made a little more sensuous, a little less subtle and idyllic, was to become the inspiration for Boucher, Fragonard, and a host of 18th-century painters. Years later, after the Revolution, when aristocracy had passed away and only the *bourgeoisie* remained, a group of painters such as Sisley, Signac, and Monet were to paint the landscapes alone, with all their sparkle of light and color. Watteau's composition schemes are those of the realist, close to Vermeer and Rembrandt.

The Rococo of Boucher and Fragonard. Under the influence of Madame de Pompadour,

Watteau's followers, artists connected with the court of Louis XV, particularly Fragonard and Boucher, turned to the classical mythological subject matter of the Academy, which they rendered in delicate baroque composition schemes. Boucher's Cupid a Captive (Fig. 518) is a wall panel painted for a rococo palace. In both the drawing and the coloring of these figures, the tenderness of childhood and maidenhood has been accentuated. The wealth of sweet-smelling flowers, particularly roses, in the foreground and the soft silken robes suggest feminine luxury. The composition has been ordered on three planes, the first proceeding from right to left, the second from the figure of the nymph in the center of the picture back toward the right, and the third up the trunk and branches of the tree. A composition scheme which one hundred years earlier would have symbolized some religious emotion or ecstasy now is associated by the artist with the delights of the boudoir. No wonder the proletarian revolutionaries at the end of the century considered the rococo a symbol of all that was degenerate in the life of aristocratic society.

Academic Realism in the Late 18th Century. During the late 18th century, with the widening of a rift between the aristocracy and the masses led by the intellectuals, a number of painters sought realistic subject matter, which gradually came to characterize the revolutionary movement. Diderot, the critic, fulminated against the art of Boucher and Fragonard on the grounds of its antisocial subject matter. Greuze, an academician, found his subjects in genre scenes, which he handled with rococo delicacy. Chardin created groups of still life, unsurpassed for their perfect balance of formal values except in the art of Vermeer. Naturally, realism availed itself of the methods of the Academy and the best known French realist during the last quarter of the century was Louis David (1748–1825).

David's first passion was the Neo-Classical revival taught in Rome by Raphael Mengs and the archaeologist Winckelmann. This became popular in France on the eve of the Revolution, as the republican spirit among the intellectuals replaced the more aristocratic academicism of the 17th century. David's earliest painting in

Fig. 519.—Oath of the Horatii, by Jacques Louis David, 1784. Oil on canvas (Louvre Museum). Compare with the more realistic representation by Daumier at the end of the French Revolution, Fig. 567, Chap. XVIII. (*Courtesy of Metropolitan Museum of Art.*)

the Neo-Classical style shows Belisarius, the ancient Goth, begging in the streets of Rome. It was said that he had created the work to shame "ungrateful tyrants." The intellectuals, who were then condemning the decadent monarchy, hailed the picture as a revelation. The Count d'Angiviller, a leader of the republicans and a director of the Academy, commissioned David to paint The Oath of the Horatii (Fig. 519), which was later sold to the king. Here was a perfect dramatic presentation of ancient Roman heroism set in an appropriate archaeological frame. The composition is academic and Classical in its simplicity, the figures are sculpturesque and obviously posed, the color is cool and intellectual. However, the work is so realistic that antiquity seemed to live again. In 1787, his Socrates Taking the Poison and, in 1789, Brutus Condemning His Sons for Having Conspired against Roman Liberty ended the period of republicanism and ushered in the Revolution. David's first thought on becoming a political power in the Revolutionary Tribunal was to dissolve the Royal Academy and to abolish the free salons, which had been fostered by the wealthy *bourgeoisie*.

The Oath of the Horatii shows a return to the balanced, frontal composition associated with the art of Raphael. The room in which the action takes place is square, with three arches in the rear. The center arch frames Brutus, the left his sons, and the right their womenfolk. So strong is the individual power of expression that each group seems capable of standing by itself, yet each takes its place as part of a whole. The attention is allowed to wander very little, for the story is straightforward and the associational values aroused by the subject matter dominate the formal values. How little is left of the baroque may be noticed by anyone who wishes to find an escape through the background of the picture. The one simple exit, backstage left, was associated with danger and defeat on the classical stage of the time. So the picture has a sinister dramatic quality, which is heightened by the strongly cast tragic shadows. The same tragic tone sounds in David's Return of the Dead Sons of Brutus and other pictures painted just before the outbreak of the Revolution.

Selected by the Revolutionary Assembly as the official painter of the communes, David became the leader of an insurgent group within the Academy which overthrew the "tyrants" (directors), among whom was the Count d'Angiviller, his first commissioner. As a revolutionary painter, David created the most realistic of his canvases, La Maraichère, a woman of the Revolution. She is a fit companion, in a less sketchy style, for Franz Hals's Hille Bobbe. The Death of Marat, a photographic picture of the revolutionary tyrant stabbed and bleeding in his bath, shows the innate quality of the painter. Shortly after he finished the Marat, another turn of the revolutionary wheel almost cost David his life, when his friends in the Jacobin party were "purged" with the help of the guillotine. During the empire of Napoleon, David's painting again became the vogue and the painter composed a monumental piece

called Le Sacre, showing the crowning of the dictator. The last phase of David's activity saw him in exile after the return of the monarchy. In Belgium, he founded a realistic school of painting, *verisme*, with "fidelity to nature" as its watchword.

David's activity furthered two movements in modern art, the one from his classical mode leading the neoclassical style of the revived Academy; the other, realism, leading to photography. For a time the realists, who called themselves "mediators" because their imitations introduced man to nature, proclaimed the superiority of inspiration, the revolutionary element in art, over the authority of all formal values. With this destruction of formal criteria came a complete renunciation of all standards of criticism. The pleasure of the individuals served as the sole basis for judgment, some enjoying pictures for their fidelity to nature; others, for the strong social and moral messages preached. Anyone who would profess to a liking for the idyllic visions of a Watteau or for rococo pictures, with their wealth of formal values which had no conceivable purpose, might find himself condemned to the guillotine as an aristocrat.

The Apotheosis of Homer by Ingres and the Neo-Classic Academy. The Neo-Classical tradition derived from David continued in the works of Wicar, Fabre, Granet, and Ingres. These were called the "primitives" because they found, through the French Academy of Rome, fresh archaeological interest for the primitive beginnings of classical sculpture and Italian painting. Jean Auguste Dominique Ingres, son of an ornamental sculptor and painter of miniature landscapes, was at first looked upon with suspicion because of his interest in ancient illumination, which seemed to be a Gothic style dependent more upon color than line. During his long sojourn in Italy, Ingres found, through his study of the drawings of Pisanello and Filippo Lippi, a linear style acceptable to the Neo-Classicists. For a time he painted scenes of Greco-Roman mythology and history. He also took Renaissance and modern subject matter, composing for Roman patrons pictures of Pope Pius VII in the Sistine Chapel and Raphael Receiving Cardinal Bibbiena. Next, like those Francesca da Rimini and Malatesta. These literary associations in the earlier works of the young classicist deserve notice because, as was pointed out, from that period on, no artist

FIG. 520.—Apotheosis of Homer, by Jean Auguste Ingres, 1827. Oil on canvas, height 12 feet 8 inches. (Louvre Museum). (*Courtesy of Lesch-Carnegie.*)

Romantics whom he in after years condemned, he turned toward the Orient.

When, as Chateaubriand wrote, Rome under Napoleon had become "A French town, capital of the department of the Tiber," Ingres became the favorite portraitist of the bourgeois officialdom appointed to rule the city. From that time date many of his finest portrait groups in silver point and pencil, studies that show his mastery of composition, line, and characteristic physiognomy. During that period he painted many small panels showing the lives of Romantic heroes from the *chanson de geste*, such as Roger and Angelica, and from the Italian *novelle*,

worked singleheartedly on any one theme or in any one style. It marks the beginning of the split character patterns associated with modern living. The portrait of Ingres (Fig. 543) at that time shows him to have been a typical young Romantic, like Goethe or Delacroix (Fig. 520).

In 1824, after an exile of eighteen years, Ingres returned to France, where he became the leader of the neoclassicists, at that time battling with what they called the "romantic hordes," led by Delacroix and Victor Hugo. The Apotheosis of Homer is the work of the finished artist—the "classicist pope," as he had come to be called. This picture ends the program of the Academy, for its static composition, its realistic draftsmanship, and its cold, almost unpleasant color embalm the portraits of Molière, Racine, Corneille, Dante, Vergil,

FIG. 521a.—Royalty, Episcopacy and Law, Inhabitants of the Moon, engraving by William Hogarth, c. 1752. This early example of surrealism displays the essential character of Hogarth's satire.

Raphael, and a host of other geniuses, all paying homage to Homer, who sits in front of an almost perfect reconstruction of a Greek Ionic temple with a Roman pediment. Ingres realized in this design the static quality which the academicians felt to be the essence of ancient art. From this effort arose a whole school of mural painters who decorated the walls of government buildings in France, Germany, England and even America. The picture symbolized not only the triumph of Homer but the triumph of the idea of law-abiding Beauty on an almost prosaic level.

William Hogarth and the Idealistic Realism of English Painting. English painting during the 18th century exhibits one outstanding characteristic that differentiates it from most Continental art of the time. The English, a nation of home lovers destined to empire, by nature appreciated art like that of the "Little Dutch

Masters." In the 17th century, during the period of their greatest expansion, they produced no significant painter. The first master of genius, William Hogarth (1697–1764), was the son of

FIG. 521b.—The Shrimp Girl, by William Hogarth. Oil on canvas, height 2 feet 1 inch (National Gallery, London). (*Courtesy of Lesch-Carnegie.*)

a cultured printer. Raised with an engraver's burin in his hand, Hogarth early learned draftsmanship by illustrating the *Golden Ass* of Apuleius and the *Hudibras* of Samuel Butler. His three great series of engravings—The Harlot's Progress, A Rake's Progress, and Marriage à la Mode—show all the pitiless detail and penetrating descriptive quality found in the novels of his contemporary, Fielding. The realism of Hogarth has the added point of the typically English moral purpose, coupled with satire. His engravings are sermons pointing to and ridiculing the degenerate human soul, but he lacks the pessimism and suggestion of cruelty found in the parallel works of the Spaniard, Goya (Fig. 521a).

Hogarth's picture of the Shrimp Girl (Fig. 521b) is a quick masterful impression of an English type, far more charming than Hals's Hille Bobbe or David's La Maraichère, quite perfect in technique and composition. Like

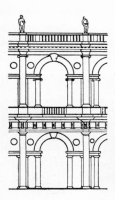

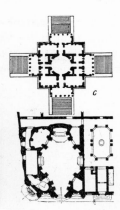

a   *b*   *d*

FIG. 522.—*a*, the Palladian motif, two bays of façade, Basilica Vicenza, 1549; *b*, Villa Capra or the Rotunda, Vicenza, 1570; *c*, plan of Villa Capra; *d*, plan of San Carlo allo Quattro Fontani, Rome, by Borromini (1660–1667).

Rembrandt's Syndics of the Cloth Guild, it suggests an essential quality, the portrait of a people. The same quality can be found in most of the works of the academicians, Sir Joshua Reynolds, Thomas Gainsborough, George Romney, Raeburn, and the other excellent portraitists who followed Hogarth. Although related under the skin. The English love for nature expressed in landscapes by Old Crome, Cotman, David Cox, and the Scot, Richard Wilson, rivals the efforts of the Dutch landscapists, Ruisdael and Hobbema. In the works of all these men appears an expression of the spirit which found its fullest development in

a   *b*   *c*

FIG. 523.—*a*, façade of SS. Vicenzo and Anastasio, Rome, by Martino Longhi, about 1600 (*courtesy of Lesch*); *b*, interior of Il Gesù, Rome, by Vignola and della Porta, 1568–1575, width 55 feet (*courtesy of Lesch-Carnegie*); *c*, detail of façade of San Carlo alle Quattro Fontane, Rome, by Francesco Borromini, 1660–1667 (*courtesy of La Porte*).

the essential may be overlaid at times with the velvets of fashion or framed with romantic rococo backgrounds, like "Judy O'Grady and the Colonel's lady," all English portraits are the realism of the 18th-century novel and the poetry of the Lake school.

Throughout this survey one is made continually aware of the tremendous part played in the enjoyment of baroque, classical, academic, and realistic painting by the associational, or literary, values. At every step of the development formal values have been subordinated to the

Fig. 524.—Pavilion of the Zwinger Palace, Dresden, by Daniel Poppelmann, 1711. (*Photograph by Edwards.*)

others. In architecture and sculpture the same holds true and, although these arts show far less fertility or invention, a brief examination of a few significant monuments in both is necessary to show the dominance of concepts derived essentially from literature and music. Formalism for its own sake has practically no place in these styles.

Architecture

Throughout the Italian Renaissance two tendencies in building contest each other. The great geniuses of the 15th and 16th centuries thought in terms of room spaces and, in the case of Michelangelo at least, in terms of an impressive arrangement of masses. The lesser men, mere decorators, interested themselves in the design of pictorial façades with properly proportioned and appropriate classic orders.

The Classical Style of Palladio. Starting with the buildings of Palladio, in the latter part of the 16th century, one can discover a new formal arrangement of parts related definitely to the underlying fundamentals of classical building as explained by Vitruvius, and at the same time

using static masses, including the dome and temple-formed prisms. From Palladio's atelier came buildings copied for 300 years afterward by exponents of academic classicism.

Fig. 525.—Château d'Azay-le-Rideau, Loire valley, 1518–1524. (*Courtesy of Metropolitan Museum of Art.*)

Andrea Palladio (1518–1580), the greatest architect of the later Renaissance, is best represented by the buildings he planned and erected in his native city, Vicenza, and in Venice. How accurately he studied and measured the architectural works of antiquity can be seen in his published drawings, *I quattro libri dell' architectura.* The results of his research evidenced in his completed buildings had less direct influence on later French, English, and American classicism than had this publication.

That system consisting of an arcade with a large order under the main entablature framing an arch supported on smaller freestanding, twin columns has come to be known as the "Palladian motif" (Fig. 522*a*). His Villa Capra (the Rotunda) in Vicenza, is most important for its influence on succeeding styles (Fig. 522*b*). It is a square building with a pillared portico on each face, giving the feeling of a cruciform plan (Fig. 522*c*). The circular hall is expressed on the exterior by the central dome. This design, first copied in England, later came to America, where it has been utilized in mansions and public buildings.

The Early Baroque in Italy. In the late 16th

century and in the 17th, the desire to arrange dynamic building masses impressively, so they would suggest the energy of the Roman Church militant, led to the creation of the baroque

FIG. 526.—East façade of the Louvre, Paris, by Claude Perrault, 1667–1674, length about 600 feet. (*Photograph by Hall.*)

style. This employed the decorative elements of the classic orders without primary regard to their significance as architectonic functional units. To designers thinking primarily of pictorial composition, they appeared valuable as part of a pattern of light and shade (Fig. 523*c*). A study of the façade of the Roman Church of SS. Vicenzo and Anastasio by Martino Longhi, built about 1600, demonstrates an early stage in the development (Fig. 523*a*), which is even more apparent in the church plans of the time (Fig. 522*d*).

This baroque façade, still architectonic in character, shows a beginning of the dramatic sculpturesque use of architectural detail. The lower story, with its modified, ornate Corinthian columns, supports an entablature broken in a completely unstructural fashion. The central portion of the entablature directly above the doorway, contains an intricate combination of dependant keystone, conched arched pediment, and superimposed broken pediments. These frame a central bust, with depending garlands, placed upon the plinth of the second story. Above, in the central portion, rises a high

columnar structure buttressed by reversed garlanded scrolls and atlantes. These human figures and the corresponding caryatids appear very often as ornaments in baroque design. The

FIG. 527.—Rococo decoration, woodwork and plaster of Paris with light neutral background and gilded ornament, regency, early Louis XV, 1720–1725, console table c. 1700. On the table is a Chinese vase of K'ang Hsi period, imported at the time. (Morgan Collection, Metropolitan Museum of Art). (*Courtesy of Metropolitan Museum of Art.*)

entire upper structure functions like a plastic relief for the ornate window frame, which acts as a pedestal for the cardinal's cap and coat of arms. These are further decorated by *putti* and angels, who seem to have alighted momentarily upon the architectural details.

One must admire the genial way in which the architect, functioning as sculptor and painter, has woven together the parts of this façade, forcing the eye to move restlessly over its surface. Should architecture, following the Neo-

Platonic tradition, strive to become "frozen music," then this façade is like a chorus by Longhi's contemporary, Palestrina. Later German rococo façades may be said to parallel the

The Late Baroque. The final development of the overornamented baroque style comes in Spanish and German churches and palaces. In these lands, where medievalism and the

FIG. 528.—Stairway and Fountain of the Dragons, Villa d'Este, Tivoli, by Piero Ligorio, 16th century. (*Courtesy of Lesch.*)

fugues of Bach. Whoever follows this style of development will eventually reach a type of building in Spain that gives almost the same pictorial impression as a Hindu temple. Here, as in the Orient, this style of exterior accompanies interiors like that of Il Gesù, designed by Vignola in Rome to be the mother church of the Jesuit order (Fig. 523*b*). Most Jesuit churches, incorporating the dome and long-naved form, have an arrangement of interior parts suggesting endless vistas and an unarchitectonic, musical quality. The mural decorations, designed further to open the wall space, lend to relatively small buildings the feeling of expansiveness. The sculptural decoration, like the pulpit in the Church of St. Gudules, Brussels (Fig. 531), suggests a transcendental quality proper to painting rather than stone.

Gothic style persisted late into the 17th century, details of the classical orders were almost completely transformed into flowing baroque scrolls, draperies, and volutes set on edge. The portal of the Provincial Hospital at Madrid, by Pedro Ribera, with its intricate pattern of interwoven fruit, flowers, and shells is what was called the *Churrigueresque* manner, named after José Churriguera, whose new cathedral at Salamanca culminated the Spanish Renaissance.

Daniel Poppelmann's pavilion of the Zwinger Palace (1711–1722) in Dresden (Fig. 524) is a typical monument of the northern rococo. On a festival occasion, Poppelmann created this pleasure palace in a unique style, enchanting in its consistent combination of masses, dynamic forms, and interwoven flowing lines. All the parts contribute to a feeling of exuberant fantasy. In richness of detail, in carefully planned perspective vistas, in remarkable silhouette and gay coloring, this pavilion lacks all useful values. Here one sees an almost completely formal, architectural composition built for its own sake, satisfying for its purpose—which was wholly festive.

Classicism in French Architecture. From the beginning of the 16th to the 17th century, Italian Renaissance details had gradually filtered into French design, but were applied only in combinations with Gothic features. Since there were already enough medieval churches, early efforts were restricted to homes and palaces for the wealthy, such as the Château d'Azay-le-Rideau. This charming, picturesque, country home adheres to medievalism with its turrets, high roof, and gables, but its borrowed decorative scrolls and pilaster forms around the gables and windows point to the Italian influence (Fig. 525).

Toward the middle of the 16th century, in French churches, which maintained medieval roofs, tracery, and buttressing, the contemporaneous Italian baroque appeared, to clothe them with Renaissance details and classical façades. However, these works lack freshness and originality. Other buildings show better understanding of the principles and proportions of classic architecture. This led to the strength, fine composition, and scale of the later classical period, which manifests itself in the more dignified style of the 17th-century academicians.

An almost complete summary of these transitional styles can be discerned in many parts of the Louvre (1546–1878). Here the fineness of Perrault's classical east façade (Fig. 526) dominates all others. The correct use of Palladian principles influenced him in building the monumental colonnade supported on a heavy basement. The freestanding Corinthian columns seem to march down the façade, becoming more static at the pedimented center piece, where they are no longer completely free of the wall. They finally come to rest on the side wings, where they are transformed into attached pi-

lasters (Fig. 522*a*). Development of the French châteaux, culminating in Versailles and Fontainebleau, represents every stage in the transition from a weak Renaissance to a strong

Fig. 529.—Grotesque from fountain, Boboli Gardens, Florence, c. 1600. (*Photograph by Paul La Porte.*)

classicism. The great builders, Lescot, de L'Orme, the Mansarts, and Le Mercier (city planner for Cardinal Richelieu), are men noted for the construction of the many palaces, civic buildings, and churches of the 17th and 18th centuries.

The interior of a room in a palace of the 18th century shows the final French development of the baroque in that style called the "rococo" (Fig. 527). For Louis XV and his courtiers, interested in salon and boudoir decoration, many elliptical and curved interiors were designed, like the Zwinger gate, but with more delicate decoration and furniture.

Fortunes of the Classical Style in England. In England, the architects followed with reservations all the modes that the Continent had carried to extremes. English builders held closely to the classical style for public buildings and palaces, as taught in Palladio's treatises on architecture. Inigo Jones, John Webb, and Sir Christopher Wren also constructed many churches remarkable for a refined use of the classical orders and for the ingenuity with

Fig. 530.—Three garden vistas with corresponding pictorial compositions. *a*, Villa d'Este (baroque); *a'*, Titian, Madonna Pesaro; *b*, Versailles (classicist); *b'*, Ingres, Apotheosis of Homer; *c*, England (realist); *c'*, Corot, landscape.

which classical details were adapted to Gothic towers. Wren's St. Paul's in London, although smaller than St. Peter's in Rome, after which it was modeled, in some ways seems more complete and refined.

This summary survey of architecture appears brief, in consideration of the tremendous number of buildings constructed, chiefly because, outside of the baroque, few new forms were invented. Historically the period has great significance, particularly with respect to the development of American colonial architecture, churches, and civic buildings of the 18th and 19th centuries. The Spanish style, carried by the missionizing Franciscan and Jesuit fathers, reached those parts of the Americas settled by Latins. The Palladian classicism of England influenced building in those colonies founded by the English. Lord Burlington at Chiswick and Colin Campbell at Mereworth Castle utilized the Villa Capra Palladian style.

The Art of the Garden. The formally planned garden as a work of art increased in charm and dramatic power with the northward extension of the Renaissance spirit. A 16th-century garden on the hillside in front of the Villa d'Este at Tivoli near Rome, with its arrangement of descending terraces, was the model for many baroque plans. Here the mountain stream running below the palace has been channeled into innumerable fountains and long basins bordered with cypresses, so that the purling sound of water enhances the many shady vistas. In a number of baroque gardens, provision was made for jets of water tuned to give harmonious sounds. In some, water organs, built like those described by Vitruvius, added their music to the scene.

The garden plan of the Villa d'Este, following that of the ancient Roman villa of Hadrian, on the plain just below, is distinctly formal. The terrace avenues lead off at right angles from a central axis drawn directly in front of the building. The stairways descending from one level to another (Fig. 528) have been designed in the great swinging lines of the baroque picture, following the plan suggested by Michelangelo in his entrance stairway to the Laurentian Library at Florence.

The arrangement seen in this illustration, showing the Fountain of the Dragons and the ramped stairway, is typical of the baroque garden. Here marble structures and open spaces contrast with the heavy shadows of grottoes and trees. The statues of giants carved within the dark grottoes so that they appear to be just emerging from their native rocky element gave birth to the term *grottesco*. This term applied to figures means strictly those forms half hidden in darkness. As the subject matter of grotesque sculpture includes satyrs, hamadryads, centaurs, and other half-human mythological figures of classical origin, the term "grotesque" gradually came to mean animallike human forms. From classical antiquity the baroque garden also took the hermes, a stone pillar capped by a head of Hermes or some other nature spirit (Fig. 529).

In France, during the 17th and 18th centuries, the garden plan opened to include wide spaces, or esplanades, with formal flower beds planted to simulate the woven patterns of great baroque rugs. (The Italians had used no flowers.) The plans of Versailles and Fontainebleau, the most famous in France, stimulated the designer of the parks of Castle Schönbrunn in Austria and Potsdam in Germany. These gardens correspond in composition to academic painting, where contrast of light and shade is sacrificed to perspective vistas with formal classical architecture for the pavilions.

The third style of garden, corresponding to the realistic painting, was developed in England, where the parks and forests surrounding the castles retained the natural appearance of grassy meadows with their winding serpentine paths, their unclipped bushes and trees. The English gardener attempted to suggest that nature guides rather than is guided. In contrast, the Italian gardeners arranged the tall cypresses or heavy plane trees, which added strongly vertical lines to the composition. The military precision of the closely cropped hedges in the classical gardens helped to stress the horizontal composition. The English realist gardeners combine the two methods. As can be seen, each of these duplicates one of the three types of pictorial composition (Fig. 530) peculiar to the times.

Sculpture

Sculptors following Michelangelo inherited his methods for representing the human form in those endless dynamic positions that suggested the explosive energy generated by their tumultuous passions. Baroque sculptors strove to rival the painters and confused their figures, writhing in ecstasy or tortured by the pangs of conscience, with the living forms of trees,

FIG. 531.—The Pulpit of Truth, Church of St. Gudules, Brussels. (*Courtesy of Lesch.*)

clouds, and rocks (Fig. 531). In baroque compositions the carved draperies appear to detach themselves and in Gothic fashion to move as though animated by a life of their own.

The pulpit in the Gothic church of St. Gudules, Brussels, clearly indicates all the characteristics of the type. Here the entire structure has been conceived as the Tree of Life. In the lower part, Adam and Eve are being banished from the Garden of Eden, pursued by the skeleton Death, a figure dear to baroque sculptors. The balustrades, naturalistically carved to represent vines with thousands of twigs and leaves, hold all manner of birds and animals. Above the steps the tree eventually branches into a canopy hung on carved clouds, among which can be seen angels and cherubs flying off in all directions. The ensemble blossoms into a glorious figure of the Madonna, floating down upon the crescent moon. Details of the figures are so modeled as

Fig. 532.—Apollo and Daphne, by Lorenzo Bernini, 1620. Marble figures, life size (Borghese Palace, Rome). (*Courtesy of Lesch-Carnegie.*)

to produce the strongest possible contrast of light and shade. The human beings are portrayed with the greatest naturalism, the saint with the greatest degree of expression, necessary to show theatrically strong inner emotion. Baroque compositions often gain in magnificence because of the suggestive power of their elaborate detail, the skill required for their execution, and the startling novel contrapuntal

arrangement of contrasting forms. These usually suggest the musical scenic effects developed in the opera of the period (Fig. 532).

Classical associational values in baroque art can nowhere be better demonstrated than in the Apollo and Daphne by Giovanni Lorenzo Bernini (1598–1680), an artist known for his contributions in architecture as well as sculpture. This group, in the Villa Borghese at Rome, embodies a mood greatly loved by baroque artists. It symbolizes the metamorphic or changeful aspect of existence. The nymph, pursued by Apollo, is shown at the moment when she began to change into a tree. This scene, too Oriental for a purely Classical artist, too unarchitectonic for a Gothic craftsman, seems completely apropos to the musical changes in dissolving chords and varying cadences. Evidence of Bernini's realism appears in the skill with which he has rendered the flesh of Daphne at the point where it turns into bark. His dependence upon a classical model, the Apollo Belvedere, is shown by the pose and proportions of the sun-god. Finally, this group, more appropriate to expression in a ballet or a musical suite than in stone, seems plausibly held together by the graceful rhythm of the bodies.

Bernini's musical fantasy appears at its best in his many fountains where splashing, bubbling streams harmonize sea-gods, grotesque fish, and spiraling shells. The Fountain of the Triton in the Piazza Barberini and that of the Four River-gods in the Piazza Navona, in Rome, epitomize an art which reached its fullest development in connection with the perfection of baroque garden and city planning.

Like most of the baroque sculptors who followed him, Bernini, as he aged, graduated from a humanist period to one of Gothic preoccupation with death. His tomb figures have a rarely equaled realism and dramatic continuity with the type of structure to be decorated and his religious works clearly portray the ecstasy of the saints. Bernini's most famous statue—that of Thérèse transfixed by the arrow of death—shows the saint, with heavenward

FIG. 533.—Comtesse du Cayla, detail of head and shoulders, by Jean Antoine Houdon. Marble, life size (Frick Collection, New York). (*Courtesy of Frick Collection.*)

rolling eyes, at the moment of transfiguration. She seems to be caught upon the many folds of flying draperies and restless cloud forms, all superbly staged in the theatrical light which pours down over the composition from a window properly arranged above. This gilded, glittering group in the Roman Church of Santa Maria della Vittoria, aptly carries that message of faith most desirable to the missionizing fathers of the Counter Reformation.

The bust of the Comtesse du Cayla (Fig. 533), by Jean Antoine Houdon (1741–1828), unites the rococo sensist style with the fundamental bourgeois realism of the Revolution. Many of Houdon's busts, including the well-known portraits of Franklin and Washington, are in his most severe realistic manner. Better than any other sculptor of the 18th century, Houdon knew how to capture the fundamental characteristics of his sitters. Despite their naturalism, a careful study of his portraits reveals that the sculptor has carefully eliminated many irrelevant details. Breaking no laws of form, the resulting creation incorporates the ideal and the real, the universal and the particular. That Houdon's works contain another quality, an element of willed selection or design appropriate to his own character, nowhere appears more clearly than in the charming head of the comtesse. This exquisite personality is more than a person and, like Michelangelo's Moses, epitomizes a period. Her pose, as well as the arrangement of her hair and clothing, endows her with a quality similar to that which makes Houdon's seated statue of Voltaire in the Théâtre Français one of the finest portraits of all time.

Aesthetic Criticism during the Seventeenth and Eighteenth Centuries

The previous chapter demonstrated the tendency on the part of Renaissance artists to discover a rationale for their work. From the guild workshop came recipe books dealing with those advances in the technique of painting calculated to aid in achieving the greatest possible realism. From the academic societies, such as that founded by the Medici, came a more literary idea of art discussing formal and associational values as they could be discovered in the writings of the critics of antiquity. Great artistic minds of the Renaissance combined the two modes of thinking, thus wedding practice to the theory of the Beautiful.

The 17th and 18th centuries, an age of aesthetic criticism par excellence, drew out from the Renaissance treatises their main threads of discourse, elaborating each subject earlier dealt with by adding the fruits of new archaeological research and the translations of such books as Aristotle's *Poetics*. The critics evolved three modes of criticism to explain the main tendencies in European painting. The first, called "classicism," corresponded to academic art; the second, called "aesthetic sensism," corresponded to the baroque; and the third, "realism," attempted to explain the revival of primitive naturalism that accompanied the growing religious, social, and political revolution. It should be noticed that this new meaning of realism (naturalism) differs considerably from medieval "realism," being closely allied to medieval nominalism. In philosophy, medieval realism now becomes "idealism."

Academic Criticism or Classicism. Two Italians, the Abbot Belori and the Cardinal Ludovico Muratori, first linked the intellectual mode of criticism with those literary ideals taught by Plato which were acceptable to the church. For these clerics, good art must be a revelation of some ideal moral beauty. Its study was arranged in a hierarchy of values beginning with the associational and ending with the technical. These church scholars stressed drawing and geometric composition among the formal values, in contrast to the more senuous color and chiaroscuro.

Charles Dufresnoy, the architect Charles Perrault, and Fréart de Chambray—French acade-

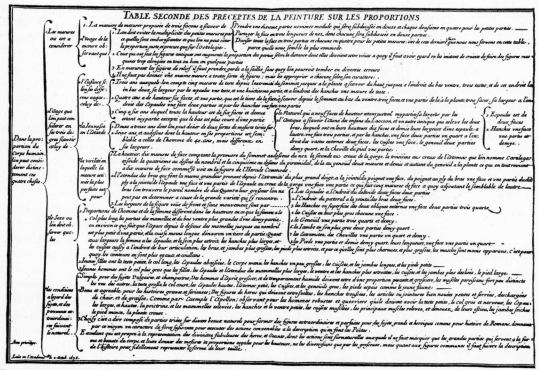

Fig. 534.—Page from *Treatise on the Practice of Painting and Sculpture*, by Henry Testelin, 1696. (*Courtesy of British Museum and F. P. Chambers, History of Taste, pp. 96ff.*)

micians—departed somewhat from the Italian position by examining the disposition of light and shade in the picture. These men also sought the ultimate sources of design beyond the works of Italian Renaissance masters in those of antiquity. They made a meticulous study of proportion in ancient art, deriving therefrom an aesthetic mean which they held up as a standard of good taste. The infallibility of the French academies, which symbolized the centralized authority of the monarchy, was made available in enormous publications covering explicitly every phase of the spatial arts. For example, the province of painting was divided into six parts. Drawing, the intellectualization of nature, appeared first, followed by its rationalization, proportion. Expression, third on the list, signified dramatic arrangement to clarify some literary idea. Rendering in light and shade came next, followed by ordonnance, an ar-

rangement of parts such as to gain the most pleasing effect. Finally, the academicians mentioned color, the most pleasurable element in painting. The thoroughness of academic studies can be judged by an examination of Fig. 534, the second page from Henry Testelin's *Treatise on the Practise of Painting and Sculpture*, published in 1696. This page deals with the study of proportion alone. Poussin's picture Arcadia (Fig. 512) best illustrates all the points stressed by the academician Dufresnoy in his didactic poem *De arte graphica*.

The English academicians, led by Sir Francis Bacon, stressed appropriateness and refinement in art. In his essay, *Proficience and Advancement of Learning* (1605), Bacon advocated that the subject matter of poetry should be chosen because of its heroic, noble character. For Bacon, art's greatest virtue lay in its ability to choose and refine the best moments of man's life to a rare essence, which he called "Strangeness." Of course, the refining process of artistic vision appeared at its best when placed at the service of morality. The English Bishop Berkeley in his *New Alciphron* (1732) likened Beauty to appropriateness, very much as had Socrates. Berkeley approached what we shall call the realistic position by comparing the dynamic beauty of a living horse, based upon his courage, strength, and speed, with the static beauty of a graceful Greek column, which pleases by its relationship to its entablature. Berkeley's rule, "Beauty consists of a proportion pleasing to the eye, considering by means of the judgment whether the object is appropriate to its use," is also seen to be more realistic than the strict religious academicism, which held that Beauty depends upon the moral worth of the subject matter.

Outgrowing the moralistic Platonic tradition fostered by the church, some late academicians eventually reached a Neo-Platonic position and sought to explain genius, or the inspirational element in art. In his *Discourses*, the painter Sir Joshua Reynolds sums up the most tolerant and universal academic teachings. Apparently inspired by Longinus, Reynolds advised the student to create as though the great masters Michelangelo and Raphael were to judge the excellence of his work. When the student had derived from these masters the general principles of artistic construction, he should seek their application in nature. Reynolds also valued the power of imagination, observing that slight sketches often give more delight than finished pictures, a fact particularly noticeable in Chinese painting and in the drawings of the masters. Following Longinus, Reynolds also held that genius seems to have an inherited talent for selection, so that the suggestive artistic essence was concentrated in one stroke of the brush. Genius, Reynolds defined as the capacity for long, constant work and the slow process of self-education when enlightened by an inherited power to profit quickly by one's mistakes.

Baroque or Sensist Criticism. The second or sensist mode of criticism, important for an understanding of the modern romantic attitude, centered around those formal values—color, chiaroscuro, and sound—which most immediately affect the senses. The sensists, led by the Venetian Marco Boschini, the Frenchmen Franciscus Junius and the Abbé Du Bos, sought to define those elements that lend charm to a work of art. They also advocated the primacy of inspiration, or genius. Since the genius always seems to transcend the acceptable formal patterns of a period, there will always be in his work an indefinable element which the sensists called the *je ne sais quoi*. However, they made no attempt to analyze this psychologically, merely giving as a *raison d'être* for the lawbreaking or revolutionary function of art, its similarity to religious mystical inspiration or saintly ecstasy, which should be used by the church in stirring people's emotions. The ideal sensist picture would be one of the works of Rubens (Fig. 507) or perhaps of El Greco (Fig. 503).

Roger de Piles, one of the best known critics advocating the sensist point of view, attempted in his *Abrégé* (*The Abstract*, or *Abridgment*) to unite the intellectual academic and emotional baroque systems. He was perhaps the first to warn that "Only great genius is above rules, knowing when to properly use its license." De Piles's work is of the highest value for understanding the succeeding realist criticism.

The Realistic Critical Position. Realistic criticism embraces those elements of the academic and sensist critical doctrines which tend to stress the power of man's mind to evaluate and to reorder the knowledge gained by research and to explain the new creations of genius. Realistic criticism in art accompanies the growth of the scientific point of view. It is based in part on Descartes's sentence, "I think, therefore I am," in part upon the belief of Leibnitz that all knowledge arises from self-moving atoms, or monads, each of which has a characteristic form. This emphasis upon the particular moment or "thing-in-itself" might be likened to medieval nominalism. Realism at its best may be visualized in the sculpture of Houdon, whose busts of Franklin and Washington are well known to all Americans, or in our Fig. 533. Here Houdon's realism leans slightly toward the sensist tradition of color and charm.

With the growth of realistic criticism, one finds its chief exponents—Count Caylus, La Fonte de St. Yenne, and Diderot—seeking out the artists in the great academic salons, questioning them about their work, and finally publishing the results of this research into the meaning of art. They came to the conclusion that every man must be his own critic. Here, and not in the romantic sensist tradition was the real revolution, for with this belief both the state-supported academy and the church lost their hold upon men's standards of taste.

The most complete program of realistic criticism appears in the French *Encyclopédie*, founded by Diderot. Here was a revival of the comprehensive Aristotelian critical attitude, the birth of a new scientific experimental method, and the substitution of the Promethean revolutionary belief in the nobility of man for the Platonic belief in the supremacy of the idea. Diderot, like de Piles, found in the work of art imaginative creative use of symbolic values, composition, and a power of expression stemming from mastery of technique. Diderot's philosophy lacks any decisive definition of his own ideal goal, probably because such a definition would seem static, and his revolutionary mentality demanded an active state of mind outside the confining borders of a definite program.

Parallel with the growth of the journalistic realism of Diderot and St. Yenne, went a more academic sort pursued by the savants. The philosopher Alexander Baumgarten (1714–1762) founded aesthetics as a branch of philosophy, deriving the term from the Greek word *aistheta* meaning "knowledge about imaginative things." He contrasted this with *noeta*, which he considered a higher knowledge, consisting of such objects of thought as were amenable to the rules of logic. Opposed to Baumgarten,

whose underlying philosophy is sensist and romantic, were the archaeologists Winckelmann and Luigi Lanzi, who sought to found systems of criticism based upon the study of art history and the development of cycles of style.

Winckelmann's *History of Art* written in 1764 was based chiefly on studies of Greek artists from Praxiteles through Lysippus. He differentiated among four periods of Greek art—the first, which he called religious, reaching to the time of Phidias. Following Philostratus, Winckelmann called the art of Phidias, "the Sublime." The art of Praxiteles was "beautiful," and that from Lysippus on through Roman times was "imitative." Winckelmann's classification has greatly affected 20th-century art criticism. Lost in his admiration of the static, beautiful antique, Winckelmann completely ignored the more comprehensive Sublime, and the Energetic in the Gothic architecture around him, or in the music of his contemporaries, Bach and Haydn.

The poet Lessing, in his famous critical essay *Laocoön*, took for his subject a late Greek sculpture condemned by Winckelmann as of inferior, imitative quality. Here Lessing significantly stressed the difference between poetry and painting, thus reviving the centuries-old debate. Lessing defined poetry as an art depending for its effect upon progression. Painting draws strength from its static character. He differentiated between "pictorial" and "temporal" arts, overthrowing the French academic term "fine arts," which had condemned literature and music to a place outside the sacred aesthetic hierarchy.

To conclude, the realists, whether stimulated by archaeological research, an unbiased spirit of inquiry, or their love of reality in nature and man, rediscovered something like Socrates's point of view. This was, loosely, a system of relativity in which a fine sense of appropriateness called for differing treatments of different subjects using the more subtle formal designs discoverable in natural phenomena. Stimulated by the realists, the salons of painting first created by the aristocratic Academy gradually became the public exhibitions. These critics further popularized the aristocratic arts for the masses by suggesting that insight on the part of ordinary individuals might have as much weight in judging art as academic theory. Realistic criticism further tended to separate the literary theory of the Beautiful from the study of formal values in pictorial art and to discover the sources of artistic genius, not in divine ideas but in the characteristically energetic aspects of nature or in the Sublime. From realism eventually came the doctrine of the 20th-century critic, Goyau, who summed up this eclectic attitude by defining art as "A manner of enlarging experience through extension of our contacts with other men beyond the confines of our own egos." This idea of art as a means of expanding the soul corresponds to the American position of such realistic philosophers as William James and John Dewey.

Development of New Literary Forms

Comparable to the realistic movement in painting that took place in the 17th and 18th centuries was the development of the youngest literary form, the novel. Prose fiction, the language of the novel, differs from its closest poetic relative, epic verse, chiefly in its longer rhythms and its use of words which describe, more than they suggest meaning. Thus the novel seems the most appropriate vehicle for expressing the moods and reactions of people during the journey of life. Chaucer's medieval Canterbury pilgrims with their many stories or *novelle* patterned after Italian tales, the travels of Sir John Mandeville and Marco Polo, Caxton's *Recuyell of the Histories of Troy*, and the chansons of trouvères or the Italian *canzonieri* are the medieval antecedents of the novel. Two of the most significant novels ever written, the *Gargantua* of Rabelais and the *Don Quixote* of Cervantes, appear as connecting links between medieval and modern forms.

The Artistic Media of Prose Fiction. The novel achieves its rhythmical sweep through alternating passages of dramatic and descriptive character. The latter fluctuates between objective description of the world seen and subjective description of the emotional reactions of the protagonists. Both may at times reach almost lyric poetic heights. The ability of the novelist to suggest universal rhythms leads eventually to the Sublime. Such works as *Don Quixote* and Victor Hugo's *Toilers of the Sea* have in them a grandeur approaching the infinite. So the novel, essentially a narrative form suggesting action, must be judged in terms of its power to stimulate or achieve a state of equilibrium within the mind of the reader. The time necessary to experience a novel is longer than that of any other art form and so must carry through a variation of moods. Further, the changing actions and thoughts of the chief characters must suggest like variations in the mind of the reader throughout the days or weeks necessary for reading. Properly to analyze a novel, one should proceed along lines suggested by Longinus and Aristotle. Good prose fiction is completely described poetry and drama.

The Gargantua of Rabelais as the Earliest Introspective Novel. The prototype of the introspective novel is the magnificent tale, *Gargantua*, written between 1560 and 1568 by the physician François Rabelais, who likened himself to Socrates. Fresh from the cloistered world of the monastery in which he had been educated, Rabelais recorded in his spare time the marvelous adventures of two giants, Gargantua and Pantagruel. These, with two smaller human beings, Friar John and Panurge, explored the world through the sharp eyes of Renaissance youth. Rabelais's purpose, expressed in the prologues of his five books, was simply to entertain his patients. Protected by royal patronage, the audacious doctor cheerfully satirized the most cherished superstitions held by ecclesiastical and humanist scholars of his time, combining philosophy, description, and action within the loose adventurous plot of his philosophical life journey.

Pantagruelism, Rabelais's recipe for those

who are sick, he describes in the prologue to his fourth book as "A certain jollity of mind pickled in the scorn of fortune." In these books, Rabelais, seeking a new, more expressive vocabulary, gave to the French language a treasure house from which three succeeding centuries of authors drew. The novelist more than any other writer likes to play with words for their own sake, trying the contrasting effects of harsh and subdued, soft and crackling, harmonious and cacophonous sounds with which he may charm or excite the reader. In general, novels must be read by oneself to be appreciated. Unlike poetry, they can rarely be recited aloud to others.

The Don Quixote of Cervantes as a Prototype of the Objective Novel. In his preface to *Don Quixote*, Miguel de Cervantes informs us that he has thrown away the affectation of humanistic knowledge. As he tells a straightforward, truthful tale, he needs no scholarly compendium for his subject. A satire on knight-errantry is something so new that Aristotle, St. Basil, and Cicero never dreamt of it. "Nothing but pure nature is your business; her you must consult, and the closer you can imitate, your picture is the better." There follows in a sentence the whole program of the realistic novel. "Do but take care to express yourself in a plain easy manner in well-chosen, significant and decent terms, and to give an harmonious and pleasing turn to your periods."

The retrospective Don Quixote of Cervantes stands in contrast to the introspective and forward-looking Gargantua of Rabelais. Rabelais, discovering himself, could laugh at the world, Cervantes, having discovered the world, laughed at himself. The story of Don Quixote tells of a man, by nature kindhearted, who finds himself thwarted in every attempt at knightly action whenever he undertakes to act according to the outmoded codes of chivalry. The romantic heroism of the knight-errant, so proper to the time of the crusades, no longer fitted the realistic world of the 17th century. By that time a few men had begun to see that all wars were nothing more than a brutal struggle for gold and power. However, Don Quixote is presented as hopelessly conservative, a man who refuses to forsake his dreams. To those around him he appears so unrealistic as to be considered insane. Only his goodhearted servant appreciates the innate fineness of a character still living as in the Middle Ages.

Subtly mixing fact and religious tradition with fiction, Don Quixote can easily convince himself that he is right. So he embarks on a series of unfortunate adventures in the field of romance. Thus Cervantes, the realist, advances the life of reason by slowly demolishing every pretension of medieval thought. He, more than Rabelais, relies upon colorful descriptions of actual scenes which he must have witnessed. In contrast, Rabelais appealed to the more intimate bodily sensations, by using words that recall specific emotional states. The two novels provided a means of expression particularly suited to the needs of that bourgeois class whose romance had to be found in the affairs of the counting house instead of in the court of love or on the field of battle. With the passage of the 18th and 19th centuries, this became the prevailing class, printing became cheaper, and novel writing flourished accordingly.

A Brief Excursion through the Realm of English Literature. The period of artistic self-revelation or enlightenment so aptly described in Alexander Pope's *Essay on Man* begins with the *Faerie Queen* of Edmund Spenser and the Sonnets of William Shakespeare. Spenser's rambling allegorical poem unites Arthurian legends, Christian medieval mystical thought, and classical lore. Its charming passages and rich suggestive words furnish a basis for modern English style, much as Rabelais's *Gargantua* does for the French.

The succinct expression of Shakespeare's sonnets concentrates in a classical form the widest range of human emotion. The difference in rhyme between these and the Petrarchan sonnets lends to them an air of greater finality. By having three sets of four-line stanzas rhymed alternately, followed by a concluding rhymed couplet, Shakespeare achieves a simpler formal unity. One of the finest sonnets suffices to demonstrate the felicity of Shakespeare's style.

THE CONSOLATIONS OF REMEMBRANCE

When, in disgrace with Fortune and men's eyes,
I all alone beweep my outcast state,
And trouble deaf Heaven with my bootless cries,
And look upon myself, and curse my fate,
Wishing me like to one more rich in hope,
Featured like him, like him with friends possessed,
Desiring this man's art and that man's scope,
With what I most enjoy contented least;
Yet in these thoughts myself almost despising,
Haply I think on thee, and then my state,
Like to the lark at break of day arising,
From sullen earth, sings hymns at Heaven's gate;
   For thy sweet love remembered such wealth brings
   That then I scorn to change my state with kings.

The Renaissance spirit, grown a little older and a little less dignified, appears in the poetry of the Caroline lyricists, Suckling, Lovelace, Dunn, Carew, and Herrick. The gay love-making cavaliers sing in Herrick's charming lines "To the Virgins, to Make Much of Time."

   Gather ye rosebuds while ye may,
     Old Time is still a-flying;
   And this same flower that smiles to-day
     To-morrow will be dying.

   The glorious lamp of heaven, the sun,
     The higher he's a-getting,
   The sooner will his race be run,
     And nearer he's to setting.

   That age is best which is the first,
     When youth and blood are warmer;
   But being spent, the worse, and worst
     Times still succeed the former.

   Then be not coy, but use your time,
     And while ye may, go marry:
   For having lost but once your prime
     You may for ever tarry.

While cavaliers sang their rollicking songs, bourgeois England in the person of Izaak Walton wrote his *Compleat Angler*, scholars translated into melodious prose that version of the Bible named after King James, and Sir Thomas Browne finished his *Urn Burial*.

[1] *Paradise Lost*, Book IV, line 159.

Following the revolution led by Oliver Cromwell, when republican England replaced the Stuart kings, a humble artisan, John Bunyan, piously retold the tale of Everyman in *Pilgrim's Progress*. The blind John Milton, trained as a humanist, who had earlier written "L'Allegro" and "Il Penseroso" in the Renaissance spirit, dictated the more somber epic of Protestantism, *Paradise Lost*. In magnificent, cadenced verse Milton tells the story of Lucifer, Prince of Darkness, who warred with the God of Light. Here at last the old Manichaean story of the endless battle between good and evil found its greatest poetic expression.

Milton's lines suggest his spirit of adventure in an age of exploration, longing for far-off lands:

      As when to them who sail
Beyond the Cape of Hope, and now are past
Mozambic, off at sea north-east winds blow
Sabean odours from the spicy shore
Of Araby the Blest, with such delay
Well pleased they slack their course, and many a league
Cheered with the grateful smell old Ocean smiles; . . . [1]

Infinite distances, discovered in a new astronomical concept of the universe, suggest better than almost any other lines in our language the Sublime:

The secrets of the hoary Deep—a dark
Illimitable ocean, without bound,
Without dimension; where length, breadth, and highth,
And time, and place, are lost; where eldest Night
And Chaos, ancestors of Nature, hold
Eternal anarchy, . . . [2]

Most significant of all in Milton's poetry is the magnificent sweep of his stanzas with their long periods. The classicist grammarian, Samuel Johnson, author of the first English dictionary, in his essay from *The Rambler* on "heroic verse," praises Milton's use of the "mixed measure." This, says Johnson, though it injures the harmony of the line, considered by itself, "yet compensates the loss by relieving us from the continual tyranny of the same sound." Note that the fifth and ninth lines, which we have

[2] *Paradise Lost*, Book II, line 890.

italicized, in the following selection from Milton's *Paradise Lost* have all their accents falling upon the second syllables. These lines have a regular beat, contrasting with the more or less irregular beat of the others.

Thus at their shady lodge arrived, both stood,
Both turned, and under open sky adored
The God that made both Sky, Air, Earth and Heaven,
Which they beheld, the Moon's resplendent globe,
And starry Pole:—"*Thou also madest the Night,*
Maker Omnipotent; and thou the Day,
Which we, in our appointed work imploy'd,
Have finished, happy in our mutual help
And mutual love, the crown of all our bliss   •
Ordained by Thee; . . . "[1]

John Dryden, a classicist critic whose poetry is unsurpassed for polish, although cold in temper, should be studied because of the perfection of his form. His three satires in verse, *Absalom and Achitophel*, *Religio Laici*, and *The Hind and the Panther*, mark the Restoration and the beginning of an academicism associated with the Jesuit Counter Reformation. This somewhat influenced English literature for a short time after the return of the Stuart kings. Dryden's most significant contribution to the form of English verse may be studied in the superb meter of his "Alexander's Feast." Here, as in Dryden's plays, one notices colorful, swinging lines suggestive of the sweeping baroque pictorial and sculptural compositions used to express the same ideas in the spatial arts. The melodic quality of the ode, also entitled "The Power of Music," appealed so much to the composers Clarke, Clayton, and Handel that each set it to music.

After the Restoration, Samuel Butler's *Hudibras* appeared in three parts, reciting in mock epic style the adventures of a Quixotic figure, Sir Hudibras. This Presbyterian justice of the peace, prototype of all rabid prohibitionists, tried in vain to reform the England of the Restoration. Jonathan Swift, an Irish satirist contemporaneous with Butler, combined the figures of Gargantua and Morgante in his *Gulliver's Travels*. The *Spectator Papers* by Addison

[1] *Paradise Lost*, Book IV.

and Steele developed the English essay around homely, genre subjects, stimulating a realism which eventuated in the novel. Samuel Richardson began English prose novel writing with the fortunes of feminine virtue as a subject in *Pamela*, and in *Clarissa Harlowe*. Henry Fielding, striving to burlesque Richardson's *Pamela*, developed novels around two masculine characters, Joseph Andrews and Tom Jones, lusty Don Juans in bourgeois dress. Fielding's Rabelaisian humor has a realistic turn, appealing to the adventurous English aristocracy of the 18th century. Oliver Goldsmith's *Vicar of Wakefield* and Daniel Defoe's *Robinson Crusoe* are also among the most interesting realistic novels of the time. With the novels of Smollett and Sterne, this style of literature gradually came to replace the more poetic literary forms of the 17th century. The magnificence of the classicist-historical style appears in Gibbons's *Decline and Fall of the Roman Empire*.

In this all too brief review of European literature can be perceived, with the growth of a leisure middle class, the entrance of a prosaic, realistic, and puritanical spirit. This gradually dominated the literary arts, as there expanded within the consciousness of northern Gothic man a philosophy of life, Aristotelian in scope, historical and scientific in mood. The concept of evolution, doubly strong because of its origins in Aristotle and partly traceable to a classic revival of the philosophy of Lucretius, finds echo in further lines from Pope's deistic poem, *An Essay on Man:*

See him from Nature rising slow to art!
To copy instinct then was reason's part;
Thus, then, to man the voice of Nature spake—
"Go, from the creatures thy instructions take: . . .
Thy arts of building from the bee receive;
Learn of the mole to plough, the worm to weave;
Learn of the little nautilus to sail,
Spread the thin oar, and catch the driving gale.
Here, too, all forms of social union find,
And hence let reason, late, instruct mankind; . . ."

That spirit of human brotherhood sought for by Rousseau and the French encyclopedists of "the Age of Enlightenment" also appears in Pope's lines which begin:

> Hope springs eternal in the human breast,
> Man never *is*, but always *to be*, blest.

This enlightened deistic philosophy ushers in the social revolution and the nature romanticism of the 19th century. That Pope brought all his philosophy into harmony with a deistic realism, Gothic in mood, may be seen in his lines:

> All are but parts of one stupendous whole,
> Whose body Nature is, and God the soul. . . .

> . . . God loves from whole to parts; but human soul
> Must rise from individual to the whole. . . .

> . . . Earth smiles around, with boundless bounty blest,
> And Heav'n beholds its image in his breast.

The Development of the Theater

Three main tendencies characterize European drama after the 16th century, corresponding to similar styles in the development of the graphic and plastic arts. (1) Elements from the medieval drama account for melodramatic, romantic, sensist effects, particularly in the historical plays. (2) Classical elements influence the structure of the plays toward greater simplicity and unity. (3) A spirit of realism proper to the French and English peoples inspires greater naturalness in depiction of character. The greatest dramatists, Shakespeare and Molière, are realists who employ the other two elements.

In Southern Europe, the Italy of the late Renaissance gave birth to Arcadian-romantic adventure plays such as Tasso's *Aminta*. The Spaniard, Lope de Vega, during his long life produced over 2,000 plays, including medieval-romantic and Renaissance-classical subject matter. His work corresponds to that of Shakespeare in England.

In northern lands, throughout the 16th and 17th century, organized craft guilds, such as the Meistersinger in Germany and the Passion

Brothers in France, continued their productions of miracle, mystery, and eventually morality plays, in connection with church festivals. One of the first great European dramatists, Hans Sachs, the cobbler and Meistersinger of Nuremberg, grew up in this tradition. Led by playwrights who were like Hans Sachs, the Parisian Passion Brothers controlled the dramatic performances of that city under a charter operative between 1402 and 1677. Their playhouse, the Hôtel Bourgogne, had a monopoly over French dramatic performances until the time of Molière (Fig. 535).

The Commedia dell' Arte. Throughout the Middle Ages companies of professional actors, the jongleurs, histriones, and mimes playing at the fairs or for the nobles, were often paid as leading actors in the mystery plays. They preserved until after the Renaissance many of the traditions of the ancient Roman theater. With the 16th-century revival in Italy of comedies by Plautus and Terence, there came into being among these professional entertainers a distinct type of original performance called the *commedia dell' arte*. The actors of the *commedia* utilized scenarios of ancient comic plots from the Atellanae and a few essential situations from morality plays like *Everyman*, which they expanded, improvising as they played. Certain stock characters, such as Harlequin, Punch, Capitano, and Pantalone, whose masks, voices, and gestures became fixed types; shaped the dialogue to the desires and quality of their audience. The *commedia dell' arte*, thus marks a return to the almost primitive conditions in which Greek drama started. Among the many plots taken from the *commedia*, the most notable are those of *Dr. Faustus, The Harlequin Necromancer* or *The Sorcerer's Apprentice*, and *Don Giovanni*.

The story of Dr. Faustus tells of a famous savant who, like Renaissance man, desires all knowledge, and to attain his wish sells his soul to the devil. *The Sorcerer's Apprentice* tells of an unworthy servant who, misappropriating the magic spells of his alchemist master, soon finds

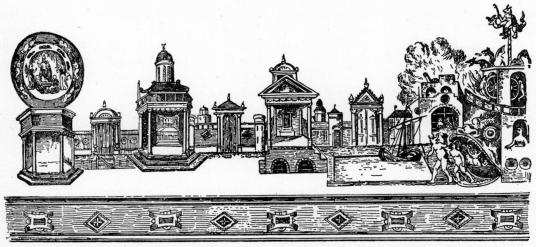

Fig. 535.—Setting of the Valenciennes mystery play, c. 1550. Note that, although the Mansions of Paradise are classical in style, Hell at the right remains medieval. (*From K. Mantzius, A History of Theatrical Art in Ancient and Modern Time*s, *Peter Smith, Pub.*)

himself frantically trying to escape the mischief created by the misuse of them. Both of these plots carry something of the element of tragic fear. In them scientific pioneer investigators of the 17th and 18th centuries were seen to face the uncertainty of ultimate destruction through their own efforts. The plot of *Don Giovanni* is a kind of "harrowing of hell," telling how a cruel, rather thoughtless, but witty rascal gets his just deserts.

In epic medieval tragic plots, derived from miracle, mystery, and morality plays; in the medievalized Latin and Gallic character types of the *commedia dell' arte;* and in the revival of Senecan tragedy, which followed the translations of Renaissance humanists, lies the background of modern drama that lends richness to the works of Shakespeare and Molière. The ultimate analyses of the variety of literary forms presented by this background are usually made in the teaching of English or French literature, so they will be omitted here. In the realm of dramatic action a study of the productions of Shakespeare and Molière will, however, furnish the basis for all modern dramatic form.

The Backgrounds of Shakespeare's Drama. The variety and universality of Shakespeare's plays arises from their synthesis of legends and associational overtones derived from several distinguishable sources. Many of his plays adapt medieval versions of classical stories. The forms are greatly influenced by the Senecan revivals of the University Wits, a group of Shakespeare's contemporaries who enjoyed Roman tragedies with their ghostly apparitions and antique conception of the Fates. From these ultimately came those stories of revenge which play a great part in Shakespeare's creations.

The patriotic note appears in English drama after the destruction of the Spanish Armada, when the adventurous exploits of English seamen and soldiers brought about a revival of historical chronicles from British history. These, rendered into prose by Sackville in his *Mirror for Magistrates*, became a prime source book. From Higgins's lives of ancient British heroes, Sackville and Norton took their story of *King Gorboduc*. From the same source and from Holinshed's chronicle came the Shakespearean historical plays. Translations of the medieval Continental history of Trojan heroes in the *Recuyell of the Histories of Troy* gave Shakespeare such stories as *Troilus and Cressida*. From Renaissance sources in the *novelle* of Bandello and

Boccaccio came Brooke's dramatic poem *Romeus and Juliet*. Plots from these Italian sources told of the Oriental monarchs, Cambyses and Darius, who rose to great heights and, with the turn of fortune's wheel or because of their own misdeeds, were later destroyed. These tales parallel the inner plots of such characters as Shakespeare's Macbeth and King Lear.

Behind these primary stories, all of which had been dramatized by Shakespeare's immediate predecessors in the 16th century, lay other deeper religious and philosophic associational plots distinctly Gothic and medieval in character. A study of Marlowe's story, *Dr. Faustus*, or of *The Sorcerer's Apprentice* will furnish clews to a new concept of life's tragedy which underlay most of Shakespeare's productions. Briefly, the northern, Gothic man, while going through a Renaissance period of his development, without full mental cognizance, conceived his soul as a battleground between the powers of light and of darkness. In his character, that warfare between the virtues and vices recounted in Prudentius' *Psychomachia* creates the dramatic tensions. The Gothic sense of tragedy arises from the knowledge that man can never be absolutely certain as to which of his gifts are virtues and which vices, or by means of which plan of battle he may win the victory for goodness.

This Gothic tragic sense has slight kinship with the Greek tragic sense, in which the struggle between two groups of deities engulfs man. The difference lies in the fact that in Greek tragedy what man does seems to have little effect upon the struggle. Man's resulting attitude is outspokenly fatalistic. In Gothic tragedy the inheritance of the Neo-Platonic Augustinian philosophy leads man to feel that he is a necessary part of God. So, his victory or his defeat means to some extent the victory or the defeat of the Good, that is, of God Himself. That is why Hamlet, defeated by his own indolence or indecision, makes us feel more deeply his tragic circumstance than does Orestes. That is why Lear, slowly gaining new spiritual insight under

increasing adversity, carries mankind with him into deeper psychological waters, with a correspondingly deeper sense of comfort than Oedipus. Shakespeare's King Lear more closely parallels, as a character, the sublime grandeur of Aeschylus's Prometheus.

Shakespeare, the realist, drew from the world around him many Gothic and Renaissance characters who appeared true to life for the essentially Gothic people of England. Bottom the Weaver, Sir John Falstaff, Shylock, Richard III, and Hamlet were very definite medieval types, such as one may find in the pages of Chaucer's *Canterbury Tales* or the morality plays. So Shakespeare stands to the modern drama as Aeschylus to the Greek. His lines incorporate the medieval Gothic and the Renaissance Classical heritage, which comes to life in the clearly drawn characters of the Englishmen—heroes who are never demigods, but men striving in vain to reach the Sublime. Their tragedy rises from the fact that their ideals are too high or too inclusive. Since a study of Shakespeare's plays is an accompaniment of our common English literary heritage, compulsory in all schools, it seems unnecessary here to do more than suggest those periods in his personal development which led to the perfection of his style.

Shakespeare's Plays. In the early part of his life, beginning with *Henry VI* in 1592, Shakespeare wrote a number of chronicle plays— *Richard III* (1593); a patriotic play, *King John* (1594); *Richard II* (1595); *Henry IV*, Part I (1596); Part II, with its creation of the character of Falstaff (1597–1598); and *Henry V*, with the death of Falstaff (1599). His great tragedies began in 1594 with *Titus Andronicus*, a melodramatic horror tale; continued in 1595 with *Romeo and Juliet*, a story derived from a *novelle* of Bandello through the poem *Romeus and Juliet* by Brooke. *Julius Caesar*, in 1599, and *Hamlet*, in 1601, mark the invention of two of his greatest tragic characters, Brutus and the melancholy Danish prince. In these the combination of tragic forces generated by interaction of struggling human frailty and fate reach a balance similar to that found in the works of Sophocles. The late tragedies, which follow—*Troilus and Cressida* (1602), *Othello* (1604), *King Lear* (1605), *Macbeth, Antony and Cleopatra, Coriolanus* (1606), and *Timon of Athens* (1607)—contain tragic characters as great as those of Aeschylus. Shakespeare's other plays—masques like *The Tempest* and *A Midsummer Night's Dream*, comedies like *The Taming of the Shrew, The Merchant of Venice, Two Gentlemen of Verona, A Comedy of Errors, Love's Labour's Lost*, and *All's Well that Ends Well*—were scattered throughout his long productive career.

To summarize: the sources of Shakespeare's comedy lie in medieval pageants with their rustic folk characters and in situations suggested by the *commedia dell' arte* or by translations of Roman comedies. His tragedies arise because his heroes, gifted with character and capable of perceiving the right, are unable to achieve success by reason of their unfortunate position on the turning wheel of fortune. Although these heroes form centers of melodramatic action which moves quickly around them, this activity accompanies an exposition of violent mental conflict. Unlike the Greek heroes, Shakespearean heroes are in no sense demigods. Thus their tragedy is heightened by the fact that we feel more for them as superior human beings, deserving a better fate because of their gifts of superior insight. The greatness of Shakespeare's tragic characters comes from the plausible union of their thoughts and actions with their emotions. Important to remember as differentiating Shakespeare's tragedy from that of his contemporaries is the fact that it practically never results from excesses of love. As Hazlitt justly remarked, the peculiar quality of Shakespeare's mind lay in its universality and its tremendous power of communication with other minds. Shakespeare approached the world much as Rabelais, but his Gargantuan appetite for knowledge and his Pantagruelian zest for life were refined by a mastery of poetic and dramatic form and by the necessity of a performance time that made him condense his material into concrete packages. In the hundred years between Rabelais and Shakespeare, the Classical conception of what constitutes good drama, inherited through revivals of Seneca's plays, had created a new form, which asked that the Gothic wealth of detail be confined to a classical structure. Although Shakespeare, comparable in many respects to Leonardo da Vinci, seems to have explored every condition of mankind, he remains so humble and unegotistical, so true to the medieval type, that we know practically nothing about him personally. So, his whole life must be reconstructed from his artistic creations.

The Theater in Paris from 1634 *to* 1673. In 1634 Paris supported two theatrical troupes. One company, The Royal Players, had quarters in the Hôtel Bourgogne, which was rented from the Passion Brothers; the other, The Prince of Orange Players, was established in the covered tennis court of Marais. The more significant, the Marais troupe, which was supported in part by the powerful Cardinal Richelieu, fortunately had discovered the playwright Pierre Corneille and produced his comedy *Mélite* in 1629. They also mounted Corneille's *La Veuve, La Galerie du Palais, La Place royale, L'Illusion comique*, and eventually his two great tragedies *Médée* and *Le Cid. Médée* dealt with classical, *Le Cid* with medieval romantic subject matter.

More important, however, to the development of French drama than either of these companies was a third, little-known, outcast group calling themselves "Les Enfants de Famille." They played in another tennis court, where the Institut de France now stands. After 1644 this company was managed by one Poquelin, a law student, who had adopted the name M. D. Molière. Following the collapse of his company in its first year, after he had been released from the debtors' prison, Molière took the troupe for a twelve years' tour of the provinces. Here, on the road, his genius slowly developed. Molière's first successful play, *L'Étourdi*

(*The Blunderer*), was produced in Lyons in 1653. In 1658 the troupe returned to Paris, where it soon found favor with the youthful King Louis XIV, who allowed the players to share the theatrical hall of the Petit Bourbon Palace with some Italian comedians. Here, poking fun at society and the rival troupes of the Bourgogne and the Marais, who specialized in classical tragedy, Molière produced some of his best known comedies. The final move was to the old Palais Royale Theater of Richelieu in 1660.

The Contribution of Molière to Modern Drama. Molière's chief contribution to dramatic art was that he drew into close union the panto- mime and the actions of the characters, their positions on the stage, and the inflections of their voices, so as to create effects of contrast or harmony. This greatly heightened the inten- sity of the performance. Molière's plot and his separate characters hold our interest equally, by reason of their realistic quality. Unlike Shakespeare, Molière seems to have been in- capable of developing those elements of the human character which led to tragic sublimity.

Molière burlesqued contemporaneous clas- sical revivals of the Senecan style, with their chanting declamation and imitations of the Greek choruses, as then played at the Hotel Burgogne. In his only attempt at tragedy, *Don Garcie de Navarre*, Molière's strong sense of real- ism, which might have succeeded in contem- poraneous England, appeared crude to the French literati, who were biased by the Neo- Classical academic rules of criticism that came from Aristotle, Horace, and Longinus. Having too great a sense of the theater to enjoy purely literary drama, Molière followed his genius for realism. He achieved success in *L'École des fem- mes* (*The School for Wives*) by raising comedy to the level of the tragedy of his time. He did this by portraying the *esprit de Gaul*—a compound of pungent wit, Gothic grotesquery, and a satir- ical view of serious things characteristically French. This witty French point of view, ex- pressing itself naturally in Molière's lines, forced even his bitterest critic, de Vise, to exclaim in admiration "Some parts of *L'École des femmes* are written as though by Nature herself, and certain inimitable passages are so exactly ex- pressed that no critical words suffice to explain them."

Molière also excelled in the art of the ensem- ble, that is, the proper timing of entrances and exits, the discovery and use of a fundamental rhythm by which actions and speeches must be regulated so as to gain the greatest dramatic effect. Of this de Vise wrote, "Every one of his actors knows the exact number of his steps, the exact direction of every glance."

Molière analyzed his own methods in a shorter play, *The Criticism of the School for Wives*, whose characters demonstrate the superiority of this type of comedy over the tragedy of the time. In this critique he presents the following statement of faith, followed today by most pro- ponents of realistic drama:

It is a great deal easier to express deep feeling, to harangue fortune in verse, to rail at destiny and re- proach the gods, than to enter familiarly into the ridiculous situations of life. When you depict heroes, you can do as you like. You have but to follow the natural flight of your imagination, which often drops truth to snatch at the marvelous. But when you de- pict men, it must be done faithfully; such portraits must resemble men and women, they are useless unless the men and women of your own times are recognizable therein.[1]

Satirizing Molière, the Bourgogne produced a counter-critique in *The Painter's Portrait*, to which Molière replied with the *Impromptu de Versailles*, a burlesque of the preparations in a classical troupe for a tragic production. Here he ridiculed the affected style of the Bourgogne tragedians. At that time Jean Racine, who had written *Le Thébaïde* and *Alexandre* for Molière, deserted to the Bourgogne, taking with him Mademoiselle du Parc, the troupe's chief tragic actress.

The three Molière plays *L'École des femmes*,

[1] KARL MANTZIUS, *History of Theatrical Art*, Vol. IV, p. 148, Peter Smith, Pub., New York, 1937.

Critique de l'école des femmes and *L'Impromptu de Versailles* furnish a complete textbook for the modern theater. With his principles laid out before him, Molière embarked upon the last stage of his career, writing his greatest plays— *Tartufe* (*The Hypocrite*), *Amphitryon*, *Don Juan*, *Le Misanthrope*, and *Le Malade imaginaire*. For potboilers he wrote a number of ballets, one of which, *Psyche*, was produced with music by Lully.

In *Tartufe* Molière satirized one of the many religious missions which had sprung up as part of the church's apparatus for the Counter Reformation. This Society of the Holy Sacrament, while in its inception noble, had degenerated after some years of service to become a refuge for hypocritical prohibitionists masking their nefarious activities behind a cloak of piety. Molière's characters set the types of hypocrisy for all time. Orgon, a blindly intemperate reformer; Madame Pernelle, his mother, a symbol of bigoted old age; Mr. Loyal, a professional hypocrite; and Tartufe, who seems to enjoy his hypocrisy for its own sake, while indulging his worldliness behind a puritanical garb, comprise as mean a group of human creatures as it is possible to conceive.

In *Tartufe* Molière's satire was so keen that only the protection of the king, who enjoyed a private court performance, made it possible for the actor playwright to continue on the stage. Powerful members of the Society of the Holy Sacrament made public production of the play impossible for five years and some of its reforming priests accused the author of being a heretic, recommending death at the stake. Molière, refusing to be silenced, made his next great character Don Juan avow his intentions to become a professional hypocrite as the best way of getting along in the world. This Don Juan was, more than Tartufe, a revival of the medieval belief in the last judgment for evildoers, brought to its final degree of perfection.

Molière's last play, *Le Malade imaginaire*, produced in 1673, was written as the actor was dying. In this play he had a final jest at the expense of all doctors and peddlers of medicine. Actually, Molière collapsed on the stage in the final scene where he showed the death of the leading character. His friends found that the parish priest would not shrive him because of *Tartufe*, and the Bishop of Paris allowed him to be buried in hallowed ground only at the command of his old protector, the king. So passed a man gifted with supreme insight into human character and a ready wit for exposing the weaknesses of society. With his knowledge of life, out of an overwhelming repertoire of French and Italian comic folk plots, Molière brought to perfection a few of the world's greatest dramas.

After his death Molière's company united with their rivals of the Hôtel Bourgogne, and by 1680 had become organized as the *Comédie-Française*. So, in a way, Molière may be spoken of as the founder of French drama, as Shakespeare was of the English. Each, essentially a realist, used Romantic and classical plots, but found more in contemporaneous human comedy than in Neo-Classical revivals.

Melodrama in England. In Shakespeare's later years a great number of productive playwrights, particularly Beaumont and Fletcher, John Webster, Massinger, Middleton, Ford, Shirley, and Rawley created endless dramas of revenge, horror, and mystery. They left behind a welter of plots from which Restoration dramatists, Romantic novelists, and mystery story writers drew heavily in later times. The Elizabethans, interested in the display of melancholy mentalities, enjoyed those horrific ghosts, sired in antiquity by Sophocles and Seneca, and all the tortuous villainies of which Orestes and Atreus were capable. Following Kyd's *Spanish Tragedy* and Marlowe's *Jew of Malta* in the 16th century, Beaumont and Fletcher wrote *The Maid's Tragedy*, and Webster, *The Duchess of Malfi*, both typical revenge plays. Ford's *The Broken Heart* and Massinger's *The Virgin Martyr* furnish examples of the horror play.

All these tragedies suffer from a common fault; the plethora of unpleasant situations lacks a consistent heightening of dramatic tone leading to one great climax. Great tragedy needs a succession of incidents so directed that each rises to a climax a little higher than the one

FIG. 536.—The Olympian Theater at Vicenza, by Palladio, 1565. (*Courtesy of Metropolitan Museum of Art.*)

preceding, each contributing greater dynamic tensions to following climaxes. The horror plays, by realistically exploring all the passages of frenzy, cruelty, and passionate love, soon glut the imagination. By 1640 the Puritans put an end to this type of drama and Parliament ordered the theaters closed. A few strolling companies of players still mounted small comic or tragic sections from plays of Shakespeare such as the Pyramis and Thisbe scene from *A Midsummer Night's Dream*, at the village fairs. These one-act plays were called "drolls." Those Cavaliers who did not follow Charles II into exile retired to their castles, where masques and pageants were still held.

The Masques, Restoration Tragedies, Comedies, and Burlesques. The best known masques, by the comedian Ben Jonson, include the *Masque of Blacknesse*, staged by the architect Inigo Jones, and the *Masque of Queens*. In the latter, Jonson adds to the usual beautifully costumed dance with music a grotesque, satiric antimasque. He followed the custom of the Greeks, who balanced each dignified tragic performance with one of grotesque character. In Shakespeare's

Midsummer Night's Dream the burlesque tragic plot of Bottom and his friends runs within the masque plot of Titania and Oberon. One of the best known masques is the *Comus* of Milton, who wrote in his youth as a humanist, in old age as a Puritan.

The elaborately staged masque, played in castle halls or gardens, shows a longing for a return of those great spectacles in the medieval cycle production. It called for new types of scenery, many of which were brought to the English stage from the court productions of France and Italy. Combined with the old melodrama, the spectacular masque contributed to the heroic Restoration "tragedies of honor," almost operatic in style, produced after the return of Charles II, in 1660. The two classicists, Settle and Dryden, influenced by the neoclassic French tragedies, wrote many of these. Settle's *Cambyses, King of Persia* and *The Empress of Morocco* brought a new pompous note to English melodrama. Dryden, whose critical sense unfitted him for emotional tragedy, wrote *The Indian Queen, All for Love, The Conquest of Mexico*, and *The Conquest of Granada*. In all these tragedies, where love conflicting with honor furnished the keynote of action, unconvincing heroes of superhuman strength and impossibly high ideals fight for heroines impossibly virtuous, constant, and beautiful. With this last faint echo of the French *chansons de geste* and the *Orlando Furioso*, chivalry passed from the stage in England. The comedians who followed in the next century produced a number of burlesques or mock-heroic dramas before a new realism set in.

The "comedies of humor," by Ben Jonson, Wycherley, Etherege, and Congreve, gave place to "comedies of manners," holding up a mirror to reflect the sophisticated dilettante court surrounding Charles II. Sir George Etherege's *She Would If She Could*, Wycherley's *Plain Dealer*, and Congreve's *The Old Bachelor*, in the 17th century, set the stage for the perfected comedy of manners in Goldsmith's *She Stoops to Conquer*, Sheridan's *The Rivals* and *The School for Scandal* in the 18th. While the comedy of manners grew to supply the needs of the court, farce comedies and burlesques appealed to the masses. The heroic-romantic operas for the aristocrats were countered by burlesques such as John Gay's *Beggar's Opera* for the multiplying middle class.

The Development of Stage Architecture. Between the 16th and the 18th century the stage developed to answer the needs of the rapidly changing dramatic form. From the Passion and miracle plays, with their separate mansions arranged around the city squares, later scene designers adopted many details. From castle and monastery halls with small, temporary platform stages built by the jongleurs, the craftsmen of Shakespeare's time took certain conventions. These included the inner and outer stage, which they mistook from medieval illuminated manuscripts of Terence for classical stages. Finally, in Italy, from the publication of Vitruvian treatises on architecture the classicist architects took the shape of the 17th-century Palladian theater, which, uniting with the others, eventually became the 18th- and 19th-century opera house and playhouse.

The Classical Tradition in Staging. The classical tradition in staging plays accompanied a widespread revival of the Senecan tragedy and the comedies of Plautus and Terence. Such Italian architects as Palladio and Serlio designed stages closely following Roman models. The Olympian Theater at Vicenza, built by Palladio in 1565 (Fig. 536), has for its permanent scene the façade of a Roman palace transformed into a kind of triumphal arch. Through the three large openings of the arch can be glimpsed street scenes modeled in perspective. Serlio tells us that the three types of scene visible through the arches could be used for all kinds of drama. The narrow, deep street scene with its shops and signs was considered appropriate for comedy. The great piazza scene, through the central arch, and the right-hand vista served for tragedy. A third, wooded scene or park sufficed for ballets.

The Platform Stage of the Realist Tradition. The new drama, inherently realistic, incorporating the two other traditions, called for a third type of stage. This developed naturally, as had the earliest Greek stages, from wooden platforms

FIG. 537.—Drawing of the Swan Theater by Thomas Witt, c. 1600. (*Courtesy of Yale School of Drama.*)

erected at the fairs or in innyards, where strolling Italian and Spanish players stopped overnight. The simplest platform stage, an extension perhaps of the medieval mystery wagon, had a robing room behind a curtain. These curtains, painted in some cases by such famous artists as Mantegna, suggested tapestried halls or sylvan vistas. In England, where the drama first escaped the monopoly of guild or court productions, a number of players' companies, formed during the last half of the 16th century, settled in Shoreditch and Bankside, suburbs of London. Here the showmen had erected galleried amphitheaters of wood and brick for bull- and bear-baiting, medieval sports that had taken the

FIG. 538.—Late 17th-century picture-frame stage with set for *Agarite* as designed by Mahelot. The stage is in three levels called *plans*. At the right, lower *plan* the cavern replaces Hell; at the left, the painter's studio replaces a mansion of Paradise. The second *plan* contains a churchyard (medieval purgatory), at the right, and a garden, left. The bedroom, rear, has a great bed replacing the medieval throne of judgment. The kings of that time habitually administered justice from the *Lit de Justice*, which was an Oriental importation from Persia.

place of the Roman gladiatorial combats. Into such a building, by 1576, some unknown genius had brought the platform stage.

This Elizabethan theater for the masses—the theater of Shakespeare and Marlowe—as shown in a drawing of "The Swan" (Fig. 537) by a Hollander, Thomas Witt, consisted of a great open court bordered by three rows of balconies. A roofed stage at one end projected into the court. Under the roof at the rear of the platform were two exits to a robing room. Above them a balcony was used by both actors and patrons. Probably curtains, hung inside the columns supporting the stage roof, were drawn at times. On such a stage there could be no room for scenery in the modern sense, but the symbolic properties of the mystery plays—a single tree for a forest, a painted flat for the town of Rome, a few chairs, a bed and a table—served, along with signs or prologue descriptions in the plays, to indicate the locale.

The Fusion of the Three Types of Stage and the Appearance of the Modern Proscenium. Gradually, during the 17th century, the medieval, the classical, and the realistic platform stages fused, to become the stage as it appears today. In France, Cardinal Richelieu had a theater constructed in one of the halls of the Palais Royal, a part of the Louvre. Here the great triumphal arch of the Palladian theater was moved so far forward that it became a sort of picture frame or proscenium for a curtained stage.

In the meantime, at the old Hotel Bourgogne, the designers compressed the mystery-play sets into one scene, which could be arranged within the frame. Mahelot, a French scenic architect, describes a set for the romantic play *Agarite* produced in 1673 (Fig. 538). Mahelot's stage arrangement has become conventional for most romantic settings in the modern theater. Prison and defeat are on the right (stage left) and victory on the left (stage right).

Contrasting with this romantic set, in the 18th century the various details of the old Palladian scenery were enlarged and arranged as single pictures with compositions comparable to the baroque and classicist paintings of the time. The architect Inigo Jones first brought to England from France scenery flats that could be pushed in from the wings of a proscenium stage. They furnished a narrow street scene for comedy, a public place or square for tragedy, a classic colonnade, a forest for ballets, and a large room with five doors. Such classical scenes were used by Molière in his greatest plays, *Tartufe*, *Le Misanthrope*, and *L'Avare*.

After this time the romantic plays developed great ceremonial baroque stairways and Oriental harem scenes or arcaded rooms set on a diagonal to the proscenium so that the attention of the audience could be thrown by the lighting and action strongly to left or right (Fig. 539). With the development of the enclosed stages came the necessity for indoor lighting, particularly as during the 18th century the time of performance gradually moved from the afternoon toward the evening. Chandeliers from the ceilings and lights in brackets just behind the proscenium illuminated the actors. The fact that the oil lamps and tapers which furnished the light could not have been strong enough to provide complete illumination of the scene probably heightened the dramatic effect by stimulating the imagination.

Summary

During the period studied, a spiritual expansion of the European mind accompanied the physical exploration of the earth, the discovery of hitherto unknown primitive races, and an objective examination of natural phenomena. This scientific objective interest inevitably led to the formation of new faiths linking themselves to the rapidly developing Protestant Reformation which had begun simply as a dynamic manifestation of the northerner's revolt against the southern Roman Church. The resultant freeing of the soul from many medieval superstitions led to new types of artistic production, most important of which were the developments in music, literature, and the drama.

The northern Gothic people enjoyed a widespread dispersion of the Bible, which followed the invention of printing. The growth of science

accompanied a revival of a religious philosophy similar to that of the Manichaeans, who conceived life to be a struggle between powers of light and of darkness. Thus a heresy long com-

FIG. 539.—Design for Italian baroque stage setting, by Stefano Orlandi, 1681–1760. This is supposed to represent ancient Roman baths.

bated by the Roman Church at last flowered into a powerful religion, officially recognized by many of the newly developed nationalistic states. Nationalists used Protestantism as a weapon in their conflict with the Empire or with the Roman Church considered as a temporal kingdom. The new dynamic revolutionary religion emphasized the Celto-Germanic or mystical Oriental elements in Christian character. At first, like the early Church Fathers, Protestants frowned upon all representative arts, while accepting and furthering music. In contrast, the Roman Church in its Counter Reformation supported the spatial arts, stressing their theatrical and ecstatic elements with charming color and sensist appeal. It also encouraged the mass and the oratorio, forms of music useful in the service.

The rise of nationalism led, in the case of France and England, to the formation of art academies, planned like those academies supported by Italian despots. Academicism stressed stability in politics and science as well as in art. Accompanying academicism went a belief in a unified universe capable of complete geometric arrangement.

Freed by the theological battles of the Reformation and the Counter Reformation, some thinkers turned to empirical observational science and, following Francis Bacon, Locke, and Diderot, eventually advocated realism in the spatial arts. On the other hand, rationalistic scientists like Descartes and Newton, using mathematical measurement to explain all phenomena, turned to formal academicism as a method for self-expression.

From these freethinkers, mostly deists, eventually came a religion of science which conceived the universe to be either an orderly machine, in which case the Deity was constructive intelligence or as a gradually unfolding evolutionary process. Skeptics, unwilling to accept either view, turned to social revolution as an outlet for their energies. These advocated the overthrow of national feudalities, the formation of a world brotherhood, and the wide spread of humanism.

Seeking an appropriate art to express the flux of societal and universal life, the greatest creative artists of the period found in the new contrapuntal music which emphasized the contrast between static chords and dynamic melodies, between instrumental tones and human voices, the most perfect medium. In oratorio, cantata, opera, sonata, and symphony, masters such as Palestrina, Cavalieri, Monteverdi, Scarlatti, Bach, Handel, Haydn, and Mozart brought music from its simple medieval forms to the complex, architectonic structures of the present day. Particularly important in this development was a recognition of the parts played by harmonic chords, the perfection of new instruments like the violin and harpsichord, the arrangement of the tempered scale, and the development of sonata or symphonic forms.

In the realm of painting, one finds the baroque style, started in Venice during the 16th century, moving to Rome, Spain, and France. Here it was used to decorate aristocratic palaces and Jesuit churches with great mural canvases preaching the story of a reformed Roman religion. Tintoretto, the first outstanding master of the baroque sensist style, composed masses so as to suggest a movement of volumes in space. El Greco's ecstatic figures followed Gothic and Byzantine Oriental composition lines. In 16th-century Rome, great baroque ceiling decorations vied for a time with the condemned realism of Correggio and the academicism of the Caracci. In France the followers of Poussin, who inspired the Academy, and the baroque master Rubens, supported respectively by French royalty and the church, made some advances in the pictorial art by uniting their inheritance from Venetian and Roman masters with the Flemish love of color.

Contrasting with the Romanist baroque and nationalist academic art, there grew in the bourgeois countries of the north, particularly Holland, a realistic type of genre painting, characterized by the works of Hals, Rembrandt, and Vermeer. From all three directions came an interest in landscape composition for its own sake, which accompanied the development of natural science. Velázquez, the Spaniard, supported by a royal family, displayed a skill in realistic painting unsurpassed by other European masters. French rococo painters, such as Watteau and Boucher, discovered new color techniques tending toward a more interesting interpretation of atmospheric effects and developed more delicate baroque color schemes, which contributed to the growing Romantic feeling. Realism returned for a time as the dominant style for the lower classes during the Revolution and a belated academic classicism became the official style of the Napoleonic empire.

In architecture, classical academic formalism, based upon the writings of Palladio and Perrault, and baroque theatricalism vied with each other through three centuries. The classical style dominated in 18th-century France and England. Germany, France, and Holland developed a delicate baroque style, the rococo, out of the interior decoration associated with the French palatial architecture. Garden architecture and city planning accompanied nationalistic developments and the creation of great palaces in France, England, and Germany.

The sculptor's art, definitely dominated by theatrical and pictorial concepts, became with the baroque works of Bernini something that belied its original formal character. Like all the other spatial arts, sculpture may be said to have come under the influence of a strongly temporal or musical concept of form.

The 17th and 18th centuries constitute a period of art criticism par excellence. Logically constructed formal systems of criticism published by the French academies perhaps had the widest circulation. In architecture, Vitruvianism and Palladianism reigned supreme. In painting, baroque sensist criticism, at first supported by the church, enlivened the more formal academic modes, which were based in part on formulae derived from ancient writers or in part on the painting books of Renaissance masters like Alberti, Leonardo, and Lomazzo. From sensist and academic criticism eventually arose, in the 18th century, a new realistic academicism based upon objective archaeological research and art history. From the spirit of Baconian empiricism came a tendency to examine all critical theories critically and to collect in the encyclopedia the observations of a new realistic criticism which should consider of primary importance the useful values or appropriateness of the art work.

The novel and the essay, literary forms reaching a high degree of perfection, appealed particularly to the *bourgeoisie* and to the scientific deists. In the realm of the theater a new type of drama came from the efforts of great realists, such as Shakespeare and Molière. This dramatic art could be called neither tragedy nor comedy in the old classical sense, but a new type, which compressed the medieval cyclical drama into a classical form. Visually, the action of the drama, compressed within the walls of a small indoor theater framed by a proscenium and limited in time and place to a more compact unity, had to express man's struggle to break the confines of his own sloth and ignorance. Life was conceived by the dramatist to be a struggle within the soul of man between his narrow egotistic desires and his universal possibilities. The ultimate tragedy of life was considered to be the inability of a man, because of either physical or moral weakness, to express himself in good actions of universal significance. In short, man appeared as a protagonist in the struggle between the powers of light and of darkness. Thus the dramatist presented not the *Divine Comedy* of Dante but the human comedy of Cervantes and Rabelais. Man, as expressed by the artists of this period, was, in the words of Pope with which the chapter began, "The glory, jest, and riddle of the world."

Bibliography

WOELFFLIN, HEINRICH: *Principles of Art History*, translated by M. D. Hottinger, Henry Holt & Company, Inc., New York, 1932.

VENTURI, LEONELLO: *History of Art Criticism*, E. P. Dutton & Company, Inc., New York, 1936.

CHAMBERS, FRANK P.: *The History of Taste*, Columbia University Press, New York, 1932.

SITWELL, SACHEVERELL: *Southern Baroque Art*, Alfred A. Knopf, Inc., New York, 1924.

BLOOMFIELD, REGINALD: *A History of French Architecture*, 2 vols., George Bell & Sons, Ltd., London, 1911.

French Painting and Sculpture of the XVIII Century, Metropolitan Museum of Art publication, New York, 1935.

MANTZIUS, KARL: *A History of Theatrical Art*, Vol. IV, translated by Louise von Cossel, Peter Smith, Publisher, New York, 1937.

BAKER, GEORGE PIERCE: *The Development of Shakespeare as a Dramatist*, The Macmillan Company, New York, 1907.

MOWAT, R. B.: *The Age of Reason*, Houghton Mifflin Company, Boston, 1934.

SPAETH, SIGMUND: *The Art of Enjoying Music*, Whittlesey House, McGraw-Hill Book Company, Inc., 1933.

LEICHENTRITT, HUGO: *Music, History, and Ideas*, Harvard University Press, Cambridge, Mass., 1938.

PARRY, SIR C. H. H.: *The Evolution of the Art of Music*, D. Appleton-Century Company, Inc., New York, 1932.

PARRY, SIR C. H. H.: *Johann Sebastian Bach*, G. P. Putnam's Sons, New York, 1934.

DOWNES, OLIN: *Symphonic Masterpieces*, Dial Press (Lincoln MacVeagh), Inc., New York, 1935.

Davenport, Marcia: *Mozart*, Charles Scribner's Sons, New York, 1932.

Rabelais, François: *Gargantua and Pantagruel*, American Library, Albert and Charles Boni, Inc., New York, 1925.

Cervantes, Miguel de: *Don Quixote*, translated by J. W. Clark, Hogarth Press, London.

Reynolds, Sir Joshua: *Discourses*, Everyman's Library, E. P. Dutton & Company, Inc., New York, 1907.

Frank, Bruno: *A Man Called Cervantes* (novel), translated by H. T. Lowe-Porter, Viking Press, Inc., New York, 1935.

Van Loon, Hendrik Willem: *Rembrandt van Rijn*, Garden City Publishing Company, Inc., New York, 1937.

Recordings

Palestrina:

Gloria, *Kyrie*, and *Sanctus*, V 20897, V 35941.

Schutz:

Motet—chorale, Decca 20165 a.

Early Opera:

Peri and Caccini V 21752.
Purcell V 4009.

Byrd:

Sellinger's Round—harpsichord—Decca 20163 a.

Franck, Melchior:

Pavane, Quintet of viols, Decca 20163 b.

Rameau:

Harpsichord solo, Decca 20167 a.
Rigadoon (dance) from *Dardanus*, Polydor 522420.

Lully:

Minuet from *Bourgeois Gentilhomme*, Polydor, 522420.

Scarlatti:

G minor sonatina—Longo 497 (The Cat's Fugue), V 1664.

Early Instrumental Music:
Columbia Music History, Vol. II. Ed. Dolmetsch.

Bach:

Das wohltemperirte Klavier, Prelude in B minor, Book 1, No. 24, V 7316.
Fugue from the *Burial Motet* (1729), Decca 20166.
Sonata No. 2 for violin and harpsichord, Decca 20166 a.
French Suite in G minor—*Sarabande* and *Gavotte*, Decca 20167 b.
Fugue No. 4, C-sharp minor, Das wohltemperirte Klavier, G-C 2391, CM 120—alb. 120.
Chorale, *O Haupt voll Blut und Wunden*, B 90091.
Sonata, 3rd movement (Courante), arranged for guitar by Segovia, V 1298.
Chorale, *Komm Süsser Tod*, V 8496.
English Suite, Sarabande, V 8496.
Organ Fugue in E minor, V 9741.

Handel:

Quartet in C major, opus 76 No. 3, "The Emperor," CM 246 (alb.).

Haydn:

Symphony in E-flat major, CM 221 (alb.).

Gluck:

Che faro senza Euridice, from *Orfeo ed Euridice*, V 6803.

Mozart:

Non piu andrai and *Se vuol ballare*, from *Le Nozze di Figaro*, CL 2185.
Overture to *Le Nozze di Figaro, Die Entführung aus dem Serail*, V 11142.
Overture to *Le Nozze di Figaro, Voi che Sapete*, V 7822.
Overture to *Die Zauberflöte*, V 1486.
Symphony No. 41—C major, K 551, CM 194 (alb.).
Symphony No. 40—G minor, VM 109 (alb.).

CHAPTER XVII

Romanticism in the Nineteenth Century

We are the music-makers,
  And we are the dreamers of dreams,
Wandering by lone sea-breakers,
  And sitting by desolate streams;
World-losers and world forsakers,
  On whom the pale moon gleams;
Yet we are the movers and shakers
  Of the world for ever, it seems.

With wonderful deathless ditties
We build up the world's great cities,
  And out of a fabulous story
  We fashion an empire's glory;
One man with a dream, at pleasure,
  Shall go forth and conquer a crown;
And three with a new song's measure
  Can trample an empire down.

We, in the ages lying
  In the buried past of the earth,
Built Nineveh with our sighing,
  And Babel itself with our mirth;
And o'erthrew them with prophesying
  To the old of the new World's worth;
For each age is a dream that is dying,
  Or one that is coming to birth.[1]

ROMANTICISM is that movement in 19th-century European art which indulges man's propensity for dreaming. Romantic artistic productions aim to carry him away from present-day actualities into scenes of past or future glory, helping him to reconstruct in his fancy the environment of the past, with particular reference to the Middle Ages and the ancient East. Design patterns are characterized by an attempted return to Gothic modes of expression and energized forms suggestive of the baroque, by which the artists strive to break the barriers of convention with a revolutionary zeal.

At a time when the discoveries of science had made possible that industrial revolution which was to overturn the economic and political foundations of the Western world, men dreamed great dreams, and the artists considered it their function to present these dreams in aesthetic form. Patterning himself after his hero, the military genius Napoleon, man thought himself a conqueror, and woman, observing Queen Victoria, moved toward emancipation from her inferior position in a patriarchal society. Carried by his research far out into the infinity of stars, man found in the universe ever new aspects of his own soul revealed in nature; thus his painters sought to express themselves through the medium of landscapes; his musicians, through a music that consciously imitated nature's sounds. Faced by the ugly slums

[1] From an ode (1874) by Arthur William Edgar O'Shaughnessy (Romantic poet).

spawned in factory towns, man dreamed Utopias and planned sanitary, aesthetic cities for a future in which peaceful industry would free him from many of the burdens of the struggle for existence. Thwarted in his normal expression of love by a Puritan conscience bred from ancient patriarchal Mesopotamian ideologies in a dominant Protestant church, man returned to a worship of Ishtar, the fatal goddess, and visualized her as Proserpine, the queen of death, or *la belle dame sans merci*. When thwarted by the actuality of living in an imperialistic world or caught by economic rivalries leading to inevitable wars, Romantic artists created phantom forms and symbols expressive of the wish for death. The youth of the 20th century has left romanticism behind, but the teachers of 20th-century youth, for the most part romantic idealists intent on saving the valuable parts of the Romantic's dreams, stress the fact that man can control his own destiny insofar as that destiny has to do with his relationships to his fellow man. This spiritual essence of romanticism accounts for whatever elements of strength we may find in Romantic art. To understand it, one must examine the backgrounds of the period.

The Growth of Tolerance. Accompanying the scientific discoveries of the 18th century came a more tolerant attitude in political, moral, and religious thought. This inevitably led freethinking artists to express themselves in the widest divergence of styles. A new freedom of conscience accompanied the progress of constitutional, representative government, which came to be known as "democracy." Far-flung commercial enterprise resulting from the capitalistic industrial revolution furnished channels for an accelerated interchange of Asiatic, American, and European ideas which overcame the intolerance of provinciality. Freedom of worship for all faiths, with concomitant lightening of censorship and freedom of the press, marked the final emancipation of man's conscience from imposed ethical and aesthetic ideas.

Tolerance of oneself and of others, accompanied as it was by a growing skepticism and widespread divergence from the old mores, led in many cases to a certain weakening of man's expressive energies. Empirical social sciences displaced in part belief in the superior value of the classical humanities. With the fall of the Copernican system of astronomy came a scientific revelation that led many individuals to doubt their own spiritual substance. Answering man's doubts, Descartes had found the reason for his existence in the formula "I think, therefore I am." Kant substituted the rather cold categorical imperative, "Act as though by your action what you do becomes a law of the universe," for a more social-minded group ethics.

Psychologically, both his doubts and his rather lonesome, though brave, individualistic position caused man, as an empirical scientist, to renounce all ancient values. At the same time he must consider all his personal dreams and experiments equally valid until each had been tested through experience. Consequently, in Romantic art the greatest diversity of ideas clamored for uncensored expression. To an objective observer the youthful Romantic might seem to be acting paradoxically in the course of proving all values through first-hand experiment. For example, the arch-Romantic Lord Byron, although narrowly egotistic when interested in his personal development, was at the same time a champion of freedom; altruistic to the point of self-sacrifice. Thus the new tolerance in many cases resulted in a seemingly dispersed life and art.

The Idea of Evolution. Comprehending all previous cultural attitudes and religions, the Romantic thinker, half unconsciously, introduced his philosophies into his artistic and scientific expressions. During the life of any given Romantic creator, we find him developing through all the former periods of man's growth. If, on the whole, he followed Plato, he became known as an idealist and stressed formal beauty. If he followed Aristotle, he turned toward the Middle Ages, striving to grasp some aspect of their dynamic modes of expression. A few great Romantics, men of genius, like Goethe, Hugo, and Wagner, foresaw dimly the idea of development or evolution, popularized by Darwin and Huxley in the scientific world. In their lives, we find both Classical and Gothic modes of expression consciously used. The great philosophic task of their lives remained that of the Renaissance man, who strove to unite love and power, the Beautiful, the Energetic, and the Sublime. However, the Romantics differed from the men of the Renaissance in having behind them most of the revelations of science. William Blake, a poor, unlettered, Romantic near-genius, considered half mad in his own day, came close to making this union which should lead the way to the philosophy of the 20th century, in his mystical definition of art:

> To see the world in a grain of sand,
> Infinity in a wild flower,
> To hold the earth in the palm of your hand
> And Eternity in an hour.

Here, the classical-minded Blake stresses the idea of the particular as an expression of the universal or ideal. In another, more dynamic mood he wrote: "I must create a system or be enslaved by another man's." Yet Blake, like all the Romantics, never succeeded in combining the Classical, or ordered, art of his nature (the conscious mind) with the transcendental, or uncontrolled, part of his nature (the unconscious mind). Goethe, the German poet-philosopher and scientist, came closer to this in his life poem, *The Faust*.

Because of the tremendous scope of his thought, the associational patterns in the art of the Romantic are the most difficult to explain briefly. The productions of one individual may vary as much as the product of the many schools of Hellenistic art under the Roman Empire. However, three general moods of thinking emerge from this chaos of the Romantic mind: (1) Utopian idealism, suggesting a plan for man's destinies; (2) the idea of evolution, which proposes a plan continually modifying itself according to discoverable laws; (3) a materialistic mechanism which allows man control of the dynamic forces of nature in order to achieve freedom from physical want.

Historical and Political Backgrounds

The revolt from authority, a fundamental part of the Romantic creed, inheres in the human spirit. History records many instances of revolt, political and religious. The latter part of the 18th century and the beginnings of the 19th witnessed entire social groups within given nations or imperial systems, revolting against unjust taxation and loss of civil liberties. This followed as a natural result of the religious revolt, called the "Protestant heresy," of northern, or Gothic, churches, from the dominance of the centralized, Classical church at Rome. The discovery and exploration of the Western Hemisphere bred, particularly among the Celto-Germanic peoples, a race of revolters. Wherever incipient revolution reared its head in Europe, the exploits of the American colonists in their war against England were recited. To America came the Romantic revolutionaries from all Europe. From America came those exponents of freedom who helped in the French Revolution. Russia freed her serfs. Germany won her freedom from Austria, and the German people strove in vain to found a republic, while all of Europe fought the tyranny of the imperialistic Napoleon. The noblest expression of the political revolution on American soil was Roger Williams's principle that the power of the church should be forever separated from the power of the state. This freed man from a dual domination which alone could completely enslave him.

The Industrial Revolution. The industrial revolution brought about by the introduction of scientifically conceived machines accelerated economic production, and promised to gain for man increased leisure time in which to enjoy art. Unfortunately, up until the 20th century, man had not discovered how to free these machines from the imperialistic control of some individuals unequipped morally to manage them for mankind's good. Here is a case of abortive revolution. The political revolution, significant as it was, had its sinister

Fig. 540.—Interior of the painter Makart's studio, 1881. (*American Art Journal.*)

aspects. Revolution often gives the unsocial egotist an opportunity to mislead people inflamed by their war for freedom. Napoleon, a romantic figure in the worst sense of the term, told his followers that every soldier of France carried a marshal's baton in his knapsack. The Napoleonic pattern of thought in some degree dominated several 19th-century leaders of the industrial revolution.

Rugged Individualism, the "Nouveaux Riches" and Their Standards of Taste. The consequences of a new distribution of wealth among the bourgeois, or middle, classes and the growth of a new aristocracy based upon the emergence of this industrial class, led to the growth of more rugged individuals, on the Renaissance model, throughout France, Germany, England, and America—the most productive countries of the Romantic movement. This class was called by the French critics the *nouveaux riches*. Lacking the background of taste fundamental to the old aristocracy, a *nouveau riche* was incapable of distinguishing between the genuine and the spuri-

ous in art. Stimulated by a desire to appear cultured, the members of this class paid heavily for reproductions of antique Gothic furniture and architecture, for chairs and picture frames that would look as though they had come from the palace of the Sun King at Versailles. The new moneyed class had little respect for the artists of its own day, deeming more impressive a romantic vision of the past. So the Victorian living room became a museum of artistic curios. No better commentary on the aesthetic background of the people who sometimes bought the panel paintings of the Romantic artists, or who attended the opera as some social function, can be given than Fig. 540, showing the studio interior of the Austrian court painter Makart, in Vienna. A reporter for the *American Art Journal*, in 1881, thus described a visit to that studio.

The most interesting thing you have shown me is without doubt Franz Makart's studio. It is one of the chief attractions of Vienna . . . Rich velvet curtains are withdrawn as we pass out of this studio into the anteroom, where a few knight's armours seem to keep watch before a heavily curtained door . . . On the left side, opposite the picture wall, there is an old fireplace with its mantelpiece, and torchlight bearers very nearly reach the ceiling. In front of it is an old iron grate of fine design taken from the grave of two nuns in a French cemetery, and holding rare old pottery in the iron basins that were once filled with hallowed water. To the right and left of the chimney stand old candelabra ten feet high, with beautiful modeled urchins in every position. One of the little cupids has an old straw hat on his head, another two or three chains with rare coins round his neck; another has the iron gloves of a knight on his tiny hands and another supports a Chinese parasol with his tiny arms. Not far from the chimney is a piano, covered with Gobelin tapestry to conceal its all too modern beauty.

The Ideal of the Natural Man and the Writings of Rousseau. Descartes, the mathematical philosopher, freed the Romantic intellectually with his reasoned argument for being. Another philosopher, Jean Jacques Rousseau, living in the

Age of Reason, epitomizes the emotional, free-thinking, progressive Romantic, who, because of a sensitive temperament, was forced to affirm his lack of faith in mere logic and reason. In his *Confessions*, an autobiography, Rousseau reaffirmed the importance of the inspirational moments in man's living. The *Confessions* described the romance of a self-educated individual, growing up without roots in the past, seeking to discover in his own nature by empirical means such universal qualities as are common to all mankind. Rousseau's philosophy, which was to become the dominant philosophy of the revolutionary world, asserted optimistically that man, evolving from nature, brought with him impulses fundamentally good.

At heart an idealist, after the manner of Plato, Rousseau maintained, in his *Émile*, that the natural man could be educated by means of art to expand his natural instincts so that the cultured total personality would become one with the perfect social personality or state. Like the Renaissance humanists, Rousseau believed in the religion of nature. Unlike them, he attempted to practice it, preaching that men should lose themselves in nature, and, returning to the natural state of being, find the sources of the Good. Promising that a new education in a new environment would create a better race of men, he promulgated those ideas that sent bands of romantic idealists to America, where they hoped to create a democratic nation. Almost all modern American theories of government and education stem from Plato through Rousseau. Rousseau's definition of liberty, in his *Social Contract*, holds that "Slavery arises in following the impulses of appetite; liberty in the obedience to a self-prescribed law."[1]

Rousseau's primary assumption of a beneficent Deity in nature, working through human beings, was a Utopian projection of the essentials of democracy. It came to its fullest expression in the American Jeffersonian sentence:

[1] Jean Jacques Rousseau, *Social Contract*, Book I, Chap. VIII.

"That form of government is the best which provides most effectively for a wise selection of these natural *aristoi* into the offices of government." That is, allowing all men an equal opportunity to develop their talents under a system of education which helps all to discover their own fundamental goodness, men will inevitably choose, as heads of their government, those of their number naturally talented in the business of governing. This idealistic belief inspired schools of Romantic painters, such as the Nazarenes and the Pre-Raphaelites. It influenced the arts and crafts movements of 19th-century England and the social philosophy of the art critic Ruskin.

Literary Backgrounds

In the social background of the 19th century, two forces dominated: the one, ideal and progressive; the other, reactionary and materialistic. These alternately accounted for most of the economic and political movements of this period, which has often been called "the Age of Enlightenment." Foremost among the former were spirits like Beethoven and Johann Wolfgang von Goethe; among the latter, Napoleon and Bismark.

The Romantic's Philosophy in the Works of Goethe. The new man who stood revealed to himself in the last phases of the Renaissance, the Age of Reason, and the beginning of the period of enlightenment, was, in one respect, a counterpart of sophistic man, "the measure of all things," lacking the Classical sense of the finite. In his own imagination, the Romantic considered himself a natural microcosm with limitless possibilities for development, a paradoxical world "with a beginning but without an end." Goethe accepted this point of view. His literature can be understood primarily in terms of the expression of one naturally desiring academic certitude, but of one who was, at the same time, jealous for his Gothic power of creation.

Goethe's life began before the French Revolution, in a home atmosphere created by a puritanical lawyer father and an artistically creative actress mother. Goethe, maturing during Na-

Fig. 541.—Goethe on the Roman Campagna, by Johann Tischbein (Darmstadt Museum). (*Courtesy of Lesch.*)

poleonic times, attempted plays on Alexander the Great and Julius Caesar. During this period of his life he analyzed the architecture of the Gothic cathedral at Strasbourg, and eventually found as his first successful hero not a man on the Classical Napoleonic model, but a German Gothic Robin Hood—the more democratic Götz von Berlichingen, about whom he wrote a play.

In later life, observing natural phenomena with all the powers of his intellect, Goethe made significant contributions to the sciences of comparative anatomy and botany. On the other hand, in the field of optics, unconsciously influenced by his own Gothic, Romantic soul Goethe ignored Newton's scientific discoveries in the physics of color, devising a theory of color artistically significant but medieval in its pattern. He based his theory of color on the real contrast between light and shade, ignoring the spectral analysis of color based upon the composition of light alone.

Again, under the influence of classical scholars in the university, the young Goethe tried to formulate an absolute aesthetic criticism founded on an assumed evolution of all European art styles from the Greeks. He hoped thus to discover an absolute aesthetics transcending all national feeling. His aims were universal; his means, however, limited. Goethe's appreciation of the classical style was not based on an accurate archaeological knowledge of the superior creations of Phidias and Praxiteles, but on Roman copies of Hellenistic sculpture.

The Romantic Goethe, when he reached the fields of Greece and the Roman Campagna (Fig. 541), was not interested primarily, like the Renaissance humanists, in scientific excavation, but in attempting to recapture nostalgically the essence of an Arcadian past. In his novel, *The Sorrows of Young Werther*, Goethe revealed the soul of the youthful Romantic, always seeking release from present-day troubles in some far-off land. Werther's last escape from reality lay in suicide. But the young Goethe himself, touring the classic lands, found a pleasure which he expressed in Mignon's song:

Do you know the land where the lemon flowers grow,
In arbors of shade, the gold oranges glow,
Where gentle wind from Heaven blue descends
The myrtles stand, with laurel incense blend?
Do you know that fair land? Then quickly away,
With you, love, forever and ever I'd stay.

Mignon's song continues, telling of a house with a roof resting on polished, glittering columns, girt with marble statues. In this lovely place, writes Goethe, "You and I, poor child, may go and be sheltered." In this flight from the harshness of the world to a classical Arcadia, Goethe's escape may be compared to Rousseau's search for the pure natural man in a primitive paradise.

Goethe and the "Storm and Stress" Movement. The young Goethe, caught between the Christian and the pagan ideologies, the northern desire for expression and the southern desire for form, was like the great geniuses of the Italian Renaissance. He differed from them, however, in that he matured more quickly, passing through the Renaissance period of his life in the years between twenty and thirty. These were known as the *Sturm und Drang* years. All of Northern Europe went through this period of "Storm and Stress" with Goethe. Through it political and social upheaval became audible in literature.

Goethe's play *Götz von Berlichingen* symbolized the revolt of the German people. Schiller's dramas, *William Tell* and *The Robbers*, expressed similar revolutionary themes. In England, "Storm and Stress," portrayed in a less dramatic form, can be found in Shelley's *Prometheus Unbound*, Wordsworth's poem "On the French Revolution," and Coleridge's "Ode to France." These and many other literary works, including the social novels of Victor Hugo, particularly *Les Misérables*, portray the Promethean social titan of the times.

Still greater artistic expressions of the period of "Storm and Stress" can be found in the field of music, particularly in the symphonies and quartets of Beethoven. Goethe escaped from his period of "Storm and Stress" in two ways. (1) He created the heroic figure of Faust, a man of the enlightenment, caught in the eternal strife between God and the devil, seeking redemption through love, and salvation by good works. In his Faust story, Goethe came close to the ideals of the leaders of the industrial revolution, and he thus epitomizes the active elements in romanticism. (2) His other escape was into a quasi-Oriental philosophy, written in his series of essays, *The West-Eastern Divan*.

Psychological Self-analysis in Romantic Fiction. Throughout Goethe's literary works, one discovers the growing interest in self-analysis, which, starting in the Renaissance, was to reach its final culmination in the late Romantic writings of the 19th-century symbolists, and its eventual scientific explanation by the discovery of the theory of the unconscious mind in the Romantic scientific writings of the psychoanalysts.

Throughout the story of Faust, one feels that Goethe is attempting to discover himself in relation to his dreams of two types of beautiful women, recognizing at the same time that a rest from his soul struggles can come only with his descent into the grave, which may mark his eventual victory or defeat, depending on how well he has played the part of a man. The Romantics, overburdened with man's knowledge, feeling their impotence before the rising forces of destruction and universal warfare inherent to the unbridled excesses of the industrial revolution and national imperialistic expansion, were all more or less haunted by death fantasies.

The macabre, a characteristic motif of Romantic art, stemming in part from medieval visions of the Doom, expressed itself in Goethe's fantasy as the "witches' Sabbath scene" from Faust. Seeking love, Faust must descend to a "sphere by dreams enchanted" and, floating through a weird, abysmal land, is carried hither and yon by a wind which "whistles and surges over rock-strewn gorges." Here, Faust, guided by Mephistopheles, meets a bloodless, phantom girl whose Gorgon glance can turn the blood to stone. Desiring her, Faust is warned that every man sees in this doll his own love. Faust replies that he has fallen beneath her fatal spell. Thus Goethe recognizes that profound love for some unworthy woman or vampire can easily result in artistic impotence and the loss of the sources of an artist's life. Man's unconscious fear of the mystifying elements in the eternal feminine, early found in the Ishtar legend of Babylon and in the plays of Euripides, here begin to have their psychological explanation. As we shall see, most Romantic poets as well as many Romantic painters were preoccupied with the problem of the relationship of the creative man to the fatal woman—*la belle dame sans merci.*

The Romantic Novels. The Romantic novels comprise three sorts: (1) works describing the effects of unrequited love in realistic fashion—books like *The Sorrows of Young Werther;* (2) books of weird mystery and horror, such as Mary Shelley's *Frankenstein*, Hugo's *Bug Jargal*, or his *L'Homme qui rit;* (3) what might be called archaeological novels. In England, following the publication of McPherson's collection of legends attributed to the bard Ossian, Walter Scott wrote *Waverley*, *The Bride of Lammermoor*,

Ivanhoe, and *Quentin Durward*. Horace Walpole's *Castle of Otranto* combines the medieval scene with those elements of horror deemed necessary for a good romance. The French revived many medieval romances, particularly the *Four Sons of Aymon*, *Genevieve of Brabant*, *Jean of Paris*, and *Amadis of Gaul*. Victor Hugo's masterful description of the medieval scene in *Notre Dame de Paris* followed, along with the ever-popular *Three Musketeers* of Alexandre Dumas. The writings of the last-named master, because of their swift dramatic action, lend themselves most easily to 20th-century motion-picture production.

Chateaubriand, the ideal Romantic novelist, carried his readers to America in *Natchez*, to the Orient in his *Itinerary from Paris to Jerusalem*. In his book, *The Martyrs*, he reconstructed the life of the primitive Celto-Germans. In his *Genius of Christianity*, combining the language of orator and poet, he attempted to define, in terms of the revived Christian mythology, the spiritual essence of medieval faith. His studies led directly to the archaeological reconstructions of his contemporary, Viollet-le-Duc, who rebuilt the ancient castles and churches of France at the behest of Bourbon king and Napoleonic emperor alike. Faguet thus described Chateaubriand:

> He loved passionately all orders of beauty, was an enraptured admirer of the solitudes of the new world, the Orient, Greece, Rome, and Italy. Versed in Greek and Latin antiquity, he read Homer with delicacy and Virgil with charm. He understood by instinct and intuition the Middle Ages with Dante, the Renaissance with Petrarch, and better than any one else, the true and solid beauty of the seventeenth-century classics. Thus equipped he revealed to his compatriots a new world which was the whole world.

In contrast, the more realistic scholar of the 20th century sees the past with a scientifically trained historical vision. Unlike the Romantic, he can no longer consider "all primitivism lyric poetry, all Classical culture epic in quality," as did Victor Hugo.

Lord Byron and "l'homme fatal." Corresponding to man's perennial dream of the "fatal woman," which accounts for many of the types pictured by Romantic artists, was a literary concept of man, partly originating in the poem *Don Juan*, by Lord Byron. The Romantic adventurous poet, the "dangerous man," had an appeal, as a sort of dream lover, for the Victorian lady. *Childe Harold's Pilgrimage*, a poem of epic proportions describing Byron's romantic wanderings through the classical lands, tells of a Gothic soul striving to recapture an ideal of liberty among the ruins of ancient Greece. The active, clubfooted Byron, galloping over the sands of the Lido, wooing his lady in a palace of Ravenna, and eventually dying in the Greek war for freedom, on the plains of Missolonghi, set the type of hero popularized by Victorian novels and the English stage.

Robert Browning and the Romantic's Aesthetic Dilemma. The plays and poems of the Englishman, Robert Browning, who spent much of his life wandering about Italy, disclose the aesthetic eclecticism of the Romantic striving for an Oriental synthesis. The painter, in Browning's "Andrea del Sarto," warns, in Gothic thought pattern, "A man's reach should exceed his grasp, or what's a heaven for?" The mature Renaissance painter Lippi, speaking as a Classical man or a humanist, asks

> Can't I take breath and try to add life's flash,
> And then add soul and heighten them threefold?
> Or say there's beauty with no soul at all
> (I never saw it—put the case the same)
> If you get simple beauty and naught else,
> You get about the best thing God invents.

This is his answer to the Prior's remarks in Gothic mood:

> Your business is not to catch men with show
> With homage to the perishable clay
> But lift them over it, ignore it all,
> Make them forget there's such a thing as flesh.
> Your business is to paint the souls of men—
> . . . .
> Give us no more of body than shows soul!

The Love of Nature and the Growth of Symbolic Imagery. Attention has been called to the development after the Middle Ages of the medieval dream of the City of God, which the Romantic Blake called "the new Jerusalem." This was allied to another Utopian dream, the Arcadia. Sannazaro's *Arcadia* contained passages of colorful, natural beauty. Rousseauism sought in primitivism and nature some elementary law-abiding sense possessing in itself an ethical content. The English poet Matthew Arnold expresses this love of nature to the exclusion of human values, in the following lines:

> And with joy the stars perform their shining,
>   And the sea its long moon-silvered roll,
> For self-poised they live, nor pine with noting
>   All the fever of some differing soul.

The poetry of the Romantics, particularly Coleridge, Wordsworth, and Swinburne, abounds with rich, new word sounds, expressive of onomatopoetic natural effects. Thus began a movement in poetry, "Symbolism," which was to lead out through Coleridge's pictures in *The Ancient Mariner* and Robert Browning's descriptions of nature on the Roman Campagna to a sensism in which word sounds were enjoyed almost solely for their own sake.

Seeking ultimate good in nature, some of the early Romantics reached mysticism by middle age and retreated from the world into a purple-shadowed realm where art, like some rare orchid, grew upon the air. Wordsworth became a mystic, as had Blake. But the unhappy Oscar Wilde, one of the last of the Romantics, coming at the end of this movement, never matured beyond his own "Storm and Stress" period. Overwhelmed by the bitterness of the struggle for existence which he found in nature, he wrote pessimistically

> Art is our spirited protest, our gallant attempt to teach nature her proper place. . . . Whenever I am walking in the park here I always feel that I am not more to her than the cattle that browse on the slope, or the burdock that blooms in the ditch. Nothing is more evident than that Nature hates Mind.

Wilde's thought leads to 20th-century Bohemian attitudes.

The Retreat into the Realm of Dreams and the Influence of "la belle dame sans merci." In the latter half of the 19th century, Algernon Swinburne and Dante Gabriel Rossetti, along with many of the French symbolist poets, including Paul Verlaine, found in the realm of dreams Proserpine, the goddess of death. Their concepts of womanhood influenced the style of painting affected by the significant school of the Pre-Raphaelites in England, and by Romantic painters such as Moreau, in France, or Böcklin, in Switzerland.

Walter Pater, the Oxford Platonist, saw this type in the portrait of Isabella d'Este, usually called the Mona Lisa, in the Louvre. A paragraph on the subject of Leonardo's picture, important enough to be quoted in full, shows to what extent the Romantic literary critical fantasy could transform an otherwise fairly objective picture. Interestingly enough, most of our ideas concerning this portrait come from Pater's description rather than from the original painting.

The presence that rose thus so strangely beside the waters, is expressive of what in the ways of a thousand years men had come to desire. Here is the head upon which all "the ends of the world are come," and the eyelids are a little weary. It is a beauty wrought out from within upon the flesh, the deposit, little cell by cell, of strange thoughts and fantastic reveries and exquisite passions. Set it for a moment beside one of those white Greek goddesses or beautiful women of antiquity, and how would they be troubled by this beauty into which the soul with all its maladies has passed! All the thoughts and experience of the world have etched and moulded there, in that which they have of power to refine and make expressive the outward form, the animalism of Greece, the lust of Rome, the mysticism of the Middle Ages with its spiritual ambition and imaginative loves, the return of the Pagan world, the sins of the Borgias. She is older than the rocks among which she sits; like the vampire she has been dead many times, and learned the secrets of the grave; and has been a diver in deep seas, and keeps their fallen day about her; and trafficked for strange webs with Eastern merchants, and, as Leda, was the mother of Helen of Troy, and, as Saint Anne, the mother of Mary; and all this has been to her but as the sound of lyres and flutes, and lives only in the delicacy with which it has moulded the changing lineaments, and tinged the eyelids and the hands. The fancy of a perpetual life, sweeping together ten thousand experiences, is an old one; and modern philosophy has conceived the idea of humanity as wrought upon by, and summing up in itself, all modes of thought and life. Certainly Lady Lisa might stand as the embodiment of the old fancy, the symbol of the modern idea.[1]

Praz points out that the family likeness between this portrait and the fatal women of Gautier, Flaubert, and Swinburne strikes one immediately. She is, like Swinburne's Faustine, vampirous. How deeply Victorian literary Europe was preoccupied by the vagaries of the subconscious, the forbidden delights of the flesh, and the macabre, one detects even in the works of a writer relatively so objective as the poet laureate of England, Alfred Lord Tennyson. In "A Dream of Fair Women" (1832) he conjured from the realm of Dis, Helen of Troy, Iphigenia, Cleopatra, Rosamond, and Jephthah's daughter. To these disquieting women he later added the Lady of Shalott, Clara Vere de Vere, the May Queen, Guinevere, Elaine, and Maud—all more or less phantom loves. Tennyson described in "The Palace of Art" (1832), a phantom underworld like the gloomy Aralu ruled by Queen Ereshkigal, where

> . . . in dark corners of her palace stood
>   Uncertain shapes; and unawares
> On white-eyed phantasms weeping tears of blood,
>   And horrible nightmares,
> And hollow shades enclosing hearts of flame,
> . . . .
> On corpses three-months-old at noon she came,
> . . . .

Here, as in Tennyson's poem "The Vision of Sin," written in 1842, one finds pictured in literary form not only the foreboding landscapes of Böcklin but also certain passages of 20th-century surrealist painting.

Literature, the art of art criticism, and the graphic arts were so closely bound together, and the power of the literary arts was so much greater than the painting of most of the Pre-Raphaelites that much 20th-century art criticism is still phrased in the suggestive but inaccurate terms invented by the Romantics. It is only by examining, as has been done here, the writings of two or more critics on one artist that one may escape to a more objective view of the period.

The sonnet *"Mon rêve familier"* by Paul Verlaine will illustrate a French example of the Romantic preoccupation with voices from the grave.

> Often I have that strange and poignant dream
>   Of some unknown who meets my flame with flame—
>   Who, with each time, is never quite the same,
> Yet never wholly different does she seem.
> She understands me! Every fitful gleam
>   Troubling my heart, she reads aright somehow:
>   Even the sweat upon my pallid brow
> She soothes with tears, a cool and freshening stream.
> If she is dark or fair? I do not know—
> Her name? Only that it is sweet and low,
>   Like those of loved ones who have long since died.
> Her look is like a statue's, kind and clear;
>   And her calm voice, distant and dignified,
> Like those hushed voices that I loved to hear.[2]

Poe's "Helen" is the best-known American example.

The Escape from the Romantic's Dilemma in the Poems of Blake. The escape from the philosophical dilemmas and the morbid fantasies of the Romantic artist—one which would help him to overcome both the evils of the misused industrial revolution and his inherent tendency to flee reality into the realm of dreams—was foreseen by the first Romantic poet, William Blake. In his poem, "Jerusalem," Blake wrote

> Oh, divine spirit, sustain me on thy wings,
> That I may awake Albion from his long and cold repose:

[1] WALTER PATER, *The Renaissance*.
[2] "My Familiar Dream," by Paul Verlaine, translated by Louis Untermeyer. (*Courtesy of translator.*)

For Bacon and Newton, sheathed in dismal steel, their
    terrors hang
Like iron scourges over Albion; Reasonings like vast
    Serpents
Infold around my limbs, bruising my minute articula-
    tions.
I turn my eyes to the Schools and Universities of Europe
And there behold the Loom of Locke, whose woof rages
    dire,
Washed by the capital water wheels of Newton; black
    the cloth
In heavy wreaths fold over every Nation; cruel Works
Of many Wheels I view, wheel without wheel, with
    cogs tyrannic
Moving by compulsion each other, not as those in
    Eden, which
Wheel within Wheel, in freedom revolve in harmony
    and peace.

Man can escape the Frankenstein monster—
the system of science and industry that was
then being created—only by creating another
system, says the Romantic Blake.

I must create a system or be enslaved by another man's.
I will not reason and compare; my business is to create.

The Socio-critical Essays of Ruskin and Morris.
John Ruskin, perhaps the most voluminous art
critic the world has known, dedicated his *Modern Painters* to an analysis of the work of Turner
as compared with the entire history of painting.
His masterful analyses of Gothic and Byzantine
architecture in *The Stones of Venice* and *St.
Mark's Rest* remain textbooks of criticism.
Forced by a spirit of Gothic realism to face the
fact that under the industrial revolution art
seemed to lose both its integrity and its craft,
Ruskin turned to Socialism, a doctrine at that
time propounded by a German revolutionary
exile, Karl Marx, in his book *Das Kapital*. There
resulted a series of socio-critical essays of which
the best known are *Unto This Last* and *Munera
Pulveris*. Despairingly Ruskin wrote: "There is
hardly a thing in the world that some man
cannot make or do a little worse and sell a
little cheaper, and people who consider price
only are this man's lawful prey."

Another painter and printer, William Morris,
pointed the way to the eventual 20th-century
escape from a regressive romanticism by suggesting that industry should, through its own
processes, create a new art, based upon craftsmanship. Morris, willing to accept the actuality
of the industrial revolution, asked:

Is money to be gathered? Cut down the pleasant
trees along the houses, pull down ancient and
venerable buildings, for the money that a few square
yards of London dirt will fetch; blacken rivers, hide
the sun and poison the air with smoke and worse,
and it's nobody's business to see to it nor to mind it;
that is all that modern commerce, the counting
house forgetful of the workshop, will do for us herein.

And Science—we have loved her well, and followed her diligently—what will she do? I fear she
is so much in the pay of the counting house and the
drill sergeant, that she is too busy and will for the
present do nothing. Yet there are matters which I
should have thought easy for her; say, for example,
teaching Manchester how to consume its own
smoke, or Leeds how to get rid of its superfluous
black dye without turning it into the river, which
would be as much worth her attention as the production of the heaviest of heavy black silks, or the
biggest of useless guns. Anyhow, however it be
done, unless people care about carrying on their
business without making the world hideous, how
can they care about art?

Growing out of this pessimism finally came
the doctrine of the aesthetic value as the highest
ethical ideal. Morris thus answered his own
question.

There is an art of which the old architect who
built New College at Oxford was thinking when he
took for his motto "Manners maketh Man." He
meant by manners the art of morals, the art of living
worthily and like a man. I must needs claim this
art also as dealing with my subject.

Morris and Ruskin preached that an aesthetic philosophy of honest craftsmanship,
measure for measure, was the highest ethical
concept. Correct design in line and form was
carefully studied and explained in the works of
Walter Crane, who also published his famous
Cantor lectures on the decorative illustration of
books. The page of printing by Morris introduced here (Fig. 542), if diligently scanned for
aesthetic form and philosophical content, marks

HERE BEGIN POEMS BY THE
WAY. WRITTEN BY WILLIAM
MORRIS.   AND FIRST IS THE
POEM CALLED FROM THE UP-
LAND TO THE SEA.

HALL WE
WAKE ONE
MORN OF
SPRING,
GLAD AT
HEART OF
EVERY-
THING,
YET PEN-
SIVE WITH
THE THOUGHT OF EVE?
Then the white house shall we leave,
Pass the wind-flowers and the bays,
Through the garth, and go our ways,
Wandering down among the meads
Till our very joyance needs
Rest at last; till we shall come
To that Sun-god's lonely home,
Lonely on the hill-side grey,
Whence the sheep have gone away;
Lonely till the feast-time is,
When with prayer and praise of bliss,
Thither comes the country side.

FIG. 542.—Initial page of *Poems by the Way*, by William Morris, printed at Kelmscott Press, September, 1891.
Note revival of quasi-Romanesque ornamental style.

a fitting conclusion for this brief study of the literary aspects of the movement.

Reviewing the social, political, and literary backgrounds of the visual arts in the Romantic 19th century, one finds many broadly cultured individuals expressing the desirability of a Promethean vision with revolution in every field of social intercourse as significant as the revolutions in scientific, economic, and political fields. Like the ill-fated Cassandra of Aeschylus's play, most Romantics found themselves able to prophesy but unable to bring about significant action. Perhaps because they were too early, their art could contribute very little to the active life of their time. With longing, many strove to return to an earlier age of faith in the Middle Ages or else, if too realistic, to nature. As individualists, many lost themselves in a Neo-Platonic half-mystical worship of formal art values for their own sake. A few, turning inward, began that self-analysis through an introspective contemplation of their created art symbols which, in the 20th century, was to eventuate in the literary pseudoscientific psychoanalysis.

French Painting

A Self-portrait of Ingres in His Romantic Style. The Romantic revolt began in French painting after the fall of Napoleon. Although cutting off the baroque and the rococo, the French Revolution did not immediately establish romanticism in art. The Empire, in fact, enlisted the services of David, Ingres, and Drouais—three Academy painters—to assist in glorifying Napoleon and the new France, much in the same way as the Second Empire was to enlist the thoroughly Romantic painters of that period.

To what extent romanticism affected even the Academy may be seen by the classicist Ingres's self-portrait (Fig. 543). Here there is a Romantic picturesqueness in the way the painter's cloak is thrown back from the shoulders. The sleeve of the cloak at the right has a line

unconsciously felt along the right arm, which partly frees itself from the garment as the hand reaches toward the canvas with a palette knife. The line is repeated in the left arm, with the

Fig. 543.—Self-portrait of Ingres as a Youth, Salon of 1806. (*Courtesy of Lesch.*)

left hand cleaning the canvas. Implied in these three lines—that of the cloak and the two arms —is a movement toward the canvas, coming out from a central position just below the head. Here combine all the aspects of typical Romantic subject matter—in the portrait of a youth approaching the canvas of life. What will he make of it? Ingres, forsaking romanticism, followed in the footsteps of David, became the head of the Academy, and spent a comfortable life picturing the *haut monde*. His compositions became nicely balanced, gained in form, finish, and delicacy of line, but lost their energy (Fig. 520, Chap. XVI).

Romance and Realism in Géricault's Raft of the Medusa. A further illustration of the developing Romantic spirit can be found in a painting by Géricault. The French, exceedingly pragmatic, built their romanticism upon a study of observed phenomena. The Frenchman always, to some extent, appreciates formalized academic art, and in escaping from a formularized tech-

Fig. 544.—Raft of the Medusa, by Jean Louis Géricault, 1819. Oil on canvas, height 16 feet 1½ inches (Louvre Museum). (*Courtesy of Lesch-Carnegie.*)

nique, like Géricault in his famous Raft of the Medusa (Fig. 544), will carry the study of psychological expression and natural muscle movement to the extent of photographic naturalism. Géricault studied as a youth under the classicists, Vernet and Guérin. When he heard of the wreck of the *Medusa*, being morbidly intrigued by the horror of the event, he reconstructed, as far as he was able, the episodes in the desertion of the raft—the 150 survivors, the attempted escape by the ship's boats, and the subsequent rescue after most of the passengers had perished. The final dramatic moment —the time when the rescuing ship was sighted —became the subject of Géricault's canvas, first exhibited in 1819.

The compositions of Poussin and the academic painters all have definite pictorial centers which draw the attention. In Géricault's painting the raft comprises such a center— the culmination of the tremendous upsurge of the waves which bear it. However—and this is significantly characteristic of most Romantic art—the attention is not continually held upon this center but is distracted to other parts of the composition by the explosive movement of the writhing forms, those tortured survivors

who sight the rescuing frigate far in the distance. Géricault's color scheme here is browned and academic. For that reason the painting is more realistic than Delacroix's Bark of Dante, which

Fig. 545.—Dante and Vergil in Hell, by Eugène Delacroix, 1822. Oil on canvas, height 5 feet 11 inches (Louvre Museum). (*Courtesy of Lesch-Carnegie.*)

followed three years later. The colors in midocean are not particularly chromatic, but under a tropical sun details stand out in light and shade with horrifying clearness. In Géricault's picture man is overwhelmed by the immensity of nature. So, this canvas belongs to the naturalistic movement in French art as well as to romanticism. When the richer colors and less careful drawing of Delacroix are reached, one faces the complete Romantic production.

Delacroix and The Bark of Dante. What Géricault left incomplete in the direction to which he had aspired was later completed by Eugène Delacroix, the greatest Romantic painter of the 19th century in France. The entire reaction against Neo-Classicism in painting descended on the shoulders of this man, who, as a boy, had been raised during the Revolution by parents thoroughly in sympathy with revolutionary ideals. Emotional by nature, widely schooled, and with brilliant artistic talents, young Delacroix made no compromises with the Academy —which persisted through the first half of the 19th century. An associate of Géricault in the atelier of Guérin and, like him an admirer of

Rubens, Delacroix could have had no more favorable opportunity to adapt his temperament and ideas to the new spirit of the day. Like many Romantic painters, he built his subjects around literary allusions. Of that type was his first Salon picture, exhibited in 1822—Dante and Vergil in Hell, known as The Bark of Dante (Fig. 545). This painting raised a storm of controversy and its author became the recipient of some of the most immoderate criticism of the times on the part of the Academy.

Delacroix, shortly afterward, saw Constable and Turner's paintings in England and began a lifelong association with the English romanticists. He traveled subsequently in the Near East, sought out the color and exoticism of that part of the world, did a series of Oriental scenes, infused vigor and imagination into his work, and pursued in his own words the "Grand Style." It remained for Delacroix to discover that the painter who would break away from the academic formulae needed more than a changed style. It was necessary to adopt new literary associations, create the art around familiar themes, much as the classical painters had done, in order to realize the potential values of the Romantic temperament. In short, romanticism could not operate in a vacuum; neither Gros nor Géricault found the commemoration of current events congenial themes for nonclassical painting, and Delacroix alone, going back to Dante, was to solve the problem.

The Bark of Dante demonstrates the way in which this painter used the Gothic "struggle" theme for an expression of the Romantic attitude. The composition of the painting centers on the figure of Dante, which is practically one with the figure of Vergil. These two monumental shapes, painted with broad, flowing strokes of color, stand in a boat around which move the tortured bodies of unfortunate sufferers in the River Styx. Dimly discernible through the smoke, the flames of hell appear. In this composition all moves around one center and, although the human bodies are muscu-

lar in the extreme, they seem but so many animated masses of color.

The Romantic school inherited from the baroque facility of brush stroke and a desire for

FIG. 546.—Dance of the Nymphs, by Jean Baptiste Corot, 1851. Oil on canvas, height 3 feet 2¼ inches (Louvre Museum). (*Courtesy of Lesch-Carnegie.*)

intense color. The human form was studied not for its own sake, but simply to get enough verisimilitude so that one might feel the emotional effects of moving masses. The Bark of Dante can be well compared with the Pergamum altar, of late Hellenistic times (Fig. 219, Chap. IX). It is essentially dramatic art in painting—not the deep, spiritual drama of Botticelli's painting, but a superficial dramatization. It looks to the Middle Ages, not as an abode of saints and martyrs, but rather as a colorful and glamorous era.

Return to Nature by the Barbizon School and Corot's Dance of the Nymphs. The possibilities of nature as the sole subject for art, beautiful in its idealized, dreamy aspect, were realized by a group of painters who settled in Barbizon, a quiet village some 20 miles south of Paris. The realist, Courbet, and the Romantics, Daubigny, Rousseau, and Corot, specialized in making complete studies of nature, much after the manner of the Dutch painters. They not only studied the inner structures of trees as carefully as though they were studying personalities, but they also observed the effects of different natural lighting upon leaves and shadows. The fine points of the Barbizon painters may be understood by studying the ever-popular Dance of the Nymphs (Fig. 546), painted in 1851 by Jean Baptiste Camille Corot

Fig. 547.—The Gleaners, by Jean François Millet, 1857. Oil on canvas, height 2 feet 9 inches (Louvre Museum). (*Courtesy of Lesch-Carnegie.*)

(1796–1875). Corot was trained in the classical school, and traveled to Rome in 1825. There he painted a series of classical landscapes showing the city and the Campagna, very much in the style of the academician, Horace Vernet. Two other trips to Rome brought the same results—careful, classical drawings and exact studies.

In his later years, however, when he had come under the influence of romanticism, Corot discovered that he could achieve a freedom of expression by studying carefully the effects of atmospheric depth, as attained by making brush strokes feather out over indefinite contour lines. Corot understood how the eyes are so tricked by nature that it is only when we focus them on some object in the picture that we see it sharply; all other objects are slightly hazy and do not immediately strike the perception. He succeeded in making a sharply perceived object indistinct on one side so that it would seem to connect with some distinct plane of the picture. Then, too, Corot by blurring the outlines of objects in the distance, with what Leonardo da Vinci called *sfumato*, suggested their greater removal from the front of the picture plane. In the Dance of the Nymphs, the group of sprightly figures under the trees are distinct enough to be recognizable, and yet indistinct enough so that we may imagine them part of the flicker of sunlight on the leaves. The golden sun's beams sifting through the dusty air make the entire scene almost dreamlike in quality. Similar effects can be found in the canvases of Titian and Correggio, as well as other late Venetian painters.

The literary quality of Corot's painting can be gathered from one of his letters to a friend. Here he tells of his impressions on going out early in the morning to paint a landscape.

There is nothing remarkable to see at first. Nature looks like a white tablecloth where one barely distinguishes the outline of a few masses. Everything is scented; everything trembles in the fresh breeze of early dawn—the sun shines out, but has not yet dispelled the mist that hides plains, valleys, and hills on the horizon. The nocturnal vapors still float like silver clouds over the sleeping vegetation. Bing! Bing!—the first ray of the sun, the second ray, the tiny flowers seem to awake joyously. Each has its dewdrop that trembles. The leaves shiver in the morning breeze. Unseen birds are chirping among the foliage, and it is as if the flowers were offering prayers.

For many pages Corot continues the description of the changing aspects of nature throughout the day. Always one hears music and realizes that during those years while Corot was painting, Wagner wrote the *Forest Murmurs Music* of *Siegfried*. Debussy, coming later in the century, was to adopt this Impressionism and compose *The Afternoon of a Faun*. Ruskin in England could write, at the same time, that architecture must be "frozen music"; and Schopenhauer, following Plato, "that all art aspires to the condition of music." The barriers between the arts were breaking down, as Corot's pictures attempted to show in graphic form the harmonious, odorous effects of woodland scents and melodies.

Millet's Gleaners. Another aspect of nature painting in 19th-century France appears in the works of Jean François Millet (1814–1875), also of the Barbizon school. Millet's work treats the less lyric and sometimes more somber sides of the landscape, as well as the peasant who is so much a part of it. His well-known painting, The Gleaners (Fig. 547), illustrates the union of a desire to understand human life with a study of the rich color effects in nature. Millet, himself a peasant and a product of Normandy, was convinced that the peasant toiling in the fields was the very heart of France. Critics have at times attempted to read into his paintings a socialistic regard for the fortunes of the peasants; however, Millet himself on one occasion disclaimed any such intent. It was enough for him, he said, to catch the characteristic scenes of true peasant life, letting them speak for themselves.

In The Gleaners one feels the heat of the sun beating down on the laboring farmers. Like Giorgione in his Concert (Fig. 477, Chap. XV), Millet has brought the sun in from the left, making that side of the picture a bit lighter than the right. He also leads the attention, moving from the lower left diagonally up through the body of the third gleaner toward the village at the right and then back again along the line of the horizon and into the sky. When Millet has intrigued the observer into the picture, he allows the combination of red, blue, and yellow to blend in the sunlight, thus giving the feeling of the hot, misty atmosphere. Observing the black-and-white reproduction, one may focus upon the literary message, feeling sorry for the hard-working peasant. Before the colorful original, one more simply enjoys the skill of the painter who can make him feel that even this world of labor has an artistic integrity of its own.

Another aesthetic effect can be noticed in the many works by Millet. Géricault's raft was lifted up by, and continues with, the great mass of the wave, so that the survivors partook of the elemental force of nature. All of Millet's types have this same characteristic, as does the famous figure of the Philosopher by Manet and the little bronze studies of working men by the Belgian Meunier. These Romantic realists had begun to discover that man has grown out of and is a part of the mass of nature. Millet's peasants in The Gleaners have arisen from the soil. Compare with Fig. 567, Chap. XVIII.

The Growth of Natural Realism and the Invention of the Camera. In contrast to Corot's treatment of nature as beautiful in its own right, and Millet's introduction of the peasant as a consistent and logical outgrowth of nature, there developed further that naturalism, earlier called "realism" in painting. This found its chief exponent in Gustave Courbet (1819–1877) and resulted in the narrative, natural, military panoramas of Detaille and Meissonier. Eventually, it reached a climax in the invention of the photograph.

Courbet lived in Paris and painted urban scenes of factories and railway stations, typical of the coming age of iron and steel. His realism attempted to show the peasant and the worker not as a true growth of the soil but as men chained to an infinite force of hard labor; thus Courbet consciously portrayed social phenomena which demanded redress. He pictured not only normal people of the lower classes but the idiot and the unfortunate. His realism succeeded in embittering the artists who clung to a Romantic interpretation of reality or the late classicists who inflated the past with hollow meanings. Aesthetically, his studies and compositions in terms of planes of color were to be of value later in the century to the expressionist school. The tendency toward realism which Courbet expressed is mentioned here because it resulted in the collaboration of the engraver, Niepce, and a young painter, Daguerre, who together developed the photograph, or daguerreotype, in an effort to get an exact transcription of reality. When these inventive artists discovered that certain silver salts might be acted upon by light and deposited on a copper plate so as to make a facsimile reproduction of nature, they were at first convinced that this method of recording reality could take the place of the painter's art. If one wishes unselective realism, no artist's brush or pen can possibly rival the camera plate. In later life Daguerre returned to painting, con-

Daguerre. The final direction taken by 19th-century painters in France was a further development of romanticism, which found its métier in an alliance with symbolic literature,

Fig. 548.—Portrait of Alphonse Daudet and Daughter, by Eugène Carrière. Oil on canvas, height about 2 feet (Palais des Beaux-Arts, Paris). (*Courtesy of Lesch.*)

vinced that he lost something in the photographic process.

Four movements appear in 19th-century French art: the persistence of the academic style, on the part of such painters as Ingres; the development of Romantic compositions around literary association, expressed chiefly through the works of Delacroix; the growth of nature and landscape painting, both with and without the introduction of the human element, as exemplified by the Barbizon school; and the rise of natural realism in art, first in the works of Géricault, and later through Courbet and

and endeavored to depict the vagaries of the artistic soul.

The Dream Art of Eugène Carrière. After Corot, it became conventional to represent all of life, even the human face, as though appearing from a haze. The remarkable portrait of Alphonse Daudet (Fig. 548) and his daughter, by Eugène Carrière, shows that in the last stage of this part of romanticism painting was possible without even a thought of geometric composition. Here the two figures appear as disembodied personalities floating out of space. Like so much spiritualistic ectoplasm, they move from right to left in a long attenuated sweep. Everything is concentrated on the essential elements of the two personalities, as portrayed in the faces, but each face in itself appears as a simple collection of relationship between eyes, nose, mouth, without a well-defined border. From time to time in one's dreams, faces appear like this.

Moreau's Salome and the Growth of Symbolism. Moreau's Salome (Fig. 549) shows the fatal dancer as she beholds, floating above her, the haloed head of the decapitated John. The painting has a hypnotic power (1) because of the gruesomeness of the story; (2) because the technique employed gives the indefinite effect noticed in the work of Corot and Carrière; and (3) because, in the mind of the Romantic artist of the time, there persisted an almost neurotic fantasy linked with the idea of *la belle dame sans merci,* the fatal woman. Salome is such a person. Despite the arguments of certain realistic critics, the Romantic artist believes that a work of art may have associational literary values that cannot be wholly separated from purely objective formal values. Moreau's paintings, like most of the work of the Pre-Raphaelites in England, were woven around these symbolist legends and are best understood when the literary implications are familiar. Recollection shows the formal composition of the Salome to have been taken from Rembrandt (Fig. 510), whose painting technique was also reborn in the works of Moreau. The Salome painting has elements of geometric strength toned down by the golden light which bathes the lurid subject, thus uniting the macabre suggestiveness with the purely formal values.

German Painting

Romantic painting in Germany stressed the natural scene and the archaeological reconstruction of Germanic mythology or fairy tales. The former may be demonstrated in the canvases of men like Friedrich, Runge, and Aschenbach. The famous painting *Northern Lights* (Fig. 550), by Caspar David Friedrich, in the collection of Professor Harold Friedrich of Hanover, typifies German nature Romanticism.

Fig. 549.—The Apparition, by Gustave Moreau, oil on canvas. (*Courtesy of Lesch.*)

The Return to Nature and Friedrich's Northern Lights. In Friedrich's painting of the northern lights there rise from misty vales, jagged, lone peaks of earth-born rock, swept round by magic fires in flickering light. The aurora swings from the distant lower right, up through the sky, and out toward the left, then back again, until it blends at last into the blue of the night. Nature seems remote, alone, as before man came. One hardly notices two tiny human forms. A few leafless trees silhouetted against the light accentuate the eerie impression made by the painting.

In another picture, where a white-capped,

sultry sea is breaking along the sandy dunes, Friedrich placed a small, solitary figure of a woman. This gives the greatest possible feeling of loneliness—an effect to which the Celto-

FIG. 550.—The Northern Lights, by Caspar David Friedrich, oil on canvas (Hanover, Germany). (*Courtesy of Lesch.*)

Germanic soul seems predisposed. For the Germans there is, apparently, an almost enjoyable sadness in feeling oneself lost. This attitude is further expressed in one of Goethe's poems which was set to music by the Russian Romantic, Tschaikowsky. The resulting song, *Nur wer die Sehnsucht kennt weiss was ich leide* ("None but the lonely heart can know my sorrow"), admirably illustrates this mood in German romanticism.

Medievalism and Religious Romanticism in Germany. Two other movements in German Romantic painting deserve notice, not because they solve any new formal, aesthetic problems, but because of their literary subject matter. With the rising tide of German nationalism there came a revival of interest in the German

Middle Ages. In England, Germany, and France the 19th century saw the reconstruction of much medieval architecture, and in Germany painters such as Moritz von Schwind and

FIG. 551.—Crossing the River, by Ludwig Richter. Oil on canvas, height about 3 feet (Civic Painting Gallery, Dresden). (*Courtesy of Lesch.*)

Wilhelm von Kaulbach painted scenes of medieval life, particularly illustrative of romantic fairy tales. Another group of German painters, including Peter Cornelius, and Friedrich Overbeck, were known as the Nazarenes, because of their interest in art as a revelation of Christian faith. Ludwig Richter's Crossing the River (Fig. 551) illustrates all the elements proper to German romanticism and serves to illustrate the style of the other men.

The Retreat from Life in Böcklin's Island of the Dead. The finest of the works of the illustrative Romantics, however, is the famous Island of the Dead (Fig. 552) by Arnold Böcklin (1827–1901), a Swiss painter who spent most of his life in Germany and Italy and whose work, although built around classic mythology, has the quality of melancholy and sorrow peculiar to the Romantics. All of the sorrow which Böcklin must have found as he surveyed the ruins of the antique world was put into the picture for which he is most noted—Island of the Dead. Here he succeeds in bringing together in one tiny world of stone and cypress trees and tombs the inevitable destination of mortals. The island floats in a wide sea which stretches on either side. The composition is essentially that of Poussin's Arcadia and Delacroix's Bark of Dante. It is perhaps significant that this painting, which was copied four times

calling up the feeling of sorrow. When the Romantic allows nature to overtake the human creature, as Wilde maintained, it is with fear of ultimate extermination.

FIG. 552.—The Island of the Dead, by Arnold Böcklin, 1880. Oil and varnish on wood, height about 3 feet (Civic Art Gallery, Dresden). Compare with example in the Metropolitan Museum of Art. (*Courtesy of Lesch.*)

with slight deviations in composition, was done at the instigation of the deeply intuitive Countess Oriola. Two months after she begged him to paint the picture, in 1880, Böcklin brought her the finished composition. "You have what you wished," he is reported to have told her, "a picture for dreaming. It must work upon your senses so deeply that you will be frightened if one knocks on the door." It is difficult to imagine any other picture in which almost pure landscape can react so deeply upon the human spirit. It was given a commentary in music by Sergei Rachmaninov, who wrote the tone poem *Island of the Dead* about it.

In Grünewald's Christ (Fig. 394, Chap. XIII) inner anguish was expressed through the bodies. In Giorgione's work there appeared a fine balance between landscape and human life. Here one feels, as in Chinese painting, that the human element is subordinated to the landscape, with this great difference, the Oriental succeeds in subordinating man without

English Painting

In contrast with German Romantic painting, which unconsciously carried the soul of man out in abstract philosophical concepts, and French romanticism, which tended toward dramatic realism, the English Romantics, following Blake, allowed a social message to animate their art or, following Turner, enjoyed natural effects in their sublime aspect for their own sake.

God Measuring the Universe, or The Ancient of Days, by Blake. Blake's painting, The Ancient of Days (Fig. 553), which has recently been used as the basis of a central sculptural composition on a façade in Rockefeller Center, New York, expresses the tremendous vision necessary to a new idealism, conceiving of the universe millions of light-years deep and controlled by something paralleling the human spirit.

Beginnings of Impressionism in the Landscapes of

Constable and Turner. Nature itself, when made over artistically, becomes a symbol of the inner life. Upon this foundation, in the 20th century, the doctrine of the expressionists was built. But

FIG. 553.—The Ancient of Days, by William Blake, water color (British Museum). (*Courtesy of British Museum*.)

in the early 19th century the inner energy found its release in landscape painting, notably in the works of Constable and Turner, in England, and on the canvases of the Barbizon school in France, already considered. John Constable (1776–1837) discovered that new power might be achieved by placing contrasting colors side by side so that greater depth of the whole was gained (Fig. 555). Disregarding the methods of the Academy painters, Constable studied colors directly from nature, finding that brilliant greens, oranges, and purples would give a more exciting effect than the conventional brown tones formerly used by the Hollanders. Another aesthetic advance that may be credited to Constable was his accenting of the planes within a picture, so that one plane cut into another, throwing the eye back into the distance. Along with this he achieved an interweave of trees, clouds, and fields, which did much to make the work of Corot and the Barbizon painters possible.

Constable's influence on landscape painting, in both Europe and America, would be hard to overestimate. His contemporary, Joseph Mallord William Turner (1775–1851), approached nature from an entirely different point of view, attempting to capture broad impressions rather than realistic particulars. Turner, trained in Royal Academy schools, throughout his life had a penchant for painting classical mythology—not, as Böcklin did, in realistic terms, but in a style so original and poetic that one never feels the myth to be impossible. Like most Romantics, Turner did not care for academic "draftmanship" in art. His interest in the total dramatic effect of a world of color, bathed in streams of fluctuating light, developed, perhaps, from an early acquaintance with Claude Lorrain, was united with a superb sense of composition. His paintings are like the work of a stage impresario, more rococo than baroque in style, with lines of force running centripetally through the composition toward some central object or, in some cases, toward a misty, ill-defined region near the center of the canvas (Fig. 554).

Strife of the Critics around Turner's Art. Turner's originality in the use of color, his foreshadowing of Impressionism, his poetic interpretations of nature seemed so unusual that at first the British public did not care for his work. It remained for John Ruskin, writing some years after Turner had begun painting, to recognize his genius and defend him to the public in a treatise on *The Art of Painting*. Ruskin wrote particularly of Turner's "truthfulness" and recognized that the painter had discovered that light was a spectroscopic phenomenon. Turner flooded his

FIG. 554.—The Sun of Venice (Going to Sea), by Joseph M. W. Turner (1775–1851), oil on canvas (National Gallery, London).
(Courtesy of Lesch.)

canvases with light, like some medieval aesthete who wished to demonstrate how the physical light from God illumined the world.

Ruskin defended Turner and his use of Im-

any prescribed form, he painted what he believed to be pre-eminently the beautiful and in so doing consulted naught but his own genius and innate taste. Thus it happens that, in spite of sublime pro-

Fig. 555.—Salisbury Cathedral, by John Constable, 1823. Oil on canvas, height 2 feet 10 inches (Victoria and Albert Museum, London). Note Gothic cathedral, castle, stream, and expanse of fields—all Romantic subject matter. The rainbow suggests the awakening interest in the phenomena of light and color which was to eventuate in late 19th-century Impressionism. (*Courtesy of Leach-Carengie.*)

pressionism in colors, stressing the fact that he saw nature more naturally than did the academicians who emphasized brown and black in their canvases. A less sympathetic critic, Ernest Chesnau, attacked Turner from the academic point of view and saw, rather than truthfulness, a fundamental dishonesty in Turner's approach to nature.

Turner [he wrote] in love with the sun, did not represent it as he saw it with his material eyes but as he viewed it in his dreams; utterly regardless of

ductions, he is sometimes misled, and this is the case with all those who dwell too much within themselves.

Chesnau finished by suggesting that Turner had forsaken Nature, the foster mother of art. Here, among the 19th-century critics, is Augustine's old conflict between the two conceptions of art: "The Fair" and "The Fit."

The Romantic Revolt of the Pre-Raphaelite Brotherhood. Conservative, imperialistic England, unmoved by the Continental revolutions, had an academy more firmly entrenched than that of the French. A few painters who sought to escape its influence organized themselves into the Pre-Raphaelite Brotherhood. Acutely aware of the stultifying effects of the new industrial-

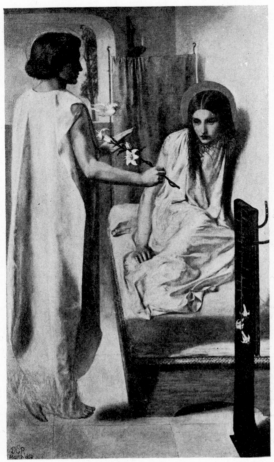

Fig. 556.—The Annunciation, by Dante Gabriel Rossetti, 1850. Oil on canvas (National Gallery, London). (*Courtesy of Lesch.*)

ism, these men, particularly Dante Gabriel Rossetti, Holman Hunt, and Burne-Jones, with Walter Crane and William Morris, agreed on the principle of human and ethical values as the great end of society. They sought to restore the medieval methods of the handicraft arts as a corrective to the mechanical coercion of an industrialist society. Their chief literary exponent, the critic John Ruskin, who had de-

fended Turner, found in his studies on the nature of Gothic architecture much to support their point of view. Considering Raphael to have been the instigator of academicism, they adopted as a watchword, "Nothing good has been painted since Raphael." The Pre-Raphaelites studied the works of Leonardo da Vinci, Botticelli, and Mantegna, opposing the early Florentine and Venetian schools to the later Roman aspect of the Renaissance. With them began a retreat of English painters and writers to Florence as the artistic center of the world. Similarly, the German Nazarenes, becoming converts to Catholicism, retired to Rome, where they lived like monks on the Pincio.

The Pre-Raphaelites, interested more in the associational values of art than in the doctrine of "art for art's sake," which would have led them to an exploration of formal, aesthetic values, painted with all the careful drawing of the 15th-century Florentines. Ignoring the advances in color made by the baroque masters, their works show a lack of interest (with often very unpleasant results) in the problem of color harmony, which chiefly lends emotional overtones to painting. Retreating from the world into a detached medieval existence, all but Crane and Morris created works of art that had a distinct flavor of unreality.

An Annunciation by Dante Gabriel Rossetti. In painting, the works of G. F. Watts, Hunt, Burne-Jones, and the Rossettis are significant. Here, the use of white, with pale colors—like the Florentine primitives, Botticelli and Fra Angelico—carries the observer back to the dreamy, half-legendary world of the late Middle Ages and early Renaissance. Dante Gabriel Rossetti's Annunciation (Fig. 556), perhaps his best known painting, is important in its contrast with the classical Annunciations of the Renaissance masters.

A study of his Annunciation reveals the reasons for its pleasing effects, principally in the refined silvery tones of robes and walls, with not too bright red and blue, and the golden halos. The subject matter is taken care of by two semirealistic figures; the head of the angel is strong and well modeled, but the lower part of the body seems vague and unsubstantial. The Virgin on the couch, drawing back, looks pale and wistful, half frightened. Here is an attempt at a psychological understanding of the situation, with an expression almost impossible to conceive in an earlier age. The strong red in the foreground gives greater distance to the blue in the background; thus the picture achieves depth. This, one of the best of the Pre-Raphaelite paintings, is based upon the persistent memory of a legend, rather than something wholeheartedly believed in.

Rossetti's Studies of Women. In Rossetti's many studies of women—particularly in his Proserpine, Rosamond, Beatrice, and Lilith—appears *la belle dame sans merci.* These women are all of a type. Approach them by studying the contour of the face of the Virgin in The Annunciation, with its high forehead, its delicate but firm chin setting off lips that are small and slightly pouting but carefully modeled. Attention is directed especially to the eyes, which appear large, a bit deep-set and slightly staring, as though the revelation of the angel, symbolized in the lily branch, has had an almost hypnotic power over her. The composition scheme of most of Rossetti's feminine portraits may be found in the diagrammatic sketch of the Proserpine (Fig. 557), showing how the lines of drapery and limbs lead up to the face, where the flowing hair masses call attention to the eyes.

The human eye, as Leonardo said, is "the window of the soul." The eyes of Proserpine seem to be staring out beyond the grave. Rossetti paints the eyes of Beatrice with the lids drawn down and with her lips half-open, as though waiting for her lover's kiss. She carries associational values that unconsciously affect most of us. The Blessed Damozel looks out from her "gold bar of heaven" with eyes half-closed, as though in her turn dreaming of the lover who sleeps, on earth.

Thus romanticism in England ends on a weird note, the property chiefly of literature rather than the graphic arts, with criticism playing perhaps the most important role of all. Romanticism died of its own feebleness.

Fig. 557.—Proserpine, by Dante Gabriel Rossetti, with diagram of formal composition. Compare with Fig. 303*e*.

The poverty of new ideas and themes, the confession of inadequacy in a new world, the loss of vigor, the disappearance of original sources, all contributed to the decline of romanticism in the art of the 20th century as an *ideé fixe.* Romantic expression, in Europe, found its strongest utterance in different arts in the various countries—music in Germany, painting in France, and literature in England. It is necessary now to consider the development of architecture and sculpture, as well as music, in 19th-century European culture.

Sculpture

Sculpture during the early development of romanticism, like painting, was allied to the baroque and is not especially important from the standpoint of formal results. The academic ideal, however, persisted well into the 19th century. A contrast between it and the Romantic is well illustrated in two reliefs on Napoleon's Arc de Triomphe, erected in Paris, 1806–1836. The two reliefs are, respectively, by one of the old Roman lawgivers. The whole attitude, conventionally classic, is well known throughout the temperate zone, where similar statues of beneficent dictators, politicians, and

FIG. 558.—Reliefs on the Arc de Triomphe, marble, heroic size, Paris, finished in 1837. *a, Le Triomphe*, by Cortot; *b, Le Chant du départ*, by Rude. *(Courtesy of Lesch.)*

Cortot, an academician, and François Rude, a romanticist. The illustrations included here serve to show how far the Romantic artist of the 19th century in France had departed from the classical definitions of the Academy.

Comparison of Classical and Romantic Sculpture on the Arc de Triomphe. Cortot's relief, *Le Triomphe* (Fig. 558a), on the left side of the arch, like Ingres's Apotheosis of Homer, is built up around a central personality, the figure of Napoleon, who stands in the pose and wears the robes of a Roman emperor. He is being crowned by a figure on his left (obviously a copy of the Venus de Milo with its arms replaced), who represents the spirit of France. The conqueror, too, in his toga has a pose copied from a statue of

commencement-day orators have been spawned by the thousand. The balance of masses is perfect, and the group as a whole has a comfortable, static quality which meets all the requirements of classical art.

Were the arch a consistent structure, the opposite side would carry an equally static group designed to heighten the feeling of order and stability. The sculptor Rude, however, saw not the classical glorification of the Empire as had Cortot, but the romance of France's dream of empire, with its political and aesthetic revolution. In expressing this, he negated everything that Cortot had said on the left side.

Rude's relief, sometimes called *Le Chant du départ* (Fig. 558b), is almost shocking in its dynamic quality, in its active, militant representation of the fighting spirit of France. There is no central figure here, as in Cortot's group, but five figures woven together in a fighting front, almost a part of the flying fury, *La Gloire*, above. Like the opening crescendo of *La Marseillaise*, for which the relief was popularly named, all the limbs and drapery lines contribute to an irresistible movement forward and upward. Here in graphic form is the Romantic drama of military life and eternal revolution.

Rodin's Burghers of Calais. The study of Rude's Marseillaise leads inevitably to a consideration of the work of Auguste Rodin (1840–1917), greatest of the Romantic sculptors in France. Rodin himself compared Rude's relief with a great tragedy by Corneille. Calling attention to it he said, "You will no longer say, I think, that sculpture and painting are unable to compete with the theater."[1] Rodin emphasized the pictorial and dramatic qualities of his medium and believed that his own work was a further development of the spirit displayed in The Marseillaise. Because his efforts resulted in deeper emotional tone, he believed them greater than Rude's work. The Burghers of Calais (Fig. 559), perhaps Rodin's most successful creation, unites six massive figures, earthbound and in chains, who offered their lives to the English king, Edward III, in sacrifice for their city. In his book *L'Art*, Rodin discusses his intention concerning this group, telling that he planned to have the figures placed in a row proceeding from the municipal building at Calais toward the site of the English camp, so that "the people of Calais of today, almost elbowing them, would have felt more deeply the tradition of solidarity which unites them to these heroes." His proposal was rejected by the people of Calais, "and they insisted upon a pedestal which is as unsightly as it is unnecessary." Rodin here shows that he wished his art not to be enshrined in the Classical fashion, but to appear to grow out of the lives of the people, as had Millet

before him. This aspect of romanticism, which is very close to the Oriental, appears with even greater force in later American sculpture.

Studying the group, one observes that Rodin

Fig. 559.—The Burghers of Calais, by Auguste Rodin, bronze, over life size, Calais. (*Courtesy of Lesch.*)

has done here in sculpture essentially what Géricault did in painting his Raft of the Medusa. He studied realistically all the muscles and limbs and then broke his sculptural surfaces plausibly—at first glance, overrealistically—into areas that give the feeling of great stress. He made the weight of clothing and limbs so heavy that one almost feels the agony of this slow parade toward destruction. Rodin definitely stated that he wanted the citizens of today to feel more deeply for those who have passed. In this lies the difference between the aesthetics of the Romantic, Rodin, and the moralist, Plato. Plato was interested simply in using art to teach. Rodin, in all his work, seems to be more interested in having people feel deeply.

Rodin's Feeling in Le Poète et la muse. Since feeling is what Rodin would have us get from his work, there is no better person for the young sculptor to study if he wishes to be successful in displaying feeling through the medium of form. Rodin investigated carefully the natural char-

[1] From *Art*, by Auguste Rodin, translated by Mrs. Romilly Fedden, Dodd, Mead & Company, Inc., New York, 1912.

acteristics of the various media with which he worked. Like Praxiteles, he understood the soothing effects of rounded surfaces and rich, cool marble. Like Donatello and Ghiberti, he

Fig. 561.—Church of the Madeleine, Paris, from the southwest, by D'Ivry (1764), Vignon, and Huvé, 1764–1852. Stone, length 354 feet, width 141 feet, height 100 feet. The exterior was transformed by Napoleon in 1806. (*Courtesy of Lesch-Carnegie.*)

Fig. 560.—*Le Poète et la muse*, by Auguste Rodin, marble (Musée Rodin, Paris). (*Courtesy of Lesch.*)

knew the effect of lively, disturbed surfaces in bronze and used these particularly on statues such as John the Baptist, *La Vieille heaulmière*, and The Thinker. From medieval wood carving, Rodin borrowed the effect of the counterpoint of rounded surfaces with sharp planes. He used this device particularly in modeling the drapery of his Burghers. Finally, having studied Michelangelo's Bound Slaves and Titans, he adopted the use of the unfinished form, and gave to the world hundreds of dream figures, partly emerging from clouds of marble (Fig. 560). Thus in his sculpture he reached an effect similar to that in the paintings of Carrière and Rossetti; and thus was the Romantic

sculptor revealed to himself in his dreams and to us in *Le Poète et la muse*.

Two other artists of the 19th century succeeded in capturing the underlying revolutionary struggle in forms which transcend the realm of the purely dramatic, or the dream. The first of these was the newspaper artist, Daumier; the second, the Belgian sculptor, Meunier. Although both had contacts with Romantics and academicians, they followed neither, nor were they photographic realists. They must be considered, because of the universal quality of their work, as transcending the purely Romantic style. They are not to be classified easily and will be dealt with in the discussion of the art of the 20th century, upon which they had considerable influence.

Architecture

The architecture of romanticism results from a desire to have something "just as good." In France it took the form, originally, of a revival by Napoleon of Roman classical styles, embodying what was really a Romantic dream of world empire. This eventuated in the Arc de Triomphe and the Church of the Madeleine (Fig. 561)—the latter, a peripteral temple in the Corinthian style dedicated to *La Gloire*. There is nothing new in Cortot's relief, the arch, or the temple. They are simply larger than similar Roman sculpture and buildings.

Art, and with the development of German nationalism there came a proud affirmation of the importance of the Goths in the cultural development of Europe, the exponents of the

Fig. 562.—Romanticism in industrial design. Railroad bridge over the Rhine, at Strasbourg.

However, the Romantic architectural form of the 19th century in France, as well as in England and Germany, was a revival of the Gothic style.

The Gothic Revival. The revival of interest in Gothic architecture was inspired in part by Victor Hugo's *Notre Dame de Paris*, written in 1831, a production itself as monumental as a Gothic cathedral and an excellent essay on the medieval mind. Equally important in this trend is the work of Viollet-le-Duc, a military architect and engineer of note, as well as an authority on archaeological research and a professor in l'École des beaux-arts. In 1860, Viollet-le-Duc wrote an encyclopedic *Dictionaire de l'architecture française de l'onzième au seizième siècle* (*Dictionary of French Architecture from the 11th to the 16th Century*). As the agent of the government, he restored many churches, as well as the walled town of Carcassonne, not without some unscientific blundering. Like his English contemporary, Ruskin, Viollet-le-Duc, however, tried to show that the principles underlying Gothic architecture were essentially logical (Fig. 356, Chap. XIII).

In Germany, the philosopher Herder published his essay *Concerning the German Style and*

style glorying in what they called their *verwilderungs* period, the return to the primitive (Fig. 562). The effort of King Louis II of Bavaria to reconstruct the Gothic style in his own country best illustrates this tendency. He not only built himself an imitation rococo Versailles at Herrenchiemsee, but restored on the ruins of Hohenschwangau a Romantic castle, Neuschwanstein.

This remarkable structure, with a mixture of both Flemish and German Gothic for exterior details, has many rooms in the Romanesque style, great canopied Gothic beds, and a host of wall paintings in a monumental Romantic vein, done in greater part by members of the Nazarene school. Following the example of this Louis of Bavaria, it became the fashion to restore ruined castles and build new ones where none had existed before. A new Gothic cathedral was proposed for Berlin in 1819, following, perhaps, an impetus started by Goethe's youthful essay on the Gothic cathedral of Strasbourg. The Werder Church in Berlin was built in the Gothic style in 1825, and in Vienna, between 1853 and 1879, Ferstel built the Votive Church on the plan of a Gothic cathedral. Later, the German emperor, William II, had the old Romanesque chapel of Charlemagne at Aix-La-Chapelle restored, and gave money to finish the second tower on the Gothic Cathedral of Cologne. The second being erected in exact

Fig. 563.—Houses of Parliament, by Sir Charles Barry, London, 1840–1860. (*Courtesy of Metropolitan Museum of Art.*)

duplication of the first tower, this is almost the only large Continental Gothic cathedral that is completely balanced in all details. It has, therefore, a finished appearance lacking in most of the other Gothic churches.

Pseudo-Gothic Architecture in England. In England the origins of Romantic architecture differ from those of France and Germany in that they resulted largely from antiquarian research on the part of literary men. Moreover, the Gothic style had persisted, both in the abbeys destroyed by Henry VIII and in the English imagination, as symbols of the freedom that had existed for the English country gentleman, previous to the industrial revolution. Early in

the century, many individual publications dealing with the history of separate towns and cathedrals appeared, and Horace Walpole's novel, *The Castle of Otranto*, subtitled *A Gothic Tale*, was extremely popular.

Walpole became, in the 18th century, the most famous exponent of the Gothic style in England. In his own dwelling, Strawberry Hill, he surrounded himself with the kind of life which his imagination constructed in his literary works. While he was writing his novel, he had his villa remodeled with turrets, doors, ceilings, and chimney pots taken from miscellaneous ruins, without great regard for their original style. The result was a fantastic creation, the "castellated Gothic" (Fig. 611). As the century advanced, a more accurate reconstruction of the true Gothic, based on English models, took place. Churches, which formerly had been built in the classical style, were now commissioned in the Gothic; and, to cap the climax, in 1836 a commission for the rebuilding of the new Houses of Parliament in the Gothic style was given to Sir Charles Barry (Fig. 563).

In both England and America, where the *nouveaux riches* developed a passion for collecting culture rather than creating it, parks were laid out with purposely built Romantic ruins as centers of attraction. Among the most humorous and delightful manifestations of this desire for the trappings of the Middle Ages were advertisements in the newspapers, asking for hermits to inhabit the ruined cloisters. No truly Romantic landscape was complete, it seems, without a cell in which some anchorite, who had taken the vows of silence, could be kept in captivity.

One may account in part for the poverty of great architecture during the 19th century, especially in England and America, by the preoccupation of its genius with scientific and industrial advancement, rather than art. Both Samuel Morse and Robert Fulton, widely known as inventors, began life as artists. How much genuine artistic talent was drawn into the channels of business and industry will never be known. Probably the absence of originality in the architecture of the last century is in no small degree due to the preempting of creative ability by the new industrialism whose first significant buildings, as will appear in the next chapter, were designed by realistic engineers rather than Classical or Romantic architects.

The Baroque Revival in the Art of the Theater. The most inspiring and perhaps the most inspired buildings during the entire Romantic period belong to the world of the theater. Significant is the Paris Opera (Fig. 564), designed by Charles Garnier. Its styles include late Venetian Renaissance for the exterior and Roman baroque within. The magnificent grand staircase is a pure Romantic construction on baroque models. This structure, in the well-planned relationship between its three chief parts—stage structure, auditorium, and vestibules—its splendid disposition of masses in elevation, and its stage mechanisms, has furnished the prototype for many opera houses and theaters the world over.

Another of the great buildings dating from that time was the Bayreuth Festival Theater, built by the romantic king of Bavaria, Louis II, for the operas of Richard Wagner.

Music

Music, while stimulating the imagination and allowing the greatest possible freedom of expression, stresses those dynamic elements of art form most necessary to strengthen that expression. Therefore, it must seem to be the art par excellence for the Romantic soul. The associational overtones of music, because of their indeterminate quality, allow a greater variety of interpretation than those of the other arts; therefore, a greater variety of differing temperaments may gain satisfaction from them.

The Romantic composers, Schubert, Beethoven, Mendelssohn, Schumann, Chopin, Liszt, Berlioz, and Wagner, with a host of other brilliant artists, enriched their century with remarkably varied inventions. Since their pro-

duction was so fertile and inspiring, it demands a descriptive analysis far beyond the compass of this book. Here only a few of the main *literary* trends in the development of Romantic

Fig. 564 —The grand staircase in the Paris Opera, by Charles Garnier, marble and bronze with gilt fixtures, 1861–1874. (*Courtesy of Lesch.*)

music can be suggested. The student should explore further, using phonograph recordings and histories of the formal values of the art, and should examine into the aesthetics of music —a subject which has been working out only during the past few years. This field has had less scientific exploration than the other arts, chiefly because accurately recorded music, making possible a comparison of styles, is a comparatively recent thing.

One is tempted to speak of the development of Romantic music as an almost specific invention of the Celto-Germanic people. Its area of geographic distribution follows very closely that of the distribution of Gothic cathedrals. While Paris, Milan, and Naples became the centers for the classical composers, with their operas built around ancient dramatic plots and the pageantlike movements of the ballet, the Germans, particularly the Viennese, perfected the rich interweave of melodic lines and harmonic instrumental chords, which revealed depths of feeling incomprehensible to Classical man. In Germany and in France the course of European music during the 19th century tends away from the objective, balanced sonata forms of the 18th, toward those indefinite dream fantasies which, inappropriate to sculpture and painting, reach an appropriate expression in the most intangible of the arts. Striving to visualize the difference between Romantic and Classical music, one may say that the works of the Romantic Wagner, on the whole, bear the same relation to those of Handel as does the relief by Rude on the Arc de Triomphe to its companion relief by Cortot. Classicism in music, of course, continues throughout the century in the works of such a composer as Brahms. Even his lieder, however, bear the imprint of romanticism.

The Significance of Beethoven. Beethoven's musical development parallels the literary development of Goethe. Having their origins in the classical sonatas of Karl Philipp Emanuel Bach, Handel, and Mozart, Beethoven's early sonatas display such exact balance of parts that one may diagram them as one would plot a classical drama or design a pedimental sculpture. Beethoven early broke through the boundaries in the classic formulae set for him by his first Viennese teachers. Becoming romantically individualistic, he gave free rein to the emotions in his later sonatas, composed between 1800 and 1803, and in his *Third Symphony*.

In his first and second symphonies, Beethoven had followed Mozart. In the third, the *Eroica*, written about 1803, he proposed a work dedicated to the early Napoleon—that revolutionary lieutenant of the barricades who championed the cause of liberty. By the time the symphony reached completion, Napoleon had been elected emperor. Beethoven then tore off the title page and trampled on it.

Beethoven's *Fourth Symphony*, expressing great depth of subjective feeling, led to the fifth, in C minor. Here, as Beethoven himself wrote, the "heavy hand of fate" is heard as a theme in the opening bars, to be answered as the music develops. The *Sixth Symphony*, called the *Pastoral*, includes many passages suggestive of sounds in nature. Beethoven's *Ninth Symphony*, in D minor, his great choral symphony, unites all the resources of musical style with an augmented orchestra and a chorus of human voices singing parts of Schiller's *Ode to Joy*, set to a theme which appears again and again throughout the composition. Beethoven's treatment of a theme with a definite literary association leads the way to the later leitmotiv of Richard Wagner. His consideration of the human voice as an extra member of the orchestra also leads to the later concept of the interrelationship of voice, music, and pageantry, mastered in Wagner's operas.

The structure of a Romantic musical composition is usually of such magnitude that only the smallest hint of its aesthetic qualities can be given here. In Beethoven's relatively simple sonatas, short themes contrast with counterthemes in a question-answer relationship. From part to part, organic transitions using these themes lead the reveries of the listener so smoothly that one is unconscious of the means by which great climaxes of emotion are built up. Many original rhythms contribute to the effect of dramatic intensity. The listener is carried from deeply felt slow movements, in the form of rondos, to quicker minuets or scherzos. Beethoven can make the four stringed instruments of the quartet—the two violins, the viola, and the cello—suggest an entire orchestra, and his quartets have often been expanded into full symphonic arrangements.

Two Quartets by Beethoven as Ultimate Creations of the Musician's Art. A consideration of two compositions—the *Quartet in B-flat major* (opus 130) and the *Quartet in A minor* (opus 131)—serves to demonstrate Beethoven's remarkable mastery of both the Classical and the Romantic side of his nature. In the first of the quartets, a number of pleasant dance tunes and melodies are neatly placed one after another. Among the melodies, one can distinguish many used as the bases for the lieder, or art songs, of Romantic composers; for example, Schubert's *Ave Maria*, Tosti's *Good-bye*, and Tschaikowsky's setting of Goethe's poem in the song, *None but the Lonely Heart*.

In contrast with this beautiful succession of Romantic melodies, the *A minor Quartet* appears like the sum total of all the visual effects earlier associated with the structure and color of a great cathedral. Of this quartet, Wagner wrote, "The aesthetic idea of the sublime is alone applicable here; for the effect of serenity passes at once far beyond the satisfaction to be derived from mere beauty." The first movement of this magnificent interweave creates a mood of philosophical questioning which breaks, in the second movement, into a number of discords resolving into weird, Oriental melodies like the *Kol Nidre* of the Jewish religious service. Throughout the other movements, there come many remarkable enharmonic transitions from key to key, carrying the soul into a rich maze of sound suggesting infinite possibilities for the development of the human spirit.

The Songs, or Lieder, of Schubert. After Beethoven, Franz Schubert departed still further from the classical tradition. He is best remembered for his many spontaneous songs, or lieder, of which he often composed several in a single day. These songs contain melodic gems which had been passed down from minnesinger and Meistersinger and were arranged by Schubert in three different ways. In the first, called *Volksweise*, or folk songs, each verse of a poem has the same tune. In the second, called the *Durchkomponiertes*, the melody follows the words. The third type, which revives the ballad, tells a story.

In all Schubert's lieder, the composer identifies himself with the object. *The Trout* and *The Linden Tree*, two of the most famous lieder (obtainable on phonograph records), serve to demonstrate the style. *The Linden Tree* furnishes

an example of a song combining the first two manners. The two first lines of the third verse, which call for a particular expression of loneliness, have been changed from a major to a minor key. The poem, by Heine, in English translation below, also shows the German Romantic's identification of himself with a natural object, the tree, a cult object of the early Celto-Germans.

Beside the gateway fountain, a linden tree doth stand;
  I dreamed within its shadows of other fairer lands.
And often to its branches I sang my hopes and fears,
  And so its love gave shelter, it drew me ever near.

Today, alas I wander, afar in deepest night,
  And yet I see its shadow, with fading, longing sight.
I hear its branches rustling, as if they called to me,
  Come back to us and trusting, will all your sorrows flee.

The winter winds are blowing; chill, deep within my heart.
  They leave me 'lorn and friendless, by anguish torn apart.
And now, alas, I've wandered, so far from that release
  And still I hear it calling, come back and find your peace.

Of Schubert's ten symphonies, two—the one in C major, and the so-called *Unfinished Symphony*, in C minor, have enriched man's culture with haunting melodies and passages of deepest feeling suggesting the sublime. To discover the purely stylistic attributes of musical romanticism one should examine the works of some less significant musician such as Hector Berlioz.

The Fantastic Symphony of Berlioz as the Essence of Romanticism. One dramatic French composer, Hector Berlioz, in his *Fantastic Symphony*, in C major, furnishes the most complete revelation of the Romantic spirit in music. Berlioz himself explained the occasion for this composition as being the outpouring of his soul during his love affair with an Irish actress, when he was twenty-seven years old. The symphony contains two significant advances in the dramatic musical style, which were to influence 20th-century music. The first of these is the further employment of a set theme, here *l'idée fixe*, or obsession, which stands for the almost insane love felt by the composer. The second is the form of two themes—one, the *Dies Irae*, a medieval motif, and the other a *ronde du sabbat*, a witches' dance—so arranged that they create a macabre syncopation very much like 20th-century jazz music. Berlioz also experimented with new instruments and tonal effects, covering his horns with bags and muffling his drumsticks with sponges. Since the literary and associational effects deemed desirable by Berlioz are so clear, we may accept his written interpretation as decisive for what he tried to say.

The composer explained that his music told how he sought his beloved in the realm of dreams. Drugged with opium, he imagined that this loved one would eventually cause his death. At first, her spirit appears in the shape of the slow, soft melody of *l'idée fixe*. This melody, in many variations, weaves like a haunting wraith through all the succeeding passages. As love grew upon the young artist, completely absorbing him, his passion turned to fear, jealousy, renewed love, and finally a turning to religion for refuge from the results of his passion.

In the second movement, to be played in a mood "not too joyous"—*allegro non troppo*, A major, three-eight time—the lover follows his loved one to a ball where, listening to the strains of a gay, melodious waltz, his jealous eyes follow her. She is the center of attraction, entrancing all men, while he feels inferior and forsaken. It must be noticed in passing that the waltz furnishes the significant rhythm for the entire Romantic mood.

In the third movement, written slow—*adagio*, F major, six-eight time—the artist seeks relief from his melancholy thoughts in the fields where he wanders of a summer evening. There he hears two shepherds playing to each other simple melodies such as are used by the Alpine shepherds to call their flocks. One melody is played on the oboe, the other upon the English horn—both instruments whose tone color suggests sadness.

In the fourth movement of the symphony, written "not too joyfully"—*allegretto non troppo*,

in the minor key of G and in B-flat major, to four-four or march time—the hero imagines that he has killed his loved one. Now, condemned to death, he is on his way to the scaffold accompanied by a jeering crowd who move along with him to the music of a death march.

After death, in the fifth movement, the artist sees the witches dancing, accompanied by terrifying shrieks and demoniac laughter. Again the leitmotiv of the loved one sounds, but changed into a different time, so that it seems like a bawdy dance. Now the poet realizes he has been in love with a witch and he can see her dancing with the other witches. Finally, the death-bells toll, first leading into the majestic melody of the medieval hymn, the *Dies Irae*. Even this hymn of the Last Judgment soon partakes of the character of the witches' dance, now almost a march. The two rhythmical themes are so arranged contrapuntally that there results a syncopation. Thus, in the end, the witches' dance and the medieval hymn fuse into a new tempo, a funeral march, which sounds like 20th-century jazz.

The suggestive power of the music, which runs from one theme to another as aimlessly as the figures in a dream, displays many elements borrowed from the subject matter of Romantic painting and literature. We recognize the summer evening, with the shepherds and the thunderstorm, as corresponding to the work of such nature Romantics as Constable, Turner, and Millet.

In Berlioz's symphony one recognizes the full development of what came to be called "program music." Program music is music that tells a story through symbolic tone colors and melodies. The relation of program music to the old classical, formal music is the same as that of the long, narrative, epic poem to the lyric or to the completely balanced dramatic poem. Being in what might be called free form, it relies upon suggestive passages that call to mind visual images, rather than upon the deeper emotional tone aroused by a formal relationship of harmony, rhythm, and melody.

Synthesis of Classical and Romantic Elements in the Music of Brahms. Johannes Brahms, like Bach and Beethoven (the three are the "three B's" who represent the peak of European musical development), transcends the category of any one style. In his work classicist and Romantic elements form that contrast necessary to an equilibrated musical synthesis of a universal order. Brahms's orchestral *Variations on a Theme from Haydn* represents his classicist character; the rhapsodic gypsy melodies in his Hungarian dances, a more Romantic side of his nature. The Adagio movement of his *Quintet in B minor for Clarinet and Strings* (opus 115) reveals, as a dreamy revery, an indescribable new combination of muted viola and clarinet in passages of sensuous beauty, which elevates the "Flutes of Ishtar" toward the condition of the Sublime. The third movement of the massive *Symphony Number One in C minor* (opus 63)— *un poco allegretto e grazioso*—unites inspirational and formal elements to create a fresh vision of noble beauty. In contrast, the second movement of the *Concerto in B-flat major* (opus 83)— *allegro appassionato*—reveals a continuous fire of inventive genius through its intricate syncopated rhythm, which connects the grandeur of Beethoven's melodic phrases with the New World music of the 20th century.

Nationalism in Music. As in architecture, the growth of nationalism brought about a revival of the past in the form of old folk songs. In Germany they appear in the compositions of Schubert, Schumann, Brahms, and Wolf. These songs were made centers of operatic compositions, and often folk dances were used for ballets. Humperdinck's *Hansel and Gretel* matches the fairy-story painting of Moritz von Schwind, using folk songs for its chief melodies. Weber's *Der Freischütz* was the first opera in which the folk song, the supernatural element, and the national legend were combined. Similarly, Romantic opera composers in France and even Gilbert and Sullivan in England drew upon folk music.

In instrumental music also this tendency became apparent. Dvořák produced a nationalist style, using the material of his own country as in his *Slavonic Dances* and the Bohemian dance movements of his symphonies. In the *New World Symphony*, he gave to America, as well, a national work, greater than any native composer had yet produced. Liszt contributed works for both piano and orchestra in his *Hungarian Fantasy*, *Hungarian Rhapsodies*, smaller songs, and choruses. Chopin, the piano composer par excellence, was above all the nationalist, the patriot devoting himself to the dances and folk tunes of his own country. His mazurkas and his polonaises are his most characteristic compositions. Tschaikowsky also used nationalistic folk tunes, as in his *1812 Overture*, where he combined the French *Marseillaise* and the Russian hymn *God Save Our Noble Czar*.

The Development of Macabre Themes. Something similar to the morbid interests of the Romantic painters appeared musically in the large number of funeral marches which became characteristic forms of the 19th century. *Siegfried's Funeral March* in Wagner's opera, *Götterdämmerung*, is the best known, but Beethoven contributed two, one in his *Eroica Symphony* and one in his piano *Sonata* (opus 26). Rachmaninov's tone poem *Island of the Dead* has already been mentioned.

The Music Dramas of Richard Wagner. One man, the greatest musico-dramatic genius of his time, united all the inventions of his contemporaries in his struggle to find an integrated soul through his art. Richard Wagner early noticed that music depends for its emotional effects on its contrast between dissonant and consonant chords, between the tone color of one instrument and that of another. His earliest attempts taught him that he must master the classical operatic style. His overture to *Rienzi*, finished in his twenty-seventh year, would have made him the head of the classicists. Like Delacroix in painting, he turned away from the classical subject matter and dramatic methods for his next opera to the story of the phantom Flying Dutchman, a man cursed to endless voyaging, until he should be rescued by the love of some virtuous maiden. The opera is a study of the bewitching spell which the Dutchman casts over the maiden, Senta. During the

Fig. 565.—Scene from *Parsifal* as staged in Bayreuth. (*Courtesy of Lesch.*)

course of the drama Wagner developed certain musical motifs which stood for *Senta normal* and *Senta bewitched*. Throughout Wagner's musical career we may trace these two motifs, until they become, later, the magnificently involved orchestration in the *Ride of the Valkyries* and the final cry of Kundry in *Parsifal*. Wagner later developed more of these melodic symbols, or leitmotiv.

At times these motifs are interwoven into long themes, often lacking any sense of measure. This led to an unending melody such as Wagner's *Träume*, which was the preliminary sketch for the love music of *Tristan and Isolde*. Here a seeming improvisation brought music nearer to realism, thus breaking the conventions of Wagner's predecessors and opening up the way for his followers. But Wagner did more than this. He completed certain experiments, begun by Beethoven and Schubert, in harmony, using dissonant chords along with developments in orchestration. He added more brasses and wind instruments to his ensembles, thus getting golden baroque effects, which he made subservient to the Romantic ideals of the theater.

Wagner had, in general, two types of subject matter for his musical moods. The first of these was the conflict between the medieval and the classical vision of beauty; the second, the story of the greatness of Germanic heroes, a battle of gods and giants, which might some day bring into the world a new era and a finer race of men. Both of these stories were on the way to solution in the Romantic *Parsifal* (Fig. 565) where, in an atmosphere of medieval mystery, the Holy Grail was uncovered for the salvation of mankind. Here Kundry, the woman possessed, at last finds salvation in a vision of "service," an ideal under which the Celto-German creates at his best.

This is the thought, expressed by the Germans, similar to that of the Pre-Raphaelites in England, who wished for a perfect Christian concept of the state, something like the ideal "City of God."

Drama

The brief survey of the spatial and temporal arts has demonstrated that the essence of romanticism consists of its literary dramatic value in the melodramatic sense. Paris, the center of dramatic art in the 18th and 19th centuries, was the battleground for two types of stage production. Late in the 18th century, the actor Garrick took the plays of Shakespeare to France, and a Scotch poet, McPherson, writing under the name of Ossian, published a book purporting to be the original legends of the bards, set in a Romantic landscape of weird, ancestral splendor. The combination of these two influences, avidly devoured by the young Romantics, Victor Hugo and Alexandre Dumas in France, Goethe and Schiller in Germany, stimulated the production of a number of plays whose bases lay in medieval or Renaissance characters. In Shakespeare's *King Lear*, in his *Romeo and Juliet*, and more particularly in his *Othello*, the young Romantics found those elements of horror and of dramatic denouement necessary to stimulate an audience already satiated with the dramatic events of the Revolution and the Napoleonic Wars.

The opening gun of the Romantic campaign against the academic *Comédie-Française* was *Henry III and his Court*, by Alexandre Dumas. There followed Hugo's *Cromwell, Marion de Lorme, Hernani, Le Roi s'amuse, Lucrezia Borgia, Mary Tudor, Angelo*, and *Ruy Blas*. In Germany, Goethe wrote *Götz von Berlichingen, Torquato Tasso, Egmont, Iphigenia in Aulis;* and Schiller, *The Robbers, The Maid of Orleans, Wilhelm Tell, Wallenstein*, and *The Bride of Messina*. Victor Hugo's preface to *Cromwell*, published in 1827, summarizes the Romantic's ideals for the drama. He wrote

Poetry has three ages, the ode, the epic, and the drama, each corresponding to a period in the development of society. Primitivism is lyric; antiquity, epic; but modern times are romantic. Drama alone is complete poetry. In the drama one may best express modern thought, for the character of drama is the real. Reality results from a combination of all natural phenomena in two types, the sublime and the grotesque, and these unite in the drama, as they unite in life and in creation, for true complete poetry results from a harmony of opposites. All of that which is in nature is in art.

Three significant Romantic attitudes appear in this quotation. (1) Art consists of a combination of the Sublime and the Grotesque, Beauty being absent. (2) The Romantics were striving to achieve realism, although from the distance of a century we know them to have been far from reality. (3) In medieval fashion, Hugo had adopted Aristotle as his master, using Aristotle's original three poetic types, which he united with the growing concept of the evolution of society from a primitive toward a modern cultured state. To the Romantic the life of *l'homme naturel* naturally seems of lyric sweetness, all of antiquity, heroic and classically measured. Only the revolutionary, dynamic present has in it the true elements of tragic struggle. The Romantic must clothe his characters in the garments of other times, simply because the age of universal warfare and bloody revolution in which he lived was too cruel to be represented on the stage. Hugo appropriately left his pictures of the contemporary scene to his realistic novels, *Les Misérables* and *Toilers of the Sea*.

Aesthetic Theories

Romanticism, with its intensely personal forms of art expression and its Gothic propensity for investigation into the sources of its own emotional drives, gave to the world an abundance of aesthetic theories. In a way, these productions parallel the productions of the late Greco-Roman and Alexandrian philosophers and critics, but with an essential difference: the arts of music, painting, and architecture had, through the Christian centuries, developed so far beyond anything which ancient man could have conceived that they lent an entirely different tone to aesthetic theories. The writings of Plotinus showed a tendency, inherited from Plato, to dissociate the actual works of art from the ideal of beauty. The Romantic attempted to define the ideal of beauty in terms of its dynamic power to vitalize the work of art. Through the theories of Kant, Schopenhauer, Schelling, and Hegel, the Romantics developed a line of reasoning intended to demonstrate the manner in which this took place. Unfortunately, most of these metaphysicians or professional philosophers theorized without exploring art from either the historical or the creative point of view. One man alone, John Ruskin, coming at the end of the period, undertook to evaluate art empirically. The Romantic philosophers, excluding Ruskin, attempted to define art in the abstract. This led to an aesthetics of "art for art's sake."

Kant's Analysis of the Beautiful. Immanuel Kant discriminated between two types of beauty, which he characterized as "free beauty" and "dependent beauty." Free beauty, which might be called "art for art's sake," included the fantasies of art and abstract designs, roughly corresponding to the "imaginative art" of Muratori. These forms of art had no meaning beyond themselves, because they represented no definite conceptions. Music without words to Kant typified such "free beauty."

All beauty that has to do with man and everything that arises from some purpose could be classified as "dependent beauty." Kant unconsciously adopted Vincent's earlier idea of medieval ornamental beauty as the purest form. With this concept begins aesthetic individualism and the philosophy underlying practically all the nonrepresentational art movements after the 19th century. It found ultimate realization in the 20th century in the triumph of individualism and professional specialization which came after the industrial revolution.

The entire Romantic dichotomy of thought arose from the fact that some philosophers persisted in seeing beauty as the moment of greatest freedom from reality, whereas others held it to be the moment of greatest union with reality. The idealist, always following the strict course of logic, was in the position of Kant or Plotinus, who denied superior beauty access to the flesh and bones of physical human existence. Kant held that one must strive to separate the beauty of pure form from the sensually pleasant elements. Here, following earlier idealists, Kant thought the highest art to be that which approached the condition of music.

Kant's Theory of the Sublime. Kant, differentiating between the Beautiful and the Sublime, wrote that the true satisfaction in the former was connected with the idea of quality, whereas that of the latter was connected with quantity. He said that the Beautiful in nature belongs to the form of a thing, which consists of its boundaries. The Sublime, in contrast, can be found even in a formless thing, insofar as one finds through it an idea of infinity, while attaching to it the thought of unity.

Considering art as a type of expression that demands a certain degree of dynamic power, Kant advanced the definition of art by indi-

[1] IMMANUEL KANT, *The Critique of Reason.*

cating that the *quality* of expressive energy created beauty and the *quantity* of that energy created the Sublime. Further, beauty for Kant, was associated with charm. Sublimity he held to be something that first checks all the vital powers and then, releasing them, causes them to flow more strongly. Finally, the epitome of beauty would seem to be the measurable art of sculpture; that of the Sublime, the measureless art of music.

The feelings of sublimity, being aroused in us by vaguer perceptions, without reasoning, produce forms ill fitted to our judgment, that is, intangible. Anything that looks natural, therefore, being measurable in formal terms, cannot be sublime. Kant analyzed the concept of the Sublime by dividing it into two kinds, the mathematical and the dynamic. Concerning the mathematically Sublime Kant wrote that the imagination striving for progress toward the Infinite is checked by the reason which demands a complete whole as an idea to be realized. The more dynamic Sublime causes man to consider nature as something fearful or awe-inspiring without causing him to have very definite emotions of fear toward it.

Influence of Kant upon 20th-century Aesthetics. "Estimating beauty one never seeks to criticize from experience; instead he judges for himself in terms of formal aesthetic values whether things are beautiful. In this way the aesthetic process of judgment has created its own laws."[1] With these words, Kant expressed the credo of the modern artist, setting the stage for that type of aesthetic criticism which attempts completely to eliminate associational and formal values in discussing the work of art. However, the formal and associational values still persist, being inherent in every actual work of art that has the power to interest people. Probably the aesthetic of the future should be based on some sort of formula that helps man to judge how well or how poorly the formal values have been used to express the associational or to enhance the useful. Such, of course, would be an aesthetic of relativity, more realistic and pragmatic in character.

Schopenhauer's Philosophy of Art as an Escape. With Schopenhauer begins the idea of "aesthetic detachment" stressed in most modern definitions of art. The true work of art, according to Schopenhauer, leads to a state of complete self-detachment not only the artist who creates it, but anyone who enjoys it.

Schopenhauer held that aesthetic pleasure can be the same with regard to phenomena in nature as well as in art. The work of art simply facilitates our gaining knowledge, in which alone true pleasure consists. Copying Longinus and Bacon, Schopenhauer maintained that the Idea appears more clearly in the work of art because there the artist has abstracted the ideal from the actuality, omitting all disturbing incidents.

Schopenhauer examined the psychology of aesthetic contemplation and found it consisting of two inseparable parts. The first was a sort of inspired knowledge of the object as part of the universal Idea; the second, the self-consciousness of the knowing person, not as an individual but as a pure will-less subject of knowledge. For Schopenhauer, as for Plotinus, the individual contemplating any work of art must have within himself a spiritual knowledge corresponding exactly to the aspect of the idea that impelled the artist to create. Also—and this seems to be a new contribution—he must be completely receptive to the means which the artist employed to express the idea. That is, he must enjoy the very same sounds, colors, or forms. In going to any work of art, we may gain pleasure from either the idea or the means by which it is expressed. In terms employed throughout this book, one may, depending on his individual nature, enjoy either the physioplastic or the ideoplastic aspect of art.

Schopenhauer found that at times some external cause or inner disposition has the power to lift man suddenly out of the endless stream of *willing*, so that as he attains objectivity there comes to him a certain feeling of peace. Then "one loses himself in the art object, forgetting his individuality." Here in Schopenhauer one finds a complete union of the Indian doctrine of yoga and the Gothic interest in medieval realism. As an example of his position, Schopenhauer cited the utter peacefulness of Dutch still-life painting, which arose from purely objective perception of the most insignificant objects, disclosing the peaceful mind of the artist who made it (Fig. 516, Chap. XVI).

Allied to Schopenhauer's belief that the art of painting might lead to freedom from demands of the flesh (will) is his theory of tragedy. This art by presenting a spectacle of suffering leads to acceptance of pain and resignation to one's lot.

Schopenhauer, like all idealists, was forced to conclude that the most abstract art had the greatest value, so he maintained that music is as direct an objectification or copy of the entire Will as is the actual world itself. He even believed that music could portray directly those Ideas which combine to form the world of individual things. Music is, thus, by no means like the other arts, the copy of the ideas, but the copy of the Will itself, and an objectification of the Ideas. This is why the effect of music is so much more powerful and penetrating than that of the other arts. Sculpture and painting only copy shadows of the Idea, but music speaks of the thing itself. The entire discussion, as in most idealistic art theorizing, tends toward mysticism.

Schelling and the Creative Approach to Art. In Schelling's essay, *The Relation of the Arts of Form to Nature*, appears the thought that the observer must read into the empty shapes of things the visions of his own soul. From this doctrine arose the idea that the appreciation of art called forth a certain degree of creativity, eventually called *Einfühlung*. For Schelling, works of art that contain nothing more than shape—that is, a purely physioplastic appearance—are empty and the artist must strive to abstract the essence or spirit that animates them.

Hegel and the Idea of Cultural Categories. Hegel, carrying the philosophy of Schelling further, held beauty to be a synthesis of the abstract concept and the sensate material. Also in Hegel's philosophy of art may be found for the first time the observation that at least three general psychosociological art types exist. The first of these, symbolic art, corresponds to the work of the Orientals. Hegel held that Eastern artistic pantheism, which he thought of as simply primitive, either embodies the most fundamental meaning in the most ordinary objects or violently distorts natural appearances to express its conception of reality so that it has both the quality of yearning and an unclear sublimity. Such art is symbolic. Hegel's insight was remarkably keen, but having decided, a priori, in favor of Classical art, he failed to observe empirically that Oriental art consists of two kinds —one primitive, the other highly cultured.

Hegel believed that Classical art is more perfect than the symbolic Oriental, because it contains a natural, adequate expression of some spiritual reality in a form peculiarly and essentially appropriate to its own inner meaning. Here form and spiritual content unite in perfect harmony. The subject matter of Classical art has a peculiarly concrete reality approximating a state of equilibrium. Hegel considered the classical to be the most beautiful type of art because it reaches a perfection of sensuous presentation.

Higher still was the third, or Romantic type, in which, Hegel suggested, art passes beyond its proper nature, though retaining the form of art and working necessarily within some limits. Therefore, Romantic art reaches more subjective associational states than does the Classical.

Hegel considered architecture to be the typically Oriental or symbolic art; sculpture, the Classical type; and painting, music and poetry, the Romantic. For him, music seemed to spiritualize the more sensuous elements. Following Plato (with modifications), Hegel was declaring that painting and sculpture imitate things, music influences the state of mind, and architecture expresses in symbolic form the essential structural plan of life.

John Ruskin endeavored to unite all these points of view in an encyclopedic system by examining closely the effects of art upon the artist and the beholder. The practical scientist, Herbert Spencer, held that art arises as excess energy in play, thus deducing its inevitability in any culture after the physical demands of commercial activity have been met. Twentieth-century followers of these men have assumed that there is in man a separate aesthetic instinct, which can be measured.

Reviewing Romantic aesthetic theory, we find the philosophers, like the thinkers of the late Greco-Roman world, turning to the problems of artistic production. Finding interesting psychological effects, they eventually developed a theory of expression. They held art to be the result of an excess of playful energy, capable of abstracting the spiritual essence of life and giving it form in order that man might be freed from physical reality. For them the highest type of art production, like the superbeautiful beauty of Plotinus or the pure ideas of Plato, came to be detached from the rest of man's thoughts. The act of artistic expression, also appearing to differ from all other activity must, therefore, proceed according to its own laws. Its purpose came to be not so much an acceptance of, but an escape from reality— "art for art's sake."

Summary

A thorough study of the creative methods of Goethe and Blake in literature, or Turner, Delacroix, Rodin, and Wagner in the other arts would reveal completely the spiritual contribution of romanticism to modern thought. In terms of new aesthetic discoveries, romanticism has little to give the world except in music. Painting received some new advances in coloring and composition, but the techniques used are those of Titian, Rembrandt, and Rubens. In sculpture, Rodin called attention to the use of variable surface modeling to produce more dramatic effects. In music, as we have seen, new tone colors were introduced in the orchestra, and contrapuntal composition was brought to its greatest development.

In summing up romanticism and its contribution to the culture of the Western world, one may, like Wagner, find certain characteristic leitmotivs. To these art symbols set techniques and conventions were attached, until Romantic art, like Oriental and Classical, recognized constant modes of expression connected with an accepted subject matter.

In France the subject of nationalism, built around the concept of *la gloire*, used as its chief actors Napoleon, the Old Guard, and the soldier with his marshal's baton. To these must be added the victorious battle flags, the *Croix de guerre*, and the decorations of the Academy. This military glorification as a symbol of romanticism was expanded to include the Arc de Triomphe, cenotaphs, memorial days, and later, the Unknown Soldier. In Germany, England and France the romantic spirit created a revival of medieval glories, chiefly in Gothic architecture and folk music.

Following the Revolution, the theme of the dignity of man—expressed in the slogan "Liberty, equality, fraternity"—was used by the artists as an aspect of Romantic painting, which recognized the social value of the common individual to be seen in the works of Géricault and Millet. Daumier and Meunier have been excluded from this chapter because romanticism is seldom bitter, nor is it consciously propagandist. Romanticism worships individual freedom rather than communal action and believes in art for art's sake.

The return to nature, another aesthetic symbol of romanticism following Rousseau's philosophy in France, led to the landscapes of the Barbizon school. Friedrich in Germany, Constable and Turner in England also sought to avoid social and human implications in a study of landscapes. In Germany particularly, a sentimental attachment for nature pictured man as philosophizing upon the inevitability of final extinction in nature. This dramatic idea led to the creation of mood pictures in music and to the Wagnerian concept of the music drama.

Into all the arts a strain of weirdness found its way, expressed chiefly as the "fatal woman" in England, the dream fantasy in France, the grotesque in Spain, and the macabre in Germany, furnishing roots of that movement in 20th-century art known as surrealism.

In England, a strongly commercial country, under the industrial revolution the Romantic movement produced least in art and most in the criticism of art. Turner, living in the early part of the century, made all the definitive advances in color and compositional painting, as well as in the observation of light effects. The Pre-Raphaelites withdrew into their "ivory towers" and painted rather ineffectively. The most robust of this group, William Morris, was alone willing to face the actuality of the industrial revolution and placed the question of the work of art in society squarely before the people of his country. The efforts of Morris, Ruskin, and Crane made possible a desire for better design in 20th-century industrial art. Thus their philosophy underlies almost every movement for civic betterment among the industrial philanthropists of the New World.

In music, romanticism advocated a freedom from old classical restriction of form and eventuated in the "program music" of Berlioz and Liszt. This term, coined in derision by exponents of classicism, means simply that in their endeavor to describe realistically the effects of nature the Romantics wrote their music as tone poems. The Romantic composers also used folk melodies with set emotional appeal, to stimulate feelings of nationalism. Romantic music strives to suggest aspirations rather than completion.

Finally, in philosophy the end of the Romantic development sees both Plato's idea of art as something serving the state, and Socrates's idea of superior craftsmanship resulting in beauty, held along with the Neo-Platonic doctrine of expression for expression's sake.

Bibliography

CLUTTON-BROCK, ALAN: *An Introduction to French Painting*, Henry Holt & Company, Inc., New York, 1932.

CLARK, KENNETH: *The Gothic Revival*, Charles Scribner's Sons, New York, 1928.

GOETHE, JOHANN WOLFGANG VON: *Faust*, Modern Library, Inc., New York, 1930.

BROWNING, ROBERT: *Complete Poetic and Dramatic Works*, Harvard University Press, Cambridge, Mass., 1895.

ROUSSEAU, JEAN JACQUES: *Confessions* and *Social Contract*, Book I, translated by Edmund Wilson, Alfred A. Knopf, Inc., New York, 1923.

RUSKIN, JOHN: *Modern Painters*, Everyman's Library, E. P. Dutton & Company, Inc., New York, 1906.

RUSKIN, JOHN: *Unto This Last* and *Munera Pulveris*, World's Classics, Oxford University Press, New York, 1906.

MORRIS, WILLIAM: *Hopes and Fears for Art*, Longmans, Green & Company, New York, 1917.

PRAZ, MARIO: *The Romantic Agony*, Oxford University Press, New York, 1933.

RODIN, AUGUSTE: *Art*, Dodd, Mead & Company, Inc., New York, 1912.

The Journals of Eugène Delacroix, edited and translated by Walter Pach, Covici, Friede, Inc., New York, 1937.

WAGNER, RICHARD: *My Life*, Tudor Publishing Company, New York.

CARRITT, EDGAR F.: *Theories of Beauty*, The Macmillan Company, New York, 1914.

BEKKER, PAUL: *Beethoven*, E. P. Dutton & Company, Inc., New York, 1932.

HOEBER, ARTHUR: *The Barbizon Painters*, Frederick A. Stokes Company, New York, 1915.

BICKLEY, F. L.: *The Pre-Raphaelite Comedy*, Henry Holt & Company, Inc., New York, 1933.

MOUREY, GABRIEL: *French Art in the 19th Century*, Studio Publications, London, 1928.

Recordings

BEETHOVEN:

Eroica Symphony—VM 263 (alb.).
Fourth Symphony—VM 274 (alb.).
Fifth Symphony—VM 245 (alb.).
Sixth Symphony—VM 50 (alb.).
Ninth Symphony—VM 236 (alb.).
Quartet in B-flat major, opus 130—CM 70 (alb.).
Quartet in A minor, opus 131—CM 273 (alb.).

BERLIOZ:

Fantastic Symphony—VM 111 (alb.).

DVOŘÁK:

Slavonic Dances—V 6649.

LISZT:

Hungarian Rhapsodies—No. 2, C-sharp major—V 6652.

RACHMANINOV:

Island of the Dead—VM 75 (alb.).

WAGNER:

Götterdämmerung, Siegfried's Funeral March—V 6860.
Siegfried, Waldweben—V 7192.
Rienzi—V 6624.
Ride of the Valkyries—V 9163 a.
Parsifal—V 6861/2.
Tristan and Isolde—CM 101 (alb.).
Träume, and *Senta's ballad* from *The Flying Dutchman*—V 2577 a & b.

BRAHMS:

Quintet for Clarinet and Strings, B minor, opus 115—CM 118 (alb.).
Symphony No. 1—E minor, opus 68—VM 301 (alb.).
Concerto No. 2—B-flat major, opus 83—VM 305 (alb.).
Variations on a Theme by Haydn, opus 56a—V 9287/9.

CHAPTER XVIII

The Art of the Twentieth Century

The dramatic form is reached when the vitality which has flowed and eddied round each person fills every person with such vital force that he or she assumes a proper and intangible esthetic life. The personality of the artist, at first a cry or a cadence or a mood and then a fluid and lambent narrative, finally refines itself out of existence, impersonalizes itself, so to speak. The es-thetic image in the dramatic form is life purified in and reprojected from the human imagination. The mystery of esthetic like that of material creation is accomplished. The artist, like the God of the creation, remains within or behind or beyond or above his handiwork, invisible, refined out of existence, indifferent, paring his fingernails. . . . [1]

A rose, is a rose, is a rose.[2]

A WORLD which had lost its faith successively in the church, progressive evolutionary theories, and the benefits of science presented itself to the artist for interpretation and expression after the philosophers, politicians, and industrialists had failed with it. The artist, usually considered a social outcast, in the meantime had decided that he could have faith only in himself. With the ideal of self-expressive creation as their ultimate goal, these artists furiously attacked the problem of decorative *form* in all the arts, rejecting useful and associational values as completely as possible, chiefly because these values seemed to symbolize industrialism or vested religious and political interests. In this chapter it becomes necessary to observe how well the 20th-century artist succeeded in creating an art of pure form and to what extent the art that he created answered the needs of the society around him.

Painting

Impressionism vs. Expressionism. The two fundamental attitudes dominating artistic production in the last part of the 19th century and the first quarter of the 20th remained the same as those discussed throughout the long evolution of Occidental art. In terms of painting, most easily described because most easily seen, physioplastic and ideoplastic art, in their purest forms, persisted to inspire definite schools of painters, called "impressionists" and "expressionists." The contrast can most clearly be pointed out in the two paintings in color (Fig. 554, Chap. XVII), by Turner and (Fig. 577) by Franz Marc. Turner, although a forerunner of the impressionists, cannot be listed categorically under the school active in France and Germany from 1874 to 1910. Marc, who was killed in 1916 at Verdun, definitely belonged, with Kandinsky, Feininger, Klee, Arp, and others, to those Germans narrowly called the "Blue Rider Group" of Munich expressionists.

The two terms "impressionist" and "expressionist" here are used to define generally two opposing tendencies in the art of our times. Later they appear historically and specifically to describe the schools that, with the pointillists, cubists, futurists, syntheticists, vorticists, Dadaists, suprematists, and surrealists, include most of the leading groups of the last fifty years. All the schools that came after historical Impressionism show a progressive movement away

[1] From *A Portrait of the Artist as a Young Man*, by James Joyce, copyright 1916, by B. W. Huebsch. By permission of The Viking Press, Inc., New York.   [2] By Gertrude Stein.

FIG. 566.—*a*, lines of force in Turner's painting, The Sun of Venice, Chap. XVII, Fig. 554; *b*, color areas in Monet's Haystacks, 1891 (Metropolitan Museum of Art); *c*, synthesis of color and linear patterns in a canvas by Cézanne.

from photographic realism and a definite intention to create an abstract art.

The painting by Turner reveals nature in many misty vistas which glisten with all the colors of the rainbow. In his work nature seems changeable as a dream. An analysis of Turner's creation will clarify the relationship of the impressionists to the expressionists, and between these two extremes range all the other groups.

The great work of art always contains a geometric, underlying symbolic construction, clothed with a realistic impression that carries the verisimilitude necessary to impress the beholder. Turner, being a complete genius, left a picture in which we, like Ruskin, can find the lines of force indicated in Fig. 566*a*. An expressionist painter, like Marc, simply emphasizes these lines, thus affirming his belief in the dynamics of existence. An impressionist painter such as Monet concerns himself with the indistinct pattern of color areas (Fig. 566*b*), omitting the dynamic lines of force and losing himself in an almost mystical adoration of the static, fluid, opalescent light. As we shall see, Cézanne strove to make the color dynamic and to get a synthesis between the two (Fig. 566*c*). One general rule dominates both impressionists and expressionists—literary subject matter with associational values shall be reduced to a minimum. In this way both Monet and Marc usually differ from Turner.

Salon des Refusés—1863. During the middle decades of the 19th century, official French art, which received the approbation of the late imperial or republican forms of government, remained under the domination of a tradition characterized by the classicist Ingres or the venerable realist David. Courbet, the realist, caught the public fancy by giving the matter-of-fact man in the street that enjoyment in recognizing objects which he mistook for the more subtle forms of aesthetic pleasure. The nature Romantics of the Barbizon school, Rousseau and Corot, carried this realism into the realm of landscape painting, busying themselves with the study of atmospheric perspective. Daguerre and Meissonier, striving for more exact realistic vision, busied themselves with the invention of photography and the motion picture. Among the individualist groups at the time of Napoleon III, in 1863, some were to distinguish themselves by discovering new aesthetic pleasures in a type of painting arranged in flat, almost Oriental patterns. These young insurgents, led by Edouard Manet, came to be known as the "impressionists"—because one of Manet's little landscapes was entitled "Impression."

At first the impressionists announced as their intention simply the achievement of a more realistic rendition of color than that of the classicists, who used brown pigment for their shadows, or of the realists and Romantics, who used blacks. There seems to us nothing very revolutionary in this. However, the impressionist insisted that when a man painted a picture out-of-doors he could often see purple, blue, and green reflex tones of color in shadowy parts, or if he painted in his studio with gray walls, his shadows would appear black. This one observation alone did not condemn the impressionists in the eyes of contemporary critics. However, in one painting by Manet—The Picnic—there appeared two nude female figures which had no possible allegorical meaning.

of the academicians. The critics, had they been brilliant enough, might have noticed that Delacroix, the Romantic leader, had here and there discovered the first effect and Leonardo da

a   *b*   *c*

FIG. 567.—*a*, The Philosopher, by Manet (*courtesy of Chicago Art Institute*); *b*, The Uprising, by Honoré Daumier 1808–1879, oil on canvas, height 2 feet 10½ inches (Phillips Gallery, Washington) (*courtesy of Lesch-Carnegie*); *c*, The Stevedore, by Constantin Meunier, 1890, bronze, height 19¼ inches (Luxembourg, Paris) (*courtesy of Lesch-Carnegie*).

Here was realism, naked and unashamed, art stripped of all pretense other than that gained by the purely simple enjoyment of light playing over the surface of a female body. Having no definite social purpose, painted in a technique which broke the tradition of the classical Academy, the picture and the associated works of Manet's friends outraged both the sensitive Victorian public and the critics, who decried the work as too revolutionary.

As the doctrine of "art for art's sake" had not yet emerged in 19th-century criticism and the critics had not been trained to observe objectively new formal values, they missed the chief point—that Manet had placed one bright area of color next another without transitional tones, thus getting a more exciting type of painting. Manet broke up the unity of sense impressions by doing this, and his canvas appeared more lively—that is, a little nearer what one actually experiences in real life. The use of the colored shadows also made the canvas more dynamic than the nicely modulated works

Vinci, the reflected colors in the shadows. An official decree by the Emperor Napoleon III set aside a new show place, the Salon des refusés, where Manet and his friends might exhibit.

Almost everyone laughed at the paintings in the Salon des refusés. Manet continued painting splendid animated versions of bourgeois French types, all of which suggest, not so much that the Frenchman is by nature a revolutionary as they do that he is simply a very interesting person. A favorite among Manet's paintings is the young fifer in the uniform of Napoleon's Zouaves. One of the strongest of Manet's works in America is the figure of the philosopher in the Chicago Art Institute (Fig. 567*a*), which is almost devoid of color interest.

Similar figures by the Belgian sculptor Meunier and Daumier's strong paintings of proletarian types (Fig. 567*b*) furnish fit companion pieces for this champion of the rights of the people. Manet, the first impressionist, who was also a great expressive realist, examined with a creative vision the life of the common man, until, becoming rather famous as he aged, he accumulated wealth, which gave him more and more time for picnicking. Then turning from his revolutionary realism, he led the group of impressionists into a simple study of the play of colored lights over pleasant landscape vistas along the Seine. The critics still condemned these harmless impressionist studies as "revolutionary."

Monet and Pointillism. Monet, a friend of Manet, surpassed the greater artist in his analysis of color phenomena. He and his contemporaries Sisley and Pissarro confined themselves almost completely to the study of small scenes, endeavoring to make each canvas painted reflect so much colored light that it would almost rival the effects of sunlight upon the objects seen. These impressionists studied closely the techniques of Constable and Turner whose works were exhibited in Paris by adherents of the Romantic school. Both Constable and Turner had found that tiny brush strokes of yellow and blue pigment, for example, dragged close together over the canvas without mixing, gave a much more vibrant impression of green than could be gained by completely mixing yellow and blue pigment on the palette and applying it as a flat green paint. They also discovered, perhaps from medieval stained glass, that dots of pure blue and red laid close together gave a purple effect, more brilliant than that to be gained by a natural purple-lake pigment. This technique takes advantage of an optical illusion to get a more realistic rendition of color than that gained by the conventional method of allowing unmixed green pigment to stand for nature's green or unmixed purple dye to stand for nature's purple.

Two painters, Seurat and Signac, who made a sort of fetish of the new technique, labored for years upon mosaiclike canvases. They came to be known as "pointillists." Curiously, these two later men, stressing each dot of color by itself, lost the illusionistic effect desired by the impressionists and emerged as highly decorative painters interested in abstract design. Mo-

net became famous for his studies of light flooding over the façades of lacy Gothic cathedrals and for his careful impressions of lily ponds or haystacks under various conditions of atmosphere and at different hours of day or night. Sisley and Pissarro favored fields and orchards with brilliant-colored houses.

The causes that led these men to explore so thoroughly such tiny, meaningless sections of reality are as complex as the modern mind. (1) There is the rising belief in specialism fostered by some research scientists. These impressionists who specialized in light reached toward an ideal that is achieved today by means of photography in color. (2) From a social side these men could be considered as nature Romantics lost in the mystical contemplation of that moment when the deity of light embraced the tangible object. (3) From an economic angle these men can be shown to have been typical, well-fed burghers producing an art of picnics, vistas, even industrial subjects, such as railway stations or city streets, which lack thought-stimulating, associational values. These agreeably tickled the sensibilities of a *bourgeoisie* that no longer wished to think beyond the pleasures of the Saturday and Sunday holidays. This last explanation appeals particularly to those who assume that art arises simply in connection with economic causes.

Two Mature Impressionists—Degas and Renoir. Among the impressionists, two—Degas and Renoir—consistently avoid all revolutionary social themes. The sophisticated dandies of Impressionism, they are by far her most accomplished artists. Degas, using the technique of pointillism, studied Parisian night life, the race course, and the *corps de ballet.* His delightful studies of life backstage among the ballet dancers of the Paris Opera have a quality of charm as typical in painting as that of the late Greek sculpture after Praxiteles. Renoir, perhaps the most nearly universal artist among the late impressionists, occupies our attention with views of the wealthy *bourgeoisie* as they enjoy themselves at the opera, houseboating on the Seine, or dining along the boulevards and in the cafés. However one may try, it is difficult to find in the pleasant canvases of Renoir anything of the revolutionary.

For correct understanding of the full aesthetic significance of mature Impressionism and its influence on the later postimpressionists, it should be seen through the eyes of the great contemporary nonimpressionist painters. Daumier, reviewing the works of Manet, once remarked, "I am not a very great admirer of his work, but I find it has this much quality. It is helping bring art back to the simplicity of playing cards." This statement may be taken either as a sharp observation of certain formal values in Impressionism or as a satirical thrust at the impressionist lack of interest in associational values.

An Oriental influence derived directly from Japanese wood blocks, collected by the impressionists and postimpressionists, sometimes accounts for the well-balanced, flat color patterns seen in such works as Manet's Olympia and less obviously in the portrait group of Madame Charpentier and her children (Fig. 568), painted by Renoir while he was still under forty for the *Salon* of 1879. This Oriental influence touched not only the experimental impressionists but the conservative, acknowledged leader of the late classicists, Puvis de Chavannes, who used it significantly and correctly in the formation of a monumental mural style reminiscent of the great Oriental wall paintings of the Far East.

Oriental Influences in the Paintings of Renoir and Puvis de Chavannes. One must compare Chavannes's Poor Fisherman and His Family (Fig. 569) with Renoir's Madame Charpentier to see that the same geometric, flat, Oriental composition scheme underlies the work of both great masters. The impressionists inherited a color scheme and a flow of well-modeled forms from the great baroque painters. Chavannes derived his careful drawing with a blue-gray, green color scheme from the classicists. In this way, transcending all the little efforts and styles

of the two opposing schools, there gradually crept into European art an awareness of the peculiar decorative quality of Oriental painting which, as we have seen, symbolized either

FIG. 568.—Madame Charpentier and Children, by Auguste Renoir, 1878. Oil on canvas, height 5½ feet. (Metropolitan Museum). (*Courtesy of Lesch-Carnegie.*)

a quietistic state of mind or an acceptance of the paradoxical elements in man's existence. Curiously, the effort of Chavannes is closer in spirit to the actual Japanese wood blocks. However, Renoir's painting acknowledges openly, in the Japanese screen with its peacocks and the hanging Japanese print in the right rear, this particular background of late 19th-century European culture. Approaching from an economic standpoint, one must remember that at this time the French and English were developing a trade with the Orient, particularly Indo-China and Japan.

To see Renoir's paintings, or for that matter any of the paintings of the impressionists, without their color is to lose most of their formal, aesthetic value. The picture by Chavannes has lost very little in the black-and-white reproduction; Renoir's, of Madame Charpentier, on the other hand, has lost much. The vibrating energy given by Renoir's pointillistic brush strokes and all the splendor of his color, which make the soft hair of the little girls call for tender caresses, is almost lacking in the black-

and-white reproduction. So it is with his nude figures, with his scenes of Parisian streets, with his tinkling glasses and happy groups of diners in open-air cafés. A certain rococo joyousness net and Pissarro. The use of newly invented tube colors, many of them fleeting in chromatic value, has robbed of their original splendor these hastily painted impressions. A less for-

FIG. 569.—The Poor Fisherman and his Family, by Puvis de Chavannes, 1881. Oil on canvas, height 5 feet (Luxembourg, Paris). (*Courtesy of Lesch-Carnegie.*)

scintillates on every square inch of his canvas, and this formal value seems to suggest that life for the French middle classes of the late 19th century and the early 20th was the "Best possible in the best of all possible worlds."

Puvis de Chavannes, an officially recognized artist who covered thousands of square feet of wall surface in the public buildings of France with finely designed murals, mixed his pigments thinly. He used many of the new coaltar colors, which soon blackened in the sulphurous air of the cities. So it is with the works of some of the impressionists, particularly Mo-

tunate group of experimenters—the postimpressionists, of whom Cézanne, Gauguin, and Van Gogh will be studied here—were not content with playing-card patterns, the rendition of colored light, or the simple joys of middleclass life.

Paul Cézanne and the Return to Depth in Pictorial Structure. The artist, Paul Cézanne, who was born in Aix-en-Provence, in 1839, lived there for a great part of his life and died there in 1906. He came to be known as the Primitive of the Moderns. This curious, conservative, stubborn bourgeois from the provinces preferred antiquated oil lamps to the brilliant electric lights in the Paris streets. His attitude toward all social development was completely reactionary and he repudiated "The Kingdom of Engineers." However, so completely did he dominate the imagination of early 20th-century Bohemian artists, that they almost enshrined him as a god. Examining large numbers of Cézanne's canvases, the uninitiated is liable to ask at first what all the tumult was about, for they seem singularly unintelligible beside the works of the impressionists. They lack the clean-cut, dynamic composition of the later futurists. Cézanne's importance lies in the fact that he was a transitional figure, a pioneer and experimenter.

To the psychologist, much of Cézanne's attitude toward life appears to have resulted from a certain obstinacy coupled with revolt against a banker father determined to make a lawyer of him. His slowness in painting was proverbial, his reliance upon a few models, such as the inert mass of a mountain, some fruit, a tablecloth, or now and then a human being willing to sit for a hundred hours or more, indicates a man singularly lacking in literary creative imagination. Living alone in the country, Cézanne employed himself with the simple problem of trying to paint a movement from realistic, rounded objects to flat, decorative areas, in terms of color, excluding as far as possible correct linear perspective and accurate, realistic modeling in light and shade.

Cézanne repeated, without knowing anything about it, the famous sentence of the Egyptian artist who wrote, "all art consists of a combination of cones, squares and cubes." He never attempted to construct literally a plastic vision of the world in terms of cones, squares, and cubes, leaving that for his followers.

Either in his early training Cézanne never learned to draw consistently in correct linear perspective or, in an attitude of protest, he accepted definitely the problem of pattern and design as being more worthy of his attention. He could and did draw casts in the Louvre in correct chiaroscuro, and, under the rigorous guild training of the late Renaissance, he probably would have been a painter very much like Rubens, if he can be judged by the excellence of his earliest figure studies. He seems to have been without a sense of appropriateness or a desire for decorative unity over large areas. His murals painted on canvas or directly on the plaster walls of his father's house, Jas de Bouffan, between 1862 and 1869, definitely indicate this. Panels showing the seasons, symbolized by four women, were done in the old academic manner and playfully signed "Ingres." On one wall a canvas with a landscape was done in the style of the painter Lancret, an older academician, whose works look like those of Watteau. Still a third style, that of Sebastiano del Piombo, dominates another panel. Finally, in the center of all is the rough, almost brutal, geometric portrait of Cézanne's father in that style which we know as Cézanne's own, opposite a picture of the dwarf, Achille Empereur. The last was painted under the influence of the Romantic, Delacroix. Had this mélange come from a sophisticated modern after 1900, we should call it satire, but for Cézanne it was an honest attempt to find himself through copying the style of a number of older masters and then registering his "protest" in another style so novel, so primitive, that he could call it his very own.

The still life (Fig. 570) in the Lillie P. Bliss Collection of the Museum of Modern Art, in New York, indicates even in black and white the innovation for which Cézanne has become famous. The total effect is more geometric and abstract than realistic. In order to get a better area of design in the upper right part of the picture, the artist modified his perspective in several places, particularly in the drawing of the ellipses at the top of the bowl and the decanter (compare with Fig. 508, Chap. XVI). He modeled the fruit with brilliant colors rather than with light and shade, often painting an apple green in shadow, yellow-green where the shadow emerges into the light, and yellow in the high light. Sometimes an orange is red in the shadow, yellow-red on the turn, and yellow in the high light. Cast shadows are usually made purple, blue, or green, often brown, rarely

FIG. 570.—The Decanter, by Paul Cézanne (Bliss Collection, Museum of Modern Art). (*Courtesy of Museum of Modern Art.*)

black or gray. Cézanne nullifies the elementary laws of the psychology of color, placing an apple predominantly blue or green in front of another apple in brilliant red. A fold of drapery that retreats from the eye in linear perspective will be colored blue at the front and yellow white at the back. One concludes either that Cézanne was not trying to model in color, or else that he fumbled a great deal.

He himself tells us that he did not wish to paint in flat decorative areas, and he definitely expressed his dislike for Byzantine art. So his pictures display both roundness and flatness, an indeterminate quality like a Celtic inter-weave, a discontinuous arabesque of form, line, and flat color areas which express clearly the fluctuating state of mind of the amateur who would like to become a painter, whose paint-ings hardly ever sold, and whose obstinacy kept him at his chosen task until he had created a few consistent panels in a new style. When this integrity of his character at last became known, toward the close of his life, Cézanne's old friends —men like Zola—had become wealthy and passed on. But the revolutionary younger gen-eration who surpassed his experiments praised

him as their leader, and the art dealers who had bought up his countless studies for little or nothing, profiting by the just acclaim of his few fine works, sold many aesthetically worth-less trials for exorbitant prices to the *nouveaux riches* who wished to be considered cultured.

Gauguin and the Return to Imaginative Painting. Paul Gauguin was born in 1849, the son of a radical journalist and a socialist mother, the latter known as a pioneer in the woman-suf-frage movement and trade-unionism. From his father he seems to have inherited a violent temper and a headstrong disposition; from his mother, a passionate desire for personal free-dom. After a very romantic *Wanderjahr*, at the age of thirty-two, he entered the banking house of Bertin, in Paris, and shortly amassed a fortune in the stock market, which enabled him to marry the daughter of a Swedish Protestant clergyman.

Finding among the friends of his wife a num-ber of painters and others interested in art, Gauguin began to spend his holidays painting for amusement. Not satisfied with work in color, he essayed sculpture in stone, clay, and wood, and tried his hand at poetic literature, as well. These biographical details have importance not only for the art of Gauguin but for much of 20th-century art. The ideal of the wealthy dil-ettante, inherited from the Renaissance and from the critical amateur of the 18th and 19th centuries, now descended upon the *bourgeoisie*.

In this age of aesthetic anarchism, the im-pressionist, Camille Pissarro, soon initiated Gauguin into the mystery of the pointillist tech-nique and he turned out some creditable sketches in this style. By 1883 the primitive and artist had triumphed over the banker and hus-band. Not without the encouragement of his wife, Gauguin left her and their five children. Between 1885 and 1889 he lived in Paris, rent-ing a small studio, attempting unsuccessfully to support himself by his art, and frequenting chiefly the Oriental collections of the city, as he was drawn by a desire to study decorative design. He actively sought to express himself in patterns suggested by Byzantine mosaic enamels and stained-glass designs. He tried to create pictures that would have unity and some harmonious expression of a definite emotional tone. Although he experimented with true impressionist techniques, he can be seen to have been continually marking off color areas by strongly drawn lines.

Gauguin showed himself a most complete egotist in relation to his two friends Van Gogh and Schuffenecher. In comparison with his utter selfishness, he expressed at times sentiments tending to show that he thought his art must be a great gift to mankind. In this he follows the pattern of such Romantics as Lord Byron and Richard Wagner. Curiously, although he was utterly egotistic, his art expresses in its flat patterns a negation of the dynamic egotistic elements. In contrast, Van Gogh, who was the humblest of mortals, shows in his painting the most dynamic self-assertion. The psychologist observing this phenomenon generalizes by saying that for these men art was an escape from their habitual daily attitudes. Almost on his deathbed, Gauguin finally realized that his art had been simply a great protest and outward manifestation of some revolt within his own soul. He maintained that he had fought against the moral degradation and the hypocrisy of European society. The playwright Strindberg, both friend and critic, wrote of him:

He is the savage who hates a commercialistic civilization, something of a Titan who, jealous of his creator, in his idle moments makes his own little creation; a child who breaks up his toys to make others, he who denies and defies the rabble, preferring to see the sky red rather than blue as they do.[1]

Gauguin, fleeing European society to paint in the South Sea Islands, strove to be a Buddhist in thought, losing himself in a return to the primitive conditions of Rousseau's *l'homme naturel* (Fig. 571). Once on Tahiti, in a society

of degenerate natives who had been spoiled by contacts with Europeans, Gauguin found a measure of peace in what was left of their fine civilization and wrote the story of his conver-

Fig. 571.—Barbaric Poems, by Paul Gauguin, oil on canvas, 25½ by 19 inches (Goodyear Collection, New York). (*Courtesy of A. Conger Goodyear.*)

sion to savagery in the almost poetic tale, *Noa-Noa*. Perhaps the entire center of Gauguin's difficulty with life is expressed in his account of his meeting with the islander Totefa. He writes:

Totefa showed me that I was a better man than most of the others because I could make things in art and that art is useful. I indeed believe Totefa is the first human being in the world who used such words toward me. It was the language of a savage or a child, for one must be either one of them, must one not, to imagine that an artist might be a useful human being.[2]

Here was an intensely dynamic personality

[1] J. G. FLETCHER, *Paul Gauguin, His Life and Art*, p. 137, Frank-Maurice, Inc., New York, 1921.
[2] PAUL GAUGUIN, *Noa-Noa*, translated by Theis, Greenberg, Publisher, Inc., New York, 1927.

that created an art which, much more than the art of Cézanne or Van Gogh, strove for a decorative restfulness. Gauguin worked for a time with a group of artists who called them-

Fig. 572.—Portrait of an Actor, by Vincent Van Gogh, 1888. Oil on canvas, about 24 by 20 inches (Collection of Mrs. H. Kroller-Müller, The Hague). (*After Vincent Van Gogh, the Phaidon Press.*)

selves "syntheticists." One of them, Maurice Denis, wrote: "A picture before being a force, a nude form or some story is in essence a flat surface covered with a certain arrangement of colors." This almost exactly describes the formal, aesthetic effect of Gauguin's pictures, which show Oriental arabesques and decorative spacing of balanced color and form. So he and Cézanne are venerated as pioneers in the movement toward analytical abstraction of line, color, and form which was to eventuate in the schools of futurism, cubism, expressionism, and vorticism.

The Energetic Painting of Vincent Van Gogh. The third of the great postimpressionists, Vincent Van Gogh, was a Hollander from the town of Zundert in northern Brabant. He in-

herited from a pastor father a desire to be an evangelical preacher. With the clear mystical vision of an early Christian saint and an unsophisticated, childlike, literal belief in the innate goodness of man, Van Gogh was completely unfitted for the age and society in which he was born. Had he appeared in the Middle Ages, he could have been a highly respected master, honored for his piety; had he been born thirty years later, he would have been eagerly seized upon by some psychoanalyst and a progressive art dealer who between them would have advertised and sold his work. This success might have saved him from insanity.

Van Gogh recorded that he undertook painting as had Millet, with somewhat of a religious feeling. He definitely hoped to win the world to a recognition of his usefulness by giving it his painting. Perhaps, he thought, if he demonstrated how the whole world was alive with the color and energy of God, people would turn from lives of indifference and sin to a worship of the great Creator. Sincerely believing that man might find his own soul through creating anew in art what nature brought to his senses, Van Gogh went to Paris, taking with him a style of drawing closely resembling that of Millet, whose compositions he had copied. From Millet, too, he inherited the essentials of Impressionism, for Millet, like Constable and Turner, had gained effects of vibration in colored light. In Paris Van Gogh found the pointillism of Seurat, with its square dots of color, a ruling fashion. He changed the mosaic of these dots, making of them elongated, twisting brush strokes following the vital naturalistic lines of growth, which he wove together into a tapestry like a Celtic interweave. The large composition of the picture, like the pictures of his predecessors, showed derivations from either Japanese print designs or the 13th-century stained glass that he may have studied.

Van Gogh's energetic, sometimes incoherent, evangelical nature made him unacceptable to the sophisticated, pleasure-loving impressionists and pointillists. Obviously, this country fellow from the mining towns of the north did not belong to their "set." So, like Cézanne and Gauguin, he fled the city, at the age of thirty-five, settling at Arles. For two feverish years he painted like one possessed, sometimes two canvases a day, in the blazing sun. His portraits, landscapes, still lifes, and interiors revealed that all life was light and heat, color and darting, flamelike lines. In 1890, during a fit of madness and despondency, he shot himself.

To the later expressionists Van Gogh appeared almost godlike, and he was considered the founder of their movement. In his portrait of a man (Fig. 572) one may observe the utmost limits to which a human face can be drawn while still keeping recognizably human and sane. All great portraitists subtly modify the proportions of various parts of a face in order to express the characteristics of the sitter. Van Gogh has gone beyond this and brought into the face of the man portrayed his own inner struggle.

Unity has been achieved by a refined balance of large areas in counterpoint to the brush strokes with which the features of the face are modeled. The final decorative unity, only suggested here, comes through the color scheme, which remains the same throughout all of Van Gogh's works. Against backgrounds of limpid blues or turquoise greens Van Gogh painted violent yellows and violets, pinks and reds, with here and there small areas of light brown and earth colors tending toward orange; rarely was there a stroke of pure black. The color areas were usually bounded with heavy lines, so that their Oriental flatness counterbalances, here and there, an object drawn in correct perspective of line but incorrect color perspective. The resultant picture appears as a Gothicized version, boldly enlarged, of a Persian miniature.

Had Van Gogh been able through his art to reach a completely Oriental synthesis of character, a sanity would have probably resulted which would have carried him far beyond his time. Like his friend Gauguin, whose unsocial egotism may have helped to drive Van Gogh insane, the Dutch artist was seeking such an Oriental synthesis. Unlike Gauguin, Van Gogh lacked the ruthlessness necessary to enable him to escape to a more primitive environment, where his energy could have been released without precipitating social punishments.

Bohemia, and the Genre Art of "les Fauves." The interrelationship between environment and art can nowhere be more clearly demonstrated than in the lives and dwelling places of the Bohemian artists, *les Fauves*, or the "wild men," as they called themselves, who lived in Paris during the first decade of the 20th century. The Pre-Raphaelites of England created for themselves a medieval scene. The impressionists in France enjoyed suburban life and the postimpressionist adventurers fled the city to live in the provinces. The "wild men," needing the stimulation of the Latin Quarter on the Left Bank of the Seine, the more romantic, dimly lighted streets of Montparnasse, or the underworld society of Montmartre, congregated in the slums, frequented the cheap cafés, lived in garret studios, or haunted the stage and the circus.

Mürger's novel, *La Vie de Bohème*, popularized by the opera *La Bohème*, describes the life of those artists whose superior wit enabled them to live upon the foibles of the stodgy *bourgeoisie* while pursuing love affairs with their models or portraying their own souls. The dweller in Bohemia, a Till Eulenspiegel, alive in a world of puppets was at once mountebank and cardsharp, perhaps a satirical clown living almost at war with society. He was tolerated chiefly because almost every Parisian fancied himself a potential artist or amateur. It was perhaps as such a Bohemian that Picasso could write, "All art is a lie."

Much of this "Bohemian" art cannot be taken too seriously for either its aesthetic quality or its social value, because it has been created "tongue in cheek," as a gesture of defiance toward an unsympathetic world. The subject matter of Bohemian art, for the greater part, includes objects unassociated with charm or pleasantness. Perhaps some onions and moldy cheese, a bottle of villainous-looking wine, a cast-off shoe, or a broken chair will be arranged and so painted that, despite our natural disgust, we are inclined to admit the power of

Fig. 573.—The Dance, by Henri Matisse, 1910. Oil on canvas, height about 15 inches (Stchoukine Collection, Moscow). (*Courtesy of Lesch-Carnegie.*)

art to create an interesting effect where actually none exists. So the Fauvists sought an unattractive environment as a milieu out of which to create, in a revival of genre painting, a more significant design.

Here, first the unhappy Gauguin, then the misshapen dwarf Toulouse-Lautrec, using the techniques of the fantast Moreau, sought significance in the castoffs of society. Roualt, designing with the rich reds, purples, and greens of stained-glass windows, caught underworld characters in designs strongly reminiscent of Romanesque fresco painting. Matisse, enamored of odalisques, sketched whirling dancers (Fig. 573) and goldfish in arabesques of lines balanced by flat areas of pink, yellow, and red. Derain, who escaped at times to the country, took with him all the hard realism of a city dweller, painting with that naïveté always shown by an urban soul when visiting the barnyard.

In the works of Derain black tree trunks, carelessly drawn without much knowledge of nature's vital lines, feather out into delicate impressionistic greens and pinks against skies of cerulean blue or flat tan fields. Utrillo, approaching his canvas like a house painter, strove to imitate the precise effects of the medieval French miniaturists. Henri Rousseau, a retired customhouse officer, likewise saw life through the less sophisticated eyes of a middle-class Parisian. In youth, during his army service, Rousseau had served under the ill-fated Maximilian in Mexico, whence he brought back a few naïve visions of tropical life. These haunted him, until at last as a *pensionnaire* he could spend a leisurely old age arranging them on canvas. These jungle visions, which would delight the heart of a child, rendered with exquisite craftsmanship by a frightened city primitive, have become highly prized items in postwar collections of wealthy businessmen. A curious group of individualists were these "wild men," whose lives as painters were made possible simply because each specialized in some aspect of modern everyday life, presented in a novel mode of painting succinctly expressing its genre subject matter.

Picasso and the Rise of Cubism. Out of the efforts of the Fauvists arose at least one new movement in painting that could be dignified by being named a school; this was cubism, founded almost unaided by Pablo Picasso, a young Spaniard from Barcelona. With Picasso's cubist compositions begins a definite tendency to formulate a new and completely abstract art, depending chiefly upon arrangement of forms, lines and colors for the achievement of aesthetic effects lacking associational and useful values. Picasso's earliest development shows definite influence by the paintings of El Greco and other Spanish baroque masters. As a boy, having copied very carefully casts and pictures in the museums, he began to paint original, relatively physioplastic compositions in various shades of blue.

The admirable example of the emaciated guitar player, in the Chicago Art Institute, a very figure of death and decomposition, came at the end of the blue period. In the next phase of his development, Picasso chose more cheerful subjects, including feminine figures, which he painted in shades of pink. This was followed by a white period, characterized by arabesque, baroque, linear studies of horses; then by a circus period, in which the painter used as his chief subject the shabby, tinsel life of the clown, who gradually emerged as a tragic figure like Pagliacci, a man with an unhappy soul behind a grinning mask.

Having revealed man as a mask, Picasso reached a definite turning point in his life and abandoned objective painting for the construction of abstract forms which should express in geometric terms the inner structure of all reality. With his friend Max Jacob, an amateur poet and painter, and the symbolist poet Apollinaire, Picasso dined one evening in the apartment of Matisse. Here Picasso saw for the first time an example of African Negro sculpture. All the evening, the artist sat with it in his hand, as though hypnotized. The following morning, Jacob found Picasso in his studio, where he had spent the entire night drawing a woman's face dominated by a long nose joined to the mouth around a single eye. Next, many versions of this grotesque face, obviously in the style of the African sculpture, appeared on a single enormous canvas, which he called The Young Ladies of Avignon (Fig. 574). Here was a series of angular nude forms, disjointed, and shuffled like a pack of playing cards. Thus was cubism born.

By 1907 Picasso's studies had incorporated Cézanne's formula that all nature should be represented in terms of cubes, cones, and cylinders. Other painters, notably Braque and Leger, adopted the new style between 1908 and 1910. Consciously studying Cézanne, these three painters soon surpassed him in achieving unified compositions with dominating geometric elements. In many cases they obtained finely balanced decorative canvases with the essentials of geometricity found in earlier Egyptian and Byzantine art, in Romanesque sculpture, and in the carvings of aboriginal peoples. The element of free and joyful play, which determined the fortuitous structure of the cubist compositions, was echoed in the critical formula that a picture should make a pleasant appearance,

even when hung on its side or upside down. Maurice Denis and other champions of the new abstract art held that the prime function of any work of art lay simply in presenting an

FIG. 574.—The Young Ladies of Avignon, by Pablo Picasso, 1906–1907. Oil on canvas, 96 by 92 inches (Museum of Modern Art). (*Courtesy of Museum of Modern Art.*)

organization of light and shade, line and color; "pure, unadulterated art, the art of abstraction, is necessary in a world of specialization." So the abstract artist recalled two passages from Plato, one suggesting that "the most beautiful shapes were those which had no sensuous associations," that is, purely mathematical shapes, the other that "all art should approach the condition of music," in which harmony and rhythmic repetition or melody would be the dominant sensations experienced.

In the works of Picasso and his immediate followers, as well as in the works of the futurist groups shortly to be described, attention was still given, particularly through names assigned to the canvases, to some associational values. In greater part, the painters of this group, like true Fauvists, used in their compositions playing cards, bottles, musical instruments, the names of daily newspapers, and advertisements for cognac and cocoa. These they combined with word fragments, such as *étude*, *Bal*, and Bach, which have artistic connotations. The figures portrayed are those of Pierrot and Har-

FIG. 575.—Head of a Woman, by Pablo Picasso, 1908–1909. Oil on canvas (Collection Guillaume, Paris). (*Courtesy of Museum of Modern Art.*)

lequin, or some subject intimately connected with the detached Bohemian milieu, almost utterly lacking in universal social values.

The Head of a Woman, by Picasso (Fig. 575), painted in 1909, not only demonstrates the chief elements of his cubist style, but forms a point of transition to two later movements in 20th-century painting, futurism and surrealism. On first observing this picture, one is impressed, if not by its abstract pattern—which suffers in the black-and-white reproduction— then by its association with a mask. The face is composed of a combination of pyramidal forms suggesting the bone and muscle structure. This much is cubism; but by the stress given to the relatively bold spherical shapes on the right side of the head, the attention of the observer is made to move unconsciously from

lower right, up and over toward the left, and then down to the ear, at which point the strong angle of head and shoulder forces the attention in again toward the right. Thus one has a strong empathic feeling, as though the head were in movement. The attempt to simulate movement by a composition of abstract, rhythmical lines is known as "futurism." Finally, looking at the picture once more, one sees that the right side of the head may be detached from the rest of the face, to become a second distinct profile head. So where there first appeared to be only one face, two can now be seen. This picture, which unites two concepts in one, presents the essence of the surrealist style.

The Futurists of Italy and the Expressionists of Germany. In 1909 Marinetti, an Italian painter with a social program, published the first "Manifesto of Futurism" in the Parisian newspaper *Figaro.* There followed in 1910 at Milan his second "Manifesto of Futurist Painting," accepted by five painters—Balla, Russolo, Carra, Boccioni, and Severini. These friends united to conceive an art which would express on canvas the dynamic motion of moving figures, mechanical vehicles, and flying birds by means of abstract lines and forms. The intellectual quality of this art is shown by the fact that the program preceded the painting in true classical fashion. It was to be a rebellion against the concepts of "harmony and good taste," a celebration of all the inventions of modern science. To Marinetti a speeding automobile held more of beauty than did the Victory of Samothrace.

In their paintings, the futurists used both the techniques of color analysis devised by the impressionists and the analysis of forms invented by the cubists. Arranging these symbols of dynamic light and movement around the object portrayed, the futurists showed successive steps in the progression of that object. Balla painted a Dog on a Leash, with nine positions of the tail and innumerable positions of the legs, so that he would appear to be running. Exactly the same effect could have been achieved by printing twenty frames of motion-picture

FIG. 577.—Gazelle, by Franz Marc, watercolor. (*Courtesy of Lesch.*)

negative upon a single positive. Naturally, in getting this effect the futurists made some very striking designs in color and line. The dynamism of Russolo's Automobile and Severini's Armored Train, painted during the World War, in 1915, suggest the explosive force of the movement, which spread to Russia and Germany after the war.

Lyonel Feininger and the Development of Expressionism. The example of futurist painting entitled Side Wheeler (Fig. 576), by Lyonel Feininger (now in the Detroit Institute of Art), furnishes one of the finest examples of the style, here chosen because of its transitional character to that related movement in German art known as "abstract expressionism." In Side Wheeler, interweaving angular planes of color finely balanced in harmonious grays, greens, and purples, unite to give a dynamic impression of a steamboat riding through a storm. From all directions the lines of force react upon the boat so that it seems held stationary for a moment, though inevitably moving from left to right. The fact that the forms of the waves, the shape of the boat, its masts and wheels and the billowing smoke all dissolve into abstract angular patterns without plasticity, suggests a further development at the hands of Kandinsky, Franz Marc, Arp, and Klee. In this abstractionism, fluid forms would eventually flow into each other and partially naturalistic objects would change before our eyes into cubistic patterns.

Kandinsky, the leader of the expressionist school, which started in 1911, wrote a manifesto in 1912 entitled "Upon the Spiritual in Art." He explained that he wished to paint the representation not of objects but of moods. He used the principle of free association in composing his pictures, allowing the brush to proceed haphazardly with its drawing from one part of the canvas to another. The results he labeled "Improvisations" and "Compositions," much as though he were a musician idly playing scraps of melody and harmony upon the piano.

Of all the expressionists, most successful for his ability to unite a futurist or a cubist technique with natural objects carrying associational romantic overtones was Franz Marc,

FIG. 576.—Side Wheeler, by Lyonel Feininger (Detroit Institute of Art). (*Courtesy of Detroit Institute of Art.*)

whose Gazelle in water color (Fig. 577) presents the characteristic color scheme of most abstract painting. The two crystalline forms on the right of the composition have enough plasticity to recall the beginnings of the expressionist movement in the works of Cézanne. The upper left part of the body of the gazelle likewise has enough modeling to suggest a rounded form. The rear of the gazelle's body, with its five triangular black strokes, seems flat. The pink area between the legs of the gazelle suggests a connection with the pink upper border of the large left triangle and the direction of this movement. Thus this static picture, like the Side Wheeler of Feininger, is strongly dynamic. This plastic Gazelle is also decoratively flat. At no place on the entire surface can the gaze rest except in the eye of the animal. Around that occult center one moves from prismatic to suggested spherical forms. There results one of the most significant paintings of 20th-century abstract art.

Paul Klee and Dadaism. Paul Klee, with Kandinsky and Marc, published a magazine, *The Blue Rider*, from which the three received the name of the "Blue Rider Group." An examination of Klee's many drawings in the pages of this publication shows that he studied not only primitive and curious forms of medieval art

FIG. 578.—The Twittering Machine, by Paul Klee, 1922 (National Gallery, Berlin). (*Courtesy of Museum of Modern Art.*)

but also the creations of the insane and of children. His picture The Twittering Machine (Fig. 578), drawn in 1922 and now in the National Gallery at Berlin, demonstrates the ultimate phase of abstractionist painting outside of the pure geometric figures of the suprematist school or the compositions of Dutch abstractionists known as *de Stijl*. The Twittering Machine might almost have been the result of a child's dream, pictured by a child. During the war years, Klee, Ernst, Picabia, Duchamp, and Man Ray invented Dadaism, an art which, they explained, "meant absolutely nothing."

The Dadaists proposed to create a specifically unintelligible form that would symbolize the unintelligibility of the World War from which they had escaped to Switzerland in 1916. Pasting together haphazardly scraps of paper, twine, and other objects that might suggest the debris of modern life, they hoped to convince mankind of its lunacy. Picasso, passing through something like Dadaism on the way to a surrealist stage of development is reported to have said, that a true artist never copies nature, neither does he imitate it; he merely allows imaginary objects to clothe themselves with the appearance of things real. For art is not truth; it is merely a lie which makes our dreams come true.[1]

George Grosz and the Coming of Surrealism. Another German, George Grosz, who belonged to no school, as a pacifist fought the war spirit in a series of satirical grotesques not unlike the style of Klee and the Dadaists. Forced into the front-line trenches, he retaliated by storing up in his mind nightmarish visions of the holocaust, so powerful that their expression after the war led to his banishment by the Nazis. His most powerful cartoons (Fig. 579) link him closely with the Gothic artists Breughel and Grünewald. The persistence of the disintegrating nightmarish visions in the artist's mind can be seen in his canvas, Piece of My World (1939). This shows the effect upon human nature of a war so long that only corpses remain to carry it on. Through dirty-gray gaseous mists stumble a number of tattered grisly forms among fragments of a ruined world, accompanied by an army of enormous trench rats, who may have fattened upon the dead.

Any efforts toward self-analysis through the medium of art lead eventually to the lowest childhood levels of the subconscious mind, where expression reaches the condition of almost complete unintelligibility. Suggestive scraps of symbolism composed of nonsense rhymes like those in *Alice in Wonderland*, formless ethereal figures, or such playful diagram-

[1] For elaboration of this theme read *The Decay of Lying*, by Oscar Wilde.

matic constructions as the birds in The Twittering Machine characterize Klee's art. From it and similar subconscious experiments by the Italian artist Giorgio de Chirico, the Russian

FIG. 579.—Crucifixion, by George Grosz, lithograph, after drawing, c. 1917 from *Interregnum*. (*Courtesy of George Grosz and Black Sun Press.*)

Chagall, the Spaniard Salvador Dali, and the Frenchmen Miro and Masson arose that art known as surrealism.

Salvador Dali, most widely publicized and probably the most talented, inventive painter of this school, as well as its finest craftsman, suggests in his small book, *The Conquest of the Irrational*, that surrealism attempts to show the seemingly irrational dream images of the subconscious mind painted so that they appear real. The surrealists accept as definitive that illusionistic technique employed by the primitive Alaskan Indian, who drew the bear so that one might see both the front and profile views (Fig.

43a, Chap. III) and the element in Picasso's painting (Fig. 575) which likewise unites two symbols in one. They paint, as can be seen in the example by Dali (Fig. 580), pictures that

FIG. 580.—Paranoiac Face, by Salvador Dali, 1935. Oil on wood (Collection of Edward James, London). (*Courtesy of Levy Galleries and Museum of Modern Art.*)

reveal, when studied, not a single impression of life but a double image. So the African kraal on the desert with a number of savages seated about it, studied intently, becomes a face lying on its side. The leaning figure second from the left in the front row forms in silhouette the bridge of the nose. The jug slightly off the center is the chin of the woman whose hair appears as the trees. Compare with Fig. 1, Introduction. A number of such creations appeared in the American humorous magazine *Life* around 1905.

Most surrealist paintings supply rather boldly images readily available for interpretation by the psychiatrists. Unlike the pictures of the insane, they are the issue of a conscious desire on the part of the mind to free itself from its soul-destroying fantasies by objectifying them. Usually the pictures are very high in associational value and exceedingly low in formal, aesthetic value. In this way the painting records a return on the part of the artist to literary interests, although those interests, like the poetry of Gertrude Stein and the writings of James Joyce, lose somewhat in effectiveness because of their tedious quality. Almost everyone knows now that the world is capable of going into periods of murderous insanity. The

Fig. 581a.—Bibliothèque Sainte Geneviève, by Labrouste, Paris, 1845, height about 40 feet. (*Courtesy of Professor Siegfried Giedion.*)

need is for an art which suggests that something can be done about it. Surrealism merely records the *status quo*.

Architecture

Industrial inventions, the needs of a manufacturing society, and new facilities for the large-scale production of iron, steel, glass, hollow tile, and cement, placed in the hands of the builders of the middle 19th century appropriate materials for the creation of a new, distinctive, functional style of architecture.

Pragmatic Methods of Modern Architectural Design. The use of cast iron in building construction after 1840 and the large-scale production of steel after 1890 were perhaps the most decisive factors in the eventual appearance of the new architecture. As the Assyrian palaces, of brick, predetermined the Mesopotamian design, and the concrete baths and basilicas influenced the Romans, so one may say that the architecture of the 20th century derived di-

rectly from the ferroconcrete-and-glass factory and railway station.

The greatest German architect of the late Neo-Classical revival, Karl Friedrich Schinkel, who in 1824 designed the Greek columnar façade of the Berlin Museum, later visited the factory towns of England. He recorded the shocked surprise with which he first saw the great masses of brick and glass housing the new machines of the industrial revolution, designed not by trained architects but by contractors and foremen. After his return to Germany, it gradually dawned on Schinkel that these were the precursors of a new style, and he began to theorize as to how something might be built to epitomize his age. Having faced the problem, Schinkel first suggested that the new architecture should emphasize constructive or functional elements, using the new materials boldly, without employing useless antique decoration.

Significant Early Buildings in the Functional Style of Architecture. With the rapid growth of the railroads, in the middle decades of the 19th century, European engineers devising trussed structures for bridges were asked to contribute their knowledge of iron construction to the building of train sheds, in which light and a wide, fireproof span of roof were needed. By the middle of the century a number of significant exhibition halls were built for expositions in Paris and London (Fig. 581a).

An engineer architect, Henri Labrouste, first used iron construction for a noncommercial building on a large scale in the library in Paris—Bibliothèque Sainte Geneviève. Truly advanced in spirit, Labrouste began with a central skeleton of tall cast-iron columns, from which sprang round arches like those of the nave arcade in a medieval cathedral. Above them two large barrel vaults of iron covered the central space. This framework was roofed with glass. On the exterior of the building the engineer gave way to the architect, as though that individual feared to submit his radical construction to the gaze of the critic. The building has a façade in the classical manner. From the point of view of the development of style, the form of the modern skyscraper arises naturally from the wooden Gothic structures and, projecting height rather than horizontality as engineer Cottancin and the architect Dutert (Fig. 581b). The Eiffel Tower, which still stands, is the father of all skyscrapers. Unlike later skyscrapers, it has no use value, being a simple,

FIG. 581b.—Galerie des Machines, by Cottancin (engineer) and Dutert (architect), 1889, Paris. (*Courtesy of Professor Siegfried Giedion.*)

the ideal, can more naturally be associated with Gothic than with classical decorative elements.

In 1851 Joseph Paxton, a designer of greenhouses, built a supergreenhouse, the Crystal Palace, for the great International Exhibition in London. He copied the plan and elevation of the Roman basilica, using a great central barrel vault over a cruciform building with side aisles, all constructed of iron and glass. Both these earliest attempts to use the new material adopted ancient architectural styles.

The first truly original constructions in the new medium arose in connection with the Paris Exposition of 1889; these were the famous tower constructed by the engineer Gustave Eiffel and the great Galerie des Machines designed by the

bold monument, soaring 1,000 feet into the clouds in long sweeping curves. The other building, unfortunately dismantled after the exhibition, was 1,377 feet long, 377 feet wide and 147 feet high. This 19th-century masterpiece, the first significant building in a style expressive of material and function, was described by a contemporary, P. Morton Shand, in the following terms.

Steel has found its form at last. Construction had once again become its own expression, its own "style." Cottancin's Galerie des Machines was one of the loveliest shapes in which man has ever enclosed space; but whereas hitherto it had always been imprisoned like a bird in a cage, here it floated free as the circumambient air.

This hall and a similar structure built in 1898 for the Columbian Exposition at Chicago were probably the two most satisfying structures in steel and glass built since the invention of the

FIG. 582.—Interior in style of *l'art nouveau*, by Raymond Hood, from exhibition in Metropolitan Museum of Art. Note use of abstract plant lines combined with metal in decoration. (*Courtesy of Metropolitan Museum of Art.*)

new form. They furnished the models for the great European railway stations of the early 20th century.

In the first years of the 20th century, the introduction of steel and reinforced concrete, particularly at the hands of American factory builders, began to influence European engineers and architects, who now designed buildings with an inner skeleton of concrete columns and floors, from which were hung walls of glass with spandrels between. This new system of construction, so common to all Americans as to hardly warrant consideration as art, was widely proclaimed in Europe as a new, distinctive style, when taken over by the cubist designers in Holland, Germany, and Paris.

L'Art Nouveau, De Stijl, the Bauhaus, and the New Domestic Architecture. Indicative of the lack of cooperation accompanying the individualistic creations of an industrial age was the circuitous process by which the new functional style of commercial building eventually developed its own system of ornament and became adapted to domestic architecture. William

Morris and his friends endeavored to build a new system of domestic architecture uniting modern industrial forms with Gothic roofs. Gradually, they devised a system of ornament

FIG. 583.—Hall of country home, Noordwijkerhout, Holland, by J. J. P. Oud (architect) and Theo van Doesburg (painter), 1917. (*After Albert Morancé, L'Architecture vivant, Automne, 1925; courtesy of Museum of Modern Art.*)

based upon a study of plant forms which suggested in a way the very constructive line of the great steel-and-glass exhibition halls.

In Belgium and Holland a number of painters, led by Henry Van de Velde, declared their intention to further this work by inventing a new elementary form that should arise from the creations of modern technique. Most of Van de Velde's followers—men like Otto Eckman and Peter Behrens—had been painters of the late Romantic school. In Germany and France such men created a style employing basic plant forms, called *l'art nouveau* (Fig. 582). Like Morris, they attempted to dramatize by an abstract ornament, suggesting the original Celtic interweave, the various functions of support, tension, suspension, and bracing—the dynamic lines of the new steel structures. The finest examples of this ornament still to be seen in America are those developed by Louis Sullivan (Fig. 614, Chap. XIX). The ornament of Morris and the exponents of the *art nouveau*, coming twenty years too soon, died out, lacking suitable structures to decorate.

Another, more geometric, ornament, which had to arise as a technomorphic design in con-

tecture with the advent of Doesburg into the group. The most significant buildings in the new style remained those of the Dutch architect J. J. P. Oud, whose workmen's houses

FIG. 584.—Workmen's Houses, by Oud, Hook of Holland, 1926.

nection with building of angular technical character, found its designers among the cubists, Mondrian and Doesburg, who, with the architect J. J. P. Oud, formed in Holland during the World War a group called *de Stijl*, after their magazine. Oud and Doesburg collaborated in designing the interior of a house at Noordwijkerhout (Fig. 583). The illustration shows that the ornament grows from a repetition of the right-angular form of the simple cast-concrete construction; the walls, receiving varied lights, are painted in different hues.

In 1919 Feininger, who had visited the members of *de Stijl* in Holland during the war, brought back to Weimar in Germany the influence of this new type of design. Here the architect Gropius united with the expressionists, Klee, Feininger and Kandinsky, to form the Bauhaus Group. Gropius at first had a tendency toward picturesqueness which was modified to a more functional type of archi-

on the Hook of Holland, built in 1926 and 1927 show a union of the forms derived from the new construction with lines suggestive of the streamlining of airplanes and motorcars (Fig. 584).

In the Scandinavian countries, where the cooperative movement was strong, and in the new socialist republics of Germany and Austria, many government-subsidized architectural projects developed designs as fine as those of Oud. Each was distinctive of its own social background (Fig. 585). The Grundtvig Memorial Church built by Klint in 1926 at Copenhagen, Denmark, presents a modification of the modern style in which the late Gothic forms of the near-by dwelling houses, abstracted and refined, have been used as chief decorative elements in the façade of the central church. This entire structure, in which an almost Romanesque form emerges from a concrete construction, suggests that aesthetic element most dominant in the northern Protestant religious service, the choral organ music. A number of churches in Germany and France, built of concrete, steel, and glass, deserve intensive study for their splendid unity of design, construction,

FIG. 585.—Grundtvig Memorial Church, by Klint, Copenhagen, 1926. (*Courtesy of Lesch.*)

symbolic function, and architectonic decoration (Fig. 586).

Sculpture

The development of sculpture in the 20th century parallels closely developments in painting. Two distinct styles exist—one, individualistic and highly expressionistic; the other, communal, architectonic, and more physioplastic or decorative. The tendency to create a new architectural sculpture came at first from the members of the *art nouveau* group. They attempted to express the fundamental stresses in industrial productions by long, curvilinear designs. The most pertinent example of this work, the sculpture of the Battle of Nations Monument near Leipzig, symbolizing the movement of the democracies against Napoleonic imperialism, was by Christian Behrens and Franz Metzner (Fig. 587). The strong union of architecture and sculpture here displayed in-

fluenced the design of many 20th-century creators, such as Bourdelle and Mestrovic.

Decorative Sculpture and Antoine Bourdelle. The first truly significant piece of architectural sculpture whose designs definitely enhance the appearance of a modern building was Antoine Bourdelle's relief of Apollo and the Muses for the Théâtre des Champs-Élysées (Fig. 588). This attempt, somewhat suggestive of Burgundian Romanesque sculpture and of futurist painting, followed the cubist sculpture by the individualist experimenter Picasso and the earlier attempts in the carver's medium by Boccioni. Boccioni the futurist and Picasso the cubist were interested in a type of sculpture that should express the dynamic movement characteristic of the 20th century. The new building was strictly functional. In Bourdelle's

FIG. 586.—The Pallotiner Church, Limburg, by J. H. Pinand, architect. (*From F. S. Onderdonk, The Church of Infinity, The Architectural Forum, August, 1929, by permission.*)

sculpture for the first time in the 20th century the new dynamic symbol and the functional building united, but—and this is most important—the type of sculpture did not seem improper because the people who daily beheld it were used to Romanesque and Gothic sculpture in which an interest had been aroused through the government restoration of French cathedrals and a Romantic interest in medievalism.

The Futurist Sculpture of Boccioni. Boccioni in April 1912 wrote his "Manifesto of Futurist Sculpture." He explained that a work of sculpture should express the inner life of an object by indicating its connection with the space around it. Following the futurist program for painting, Boccioni suggested that one should use in futurist sculptural composition not only stationary planes of wood or metal but also objects pivoted or suspended so that they might actually move (mobiles). Finally, he tried to free sculpture from the values associated with bronze and marble, and advocated experimenting in glass, cement, iron, and cardboard, using mirrors and electric lights for effect. In 1913 Boccioni carved his statue, Unique Forms of Continuity in Space (Fig. 589). In this piece he tried to show in abstract form the dynamic actions of the various muscles of the body, the entire composition standing for the actions of the body as a whole. The chief lines of force appear as a number of progressing streamline shapes—the very essence of the baroque "twisting of muscles" which Boccioni decried. The illustration shows that the total effect of Boccioni's streaming forms is not unlike that of the drapery of the Winged Victory of Samothrace. In contrast with Boccioni's creation, the one long, connected line of breast, torso, and limb on the Victory of Samothrace suggests a movement forward engaged in by the entire figure. Since both sculptures are intended to suggest movement, the futurist gives us an explosive energy in all directions, which is of course one type of motion; the Greek masterpiece suggests an integrated forward thrust.

Union of Decorative and Individualistic Character in the Debussy Monument. The final union of decorative architectonic sculpture with technical expressive advances made by the futurists

Fig. 587.—Interior of "Battle of the Nations" Monument, Leipzig. Detail, Masks and Mourning Knights, by Franz Metzner, c. 1905.

may be found in the monument to the musician Claude Debussy, cast in yellow-rose cement for the city of Paris (Fig. 590). The two sculptors Joel and Jan Martel had as a definite commission that very ideal toward which Neo-Platonic Romantic art criticism had always striven—to make all arts approach the condition of music. Their difficulties were not lightened by the fact that the music of Debussy abounds in concrete images and lacks, relatively, the element of rhythm. Its chief characteristic lies in its remarkably harmonious chords. Using as pictorial subjects Debussy's chief tone poems—*The Sunken Cathedral, The*

Afternoon of a Faun, Pelleas and Melisande, and *St. Sebastian*—the Martels succeeded in gently weaving shallow planes of abstract technomorphic designs like those in colorful stained glass.

music, action, poetic diction, and staging could each contribute equally to the ensemble. Nietzsche's theory of drama, derived in part from Schopenhauer, considered music as the dy-

FIG. 588.—Apollo and the Muses, by Antoine Bourdelle, Théâtre des Champs-Élysées, 1912. (*Photograph by Hachette.*)

Thus one area seems to dissolve into another, as do musical chords. Compare this with the Gothic sculpture (Fig. 374, Chap. XIII) which has similar intent and effect. It would be hard to imagine plastic form coming any closer than this to the mystical lyricism of the composer.

Drama

The New Concept of Drama. Realism, as defined in the medieval Scholastic sense, becoming the dominant dramatic style at the close of the 19th century, still saw a possible ideal future for struggling man. When realists, following the paths of introspective analysis, focused the spotlight upon evils caused by man's inability to overcome inherited thought patterns or to transcend an unfavorable spiritual environment, they were known as "naturalists." The 20th-century plays of the great realist and naturalist writers could not have been produced without the formation in Paris and Germany of many new theatrical enterprises which strove to produce experimentally plays whose plots had a distinct social message.

The two most influential persons in the formation of 20th-century theatrical style were the composer Wagner and his critic, the philosopher Nietzsche. The latter thought of himself as a tragedian. With these two dynamic individuals there came into the theater a desire to revive the ancient Greek type of performance, in which

namic soul or will which should generate the action or the rhythm moving the characters. Music, according to Wagner, needed most of all appropriate scenery and lighting that would aid in visualizing dramatic tensions. Eventually, rhythmical color-lighting effects and scenery changes came to have value as high as the action and poetry, thus changing the relative values given to these parts by Aristotle.

The first two great scenic artists to grasp the principles of Wagner and Nietzsche were Adolph Appia and Gordon Craig. Appia staged many Wagnerian operas, while Craig brought the plays of Shakespeare and Ibsen to a peak of effectiveness never before experienced. Both Appia and Craig reduced scenic details to a few essential monumental forms. Craig explained his method, which underlies most realistic and expressionistic staging, in his book *On the Art of the Theatre*. To be effective, Craig advised the designer to study the play carefully for a full understanding of the poet's meaning, afterward allowing the scenery to grow out of the universal thought passages which it stimulates. Craig said that *Macbeth* calls for high rocks and fierce, warlike men, with a gray mist enveloping all (Fig. 591). In his production of Ibsen's *Brand,* the sublime rugged contour of the fjords was used to symbolize the flinty character of the hero. After Craig, it became a rule that scenery must enhance the play by its symbolic value. Lighting also played a great part in the work of Craig and continued to do so thereafter. The abstract, vanishing lines of a Gothic cathedral could in one colorful lighting suggest, under rainbow hues, man's aspiration.

Fig. 589.—Unique Forms of Continuity in Space, by Umberto Boccioni, 1913. Bronze, height 40 inches (Museum of Modern Art). (*Courtesy of Museum of Modern Art.*)

Differently lighted, with dark purples, these same lines might be made to appear depressing, suggestive of horror and mystery. Craig also taught in his Florentine school of theatrical art, what he thought to be his new concept of the *régisseur*—a director who would be at the same time poet, scenic artist, musician, and actor. The first great practical *régisseur* was the Austrian, Max Reinhardt, who tempered symbolism in staging with naturalism. His early, well-known productions were Oscar Wilde's *Salome*, afterward set to music by Richard Strauss, and Tolstoy's *The Living Corpse*. Later, he was active as a theatrical revolutionary,

Fig. 590—*Below*, Debussy Monument, by Jan and Joel Martel, Paris (*photograph by Reifenberg*); *above*, detail (*photograph by Debretagne, after Agard, The New Architectural Sculpture*).

building the great theater (Grosses Schauspiel-haus) of Berlin, in 1919.

In France a number of little art theaters grew up about 1890. The best known were the

FIG. 591.—Scene for a Shakespearean drama, after the manner of Gordon Craig.

Théâtre Libré of André Antoine and the Théâtre de l'Oeuvre of Lugné Poe. These produced hundreds of experimental plays. Jacques Copeau's Théâtre du Vieux-Colombier (Fig. 592) had a very significant, intimate stage, which seemed to grow out of the audience room. In Germany, about 1890, revolutionary movements created the *Freie Volksbühne*, or People's Free Theater. After the war, German revolutionary groups called the Spartacus Bund produced, before an audience of 50,000, such mass dramas of revolt as *Der Arme Conrad*, a story of an uprising of peasants in 1514. Many of these vitalizing experiments employed staging devices and electric lighting tending to more closely identify the actors with the audience.

In Russia the Moscow Art Theater of Constantin Stanislavski and the Imperial Theater and Opera House in St. Petersburg, under Meyerhold, developed many remarkable sym-

bolic dramas, such as Maeterlinck's *Death of Tintagiles* and *The Blue Bird*, and Gordon Craig's production of *Hamlet*. Founded in the nineties, the Moscow Art Theater first produced the

FIG. 592.—The "intimate" stage of the Vieux-Colombier Théâtre, Paris. (*Courtesy of Yale University School of Drama.*)

plays of the naturalists, Maxim Gorki, Hauptmann, and Chekhov. Stanislavski perfected a remarkable rhythmical style in acting, combining a revival of Molière's techniques with naturalistic drama.

Social and Psychological Backgrounds. Modern European drama has its chief roots in industrial unrest, commercial wars, and a continuation of 19th-century Romantic individualism. Thus 20th-century drama, like that of the great Greek tragedians, of Shakespeare, and Molière, clearly parallels the other significant artistic discoveries of the period. Most critics differentiate between realistic, naturalist, symbolic, and expressionistic dramas. To these should perhaps be added an impressionistic drama in the works of Vildrac. Romanticism persists as a mood derived from earlier centuries, being continually present as an escape into a more heroic existence.

Realism and the Plays of Henrik Ibsen. Insofar as it contrasts with the prevailing Romantic mood of the 19th century, the roots of 20th-century drama can be found in the plays of Henrik Ibsen. His realistic drama, usually proposing a problem to be solved, can be considered as the logical descendant of the medieval morality play. In Ibsen's strongly autobiographical *Peer Gynt*, one sees the Viking individualist fated, like Wagner's Flying Dutchman, to endless journeying around the world in search of his own salvation. Nora, in *A Doll's House*, is a woman fighting against the conventions of the Victorian home to achieve status as a personality. Through other of Ibsen's plays —*Ghosts*, *The Master Builder*, *When We Dead Awaken*—interest is held not only by the portrayal of character but by dramatic tensions rising from the display of a thesis, determination to overcome poor heredity and environment, with its antithesis, one's own defects. The tragedy usually results through inability to make a happy synthesis.

Under Ibsen's influence, at the beginning of the century his compatriot Björnstjerne Björnson, as well as the British writers Arthur Wing Pinero, Henry Arthur Jones, Bernard Shaw, and John Masefield; the German Gerhart Hauptmann; and the Frenchman Henri Becque, also wrote realistic dramas. In Italy Roberto Bracco carried on the tradition. The method of the realist appears at its best in Björnson's play *Beyond Our Power*, written in 1883, first performed in the Parisian Théâtre Libré in 1893. Here ultimate healing for human woes was sought through the miraculous.

Björnson's Play, Beyond Our Power, as a Typical Realistic Drama. In *Beyond Our Power*, a Norwegian pastor, Adolf Sang, has found that his great faith can work miracles. His ailing wife, Clara, alone can find no cure, but seems fated to suffer throughout the play in order that she may finally bear witness to some supermiracle that will make the entire world return to its belief in God. Finally, in bringing about the miracle that cures the wife of her illness before great crowds of pilgrims, both Sang and Clara are killed.

The aesthetic philosophy implied in realistic plays is that of Hegel, who held that a truly dramatic character is one suffering chiefly because of his own misdeeds and his inability to reach the ultimate perfection in a higher order of things. Napoleon, in Thomas Hardy's epic drama *The Dynasts*, is such a tragic character. Though desirous of bringing the entire world into one orderly state, Napoleon is continually defeated, inwardly by his own imperfections and outwardly by the English prime ministers. In order to gain effect, most realistic playwrights like Ibsen, Björnson, and Shaw use long monologues that are interesting, often witty, explanations of their ideas. The plays are correspondingly weak in action and many of them can be read with almost as much pleasure as they can be seen. In this they contrast with the naturalistic drama, which is more interesting when produced.

The Naturalists. The naturalistic drama developed out of the realistic early in the 20th century. In it man appears to seek salvation, not from the terrors of nature or a physical death, but from the horrors of self-murder and that pessimism which accompanies his futile struggle with his inherited defects and unfavorable spiritual environment. In the realm of prose fiction, the greatest naturalistic novel early in the century is Dostoyevsky's *The Idiot*. It presents a careful psychological analysis of the way in which a series of lies can undermine a character, causing what the psychiatrist knows as "schizophrenia," or a split personality.

The most brilliant naturalist playwrights were the Russians Count Ilya Tolstoy, Maxim Gorki, Anton Chekhov, and the German Gerhart Hauptmann. The philosophy underlying the naturalistic play may be found in Tolstoy's essay *What Is Art?* and in his novel *The Kreutzer Sonata*, where the thesis is held that art should no longer, like the academic art of official Russia, be "the opiate of the people" or a vain pursuit of beauty, but a means of quickening human sympathy. The naturalist believes that man's abnormalities can be overcome by exposing their sources in mistaken ideas. His tragedy arises from the fact that the enlightenment comes too late to prevent crime. The course of naturalistic tragedy is thus inevitably downward in its tone and completely pessimistic.

The Eclecticism of Gerhart Hauptmann. The greatest German naturalist playwright was a leader of the *Freie Volksbühne*—Gerhart Hauptmann. In attempting to show that the lives of the lower classes hold as much, if not more, tragic material than those of the upper classes, Hauptmann subordinated strength of plot to the development of character. He discovered, as Aristotle had years before, that people of all classes are interested in observation and recognition for their own sake. He chose as his subject the everyday doings of ordinary people, and saw the human tragedy resulting from heredity reacted upon by environment. In his best known social drama, *The Weavers*, Hauptmann tells of the struggle of oppressed workers against dominating industrialists. His hero is no one person, but the mass action of the strike. As he grew older, this successful playwright posed as a reincarnation of Goethe, so instead of finding expressionism, as more alert individuals were doing, he embraced Neo-Romanticism and lived in the gold-and-ivory tower of success.

Impressionism; the Plays of Vildrac and Wedekind. In the field of drama, one type of naturalism which required great skill in the depiction of character or description of scene led to a theory that drama had as its sole purpose an entertainment through the simple display of a number of interesting situations. From this philosophy there resulted plays lacking in active plot and ideational content, often quite charming, which might be called impressionist dramas. Many of the works of Claudel, Duhamel, Lenormand, and Charles Vildrac represent this impressionist movement—for the greater part, French in origin—whose productions were associated particularly with the Théâtre du Vieux-Colombier in Paris.

The impressionistic drama rubs elbows with another more intellectual type—the symbolic play. When a playwright such as Paul Claudel dips into the Romantic subject matter of the Middle Ages as in *The Tidings Brought to Mary*, Impressionism under the changing magic of stage lighting appears as symbolic drama. Here all the naturalistic characters have dual meaning as symbols.

The impressionist critic, at times asserting that the chief purpose of drama is simply to amuse, can be found, like the weathercock usually turning in the opposite direction, to hope that his amusement may aid society by making the audience feel compassion for their fellow men. Here is a sort of analogy to Aristotle's theory of catharsis. The stage characters of Claudel, Maeterlinck, Andreyev, and Pirandello—all Symbolists—present the essence of human frustration on a naturalistic level while speaking in poetic overtones suggesting an unrealistic dream life. Close to the plays of Vildrac and Claudel are those of the German Franz Wedekind—*The Awakening of Spring*, *Earth Spirit*, *The Heart of a Tenor*, *Pandora's Box*, and *Such Is Life*.

Symbolist Drama; the Plays of Maeterlinck and Pirandello. Symbolist drama finds in every action and thought a double meaning. Like the symbolic realism of the Middle Ages, it considers every object to be not only a natural appearance but the image of some greater power. In Symbolic drama man appears to be always on the border of another world, so that he has two aspects like the objects in surrealist painting. The greatest dramatist in this field was the Belgian mystic poet and empirical scientist, Maurice Maeterlinck, who as the leader of the Symbolist poets spent most of his life in Paris. For melodramatic action, which he considered detrimental, Maeterlinck substituted an interaction of emotional states symbolized by dream images of universal significance. That he actually dramatized the subconscious mind can be seen in his plays, *The Blind*, *Intruder*, *The Death of Tintagiles*, and *Pelleas and Melisande*.

In *Pelleas and Melisande*, a charming, half-awakened, timid girl gradually falls in love with her brother-in-law. Her husband, King Golaud, after destroying both his brother and his wife, is eventually overcome by his own jealousy. Most of the speeches and situations in this play are rich in the *double entendre* of Molière, which here appears in a new form as Symbolism.

In the dramas of Pirandello, another Symbolist, one seems to move with Lewis Carroll's heroine Alice through a looking-glass world. Naturally, for such drama one needs settings and improved lighting facilities that suggest, rather than depict actualities. The Symbolists first used changeable stage paints which, under one lighting, showed a forest scene and, under another, a palace interior. They also used the music of Debussy and other impressionists to charm the audience into ready acquiescence with a dreamlike mood. Thus the efforts of the Symbolists can be closely seen to follow the experiments of the Romantic Wagner.

The final development of Symbolism, in which all actions had a double meaning, depicted man as a multiple personality. In Italy, following Marinetti's "Futurist Manifesto" of 1909, several Italian playwrights used grotesquerie and the expressionistic effects of unrelated word passages or actions to symbolize a growing skepticism and revolt. These futurists sought to show that no clear line of demarcation exists between the normal and the abnormal. They were greatly influenced in their psychology by the theories of the Italian criminologist Lombroso, the French critic Max Nordau, and the Viennese psychiatrist Sigmund Freud.

Pirandello's *Henry IV* depicts an insane man who, having suddenly become sane, is forced to continue feigning insanity in order to gain protection from a sane world, which threatens to destroy him. In *Six Characters in Search of an Author*, Pirandello made the characters appear more real than either the man who brings them together or the audience that watches them. In the works of Pirandello one finds graphic presentation of Oscar Wilde's doctrine that "Art makes life." Such playwrights consider that the theater has a greater reality than life itself, perhaps because the play is a unified performance, while incomprehensible life is only "an evil dream."

Expressionism in Modern Drama. Expressionism began in the naturalist works of Strindberg and Andreyev. It reached its height in the plays of Capek, Kaiser, and Chlumberg, with the central thesis that unless man can actively remake his social order he must inevitably destroy himself. That expressionism seems revolutionary and dangerous can be seen by the fact that the totalitarian states have forbidden it. It died out in Russia as Communism gave way to ruthless despotism.

By most critics the Swedish playwright August Strindberg is considered the author of expressionism in modern drama. Strindberg, a singularly unhappy individual whose life bordered upon insanity, experimented, much as Picasso did in painting, with all types of dramatic production from realism through Symbolism. More than any other dramatist, Strindberg consciously used the stage as an instrument for expressing his own inner conflicts. Thus his plays illustrate the fundamental aesthetic ideal of the Italian philosopher Benedetto Croce, who considered art to be primarily a matter of self-expression. Strindberg's expressionistic mood appears in his trilogy, *Toward Damascus*, and in *The Spook Sonata*.

Leonid Andreyev's *The Red Laugh*, a short novel about the battlefields of the Russo-Japanese War, is the first dramatic narrative to describe man's spiritual disintegration under the impact of mechanized mass murder. Andreyev's plays present no new plot. His clown He, in *He Who Gets Slapped*, decides to mock the world by laughing at it, but losing his real personality, finally escapes all contact with life. The man-as-clown symbol (Pagliacci) unites with the idea of the puppet woman, half doll, half human, earlier found in *The Tales of Hoffmann*. The two symbols appear more powerful because the clown and the doll from time to time almost escape their environment into a world of poetic idealism where they show their highest potentialities. Bits from Andreyev's dialogue show an awareness of the complete upset of values in modern art and life.

The clown, on first entering his new world, says "How strange it all is!" and is answered by another clown, "Here all is strange." After living in this unreal world for a time, He, when asked for a reason for his actions, simply puts his fingers to his nose, saying "This is my reason." Here a Dadaist element expresses succinctly that proposition of the modern sophisticated artist which makes of art a childish protest. The last scene, when He poisons the bareback rider Consuelo and himself, simply recapitulates Wagner's love-death scene from *Tristan and Isolde*, in a jazz environment.

The Works of Kaiser; Man-and-Machine Drama. The most powerful expressionist dramas—those of Karel Capek, Hans Chlumberg, and George Kaiser—deal with the problem of war and peace, man's struggle with the machine, or his attempts to cope with all the disintegrative forces of industrialism at once. Karel Capek's *R U R*, or *Rossum's Universal Robots*, describes half-human mechanical monsters who eventually destroy humanity. In this play the author contrasts the willed actions of human beings with the mechanical will-less action of the Robots. In Hans Chlumberg's *Miracle of Verdun*, the dead of the World War return to life to find themselves unwanted. Here the actions of the ghosts are mechanical and aimless; their speeches, disconnected, so that they contrast with the more passionate utterances and actions of the living. In George Kaiser's trilogy, *Coral*, *Gas I*, and *Gas II*, the mood of the successive plays changes from symbolic naturalism to almost complete expressionism. Kaiser uses all the tricks of staging and melodrama to depict a world which, dominated by an industrial machine, finally goes mad and destroys itself.

Neo-Romanticism. Escaping from the realities presented by expressionist plays, the Neo-Romantics allowed themselves to use the old Romantic subject matter with a modicum of realism and humor, in order to provide amusing tragicomedies. The first and greatest of the Neo-Romantics, Edmond Rostand, started the century with *Cyrano de Bergerac*, the story of an inspired poet and brave soldier cursed with a nose so large that he was the jest of all who knew him. Because every modern feels himself to have some tragic defect, symbolized by the nose of Cyrano, Rostand's was the most successful play at the turn of the century. In *L'Aiglon*, the story of Napoleon's son, he tells of a youth who hopelessly strove to be as great a man as his father. This tale had a source of tragedy almost universal in the homes of industrial leaders. Both plays, ministering to a universal inferiority complex, also contain splendid stage devices, making certain audience reaction, and both have admirable construction. In *Chantecler* birds and animals with human failings satirize the human race as did those in Aristophanes' drama, *The Birds*.

Other typical Neo-Romantic plays were d'Annunzio's *Francesca da Rimini* and Vollmöller's *The Miracle*. Ferenc Molnar, a Hungarian writer, had a Neo-Romanticism with a satirical naturalistic flavor desired by postwar audiences. *The Swan* introduces a new sentimental character type, the beloved old philanthropist, usually a retired banker or "The Man Who Played God." In Neo-Romanticism one also finds, as in Cyrsky's *The Dybbuk*, a girl possessed by a phantom lover. There are other plays about vampirous individuals, such as *Dracula* and *Death Takes a Holiday*. Molnar's *Carnival*, *Liliom*, *The Guardsman*, and *The Red Mill* all have a delightful wit, which for their writer spelled financial success.

The New Comedies of Manners. Outside the above category are the works of a number of brilliant playwrights successful primarily not because of any depth of thought or feeling but because of a sophisticated wit. Most representative was the Viennese physician, Arthur Schnitzler. He, like Rabelais, had leisure to describe the human comedy. A naturalist without a thesis, Schnitzler is gently cynical, an impressionist in manner. In *Anatol*, *The Lonely Way*, and *Light of Love*, he pictures the blasé who already have begun to show a lack of driving will or direction because of their moral laxity. Schnitzler invented a new dramatic form, the one-act play, in which brilliant dialogue and concentrated action lead to a good curtain at the end of half an hour.

Schnitzler suggested delicately the motives which the Frenchman Henri René Lenormand boldly put into his plays, *The Coward, Possessed, The Dreamer of Dreams*, and *Man and His Phantoms*. The last was a psychoanalysis of Don Juan, more subjective than Rostand's. Lenormand's personality closely paralleled that of Gauguin and most of his work concerns the erotic fantasy of his own mind.

Modern Drama in England. Two admirers of Henrik Ibsen—Arthur Wing Pinero and Henry Arthur Jones—presented the English stage with its first vital drama after Sheridan's *School for Scandal. Saints and Sinners*, produced by Jones in 1884, gave England its first problem play. Pinero, a master of stagecraft, through *The Second Mrs. Tanqueray* told the story of a woman striving vainly to escape an unsavory past. The social satire of Pinero is but a short step from the infinitely more interesting comedies of George Bernard Shaw.

Shaw, a Fabian socialist and literary propagandist, brilliantly presents his advanced ideas through witty plays abounding in long philosophical monologues. If Ibsen could be called the Aeschylus of modern drama, Shaw would certainly be its Aristophanes. His first great thesis play, *Mrs. Warren's Profession*, tells the story of people influenced by an unsocial environment or striving to escape one. In *Candida*, the reformer, in the person of the Reverend James Morrell, is held up for inspection. The thesis that true nobility can rise from even gutter society is ably defended in *Pygmalion*, eventually produced by Shaw as a remarkable motion picture. In a host of successive plays Shaw developed a realism more balanced and less tragic than that of Ibsen.

Possibly of even more importance as an all-round dramatic genius is Sir James Barrie, whose comedy *What Every Woman Knows* presents the first example of the eternal triangle play. The success of his *Peter Pan*—a romantic,

whimsical, child's play akin to Maeterlinck's *Blue Bird* and Humperdinck's opera *Hansel and Gretel*—bears witness to a strange tendency on the part of mature 20th-century minds to find delight in sentimental fairy tales written primarily for children. *The Admirable Crichton* sets forth that even servants may be human. Here the most perfect butler ever conceived, cast away with his "betters" in primitive surroundings, rises above them by means of his native talents and greater presence of mind. This play cleverly combines romance, comedy, and social satire.

John Galsworthy, the novelist, presented great thesis dramas in *Strife* and *Justice*. John Masefield, the poet, wrote *The Tragedy of Nan* and *Melloney Hotspur*. Somerset Maugham, a third novelist, produced *The Constant Wife* and *The Sacred Flame*. John Drinkwater, a writer of historical plays, is best known for his *Abraham Lincoln*. Noel Coward brought the comedy of manners up to date with brilliant dialogue and catchy music in *Design for Living* and *Private Lives*, both of which deal in new ways with the problem of the eternal triangle and divorce. His more serious *Cavalcade* dwells upon English history from the Boer War to recent events. In general, Coward's world and characters—the smart set of London and a sophisticated society whose delight is in clever cynicism—are the English counterpart of Schnitzler's.

One great English tragedy comparable to the works of Shakespeare and Ibsen arose from the World War scene in Robert Cedric Sheriff's *Journey's End*. This tells the story of a heroic group of doomed English officers in the trenches. The naturalistic depth and keen knowledge of human character in this play furnished a note of sobriety in the jazz world.

Music

Before the 19th century music shows little interest either in dramatic tensions set up by the addition of new instrumental tones to the orchestras or the planned use of dissonant and complex chords. Wagner's dramatic music marked a beginning of the use of contrasting tones, without progressing so far as to create unsupportable dynamic tensions, or over-naturalistic effects.

The Importance of Instrumental Timbre. During the Romantic development, musicians became increasingly aware of the value of distinctive tone, or instrumental timbre. For the Romantic, these tones were still bound to old associational values from folk melodies or animal cries. Musicians such as Berlioz and Liszt used timbre in the more suggestive passages of their newly developed free-musical forms, such as the symphonic poems. Twentieth-century writers, hearing a whole new world of sound from industrial life, found instrumental timbres to suggest not only pleasant sounds but cacophonies and noises. Thus instrumental timbre may be said to have become detached from its primary context in order that it might create new expressionistic effects.

An illustration of separate instrumental effects can be found on the specially prepared Victor phonograph records 20522A, 20523A, 20150A and B. The first and second reproduce modern orchestral instruments, the third and fourth present combinations that sound pleasant. Two instruments sound pleasant or unpleasant together depending on whether their overtones blend easily or not. Where effects of harmony and unity (in the greater sense) are desired, instruments are chosen whose overtones blend. Where effects of contrast and power are desired, instruments of dissimilar timbre must be chosen. Actually, any combination of instruments may be used effectively, providing that the amount of each timbre used, or its loudness when played, is taken into account by the composer.

After playing the above four records the student should listen to the various effects gained by different instruments considered as parts of complete compositions. The following selections have been found helpful. For plucked strings, or pizzicato effects, suggestive of lutes,

mandolins, or Russian balalaikas, the Scherzo of Tschaikowsky's *Fourth Symphony* will serve; for muted strings, the slow movement of the Debussy *Quartet in G minor.* Perhaps the most beautiful combination of muted violas and clarinet known is to be found in the second movement of Brahms's *Quintet in B minor* for clarinet and strings, opus 115. The Scherzo from Beethoven's *Fifth Symphony* shows what can be done with the double bass.

Among the wind instruments, flutes play an important part in the *Dance of the Mirlitons* from Tschaikowsky's *Nutcracker Suite.* The opening movement of Dvořák's *New World Symphony* has a splendid passage for the English horn, a species of double-reed instrument. The oboe, another double-reed instrument, descended from the ancient Greek *aulos*, plays a most important part in the last movement of Brahms's *Fourth Symphony.* The bassoon, considered to have a humorous quality, shows best in the Mozart *Concerto for Bassoon and Orchestra.* The French horn, an enlarged trumpet form, appears in the Nocturne from Mendelssohn's *Midsummer Night's Dream Overture.* A muted trumpet has been used effectively in Wagner's *Ride of the Valkyries* and in the *Till Eulenspiegel* of Richard Strauss.

Kettledrums serve only to introduce the first movement of Brahms's *First Symphony,* but Ravel, a 20th-century composer, used them persistently throughout his *Bolero.* Modern composers on the whole magnify and overstress the single effects, while the older men save these effects for dramatic heightening in some part of a monumentally conceived work. Composers like Debussy and Strauss, who stand between the romanticism of the 19th and the realism of the 20th century, started with strong form or structure, like the older composers, but used increasingly the dramatic effects of timbre as their art developed. This movement in music corresponds to the rise of Impressionism in painting. The little section for the harp and the flute in Debussy's *Afternoon of a Faun* or the tones of the celesta in the *Dance of the Sugarplum*

FIG. 593.—Chord with dissonance from the Passion music by Johann Sebastian Bach.

Fairy from Tschaikowsky's *Nutcracker Suite* will serve to demonstrate how timbre may be used in Impressionism. Before studying further in 20th-century music one should listen carefully to the above or similar timbre effects. He should then be prepared to observe how most modern composers have removed these effects from their original context to use them as bright spots of color either in an impression of the new industrial world or as an expression of revolt from it. Parts of Stravinsky's *Rite of Spring* and Arthur Honneger's *Pacific 231*—the former, a primitive nature dance; the latter, a locomotive effect—sound almost alike. The first is an example of modern Expressionism; the second, of Impressionism.

Changes in Structure Due to the Rise of the Concept of the Expanding Chord. In the works of such masters as Bach and Handel the various melodies moving along in contrapuntal arrangement keep a relatively thin linear character which stresses the tone of each instrument. This demands on the part of the hearer an almost intellectual regard for the quality and combination of tones produced. As their music progressed, contrast in the relative distance between outside voices, or the loudness of the tones produced was limited. However, in the great choral works of these masters, dramatic effects are sometimes achieved by volume of sound. Finally, the cadence appeared simply as a necessary termination to the melody, when the composer considered that his fugue was ended.

As the symphony developed, more attention was given to that contrast achieved by considering some chords as rich expansive sets of overtones, produced by as many as twenty instruments at once, and weaker chords of only a few notes, played upon two or three instruments. Romantic music in its striving for dramatic effect conceived the chord as an expanding dynamic thing which reached its greatest climax in a rich, full volume of sound, capable of stirring or even shattering the emotion. The chord might eventually be resolved in a cadence which would rest the senses by suggesting peace or, more often, allowed to suggest still further expansion or aspiration by being left unresolved, as in the Prelude to *Lohengrin.*

The final stage in the development of European music came with the recognition that the dynamic chords, with their varying degrees of contrast between harmonic unity or disharmonic cacophony, could be employed in any composition. The theory underlying this type of music can be found in the writings of Scriabin, Schönberg, and the American critic Ezra Pound, who held that "There are no two chords which may not follow each other, if the sequence of time intervals and durations is correct."[1] The late Romantic musicians of the 19th and 20th centuries also discovered that

[1] EZRA POUND, *Antheil*, Pascal Covici, Pub., Chicago, 1927.

FIG. 594a.—Chromatic passage by Schubert.

unpleasant sounds could make pleasant sounds appear of greater value by contrast. That this was no new thing we may be sure, when we notice that Bach in the Passion music used chords such as Fig. 593 to describe the intense anguish of Christ. The difference is that modern musicians, living in an unmusical world of machinery driven to express disharmony, have used far greater numbers of such chords and more violent contrasts.

The Chromatic Progressions of César Franck. With César Franck began a movement away from the theatricalism of Richard Wagner and back toward the interweave of voices that characterizes the work of Bach. Franck, a Belgian organist who spent most of his life in Paris, derived from his studies of Bach, Beethoven, and Wagner a combination style. In Franck's work delicate voices gradually expand like opening flowers into tonal harmonies which resolve into other flowering, delicate structures,

until the composition seems like a richly embroidered tapestry of sound. The chief means used by César Franck to gain an effect in music which parallels that of the impressionists Monet and Renoir in painting was a conception of modulation borrowed from Schubert, Fig. 594a.

Schubert and Beethoven developed several ways of modulating by means of chords, with one or two elements from the old key moving over gradually toward the new key, in order to make a smooth, pleasant transition necessary for the development of a sonata or a symphony. Franck discovered that a strong assertion of tone in a full chord of the new key could be made without the intervening modulations, providing that it followed a thin tone in a previous key. For years new conceptions of modulation drew from the critics an echo of Gounod's words on first hearing them, "They result simply from incompetence or weakness." Actually, it seems now as though Franck had

FIG. 594b.—César Franck passage from D minor Symphony.

begun to discover what Pound expressed, or perhaps to rediscover an old law, namely, that the most discordant intervals possible might be played successively, provided that one had the proper time interval to allow the overtones to blend, or provided that the attention were taken from the discord by a striking rhythmical effect. Playing these passages (Fig. 594b) over will show their close approximation to what is known as American "swing" time or "blues" playing.

It must not be thought that Franck's music, because of its tendency toward impressionistic colorful romantic passages, lacks the firm structure of the dramatic symphonic form. Franck's great *Symphony in D minor*, a composition worthy of Beethoven, proved to be an inspiration for most of the impressionists who followed. Few of these ever reached the sublimity and firmness of Franck's mighty composition.

Claude Debussy and the Impressionists. Possibly influenced by Franck's masterly employment of chromatic progressions, Claude Debussy, a French musician interested in the Symbolist poetry of Mallarmé, completely developed what is usually known as Impressionism in music. Imagining the various scales as differing colors in a palette, Debussy perceived that to depict such effects in nature as those described by Corot or painted by such men as Monet and Manet, he must be able to move freely from one scale to another without any set system of modulation. His music, like the canvases of the impressionists, must suggest not structural form but a world saturated with color. Debussy achieved a full palette by combining the whole-tone scale with pentatonic scales and the ordi-

nary scales, to paint a number of tone pictures which he, following the example of Monet, entitled *Impressions.* Among these one finds for the orchestra *The Clouds;* for the piano, *Gardens in the Rain, Mists, Reflections in the Water,* and *Footsteps in the Snow* (Fig. 594c).

With Debussy there came into music a further development of Liszt and Berlioz's idea of the symphonic tone poem. Best known are his series of three symphonic sketches, *The Sea, Iberia,* and *Prelude to the Afternoon of a Faun. The Sea* includes in its first part a view *From Dawn till Noon;* in the second part, *The Play of the Waves;* and in the third part, a *Dialogue between the Wind and the Sea.* His *Iberia* first describes the *Streets and Pathways;* next, *The Perfumes of the Night;* and third, *The Festival Morning.*

Two works by Debussy, which best illustrate his connection with the Symbolist school of poets, his *Prelude to the Afternoon of a Faun* and his opera *Pelleas and Melisande,* have a complex structure. In them he uses not only his whole-tone scale but also whatever effects he needs of a rhythmical or a melodic nature from the various types of music that preceded his. Debussy's music, having to do with vague, almost ethereal effects, does not rely upon any strict

p très doux
(very sweet)

FIG. 594c.—Debussy passage using whole-tone scale.

form, like the sonata form underlying the symphony.

In striving to differentiate among 20th-century composers, one discovers each of them either unconsciously or consciously striving for an individualistic style, which in a way indicates a revolt from some previous style. Paul Dukas, although influenced by the impressionist Debussy, belongs to what might be called an expressionist school, comparable to painters like Cézanne and Van Gogh. Dukas's *Sorcerer's Apprentice* introduces again a strong element of naturalism, using clashing tones and harsh descriptive effects such as are found in the works of Berlioz. Of this particular mode of composition, the greatest exponent among French composers is Maurice Ravel; among Germans, Richard Strauss; and among Russians, Scriabin and Stravinsky. Dukas was noted for a certain piquant quality of his orchestration. Ravel excels through judicious use of tone color woven about a number of early Provençal, Basque, or Spanish dance forms, such as the bolero, the pavane, and the saraband. He also uses impressionistic passages comparable to those of Debussy.

The final degree of Impressionism in French music can be found in the works of Arthur Honneger, whose *Pacific 231* gives a description of a locomotive. This unites the noises of escaping steam, rhythms suggestive of flashing piston rods, and the dynamic rush of an iron monster.

Dynamic Naturalism and the Expressionism of Richard Strauss. Richard Strauss, the most powerful of the expressionist musicians, started as a direct follower of Richard Wagner, developing the symphonic poem to its greatest extent by applying the idea of the leitmotiv to this Romantic substitute for the symphony. With a mastery of orchestration and a knowledge of symphonic form as great as that of Beethoven, Strauss duplicated the discoveries of Debussy and Franck by weaving together a magnificent contrapuntal arrangement, which seemed to move through a series of discordant sounds. Actually, Strauss's music has periods of discord followed by short periods of concord, so that one seems to recognize little melodies, which never quite come to any conclusion. This was

no new thing; the Prelude to Wagner's *Tristan and Isolde* has practically no long periods of concord, but is simply an enormously expanded fugue.

To suggest action, humor, horror, delight, or disgust, Strauss uses harmonic progressions completely at variance with all the established rules. He has no aversion to playing one melody of counterpoint in one key and the other in a different key. His tone poem *Also sprach Zarathustra* ends in both B major and C major. Strauss's best known works include the symphonic fantasies, *Aus Italien, Macbeth, Don Juan, Tod und Verklärung, Till Eulenspiegel, Also sprach Zarathustra, Don Quixote* and *Ein Heldenleben*. *Till Eulenspiegel* tells the story of a merry baker's apprentice whose pranks eventually get him into trouble. *Also sprach Zarathustra* tells of the daring philosophy of the superman. Debussy needed for his expression a whole-tone scale which gave a definite mood value like a Greek musical mode. Strauss wanders at will through all the scales, dominated by strong rhythmic modulations of concord and discord. His work, although it has fewer charming passages, can be compared closely with Franck's symphony.

In the Nietzschean tone poem, *Also sprach Zarathustra*, Strauss was essentially the philosopher. In *Till Eulenspiegel, Don Quixote*, and *Ein Heldenleben* he shows his Romantic side. A third Strauss can be found in his *Domestic Symphony*. Here the naturalist uses his Gargantuan orchestra to tell a humorous story of the household. In his operas, *Salome* and *Elektra*, the new sound media are used to express the morbid visions of Wilde and the primitive savagery of the vengeful Elektra. This last opera comes nearest to Nietzsche and Richard Wagner's dream of dynamic music, words, action, and scenery, together expressing the same theme.

Its shocking character appears from the start in the shrieking, dissonant chord on which the curtain rises. With a tempo rivaling that of the most thrilling screen gangster story, there follows for an hour and a half the cruel revenge of King Agamemnon's half-mad daughter. The effect of insanity is achieved by using broken melodies, partly joined, only to be again separated. The most restful part of the entire opera is the love duet between Elektra and her brother Orestes, which seems like a tabloid version of Wagner's *Tristan and Isolde*.

Schönberg and the Intellectualization of Music. If Franck and Debussy may be considered the impressionists of music, Strauss and Ravel its expressionists, then Schönberg and Scriabin can be thought of as its cubists and suprematists, the men who seek to express themselves through geometric figures. Schönberg's monumental *Theory of Harmony* attempts to show that logically the postimpressionists of music used such advanced chords as the ninth, tenth, eleventh and the thirteenth, allowing the composer to combine any sets of sounds. Schönberg noticed that in the beginnings of theoretical harmony convention allowed only the octave and the fifth and that as music progressed composers consistently used smaller and smaller harmonic intervals. Each new invention was at first condemned and then accepted by the critical writers.

The theory underlying the first part of Schönberg's *Theory of Harmony* recapitulates the development of the chord from Bach to Wagner. It is valuable in pointing out that the strongest possible movement of contrapuntal melodies proceeds according to almost mathematically necessary laws. In the second part of his work, Schönberg proposed that since the chords may theoretically be of any degree, obviously scales can be built upon any intervals. He suggested a system of chords using superposed fourths instead of thirds. Keeping to this rigid geometric formula, Schönberg produced music with a structure of sounds so complex that only dissonances result.

Schönberg and his followers at first strove to write their music by rule, without respect to the sounds produced. Obsessed with the old Platonic idea that music is closely allied to mathematics, they produced such a work as *Pierrot Lunaire*, which almost corresponds to futurism

or the works of Picasso and Kandinsky. Schönberg's experiments led to the foundation of a new twelve-tone scale similar to some of the Indian Ragas, with no leading or tonic note and no internal relationship. His most understandable work, the *Verklärte Nacht*, is an example of romanticism before he followed his own teachings to their logical conclusion. The *Gurrelieder* written in his later style, has 114 orchestral parts and two choruses, one of eight, the other of twelve parts, with five solo voices and a reader.

Schönberg's theories reach their consummation in the works of his followers—Alban Berg, Paul Hindemith, and Anton von Webern in Germany; Darius Milhaud in France; and Manuel de Falla in Spain.

In his proletarian opera *Wozzeck*, Berg arranged a recitative accompanied by an orchestra which uses the conventional forms of the fugue and variations. This he combines with Schönberg's atonal scale. The chords produced are so powerful and so freed from all pleasant associations as to make the hearer deeply unhappy. They definitely express the filth and terror of a sordid life in the slums, surpassing the most disagreeable passages in Strauss's *Elektra*.

Hindemith, more than any other of Schönberg's followers, shows the greatest personal development. His early works were strongly influenced by the masterful musical structures of Brahms. Next he experimented with the atonality of Debussy and Schönberg, while returning to Bach for strength in counterpoint and fugue. His one-act operas *St. Suzanna* and *Murder, Hope of Women* have a gripping power. To these he has added the strongly syncopated rhythms of American music, which he uses for an energetic display of the ugly and morbid side of life. His opera *Neues vom Tage* and Krenek's *Jonny Spielt Auf* characterize the jazz era of German life shortly after the World War. The latter deals with the ballroom adventures of a Negro orchestra leader.

Manuel de Falla's *Don Quixote* and Carrillo's

Cristobal Colón suggest fire sirens, with notes running through all the known scales, as well as a quarter-tone scale. Von Webern, who has been called the "master of the pianissimo," adopted Schönberg's principles, which he used with the greatest delicacy. His short pieces, like Debussy's *Preludes* and *Scenes*, include several *Impressions* for string quartets and trios.

The Russian Influence. Russia, with its diverse peoples, had, in contrast to European nations, the greatest background of folk melodies and the greatest variety of primitive scales. During the 19th century a national school of composers drew heavily upon these folk backgrounds with their indefinite melodic patterns. One of the early composers, Glinka, used the whole-tone scale, later developed by Debussy. Peter Ilyitch Tschaikowsky, trained in the German school and greatly influenced by Beethoven, used powerful primitive rhythmical effects and melodies from Slavic folk songs. Although he developed no new musical inventions, Tschaikowsky's well-constructed symphonies introduced the music of Russia to the Western world.

Like Tschaikowsky, Rimski-Korsakov, another Russian of Romantic temper, added little new to the development of music, although his experiments with musical timbre are worthy of notice as comparable to the work of Berlioz and Wagner. Rimski-Korsakov employed intricate Spanish rhythms and melodic themes in the *Capriccio Espagnol*, and Oriental scales to give atmosphere in the *Scheherezade*. Moussorgsky, whose nationalistic opera *Boris Godounoff* approximates the works of Wagner, proved an innovator with his impressionistic suite entitled *Pictures at an Exhibition*. Using the techniques of Debussy, Moussorgsky here reproduced a number of scenes from Russian life. Borodin, significant in the field of opera writing, produced *Prince Igor*. In this a number of dance rhythms called the *Polovetsian Dances*, from the steppes of Central Asia, played an important part in the development of modern rhythmical patterns. Rimski-Korsakov, Moussorgsky, and Borodin,

along with Balakireff and César Cui, formed a group called the "famous five" during the 1860's, to develop a Russian national style. Their works constitute a necessary background for the understanding of 20th-century music.

Following the lead of Glinka, Scriabin broke with these Romantics, using a chord structure based neither on the usual thirds nor upon Schönberg's superposed fourths, but upon fifths. In his *Prometheus* he attempted to unite music with color effect, using a specially constructed color organ for the purpose.

Scriabin was followed by Igor Stravinsky, who attacked music with the energy and joy of a primitive. Stravinsky brought to the most elemental, instinctive musical effects and folk melodies all the resources of the modern orchestra. Absorbing most of the modern ideas of Franck, Schönberg, Scriabin, and Debussy, Stravinsky produced a number of ballets, including *Petrouschka*, *The Fire Bird*, and the *Sacre du Printemps*.

Nationalism in 20th-century Music. The feeling of nationalism early discernible in 19th-century German, Polish, and Russian music accompanied the rediscovery of folk tunes, rhythms, and primitive scales. These played an increasingly important part in the development of 20th-century music. Smetana, a Czech composer living in the Austrian province of Bohemia, was known for his opera *The Bartered Bride* as well as for his impressive description of *The River Moldau*. The rhythm of the old Slavic folk dances animates all his music. Anton Bruckner, the Austrian composer, based many of his works upon the folk songs of his land. Karl Goldmark, the Hungarian, likewise used the rhythms of the czardas in his operas. Anton Dvořák, another Czech, uses Slavic rhythms and, in his *New World Symphony*, scales and rhythms suggestive of primitive American life. The Rumanian composer Georges Enesco is the latest of the moderns to use folk melodies. His *Rumanian Rhapsody* contains many strains derived from age-old Balkan dances, including the Ratta.

In Scandinavia, Edvard Grieg was the first to attempt well-composed symphonic structures based upon Norwegian folk music. In Finland, Jean Sibelius, trained in the strong German tradition of Brahms, wove many folk songs into such national epic works as *Finlandia*, *En Saga*, and *The Swan of Tuonela*.

The Spaniards, Isaac Albeniz and Enrique Granados, used native dances, many of which had their roots in Moorish music. Comparable to the work of these nationalists are the tuneful English operas of Sir Arthur Sullivan, based upon folk music, and the works of Vaughan Williams, who uses English modal folk songs.

Other representative composers in the modern style, who cannot be considered nationalists, are the Austrian Gustav Mahler, the Italian Ottorino Respighi, and the Englishman Edward Elgar. Mahler, following in the tradition of Brahms and Bruckner, created symphonies of tremendous scope. Respighi, in the tradition of Franck and Debussy, has composed many impressions, such as the *Pines of Rome*, which show the power of modern orchestration. The Englishman Cyril Scott, also following Debussy, like Anton von Webern exhibits a great delicacy in a number of impressionistic piano pieces with shifting tonalities. These bits of music have much the same spirit as Chinese lyric poetry.

Aesthetic Directions of the 20th Century

Twentieth-century creative individuals, striving to overcome the dichotomy of modern thought, labored with minds torn between a desire for absolute freedom and the necessity for spiritual cooperation. They hoped to get this by creating art which called for a self-discipline imposed by the formal nature of their creations. At the same time, they were loath to forsake the premise that the primary function of imaginative genius was to break the barriers of form. Faced by the unsatisfactory results of such unclarified purpose in modern art, the philosophical critics produced no coordinated, satisfying theory which could explain art's function and unique significance.

The various theories produced may be grouped in three classes—two distinctly unsocietal; the third, societal. This last is a historical evolutionary theory not yet completely formulated. The first of the two former, an experiential theory, holds that art is pure expression, inspiration, or any issue of the imagination. This, a Dionysian outlook, is allied with one phase of Nietzsche's thought. The second, an intellectual theory that art is pure form, is connected in modern times with the Apollonian aspect of Nietzsche's philosophy. The first appears as a survival of romanticism and the northern Gothic spirit; the second, as classical academicism and mathematical idealism. Visibly, the first appeared in expressionist and futurist art; the second, in cubism.

Several culture historians—notably Spengler, Wells, and Friedel—accepting general premises laid down by Hegel and Spencer, sought for new meaning in the relationship between developing styles and the evolution of human culture. Noteworthy among the aestheticians who took this historical point of view were Verworn, Worringer, Alois Riegl, and H. Woelfflin. None of these modern critics seemed to grasp the idea that the great work of art had a significance that must be approached by all three methods if it was to be completely understood. Behind 20th-century aesthetic theories lay a world of unclear assumptions and partly explained meanings, each with its peculiar associations, each in part valid, but none completely satisfying.

The sociohistorical critics considered the work of art primarily as the revelation of some great plan that could be understood on an intellectual level also. This idea underlies the monumental idealistic aesthetics of Hegel's follower, Bernard Bosanquet. Schopenhauer considered art partly as revealing the meaning of a dynamic will to live and partly as an opiate, making man's lot easier, thus combining the idealistic aesthetics with a hedonistic aesthetics, that is, one which eventually would concede that the chief purpose of art is to give pleasure. Walter Pater, the Oxford Neo-Platonist, held a quasi-mystical point of view in which art was thought of as an objectification of the Super-beautiful—a doctrine stressing the element of inspiration but also allowing possibly for the mathematical interpretation in an unrealistic sense.

The Significance of Nietzsche as a Prototype of the Modern Aesthetician. Nietzsche, interested in the developmental theories of Darwin and Spencer, and partly convinced of the idealistic theories which assigned meaning to historical processes, was by nature a poet. He had the grave misfortune to suffer from an incurable social disease. As he aged, Nietzsche became an adherent of Schopenhauer. At the same time, he felt that man could conquer all human evils only by living heroically and dangerously. Nietzsche saw in art at its best man's revolt against all negative social forces by means of the imagination, which he considered an expression of the pure ego. Art, then, for him had as its ultimate purpose bringing man to a higher degree of sanity, not through an acceptance of ordinary ethical meaning, but through emotional and intuitive broadening of the humane instincts.

Tolstoy, Croce, and the English Aestheticians. The more intuitive systems of aesthetics are those associated with the names of the Russian, Count Tolstoy, and the Italian, Benedetto Croce. Tolstoy pessimistically called the academic art of czarist Russia, the opiate of the people. He insisted, in his essay *What is Art?* that art should be the means of uniting man more closely with the divine idea and with humanity. In contrast, Croce thought of art as an issue of pure imaginative expression, valuable only for itself. Allied to the expressionist theory of Croce is that of the Spaniard Santayana, who taught that art is something produced simply to objectify the reason. An Italian philosopher, Giovanni Gentile, suggested that the prime function of art is to induce simply a state of alertness or superawareness to all of life,

without, as Tolstoy would have it, any particular awareness of humane, social values.

Henri Bergson, a Frenchman, noticed, as had Herbert Spencer, that much of man's excess energy appears in the form of art. Considering this energy mystically as part of a universal rhythmical pulsation—the *élan vital*—Bergson noticed that certain human motions appear laughable in direct proportion as they approach the actions of a machine. The idea of the unexpected or inappropriate here is used to explain the humorous. Thus Bergson gave to his type of expressionism a bias toward the appropriateness of Socrates.

A number of British writers on aesthetics were among the first to consider the possibility of uniting the purely intellectual or mystical points of view with the sociohistorical. These were stimulated by the French critic, Taine, who in his monumental history of English literature strove to derive the peculiarities of the English style from a definition of English geographic, racial, and cultural characteristics, and in part by the efforts of Darwin and Spencer to formulate a theory of historical evolution and by Ruskin.

In Austria, Josef Strygowski began empirically to evaluate all the data on the graphic and plastic arts. In Italy, Lionello Venturi built upon the efforts of several generations of art historians his highly significant *History of Art Criticism*, which should be studied along with Chambers's *History of Taste*, Carritt's *Theories of Beauty*, and Saintsbury's *Loci Critici*. The material gained from a coordination of the data in these books and an objective history of all the arts, including music and drama as well as the graphic and plastic arts, alone would constitute a fitting background for a modern critic of art. Such a coordination would seem to be beyond the powers of any single individual and could arise only from the cooperative efforts of a group of scholars working together. Such a group are Ogden, Richards, and Wood.

The Foundations of Aesthetics, by Ogden, Richards, and Wood. C. K. Ogden, noted as the editor of

Psyche and as the author of *History of Civilization*, I. A. Richards, a lecturer on art, and author of the *Meaning of Meaning*, and James Wood, a painter, in their stimulating essay *The Foundations of Aesthetics*, published in 1925, undertook to review briefly sixteen varying "meanings of beauty." Unfortunately, these scholars made little attempt to point out the primary sources of each definition. To the list that follows have been added more complete references, giving the historical sources of the various meanings. Thus, the student may remember the associational overtones that cluster about each. The list, then, may serve as a partial survey of the critical theories discussed throughout our book.

1. The first definition holds anything to be beautiful which possesses the simple quality of beauty. This mystical definition, which arose first with Plotinus, explains nothing. The term always suggests, as we have found, overtones of charming humanity with balanced proportions and features supposed to indicate goodness and truth.

2. Rejecting the first, the three scholars turned to the definition: "The Beautiful is that which has a specified form." This derives from Aristotle and suggests the more naturalistic art embodied in the theory of the characteristic held in the Middle Ages. This is rejected on the grounds that tastes in the characteristic differ and so there can be no absolute meaning of the term.

3. The third theory of beauty, also stemming in part from Aristotle is very primitive. It holds that any article that successfully imitates any other must be beautiful. The pleasure of recognition, not necessarily aesthetic, here requires that the theory be rejected. Ogden, Richards, and Woods, however, fail to consider that skill in copying, resulting in accurate re-creation, might have something of an aesthetic element in it. Much late Roman and Renaissance art theory places successful imitation very high in the judgment of beauty.

4. The next theory of beauty—one particularly fostered by baroque critics—is that man gets a feeling of pleasure through the successful exploitation of a medium. This must be rejected on the grounds that skill can also be found in games, as well as in the exploitation of many media which obviously have nothing to do with art.

5. The idea that any creation by a genius must be beautiful, can be found in Plotinus, Kant, Schopenhauer, Nietzsche, and many of the Romantic critics. This doctrine, particularly flattering to many 20th-century artists who consider themselves geniuses, likewise fails, obviously because not all genius is interested in artistic production.

6. Beauty as the effusion of genius is closely allied to an idea from Plato, that without genial inspiration or revelation there can be no art. This leads to the sixth meaning of beauty, which holds that any work of art that reveals Truth, the Spirit of Nature, the Ideal, the Universal, Divine Goodness, or the Typical, is beautiful. This thought, particularly strong in all religious art, can be found in most of the classical theories, from Socrates on, as well as in the writings of the Hindus and of most medieval scholars. Its final development, as we have seen, came with idealistic Romantic artists, such as the German Nazarenes, the Englishmen Morris and Ruskin, the Russian Tolstoy, and the Frenchman Bergson. To the three Englishmen this almost universally accepted meaning of beauty seems too indefinite and overmystical. Possibly they were unconsciously loath to accept it as stressing strongly the associational or overtone values of art. Any theory of this kind is unpopular among 20th-century professional aestheticians. The scholars pointed out that the theory is closely allied to the nature romanticism of Coleridge, but neglected to mention that it is very close to Longinus' *Essay on the Sublime*. However, the idea of revelation as a meaning of beauty is related to the definition that they eventually proposed.

7. The next meaning of beauty is that which stresses its power to produce an illusion. This attitude was fostered by late Roman critics and baroque masters. Many of the moderns, following Picasso, hold that "all art is a lie." Such a misanthropic thesis is avoided by Ogden, Richards, and Wood as unworthy of the highest meaning of beauty. This shows that there are some social implications unconsciously inherent in their philosophy.

8. The eighth definition holds that anything is beautiful which has desirable social effects. This, which is very close to the sixth, arises in the theories of Plato and was stressed by the Jesuit writers in the College of Propaganda. It has also been held in modern times by communist artists. It is rejected because any mere statement of truth without

emotional overtones might affect society without being art.

9. The idea that beauty is expression—the ninth meaning—first found in Socrates, Aristotle, Plotinus, and the Romantic writers, eventually ends in the theory of Croce and his English follower Carritt. Obviously, expression takes many forms, some of which suggest the opposite of the generally accepted Classical meaning of beauty. In fact, expression as the dynamic element in art seems the very opposite of those formal values necessary for completion. Under expressionistic theories, one may consider all those which arise from primitive instincts, such as self-preservation and procreation, as well as the ethically higher expressions of ideal or religious goals. So the thoughts of Croce, Bosanquet, the Freudians, and Grant Allen—author of a book on the physiological basis of aesthetics—as well as the progenitor of them all, Herbert Spencer, would be rejected together by these critics. Spencer maintained that art is a sort of play, or the result of excess energy expressing whatever state of mind dominates the artist.

10. The hedonistic, or pleasure, theory of beauty, also arising in the baroque and fostered by church humanists and Classical academicians, descended to the Spaniard Santayana. Pleasure alone cannot describe the greatest works of art and many objects of purely sensual attraction are inartistic.

11. This leads to a consideration of the idea that anything is beautiful which simply excites the emotions. This theory, too, which could have risen in the most primitive states of mind, must be rejected for the same reason as that preceding.

12. The theory that "anything is beautiful which excites specific emotion," like Clive Bell's theory of "significant form," seeks a specific aesthetic emotion and must be rejected as lacking physical basis. The scholars recognize that the words are suggestive of meaning (that is, have associational values) without having any specific meaning.

13. Much closer to the ultimate truth proposed by the three scholars is the theory that any arrangement of elements which makes an observer want to move with the work of art or feel for it is beautiful. This is the theory of empathy, or *einfühling*. Our study of great works of art has shown that each was strong in some indefinite quality which carried us out of ourselves into the art object. As a doctrine this was suggested by Aristotle and later by baroque writers, being most completely explained scientifically by the Germans, Lipps and Lotze. Empathy, although very close to the true meaning of beauty, must be rejected because it is simply another aspect of the doctrine of pleasure though a little less consistent. The idea of empathy, however, has some importance in suggesting that in its final definition beauty must take the observer out of himself into a more balanced or contained condition, like that which is inherent in the work of art.

14. The fourteenth point, closely allied to the theory of empathy, is that the Beautiful heightens one's feeling of vitality. This aspect of art, which can be found in primitive animal drawings as well as in the hunting scenes of Assyrian kings or the figures of Greek athletes, arose with Socrates and finds its most modern adherent in Gentile, who expected the Beautiful to give one a quickening feeling of "greater awareness."

15. When greater awareness has brought the observer into touch with the great personality who created the work of art, he has an example of the fifteenth meaning of beauty—one to be found in Longinus. Since the artist has made in his work a selection from a great number of possible elements, we must accept his personality, although we need not necessarily experience the Beautiful when we do so; our attitude has become impersonal. The artist has succeeded in taking us out of ourselves and making us agree, not with his ideas, but with his feeling.

Synaesthesis as the Final European Meaning of Beauty. When all the elements selected by the artist are harmonious, the observer reaches a "state of equilibrium," which appears to the English scholars as the most universal definition of beauty. To this they give the name "synaesthesis." Synaesthesis means simply a union of all the contributing aesthetic factors in a work of art. This doctrine, derived from Confucius, describes a state of equilibrium that is not passive, inert, inspiring, or conflicting. It cannot be completely identified with harmony, at oneness with nature (Longinus' the Sublime), mystical ecstasy, the Oriental Nirvana, or the Freudian Sublimation (Fig. 595).

Criticism of the Term "Synaesthesis." Unfortunately, like many less empirical philosophers, whom they have criticized, the English scholars have assumed, a priori, that the ultimate goal of all art is Beauty. The people who built Gothic cathedrals obviously had as an end goal something different from those who constructed the Parthenon; the Hindu creator of the Siva statue, something different from Phidias. If synaesthesis is that which describes or explains Beauty, one still has to explain the more universal term "the Sublime," which has overtones of the dynamic inspirational element of art. If the great work of art can be shown to have in it an element which stimulates the imagination so that the observer is not completely quiescent but must allow his own imagination to become active, then a term with a slightly more dynamic meaning would seem to be indicated. As our revolutionary times demand an examination of both aspects of art, the ultimate meaning should probably have overtones of the generally accepted meanings of both the Beautiful and the Sublime.

Summary

European arts in the 20th century had no universal theme to celebrate. Those forces in modern life which made it impossible for artists to create in universal terms were the unbalanced forces of fascist nationalism, revolutionary communism, or unenlightened industrial feudalism. Most of the popular, widely advertised artistic effects were little more than a series of highly individualistic expressions of the unintelligibility of natural and social phenomena, affirmations of revolt against existing spiritual and economic conditions, or simply the means for escape from reality.

If a few works have any particular appeal or significance, it comes because they can be seen to broaden man's outlook and to help him understand the spiritual struggles of his fellow men. For the European philosopher, the highest value of this art is that it may induce a state of equilibrium in which all of man's tortured senses may at last come to rest. To this meaning

of Beauty European scholars gave the name "synaesthesis," a term slightly suggestive of anaesthesia. It becomes our task in the concluding chapter to suggest how American art may

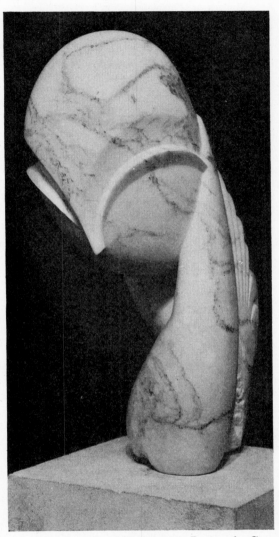

Fig. 595.—Portrait of Mademoiselle **Pogany**, by Constantin Brancusi, Rumanian. Marble, life size. (*Courtesy of Lesch-Carnegie.*)

transcend the incomplete experiments of the early 20th century so that a universal art and a more comprehensive meaning may be created for mankind's future.

Bibliography

DURET, THÉODORE: *Manet and the French Impressionists*, J. B. Lippincott Company, Philadelphia, 1910.

BARR, A. H.: *Cubism and Abstract Art*, Museum of Modern Art Publication, New York, 1936.

Modern Architecture, Museum of Modern Art Publication, New York, 1932.

BEHRENDT, WALTER CURT: *Modern Building*, Harcourt, Brace & Company, Inc., New York, 1937.

AGARD, W. R.: *New Architectural Sculpture*, Oxford University Press, New York, 1935.

OZENFANT, AMÉDÉE: *Foundations of Modern Art*, Harcourt, Brace & Company, Inc., New York, 1931.

SWEENEY, JAMES JOHNSON: *Plastic Redirections in 20th Century Painting*, University of Chicago Press, Chicago, 1934.

ROTHSCHILD, L. F.: *The Meaning of Unintelligibility in Modern Art*, University of Chicago Press, Chicago, 1935.

GAUGUIN, PAUL: *Noa-Noa*, translated by Theis, Greenberg, Publisher, Inc., New York, 1927.

VAN GOGH, VINCENT:
Dear Theo: The Autobiography of Vincent Van Gogh, edited by Irving Stone, Houghton Mifflin Company, Boston, 1937.

DALI, SALVADOR: *Conquest of the Irrational*, Julian Levy, Publisher, New York, 1935.

WILDE, OSCAR: *Decay of Lying*, Haldeman Julius Co., Girard, Kansas.

ANDREYEV, LEONID: *The Red Laugh*, T. Fisher Unwin, London, 1915.

ELIOT, T. S.: *Collected Poems*, Harcourt Brace & Company, Inc., New York, 1930.

NIETZSCHE, FRIEDRICH WILHELM: *Thus Spake Zarathustra*, translated by A. Tille, Everyman's Library, E. P. Dutton & Company, Inc., New York, 1933.

MURGER, HENRI: *La Vie de Bohème* (novel), translated by E. W. Hughes, Jarrolds, London, 1931.

DICKINSON, THOMAS H.: *The Theatre in Changing Europe*, Henry Holt & Company, Inc., New York, 1937.

CRAIG, GORDON: *On the Art of the Theatre*, Small, Maynard & Co., Boston, 1911.

CHANDLER, FRANK W., and RICHARD A. CORDELL: *Twentieth Century Plays*, Thomas Nelson & Sons, New York, 1934.

DICKINSON, THOMAS H.: *Chief Contemporary Dramatists*, Third Series, Riverside Press, Cambridge, Houghton Mifflin Company, Boston, 1930.

LANGFELD, H. S.: *The Aesthetic Attitude*, Harcourt, Brace & Company, Inc., New York, 1920.

OGDEN, C. K., I. A. RICHARDS, and J. WOOD: *The Foundations of Aesthetics*, International Publishers Co., Inc., New York, 1925.

Recordings

FRANCK, CÉSAR:
Symphony in D minor—VM 22 (alb.).

DEBUSSY, CLAUDE:
Pelléas and Mélisande—VM 68 (alb.).
Reflections on the Water—V 6633.
Boating—V 1358.
Iberia—Decca 25558.
Golliwogg's Cakewalk and *Clair de lune*—Decca 25934D.
Prelude to the Afternoon of a Faun—V 6696.

HONNEGER, ARTHUR:
Selections from *King David*—C 8865.
Pacific 231—Decca 25206.

STRAUSS, RICHARD:
Also sprach Zarathustra, op. 30—VM 257 (alb.).
Don Juan—B 90046/7.
Tod und Verklärung—VM 217 (alb.).
Till Eulenspiegel—B 90044/5.
Don Quixote—VM 144 (alb.).
Ein Heldenleben—VM 44 (alb.).

MOUSSORGSKY, MODEST:
Opening chorus of *Boris Godounoff*—C-G7273M.
Pictures at an Exhibition—VM 102 (alb.).

BORODIN, ALEXANDER:
Polovetsian Dances from *Prince Igor*—C-68384/5d.

STRAVINSKY, IGOR:
Petrouschka—CM 109 (alb.).
The Fire Bird—VM 291 (alb.).
Sacre du printemps—CM 129 (alb.).
Symphony of Psalms—CM 162 (alb.).

SMETANA, BEDRICK:
The Bartered Bride—VM 193 (alb.).
The Moldau—V 11434/5.

ENESCO, GEORGES:
Rumanian Rhapsody—V 1701/2.

RAVEL, MAURICE:
Pavane for a Dead Princess—C 4082M.
Bolero—V 7251/2.

SIBELIUS, JEAN:
Finlandia—V 7412.
En Saga, op. 9—V 9925/6.
The Swan of Tuonela—V 7251/2.

TWENTIETH CENTURY:
Columbia History of Music, Vol V., edited by Percy Scholes—CM 361.

CHAPTER XIX

The Art of the Americans

We live under a form of government called Democracy. It is of the essence of Democracy that the individual man is free in his body and free in his soul. It is a corollary therefrom, that he must govern or restrain himself, both as to bodily acts and mental acts;—that in short he must set up a responsible government within his own individual person. . . . [1]

Have the elder races halted?
Do they droop and end their lesson, wearied over there beyond the seas?
We take up the task eternal, and the burden and the lesson,
        Pioneers! O pioneers! . . .

All the pulses of the world,
Falling in they beat for us, with the Western movement beat,
Holding single or together, steady moving to the front, all for us,
        Pioneers! O pioneers! . . .

Minstrels latent on the prairies!
(Shrouded bards of other lands, you may rest, you have done your work,)
Soon I hear you coming warbling, soon you rise and tramp amid us,
        Pioneers! O pioneers! . . .
                                        "PIONEERS! O PIONEERS." [2]

Art acquaints us with the wonderful translations of the same thought into the several languages of drawing, of sculpture, of music, of poetry, of architecture. . . . [3]

Beauty is the moment of transition, as if the form were just ready to flow into other forms. [4]

AMERICAN art, now in the process of creation, belongs to the future. If to its creation one brings knowledge gained from a study of the past, he bequeaths to posterity new cultural inventions distinctly his own, yet rich in the more universal values which bind him to the entire human race. In light of the preceding review of culture one perceives that American art is a fresh, vigorous creation of a new form rapidly approaching maturity, perhaps its Golden Age and its sublime style. Having gained some sense of detachment from this objective, historical study of other cultures, one may turn to his own prepared to discover the unique characteristics for which it will be marked in the future.

Europeans hold two points of view concerning American art. In *The Decline of the West*, Oswald Spengler, the German sociologist, characterized American culture as the decadent end of the European civilization. Many European critics point to our academic art schools, teaching in the tradition of the Renaissance and French court artists, or to our art museums, usually built in a pseudoclassical style, as evidence of our lack of creative imagination.

---

[1] LOUIS H. SULLIVAN, "The Young Man in Architecture," *Brickbuilder*, Vol. IX, No. 6, pp. 115–119, June, 1900, by permission of *The Architectural Forum*.
[2] WALT WHITMAN, *Leaves of Grass*, Rees Welsh and Co., Philadelphia, 1882.
[3] RALPH WALDO EMERSON, *Journals*, Vol. VII, pp. 173–174, Houghton Mifflin Company, Boston, 1914.
[4] RALPH WALDO EMERSON, *The Complete Works*, Vol. VI, p. 292, Houghton Mifflin Company, Boston, 1904.

Others, who wish to find us decadent, discover in the ballyhoo of our bathing-beauty contests and supercolossal film spectacles, in the countless towering skyscrapers erected between 1910 and 1930, in overcrowded radio programs, and the mass production of poorly designed household utensils, evidence enough to indicate that the Americans lack a refined aesthetic sense. The question still remains whether this is due to a degenerate weakening of the creative powers or a primitive superabundant production of articles seeking to express some new form appropriate to a young, virile people.

European artists, on the other hand, agree with Paul Claudel, for many years French Ambassador to the United States, who wrote:

There is in the American temperament a quality which they express over there by the word resiliency . . . the word suggests at once elasticity, energy, resourcefulness and good humor . . . The great strength of a man over there lies in his feeling the solid earth under his feet, and in his having space at his disposal. . . .

Experience does not have in America the same meaning as in Europe. It is not a matter of wisdom won from the past but of an adventure with the future. . . . The American needs horizons, and he needs to be surrounded by friends. And then forward! Once again he commences to hear the fife and drum, and his feet begin to move in time with the music.

Clear through American life you feel this nervous rhythmical beat, like the pistons of a steam engine interrupting the cyclical continuous roar of the dynamo. . . .[1]

For astute observers like Claudel, American revival meetings, the great athletic contests with their snake dances, and the crowds of dancers around the jazz orchestra or swing band in some enormous hall seem phenomena closely linked to primitive Indian ceremonies. The museums, donated in part by American industrialists, in part supported by contributions from the mass of citizens, house within their somewhat cold exteriors friendly groups from all classes of society who at times enjoy symphonies played by orchestras or the music from great pipe organs. Through the week, these museums become art schools in which quite modern functional designing and primitive American decorative forms are taught. Such arts as the motion picture display new combinations of dramatic musical form, while the comic strips and Silly Symphonies of Walt Disney show the primitive beginnings of a new type of design. This tremendously rich productive stream originated in all the continents. From a purely historical point of view alone it cannot be fully understood in terms of either Classical or Gothic European developments.

Literature

The taproots of American productions in both continents go deep into the Indian culture. In South America and in North America south of the Rio Grande, the native Indian population is ethnically the largest group. Into this great underlying stratum of indigenous American culture flowed first, in Central and South America, a Spanish strain. Before 1800, to the more sparsely populated North America came French, English, Dutch, and German groups. These were followed by German revolutionaries, the Irish, the Italians, and from 1910 on, by great Slavic migrations, bringing their colorful folk arts from the Balkans and Western Asia. All through these years the Africans brought into our literature and music their rich underlying rhythms and soft harmonious speech.

Although the majority population in the United States is of Celto-Germanic origin, it has assimilated elements from Indian, African, and Mediterranean cultures, so that the fundamentally Gothic art which it would naturally have created has been transformed into a new form, more nearly universal in style and inter-

---

[1] PAUL CLAUDEL, *The Rhythm of the Dynamo*, from the *Paris Soir*, translation from *The Living Age*, Vol. CCCLI, September, 1936–February, 1937.

national in its message. This poetic ideology, expressed in the four quotations heading this chapter, has not yet found its expression in a satisfactory graphic and plastic form necessary for complete definition of the American idea of beauty. One cannot fully visualize the American art of the future until he has examined the folk legends and mythology of the various groups represented. Considering these legends and the primitive rhythms of the dances accompanying them, one gains a new conception of the meaning of American art. It is broader than that presented by Paul Claudel, who derived all from the dynamo. The inventive American, although capable of creating the dynamo, enjoys a feeling of power transcending the monotony of the assembly line. His construction of the machine, undertaken partly for the joy of creating new sources of power, also predestines him for the creation of a spatial art, energetic as the early Celto-Germanic interweave. (Fig. 306, Chap. XII and Fig. 614. Design by Sullivan.) Throughout American mythology one also finds a Promethean spirit, at times rough and humorous, at times melancholy and musical, which seeks expression in the temporal arts.

Indigenous Origins of American Literature. The earliest Indian legends bear close resemblance to those of China and East India. In Central America, the figure of the savior-god Quetzalcoatl corresponds to the Great Man Panku of the Chinese or the Purusa of the Hindus. The American savior-god, like the sun-god Mithras of the Persians, battles an evil spirit or magician. Like the Greek Orpheus, Quetzalcoatl has the power to charm all nature of which he is a part. His song begins with a remarkable invocation to nature's beauty, differing in this from the European epics. The god sings

> As I wander through the forest
> There I hear the rocks replying
> To the sweetly-singing flowers;

> And the gleaming, chatting water
> Makes its answer to the fountain,
> To the ever-shining fountain,
> Sweetly singing, forward springing,
> Ever lilting its new song.

There he envisions a land.

> Land where there is no affliction;
> Land where no one serves a master,
> If on earth we ever reach it
> 'Twill be only through submission
> To the Author of Our Being.[1]

Quetzalcoatl, we are told, taught his people all the arts and crafts. Together they built wondrous houses adorned with coral and sea-shells, emeralds, gold, and silver. They had chocolate plantations and untold wealth. They lacked nothing in their households, and hunger never dwelt among them. The small ears of corn they never had to grind, but used them for heating their baths. Many are the songs which Quetzalcoatl left to his people. Almost all the North American Indian tribes had stories which can be connected with him.

Chief among the stories of the Iroquoian nations was that of Hiawatha, who united them in a confederacy under a rule of law. The Great Spirit or the Indian's Manitou still persists in many forms as an underlying concept of the Deity for most people of Indian background. Several totemistic legends concerning the animals related to the various tribes have come down in the "Brer Rabbit Tales" of Uncle Remus. Many American fraternal organizations (for which the Europeans have no counterparts) include various lodges called the Eagles, Elks, Owls, and Redmen, which have adopted Indian ceremonial rites.

Stories of giants characterize the mythology of all primitive peoples who are forced to wrestle with a powerful natural environment for their existence. The Cherokee Indian has the tale of Tsul Kalu, a slant-eyed giant whose many marvelous exploits are almost completely duplicated by the frontiersman Davy Crockett, the lumberjack Paul Bunyan with his Swedish

---

[1] JOHN HUBERT CORNYN, *The Song of Quetzalcoatl,* translated from the Aztec, The Antioch Press, Yellow Springs, Ohio, 1930.

foreman Ole Olsen, and the Mississippi Negro stevedore, John Henry. American humor, relying for much of its expansive effect upon the narration of highly improbable or "tall" stories, incomprehensible to most Europeans, bears direct relationship to the primitive vigor of the pioneers. This accounts in part for the "resiliency" mentioned by Paul Claudel.

Americans of both continents tend to glorify their heroic democratic leaders—Washington, Jefferson, Bolivar, San Martin, Juarez, and Lincoln—conceiving of them not in any sense as deities, but as men of gigantic stature and superhuman achievements. Personification of the various American ideals can be found in the tall figure of Uncle Sam, suggestive of Yankee ingenuity, and in the Goddess of Liberty. The Mexicans have recently pictured Quetzalcoatl, and the Peruvians have their Inca general, Ollantay.

The White Folk Legends. The northern groups brought in, besides the Elizabethan folk legends, much material from the medieval morality plays found in the stories of *Pilgrim's Progress* or the poetry of Milton. With the development of an aristocracy in New Orleans, New York, and Virginia, there came during the last years of the 18th century the classical legends of Greece and Rome. These were taught as part of the body of humanist culture in the newly founded colleges. During the 19th century, many of these legends, with the fairy tales of the Dutch, Germans, and Scandinavians, furnished much of the grade-textbook material.

The Germanic legends have come mostly through the folk stories of the brothers Grimm and of Hans Christian Andersen, introduced during the 19th century. Among them, a famous plot much used in American dramatic literature is the story of Hans the Swineherd, who grew up to marry the king's daughter. This, the first success story, was popularized in the tales of Horatio Alger, considered indispensable reading by the developing youth in the last half of the 19th century and the early 20th. Another legend, which runs through most of

the American idealistic philosophy, includes the thought that inventive ability used for the good of society eventually brings recognition and riches. Riches, in turn, bring leisure time which can be spent in healthy sport and aesthetic pursuits. Throughout all American legendry runs a large strain of Utopianism. The Americans unconsciously believe in an aesthetically planned society where all the component parts move with the minimum amount of friction and where the maximum of lasting enjoyment can be got with a minimum of labor. This legendary plot material from which all American art forms arise is usually portrayed with humor. The American tragic sense appears when the individual feels thwarted in his attempts to achieve this expanding life or when, having achieved it too late, he has forgotten how to use it.

A Literary Portrait of America

Colonial Times. Colonial literature in the 17th and 18th centuries retained much of its Elizabethan flavor, which still persists among writers from the mountains and prairies. Half of the matter in this vigorous style had to do with religious subjects; the rest, with history. During this period the witchcraft trials and the struggles against persecution by Roger Williams and the Quakers had built up a considerable background of dramatic historical material.

In the period between 1700 and 1776, despite the unfortunate attitude of the Puritanical priestcraft in New England, and the determination on the part of such provincial leaders as Governor Berkeley of Virginia to keep the people ignorant by forbidding free schools and printing, there had grown up a strong spirit of liberal idealism, which can be detected in the writings of Jonathan Edwards. Edwards's *Essay on Beauty* presents a definition which displays both the strength and the weakness of the Puritan's position—that beauty is similarity, regularity, or mutual accord, that is, conformity.

Benjamin Franklin, the most typical 18th-century literary figure, educated himself with Bunyan's *Pilgrim's Progress*, the writings of Daniel Defoe, *The Spectator Papers*, Plutarch's *Lives*, and the powerful sermons of Cotton Mather. From this balanced humanistic-medieval background arose a liberal, witty personality with a pragmatic philosophy. Franklin's *Autobiography* presents the first authentic American self-portrait.

The spirit of the Revolution, clearly presaged in the writings of Paine, Jefferson, and other patriots, is closely related to the deism and the social pamphlets of Rousseau and Voltaire. Clarity and fineness of expression in American statecraft is a tradition which found its epitome in the *Declaration of Independence* and the *Preamble to the Constitution*, as well as in the state papers of Abraham Lincoln.

The Early Republic. The early years of the 19th century saw the beginnings of westward expansion, accompanied by the growth of the merchant marine, steamboat travel on the inland rivers, and the building of canals and railways. New England and New York at that time were the acknowledged centers of cultural activity. Washington Irving's *Tales of a Traveller*, *Sketch Book*, and *Knickerbocker's History of New York* carry forward the tradition of Elizabethan style untempered by sober puritanism. Irving also wrote the *Conquest of Granada* and *The Alhambra*. The energy of the American spirit, with its love of adventure and the sea, is nowhere better expressed than in Herman Melville's great novel, *Moby Dick*, the story of the revengeful Captain Ahab and the whale Moby Dick, or in *Two Years before the Mast*, by Richard Henry Dana.

In a more romantic vein, James Fenimore Cooper's *Leatherstocking Tales* told the story of frontier heroes and Indians. George Catlin wrote and illustrated careful scientific monographs on the Indians, while Henry Rowe Schoolcraft collected their legends directly from the tribal storytellers. With a romantic's love of nature, and with Rousseau's determination to live free from the bonds of civilization, Henry David Thoreau built his cabin by Walden Pond and wrote his essays to prove that simple living under the beneficent influence of nature nourishes the soul of man more than can material success. In New England an intellectual attitude grew up which was characterized by Oliver Wendell Holmes as "Brahminism."

The Brahmins were those literary artists who acknowledged inherited backgrounds of European culture. Most of them had university training and some had traveled abroad. The philosopher Emerson, author of the poem *Brahma*, led the group, which included Longfellow, Lowell, and Holmes himself. Contrasting with the Brahmins, Holmes found less cultured, virile men whose provinciality led them to ignore Continental backgrounds. Although he wrote only in jest, Dr. Holmes characterized two definite tendencies in American artistic thought. The "Brahmins" for all their inheritance, never reached the primitive virility and revolutionary fervor of their contemporaries—Thoreau, Whittier, Edgar Allan Poe, and later, Walt Whitman and Mark Twain. Two women—Louisa May Alcott and Harriet Beecher Stowe—reached wide audiences, respectively, with *Little Women* and *Uncle Tom's Cabin*.

Nathaniel Hawthorne is remembered for his short stories, and his well-constructed novels, *The Scarlet Letter*, *The Marble Faun*, and *The House of the Seven Gables*. These are distinguished by writing of great suggestive power and well-drawn characters, presented together with a fine psychological analysis of the inner motives of their actions. Henry Wadsworth Longfellow, who translated both the *Niebelungen Lied* and Dante's *Inferno*, is best remembered for his romantic minor epics *Hiawatha* and *Evangeline*, his *Tales of a Wayside Inn*, and *The Courtship of Miles Standish*. Ralph Waldo Emerson, a philosopher in the deist tradition of Pope, although he was the leader of the "Brahmins," believed that American literature should be based directly upon American life. The exuberance of the unformed American spirit lives in all Emer-

son's essays. Particularly in his attempted definitions of beauty one finds that he includes
all nature and suggests universal associational
patterns.

The natural depth of American character,
already demonstrated in the early years of the
19th century by such poems as Bryant's *A Forest
Hymn*, *The Prairies*, and *Thanatopsis*, emerged
again in Whittier's *Snowbound*, in the vast
reaches of Whitman's descriptive verse and the
Marshes of Glynn and other poems by Sidney
Lanier. A vein of utopianism runs through the
writings of all these men, as it had in those of
Emerson's friend, Thoreau. Those were the
days of many experiments in communal living.
Hawthorne, for a time, lived at Brook Farm, a
Utopian community, but found that intellectual
life could not easily be combined with the hard
manual labor of the pioneer. Americans must
experiment with ways for improving man's lot
or else they belie the premises of their Declaration of Independence. Underlying the writings
of most philosophic American literary men is
that belief expressed in Lowell's essay *On a
Certain Condescension in Foreigners*, "There never
was a colony save this that went forth not to
seek gold but God."

Edgar Allan Poe, the most brilliant writer
of prose fiction during the first half of the century, alone among the early Americans discovered the romantic formula that the primary
purpose of art is pure sense impression. Lacking
stability of character and great social integrity,
Poe had to believe that the primary purpose of
art is amusement. His Symbolist verse and his
exciting, macabre short stories made him a
Continental literary figure long before his compatriots were so accepted. Walt Whitman, another pioneer in the field of expressionism, wove
Emerson's philosophy into a mighty, expansive,
rhythmical verse of epic grandeur.

The Late 19th Century. Mark Twain (Samuel
L. Clemens), a Missourian, the most significant writer in the latter half of the 19th century,
began his adventurous life as a steamboat pilot
on the Mississippi. Here he absorbed the legendry of the early Midwestern frontier. After a
few months spent as a soldier of the Confederacy, he became a Union sympathizer and
spent his next years in the gold camps of the
West. The rest of his life, when he was not
lecturing, was spent in traveling and writing in
bed. Mark Twain's *Tom Sawyer*, *Huckleberry
Finn*, and *Life on the Mississippi* hold much of
the romance of the old South. *Roughing It* tells
of the pioneer West. The *Jumping Frog* story is a
classic of American humor. *Innocents Abroad*, *The
Man That Corrupted Hadleyburg*, and *A Connecticut Yankee in King Arthur's Court* display the
writer's satire at its best.

Other writers who caught the spirit of the
West were Bret Harte and Edward Eggleston.
The latter told, in *The Circuit Rider* and *The
Hoosier Schoolmaster*, of the early settlements in
Indiana. Hamlin Garland, following this tradi-
tion, later wrote *A Son of the Middle Border*.
Shortly after the Civil War, these writers and
others awakened a strong interest in local color.
In *Deephaven*, Sarah Orne Jewett characterized
the little New England seaport town; in his
Old Creole Days, George W. Cable told of New
Orleans; and in his book, *In Old Virginia*,
Thomas Nelson Page characterized the South.
The New England businessman furnished the
subject of William Dean Howells's *The Rise of
Silas Lapham*.

Henry James, a "Brahmin," saw this same
American businessman rather satirically in *The
American*. In his *Daisy Miller* he described the
unconventional young American girl. Fleeing
the aesthetic crudities of American life, Henry
James, after living in Europe for years, wrote
several novels in almost perfect form. Best
known among them are *The Ambassadors* and
The Wings of the Dove. In all his works the
American is seen as an individual who, discontented with his own lack of spirituality,
seeks for a more complete development through
a greater knowledge of European culture. While
Henry James strove for an understanding of the
soul of the New England "Brahmin" type
through literary expression, his brother Wil-

liam characterized it through his studies in psychology and philosophy. He founded the philosophical school known as "American pragmatism," which maintains that ideals should be checked with social experience and are most valuable when socially effective.

Another New England scholar whose historical writings and literary self-analysis have the greatest value for the understanding of American character is Henry Adams. His description of the medieval point of view in *Mont-Saint-Michel and Chartres* has had great influence in stimulating interest in the field of medieval studies. With his *History of the United States during the Administrations of Jefferson and Madison* and *America*, Adams represents the last of a line of literary historians which began with William H. Prescott, author of *The Conquest of Peru* and other works, and John Lothrop Motley, who wrote *The Rise of the Dutch Republic*. Edward Bellamy, a leader of the Populist movement, in *Looking Backward* and *Equality* strove to chart the future, prophesying the phonograph and the radio.

Joel Chandler Harris, a Southerner, recorded the poetry and songs of the Negroes in *Uncle Remus, His Songs and Sayings*. The introduction to this book includes a significant study of those primitive rhythms which later greatly influenced American poetry and music. Sidney Lanier, particularly interested in music, regarded all his verse as having a melodic background. He contributed to American aesthetic theory in *The Science of English Verse*. James Whitcomb Riley, the Hoosier poet, like Whittier before him, was interested in home life. Lyric poets such as Joaquin Miller, Emily Dickinson, and Walt Whitman, although creating in the nineteenth century, had their greatest influence just before the World War. In all their works lives a strong suggestion of the great expanse of the American soul, its incompleteness, its exuberance, and at times its sadness.

The Early 20th Century. By the end of the 19th century there rose in American life a consciousness of having come of age. Richard

Harding Davis, Jack London, and O. Henry wrote completely without the "Brahmin's" interest in European culture. Encouraged by the example of the greatest American literary figure, Mark Twain, these local colorists and a host of writers without self-consciousness then created the most significant novels of the American scene. Most of these, nevertheless, still retain their Puritan inheritance—a sense of social significance. In their methods they fluctuate between realism and naturalism, most being influenced by the prevailing methods in literary style of the American press. In 1915, Theodore Dreiser wrote *The Genius*, analyzing the egotistic selfishness of the romantic creative individualist. His *An American Tragedy* (1925) tells with the minutest detail of the way in which a crime may overtake almost anyone in modern society who is without a sense of direction. Sherwood Anderson in *Dark Laughter* shows the American businessman, who, like Thoreau, desires to escape social obligations.

Sinclair Lewis, like Dreiser essentially a news reporter, in *Main Street* and *Babbitt* shows the frustration caused in the human soul by provincialism, the demands of the race for material success, and inability of the American middle class to achieve spiritual freedom. Carol Kennicott in *Main Street* and George F. Babbitt in *Babbitt* were to see their isolationist world blasted by the World War, to witness their children in the jazz age from 1920 to 1930 finding an illusion of freedom in the "speak-easy." Lewis, like most naturalists, gains an effect almost of caricature by carefully reporting many details. In *Arrowsmith* he portrays a young idealistic physician thwarted by commercialism, or industrialism, in his task of helping mankind. In the name character of *Elmer Gantry*, Lewis concentrates all the habits and attitudes of revivalist preachers. In *It Can't Happen Here*, he pictures the struggle of a patriotic newspaper editor against the American equivalent of a Fascist dictator.

Edith Wharton's Undine Spragg in *The Custom of the Country* characterizes the ambitious young American woman without moral guidance; and in *Ethan Frome* Mrs. Wharton tells of New England's frustrated souls. In contrast, Willa Cather, living among the Norwegian pioneers of the Middle West, affirms in *O Pioneers*, *The Song of the Lark*, and *My Antonia* the ability of the American woman's creative spirit to overcome the greatest handicaps. O. F. Rolvaag, in his *Giants in the Earth* and *Peder Victorious*, likewise tells of hardy Scandinavians pioneering in a new world.

In a vein akin to the spirit of these novelists is the poetic *Spoon River Anthology* of Edgar Lee Masters, with its somewhat pessimistic revelation of unheroic American lives. Carl Sandburg deals boldly and gladly with American industry in *Chicago*, *Corn Huskers*, and *Smoke and Steel*. Vachel Lindsay, catching the rhythms of Negro life, of frontier camp meetings, and the industrial machine, creates an expressionist poetry in "General William Booth Enters into Heaven," "The Congo," and "The Kallyope Yell." For years Lindsay, like some inspired bard of the Middle Ages, wandered from town to town preaching a gospel of beauty and regeneration through art. Sandburg, too, with his guitar inspired those who heard him. Like Lindsay, Robert Frost describes farm life, but his scene is New England rather than the Middle West.

The period shortly before and immediately after the World War brought to the "Brahmins" an interest in Symbolism, expressionism, and introspective analysis which had earlier found its verse forms in the works of Walt Whitman and Emily Dickinson. Edna St. Vincent Millay, Amy Lowell, T. S. Eliot, and Edward Arlington Robinson carry introspective analysis further and approach the techniques of such stream-of-consciousness writers as E. E. Cummings and Gertrude Stein. All of these, like late English Romantics, the French Symbolists, and Edgar Allan Poe, have an interest in the effectiveness of words or rhythmical patterns for their own sake or as an aid to self-revelation. Most of them, cut off from the American

Utopian vision or disillusioned by the apparent triumph of materialism during the war years, can be considered as thwarted individuals seeking an escape through their art.

After the war of 1917–1918, many Americans retreated into mysticism or nature worship. It is perhaps significant that a poem like Joyce Kilmer's "Trees" became the favorite of Rotary and other social service clubs where American businessmen strove to recapture some vision of Utopia. The paradox of the American as revealed by his literary portrait is that he wants freedom from domination, wants escape from his loneliness, yet fears to take his place as a citizen of the world. Today he is being forced to see that he cannot escape wholly either the culture or the consequences of his background.

In his attempt to mature quickly after the World War, the American turned to many popular semiliterary accounts of scientific accomplishment, first pausing, with Gamaliel Bradford, to debunk his heroes, in thoughtful *American Portraits*. Edward Bok, Michael Pupin, and Mary Antin wrote autobiographies that told what the latest immigrants hoped to achieve in America. In Jane Addams's *Twenty Years at Hull House* are skillfully portrayed the problems of Americanization.

Always eager students, the average Americans turn to the idealistic Englishman H. G. Wells for a popular historical outline. Edwin E. Slosson's *Creative Chemistry*, Paul deKruif's *Microbe Hunters*, Will Durant's *Story of Philosophy*, Harry Overstreet's *About Ourselves*, Lewis Mumford's *Technics and Civilization*, and the pseudo-anthropological writings of Freud, Adler, and Jung take the place of Benjamin Franklin's humanist and Biblical backgrounds. For his economic and political theory the American depends too greatly upon the daily press and the radio. The actual drama of modern life has become so thrilling that the arts pale by comparison. In 1939 a radio drama telling of the invasion of this world by people from Mars appeared to be so real that many could not distinguish it from actual reports of armies in Europe about to destroy civilization.

Prehistoric Origins of American Design

The first Americans, a few wandering hunters on the paleolithic culture level, probably reached this continent about 7,000 years ago. Archaeologists in general agree that these primitive people either crossed the frozen ice or a land bridge then connecting Alaska with Siberia. During succeeding centuries, other groups followed in canoes traveling along the coast or using the old route. Throughout the North, where a rigorous climate prevented cultural development, the various Asiatic people now known to us as Eskimos and Indians remained on a paleolithic hunting level.

Their Central American relatives gradually developed agriculture during the thousand years before Christ. Baked painted pottery, weaving, and basketry appear at that time, along with those crude clay figurines from which this culture takes the name "archaic." By the first century before Christ, the archaic culture can be found from northwestern Mexico throughout Central America and as far south as Colombia, Venezuela, and Ecuador. The faces of the figurines indicate that their creators included a diversity of Asiatic and Oceanic ethnical types. Most of them have the slant eyes, round faces, and thin lips of the Mongoloid people (Fig. 596). Many either have profiles with retreating brows and chins, like those of the Javanese, or are bearded, like some of the Polynesians and Chinese. Some of the earliest archaic figures are clothed with turbans and skirts; others have hair styles like those shown on early Hindu sculpture. Some wear bird's-head helmets, like the wooden masks of the Alaskan Indians; but few have the elaborate feathered headdress later associated with Mayan and Aztec cultures. The archaic people

also worked shell and precious stones for their jewelry. Pottery whorls for spinning, as well as bone and stone implements, abound. Archaic pottery made of coarsely kneaded clay, baked

FIG. 596.—*a*, archaic figurines, representing prehistoric American types, early period, mostly from Zacatenco, Valley of Mexico (*after Vaillant, Natural History, Vol. 29, No. 5; courtesy of American Museum of Natural History*); *b*, wooden lintel in early Mayan temple, Tikal, about A.D. 100; *c*, stone heads and pottery mask of Indo-Chinese character from Temple A and structure B, Quirigua, early Mayan, A.D. 300–600 (*after S. G. Morley, National Geographic Magazine, March*, 1913).

to a reddish brown, repeats most of the shapes found in Chinese neolithic ware. The decoration is in red, white, or black geometric lines.[1]

Until the 1st century B.C., archaic art shows little sign of aesthetic development, remaining upon a level as low as that of the earliest Susian or predynastic Egyptian. There exist no signs from which the complicated hieroglyphic system of the Mayans could have been evolved. Overnight, so it seems, a rich culture appeared in Central America. Almost simultaneously, the Chimu and Nazca cultures arose along the coast of Peru.

[1] GEORGE C. VAILLANT, "On the Threshold of Native American Civilization," from *Natural History*, the journal of the American Museum of Natural History, Vol. XXIX, September–October, 1929, No. 5.

Despite the remarkable evidence of this unexplained appearance of complex culture forms and design motives so closely paralleling those of contemporaneous Southeastern Asia, most

fact that Shih Huang Ti, the Ts'in emperor, who built the Great Wall of China, sent expeditions across the eastern sea for the drug of immortality, which supposedly grew on the

FIG. 597.—Early Mayan city of Palenque, Chiapas, Mexico, about A.D. 300–600. Painting by Carlos Vierras. The pagodalike structures and pyramids correspond to contemporaneous buildings in Indo-China. (*Courtesy of San Diego Museum.*)

American archaeologists persist, as the ethnologists did for many years before them, in trying to interpret all Indian design in terms of a wholly indigenous development, pointing to the great divergence of styles as against any single Asiatic origin. European ethnologists and archaeologists explain this divergence of types by pointing out that as in historic times there have been several well-known instances of boats and canoes being carried by the Japanese current down the west coast of America, so probably at various times in the last 3,000 years small groups of people from Polynesia, Indo-China, China, Korea, and Mongolia reached the American shores by the water route. These brought a few designed articles, with various techniques like bronze casting, pottery inlaying, and wood carving, as well as their Asiatic customs and gods. The earliest and most obviously Asiatic designs disappeared because carried by people who, like the present-day Indian tribes of the Northwest coast, carved their totem poles, great war canoes, thrones, and chests in wood, which disintegrated in the moist climate of the tropics.

Some European scholars suggest definite cultural influences from China, pointing to the

legendary three islands of the blest. Between 140 and 85 B.C., the Han emperor Wu Ti also sent out expeditions over the eastern sea. Considering that some of these expeditions might have missed the blessed islands and been caught in the Japanese current, it is conceivable that one or more ships manned by highly intelligent, cultured people could have reached the western shores of Mexico, Guatemala, Colombia, and Peru just before the time of Christ.

These men would have understood the art of bronze casting by the lost wax process, the art of building great walled cities, circular and square pagodas, pyramids like those of Indo-China, with sky temples. They would have brought with them a pantheon, including the winged skyserpent, the feline goddess with the serpents, or the Tao Tieh mask and more humane conceptions of the Deity associated with Confucianism and Taoism. They would also have had an elementary system of writing, with signs designed like those on Chou-dynasty bronzes. Most of these things appear in prehistoric American art after the first century.

Important it is to notice that in both the South American and the Central American cultures the quality of the aesthetic production slowly degenerated after the first two or three hundred years of the first millennium. In so elementary a study as ours, there can be no room for more than a glimpse into this fasci-

several stories in height, passageways covered with horseshoe vaults similar to those in the Hindu cave temples, and other advanced refinements of the builder's art. The appropriate,

FIG. 598.—*a*, altar front, La Venta, Tabasco, Mexico, Olmec culture, 91 B.C.–A.D. 466 (Thompson's correlation); probably the earliest known version of Quetzalcoatl as serpent king seated at mouth of underworld goddess (*courtesy of the National Geographic Society*); *b*, ceremonial receptacle with masks of death-goddess Cihuacohuatl and battling warriors, Tres Zapotes, Vera Cruz, Mexico (*courtesy of the National Geographic Society*); *c*, entrance to sacred kiva or underworld temple through gorgoneion mask of serpent-goddess Cihuacohuatl, Malinalco, Mexico, Matlazincan culture, about A.D. 700 (?) (*after Mexican Art and Life, April*, 1938). Excavations by the National Geographic Society, Smithsonian Institution Expeditions led by Matthew W. Stirling (*National Geographic Magazine*, August, 1939, and September, 1940) and the Mexican Government Expedition by Professor José García Payón in the rock-cut temples of Malinalco furnish many parallels with Pre-Vedic East Indian, Japanese, and Korean ancestral worship and its underworld guardian serpent.

nating field, the last frontier of archaeological research where the great problems of the origin of the American style are still to be solved.[1]

Archaeologists differ as to the exact time when the Chimu and Nazca cultures appeared in Peru. S. G. Morley and D. Herbert Spinden would date the statuette from Tuxtla, an early Mayan monument, around 100 B.C.; others, like J. Eric Thompson, around 60 A.D. Throughout this chapter the later dates will be used. The first datable city, Uaxactun in Guatemala, was built between A.D. 160 and 320. Shortly after that time, the Mayans had cities at Palenque in Southern Mexico and at Tikal, Copan, Piedras Negras, and Quirigua.

The earliest cities of the old Mayan empire, like Palenque (Fig. 597), show that the Mayan architects had an excellent feeling for mass, a genius for designing great complex structures, and a sense for city planning. The buildings of Palenque include ziggurats, pagodalike towers

skillful design of the architectural sculpture so quickly reached a state of perfection in the earliest stone buildings of the old Mayan cities that one concludes it followed a long practice in wooden sculpture, now lost, or else that seafaring people related to the Polynesians, with skill in wood carving and many advanced motifs, brought new ideas to the receptive archaic culture, along with the advanced hieroglyphic writing which then appears in stone (Fig. 598).

In several of the cities, particularly Yaxchilan and Tikal, fragmentary remains of richly carved wooden lintels and doorposts have been found. One from Tikal (Fig. 596*b*) pictures in complex form the feathered serpent associated with the worship of Quetzalcoatl. It is similar in many points to the Tao-Tieh mask on Chou-dynasty bronzes. All the spaces are completely filled with an intricate interweave of colored areas in absolute balance. Most Mayan sculpture, like this lintel from Tikal, is carved in low relief, so

[1] Dr. Robert von Heine-Geldern, Research Associate in Anthropology of the American Museum of Natural History, has been able to show close affinities between the Uloa Valley and Totonac designs of Mexico and those of the late Chou dynasty in China.

as to harmonize with the surfaces of the rectangular structures. Some of the architects developed a degree of refinement in their design which called for less primitive conceptions than

The Copan Head. Rarely did the Mayan sculptors essay figures in the round. The Copan head of the maize goddess (Fig. 601), carved in the 6th century, indicates by its sensitive

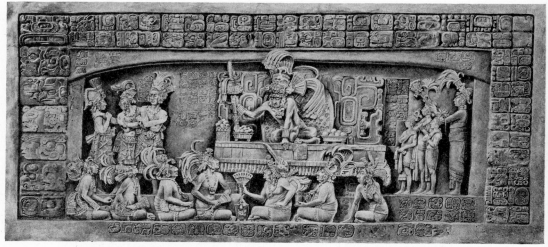

FIG. 599.—Restoration of lintel 3, Piedras Negras, Guatemala, early Mayan, about A.D. 400. Stone, length about 4½ feet (University of Pennsylvania Museum). (*Courtesy of University of Pennsylvania Museum.*)

this, as can be seen by studying some of the early pottery and the relief panel from Piedras Negras (Fig. 599).

Refined Space Designing of the Old Mayans. Early Mayan pottery, such as the two bowls from Holmul and Uaxactum (Fig. 600), rival for sophistication the tile paintings of the Chinese Han dynasty. The temple of the cross at Palenque and some of the buildings at Piedras Negras have great colored mural carvings in low relief as well composed as the plate from Holmul. The other plate, from Uaxactun, has an abstract quality in its lines like that of Chinese brushwork. The fine balance of its spaces rivals that of the best Greek pottery.

The lintel from Piedras Negras, perhaps the finest mural design of ancient American art, arises from hands as skilled as those that painted the two plates. The sculptor surpasses the painter here in his plausible indication of perspective depth, in the foreshortening of his figures, the naturalness of their poses, and the knowledge of anatomy.

modeling and its fine balance of decorative character and humane picturization, the highest degree of mastery achieved in the sculptor's art. In many respects this head has a Gothic and an archaic Greek quality. Unlike the art of the European sculptors, the indigenous art of America has a detached and impersonal repose comparable to that in most Buddhistic art. Prehistoric American sculpture as a whole lacks the sensual and emotional features that characterize the individualistic European creations. Like the art of the Egyptians, it is essentially religious and architectonic.

The South American Cultures. While the Mayan culture developed in Central America, other great cultures arose along the seacoast of Peru at Nazca and Trujillo. According to the ancient legends, their development came with the advent of people in ships. Similarly, the Mayan legends concerning Quetzalcoatl tell of his coming in a ship. From the beginning, the early Chimu culture, centered around Trujillo, had an advanced complex social structure, with war chiefs and priests ruling over the lower classes of warriors, artisans, and slaves.

The early Chimu had fine red pottery covered with a white slip decorated in black, red, yellow, and orange figures, showing helmeted warriors, fish, birds, and flowers. Vases in the form of human faces as well modeled as the Copan head have been found in early Chimu levels. Contemporaneous with the Chimu, the early Nazca—farther south in Peru—developed polychrome ware (Fig. 602) suggestive of lacquered inlay, with patterns similar to those on some of the Han-dynasty bronzes.

Following the Chimu and Nazca, other cultures grew up at Tiahuanaco and Chavin. The Tiahuanaco culture or its predecessors perfected architecture and casting in bronze. Like the Mayans, the early Peruvians built great ziggurats, constructing both round and square buildings with corbeled stone domical roofs. They planned their abundantly irrigated cities with much skill. Archaeologists differentiate between Epigonal, Chavin, late Chimu, and Inca cultures, which followed each other with a gradual degeneration of the arts until about

FIG. 600*a*.—Mortuary bowl, Uaxactun, early Mayan, about A.D. 320 (?). (*After Smith; courtesy of Carnegie Institution of Washington and University of Pennsylvania Museum.*)

1000 A.D. At that time the Quechuas, a highland tribe under their ruler, the Inca Manco Capac, began to conquer and coordinate all the tribes from Colombia to the Argentine, a

FIG. 600*b*.—Center of plate from Holmul, Guatemala, early Mayan, polychrome. (*Courtesy of George C. Vaillant and Peabody Museum.*)

process which continued over the next 500 years. Making their capital at Cuzco in Peru, the Incas united their empire with well-constructed roads carried over chasms on suspension bridges. They built many great cities, temples, and fortresses, notably Ollantaytambo, Macchu Picchu, Cuzco, and Sacsahuaman.

Through all the South American cultures, as well as those in Central America, the influence of technomorphic designs created first in weaving plays a great part in the architectural decoration. A comparison of a section of decorated wall in an Inca room at La Centinela (Fig. 603), part of the wall from the late Mayan temple at Mitla, and a design by a 20th-century architect on the Furniture Exchange in New York City, indicates the appropriateness of this primitive, indigenous design when applied in our own day. It is important to notice that in all the American cultures the high quality and humanistic character of the earlier

FIG. 601.—Head of Maize Goddess, Copan, Honduras, about A.D. 515. Trachyte stone, height about 1 foot 6 inches. Note that head combines Indo-Chinese and indigenous characteristics shown in archaic terra cottas (Fig. 596, *a* and *c*). (*Courtesy of Peabody Museum, Harvard University; photograph by Clarence Kennedy.*)

work gave way, as the cultures aged, to more massive architectural construction and more profuse decoration of a primitive, geometric character.

Late Mayan and Aztec Art. In Central America the well-ordered, relatively peaceful old Mayan empire passed away by 870. Before that time, the Itzas, a colonizing tribe of Mayans, founded the city of Chichen Itza in Yucatan. Other Mayans colonized Coba and Tulum near the eastern seacoast, perhaps going north toward the valley of Mexico, where they joined the growing Toltec culture which was emerging from the archaic there. Until about 1250, the new Mayans seem to have lived in an unproductive state. At that time there came a revival of culture at Chichen Itza, Mayapan, Uxmal, Labna, and other cities in Yucatan. The Caracol, a circular astronomical observatory or temple, is one of hundreds of well-planned buildings from this second or late Mayan empire (Fig. 604). The ziggurats of that period are much steeper than the early ones. They have high, combed stone cult-houses and suggest skyscraper cities with stepped-back buildings. In every way, the artistic productions of the late Mayans, as well as the Toltecs and the Aztecs who lived in the highlands of Mexico after A.D. 1300, are inferior to the work of the early Mayan empire. This is particularly noticeable in the case of Aztec temple sculpture and late Mayan wall painting. Both the late Mayans and the Aztecs painted codices telling the history of their people after the coming of the Spaniards. These approximate the cartoons of the later American comic strips or, if one believes in the continued influence of our indigenous art, the comic strips can be said to approximate late Mayan and Aztec painting. Central American influences carried by Mayan or Aztec colonists found their way up the Mississippi River valley, appearing in the pyramids of the Mound Builders.

Surveying indigenous American culture, one becomes convinced that Asiatic influences which may have contributed to its rapid flowering at the time of Christ were either so small, or the native American primitivism was so great, that humanistic characteristics soon became lost in a jungle of primitive geometric

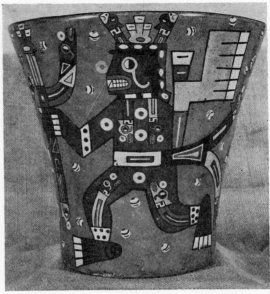

FIG. 602.—Polychrome ware, early Nazca, Peru. Although the inlay type of decoration imitated here is similar to that found on late Chou-dynasty bronzes, the formal characteristics are similar to later Aztec work when Oriental influences had died out. (*Courtesy of John Wise; photograph from Fogg Museum.*)

designs. In the later Mayan, Inca, and Aztec art any foreign influences had practically disappeared, transformed into designs only quasi-Oriental and distinctively American. An American style of architecture, sculpture, and painting had spread over the two continents when the Europeans arrived. To something like that style the Americans of the 20th century may be gradually changing all the European contributions made during the last 200 years. Our Gothic inheritance, vying with the humanist Classical tradition of simplicity and balance, may find in the quasi-Oriental Indian styles (Fig. 605) the form most appropriate to the expression of our American culture. If there be any tendency in this direction, it can be discovered in a brief survey of the fortunes of

a   *b*   *c*

FIG. 603.—*a*, carved design on wall of room, La Centinela, Peru, Inca or Chincha, about A.D. 600; compare with Fig. 33, Chap. III; *b*, decorated wall from Mayan temple, Mitla; *c*, architectural detail, Number Two Park Avenue, New York, by Bochman and Kahn.

the European styles on the American continents between 1700 and 1930.

Architecture

Earliest Colonial Buildings. The earliest colonial monumental stone structures on the American continent are the 16th- and 17th-century baroque churches of Central and South America (Fig. 606*a*). Decorated with lacy, intricate, carved stonework under the direction of Jesuit or Franciscan architects, these *Churrigueresque*

baroque changed to a more geometric, blocky line which reduces the vitality of the interweave to an emotionless pattern, similar in some respects to early Eastern Christian carving, in others to the plant ornament on the East Indian temples of Ajanta. A section from the façade of the early church at Taxco shows this new American style (Fig. 606*b*). Notice particularly the difference between the central grotesque face and earlier European grotesques, as well as the geometric windmill effect of the carved rosettes.

FIG. 604.—Caracol tower from west, Chichen Itza, Yucatan, about A.D. 1250. (*Courtesy of Carnegie Institution of Washington.*)

buildings were constructed in great part by the enslaved Indians. Here for the first time can be seen the effects of the union of Indian and European styles. The flamboyant lines of the

The English emigrants at Jamestown, Virginia, and in New England found the Indians living in long houses built of bowed tree branches covered with bark. Many of the settlers lived in dugouts, others in conical huts of branches, rushes, and turf. The church at Jamestown was a frame structure like an Eng-

FIG. 605.—Cheyenne Dog Soldiers, water color by Monroe Tsa Toke, Osage Indian student, University of Oklahoma, 1929. (*Courtesy of Oscar B. Jacobson.*)

lish barn, covered with wattling, grass, and earth. The earliest houses at Plymouth seem to have been made of hewn planks set vertically in the ground like palisades and covered with a thatched roof, perhaps plastered inside. The first log houses of the type used by the Midwestern pioneers appear relatively late (1669) and seem to have been brought into America by the Swedes and Finns who settled along the Delaware River.

The most popular houses among the wealthier New England colonists, such as the Capen house built in 1683 at Topsfield, Massachusetts, were framed structures covered with clapboards (Fig. 607). In appearance this structure followed closely that of late medieval English city houses, with overhanging stories and high peaked roof. The simple, almost primitive plan shows an entrance in the center of the long side, with a steep staircase, which is placed against the wall of a large, central chimney built to accommodate fireplaces in the great rooms to right and left. The side frames for the house, usually fabricated on the ground by shipwrights or carpenters, were raised into place by the combined efforts of neighbors. Intermediate posts and girders spanning the frame

received joists on which the floors were laid with boards of random width. The windows, often swung on hinges, had small diamond-

a

b

FIG. 606.—*a*, baroque church portal, Arequipa, Peru, 17th century (*after M. Mancitta*); *b*, ornament from façade of church at Taxco, Mexico, 17th century (*after photograph by A. Henderson*). The Spanish baroque style combining with primitive Indian form creates here a new ornament almost Oriental in appearance but definitely American. Compare with later designs by Sullivan and with mural painting by Rivera.

shaped glass panes brought from England. The interior walls of the New England houses were sometimes built of brick or of daubed wattle, which in time gave place to lath and plaster.

FIG. 607.—The front of the Capen house, Topsfield, Massachusetts, 1683. Wood with brick chimney, length 44 feet, width 20 feet, height 30 feet. (*Courtesy of Lesch-Carnegie and Topsfield Historic Society.*)

The ornamental features of the Capen house are the Tudor chimney and the lower end of the second-story posts carved into pendants. Other famous houses in the early New England medieval tradition are the Fairbanks house in Dedham, the Ward house and the House of Seven Gables in Salem, Massachusetts—all built prior to 1684.

The Renaissance Georgian Style. The Craigie house, in Cambridge, Massachusetts, typical of those built by wealthy merchants in the 18th century, shows a refined English Renaissance decorative style, known as the Georgian, characterized by well-modeled moldings and beautifully carved cornices (Fig. 608). The method of construction remains the same as that of the Capen house, but the plan differs by approaching the square, with a great central transverse hall dividing two separate sections, each with a central chimney. Both of these parts have the plan of the Capen house. Thus this colonial mansion has four rooms instead of two, on the main floor. Such a scheme descended from Palladio by way of Gibbs's *Book of Architecture*—

a handbook of construction frequently employed by the colonial builders. Other houses in the Georgian colonial style are the Hancock house in Boston, and the Miles Brewton house

FIG. 608a.—Craigie house (Vassall or Longfellow House), Cambridge, Massachusetts, 1759. (*Courtesy of Harvard Film Service.*)

in Charleston. Variations are the Governor's palace at Williamsburg, Virginia, and Cliveden at Germantown, Pennsylvania. In the 18th century many churches were built in this style, notably the Old North Church in Boston, St. Paul's Chapel in New York City, and Christ Church in Philadelphia (Fig. 608*b*).

Farms and city houses in the Central Atlantic states show Dutch and German influence. Here the inhabitants of New York, New Jersey, and Pennsylvania developed a brickmaking industry and discovered easily worked stone. This had such influence upon the decorative details that 18th-century houses in the Middle States lack many of the classical refinements.

The most expansive palatial examples of the Georgian style appear in the great feudal estates of the Southern colonies. Most characteristic of these Southern mansions were loggias connecting the central dwelling with balanced outbuildings, an idea taken from James Gibbs's designs of English country houses. Among the best examples of this style are Westover, built in 1730, and Mount Airy, in 1758, in Virginia. Notable in all the Georgian houses are the refined Renaissance doorways, some with broken pediments, others with rich cornices, and many with fanlights and flanking engaged pilasters or columns. After 1735, tall pilasters and sometimes rusticated enframements were applied to the corners of the houses. The finely carved wooden paneling of the interiors showed sometimes baroque, sometimes French neo-classical influence; the latter, particularly in plantations near New Orleans.

The Classical Revival. Shortly before the American Revolution, Peter Harrison—the first American professional architect—built the Redwood Library in Newport, Rhode Island. Here the Roman Doric portico, with its four columns raised upon a high porch, presents the appearance of a temple façade. Only the wings on either side of this façade prevent it from appearing like the imitation Roman temples being built at that time in English gardens. After the Revolution, that universal genius, the statesman Thomas Jefferson, designed one of the first governmental buildings of the new republic, the state capitol at Richmond, Virginia. Jefferson, convinced that the republican form of government had its origin in antiquity, considered that the style appropriate to the new nation should stem directly from classical examples. With that in mind, he adopted for his model the Maison Carrée at Nîmes, substituting the Ionic order in place of the Corinthian for the portico, and windows pierced in the cella walls in place of the engaged pilasters.

Jefferson planned Monticello, his own home, with a raised central dome, a Doric portico, and great side halls like those in the original Georgian houses that had been taken from Palladio's Villa Capra. The final development of Jefferson's plan was reached in the University of Virginia at Charlottesville. Here, at the end of a long central court flanked on either side by colonnades, connecting rows of Georgian houses with high porticos, stands a replica of the Roman Pantheon (Fig. 609).

A combination of the classic and the Palladian academic influence with the high central dome can be seen in the Massachusetts State House in Boston (1795–1798), by Charles Bulfinch. Its tall dome rises from an attic over a Corinthian colonnade based upon an arched loggia. The culminating result in the union of

Fig. 608*b*.—Congregational Church, Southbury, Connecticut, founded 1732. Every New England town had one or more churches of this type, often presenting charming refined variations of the Continental tradition and constituting a distinctive new style.

plans influenced by the academicism of Jefferson and Bulfinch and the classical revival, is the United States Capitol at Washington (Fig. 610). A study of the competitive drawings made in 1793 and that stage of the building completed by Walter in 1865 shows a continual fluctuation between pure classicism and Palladian academicism. From the first, both William Thornton and the French architect Steven Hallet had in mind a central dome. This gradually rose from a low, round form, to the high shape suggestive of St. Paul's in London and the Panthéon in Paris.

During the early years of the Republic many other buildings imitated as closely as possible Greek or Roman originals. Noteworthy is the Bank of the United States, or Custom House, Columbian Exposition, in 1893. Architects such as Richard Morris Hunt, influenced by French academicism, started the vogue of designing art museums in the classical style. McKim,

FIG. 609.—University of Virginia, the lawn and rotunda, by Thomas Jefferson. (*Courtesy of Frank J. Roos, Jr.*)

in Philadelphia. Built in 1819 by Benjamin Latrobe, it has the form of a Doric temple. Beginning with this bank, the Greek revival spread rapidly from Georgia to Michigan, until Greek temples in all the orders, used as dwelling houses, dominated the great estates. Stimulated by the Greek war for independence, 1821–1827, the frontier states named their towns Ypsilanti, Byron, Sparta, Troy, Syracuse, and Athens. Here they built their temples alongside the log cabins of the first settlers. Using handbooks such as Minard Lafever's *Modern Builders' Guide*, published in 1833, these amateurs soon substituted square pillars of wood and stock moldings for the finely wrought Greek columns with their refined entasis. The new style resulting in western New York, Ohio, and the Middle Western states had a distinctive charm of its own.

The classical tradition in American building early became associated particularly with governmental and academic buildings or libraries. Dying down for a time during the Romantic era after 1850, it returned to culminate in the buildings of the Chicago World's Fair, the

Mead, and White—a firm founded in 1879—employed refined Renaissance classical forms in the Boston Public Library and the Morgan Library, New York. The same firm designed the Pennsylvania Railroad Station in New York on the plan of a Roman bath, and inaugurated an era of classical station construction. Other architects in the classicist tradition are Carrère and Hastings, with the New York Public Library; John Russell Pope, with the Temple of the Scottish Rite in Washington, built as a reconstruction of the Mausoleum at Halicarnassus; and Henry Bacon, whose Lincoln Memorial in Washington achieves something more original, albeit using the classical order.

The Romantic Gothic Revival. Both Jefferson and Latrobe, although primarily builders in the classical style, were interested in that Gothic revival which accompanied the birth of the Romantic movement on the Continent. About 1840, Richard Upjohn planned Trinity Church in New York City on a design copied from English examples. James Renwick built St. Patrick's Cathedral in New York between 1850 and 1879. As Gothic detail more easily lent itself to the prevailing wooden house construction than did Greek classicism, there were built after 1840 a succession of domestic buildings in various medieval styles (Fig. 611). Small frame churches were designed with pointed windows and spires. The invention of the jigsaw and its use by romantically inclined builders led to the adoptions of an ornament suggestive of the old-fashioned lacy valentines. Steamboats that plied the great inland waterways carried this flamboyant ornament through the Middle West.

The most appropriate use of the Gothic appears in a number of modern churches—particularly the Cathedral of St. John the Divine, in New York, by Ralph Adams Cram; the National Cathedral at Washington, by Vaughn, Bodley, and Frohman; and the Riverside Church in New York, by Henry C. Pelton, Allen, and Collens. Several of the large universities, notably Princeton, Yale, and Chicago, have attempted an adaptation of the English Collegiate Gothic, designed to lend to the halls of learning a proper atmosphere of medieval enlightenment.

The end of the Civil War found an eclecticism in American architectural styles such as no other culture had ever faced. Houses were hastily thrown together by contractors without professional training, who used stock patterns turned out en masse by the planing mills. They catered to the individual desires of the highly imaginative Americans, each of whom considered himself an architect. As a result, in the new, rapidly developing communities of the Middle West and the suburbs of the Eastern cities, many streets furnished complete museums of building styles. These included Swiss villas, Egyptian or Greek temples, and Romanesque castles. The Queen Anne style and the Italian Gothic vied with Elizabethan and Renaissance.

Richardson and the Romanesque Revival. Henry Hobson Richardson, the dominating figure of late 19th-century American architecture, with Richard Morris Hunt, was one of the first men

to study abroad at the École des beaux-arts. Unlike Hunt, Richardson cared little for the French Renaissance. Observing the difficulties in getting skilled carvers for detailed stone-

Fig. 610.—The Capitol, Washington, D.C., by Thornton, Hallet, and Latrobe, 1792–1830. (*Photograph by Hanauer.*)

work, he chose the Romanesque style as particularly appropriate to American needs. His first large commission, Trinity Church in Boston, was planned for a small, almost square plot. This precluded the use of a deep Gothic nave. Forced by a condition that was to become common in later American urban construction, Richardson constructed a high church on a cruciform plan, not unlike the early German Romanesque (Fig. 612). Above broad naves he built a massive tower of polychrome sandstone. Simple decoration was confined, as in true Romanesque buildings, to engaged colonnettes, window moldings, and borders. Richardson found that the various Romanesque styles allowed for an elasticity of plan and a picturesque massing of parts as interesting as the Gothic and easily adaptable to civic buildings, factories, and stores, as well as office buildings. Further, Richardson discovered that the interior space could be translated into well-designed exteriors, thus uniting efficient construction and good composition. Following Trinity Church in Boston, Richardson designed the City Hall in Albany, the Courthouse at Pittsburgh, and many railway stations, libraries, and smaller

Fig. 611.—Little Antioch, frame construction, Yellow Springs, Ohio, 1860–1870, one of the earliest Academic buildings in the castellated Gothic style. Many of these structures copied the Smithsonian Institution in Washington.

churches. Before his death in 1886, Richardson was building iron-frame structures bolted to transverse rails set in concrete. He is thus one of the originators of skyscraper construction.

The Origins of the Skyscraper. For many observers our sole original contribution to the spatial arts is the alternately praised and condemned skyscraper. Foreign critics find in this typically American construction either a triumph of engineering skill comparable to the Roman amphitheaters and baths, or a poorly designed architectural monstrosity. Most agree that few buildings of this type have reached the

[1] Courtesy of E. M. Upjohn and *College Art Bulletin.*

excellence of design to be found in American motorcars. Curiously, one of the first skyscrapers designed, a twenty-eight story building by L. S. Buffington, of Minneapolis, was developed from

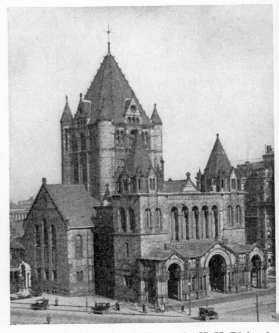

Fig. 612.—Trinity Church, Boston, by H. H. Richardson, 1877. (*Courtesy of Lesch-Carnegie.*)

a modification of Richardson's Romanesque forms into an original structure of more than average dignity (Fig. 613). This edifice, although completed only on paper, seems to have influenced contemporary builders through the unique quality of its interior construction. Buffington, its inventor, defined the skyscraper as "composed of a braced skeleton of steel with (masonry) veneer supported on shelves fastened to the skeleton at each story." His plans for the new building showed square cast-iron columns anchored to a foundation of concrete reinforced with I beams.[1]

During the years when Buffington dreamed of his building and used a modification of this same system of construction in the West Hotel at Minneapolis, Colonel W. L. B. Jenney built the Home Insurance Building in Chicago. In 1886 Burnham and Root built the sixteen-story Monadnock Building, also in Chicago. In 1891 they used the first riveted steel frame, there-emphasize in its exterior design the greater weight carried by the vertical members. The frame was cased with terra-cotta tiles delicately colored with intricate design (Fig. 614*b*). Sul-

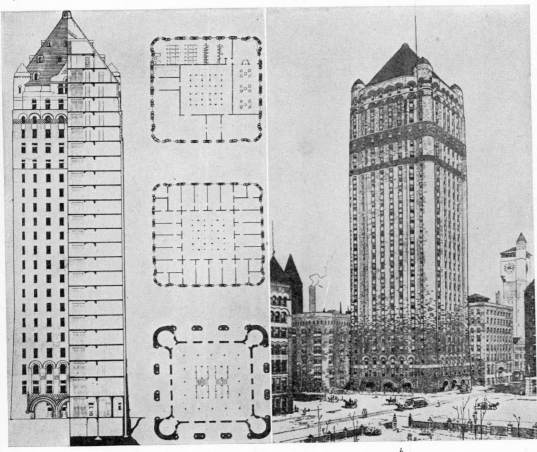

a   *b*

FIG. 613.—*a*, first plans for skyscraper, by L. S. Buffington, 1883; *b*, finished drawing of Buffington skyscraper by Harvey Ellis, *Inland Architect and News Record*, July, 1888. (*After E. M. Upjohn, College Art Bulletin, March,* 1935.)

after called "Burnham construction," in Chicago's twenty-story Masonic Temple.

Buffington was followed among the earliest builders of skyscrapers by Louis Sullivan, who not only showed great originality in the new style of construction, but also in the invention of an appropriate form of ornament. Sullivan quickly recognized the decorative possibilities in steel construction and designed the Guarantee (Prudential) Building in Buffalo so as to

livan's original influence, one of the most powerful in the development of 20th-century American architecture, made itself felt through the Transportation and Fisheries Buildings at the Chicago Exposition and later in the works of his pupil, Frank Lloyd Wright.

Although the chief considerations in the design of skyscrapers are necessarily utilitarian, distinct advances in their formal design have been made during the past twenty years. To the practical Americans, the primary appeal of the earliest skyscrapers was that of economy. Such a building was designed to give a maximum rental capacity on a minimum of ground

the Loop section of Chicago too many high buildings reduced the light in the streets and the lower stories. Then increased lighting bills added to the maintenance costs. At this stage,

FIG. 614a.—Guarantee (Prudential) Building, Buffalo, N. Y., by L. H. Sullivan, 1896, after architect's drawing. Terra cotta on steel frame, length 116 feet, width 93 feet, height 163 feet. (*Courtesy of Lesch-Carnegie.*)

FIG. 614b.—Sullivan design called Impromptu, from L. H. Sullivan, *A System of Architectural Ornament*, 1924. (*Courtesy of American Institute of Architects.*)

area. With technical improvements in steel construction, it would seem as though no limit need be put to the number of stories, which like horizontal cells cluster around the elevator shafts.

The first thirty years of skyscraper building convinced designers that above a certain height the maintenance costs must exceed rental income. Engineers skilled in mechanical appliances, electricity, traffic control, water supply, and heating designed the successful skyscrapers of the thirties. The skyscraper suffered in formal quality because of the primary interest in utility. Experience soon showed that in such crowded centers as downtown Manhattan and

it was found advisable to pass laws making setback construction a requirement. This forced the builders to use more interesting masses, which soon came to play a decorative role, as in the French Building on upper Fifth Avenue, New York. Here the recessed upper floors lend a dynamic effect to the tower, which seems to gather momentum from the steps to push skyward, like the Central American pyramid temples (Fig. 615).

Since the simple, unbroken repetition of windows gives an unpleasing, monotonous effect, designers following Buffington and Sullivan soon learned to stress the vertical lines in the exterior construction, to decorate the tops of the setbacks and the termination of the building with bold flat ornament. Architects like Cass Gilbert, in the Woolworth tower, and Raymond Hood, in the Chicago Tribune tower, searching for a suitable type of design, employed Gothic detail. Among the many plans for the widely advertised Chicago Tribune competition, the unbuilt design by the Finnish architect Eliel Saarinen, like Buffington's design forty years earlier, was the one which had the greatest influence upon the ensuing building development (Fig. 616). It stressed the verticality of the building by simplifying detail and employing setback construction for its aesthetic effect. Raymond M. Hood, the builder of the Chicago Tribune tower, profiting by Saarinen's suggestions, improved his design in the New York American Radiator building, where he not only used setback construction but employed colors.

The chief rule of the skyscraper architect, proposed by Sullivan and stressed by Wright, Saarinen, and Hood, was that the form of the building should follow its function. This raised the question whether the chief function of the skyscraper is to appear vertical or to suggest the presence of a number of horizontal floors supporting people, machinery, and manufactured products. Raymond Hood, having perfected the News Building (Fig. 616b), which better than any other stressed verticality, turned to the design of a building which would bring verticality and horizontality into a perfect equilibrium; a building which should interest because of its color and give the maximum of light and floor space for the minimum of maintenance cost. About his McGraw-Hill Building (Fig. 616c), in New York, Hood wrote:

The concept of architecture as a logic does not in any sense imply the neglect of appearance, but, on the contrary, logic and knowledge always have been the road to beauty . . .

A logically designed plan is nearly always capable of producing an acceptable form or mass and an

outward appearance that satisfies aesthetic demands. The materials, their color and texture, and details of elaboration also contribute to appearance and are largely matters of choice. The "progress photo-

Fig. 615.—The Fred F. French Building, Fifth Avenue, New York. (*Photograph by J. T. Wood.*)

graph" of the McGraw-Hill Building, included in the illustrations, shows the practical development of and relation between the structural construction and the enclosing walls of the façades. These enclosing walls are analogous, may we say, to a glove that is slipped on the hand to shelter and protect.[1]

After the depression of 1929, when American businessmen found that the highest skyscrapers could not pay, architects turned to the design of smaller buildings with greater refinement. The discovery of new materials, particularly glass brick and weatherproof metal alloys, and the development of air conditioning led to the design of new building types. The Corning Glass Works Building (Fig. 617) at 718 Fifth Avenue, New York City, with sculptured details by Sidney Waugh, marks a step forward in design. Here modern American architectural form reaches a state of refinement comparable to that achieved by the designers of late American motorcars. The function of this

[1] RAYMOND M. HOOD, *Contemporary American Architects—Raymond M. Hood*, Whittlesey House, McGraw-Hill Book Company, Inc., New York, 1931.

building as a display room and offices for Steuben glassware is completely expressed by the immaculate design. Its sparkling glass units, framed in bars of Indiana limestone and nickel ations of the German Bauhaus, the Dutch architect Mies van der Rohe, and the French architect Corbusier. These houses have large window spaces and rooms opening upon gar-

a *b* *c* *d*

FIG. 616.—Solutions of the skyscraper problem. *a*, design for Chicago Tribune Building, by Eliel Saarinen, 1923; *b*, News Building, New York, by Raymond Hood, 1930; *c*, progress photograph, the McGraw-Hill Building, New York, by Raymond Hood, 1931; *d*, Philadelphia Savings Fund Society Building, by Howe and Lescaze, 1931–1932.

silver, suggest the skilled workmanship in the product sold.

Late Domestic Architecture. The influence of Louis Sullivan, perpetuated in the buildings and writings of Frank Lloyd Wright, one of the most creative and stimulating architects of the 20th century, found expression particularly in domestic architecture. After his Larkin Soap Building, built in 1904, and his earthquake-proof Tokio hotel in 1916–1920, Wright turned to the problem of reinforced-concrete construction and to the design of dwelling houses. His earliest creations made use of Mayan and Aztec forms for a desert environment and long, horizontal structures for the Western prairies. Specifically, Wright's idea is that American house construction should appear appropriate to the environment. Influenced by his studies in Japan, Wright suggested the use of Japanese house designs that closely approximate the cre-

dens. Wright, with his colony of apprentices at Taliesin, epitomizes the American desire to commune with nature. His dreams for the city of the future with plenty of air space and sunlight, horizontal in its aspect instead of vertical and cramped as at present, have already begun to find expression in many national civic planning developments.

Modern Industrial Buildings and Fairs. The pure functionalism of the factory and skyscraper designer gives way in the Cincinnati Union Terminal (Fig. 618*a*), by Fellheimer and Wagner, to the decorative functionalism which combines well-placed masses with steel construction, decorative sculpture, texture, color, and the rhythmic arrangement of accents. The terminal, perfectly designed with relation to the tracks of four railway systems, has a comfortable waiting room decorated with great mosaic murals of the city's various industries by

Winold Reiss. The central steel half dome joining the waiting room to the city has a façade
suggesting subtly by its lines the movement of
the trains and the structure of the bridges on
all the great systems it serves. Before the station, a fountain with colored lights terminates
a central boulevard 1,000 yards long. On either
side of this are being erected great municipal apartment houses. When finished, the entire group of buildings will form one of the
most inspiring civic plans in the world, impressive as a monument to enlightened industrial democracy.

America's most advanced ideas in architectural construction have found their widest dissemination through a series of great industrial
exhibitions or fairs, beginning with New York's
Crystal Palace Fair of 1853 and the Centennial
Exposition in Philadelphia in 1876. In these
early fairs a number of greenhouses constructed
of glass and iron introduced Americans to the
possibilities of metal construction such as that
in Labrouste's Bibliothèque Sainte Geneviève
and Paxton's London Crystal Palace.

The Columbian Exposition of 1893–1894, not
only gave Sullivan an opportunity to show the
excellence of his design, but even more strikingly, through its great "Hall of Science," copied after the French Hall of Science, impressed
upon the people the possibilities in well-designed truss construction. That Chicago fair
was still more important for its influence upon
city planning. Its architects, many of whom had
been trained in Paris, had an eye to vistas and
placed their chief monuments at significant
focal points. The system of parks that grew
out of that exposition definitely benefited the
city where it was held. Other expositions—
in Buffalo, St. Louis, San Diego, and San
Francisco—gave many of the better known
American architects opportunities to influence
American taste.

The Chicago Century of Progress fair, in
1933, introduced many novel schemes of construction, most of which were too bizarre to
be practical. The chief advantage to be gained

from a study of this Chicago fair lay in the
use of color in architecture and in the development of lighting effects, which began to play
an increasingly extensive role in the design of

Fig. 617.—Corning Glass Works Building, Fifth Ave.,
New York, W. and G. Platt and J. M. Gates, architects,
and Sidney Waugh, sculptor, 1937. This structure
illustrates complete union of form, function, and decoration where sculptor and architect work in cooperation.
(*Courtesy of Corning Glass; Photograph by Brown Bros.*)

buildings after 1930. The New York World of
Tomorrow fair of 1939–1940 showed increasing
skill in functional design and a renewed interest in group planning. The model city exhibit
in the Perisphere unites the best of the practical
suggestions resulting from the last fifty years of
city planning (Fig. 619a). The contemporaneous
Golden Gate Exposition at San Francisco, on
the other hand, stressed highly decorated Pacific aboriginal and Indian styles.

City Planning. Two of the earliest colonial
leaders in America, General Oglethorpe and
William Penn, laid down plans for cities which
today place Oglethorpe, Georgia, and Phila-

delphia far ahead of such haphazard developments as Boston. The nation's capital, designed by Major L'Enfant, has a number of radiating avenues converging upon the central dome of

part of the long-range planning for a stable industrial civilization.

Since each community represents a tremendous capital investment owned by countless

Fig. 618a.—Cincinnati Union Terminal, 1933. (*Courtesy of Cincinnati Terminal Corp.*)

the Capitol. Although his plan was forgotten for many years, interest in it was revived during the administration of President Wilson, when new buildings had to be constructed to accommodate the increased governmental activity.

The prime difficulty in most city planning until the 20th century was due to the fact that too few trained individuals had given specific thought to such problems as the regulation of traffic, control of the ingress of food stuffs, and the elimination of waste material. No one had considered the city as a greatly magnified human being which needed light, air, and exercise, as well as protection from the smoke and noise of the machine. As cities simply grew, with the great concentration of population in the slums and with the advent of the skyscrapers, daily drawing their thousands of occupants from suburban areas, the problems of congestion and health control eventually forced the architects to think in terms of the efficiently planned metropolis. In the 20th century, a few enlightened industrialists also began to perceive that well-housed, healthy workers are a necessary

individuals, many of whom will be affected adversely by any change proposed, the problem of city planning in the towns already built becomes primarily one of a social and political nature. New laws must be passed enabling local governments to condemn unsafe and unsanitary areas. New funds must be voted to buy land on which to construct high-speed roadways or the necessary parks to accommodate great populations. The chief problems of city planning for the latter half of the 20th century continue to be those of slum clearance, adequate housing for the lower salaried classes, more rapid and efficient means of communication for traffic and commodities, and the making available of adequate healthy recreational centers for anemic city dwellers (Fig. 619*b*).

The practical city, of necessity, looks well. The grouping or zoning of the city's various functions necessitates that those buildings which have to do with government and the commercial life be arranged in the center, like the medieval *Rathäuser* and the guildhalls. From this center the brain of the city can most easily control the industrial and transportational developments that connect it with the outside world. Naturally, the problems differ somewhat between seaport and inland towns. Residen-

Garden City and Suburban Planning. With the Arcadian and Utopian idea continually before him, the average American considers the ideal living conditions to be such as will allow him a

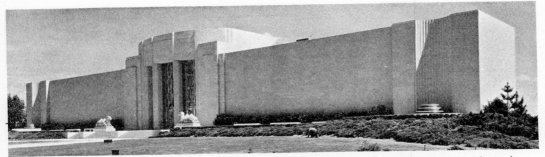

FIG. 618*b*.—Seattle Art Museum, Bebb and Gould, architects, 1933. (*Courtesy of Seattle Art Museum.*)

tial facilities must be regulated by the presence or absence of nuisance factors, such as smoke, noise, and poisonous fumes, connected with the city's industrial plants.

Many city governments or groups of businessmen interested in real estate engaged architects to study the problems of city planning after the Chicago World's Fair of 1893. New York passed her tenement-house act in 1900, after many surveys showed that conditions were rapidly growing worse. Chicago and San Francisco developed city plans for further development in 1910; Cleveland and Philadelphia followed. In most of these plans definite attempts were made to arrange governmental office sections with regard to monumental groupings of buildings, the employment of vistas, focal points of interest, and the regulation of monuments along lines laid down by the Parisian city planners during the Napoleonic Empire. These had already been partially successful in the case of Washington and Philadelphia. New York, Philadelphia, and Chicago becoming increasingly conscious of the necessity for adequate parkways and recreation centers, developed the terminal facilities of their railways and motor roads to care for the increased suburban commuting populations, many of whom traveled as much as 80 miles a day to and from work.

maximum of space in an individual home, preferably in the suburbs. Beginning with the town of Pullman, founded in 1880 at Gary, Indiana, there rose in America several privately planned suburban real-estate developments. Following that start, a number of industrial towns like Walpole, Massachusetts, and Overlook County Colony, planned for the General Chemical Company near Wilmington, Delaware, were patterned after Letchworth, the first garden city of England, Tours in France, or Emden in Germany.

During the World War and shortly afterward a number of industrial villages were planned by the federal government. Three, in particular, deserve mention: Union Park Gardens, Wilmington, Delaware, built for shipworkers; one near Bridgeport, Connecticut, for munitions workers; and Yorkship Village near Camden, New Jersey. These garden cities are so arranged that houses and apartments are convenient to through traffic streets and car lines without being directly on them. Each town has a community center with school, city hall, stores, and recreation areas. Considerable attention is given in all these projects to landscaping, the houses being arranged in irregular building lines along curved roadways, so that the owner of each, on approaching his home, gains a distinctive pictorial impression.

In most garden cities frame houses built in a style derived from a combination of the early New England frame, gable construction, with irregular ground plan, are the rule. Since such

(1) garden cities for the lower salaried professional class; (2) large apartment-house developments for industrial workers. Of the former, Norris, Tennessee, and Greenbelt, Maryland,

FIG. 619a.—Centerton, the heart of the Democracity of the future as visualized by the designer, Henry Dreyfuss, for the World of Tomorrow, New York World's Fair, 1939. The planned City of the Future consists of a central business, governmental, social, educational, and cultural section shown here. Its designer describes it as "a center built in greenery with a perfect traffic system, and surrounding it, separated by a green belt, are industrial and residential towns—and all these towns, with the business and social section at the center, together constitute Democracity." (Photo Garrison.) (*Courtesy of Rogers-Kellogg-Stillson, Inc., and New York World's Fair, 1939.*)

houses appear best in combination with elms and maples, the streets are planted with these trees, whose lines carry the impression of the central parkway with its brook over into the residence area. Lawns without fences or hedges lend an air of continuity and friendliness to the community. Obviously, the cost of such houses as described, coupled with high commutation rates, make these developments available to only the high-salaried classes. Underpaid factory workers or people in the seasonal industries, without steady employment, are obliged to live in the abandoned small tenement houses or flats nearer the centers of industry.

After 1929, the federal government allocated funds for two types of housing developments:

are leading examples. Detroit, Cleveland, and New York have begun the construction of a number of community apartment houses like the Karl Marx Apartment in Vienna, which will eventually give to the underprivileged classes rooms renting from six to ten dollars a month. In some cases, trade guilds such as the Stocking Makers' Union in Philadelphia and the Tailors' Union in New York City have undertaken the construction of well-equipped apartments to rent for reasonable rates. These apartments are planned with outside windows. They have good cross ventilation, a modicum of privacy, standardized sanitary and heating equipment. Some have balconies, porches, and roof facilities for sunshine and recreation. In their fireproof construction, the newest types of insulated noiseproof walls and in some cases glass bricks are being used. A comparison of any of these examples with any slum will con-

of the real combined with the romantic urge to forceful expression, gradually revealing a refined, almost Oriental feeling for occult balance (Fig. 620). American painting as it emerges

FIG. 619*b*.—Democracity emerging. A cooperative U. S. government and municipal housing project, Lakeview Terrace, Cleveland, Ohio, 1939. (*Courtesy of PWA.*)

vince one that only from such surroundings as those provided by these new, clean homes can we hope to gain a healthy democracy, capable of producing an art of refinement and distinction. Cleanliness is next to godliness, and beauty rarely comes from homes of squalor (Fig. 619*c*).

Painting

A distinctly American style of painting worthy to rank with the works of the great European masters developed but slowly before the 20th century. However, a few vigorous, colorful pictures, distinguishable from European paintings, can be found even in the 19th century. In these, characteristic idealizations

during the 20th century makes a new, definite contribution to the world's art still undiscernible to most Continental critics. To understand this American style one must study significant monuments of its development, keeping in mind that the painter unconsciously strove to express in terms of paint, mass, and line, emotions similar to those occasioned by the mysticism of a Whittier or a Whitman, the gusty humor of Mark Twain, and the idealism of Emerson, through a realism related to that of Breughel, Rembrandt, and Hogarth.

English Academic Influence in Colonial Art. The usual plaint of the European critic that all American painting derives from Old World sources, appears most correct when one considers the influence of the English Academy with its rococo tendencies on the professional colonial artist. Corresponding to the practice of building aristocratic homes in the Georgian style, there was a desire among the wealthier

Revolutionary War. Trumbull's art education started with books on art in the college library. He copied Italian landscapes, Coypel's Rebecca at the Well, Van Dyck's Cardinal Bentivoglio,

Fig. 619c.—Close-up of Democracity. View of court and inexpensive appropriate sculpture in concrete. Cooperative municipal and U. S. government housing project. Willert's Park, Buffalo, New York, 1939. (*Courtesy of PWA.*)

colonists for portraits painted in the English court manner. Two of the most talented painters—John Singleton Copley of Boston and Benjamin West of Philadelphia—followed this prevailing English mode. West, who spent the greater part of his life in England, succeeded Sir Joshua Reynolds as president of the Royal Academy in 1792.

Copley, John Trumbull, Charles Willson Peale, and Washington Allston, all studied in Boston the same copy of Van Dyck's baroque Cardinal Bentivoglio. These men were but a few of the more talented members of a large class of itinerant painters who earned a living decorating stagecoaches and painting signboards for shop- and innkeepers. The works of the lesser members of this group indicate that most of them had a style in which color played the most important role, as in the work of 15th-century Dutch and Flemish primitives.

John Trumbull (1756–1843), who graduated from Harvard at the age of seventeen, served as an aide-de-camp to Washington through the

and later, one of the works of Raphael. Trumbull's original compositions include a number of small historical scenes, notably the Battle of Bunker Hill, the Signing of the Declaration of Independence, and the Surrender at Yorktown —familiar to all Americans as the earliest narrative paintings of national history. These are noteworthy for the fine quality of their realistic miniature portraiture. Trumbull's work, like that of all the other colonial painters, shows a love of brilliant color, more exciting or Gothic than that of his English contemporaries.

Refinement and delicacy of the American color sense begins with the work of Gilbert Stuart (1755–1828). Although he studied with West for a time in London, Stuart spent most of his life in the colonies. His many portraits of George Washington show the skill of his brushwork, the richness of his flesh tones, and his ability in anatomical construction. The exuberance and vitality of his own character found its way into Stuart's portraits, which rival those of his English contemporaries, Gainsborough and Romney. He adhered to the rococo color scheme which charms through its use of pleasing warm shades of orange and pink, with lavender shadows. This tradition, supported

cating various brands of tobacco and other commodities.

Realism in Early American Painting. In their earliest compositions, painted before studying

Fig. 620.—Fur Traders Descending the Missouri, by George Caleb Bingham, 1845. Oil on canvas, height 29¼ inches, width 36¼ inches. (*Courtesy of Metropolitan Museum of Art.*)

by the Philadelphia portraitist Charles Willson Peale (1741–1827), eventuated in the Philadelphia Art Academy. Thomas Sully (1783–1872), the most facile painter of this academic group, gained such skill as a portraitist that in 1838 he was commissioned to paint a portrait of Queen Victoria. His tradition has continued in the American commercial art schools. It accounts for most of the idealized types with pretty faces on American magazine covers and in enormous billboard advertisements advo-

in Europe, Matthew Pratt (1734–1805) and John Singleton Copley (1737–1815) showed intense realism similar to that found in the Flemish primitives. Copley's style is said to have influenced even David toward his most realistic creation, The Death of arat. Matthew Pratt's The American School, in the Metropolitan Museum of Art, and Copley's historical portrait compositions have a style close to that of Hogarth. George Catlin's drawings of the American Indians and John James Audubon's paintings of American birds indicate that the realistic tendency in American art lay close to the pioneer scientific spirit. Catlin the lawyer, and Audubon the naturalist, like Caleb Bing-

Fig. 621.—Marquis de Lafayette, by Samuel F. B. Morse, 1824. Oil on canvas, height 8 feet (New York City Hall). (*Courtesy of Lesch-Carnegie.*)

ham, a Missouri politician, turned toward the frontier for their subject matter. To these should be added William Sidney Mount, active in the middle decades of the 19th century.

Bingham's many paintings of political life, such as The Verdict of the People in the St. Louis Mercantile Library Association Building, show that artist to have been one who emerged from the old sign-painting tradition. However, Bingham's sense for composition far surpassed anything known in Europe in the middle of the century, with the possible exception of the work of Friedrich, the German Romantic landscapist. Bingham's Fur Traders

Descending the Missouri (Fig. 620) marks the first appearance of a style in which humane characteristic personality, realistically portrayed, blends with a mystical, Oriental background in a composition whose occult construction rivals that of the best Chinese painters. This tour de force, an isolated phenomenon in 1845, was to become the rule in the art of one of the greatest American painters, J. M. Whistler. The warm yellow-green and ocher tones of this picture of Bingham's completely express the atmosphere of the foggy river in the early morning sunlight. Twenty years were to elapse before Corot would discover similar effects, with less refinement and monumentality, in French landscape.

Robert Fulton, another early American realist, better known as the inventor of the steamboat, had some success as a miniaturist. His painting was excelled by that of a second inventor, Samuel F. B. Morse, who became the first president of the National Academy of Design. Morse's portrait of the Marquis de Lafayette (Fig. 621) combines realism in portraiture with an expressionism in the folds of the cloak and the swirl of the clouds suggesting a Romantic element, partly inherited from the rococo, partly stimulated by memories of the Revolution. The classical movement, associated with the ideals of Jefferson and Washington is suggested by the balustrade, the wreathed pedestal at the left, and Houdon's portrait busts of Washington and Franklin. Each detail of this mural-size composition is rendered with extreme fidelity to nature.

Romantic Landscapists and the Problem of Distance. Broadening horizons call for adventurous spirits. Beyond the Appalachians, pioneers with their covered wagons had already opened the West when the first romantic paintings appeared in the long-settled farm country of the Hudson River valley. While the Erie Canal was connecting New York with the Great Lakes, while the river steamboats carried commerce north and south between the Lakes and the Gulf and even as the first railway lines pushed out across the prairies, the romantic spirit in American architecture and painting dominated among the stay-at-homes of the East.

Thomas Cole, Asher B. Durand, J. F. Ken-

as the Eastern Americans, conceived to lie beyond the prairies of the West (Fig. 622).

A certain feeling of inferiority and lack of culture, which forced the "Brahmins" to seek

FIG. 622.—Dream of Arcadia, by Thomas Cole, c. 1840. Oil on canvas, 48 by 72 inches (Toledo Museum). (*Courtesy of Toledo Museum.*)

sett, John Casilear, Robert Swain Gifford, Charles Melville Dewey, and George Inness are some representatives of that Romantic group of landscapists called the Hudson River School. Thomas Cole (1801–1848), one of the last signboard painters, who traveled with brushes and paints in his knapsack and a flute for his companion, was in many ways more poet than painter. In early life, a brief journey to England acquainted him with the works of Turner and Constable. Influenced by Turner, he sought the rocky glens of the Catskills, introducing them into a series of paintings called "The Voyage of Life." There he portrays the journey of man through an Arcadian wilderness such as all true Romantics in Europe, as well

instruction from European masters, impelled many of the Hudson River painters to study abroad. In the field of landscape painting, which depends for its power on the way in which the artist captures the *genius loci* in a new form appropriate to the new subject matter, Americans gained least from Europe. In the works of the Ohio painter, A. H. Wyant, the river scenes by Bingham, the gigantic compositions of Albert Bierstadt, J. W. Hill, F. E. Church, and Thomas Moran, the American painters discarded the sentimentality of the European Romantics. These adventurous explorers spent the greater part of their lives painting the sublime scenery of the deserts, the Rocky Mountains, and the canyons of the

West. Not contented with the northern continent Church explored the mountains of South America, painting Chimborazo, Cotopaxi, and the Andes of Ecuador. Throughout the work of

romantic mood to wrestle with the reality of nature. By the end of the 19th century, other American painters, such as Winslow Homer and Rockwell Kent, again approached this dy-

FIG. 623.—The Grand Canyon of the Colorado, by Thomas Moran, 1873. Oil on canvas (United States Capitol). (*Courtesy of Handy Studios.*)

all these men one finds brilliant rainbow effects, dramatically illuminated peaks, a feeling for the mass or structure of the hills, and the immensity of the sky. They seem to say that this land of ours is worthy of greathearted souls like those who speak through the verses of Whitman and Lanier.

The Grand Canyon of the Colorado (Fig. 623), by Thomas Moran (1837–1926), displays a knowledge of perspective and a grasp of the power in landscape unknown to most Europeans. Moran, who had studied the works of Turner, developed the program already suggested by Cole, enlarging the Arcadian vistas of the Hudson River to the still grander dimensions of the Western American scene. His skillful dynamic composition, his mastery of light and shade, and his knowledge of the structure of rocks and trees carried his spirit out of the

namic aspect of nature with a certain rugged joy and healthy gusto.

The last and best known member of the Hudson River School, George Inness (1825–1894), mastered atmospheric painting. He studied light as had Turner and Constable, anticipating in his luminous canvases many of the effects of the French Impressionists. Inness expresses in his poetic, colorful landscapes an almost mystical, musical note in American life. The very subjects of his pictures—Sunset on the Passaic, The Delaware Valley, Winter Morning at Montclair, and Georgia Pines—suggest his love of the Eastern pastoral scene.

Commercial Artists and Spiritual Adventurers during the Age of Industrial Expansion. The American artist-adventurer during the latter half of the 19th century was of two sorts—one the illustrator, journalist, or commercial artist who placed his interest in the American scene above his desire for immediate perfection in art; the other, a "Brahmin" refugee who lived in Europe. Such men as Winslow Homer, Thomas fisherfolk of New England. In all his late compositions Homer reaches a scheme of occult balance like that of Bingham's Fur Traders (Fig. 624).

Fig. 624.—Gulf Stream, by Winslow Homer, 1899. Oil on canvas, height 2 feet 5 inches (Metropolitan Museum of Art). (*Courtesy of Lesch-Carnegie.*)

Eakins, and George Wesley Bellows, in the first category, managed to make a living in an atmosphere uncongenial to aesthetic exploration. James McNeill Whistler and John Singer Sargent spent most of their time in England or Paris, where a cultured bourgeois and aristocratic class supported their more refined art with a keener criticism, as well as an abundance of commissions. Both the commercial artists at home and the pioneer Americans abroad reached a style that differentiates their art from that of the Europeans. Winslow Homer (1836–1910), whose work as a lithographer and an illustrator of the Civil War drew him close to such French realists as Meissonier, Detaille, and Daguerre, as can be seen in his Prisoners from the Front in the Metropolitan Museum, developed an almost photographic eye. This he eventually focused upon seascapes and the

Another well-known realist, the Philadelphian, Thomas Eakins (1844–1916), whose paintings presage the art of the colored camera, also developed this sense of occult balance. Not all the artists who stayed in America were so well equipped as Homer and Eakins with a tough nervous fiber to withstand the tremendous pressure for materialistic expansion which dominated American life in the last quarter of the 19th century. The mystic, Albert P. Ryder (1847–1917), whose dream pictures might have developed still further the style of Inness and Cole, lived the life of an animal. Blakelock, another nature mystic with a message of beauty, after years of neglect and a period in an insane asylum, died in 1919 shortly after his tardy recognition.

James McNeill Whistler (1834–1903) escaped the fate of Ryder and Blakelock by spending most of his life in London. Although born in Massachusetts, Whistler, when a child, lived in Russia, where he came in contact with the Orient. As a young man, he returned to

Fig. 625.—Portrait of Carlyle, by J. A. McNeill Whistler, 1872. Oil on canvas, 5 feet 7 inches (Corporation Art Gallery, Glasgow). Note the butterfly with which Whistler signed his paintings. This symbolized the Soul to the ancient Greeks and the Chinese. (*Courtesy of Lesch-Carnegie.*)

America and spent a short time at West Point, preparing for an army career. Forsaking the profession of arms, however, he studied in the Paris studio of Gleyre with Degas, and in 1863 had his first pictures exhibited along with those of the Impressionists. Throughout the rest of his artistic career, which he spent in London and Venice, Whistler remained an American in his outlook, considered *l'enfant terrible* in the courts of European art. He was even better known for his battles with European critics, particularly John Ruskin, than for his highly individualistic style of painting. Like Oscar Wilde and the French Symbolists, Whistler naturally supported the Bohemian point of

view, which enabled the artist to retain his self-respect in a world submerged by materialistic values. In London during the late sixties, Whistler began to create in a style influenced by Japanese painting. Perhaps his greatest new contribution to American art was the attention he directed to refined color arrangement.

Like most of his countrymen who preceded him, Whistler had a special interest in the playful arrangement of flat areas of color. Through a multitude of experiments entitled simply "Arrangements," Whistler rendered the river landscapes of London and created many portraits in gray and yellow, gray and black, flesh color and green, flesh color and red, silver and blue. Whistler's intent seems to have been to discover a new type of painting that should unite the refinement of the delicate Oriental design with the individualistic realism of the Western character. What he was trying to say, in point of aesthetic form, was that a new style might come into being, suggestive of change or motion from the tangible to the intangible. His new inventions were to influence strongly American photography, as well as painting, and eventually the American mural design of the 20th century.

Whistler's new arrangement of color areas and tones, which the Japanese called "notan," helped to incorporate the human personality in a decorative scheme that made of it a symbol. His portrait study of his mother stands for calm assurance. In his presentation, the philosopher Carlyle (Fig. 625) is a man detached from the world, eeing with comprehensive vision the meaning of the dream stuff in life. In Whistler the mysticism of Whittier and Whitman leaves the dynamic romanticism of Ryder and comes to an orderly, though infinitely subtle, arrangement. The arrangement is definitely one suggesting an equilibrium between the static and the dynamic. In Whistler's art the American spirit comes of age.

The Dynamic Quality of the Youthful Sargent. John Singer Sargent (1856–1925), who like Benjamin West before him eventually became best known as an English painter, showed in his earlier days the same interest in occult spacing of color as did Whistler. Sargent's hearty young realistic blood is represented in his magnificent

jects in nature found a congenial atmosphere in the Impressionist schools of France. Childe Hassam and Mary Cassatt helped to popularize Impressionism as an academic mode

FIG. 626.—El Jaleo, by John Singer Sargent, 1882. Oil on canvas, height 7 feet 7½ inches (Gardner Museum, Boston). (*Courtesy of Lesch-Carnegie.*)

mural canvas of the Spanish dancer, El Jaleo (Fig. 626), easily one of the great masterpieces of American art. The row of musicians and women seated against the white wall in the rear of the room suggests a definite, accented beat against which the swiftly whirling dancer, caught for a moment in a characteristic tango or rhumba pose, captures the intricate rhythm of life. Here energy, displayed in snapping lines, combined with definite formal accents of color, carries the composition scheme of Whistler back into the realm of dynamic expression.

During the early decades of the 20th century, those Americans who would have followed Inness by exploring the effects of light on ob-

taught in most American art schools from 1910 to 1930.

Other American wanderers in Europe were the Impressionist, Gari Melchers, who developed a flat, mural style, using vibrant colors, and the mystic Arthur B. Davies, whose Maya, Mirror of Illusions, in the Chicago Art Institute, and whose Unicorns, in the Metropolitan Museum, mark him as a true Romantic.

Other artists of the earlier 20th century whose eyes no longer turned toward Europe, inherited the strength of Homer and the formal advances made by Whistler and Sargent. In the vital works of such a painter as George Wesley Bellows (1882–1925), the rush and vigor of the American scene is caught with full-colored pigment balanced against deep darks and grays. Here the realistic, dramatic painter, with the quick brush strokes of a Hals and the psychological insight of a Rembrandt, has

Fig. 627.—Stag at Sharkey's, by George Bellows, 1907. Oil on canvas, 36¼ by 48¼ inches (Cleveland Museum of Art). (*Courtesy of Cleveland Museum of Art.*)

been skillful in effecting a counterpoint between active curves and the straight angles of a mechanical environment. His painting, A Stag at Sharkey's (Fig. 627), combines the bodily, dynamic expression in American realism and a new primitive, geometric feeling which expanded in Europe with cubism and expressionism.

Postimpressionist Influences in American Painting. An American who mastered cubism and expressionism, carrying these styles beyond their European horizons into something as fine as the composition and color of Whistler, and at the same time suggestive of dynamic action, was Lionel Feininger, one of the members of the German Blue-Rider Group. Feininger's Rainbow, painted in 1927, stresses the immense loneliness of the human being lost at that point in space where the dynamic force of the cloud-swept headland meets the calm of the sea, while land and water, crystal and fluid, evanesce to the sparkling hues of the spectrum. Within the United States, the earliest exponent of expressionist and abstractionist art was the photographer Alfred Stieglitz, who encouraged

the young painter Georgia O'Keeffe and the water-colorist John Marin, as well as the Frenchman Matisse and the Spaniard Picasso.

Many postimpressionists followed the illustrators, George T. Cole, Irving Couse, Ernest Blumenschein, and Walter Ufer, to Taos, an Indian pueblo town in New Mexico. There Dazburg, Nordfelt, Applegate, and Sloan studied the desert with its brilliant colors and clear perspective views, its luminous shadows and structural rock formations, its primitive inhabitants and adobe houses.

Emergence of an American Style. The history of the rediscovery of primitive American art begins in Paris with the Fauvists and the cubists, who found that the Peruvian and Central American textiles, sculptures, and painting displayed in the Trocadero Collection suggested means for uniting realism and abstraction, more colorful and direct than those made by Whistler and Feininger. Around 1910, artists began to study Mexican and Peruvian art in the American Museum of Natural History in New York. There, students of design from the art schools adapted motifs from ancient American art to textiles, ceramics and interior decoration.

In the South American countries during the early 1920's, artists—many of whom had Indian blood—began to take a proud interest in the work of their ancestors. In 1921, following David Siqueiros, a number of painters, including Carlos Orozco, Romero, Diego Rivera, Jean Charlot, and Carlos Merida, founded the Syndicate of Painters and Sculptors, which had for its express purpose the stimulation of interest in Mexican folk arts. These men were no romantics interested in archaeological reconstructions, but tremendously productive artists whose creations, rooted deep in native soil, flowered profusely and bore abundant fruit. Following their experiments, three similar art styles united. The first was the decorative, illustrative sign-painting tradition in the folk art beloved of the masses, proper to the comic papers, which has finally been transposed to the motion pictures in the colored animations of Walt Disney. The second included the end results of the experiments of Whistler, Feininger, and the followers of the abstractionists and expressionists. The third was indigenous

FIG. 628.—Into the World There Came a Soul Called Ida, by Ivan L. L. Albright. Oil on canvas, about 4 feet 6 inches by 3 feet 6 inches. (*Courtesy of Ivan L. L. Albright.*)

Indian folk art. The art historian interested particularly in folk art can trace this development in the comic papers alone, beginning with Opper's creation of Happy Hooligan, that cheerful hobo and exponent of rugged individualism, the futurist adventures of Little Nemo with Flip and his other friends, and McManus' Bringing Up Father. In these works one finds composition schemes closely approaching those of the Indians. In Polly and her Pals one sees stronger geometric motifs. Other forms of primitivism appear in the adventures of Barney Google and of Mickey Mouse. Critics of classical training persist in seeing in this rich folk art, which unconsciously influences the mass of Americans, simply degenerate forms of European design. The mural

creations after 1920 using this style seem to indicate that it is the starting point for a new monumental art.

The disillusioning years of the World War

FIG. 629.—Suicide in Costume, by Franklin C. Watkins. Oil on canvas, width about 4 feet. (*Courtesy of Estate of A. C. Lehman, and Carnegie Institute, Pittsburgh.*)

led some to an expression of pessimistic naturalism, such as that found in the pictures of Lorraine Albright. Albright's Into the World There Came a Soul Called Ida (Fig. 628) and God Created Man in His Own Image, reproduced in black and white, denote a depth of pessimism darker than that in the gloomiest Russian novels. Only Albright's remarkably fine color sense brings these pictures into a psychical balance which allows for some hope in life.

Active work along the lines of research into the meaning of form and structure in art carried on by a number of aestheticians directed by Dr. Albert Barnes of the Barnes's Foundation in Merion, Pennsylvania, led to the production in 1932 of the famous Suicide in Costume (Fig. 629), awarded first prize at the Carnegie International Exposition of Pittsburgh. This abstractionist painting of a clown whose body, following suicide, has begun to disintegrate, suggests the end of a social and economic era characterized by the romantic label "rugged individualism."

The picture arose in the mind of an artist

haunted by a tragedy connected with the industrial crisis of 1929. It shows the regression which takes place as the American artist faces the lack of appreciation for his spiritual adventuring which drove Whistler, Sargent, and Feininger away from our shores. From such mental depression the only healthy solution is to be found by immersing oneself in the stream of folk art. One must turn to sign painting, to the humorous aspects of American life, or to such mural decoration as that which is needed to make more interesting the walls of our churches, community buildings, schools, and colleges. This solution was found by thousands of artists after 1930 and resulted in a wide-scale production of murals ,painted under supervision of the government for the Works Progress Administration. To understand the aesthetic value of the American mural production which is based upon the factors already discussed in this brief survey of American painting, one must study a number of previous murals painted by Orozco, Rivera, and Thomas Benton during the twenties.

Growth of a Monumental Mural Style. Before the experience of concerted effort necessary to carry on the World War, leading American artists habitually painted uncommissioned pictures. A monumental mural style can grow up only when artists are subsidized by church, state, or an intelligent democracy. In order to be most effective, this type of painting takes time and security for planning and execution. Every mural worthy of the name is the exposition of an idea of such grandeur that it needs time to mature. In it the narrative element must be strong, and the details must be interwoven with some significant symbolic composition scheme.

In the early years of the 19th century, no Americans seem to have been capable muralists. The first monumental murals by an American artist were those of John La Farge. These show little more of a mural concept than some of the works of Titian. They mostly approximate a late Renaissance style.

The Chicago Columbian Exposition of 1893–1894 stimulated mural painting by giving opportunities to Edwin H. Blashfield, J. Alden Weir, Robert Reid, and others. Their murals, for the most part, were conceived in terms of the classical French school. Most of them remind one of Ingres's Apotheosis of Homer. In the following two decades, museums, libraries, and banks, as well as many of the state capitols, were built in a style set by the powerful firm of McKim, Mead and White. These architects usually preferred rich marbles and bronze or gilded decorations to mural painting.

In the Boston Public Library, a number of painters, including Sargent and Edwin Austin Abbey, were asked to decorate the various rooms. Abbey's romantic illustrations of the Arthurian legend, although very small panels, have a truly monumental effect. Sargent's enormous Prophets in the front hall, if reduced to simple, brilliant color patterns without their fancy gilding, would be seen to approximate a style later developed by Rivera. The most successful treatment of the wall surfaces is that by Puvis de Chavannes, who never saw the building. None of these murals can approach the integrity of style and architecture developed by later painters.

Rivera, Orozco, and Benton. The greatest change in American mural painting came in the decade immediately following the World War. At that time a strongly communal feeling and a belief in an international society as the necessary basis from which a monumental art could spring became the common inheritance for all Americans who had taken part in the war. The lower classes in Mexico gave America an indigenous style in the works of Diego Rivera and J. C. Orozco. Both of these men united the experiments of the postimpressionists, the color schemes of the Aztecs and Mayans, and an ideology stemming from the Russian Revolution or the Promethean philosophy of Nietzsche.

Diego Rivera has a style closely approximating the Oriental frescoes of Sirigya and Ajanta in India, picturing human forms much as they were drawn in the early Mayan art. He accepts the machine as a necessary part of 20th-century civilization and uses it as a means to gain a more abundant life for mankind (Fig. 630).

business executives at their desks—all happy in their work. With joyous color schemes like those in the comic strips, Rivera wove a tapestry of form and movement. His superb decora-

FIG. 630.—Frescoes by Diego Rivera, south wall, Detroit Museum, height about 36 feet. Center panel: interior of automobile factory with presses, polishers, and assembly line. Center top panel: left, the white race with lime crystals, symbolic of organizing ability; right, the yellow race, with earth, symbolic of ancient wisdom. Narrow band beneath: the geologic origins of coal, sand, and limestone. Upper left, small panels: drug industries of Detroit, with surgery directly beneath. Upper right, small panels: processes of the foundry, with fiery union of the minerals beneath. Six small panels at bottom: mechanized agriculture, a sawmill, a training class, glass manufacture, and workers leaving the plant. (*Courtesy of Detroit Museum.*)

Underlying Rivera's murals in the Detroit Museum of Fine Arts, probably his finest work, is the idea that the fundamental energies of earth's mighty forces unite with the intelligence of man to create a more abundant life. Rivera here came to the modern industrial world with the keen interest of a primitive. He found the scientist in his laboratory, the mechanic at his machine, the workers in the fields, and the

tive effects blend appropriately with the difficult baroque architecture of the museum court. Above all this activity and greater than any of it appear the four races of mankind which have combined to produce American life, each symbolizing some significant aspect of our mentality. Rarely can a finer combination of symbolism, decorative color quality, strong composition, and realism be found.

Following successful completion of the Detroit commission Rivera painted the central lobby panel of the RCA Building in Rockefeller Center, immediately behind the portal,

Fig. 631.—Modern Migration of the Spirit, fresco, fourteenth panel of mural entitled An Epic of American Civilization, by J. C. Orozco, Baker Library, Dartmouth College 1934. Height about 10 feet. Compare with Last Judgment, Fig. 291, Chap. XI. (*Courtesy of Dartmouth College.*)

where Lee Lawrie pictured Wisdom Guiding the Universe (Fig. 636). Here Rivera surpassed his Detroit work in a picture almost rivaling for its spiritual integrity, craftsmanship, and composition the works of Leonardo da Vinci and Michelangelo. He painted, as a continuation of the monumental form of the building, the tube of an enormous telescope, which appeared as an apparatus capable of exploring the macrocosm and microcosm. Rockefeller Center, as the meeting place of the various scientific philanthropies representing the constructive side of our economic system, is essentially just such a telescope. As the center of the great radio industry, it may be considered a meeting place to which all human knowledge

may flow. Here an idealized figure of a man, who controlled the telescope, stood at the intersection of four great rays, cast by its two reflecting mirrors. In one ray appeared the nebulae and the worlds in process of ceaseless becoming, as evidence of that dynamic power implicit in the universe. In the other appeared the minute cells of life, the bacteria and tissues which transform cosmic energy for human good.

Through other details in the picture Rivera conveyed the thought that unintelligent wastrels allow God's universal benefits to be used for destructive purposes. Only through peaceful, cooperative action can mankind continue happily moving toward a better social order. Unfortunately, to Rivera, interested in the Russian Revolution, a portrait of Lenin, on the right, seemed the most fitting symbol of this new world order. So the mural, which was to have been unveiled early in 1930, was first covered and then destroyed. In its place Sert, the Spanish muralist, has created a picture whose structure has a less fortunate relationship to its architectural setting.

The second great American muralist, J. C. Orozco, began in 1932 to create on the walls of the library in Dartmouth College the epic story of the entire American civilization. His two central religious figures, Quetzalcoatl and Christ, represented in a series of dynamic panels, struggle to overcome the ancient and the modern superstitions of human sacrifice. In the first series, as Quetzalcoatl departs from his people prophesying his eventual return with a new concept of civilization, so in the second series, Christ overthrows the false gods of industrialism which led man to the needless slaughter of the World War. Orozco's concluding panel, Modern Migration of the Spirit, here reproduced (Fig. 631), shows a dynamic Byzantine, Promethean Christ. He destroys His own cross along with the other symbols of superstitious religions and those war materials which represent the violence so often invoked in His name. Orozco's essentially Nietzschean philosophy suggests that only through spiritual revolution can man overcome the primitivism of a purely material concept of life.

Thomas Benton, the third great American muralist, is known as one of a group of Mid-

baroque composition giving an interweave in depth.

The works of the three great muralists here described and the many splendid murals

FIG. 632.—Abe Lincoln in Indiana, details from mural by Thomas Benton, Indiana Building, World's Fair, Chicago, 1933. Oil on canvas, height about 12 feet. (*Courtesy of Kaufmann-Fabry, Photographers.*)

western painters which includes Grant Wood, John Stewart Curry, and Charles Burchfield. These, with Albright and Bohrod of Chicago, Reginald Marsh of New York, and Sheeler of Philadelphia, have characterized in many genial works the American scene north of the Rio Grande. Benton's murals for the Indiana Building of the Chicago World's Fair embody the spirit that runs through Walt Whitman's poetry (Fig. 632). In later murals for the New School of Social Research, the Whitney Museum in New York City, and the State Capitol at Jefferson City, Missouri, Benton reiterates his central theme that American life is virile and crudely passionate. More than the work of either Orozco or Rivera, Benton's paintings demonstrate the energetic, Celto-Germanic line inspiriting dynamic human forms. He also uses

painted for federal buildings after 1934 would not have been possible without a great deal of experimentation on the part of such American postimpressionists as Maurice Stern, John Marin, A. G. Dove (Fig. 633a), and Arthur B. Davies in the last years of his life. These came so close to the primitive Indian patterns and to the universally accepted folk art of the comic strips that a style which unites all these attributes seems somehow familiar and has been accepted by all but the oldest academicians.

These artists all show particularly that quality of action and color design made popular through the motion pictures of Walt Disney (Fig. 633b). The work of the government in fostering the arts after 1930 surpassed in magnitude anything attempted in ancient Athens under Pericles or in Florence under the Medici.

Freedom is the keynote of the earliest expression in this new unique American style. As it matures, the artists improve in craftsmanship and in the ability to design their work so that it is more appropriate to the buildings decorated.

Sculpture

The Pioneers. The earliest North American sculptors from colonial times until the middle of the 19th century worked in the Italian neo-

FIG. 633.—*a*, abstract landscape, Thunderstorm, by A. G. Dove, 1921, height 21⅝ inches, width 18⅛ inches (Columbus Museum) (*courtesy of Columbus Museum*); *b*, still from "The Three Little Pigs" by Walt Disney (*courtesy of Walt Disney*); *c*, detail from mural by Gilbert Wilson, High School, Terre Haute, Indiana, 1936 (*courtesy of Gilbert Wilson*).

This may be aptly demonstrated by even a brief examination of some of the most significant murals created for federal buildings after 1932, through the Works Progress Administration. Such creations as Frank W. Long's panels for the post office in Louisville, Kentucky, John F. Holmer's friezes in the Cincinnati post office, and Thomas La Farge's panels in the post office at New London, Connecticut, all show action and color design in our distinctive new style. The compositions of Reginald Marsh in Washington and New York, Frank Mechau's Pony Express in the Washington Post Office Building, and Maurice Stern's library murals in the Department of Justice Building have received such widespread acclaim as to make their mention seem almost superfluous.

To summarize, the new American style, as revealed by the above muralists, has a dynamic interweave, brilliant color, dramatic action of forms in and out of the picture plane, and figures which contribute to an action suggestive of our motion pictures. The latest murals unite those aspects of art known as the Decorative, the Energetic, the Beautiful, and the Sublime.

classic tradition, popularized in Europe by Canova and Thorvaldsen. Among these, Henry Kirke Brown, Thomas Ball, and John Quincy Adams Ward were noted for a number of statues of Washington, who at that time symbolized the aristocratic ideal of the Republic's leadership. Shortly after the Civil War, these sculptors designed a type of monument unknown on the Continent—the Soldiers and Sailors Monument, one of which can be found in almost every American city. The first of them was built by Martin Milmore, a pupil of Ball, on Boston Common, in 1874. This type of monument consists of a high base, often with a column supporting a statue of Liberty or Victory guarded by soldiers and sailors. Seldom has one of these monuments a completely satisfying mass, since the supernumerary figures usually project too far from the central pyramid.

Contemporaneously with Milmore, the sculptor John Rogers worked, creating his little genre groups immensely popular about the middle of the century. Such subjects as Coming to the Parson, Weighing the Baby, and The Volunteer's Return were presented in groups of small figures which, although poorly designed, serve to illustrate Rogers's Victorian penchant for descriptive details. Such sculpture and other small objects collected as souvenirs to grace the

with a knowledge of composition and anatomy equal to that of most Renaissance masters. All, at times, like Rogers, fell to the level of the anecdotal or the sentimental, something not

FIG. 634.—Fountain of Time, Chicago, by Lorado Taft, 1913–1920. Cement of colored stones, figures about life size. (*Courtesy of Lorado Taft.*)

parlors of the *nouveaux riches* were given the name "bric-a-brac." Romantic sentimentality in associational, literary values and poor formal arrangement characterize the style.

Literary Styles of the 19th Century. After the Philadelphia Centennial Exposition in 1876, romantic Americans who traveled abroad to study sculpture, substituted for the Italian schools the ateliers of the French realists. In the resulting work, formal quality improved considerably, without the Romantic literary flavor's ever completely disappearing. Olin Warner, known for the bronze doors on the Congressional Library, and Herbert Adams, whose Bryant appears on the west side of the New York Public Library, with Solon and Gutzon Borglum, Augustus Saint-Gaudens, George Grey Barnard, Frederick MacMonnies, Paul Bartlett, Cyrus Dallin, Malvina Hoffman, Anna Hyatt Huntington, Daniel Chester French, and Lorado Taft, represent the best of the Romantic literary tradition as it turns toward realism. All these were skillful modelers

wholly appropriate to simple sculptural form. Following an example set by Augustus Saint-Gaudens, each of these sculptors showed himself at his best when designing a new, distinctly American type of monument with an exedra or architectural setting composed so as to connect ideal or realistic figures with some pleasing landscape vista. The best known commemorative pieces of this type are Saint-Gaudens' Shaw Memorial in Boston and Farragut Monument in New York City. In the face of his angel for the Sherman Monument, Saint-Gaudens created the ideal American feminine profile which has been adopted for our coinage.

Lorado Taft, whose workshop, like some Renaissance *bottega*, was a meeting ground and training place for many young artists in the Middle West, inherited the Italian classical and French baroque styles, which he united with the American tendency toward the anecdotal and the idealistic realism of Rodin. His fountain of the Great Lakes at the side of the Art Institute in Chicago, and his Columbus fountain before the Union Station in Washington display the neoclassical side of Taft's nature. His monumental, concrete statue of Black Hawk on the bluffs overlooking Rock River

figures of China and the Egyptian Sphinx. The attempt to link the human being with natural forces and the tendency to consider the personal in terms of the Sublime are prime character-

a   b   c   d

Fig. 635.—Lincoln—the democratic ideal in sculpture. *a*, Augustus Saint-Gaudens, Lincoln Park, Chicago, c. 1900, bronze, height about 8 feet (*photograph by Ianelli*); *b*, Gutzon Borglum, Newark, N. J., c. 1910, bronze, height about 5 feet (*photograph by Wood*); *c*, George Grey Barnard, Lytle Park, Cincinnati, c. 1925, bronze, height about 8 feet (*photograph by Kosman*); *d*, Daniel Chester French, Lincoln Memorial, Washington, D.C., c. 1918–1920, marble, height about 20 feet (*photograph by Veal*).

just south of Eagles' Nest Camp, Illinois, is dignified and noble in its simplicity.

Taft's Fountain of Time (Fig. 634), on the Chicago Midway Plaisance, is his most significant work. It preserves the exedra form, within which a group of figures symbolic of the various conditions of mankind rise from the ground, pass in review, and sink back again into the earth before the brooding figure symbolizing Eternity. The rhythmical wave motion of surging life, rising and falling without meaning other than the pathos of life itself, can be compared with the naturalistic drama of Tolstoy or the symbolic impressionism of Maeterlinck and Vildrac.

Other attempts to unite man with nature are the gigantic mountain carvings of Gutzon Borglum. His heads of Lincoln, Washington, Jefferson, and Theodore Roosevelt have been gradually emerging from Mount Rushmore in the Black Hills of South Dakota. These can be compared only with the gigantic Buddhistic

istics of American idealism earlier described in Hawthorne's story *The Great Stone Face*.

Four Studies of Lincoln as the Ideal American. The American, despite his tendency to ally himself with the forces of nature, never loses his sense of the actual worth of man. The work of Saint-Gaudens, French, and Barnard particularly shows a careful study of the new ethnic type compounded of many races, which eventually appears as the American ideal. The pioneer figure of Abraham Lincoln, foremost product of Jeffersonian democracy, dominated the sculptor's imagination during the early years of the 20th century. By that time the statesmanship, humor, and kindliness of the great emancipator had assumed superhuman proportions. Saint-Gaudens' statue in Lincoln Park, Chicago (Fig. 635a), appears that of a dignified statesman, refined, pensive and still humane, ennobled by the office of president.

The Lincoln of Gutzon Borglum, in a Newark Park (Fig. 635b), sits on a bench, accessible to the crowd, and, being little more than a man, appeals with friendly sentiment to children, who can usually be seen playing about his knees.

The third Lincoln, by Daniel Chester French (Fig. 635d), like Phidias's seated figure of Zeus at Olympia, is a cult statue in a national shrine. As part of an impressive neoclassic edifice looking beyond the lagoon, past the Washington monument, to the distant Capitol, this powerful, brooding figure symbolizes the innate sadness and loneliness of the American character, usually covered over in most of us by a rather light or humorous attitude.

The fourth Lincoln (Fig. 635c), by George Grey Barnard, stands in Lytle Park, Cincinnati. This, the proletarian Lincoln, is a gaunt, awkward figure, with only the dignity of his face to draw him away from the soil. Closely allied to Rodin or Meunier's realistic figures, Barnard's Promethean statue bespeaks a surging, elemental force arising from the creation of a new race and culture, which so long as it continues to grow will feed the productive fires of American genius. This spirit in American sculpture has been caught and furthered by the Swedish Carl Milles whose many magnificent designs found appropriate place in many of our homes and parks after 1920.

Decorative and Architectural Sculpture. Paul Manship, a leader in the field of decorative sculpture, is known for his figure of Night and his Dancer and Gazelles, as well as a host of other pieces characterized by flowing lines and a somewhat archaistic manner. An expert craftsman, Manship shows thorough acquaintance with the techniques of bronze casting and with Oriental motifs particularly suited to his medium.

During the third decade of the present century a number of sculptors— particularly Leo Friedlander, Ulric Ellerhusen, Katherine Lane, Alfonzo Ianelli, René Chambellan, the architect Ely Jacques Kahn, and Lee Lawrie— created a style of architectural sculpture most appropriate to the new skyscraper construc-

tion. Lee Lawrie's treatment of the entrance to the RCA Building in Rockefeller Center may be taken as the epitome of this style. The central figure, Wisdom (Fig. 636), modeled

FIG. 636.—Wisdom, by Lee Lawrie, entrance of RCA Building, Rockefeller Center, New York, c. 1929. Stone painted in red, gold, and black, height about 10 feet. (*Courtesy of Photographic Department, Rockefeller Center.*)

after an idea drawn by Blake (Fig. 553) emerges in unfolding planes on an oblique angle above a great panel of molded glass. The compass of The Ancient of Days, spreads out to include the glass designs, which suggest the courses of the planets. For appropriateness, symbolic significance, and construction this figure compares to the portal sculptures of Chartres. It completely expresses the function of the building in an appropriate architectonic design.

An increasing tendency on the part of architects and sculptors to use color is well demonstrated by Lee Lawrie's Wisdom. The background of the panel is in salmon pink, with details of the compass, the drapery, and the edges of the clouds in gold and blue. On either side of the central doorway, figures representing Light and Wind carry out the motif of the central design. Among all the sculptural decorations in Rockefeller Center—more than on any of the other skyscrapers—this by Lee Lawrie is the most fitting. More examples of Lawrie's work, inspired by the architect Bertram Goodhue, may be studied on the Nebraska State Capitol and the Church of the Heavenly Rest, New York City.

Music

The fundamental rhythm of American music arises from a combination of Indian, African, and European dance forms. Syncopation, a quality common in popular American music, can be found in all primitive cultures. The complicated improvised rhythm of American music at various times called "ragtime," "jazz," and "swing" has a distinctive manner unanticipated by European musicians. American melodies also are derived, in part, from primitive Indian and Negro sources, but for the greater part come from European folk songs.

Primitive Rhythms and Melodies. The earliest recorded American music consists of the *Harawi* or Inca melodies incorporated by the Peruvian composer Valle Riestra in his operatic treatment of the Inca folk drama, *Ollanta.* Many Indian melodies common to the Mexicans and the other North American tribes appear as basic components of Carlos Chavez's *Sinfonia India.* Other melodies, generally considered Negro in origin were taken by the Negroes from the Indians, who worked with them as slaves in the fields early in the 19th century. A well-known example, *Water Boy*, is derived from a Cherokee Indian song. All of these employ both pentatonic and heptatonic scales, sometimes with quarter-tone intervals like those in East Indian music. Early American Romantic composers drew heavily upon aboriginal sources, but without ever coming so close to the original rhythms as did Dvořák.

Negro influence in American music is important chiefly because the Afro-American, by nature a social individual, has assimilated most of the melodies of other folk groups and re-created them in terms of his own intense rhythmical desire for musical expression. The Negro has contributed such happy strains as *I've Been Working on the Levee, Good News*, and *Golden Slippers.* His lullabies have become the crooning associated with American popular love tunes. His spirituals, because of their melancholy strain also common to the Celto-Germanic temperament, have been accepted as modifying the stricter Protestant hymn forms. The Negro harmonizes his spirituals and "blues" in irregular canonical form with intricate polyrhythmic accompaniments of odd words forced to fit the tunes. This most significant rhythmic melodic synthesis dominates the orchestral style of such modern composers as Ferde Grofé, George Gershwin, and John Alden Carpenter. A description of the part played by the Negro in the development of swing can be found in Louis Armstrong's book *Swing That Music.*

Pioneer Folk Songs. In early colonial times, the settlers of Maine and Vermont sang many work songs brought from England and France. Our sailors picked up chanteys, which became popular throughout the United States during the days of the clipper ships. From Ireland and Scotland came the jig, the reel, and other round and square dances. With many Elizabethan, Anglo-Saxon, Scotch, and Irish ballads, these dances passed into the mountains of Kentucky, Tennessee, the Carolinas, and Arkansas, where they persist as the dominant musical form today. For example, *Barbara Allen, Sweet William and Fair Ellen, Will the Weaver*, and *Pretty Polly* are favorites in Kentucky. Mississippi River boatmen and the cowboys developed innumerable work songs, with cries, cheers, and curious ballad refrains (see Carl Sandburg's *The Songbag*). After 1812 and throughout the Civil War days, many patriotic marching songs were written and sung by the minstrel showmen. By always appearing in blackface, these showmen recognized the importance of the colored race in creating American humor. The Two Black Crows and Amos 'n' Andy carried on the tradition.

The American folk song reached its greatest refinement and its epitome in the work of Stephen Collins Foster. In his short life, Foster composed over 150 art songs, most of which seem to arise from primitive folk melodies. His *Old Black Joe, Swanee River*, and *My Old Kentucky Home* are truly American, different in spirit from European music.

Romanticism and Classicism after 1870. The tradition of early universal musical educators, such as Lowell and William Mason, has been taken over by Walter Damrosch and Deems Taylor, both of whom are known for their admirable radio talks as well as for their orchestral and operatic compositions.

Horatio Parker, a distinguished musical educator, on the faculty at Yale University until 1910, is widely known for his noble choral music, particularly the oratorio, *Hora Novissima*, and an opera, *Mona*. In the latter, Parker used Indian Melodies. Edward MacDowell who taught first in Boston and later at Columbia University produced a number of orchestral and piano works, including a famous *Indian Suite*. In his many songs and his "Impressions" entitled *Woodland Sketches, Sea Pieces*, and *New England Idylls*, MacDowell created tender love lyrics and short lyric pieces suggestive of nature —moods of the sea or reveries in forest and farmland. His style has a delicacy almost Oriental in quality. Better than any other composer, he captures Indian and Negro folk music in almost poetic forms. Ethelbert Nevin's short piano lyrics and songs hold many fresh romantic melodies, similar in style to the works of MacDowell.

Charles Wakefield Cadman adapted Indian music in several operas and orchestral suites. His suite of four American Indian Songs and his opera *Shanewis* furnish typical examples of the romantic transposition of original Indian themes to highly sophisticated forms quite dis-

similar to their rhythmical structure. Other composers working under more modern European influences are Mrs. H. H. Beach, noted for her *Gaelic Symphony*, and Leo Ornstein, a pioneer of expressionism in America, who wrote *Impressions of Chinatown*.

During the early part of the 20th century, the most popular writers of music were John Philip Sousa, the march king, and Victor Herbert, who composed many operettas and symphonic poems, and some orchestral and chamber music. Reginald De Koven, author of the light opera *Robin Hood*, wrote a number of such ballads as the perennial favorite, *O Promise Me*. Jerome Kern and Sigmund Romberg have contributed greatly to modern popular music, with many tunes of more than passing interest. Most of the work of these men has found its way into the motion pictures.

Expressionism in Music. John Alden Carpenter has dedicated compositions to skyscrapers and Krazy Kat. With refined musicianship Carpenter combines expressionistic effects and typically American rhythms, in many piano pieces, sonatas, and symphonies. Lamar Stringfield, in *The Moods of a Moonshiner*, allows the folk melodies and rhythms of the Cherokees to grip the entire orchestra for long sustained passages.

The most successful exponent of that combination of international folk melodies rendered in swing time was George B. Gershwin, whose first successful orchestral work, *The Rhapsody in Blue*, is now seen to have been as fine in its way as many of the compositions of Debussy and Strauss. His opera *Porgy and Bess*, with its splendid orchestration of folk tunes, is one of the most significant contributions to native American music. The direction in which our new musical style may proceed can be heard in the composition *Grand Canyon Suite* by Ferde Grofé, a musician trained in the Wagnerian idiom who has begun to understand the need for a return to the simplicity and fineness of Bach's melodic line and the intricate polyrhythms of the Indians. The humorous element common to most modern American popular music appears at its best in Raymond Scott's *The Penguin* and *War Dance for Wooden Indians*. The musical idiom called "swing" is most pleasing in Lou Singer's arrangement of an old folk ballad, *The Keeper*, under the name of "Jackie Boy," as sung by Maxine Sullivan, and in *Blues in C-sharp minor* by Teddy Wilson.

In 1940, the well-known musicologist Marion Bauer listed for their American quality several compositions besides those already mentioned. These include the *Concord Sonata* by Charles Ives, *Horizons* by Arthur Shepherd, John Powell's *Negro Rhapsody*, Louis Gruenberg's *Daniel Jazz*, Nathaniel Dett's *The Ordering of Moses*, Henry S. Gilbert's *Dance in Place Congo*, Aaron Copland's *Outdoor Adventure*, Roy Harris's *Song for Occupations*, and Philip James's *Station WGBX*. These compositions are as typically American as the works of the contemporary painters Grant, Benton, Curry, and Wood. In order that the qualities that differentiate them from Old World creations may be clearly defined, they should be compared with the work of such European composers as Honneger, Hindemith, Schönberg, and Ravel.

The Drama

During the first half of the 19th century, drama rarely escaped the primitive level of the medicine show, the circus, or the melodramatic showboat performance. During the latter half of the century, the Civil War scene gave rise to Bronson Howard's *Shenandoah*, William Gillette's *Secret Service*, and Clyde Fitch's *Barbara Frietchie*. Other plays by Fitch, such as *The City* and *The Truth*, were not only better constructed than the first, but presented more natural characterizations of American life. William Vaughn Moody's *The Faith Healer* and *The Great Divide* had a considerable vogue in the first years of the 20th century. These early playwrights in the late European Romantic tradition rarely approached the power of later writers.

European post-Ibsen experiments in naturalistic drama could be performed only after the reformation of the theaters. Similarly in America, the work of Elmer Rice, Marc Connelly, Eugene O'Neill, and other pioneers depended to a great extent upon the foundation between 1913 and 1915 of Maurice Browne's Little Theatre in Chicago, the Provincetown Theatre, the Washington Square Players, and the New York Neighborhood Players. The most talented playwright to benefit by these new theatrical groups, whose cooperative spirit made possible experiments too radical for the organized commercial theater, was Eugene O'Neill.

In O'Neill's plays one may find all the advances of naturalism, expressionism, and symbolism made in the theater from Ibsen on. All his plays have a high degree of social significance, probing deeply into the motives of every one of the American literary types. Each play has a form expressive of some fundamental American rhythm. The tremendous primitive vitality of *The Hairy Ape* comes from the depths. In *Emperor Jones*, O'Neill shows the primitive Negro folk soul. *Anna Christie*, *Lazarus Laughed*, and *The Great God Brown* are symbolic dramas. *Desire under the Elms*, *Strange Interlude*, and *Mourning becomes Electra* explore the unconscious thought patterns underlying the actions of more or less repressed American types. The latter, particularly, combines the ancient Greek Electra story and the American scene with a Freudian interpretation.

Sidney Howard, whose realism grows out of vast introspective backgrounds, produced *The Silver Cord*, a story of unwise mother love. Robert Sherwood, like Schnitzler before him, specialized in satires, the best known of which is *Reunion in Vienna*. George Kaufman used expressionistic techniques for *Beggar on Horseback;* uniting with Morrie Ryskind, he produced a number of comedies on the political scene, including *Of Thee I Sing*. Elmer Rice's *Street Scene*, *Counselor at Law*, and *We the People* are realistic dramas of city life. In contrast to these, Marc Connelly characterized the pious depths of the Negro soul in *The Green Pastures*. This appealed to all classes of Americans because of its sincere religious feeling, its splendid spirituals, and fine rhythmical structure.

The Radio Drama. A new form of drama, written without visual staging, particularly for the radio, became popular in the fourth decade of the 20th century. Archibald MacLeish brought poetic literary accounts of destructive wars to the air waves with *Air Raid* and *The Fall of the City.* For pure radio-dramatic effect, Orson Welles's expressionistic-naturalistic account of the invasion of New Jersey by the men from Mars delivered in the same way as a regular news broadcast remains unsurpassed. So close at that time was the highly startling fiction of Welles to the drama of life as reported weekly from the European countries, that laws were passed forbidding naturalistic dramatic performance over the air concerning modern warfare. No recital of American visual, musical, literary, or dramatic art can be complete without a study of our most lively new synthetic art form, the talking motion pictures. Future generations will probably be able to see more clearly than we today just how great the influence of the cinema has been upon all other art forms. Without a brief critique of the motion picture one cannot understand the unique characteristics of American art.

The Motion Picture

Before 1930 most critics, unable to classify the motion picture definitely either as a graphic or as a literary dramatic art, avoided mentioning it. The growing effectiveness of the motion picture as an art medium and its increasing social significance eventually led Harvard and Yale universities to acknowledge its importance in 1938 by granting honorary degrees to Walt Disney, creator of *Mickey Mouse* and the *Silly Symphonies.* Thus the academic world accepted the motion picture as an art comparable to the stage drama, mural painting, and the symphony.

Economically, the motion picture today surpasses all other arts in its widespread distribution and the commercial value of its productions. The film play stands in the same relation to other 20th-century arts as did the cathedral to medieval art. Its influence upon speech, fashions, and mores is apparent. Further, the motion picture succinctly expresses the composite active character of the 20th-century American. Today the static arts of sculpture and painting have given ground to the more dynamic dance, music, and drama in a development which has come, through the music dramas of Wagner and Strauss, to find its most satisfying synthesis in the colored talking motion picture. In creation, this art proceeds from artist-directors, or *régisseurs,* who employ hosts of painters, architects, composers, dancers, and musicians, as well as playwrights and photographers, in order to achieve their monumental effects. The *régisseur,* or director, in the last analysis responsible for the entire filmic production, must understand the laws by which each component element of the film play can reach its greatest effectiveness. The effects peculiar to the new art differ from their antecedent simpler components because they depend primarily upon a series of contrasts between dynamic and static moments. Allardyce Nicoll has called this "filmic rhythm."

After the director, the most important motion-picture artist is the cameraman, who borrows from Renaissance and baroque painters, pictorial devices such as chiaroscuro, or plastic modeling using light and shadow, and *sfumato,* or soft and sharp focus. These and other mechanical effects, such as the halation of the film when shiny objects are photographed, can be used to suggest contrasting emotional states, even in still photography.

Essential Techniques of the Motion-picture Art. The fundamental of all filmic art is an appropriate interaction of characters and environment. In still pictures only given amounts of each appear, but in the film one can show the action of a character large in the front of the field or, by moving it backward into the picture, can reveal increasing amounts of the environment. This carries the emotions from the personal to the impersonal. In the earliest films, with a stationary camera, all action took

Fig. 637.—Still of first close-up, *The Birth of a Nation*, D. W. Griffith, director, c. 1916. (*Courtesy of New York Public Library.*)

place in a sight triangle directly before a single point. The characters, advancing or retreating, moved to right or left as they do upon the stage. An essential difference between stage and screen effects at once became apparent; for an actor, advancing toward the camera, could come so far forward as to fill the screen completely. This created an overpowering effect. Advantage was early taken of this technique to get a greater degree of emotional contrast.

In one of the earliest films, a man walking over Brooklyn Bridge came so close to the lens that his open mouth appeared to swallow the camera. At this point the first "shot,"[1] which consisted of this simple action in walking toward the camera, ended. When the film was started again, the actor had stepped from in front of the camera and other people were seen walking on the bridge where he had been. These two shots together constituted a sequence. Such a sequence, made of two or more shots, opens the possibility for greater rhythmical expression of pictorial contrast.

The Discoveries of George Melies, the First Filmic Artist. The Frenchman George Melies, who produced a number of fantastic pictures early in the present century, was the first to understand the film as a new art medium. Melies saw in the camera greater possibilities than the simple copying of stage plays or the recording of objective effects in nature. In his films of *Cinderella* and *The Trip to the Moon* Melies demonstrated the artistic effects created by manipulating the lens opening, shutter, and diaphragm. By closing the diaphragm as he ground the crank, he found that the projected subject could be made gradually to "fade out." Reversing this process, the object would fade in. By "splicing," or printing over the fade-out of the first shot with the fade-in of the second, Melies got a sequence in which one object appeared to change into another. This trick was called the "overlapped dissolve."

Melies also found that the action of a character might be filmed on one half of the frame (a single snapshot section of the continuous film) while the other was left unexposed. The actor whose motions were properly synchronized could then be rephotographed on the unexposed side of the frame. When projected, the character would appear to be acting with himself. This was called "double exposure." Melies invented a trick now used as the basis for making Walt Disney's "animations" (Fig. 633). By exposing one frame at a time while the camera was pointed at an inanimate object, and by changing the position of that object slightly between frames, the resulting sequence would show the object apparently moving without aid. These tricks demonstrated conclusively that the motion picture, more than a copy of nature or the stage, is a unique new means of expression. Following the production simultaneously in New York, London, and Paris of Melies's *Kingdom of the Fairies*, which had its own musical score, the motion picture was first mentioned as an "international art" by a few critics such as Vachel Lindsay and H. G. Wells.

[1] Any action which can be photographed uninterrupted by stoppage of the film is called a "shot."

D. W. Griffith and the Growth of Filmic Symbolism in Close-ups, Flash Backs, and Parallel Action. Between 1910 and 1914 a number of narrative epic dramas were filmed abroad. Soon an American, D. W. Griffith, brought to these epic stories all the resources of the newly discovered motion-picture techniques, adding many inventions of his own for greater suggestive power. In his picture, *The Birth of a Nation*, not content with magnificent distance shots of riding figures, Griffith found that quick movement from a wide-expanse to a close-up study of the human emotions induced a new contrasting dramatic effect. Figure 637 shows a still shot of the first close-up. Here a sentry on duty at the entrance to a hospital ward symbolizes the horrors of war. The actress Lillian Gish, who has just come through the portals, stands for the tenderness of feminine character and the peace of home life. In this action the soldier sighed as she passed and longingly followed her with his eyes. This particularly poignant combination of comedy and tragedy, seen close up, added new interest to the film play.

In *The Birth of a Nation* Griffith also developed what is called "parallel action" in the plot. Shakespeare's plays often have interwoven plots which eventually terminate in a single goal. Griffith found that the dual plot had more powerful possibilities in the motion picture because the camera could move quickly from an episode in one plot to a similar episode in another. Before this, it had been noticed that a last-minute rescue appeared more effective if the camera were switched from a shot of the heroine in the toils of a villain to another of the hero galloping over the plains to her rescue. Griffith applied the technique of his close-up to this "flash back," as it is called.

He added one other type of action to the film. In a technique called "panning" (from the word panorama), Griffith mounted the camera on a swivel and followed the movement of the chief character with its lens. Today's playgoer has Griffith to thank for at least four new aesthetic techniques—panning, the close-up for recording emotion, the use of close-ups to speed parallel action, and the use of close-ups and flash backs to gain a greater degree of filmic symbolism.

FIG. 638.—Still, showing early use of angle shots, *The Cabinet of Dr. Caligari*, by Ufa, c. 1920. (*Courtesy of New York Public Library.*)

Expressionism, Distortion, and the Subjective Effects of the Moving Camera. After the World War, rapidly developing expressionistic stage techniques and those advances in scenic design known as the "plastic stage" found their way into the film. These were all heightened in distortion effects produced by tilting the camera for new "angle shots"—shots that negate the usual vertical picture plane. A German picture, *The Cabinet of Dr. Caligari* (Fig. 638), made in 1920, attempted to show the feverish visions of a madman. To such a person, as to the drunkard and the semiconscious, the objects might appear leaning at peculiar angles. In this film, not only the scenery but the clothing and make-up of the actors were exaggerated. Ernst Lubitsch made a final development in the use of the moving camera by mounting it upon a traveling crane or dolly. By this means, the lens can follow the most intricate rhythmical movements of a dancing couple, taking in the changing environment around them and their varying motions as they move through space and time.

Avant-garde vs. Documentary Films. From 1920 to 1930 critics discerned two tendencies in the filmic art. Artists who stressed the symbolic value of movement and expressionism called

Fig. 639.—Still, suggesting quality of filmic rhythm, from *Armored Cruiser Potemkin*, by Eisenstein, c. 1925. (*Courtesy of New York Public Library.*)

themselves the *avant-garde* or "film of the future." Another group, made up of newsreel cameramen interested in the more objective recording of facts or nature adopted the name "documentary film." Among significant *avant-garde* films one finds Miklos Bandy's *Hands* (*Fama*), 1929, and Dr. Sibley Watson's *Fall of the House of Usher*, 1928, and *Lot in Sodom*, 1930. Significant documentary films are James Flaherty's *Grass, Chang,* and *Man of Aran;* Eisenstein's *Thunder over Mexico;* John Grierson's *The Drifters;* Paul Strand's *The Wave;* and Pare Lorentz's U. S. Government films *The Plow That Broke the Plains* and *The River.* The best techniques discovered by the two schools were quickly adapted to Hollywood needs. For example, *The Covered Wagon* and *The Iron Horse* were documentary in nature; Reinhardt's *Midsummer Night's Dream* took much from the *avant-garde.*

The Coming of Montage as a Means to Filmic Rhythm. Between 1920 and 1930 a number of Russian and American directors, particularly Pudovkin, Lubitsch, and Eisenstein, discovered that scraps of newsreel material interspersed with individual actions and shots of moving machinery could be made more effective if cut and spliced so that their realistic and expressionistic effects would induce contrasting objective and subjective states of feeling. A filmic sequence is more powerful if the types of action are arranged to build up within the spectator tensions like those built up in a stage play by means of words.

The classic example of a film built up by the montage process is Eisenstein's *Armored Cruiser Potemkin* (Fig. 639). Something of the effect of tensions set up by the movement within this remarkable film has even reached the still shot presented here. In it the mass of people, broken up into three streams, moves in different directions in and out of the picture plane, the lighter stream marching across the bridge from right to left. Like a mountain freshet the processions gather force with added numbers as they come down the alley from the left and out toward front right. From front left, a still larger stream moves in (we seem to be part of the stream), carrying our attention toward the rear right, where we the people will soon see the cruiser *Potemkin* bombard the Cossacks of the Czar. Here a type of movement taken from the canvases of the baroque painters comes to life with great effectiveness in a screen shot.

The Importance of Sound. In 1927, sound came to augment pictorial rhythm with soft or harsh, muffled or clear tones, accompanied by instruments and voices carrying endless new associational values. In an early Lubitsch sound film, *Monte Carlo,* appeared a most effective shot showing a locomotive's driving wheels with the hiss and roar of escaping steam. The flash of the piston and the click of the rails made a polyrhythmic accompaniment from which gradually emerged a melodic thread. Finally, including the blasts of the locomotive whistle, this expanded to a full orchestra creating a song to which words were added by one of the chief characters. The capacity for uniting musical sounds and industrial noises with pictorial sequences would have been impossible without the orchestral groundwork in the operas of Berlioz, Wagner, and Strauss or the modern compositions of Carpenter, Honneger, and Gershwin. A classic example of expressionistic symbolism in sound accompaniment may be found in Charlie Chaplin's film, *Modern Times.*

plays as *The Informer* by John Ford, *Modern Times* by Charles Chaplin, *Blue Angel* by Joseph von Sternberg, *Henry VIII* and *Rembrandt* by Alexander Korda, *Mutiny on the Bounty* by Irv-

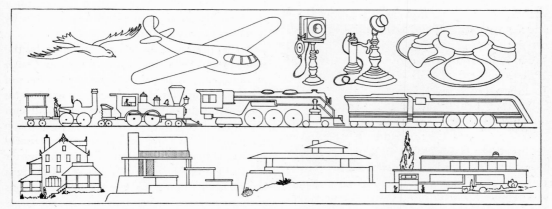

Fig. 640.—"Streamlining" or "form follows function." See Emerson's definition of art on page 825.

The work of Disney is even more significant in this respect.

Most pictures are now made with the help of a musical composer and a sound director who combines a knowledge of electricity with that of the physics of sound. Significant sound effects can be found in Erich Korngold's adaptation of Mendelssohn's music for *Midsummer Night's Dream*, Antheil's music in De Mille's filming of Cooper's novel *The Plainsman*, and Arthur Honneger's music for Shaw's *Pygmalion*.

An excellent didactic film, *The City*, resulted in 1939 from the combined efforts of the musician Aaron Copland, the architect-writer Lewis Mumford, and the documentary photographer Pare Lorentz. This film not only excels in form but suggests the ideal American goals for a wider spread of a more abundant life.

A Basis for Criticism of the New Filmic Art. This brief historical review has shown that the basic element of the film play consists of sequential contrasting actions expressing inner tensions induced during the narration of a legend. The ideal film combines both spatial and temporal artistic elements in good balance. Such film

ing Thalberg, *Mr. Deeds Goes to Town* and *It Happened One Night* by Frank Capra, and *Snow White and the Seven Dwarfs* by Walt Disney, demonstrate the ideal relationship of parts. Thalberg's M. G. M. production of *Romeo and Juliet*, with Leslie Howard and Norma Shearer in the title roles, demonstrates excellently how the mood values arise in a filmic rhythm created by the interaction of pantomime, sound, environment and poetic words. The artists taking part have recorded in their book *Romeo and Juliet* much of the data concerning this production, including the film play itself for comparison with Shakespeare's original script. It is thus of the highest value for pedagogic purposes.

American Aesthetic Theories

John Dewey has wisely observed that "Without a unifying point of view, based on the objective form in a work of art, criticism ends in enumeration of details."[1] Our previous review of man's cultural activities has demonstrated that critical theories arose in each period only

[1] John Dewey, *Art as Experience*, G. P. Putnam's Sons, New York, 1934.

after the arts of that period had suggested ideal definitions. American criticism, no exception to this general rule, has not yet reached a definiteness apart from European traditions, chiefly perhaps because the critics have not yet seen that the motion picture and the sky-scraper are probably the most definitive American art forms (Fig. 640).

Throughout the 19th century and early in the 20th three general critical theories appeared. Jonathan Edwards, a formalist, attempted to show that beauty arises from regularity of design. This type of criticism, stressing formal values, tends to find the ultimate meaning of art in pattern. James McNeill Whistler, Arthur Dow, J. J. Hambidge, Professor Birkhoff, and Denman Ross all offer various formalistic theories. The latest book in this tradition is Abell's *Representation and Form.*

A second point of view, found in the intensely personal critical essays of Edgar Allan Poe, borrows from Sir Francis Bacon the idea that "There is no exquisite beauty without some strangeness in proportion." Whereas the formalists stress regularity, Poe advocates irregularity. He indicates that this accounts for the most significant quality of Hawthorne's *Twice Told Tales*, their suggestive power. This Dionysian expressive element in art, a final development of the Neo-Platonic ideal which permeates most romanticism, finds art's chief significance in emotional intensity rather than in the unity of formal design. Among Americans following this tradition are Gilbert Seldes, Sheldon Cheney, and Walter Pach. A romanticist who attempts to unite the two schools very much as had the baroque critics of the 17th and 18th centuries is W. H. Wright, who in his *Modern Painting* constructs a hierarchical scale of aesthetic values.

Form in painting [he writes] like the eternal readjustments and equilibria of life, is but an approximation to stability. The forces in all art are the forces of life coordinated and organized. No plastic form can exist without rhythm; not rhythm in the super-ficial harmonic sense, but the rhythm which underlies the great fluctuating and equalizing forces of material existence. Such rhythm is symmetry in movement. On it all form, both in art and life, is founded.[1]

Both formalistic and expressionistic approaches to art have been recognized in critical patterns prior to the American. The three English scholars, Ogden, Richards, and Wood, suggested as the primary function of the work of art *synaesthesis*. The work of these three scholars has been duplicated recently by two American philosophers. Professor Philip Mac-Mahon in *The Meaning of Art* leans slightly toward Neo-Platonism, stressing intensity of expression. John Dewey in *Art and Experience* stresses art's function as self-revelation. Neither of these men nor any of the other American critics, with the exception of the poet Vachel Lindsay, seems to recognize that our new dominant art form from which a unified criticism may be derived is probably the motion picture. However, both these men have come closer to making a critical examination that will enable us to understand the motion-picture art than have any of the others.

The third approach to criticism in American culture, similar to that of Ruskin in Europe, is symbolized by Emerson, who first presented an aggregate of theories from which a well-balanced criticism might be taken. In Emerson's *Essay on Beauty*, the following sentences include most of the types and ultimate goals previously discussed.

. . . We ascribe beauty to that which is simple; which has no superfluous parts; which exactly answers its end; which stands related to all things; which is the mean of many extremes. . . .

The lesson taught by the study of Greek and of Gothic art, of antique and of Pre-Raphaelite painting, was worth all the research,—namely, that all beauty must be organic; that outside embellishment is deformity. . . . The tint of the flower proceeds from its root, and the lustres of the sea-shell begin with its existence.

[1] Willard Huntington Wright, *Modern Painting*, p. 18, Dodd, Mead & Company Inc., New York, 1923.

. . . Beautiful as is the symmetry of any form, if the form can move we seek a more excellent symmetry. The interruption of equilibrium stimulates the eye to desire the restoration of symmetry, and to watch the steps through which it is attained. This is the charm of running water, sea-waves, the flight of birds and the locomotion of animals. This is the theory of dancing, to recover continually in changes the lost equilibrium, not by abrupt and angular but by gradual and curving movements. . . . To this streaming or flowing belongs the beauty that all circular movement has; as the circulation of waters, the circulation of the blood, the periodical motion of planets, the annual wave of vegetation, the action and reaction of Nature; and if we follow it out, this demand in or thought for an ever-onward action is the argument for the immortality.

The felicities of design in art or in works of Nature are shadows or forerunners of that beauty which reaches its perfection in the human form. . . .

That Beauty is the normal state is shown by the perpetual effort of Nature to attain it. . . .

. . . Things are pretty, graceful, rich, elegant, handsome, but, until they speak to the imagination, not yet beautiful. This is the reason why beauty is still escaping out of all analysis. . . . The new virtue which constitutes a thing beautiful is a certain cosmical quality, or a power to suggest relation to the whole world, and so lift the object out of a pitiful individuality. . . .

All high beauty has a moral element in it, and I find the antique sculpture as ethical as Marcus Antoninus; and the beauty ever in proportion to the depth of thought. . . . [1]

The preceding sentences, with the two lines quoted at the head of the chapter, suggest an average American's unconsciously held idea of Beauty. Emerson, accepting most of the ideas of Plotinus, Longinus, and the formalists, suggests that art, to him one with Beauty, has as its greatest purpose making man more humane. It does this by condensing in a single work the abstract quality of not only the human but the natural world. Nature, although apparently infinite, has one universal principle inherent in a landscape and a sunbeam, appearing also in the simple structure of a leaf. The quality common to all is a perfection

[1] *Essay on Beauty*, by Ralph Waldo Emerson.

of organic unity. This indefinite standard of beauty seems so broad as to include the infinite variety of nature. Emerson, like the medieval mystic, tells us that nothing is beautiful alone, but has its power because it is able to suggest some divine grace. The true artist is one who can focus the universal in the particular form, and the work of art is all of nature seen through a temperament. Truth, Goodness, and Beauty are, then, simply different aspects of the Eternal. Emerson's all-inclusive sentences, like the inspired critical thoughts of Socrates, contain the germs of all aesthetic theorizing and closely approximate the Oriental philosophy of art.

The same ground, reworked by Professor Dewey, leads him to conclude that all art shows two general tendencies, one toward the concrete, the other toward the abstract; one frankly open and representative, the other symbolic and ideational. He concludes "but each is justified when form and matter reach equilibrium." Dewey's philosophy, based upon the pragmatic psychological methods of James, thus leads him to the same conclusion as Ogden, Richards, and Wood.

Corresponding to the historical approach of Carritt, Chambers, and Venturi, two American scholars, K. E. Gilbert and Helmut Kuhn, in 1939 published a significant work on the history of aesthetics. Although ignoring the full implications of the work of Ogden, Richards, and Wood, and their meaning of the doctrine of synaesthesis, Gilbert and Kuhn conclude, as we shall here, that the end of the Crocean aesthetic is a complete estrangement of art from its sources of power in life. Further, the associational overtones of their concluding paragraph suggest *equilibrium* as a condition of harmony between the artist and philosopher, without specifically mentioning it. From this somewhat cryptic ending one may infer that the prophetic philosopher and the form-creating artist must somehow unite in order to achieve the new art of the future. Thus, as we have seen, the inspirational and formal elements have always had to unite for any creation of universal import.

Psychological Aesthetics. In many colleges and universities, experiments are continually being made which have found their way into elementary art pedagogy. Using techniques developed in the natural sciences, hundreds of psychologists, yearning for art, have followed the Germans Fechner, Lipps, and Carl Stumpf. They proceed from the a priori ground that the aesthetic intuition can be isolated, unified, and significant for itself, and have tried to separate it into its component parts as sense impression. Most psychologists assume that the purpose of art is to induce pleasurable states. They contrast aesthetic effects with other sense impressions which together build up to bodily, practical, and intellectual needs. Significant work in this field has been done by Max Schoen, H. L. Langfeld, C. W. Valentine, and E. L. Thorndike.

Some psychological experiments, such as the Seashore music tests, have been made upon the basis of purely physical sense reactions. Other experiments, like those suggested by MacMahon in his *Art of Enjoying Art*, are made upon a combination of various sense reactions with reference to spatial arrangement. Still a third method is to examine group concepts objectively and with some control, as suggested by the Gestalt psychologists. The fourth psychological method, introspective and with little control, employs psychoanalytic techniques.

Art as Communication and Expression. When the sum of all reactions caused by the work of art has been considered, one must turn to experimentation through recreation. This method of approach, combined with an examination of cultural backgrounds and a study of the history of the arts, leads people like Professor Dewey to feel that the unique purpose of art is to make human nature intelligible to itself by objectifying its dreams, a conclusion also reached by the aesthetician De Witt Parker. These and other critics, like F. J. Mather, insist that art is a way of communicating knowledge about

a mystical reality greater than that charted mathematically in the natural sciences. This *aistheta*, like Baumgarten's, includes unanalyzable emotional states. These men approach closely to the old revelation-idealistic theory, without assuming a divine plan. The Orientals perceived that any given work must be capable of imparting its life to the people who experience it. Obviously, such works cannot be completely analyzed on purely Apollonian formal grounds alone. To appreciate them one must bring to them greathearted, humane personal experience, with wide natural and cultural backgrounds, as well as a lively Dionysian creative imagination. Any method of art appreciation, to be effective, must develop all these qualities with respect to works of art.

Bibliography

CORNYN, JOHN HUBER: *The Song of Quetzalcoatl*, Antioch Press, Yellow Springs, Ohio, 1930.

PARKER, ARTHUR: *Seneca Folk Tales*, Buffalo Historical Society, 1923.

THOMPSON, J. ERIC: *The Civilization of the Mayas*, Anthropology Leaflet 25, Field Museum of Natural History, Chicago.

JOYCE, T. A.: *South American Archaeology*, G. P. Putnam's Sons, New York, 1912.

VAILLANT, GEORGE C.: *Indian Arts in North America*, Harper & Brothers, New York, 1939.

BRENNER, ANITA: *Idols behind Altars*, Parson and Clarke Ltd., New York, 1929.

PARRINGTON, H.: *Main Currents in American Thought: An Interpretation of American Literature*, Harcourt, Brace & Company, Inc., New York, 1930.

WHITMAN, WALT: *Leaves of Grass*, Rees, Welsh & Co. Philadelphia, 1882.

JACKMAN, RILLA EVELYN: *American Arts*, Rand McNally & Company, Chicago, 1928.

BOSWELL, PEYTON: *American Painting*, Dodd, Mead & Company, Inc., New York, 1939.

BRUCE, EDWARD, and FORBES WATSON: *Art in Federal Buildings*, Art in Federal Buildings, Incorporated, Washington, D. C., 1936.

CAHILL, HOLGER: *American Sources of Modern Art*, Museum of Modern Art, New York, 1936.

CAHILL, HOLGER: *New Horizons in American Art*, Museum of Modern Art, New York, 1936.

RIVERA, DIEGO, and B. D. WOLFE: *Portrait of Mexico*, Covici, Friede, Inc., New York, 1937.

HITCHCOCK, H. R., and P. JOHNSON: *The International Style; Architecture since 1922*, W. W. Norton & Company, Inc., New York, 1932.

CHANDLER, F. W., and R. A. CORDELL: *20th Century Plays*, Thomas Nelson & Sons, New York, 1934.

KIMBALL, FISKE: *Domestic Architecture of the American Colonies and the Early Republic*, Charles Scribner's Sons, New York, 1922.

REED, WILLIAM V., and ELIZABETH OGG: *New Homes for Old*, The Foreign Policy Association, New York, 1940.

MUMFORD, LEWIS: *Technics and Civilization*, Harcourt, Brace & Company, Inc., New York, 1934.

MUMFORD, LEWIS: *The Culture of Cities*, Harcourt, Brace & Company, Inc., New York, 1938.

ARONOVICI, CAROL: *Housing the Masses*, John Wiley & Sons, Inc., New York, 1939.

KEPPEL, FREDERICK P., and R. L. DUFFUS: *The Arts in American Life*, McGraw-Hill Book Company, Inc., New York, 1933.

OVERMYER, GRACE: *Government and the Arts*, W. W. Norton & Company, Inc., New York, 1939.

CHENEY, S., and M. C. CHENEY: *Art and the Machine*, Whittlesey House, McGraw-Hill Book Company, Inc., New York, 1936.

VAN DOREN, HAROLD: *Industrial Design*, McGraw-Hill Book Company, Inc., New York, 1940.

KAHN, E. J.: *Design in Art and Industry*, Charles Scribner's Sons, New York, 1935.

WAUGH, ALICE: *Planning the Little House*, McGraw-Hill Book Company, Inc., New York, 1939.

MORRISON, HUGH: *Louis Sullivan*, Museum of Modern Art and W. W. Norton & Company, Inc., New York, 1935.

WINSLOW, LEON L.: *The Integrated School Art Program*, McGraw-Hill Book Company, Inc., New York, 1939.

HUGHES, R. M.: *Dance as an Art Form*, A. S. Barnes & Co., New York, 1936.

HOWARD, J. T.: *Our American Music*, The Thomas Y. Crowell Company, New York, 1939.

LINDSAY, VACHEL: *The Art of the Moving Picture*, The Macmillan Company, New York, 1922.

NICOLL, ALLARDYCE: *Film and Theatre*, The Thomas Y. Crowell Company, New York, 1936.

BARDECHE, M., and R. BRASILLACH: *The History of Motion Pictures*, W. W. Norton & Company, Inc., New York, 1938.

LEWIN, WILLIAM: *Photoplay Studies*, Educational and Recreational Guides, Inc., Newark, 1937.

ROTHA, PAUL: *Movie Parade*, Studio Publications, Inc., New York, 1937.

Romeo and Juliet, A Motion Picture Edition, Random House, Inc., New York, 1936.

EMERSON, RALPH WALDO: *Complete Works and Journals*, Houghton Mifflin Company, Boston, 1926.

McMAHON, A. PHILIP: *The Meaning of Art*, W. W. Norton & Company, Inc., New York, 1930.

DEWEY, BARNES, BUERMEYER, MUNRO, GUILLAUME, MULLER, and DeMAZIA: *Essays on Art and Education*, Barnes Foundation Press, Merion, Pennsylvania, 1929.

SEASHORE, CARL E.: *Psychology of Music*, McGraw-Hill Book Company, Inc., 1938.

RYAN, GRACE: *Dances of Our Pioneers*, A. S. Barnes & Company, New York, 1929.

SANDBURG, CARL: *American Songbag*, Harcourt, Brace & Co., Inc., New York, 1927.

SHARP, CECIL: *English Folk Songs from the Southern Appalachians*, Oxford University Press, London, 1932.

KRENEK, ERNST: *Music Here and Now*, W. W. Norton & Company, Inc., New York, 1940.

DREISER, THEODORE: *The Genius* (novel), Liveright Publishing Corporation, New York, 1923.

LEWIS, SINCLAIR: *Work of Art* (novel), Doubleday, Doran & Company, Inc., New York, 1934.

Recordings

CHAVEZ, CARLOS:

Sinfonia India, V-122337/8, a program of Mexican music, Columbia M 414.

GRUENBERG, LOUIS:

Emperor Jones—V 7959.

HANSON, HOWARD:

Merrymount—V 7959.

HARRIS, ROY:

Song for Occupations—C-68347/8D.
Overture to *When Johnny Comes Marching Home*—V-8692.

GERSHWIN, GEORGE:

Rhapsody in Blue—V-35822.
Porgy and Bess—VM-C-25 (alb.).

CARPENTER, JOHN ALDEN:

Skyscrapers—VM-130 (alb.).

GROFÉ, FERDE:

Mississippi Suite—V-35859.
Grand Canyon Suite—VM-C18.

GUION, DAVID:

Home on the Range—V-1525.

IVES, CHARLES:

General Booth Enters Heaven, New Home Quarterly Recording—1-5 & 1-11.

MacDOWELL, EDWARD:

Suite No. 2 (Indian)—V-20342.
Peruvian music, Decca 20329.
Inca Music, *Religious Dance Song* (*Huachitorito*), Decca 20388.
Jackie Boy (*The Keeper*), arranged by L. Singer, as sung by Maxine Sullivan and orchestra, V 26372 A.

SCOTT, RAYMOND:

The Penguin—M 8058 (M 703).
War Dance for Wooden Indians—M 8058 (M 702).

Conclusion

IN FINAL analysis the work of art presents the total measure of man. Its unique value consists in its power to strengthen the individual's ego-centered self, giving him confidence, while at the same time it increases his value for society.

The Artist and Society. As a living organism man exists by reason of his ability to preserve his entity while reproducing his kind. The interaction of these two primary drives generates a third, spiritualizing instinct proper to the human. This functions by creating a record of the interaction of the first two. Art, the refined moment of synthesis, carries in its associational overtones a reservoir of healing energy. It also furnishes a symbol of man's ability to resolve his conflicts. Thus every work of art symbolizes in some degree the union of man and his environment, and these two factors achieve equilibrium through their expression.

The most effective art is that which unites the greatest possible diversity of interests in the most unified, restful synthesis. Such art has power strongly to stir the imagination while it appeases the senses. In every great work there appears evidence of a peaceful victory for the human race. Such a victory gladdens life and raises no thoughts of revenge: in it, the free-willed, productive ego and the society-conserving group have united for common celebration of a moment which contains the maximum significance for both.

The Ultimate Meaning of the Symbol. All human expression seeks arrangement under three general categories, each symbolized by a simple design growing out of the primary attributes of matter. These schematic designs, already presented in the preface, were there derived from the basic composition forms in the various historical styles. They have, however, a more fundamental basis in the nature of all reality. Every living organism needs pause or rest from outward activity in order that its inner forces may concentrate their energy for further progress. The moment of rest is best pictured symbolically as an equilateral triangle or pyramid. The dynamic moment of progressive extension and growth naturally appears as a spiraling dynamic line or as an endless interweave—the latter, a figure to which the Buddhists impute "infinite happiness." The third moment, rare indeed in our consciousness, is that in which the static and dynamic elements reach a state of equilibrium. Such a moment suggests the symmetrical circle or sphere—with any interior arrangement of lines in absolute balance if it is to suggest the static; enclosing one or more spirals if it is slightly dynamic.

The three symbolic composition forms, arising in nature, were early adopted by primitive man, who of necessity attributed to each its proper significance. As the mind became cultured, an unknown Egyptian sculptor dimly perceived that all art consisted of an arrangement of such symbolic forms. He chose in particular the more static cones, squares, and cubes. Heraclitus, conceiving the basis of matter to be more dynamic, stressed the line of flame, later known as the Praxitelean curve of beauty. Parmenides chose the more static yet equilibrated sphere. Pythagoras, interested in musical progression, found number and geometric relationships to be the controlling factors in all life. Although Plato considered the soul of beauty to be a static triangle, his follower Plotinus again needed the flame. Each of these philosophers, in poetic fashion, thus affirmed the primary importance of one of the three moods of conceiving life. All the various theories of art's highest excellence, discussed at the end of Chap. XVIII, may be subsumed under these three.

Throughout the Middle Ages mystics conceived God (the whole) as a sphere, into which or upon which was placed the cross, a symbol standing for the moment of birth, or genesis from the Mother. The cross combined with its active correlate, the fylfot or swastika, in a way suggests equilibrium. Within the circle, the cross seems completely equilibrated. The Celts, combining the triangle with the dynamic principle of the fylfot to produce the triquetrum, willed the dynamic in art. Early in the development of Chinese culture the circle was divided by spiraling lines into the yang and the yin. Around this figure eight elements, each made up of horizontal lines, were so arranged that the entire sign came to stand for the equilibrium of the universe. Every normal man seems obliged by the complete need of his logical nature to group his thoughts so that they will fall into some relationship like the above equilibrated grouping.

Fortunes of the Symbols. Briefly summarizing the history of man's cultural development (see Chart, pp. 834–835), it becomes apparent that a certain grouping of cultures—including the Egyptian, early Greek, Byzantine, early Renaissance, and Neoclassical—tend to use the static composition form. A second group of cultures—including the Assyrian, late Greek, pre-Romanesque, late Gothic, baroque, and Romantic—tend to use the second, or dynamic, composition form. In the cultures of the Fourteenth dynasty in Egypt, the Golden Age of Pericles in Athens, the 13th-century Gothic, and of 15th-century Florence, as in the best of Chinese art, the two general composition forms unite in a synaeresis, approximating the third symbolic complex. When two composition forms are consciously placed beside each other in a given work, eclecticism results and something similar to primitive space filling appears.

Only such excellent compositions as the sculpture of the Parthenon pediments; the Last Supper, by Leonardo; several works by Michelangelo; paintings by Rembrandt, Giorgione, Vermeer, and several of the Chinese landscapists furnish a satisfying equilibrium, so subtle that it eludes easy analysis into its contrasting moments. The equilibrium of formal values in these works is accompanied by an equilibrium of associational values. They also have an equilibrium between the use (healing), associational (commemorative), and formal (sensate) values. Such works contain a reservoir of static and dynamic strength from which all conditions of people may draw inspiration or in which all may find rest. Since the works themselves have a quality which man must impute to the universe as a whole, their significance is universal.

Place of the Artist in the Society of the Future. As a growing organic part of an educational program, this study may not be summarily brought to an end. The American chapter noticeably remains without a conclusion, chiefly because this culture has not yet attained its definitive style. Similarly, the book of man's creative life has not reached an aesthetic synthesis revealing man's most universal concept of perfection. Nor can such art appear until the peoples of the earth have created a truly cooperative world culture. Any possible suggestion concerning the future fortunes of the artist must arise from our knowledge of the past. A factual résumé of our study may here be gained by coordinating the summaries at the ends of all the chapters, and the maps, with the chart on pages 834–835.

The conclusions reached above concerning art's ultimate symbolic meaning were implicit in the a priori grounds with which we began. Art to the author, after 20 years, still remains a symbol of the self-healing factors in human nature. In its most characteristic moments, art unites the will to preserve the race and the revelations of her greatest prophets. The artist as prophet symbolically presents our common goals for eventual unity, at times even suggesting those cooperative attitudes necessary to achieve this unity. Men are now much closer to achieving an ultimate cooperative society than they know. During the past 20 years the arts have approached a condition of international and interracial appeal never before reached. The motion pictures, the 20th-century mural style, new communal housing developments for the working classes, as well as the functional character of the new world architecture, all hold for man a fresh vision of his fundamental humanity. Only those forces which today tend to retard the democratic confederation of peoples still employ Romantic 19th-century art forms, which present little more than revivals of the Romanesque or the Roman Imperial style.

Even the present struggle in Europe and Asia presents one aspect of man's desire for ultimate unity, for each of the warring nations considers that it is destined to bring that unity to mankind. The essential difference between them is not concerning the goal but concerning the means of reaching it. One group maintains that unity must come from the top down, by divine right. This kind of political belief, as we have seen it paralleled in the aesthetic field, creates the so-called classical, academic style. Corresponding to medieval realism, it stems ideologically in great part from Plato's first Spartan Utopia. In contrast, the other political group inclines to the view that human unity must come from the free-willed cooperation of characteristic individuals, from the bottom up, as Aristotle might say. This approach to unity corresponds to the Gothic nominalistic conception and to some aspects of the ancient Athenian vision of democracy. An effective modern democracy, of course, presents that paradox, a state which functions in both ways. Seen in the light of history, it is apparent that we in America stand to the conflicting nations of the world of our day much as democratic Athens did to the Hellenic world under the leadership of Pericles just before the Peloponnesian War. Our culture and politics may be favorably compared to that of republican Rome before the advent of the Caesars or to Florence and Venice in 15th-century Italy. Our arts have today almost reached an excellence corresponding to the greatest art of those democracies.

Obviously, the future of the human race belongs to us. What we make of it depends upon the general level of intelligence of every citizen and upon the inspired imagination of those whom we elect to lead our common endeavors. So far, the evidence presented to the historian by the great housing developments, by the growth of cooperative industrial enterprise, by the character of our motion pictures, and by the significant civic arts program fostered during the last 10 years indicates a degree of constructive imagination surpassing any display by the leaders of prior democracies. If this spirit can be kept alive, if by astute statesmanship we can somehow manage to avoid the devastation of a war, then like master artists, we can help in the molding of a more peaceful world. Only then shall we have fulfilled a destiny indicated in the following words by George Washington:

I consider how mankind may be connected, like one great family, in fraternal ties. I indulge a fond, perhaps an enthusiastic idea, that as the world is much less barbarous than it has been, its melioration must still be progressive . . . that the period is not very remote when the benefits of a liberal and free commerce will pretty generally succeed to the devastations and horrors of war. And I most sincerely and devoutly wish that the exertions of those having this view may effect what human nature cries aloud for—general peace.

The thought of Washington, embodying the ideal goals of our nation, finds even more significant arrangement and sublimity in the lines of Lincoln and Whitman. A fitting conclusion is reached in the words of Wilson that we must save the world for democracy. These and the expression of Sullivan quoted at the beginning of the American Chapter provide us with the sociopolitical philosophy out of which arise the associational values of our most characteristic art. Besides these ideals, we need clear vision as to the future possibilities in world political developments. These I shall attempt to give in terms of man's artistic symbols and in light of what we have discovered through the pages of this book.

Art and the Totalitarian State. The aesthetic productions of the next great world culture period will be determined by one of four social political situations to which the mind of the artists must react. If the world as a whole accepts the type of government represented by the Third Reich in Germany, based upon conquests by a group considering themselves superior to the rest of the human race, with a strongly organized central government conceived in terms of a religion of power, the aesthetic styles will approximate those of ancient Mesopotamia, Imperial Rome, and the Romanesque period of Europe. Between 1934 and 1940 most of the buildings constructed in Germany and Italy evidence this style.[1] In such a culture the representative arts will approximate the classical, academic style with a return to the painting methods of Ingres. The motion pictures will have a strongly didactic character, with a revival of epic themes from Germanic and Roman history conceived after the manner of Richard Wagner. Abstract and purely playful art will be banished as a symbol of revolt against the central authority, or as escape from reality.

International Anarchy and Art for Art's Sake. The second sociopolitical possibility is one leading to some sort of international anarchy, with a continuation of national rivalries like those prior to the World War, or in the decade between 1930 and 1940. In this case there will be a further development of strongly local art styles displaying the greatest possible diversity.[2] The more inspired creators will either, if they are philosophers, create a semimystical, surrealistic art or, if they are virtuosos, produce an eclecticism like that of the Hellenistic period between the dissolution of Alexander's world-state and the rise of the Roman Empire. Many individual art cliques, seeking escape from reality, will arise under the lead of vital artist-personalities; the bizarre or the macabre will be highly valued and there will be a further orchidaceous growth of aestheticism.

Political Rivalry and the Schizophrenic Artist. The third possibility would be some sort of political union between the separate parts of the British Empire, the United States, and various other small states, opposed by the combined forces of Japan, Italy, Germany, and other small states, possibly in league with Russia and dominated by either Moscow or Berlin. Two such powerful combinations would be able to carry out a long, exhaustive war. In such a case, the artist in each culture would create under a high degree of emotional pressure, dominated by a strong complex of fear. Artists in the Anglo-Saxon group would probably inherit a combination of the Celto-Germanic interweave, abstractionist tendencies in graphic design, and an architectural style frozen into an official government neoclassicism. The artistic results of this eclecticism would lack integrity and would reecho the gradual shattering of man's mind, with a return to primitivism. In either case, the artist, having little personal freedom, would tend severely to formalize his work and to produce an exposition of "safe" subject matter. Domestic architecture would, perforce, approximate the fortresslike, and much of the building would be of cavate construction.

Art in a World Democracy. The fourth possibility is that, taking advantage of the many military and political accidents that are bound to occur in the next few years and recognizing man's will eventually to overcome the disease

---

[1] See *Architektur and bauplastik der gegenwart* by W. Rittich, Berlin, 1938.
[2] See *Public Buildings—Architecture under the Public Works Administration*, 1933–1939, U.S. Government Printing Office, 1939.

of warfare, we shall be able to unite on an effective cooperative league of nations, or better, expanding our American idea of government, a United States of the World. How soon this will come about depends on so many diverse factors that anyone would be foolish to prophesy. However, since it must eventually arrive, we who take the long-time, realistic, historical view of the ultimate destiny of the race may as well consider what the artistic production would be like under such a government.

There will be further growth and refinement of the democratic styles reached in the Pan-American productions between 1930 and 1940. Art, being considered an ever more necessary part of daily living, will be strong in use values; therefore, the refining principles of streamlining and functional design must find their way into the figurative arts. The associational overtones of musical and graphic arts will suggest either cooperation and human brotherhood or the eternal warfare that man must carry on against the forces of disease and decay in nature. The pattern of the representative arts should reach a refined synaesthesis between the Classical and Gothic forms approximating the equilibrium of the most characteristic Oriental works.

For the first years in the development of this international style the dynamic elements in the composition will somewhat dominate, chiefly because there is a suggestion of physical work to be done, rebuilding war-torn Europe and China, clearing the slums, and conserving our natural resources. The artists, feeling this need, must suggest in their design the challenge of the new undertaking. Mural painting, like many recent government murals, and student work in the colleges of Midwestern America, will be somewhat crude but correspondingly sincere. Greater integration and refinement will inevitably appear in the second generation of artists working under this program, whose results must stem from the vital primitive energies of our present archaic style.

In the field of the motion picture, the documentary type of film will grow, chiefly because the inhabitants of the new world democracy will be interested in getting acquainted with all conditions of mankind. The musical accompaniment for such films will be simple, with fundamental, almost primitive effects of harmony and rhythm, understandable by all in the new world-state. However, each nation will proudly embellish its own folk art, which it will display at great contests similar to the poetic and musical contests of ancient Greece and medieval Europe. The Christian concept of the "City of God" has been a long time on the way, probably because too often overshadowed by the pagan Plato's Republic. Actually, however, the process of cultural cooperation has been so accelerated by man's inventions during the past four decades that we may realistically expect great strides to be made as soon as the present war is ended. The words of George Washington are now more true than ever. The spirit of Lincoln is stronger in the world today than in the years just following the War between the States. Here in our democracy each citizen has as his first creative task an understanding of the world which he must help toward a federal union, similar to that which our very creative revolutionary ancestors brought together 200 years ago. Obviously, such a world picture as this demands an aesthetic formula with an overtone of imagination not suggested by the word "synaesthesis." The work of art, like the finest prophetic works just studied, must always have a dynamic life of its own, capable of inspiring the beholder to further artistic creation. To describe such a work I have suggested the word "synaeresis," which refines and compresses imaginative energy into a small compass out of the purely descriptive passages of nature. Here the aspect of the Sublime is condensed to the condition of the Beautiful without becoming static, that is, without losing the Energetic. Such a term precisely describes the finest film plays, the symphonies of Beethoven or the pictures of Rembrandt and Leonardo.

Throughout this extended essay on the relation of the arts to man we have tried to experience vicariously the great creations of the past by re-creating them in our minds and with our hands. As a final illustration of art's meaning, we should consider together some elementary symbol for the future of mankind. Such a symbol might be a flag under which the separate states of the world could unite. Being Americans, naturally we cannot help taking as a foundation plan something from the design of the "Star-Spangled Banner," which symbolizes our most immediate experience of democracy. Since the United States of the World would consist of nations on five continents, distributed over the globe in the four regions indicated by the compass, let us construct a cross, symbol of the ancient mother goddess of nature. The cross should be of five alternate red and white stripes

with associational values like those of the stripes in "Old Glory." The associational value of the cross carries over from the words of the Iroquois "Little Waters" medicine ceremony:

> Under the four heavens journeying
> All men are brothers.

These words, which may have come to America with Quetzalcoatl, were also the words of Buddha, of Confucius, and of the Christ. Within the four fields created by the cross, the flag would show the stars of the various democratic member nations of the world confederation. Upon the cross a central globe of green might hold the intimate symbol of the particular nation over which the flag would be flown; for example, the music of Ireland, symbolized by its golden harp, or the torch of liberty as the emblem of our own United States.

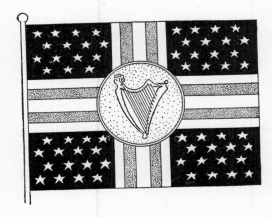

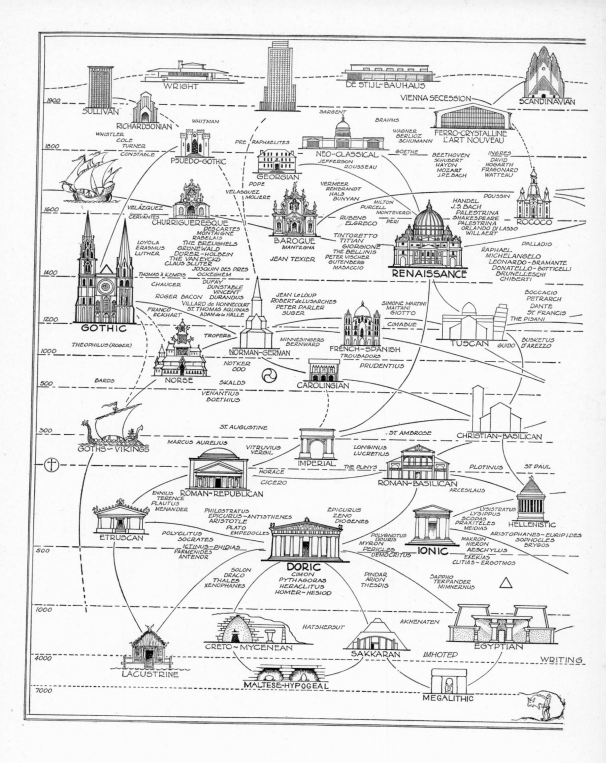

1900

WRIGHT

DE STIJL-BAUHAUS

VIENNA SECESSION

SCANDINAVIAN

SULLIVAN

RICHARDSONIAN

WHITMAN

SARGENT

BRAHMS

FERRO-CRYSTALLINE
L'ART NOUVEAU

WAGNER
BERLIOZ
SCHUMANN

1800

WHISTLER
COLE
TURNER
CONSTABLE

PRE RAPHAELITES

NEO-CLASSICAL

GOETHE

BEETHOVEN
SCHUBERT
HAYDN
MOZART
J.P.E.BACH

INGRES
DAVID
HOGARTH
FRAGONARD
WATTEAU

PSUEDO-GOTHIC

GEORGIAN

JEFFERSON
ROUSSEAU

POPE

VELASQUEZ
MOLIERE

VERMEER
REMBRANDT
HALS
BUNYAN

DOUSSIN

HANDEL
J.S.BACH
PALESTRINA
SHAKESPEARE
PALESTRINA
ORLANDO DI LASSO
WILLAERT

ROCOCO

1600

VELÁZQUEZ

CERVANTES

CHURRIGUERESQUE

DESCARTES
MONTAIGNE
RABELAIS
THE BREUGHELS
GRUNEWALD
DURER-HOLBEIN
THE VAN EYCKS
CLAUS SLUTER

RUBENS
ELGRECO

MILTON
PURCELL
MONTEVERDI

PERI

TINTORETTO
TITIAN
GIORGIONE
THE BELLINIS
PETER VISCHER
GUTENBERG
MASACCIO

BAROQUE

MANTEGNA

JEAN TEXIER

RENAISSANCE

RAPHAEL
MICHELANGELO
LEONARDO - BRAMANTE
DONATELLO - BOTTICELLI
BRUNELLESCHI
CHIBERTI

PALLADIO

LOYOLA
ERASMUS
LUTHER

JOSQUIN DES PRES
OCKEGHEM

THOMAS à KEMPIS

CHAUCER

DUFAY
DUNSTABLE
VINCENT

BOCCACIO
PETRARCH
DANTE
ST. FRANCIS
THE PISANI

1400

ROGER BACON DURANDUS

VILLARD de HONNECOURT
ST. THOMAS AQUINAS
ADAM de la HALLE

JEAN Le LOUP
ROBERT de LUSARCHES
PETER PARLER
SUGER

SIMONE MARTINI
MAITANI
GIOTTO

FRANCO
ECKHART

CIMABUE

1200

GOTHIC

TROPERS

MINNESINGERS
BERNWARD

FRENCH-SPANISH

TROUBADORS

TUSCAN

GUIDO

BUSKETUS
D'AREZZO

THEOPHILUS (ROGER)

NORMAN-GERMAN

PRUDENTIUS

1000

BARDS

NORSE

NOTKER
ODO

SKALDS

CAROLINGIAN

500

VENANTIUS
BOETHIUS

300

ST. AUGUSTINE

ST. AMBROSE

CHRISTIAN-BASILICAN

GOTHS-VIKINGS

MARCUS AURELIUS

VITRUVIUS
VERGIL

IMPERIAL

LONGINUS
LUCRETIUS

PLOTINUS

ST. PAUL

HORACE

THE PLINYS

CICERO

ROMAN-BASILICAN

ARCESILAUS

ENNIUS
TERENCE
PLAUTUS
MENANDER

ROMAN-REPUBLIC

EPICURUS
ZENO
DIOGENES

LYSISTRATUS
LYSIPPUS
SCOPAS
PRAXITELES
MEIDIAS

HELLENISTIC

PHILOSTRATUS
EPICURUS-ANTISTHENES
ARISTOTLE
PLATO
EMPEDOCLES

MAKRON
HIERON

ARISTOPHANES~EURIPIDES
SOPHOCLES
BRYGOS

ETRUSCAN

POLYCLITUS
SOCRATES
ICTINUS-PHIDIAS
PARMENIDES
ANTENOR

POLYGNOTUS
DOURIS
MYRON
PERICLES
DEMOCRITUS

EXEKIAS
CLITIAS ~ ERGOTMOS

IONIC

500

SOLON
DRACO
PYTHAGORAS
THALES
XENOPHANES

DORIC

CIMON
PYTHAGORAS
HERACLITUS
HOMER ~ HESIOD

PINDAR
ARION
THESPIS

SAPPHO
TERPANDER
MIMNERNUS

1000

HATSHEPSUT

AKHENATEN

LACUSTRINE

CRETO~MYCENEAN

SAKKARAN

IMHOTEP

EGYPTIAN

WRITING

4000

MALTESE-HYPOGEAL

7000

MEGALITHIC

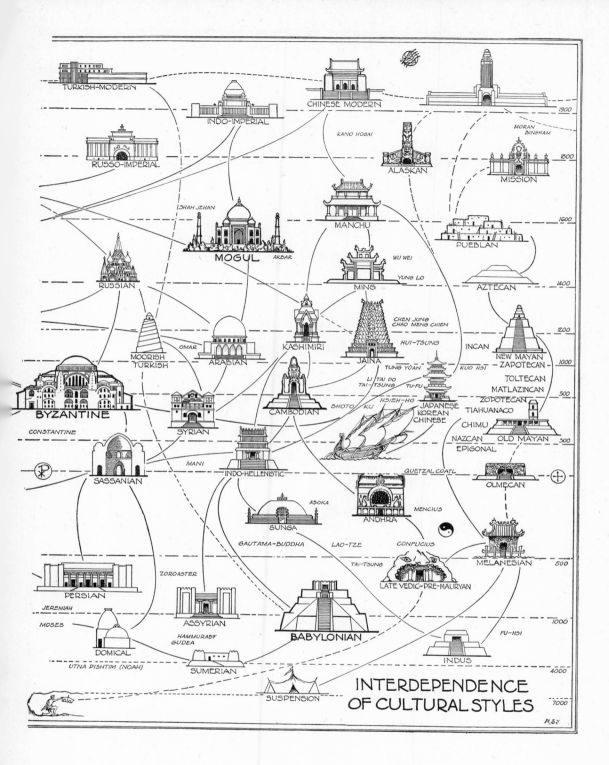

INTERDEPENDENCE
OF CULTURAL STYLES

835

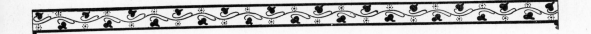

Index

Italic type refers to illustrations; **boldface** indicates definitions